# Praise for *Positive Psychology in Practice*, Second Edition

"When the first edition of *Positive Psychology in Practice* arrived in 2004, it was an early and authoritative reference for an emerging science and its application. Now, a decade later, we are graced with a second edition. Here, you will find updated chapters and all new content. This book provides a deep dive into current trends in research and practice for anyone interested in positive psychology."

—Dr. Robert Biswas-Diener, author of *The Upside of Your Dark Side* and *The Courage Quotient* and Professor at Portland State University

"One of psychology's best books just got better. Experts, evidence, applications—exactly what you need to make positive psychology work in practice, and work well. A definite resource addition to my own library and practice."

—George Burns, Adjunct Professor of Psychology at the Cairnmillar Institute in Australia and author of *101 Healing Stories* and *Happiness, Healing, Enhancement*

"For each of the past 10 years, I have assigned *Positive Psychology in Practice* as required reading for my course on positive interventions in the Master of Applied Positive Psychology (MAPP) program at the University of Pennsylvania. I am delighted to see this second edition, which expands the content in exciting new directions and brings the chapters up to date. My students and I are grateful to Stephen Joseph and the many chapter authors for this valuable contribution to the field."

—James O. Pawelski, Director of Education and Senior Scholar, Positive Psychology Center, University of Pennsylvania

"This book is a critical companion for anyone who works for the betterment of others, be they an educator, a consultant, a coach, a health professional of some kind, or an applied researcher. Stephen Joseph set out to assemble a volume of wide-ranging appeal and he has delivered precisely that. It expands wonderfully on the first edition, capturing much of what has transpired in the field over the past decade. My first edition copy will finally get a well-deserved rest!"

—Dr. Gordon Spence, Program Director, Master of Business Coaching, Sydney Business School, University of Wollongon, Australia

"This is an excellent book that provides an up-to-date, accessible, and comprehensive overview of the best positive psychology interventions that are currently available. It reflects a deep understanding of positive psychology, as it not only gives an accurate account of the field's growing complexities but also addresses the movement's roots within the history of psychology."

—Carmelo Vázquez, Complutense University,
Madrid, Spain, and President of the
International Positive Psychology Association

"*Positive Psychology in Practice, 2e* is a milestone in the annals of texts detailing the intricacies of positive psychological inquiry. Its stress on the social implications of positive psychology, for example, makes it not only relevant to public policy but also to the kind of society, and indeed world, we wish to foster. Furthermore, its coverage of humanistic and existential perspectives on positive psychological practice will be greatly welcomed in those areas of our profession that have been skeptical of conventional positive psychological emphases on the 'good life' with relatively less emphasis on the 'full' or 'vital' life. These existential and humanistic dimensions add notably to our deepening knowledge of such areas as resilience, posttraumatic growth, and qualitative/subjective experiences of what it means to flourish. In short, I highly recommend *Positive Psychology in Practice, 2e* as a rigorous and humanizing exploration of the vital life."

—Kirk Schneider, PhD, adjunct faculty member at Saybrook University
and Teachers College, Columbia University,
and author of *Existential-Humanistic Therapy*,
*The Handbook of Humanistic Psychology*, and *The Polarized Mind*

# Positive Psychology in Practice

Promoting Human Flourishing
in Work, Health, Education,
and Everyday Life

Second Edition

Edited by

Stephen Joseph

## WILEY

*In memory of Christopher Peterson (1950–2012),*
*who reminded us that "Other People Matter"*

# Contents

Preface     xi

Acknowledgments     xv

1   Applied Positive Psychology 10 Years On     1
    *Stephen Joseph*

PART I   HISTORICAL AND PHILOSOPHICAL FOUNDATIONS

2   Historical, Philosophical, and Epistemological Perspectives     9
    *Hilde Eileen Nafstad*

3   Building Bridges Between Humanistic and Positive Psychology     31
    *Brent Dean Robbins*

4   Existential Dimensions of Positive Psychology     47
    *Roger Bretherton*

5   The Salutogenic Paradigm     61
    *Shifra Sagy, Monica Eriksson, and Orna Braun-Lewensohn*

PART II   VALUES AND CHOICES IN PURSUIT OF THE GOOD LIFE

6   The Science of Values in the Culture of Consumption     83
    *Tim Kasser*

7   Values and Well-Being     103
    *Lilach Sagiv, Sonia Roccas, and Shani Oppenheim-Weller*

8   The Paradox of Choice     121
    *Barry Schwartz*

9   A Self-Determination Theory Perspective on Fostering Healthy
    Self-Regulation From Within and Without     139
    *Kirk Warren Brown and Richard M. Ryan*

10   The Complementary Roles of Eudaimonia and Hedonia
    and How They Can Be Pursued in Practice     159
    *Veronika Huta*

PART III   PRACTICES FOR HEALTH AND WELL-BEING

11   The Prospects, Practices, and Prescriptions for the Pursuit of Happiness     185
    *Kristin Layous, Kennon M. Sheldon, and Sonja Lyubomirsky*

12   Putting Positive Psychology Into Motion Through Physical Activity     207
    *Guy Faulkner, Kate Hefferon, and Nanette Mutrie*

13  Balancing Time Perspective in Pursuit of Optimal Functioning          223
      *Ilona Boniwell and Philip G. Zimbardo*
14  Putting Positive Psychology Into Practice via Self-Help               237
      *Acacia C. Parks*
15  Positive Psychology and Life Coaching                                 249
      *Margarita Tarragona*

PART IV   METHODS AND PROCESSES OF TEACHING AND LEARNING

16  Different Approaches to Teaching Positive Psychology                  267
      *Amy C. Fineburg and Andrew Monk*
17  Positively Transforming Classroom Practice Through
      Dialogic Teaching                                                   279
      *Alina Reznitskaya and Ian A. G. Wilkinson*
18  Teaching Well-Being and Resilience in Primary and Secondary School    297
      *Chieko Kibe and Ilona Boniwell*
19  Cultivating Adolescents' Motivation                                   313
      *Reed W. Larson and Nickki Pearce Dawes*

PART V   POSITIVE PSYCHOLOGY AT WORK

20  Bringing Positive Psychology to Organizational Psychology             329
      *Sarah Lewis*
21  Improving Follower Well-Being With Transformational Leadership         341
      *Heather M. Clarke, Kara A. Arnold, and Catherine E. Connelly*
22  Applications of Positive Approaches in Organizations                  357
      *Jane Henry*
23  Leadership Coaching and Positive Psychology                           377
      *Carol Kauffman, Stephen Joseph, and Anne Scoular*

PART VI   HEALTH, CLINICAL, COUNSELING, AND REHABILITATION

24  Complementary Strengths of Health Psychology and
      Positive Psychology                                                 393
      *John M. Salsman and Judith T. Moskowitz*
25  Deconstructing the Illness Ideology and Constructing an Ideology
      of Human Strengths and Potential in Clinical Psychology             411
      *James E. Maddux and Shane J. Lopez*
26  The Relationship Between Counseling Psychology
      and Positive Psychology                                             429
      *Andreas Vossler, Edith Steffen, and Stephen Joseph*
27  Positive Psychology in Rehabilitation Psychology Research
      and Practice                                                        443
      *Claudio Peter, Szilvia Geyh, Dawn M. Ehde, Rachel Müller,
      and Mark P. Jensen*

PART VII   CONTEXTS OF CLINICAL PRACTICE

28  Clinical Applications of Well-Being Therapy                           463
      *Chiara Ruini and Giovanni A. Fava*
29  Strategies for Accentuating Hope                                      483
      *Jeana L. Magyar-Moe and Shane J. Lopez*

30  Clinical Applications of Posttraumatic Growth                                    503
      *Richard G. Tedeschi, Lawrence G. Calhoun, and Jessica M. Groleau*
31  Strength-Based Assessment                                                          519
      *Tayyab Rashid*

PART VIII   INNER RESOURCES AND POSITIVE DEVELOPMENT ACROSS
                  THE LIFE SPAN

32  The Ability Model of Emotional Intelligence                              545
      *David R. Caruso, Peter Salovey, Marc Brackett, and John D. Mayer*
33  The Power and Practice of Gratitude                                          559
      *Giacomo Bono, Mikki Krakauer, and Jeffrey J. Froh*
34  Wisdom-Related Knowledge Across the Life Span                     577
      *Ute Kunzmann and Stefanie Thomas*
35  Positive Aging                                                                         595
      *George E. Vaillant*

PART IX   BUILDING COMMUNITY THROUGH INTEGRATION
                AND REGENERATION

36  Psychological and Relational Resources in the Experience of Disability
      and Caregiving                                                                      615
      *Antonella Delle Fave, Andrea Fianco, and Raffaela D. G. Sartori*
37  Good Lives and the Rehabilitation of Sex Offenders               635
      *Clare-Ann Fortune, Tony Ward, and Ruth Mann*
38  Facilitating Forgiveness Using Group and Community Interventions   659
      *Frank D. Fincham*
39  The Interface Between Positive Psychology and Social Work in Theory
      and Practice                                                                        681
      *Rachel Dekel and Orit Taubman–Ben-Ari*
40  Building Recovery-Oriented Service Systems Through Positive
      Psychology                                                                          695
      *Sandra G. Resnick and Meaghan A. Leddy*

PART X   PUBLIC POLICY AND SYSTEMS FOR RESILIENCE
               AND SOCIAL PLANNING

41  Balancing Individuality and Community in Public Policy          713
      *David G. Myers*
42  Happiness as a Priority in Public Policy                                  731
      *Ruut Veenhoven*
43  Positive Social Planning                                                         751
      *Neil Thin*
44  Resilience Theory and the Practice of Positive Psychology From
      Individuals to Societies                                                        773
      *Tuppett M. Yates, Fanita A. Tyrell, and Ann S. Masten*

PART XI   SIGNPOSTS FOR THE PRACTICE OF POSITIVE PSYCHOLOGY

45  The Role of Embodiment in Optimal Functioning                   791
      *Kate Hefferon*

46  The Uneasy—and Necessary—Role of the Negative
in Positive Psychology                                          807
    *Brian G. Pauwels*
47  The Future of Positive Psychology in Practice                823
    *Stephen Joseph*

About the Editor                                                829

Contributors                                                    831

Author Index                                                    835

Subject Index                                                   859

# Preface

POSITIVE PSYCHOLOGY HAS captured the interest and imagination of scholars and led to a new vision for what psychology has to offer as both an academic and a professional discipline. This has promoted a growing interest among practitioners about real-world applications.

The first edition of this book provided a comprehensive resource to which practitioners and academics with applied interests could turn. Ten years on from the first edition, positive psychology has matured, developed a solid evidence base, and is now better equipped to put its vision into practice. This new expanded edition builds on the previous edition. Like the first edition, it focuses on the actual and potential interventions and applications that have been developed from research within positive psychology. It provides a compendium of scientific evidence that supports the application of positive psychology, proposes new theoretical frameworks that will guide the advance of positive psychology research, and engages with applied psychologists and other practitioners and policy specialists in showing how positive psychology can contribute to health, happiness, and human flourishing.

The importance of this book is that it shows us how to move from the theoretical to put the vision into practice. In addition to considerations of how positive psychology can help individuals, this edition considers in more depth the application of positive psychology to institutions and policy. It raises questions about the sort of society we want to live in and it does not shy from the realities of life and its inevitable hardships and misfortunes. It is a vision for individuals, communities, and societies to function at their most optimal.

This volume is a necessary addition to any positive psychology collection, containing as it does the most up-to-date and cutting-edge scholarly work from leading experts. Throughout the book, there is information, guidance, and suggestions that practitioners can take away and put into practice. The authors review the state of research on each topic, discuss how it has been applied in practice, and consider new ideas for how and where it might be applied and what future research should be undertaken, always keeping in mind that the intended audience is professional psychologists who will be most interested in how to use the research findings in their professional practice.

In this edition, I say goodbye to Alex Linley, who coedited the first edition but whose commitments prevented him from being part of this edition. My best wishes to Alex in his new endeavors. I also say goodbye to some authors who were unable to contribute this time, and particularly with sadness note the death of Chris Peterson, one of the founders of positive psychology. His contributions to positive psychology were immense: He developed the character strengths and virtues perspective at the heart of positive psychology and emphasized the importance of human relationships with his phrase "other people matter." His influence can be seen throughout the chapters of this book.

I also welcome new authors. When I began selecting new chapters for this edition, I wanted it to remain fresh and challenging and provide the best of positive psychology. This edition contains new chapters from scholars and practitioners at the cutting edge of the most vibrant areas of positive psychology today, such as eudaimonia, assessment and policy, and in areas of application such as coaching, occupational psychology, and self-help. At the same time, I also wanted to surprise readers with the unexpected and include applications of positive psychology to novel areas such as social work, social planning, rehabilitation, and recovery, and I wanted to make greater space for consideration of how positive psychology addresses the dark side of life, its historical and philosophical roots, and dialogue with humanistic psychology.

As with the previous edition, in establishing the aims of the volume, I was faced with the daunting task of providing state-of-the-art research evidence that underpinned practical recommendations for professional psychologists while at the same time defining the parameters for future academic research. The result is a volume that bridges the theory, research, and applications of positive psychology. The book draws on cutting-edge scientific research that is leading the development of positive psychology. Contributors are all experts in their fields who have been selected on the basis of their empirical, theoretical, and applied contributions to psychological knowledge. They have been invited to review the state-of-the-art empirical evidence with regard to the application of positive psychology and to discuss their own experiences of using positive psychology in their practice. Further, the contributors were invited to consider what new research is required to enable professional psychologists to use positive psychology within applied work.

Positive psychology has its origins in the United States, but its popularity has spread internationally to capture the interest of psychologists elsewhere; for this reason, authors are drawn not only from the United States but also from Australia, Canada, France, Germany, Israel, Italy, Japan, Mexico, Netherlands, New Zealand, Norway, South Africa, Sweden, Switzerland, and the United Kingdom.

The main aim of this second edition is to provide an overview of the current state of the art in applied positive psychology and to look to its future development. At the beginning of the positive psychology movement, a critical question was how positive psychology could be applied in real-world settings. The 2004 edition of this volume was the first to specialize in the applications of positive psychology. It was a landmark that helped to create the subsequent interest in the field and its applications. It is my hope that this second edition will similarly serve as a landmark work to stimulate future developments in research and theory, and that it will fuel continued interest in applied positive psychology. Specifically, my hope is that this edition will reach out not only to those who already identify as positive psychologists, but also to a new and wider audience of scholars and practitioners yet to discover how the ideas and research of positive psychology may transform their ways of working.

As such, the subtitle, *Promoting Human Flourishing in Work, Health, Education, and Everyday Life*, was chosen to make explicit the relevance of this volume to the wider professional audience of leaders, health-care professionals, and educators. I wanted the title to prompt new readers who are less familiar with positive psychology to understand that positive psychology is not a happiology urging us to smile in the face of adversity and to ignore the real problems that confront us all. It is a serious scholarly pursuit to understand the causes and consequences of optimal functioning and their application to real-world issues. Positive psychology can help us manage and succeed in the workplace, deliver better and more compassionate health care, and provide effective and engaging education in ways that optimize achievement, well-being, and the development of community.

Other professionals who are not psychologists will find much that can inform their practice within the domains of business, management, counseling, psychotherapy, economics, the criminal justice system, medical settings, social work, and social and public policy. Positive psychology is not only concerned with one-to-one interventions but is also relevant for individuals, groups, organizations, and societies. This book is an invitation to become part of the future of positive psychology and to help put it into practice.

Chapters are arranged thematically, beginning with an excursion into the history and philosophy of positive psychology, moving through applications in work, health, education, and everyday life, and finally, the directions for the future of positive psychology. But readers will find that there are consistent themes throughout the volume that cut across disciplinary divides; where this is apparent, I have made cross-cutting references to help readers see how the chapters interrelate. I trust that readers will explore the book in ways that best suit them, whether it is moving through it chapter to chapter or jumping from topic to topic as their interest motivates them. Readers new to positive psychology may find my introduction chapter provides a useful summary and map of the book, and they may proceed from there in whichever way they prefer. In this edition, I have also asked all authors to conclude their chapters with a short list of summary points so that readers can see at a glance the practical implications.

This book stands for me as an assertion of the human capacity for growth. It is my hope that academics, practitioners, and students find the learning and wisdom in this book to be of value.

STEPHEN JOSEPH
April, 2014

# Acknowledgments

Editing this book has been a pleasure, in no small part due to my editor Rachel Livsey at John Wiley & Sons and her enthusiasm for the second edition; editorial assistant Amanda Orenstein and senior editorial assistant Melinda Noack for their help and guidance throughout; and the staff at Cape Cod Compositors for making the production process run so smoothly. Thanks also to Kate Hefferon for her advice and to George Burns and Robert Biswas-Diener for their helpful suggestions at the outset. Most of all my thanks to the authors themselves for taking the time to share their expertise and experience and be part of this volume. Finally, my thanks to Barry Joseph and Rosemary McCluskey for their support.

# CHAPTER 1

# Applied Positive Psychology 10 Years On

STEPHEN JOSEPH

THE FIRST EDITION of this handbook was published in 2004. The title of the introduction chapter was "Applied Positive Psychology: A New Perspective for Professional Practice." In that chapter, the authors argued for the need for applied positive psychology. It had only been a few years since positive psychology had first come to widespread attention following Seligman and Csikszentmihalyi's (2000) special issue of the *American Psychologist*. Positive psychology was still a fledgling discipline and scholars were beginning to coalesce around this exciting new idea. Applications of positive psychology were in their infancy.

A decade later, positive psychology is no longer new. The ideas of positive psychology have now firmly taken root within professional psychological practice. In the intervening years, there have been applications in the contexts of work, health, organizations, counseling, and coaching, as well as in professional disciplines outside psychology such as sociology, social work, education, and public policy. There seems little need 10 years on to argue the case for positive psychology. The notion that psychology had focused too much on the alleviation of problems with scant attention to what goes right in life is no longer controversial. It is now widely accepted that it is of equal value to attend to what makes life worth living as it is to what goes wrong, and it is important to look for ways to help people lead lives in which they are happier, have a sense of meaning and purpose, and come closer to fulfilling their potential. These are the aims of positive psychology, which broadly expressed can be said to be "the study of the conditions and processes that contribute to the flourishing or optimal functioning of people, groups, and institutions" (Gable & Haidt, 2005, p. 104).

Since 2004, research output in positive psychology has continued apace, not only in the dedicated journals of positive psychology, well-being, and happiness, but also in the wider literature. Research with a positive psychology emphasis is now regularly published in the journals of social, personality, and clinical psychology, as well as in the flagship journals of the leading professional associations. Many new books have appeared in the intervening years, including major scholarly volumes (e.g., Csikszentmihalyi & Csikszentmihalyi, 2006; David, Boniwell, & Conley-Ayers, 2012; Lopez & Snyder, 2011), an encyclopedia (Lopez, 2009), and introductory level textbooks (e.g., Hefferon & Boniwell, 2011; Peterson, 2006), which demonstrate the breadth of the topic and its appeal.

It is beyond doubt that positive psychology deserves to be a major force in contemporary psychology. Across the globe, there are now dedicated courses in positive psychology as part of the undergraduate curriculum and postgraduate-level courses specializing in positive psychology, and since 2004 a new generation of scholars with doctorates in positive psychology has emerged. Many more scholars and practitioners now identify themselves with positive psychology.

Positive psychology provides a common identity for all scholars and practitioners interested in human flourishing and well-being. Some may identify themselves primarily as positive psychologists, particularly those who have graduated from the new courses over the past decade or gained doctorates in positive psychology topics. For others, positive psychology may be a secondary identity because they view themselves first and foremost as clinical, counseling, developmental, educational, forensic, health, management, occupational, personality, or social psychologists. They may be academics or practitioners, but all share the same concern in what makes for a good life, but in a way that now encompasses the idea that we ought to be interested not only in the alleviation of problems but also the promotion of optimal functioning. For some, positive psychology has been a new way of thinking altogether. For others, it has provided a way to understand and give voice to what it was they always aspired to achieve.

Positive psychology has also attracted interest from the general public eager to find out what the science can contribute to their lives. In the bookstores, positive psychology is well-represented by a number of books written for the general public (e.g., Froh & Bono, 2014; Joseph, 2011; Lyubomirsky, 2008; Seligman, 2011). Unlike many of the traditional areas of psychology, positive psychology has clear and direct applications to everyday life. As human beings, we are motivated to fulfil our potential, function at optimal levels, and achieve a pleasurable and meaningful life. Positive psychology is concerned with how best to support these aspirations in us in ways that are both good for us and those around us.

## THE CONTENT OF THIS VOLUME

Any volume such as this inevitably reflects the interests and biases of its editor. I have endeavored to provide coverage of the range of activity in positive psychology and to maintain the book's cutting-edge appeal. I was also interested in strengthening the historical, theoretical, and philosophical perspectives. There is a famous quote from Kurt Lewin: "There is nothing so practical as a good theory" (Lewin, 1951, p. 169). To me this quote sums up the essential ingredient of good practice. No matter what one's practice specialty, whether it is in coaching, counseling, clinical, or health psychology, the most important thing is to understand how what you do relates to and emerges from theory. There is much that is directly practical in this volume, but it is also a book that is rich in ideas. In this respect, one of the key developments over the past 10 years has been the shift in emphasis from hedonistic well-being to eudaimonic well-being.

The importance of this development of interest in eudaimonia is twofold. First, it has widened the scope of positive psychology so that it is no longer as concerned with happiness in the traditional sense of joy and pleasure but also with the existential concerns of meaning and purpose. This has given positive psychology greater depth and provided a counterbalance to those critics who saw it as little more than happiology. Second, it has allowed positive psychology to build bridges toward humanistic psychology. Initially, positive psychology distanced itself from humanistic psychology. But as positive psychologists have shifted toward a greater appreciation of the eudaimonic perspective, it has become clearer that there is much to be valued in the earlier writings of the humanistic psychologists. As will be clear in this volume, the two disciplines have come closer together, and many of the ideas in humanistic psychology have now become part of the scope of positive psychology. Positive psychologists did not invent the study of well-being. It is now acknowledged that the pioneers of humanistic psychology, such as Maslow (1968) and Rogers (1963), also offered perspectives that were positive psychologies. It is useful to see the links between disciplines and for their forces to combine in creating a better understanding of what makes for a good life. Positive psychology must recognize that its topics of interest date back to humanistic psychology and even beyond to the origins of psychology itself. This has led to deeper philosophical considerations and a more thoughtful and sophisticated approach to what it means to promote human flourishing.

In Part I (Historical and Philosophical Foundations), Hilde Nafstad (Chapter 2) deals with a number of antecedent developments in the history of psychology and science that have informed the development and epistemology of today's positive psychology. Specifically, Nafstad discusses the Aristotelian philosophical position that has attracted increasing attention over the past decade. It is important to understand that practice is always rooted philosophically. Despite a contentious early relationship, the past 10 years have seen much rapprochement between positive psychology and humanistic psychology. Humanistic psychology has long recognized the importance of one's philosophical position. As such, a new chapter from Brent Robbins (Chapter 3) is included that continues this theme of understanding our history, the Aristotelian tradition, and further builds bridges between humanistic and positive psychology. Roger Bretherton deepens this line of enquiry even further in Chapter 4 with an exploration of how positive psychology can learn from existential thinking with its focus on the person's inherent strengths and capacities. Finally, concluding this section is another new chapter by Shifra Sagy, Monica Eriksson, and Orna Braun-Lewensohn (Chapter 5) on Antonovsky's concept of salutogenesis. Most positive psychologists will have heard the term *salutogenesis*, but this is a concept that deserves to be more widely understood than it is, particularly the profound notion that entropy is the natural state of being human.

In Part II (Values and Choices in Pursuit of the Good Life), Tim Kasser (Chapter 6) examines the question of our pursuit of "the good life or the goods life"—that is, psychological satisfaction or material success and its implications for personal and social well-being. Lilach Sagiv, Sonia Roccas, and Shani Oppenheim-Weller (Chapter 7) consider three value pathways to fulfillment, looking specifically at the roles of healthy values, valued goal attainment, and the congruence between our own values and the values supported by our environment. Barry Schwartz (Chapter 8) addresses the paradox of choice, that is, how it can be that more choice is actually bad for us, and suggests ways in which we can act to counter this maladaptive influence. This theme is reflected by Kirk Warren Brown and Richard Ryan (Chapter 9) who discuss developments in self-determination theory and how adopting an attitude of mindfulness can facilitate autonomous thought and behavior that serves to foster more fully informed decisions and intrinsic values and goals with attendant positive psychological outcomes. As already mentioned, one of the key developments in the past 10 years has been the increased attention to Aristotelian philosophy and rapprochement with humanistic psychology. Veronika Huta (Chapter 10) concludes this section with a new discussion of eudaimonic and hedonic pursuits. Huta shows how these ideas are now being taken forward conceptually and empirically, and how specific activities and practices can bring more eudaimonia and hedonia into a person's life.

In Part III (Practices for Health and Well-Being), Kristin Layous, Kennon Sheldon, and Sonja Lyubomirsky (Chapter 11) discuss strategies for achieving sustained gains in happiness and well-being, noting that intentional activities may hold the key to this elusive pursuit. The role of physical activity in promoting both physical and psychological health is discussed by Guy Faulkner, Kate Hefferon, and Nanette Mutrie (Chapter 12), who show that relatively simple and available physical activity strategies can convey substantial benefits for well-being. Ilona Boniwell and Philip Zimbardo (Chapter 13) explore how the way in which we relate to the temporal aspects of our lives influences our choices, intentions, and behaviors, and discuss what we can do to try to achieve a more optimal balanced time perspective. The lesson is that if we choose to, we can do things to facilitate our well-being. Concluding this section are two new chapters by Acacia Parks (Chapter 14) on self-help and Margarita Tarragona (Chapter 15) on life coaching, showing how the ideas of positive psychology can be put into practice in everyday life.

In Part IV (Methods and Processes of Teaching and Learning), Amy Fineburg and Andrew Monk (Chapter 16) show the value of introducing positive psychology to students and the different ways this can be achieved. Alina Reznitskaya and Ian Wilkinson (Chapter 17) build on their chapter in the previous volume with an overview of the dialogical approach to education. Recognizing that education is one of the most important and flourishing areas of application, a new chapter from Chieko Kibe and Ilona Boniwell (Chapter 18) discusses positive education in primary and secondary schools. Finally, concluding this section, Reed Larson and Nickki Dawes (Chapter 19) describe their work in documenting what practices in adult leaders are effective in youth development programs and facilitating motivation of young people.

Part V (Positive Psychology at Work) opens with a new chapter by Sarah Lewis (Chapter 20) on the relationship between organizational psychology and positive psychology. Heather Clarke, Kara Arnold, and Catherine Connelly (Chapter 21) show how transformational leadership can positively affect all levels of an organization, from its employees and culture through to its leaders themselves. The culture and functions of positive and creative organizations are discussed by Jane Henry (Chapter 22), who describes how positive working practices can be fostered from the top down. Carol Kauffman, Stephen Joseph, and Anne Scoular (Chapter 23) review executive coaching through the lens of positive psychology and note the many possibilities for further research in this area.

In Part VI (Health, Clinical, Counseling, and Rehabilitation), John Salsman and Judith Moskowitz (Chapter 24) elaborate on the integration of positive psychology and health psychology, showing how health psychologists have often worked in ways typical of positive psychological practice. James Maddux and Shane Lopez (Chapter 25) critique the dominance of the *DSM* diagnostic system within clinical psychology and provide recommendations for the development and practice of a positive clinical psychology. In a new chapter, Andreas Vossler, Edith Steffen, and Stephen Joseph (Chapter 26) continue this theme within the domain of counseling, showing how counseling psychology can benefit from the theorizing and applications of positive psychology. Finally, concluding this section with another new chapter, Claudio Peter, Szilvia Geyh, Dawn Ehde, Rachel Müller, and Mark Jensen (Chapter 27) consider rehabilitation psychology from the positive psychology perspective.

In Part VII (Contexts of Clinical Practice), Chiara Ruini and Giovanni Fava (Chapter 28) update their review of well-being therapy, a psychotherapeutic approach that aims to facilitate sustainable increases in psychological well-being that go beyond the more traditional focus on just the treatment of presenting psychopathology. Jeana Magyar-Moe and Shane Lopez (Chapter 29) examine the role of hope as an agent of positive change and focus on how hope might be facilitated within the consulting room and beyond. Dealing with the aftermath of trauma and adversity from a positive, growth-oriented perspective is the focus of Richard Tedeschi, Lawrence Calhoun, and Jessica Groleau's chapter (Chapter 30) on posttraumatic growth. Concluding this section is a new chapter by Tayyab Rashid (Chapter 31) on strength-based assessment. Importantly, Rashid opens up discussion on how we can understand distress and dysfunction as the opposite or absence of the positive.

In Part VIII (Inner Resources and Positive Development Across the Life Span), David Caruso, Peter Salovey, Marc Brackett, and John Mayer (Chapter 32) update their review of their work on emotional intelligence and its role in relationships, working environments, education, human resources, and executive coaching. Giacomo Bono, Mikki Krakauer, and Jeffrey Froh (Chapter 33) survey the role of gratitude in practice, demonstrating how it is a character strength reliably related to positive psychological outcomes and good lives in both adults and young people. Ute Kunzmann and Stefanie Thomas (Chapter 34) describe their work on the emotional-motivational side of wisdom. Concluding this section, George Vaillant (Chapter 35) moves the focus toward the end of life with his analysis of what constitutes and facilitates positive aging—factors that are pertinent and applicable throughout the life span.

In Part IX (Building Community Through Integration and Regeneration), Antonella Delle Fave, Andrea Fianco, and Raffaela Sartori (Chapter 36) look at the role of optimal experiences in adjusting to and living with disability and the role of caregivers, demonstrating that to be disabled in no way represents the end of opportunities for optimal living. Clare-Ann Fortune, Tony Ward, and Ruth Mann (Chapter 37) address positive treatment approaches with sex offenders, conveying how interventions that respect them as individuals lead to improved treatment compliance and lower recidivism. Frank Fincham (Chapter 38) explores the role of forgiveness at group and community levels, offering a range of ways in which forgiveness can be facilitated to promote group and community healing and integration. Two new chapters end this section on how positive psychology is relevant to professional practices in the community; the first by Rachel Dekel and Orit Taubman–Ben-Ari (Chapter 39) on social work, and the second by Sandra Resnick and Meaghan Leddy (Chapter 40) on the recovery movement.

In Part X (Public Policy and Systems for Resilience and Social Planning), David Myers (Chapter 41) explores the tension between individualism and community in facilitating good human connections and the attendant implications for public policy. Ruut Veenhoven (Chapter 42) outlines and debunks the objections to the greatest happiness principle, showing that greater happiness for people is a legitimate and achievable public policy aim. In a new chapter, Neil Thin (Chapter 43) discusses social planning. Finally, Tuppett Yates, Fanita Tyrell, and Ann Masten (Chapter 44) explore the role of resilience theory in the practice of positive psychology and the need for a systems-based approach.

Finally, in Part XI (Signposts for the Practice of Positive Psychology), two new chapters introduce signposts for the future. Kate Hefferon (Chapter 45) discusses the need for positive psychology to pay much greater attention to the fact of our embodiment as human beings. Brian Pauwels (Chapter 46) discusses what is meant by the term *positive* in positive psychology and its relation with the negative. Finally, Stephen Joseph (Chapter 47) concludes the volume by reviewing some of the key issues and implications facing applied positive psychology.

The sections of the book organize the chapters in a coherent way and provide structure, but there are also consistent themes throughout the book that cut across the sections and contexts of application. Practitioners of all persuasions will find riches in the sections on values and choices and on lifestyle practices.

This volume promises to be a valuable resource in the further development and evolution of applied positive psychology and in bringing it to the attention of new scholars and practitioners. In doing so, it is my hope that we will move closer to the vision that one day all psychologists will embrace the idea of positive psychology. Finally, it has been my great pleasure to work with these authors in the development of this volume, and I hope you will enjoy reading it and will learn as much as I have learned in its preparation.

## REFERENCES

Csikszentmihalyi, M., & Csikszentmihalyi, I. S. (Eds.). (2006). *A life worth living: Contributions to positive psychology.* New York, NY: Oxford University Press.

David, S., Boniwell, I., & Conley-Ayers, A. (Eds.). (2012). *Oxford handbook of happiness.* Oxford, England: Oxford University Press.

Froh, J., & Bono, G. (2014). *Making grateful kids: The science of building character.* New York, NY: Templeton Press.

Gable, S. L., & Haidt, J. (2005). What (and why) is positive psychology? *Review of General Psychology, 9,* 103–110.

Hefferon, K., & Boniwell, I. (2011). *Positive psychology: Theory, research and applications.* Berkshire, England: Open University Press.

Joseph, S. (2011). *What doesn't kill us: The new psychology of posttraumatic growth.* New York, NY: Basic Books.

Lewin, K. (1951). *Field theory in social science: Selected theoretical papers.* New York, NY: Harper & Row.

Lopez, S. J. (Ed.). (2009). *The encyclopedia of positive psychology.* New York, NY: Wiley-Blackwell.

Lopez, S. J., & Snyder, C. R. (Eds.). (2011). *The Oxford handbook of positive psychology* (2nd ed.). New York, NY: Oxford University Press.

Lyubomirsky, S. (2008). *The how of happiness: A practical guide to getting the life you want.* New York, NY: Penguin Press.

Maslow, A. H. (1968). *Toward a psychology of being* (2nd ed.). New York, NY: Van Nostrand Reinhold.

Peterson, C. (2006). *A primer in positive psychology.* New York, NY: Oxford University Press.

Rogers, C. R. (1963). The concept of the fully functioning person. *Psychotherapy: Theory, Research and Practice, 1,* 17–26.

Seligman, M. E. P. (2011). *Flourish: A new understanding of happiness and well-being—and how to achieve them.* London, England: Nicholas Brealey.

Seligman, M. E. P., & Csikszentmihalyi, M. (2000). Positive psychology: An introduction. *American Psychologist, 55,* 5–14.

PART I

# HISTORICAL AND PHILOSOPHICAL FOUNDATIONS

# Historical, Philosophical, and Epistemological Perspectives

HILDE EILEEN NAFSTAD

T HE PURPOSE OF RESEARCH, the renowned experimental social psychologist McGuire (2004) argued in one of his influential articles on epistemology, is to discover "which are the crucial perspectives," not whether one hypothesis or theory is true or false, as "all hypotheses and theories are true, as all are false, *depending on the perspective* from which they are viewed" (p. 173; italics added). For a long time, mainstream psychology has neglected and down-prioritized discussions of paradigms—paradigms that stake out perspectives and development of theories within the different fields of research and practice. Neither has mainstream psychology been spending much effort on the important issue of how and to what extent the a priori assumptions and values in psychological research and theory are interwoven with prevailing and predominant values and ideologies in the culture and society at large. Condor (1997) critically maintained that contemporary psychology in fact too often considered its positions as "indisputable universally true facts" (p. 136). Not to discuss horizons and perspectives is a detrimental state, in particular in our time when scientific psychological knowledge for many people in various cultures constitutes a considerable part of their meaning structure of what it implies to be a human being (Miller, 1999; Nafstad, 2002, 2005; Slife, Reber, & Richardson, 2005). Critical reflection over psychology's a priori assumptions, positions, values, norms, and perspectives should constitute a highly prioritized area within research. Slife and Williams (1997) expressed the necessity or value of such analyses: "The essence of the discussion would be a careful clarification of the issues involved, along with an evaluation of outcomes and consequences, pragmatic as well as rational and moral" (p. 121).

Positive psychology started as a protest against some of the predominant taken-for-granted assumptions in mainstream psychology. Seligman and Csikszentmihalyi (2000) critically maintained that contemporary psychology gives priority to a conception of human beings that to too great a degree is based on pathology, faults, and dysfunctions—that is, a medically oriented psychology. Other horizons than those that focus on lacks, dysfunctions, and crises have been given little possibility to direct and form contemporary (clinical) research and practice. The ideology of illness is thus a priori given priority within today's psychology. Positive psychology's aim is to be an important corrective, and it demands of predominant mainstream psychology not to continue to marginalize or exclude, but bring in again and revitalize the positive aspects of human nature: *Positive subjective experiences, positive individual traits,* and *civic virtues* (Seligman & Csikszentmihalyi, 2000). Rather than taking the medically oriented model as given, the human being should, as Seligman and Csikszentmihalyi (2000) maintain, be conceptualized and understood as a being with inherent potentials for developing positive character traits or virtues.

Seligman (2002a) formulated what became the basic assumptions of positive psychology:

- That there is a human "nature."
- That action proceeds from character.
- That character comes in two forms, both equally fundamental—bad character and good virtuous (*angelic*) character. (p. 125)

Seligman (2002a), moreover, asserted the following about the current status of these assumptions in mainstream psychology:

Because all of these assumptions have almost disappeared from the psychology of the 20th century, the story of their rise and fall is the backdrop for my renewing the notion of good character as a core assumption of positive psychology. (p. 125)

Positive psychology thus aimed at renewing the perspective of the human being. Seligman (2002a) also argued positive psychology's perspective by claiming that "Any science that does not use character as a basic idea (or at least explain character and choice away successfully) will never be accepted as a useful account of human behavior" (p. 128).

Formally launched in the millennium issue of *American Psychologist* (edited by Seligman & Csikszentmihalyi, 2000) the movement of positive psychology offered and encouraged necessary discussions and analyses of assumptions and perspectives taken for granted within mainstream psychology. As Csikszentmihalyi and Nakamura (2011) a decade later in retrospect formulated this protest against assumptions, there were discussions of what "should be done to redress the imbalance between negative and positive perspectives in psychology" (p. 5). However, these discussions were most probably not undertaken only as a potential enrichment for psychology in general. To develop positive psychology as a scientific field, it was a mandatory task to systematically discover which are the crucial perspectives for positive psychology, that is, which are the perspectives and theories that cannot be neglected or dismissed in shaping and forming this new field of psychology.

In our chapter in the original edition of *Positive Psychology in Practice* (Jørgensen & Nafstad, 2004), we reflected on historical, philosophical, and epistemological roots of this new movement. In the present chapter, I draw upon this analysis because the major historical roots for positive psychology are evidently still the same. However, for almost 15 years now, positive psychology has moved on and constitutes a vital, active, powerful, and influential field of research within psychology. Therefore, this chapter also considers aspects of positive psychology in this new phase, often contrasting positive and mainstream psychology to more clearly illuminate the foundations, horizons, and values of positive psychology.

## THE AGENDA OF POSITIVE PSYCHOLOGY

Multiple paradigms and multiple theories within each of the paradigms give positive psychology an array of horizons and assumptions from which to protest. At the Akumal 1 meeting in January 1999, a manifesto for positive psychology was formulated. Here it was stated that "Positive psychology is the scientific study of optimal functioning. It aims to discover and promote the factors that allow individuals and communities to thrive" (Sheldon, Fredrickson, Rathumnde, Csikszentmihalyi, & Haidt, 1999, p. 1). The manifesto, moreover, stated that positive psychology "must consider optimal functioning at multiple levels, including biological, experiential, personal, relational, institutional, cultural, and global" (Sheldon et al., 1999, p. 1).

The first *Handbook of Positive Psychology* (Seligman, 2002b) gives a more comprehensive definition:

We have discovered that there are human strengths that act as buffers against mental illness: courage, future-mindedness, optimism, interpersonal skill, faith, work ethic, hope, honesty, perseverance, the capacity for flow and insight, to name several. Much of the task of prevention in this new century will be *to create a science of human strength* whose mission will be to understand and learn how to foster these virtues in young people. (p. 5; italics added)

Furthermore, Seligman (2002b) underlines, "We now need to call for massive research on human strength and virtue" (p. 5). And he concludes, "We need to do the appropriate longitudinal studies and experiments to understand how these strengths grow (or are stunted; Vaillant, 2000). We need to develop and test interventions to build these strengths" (Seligman, 2002b, p. 5). That positive psychology was launched as a protest against some of the predominant taken-for-granted assumptions in mainstream psychology is clearly reflected in the introductory sentence in Seligman's (2002b) article, where he points out:

Psychology after World War II became a clinical psychology largely devoted to healing. It concentrated on repairing damage using a disease model of human functioning. This almost exclusive attention to pathology neglected the idea of a fulfilled individual and a thriving community, and it neglected the possibility that building strength is the most potent weapon in the arsenal of therapy. (p. 3)

Maddux (2002) corroborated this corrective protest when he pointed out that mainstream psychology was not aware of how "powerful sociocultural, political, professional, and economic forces built the illness ideology and the *DSM* and continue to sustain them" (p. 15; see also Maddux & Lopez, Chapter 25, this volume). With this approach and research agenda of optimal functioning and human strengths and virtues, positive psychology placed itself clearly within an Aristotelian approach to human development (Jørgensen & Nafstad, 2004). To understand the science and movement of positive psychology, therefore, I will also start this time by looking through Aristotle's model of human nature and development. As Waterman (2013a) concludes on the basis of his analysis of positive psychology's and humanistic psychology's respective philosophical foundations, Aristotle is the philosopher "most consistently cited in the writings of positive psychologists" (p. 126; see also Robbins, Chapter 3, this volume).

## POSITIVE PSYCHOLOGY AND THE ARISTOTELIAN FOUNDATION

The most fundamental assumption about human nature and functioning from the Aristotelian perspective is the teleological idea that human life and human well-being consist in nature-fulfillment and the human being as inwardly driven by a dynamic of ever more optimal functioning. Within the Aristotelian model, with its four causal factors (*causa materialis, causa formalis, causa efficiens*, and *causa finalis*), *growth* or *change* becomes the fundamental dimension of the object or phenomenon. The human being is thus understood as a being constantly driven forward by a dynamic principle toward what is better or more perfect. In Book I of the *Nicomachean Ethics*, Aristotle (trans. 2000) clarifies his optimal functioning or perfectionism concept: "Every craft and every line of inquiry, and likewise every action and decision, seems to seek some good; that is why some people were right to describe the good as what everything seeks" (Morgan, 2001, p. 195). Thus the Aristotelian frame of understanding represents a perspective of a core human nature in which change toward something good, better, or more perfect comprises the fundamental aspect. The good is what everything strives toward. The individual is hence a being who will introduce positive goals and values and strive to realize and reach them. The Aristotelian model then takes into account teleological goals: the individual as a being that lives a life in which thoughts and ideas about future positive goals—not only present and past—also influence the direction of actions here and now.

The Aristotelian model introduces a distinction between the individual's *possibilities* or *potentials* on the one hand, and the individual's *factual* characteristics or *realization* of these potentials on the other hand. In fact, Aristotle's entire metaphysics and psychology are elaborated "from a developmental perspective in which the concepts of potentiality and actuality are fundamental" (Bernstein, 1986, p. 2). The individual is, moreover, according to Aristotle, a being who is characterized by experiencing joy when exercising his or her inherent or acquired abilities and is striving toward realizing them in ways that are experienced as better, more complex, or more perfect. As the philosopher Rawls (1976) states about this strongly positive motivational dynamic principle of human beings that Aristotle formulated, "The Aristotelian Principle runs as follows: other things equal, human beings enjoy the exercise of their realized capacities (their innate or trained abilities), and this enjoyment increases the more the capacity is realized, or the greater the complexity" (p. 426). The Aristotelian model then holds that we will be happy when fulfilling our destiny as good humans and it is the *process* of exercising itself that is central to the experience of enjoyment. Furthermore, Aristotle's idea is that one should habituate people to realization of their positive virtues in more perfect or complex ways, with the purpose that moral goodness becomes almost instinctive.

Positive psychology is clearly inspired by the Aristotelian model of human nature: To grow, improve, and function optimally is for positive psychology a fundamental or core concept. Positive psychology also strongly draws on the concept of exercise and practice. As Seligman and Csikszentmihalyi (2000) adopt and reformulate this Aristotelian view on joy and exercise:

> Enjoyment, on the other hand, refers to the good feelings people experience when they break through the limits of homeostasis—when they do something that stretches them beyond what they were—in an athletic event, an artistic performance, a good deed, a stimulating conversation. Enjoyment, rather than pleasure, is what leads to personal growth and long-term happiness. (p. 12)

Within (developmental) psychology there are three types of theories explaining human development. First, endogenous or essential theories—such as the Aristotelian—describe and explain development as predominantly a result of internal influences. The emphasis is on the organism's internal nature and the theory locates change and development mechanisms within the internal component of the organism (software/blueprint for growth, hereditary plan, etc.). Second, there are theories anchored in the exogenous paradigm that explain development as a result of specific environmental factors external to the individual or organism. The third type, constructivist theories, rather than arguing development as being either innately or environmentally determined, view development as a synthesis of progressive organizations and reorganizations constructed, formed, and shaped in the process of the human individual adapting to and interacting with the external world (Green & Piel, 2002).

As now shown, positive psychology clearly adopts and revitalizes an Aristotelian frame of reference and argues that the science of psychology should once again include assumptions about the essence-driven motivation toward something better—that is, more optimal functioning. In accordance with the Aristotelian root—an essential or endogenous developmental theory—positive psychology, moreover, as a consequence takes as its point of departure that the human being is "preprogrammed" with moral "software" of justice, courage, fairness, and so on. The Aristotelian model—an essentialist theory—holds that development of any organism, including human beings, is the unfolding of natural, fixed, or innate potentialities. Within the Aristotelian model of development, therefore, there is a right, optimal, or perfect functioning that is teleologically fixed as the realization of innate patterns of growth. The Aristotelian model, moreover, clearly underlines how the developmental process of fulfilling human nature results in well-being. Or as Haybron (2008) points out, "In broad terms, Aristotelian theories identify well-being with 'well-functioning,' which is to say functioning or living well as a human being: the fulfillment of nature" (p. 35). The Aristotelian approach is, as Haybron (2008) formulates it, "The teleological idea that well-being consists in *nature fulfillment*" (p. 35; italics in the original). Dynamic teleological determinism is thereby, as shown, concerned with describing and explaining where the organism is going rather than where it has come from (Hopkins & Butterworth, 1990).

For positive psychology, in congruence with the Aristotelian model, goodness and morality thus do not come from outside the person. They do not arise from cultural sources or from the moral rules of society, but from the potentials of the human being him- or herself. Aristotle also claims that "none of the virtues of character arise in us naturally. . . . Rather we are by nature able to acquire them, and we are completed through habit" (Morgan, 2001, p. 206). Thus, it is up to the individual to realize his or her full potential. Positive psychology also argues that strengths and virtues can be and must be cultivated, and their development and realization is the route to happiness and well-being (Peterson, Ruch, Beermann, Park, & Seligman, 2007; Ryff & Singer, 2006; Seligman, 2002b; Waterman, 2013b). As a consequence, a most particular aim for positive psychology is to develop and test interventions to build these strengths (Seligman, 2002b; Wong, 2006).

As shown, the Aristotelian model focuses on the virtuous individual and those inner traits, dispositions, and motives that qualify the individual to be virtuous. Within the Aristotelian model, the virtues of the soul are of two sorts: virtue of thought and virtue of character. "Virtue of thought arises and grows mostly from teaching; that is why it needs experience and time. Virtue of character (i.e., of *ethos*) results from habit (ethos)" (Morgan, 2001, pp. 205–206). Hence it is also clear, as

Aristotle states, that both types of virtues have to be cultivated—"none of the virtues of character arise in us naturally" (Morgan, 2001, p. 206). The topic of intellectual activities, giftedness, creativity, and exceptional cognitive performance is central to positive psychology. But equally important, as now shown, positive psychology stresses that there are virtues of a different kind: The concept of *good character* constitutes one of the other conceptual cornerstones of positive psychology. In the course of past decades, ethical theory in philosophy has focused increasingly on the assumption of the individual as having virtuous motives (Baron, Petit, & Slote, 1997) and positive psychology tries to revitalize this idea of human nature. Positive psychology, wisdom, courage, humanity, gratitude, justice, temperance, and transcendence, for example, are categories of virtue that are postulated to be universal virtues (Dahlsgaard, Peterson, & Seligman, 2001; Emmons & McCullough, 2004; Peterson & Seligman, 2004; Seligman, 2002b).

To sum up, by placing itself clearly within the Aristotelian model, positive psychology argues the view of the good person; the idea of the individual with a positive character, strengths, and given virtues; and the idea of the basic distinction between "man as he happens to be" and "man as he could be if he realized his essential nature" (MacIntyre, 1984, p. 52). As shown, the Aristotelian model also combines realizing human teleos and happiness: "Since happiness is a certain sort of activity of the social in accord with complete virtue, we must examine virtue, for that will perhaps also be a way to study happiness better" (Morgan, 2001, p. 204). These ideas of a common core nature for all human beings and continuous development and realization of these human potentials as the source of well-being and happiness constitute the central agenda for positive psychology.

Teleological determinism, which relates to the Aristotelian idea of final cause, strongly argues a preprogrammed directiveness to human development. However, notions or ideas of ideal teleos are in the end created and formed in a subtle interplay with values and ideals in society. We will later come back to this issue.

## THE PLACE OF SOCIAL AND MORAL MOTIVATION WITHIN POSITIVE PSYCHOLOGY

Positive psychology articulates the presumptions of the Aristotelian approach to human nature and development, and this includes the view of the good person—the idea of the individual with a positive character, strengths, and given virtues. The basic starting point for positive psychology then is that the human being has given dynamic potentials for positive virtues or character.

Science may, in many ways, be considered what the philosophically and ecologically oriented psychologist Howard (1985) terms a "witch's caldron" in which different a priori starting points, values, axioms, and basic assumptions, as well as different concrete theories, "boil" and vie for dominance. Every position and concrete theory thus wishes to become the one recognized, the one accepted as the truth and an expression of reality. Another more systematic way to explicate positive psychology's assumptions and foundations is therefore to ask what kind of theories of human motivations mainstream psychology puts into the "witch's caldron" as compared with the questions that positive psychology raises.

The concept of relationship is one of the most used in psychology and the social sciences. As Noam and Fischer (1996) point out, "Many of the most important classic works in social science, including psychology and philosophy, have recognized the foundational role of relationships" (p. ix). Social relationships thus comprise one of today's most central concepts in analyses of human motivation and the individual as a social and moral being. It is therefore natural to go to the huge field of social relationships where social motivation and human morality are core issues to more systematically answer this question of human motivation.

Fiske (1992) maintains, concerning today's situation in mainstream psychology about social relationships and human social motivation:

> From Freud to contemporary sociobiologists, from Skinner to social cognitionists, from Goffman to game theorists, the prevailing assumption in Western psychology has been that humans are by nature asocial individualists. Psychologists (and most other social scientists) then usually explain social relationships as instrumental means to extrinsic, non-social ends, or as constraints on the satisfaction of individual desires. (p. 689)

And van Lange (2000) points out,

> Within the domain of psychological theory, this assumption of rational self-interest is embedded in several key constructs, such as reinforcement, the pursuit of pleasure, utility maximization (as developed in the context of behavioristic theory, including social learning theory), psychoanalytic theory, and theories of social decision making. (p. 299)

Nafstad (2002) concludes, "Fundamentally viewed, within mainstream psychology, the person has thus one goal for own actions also in social relations: Consideration for oneself" (p. 6). This goal or teleos for human development represents, therefore, an integral component of today's Western motivation theories and thereby also theories of morality. As this shows, in mainstream psychology as well as in the other social sciences, the axiomatic postulate of human beings as asocial and egoistic individuals is the prioritized and tacitly taken-for-granted perspective.

Within contemporary psychology and the other social sciences, the individual is thus often a priori limited to being constantly motivated by consuming the social and material world, with the goal of attaining the best possible benefits for him- or herself. To keep order in a society made up of individuals who are strongly motivated by individual desires, hedonism, and consumption, society needs norms and rules of morality. Without such moral rules or social norms, the individual as acting subject would not give any consideration to others as long as this might be unpleasant and affect his or her own comfort negatively. It was the English philosopher Thomas Hobbes (1651) who was first to argue in favor of such a view of human nature, a position that has predominated modern psychology's view of human motivation. The Greek philosophy that prevailed before Hobbes, however, held the view that human beings were positive and fundamentally social by nature. Hobbes launched the doctrine that maintained that human beings were basically bad, and not much may be done about it. Thus morality cannot be anything but social contracts between self-seeking, hedonistic, and ruthless human beings. Morality therefore became the same as obedience to law. This is a deeply negative view of human nature—a human nature without given positive virtue potentials.

The doctrine opposed to that of Hobbes, the view that human beings are born as moral beings with a dynamic potential for goodness, was proposed by Rousseau (1762). Within psychology, Spencer (1870, 1872) and McDougall (1908, 1932) around the turn of the previous century also attempted to oppose this predominating negative position of psychological egoism and hedonism within psychology. McDougall (1908) argued in fact that human beings have an empathic instinct. However, this view did not gain approval. According to mainstream psychology at that time as well as today, the individual has only one motivation system (Darley, 1991; Nafstad, 2002, 2004). *Self-interest* is regarded as the primary and true motivation, the one from which other motives, including moral and social ones, derive. Thus human beings as simply pleasure-pain organisms is modern psychology's predominant assumption about human motivation, from which a variety of different more negative self-interest motivation theories have been developed (Dovidio, Piliavin, Schroeder, & Penner, 2006). Within social and developmental psychology, however, there has been research on prosocial behavior, opening the way for more complex motivation systems (Batson, 1991; Batson, Ahmad, Lishner, & Tsang, 2002; Eisenberg, 1982, 1986; Hoffman, 1975, 2000; for a review, see Mikulincer & Shaver, 2010). In fact, in 1751, the philosopher Hume suggested that sympathy and empathy play a major role in altruistic or sympathetic behavior. The modern philosopher Blum (1980) also strongly argued this perspective that altruistic behavior is often motivated by altruistic emotions such as compassion or sympathy. Furthermore, modern humanistic and existential personality theorists took as their point of departure that the human nature is basically benign (Frankl, 1967; Maslow, 1954; May, 1966; Rogers, 1961).

Adopting an Aristotelian perspective, positive psychology clearly opposes mainstream psychology's predominant negative assumption of human motivational nature. Positive psychology takes as its starting point that the individual is a socially and morally motivated being. Seligman (2002a) argued this position very strongly: "Current dogma may say that negative motivation is fundamental to human nature and positive motivation merely derives from it, but I have not seen a shred of evidence that compels us to believe this" (p. 211). As Seligman (2002a) formulates this claim of an alternative to the "witch's caldron" about the human being as a social and moral individual: "This unpacks the meaning of the claim that human beings are moral animals" (p. 133). In addition, positive psychology underlines that humans have capacity for both good and evil: "Evolution has selected both sorts of traits, and any number of niches support morality, cooperation, altruism, and goodness, just as any number support murder, theft, self-seeking, and badness" (p. 211).

By taking the standpoint that humans are fundamentally social and moral, positive psychology again places itself clearly in the midst of the Greek tradition and virtue ethics. In Greek philosophy, the individual was not considered to be an enough-unto-itself-being, an individual concerned only with taking care of his or her own interests. Goods, resources, and advantages, Aristotle maintained (Barnes, 1984), were not the property of individuals to such a great degree as is implied in our social time and culture. Within the Aristotelian frame of reference, the person who acts egoistically is making a fundamental error, which in practice excludes the person from social relationships and therefore also from well-being and the good life. Social relationships were concerned with sharing, giving, and taking care of others (Vetlesen, 1994). Within the Aristotelian frame of understanding, a friendship was a relationship of equality and mutuality, not a "one-way affair" (Vetlesen & Nortvedt, 2000) in which other people are considered a means for gain or becoming better off. As Vetlesen and Nortvedt (2000) described the social relationship of friendship within the Aristotelian approach, "Friendship is inseparable from sharing with the other and reciprocating the feelings received" (p. 23). Within the Aristotelian model, the individual thus has both characteristics that serve to preserve his own welfare, as well as *civic virtues* that are concerned with preserving the welfare of others. Central to Aristotle's philosophy of human nature, therefore, is that there is a human core nature that entails positive relations and communal responsibility. Building on the Aristotelian model, positive psychology today revitalizes within psychology the very idea of the moral and good motivated human being and the idea of the individual also being a good citizen. Thus positive psychology clearly adopts and revitalizes this Aristotelian frame of reference for our time and argues that the science of psychology should once again include assumptions about the good or essence-driven motivation and the good person within its core assumptions of what a human being is.

For positive psychology, in congruence with the Aristotelian model, goodness and morality, to sum up, do not come from outside the person. They do not arise from cultural sources or from the moral rules of society, but from the potentials of the human being him- or herself. Positive psychology, in accordance with the Aristotelian root, takes as its point of departure that the human being is "preprogrammed" with moral "software" of justice, courage, fairness, and so on. Aristotle claims, however, that "none of the virtues of character arise in us naturally. . . . Rather we are by nature able to acquire them, and we are completed through habit" (Morgan, 2001, p. 206). As Vetlesen (1994) formulates this Aristotelian view of human nature, "It is only through such an ongoing process of education and habituation that the individual acquires the virtues" (p. 30). Thus, it is up to the individual to realize his or her full potential. People have an inherent capacity for constructive growth, for kindness, generosity, and so on. But it needs to be continuously exercised. To use Seligman's (2002b) concept, "fostering these virtues" (p. 5) is therefore a central aim for positive psychology. Strength interventions and strength therapy are also one of the central parts of positive psychology's research and applied agenda today (Linley & Joseph, 2004; Wong, 2006).

## POSITIVE PSYCHOLOGY AND THE UNIVERSALISTIC PERSPECTIVE

Positive psychology and the Aristotelian model, with its teleological determinism, is an endogenous theory and, as mentioned, inevitably faces a challenge when answering what is better, more optimal, more excellent. It can be argued that against all definitions of goals and teleos, critical objections may be raised: Notions or ideas about ideal teleos are in the end inevitably created and formed in a subtle interplay between the values and ideals in society, the social and cultural conditions within which the researcher in question works, as well as the traditions of the discipline (Baumrind, 1982; Bruner, 1986; Cirillo & Wapner, 1986). Maintaining and giving priority to certain developmental goals and not others will thus be an expression of the predominant values and power structures of the culture and time period in question (Bruner, 1986; Cirillo & Wapner, 1986; Foucault, 1972, 1980; Gergen, 1989, 1991). Seligman (2002a) also argues that "fully functioning" is a culture-bound concept.

Humans are born into a sociocultural world defining and valuing what is important in life (Bronfenbrenner, 1979). In fact, the concept of optimal or "fully" functioning must be defined and analyzed in terms of five elements or dimensions: *motivation, action, goals, physical and psychological context,* and *(social) time.* So far, optimal functioning has been discussed from a motivation, action, and goal perspective. But physical and psychological context and (social) time also have to be part of the analysis. Hence, when conceptualizing in terms of what is optimal, good or bad, wise or not wise, noble or ignoble, admirable or deplorable, positive psychology must decide how to deal with the influences of culture and social or historical time. In the end, in fact, almost all discussions about approaches and paradigms in psychology are related in some way or another to this theme of the individual, history, social context(s), and/or the interaction between them (Bronfenbrenner, 1979, 1992; Lewin, 1935; Petti-grew, 1997; Walsh, Craik, & Price, 1992). Thus, a most crucial question for psychology throughout its history has been: Where are the defining and stabilizing forces of indi-vidual functioning to be found? Mostly in the individual? Primarily in the contexts? Or in the interactions between them? Within psychology there are three types of the-ories offering different approaches and answers to this question: the endogenous, the exogenous, and the constructive theories. How universalistic then is positive psychol-ogy's approach? Or formulated differently, because endogenous theories emphasize environment differently, is positive psychology arguing in favor of a strong or a more "soft" universal psychology?

Let us once more start our analysis by examining Aristotle's position. Aristotle argues that when we travel and meet people in different cultures, we nevertheless "can see how *every human being* is akin and beloved to a human being" (Morgan, 2001, p. 268; italics added). Aristotle thus argues the position of common human features in different cultural groups. Parts of psychology and other social sciences have always taken as a starting point that people in the past, present, and future have some given common capacities or characteristics. Furthermore, it has been assumed that *existing* and *adapting* are experiences that also give common characteristics and similarities (see Darwin, 1859). The task then becomes to describe validly that which is common or universal to human beings. Within such a universalist approach, groups of peo-ple are thus compared in order to illuminate aspects of the assumed common and homogeneous core. As Rohner (1975) formulated the universalist position, "The uni-versalist approach asks about the nature of human nature, or, more specifically, about researchable features of 'human nature'" (p. 2).

Within psychology and the other social sciences, however, researchers have also adopted a fundamentally different point of departure on the human being: Every individual, every society is unique and different from all others. This assumption, the *idiographic tradition*, takes its principal arguments from, among others, Kierkegaard's philosophy. Kierkegaard's (1843/1962, 1846/1968) philosophy did indeed represent a protest against the philosophy of his time, which was concerned only with what was common to all human beings. Kierkegaard's idea was, on the contrary, that it is the individual, the single person, who must be the frame of reference. Moreover, the individual as he or she exists and lives is more than the universal human being. The individual is thus a uniquely existing being. Consequently, it is not the species of mankind, but the single individual with whom we should be concerned. When one studies human life and development, one must start with the individual or the person. All human beings are committed to their subjective truths, and it is always only the single individual who acts.

The idiographic position, with the idea of uniquely subjective experience as the basis of human actions, thus constitutes another important and central approach within psychological research. The influential psychologist Gordon Allport was the first to be associated with this debate between nomothetic versus idiographic approaches within psychology. Allport (1937/1961, 1946, 1960) maintained that both perspectives were legitimate, but that an idiographic basis was to be preferred in studies of personality. As Allport (1937/1961) formulated his position of the human person, "He is more than a representative of his species, more than a citizen, more than an incident in the movements of mankind. He transcends them all" (p. 573).

Eysenck (1947, 1955, 1956, 1967) held, on the other hand, the opposite standpoint: Personality psychology, too, must be nomothetically oriented. Thus the debate between a nomothetic versus idiographic approach in psychology was primarily raised in the field of personality psychology.

Within anthropology, the unique or radical relativistic approach has maintained that no cultures are alike. Consequently, it is not possible to make generalizations. Hypotheses about cross-cultural or universal similarities and possible common claims of cause and effect are impossible (Benedict, 1934, 1946). Each culture must be considered as a unique configuration and may only be understood in its totality. A cultural element has no meaning except in its context. The single elements may be understood, and can only be understood, within the network of interpretations that the culture itself represents. The task of seeking what is common is thus meaningless. All cultures are special and unique. Nomothetically oriented psychology and social science consequently represent an impossible idea.

Within contemporary philosophy and psychology there are also many who argue that it is difficult or impossible to hold on to this idea of human nature having any such common core potentials (Bruner, 1986, 1990; Gergen, 1991, 1994; Kvale, 1992; Shotter & Gergen, 1989). The Aristotelian idea that the human being is "preprogrammed" with a personal and moral "software" of justice, wisdom, and so on, and that such dispositions are up to the individual to realize, is according to these scholars not at all reasonable. Gergen (1982, 1994) therefore argues in favor of a psychology concerned with understanding and attempting to account for social processes in terms of social contexts and social and historical time, which create and fill a culture's concepts, for example, the concepts of human nature, the nature of human motivation, our personality or our self, and so on. Each culture thus creates at all times its own content of truth as to what human nature and good life contains. The descriptions and concepts that psychology has at its disposal must not then be understood as anything but what they indeed are: cultural and historical objects. Every culture and every historical epoch creates its discourses, its forms of understanding, and its truths; for example, about the concept of human nature and human virtues, and motivation. The nomenclature of psychology is thus not given its content through some form of more independent reality about how human nature "really" is. Consequently, the task of seeking the common virtuous being, what is common and similar among individuals, is not meaningful. Every culture will create its own content of meaning as to what human nature is. Human nature, virtues, and individuality are thus created by the prevailing concrete cultural patterns. People must adapt to, maintain, and reproduce this pattern of cultural values and images about what human nature and personality are and should be.

Thus, the historical-cultural approach argued by the social constructivists (e.g., Cushman, 1990; Gergen, 1989, 1994; Kvale, 1992; Shotter & Gergen, 1989) maintains that it is not a meaningful research issue to seek what is universal, common, and similar. The idea of ordered development, for example from the simple to the more complex and excellent (Werner, 1926/1957a, 1957b), therefore is rejected as being a typical idea from the romantic and humanistic tradition in Western culture. And what would be, in any case, better or more perfect functioning?

Positive psychology argues, in the same way as Aristotle, that there are some common dimensions or dispositions in core human nature. However, this does not imply that positive psychology does not accept the idea that human nature also is a product of history and cultural environment. As Seligman and Csikszentmihalyi (2001) contended, "We are acutely aware that what one considers positive is, in part, a function of one's particular ethnic tradition and social condition" (p. 90). However, Seligman and Csikszentmihalyi (2001) also stressed that:

> We believe that our common humanity is strong enough to suggest psychological goals to strive for that cut across social and cultural divides. Just as physical health, adequate nutrition, and freedom from harm and exploitation are universally valued, so must psychologists ultimately aim to understand the positive states, traits, and institutions that all cultures value. (p. 90)

Going back to the Aristotelian position, Seligman and Csikszentmihalyi (2001) thus take as given and embrace the Aristotelian basic position that (a) "what I strive toward as an individual is the perfection of what it means to be a man" (Vetlesen, 1994, p. 30), and (b) what is good for me as a unique person is what is good for humans as universal beings. As a consequence, social practices for positive psychology will be compared to and evaluated in the light of a core human nature of virtues that may, and should, be developed and realized. We might therefore conclude that positive psychology does not only revitalize the Aristotelian idea of the positive individual, but also the view of a more universal individual. Positive psychology then takes as point of departure that it is possible to compare psychological constructs across cultures, and most of positive psychology's ongoing studies are cross-cultural, not studies of one particular culture (Gelfand, Chiu, & Hong, 2011). For example, currently there exists within positive psychology a huge body of cross-cultural research analyzing the meaning and value of happiness across the world (Delle Fave, 2013; Delle Fave, Brdar, Freire, Vella-Brodrick, & Wissing, 2011; Selin & Davey, 2012; Veenhoven, 2010). A prioritized approach to the concept of happiness within positive psychology, therefore, is the position that people in one way or another seek happiness. However, what constitutes happiness may be markedly different in different cultures and needs to be explored.

## POSITIVE PSYCHOLOGY AND HUMANISTIC AND EXISTENTIAL PSYCHOLOGY

Through the history of any scientific field, successive bodies of theoretical and empirical knowledge are established and constitute a foundation for succeeding generation(s). What then about positive psychology and its relations to the previous traditions of modern humanistic and existential psychology, which also hold a more positive view of the human being? Psychology was in the last century characterized by grand theories. The grand theories within humanistic and existential psychology were preoccupied by the same idea of the basically positive nature of the human being as is positive psychology today (Frankl, 1967; Maslow, 1954; May, 1966; Rogers, 1961). The grand humanistic and existential theories of personality were also to a large extent theories of human motivation. Moreover, existential and humanistic personality theories were developed as critical alternatives to that time's predominant psychoanalytic framework, and psychoanalytic psychology held a strongly negative view of human motivation. The psychoanalytic horizon and theories were at the time the study of negative, often strongly perverse human nature. Roudinesco (2009) in her study of perversity as an aspect of human psychology from the Middle Ages up to the era of Nazism in the 20th century in fact starts her presentation by noting "as for the word structure or term 'perversion,' it has been studied only by psychoanalysts" (p. 1).

Maslow (1954, 1968) and Rogers (1951, 1961), in opposition to the dominating psychoanalytic view at that time, asserted that human nature is positive; that human beings strive to fulfill benign potentials. According to Rogers (1951, 1961), the human being is motivated by a single positive force: an innate tendency to develop constructive and healthy capacities. Furthermore, Rogers takes a teleological perspective on human nature. Maslow shares Rogers's view that human innate dynamic tendencies are predominantly constructive and benign. Maslow's (1954, 1968) theory is a dualistic theory of motivation including both deficiency and growth motives. Growth motives include development and fulfillment of one's own inner potentials and capacities as well as nonpossessive and unselfish caregiving and love to others. As Maslow (1968) pointed out, "Satisfying deficiencies avoids illness; growth satisfactions produce positive health" (p. 32). For the existentialist clinical psychologist May (1967), life is also about fulfilling one's own innate potentials. But this is a continuous fight; we are all too vulnerable to potential nonbeing. Therefore, May (1967) argues, "The aim of therapy is that the patient experiences his existence as real . . . which includes becoming aware of his potentials, and becoming able to act on the basis of them" (p. 85).

Each of these grand humanistic or existentialist personality theories was developed in opposition to and as a critique of the predominant strongly negative and destructive perspective on human motivation and human behavior stemming from psychoanalytic theory as caused only by childhood experiences. As we have now seen, modern humanistic and existential psychology on one hand and the movement of positive psychology on the other are both trying to open up the horizon for the positively motivated and benign human being. Also, Seligman (2002b) remarks that "I well recognize that positive psychology is not a new idea. It has many distinguished ancestors (e.g., Allport, 1961; Maslow, 1971)" (p. 7). But Seligman (2002b) comments critically about these ancestors: "But they somehow failed to attract a cumulative and empirical body of research to ground their ideas" (p. 7).

Science may be divided into separate but related levels of activity. A pragmatic division of scientific levels of activity is used to distinguish between (a) metatheory, (b) theory, (c) design, (d) primary method, (e) data, and (f) phenomenon. Compared to the traditions of humanistic and existential psychology, positive psychology has, as Seligman (2002b) clearly stated, decided on other approaches with regard to theory development, design, and methodology. Waterman (2013a) also concluded his comparative analysis of positive psychology and humanistic psychology: Humanistic psychology has a phenomenological and ideographic underpinning and prefers qualitative methodological research. Positive psychology on the other hand prioritizes quantitative design: the experiment and survey design. Thus positive psychology argues for and uses design and methods in accordance with quantitative methodology and the logical positivistic paradigm of research. Mainstream psychology has, however, for some time now argued for the necessity of using mixed design; both qualitative and quantitative approaches, a both/and approach (Teddlie & Tashakkori, 2003). Also within positive psychology there is now an opening for qualitative methodology (Linley & Joseph, 2004), and in the most recent phase of positive psychology, empirical research combining quantitative and qualitative methodology is being conducted (e.g., Delle Fave et al., 2011). Let it also be mentioned that there might be more acceptance for combining qualitative and quantitative methodologies within psychology in Europe as compared to North America. In Europe, the strong influence of Piaget (1960; see also Dasen, 1972), who used clinical interviews and standard stimulus tasks to map out universal developmental patterns, clearly challenged the assumption that experimental control and quantitative measurements represent the only approach to studies of general principles of human (optimal) functioning.

Modern humanistic psychology is concerned with the more philosophical questions of how to manage apparent meanings of life and what it means to exist at one moment and place in an eternity of time. This is clearly different from positive psychology as Waterman (2013a) concludes: "Rather, the philosophical assumptions underlying positive psychology interventions are based on pragmatics, that is, directing the client's attention to what can be done now to make incremental improvements in quality of life" (p. 129). Compared to humanistic and existentialist psychology, positive psychology then is more preoccupied with the pragmatics of daily life. King (2011) expresses this pragmatic approach of positive psychology as follows:

> I would hope that positive psychology stays relevant to everyday human experience, in theory, methods, and applications. Positive psychology would do well to emerge as the scientific study of the ordinary and the simple that are, simultaneously, the graceful, the beautiful, and the wondrous that we see in everyday human life. (p. 444)

However, in the current phase of positive psychology, we see systematic debates of the conceptual and theoretical links between humanistic and positive psychology (Joseph & Murphy, 2013; Linley, 2013; Linley, Joseph, Harrington, & Wood, 2006; Waterman, 2013b).

## THE PARADIGM OF GROWTH AND OPTIMAL FUNCTIONING AND POSITIVE PSYCHOLOGY'S RESEARCH AND PRACTICE: CONCLUDING REMARKS

Stretching back over at least 15 years, positive psychology does not recognize disciplinary boundaries, but has prioritized and offered a growth and optimal functioning paradigm to all subdisciplines of psychology, arguing that such a paradigm will enrich psychology as a science both in theory as well as in practice. Consequently, positive psychology as a field of research and practice cannot be defined to belong to any one of mainstream psychology's different subdisciplines, such as social psychology, cognitive psychology, developmental psychology, or personality psychology. Thereby, positive psychology has from 2000 on initiated an academic and applied agenda across psychology's different subdisciplines, analyzing the mechanisms, structures, and processes accounting for growth and development at the individual and social levels. In this period, positive psychology has been focusing on the issue of how to enable individuals to develop their capacities to a more optimal level so that they can grow intellectually as well as socially and morally and achieve optimal functioning and well-being (Linley & Joseph, 2004; Sheldon, Kashdan, & Steger, 2011; Snyder & Lopez, 2002). In tune with this perspective of growth and more optimal functioning, positive psychology's research and practice above all have turned their focus to nonclinical areas of psychology, especially education and training and lifestyle programs. How to foster positive emotions, positive traits, and positive social relationships in life (for example, how colleges and universities can equip young people with the understanding and skills of responsible citizenship), has thus been an issue (Colby, Beaumont, Ehrlich, & Corngold, 2007). Currently, positive training programs to build emotional, social, and spiritual fitness are also offered on a large scale in the military, not only for all ranks of soldiers, but also for their families (Cornum, Matthews, & Seligman, 2011). Positive psychology is also offering the growth paradigm to the subdiscipline of clinical psychology and psychotherapy. Positive psychology is therefore now facing the problem of how not only to increase psychological growth but also to relieve suffering—an endeavor person-centered therapy has been addressing for a long time (Joseph & Murphy, 2013). Paradigmatic metadiscussions, moreover, are still very active: Some point out, for example, that positive psychology too often has relied on individual happiness as the ultimate outcome criterion of human fulfillment (Kashdan & Steger, 2011). Others claim that the outcome of interest for positive psychology ought not to be simply happiness, but the one that emerges from doing good acts (see King, 2011; Tiberius, 2013.) Another claim is that positive psychology is facing the problem of a language of constraint in studying growth and optimal or full functioning; the illness ideology and pathological language are still too dominating (Joseph & Murphy, 2013; Maddux, 2002). Still others are discussing that positive psychology in this phase, as in Western mainstream psychology, has prioritized the individual at the cost of the societal level as the basic unit of analysis and practice (Biswas-Diener, Linley, Govindji, & Woolston, 2011). As a consequence, the well-being of community and society is neglected. Another relevant discussion is that positive psychology as currently developed has not addressed more systematically the complex issue of how sociocultural contexts, institutions, and public policy sometimes do not create or recreate experiences that can enhance individual positive growth and quality of life (Duncan, 2010; Myers, 2004; Selin & Davey, 2012). However, looking back on these 15 years, one can conclude that leading psychologists around the world within psychology's various subdisciplines are involved in doing basic and applied research and practice inspired by Aristotelian models of growth and optimal functioning, thereby strongly broadening the scope of today's psychological science and practice.

Howard (1985) concludes by referring to Mahatma Gandhi, who argued that there are seven sins in the world: wealth without work, pleasure without conscience, knowledge without character, commerce without morality, science without humanity, worship without sacrifice, and politics without principle. What did Gandhi mean by science without humanity? The meaning might be very different for every science. Given the subject of psychology, the human being, the answer is of course critical. I agree with Howard (1985) when he concluded, "Our legacy could be an impoverished vision of humanity. By viewing humans from an unduly narrow perspective, we may perpetuate a paralyzing myopia that serves to diminish rather than expand humans' potential as individuals and as species" (p. 264). I also endorse Howard's (1985) formulation of the challenge for psychology: "Our challenge, then, is to construct a science of humans built upon an image of humanity that reflects and reveres human nature in all its diversity, complexity, and subtlety" (p. 264).

Since its launch in 2000, positive psychology has represented a dynamic and strong revitalization of paradigmatic discussions within psychology. Positive psychology has initiated and established new and vital empirical research and practice fields of growth, virtues, strengths, engagement, and different ways or routes to how to live a good life. Maybe future psychologists will look back on this time as a turning point—the point of time when psychology in research and practice with strong consequences for promoting individual and community well-being paradigmatically reinvented the human being as a genuinely good, socially responsible, and virtuous organism.

## SUMMARY POINTS

- Paradigms stake out perspectives and development of theories and thereby decide what it implies to be a human being. As scientists, practitioners, and students, we therefore all have an obligation continuously to analyze and discuss horizons and paradigms in our different disciplines and fields of research.
- In practice, it is most important to know the intellectual roots and the implicitly taken-for-granted assumptions in our field.
- Within science every paradigm with its concrete theories wishes to become the one accepted as being the truth and an expression of reality. A strong obligation for science is therefore to identify ignored, neglected, or even excluded perspectives and positions about human nature.
- Positive psychology started as a protest against predominating and taken-for-granted assumptions in mainstream psychology: the ideology of illness, of pathology, faults, and dysfunctions, as well as the paradigmatic assumption that humans have only one motivation system: asocial self-interest.
- Inspired by the Aristotelian model of human nature, positive psychology revitalized the idea of the human being with a positive character, strengths, and given virtues. Positive psychology takes a point of departure that realization of human potentials is the source of well-being and happiness.
- Since its launch in 2000, positive psychology has initiated and established a vital and disciplined empirical research field of virtues, strengths, engagement, and different ways or routes to how to live a good life.
- To conclude: As scientific knowledge shapes and forms peoples' meaning structure of what it means to be a human being, it is an ethical obligation of researchers, practitioners, and students to discuss what it means to be a human being.

## REFERENCES

Allport, G. W. (1946). Geneticism versus ego-structure in theories of personality. *British Journal of Educational Psychology, 16,* 57–58.

Allport, G. W. (1960). *Personality and social encounter.* Boston, MA: Beacon Press.

Allport, G. W. (1961). *Pattern and growth in personality.* New York, NY: Holt, Rinehart & Winston. (Original work published 1937)

Barnes, J. (Ed.). (1984). *The complete works of Aristotle* (Vols. 1–2). Princeton, NJ: Princeton University Press.

Baron, M. W., Petit, P., & Slote, M. (Eds.). (1997). *Three methods of ethics.* Malden, MA: Blackwell.

Batson, C. D. (1991). *The altruism question. Toward a social-psychological answer.* Hillsdale, NJ: Erlbaum.

Batson, C. D., Ahmad, N., Lishner, D. A., & Tsang, J. A. (2002). Empathy and altruism. In C. R. Snyder & S. J. Lopez (Eds.), *Handbook of positive psychology* (pp. 485–497). New York, NY: Oxford University Press.

Baumrind, D. (1982). Adolescent sexuality: Comments on William's and Silka's comments on Baumrind. *American Psychologist, 37,* 1402–1403.

Benedict, R. (1934). *Patterns of culture.* Boston, MA: Houghton Mifflin.

Benedict, R. (1946). *The chrysanthemum and the sword: Patterns of Japanese culture.* Boston, MA: Houghton Mifflin.

Bernstein, R. J. (1986). The question of moral and social development. In L. Cirillo & S. Wapner (Eds.), *Value propositions in theories of human development* (pp. 1–12). Hillsdale, NJ: Erlbaum.

Biswas-Diener, R., Linley, P. A., Govindji, R., & Woolston, L. (2011). Positive psychology as a force for social change. In K. M. Sheldon, T. B. Kashdan, & M. F. Steger (Eds.), *Designing positive psychology. Taking stock and moving forward* (pp. 410–418). Oxford, England: Oxford University Press.

Blum, L. A. (1980). *Friendship, altruism and morality.* London, England: Routledge & Kegan Paul.

Bronfenbrenner, U. (1979). *The ecology of human development. Experiments by nature and design.* Cambridge, MA: Harvard University Press.

Bronfenbrenner, U. (1992). Ecological systems theory. In R. Vasta (Ed.), *Six theories of child development* (pp. 185–246). Greenwich, CT: JAI Press.

Bruner, J. (1986). Value prepositions of developmental theory. In L. Cirillo & S. Wapner (Eds.), *Value presuppositions in theories of human development* (pp. 19–28). Hillsdale, NJ: Erlbaum.

Bruner, J. (1990). *Acts of meaning.* Cambridge, MA: Harvard University Press.

Cirillo, L., & Wapner, S. (Eds.). (1986). *Value presuppositions in theories of human development.* Hillsdale, NJ: Erlbaum.

Colby, A., Beaumont, E., Ehrlich, T., & Corngold, J. (2007). *Educating for democracy. Preparing undergraduates for responsible political engagement.* San Francisco, CA: Jossey-Bass.

Condor, S. (1997). And so say all of us? Some thoughts on "experimental democratization" as an aim for critical social psychologists. In T. Ibanez & L. Iniguez (Eds.), *Critical social psychology* (pp. 111–146). London, England: Sage.

Cornum, R., Matthews, M. D., & Seligman, M. E. P. (Eds.). (2011). Comprehensive soldier fitness. *American Psychologist, 66*(1), 4–9.

Csikszentmihalyi, M., & Nakamura, J. (2011). Positive psychology: Where did it come from, where is it going? In K. M. Sheldon, T. B. Kashdan, & M. F. Steger (Eds.), *Designing positive psychology. Taking stock and moving forward* (pp. 3–8). New York, NY: Oxford University Press.

Cushman, P. (1990). Why the self is empty: Toward a historically situated psychology. *American Psychologist, 45,* 599–611.

Dahlsgaard, K. A., Peterson, C., & Seligman, M. E. P. (2001). *Toward a classification of strengths and virtues: Lessons from history.* Unpublished manuscript, University of Pennsylvania.

Darley, J. M. (1991). Altruism and prosocial behavior research: Reflections and prospects. In M. S. Clark (Ed.), *Prosocial behavior* (pp. 312–327). Newbury Park, CA: Sage.

Darwin, C. (1859). *On the origin of species.* London, England: Murray.

Dasen, P. R. (1972). Cross-cultural Piagetian research: A summary. *Journal of Cross-Cultural Research, 3,* 23–29.

Delle Fave, A. (Ed.). (2013). *The exploration of happiness. Present and future perspectives.* Dordrecht, The Netherlands: Springer Science + Business Media B.V.

Delle Fave, A., Brdar, I., Freire, T., Vella-Brodrick, D., & Wissing, M. P. (2011). The eudaimonic and hedonic components of happiness: Qualitative and quantitative findings. *Social Indicators Research, 100,* 185–207.

Dovidio, J. F., Piliavin, J. A., Schroeder, D. A., & Penner, L. A. (2006). *The social psychology of prosocial behavior.* Mahwah, NJ: Erlbaum.

Duncan, G. (2010). Should happiness maximization be the goal of government? *Journal of Happiness Studies, 11,* 163–178.

Eisenberg, N. (Ed.). (1982). *The development of prosocial behavior.* New York, NY: Academic Press.

Eisenberg, N. (1986). *Altruistic emotion, cognition and behavior.* Hillsdale, NJ: Erlbaum.

Emmons, R. A., & McCullough, M. E. (Eds.). (2004). *The psychology of gratitude.* Oxford, England: Oxford University Press.

Eysenck, H. J. (1947). *Dimensions of personality.* London, England: Routledge & Keagan Paul.

Eysenck, H. J. (1955). The science of personality: Nomothetic! *Psychological Review, 61,* 339–342.

Eysenck, H. J. (1956). The inheritance of extraversion-introversion. *Acta Psychologica, 12,* 95–112.

Eysenck, H. J. (1967). *The biological basis of personality.* Springfield, IL: Thomas.

Fiske, A. P. (1992). The four elementary forms of sociality: Framework for a unified theory of social relations. *Psychological Review, 99*, 689–723.

Foucault, M. (1972). *The archeology of knowledge.* New York, NY: Harper Colophon.

Foucault, M. (1980). *Power/knowledge.* New York, NY: Pantheon.

Frankl, V. (1967). *Psychotherapy and existentialism.* New York, NY: Simon & Schuster.

Gelfand, M. J., Chiu, C.-Y., & Hong, Y.-Y. (Eds). (2011). *Advances in culture psychology.* Oxford, England: Oxford University Press.

Gergen, K. J. (1982). *Toward transformation in social knowledge.* New York, NY: Springer Verlag.

Gergen, K. J. (1989). Social psychology and the wrong revolution. *European Journal of Social Psychology, 19*, 463–484.

Gergen, K. J. (1991). *The saturated self: Dilemmas of identity in contemporary life.* New York, NY: Basic Books.

Gergen, K. J. (1994). *Realities and relationships: Soundings in social construction.* Cambridge, MA: Harvard University Press.

Green, M., & Piel, J. A. (2002). *Theories of human development. A comaparative approach.* Boston, MA: Allyn & Bacon.

Haybron, D. M. (2008). *The pursuit of happiness. The elusive psychology of well-being.* Oxford, England: Oxford University Press.

Hobbes, T. (1651). Leviathan (Chapters 1–15). In M. L. Morgan (2001), *Classics of moral and political theory* (pp. 491–671). Cambridge, MA: Hackett.

Hoffman, M. L. (1975). Developmental synthesis of affect and cognition and its implications for altruistic motivation. *Developmental Psychology, 11*, 607–622.

Hoffman, M. L. (2000). *Empathy and moral development. Implications for caring and justice.* Cambridge, England: Cambridge University Press.

Hopkins, B., & Butterworth, G. (1990). Concepts of causality in explanations of development. In G. Butterworth & P. Bryant (Eds.), *Causes of development. Interdisciplinary perspectives* (pp. 3–32). Hertfordshire, England: Harvester Wheatsheaf.

Howard, G. S. (1985). The role of values in the science of psychology. *American Psychologist, 40*, 255–265.

Hume, D. (1751). *Enqueries concerning the principles of morals.* Oxford, England: A. Millar.

Jørgensen, I. S., & Nafstad, H. E. (2004). Positive psychology: Historical, philosophical and epistemological perspectives. In P. A. Linley & S. Joseph (Eds.), *Positive psychology in practice* (pp. 15–34). Hoboken, NJ: Wiley.

Joseph, S., & Murphy, D. (2013). Person-centered theory encountering mainstream psychology: Building bridges and looking to the future. In J. H. D. Cornelius-White, R. Motschnig-Pitrik, & M. Lux (Eds.), *Interdisciplinary handbook of the person-centered approach: Research and theory* (pp. 213–226). New York, NY: Springer.

Kashdan, T. B., & Steger, M. F. (2011). Challenges, pitfalls, and aspirations for positive psychology. In K. M. Sheldon, T. B. Kashdan, & M. F. Steger (Eds.), *Designing positive psychology. Taking stock and moving forward* (pp. 9–21). Oxford, England: Oxford University Press.

Kierkegaard, S. (1962). *Either/or* (Vol. 1). Princeton, NJ: Princeton University Press. (Original work published 1843)

Kierkegaard, S. (1968). *Concluding unscientific postscript.* Princeton, NJ: Princeton University Press. (Original work published 1846)

King, L. A. (2011). Are we there yet? What happened on the way to the demise of positive psychology? In K. M. Sheldon, T. B. Kashdan, & M. F. Steger (Eds.), *Designing positive psychology. Taking stock and moving forward* (pp. 439–446). Oxford, England: Oxford University Press

Kvale, S. (Ed.). (1992). *Psychology and postmodernism.* Newbury Park, CA: Sage.

Lewin, K. (1935). *A dynamic theory of personality.* New York, NY: McGraw-Hill.

Linley, P. A. (2013). Human strengths and well-being: Finding the best within us at the intersection of eudaimonic philosophy, humanistic psychology, and positive psychology.

In A. S. Waterman (Ed.), *The best within us: Positive psychology perspectives on eudaimonia* (pp. 269–285). Washington, DC: American Psychological Association.

Linley, P. A., & Joseph, S. (2004). Applied positive psychology: A new perspective for professional practice. In P. A. Linley & S. Joseph (Eds.), *Positive psychology in practice* (pp. 3–12). Hoboken, NJ: Wiley.

Linley, P. A., Joseph, S., Harrington, S., & Wood, A. M. (2006). Positive psychology: Past, present and (possible) future. *Journal of Positive Psychology, 1,* 3–16.

MacIntyre, A. (1984). *After virtue. A study in moral theory.* Notre Dame, IN: University of Notre Dame Press.

Maddux, J. E. (2002). Stopping the "madness": Positive psychology and the deconstruction of the illness ideology and DSM. In C. R. Snyder & S. J. Lopez (Eds.), *Handbook of positive psychology* (pp. 13–25). New York, NY: Oxford University Press.

Maslow, A. H. (1954). *Motivation and personality.* New York, NY: Harper & Row.

Maslow, A. H. (1968). *Toward a psychology of being* (2nd ed.). New York, NY: Van Nostrand Reinhold.

Maslow, A. H. (1971). *The farthest reaches of human nature.* New York, NY: Viking.

May, R. (1966). *Love and will.* New York, NY: Norton.

May, R. (1967). Contributions of existential psychotherapy. In R. May, E. Angel, & H. F. Ellenberger (Eds.), *Existence: A new dimension in psychiatry and psychology* (pp. 37–91). New York, NY: Touchstone Books.

McDougall, W. (1908). *An introduction to social psychology.* London, England: Methuen.

McDougall, W. (1932). *The energies of men.* London, England: Methuen.

McGuire, W. J. (2004). A perspectivist approach to theory construction. *Personality and Social Psychology Review, 8,* 173–182.

Mikulincer, M., & Shaver, P. R. (Eds.). (2010). *Prosocial motives, emotions, and behavior. The better angels of our nature.* Washington, DC: American Psychological Association.

Miller, D. T. (1999). The norm of self-interest. *American Psychologist, 54,* 1053–1060.

Morgan, M. L. (2001). *Classics of moral and political theory.* Cambridge, MA: Hackett.

Myers, D. G. (2004). Human connections and the good life: Balancing individuality and community in public policy. In P. A. Linley & S. Joseph (Eds.), *Positive psychology in practice* (pp. 641–657). Hoboken, NJ: Wiley.

Nafstad, H. E. (2002). The neo-liberal ideology and the self-interest paradigm as resistance to change. *Radical Psychology, 3,* 1–13.

Nafstad, H. E. (2004). Mennesket—egoistisk ja, men også altruistisk [The human being—egoistic yes, but also altruistic]. In H. E. Nafstad (Ed.), *Det omsorgsfulle mennesket* [*The caring human being*]. Oslo, Norway: Gyldendal Akademisk.

Nafstad, H. E. (2005). Assumptions and values in the production of knowledge: Towards an area ethics of psychology and the social sciences. In S. Robinson & C. Katulushi (Eds.), *Values in higher education* (pp. 150–158). Vale of Glamorgan, Wales: Aureus.

Noam, G. G., & Fisher, K. W. (1996). Introduction: The foundational role of relationships in human development. In G. G. Noam & K. W. Fisher (Eds.), *Development and vulnerability in close relationships* (pp. ix–xx). Mahwah, NJ: Erlbaum.

Peterson, C., Ruch, W., Beermann, U., Park, N., & Seligman, M. E. P. (2007). Strengths of character, orientations to happiness, and life satisfaction. *Journal of Positive Psychology, 2,* 149–156.

Peterson, C., & Seligman, M. E. P. (2004). *Character strengths and virtues: A handbook and classification.* Oxford, England: Oxford University Press.

Pettigrew, T. F. (1997). Personality and social structure. Social psychological contributions. In R. Hogan, J. Johnson, & S. Briggs (Eds.), *Handbook of personality psychology* (pp. 417–438). New York, NY: Academic Press.

Piaget, J. (1960). *The child's conception of the world.* New York, NY: Basic Books.

Rawls, J. (1976). *A theory of justice.* Oxford, England: Oxford University Press.

Rogers, C. R. (1951). *Client-centered therapy: Its current practice, implications and theory*. Boston, MA: Houghton Mifflin.

Rogers, C. R. (1961). *On becoming a person: A therapist's view of psychotherapy*. Boston, MA: Houghton Mifflin.

Rohner, R. P. (1975). *They love me, they love me not: A worldwide study of the effects of parental acceptance and rejection*. New Haven, CT: HRAF Press.

Roudinesco, E. (2009). *Our dark side. A history of perversion*. Cambridge, England: Polity Press.

Rousseau, J.-J. (1762). On the social contract. In M. L. Morgan (2001), *Classics of moral and political theory* (pp. 771–830). Cambridge, MA: Hackett.

Ryff, C. D., & Singer, B. H. (2006). Know thyself and become what you are: A eudaimonic approach to psychological well-being. *Journal of Happiness Studies, 9*, 13–39.

Seligman, M. E. P. (2002a). *Authentic happiness*. New York, NY: The Free Press.

Seligman, M. E. P. (2002b). Positive psychology, positive prevention, and positive therapy. In C. R. Snyder & S. J. Lopez (Eds.), *Handbook of positive psychology* (pp. 3–9). New York, NY: Oxford University Press.

Seligman, M. E. P., & Csikszentmihalyi, M. (Eds.). (2000). Positive psychology. *American Psychologist, 55*(1), 5–14.

Seligman M. E. P., & Csikszentmihalyi, M. (2001). Reply to comments. *American Psychologist, 56*, 89–90.

Selin, H., & Davey, G. (Eds.). (2012). *Happiness across cultures. Views of happiness and quality of life in non-Western cultures*. Dordrecht, The Netherlands: Springer Science + Business Media B.V.

Sheldon, K., Fredrickson, B., Rathumnde, K., Csikszentmihalyi, M., & Haidt, J. (1999). *Akumal Manifesto*. Retrieved from http://www.ppc.sas.upenn.edu/akumalmanifesto.htm

Sheldon, K. M., Kashdan, T. B., & Steger, M. F. (Eds.). (2011). *Designing positive psychology: Taking stock and moving forward*. Oxford, England: Oxford University Press.

Shotter, J., & Gergen, K. J. (1989). *Texts of identity*. Newbury Park, CA: Sage.

Slife, B. D., Reber, J. S., & Richardson, F. C. (2005). *Critical thinking about psychology*. Washinton, DC: American Psychological Association.

Slife, B. D., & Williams, R. N. (1997). Toward a theoretical psychology. Should a subdiscipline be formally recognized? *American Psychologist, 52*, 117–129.

Snyder, C. R., & Lopez, S. J. (Eds.). (2002). *Handbook of positive psychology*. Oxford, England: Oxford University Press.

Spencer, H. (1870). *The principles of psychology* (Vol. 1). London, England: Williams and Norgate.

Spencer, H. (1872). *The principles of psychology* (Vol. 2). London, England: Williams and Norgate.

Teddlie, C., & Tashakkori, A. (2003). *Handbook of mixed methods in social & behavioral research*. Thousand Oaks, CA: Sage.

Tiberius, V. (2013). Recipes for a good life: Eudaimonism and the contribution of philosophy. In A. S. Waterman (Ed.), *The best within us: Positive psychology perspectives on eudaimonia* (pp. 19–38). Washington, DC: American Psychological Association.

Vaillant, G. (2000). The mature defences: Antecedents of joy. *American Psychologist, 55*, 89–98.

van Lange, P. A. M. (2000). Beyond self-interest: A set of propositions relevant to interpersonal orientations. In W. Stroebe & M. Hewstone (Eds.), *European review of social psychology* (Vol. 11, pp. 297–331). Chichester, England: Wiley.

Veenhoven, R. (2010). *World database of happiness*. Erasmus University Rotterdam, The Netherlands. Retrieved from http://worlddatabaseofhappiness.eur.nl

Vetlesen, A. J. (1994). *Perception, empathy and judgmen: An inquiry into the preconditions of moral performance*. University Park: Pennsylvania State University Press.

Vetlesen, A. J., & Nortvedt, P. (2000). *Følelser og moral* [*Emotions and morality*]. Oslo, Norway: Gyldendal Akademisk.

Walsh, W. B., Craik, K. H., & Price, R. H. (Eds.). (1992). *Person-environment psychology: Models and perspectives*. Hillsdale, NJ: Erlbaum.

Waterman, A. S. (2013a). The humanistic psychology-positive psychology divide. Contrasts in philosophical foundations. *American Psychologist, 68*, 124–133.

Waterman, A. S. (Ed.). (2013b). *The best within us: Positive psychology perspectives on eudaimonia*. Washington, DC: American Psychological Association.

Werner, H. (1957a). *Comparative psychology of mental development*. New York, NY: International Universities Press. (Original work published 1926)

Werner, H. (1957b). The concept of development from a comparative and organismic point of view. In D. B. Harris (Ed.), *The concept of development* (pp. 125–148). Minneapolis: University of Minnesota Press.

Wong, Y. J. (2006). Strength-centered therapy: A social constructionist, virtues-based psychotherapy. *Psychotherapy: Theory, Research, Practice, Training, 43*, 133–146.

# CHAPTER 3

# Building Bridges Between Humanistic and Positive Psychology

BRENT DEAN ROBBINS

T HE RELATIONSHIP BETWEEN positive psychology and humanistic psychology has been a strained one. Although positive psychology was at first warmly embraced by some humanistic psychologists as an extension of the aims of humanistic psychology (e.g., Resnick, Warmoth, & Serlin, 2001), this reception grew cold when Seligman and Csikszentmihalyi (2000) distanced positive psychology from humanistic psychology in a special issue of *American Psychologist*. Somewhat in passing and in a way that lacked supporting evidence, Seligman and Csikszentmihalhyi (2000) were harshly critical of humanistic psychology, saying that, although it offered a "generous vision" (p. 7), it lacked a cumulative research base, promoted self-help at the expense of scientific rigor, and reinforced narcissistic tendencies in individuals and the culture—all claims that were received as fallacious, straw man arguments by the humanistic camp (e.g., Bohart & Greening, 2001; Robbins, 2008; Shapiro, 2001). Since that time, many attempts at dialogue have sometimes worked toward integration (Froh, 2004; Linley & Joseph, 2004b; Linley, Joseph, Harrington, & Wood, 2006; Rathunde, 2001; Robbins, 2008; Robbins & Friedman, 2008, 2011; Schneider, 2011; Wong, 2011a, 2011b) but have been just as often marked by sharp criticism and debate (Bohart & Greening, 2001; Friedman & Robbins, 2012; Held, 2004; Rich, 2001; Shapiro, 2001; Sugarman, 2007; Sundararajan, 2005; Taylor, 2001; Woolfolk & Wasserman, 2005).

In what is perhaps one of the strangest responses from a positive psychologist, Waterman (2013) recently suggested that, because positive and humanistic psychology tend to cite different philosophers and therefore seem to have different philosophical presuppositions, they really have nothing to say to one another. This is a recommendation that, on its face, if it were taken up by psychology as a whole, would virtually end scholarly discussion and debate in almost every subdiscipline in the field. Needless to say, this seems to be a terrible idea. The fact is, all theories have hidden or implicit philosophical presuppositions, which really are the beginning and not

*Author's Note.* Portions of this chapter were previously published in "What Is the Good Life? Positive Psychology and the Renaissance of Humanistic Psychology," by B. D. Robbins, 2008, in *The Humanistic Psychologist, 36*, pp. 96–112. These portions are being republished with permission from Taylor & Francis.

the end of dialogue in the discipline (Slife & Williams, 1995). A better alternative is to seek genuine opportunities for integration and dialogue, without avoiding times when legitimate criticism is necessary, in order to move the entire field of psychology forward toward the best possible version of a psychology of human happiness, well-being, and human strengths. To make that step forward, it seems necessary to call out straw man arguments for what they are, and also to acknowledge the fact that positive psychology has deep roots in humanistic psychology.

The philosophies are not as irreconcilable as some, such as Waterman (2013), may claim. On the contrary, there are some internally incoherent positions of positive psychology as it is generally received that, when placed in dialogue with humanistic psychology, could prove to be a superior approach to the good life than either positive or humanistic psychology taken on their own.

Humanistic psychology certainly shares with positive psychology the key aims of identifying and investigating positive experiences, traits, and institutions (Robbins, 2008), which is how positive psychology was defined broadly from its very beginnings (Gillham & Seligman, 1999; Seligman & Czikszentmihalyi, 2000). Seligman, Steen, Park, and Peterson (2005) recognized the important role of Maslow (1971), Allport (1961), and other humanistic psychologists in the formation of what Seligman coined "positive psychology." Key concepts of positive psychology such as "flow" have their roots in humanistic theory of optimal experience (Nakamura & Csikszentmihalyi, 2005). Indeed, the overlap between humanistic and positive psychology seems to be much more substantial than the differences (Linley & Joseph, 2004a). An examination of the research literature reveals the unmistakable fact that in almost every major construct studied by positive psychology, humanistic psychological theory and theorists are cited as foundational to the research (Linley & Joseph, 2004b; Peterson & Seligman, 2004; Robbins, 2008).

A humanistic positive psychology is not a contradiction in terms. On the contrary, the humanistic tradition of psychology promises to assist positive psychology in resolving what may be internal contradictions in its own philosophical presuppositions, namely the odd couple of neo-Aristotelian virtue theory and positivism. The retrieval of Aristotle's virtue theory within a humanistic perspective would benefit from philosophical insights that come with phenomenology, personalism, and existential thinking, which arguably, more than any other philosophical tradition, have sought to retrieve Aristotle and ancient Greek thought for a contemporary age. To appreciate this potential contribution of humanistic psychology, however, it is important to first situate humanistic psychology within its historical context and elucidate its core principles.

## BRIEF HISTORY OF HUMANISTIC PSYCHOLOGY

Historians typically credit Abraham Maslow as the central figure who initiated the movement that would come to be designated as humanistic psychology (Decarvalho, 1990, 1991, 1994; Grogan, 2008; Robbins & McInerney, 2013; Shaffer, 1978). Due to a growing dissatisfaction with the two reigning approaches to psychology in the first half of the 20th century, behaviorism and psychoanalysis, Maslow was in search of a Third Force that could offer a viable alternative. His initiative began as a modest effort to maintain a mailing list of those who shared his dissatisfaction, and that list grew to about 125 names (Decarvalho, 1990). Maslow referred to this mailing list, in which papers were exchanged, as the "Eupsychian Network," and this group would eventually become the subscription base for the *Journal of Humanistic Psychology* in 1961 (DeCarvalho, 1992). Allport and Rogers were two important influences on Maslow at this time. One of Maslow's primary concerns with psychoanalysis was its tendency to build psychological theory on the basis of case studies of people who were clearly dysfunctional. He strove to create a psychology that would be based not only on those who were dysfunctional, but also upon those who were fully living the extent of their human potential (Maslow, 1973). It was this effort to scientifically describe the optimal potential of the person that Maslow (1987) himself coined "positive psychology" four decades prior to Seligman's use of that term.

A key moment in the development of humanistic psychology was the formation of the American Association for Humanistic Psychology (AAHP) in 1962 (Schulz & Schulz, 2011) and shortly thereafter the Old Saybrook Conference, which was held in Connecticut and included key figures such as Gordon Allport, Carl Rogers, James Bugental, Abraham Maslow, Rollo May, Charlotte Bühler, George Kelly, Clark Moustakas, and Henry Murray, among others (DeCarvalho, 1990). On the tails of these developments came the formation of various graduate programs with humanistic orientations, such as at Sonoma State University and Duquesne University, and finally, the founding of Division 32 of the American Psychological Association, now known as the Society for Humanistic Psychology.

Through the early figures of humanistic psychology, it is possible to trace the most seminal theoretical roots of the movement. These strands include phenomenology, personalism, and existentialism (Robbins & McInerney, 2013). These were European philosophical movements that at the time were just beginning to have an impact in the United States.

PHENOMENOLOGY

As early as 1965, Carl Rogers identified phenomenology as the essential core of the Third Force. The emphasis on phenomenology highlights the centrality of meaning as it is given to perceptual experience, which for humanistic psychology was foundational to its scientific endeavors. In contrast, behaviorism emphasized a third-person perspective of the individual, which was reduced to discrete, quantifiable behaviors. Psychoanalysis on the other hand saw experience as fundamentally distorted by defense mechanisms, and so access to the truth of one's inner reality required a skepticism toward one's perception in favor of hidden meanings that psychoanalysis promised to decode through a long, arduous process. Influential figures on the humanistic viewpoint, which privileged lived, conscious meanings that are experienced explicitly and implicitly, included Eugene Gendlin (1962), whose background in philosophy equipped him with the tools to establish an experiential theory rooted in a rigorous phenomenological and existential philosophical foundation, which drew upon the work of continental thinkers such as Edmund Husserl, Jean-Paul Sartre, and Maurice Merleau-Ponty (Spiegelberg, 1972).

Rollo May helped to bring existential psychology from Europe to the United Sates through his edited volume *Existence* (May, Angel, & Ellenberger, 1958). At Duquesne University, the psychology program explicitly developed a phenomenological psychology that was to be the epistemological orientation for the new and emerging humanistic movement. This movement could be traced back as far as Goethe's more qualitative and holistic alternative to science as compared to the mechanistic science of Isaac Newton (Robbins, 2006b).

It is worth noting that this Goethean science had its roots in an attempt to retrieve lost elements of the Aristotelian approach to science and metaphysics that were rejected and replaced by Newton's modern scientific worldview. The latter, Newtonian approach, in terms of ancient Greek influence, was more indebted to Plato and his skepticism toward appearances in favor of mathematical abstraction (Burtt, 2003). The more Newtonian-Cartesian science grounded in positivism is characteristic of much positive psychology, but this epistemology is not entirely consistent with Aristotle's philosophy, including his ethics, which has been appropriated by positive psychology due to its virtue theory. Positivism reduces all causes to efficient causes, and therefore locates meaning in antecedent events and their consequences. In contrast, Aristotle's metaphysics recognized a wider range of qualitative meanings, such as the formal and final cause of a person's actions, which are retained within humanistic psychology through its integration of phenomenology. To recognize the formal cause of a person's behavior is to see it in a more holistic fashion, as belonging to a gestalt that includes person, others, and world in relation to one another. To recognize final causation in the person is to see the human being as an agent who gives direction and purpose to his or her own life (Slife & Williams, 1995). As we will discuss further in this chapter, these concepts of formal and final causality are implied in any valid retrieval of Aristotle's ethics, including the virtue theory that is at the heart of his ethics. To adhere strictly to positivism as an epistemology risks undermining the project of developing a fully realized virtue theory that can be applied to the lives of everyday people. Humanistic psychology, as informed by phenomenology, however, does not have this problem, and can readily draw upon Aristotle's virtue theory without contradiction.

## PERSONALISM

Personalism made inroads into humanistic psychology through virtually the same channels as phenomenology and existentialism. It was primarily a European movement with indirect influences in the United States, and its impact on humanistic psychology was felt mainly through the figures of Gordon Allport and Viktor Frankl. Although it was less directly an influence on humanistic psychology, personalism nevertheless was a profound and important inspiration and also made an impact on humanistic psychology and American culture through the philosophical basis of the nonviolent social ethics that animated Martin Luther King Jr.'s civil rights activism (Robbins, 2013a; Robbins & McInerney, 2013).

A key idea of personalism is a nonreductive approach to the person that recognizes that each person is unique, nonfungible, and has profound worth that can never be fully quantified or constrained by oversimplified constructs or abstract generalities. Personalism, as the basis of a social ethics, was the subject of Allport's (1922) dissertation under William Stern, and this had a major impact on the development of Allport's theory of personality. It was out of respect for the uniqueness of the person that Allport emphasized the importance of idiographic methods in psychology in addition to nomothetic approaches. Also, while at Harvard, Allport had been involved in regular meetings with the theologians at Boston University who were drawing upon the same influences of personalism. It was in fact at Boston University that Martin Luther King, Jr., developed his own personalist approach, which informed his activism. King was influenced by Allport and in fact cited Allport's (1979) book *The Nature of Prejudice,* as did Malcolm X.

Viktor Frankl was also influenced by personalism through a different channel—the existential personalism of Max Scheler (1973) (Henckmann, 2005). Frankl's emphasis on the nonreductive approach to the person and his stress on finding meaning or dignity through suffering are key themes drawn from the personalist tradition associated with Scheler.

## EXISTENTIALISM

In the introduction to his edited collection of primary existential texts, Walter Kaufmann (1956) wrote, "Existentialism is not a philosophy but a label for several widely different revolts against traditional philosophy" (p. 11). Existentialism does reject or critique a number of philosophical standpoints including naïve realism, idealism, and positivism, as well as Rene Descartes' mind/body ontological dualism. William Barrett (1990) described existentialism as "a philosophy that confronts the human condition in its totality to ask what the basic conditions of human existence are" (p. 126). May, influenced by the existential theologian Paul Tillich, saw existentialism as "an attitude, an approach to human beings, rather than a special school or group" (May, 1962, p. 185). Historian of psychology Daniel Burston (2003) likewise pointed out that "there has never been a stable or binding consensus regarding the leadership or the terms of membership in the existential movement, nor precisely when it took root historically" (p. 311). Figures commonly associated with existentialism include Soren Kierkegaard, Friedrich Nietzsche, Martin Heidegger, Jean-Paul Sartre, Max Scheler, and Maurice Merleau-Ponty, to name just a few. Within existential psychology, as informed by these thinkers, one common thread is a recognition of the irreducible complexity of existence as well as the limitations of human life and knowledge due to our bodily nature and mortality.

In general, existential thought tends to be suspicious of philosophies that privilege cognitive abstraction over concrete existence and experience. This is somewhat ironic because existential psychology is sometimes criticized for being difficult to understand due to its neologisms and strained ways of speaking, but the sense of alienation when reading existentialism comes from a style of writing and speaking that attempts to shake the audience's taken-for-granted assumptions about everyday meanings as a basis for profound insight. Therefore, the abstract category of "existential philosophy" as a philosophical school of thought is itself a subject of incredulity by those who are often associated with this style of thinking.

## KEY THEMES

Humanistic psychology's roots in phenomenology, personalism, and existentialism are the basis for central themes that organize the thinking, practice, and research of psychologists who identify as humanistic. The key themes of humanistic psychology include a strong phenomenological or experiential epistemology, an emphasis on the essential wholeness and integrity of human beings, the acknowledgment that humans possess essential freedom and autonomy within limits, a strong antireductionist stance, and a recognition of the dignity of human beings, including the person's transcendence and inability to be fully contained or understood by any simple, abstract formulation without losing something essential (Shaffer, 1978). In addition, humanistic psychologists tend to have a strong ethical foundation based in personalistic roots that recognize that human beings have fundamental rights that emerge from our shared humanity as beings who are vulnerable and suffer (Turner, 2006). A genuinely humanistic approach to positive psychology would adhere to these humanistic commitments, although within these limits it may take a wide variety of forms.

The close connection between a personalistic ethic and phenomenological epistemology implicates the way in which the humanistic perspective rejects the rigid fact–value dichotomy that is assumed by most scientific psychology (Robbins, 2013b). Scientific theories and approaches are always saturated by metaphysical, epistemological, and ethical presuppositions that are value-laden in their implications (Slife & Williams, 1995). Rather than denying that its worldview is value-laden, humanistic psychology strives to make its values explicit in order to subject them to critical reflection. This approach stands in contrast to positivism, which in assuming a fact–value dichotomy, often treats value-laden discourse with a false pretense of value neutrality.

The epistemological basis in phenomenology within the humanistic tradition of psychology can be understood to imply a deeper metaphysical or ontological commitment, which recognizes that human beings are different than things (Robbins, 2013b). Although it may seem obvious that human beings are quite different than rocks or a hammer, scientific research often implicitly treats these ontological realms as if they are equivalent. Within the positivism that informs behaviorism and much cognitive science today, human beings are treated as objects that are no different in kind than the objects of physics, and hence the science is unsurprisingly based on an epistemology based on Enlightenment-era physics. Within classical psychoanalysis and most neuroscience, physiological reductionism understands the meanings of lived experience to be reducible to dumb, mechanical forces that represent ultimate reality. Yet to start from this reductionistic position would, for example, make it nearly impossible to recognize the reality of a concept such as human dignity, which is fundamental to our fragile sense of human rights.

B.F. Skinner (1971) famously dismissed the concepts of human freedom and dignity as nonsense, yet humanistic psychology has never waivered in championing these core human values. To dispense with the concept of human dignity so casually is a dangerous affair, since many doctrines protecting human rights nationally and internationally are founded on the concept of dignity. For example, the United Nations' (1948) Declaration of Universal Human Rights states, "All human beings are born free and equal in dignity and rights," which is the basis upon which the U.N. declares that nation-states have a duty to protect the human rights of citizens of the global community.

The concept of human dignity was clarified by the philosopher Immanuel Kant (1785, cited in Williams, 2005), who contrasted dignity with price. When considering the realm of purpose, argued Kant, everything is either understood in terms of dignity or price. To understand something as having a price is to see it as an object that can be exchanged for something else of equal value, but if something, such as a person, has no equivalent and cannot be exchanged, we must refer instead to dignity. Thus human dignity is a way of making reference to the quality of persons as beyond price in the sense of being nonfungible and as possessing a kind of worth that cannot be estimated in quantitative terms. To have dignity is to be priceless, in other words.

A humanistic approach to positive psychology would recognize not only human potential but would also stress an appreciation of the intrinsic value and worth of persons, each of whom has dignity as a birthright. Because, after Kant, humanistic psychology recognizes the ontological dignity common to all human beings by reason of their nature or being, humanistic psychologists are committed to various ethical stances in the world. For example, humanistic psychology tends to be suspicious of all kinds of reductionism that attempt to reduce people to the properties of things. This is why humanistic psychologists get concerned and protest when a person's meaning and worth is reduced to a narrow and restricting label such as a mental health diagnosis. This is why humanistic psychology is drawn to holistic approaches to understanding the person, which appreciate that the person is always more than the sum of his or her cognitive, behavioral, and anatomical parts. This is why humanistic psychologists understand the person to not only be always situated within an interpersonal context, but also appreciate that the person should never be reduced to mere social meanings because no person is only a social construction. The person transcends reductionistic labels and simple categories by virtue of his or her dignity. To relate to the other person as a person of dignity is to engage with him or her in an I–thou encounter, as opposed to an I–it encounter, as Buber (1937/1958) described; it is to bear witness to the other as a person rather than a thing. This capacity seems to be essential for virtues such as compassion and love.

With the recognition of human rights as founded on the notion of dignity, and with the basis of this recognition grounded in the epistemological perspective of phenomenology and an appreciation of the ontological difference between persons and things, what follows from this worldview is an ethical imperative to protect basic human rights. It is important to remember that with the influence of existentialism there comes an equally important emphasis on humility with regard to the imposition of specific ethical principles, especially with caution regarding overgeneralization of moral principles without appreciation for the complexity and ambiguity inherent to messy, lived situations (Robbins, 2013b).

A positive psychology informed by humanistic psychology could benefit from the adoption of the philosophical framework that informs this psychological worldview.

## FROM HEDONIC TO EUDAIMONIC WELL-BEING

In positive psychology, the shift from a hedonic view of well-being to a eudaimonic perspective is clearly a shift in a more humanistic direction and is explicitly inspired by the humanistic philosophy of Aristotle (Ryan & Deci, 2001). Whereas hedonic well-being is defined in terms of the ratio of pleasure to pain in one's life (Diener, 2000; Kahnemann, Diener, & Schwartz, 1999), eudaimonic well-being is understood to be a reflection of a person who is flourishing in terms of his or her character strengths and virtues, including, among other things: autonomy, mastery of the environment, personal growth, positive interpersonal relationships, purpose in life, and self-acceptance (Keyes, Shmotkin, & Ryff, 2002; Ryff, 1989). The concept of eudaimonic well-being derives from Aristotelian virtue theory. Aristotle (trans. 2004) and his followers conceptualized well-being as composed of an individual's virtuous traits, and only a happiness that flows from legitimate harmony of the virtues was thought to be a genuine happiness. All other forms of happiness were understood to be superficial and fleeting.

Because positive psychology was originally identified by many psychologists as a hedonic approach to psychology, it was subject to quite a bit of criticism for being too "Pollyanna" (Lazarus, 2003), for succumbing to our culture's "tyranny of the positive attitude" (Held, 2002), and for failing to appreciate the adaptive and constructive aspects of unpleasant states of mind (Held, 2002; Lazarus, 2003; Woolfolk, 2002). Research nevertheless has suggested quite strongly that hedonic well-being and eudaimonic well-being, when measured quantitatively, are independent even if moderately correlated constructs (Compton, Smith, Cornish, & Qualls, 1996; King & Napa, 1998; McGregor & Little, 1998). To be subjectively well does not necessarily mean one has cultivated those characteristics and qualities that enable a person to live an authentically good life. If one is living an authentically good life, however, one enhances the capacity for deep, enduring, and mature expressions of happiness and joy (Robbins, 2006a).

If we look to the empirical evidence, the findings suggest that the motivation to maximize pleasure and avoid pain is, at best, a very weak predictor of well-being, whereas being engaged and immersed in one's projects and finding meaning in one's life are relatively much better at predicting well-being (Peterson, Park, & Seligman, 2005; Vella-Brodrick, 2007). To be engaged, to find meaning in that engagement, and to find pleasure through the fulfillment of that meaning and engagement is to live a "full life" rather than an "empty" one, according to Peterson et al. (2005).

By coming to this insight that eudaimonic well-being is key to any understanding of the good life, positive psychologists have more explicitly shifted to a humanistic frame of reference. What the neo-Aristotelians call "Eudaimonic well-being," Maslow (1978) and Rogers (1961) called "self-actualization" and "fully-functioning," respectively. And as humanistic psychologists have been noting for years, authentic well-being or self-actualization is far from anything resembling manic bliss or undifferentiated positive attitudes; on the contrary, it implies an individual's capacity to feel deeply the entire emotional spectrum so as to live life fully, vibrantly, and meaningfully.

## EPISTEMOLOGY AND METHODOLOGY IN POSITIVE AND HUMANISTIC PSYCHOLOGY

Although humanistic psychology is grounded within a phenomenological epistemology, this does not preclude humanistic psychology from drawing upon quantitative as well as qualitative methods of investigation. As Friedman (2008) has demonstrated, humanistic psychology does have a tendency to value qualitative methods, and positive psychology seems to emphasize quantitative methods. But mixed methods are found in both humanistic and positive psychology.

From the very beginning of humanistic psychology, Allport, Maslow, and Rogers stressed not a rejection of science, but an expanded view of science that appreciated the value of both qualitative and idiographic methods as well as quantitative and nomothetic approaches (Friedman, 2008). Within the field of humanistic psychology can be found some of the earliest quantitative approaches to the study of happiness, represented by the work of Fordyce (1977, 1983), whose measure has been found to have superior validity to other measures (Compton et al., 1996). Experimental and quantitative methods have also informed humanistic approaches to transpersonal psychology, meditation, and humanistic psychotherapy (Friedman, 2008). What makes humanistic approaches distinct is the emphasis on holism and the rejection of positivism as a reductive philosophy of science, not quantitative methods per se. Descriptive, eidetic, and hermeneutic phenomenological methods are best viewed as complementary to, rather than a replacement for, traditional empirical psychological methods. What we would want to avoid, however, is rushing too quickly to accept simple formulations of well-being that may be seductive as abstract conceptions of happiness but turn out to be false and misleading, such as the critical positivity ratio (Brown, Sokal, & Friedman, 2013).

## VIRTUE THEORY

Positive psychology has received much criticism for its sometimes incoherent and muddled considerations of its philosophical assumptions regarding the ethical foundations of its activity. Philosopher Mike W. Martin (2007) has written an especially astute commentary on the virtue hypothesis in positive psychology. The virtue hypothesis predicts that happiness is derived from the cultivation of virtue. Martin's primary concern is that Seligman's positive psychology appears to lack consistency in the way it articulates the virtue hypothesis: Sometimes positive psychologists claim value neutrality, but at other times they seem to combine science with normative ethics. Positive psychology engages in the activity of normative ethics to the extent that it aspires to a eudaimonic concept of ethics, which identifies the state of happiness with the acquisition of virtue. By taking on a eudaimonic conception of ethics, positive psychology can no longer consider itself merely a *descriptive* and *predictive* science, but should also acknowledge that it is engaged in the activity of *prescriptive* valuation. Again, positivism provides a problematic framework for the full and coherent expression of positive psychology, due to its fact–value dichotomy.

Martin (2007) seems to believe it is possible to achieve scientific neutrality in positive psychology. This can be achieved, he argues, if positive psychologists restrict definitions of happiness to a hedonic definition—essentially, subjective well-being—and then seek to identify any relationships between hedonic happiness and various character strengths and virtues. By doing so, psychologists could test the virtue hypothesis and discover whether there is a causal relationship between virtue and happiness. However, if eudaimonic happiness is used to define happiness, any suggested causal link between happiness and virtue would be tautological, because in that case virtue could not be said to be an independent variable distinct from happiness. Nevertheless, although it is true that virtue and subjective well-being can be identified as independent and related constructs, as we have already discussed, well-being itself cannot be reduced to hedonic well-being, for the reasons I have already cited.

In contrast to Martin, most humanistic psychologists hold that a value-neutral position is not a realistic aspiration for a researcher or therapist (e.g., Kottler & Hazler, 2001). Even if the researcher defines well-being in terms of hedonic well-being, the endorsement of hedonic well-being as a goal worth pursuing and the decision as to whether hedonic well-being is essential to "the good life" cannot help but become a normative ethical stance. The point is not to exclude normative ethics as a background assumption of research endeavors, as if that were possible; on the contrary, the route to integrity is to make one's ethical assumptions and codes as explicit as possible, which can serve as a means to alert colleagues and consumers of psychological science that they may exercise their own critical faculties to discern whether those normative ethics are justified. The failure to explicate one's ethical assumptions, which is the case in professed "morally neutral" positions, serves only to conceal one's moral framework. And in the hands of influential professionals with status and power, this concealment can be tyrannical and even abusive in cases in which groups are marginalized or persecuted as a result. If this stance seems misguided, consider what happened to homosexuality under the lens of the early diagnostic manuals of the American Psychiatric Association.

As it has been articulated by Seligman (2002), eudaimonic happiness is thought to derive from the identification and cultivation of signature strengths and virtues. As noted by Schwartz and Sharpe (2005), Seligman treats the virtues as if they were "logically independent" (p. 380). But, as they argue, a genuinely Aristotelian perspective demands that the virtues be understood holistically as interdependent constituents of the good life. One cannot pick and choose virtues as if from a menu; the activation of the virtues in the everyday circumstance of living requires the guidance of practical wisdom, or *phronesis*, the "master virtue, without which the other virtues will exist like well-intentioned, but unruly children" (Schwartz & Sharpe, 2005, p. 385). This holistic approach to the good life, in which virtues are understood to be interdependent, is more true to the Aristotelian roots of positive psychology and is a hallmark of humanistic psychology. The emphasis on formal and final causality in Aristotle's physics demands that virtues be understood in a way that is contextual and as having normative aims. This can be accomplished by a more holistic and nonreductive approach to the virtues. A virtue such as resilience, for example, like wisdom or phronesis, could be understood as a master virtue that becomes realized as a virtue only through it's relation to other personal strengths and when deployed toward genuinely moral ends (Robbins & Friedman, 2011).

When Carl Rogers (1961) asked about what it means to be a good therapist, he was asking both an empirical and an ethical question. He was asking, in effect, what it means to be a virtuous therapist—essentially, raising the question of optimal functioning within the specified practice of psychotherapy. However, he went about answering this question in an inductive, open-ended, and empirical way, and by doing so, he long anticipated more contemporary insights that therapeutic interventions are less important than common factors, such as client–therapist rapport, across models of treatment (Frank & Frank, 1991; Miller, Duncan, & Hubble, 2005; Wampold, 2001). Rogers (1961) found that the virtuous therapist is one who cultivates a growth-promoting climate through the acquisition of three essential traits: congruency, unconditional positive regard for the client, and empathic understanding. Notice that these virtues are interdependent. For example, empathic understanding can be used by psychopaths as a means to manipulate and control other people, but when coupled with unconditional positive regard, empathy becomes a benevolent and powerful conduit for interpersonal healing. A congruent therapist may have the integrity and honesty to confront a client about his or her faults, but without unconditional positive regard and empathy, these confrontations are likely to be harsh and damaging rather than constructive avenues for therapeutic change. Although Rogers did not explicitly recognize his approach to therapy as grounded in a neo-Aristotelian conception of virtue, his work nevertheless provides a perfect example of its application.

In addition, humanistic psychology has also been acutely aware of the importance of *idiographic* approaches to empirical and ethical questions and has repeatedly warned against the dangers of an entirely *nomothetic* approach to human behavior and experience (Wertz, 2001). If we want to derive generalities about aggregates of people, if we wish to identify relations among variables for the sake of reducing error in predictions, and if we wish to develop the ability to make causal inferences, we must rely on nomothetic, quantitative procedures, without which we would be lost. For this reason, humanistic psychology should embrace quantitative psychological research methodology. However, within the context of Aristotelian ethics, the identification of essential, interdependent virtues and their interrelations is not enough; we also need the practical wisdom (phronesis) that will allow us to understand how to utilize those virtues in particular, concrete situations. Idiographic approaches, including case studies, biographies, discourse analysis of diaries, and other qualitative approaches to data analysis, are uniquely equipped to impart the practical wisdom necessary to exercise the virtues in a way that can account for the highly contextualized particularities of specific, concrete, human problems, such as those encountered daily by psychotherapists and other clinical practitioners.

When idiographic and qualitative methods of analysis are combined with nomothetic analysis, we have a winning combination. When taken in the abstract, and especially when accounting for all of the variation among cultures and individuals, any categorical description of the virtues runs a great risk of being so generic that it becomes anemic and bereft of practical use-value. Doing so, we are in danger of taking the wonderful richness and complexity of concrete human lives and reducing their meanings to overly simplified formulas (May, 1996), in effect confusing the map with the countryside (Merleau-Ponty, 1995). Yet, when we ground the science of psychology in a philosophy that gives ontological priority to the reality of concrete lives, and in their meanings and values within the contextual significance of those lives, we are able to preserve meaning and value from getting swallowed up in a reductive scientism (Robbins, 2006b). In order to carry out such a psychology, we must take great care to avoid the tendency to reduce *multiplicity* to *uniformity* (Bortoft, 1996, p. 147). For this reason, humanistic psychologists have articulated an approach to human phenomena that, through holistic seeing, is able to capture a *multiplicity in unity* rather than an *impoverished unity*—that is, an approach that has the capability to identify general, essential categories of understanding that nevertheless preserve the integrity of, and recognize their existential debt to, the concrete particularities that give rise to those categories.

## CONCLUSION

Perhaps the greatest danger for positive psychology lies in its potential to misappropriate Aristotelian ethics within an epistemological framework that subtly and effectively undercuts the most fundamental presuppositions and requirements for a properly Aristotelian application of virtue theory for the human sciences. Humanistic psychology has much to offer positive psychologists if they are willing to more closely and seriously engage the expansive literature of humanistic psychologists in this area.

## SUMMARY POINTS

- Mutual criticisms of positive psychology and humanistic psychology are typically based mainly on straw man arguments, and when examined closely, these approaches share more in common than many may be otherwise led to believe.
- Although humanistic psychology is informed by a phenomenological epistemology and much of positive psychology operates within a positivist framework, this does not imply that differences in philosophical presuppositions should preclude meaningful dialogue between these two approaches to well-being and the good life. On the contrary, by adopting a humanistic approach to positive psychology, it may be possible for positive psychology to resolve what may be internally incoherent positions, such as the inherent discord between positivist epistemology and Aristotle's virtue theory. Phenomenology, in contrast, may be better able to appropriate Aristotle's ethical theory within a more contemporary philosophical context.
- A humanistic approach to positive psychology would draw upon the theoretical roots of humanistic psychology, including phenomenology, personalism, and existentialism. One advantage of this approach would be not only an appreciation of human potentials, such as the virtues, but also a recognition of the intrinsic worth of human beings by virtue of their dignity—a concept that has become important for preserving philosophical and legal frameworks that establish and protect human rights.
- A humanistic approach to positive psychology would tend to endorse a eudaimonic rather than a hedonistic approach to well-being. However, a humanistic approach, consistent with Aristotle's philosophy, would more heavily emphasize the holistic and integral nature of the virtues as guided by practical knowledge or wisdom.
- Both qualitative and quantitative approaches to positive psychology, informed by humanistic psychology's phenomenological epistemology, have the potential to provide internally coherent and integral approaches to investigating virtue theory and eudaimonia as the basis for a humanistic positive psychology.

- The humanistic approach to psychotherapy and clinical practice, as developed by Rogers, can be understood to be the cultivation of a virtuous therapist. In this case, however, the virtues are interdependent and work toward healing only in their combination. These virtues include unconditional positive regard, empathy, and congruency.

## REFERENCES

Allport, G. (1922). An experimental study of the traits of personality: With special reference to the problem of social diagnosis. *Harvard University Archives HU, 90.*

Allport, G. (1961). *Pattern and growth in personality.* New York, NY: Holt, Rinehart, & Winston.

Allport, G. W. (1979). *The nature of prejudice: 25th anniversary edition.* New York, NY: Basic Books.

Barrett, W. (1990). *Irrational man: A study in existential philosophy.* New York, NY: Anchor/Doubleday.

Bohart, A. C., & Greening, T. (2001). Humanistic psychology and positive psychology. *American Psychologist, 56,* 81–82.

Bortoft, H. (1996). *The wholeness of nature: Goethe's science of conscious participation in nature.* Hudson, NY: Lindisfarne Press.

Brown, J. H. L., Sokal, A. D., & Friedman, H. L. (2013). The complex dynamics of wishful thinking: The critical positivity ratio. *American Psychologist, 68,* 801–813.

Buber, M. (1958). *I and thou.* New York, NY: Scribner. (Original work published 1937)

Burston, D. (2003). Existentialism, humanism, and psychotherapy. *Existential Analysis, 142,* 309–319.

Burtt, E. A. (2003). *The metaphysical foundations of modern science.* New York, NY: Dover.

Compton, W. C., Smith, M. L., Cornish, K. A., & Qualls, D. L. (1996). Factor structure of mental health measures. *Journal of Personality and Social Psychology, 71,* 406–413.

Decarvalho, R. J. (1990). A history of the "third force" in psychology. *Journal of Humanistic Psychology, 30,* 22–44.

Decarvalho, R. J. (1991). *The founders of humanistic psychology.* New York, NY: Praeger.

Decarvalho, R. J. (1992). The institutionalization of humanistic psychology. *The Humanistic Psychologist, 20*(2–3), 124–135.

Decarvalho, R. J. (1994). The institutionalization of humanistic psychology. In F. Wertz (Ed.), *The humanistic movement: Recovering the person in psychology* (pp. 13–23). Lake Worth, FL: Gardner Press.

Diener, E. (2000). Subjective well-being: The science of happiness and a proposal for a national index. *American Psychologist, 55,* 34–43.

Fordyce, M. W. (1977). Development of a program to increase personal happiness. *Journal of Counseling Psychology, 24*(6), 511–521.

Fordyce, M. W. (1988). A review of research on the happiness measures: A sixty second index of happiness and mental health. *Social Indicators Research, 20*(4), 355–381.

Frank, J. D., & Frank, J. B. (1991). *Persuasion and healing: A comparative study of psychotherapy* (3rd ed.). Baltimore, MD: Johns Hopkins University Press.

Friedman, H. (2008). Humanistic and positive psychology: The methodological and epistemological divide. *The Humanistic Psychologist, 36,* 113–126.

Friedman, H., & Robbins, B. D. (2012). The negative shadow cast by positive psychology: Contrasting views and implications of humanistic and positive psychology on resiliency. *The Humanistic Psychologist, 40,* 87–102.

Froh, J. J. (2004). The history of positive psychology: Truth be told. *NYS Psychologist, 16,* 18–20.

Gendlin, E. (1962). *Experiencing and the creation of meaning.* Glencoe, IL: Free Press.

Gillham, J. E., & Seligman, M. E. P. (1999). Footsteps on the road to positive psychology. *Behaviour Research and Therapy, 37,* 163–173.

Grogan, J. L. (2008). *A cultural history of the humanistic psychology movement in America* (Doctoral dissertation). The University of Texas at Austin.

Held, B. S. (2002). The tyranny of the positive attitude in America: Observation and speculation. *Journal of Clinical Psychology, 58*, 965–991.

Held, B. S. (2004). The negative side of positive psychology. *Journal of Humanistic Psychology, 44*, 9–46.

Henckmann, W. (2005). "Geitige Person" bei Viktor E. Frankl und Max Scheler. In D. Batthyany & O. Zsok (Eds.), *Viktor Frankl und die philosophie* (pp. 149–162). Vienna, Austria: Springer.

Kahneman, D., Diener, E., & Schwarz, N. (Eds.). (1999). *Well-being: The foundations of hedonic psychology*. New York, NY: Russell Sage Foundation.

Kaufmann, W. (1956). *Existentialism from Dostoyevsky to Sartre*. New York, NY: New American Libraray.

Keyes, C. L., Shmotkin, D., & Ryff, C. D. (2002). Optimizing well-being: The empirical encounter of two traditions. *Journal of Personality and Social Psychology, 82*, 1007–1022.

King, L. A., & Napa, C. K. (1998). What makes life good? *Journal of Personality and Social Psychology, 75*, 156–165.

Kottler, J. A., & Hazler, R. J. (2001). The therapist as a model of humane values and humanistic behavior. In K. J. Schneider, J. F. T. Bugental, & J. Fraser Pierson (Eds.), *The handbook of humanistic psychology: Leading edges in theory, research, and practice* (pp. 355–370). Thousand Oaks, CA: Sage.

Lazarus, R. S. (2003). Does the positive psychology movement have legs? *Psychological Inquiry, 14*, 93–109.

Linley, P. A., & Joseph, S. (2004a). Applied positive psychology: A new perspective for professional practice. In P. A. Linley & S. Joseph (Eds.), *Positive psychology in practice* (pp. 3–14). Hoboken, NJ: Wiley.

Linley, P. A., & Joseph, S. (2004b). Preface. In P. A. Linley & S. Joseph (Eds.), *Positive psychology in practice* (pp. xv–xvi). Hoboken, NJ: Wiley.

Linley, P. A., Joseph, S., Harrington, S., & Wood, A. M. (2006). Positive psychology: Past, present, and (possible) future. *Journal of Positive Psychology, 1*, 3–16.

Martin, M. W. (2007). Happiness and virtue in positive psychology. *Journal for the Theory of Social Behaviour, 37*(1), 89–103.

Maslow, A. H. (1971). *The farthest reaches of human nature*. New York, NY: Viking.

Maslow, A. H. (1973). Self-actualizing people: A study of psychological health. In R. J. Lowry (Ed.), *Dominance, self-esteem, self-actualization: Germinal papers of A. H. Maslow* (pp. 177–201). Monterey, CA: Brooks/Cole.

Maslow, A. H. (1987). *Motivation and personality*. New York, NY: HarperCollins.

May, R. (1962). Dangers in the relation of existentialism to psychotherapy. In H. M. Ruitenbeek (Ed.), *Psychoanalysis and existential philosophy* (pp. 179–187). New York, NY: Dutton.

May, R. (1996). *Psychology and the human dilemma*. New York, NY: Norton.

May, R., Angel, E., & Ellenberger, H. R. (1958). *Existence*. New York, NY: Basic Books.

McGregor, I., & Little, B. R. (1998). Personal projects, happiness, and meaning: On doing well and being yourself. *Journal of Personality and Social Psychology, 74*, 494–512.

Merleau-Ponty, M. (1995). *Phenomenology of perception* (C. Smith, Trans.). London, England: Routledge.

Miller, S. D., Duncan, B. L., & Hubble, M. A. (2005). Outcome-informed work. In J. C. Norcross, & M. R. Goldfried (Eds.), *Handbook of psychotherapy integration* (2nd ed., pp. 84–102). New York, NY: Oxford University Press.

Nakamura, J., & Csikszentmihalyi, M. (2005). The concept of flow. In C. R. Snyder & S. J. Lopez (Eds.), *Handbook of positive psychology* (pp. 89–105). Oxford, England: Oxford University Press.

Peterson, C., Park, N., & Seligman, M. E. (2005). Orientations to happiness and life satisfaction: The full life versus the empty life. *Journal of Happiness Studies, 6*(1), 25–41.

Peterson, C., Seligman, M. E. (2004). *Character strengths and virtues: A handbook and classification.* Washington, DC: APA Press.

Rathunde, K. (2001). Toward a psychology of optimal functioning: What positive psychology can learn from the "experiential" turns of James, Dewey, and Maslow. *Journal of Humanistic Psychology, 41,* 135–153.

Resnick, S., Warmoth, A., & Serlin, I. A. (2001). The humanistic psychology and positive psychology connection: Implications for psychotherapy. *Journal of Humanistic Psychology, 41,* 73–101.

Rich, G. J. (2001). Positive psychology: An introduction. *Journal of Humanistic Psychology, 41,* 8–12.

Robbins, B. D. (2006a). An empirical, phenomenological study: Being joyful. In C. T. Fischer (Ed.), *Qualitative research methods for psychologists: Introduction through empirical studies* (pp. 173–211). San Diego, CA: Elsevier Academic Press.

Robbins, B. D. (2006b). The delicate empiricism of Goethe: Phenomenology as a rigorous science of nature. *Indo-Pacific Journal of Phenomenology, 6,* np. Retrieved from http://www.ipjp.org/SEmethod/Special_Edition_Method-01_Robbins.pdf

Robbins, B. D. (2008). What is the good life? Positive psychology and the renaissance of humanistic psychology. *The Humanistic Psychologist, 36,* 96–112.

Robbins, B. D. (2013a). Dignity, personalism, and humanistic psychology. *The New Existentialists.* Retrieved from http://www.saybrook.edu/newexistentialists/posts/08-16-13

Robbins, B. D. (2013b). Human dignity and humanistic values: A call to humanistic psychology's mission. *The New Existentialists.* Retrieved from http://www.saybrook.edu/newexistentialists/posts/12-19-13

Robbins, B. D., & Friedman, H. (2008). Introduction to our special issue on positive psychology. *The Humanistic Psychologist, 36,* 93–95.

Robbins, B. D., & Friedman, H. (2011). Resiliency as a virtue: Contributions from humanistic and positive psychology. In K. M. Gow & M. J. Celinski (Eds.), *Continuity versus creative response to challenge: The primacy of resilience and resourcefulness in life and therapy.* Hauppauge, NY: Nova Science.

Robbins, B. D., & McInerney, R. G. (2013). *Humanistic psychology: A brief history.* Unpublished manuscript, Point Park University, Pittsburgh, PA.

Rogers, C. R. (1961). *On becoming a person.* London, England: Constable.

Rogers, C. R. (1965). Toward a science of the person. In T. W. Mann (Ed.), *Behaviorism and phenomenology: Contrasting bases for modern psychology.* Chicago, IL: University of Chicago Press.

Ryan, R. M., & Deci, E. L. (2001). On happiness and human potentials: A review of research on hedonic and eudaimonic well-being. *Annual Review of Psychology, 52*(1), 141–166.

Ryff, C. D. (1989). Happiness is everything, or is it? Explorations on the meaning of psychological well-being. *Journal of Personality and Social Psychology, 57,* 1069–1081.

Scheler, M. (1973). *Formalism in ethics and non-formal ethics of values: A new attempt toward the foundation of an ethical personalism.* Evanston, IL: Northwestern University Press.

Schneider, K. (2011). Toward a humanistic positive psychology: Why can't we just get along? *Journal of the Society for Existential Analysis, 22*(1), 32–38.

Schulz, D. P., & Schulz, S. E. (2011). *A history of modern psychology.* Belmont, CA: Cengage Learning.

Schwartz, B., & Sharpe, K. E. (2005). Practical wisdom: Aristotle meets positive psychology. *Journal of Happiness Studies, 7,* 377–395.

Seligman, M. E. P. (2002). *Authentic happiness.* New York, NY: Free Press.

Seligman, M. E. P., & Csikszentmihalyi, M. (2000). Positive psychology: An introduction. *American Psychologist, 55,* 5–14.

Seligman, M. E. P., Steen, T. A., Park, N., & Peterson, C. (2005). Positive psychology progress: Empirical validation of interventions. *American Psychologist, 60*(5), 410.

Shaffer, J. B. P. (1978). *Humanistic psychology.* Upper Saddle River, NJ: Prentice Hall.

Shapiro, S. B. (2001). Illogical positivism. *American Psychologist, 56,* 82.

Skinner, B. F. (1971). *Beyond freedom and dignity.* New York, NY: Bantam Vintage.

Slife, B. D., & Williams, R. N. (1995). *What's behind the research? Discovering hidden assumptions in the behavioral sciences.* Thousand Oaks, CA: Sage.

Spiegelberg, H. (1972). *Phenomenology in psychology and psychiatry.* Evanston, IL: Northwestern University Press.

Sugarman, J. (2007). Practical rationality and the questionable premise of positive psychology. *Journal of Humanistic Psychology, 47,* 175–197.

Sundararajan, L. (2005). Happiness donut: A Confucian critique of positive psychology. *Journal of Theoretical and Philosophical Psychology, 25,* 35–60.

Taylor, E. (2001). Positive psychology and humanistic psychology: A reply to Seligman. *Journal of Humanistic Psychology, 41*(1), 13–29.

Turner, B. S. (2006). *Vulnerability and human rights.* University Park: The Pennsylvania State University Press.

United Nations. (1948). *The universal declaration of human rights.* Retrieved from http://www.un.org/en/documents/udhr/

Vella-Brodrick, D. A. (2007). *Orientations to happiness as predictors of subjective well-being.* Unpublished manuscript, Monash University, Melbourne, Australia.

Wampold, B. E. (2001). *The great psychotherapy debate: Models, methods, and findings.* Mahwah, NJ: Erlbaum.

Waterman, A. S. (2013) The humanistic psychology—positive psychology divine: Contrasts in philosophical foundation. *American Psychologist, 68,* 124–133.

Wertz, F. J. (2001). Humanistic psychology and the qualitative research tradition. In K. J. Schneider, J. F. T. Bugental, & J. F. Pierson (Eds.), *The handbook of humanistic psychology: Leading edges in theory, research, and practice* (pp. 231–246). Thousand Oaks, CA: Sage.

Williams, T. D. (2005). *Who is my neighbor? Personalism and the foundations of human rights.* Washington, DC: The Catholic University of America.

Wong, P. T. P. (2011a). Positive psychology 2.0: Towards a balanced interactive model of the good life. *Canadian Psychology/Psychologie canadienne, 52,* 69–81.

Wong, P. T. P. (2011b). Reclaiming positive psychology: A meaning-centered approach to sustainable growth and radical empiricism. *Journal of Humanistic Psychology, 51,* 408–412.

Woolfolk, R. L. (2002). The power of negative thinking: Truth, melancholia, and the tragic sense of life. *Journal of Theoretical and Philosophical Psychology, 22,* 19–27.

Woolfolk, R. L., & Wasserman, R. H. (2005). Count no one happy: Eudaimonia and positive psychology. *Journal of Theoretical and Philosophical Psychology, 25,* 81–90.

# CHAPTER 4

# Existential Dimensions of Positive Psychology

ROGER BRETHERTON

THIS CHAPTER ADDRESSES what may seem at first glance to be an unlikely theoretical and practical collaboration, that of existential thought with positive psychology. It argues that there are numerous correspondences and potentially fruitful connections between these two broad intellectual movements and that there is much mutual enrichment to be gained from their cross-fertilization. Indeed, as noted herein, some of the most illuminating concepts in positive psychology bear a distinctly existential inflection. Positive psychology is often at its best when it is most existential. For the sake of argument, some provisional definitions of terms may be useful at the outset.

Positive psychology in this chapter, as in much of the present volume, is taken to mean the movement initiated largely at the turn of the 21st century (though evident prior to that), spearheaded most notably by Martin Seligman during his year as president of the American Psychological Association (see Linley, Joseph, Harrington, & Wood, 2006). As frequently reiterated, positive psychology is concerned most particularly with the psychology of what makes the good, pleasurable, and meaningful life (Seligman, 2003), and is expressed in terms such as *thriving*, *flourishing*, and *happiness*. It is on the whole an empirical approach, seeking to use the research methods of mainstream psychology to investigate the length and breadth of human thriving, and therefore it submits to the received view of scientific knowledge, progressing by peer review and replication.

It could also to some extent be viewed as a protest movement against the tendency in certain forms of mainstream psychology to predominantly address psychological problems, under the assumption that it is these less salutary aspects of being human that are most essential or important for study (Jørgensen & Nafstad 2004; see also Nafstad, Chapter 2, this volume). According to Seligman (2003), "the 'rotten-to-the-core' view pervades Western thought, and if there is any doctrine positive psychology seeks to overthrow it is this one" (p. 126). Positive psychology aimed to correct this bias and, judging by the proliferation of attendant teaching, research, and writing, has to a large extent succeeded (Seligman, Steen, Park, & Peterson, 2005).

## THE INTERNAL DIVERSITY OF THE EXISTENTIAL APPROACH

The existential approach on the other hand is more problematic to define, but nevertheless, retains definite contours as a movement. Much of this chapter draws on the practitioners who have drawn on existential thinking in the development of therapeutic practice, but it could be argued that there is no single "existential psychotherapy" as such, and hence reviews of the field have taken to referring to the existential *therapies* (Cooper, 2003). Furthermore, existentially influenced practitioners are increasingly stretching their influence into areas of workplace coaching, supervision, and organizational development (e.g., Langdridge, 2012; Spinelli, 2010; van Deurzen & Hanaway 2012; van Deurzen & Young, 2009). The existential influence in psychology is broader than just psychotherapy; nevertheless, several features unify the spectrum of those who presume to call their therapeutic practice *existential*.

Primarily existential practitioners are philosophical in orientation (van Deurzen-Smith, 1984). They are interested in the ways in which a person's understanding of life influences and constructs his or her quality of living. In doing so they therefore draw on a rich philosophical background, biased most notably, but not exclusively, toward the mid-20th century "existentialists." Ironically, very few of them were willing to be called by that name, but the term is widely accepted to include Martin Buber, Martin Heidegger, Jean-Paul Sartre, Albert Camus, and Maurice Merleau-Ponty, to name but a few of them. According to Warnock (1970), the common interest that unites these philosophers is the interest in human freedom:

> For Existentialists the problem of freedom is in a sense a practical problem. They aim above all, to show people *that they are free*, to open their eyes to something which has always been true, but which for one reason or another may not always have been recognized, namely that men are free to choose, not only what to do on a specific occasion, but what to value and how to live. (Warnock, 1970, pp. 1–2)

This boom in existential thinking in the 1940s and 50s was anticipated by earlier thinkers such as Blaise Pascal (1623–1662), Søren Kierkegaard (1813–1855), and Friedrich Nietzsche (1844–1900). And they in turn reached further back to other philosophers of existential inclination (Plato, Aristotle, Saint Augustine, among others). What these earlier philosophers held in common with their 20th-century counterparts, and contemporary existential psychotherapists, was a thoughtful approach to the matters of everyday life.

From Socrates to Sartre and ever since, therefore, existential thinkers are concerned with how life is to be lived well. Their writings are therefore overtly *psychotherapeutic*, a theme developed by van Deurzen (1998) in contending that the etymology of the word *psychotherapy* leads to a literal translation of *care for the soul*, "for in ancient Greek the noun *psyche* means soul or life force and the verb *therapeuo* means to care for or to serve . . . to the notion of caring or looking after" (p. 134). Existential thinkers write and speak to challenge their audience, to change and awaken them. They address us directly about our "existence," that is, the way in which we (you and I) as human beings emerge, stand out, and take responsibility for our living.

This chapter therefore draws from across the range of contemporary existential thought and therapy. While the author is most influenced by the ever-broadening British school of existential therapy (Adams, 2013; Langdridge, 2013; Spinelli, 2007;

van Deurzen, 2012), the term *existential approach* will be used to denote concepts or practices derived from theorists and therapists from the existential tradition in its broadest sense.

## THE DIFFUSE INFLUENCE OF EXISTENTIAL THINKING

There is a further reason, however, beyond its wide-ranging internal diversity, that makes a definition of the existential approach difficult to pin down: the surprisingly large swath of its influence in modern therapeutic psychology. It was once said of Carl Rogers that his impact on the fields of psychology, psychotherapy, education, and human relations could be variously described as "momentous, persuasive, indirect or elusive" (Thorne, 2003, p. 44). The same could be said of existential thinking; its influence is ubiquitous in therapeutic psychology, but often anonymous.

First, there are numerous instances in which existential therapy, rather than standing alone, has been merged with other therapeutic approaches. Perhaps the first example of such occurred in 1929 when Ludwig Binswanger, a psychiatrist and lifelong friend of Sigmund Freud, first met Martin Heidegger and initiated the development of an approach designed to analyze a person's existential position via psychoanalytic methodology (Cohn, 2002). Three decades later, R. D. Laing's (1960) infamous early phenomenology of schizophrenia drew on a creative synthesis of existential concepts and developmental psychology (Laing, 1960; Laing & Esterson, 1964), and subsequently paved the way for contemporary psychological understandings of psychosis (Bentall, 2004). In the United States, the existential approach to psychotherapy achieved prominence largely due to the impressive translation into English, overseen by Rollo May, of various European scholars such as Binswanger (May, Angel, & Ellenberger, 1958). The explicitly labeled "existential psychotherapy" of May (1983) and Irvin Yalom (1980) integrated the influence of psychodynamic and humanistic psychotherapy with existential insight. Yalom drew attention to the collaborative potential of the existential approach in referring to it as the "off the record . . . throw-ins" (Yalom, 1980, p. 4) that made therapy work. His belief was that "the vast majority of experienced therapists, regardless of their adherence to some other ideological school, employ many of the existential insights I shall describe" (Yalom, 1980, p. 5).

Yalom's assertion is further borne out by an examination of the numerous approaches that carry existential assumptions implicitly without necessarily taking an existential title. Perhaps unsurprisingly, given the close association of existential psychotherapy with the humanistic perspective (Sanders, 2012), Carl Rogers expressed his indebtedness to existential thought in noting "how accurately the Danish philosopher Søren Kierkegaard pictured the dilemma of the individual more than a century ago, with keen psychological insight" (Rogers, 1961, p. 110), and how in Kierkegaard he found "deep insights and convictions which beautifully express views I have held but never been able to formulate" (p. 199). Aaron Beck, referring to the origination of cognitive therapy, acknowledged that European existential-phenomenological psychiatry had "substantially influenced the development of modern psychology in this group of psychotherapies" (Beck, Rush, Shaw, & Emery, 1979, p. 9). In addition, anyone schooled in existential thought would quickly recognize the phenomenology of awareness presented in Fritz Perls's introduction to Gestalt psychotherapy (Perls, Hefferline, & Goodman, 1951). Although these approaches may not be labeled existential as such, they nevertheless bear the mark, and thereby testify to the enormous but subtle influence of existential thinking on therapeutic psychology.

What is perhaps even more pertinent in the present context, however, is a similarly pronounced existential influence evident in positive psychology. Many prominent foci of the positive psychology movement are knowingly influenced by existential thinking. An example is the research conducted by Emmons and his collaborators. It is suffused with existential philosophy and insight. His work on strivings in human personality borrows the term "ultimate concerns" from existential theologian Paul Tillich (1957), and he even goes as far as to state that the central theme of the work can be summed up by this concept (Emmons, 1999). Similarly, his extensive research on gratitude acknowledges Heidegger's equivalence of "thinking" with "thanking" as an indication that gratitude "is not for the intellectually lethargic" (Emmons, 2007, p. 5).

Other areas of positive psychology also liberally draw on sources in the existential canon. From its outset, the posttraumatic growth literature has recognized existential themes in both theory and therapeutic outcome (Tedeschi, Park, & Calhoun, 1998; see also Tedeschi, Calhoun, & Groleau, Chapter 30, this volume), and one state-of-the-art volume on the subject quotes Nietzsche in its title (Joseph, 2011). Even more fundamentally, the continual dialogue in positive psychology circles concerning the relative costs and benefits of hedonic versus eudaimonic well-being (e.g., Biswas-Diener, Kashdan, & King, 2009; Kopperud & Vittersø, 2008; Vittersø & Søholt, 2011; Waterman, 2008; see also Huta, Chapter 10, this volume) mirrors a similarly vibrant discussion within the existential literature (van Deurzen, 2009).

It is therefore not the vagueness of the existential approach that makes it difficult to define, but rather the pervasive subtlety of its influence in psychology. Far from being absent from positive psychology, existential thinking can be found everywhere therein, and that is a good thing. Indeed, this chapter contends that paying greater attention to the existential dimensions of positive psychology enriches, expands, and deepens the field.

## THE EXISTENTIAL EMPHASIS ON TRAGEDY

Nevertheless, in spite of the conceptual interpenetration of these respective approaches, we should anticipate some objections to the notion that existential psychotherapy in its fullest sense has much to offer the field of positive psychology, not the least of which would be the dour reputation of existentialism. Whereas positive psychology has addressed itself to the happy, good, and meaningful life, existential therapy has stressed the bleaker side of life, summed up in Yalom's (1980) four ultimate concerns of death, freedom, isolation, and meaninglessness. It has sometimes been argued that, in addressing the more unpalatable domains of human living, existential thinkers and therapists have in some way magnified, exacerbated, and perhaps even celebrated the suffering involved, leading one commentator to quip that this "is what earns existentialism its reputation for being depressive, despairing, and despondent. . . . [It] certainly attracts such personality types and often makes them worse" (Marinoff, 2003, p. 35). It was perhaps for good reason that Tillich (1952) dubbed existentialism "the courage to despair." But he did not stop there; he called it "the courage to . . . despair . . . and to resist the radical threat of nonbeing by the courage to be as oneself" (Tillich, 1952, p. 140)—the courage to affirm oneself in the face of, and in spite of, despair.

It is a caricature to suggest that the existential approach is entirely gloomy. Among existential thinkers there are both optimistic and pessimistic inflections. In the domain of human relationships, for example, Sartre (1943) advocated a radically pessimistic view that arguably makes true human community nigh impossible, but others such as Martin Buber (1937, 1947) and Gabriel Marcel (1950, 1964) advocated more hopeful models of connection and commitment. Similar alternative positions can also be identified among existential thinkers as to whether meaning in life is found or created. In existential psychotherapy, this ambiguity is acknowledged by Yalom (1980) in naming his set of ultimate concerns; they could easily have been named in a more positive light. An existential approach is therefore not unanimously pessimistic, but neither is it avoidant of the tragic dimension of existence. On another occasion, Yalom (1989) phrased it as follows: "So much wanting. So much longing. And so much pain, so close to the surface, only minutes deep. Destiny pain. Existence pain. Pain that is always there, whirring continuously just beneath the membrane of life" (p. 3). It is therefore one of the contentions of existential thinking, and a fundamental tenet of its therapeutic practice, that directly facing the less glittering aspects of life can be a source of passion and courage in living. In writing of the sometimes painful process involved in this confrontation, May (1989) wrote that the client "should ordinarily go out more *courageous* after the interview, but courageous with the painful realization that his or her personality must be transformed. If the counseling has been more than superficial, he or she will feel shaken and probably unhappy" (p. 124). The existential approach suggests that a positive psychology can be found by exploring the difficulties of human living, not by avoiding them. This is not foreign territory for positive psychology; much of the psychology of hope (Snyder, 2000; see also Magyar-Moe & Lopez, Chapter 29, this volume), gratitude (Emmons & McCullough, 2004; see also Bono, Krakauer, & Froh, Chapter 33, this volume), and forgiveness (McCullough, Pargament, & Thoresen, 2001; see also Fincham, Chapter 38, this volume), for example, resonate with similar notions of human magnificence in the face of adverse circumstances. Positive psychology knows a thing or two about dealing with the darker side of life, an insight eminently compatible with an existential perspective.

## METHODOLOGICAL INCOMPATIBILITY

Perhaps a more fundamental objection to the confluence of positive psychology and existential thought lies in the perceived methodological differences that characterize the two fields. Positive psychology methodologically belongs to mainstream psychology, preferring empirical scientific methodology to establish the credibility of its field (Seligman, 2003). Existential psychotherapy on the other hand has historically preferred to analyze human existence by phenomenological methods and reflective practice, sometimes referred to as *discovery-oriented research* (Mahrer & Boulet, 2004).

This distinction, however, runs the risk of caricaturing both movements. Positive psychology embraces numerous phenomenological and hermeneutic research ventures (e.g., Krause, Evans, Powers, & Hayward, 2012), and existential research, although continuing to encourage phenomenological approaches, has broadened into a wider range of methodologies in recent years. Existential psychotherapists are prominent in researching therapeutic practice in the United Kingdom (Cooper, 2008), and several introductory texts include reviews of relevant empirical literature from mainstream psychology (Jacobsen, 2008; Langdridge, 2013). Furthermore, there is an increasing range of empirical psychology that addresses issues familiar to the existential tradition, such as death anxiety under the remit of terror management theory (TMT; Greenberg &Arndt, 2011), and several empirically based volumes on the human quest for meaning (Baumeister, 1991; Wong, 2012). The apparent methodological gulf between existentially informed research and positive psychology is therefore not as wide as initially perceived.

Related to this there is also a perceived difficulty in operationalizing what advocates of existential therapy actually do. Positive psychology tends to be attentive to the kind of predictable, replicable results that lend themselves to the design of technical interventions. Positive psychologists are not cautious about adapting their findings into short instructional manuals, a good recent example being the 21-day "emotional prosperity" program developed on the basis of gratitude research (Emmons, 2013). In contradistinction, existential psychotherapy is ambivalent about the notion of objectivized techniques. It is chary of alienating a person from his or her lived experience by the prescription of a set of objectivized skills, and it suspects that a technical approach to therapy may somehow violate the way in which the client chooses to emerge in the session (Cohn, 2002).

Nevertheless, there are several examples of existential therapists working hard to put what they do into words without necessarily naming them techniques as such. From the outset, Yalom (1980) adopted a practical onus in his elaboration of the approach and more recently condensed his profound therapeutic insight into a series of pithy chapters for would-be therapists (Yalom, 2009). Even practitioners in the British school, while acknowledging the inherent ambiguity therein, have creatively framed the practice of existential psychotherapy in terms of the skills involved (van Deurzen & Adams, 2010). It may be difficult to put what existential practitioners do into words, but it is not impossible, and this possibility clears the way for further consideration of the contribution of existential thought to positive psychological practice.

## POSITIVE PSYCHOLOGY AND EXISTENTIAL THOUGHT IN PRACTICAL COLLABORATION

The gap between theory and practice, so it is said, is much greater in practice than it is in theory. Largely due to their investment in figuring out everyday concerns, existential thinkers have abjured any clear-cut division between the theoretical and the practical. Their writings are littered with references to the sheer practicality of good thinking. Sartre rhapsodized that "the truth drags through the streets" (cited in Kearney, 1994, p. 3) and Kierkegaard (1849/1989) insisted that his writing was "like a physician's lecture beside the sick bed" (p. 35), delivered with the aim of assisting the patient. In other words, their philosophy was intended to be lived. This section addresses some specific ways in which an existential approach can collaborate with positive psychology in practice, with special reference to the burgeoning psychology of character strengths and virtues.

### The Existential Contribution to Values, Strengths, and Virtues

Given the philosophical nature of existential psychotherapy, one of the most evident areas of mutual interest with positive psychology concerns notions of moral values, strengths, and virtues, and how these can be developed in human lives. From a positive psychology point of view, the emergence of the study of strength and virtue was an important development and was central to the core of the movement. The compilation of Peterson and Seligman's (2004) taxonomy of virtues was an intentional replacement of negative diagnostic criteria of pathology with characteristics of human flourishing, or as the authors phrased it, "a manual of the sanities" (p. 3). Since then, other similar taxonomies of virtue have been developed (Linley, Willars, Biswas-Diener, Garcea, & Stairs, 2010; Post & Neimark, 2007), and a broad psychometric literature has grown up around these salutary qualities (Furnham & Lester, 2012; Linley et al., 2007; Shryack, Steger, Krueger, & Kallie, 2010; VIA Pro, 2004). As a consequence, the focus on strength and virtue, as opposed to pathology and disorder, has become one of the hallmarks of positive psychology, as evidenced in its ubiquitous application in therapeutic (Niemiec, Rashid, & Spinella, 2012) and coaching (Linley & Harrington, 2006) interventions.

Existential psychotherapy in its various guises has likewise been concerned with the strengths and virtues of human living. Similarly to this area of positive psychology, existential psychotherapy, unlike many therapeutic approaches, begins not with a model of pathology to be solved, but with the predicaments of human living to be navigated skillfully, summed up poetically by van Deurzen (1998) as the "paradox and passion" of life. It addresses itself to the question of what makes life worth living. It views living as a skill, and therapy as a tutorial or seminar in the art of living well (van Deurzen, 2012). Like many strengths interventions, it proceeds by clarifying the values by which an individual lives and thereby facilitates his or her commitment to them.

## VALUE AND VIRTUES: DISTINCT BUT LINKED

The existential vantage point therefore has a lot to offer strengths psychology. From a philosophical point of view, existential therapists would be quick to draw a distinction between the notion of value and that of virtue. In Western philosophical history, it was Nietzsche who first broached the notion of self-made "value" as an explicit repudiation of "virtue"—the "tables of ethics" handed down from previous generations (Nietzsche, 1884/1961). A similar moral vision was formerly, but independently, articulated by Kierkegaard (1843/1985) as the "teleological suspension of the ethical" (p. 83) and was latterly elaborated in the works of Sartre (1948), Camus (1955), and others. Value for the existentialists was, among other things, a challenge to take responsibility for our moral decision making.

Virtue, on the other hand, has a different philosophical genealogy. The modern revival of virtue ethics was explicitly critical of the notion of values espoused by Kierkegaard, Nietzsche, and Sartre, particularly (MacIntyre, 1985). As is well known in both positive psychology and existential therapy, the current conception of virtue emerges from Aristotle. In this tradition, virtues are "goods internal to practices . . . within an ongoing social tradition" (MacIntyre, 1985, p. 273), they are explicitly concerned with emotional regulation: feeling the right thing at the right time and embedded in a community that requires and values such virtues (Woodruff, 2001). "Virtue is the source of the feelings that prompt us to behave well. Virtue ethics takes feelings seriously because feelings affect our lives more deeply than beliefs do" (Woodruff, 2001, p. 6).

Conceptually speaking, therefore, value and virtue are distinct constructs. There is a conceptual tension here, a contradiction alluded to by MacIntyre (1985) when he posed the question, "Nietzsche or Aristotle? . . . The differences between the two run very deep" (pp. 256–259). But in practice, virtue and value are often linked; this connectedness is reflected in the psychometric literature in which the most prominent instrument for identifying strengths and virtues was originally named the Values in Action scale (VIA Pro, 2004). Virtues, it would seem, are the habits and postures we develop when pursuing that which we and/or our community value.

The existential emphasis therefore adds a note of caution to the strengths and virtues literature, a warning against reifying virtues, by treating them as entities or personality traits in their own right. It suggests that virtues are not givens but moral commitments or accomplishments, a perspective shared to some extent by much of the positive psychology literature. Failure to recognize this runs the risk of developing an inverted medical model in which diagnoses of anxiety or depression are supplanted by bestowals of humor or persistence in which virtues sound more akin to disease entities to be caught rather than the dynamic, wise practices they often are.

The existential approach therefore steers true to its philosophical roots in stressing the importance of not losing sight of human freedom in ethics and character development. It recognizes that we each have our biases and may be inclined toward certain virtues rather than others. But it also holds the door open to radical human freedom, whereby we may surprise ourselves through the development of previously unpracticed virtue, even though these breakthroughs may be accompanied by no small degree of anxiety. "The positive aspects of selfhood develop as the individual confronts, moves through, and overcomes anxiety creating experiences" (May, 1977, p. 393).

### TRADITIONS OF VIRTUE

Alongside resisting the reification of virtues, existentially informed practice would be equally quick to reemphasize the importance of acknowledging the tradition behind virtues and character strengths. An existential approach would suggest that the history of strengths and virtues is not peripheral or incidental, but an essential part of our understanding and appreciation of them. In many respects, this view of history follows Heidegger's contention that history does not so much tell us of our past as much as demonstrate human possibilities open for us in the present:

> History is concerned not with facts but with possibilities, that is to say, not with reconstructing events or chains of events in the past but with exploring the possibilities . . . that have been opened up in the course of history; and [Heidegger] claims further that history is interested not in the past but essentially in the future. It fetches from the past the authentic repeatable possibilities of existence in order to project them into the future. (Macquarrie, 1972, p. 230)

History inspires our future. The history of virtues, the various traditions in which they arise, is inextricable from our intention to develop them over the course of our lives.

In this regard, it was the existential polymath Karl Jaspers (1883–1969) who first identified the discrete portion of human history in which the first attempts at universal human virtues (ethics intended for the good of all people) arose. He named this period the Axial Age, "the years centering around 500 BC—from 800 to 200," in which "the spiritual foundations of humanity were laid, simultaneously and independently in China, India, Persia, Palestine, and Greece," and upon which "humanity still subsists today" (Jaspers, 1951/2003, p. 98). During this window of time there is evidence of the relatively simultaneous emergence of universalizing ethics in these civilizations, sometimes referred to as the Great Transformation (Armstrong, 2006) and studied particularly with regard to the roots of universal compassion (Armstrong, 2011). Jaspers (1949/1953) was bold enough to suggest that humanity as we know it emerged during this era.

But virtues with universal intent arose not in a vacuum, or even in a personal development workshop, but as a response to the existential predicaments of their time. Sociological analysis of the Axial civilizations for which we have evidence suggests that each of these "breakthroughs" occurred in response to some kind of societal "breakdown" (Bellah, 2011). Regarding virtues within the context of their historical tradition allows us to value them much more highly. Knowing that they were hard-won, costly insights for those who first stumbled over them deters us from cheapening them into Scout badges to be accumulated easily. It also underscores the aspect of the strengths literature that endorses self-regulation or willpower as the prime virtue or "moral muscle" (Baumeister & Exline, 1999, 2000). These are not characteristics to be treated lightly, sold cheaply, or earned inevitably.

The existential approach therefore finds much to celebrate in the recent elaboration of ubiquitous strengths and virtues in positive psychology. By stressing human freedom, it ensures that strengths psychology remains vibrant and dynamic and avoids viewing virtues as inert ciphers or tokens. Stressing the majestic tradition in which virtues stand ensures that character psychology retains the profundity of its subject matter and avoids the threat of superficiality. Existentially inclined practitioners, whether working as psychotherapists, coaches, or organizational consultants, view virtues not merely as relatively independent character traits, but located within the context of a person's view of the world, their "basic assumptions" (van Deurzen, 2012, p. 14), the fundamental philosophical presuppositions upon which human beings base their lives.

Perhaps the place where our character strengths and virtues become most evident is in our closest relationships—our marriages and significant partnerships. Positive psychology has a great deal to teach us in terms of what makes partnerships work (see Gottman, 1999). But there is an equally considerable existential contribution to the notion of a healthy marriage or partnership. Kierkegaard's (1843/1987) first major work, *Either/Or*, took commitment to marriage as the central motif for the psychological unity achieved through living the ethical life. Similarly, Buber's (1937) notion of the I–thou relationship in many respects expresses the avoidance of objectifying one's partner as necessary for fulfilling human contact. Marcel (1964) particularly has articulated the phenomenology of worthwhile relational commitment, which is translated from the French as "creative fidelity." According to Marcel (1964), any productive commitment requires two facets: First, that from the moment of commitment, any influence or development that would threaten the commitment "will thus be demoted to the rank of a temptation" (p. 162) to be resisted. But this is only the negative movement of commitment that Marcel labels "constancy . . . perseverance in a certain goal" (p. 153). But constancy in relationship risks emotional staleness. For a commitment to be truly life-affirming, for it to be "creative fidelity" in Marcel's terms, it requires the second positive movement. It needs hope. The belief that maintaining the commitment in some way leads to a better future for oneself and for the other, or to possibilities that would otherwise die for both if the commitment were broken. Marcel noted that the difference between constancy and fidelity was "presence" to oneself and for the other (Marcel, 1964, p. 153).

The existential literature is therefore rich in analysis and understanding of intimate relationships and has inspired various therapists to write extensively on this subject. Van Deurzen notes the importance of truthfulness:

> Couples inevitably pay the high price of fragmentation and alienation when they betray mutual trust . . . for truth is the essential ingredient of human relating and where it is shared and valued it melds people together into larger units. Where truth is not shared it pushes people apart. (van Deurzen, 1998, p. 76)

Others emphasize the required openness in committing to a person as an ever-changing process, not as an object (Amodeo & Wentworth, 1986). A process commitment is "a more flexible, but equally serious commitment to the well-being of both ourselves and others. It reflects a consistent dedication to embody factors that reliably lead to personal growth, which provides a foundation for love and intimacy" (Amodeo & Wentworth, 1986, p. 144). Again, the existential onus on freedom denotes that partners learn from one another not by merging psychologically (Fromm, 1957) but by taking responsibility for their contributions to the relationship (May, 1969).

## CONCLUSION

The existential approach, therefore, although not being a positive psychology as such, demonstrates a variety of overlapping concerns with the movement of positive psychology. It arguably has a deep awareness of its own roots in human history and can therefore act as one of the many voices that prevent positive psychology from becoming superficial psychology. Its huge stress on human freedom also maintains the notion that living the good life is a choice that cannot be coerced, and therefore stands against any sense of the good life becoming a proscribed oppressive demand. In short, whereas the existential approach is not positive psychology, positive psychology in its most dynamic forms is almost always to some extent existential.

## SUMMARY POINTS

- Taking an existential perspective can be exceptionally fruitful for both the theory and practice of positive psychology.
- Contrary to popular opinion, the existential approach is not inherently pessimistic, nor is it methodologically irreconcilable with positive psychology.
- Positive psychology is already existential; it frequently draws on existential thinkers, themes, and terminology.
- Recognizing and acknowledging this existential emphasis can add depth and clarity to various aspects of positive psychology.
- The psychology of strengths and virtues offers a major area of mutual interest for both positive psychology and existential thinking.
- Although endorsing the study of virtue in psychology, the existential perspective would be critical of separating virtuous traits too far from their original historical and philosophical context.
- The existential approach is not averse to using philosophical history in a therapeutic manner to inspire the development of similar virtue in people today.
- An existential approach can therefore make a considerable positive contribution in various therapeutic and workplace contexts, including individual and couple psychotherapy.
- By emphasizing philosophical rigor, the existential approach acts as one of the many voices that prevent positive psychology from becoming superficial psychology.

## REFERENCES

Adams, M. (2013). *A concise introduction to existential counselling*. London, England: Sage.

Amodeo, J., & Wentworth, K. (1986). *Being intimate: A guide to successful relationships*. London, England: Arkana.

Armstrong, K. (2006). *The great transformation: The world in the time of Buddha, Socrates, Confucius and Jeremiah*. New York, NY: Random House.

Armstrong, K. (2011). *Twelve steps to a compassionate life*. London, England: Bodley Head.

Baumeister, R. F. (1991). *Meanings of life*. New York, NY: Guilford Press.

Baumeister, R. F., & Exline, J. J. (1999). Virtue, personality, and social relations: Self-control as the moral muscle. *Journal of Personality, 67*, 1165–1194.

Baumeister, R. F., & Exline, J. J. (2000). Self-control, morality, and human strength. *Journal of Social and Clinical Psychology, 19*, 29–42.

Beck, A. T., Rush, A. J., Shaw, B. F., & Emery, G. (1979). *Cognitive therapy of depression*. New York, NY: Guilford Press.

Bellah, R. N. (2011). *Religion in human evolution: From the Paleolithic to the Axial age*. Cambridge, MA: Harvard University Press.

Bentall, R. P. (2004). *Madness explained: Psychosis and human nature*. London, England: Penguin.

Biswas-Diener, R., Kashdan, T. B., & King, L. A. (2009). Two traditions of happiness research, not two distinct types of happiness. *The Journal of Positive Psychology, 4*, 208–211.

Buber, M. (1937). *I and thou*. Edinburgh, Scotland: T & T Clark.

Buber, M. (1947). *Between man and man*. London, England: Routledge.

Camus, A. (1955). *The myth of Sisyphus* (J. O'Brien, Trans.). Harmondsworth, England: Penguin.

Cohn, H. W. (2002). *Heidegger and the roots of existential therapy*. London, England: Sage.

Cooper, M. (2003). *Existential therapies*. London, England: Sage.

Cooper, M. (2008). *Essential research findings in counselling and psychotherapy: The facts are friendly*. London, England: Sage.

Emmons, R. A. (1999). *The psychology of ultimate concerns: Motivation and spirituality in personality*. New York, NY: Guilford Press.

Emmons, R. A. (2007). *Thanks!: How the new science of gratitude can make you happier*. New York, NY: Houghton Mifflin.

Emmons, R. A. (2013). *Gratitude works! A 21-day program for creating emotional prosperity*. San Francisco, CA: Jossey-Bass.

Emmons, R. A., & McCullough, M. E. (Eds.). (2004). *The psychology of gratitude*. Oxford, England: Oxford University Press.

Fromm, E. (1957). *The art of loving*. Hammersmith, England: Thorsons.

Furnham, A., & Lester, D. (2012). The development of a short measure of character strength. *European Journal of Psychological Assessment, 28*, 95–101.

Gottman, J. M. (1999). *The seven principles for making marriage work*. New York, NY: Crown.

Greenberg, J., & Arndt, J. (2011). Terror management theory. In P. A. M. van Lange, A. W. Kruglanski, & E. T. Higgins (Eds.), *Handbook of theories of social psychology* (pp. 398–415). Thousand Oaks, CA: Sage.

Jacobsen, B. (2008). *Invitation to existential psychology: A psychology for the unique human being and its applications in therapy*. Chichester, England: Wiley.

Jaspers, K. (1953). *The origin and goal of history* (M. Bullock, Trans.). New Haven, CT: Yale University Press. (Original work published 1949)

Jaspers, K. (2003). *Way to wisdom: An introduction to philosophy* (R. Manheim, Trans.) (2nd ed.). London, England: Yale University Press. (Original work published 1951)

Jørgensen, I. S., & Nafstad, H. E. (2004). Positive psychology: Historical, philosophical and epistemological perspectives. In P. A. Linley & S. Joseph (Eds.), *Positive psychology in practice* (pp. 15–34). Hoboken, NJ: Wiley.

Joseph, S. (2011). *What doesn't kill us: The new psychology of posttraumatic growth*. New York, NY: Basic Books.

Kearney, R. (1994). *Modern movements in European philosophy* (2nd ed.). Manchester, England: Manchester University Press.

Kierkegaard, S. (1985). *Fear and trembling* (A. Hannay, Trans.). Harmondsworth, England: Penguin. (Original work published 1843)

Kierkegaard, S. A. (1987). *Either/Or: Part II* (H. V. Hong & E. H. Hong, Trans.). Princeton, NY: Princeton University Press. (Original work published 1843)

Kierkegaard, S. A. (1989). *The sickness unto death: A Christian psychological exposition for edification and awakening* (A. Hannay, Trans.). Harmondsworth, England: Penguin. (Original work published 1849)

Kopperud, K. H., & Vittersø, J. (2008). Distinctions between hedonic and eudaimonic wellbeing: Results from a day reconstruction study among Norwegian jobholders. *Journal of Positive Psychology, 3,* 174–181.

Krause, N., Evans, L. A., Powers, G., & Hayward, R. D. (2012). Feeling grateful to god: A qualitative inquiry. *Journal of Positive Psychology, 7,* 119–130.

Laing, R. D. (1960). *The divided self.* London, England: Penguin.

Laing, R. D., & Esterson, A. (1964). *Sanity, madness and the family.* London, England: Penguin.

Langdridge, D. (2012). Existential coaching psychology. *Coaching Psykologi: The Danish Journal of Coaching Psychology, 2,* 83–89.

Langdridge, D. (2013). *Existential counselling and psychotherapy.* London, England: Sage.

Linley, P. A., & Harrington, S. (2006). Strengths coaching: A potential-guided approach to coaching psychology. *International Coaching Psychology Review, 1,* 37–46.

Linley, P. A., Joseph, S., Harrington, S., & Wood, A. M. (2006). Positive psychology: Past, present, and (possible) future. *Journal of Positive Psychology, 1,* 3–16.

Linley, P. A., Maltby, J., Wood, A. M., Joseph, S., Harrington, S., Peterson, C., & Seligman, M. E. P. (2007). Character strengths in the United Kingdom: The VIA inventory of strengths. *Personality and Individual Differences, 43,* 341–351.

Linley, P. A., Willars, J., Biswas-Diener, R., Garcea, N., & Stairs, M. (2010). *The strengths book: Be confident, be successful and enjoy better relationships by realising the best of you.* Warwick, England: Centre for Applied Positive Psychology Press.

MacIntyre, A. (1985). *After virtue: A study in moral theory* (2nd ed.). London, England: Duckworth.

Macquarrie, J. (1972). *Existentialism.* Harmondsworth, England: Penguin.

Mahrer, A. R., & Boulet, D. B. (2004). How can existentialists do research on psychotherapy? *Existential Analysis, 15,* 15–28.

Marcel, G. (1950). *The mystery of being: Vol. 1. Reflection and mystery.* South Bend, IN: St. Augustine's Press.

Marcel, G. (1964). *Creative fidelity* (R. Rosthal, Trans.). New York, NY: Fordham University Press.

Marinoff, L. (2003). *The big questions.* London, England: Bloomsbury.

May, R. (1969). *Love and will.* London, England: Norton.

May, R. (1977). *The meaning of anxiety.* New York, NY: Norton.

May, R. (1983). *The discovery of being: Writings in existential psychology.* New York, NY: Norton.

May, R. (1989). *The art of counselling.* London, England: Souvenir Press.

May, R., Angel, E., & Ellenberger, H. F. (Eds.). (1958). *Existence.* Northvale, NJ: Aronson.

McCullough, M. E., Pargament, K. I., & Thoresen, C. E. (2001). *Forgiveness: Theory, research, and practice.* New York, NY: Guilford Press.

Niemiec, R. M., Rashid, T., & Spinella, M. (2012). Strong mindfulness: Integrating mindfulness and character strengths. *Journal of Mental Health Counselling, 34,* 240–253.

Nietzsche, F. W. (1961). *Thus spoke Zarathustra* (R. J. Hollingdale, Trans.). Harmondsworth, England: Penguin. (Original work published 1884)

Perls, F., Hefferline, R. F., & Goodman, P. (1951). *Gestalt therapy: Excitement and growth in the human personality.* London, England: Souvenir.

Peterson, C., & Seligman, M. E. P. (2004). *Character strengths and virtues: A handbook and classification.* Oxford, England: Oxford University Press.

Post, S. G., & Neimark, J. (2007). *Why good things happen to good people.* New York, NY: Broadway.

Rogers, C. R. (1961). *On becoming A person: A therapist's view of psychotherapy*. London, England: Constable.

Sanders, P. (Ed.). (2012). *The tribes of the person-centred nation: An introduction to the schools of therapy related to the person-centred approach*. Hay-on-Wye, Wales: PCCS.

Sartre, J. (1943). *Being and nothingness* (H. E. Barnes, Trans.). London, England: Routledge.

Sartre, J. (1948). *Existentialism and humanism* (P. Mairet, Trans.). London, England: Methuen.

Seligman, M. E. P. (2003). Positive psychology: Fundamental assumptions. *Psychologist, 16*, 126–127.

Seligman, M. E. P., Steen, T. A., Park, N., & Peterson, C. (2005). Positive psychology progress: Empirical validation of interventions. *American Psychologist, 60*, 410.

Shryack, J., Steger, M. F., Krueger, R. F., & Kallie, C. S. (2010). The structure of virtue: An empirical investigation of the dimensionality of the virtues in action inventory of strengths. *Personality and Individual Differences, 48*, 714–719.

Snyder, C. R. (Ed.). (2000). *Handbook of hope: Theory, measures, and applications*. San Diego, CA: Academic Press.

Spinelli, E. (2007). *Practising existential psychotherapy: The relational world*. London, England: Sage.

Spinelli, E. (2010). Existential coaching. In E. Cox, T. Bachkirova, & D. Clutterbuck (Eds.), *The complete handbook of coaching* (pp. 94–106). London, England: Sage.

Tedeschi, R. G., Park, C. L., & Calhoun, L. G. (Eds.). (1998). *Posttraumatic growth: Positive changes in the aftermath of crisis*. London, England: Erlbaum.

Thorne, B. (2003). *Carl Rogers* (2nd ed.). London, England: Sage.

Tillich, P. (1952). *The courage to be*. New Haven, CT: Nota Bene.

Tillich, P. (1957). *Dynamics of faith*. New York, NY: Harper.

van Deurzen, E. (1998). *Paradox and passion in psychotherapy: An existential approach to therapy and counselling*. Chichester, England: Wiley.

van Deurzen, E. (2009). *Psychotherapy and the quest for happiness*. London, England: Sage.

van Deurzen, E. (2012). *Existential counselling and psychotherapy in practice* (3rd ed.). London, England: Sage.

van Deurzen, E., & Adams, M. (2010). *Skills in existential counselling & psychotherapy*. London, England: Sage.

van Deurzen, E., & Hanaway, M. (Eds.). (2012). *Existential perspectives on coaching*. Basingstoke, England: Palgrave-Macmillan.

van Deurzen, E., & Young, S. (Eds.). (2009). *Existential perspectives on supervision: Widening the horizon of psychotherapy and counselling*. Basingstoke, England: Palgrave-Macmillan.

van Deurzen-Smith, E. (1984). Existential therapy. In W. Dryden (Ed.), *Individual therapy in Britain* (pp. 152–172). London, England: Harper & Row.

VIA Pro. (2004). *VIA classification of strengths*. Retrieved from http://www.viacharacter.org/www/Character-Strengths/VIA-Classification

Vittersø, J., & Søholt, Y. (2011). Life satisfaction goes with pleasure and personal growth goes with interest: Further arguments for separating hedonic and eudaimonic well-being. *The Journal of Positive Psychology, 6*, 326–335.

Warnock, M. (1970). *Existentialism* (Rev. ed.). Oxford, England: Oxford University Press.

Waterman, A. S. (2008). Reconsidering happiness: A Eudaimonist's perspective. *The Journal of Positive Psychology, 3*, 234–252.

Wong, P. T. P. (Ed.). (2012). *The human quest for meaning* (2nd ed.). New York, NY: Routledge.

Woodruff, P. (2001). *Reverence: Renewing a forgotten virtue*. New York, NY: Oxford University Press.

Yalom, I. (1980). *Existential psychotherapy*. New York, NY: Basic Books.

Yalom, I. (1989). *Love's executioner and other tales of psychotherapy*. Harmondsworth, England: Penguin.

Yalom, I. (2009). *The gift of therapy: Reflections on being a therapist*. London, England: Piatkus.

# CHAPTER 5

# The Salutogenic Paradigm

SHIFRA SAGY, MONICA ERIKSSON, and ORNA BRAUN-LEWENSOHN

I N THE LATE 1970s, Aaron Antonovsky, who was a medical sociologist, raised a new question in his book *Health, Stress, and Coping* (Antonovsky, 1979). He proposed a new way to look at health and illness, not as a dichotomy but as a continuum—the salutogenic model. Much more than the answers he supplied, the real revolution in Antonovsky's way of thinking was manifested in the questions he posed. However, in posing the question of salutogenesis, Antonovsky actually detached himself from his own past research, as well as from almost everyone else's research at that time, which focused on the need to explain pathology. This led him to feel what he described as a "strong sense of isolation" (Antonovsky, 1987). We trust that in the 21st century, these feelings have been replaced by "a strong sense of belonging" to the growing positive psychology movement (Linley, Joseph, Harrington, & Wood, 2006). Although the salutogenic theory stems from the sociology of health, it has been at the leading edge of a range of academic movements emphasizing human strengths and not just weaknesses, human capacities and not just limits, well-being and not just illness (Mittelmark, 2008). In this chapter, we aim to connect salutogenesis—which literally means the origins of health—with the positive psychology movement.

We believe that the philosophical assumptions and the conceptual background of salutogenesis can deepen our understanding of the roots of the contemporary positive psychology movement. Why was the new term, calling for a new question, the salutogenic paradigm, so revolutionary?

During the first 25 years of research in the sociology of medicine (roughly 1950–1975), many profound contributions were made. This work provided both the theoretical and the empirical basis for the biopsychosocial model. Whatever the problem studied—social class and mental illness, cultural factors and heart disease, or delay in early detection of cancer—the research of psychologists and sociologists added to the understanding of the factors that contribute to the development of disease. Disease was perceived as deviance, as the departure from the known and the normal, as what had to be explained. Medical sociologists were critical of their medical colleagues for neglecting the psychosocial factors relevant to this process. But at the same time, they accepted the pathogenic orientation of the medical paradigm. In other areas of life, some sociologists, as well as a number of psychologists, tended to see conflict, deviance, and heterostasis as immanent. However, when it came to disease, it was assumed, as in the biological sciences, that people remain healthy unless attacked by some special "bug" or combination of "bugs." This is the essential pathogenic paradigm.

Salutogenesis makes a fundamentally different philosophical assumption about the world. The basic assumption of salutogenesis is that human environments by their very nature are stressor-rich. Such stressors may be microbiological, personal, economic, social, or geopolitical. In any and every event, the human being inhabits a world in which it is impossible to avoid stressors. All human beings are subject to a stressor load. The normal state of the human organism is one of entropy, disorder, and disruption of homeostasis. The basic human condition is stressful. Anyone who has ever raised a child—as Antonovsky used to say to his students—knows, at a gut level, what this is about.

This basic assumption especially struck Antonovsky after he had analyzed life stories of Holocaust survivors (Antonovsky, 1979) and found that more than a few women among them were well-adapted, no matter how adaptation was measured. Despite having lived through the most inconceivably inhuman experience, followed by displaced persons camps, illegal immigration to Palestine, experiencing the Israeli War of Independence in 1948, and other wars and terror events in the long, violent Israeli–Palestinian conflict, as well as suffering long periods of economic austerity, a significant number of women were reasonably healthy and happy, had raised families, worked, had friends, and were involved in community activities. Following these analyses of life stories, Antonovsky's paradigm of questioning began to ask: *Whence the strength?* Only later, however, did his most striking understanding come that "not only the Holocaust or the ongoing poverty can be considered as stressors. It is the human condition itself which is stressful" (Antonovsky, 1979, p. 8).

It appears that this basic philosophical assumption of the salutogenic theory constitutes Antonovsky's most important contribution. Instead of perceiving the human system as one that is sound unless it is attacked by some pathogen, the salutogenic approach views the human system as basically unsound, continuously attacked by disturbing processes and elements that cannot be prevented. Reading the newspaper in the morning, watching TV in the evening, overload at work, raising children—all of these constitute a state of continuing pressure on *each* person. In this basic chaotic condition of the world, Antonovsky claimed, human beings have the ability to find some order. Salutogenesis, then, directs one to think about the mystery of health rather than the causes of illness. In other words, given the world as it is, the meaningful question is not how people get sick, but *how can people stay healthy?*

## TWO DIFFERENT PARADIGMS

What have been the consequences of the dominance of the pathogenic paradigm in thinking, research, and intervention? What are the consequences of adopting a salutogenic paradigm? Following Antonovsky, we will consider some of the parameters characterizing these two paradigms.

First, the pathogenic paradigm led us to think about people in an either/or framework—to classify them as either healthy or diseased. Those in the healthy category are normal; their homeostasis is undisturbed. Those in the diseased category are deviant and must be brought back to normal condition. There is, at best, only modest recognition that an intermediate condition between health and disease may exist. Our society, for example, has difficulty in conceptualizing the chronically ill, who nonetheless function in daily life tasks. Moreover, a clear distinction is made between the diseased and the healthy. The sick, who are clearly suffering and in more immediate danger, are granted a more direct claim on society's resources. Moreover, despite the emergence and the widening of the health promotion discipline in recent years, research budgets for seeking cures are still much greater than those devoted to prevention.

Salutogenesis opens the way for thinking about health and disease along a *continuum* that goes from "health-ease" to "dis-ease." In such an approach, no one is categorized as healthy or diseased. Because we are all somewhere between the imaginary poles of total wellness and total illness, the *whole population* becomes the focus of concern. Even the fully robust, energetic, symptom-free, richly functioning individual has the mark of mortality: He or she wears glasses, has moments of depression, comes down with flu, and may also have as yet nondetectable malignant cells. Even the terminal patient's brain and emotions may be fully functional. The great majority of us are somewhere between the two poles. Priority in service is justly given to those at the sicker end of the continuum. But in our thinking and our research, we should ask: How does a person—wherever he or she is on the continuum—move toward the healthy pole?

Second, thinking pathogenically, we almost inevitably focus on one specific pathogenic entity: heart disease, cancer, schizophrenia, depression. Even those of us with an interest in preventive health behavior are no different: We think in terms of preventing disease or phenomenon X, Y, or Z, studying the genetic, physical, or social risk factors that presumably led to each. The very concept of "disease," as Antonovsky noted three decades ago, suggests that there are *common factors*, both etiologic and symptomatic, to *all* the specific entities that are subsumed under the label. But specialization leads to a disregard of these common factors. In those days, theories were inflexible: Type A behavior patterns were related to coronary heart disease (Mathews, 1977); learned helplessness was related to depression (Seligman, 1972).

In his suggestion to think salutogenically, searching for the mystery of health, Antonovsky freed us, three decades ago, from the limitation of being concerned with a particular disease. In thinking salutogenically, we communicate with all others who work on health research; we deal with the generalized factors involved in movement along a continuum, not just the factors specific for one disease. Speaking of prevention, we look for common factors to prevent a variety of diseases or phenomena. Thus, education campaigns that are carried out to prevent smoking among adolescents can also be directed to preventing other social diseases: unwanted pregnancies, alcohol drinking and drug abuse, or even suicidal behavior (Antonovsky, 1993).

In parallel fashion, and here we come to Antonovsky's core idea, the pathogenic paradigm has constrained us to investigate the cause (or causes) of a specific disease. Prime attention is given to the specific "bugs" related to disease X. After all, because the organism is perceived as naturally homeostatic, we ask about the factors that disturb homeostasis. We try to understand the sick role, and why people go to the doctor. We devote our energies to the study of pathogens. Antonovsky, on the other hand, claimed that stressors, or "bugs," are omnipresent, that pathogens are endemic in human existence and open-ended in their consequences. Assuming that stressors are ubiquitous, we turn our attention away from specific potential pathogens. Instead, we concern ourselves with the resources that help an individual cope with a wide range of pathogens and stressors, actually coping with life (Antonovsky, 1987).

The question then is no longer what keeps one from getting sicker, but what facilitates one's becoming healthier? No longer do we ask how we can eradicate this or that stressor but rather, how can we learn to live, and live well, with stressors, and possibly even turn their existence to our advantage? The question is not only how some cancer patients or poor people manage to stay healthy, but how *any of us* manage to stay healthy.

Antonovsky was also interested in studying the realm of stress. In this area too, the salutogenic view led him to ask other questions than those of other stress researchers at this time. While focusing in his own work on concentration camp survivors, poor people, and African Americans in the United States, he slowly began to ask not the usual question of risk factors, but about salutary factors: What is it that enables some of the camp survivors or some of the poor people, despite the circumstances, to do well? One can also ask, Who are the elderly who succeed in staying in good health? Who are the abused children who, despite their difficult situation, do well? Assuming that risk elements surround us throughout our lives and that they are usually unavoidable, the salutogenic question is then, How is it that, despite this continual state of risk and threat around us, people are not usually in a state of illness and pathology? Salutogenesis proposes changing the question about risk factors to the question of the extent to which we know how to cope with the difficult world around us. Antonovsky considered the salutogenic orientation to be an important innovation and a necessary reorientation of stress resources (Geyer, 1997).

As mentioned earlier, by posing fundamentally new questions Antonovsky parted from his own past research and from that of his colleagues. He wrote and spoke about his sense of isolation, but it was not long-lasting. Evidently, salutogenesis was a concept whose time had come. It offered a fresh, rich, and exciting way of looking at matters that concern all those working in the health, psychology, and well-being fields. In the mid-1980s, it became clear that a radically different mode of thinking was being developed. Instead of asking about pathogens and failures in coping that led to disease, some social scientists (Bandura, 1977, 1997; Kobasa, 1982; Seligman, 1972) began to focus on explanations of successful management of stressors and maintenance of health. Since then, the positive psychology movement has expanded to become a central and important pillar in psychology research (Linley et al., 2006).

By adopting a salutogenic orientation, psychologists, therapists, and physicians have made a substantial difference in their work (Sagy, 2011). Salutogenic questions lead our study—as well as its application—to helping children, families, and communities, wherever they are on the ease/dis-ease continuum, to move toward the healthy end of the ease/dis-ease continuum.

## THE SENSE OF COHERENCE CONCEPT

Antonovsky always used to tell his students (the first author was a doctoral student of Antonovsky's) that in all fields of scientific endeavor, the question is always more important than any given answer. However, he himself not only challenged us with a new question, he also had his particular answer to the question. He was convinced that "sense of coherence" is a major determinant of maintaining one's position on the health-ease/dis-ease continuum and of movement toward the healthy end. Research data collected in the past three decades from all over the world seem to confirm this belief (Eriksson & Lindström, 2006).

Once you accept the salutogenic question, you can deal with it on varying levels of generality. Actually, considerable attention in the literature of the 1970s and 1980s had been given to a wide variety of coping variables. They have largely been conceptualized as buffers, mitigating the effect of stressors, mediating or moderating the damaging effects on health (Braun-Lewensohn & Sagy, 2011b). The list is long, ranging from money to knowledge, belief in God to certain coping styles. Social support, networks, social ties, and their relevance to health have become a broad and growing field of research (Gow & Celinski, 2011).

Antonovsky (1987), however, claimed that what characterized most of these studies was their failure to translate the variables into a higher order of abstraction that could provide a theoretical explanation of what these various coping variables have in common, leading the organism to cope successfully and to reinforce health. Thinking in these terms led Antonovsky to the sense of coherence (SOC) construct, which first appeared in *Health, Stress, and Coping* (Antonovsky, 1979). The formulation was based on the assumption that by late childhood or early adulthood (12–30), individuals develop a generalized way of looking at the world, a way of perceiving the stimuli that bombard us.

The cognitive aspect of the SOC construct is the *comprehensibility* component: the extent to which the stimuli deriving from one's internal and external environments are structured, predictable, and explicable. In other words, the world is perceived as ordered and the problems facing us are clear.

The instrumental aspect of the concept is formulated as *manageability*: the extent to which one not only understands the problem, but believes that the requisite resources to cope with the problem successfully are at one's disposal. "At one's disposal" may refer to resources under one's own control, similar to Rotter's (1966) concept, but it may also refer to resources controlled by legitimate others—friends, God, doctors, family—upon whom one can count. No implication exists that untoward things do not happen in life. They do; but when you are high on manageability, you have the sense that, aided by your own resources or by those legitimate others, you will be able to cope and not grieve endlessly.

The *meaningfulness* component of the SOC is, in a sense, the emotional counterpart of comprehensibility. When one says that something "makes sense," in cognitive terms one means that "it is logical"; but in emotional terms, one means that one cares about the problems. To be high on meaningfulness means that one feels that life makes sense emotionally and that at least some of the problems and demands posed by living are worth investing energy in and are worthy of coping, commitment, and engagement.

Much as salutogenesis is a very broad construct, seeking to understand health rather than any given diagnostic category of disease, the SOC is broader than the coping resources that have been studied. First, it is not a coping style or a substantive resource. The crucial idea is that, because people confront such a wide variety of "bugs," no specific style or resource is ever appropriate all the time. The person with a strong SOC, believing that she or he understands the problem and sees it as a challenge, will select what is believed to be the most appropriate tool for the task at hand.

Second, the SOC distills the core of specific coping or resistance resources (money, social support, mastery, a confidant, and so on) and expresses what they have in common: They enhance one's sense of comprehensibility, manageability, and meaningfulness. So replying to the salutogenic question, Antonovsky's theoretical and empirical answer was that the strength of the sense of coherence is an important, if not the decisive, factor in shaping order out of chaos.

## SENSE OF COHERENCE AND HEALTH

Wherever one is located on the health-ease/dis-ease continuum, the theory suggests that the stronger one's SOC, the more likely it is to maintain that location or improve it. But how does the SOC work? How does the SOC contribute to health?

Antonovsky suggested several ways. In this limited framework, we will mention only three of them. First, the stronger the SOC, the more one can *avoid* threat or danger. A person with a strong SOC is more likely to engage in activities that are health-promoting and avoid those that are health-endangering. Believing that life is ordered and meaningful and that you have the resources to manage provides a sound basis for such behaviors. It is worth investing in efforts to stop smoking, to exercise, and to maintain good nutrition because you believe that these efforts will pay off. You are less tempted by the "it can't happen to me" mode of thought. On the other hand, a person with a weak SOC has neither the motivational nor the cognitive basis for the active coping required by the avoidance of threat.

Second, the stronger the SOC, the more likely it is that, confronted by stimuli that cannot be avoided, one will appraise them (Lazarus & Folkman, 1984) not as threats or dangers that paralyze and lead to negative self-fulfilling prophecies, but instead, one will assess them as opportunities that offer meaningful rewards, as challenges worthy of investment of energy, and as situations that can be managed well. The recent widower who has had a happy marriage will, together with the pain and sadness, be able to go on (Parkes, 1971) and restructure his life. In other words, the person with a strong SOC, confronted with a potentially noxious situation, will be more able to define and redefine the situation as one not necessarily noxious.

There is a third way in which SOC leads to health. Whatever the possibility of avoiding threat, or of redefining situations as nonnoxious, life inevitably confronts us with noxious stimuli, with threat, with stressors. How does a strong SOC function positively in promoting health and coping with stress? Antonovsky (1987) considered this question as the heart of the matter. The crucial point is that resistance resources, defined as agencies that facilitate coping with stressors, are potentials. They must be transformed kinetically before they can function to combat and overcome pathogens. The antibiotic is of no use unless it is taken appropriately. The friend is of no use unless there is communication. Money is of no use until it is spent. Surely people differ in the potential resources available to them. But beyond this, they differ significantly in the readiness and willingness to exploit the resources that they do have at their potential disposal. It is this that distinguishes between people with a stronger and a weaker SOC. The former will search very hard for those coping resources that are potentially available; the latter are more likely to give up and say "Neither God, nor I myself, nor anyone else can help me."

In his lectures, Antonovsky used to repeat the example of the young person whose involvement in a traffic accident led to his leg amputation. With a strong SOC, he is much more likely to adopt a self-perception (and seek social reinforcement of the self-perception) as a multifaceted person, one of whose facets is a handicap—more serious than wearing glasses or needing a hearing aid, but less serious than some other handicaps. The person with a weak SOC is more likely to accept the definition, by self and others, of a one-legged person. It seems reasonable to make differential health predictions for the two.

Salutogenically oriented clinicians can indicate the health consequences of interventions such as self-help groups, active participation in transforming environmental conditions, or even faith or self-fulfilling prophecy. It certainly seems reasonable to hypothesize that one who sees life as comprehensible, manageable, and meaningful is more likely to optimally exploit potential resistance resources. This approach can also help us to theoretically explain why some prevention programs or health promotion plans tend to work well for some people but not as well for others (Sagy, 2011).

The following are short research reviews relating to several issues in the salutogenesis paradigm. We have chosen these issues with consideration given to their importance in the developing area of salutogenic research.

How Is SOC Measured?

SOC can be measured by questionnaires and by using in-depth interviews and qualitative analyses (Griffiths, Ryan, & Foster, 2011). Originally SOC was measured by 29 items reflecting a person's ability to view life as comprehensible, manageable, and meaningful (Orientation to Life Questionnaire; Antonovsky, 1987). A shorter form of 13 items (abbreviated to SOC-13) was later developed. Items on both the 29- and 13-item versions are rated on a 7-point Likert scale. Total scores are obtained by summing items such that scores have a possible range from 13–91 points (SOC-13) or 29–203 points (SOC-29). A detailed description of the questionnaire is found in Antonovsky (1987). Eleven items measure the comprehensibility dimension (five items in SOC-13); for example, "Has it happened in the past that you were surprised by the behavior of people whom you thought you knew well?" and "Do you ever have the feeling that you are in an unfamiliar situation and don't know what to do?"

The manageability dimension is measured by 10 items (4 items in SOC-13); for example, "Do you think that there will always be people whom you'll be able to count on in the future?" and "Do you have the feeling that you're being treated unfairly?" Eight items measure the meaningfulness component of the SOC (four items in SOC-13); for example, "How often do you have the feeling that there's little meaning in the things you do in your daily life?" and "How often do you have the feeling that life is full of interest or completely routine?"

The SOC questionnaire has been used in at least 49 languages in 45 countries all over the world, on all continents (not only in Western countries), in varying cultures, and on different samples such as healthy populations, groups of patients and disabled people, families and organizations (Eriksson, in press). It has also been adapted for children and adolescents. A separate questionnaire for use among children was developed (Margalit & Efrati, 1996). The Children's Sense of Coherence Scale (CSOC) consists of 16 primary items and 3 filler items (higher scores reflect more coherence) that describe children's sense of confidence in their world, as expressed in their sense of comprehensibility (understanding their environment, e.g., "I feel that I don't understand what to do in class"); sense of manageability (feelings of control and confidence that when help is needed, it will be available, e.g., "When I want something I'm sure I'll get it"); and meaningfulness (motivation and interest in investing efforts in different tasks, e.g., "I'm interested in lots of things"). The reliability of this scale has proven to be good in several studies (Margalit, 1998).

The adolescent sense of coherence scale has been adjusted to suit the adolescent stage of life. Several items were eliminated from the original 29-item scale and others were rephrased to make sure adolescents understand the idea behind the items (Antonovsky & Sagy, 1986). Since the original use of the updated scale, many studies have used this version and reliability has proved to be high (Sagy & Braun-Lewensohn, 2009).

There are several versions for the Family Sense of Coherence Scale (FSOC) to measure sense of coherence in families. One version consists of 26 items (Antonovsky & Sourani, 1988), whereas another has 12 items (Sagy & Dotan, 2001). The FSOC has been translated into Hebrew (Sagy, 1998), Chinese (Ngai & Ngu, 2012), Turkish (Cecen, 2007), and Swedish (Mosley-Hänninen, 2009) and has been used to measure family coping in a variety of samples.

Much research has been conducted on families to examine different aspects of adaptation and coping with stress by using one of the original questionnaires, SOC-29 or SOC-13 (Greeff, Vansteenwegen, & Demot, 2006). Recently, collective measures of SOC have been developed with the community as the research unit (Mana, Sagy, Srour, & Madjalli, 2013).

HOW DOES THE SENSE OF COHERENCE DEVELOP THROUGH LIFE?

Work in the past 30 years has mainly focused on SOC as an "independent variable" and health or well-being as the "dependent" variable. The question of the sources of SOC increasingly interested Antonovsky in his later years. His initial efforts in this direction are found in two papers (Antonovsky, 1991, 1993) and in three studies in which he was involved (Sagy & Antonovsky, 1996, 1999a, 1999b, 2000).

In his two articles, Antonovsky (1991, 1993) attempted, within a systems theory framework, to analyze how social structures shape the strength of the SOC. He claimed that to disregard the power of history—the generational experiences of the macropolitical events of war, depression, population shifts, and revolutions—is to disregard the context within which the strength of the SOC of each of us is molded. There is no doubt that early socialization experiences in the family are crucial. But these experiences are shaped by the broader context (Kardiner, Linton, Du Bois, & West, 1945). To write of childhood experiences without locating these in the class structure, without reference to parental occupation or to race, limits our understanding. Antonovsky (who was an enthusiastic sociologist) assumed that first and foremost, a social structure that provides a set of basic, consistent, and clear principles will in all likelihood foster individuals with strong SOC.

However, there are many roads to a strong SOC. In several joint studies (e.g., Sagy & Antonovsky, 2000), we pinpointed some of these pathways. The main life experiences during childhood and adolescence that were found relevant to developing a strong SOC were consistency, emotional load balance, and emotional relationship with a "significant other."

Beyond these life experiences, during the last decade, researchers have examined the role of several sociodemographic factors in enhancing or weakening SOC among adolescents and adults. Gender was found to be the most consistent sociodemographic factor, with men exhibiting higher SOC compared to women (Apers et al., 2013). Socioeconomic status was also found to be an important factor in building strong SOC. Thus, higher levels of parents' education were found to be predictors of strong SOC (Geckova, Tavel, Van Dijk, Abel, & Reijneveld, 2010). Family and community characteristics were examined as well in this context. Open family communication (Garcia-Moya, Rivera, Moreno, Lindström, & Jiménez-Iglesias, 2012), focused parenting, and parents' knowledge regarding their children's needs were found to be positive contributors to strong SOC (Garcia-Moya et al., 2012), as were neighborhood or community cohesion (Marsh, Clinkinbeard, Thomas, & Evans, 2007; Peled, Sagy, & Braun-Lewensohn, 2013).

Another important question relates to the stability of SOC through the life span. This was thoroughly discussed by Antonovsky (1987), who portrayed a scenario of human development in which the SOC is developed until 30 years of age, is stable until retirement, and thereafter can decrease. This assumption is not supported by empirical studies to date. Contrary to what Antonovsky assumed, SOC was found to improve with age during the whole life cycle (Eriksson & Lindström, 2011). In a random Swedish sample of about 43,000 respondents aged 18 to 85, Nilsson, Leppert, Simonsson, and Starrin (2010) showed a relationship between SOC and age, with stronger SOC in the older age groups. Other studies confirm this picture of SOC as a life orientation that can be modified by life experiences throughout the life cycle (Bental-Israeli & Sagy, 2010). The situation seems to be more complicated than Antonovsky's original assumption, and SOC can be a resource promoting resilience and health that develops and is enhanced during life.

SENSE OF COHERENCE IN CHILDHOOD AND ADOLESCENCE

In studying SOC, an area of special interest is the period of childhood and adolescence. Adolescence is a particularly important stage in the development of cognitive skills, such as SOC, because during this time advanced cognitive abilities are mastered. The advanced forms of reflection, such as the ability to consider things in hypothetical and abstract terms and the ability to monitor one's own cognitive activity during the process of thinking, enable adolescents to see an issue from the perspective of other persons, to plan ahead, to anticipate the future consequences of an action, and to offer alternative explanations of events. Cognitive mastery is therefore an important contribution to young people's ability to manage or regulate their feelings and to control their emotions and/or to avoid being overwhelmed by them (Garnefski, Kraaij, & Spinhoven, 2001).

Is SOC a stable construct during childhood and adolescence? The stability question has accompanied this construct since researchers first began to study it. Due to the developmental nature of childhood and adolescence, SOC can still be strengthened during these stages of life (Antonovsky & Sagy, 1986).

Does SOC predict or explain diverse mental health and health outcomes during childhood and adolescence? The main results of studies throughout the world reveal that, as among adults, stronger SOC is related to better perceived health in children (Braun-Lewensohn & Sagy, 2011b). Moreover, results of the various studies show that children and adolescents with higher SOC report healthier lifestyles, quality of life, and well-being (Neuner et al., 2011). The healthy lifestyle is related, on the one hand, to physical activity (Bronikowski & Bronikowska, 2009) and eating habits (Myrin & Lagerstrom, 2006) and, on the other, to smoking habits and alcohol use (Garcia-Moya, Jiménez-Iglesias, & Moreno, 2013). Psychosocial behaviors as well as school-related behaviors and achievements have also been examined. Stronger SOC has been found as a predictor of good grades and higher motivation, success in schoolwork, and social competence (Mattila et al., 2011), as well as fewer stress-related school experiences (Lackaye & Margalit, 2006).

In contrast to the basic idea of the salutogenic paradigm, SOC was also examined in relation to groups with specific health problems (e.g., Luyckx, Missotten, Goossens, & Moons, 2012). Some of the results are surprising. Adolescents with heart problems were found, for example, to have higher SOC compared to healthy adolescents. These results could be explained by the fact that youngsters with such chronic diseases have learned to cope with their problems. Those who succeed in this process increased their manageability and even their perception of meaningfulness. Moreover, it seems that a supportive home environment experienced by these adolescents emphasized specific life events as being more comprehensible, manageable, and meaningful, and through these experiences they enhanced their orientation of SOC (Luyckx et al., 2012). However, in another study of adolescents with epilepsy (Gauffin, Landtblom, & Raty, 2010), SOC was found to be weakened in the long run, and those with no seizures had higher SOC than those who suffered seizures. This finding could reflect the experience of losing control during seizures and difficulty in assessing when to expect the next seizure, which might decrease comprehensibility as well as manageability and meaningfulness.

In the area of stress and resilience, stress-related outcomes such as anxiety, anger, depression, psychological distress, and other emotional problems were examined mainly in the context of war, terror, and political violence (Braun-Lewensohn & Sagy, 2010) or with regard to extreme life experiences such as child abuse (Gustafsson,

Nelson, & Gustafsson, 2010) or juvenile delinquency (Koposov, Ruchkin, & Eise-mann, 2003). However, SOC has been constantly found as a major protecting factor in moderating stress reactions (Sagy, in press). During adolescence, chronic stress situations were found to have the potential of deteriorating SOC (Braun-Lewensohn & Sagy, 2010). In other acute situations, SOC might be weakened for a certain period of time and once the acuteness is over, it could recover (Braun-Lewensohn, Sagy, Sabato, & Galili, 2013).

In sum, a review of studies in the past decade across countries and in a variety of age groups from early childhood to adulthood shows that personal SOC is a mean-ingful resource for coping with a variety of stressful situations and is a potential protective factor for children and adolescents. It appears that during childhood and adolescence, SOC might contribute to moderating and mediating stress experiences and may also play a protective role even at a young age, similar to that of the mature adult SOC.

## WHAT IS THE COLLECTIVE SENSE OF COHERENCE?

The question of transferring the individual concept of SOC into a collective measure is another meaningful issue that Antonovsky mentioned in his 1987 book:

> A Stressor—the threat of unemployment, retirement of a family member, the breakdown of a political system, the birth of a child who has serious disability—poses a threat (or challenge) to a definable collective. On the other hand, the stressor can only be coped with successfully by a collective. This brings us to the question of whether it makes any sense to speak of a collective as perceiving the world as coherent. (p. 171)

At the philosophical level, the question is, "Does a collective—a family, a work group, a kibbutz, a social class, a nation—have a mind which perceives?" (Sagy & Antonovsky, 1992, p. 983). Can a collective have a dispositional orientation, a way of seeing the world as comprehensible, manageable, and meaningful? Can the collective SOC be more than the sum of the members' SOC? Is it possible that one member's SOC could strengthen or weaken the SOC of the others?

Although we would expect a positive correlation between a strong group SOC and the SOC of its individual members, there will not necessarily be a perfect correlation. Individuals may feel that for them personally, the world is not coherent, although they are confident that it is for the collective. We can see this in almost every beginning first-year university class. On the other hand, individuals may feel that for them the world is coherent, although they feel anxious that it is not so for the collective. We can see such examples in surveys among Israelis regarding their (high) personal and their (low) national well-being (Sagy, in press).

The question of collective SOC has hardly been addressed until recently, perhaps because it is fraught with theoretical and methodological difficulties. In the disserta-tion of the first author under the supervision of Antonovsky, she attempted to wrestle with the problem of family SOC (Sagy & Antonovsky, 1992), asking about the differ-ence it makes to the individual's health whether he or she belongs to a group (or groups) with a weak or strong SOC. Does knowing this enable any better prediction than simply knowing the individual's SOC? Actually, in that study of family coher-ence and retirement, she asked the comparative question "Do characteristics of the individual or those of the larger social system, in which the stress process occurs, contribute more to the understanding of coping with stressors and stress consequences?" The results (Sagy & Antonovsky, 1992) were unequivocal. For the sample as a whole, both individual and family orientations seemed to be of equal power in explaining adaptation to retirement. An interesting pattern, however, emerged among incongruent families, when one of the spouses had a high and the other a low SOC score. In these families, it was the score of the high-SOC spouse that was the decisive factor in predicting the retiree's adaptation. In other words, the high family score was clearly the most powerful predictor of the retiree's adaptation. These results suggest that knowing family orientation can provide a better understanding of adaptation than knowing only the orientation of the individual.

Further research on collective SOC has mostly been conducted by the first author of this chapter and her colleagues. Despite the unequivocal data (Braun-Lewensohn, Sagy, & Roth, 2011; Mana et al., 2013; Sagy, in press), we can still suggest that it is the comprehensibility, the manageability, and the meaningfulness of the network, the group, the collective, and the community that must be a central theme in the salutogenesis paradigm of research and implementation.

WHEN IS SOC NOT SIGNIFICANT IN UNDERSTANDING HEALTH AND WELL-BEING?

Having cited these very general conclusions from almost three decades of research, we would like to present two cases in which the SOC does not "work," or "works" differently, meaning that it does not contribute to moderating stress reactions or to promoting health. We trust that these two unique cases enable us to better and more deeply understand salutogenesis and the concept of SOC.

One case relates to the type of stressful situation: *When is SOC not significant in reducing emotional stress?* The other case refers to a special cultural group in which it was found that SOC does not moderate emotional distress: *For whom is the SOC irrelevant in explaining emotional reactions?*

We will start with the "when" case: Only a few models or theories on the resilience effects of stress focus on the issue of differential stress situations and their possible relations to stress reactions (Sagy, 2002). It is important to point out that the comparative question of when coping resources do or do not moderate psychological difficulties has not been systematically studied. A recent study carried out by two of the authors (Sagy & Braun-Lewensohn, 2009) examined coping resources of adolescents during two different stress experiences of political violence. The cross-situational study compared stress reactions of Israeli (Jewish and Arab) adolescents under two environmental circumstances: chronic and acute states of stress. The acute situations in the political conflict are mostly related to wars or terror attacks. They can be characterized by their intensity and unpredictability. The chronic situation is more habitual in nature. In that study, the acute situation was investigated in northern Israel, an area that was then suffering from intensive missile fire. Almost 4,000 rockets fell in the area during 1 month, approximately 200 missiles per day. There were about 900 injuries caused by the missiles in northern communities and 52 civilians were killed. The long-term chronic stress state was examined in southern Israel (the city of Sderot and kibbutz communities in the Negev), an area that, over 8 years, was exposed to frequent missile attacks, usually one or two strikes at a time, sometimes several times a day. We asked, "In which state are the coping resources more significant in reducing emotional responses?"

The significant finding of this study resides in the different magnitude of variance explanations at each state: 35% of the variance was accounted for in the chronic state, but only 16% of variance was explained in the acute stress situation. In the chronic state sample, the main predictor for the two stress reactions was SOC that contributed 15% to the variance. In the acute state sample, the exposure variable was one of the significant factors in explaining the variance (4%) and SOC contributed only 4% to the variance explanation. Overall, the findings confirm crisis theories like Caplan's (1964), which claim that the intensity of reactions in an acute situation is mainly influenced by the overwhelming nature of the situation itself. However, our findings also confirm salutogenesis, meaning that in the chronic situation, which is similar to what Antonovsky called *regular life*, the SOC is significant in reducing emotional reactions of anxiety and distress (Antonovsky, 1987).

These results support the value of developing a model that differentiates between stress situations with the aim of understanding the different patterns of salutary factors explaining the stress reactions. Our findings put greater emphasis on the chronic stressor, which was also found to have more pervasive effects, than on the dramatic, acute war situation.

Some applications for fieldwork with children and families in a conflictual area can be suggested: In an acute situation (war, terror attacks, etc.), it is much more significant to intervene at the situational level in order to minimize the exposure to stress and damage. The intervention should move away from focusing on individuals or families at risk to developing a strategy that encompasses the total population within the given acute stress state (for example, building more shelters, publishing regulatory rules on how to behave when the siren sounds). On the other hand, in chronic situations, personal or family SOC seems to moderate stress responses by increasing the ability to cope with the chronic situation. In these situations, it would be meaningful to provide interventions that strengthen resilience resources of individuals and families.

Our second case relates to the question, *For whom is SOC not significant in explaining health or emotional reactions?* This question is relevant for the wider question of culture and salutogenesis (Eriksson, Sagy, & Lindström, 2012). As a committed sociologist, Antonovsky had a deep belief in the place of culture in stress research. However, in the appendix of his second book, *Unraveling the Mystery of Health* (Antonovsky, 1987), culture is mentioned only twice, especially in connection to cultural limits for developing SOC. How can we understand this "mystery"?

The answer might lie in Antonovsky's (1987) conviction that he had succeeded in developing SOC as a cross-cultural concept. He claimed that it was only the concrete translation of SOC that could vary widely according to cultural codes. What he meant was that, in all cultures and at all stages of coping with a stressor, a person with a strong SOC is at an advantage in preventing tension from being transformed into stress. An orientation toward one's world that sees stimuli as meaningful, comprehensive, and manageable provides the motivational and cognitive basis for behavior that is more likely to resolve the problems posed by stressors than one that sees the world as burdensome, chaotic, and overwhelming.

It is only when seeking to understand *how* SOC works that it varies widely. One's culture defines which resources are appropriate and legitimate in a given situation. Thus, the hallmark of the strong-SOC person is the ability to choose what seems to be the most appropriate strategy from among the variety of potential resources. But this choice is constructed by his or her cultural manners. We always cope with stress within cultural contexts, which defines the canon, the rules. Americans will generally use primary control, whereas the Japanese will generally make use of secondary control. According to cultural rules, your confidant may be my father or your own sister, one's priest or one's rabbi. Within these cultural constraints, however, the strong-SOC person will be flexible in choosing his or her strategies and in gaining better outcomes from the coping process.

So according to the salutogenic model, culture sets limits, but within these limits, it is the level of SOC that matters. Our studies among Jewish and Arab teenagers living in northern Israel, for example, support this distinction. It was the boy or girl with strong SOC, whether Arab or Jew, who expressed less anxiety or suffered from fewer symptoms. However, the strategies of coping were quite different between Jews and Arabs, as they also were between boys and girls (Braun-Lewensohn, 2013; Braun-Lewensohn & Sagy, 2011). But does SOC matter in all cultural groups? Recent studies show that cultural and ethnic context differences indeed play a role in the process in which coping resources serve as explanatory factors of distress reactions. Among Bedouin adolescents, for example, SOC did not serve as a protecting factor when facing politically violent events (Braun-Lewensohn & Sagy, 2011b), and among Bedouin women in Israel, SOC even played a negative role by increasing depression (Daoud, Braun-Lewensohn, Eriksson, & Sagy, 2013). In sum, although we have some tentative answers, most of the research does not provide unequivocal results. The question of salutogenesis, SOC, and culture is still open and should be addressed in future research.

## PRACTICAL IMPLICATIONS

The basic idea of salutogenesis assumes stress and chaos as natural parts of life. In the fieldwork, by adopting a salutogenic orientation, psychologists, therapists, or physicians made a substantial difference in their work (Sagy, 2011). Salutogenic questions lead our study—as well as its application—to helping children, families, and communities, wherever they are on the health-ease/disease continuum, to move toward the healthy end of the continuum.

Salutogenically oriented clinicians can indicate the health consequences of interventions such as self-help groups, active participation in transforming environmental conditions, or even faith or self-fulfilling prophecy. It certainly seems reasonable to hypothesize that one who sees life as comprehensible, manageable, and meaningful is more likely to optimally exploit potential resistance resources. This approach can also help us to theoretically explain why some prevention programs or health promotion plans tend to work well for some people but not as well for others (Sagy, 2011).

The coping resource of SOC, as it appears throughout research around the world, provides significant protection for human beings. It appears that when an individual is facing a stressful event, a major resilience factor in different contexts is the personal sense of coherence. Strengthening this coping resource could enable individuals to better adapt when confronted with stress. Whether at home, at work, at school, or on a community level, it is important that individuals be included as integral parts of societal and familiar processes that could contribute to enhancing their sense of coherence. Comprehensibility could be strengthened with promotion of feelings of security and buildup of safe and respectful environments that can promote social relationships (Krause, 2011). Manageability, the individual belief that one has the resources needed to deal with situations, could be increased when the individual feels that his or her needs are being acknowledged. Therefore, experiencing self-efficacy, balance between overload and underload, acceptance and appreciation of one's individual progress and achievements, as well as recognition of his/her actions can enhance this component. Finally, meaningfulness, which is the motivational and emotional component of SOC, can be increased and promoted when individuals feel that they have real potential to influence decisions (Krause, 2011). Increasing and promoting personal

SOC could be via family or community capacities and the connections among the different ecological arches (Bronfenbrenner, 2009).

## CONCLUSION

In this chapter we have tried to describe and explain the essence of the salutogenic conceptual framework developed by Antonovsky and to suggest it as a possible philosophical basis for the contemporary positive psychology movement. The study of positive psychology—somewhat in a similar direction as salutogenesis—encourages the shift in emphasis from a preoccupation with the repair of defect and focus on disease to the building of defense and strength (Seligman, 2002). In this concluding section, we also wish to broaden the core concept of salutogenesis—the SOC construct—to other positive concepts, and to suggest salutogenesis as a possible umbrella paradigm for a variety of resource-oriented constructs (Lindstrom & Eriksson, 2011).

The positive psychology movement has produced several conceptual frameworks: cognitive, emotional, interpersonal, religious, and philosophical models (Lopez & Snyder, 2003). An array of instruments to measure human strengths have also been suggested: Optimism, hope, locus of control, creativity, self-esteem, emotional intelligence, empathy, humor, and gratitude (Lopez & Snyder, 2003) are only a few examples. Further, all these concepts can be applied in different arenas, such as educational contexts (teaching and learning) and psychological and medical practices. Moreover, community researchers and public policy planners suggest transforming positive psychology from an individual level to a societal level as well (Linley & Joseph, 2004). This is very encouraging.

Considering the salutogenic framework, a somewhat similar scenario emerges. Salutogenesis (and its core construct, the SOC) originally developed and was considered at an individual level and with its relation to health results; it is now a framework applicable to different arenas (family, neighborhood, workplaces, organizations). It has recently been discussed in an educational context as contributing to learning processes (Lindström & Eriksson, 2009), as well as in societal and political contexts (Sagy, in press).

As a former student of Antonovsky, and later as his research colleague, the first author has brought extensive knowledge of the philosophical and theoretical roots of salutogenesis to this chapter. We have emphasized the basic idea of salutogenesis that the human condition is mainly chaotic. In the very nature of human existence, stressors are omnipresent. We live in a complex world where our sets of values, formed in childhood in a local context, are challenged by the global world. Social trends point to a major upset of the traditional social structures, such as the rupture of local and intimate networks, changed function and structure of family networks, and challenges in the patterns of working life and in the political arena. The way we communicate with each other has changed because of new information technology, which presents opportunities but also challenges one's personal ability to run a coherent life. There is a risk that life becomes fragmented as our closest environment is characterized by a rapid change. A life constantly online causes a threat to one's mental and spiritual well-being in spite of the increase in material goods. Yet many people, even those with a high stressor load, survive and do well. This is what the mystery of the salutogenic orientation seeks to unravel.

Antonovsky's answer to the salutogenic question was the concept of sense of coherence. We have tried to illustrate how to measure the SOC both on the individual and collective levels. We have written a brief overview of current research, with special focus on children and adolescents, showing that a strong SOC has an impact on health and well-being. We have also indicated when, where, and for whom SOC is not associated with better well-being.

These basic ideas could perhaps be valuable for the positive psychology movement, for example, by expanding research from the strong focus on strengths as an individual characteristic to a more comprehensive perception of life orientation, as well as discussing strengths not only at the individual but also at the social level (Sagy, in press). Can we learn how to develop strong SOC and be healthier? Here we trust that positive psychology can make a meaningful contribution with its broad research on human strengths and coping resources.

To build a joint future, we must rely on historical and philosophical roots. Despite the differences between the two conceptual frameworks, we do believe that the philosophical roots are shared: The human condition is chaotic, but strengths and abilities can enable us to find some order in the chaos, some joy in the misery.

## SUMMARY POINTS

### Salutogenesis

- Assumes that stress and changes are a natural part of life.
- Raises the critical question, How do we manage stress and still feel well?
- Puts the focus on strengths and resources, on what works.
- Gives the direction for life, a life orientation.
- Relies on the core concept of sense of coherence (SOC), consisting of three dimensions (comprehensibility, manageability, and meaningfulness).
- Is more than the measuring of SOC; it is a resource-oriented approach similar to the positive psychology movement.

### Sense of Coherence

- Can be applied at an individual, group (family), community, and even societal levels.
- Has an impact on health, quality of life, and well-being among children, adolescents, and adults.
- Seems to increase with age during the whole life cycle.
- Can be learned and can be strengthened by interventions.

## REFERENCES

Antonovsky, A. (1979). *Health, stress, and coping.* San Francisco, CA: Jossey-Bass.

Antonovsky, A. (1987). *Unraveling the mystery of health. How people manage stress and stay well.* San Francisco, CA: Jossey-Bass.

Antonovsky, A. (1991). *The salutogenic approach to family system health: Promise and danger.* European Congress on "Mental Health in European Families." Retrieved from http://angelfire.com/ok/soc/agolem.html

Antonovsky, A. (1993). The structure and properties of the sense of coherence scale. *Social Science and Medicine, 36,* 725–733.

Antonovsky, A., & Sourani, T. (1988). Family sense of coherence and family adaptation. *Journal of the Marriage and the Family,* 79–92.

Antonovsky, H., & Sagy, S. (1986). The development of a sense of coherence and its impact on responses to stress situations. *Journal of Social Psychology, 126,* 213–225.

Apers, S., Moons, P., Goossens, E., Luyckx, K., Gewillig, M., Bogaerts, K. & Budts, W. (2013). Sense of coherence and perceived physical health explain the better quality of life in adolescents with congenital heart disease. *European Journal of Cardiovascular Nursing, 12*, 475–483.

Bandura, A. (1977). Self-efficacy: Toward a unifying theory of behavioral change. *Psychological Review, 84*, 191–215.

Bandura, A. (1997). *Self-efficacy. The exercise of control.* New York, NY: W. H. Freeman.

Bental-Israeli, A., & Sagy, S. (2010). Life experiences contributing to the development of a sense of coherence: Consistency and/or breakthrough experience [in Hebrew]. *Studies in Education, 1*, 215–243.

Braun-Lewensohn, O. (2013). Coping resources and stress reactions among three cultural groups one year after natural disaster. *Clinical Social Work Journal.* doi:10.1007/s10615-013-0463-0

Braun-Lewensohn, O., & Sagy, S. (2010). Sense of coherence, hope and values among adolescents under missile attacks: A longitudinal study. *International Journal of Children's Spirituality, 15*(3), 247–260.

Braun-Lewensohn, O., & Sagy, S. (2011a). Salutogenesis and culture: Personal and community sense of coherence among adolescents belonging to three different cultural groups. *International Review of Psychiatry, 23*, 533–541.

Braun-Lewensohn, O., & Sagy, S. (2011b). Coping resources as explanatory factors of stress reactions during missile attacks: Comparing Jewish & Arab adolescents in Israel. *Community Mental Health Journal, 47*, 300–310.

Braun-Lewensohn, O., Sagy, S., & Roth, G. (2011). Coping strategies as mediators of the relationship between sense of coherence and stress reactions: Israeli adolescents under missile attacks. *Anxiety, Stress & Coping, 24*, 327–341.

Braun-Lewensohn, O., Sagy, S., Sabato, H., & Galili, R. (2013). Sense of coherence and sense of community as coping resources of religious adolescents before and after the disengagement from the Gaza Strip. *Israeli Journal of Psychiatry and Related Sciences, 50*(2), 110–116.

Bronfenbrenner, U. (2009). *The ecology of human development: Experiments by nature and design.* Cambridge, MA: Harvard University Press.

Bronikowski, M., & Bronikowska, M. (2009). Salutogenesis as a framework for impoving health resources of adolescent boys. *Scandinavian Journal of Public Health, 37*, 525–531.

Caplan, G. (1964). *Principles of preventive psychiatry.* New York, NY: Basic Books.

Cecen, A. R. (2007). The Turkish version of the Family Sense of Coherence Scale—Short form (FSOC-S): Initial development and validation. *Educational Sciences: Theory & Practice, 7*, 1211–1218.

Cohen, S., & Syme, L. S. (Eds.). (1985). *Social support and health.* Orlando, FL: Academic Press.

Daoud, N., Braun-Lewensohn, O., Eriksson, M., & Sagy, S. (2013). *Sense of coherence and depressive symptoms among low income Bedouin women in the Negev Israel.* Manuscript submitted for publication.

Eriksson, M. (in press). The salutogenic framework for health promotion and disease prevention. In D. I. Mostofsky (Ed.), *Handbook of behavioral medicine.* Hoboken, NJ: Wiley.

Eriksson, M., & Lindström, B. (2005). Validity of Antonovsky's Sense of Coherence Scale: A systematic review. *Journal of Epidemiology and Community Health, 59*, 460–466.

Eriksson, M., & Lindström, B. (2006). Antonovsky's Sense of Coherence Scale and the relation with health: A systematic review. *Journal of Epidemiology and Community Health, 60*, 376–381.

Eriksson, M., & Lindström, B. (2011). Life is more than survival: Exploring links between Antonovsky's salutogenic theory and the concept of resilience. In K. M. Gow & M. J. Celinski (Eds.), *Wayfinding through life's challenges: Coping and survival.* New York, NY: Nova Science.

Eriksson, M., Sagy, S., & Lindström, B. (2012). Salutogenic perspective on mental health across the life time. Cultural aspects on the sense of coherence. In C.-H. Mayer & C. Krause (Eds.), *Exploring mental health: Theoretical and empirical discourses on salutogenesis.* Lengerich, Germany: Pabst.

Evans, W. P., Marsh, S. C., & Weigel, D. J. (2010). Promoting adolescent sense of coherence: Testing models of risk, protection, and resiliency. *Journal of Community & Applied Social Psychology, 20,* 30–43.

Garcia-Moya, I., Jiménez-Iglesias, A., & Moreno, C. (2013). Sense of coherence and substance use in Spanish adolescents. Does the effect of SOC depend on patterns of substance use in their peer group? *Adicciones, 25,* 109–117.

Garcia-Moya, I., Rivera, F., Moreno, C., Lindström, B., & Jiménez-Iglesias, A. (2012). Analysis of the importance of family in the development of sense of coherence during adolescence. *Scandinavian Journal of Public Health, 40,* 333–339.

Garnefski, N., Kraaij, V., & Spinhoven, P. (2001). Negative life events, cognitive emotion regulation and emotional problems. *Personality and Individual Differences, 30,* 1311–1327.

Gauffin, H., Landtblom, A. M., & Raty, L. (2010). Self-esteem and sense of coherence in young people with uncomplicated epilepsy: A 5-year follow-up. *Epilepsy & Behavior, 17,* 520–524.

Geckova, A. M., Tavel, P., Van Dijk, J., Abel, T., & Reijneveld, S. (2010). Factors associated with educational aspirations among adolescents: Cues to counteract socioeconomic differences? *BMC Public Health, 10,* 154.

Geyer, S. (1997). Some conceptual considerations on the sense of coherence. *Social Science & Medicine, 44,* 1771–1779.

Glanz, K., Maskarinec, G., & Carlin, L. (2005). Ethnicity, sense of coherence, and tobacco use among adolescents. *Annals of Behavioral Medicine, 29,* 192–199.

Gow, K. M., & Celinski, M. J. (Eds.). (2011). *Wayfinding through life's challenges. Coping and survival.* New York, NY: Nova Science.

Greeff, A. P., Vansteenwegen, A., & Demot, L. (2006). Resiliency in divorced families. *Social Work in Mental Health, 4,* 67–81.

Griffiths, C. A., Ryan, P., & Foster, J. H. (2011). Thematic analysis of Antonovsky's sense of coherence theory. *Scandinavian Journal of Psychology, 52,* 168–173.

Gustafsson, P. E., Nelson, N., & Gustafsson, P. A. (2010). Diurnal cortisol levels, psychiatric symptoms and sense of coherence in abused adolescents. *Nordic Journal of Psychiatry, 64,* 27–31.

Kardiner, A., Linton, R., Du Bois, C., & West, J. (1945). *The psychological frontiers of society.* New York, NY: Columbia University Press.

Kobasa, S. (1982). The hardy personality: toward a social psychology of stress and health. In G. Sanders & J. Suls (Eds.), *Social psychology of health and illness.* Hillsdale, NJ: Erlbaum.

Koposov, R. A., Ruchkin, V. V., & Eisemann, M. (2003). Sense of coherence. A mediator between violence exposure and psychopathology in Russian juvenile delinquents. *Journal of Nervous and Mental Disease, 191,* 638–644.

Krause, C. (2011). Developing sense of coherence in educational contexts: Making progress in promoting mental health in children. *International Review of Psychiatry, 23,* 525–532.

Lackaye, T. D., & Margalit, M. (2006). Comparisons of achievement, effort, and self-perceptions among students with learning disabilities and their peers from different achievement groups. *Journal of Learning Disabilities, 39,* 432–446.

Lazarus, R. S., & Folkman, S. (1984). *Stress, appraisal, and coping.* New York, NY: Springer.

Lindström, B., & Eriksson, M. (2009). The salutogenic approach to the making of HiAP/Healthy Public Policy: Illustrated by a case study. *Global Health Promotion, 16,* 17–28.

Lindström, B., & Eriksson, M. (2011). From health education to healthy learning: Implementing salutogenesis in educational science. *Scandinavian Journal of Public Health, 39*(6 Suppl.), 85–92.

Linley, P. A., & Joseph, S. (Eds.). (2004). *Positive psychology in practice.* Hoboken, NJ: Wiley.

Linley, P. A., Joseph, S., Harrington, S., & Wood, A. M. (2006). Positive psychology: Past, present, and (possible) future. *Journal of Positive Psychology, 1,* 3–16.

Lopez, S. J., & Snyder, C. R. (Eds.). (2003). *Positive psychological assessment. A handbook of models and measures*. Washington, DC: American Psychological Association.

Luyckx, K., Missotten, M. A., Goossens, E., & Moons, P. (2012). Individual and contextual determinants of quality of life in adolescents with congenital heart disease. *Journal of Adolescent Health, 51*, 122–128.

Mana, A., Sagy, S., Srour, A., & Madjalli, S. (2013). *Personal and community sense of coherence and perceptions of the "other": The case of Palestinian Muslims and Christians in Israel*. Manuscript submitted for publication.

Margalit, M. (1998). Loneliness and coherence among preschool children with learning disabilities. *Journal of Learning Disabilities, 31*, 173–180.

Margalit, M., & Efrati, M. (1996). Loneliness, coherence anad companionship among children with learning disorder. *Educational Psychology, 16*, 69–80.

Marsh, S. C., Clinkinbeard, S. S., Thomas, R. M., & Evans, W. P. (2007). Risk and protective factors predictive of sense of coherence during adolescence. *Journal of Health Psychology, 12*(2), 281–284.

Mathews, K. A. (1977). Competitive drive, pattern A, and coronary heart disease: A further analysis of some data from the Western collaborative group study. *Journal of Chronic Disease, 30*, 489–498.

Mattila, M., Rautava, P., Honkinen, P., Ojanlatva, A., Jaakkola, S., Aromaa, M., . . . Sillanpää, M. (2011). Sense of coherence and health behavior in adolescence. *Acta Paediatrica, 100*, 1590–1595.

Mittelmark, M. B. (2008). Setting an ethical agenda for health promotion. *Health Promotion International, 23*(1), 78–85.

Mosley-Hänninen, P. (2009). *Contextualising the salutogenic perspective on adolescent health and the sense of coherence in families: A study among adolescents and their families in the Swedish speaking Finland* (Master's thesis). Laurea University of Applied Sciences, Vantaa, Finland.

Myrin, B., & Lagerstrom, M. (2006). Health behaviour and sense of coherence among pupils aged 14–15. *Scandinavian Journal of Caring Sciences, 20*, 339–346.

Neuner, B., Busch, M. A., Singer, S., Moons, P., Wellmann, J., Bauer, U., . . . Hense, H. W. (2011). Sense of coherence as a predictor of quality of life in adolescents with congenital heart defects: A register-based 1-year follow-up study. *Journal of Developmental & Behavioral Pediatrics, 32*(4), 316–327.

Ngai, F. W., & Ngu, S. F. (2012). Family sense of coherence and quality of life. *Quality of Life Research*. doi: 10.1007/S11136-012-0336-Y

Nilsson, K., Leppert, J., Simonsson, B., & Starrin, B. (2010). Sense of coherence (SOC) and psychological well-being (GHQ): Improvement with age. *Journal of Epidemiology and Community Health, 64*, 347–352.

Parkes, C. M. (1971). Psycho-social transitions: A field for study. *Social Science & Medicine, 5*, 101–115.

Peled, D., Sagy, S., & Braun-Lewensohn, O. (2013). Community perception as coping resource among adolescents living under rockets fire: A salutogenic approach. *Journal of Community Positive Practices, 4*, 681–702.

Rotter, J. (1966). Generalized expectancies for internal versus external control of reinforcements. *Psychological Monographs, 80*, 1–28.

Sagy, S. (1998). Effects of personal, family, and community characteristics on emotional reactions in a stress situation. *Youth & Society, 29*, 311–330.

Sagy, S. (2002). Moderating factors explaining stress reactions: Comparing chronic-without-acute-stress and chronic-with-acute-stress situations. *Journal of Psychology, 136*, 407–419.

Sagy, S. (2011). Preventing use of psychoactive materials among children and adolescents: Where does the salutogenic model take us? [in Hebrew]. *Israeli Journal for Education and Health Promotion, 4*, 26–31.

Sagy, S. (in press). Salutogenesis: From the diary of a conflict researcher [in Hebrew]. *Israel Journal of Conflict Management*.

Sagy, S., & Antonovsky, A. (1992). The family sense of coherence and the retirement transition. *Journal of Marriage and the Family, 54*, 983–994.

Sagy, S., & Antonovsky, H. (1996). Structural sources of the sense of coherence. Two life stories of Holocaust survivors in Israel. *Israel Journal of Medical Sciences, 32*, 200–205.

Sagy, S., & Antonovsky, H. (1999a). Factors related to the development of the sense of coherence (SOC) in adolescents. A retrospective study. *Polish Psychological Bulletin, 30*, 255–262.

Sagy, S., & Antonovsky, H. (1999b). Life expereinces that contributes to development of sense of coherence: Two life stories of Holocaust survivors [in Hebrew]. *Sichot, 14*(1), 51–56.

Sagy, S., & Antonovsky, H. (2000). The development of the sense of coherence: A retrospective study of early life experiences in the family. *Journal of Aging and Human Development, 51*, 155–166.

Sagy, S., & Braun-Lewensohn, O. (2009). Adolescents under rocket fire: When are coping resources significant in reducing emotional distress? *Global Health Promotion, 16*, 5–15.

Sagy, S., & Dotan, N. (2001). Coping resources of maltreated children in the family: A salutogenic approach. *Child Abuse & Neglect, 25*, 1463–1480.

Seligman, M. E. P. (1972). Learned helplessness. *Annual Review of Medicine, 23*, 407–412.

Seligman, M. E. P. (2002). *Authentic happiness: Using the new positive psychology to realize your potential for lasting fulfillment*. New York, NY: Simon & Schuster.

Ying, Y. W., Lee, P. A., & Tsai, J. L. (2000). Cultural orientation and racial discrimination: Predictors of coherence in Chinese American young adults. *Journal of Community Psychology, 28*, 427–442.

# PART II

# VALUES AND CHOICES IN PURSUIT OF THE GOOD LIFE

## CHAPTER 6

# The Science of Values in the Culture of Consumption

TIM KASSER

O NE OF POSITIVE psychology's key achievements has been its articulation of what it means to have "a good life." Many thinkers have considered this issue over the course of recorded human thought, but positive psychology, in my mind, has made two special contributions. First, rather than assuming that a good life is defined by the absence of psychopathology, many of the leaders of positive psychology have argued that well-being is a construct to be studied in its own right. Second, positive psychologists insist that conclusions about the meaning of a good life be based on sound empirical research, rather than on anecdotal observation or philosophical speculation. Excellent early examples of the conjoining of these two threads can be seen in the January 2000 issue of the *American Psychologist*; these initial discussions have been followed by important contributions appearing in the *Journal of Positive Psychology* and other journals, as well as dozens of books that are being published with increasing rapidity. As can be gleaned from a perusal of this litera-ture, most positive psychologists seem to agree that a good life is represented via a sense of life satisfaction, pleasant affective experience, and personal meaning, and that a good life is more likely to occur when people have good relationships, pursue meaningful work, and engage in activities that provide a sense of deep involvement, vitality, choice, and competence (Csikszentmihalyi, 1999; Diener, 2000; Haidt, 2006; Lyubomirsky, 2007; Myers, 2000; Peterson, 2006; Ryan & Deci, 2000; Ryff & Keyes, 1995; Seligman, 2002).

As positive psychology continues to move forward in both the articulation and (hopefully) the eventual actualization of its vision of a good life, I believe that it is cru-cially important to recognize that an opposing, better-publicized vision of the good life vies for space in people's minds. More specifically, every day and in many ways, consumers (née people) are bombarded with powerful, psychologically sophisticated proclamations that the good life is "the goods life." The message that happiness and well-being come from the attainment of wealth and the purchase and acquisition of goods and services is a pervasive and inescapable fact of modern life across most of the planet. Such messages are found not only in increasingly omnipresent advertise-ments, but also in the subtext of political debates, business decisions, and educational practices (see, e.g., Kasser, Cohn, Kanner, & Ryan, 2007; or Schwartz, 1994).

For the past two decades, my colleagues and I have been studying the content of people's values and goals as a means of testing which of these two visions of the good life really fulfills their promises. We have reasoned that people's values and goals provide a valid means of assessing if their vision of the ideal (a standard definition of values; e.g., Rokeach, 1973) and the way they are attempting to create their lives (a standard definition of goals; e.g., Emmons, 1989) are oriented toward the good life articulated by positive psychology or the goods life encouraged by consumer culture. To reflect this distinction, we have described two types of goals and values (Grouzet et al., 2005; Kasser & Ryan, 1996). *Extrinsic* goals and values become prominent when people "buy into" the messages of consumer culture and organize their lives around the pursuit of money, possessions, image, and status. These goals are extrinsic in the sense that such pursuits are primarily focused on the attainment of external rewards and praise, and are typically means to some other end. In contrast, *intrinsic* goals and values involve striving for personal growth, intimacy, and contribution to the community. We call this latter group of aims intrinsic because they are inherently more satisfying to pursue and are more likely to satisfy the deeper psychological needs that are necessary for happiness and well-being (Kasser, 2002a; Ryan & Deci, 2000).

Substantial cross-cultural evidence supports the distinction between extrinsic and intrinsic goals. The specific aspirations representing the two types of goals fall on distinct factors in samples of students from Germany (Schmuck, Kasser, & Ryan, 2000), Russia (Ryan et al., 1999), and South Korea (Kim, Kasser, & Lee, 2003), and in samples of adults from the United States (Kasser & Ryan, 1996) and Peru (Guillen-Royo & Kasser, in press). Even more compelling evidence for the distinction between intrinsic and extrinsic aspirations derives from the work of Grouzet et al. (2005), who collected data from undergraduate students in 15 cultures (Australia, Bulgaria, Canada [Quebec], China, Colombia, the Dominican Republic, Egypt, France, Germany, Hong Kong, India, Romania, South Korea, Spain, and the United States). Using statistical techniques such as multidimensional scaling analysis and circular stochastic modeling, Grouzet et al. found evidence for a "circumplex" model of goals, in which intrinsic goals are clustered together (representing the psychological compatibility of caring about personal growth, connections with others, and helping the community) and extrinsic goals are clustered together (representing the psychological compatibility of caring about money, image, and status). Further, Grouzet et al. showed that people experience intrinsic and extrinsic goals as existing in psychological conflict with each other; that is, people find it to be relatively difficult to simultaneously prioritize an intrinsic goal (such as "being generous") and an extrinsic goal (such as "accumulating a good deal of money").

## THE ASSOCIATIONS OF INTRINSIC AND EXTRINSIC ASPIRATIONS WITH THE GOOD LIFE

Although positive psychologists have done much to articulate a coherent vision of the good life, in my opinion they far too frequently have defined the good life solely in terms of a particular person's own happiness and well-being. Such a definition gives relatively short shrift to how one's lifestyle might influence the well-being of other people, future generations of people, and other species. As Deneulin and McGregor (2010) write, it is necessary to "generate the social understandings, agreements, and institutions to live *together* in ways that do not cause us irreparable harms" (p. 511, emphasis added). Said differently, I would argue that a good life requires living in ways that support a good life for other living beings, not just for one's own person.

The available empirical evidence makes it clear that the distinction between intrinsic and extrinsic goals is among the factors predicting such a multifaceted definition of the good life. Specifically, as will be reviewed in this chapter, the relative prioritization of intrinsic goals has been shown to be associated both with higher levels of personal well-being and with the kinds of prosocial and ecologically sustainable behaviors and attitudes likely to support others' well-being. In contrast, a focus on extrinsic goals is consistently associated with lower levels of personal well-being and with attitudes and behaviors that are likely to diminish the well-being of others.

## Personal Well-Being

Across numerous studies, a large number of means of assessing well-being have been connected to the focus people place on intrinsic relative to extrinsic goals. Generally speaking, the extent to which people prioritize intrinsic over extrinsic goals has been associated with higher self-reported levels of self-actualization, vitality, life satisfaction, and pleasant affect and with lower self-reported levels of depression, anxiety, and negative affect (see Kasser, 2002b, for a review; see Dittmar, Bond, Hurst, & Kasser, in press, for a meta-analysis). People's focus on intrinsic relative to extrinsic goals also relates to diary reports of emotional experience (Kasser & Ryan, 1996; Sheldon & Kasser, 1995) and to interviewer assessments of participants' levels of social functioning, general mental health, and various forms of psychopathology (Cohen & Cohen, 1996; Kasser & Ryan, 1993).

The differential correlations between well-being and intrinsic versus extrinsic values also replicate across various participant characteristics. A strong focus on materialistic aims (one type of extrinsic goal) has been associated with lower well-being in children as young as 10 years old (Kasser, 2005; Schor, 2004) and with numerous samples of adolescents and of adults (Kasser & Ryan, 1996; Sheldon & Kasser, 2001). Findings also replicate in samples of business students and entrepreneurs (Kasser & Ahuvia, 2002; Srivastava, Locke, & Bortol, 2001), that is, individuals who exist in environments that often encourage extrinsic aims. What's more, the positive associations between personal well-being and a relative focus on intrinsic versus extrinsic goals have been reported in a variety of cultures, including the Canada, China (Lekes, Gingras, Phillipe, Koestner, & Fang, 2010), Germany (Schmuck et al., 2000), Hungary (Martos & Kopp, 2012), Peru (Guillen-Royo & Kasser, in press), Russia (Ryan et al., 1999), Singapore (Kasser & Ahuvia, 2002), South Korea (Kim et al., 2003), Spain (Romero, Gomez-Fraguela, & Villar, 2011), the United Kingdom (Chan & Joseph, 2000), and the United States (Kasser & Ryan, 1993, 1996).

Finally, some recent research has expanded beyond the cross-sectional nature of the studies just reviewed by reporting longitudinal and experimental evidence. Specifically, in samples of U.S. young adults and Icelandic adults over time spans from 6 months to 12 years, decreases in the relative prioritization of the extrinsic value of financial success are associated with decreases in levels of psychopathology and increases in levels of subjective well-being (Kasser et al., 2014). What's more, brief reminders of the extrinsic goal of financial success, compared to a control topic, are associated with decrements in mood moments later (Bauer, Wilkie, Kim, & Bodenhausen, 2012).

In sum, a large body of research supports the hypothesis that prioritization of the goals and values embodied in the "good life" articulated by positive psychology is indeed associated with higher levels of well-being, whereas focusing on the goals and values embodied in the "goods life" encouraged by consumer society is associated with lower levels of well-being and higher levels of distress.

SOCIAL WELL-BEING

Numerous studies show that one's prioritization of intrinsic relative to extrinsic values and goals also has predictable associations with how one treats other people. For example, Sheldon and Kasser (1995) found that a strong focus on extrinsic values is associated with engaging in fewer prosocial activities (like sharing and helping) and with having less empathy for others (i.e., being less interested in trying to understand another's point of view). People also tend toward more manipulative, Machiavellian, and competitive (versus cooperative) behaviors to the extent they prioritize extrinsic relative to intrinsic values (Khanna & Kasser, 1999; McHoskey, 1999; Sheldon, Sheldon, & Osbaldiston, 2000). In contrast, an intrinsic goal orientation is associated with less prejudicial attitudes about people outside of one's own group (Duriez, Vansteenkiste, Soenens, & De Witte, 2007), and, as shown by a recent meta-analysis, with a rejection of the notion that members of other groups deserve the lower status they might have (i.e., lower social dominance orientation; Onraet, Van Hiel, & Dhont, 2013).

Experimental studies complement this research by showing that activation of extrinsic values decreases how much people help others who are in need. For example, Vohs, Mead, and Goode (2006) randomly assigned U.S. college students to create phrases out of money-related words or out of neutral words; soon afterward, participants had the opportunity to behave in either a helpful or selfish manner. Those who had thoughts of money (and thus extrinsic values) spent significantly less time helping a confused person who asked for aid, were less helpful to an experimenter who had dropped some pencils, and donated less of their study honorarium to a charity. Such findings have been conceptually replicated with other means of activating values and with other measures of prosocial outcomes (Maio, Pakizeh, Cheung, & Rees, 2009). Other work shows that the activation of intrinsic values can increase concern for children in wealthy nations who are poor and for children in economically developing nations who are dying, even among people who are dispositionally prone to focus on extrinsic goals (Chilton, Crompton, Kasser, Maio, & Nolan, 2012).

In sum, the research shows that when people prioritize extrinsic values, they are likely to hold attitudes and behave in ways that undermine the well-being of other people, whereas the prioritization of intrinsic values is associated with attitudes and behaviors that are more likely to support other individuals' attempts to live a good life.

ECOLOGICAL WELL-BEING

A good life requires a healthy habitat in which to live, but the evidence shows that a relatively high focus on extrinsic compared to intrinsic values is associated with holding attitudes and behaving in ways that contribute to environmental degradation (for a review, see Crompton & Kasser, 2009; for a meta-analysis see Hurst, Dittmar, Bond, & Kasser, 2013). For example, the priority placed on materialistic (extrinsic) values by U.S. and U.K. adolescents is associated with engaging less frequently in ecologically friendly behaviors such as buying second-hand, recycling, riding a bicycle, reusing paper, and so on (Gatersleben, Meadows, Abrahamse, & Jackson, 2008; Kasser, 2005). Findings from one study of 400 North American adults showed that those who cared more about extrinsic relative to intrinsic values had substantially higher "ecological footprints," and thus used more of Earth's limited resources to meet their housing, food, and transportation lifestyle choices (Brown & Kasser, 2005). Individuals high in extrinsic values also act in greedier, more ecologically destructive, and less sustainable ways when they play forest-management simulation games in the laboratory, compared to their more intrinsically oriented counterparts (Sheldon & McGregor, 2000).

Experimental manipulations again support a causal role for values in these processes. In one study with Belgian education students (Vansteenkiste, Simons, Lens, Sheldon, & Deci, 2004), recycling was framed either as being beneficial to one's community (i.e., intrinsic values) or as likely to save money (i.e., extrinsic values). Individuals who had the behavior framed in an extrinsic fashion were subsequently less likely to take advantage of later opportunities to learn more about recycling than were those who had the behavior framed in an intrinsic fashion. Other studies with U.S. college students (Sheldon, Nichols, & Kasser, 2011) and U.K. adults (Chilton et al., 2012) have found that brief reminders of intrinsic (versus extrinsic) values improve people's expressed attitudes toward the importance of making political and lifestyle changes to combat environmental destruction.

In sum, whereas extrinsic values conduce toward environmental lifestyles and attitudes that undermine the ability of future humans and other species to live a good life, intrinsic values are associated with more ecologically sustainable approaches to living a good life.

## IMPLICATIONS FOR PRACTICE

As I hope this brief literature review demonstrates, the versions of the good life espoused by positive psychology and of the goods life encouraged by consumer culture are not only at odds, but have very different outcomes. Whereas people who organize their lives around the intrinsic values of the good life are happier, treat others in more humane ways, and pursue more ecologically sustainable lifestyles, those who focus on the extrinsic values of the goods life report more distress, treat others in more manipulative and objectifying ways, and pursue lifestyles that contribute more to ecological degradation.

Given these results, it seems to me that if positive psychology is to reach its highest potential as a scientific and practical endeavor, there is much work to do. Not only must the vision of the good life reflected in intrinsic values and positive psychology be supported, but the vision of the goods life reflected in extrinsic values and our money-driven, consumer culture must be weakened. To these ends, I discuss next a variety of different interventions and initiatives that positive psychologists might undertake, all of which have the dual purposes of dislodging the psychological and social processes that support extrinsic values and nurturing the processes that encourage intrinsic values and goals.

### CLINICAL PRACTICE

As reviewed earlier in the chapter, intrinsic and extrinsic values have been empirically associated with many of the psychological difficulties that clinicians see in their practices, including depression, anxiety, somatic complaints, personality disorders, substance abuse, and childhood disorders, not to mention the general malaise associated with diminished happiness and satisfaction with life. Value orientations are also relevant to *compulsive consumption*, which is characterized by strong, often irresistible urges to purchase goods (see Faber, 2004, for a review; see Dittmar et al., in press, for meta-analytic results).

Unfortunately, as noted by Kottler, Montgomery, and Shepard (2004), clinicians frequently overlook the many ways in which consumption, materialism, and extrinsic values interact with, and potentially cause, some of their clients' problems. This may be in part due to current diagnostic systems, such as the *Diagnostic and Statistical Manual of Mental Disorders* (American Psychiatric Association, 2013), which recognize few consumption-related issues relevant to psychopathology. Further, to my knowledge, young clinicians are rarely trained to consider consumption issues as they learn their trade, probably in part because no well-articulated clinical theories direct their practitioners to examine important aspects of life such as spending patterns, debt, or materialism. Although space precludes a longer exposition on this topic, I would like to describe two themes that might be worth exploring with clients (see Kottler et al., 2004, for more treatment ideas).

The first theme concerns people's psychological needs. Substantial theorizing and research suggests that psychological well-being is enhanced when people have experiences that satisfy four psychological needs: security and safety, competence and efficacy, connection to others, and autonomy and authenticity (see Bandura, 1977; Baumeister & Leary, 1995; Kasser, 2002b; Maslow, 1954; Ryan & Deci, 2000; Sheldon, Elliot, Kim, & Kasser, 2001). Marketers and advertisers also recognize the importance of these needs, as they frequently use psychologically sophisticated and well-researched advertisements to suggest that the acquisition of products and services will satisfy these needs. To take just the example of automobiles, common advertisement scripts suggest to viewers that a sport utility vehicle can be used to protect one from dangerous conditions (i.e., safety), to show that one has made it in life (i.e., competence), to attract members of the opposite sex (i.e., relatedness), and to escape to wherever one's heart desires (i.e., autonomy). The problem, however, is that these ads sell a false bill of goods. As I have reviewed elsewhere (Kasser, 2002b), the research shows that when people organize their lives around attaining the extrinsic goals promoted by the goods life, they actually experience lower satisfaction of needs for safety (due largely to past experiences of threat), for competence and efficacy (because they have a lower and more contingent sense of self-esteem and are exposed to more upward social comparisons that make them dissatisfied with themselves), for connection (because they have shorter, more conflictual relationships), and for autonomy and authenticity (because they often feel more controlled and less free). Even when people succeed in their pursuit of extrinsic goals, they often report relatively low satisfaction of their needs, and their well-being does not improve (Niemiec, Deci, & Ryan, 2009; Sheldon & Kasser, 1998).

The second theme concerns the fact that some people habitually use acquisition, consumption, and other extrinsically oriented activities to try to cope with feelings of insecurity and unpleasant emotional states (Kasser, 2002b), including those that might result from poor need satisfaction. Like substance use, cutting one's body, sexual promiscuity, and other high-risk behaviors, obsessive acquisition and "retail therapy" are relatively maladaptive ways that some people try to cope with their unpleasant mood states. Evidence on compulsive buying supports this claim, as compulsive buyers typically report that negative mood states precede their buying binges, and that when they feel badly, they like to shop (see Faber, 2004). Experimental manipulations similarly show that people become more materialistic and more desirous of consuming when they experience a variety of types of threats, including confronting the fact of their own mortality, being made aware that they have failed to live up to important ideals, and being reminded of feelings of isolation or meaninglessness (Braun & Wicklund, 1989; Chang & Arkin, 2002; Kasser & Sheldon, 2000; Sheldon & Kasser, 2008). Although, like drinking and cutting, shopping and acquiring might temporarily distract people from their unpleasant feelings, such consumeristic behavior does little to help them actively confront and solve the problems that brought about the negative mood states in the first place. Additionally, such behavior can lead to increased debt, family conflicts, and even poorer need satisfaction, thus diminishing quality of life.

Clinicians might raise these themes with their clients and help them to explore the irrational thoughts, unpleasant feelings, and situational reinforcements that maintain an unsatisfying extrinsic-value orientation. Once clients begin to realize that the promises of consumer culture are false and that retail therapy does little more than temporarily distract them and increase their credit card debt, they may become motivated to search out a different system of meaning in their lives. At this point, clinicians might introduce the idea of intrinsic values to help their clients reorganize their lives. For example, when stressed or insecure, clients might learn other, more adaptive coping strategies such as reaching out to other people and one's community or pursuing fun activities (like painting, exercising, or playing music) that are more likely to help them to grow as a person than will buying another sweater or pair of shoes. Switching activities in these ways should not only be effective at alleviating unpleasant feelings, but should also help to build the values of affiliation, community feeling, and personal growth that are key intrinsic values. Similarly, helping individuals learn to satisfy their psychological needs through the pursuit of self-knowledge and self-acceptance, through close relations to others, and through contribution to the community will not only work to dislodge extrinsic values, but also should increase the likelihood that people will have the types of experiences that really do satisfy their psychological needs.

In addition to exploring these themes, clinicians may want to consider having their clients engage in certain deep reflective practices that have shown promise in orienting people toward intrinsic values and away from extrinsic values. Studies show that people who have developed *mindfulness*, or the capacity to experience themselves and others in a nonjudgmental, moment-to-moment way, also report a greater preference for intrinsic relative to extrinsic values, in addition to higher levels of well-being and more ecologically sustainable lifestyles (Brown & Kasser, 2005; Brown & Ryan, 2003). What's more, an intervention designed to improve mindfulness skills increased how content participants felt with their material possessions and financial situation (i.e., extrinsic values), with consequent improvements in personal well-being (Brown, Kasser, Ryan, Linley, & Orzech, 2009). Another promising type of reflective practice involves deeply and regularly considering the fact of one's own mortality. Although some studies have shown that *brief* reminders of death typically shift people toward extrinsic values and away from intrinsic values, other studies suggest that *sustained* reflection on death shifts people toward intrinsic and away from extrinsic aims in life (Cozzolinno, Staples, Meyers, & Samboceti, 2004; Lykins, Segerstrom, Averill, Evans, & Kemeny, 2007). Two processes may explain why these types of reflective practices have beneficial effects on people's value orientation. First, rather than responding to threats by automatically endorsing extrinsic values, people who engage in reflective practices may act in less defensive and more autonomous ways, thereby derailing the largely unconscious processes that would typically push them toward money, image, and status as coping mechanisms. Second, such reflective practices may help people become more attuned to the aims in life that actually meet their psychological needs (i.e., intrinsic values), thereby improving their well-being, as well as their treatment of others and of the ecosystem.

One last point clinicians might attend to concerns relapse prevention. As they would with former alcoholics and overeaters who are tempted every day to return to their earlier problematic behaviors and thought patterns, therapists would do well to help their clients recognize that we all live in a world that is a veritable cornucopia of consumption that continually will encourage a return to an extrinsically oriented lifestyle. Discussing these issues before termination and helping clients develop ways of dealing with relapses might help ensure longer-term successes.

PREVENTION PRACTICES

Although the psychotherapeutic efforts previously described may prove helpful, it would of course be better to prevent people from undervaluing intrinsic and over-valuing extrinsic goals in the first place. Psychologists can use many of their skills to develop a variety of types of interventions in this regard. Although others could be discussed, here I focus on two broad foci of interventions.

*Children and Their Parents*    Children are a sort of holy grail for marketers and advertis-ers because young people have a relatively large percentage of disposable income, can influence their parents' purchases through whining and nagging, and might become lifelong consumers of a product if they are hooked early in their lives (Levin & Linn, 2004; Schor, 2004). Children are also particularly susceptible to messages tying secu-rity, self-worth, love, and freedom to the purchase of products, given that their cog-nitive skills are still in the process of developing and that they are often strongly motivated to fit in with their peers (Banerjee & Dittmar, 2008). Moreover, the enor-mous amount of time that children are exposed to commercial messages on television, on the radio, and on the Internet is now amplified by the spread of marketing strate-gies that connect the movies (e.g., *Star Wars*) with toys (e.g., Star Wars action figures) and food (e.g., Star Wars Happy Meals) that children are encouraged to purchase (Levin & Linn, 2004). In sum, from the time they wake up until they go to bed, chil-dren are increasingly exposed to a constant stream of psychologically sophisticated propaganda that propounds the worth of the goods life and of extrinsic values. It should thus be of little surprise that between the late 1960s and mid-2000s, increas-ingly large percentages of U.S. youth endorsed materialistic aims in life, increases that have been statistically associated with both increases in levels of youth psychopathol-ogy (Twenge et al., 2010) and the amount of advertising expenditures present in the nation (Twenge & Kasser, 2013).

How might positive psychologists help stem this rising tide? First, we must recognize that some children are at higher risk for taking on the messages of the goods life than are others. Research shows that children are more likely to emphasize extrinsic relative to intrinsic values if their parents are controlling or harsh, if they come from a divorced household, and if they are poorer (Cohen & Cohen, 1996; Kasser, Ryan, Zax, & Sameroff, 1995; Rindfleisch, Burroughs, & Denton, 1997). Addi-tionally, African Americans and young girls are particularly targeted by marketers (Kilbourne, 2004; LaPoint & Hambrick-Dixon, 2004), and unpopular children seem to believe that extrinsic pursuits will help them to fit in better (Banerjee & Dittmar, 2008). Thus, psychologists interested in prevention efforts with at-risk groups might do well to focus on these populations.

A variety of interventions might be developed and tested after choosing a par-ticular population with whom to work. Among the most often-used interventions are media literacy campaigns designed to help children understand the purposes and strategies of advertisements. Another possibility might be to "capitalize on" teenagers' sense of rebellion and educate them about the many ways that marketers attempt to manipulate and brand teens (Quart, 2003); teens' resulting anger might then be turned against the marketers to help dethrone extrinsic values. Interventions based in cognitive-dissonance theory, which are effective for behaviors such as condom use (Aronson, Fried, & Stone, 1991), might also be adapted; for example, many teens hold strong environmental beliefs, and if they can be shown how their actual consumption behavior is inconsistent with their ideals, dissonance might motivate a change in behavior. Programs that improve children's self-esteem might also decrease their materialistic values, as suggested by one experiment (Chaplin & John, 2007).

Recently we conducted an in-depth intervention with parents and teens to attempt to reduce the teens' orientation toward extrinsic, materialistic values (Kasser et al., 2014). After filling out baseline survey packets, teens and their parents were randomly assigned to a no-treatment control group or to an intervention group that underwent three 3-hour sessions based on an established program designed to help orient adolescents away from "spending" and toward "sharing" and "saving" (www.sharesavespend.com). In these sessions, parents and teens discussed a variety of topics, including the distinction between "needs" and "wants," the influence of advertisements on financial attitudes and behaviors, the importance of imitating good models of sharing and saving behaviors, and optimal strategies for giving allowances; homework assignments were also given between sessions, including tracking one's spending behavior and the advertisements to which one was exposed. When they were surveyed both 6 weeks and 8 months after the intervention ended, adolescents who underwent the intervention reported decreases in materialism (i.e., extrinsic values), relative to the control group. Further, those adolescents who began the study relatively high in materialism (extrinsic values) and who received the intervention evidenced significantly higher increases in self-esteem both 6 weeks and 8 months later than did other groups; indeed, those who began the study high in materialism and who did not receive the intervention evidenced declines in self-esteem over the time period assessed. Although these results are clearly in need of replication, they point to the possibility that interventions with parents and their teenaged children hold promise for shifting children's value orientations, to the benefit of their well-being.

Other interventions might focus more on parents, who are of course important influences on children's value systems (Kasser et al., 1995). For example, parents could be helped to examine how they may be inadvertently modeling extrinsic values to their children by each working 60 hours per week so that they can afford two large cars, a 3,500-square-foot house, and a large-screen plasma television. Such behavior clearly sends children not-so-subtle messages about what is important in life. Helping parents to model intrinsic values instead should not only increase their children's intrinsic values, but should also help to make the parents happier and healthier. Another aim of research could be to study the types of parenting practices that help build resilience in the face of consumer messages. For example, is it better to hit the mute button during commercials to demonstrate that commercials are unimportant and not worth listening to, or is it better to leave the commercials on so that the parent can critique and decode the commercial messages? Some publications provide advice about how to raise children who are living in a consumer culture (e.g., Taylor, 2003), but more empirical research and psychological theorizing are needed to help guide parents (see Buijzen & Valkenburg, 2005, for some initial steps).

*Voluntary Simplicity Interventions*    Although movements toward a more materially simple life have been notable in U.S. history since the colonial era (Shi, 1985), *voluntary simplicity* (VS) experienced a resurgence at the end of the 20th century (Etzioni, 1998) with the publication of books like *Voluntary Simplicity* by Elgin (1993), *Your Money or Your Life* by Dominguez and Robin (1992), and *The Circle of Simplicity* by Andrews

(1998). These, and other books published since, describe a lifestyle that rejects consumerism and instead focuses on a more "inwardly rich" life focused on personal growth, family, and volunteerism. Not surprisingly, then, Brown and Kasser (2005) found that, compared to a matched control group, people who self-identify as voluntary simplifiers place less emphasis on extrinsic aims and more emphasis on intrinsic aims; they also reported higher personal well-being and more ecologically responsible behaviors and lifestyles. Similar results have been reported by Boujbel and d'Astous (2012), Iwata (1999), and Leonard-Barton (1981).

Although the empirical literature on VS is relatively sparse, the self-help literature is burgeoning, and many types of workshops and programs have been designed to help people "downshift" and simplify their lives. Here, I will mention just two examples. First, working from Andrews's (1998) book, "simplicity circles" have sprouted up around the world. These essentially act as support groups for those who are trying to simplify their lives, providing a place where people can talk with like-minded others about their challenges and can share ideas and resources in the form of cooperative and barter systems. Second, many workshops based on *Your Money or Your Life* (YMYL) are presented every year. Essentially these programs teach people how to live in a more frugal manner while they save their extra earnings; eventually a point of "financial independence" is reached when individuals are spending so little money each year that they can live off of the interest of the savings that have been accumulated (which is far below what most people consider necessary to have in their individual retirement accounts). At this time, they can quit their jobs and devote their time to their own growth, their families, and the community.

Simplicity circles and YMYL programs have attracted tens of thousands of adherents and provide well-designed interventions that could be tested in randomized, controlled studies. Psychologists could study how successfully people move away from extrinsic and toward intrinsic pursuits and how their well-being changes upon simplifying. If appropriately adapted, such interventions might even be useful for high school and college students before they head out into the world of work.

## Public Policy Initiatives

Although each of the ideas suggested above has some potential, they all suffer from a problem analogous to what family therapists have recognized about therapy with children and what sociocultural theorists have recognized about psychopathology in general. Consider, for example, the likely efficacy of providing 1 hour of intervention per week to a child diagnosed with oppositional-defiant disorder who lives in an abusive home with an alcoholic father in a poverty-stricken, gang-ridden neighborhood in a nation that provides relatively few social services for the poor. So long as the broader family and social structures remain unchanged, the intervention is not likely to be very successful. In addition, acting as though the child is the one with the problem smacks of "blaming the victim," because in fact it is his family, neighborhood, and broader social environment that are actually sick and largely responsible for his problems (although each would probably deny that this is so).

Analogously, then, we must wonder about the potential efficacy of any clinical or prevention interventions so long as people live in a culture where extrinsic values are frequently encouraged, where intrinsic values are co-opted for marketing purposes, and where the media, government, and educational systems have all become outlets for materialistic interests. If this is the state of our culture, is it reasonable to say that individual citizens should be solely responsible for their value orientations? When children are targeted by marketers and pressured by peers to want the newest "in" products, is it reasonable to say that parents should just turn off the television and resist their children's complaints? In the face of the glorification of the goods life and statements by the U.S. president that people should "go shopping" after a national tragedy like 9/11 ("Excerpts," 2001), is it reasonable to believe that people can switch to a more materially simple lifestyle without being viewed as weird, unpatriotic, or subversive?

If indeed the broader social processes, structures, and agendas relevant to consumerism are important to address, psychologists must begin to overcome their disciplinary reticence to become involved in public policy issues (see Kasser & Kanner, 2004, for a discussion) and begin to work for broader structural changes. Elsewhere, I have written about a variety of areas of public policy psychologists might work on (see, e.g., Kasser, 2002b, 2011), but here I discuss two.

*The Commercialization of Childhood*  Capitalist markets must expand in order to satisfy their quest for ever-increasing profits, and in the past few decades, marketers have broken new ground by focusing on children and teens, who purchase or influence their parents' purchase of around $1.2 trillion worth of products and services annually (Robinson, 2012). Not surprisingly, marketers have consequently spent a great deal of time, effort, and money trying to influence children's desires for more stuff. Although some may claim that this is a natural and appropriate way to increase consumption and thus economic progress (i.e., extrinsic pursuits), there are good reasons to be uneasy about this development.

As has been well-documented in books by Linn (2004) and Schor (2004), a great deal of evidence suggests that many of the messages and products that are marketed to children are unhealthy in one way or another. These authors review evidence that when children consume consumer culture, they are placed at increased risk of developing eating disorders (both obesity and anorexia/bulimia), being violent and sexually promiscuous, feeling less happy, having more arguments with their families, and believing that materialistic values are important in life. Indeed, two studies of U.S. (Schor, 2004) and U.K. (Nairn, Ormrod, & Bottomley, 2007) adolescents have found support for path models showing that exposure to more media leads to high levels of "consumer involvement" and materialism, which in turn are associated with more depression, anxiety, and physical symptoms, as well as lower self-esteem. Further, as noted earlier in the chapter, time-series analyses have shown that materialism rates of teenagers are higher during times when a larger percentage of the U.S. gross domestic product comes from advertising expenditures (Twenge & Kasser, 2013).

There are other reasons to be particularly concerned about marketing to children. For one, children are often exposed to advertisements in schools; because attendance at school is compulsory, children are thus forced to see corporate banners in the hallways, study curricula sponsored by corporations, or even watch television shows such as Channel One that contain advertisements (Linn, 2004; Schor, 2004). Another problem concerns children's still-developing cognitive abilities. The American Psychological Association Task Force on Advertising and Children (2004) concluded that children under age 8 have great difficulty understanding the persuasive intent of advertising. Thus, although older children and adults typically have the cognitive capacity to become aware of how advertisements are attempting to manipulate them and can understand the biases inherent in advertising, most children (especially the very young) typically trust the messages they see in advertisements, and are thus at the mercy of those who create them.

It would be one thing if marketers had children's best interests at heart, but a quick read through the writings of Schor (2004) or Linn (2004) makes it clear that many marketers care little about the welfare of the children to whom they sell. Consider the following quote, for instance:

> Advertising at its best is making people feel that without their product, you're a loser. . . . Kids are very sensitive to that. If you tell them to buy something they are resistant, but if you tell them that they'll be a dork if they don't, you've got their attention. You open up emotional vulnerabilities, and it's very easy to do with kids because they're the most emotionally vulnerable. (Harris, 1989, p. 1)

Given the research on extrinsic aspirations previously reviewed, it is perhaps not surprising that some marketers speak about children in this way. That is, people's extrinsic pursuits are associated with caring less about others' welfare, being less empathic, and endorsing a more Machiavellian stance toward other people. It therefore logically follows that individuals who are interested in making money off of children would be willing to manipulate children, sell them unhealthy products, and promote materialism and extrinsic pursuits.

Several policy suggestions to counteract marketing to children have been proposed by Linn (2004) and Schor (2004), as well as by an organization known as Commercial Alert, which drafted a nine-point Parent's Bill of Rights (Commercial Alert, 2003). Here, I would like to highlight four sets of proposals mentioned by these sources that could work to decrease the spread of extrinsic aspirations in children, as well as to block the actions of those marketers so taken with extrinsic aspirations that they are willing to advertise harmful products and messages.

The first set of proposals concerns disclosure. Advertisements are increasingly present in television shows, movies, and video games; even chat rooms and everyday interactions have been infiltrated by actors hired to promote certain products without revealing that they are paid to do so. Clearly many of these methods involve an intent to deceive and get "below the radar screen" of the viewer/player/person. For this reason, Linn (2004), Schor (2004), and Commercial Alert (2003) all recommend that marketers must clearly state when an advertisement is occurring, and that such statements be made in age-appropriate ways so that even young children exposed to advertisements know that an advertisement is occurring. Such a policy would help decrease much of the unconscious conditioning by which marketers promote their products and extrinsic pursuits.

A second set of suggestions is to make marketing research abide by the same stringent ethical review processes that are required in academic settings. Currently, marketers conducting research do not have to follow any of the standard procedures that require academics and other researchers to obtain subjects' consent, to protect minors, or to notify subjects of potential harms that might occur from participating in the research (Jacoby, Johar, & Morrin, 1998). It is important to force marketers to operate under the same ethical standards that occur in other research settings, given the evidence that marketers often sell products that are harmful and given that they have even conducted studies designed to understand how to increase the likelihood that children's "purchase requests" (i.e., nagging) are supported by parents (i.e., the parents give) (Western Media International, 1998).

A third approach concerns reforming tax laws so as to remove existing subsidies for advertising to children. Commercial Alert (2003), for example, suggests that Congress end the practice of allowing corporations to deduct advertising expenses. An even stronger approach endorsed by both Schor (2004) and Linn (2004) is to levy a tax on advertising that is aimed at audiences with high proportions of children and teenagers. The money raised from such taxes could then be devoted to commercial-free public television, to media literacy campaigns, and to programs designed to support and encourage intrinsic values and goals. At the same time, such changes in tax laws would affect extrinsically oriented marketers and corporations in the pocketbook, thereby potentially diminishing the amount of ambient advertising in the environment.

Finally, outright bans on marketing in certain situations, marketing of certain products, marketing in certain ways, and marketing to children under certain ages have been proposed. Most activists agree that marketing in schools or on school property (including school buses) should be outlawed, given that it is inescapable and at odds with the educational mission of schools. Schor (2004) and Linn (2004) have both suggested following the lead of New Zealand by banning all advertisements of junk food. Linn (2004) also suggests banning advertisements that demean adults, or that suggest that ownership of a certain product will promote peer acceptance. Finally, many activists agree that nations concerned about the welfare of children should follow the lead of Brazil, Sweden, Norway, and the Canadian province of Quebec by banning all advertisements to children under certain ages, although disagreement exists about whether the appropriate age is 5, 8, or 12 years old.

*Time Affluence*   Contemporary society, with its capitalist economic organization dependent on consumer spending, places substantial emphasis on increasing material affluence as a barometer of progress. Given the significant psychological, social, and ecological costs associated with organizing one's life around the pursuit of the extrinsic goals embodied in material affluence, and given that in economically developed countries improvements in material affluence do not translate into improved subjective well-being (Diener & Seligman, 2004), other models of the good life are needed to supplant that of material affluence.

Time affluence is one such model. Even after controlling for feelings of material affluence, individuals who feel like they have enough time and are not overly rushed report higher levels of personal well-being (Kasser & Sheldon, 2009). Other research shows that people report higher levels of personal well-being on the weekend (i.e., when they are less likely to be working for money; Ryan, Bernstein, & Brown, 2010) and that brief reminders of time (versus money or neutral topics) increase people's happiness over the coming hours (Mogilner, 2010). Time affluence seems to provide these well-being benefits because it provides opportunities for people to pursue intrinsic aspirations (Kasser & Sheldon, 2009); to satisfy their psychological needs for autonomy, competence, and relatedness (Ryan et al., 2010); and to have social interactions with others (Mogilner, 2010). Working fewer hours is also associated with greater levels of ecological sustainability, both at the level of the person (Kasser & Brown, 2003) and at the level of the nation (Hayden & Shandra, 2009; Rosnick & Weisbrot, 2006).

Passing policies that help people to maximize their time affluence (rather than their material affluence) is thus a promising way of promoting intrinsic aspirations, undermining extrinsic aspirations, and supporting the multifaceted vision of the good life described here. Again, many scholars and activists agree on some basic policies that could be useful in this respect (see, e.g, de Graaf, 2004; Jackson, 2009; and Schor, 2010).

First, policy could improve workers' access to paid family leave. In the United States, the Family and Medical Leave Act allows workers only 12 weeks of *unpaid* leave to care for newborn children or sick relatives; this stands in contrast to the vast majority of nations of the world that provide substantially longer periods of *paid* family leave. Passing laws that support or expand paid family leave would have the important effect of allowing individuals to pursue the intrinsic aspirations of affiliation, particularly in critical moments of transition in life (e.g., births and deaths).

A second proposition concerns the minimum amount of paid vacation workers receive. The European Union requires a legal minimum of 4 weeks of paid vacation. In contrast, the United States has no law ensuring minimum paid vacation for workers; many workers do receive 2 weeks, but many other American workers, particularly low-income women, receive no paid vacation at all. By passing laws that increase vacation time, individuals would have the opportunity to pursue their personal interests, spend time with their family, and actually pause and reflect on their lives rather than continue the helter-skelter lifestyle so prominent in contemporary Western nations. Such a law might be decried by those in business who concern themselves primarily with profit, but, as noted, we must recognize that other aims in life besides money need to be supported by our legal mechanisms.

A third proposal is in regard to overtime. In the United States, there is no mandatory number of maximum hours that an employer can ask their workers to work, despite the fact that most other economically developed nations do have such maximums. Rather than being held hostage by employers who threaten the loss of job security and future raises if employees do not work more, passage of such laws would enable workers to be more in charge of their lives (thus supporting personal growth aspirations), as well as potentially have more time to spend with friends and family (i.e., affiliation aspirations) and in civic and volunteer activities (i.e., community feeling).

Finally, de Graaf (2004) proposes that the United States should "make Election Day a holiday." Voter turnout for U.S. citizens has generally been on the decline, despite the fact that the close election of 2000 showed the importance of every single vote. Voter turnout is not particularly high in other democratic nations either. Were nations to recognize that civic responsibilities (i.e., community feeling aspirations) need to be supported in the face of the press of work obligations (i.e., extrinsic pursuits), perhaps more individuals would take the time to become involved in this important aspect of democracy.

In sum, these four legislative proposals hold promise for improving "the good life" by decreasing citizens' focus on material affluence (extrinsic aspirations) and instead supporting people's efforts to pursue intrinsic aspirations by providing them with the time needed to do so.

## CONCLUSION

In summary, I have tried in this chapter to demonstrate that a large and growing body of empirical evidence suggests that consumer culture's vision of the goods life, as reflected in the pursuit of extrinsic aims for money, image, and popularity, is associated with a relatively low quality of life. In contrast, positive psychology's vision of the good life, as reflected in the pursuit of intrinsic values for personal growth, affiliation, and community contribution, seems to do substantially better at fulfilling its promises of happiness and enhanced well-being, while also promoting more prosocial and ecologically sustainable attitudes and behaviors. Psychologists might help individuals and society move away from extrinsic and toward intrinsic values by developing and testing interventions with clients, children, and adults, and by working at a policy level to end advertising to children and to provide individuals with more time affluence. Such efforts might help to loosen the grip of the goods life and free people to pursue the truly good life.

## SUMMARY POINTS

- Substantial cross-cultural evidence supports a theoretical distinction between *intrinsic goals and values* (for personal growth, affiliation, and community feeling) and *extrinsic goals and values* (for money, image, and popularity).
- Because intrinsic goals do a relatively good job of satisfying inherent psychological needs, research shows that people who focus on them generally have high levels of well-being and low levels of distress; prioritizing extrinsic goals, in contrast, is consistently associated with lower well-being and greater distress.
- Compared to those focused on extrinsic values, research shows that people who organize their lives around intrinsic values also treat others in more humane ways and pursue more ecologically sustainable lifestyles, thus supporting *others'* well-being.
- The quality of people's lives can thus be improved by encouraging the intrinsic values and goals reflected in positive psychology and by discouraging the vision of "the goods life" reflected in extrinsic values and our money-driven, consumer culture.
- One means of implementing this strategy is to develop psychotherapeutic means of helping clients prioritize intrinsic goals and deprioritize extrinsic goals.
- Preventive interventions can also be developed to help children and young people orient away from the extrinsic goals of consumer society and instead orient their lives around the pursuit of intrinsic goals.
- The possibility of fully supporting a good life, however, will also require psychologists to overcome their reticence to be involved in public policy issues, as the consumer culture in which contemporary humans exist frequently encourages extrinsic goals.
- Two such sets of policies are, first, to limit the extent to which children are exposed to advertisements, which usually encourage extrinsic goals, and, second, to promote policies that allow for greater time affluence, thereby allowing more opportunities to pursue intrinsic goals successfully.

## REFERENCES

American Psychiatric Association. (2013). *Diagnostic and statistical manual of mental disorders* (5th ed.). Washington, DC: Author.

American Psychological Association Task Force on Advertising and Children. (2004). *Psychological issues in the increasing commercialization of childhood*. Washington, DC: American Psychological Association.

Andrews, C. (1998). *The circle of simplicity*. New York, NY: Harper Collins.

Aronson, E., Fried, C., & Stone, J. (1991). Overcoming denial and increasing the intention to use condoms through the induction of hypocrisy. *American Journal of Public Health, 81,* 1636–1638.

Bandura, A. (1977). Self-efficacy: Toward a unifying theory of behavioral change. *Psychological Review, 84,* 191–215.

Banerjee, R., & Dittmar, H. (2008). Individual differences in children's materialism: The role of peer relationships. *Personality and Social Psychology Bulletin, 34,* 17–31.

Bauer, M. A., Wilkie, J. E. B., Kim, J. K., & Bodenhausen, G. B. (2012). Cuing consumerism: Situational materialism undermines personal and social well-being. *Psychological Science, 23,* 517–523.

Baumeister, R., & Leary, M. R. (1995). The need to belong: Desire for interpersonal attachments as a fundamental human motivation. *Psychological Bulletin, 117,* 497–529.

Boujbel, L., & d'Astous, A. (2012). Voluntary simplicity and life satisfaction: Exploring the mediating role of consumption desires. *Journal of Consumer Behaviour, 11*, 487–494.

Braun, O. L., & Wicklund, R. A. (1989). Psychological antecedents of conspicuous consumption. *Journal of Economic Psychology, 10*, 161–187.

Brown, K. W., & Kasser, T. (2005). Are psychological and ecological well-being compatible? The role of values, mindfulness, and lifestyle. *Social Indicators Research, 74*, 349–368.

Brown, K. W., Kasser, T., Ryan, R. M., Linley, P. A., & Orzech, K. (2009). When what one has is enough: Mindfulness, financial desire discrepancy, and subjective well-being. *Journal of Research in Personality, 43*, 727–736.

Brown, K. W., & Ryan, R. M. (2003). The benefits of being present: Mindfulness and its role in psychological well-being. *Journal of Personality and Social Psychology, 84*, 822–848.

Buijzen, M., & Valkenburg, P. M. (2005). Parental mediation of undesired advertising effects. *Journal of Broadcasting and Electronic Media, 49*, 153–165.

Chan, R., & Joseph, S. (2000). Dimensions of personality, domains of aspiration, and subjective well-being. *Personality and Individual Differences, 28*, 347–354.

Chang, L., & Arkin, R. M. (2002). Materialism as an attempt to cope with uncertainty. *Psychology and Marketing, 19*, 389–406.

Chaplin, L. N., & John, D. R. (2007). Growing up in a material world: Age differences in materialism in children and adolescents. *Journal of Consumer Research, 34*, 480–493.

Chilton, P., Crompton, T., Kasser, T., Maio, G., & Nolan, A. (2012). Communicating bigger-than-self problems to extrinsically-oriented audiences. *Common Cause Briefing.* Retrieved from valueandframes.org

Cohen, P., & Cohen, J. (1996). *Life values and adolescent mental health.* Mahwah, NJ: Erlbaum.

Commercial Alert. (2003). *Commercial Alert's parents' bill of rights.* Retrieved from http://www.commercialalert.org/pbor.pdf

Cozzolino, P., Staples, A. D., Meyers, L. S., & Samboceti, J. (2004). Greed, death, and values: From terror-management to transcendence-management theory. *Personality & Social Psychology Bulletin, 30*, 278–292.

Crompton, T., & Kasser, T. (2009). *Meeting environmental challenges: The role of human identity.* Godalming, England: WWF-UK.

Csikszentmihalyi, M. (1999). If we are so rich, why aren't we happy? *American Psychologist, 54*, 821–827.

de Graaf, J. (2004). Campaigning for time. *Yes! Magazine.* Retrieved from http://www.yesmagazine.org/issues/can-we-live-without-oil/campaigning-for-time

Deneulin, S., & McGregor, J. A. (2010). The capability approach and the politics of a social conception of well-being. *European Journal of Social Theory, 13*, 501–519.

Diener, E. (2000). Subjective well-being: The science of happiness and a proposal for a national index. *American Psychologist, 55*, 34–43.

Diener, E., & Seligman, M. E. P. (2004). Beyond money: Toward an economy of well-being. *Psychological Science in the Public Interest, 5*, 1–31.

Dittmar, H., Bond, R., Hurst, M., & Kasser, T. (in press). The relationship between materialism and personal well-being: A meta-analysis. *Journal of Personality & Social Psychology.*

Dominguez, J., & Robin, V. (1992). *Your money or your life.* New York, NY: Viking Press.

Duriez, B., Vansteenkiste, M., Soenens, B., & De Witte, H. (2007). The social costs of extrinsic relative to intrinsic goal pursuits: Their relation with social dominance and racial and ethnic prejudice. *Journal of Personality, 75*, 757–82

Elgin, D. (1993). *Voluntary simplicity* (Rev. ed.). New York, NY: Morrow.

Emmons, R. A. (1989). The personal strivings approach to personality. In L. A. Pervin (Ed.), *Goal concepts in personality and social psychology* (pp. 87–126). Hillsdale, NJ: Erlbaum.

Etzioni, A. (1998). Voluntary simplicity: Characterization, select psychological implications, and societal consequences. *Journal of Economic Psychology, 19*, 619–643.

Excerpts from the president's remarks on war on terrorism. (2001, October 12). *New York Times*, p. B4.

Faber, R. J. (2004). Self-control and compulsive buying. In T. Kasser & A. D. Kanner (Eds.), *Psychology and consumer culture: The struggle for a good life in a materialistic world* (pp. 169–187). Washington, DC: APA Press.

Gatersleben, B., Meadows, J., Abrahamse, W., & Jackson, T. (2008). *Materialism and environmental values of young people*. Unpublished manuscript, University of Surrey, United Kingdom.

Grouzet, F. M. E., Kasser, T., Ahuvia, A., Fernandez-Dols, J. M., Kim, Y., Lau, S., . . . Sheldon, K. M. (2005). The structure of goal contents across 15 cultures. *Journal of Personality and Social Psychology, 89*, 800–816.

Guillen-Royo, M., & Kasser, T. (in press). Personal goals, socio-economic context, and happiness: Studying a diverse sample in Peru. *Journal of Happiness Studies*.

Haidt, J. T., (2006). *The happiness hypothesis: Finding modern truth in ancient wisdom*. New York, NY: Basic Books.

Harris, R. (1989, November 12). Children who dress for excess: Today's youngsters have become fixated with fashion. The right look isn't enough–it also has to be expensive. *Los Angeles Times*, p. 1.

Hayden, A., & Shandra, J. S. (2009). Hours of work and the ecological footprint of nations: An exploratory analysis. *Local Environment: The International Journal of Justice & Sustainability, 14*, 575–600.

Hurst, M., Dittmar, H., Bond, R., & Kasser, T. (2013). The relationship between materialistic values and environmental attitudes and behaviors: A meta-analysis. *Journal of Environmental Psychology, 36*, 257–269.

Iwata, O. (1999). Perceptual and behavioral correlates of voluntary simplicity lifestyles. *Social Behavior & Personality, 27*, 379–386.

Jackson, T. (2009). *Prosperity without growth: Economics for a finite planet*. London, England: Earthscan.

Jacoby, J., Johar, G. V., & Morrin, M. (1998). Consumer behavior: A quadrennium. *Annual Review of Psychology, 49*, 319–344.

Kasser, T. (2002a). Sketches for a self-determination theory of values. In E. L. Deci & R. M. Ryan (Eds.), *Handbook of self-determination research* (pp. 123–140). Rochester, NY: University of Rochester Press.

Kasser, T. (2002b). *The high price of materialism*. Cambridge, MA: MIT Press.

Kasser, T. (2005). Frugality, generosity, and materialism in children and adolescents. In K. A. Moore & L. H. Lippman (Eds.), *What do children need to flourish?: Conceptualizing and measuring indicators of positive development* (pp. 357–373). New York, NY: Springer Science.

Kasser, T. (2011). *Values and human wellbeing*. Commissioned paper for The Bellagio Initiative: The Future of Philanthropy and Development in the Pursuit of Human Wellbeing. Retrieved from http://www.bellagioinitiative.org/about-us/what-is-the-bellagio-initiative/commissioned-papers/

Kasser, T., & Ahuvia, A. C. (2002). Materialistic values and well-being in business students. *European Journal of Social Psychology, 32*, 137–146.

Kasser, T., & Brown, K. W. (2003). On time, happiness, and ecological footprints. In J. DeGraaf (Ed.), *Take back your time!: Fighting overwork and time poverty in America* (pp. 107–112). San Francisco, CA: Berrett-Koehler.

Kasser, T., Cohn, S., Kanner, A. D., & Ryan, R. M. (2007). Some costs of American corporate capitalism: A psychological exploration of value and goal conflicts. *Psychological Inquiry, 18*, 1–22.

Kasser, T., & Kanner, A. D. (2004). Where is the psychology of consumer culture? In T. Kasser & A. D. Kanner (Eds.), *Psychology and consumer culture: The struggle for a good life in a materialistic world* (pp. 3–7). Washington, DC: APA Press.

Kasser, T., Rosenblum, K. L., Sameroff, A. J., Deci, E. L., Niemiec, C. P., Ryan, R. M., . . . Hawks, S. (2014). Changes in materialism, changes in psychological well-being: Evidence from three longitudinal studies and an intervention experiment. *Motivation & Emotion*, *38*, 1–22.

Kasser, T., & Ryan, R. M. (1993). A dark side of the American dream: Correlates of financial success as a central life aspiration. *Journal of Personality and Social Psychology, 65*, 410–422.

Kasser, T., & Ryan, R. M. (1996). Further examining the American dream: Differential correlates of intrinsic and extrinsic goals. *Personality and Social Psychology Bulletin, 22*, 280–287.

Kasser, T., Ryan, R. M., Zax, M., & Sameroff, A. J. (1995). The relations of maternal and social environments to late adolescents' materialistic and prosocial values. *Developmental Psychology, 31*, 907–914.

Kasser, T., & Sheldon, K. M. (2000). Of wealth and death: Materialism, mortality salience, and consumption behavior. *Psychological Science, 11*, 352–355.

Kasser, T., & Sheldon, K. M. (2009). Time affluence as a path towards personal happiness and ethical business practices: Empirical evidence from four studies. *Journal of Business Ethics, 84*, 243–255.

Khanna, S., & Kasser, T. (1999). *Materialism, objectification, and alienation: A cross-cultural investigation of U.S., Indian, and Danish college students.* Unpublished manuscript, Knox College, Galesburg, IL.

Kilbourne, J. (2004). "The more you subtract, the more you add": Cutting girls down to size. In T. Kasser & A. D. Kanner (Eds.), *Psychology and consumer culture: The struggle for a good life in a materialistic world* (pp. 251–270). Washington, DC: APA Press.

Kim, Y., Kasser, T., & Lee, H. (2003). Self-concept, aspirations, and well-being in South Korea and the United States. *Journal of Social Psychology, 143*, 277–290.

Kottler, J., Montgomery, M., & Shepard, D. (2004). Acquisitive desire: Assessment and treatment. In T. Kasser & A. D. Kanner (Eds.), *Psychology and consumer culture: The struggle for a good life in a materialistic world* (pp. 149–168). Washington, DC: APA Press.

LaPoint, V., & Hambrick-Dixon, P. J. (2004). Commercialism's influence on Black youth: The case of dress-related challenges. In T. Kasser & A. D. Kanner (Eds.), *Psychology and consumer culture: The struggle for a good life in a materialistic world* (pp. 233–250). Washington, DC: APA Press.

Lekes, N., Gingras, I., Phillipe, F. L., Koestner, R., & Fang, J. (2010). Parental autonomy-support, intrinsic life goals, and well-being among adolescents in China and North America. *Journal of Youth and Adolescence, 39*, 858–869.

Leonard-Barton, D. (1981). Voluntary simplicity lifestyles and energy conservation. *Journal of Consumer Research, 8*, 243–253.

Levin, D. E., & Linn, S. (2004). The commercialization of childhood: Understanding the problem and finding solutions. In T. Kasser & A. D. Kanner (Eds.), *Psychology and consumer culture: The struggle for a good life in a materialistic world* (pp. 213–232). Washington, DC: APA Press.

Linn, S. (2004). *Consuming kids: The hostile takeover of childhood.* New York, NY: The New Press.

Lykins, E. L. B., Segerstrom, S. C., Averill, A. J., Evans, D. R., & Kemeny, M. E. (2007). Goal shifts following reminders of mortality: Reconciling posttraumatic growth and terror management theory. *Personality & Social Psychology Bulletin, 33*, 1088–1099.

Lyubomirsky, S. (2007). *The how of happiness: A scientific approach to getting the life you want.* New York, NY: Penguin.

Maio, G. R., Pakizeh, A., Cheung, W.-Y., & Rees, K. J. (2009). Changing, priming, and acting on values: Effects via motivational relations in a circular model. *Journal of Personality and Social Psychology, 97*, 699–715.

Martos, T., & Kopp, M. S. (2012). Life goals and well-being: Does financial status matter? Evidence from a representative Hungarian sample. *Social Indicators Research, 105*, 561–568.

Maslow, A. H. (1954). *Motivation and personality.* New York, NY: Harper & Row.

McHoskey, J. W. (1999). Machiavellianism, intrinsic versus extrinsic goals, and social interest: A self-determination analysis. *Motivation and Emotion, 23*, 267–283.

Mogilner, C. (2010). The pursuit of happiness: Time, money, and social connection. *Psychological Science, 21*, 1348–1354.

Myers, D. G. (2000). The funds, friends, and faith of happy people. *American Psychologist, 55*, 56–67.

Nairn, A., Ormrod, J., & Bottomley, P. (2007). *Watching, wanting and wellbeing: Exploring the links.* London, England: National Consumer Council.

Niemiec, C. P., Ryan, R. M., & Deci, E. L. (2009). The path taken: Consequences of attaining intrinsic and extrinsic aspirations in post-college life. *Journal of Research in Personality, 43*, 291–306.

Onraet, E., Van Hiel, A., & Dhont, K. (2013). The relationship between right-wing ideological attitudes and psychological well-being. *Personality & Social Psychology Bulletin, 39*, 509–522.

Peterson, C. P. (2006). *A primer in positive psychology.* New York, NY: Oxford University Press.

Quart, A. (2003). *Branded: The buying and selling of teenagers.* Cambridge, MA: Perseus.

Rindfleisch, A., Burroughs, J. E., & Denton, F. (1997). Family structure, materialism, and compulsive consumption. *Journal of Consumer Research, 23*, 312–325.

Robinson, J. (2012, October 26). *The next generation of consumers.* BostInno. Retrieved from http://bostinno.streetwise.co/channels/the-next-generation-of-consumers/

Rokeach, M. (1973). *The nature of human values.* New York, NY: Free Press.

Romero, E., Gomez-Fraguela, J. A., & Villar, P. (2011). Life aspirations, personality traits and subjective well-being in a Spanish sample. *European Journal of Personality, 26*, 45–55.

Rosnick, D., & Weisbrot, M. (2006). *Are shorter work hours good for the environment? A comparison of U.S. and European energy consumption.* Washington, DC: Center for Economic Policy Research.

Ryan, R. M., Bernstein, J. H., & Brown, K. W. (2010). Weekends, work, and well-being: Psychological need satisfactions and day of the week effects on mood, vitality, and physical symptoms. *Journal of Social & Clinical Psychology, 29*, 95–122.

Ryan, R. M., Chirkov, V. I., Little, T. D., Sheldon, K. M., Timoshina, E., & Deci, E. L. (1999). The American dream in Russia: Extrinsic aspirations and well-being in two cultures. *Personality and Social Psychology Bulletin, 25*, 1509–1524.

Ryan, R. M., & Deci, E. L. (2000). Self-determination theory and the facilitation of intrinsic motivation, social development, and well-being. *American Psychologist, 55*, 68–78.

Ryff, C. D., & Keyes, C. L. (1995). The structure of psychological well-being revisited. *Journal of Personality and Social Psychology, 69*, 719–727.

Schmuck, P., Kasser, T., & Ryan, R. M. (2000). Intrinsic and extrinsic goals: Their structure and relationship to well-being in German and U.S. college students. *Social Indicators Research, 50*, 225–241.

Schor, J. B. (2004). *Born to buy: The commercialized child and the new consumer culture.* New York, NY: Scribner.

Schor, J. B. (2010). *Plenitude: The new economics of true wealth.* New York, NY: Penguin.

Schwartz, B. (1994). *The costs of living: How market freedom erodes the best things in life.* New York, NY: Norton.

Seligman, M. E. P. (2002). *Authentic happiness.* New York, NY: Free Press.

Sheldon, K. M., Elliot, A. J., Kim, Y., & Kasser, T. (2001). What is satisfying about satisfying events? Testing 10 candidate psychological needs. *Journal of Personality and Social Psychology, 80*, 325–339.

Sheldon, K. M., & Kasser, T. (1995). Coherence and congruence: Two aspects of personality integration. *Journal of Personality and Social Psychology, 68*, 531–543.

Sheldon, K. M., & Kasser, T. (1998). Pursuing personal goals: Skills enable progress, but not all progress is beneficial. *Personality and Social Psychology Bulletin, 24*, 1319–1331.

Sheldon, K. M., & Kasser, T. (2001). "Getting older, getting better": Personal strivings and psychological maturity across the life span. *Developmental Psychology, 37*, 491–501.

Sheldon, K. M., & Kasser, T. (2008). Psychological threat and extrinsic goal striving. *Motivation and Emotion, 32,* 37–45.

Sheldon, K. M., & McGregor, H. (2000). Extrinsic value orientation and the tragedy of the commons. *Journal of Personality, 68,* 383–411.

Sheldon, K. M., Nichols, C. P., & Kasser, T. (2011). Americans recommend smaller ecological footprints when reminded of intrinsic American values of self-expression, family, and generosity. *Ecopsychology, 3,* 97–104.

Sheldon, K. M., Sheldon, M. S., & Osbaldiston, R. (2000). Prosocial values and group assortation within an *N*-person prisoner's dilemma. *Human Nature, 11,* 387–404.

Shi, D. (1985). *The simple life.* New York, NY: Oxford University Press.

Srivastava, A., Locke, E. A., & Bortol, K. M. (2001). Money and subjective well-being: It's not the money, it's the motives. *Journal of Personality and Social Psychology, 80,* 959–971.

Taylor, B. (2003). *What kids really want that money can't buy.* New York, NY: Warner Books.

Twenge, J. M., Gentile, B., DeWall, C. N., Ma, D. S., Lacefield, K., & Schurtz, D. R. (2010). Birth cohort increases in psychopathology among young Americans, 1938–2007: A cross-temporal meta-analysis of the MMPI. *Clinical Psychology Review, 30,* 145–154.

Twenge, J. M., & Kasser, T. (2013). Generational changes in materialism and work centrality, 1976–2007: Associations with temporal changes in societal insecurity and materialistic role-modeling. *Personality and Social Psychology Bulletin, 39,* 883–897.

Vansteenkiste, M., Simons, J., Lens, W., Sheldon, K. M., & Deci, E. L. (2004). Motivating learning, performance, and persistence. The synergistic effects of intrinsic goal contents and autonomy-supportive contexts. *Journal of Personality and Social Psychology, 87,* 246–260.

Vohs, K. D., Mead, N. L., & Goode, M. R. (2006). The psychological consequences of money. *Science, 314,* 1154–1156.

Western Media International. (1998, August 11). The fine art of whining: Why nagging is a kid's best friend. *Business Wire.*

# CHAPTER 7

# Values and Well-Being

LILACH SAGIV, SONIA ROCCAS, and SHANI OPPENHEIM-WELLER

PERSONAL VALUES ARE abstract desirable goals that guide individuals throughout their lives (e.g., Kluckhohn, 1951; Rohan, 2000; Rokeach, 1973; Schwartz, 1992). People tend to be very satisfied with their values. They perceive them as close to their ideal and ought selves and do not wish to change them (Roccas, Sagiv, Oppenheim, Elster, & Gal, 2014). Values are intimately linked to well-being: It is sufficient to think about one's values in order to increase a sense of "self-integrity" (Steele, 1988). When people think about their values, they feel that they are competent and moral (e.g., Koole, Smeets, van Knippenberg, & Dijksterhuis, 1999). Thinking about one's important values improves coping with stress, reduces rumination following failure, and increases tolerance for pain (e.g., Branstetter-Rost, Cushing, & Douleh, 2009; for a review, see Sherman & Cohen, 2006). However, people differ in their personal values, and these differences predict a large variety of behaviors, attitudes, and emotions (see reviews in Hitlin & Piliavin, 2004; Maio, 2010; Roccas & Sagiv, 2010). Do people who differ in their values also differ in their well-being? Are some values especially beneficial to happiness and well-being, whereas other values risk harming it? What are the processes that link values and well-being?

Sagiv, Roccas, and Hazan (2004) proposed three perspectives that consider the relationships between values and well-being. The "healthy values" perspective focuses on the *content* of values, suggesting that endorsing some values is likely to create a positive sense of well-being, whereas endorsing other values may be detrimental for well-being. The "goal-attainment" perspective focuses on the *process* through which values are linked to well-being, suggesting that the attainment of values—any value—leads to a positive sense of well-being. Finally, the "value congruency" perspective focuses on the *context*, suggesting that values are likely to lead to well-being when they are congruent with the values that prevail in one's social environment.

In this chapter, we discuss each of the three perspectives, reviewing classic as well as recent research. We expand our discussion to include relevant research that has been conducted in various fields that add to our understanding of the multiple ways through which values are linked to well-being. Finally, we present some practical

*Authors' Note.* This project was supported by a grant to the first author from the Recanati Fund of the School of Business Administration at the Hebrew University.

implications of the three perspectives and discuss the ways in which individuals and society may rely on personal values to contribute to a positive sense of well-being.

## THE CONTENT PERSPECTIVE: HEALTHY AND UNHEALTHY VALUES

The first perspective regarding the relationships between values and well-being focuses on the content of values, positing that it is the essence of the value itself that determines its positive or negative impact on well-being.

### LIFE STRIVINGS AND WELL-BEING: THE SELF-DETERMINATION THEORY LEGACY

Drawing on humanistic perspectives, self-determination theory (SDT; Deci & Ryan, 1985, 1991, 2008; Ryan & Deci, 2000; Brown & Ryan, Chapter 9, this volume) asserts that the content of one's life-strivings affects well-being: Values that are derived from intrinsic motives and goals are inherently healthy, in the sense that they are positively associated with well-being, whereas those that are derived from extrinsic motives are inherently unhealthy and might have a negative impact on well-being.

Intrinsic motives express basic psychological needs of autonomy, relatedness, and competence and have the inherent potential to lead to independent satisfaction. They reflect psychological growth and self-actualization needs that are inherently human. Satisfying these needs is therefore a key to well-being. In contrast, extrinsic motives derive from the need to obtain other people's approval, admiration, and praise, and from the need to avoid social censure and punishment. Extrinsic motives or goals usually do not stand for themselves; rather, they are a means to obtain other goals. Striving for these goals might eventually undermine well-being because attempts to pursue them may require activities that involve high stress (Ryan, Koestner, & Deci, 1991) and excessive interpersonal comparisons (Vansteenkiste, Duriez, Simons, & Soenens, 2006).

Research stemming from SDT has provided empirical evidence for the idea that emphasizing intrinsic over extrinsic goals is likely to have a positive effect on well-being and vice versa. In pioneering research pointing to the "dark side of the American dream," American students reported the importance of their goals. The more importance they attributed to intrinsic goals, the higher was their sense of self-actualization and vitality and the lower the frequency of physical symptoms and depression. In contrast, the higher the importance attributed to extrinsic goals, the lower was the sense of self-actualization and vitality and the higher was the frequency of physical symptoms and anxiety (Kasser & Ryan, 1993, 1996; Kasser, Chapter 6, this volume).

Similar findings were obtained in other studies conducted among students in various cultures. For example, in studies on the aspirations of people from Germany, Russia, and the United States, respondents who were relatively intrinsically oriented in their aspirations reported greater self-actualization and lower anxiety (Ryan et al., 1999; Schmuck, Kasser, & Ryan, 2000). In a study of Singaporean business students, the importance attributed to materialistic aspirations correlated negatively with several indicators of positive well-being and positively with indicators of poor well-being. In contrast, a relative focus on intrinsic aspirations of self-acceptance, affiliation, or community feeling was related to some indicators of positive well-being (Kasser & Ahuvia, 2002). Similarly, among business and education students in Belgium, intrinsic aspirations of growth, affiliation, and contribution to others were positively correlated with subjective well-being, whereas extrinsic aspirations of image, fame, and financial success were negatively correlated with subjective well-being (Vansteenkiste et al., 2006).

Finally, in a series of studies among American students in various universities, Sheldon, Ryan, Deci, and Kasser (2004) asked participants to imagine that they would pursue intrinsic and extrinsic strivings. They found that thinking about an intrinsic goal (autonomy) positively predicted the happiness the participants thought they would feel. The opposite pattern was found for thinking about endorsing extrinsic goals (financial success, fame, and having an attractive image).

Consistent findings were also found in an earlier study that did not draw on the SDT theoretical framework (Emmons, 1991). Using a diary method, students reported their aspirations and several indicators of well-being. The findings indicated that power aspirations were positively correlated with psychological and physical distress and with negative affect, whereas affiliation aspirations were positively correlated with positive affect.

The studies reviewed above investigated a variety of motivations, goals, or values, both intrinsic and extrinsic. Other researchers focused specifically on the effect of holding materialistic values. Materialistic values refer to the importance people attribute to holding material possessions, such as owning expensive homes, and are by definition extrinsic. The extensive studies on the link between materialism and well-being consistently show that materialism is negatively linked to well-being (e.g., for reviews, see Deckop, Jurkiewicz, & Giacalone, 2010; Diener & Seligman, 2004; Solberg, Diener, & Robinson, 2004). The negative link between materialism and well-being is particularly strong in low-income families (Nickerson, Schwarz, Diener, & Kahneman, 2003). Thus, these studies too indicate that holding extrinsic aspirations might be harmful for well-being. In a study that focused on prosocial strivings, pleasure-based prosocial motivation (i.e., intrinsic) was found to be positively correlated with well-being indicators, whereas duty-based prosocial motivation (i.e., extrinsic) yielded the opposite pattern (Gebauer, Riketta, Broemer, & Maio, 2008).

### Personal Values and Well-Being

Direct relationships between values and well-being have also been studied within the values research framework. Schwartz's (1992) theory of the content and structure of human values is considered dominant in this field (see Rohan, 2000). Taking a cross-cultural perspective, Schwartz derived 10 distinct value types that represent 10 basic motivations, aspiring to comprehensively represent the motivational goals common across societies (Schwartz, 1992). The conflicts and compatibilities between the values yield a circular structure that can be summarized into two basic conflicts (Schwartz, 1992): self-enhancement versus self-transcendence and openness to change versus conservation. Openness to change values emphasize openness to new experiences: wish for autonomy of thought and action (self-direction) and wish for novelty and excitement (stimulation). These values conflict with conservation values that emphasize preserving the status quo: commitment to past beliefs and customs (tradition), adhering to social norms and expectations (conformity), and preference for stability and safety (security). Self-enhancement values emphasize the pursuit of self-interest by focusing on gaining control over people and resources (power) or by demonstrating ambition, competence, and success (achievement). These values conflict with self-transcendence values that emphasize concern and care for close others (benevolence) or acceptance and tolerance of all people (universalism). The theory has been tested and verified in extensive cross-cultural research (e.g., Davidov,

Schmidt, & Schwartz, 2008; Schwartz, 1992; Schwartz & Rubel, 2005; Schwartz & Sagiv, 1995; Spini, 2003).

Drawing on the SDT framework, values can be classified as reflecting either intrinsic or extrinsic strivings. Self-direction and stimulation can be viewed as largely reflecting autonomous needs, universalism and benevolence can be seen as reflecting relatedness, and achievement values reflect competence. The other value types (power, security, conformity, and tradition) can be viewed as expressing extrinsic motivation (see Bilsky & Schwartz, 1994; Sagiv & Schwartz, 2000).

Few studies have considered the direct relationships between values and well-being. Sagiv and Schwartz (2000) examined the relations of the 10 value types to measures of cognitive and affective aspects of well-being. They studied three samples of university students and three adult samples from three cultures: West Germany, the former East Germany, and Israel. Findings were highly consistent both across the three cultural groups and across the two age groups. However, they differed substantially for the cognitive and affective aspects of subjective well-being. Specifically, achievement, self-direction, and stimulation values correlated positively, and tradition conformity and security values correlated negatively, with the *affective* aspect of well-being. The correlations were relatively weak ($r = .25$ or weaker) but they were consistent across the six samples. In contrast, there was no evidence for any relations between value priorities and the cognitive aspect of subjective well-being. In a study of American students (Oishi, Diener, Sue, & Lucas, 1999), the importance attributed to achievement and benevolence values did not correlate with subjective well-being in the first part of the study. In the second part of the study, achievement values correlated positively with cognitive and affective subjective well-being. No other value type correlated significantly with any indicator of well-being. Among Turkish students, the cognitive aspect of subjective well-being was positively correlated with emphasizing benevolence, tradition, conformity, and security values, and it was negatively correlated with emphasizing self-direction and stimulation values (Karabati, & Cemalcilar, 2010). Yet a different pattern of correlations was found among students from Iran (Joshanloo & Ghaedi, 2009). The researchers examined the impact of values on four indicators of well-being. Psychological well-being, satisfaction with life, and positive (versus negative) affect yielded similar patterns, correlating positively with achievement and negatively with tradition values. In contrast, social well-being was positively correlated with benevolence and conformity values and negatively correlated with self-direction and power values.

The European Social Survey, conducted among more than 20 European cultures, provides an exceptional opportunity to investigate the relationships between values and well-being. One study (Bobowik, Basabe, Páez, Jiménez, & Bilbao, 2011) examined the simple correlations with values in an ESS sample that combined data from 22 countries in Europe, as well as in three Spanish samples and one sample of immigrants to Spain. The findings were quite consistent across the five samples: positive correlations with self-direction and stimulation values and negative correlations with conformity, tradition, and security values. The correlations, however, were very weak; most of them ranged from –.10 to .10, and none exceeded .17. Taking a different perspective, Sortheix and Lönnqvist (2014) used multilevel analysis to examine data from 25 European countries included in the ESS project. Findings indicate that benevolence and hedonism values were positively correlated with satisfaction with life across all European cultures. For all other values, however, the correlation with well-being depended on the culture in question. We refer to these findings later in this chapter.

Recent studies point to an alternative interpretation of the direct relationships observed between values and well-being. Roccas, Sagiv, Schwartz, and Knafo (2002) found that positive affect was positively correlated with self-direction, stimulation, and universalism and negatively correlated with power and conformity values. However, given the relationships between values and personality traits, the researchers hypothesized and showed that when traits were added to a regression equation predicting positive affect, the impact of values became insignificant. Investigating the relationships of traits, values, and various indicators of well-being, Haslam, Whelan, and Bastian (2009) found similar direct relationships between values and well-being. These relationships were fully mediated, however, by personality traits.

In sum, the healthy values perspective focuses on the content of values and goals, suggesting that they inherently differ in their implications for well-being. Whereas research stemming from SDT provides supporting evidence for this perspective, research using measures of values yields mixed results. Several studies confirm that there are direct relationships between the importance attributed to specific values and well-being. However, findings are not consistent across social contexts, such that in some cases a value is positively related to well-being, whereas in others it might not be related, or even be negatively related to well-being. Furthermore, the findings are not always consistent with the healthy values perspective: Values that express intrinsic, autonomous needs, such as self-direction, were found to be positively correlated with well-being in one study and negatively correlated in another. Finally, the direct relationship between value importance and well-being is generally low, and may be accounted for by confounds with other personality attributes (e.g., traits).

## THE PROCESS PERSPECTIVE: GOAL ATTAINMENT

A second perspective focuses on the process through which values are related to well-being. Researchers in this line of research suggest that well-being is affected by the extent to which people are able to attain the goals, motives, and values that are important to them. The content and the process perspectives differ in their focus: The content perspective focused on what people value, desire, and strive for; the process perspective focuses on the extent to which they can attain what they desire. The two perspectives differ because holding a value does not necessarily imply that one can attain it. For example, attributing high importance to achievement values expresses the motivation to gain personal success by demonstrating competence according to social standards. Individuals can attribute high importance to achievement values, although circumstances do not allow them to fulfill these values.

Researchers in the goal-attainment perspective agree that the more people are able to attain their needs, values, and goals, the higher their well-being (e.g., Oishi et al., 1999; Sheldon & Elliot, 1999). They diverge, however, regarding their position on whether the content of the goals and value matters. Some researchers reason that attainment of any important value or goal is beneficial to well-being, whereas others posit that there are fundamental differences between goals; attaining some goals is beneficial to well-being, whereas attaining others might be detrimental.

A seminal study in the goal-attainment approach examined students' well-being during 23 consecutive days (Oishi et al., 1999). At the beginning of the study, the students reported the importance they attributed to achievement and benevolence values. Each day, students reported how satisfied they were with their achievements and with their social life that day. To measure daily well-being, students were asked each day how good or bad that day was. Consistent with the goal-attainment perspective, participants' daily well-being was directly affected by daily satisfaction with their achievements and with their social lives.

Relations with values were more complex: Well-being did not correlate directly with the importance students attributed to achievement or benevolence values. The role of values became evident, however, when the interaction between values and satisfaction with achievements and social life was examined. Daily satisfaction with achievements was a stronger predictor of daily well-being for those who attributed high importance to achievement values than for those who attributed low importance to these values. Similarly, satisfaction with social life was a stronger predictor of well-being for those who emphasized benevolence values than for those who attributed relatively low importance to these values. Thus, individuals' day-to-day well-being was predicted by the extent to which people felt that they were able to attain their important goals.

Oishi et al. (1999) further examined the moderating role of personal values in the relations between satisfaction with specific life domains and general satisfaction. Participants reported their satisfaction with their grades, family, and social life. Again, the relations between satisfaction with a specific life domain and general satisfaction were moderated by personal values. Satisfaction with grades was a stronger predictor of general satisfaction the more important achievement values were; satisfaction with the family predicted general well-being the more important conformity values were; and satisfaction with social life affected general satisfaction more the more important benevolence values were.

A study distinguishing agentic versus communal needs provide additional support for the contention that the attainment of any value, need, or goal could lead to well-being (Brunstein, Schultheiss, & Grassmann, 1998). At the beginning of a semester, students were classified according to the extent to which they had relatively more agentic versus communal motives. During the semester, the students reported their daily emotional well-being. At the end of the semester, the students reported which goals they had attained during that period of time. Findings indicated that students who attained goals congruent with their main motive were likely to enjoy higher daily emotional well-being. That is, for students with agentic needs, well-being correlated with the attainment of agentic goals, whereas for students with communal needs, well-being correlated with the attainment of communal goals.

Support for the claim that attainment of any value has the potential to benefit well-being was also found in a study focusing on the extent to which people perceive different identities as allowing value attainment (Oppenheim-Weller, Roccas, & Kurman, 2014). The participants were asked to think about some of their important social identities and to indicate how each identity enables them to fulfill a set of values. Social identities provide opportunities and constraints for value fulfillment, hence affecting the extent to which specific values can be fulfilled. By measuring value fulfillment directly ("How much do you feel your *x* identity allows you to fulfill *y*?") the participants were directed to include the environment in which the value is being fulfilled (by directing the participant to focus on a specific identity).

The relations between subjective value fulfillment and well-being were measured in a variety of samples examining different identities: Israeli-Jewish students (examining the Israeli and the student identities), Arab-Israeli students (examining the Arab and the Israeli identities), and Druze adults (examining the Druze, Israeli, and Arab identities). The identities differed in the types of values they facilitated; for example, the student identity was perceived as enabling the fulfillment of self-direction and achievement values. In contrast, the Arab identity and Druze identities were perceived as enabling the fulfillment of conformity and tradition values.

Correlations between subjective value fulfillment and well-being were consistently positive across values and across identities. Even in identities that are controversial in a specific group, such as the Israeli identity for the Arab-Israelis, feelings of value fulfillment were positively related to well-being. A possible implication of these findings is that using the framing of value fulfillment may be useful in helping people feel positivity concerning different identities and helping people notice the positive sides in each identity.

In sum, findings of these studies suggest that attaining important values is likely to benefit well-being—regardless of the value in question. The self-concordance model (Sheldon & Elliot, 1999) presents a different perspective on the relationship of goals attainment and well-being. This model suggests that the extent to which goal satisfaction results in positive well-being depends on whether a goal is self-concordant. Self-concordant goals derive from intrinsic (also termed *identified*) motives that originate in inherent basic psychological needs. Attainment of these goals is more likely because individuals invest sustained effort in pursuing them. Moreover, their attainment contributes to one's sense of well-being more than attainment of other goals because they originate in inherent basic psychological needs.

Sheldon and Eliot (1999) conducted a longitudinal study among university students. In the beginning of the semester, students reported eight goals they had set for themselves and their motivation to pursue each goal. Three times throughout the semester, respondents reported the amount of effort put into pursuing each goal and the extent of attainment of that goal. Students put more effort into pursuing goals and were more successful in attaining them the more they were self-concordant. Goal attainment led to an experience of psychological need satisfaction, which correlated with improvement in well-being. In addition, goal attainment predicted psychological need satisfaction more, the more concordant were the goals attained. Thus, the type of goal moderated the effect of its attainment on well-being.

Sheldon and Houser-Marko (2001) replicated these findings and showed, in addition, that setting self-concordant goals at the beginning of the semester was related to setting future self-concordant goals, as long as the goals were attained. Thus, in line with the goal-attainment perspective, the self-concordance model suggests that well-being is related to the extent to which people are able to attain their important goals. However, the self-concordance model holds that the effect of value attainment depends on the value in question: Only attaining values that are self-concordant is beneficial to well-being.

Bridging these two views, Carver and Bird (1998) argued that any goal, intrinsic or extrinsic, could be self-concordant. They showed that when materialistic goals of financial success were self-concordant, they led to a positive sense of well-being. Furthermore, when the intrinsic strivings of community involvement were not self-concordant, they correlated negatively with well-being. In other words, they argued that it is the extent of self-concordance—and not the content of strivings—that lead to positive well-being.

In sum, goal attainment is a path through which values could indirectly affect well-being. Researchers differ in their view on the role that the *content* of values/goals plays in these relationships. Whereas some (e.g., Sheldon & Eliot, 1999; Sheldon et al., 2004) argue and find that it is the attainment of autonomous needs that positively affects well-being, others (e.g., Brunstein et al., 1998; Oishi et al., 1999; Oppenheim-Weller et al., 2014) show that the attainment of any values—including materialistic or conformity values—may be linked to a positive sense of well-being.

Environmental factors may play an important role in goal attainment. Ryan and Deci (2000) noted that whereas the existence of intrinsic motives is independent of environmental context, carrying them out, sustaining them, and enhancing them may well depend on circumstances. In the next section, we present a third perspective for the relations of values and well-being—the person–environment congruency perspective, which focuses on the context, suggesting that well-being is more likely the more people emphasize values that prevail in their social environment.

## THE CONTEXT PERSPECTIVE: PERSON–ENVIRONMENT VALUE CONGRUENCY

The two perspectives we discussed so far focus on the individual. A third perspective refers to the interplay between the individual and the social context. For example, in a study of 25 European countries included in the ESS project (Sortheix & Lönnqvist, 2014), the extent of societal socioeconomic development (measured with the Human Development Index [HDI]) interacted with personal values in predicting satisfaction with life. The authors found that the social context affects the relations between values and well-being, such that endorsing achievement values is positively related to well-being in societies with low HDI, where individuals have to strive to satisfy their basic requirements for living, but these values are negatively related to well-being in societies with high HDI, where basic requirements are satisfied and interpersonal relationships are likely to become more relevant to one's happiness.

A growing line of research that focuses on the context as a moderator of relationships between values and well-being investigates the fit between individuals and their social environments. Specifically, researchers posit that congruency between individuals' value hierarchies and the values that prevail in their social environments are beneficial for well-being (e.g., Chatman, 1989; Edwards, 1992; Feather, 1975; Furnham & Bochner, 1986; Segall, 1979). Research on person–environment congruency, or fit, has emerged in various areas of psychology, including social, educational, vocational, and organizational psychology. Most studies investigated the implications and outcomes of these relationships; only a few researchers considered the theoretical mechanisms that underlie and account for these outcomes (Edwards & Cable, 2009). Sagiv and Schwartz (2000) proposed three mechanisms that may explain the process through which person–environment value congruency influences the sense of well-being.

### ENVIRONMENTAL AFFORDANCES

The first mechanism focuses on the affordances for goal attainment. It considers the impact environments in which people operate have on their ability to attain their valued goals. Social environments offer sets of affordances (Gibson, 1979), of functional utilities or possibilities for action. Environments that are congruent with individuals' goals and values afford them with opportunities to attain their important goals, whereas incongruent environments do not provide people with opportunities to act on their values and hence block fulfillment of their important goals. As previously discussed, attainment of the goals underlying one's important values is likely to lead to an experience of a positive sense of well-being. The congruency perspective suggests that any type of important value or goal may lead to positive well-being, providing that it is congruent with the values prevailing in the environment.

### SOCIAL SANCTIONS

The second mechanism discussed by Sagiv and Schwartz (2000) focuses on social support. Social support is an important source of positive well-being. Extensive research points to the importance of social support in coping effectively with stressors (for reviews, see Cohen, & Wills, 1985; Uchino, Cacioppo, & Kiecolt-Glaser, 1996). Environments pose sets of expectations regarding the beliefs, values, and behaviors that are normative and desired. These expectations are backed by implicit or explicit sanctions (Getzels, 1969). In consensual environments—where most people share similar value hierarchies—clear messages are likely to be communicated regarding the values that are normative (Holland, 1985; Schneider, 1987; see also Gelfand et al., 2011). People who endorse the values prevailing in such consensual environments are likely to enjoy social support. They are likely to feel that their values are validated and that their opinions are well-founded. In contrast, individuals that express value hierarchies that oppose those prevailing in the environment are likely to experience some form of social sanctions: They may be ignored, ostracized, or punished (Holland & Gottfredson, 1976).

INTERNAL CONFLICT

Finally, the third mechanism proposed focuses on intraperson consonance. Personal well-being may be undermined by internal value conflict. This may happen when people enter new environments that differ substantially from the environments from which they came (e.g., immigrants to a new society, a person who is the first in their family to attend college). Individuals may internalize values that are advocated by their new environment, although these values may contradict values and goals they have internalized earlier. Consciously emphasizing incompatible sets of values is likely to provoke internal value conflict (Schwartz, 1992; Tetlock, 1986) because by pursing one set of values one necessarily acts in ways incompatible with the opposing set of values.

This mechanism has received support in several studies. For example, Burroughs and Rindfleisch (2002) showed that emphasizing materialism creates tension and threatens well-being only for those who also emphasize values that conflict with materialism, such as religious and family values. Similarly, studies by Emmons (1986) and Emmons and King (1988) found that poor well-being was related to both internal conflict (conceptualized as holding a goal for which attainment blocks the attainment of other goals held important) and ambivalence (conceptualized as a person's feeling that she will be simultaneously happy and unhappy if she attains that goal).

The implications of the congruency between person and environment were studied in various social contexts; employing various conceptualizations, methodologies, and instruments; and studying various outcomes and implications. The person–environment fit is a central framework in organizational research. Numerous studies have investigated the implications of the fit between individuals and their work environment (e.g., organization, job, team, or supervisor). Most of these studies investigated work-related outcomes, such as job satisfaction, organizational commitment, tenure intentions, and performance (for a meta-analysis, see Kristof-Brown, Zimmerman, & Johnson, 2005). Relatively few studies have examined the implications of value congruency on well-being.

Findings of a study focusing on the domains of work and family show that indicators of well-being are correlated with the fit between values (e.g., autonomy, relationships, security) and the extent to which the environment at work or within one's family "supplies" these values—that is, allows for their attainment (Edwards & Rothbard, 1999). In another study, fit between values and the extent to which the environment supplies them negatively predicted somatic complaints and depression, but only when job performance was low (Shaw & Gupta, 2004). Studying employees in six Chinese companies, Yang, Che, and Spector (2008) found that subjective well-being was positively correlated with the fit between striving for promotion and the extent to which the work environment "supplied" affordances for promotion.

These studies all focused on the subjective sense of congruency—the fit between one's values and the perception of the environment as supplying value-related opportunities. Focusing on objective fit, Sagiv and Schwartz (2000) explored the values prevailing in different academic departments. They measured subjective well-being and value priorities of university students who study management or psychology. They postulated that management students are exposed to an environment that promotes and encourages the attainment of power and achievement goals, but blocks the attainment of goals of benevolence and universalism values. This environment differs markedly from the environment in which psychology students study. The latter are exposed to an environment that allows for fulfillment of benevolence and universalism values, but limits or even blocks the attainment of power values. The findings indicated that different values affected students' well-being, depending on the department in which they studied: Emphasizing power values correlated negatively with subjective well-being among psychology students, but it correlated positively among management students. The opposite pattern (although weaker) was found for universalism values.

Taking a similar perspective in studying religious high-school teachers, Ivgi (2003) relied on organizational artifacts (e.g., memos, reward systems, rules, and regulations) to content-analyze the teaching profession and school environment. Ivgi hypothesized and found that satisfaction with life was positively correlated with attributing high importance to benevolence, conformity, and tradition values and low importance to power values.

Other researchers have studied value congruency in other types of social environments. For example, Nickerson et al. (2003) studied families. They found that the negative correlation between materialistic strivings and well-being was stronger the lower the income of the individual's family, and was near zero for individuals from high-income families. That is, when the social environment does not afford individuals with opportunities for financial rewards, striving for such is detrimental for one's well-being.

Another important social environment is the society to which one belongs. Recently, researchers have examined how well-being is related to the congruency between personal values and the values that prevail in the environment. For example, the fit between person and culture with regards to independence versus interdependence positively predicted subjective well-being among Chinese students (Lu, 2006). This finding emerged both when fit was assessed subjectively (by comparing what people reported about themselves to what they reported about their culture) and when fit was assessed objectively (by comparing what people reported about themselves to what their group members reported).

Employing a similar method to assess cultural values, Zilberfeld (2010) investigated person–culture value congruency among ultra-orthodox students in Israel. Compared to the general Israeli society, this group emphasizes embeddedness (versus autonomy; see Schwartz, 1999). Accordingly, Zilberfeld hypothesized that, in that cultural group, subjective well-being will be positively correlated with emphasizing conformity values and negatively correlated with emphasizing self-direction values. The findings supported these hypotheses. As expected, these patterns of relationships did not replicate in a sample of students from the general Jewish society in Israel (the correlations were near zero, in the opposite direction).

Taken together, these studies provide support to the notion that fit between person and the environment leads to positive well-being. Values that are considered unhealthy, such as power, conformity, and tradition, may be positively correlated with subjective well-being, provided that they are emphasized in the environments in which people spend their time.

The congruency perspective may shed light on some of the inconsistency found in the previously discussed studies that investigated direct relationships between values and well-being. For example, person–culture congruency may explain why conformity and security values were found to be negatively correlated with well-being in autonomous, individualistic cultures (e.g., the United States, Germany, Israel) but were found to be positively correlated with well-being in a traditional, collectivistic culture such as Turkey. Person–culture congruency cannot explain all the variation in the relationships between values and well-being (e.g., the correlations among students in Iran had the opposite pattern than among students from Turkey). A deep analysis of the environment, studied in terms of the values, may yield a better understanding of the nature of relations between values and well-being in that environment.

The studies reviewed here focused on only some of the many environments in which individuals spend time. Subjective well-being, however, is likely to be affected by the congruency between personal values and the values prevailing in the individual's family, group of close friends, social community, profession, organization, and many more. Does value congruency with each environment have equal effect on well-being? We reason that the extent to which value congruency with any one environment impacts well-being probably depends on personal and contextual factors. For example, the more important a given environment is for the person's self-identity, the stronger the impact of the congruency with this environment on that person's well-being is likely to be (Sagiv & Schwartz, 2000).

## MULTIPLE PATHS TOWARD HAPPINESS

Each of the three perspectives presented in this chapter has practical implications for both individuals and society. By integrating all three views, we may suggest more fine-tuned implications for the role that socialization agents such as parents, educators, counselors, and leaders may play in individuals' striving for happiness.

The healthy values perspective suggests a simple path toward positive well-being: Values and strivings that are intrinsic by nature (e.g., autonomy) are likely to lead to positive well-being because they reflect self-actualization needs that are inherent to human beings. Parents, teachers, leaders, and therapists may all nurture such values and strivings through modeling and reinforcement. Note, however, that external rewards may lead to introjected or internalized goals at best, but they cannot lead to intrinsic motives that are most desired according to the healthy values perspective. Parents and teachers should therefore provide children with circumstances that offer them opportunities to develop intrinsic motives.

Consider for example the case of career counseling. Sagiv (1999) proposed the distinction between two main products that counselors offer their clients: They can provide clients with direct guidance regarding the vocation most suitable to them (a process she named "giving answers"), or they can provide the clients with skills and tools that allow them to make decisions autonomously. Sagiv showed that career counselors judged counseling as more successful the more clients were oriented to search for tools (i.e., they expressed independence, activity, and insightfulness) and the less they were oriented to look for answers (i.e., acted in dependent and passive ways).

Similarly, well-being is not likely to increase when a person adapts competence strivings during therapy because she wants to please her therapist or gain the approval of her parents. Rather, a positive sense of well-being is more likely when therapy provides her with an accepting and supporting environment, where she can find out what her internal motives are and is encouraged to follow them. Correspondingly, parents may serve as models and may encourage and support their children in expressing autonomy or concern for others. Teachers may help students express independence, relatedness, or competence, and they create a learning environment that encourages students to follow their intrinsic motives and goals. Research stemming from the SDT framework has proposed interventions designed to teach and implement the principles of SDT, and hence promote the development of such learning environments (e.g., Assor, Kaplan, Feinberg, & Tal, 2009). Drawing on Schwartz's (1992) theory of values, recent research has proposed a short intervention that increases the importance of benevolence values by means of self-persuasion, without providing false information or external pressure/rewards (Arieli, Grant, & Sagiv, 2014).

A second path toward happiness is suggested by the goal-attainment perspective: According to this view, individuals should fulfill their values and attain their important goals as means for positive well-being. Consider again the example of career counseling. Consistent with the goal-attainment perspective, counselors may focus on helping clients to identify goals that they are likely to successfully attain. To identify such goals, counselors and clients may rely on intelligence and aptitude tests, on simulations, and on clients' successful past experiences. Once such desired and plausible goals have been identified, counselors may encourage clients to focus on these goals and neglect goals that are less probable.

Along these lines, societal agents and institutions may contribute to goal attainment in various ways. Parents, for example, may expose their children to suitable experiences, help them endorse those values that best suit their inner self, and encourage them to fulfill their internal goals. Education systems may be designed to allow students to identify and follow their academic interests, social perspectives, and life aspirations. Counselors or therapists could direct clients to focus on the values they can fulfill in their multiple identities and to emphasize the positive aspects of each identity. Focusing on value fulfillment can shape the perception of social identities, such that identities that are perceived mostly as restricting and impairing could become more appealing. Thus, for example, teachers could increase their personal sense of well-being by thinking about their profession as providing opportunities to promote the welfare of children (i.e., fulfillment of benevolence values) rather than thinking about the profession as restricting their opportunities for acquiring wealth (i.e., limiting the fulfillment of power values).

The third view discussed in this chapter, the person–environment congruency perspective, postulates that it is the fit between individuals and the environments they identify with that affects subjective well-being. Even truly intrinsic values may lead to a negative sense of well-being if a person holding such values highly identifies with an environment that rejects him or her. Therefore, it is not enough to internalize intrinsic strivings—individuals have to find environments that are congruent with those strivings.

Again, we can readily apply this perspective to the example of career counseling. One of the main goals of career counseling is identifying an occupational environment that fits the client's personal characteristics, values, strivings, and goals. Thus, for example, counseling may help a person who emphasizes autonomy to choose an occupation in which most people emphasize similar values and that affords many opportunities to express autonomy (e.g., artistic or investigative professions, according to Holland's [1985] typology) and to avoid occupations in which most people attribute low importance to autonomy values and that are highly structured and conservative (e.g., conventional professions).

The congruency perspective also suggests that when the environment is congruent, even extrinsic values may lead to positive well-being, because the environment offers the individual many opportunities to attain his important goals; because she may enjoy social support from those around him who endorse similar values; and because he holds a compatible set of values. This view of well-being thus underscores the importance of finding a meaningful environment (e.g., a profession, a social community, a spouse) that endorses values similar to one's own.

Individuals and societies can use two types of processes in their efforts to seek and offer congruent environments: selection or socialization processes. Selection processes allow people to search and find those conditions, situations, and environments that may ease the attainment of their goals. Autonomous individuals in a collective culture may be active in social groups that are relatively autonomous (e.g., artists), whereas conservative individuals in an autonomous culture may join conservative communities (e.g., a religious community). Society may contribute to effective selection processes too: Family members, teachers, and counselors may help individuals identify their basic motivations and recognize the circumstances that allow for their expression and attainment—the congruent schools, workplaces, social activities, family lifestyles, and so on.

Socialization processes help individuals become more congruent with their environment. Individuals may change their own value system so they come to internalize values and goals that may lead to well-being (e.g., values of autonomy or care for others). They can also adopt values and goals that are more similar to those in the environment that is important to them. Finally, individuals may create or shape the environment or social situation in which they operate. Thus, for example, managers can allow employees to shape their working environment, determine the extent of autonomy they have in carrying out their tasks, and even influence their reward system.

## CONCLUSION

Many paths may lead to happiness. In this chapter we reviewed three paths, all of which regard happiness as an objective that individuals may *actively* strive to achieve, and each entails different challenges for those who peruse it. The healthy values path requires that individuals be intrinsically motivated in their aspirations and that their aspirations be of certain form and nature. The goal-attainment path requires individuals to invest sustained effort in pursuing the attainment of their goals. Finally, the congruent environment path requires individuals to either select or adapt to the environments important to them in order to produce the congruence beneficial to them. Pursuing some or all of these challenges increases individuals' chances to be happy and satisfied with their lives.

## SUMMARY POINTS

- Drawing on Sagiv, Roccas, and Hazan (2004), we present three perspectives for the relations between values and well-being that focus on the (1) content, (2) process, and (3) context of pursuing values. For each perspective, we review past literature and discuss the main controversies.
- The healthy and unhealthy values perspective focuses on the content of values, suggesting that emphasizing some values is likely to increase well-being whereas emphasizing other values may be detrimental to well-being.

- The goal-attainment perspective focuses on the process through which pursuing values may affect well-being. This perspective suggests that it is the attainment of individuals' important values that leads to well-being.
- The person–environment value congruency perspective suggests that social contexts moderate the relations between personal values and well-being: The more individuals strive for values that are emphasized in their social environment (e.g., family, work, culture), the more likely they are to enjoy a positive sense of well-being.
- Past research found evidence supporting all three perspectives. However, studies yielded inconsistent findings regarding the content of values that lead to well-being; regarding whether attainment of any value or goal is positively related to well-being; and regarding the moderating role of the social environment. We propose that integrating the three perspectives may shed light on some of these inconsistencies.
- Building on the three perspectives, we discuss paths through which educators, leaders, and counselors can help individuals to improve their sense of well-being.
- Drawing on the healthy values perspective, teachers and counselors could create an environment that encourages individuals to follow their motivated goals and values. Social institutions can implement interventions that researchers developed to encourage intrinsic values and goals.
- Drawing on the goal-attainment perspective, parents, teachers, and therapists may encourage individuals to identify and pursue goals that they are likely to be able to successfully attain.
- The person–environment congruency perspective is especially applicable to situations of choice, such as choosing an area of study in high school or college, or during career counseling, in which individuals may be encouraged to consider the congruency between their important values and the values that are emphasized in the different learning environments, occupational fields, and organizations.

## REFERENCES

Arieli, S., Grant, A., & Sagiv, L. (2014). Convincing yourself to care about others: An intervention for enhancing benevolence values. *Journal of Personality, 82*, 15–24.

Assor, A., Kaplan, H., Feinberg, O., & Tal, K. (2009). Combining vision with voice: A learning and implementation structure promoting teachers' internalization of practices based on self-determination theory. *Theory and Research in Education 7*, 234–243.

Bilsky, W., & Schwartz, S. H. (1994). Values and personality. *European Journal of Personality, 8*, 163–181.

Bobowik, M., Basabe, N., Páez, D., Jiménez, A., & Bilbao, M. Á. (2011). Personal values and well-being among Europeans, Spanish natives and immigrants to Spain: Does the culture matter? *Journal of Happiness Studies, 12*, 401–419.

Branstetter-Rost, A., Cushing, C., & Douleh, T. (2009). Personal values and pain tolerance: Does a values intervention add to acceptance? *Journal of Pain, 10*, 887–892.

Brunstein, J. C., Schultheiss, O. C., & Grassmann, R. (1998). Personal goals and emotional well being: The moderating role of motive dispositions. *Journal of Personality and Social Psychology, 75*, 494–508.

Burroughs, J. E., & Rindfleisch, A. (2002). Materialism and well-being: A conflict value perspective. *Journal of Consumer Research, 29*, 348–370.

Carver, C. S., & Bird, E. (1998). The American dream revisited: Is it what we do or why we do it we do it that matters? *Psychological Science, 9*, 289–293.

Chatman, J. A. (1989). Matching people and organizations: Selection and socialization in public accounting firms. *Academy of Management Proceedings, 1*, 199–203.

Cohen, S., & Wills, T. A. (1985). Stress, social support, and the buffering hypothesis. *Psychological Bulletin, 98*, 310.

Davidov, E., Schmidt, P., & Schwartz, S. H. (2008). Bringing values back in the adequacy of the European Social Survey to measure values in 20 countries. *Public Opinion Quarterly, 72*, 420–445.

Deci, E. L., & Ryan, R. M. (1985). *Intrinsic motivation and self-determination in human behavior.* New York, NY: Plenum Press.

Deci, E. L., & Ryan, R. M. (1991). A motivational approach to self: Integration in personality. In R. Dienstbier (Ed.), *Nebraska symposium on motivation: Vol. 38. Perspectives on motivation* (pp. 237–288). Lincoln: University of Nebraska Press.

Deci, E. L., & Ryan, R. M. (2008). Facilitating optimal motivation and psychological well-being across life's domains. *Canadian Psychology, 49*, 14–23.

Deckop, J. R., Jurkiewicz, C. L., & Giacalone, R. A. (2010). Effects of materialism on work-related personal well-being. *Human Relations, 63*, 1007–1030.

Diener, E., & Seligman, M. E. (2004). Beyond money toward an economy of well-being. *Psychological Science in the Public Interest, 5*, 1–31.

Edwards, J. R. (1992). A cybernetic theory of stress, coping, and well-being in organizations. *Academy of Management Review, 17*, 238–274.

Edwards, J. R., & Cable, D. M. (2009). The value of value congruence. *Journal of Applied Psychology, 94*, 654.

Edwards, J. R., & Rothbard, N. P. (1999). Work and family stress and well-being: An examination of person-environment fit in the work and family domains. *Organizational Behavior and Human Decision Processes, 77*, 85–129.

Emmons, R. A. (1986). Personal strivings: An approach to personality and subjective well-being. *Journal of Personality and Social Psychology, 51*, 1058–1068.

Emmons, R. A. (1991). Personal strivings, daily life events, and psychological and physical well-being. *Journal of Personality, 59*, 453–472.

Emmons, R. A., & King, L. A. (1988). Conflict among personal strivings: Immediate and long-term implications for psychological and physical well-being. *Journal of Personality and Social Psychology, 54*, 1040–1048.

Feather, N. T. (1975). *Values in education and society.* New York, NY: Free Press.

Furnham, A., & Bochner, S. (1986). *Culture shock: Psychological reaction to unfamiliar environments.* London, England: Methuen.

Gebauer, J. E., Riketta, M., Broemer, P., & Maio, G. R. (2008). Pleasure and pressure based prosocial motivation: Divergent relations to subjective well-being. *Journal of Research in Personality, 42*, 399–420.

Gelfand, M. J., Raver, J. L., Nishii, L., Leslie, L. M., Lun, J., Lim, B. C., & Yamaguchi, S. (2011). Differences between tight and loose cultures: A 33-nation study. *Science, 332*, 1100–1104.

Getzels, J. W. (1969). A social psychology of education. In G. Lindsey & E. Aronson (Eds.), *The handbook of social psychology* (Vol. 5). Reading, MA: Addison-Wesley.

Gibson, J. (1979). *The ecological approach to visual perception.* Boston, MA: Houghton Mifflin.

Haslam, N., Whelan, J., & Bastian, B. (2009). Big five traits mediate associations between values and subjective well-being. *Personality and Individual Differences, 46*, 40–44.

Hitlin, S., & Piliavin, J. A. (2004). Values: Reviving a dormant concept. *Annual Review of Sociology, 30*, 359–393.

Holland, J. L. (1985). *Making vocational choices: A theory of careers.* Englewood Cliffs, NJ: Prentice-Hall.

Holland, J. L., & Gottfredson, G. D. (1976). Using a typology of persons and environments to explain careers: Some extensions and clarifications. *The Counseling Psychologist, 6*, 20–29.

Ivgi, I. (2003). *Value congruency of teachers: Implications for well-being* (Unpublished master's thesis). Hebrew University of Jerusalem, Israel.

Joshanloo, M., & Ghaedi, G. (2009). Value priorities as predictors of hedonic and eudaimonic aspects of well-being. *Personality and Individual Differences, 47*, 294–298.

Karabati, S., & Cemalcilar, Z. (2010). Values, materialism, and well-being: A study with Turkish university students. *Journal of Economic Psychology, 31*, 624–633.

Kasser, T., & Ahuvia, A. C. (2002). Materialistic values and well-being in business students. *European Journal of Social Psychology, 32*, 137–146.

Kasser, T., & Ryan, R. M. (1993). A dark side of the American dream: Correlates of financial success as a central life aspiration. *Journal of Personality and Social Psychology, 65*, 410–422.

Kasser, T., & Ryan, R. M. (1996). Further examining the American dream: Differential correlates of intrinsic and extrinsic goals. *Personality and Social Psychology Bulletin, 22*, 82–87.

Kluckhohn, C. (1951). Values and value orientations in the theory of action. In T. Parsons & E. Shils (Eds.), *Toward a general theory of action* (pp. 388–433). Cambridge, MA: Harvard University Press.

Koole, S., Smeets, K., van Knippenberg, A., & Dijksterhuis, A. (1999). The cessation of rumination through self-affirmation. *Journal of Personality and Social Psychology, 77*, 111–125.

Kristof-Brown, A. L., Zimmerman, R. D., & Johnson, E. C. (2005). Consequences of individuals' fit at work: A meta-analysis of person-job, person-organization, person-group, and person-supervisor fit. *Personnel Psychology, 58*, 281–342.

Lu, L. (2006). "Cultural fit": Individual and societal discrepancies in values, beliefs, and subjective well-being. *Journal of Social Psychology, 146*, 203–221.

Maio, G. R. (2010). Mental representations of social values. In M. P. Zanna (Ed.), *Advances in experimental social psychology* (Vol. 42). New York, NY: Academic Press.

Nickerson, C., Schwarz, N., Diener, E., & Kahneman, D. (2003). Zeroing in on the dark side of the American Dream: A closer look at the negative consequences of the goal for financial success. *Psychological Science, 14*, 531–536.

Oishi, S., Diener, E., Sue, E., & Lucas, R. E. (1999). Value as a moderator in subjective well-being. *Journal of Personality, 67*, 157–182.

Oppenheim-Weller, S., Roccas, S., & Kurman, J. (2014). *Value attainment through social identities.* Working paper.

Roccas, S., & Sagiv, L. (2010). Personal values and behavior: Taking the cultural context into account. *Social and Personality Psychology Compass, 4*, 30–41.

Roccas, S., Sagiv, L., Oppenheim, S., Elster, A., & Gal, A. (2014). Integrating content and structure aspects of the self: Traits, values, and self-improvement. *Journal of Personality, 82*, 144–157.

Roccas, S., Sagiv, L., Schwartz, S. H., & Knafo, A. (2002). Basic values and the five factor model of personality traits. *Personality and Social Psychology Bulletin, 28*, 789–801.

Rohan, M. J. (2000). A rose by any name? The values construct. *Personality and Social Psychology Review, 4*, 255–277.

Rokeach, M. (1973). *The nature of human values.* New York, NY: Free Press.

Ryan, R. M., Chirkov, V. I., Little, T. D., Sheldon, K. M., Timoshina, E., & Deci, E. L. (1999). The American dream in Russia: Extrinsic aspirations and well-being in two cultures. *Personality and Social Psychology Bulletin, 25*, 1509–1524.

Ryan, R. M., & Deci, E. L. (2000). Intrinsic and extrinsic motivations: Classic definitions and new directions. *Contemporary Educational Psychology, 25*, 54–67.

Ryan, R. M., Koestner, R., & Deci, E. L. (1991). Ego-involved persistence: When free-choice behavior is not intrinsically motivated. *Motivation and Emotion, 15*, 185–205.

Sagiv, L. (1999). Searching for tools versus asking for answers: A taxonomy of counselee behavioral styles during career counseling. *Journal of Career Assessment, 7*, 19–34.

Sagiv, L., Roccas, S., Hazan, O. (2004). Value pathways to well-being: Healthy values, valued goal attainment, and environmental congruence. In P. A. Linley & S. Joseph (Eds.), *Positive psychology in practice*. Hoboken, NJ: Wiley.

Sagiv, L., & Schwartz, S. H. (2000). Values priorities and subjective well-being: Direct relations and congruity effects. *European Journal of Social Psychology, 30*, 177–198.

Schmuck, P., Kasser, T., & Ryan, R. M. (2000). The relationship of well-being to intrinsic and extrinsic goals in Germany and the U.S. *Social Indicators Research, 50*, 225–241.

Schneider, B. (1987). E=f(P,B): The road to a radical approach to person-environment fit. *Journal of Vocational Behavior, 31*, 353–361.

Schwartz, S. H. (1992). Universals in the content and structure of values: Theoretical advances and empirical tests in 20 countries. In M. P. Zanna (Ed.), *Advances in experimental social psychology* (Vol. 25, pp. 1–65). New York, NY: Academic Press.

Schwartz, S. H. (1999). A theory of cultural values and some implications for work. *Applied psychology, 48*, 23–47.

Schwartz, S. H., & Rubel, T. (2005). Sex differences in value priorities: Cross-cultural and multitimethod studies. *Journal of Personality and Social Psychology, 89*, 1010–1028.

Schwartz, S. H., & Sagiv, L. (1995). Identifying culture-specifics in the content and structure of values. *Journal of Cross-Cultural Psychology, 26*, 92–116.

Segall, M. H. (1979). *Cross-cultural psychology: Human behavior in global perspective*. Monterey, CA: Brooks/Cole.

Shaw, J. D., & Gupta, N. (2004). Job complexity, performance, and well-being: When does supplies-values fit matter? *Personnel Psychology, 57*, 847–879.

Sheldon, K. M., & Elliot, A. J. (1999). Goal striving, need-satisfaction, and longitudinal well being: The self-concordance model. *Journal of Personality and Social Psychology, 76*, 482–497.

Sheldon, K. M., & Houser-Marko, L. (2001). Self-concordance, goal-attainment, and the pursuit of happiness: Can there be an upward spiral? *Journal of Personality and Social Psychology, 80*, 152–165.

Sheldon, K. M., Ryan, R. M., Deci, E. L., & Kasser, T. (2004). The independent effects of goal contents and motives on well-being: It's both what you pursue and why you pursue it. *Personality and Social Psychology Bulletin, 30*, 475–486.

Sherman, D. K., & Cohen, G. L. (2006). The psychology of self-defense: Self-affirmation theory. *Advances in Experimental Social Psychology, 38*, 183–242.

Solberg, E. C., Diener, E., & Robinson, M. (2004). Why are materialists less satisfied? In T. Kasser & A. D. Kanner (Eds.), *Psychology and consumer culture: The struggle for a good life in a materialistic world* (pp. 29–48). Washington, DC: American Psychological Association.

Sortheix, F. M., & Lönnqvist, J. E. (2014). Personal value priorities and life satisfaction in Europe: The moderating role of socioeconomic development. *Journal of Cross Cultural Psychology, 45*, 282–299.

Spini, D. (2003). Measurement equivalence of 10 value types from the Schwartz Value Survey across 21 countries. *Journal of Cross-Cultural Psychology, 34*, 3–23.

Steele, C. (1988). The psychology of self-affirmation: Sustaining the integrity of the self. In L. Berkowitz (Ed.), *Advances in experimental social psychology* (Vol. 2, pp. 181–227). San Diego, CA: Academic Press.

Tetlock, P. E. (1986). A value pluralism model of ideological reasoning. *Journal of Personality and Social Psychology, 50*, 819–827.

Uchino, B. N., Cacioppo, J. T., & Kiecolt-Glaser, J. K. (1996). The relationship between social support and physiological processes: A review with emphasis on underlying mechanisms and implications for health. *Psychological Bulletin, 119*, 488.

Vansteenkiste, M., Duriez, B., Simons, J., & Soenens, B. (2006). Materialistic values and well-being among business students: Further evidence of their detrimental effect. *Journal of Applied Social Psychology, 36,* 2892–2908.

Yang, L. Q., Che, H., & Spector, P. E. (2008). Job stress and well-being: An examination from the view of person-environment fit. *Journal of Occupational and Organizational Psychology, 81,* 567–587.

Zilberfeld, T. (2010). *Person-culture fit and subjective well-being among ultra-orthodox and secular Israelis* (Unpublished master's thesis). Hebrew University of Jerusalem, Israel.

# CHAPTER 8

# The Paradox of Choice

BARRY SCHWARTZ

WESTERN SOCIETIES ARE guided by a set of assumptions about well-being that is so deeply embedded in most of us that we don't realize either that we make these assumptions or that there is an alternative. The assumptions can be stated in the form of a rough syllogism:

The more freedom and autonomy people have, the greater their well-being.
The more choice people have, the greater their freedom and autonomy.
Therefore, the more choice people have, the greater their well-being.

It is hard to quarrel—either logically or psychologically—with this syllogism. The moral importance of freedom and autonomy is self-evident, and the psychological importance of freedom and autonomy is now amply documented (e.g., Deci & Ryan, 2000, 2002; Ryan & Deci, 2000; Seligman, 1975; see also Brown & Ryan, Chapter 9, this volume). There is also no denying that choice improves the quality of people's lives. It enables people to control their destinies and to come close to getting exactly what they want out of any situation. Choice is essential to autonomy, which is absolutely fundamental to well-being. Healthy people want and need to direct their own lives. And whereas many needs are universal (food, shelter, medical care, social support, education, and so on), much of what people need if they are to flourish is highly individualized. Choice is what enables each person to pursue precisely those objects and activities that best satisfy his or her own preferences within the limits of his or her resources. Any time choice is restricted in some way, there is bound to be someone, somewhere, who is deprived of the opportunity to pursue something of personal value.

And as important as the instrumental value of choice may be, choice reflects another value that might be even more important. Freedom to choose has *expressive* value. Choice is what enables people to tell the world who they are and what they care about. Every choice a person makes is a testament to his or her autonomy. Almost every social, moral, or polical philosopher in the Western tradition since Plato has placed a premium on such autonomy. It is difficult to imagine a single aspect of collective social life that would be recognizable if this commitment to autonomy was abandoned.

There is no denying that choice improves the quality of our lives. But this chapter argues that choice, and with it freedom, autonomy, and self-determination, can become excessive, and that when that happens, freedom can be experienced as a kind of misery-inducing tyranny. Unconstrained freedom leads to paralysis. It is self-determination within significant constraints—within "rules" of some sort—that leads to well-being, to optimal functioning. And the task for a psychology of optimal functioning is to identify which constraints on self-determination are the crucial ones. When people have no choice, life is almost unbearable. As the number of available choices increases, as it has in modern consumer cultures, the autonomy, control, and liberation that variety brings are powerful and seemingly positive. But the fact that *some* choice is good doesn't necessarily mean that *more* choice is better. As I will argue, the relation between choice and well-being is nonmonotonic (Grant & Schwartz, 2011). There is a cost to having an overabundance of choice. As the number of choices people face keeps growing, negative aspects of having a multitude of options begin to appear. As the number of choices grows further, the negatives escalate until, ultimately, choice no longer liberates, but instead debilitates.

In this chapter, I examine some of the ways in which increased opportunities for choice, coupled with the goal of getting the "best" out of any choice situation, can reduce well-being.

## CHOICE OVERLOAD AND PARALYSIS

The first demonstration that too many choices can induce decision paralysis was provided by Iyengar and Lepper (2000). They reported a series of studies that showed how choice can be "demotivating." One study was set in a gourmet food store in which the researchers set up a display featuring a line of exotic, high-quality jams. Customers who came by could taste samples, and then were given a coupon for a dollar off if they bought a jar. In one condition of the study, six varieties of the jam were available for tasting. In another, 24 varieties were available. In either case, the entire set of 24 varieties was available for purchase. The large array of jams attracted more people to the table than the small array. When it came to buying, however, 30% of people exposed to the small array of jams actually bought a jar; only 3% of those exposed to the large array of jams did so.

In a second study, this time in the laboratory, college students were asked to evaluate a variety of gourmet chocolates (6 for some participants and 30 for others). The students were then asked which chocolate—based on description and appearance—they would choose for themselves. They then tasted and rated that chocolate. Finally, in a different room, the students were offered a small box of the chocolates in lieu of cash as payment for their participation. The key results of this study were that the students faced with the small array were more satisfied with their tasting than those faced with the large array. In addition, they were four times as likely to choose chocolate rather than cash as compensation for their participation.

Since this initial demonstration, Iyengar (with various collaborators) and others have provided similar evidence from a wide variety of different domains, many of them far more consequential than jams or chocolates (e.g., Botti, & Iyengar, 2004, 2006; Hanoch & Rice, 2006; Hanoch, Rice, Cummings, & Wood, 2009; Iyengar & DeVoe, 2003; Iyengar, Jiang, & Huberman, 2004; Iyengar & Lepper, 1999, 2002). For example, adding mutual fund options to a pension plan menu *decreases* rate of participation (Iyengar et al., 2004). Participation rate drops 2% for every 10 options, even though by failing to participate employees often pass up significant amounts of matching money from their employers. Though there are no doubt limits to the choice overload phenomenon that remain to be determined, and conditions under which it does not seem to hold (Chernev, 2003; Scheibehenne, Greifeneder, & Todd, 2009), it now seems clear that under a broad range of circumstances, people find a large number of options paralyzing rather than liberating.

## THE GOALS OF CHOICE: MAXIMIZING AND SATISFICING

Half a century ago, Simon (1955, 1956, 1957) argued that in choice situations individuals will often "satisfice," that is, choose the first option that surpasses some absolute threshold of acceptability, rather than attempt to "optimize" and find the best possible choice. Such a satisficing strategy was thought to make manageable the otherwise overwhelming task of evaluating options in terms of every possible piece of information that could potentially be known about each of them. Rather than attempt to engage in an exhaustive and ultimately limitless search for complete information regarding a particular choice, satisficers would simply end their search as soon as an option was found that exceeded some criterion.

Such a strategy makes good sense in a world of ever-increasing freedom of choice. However, many would argue that attendant with increased choice has been a pressure to "maximize," that is, to seek the very best option available in a wide range of choice domains. And it may well be the case that, for certain individuals, adding more choices to an existing domain simply makes their lives more difficult because they feel pressure to choose the "best" possible option from an overwhelming array of choices rather than simply settle for "good enough." After all, as the number of choices in a domain increases, so too does the cognitive work required to compare various options, along with the possibility of making a "wrong" or suboptimal choice. Thus, if one follows such a maximizing strategy, the more choices one faces, the greater the potential to experience regret at having chosen suboptimally.

We undertook an investigation to determine whether in fact there are individual differences in the tendency to maximize, and, if so, if maximizers are more unhappy than their satisficing peers (Schwartz et al., 2002). We designed a survey instrument, the Maximization Scale, to identify both maximizers and satisficers, and then examined the potential relation between scores on the scale and a range of psychological correlates, including happiness, depression, optimism, self-esteem, perfectionism, neuroticism, and subjective well-being. We also explored whether these putative relationships might be mediated by a tendency for maximizers to experience more regret with regard to their choices than satisficers. Finally, we examined maximizers' versus satisficers' tendency to engage in social comparison. We reasoned that if maximizers are always on the lookout for the best possible option, one way to do so is to examine the choices of others, especially in domains in which no clear objective standard exists for what constitutes "the best" (Festinger, 1954).

The Maximization Scale includes 13 items that assess a range of attitudes and behaviors that together comprise a tendency to maximize rather than satisfice (for an abbreviated scale with good psychometric properties, see Nenkov, Morrin, Schwartz, Ward, & Hulland, 2008). Thus, respondents are asked to endorse statements reflecting (a) the adoption of high standards (e.g., "No matter what I do, I have the highest standards for myself"); (b) actions that are consistent with maximizing tendencies ("When I am in the car listening to the radio, I often check other stations to see if something better is playing, even if I'm relatively satisfied with what I'm listening to"); and (c) choice behaviors aimed at seeking out the "best" option ("Renting videos is really difficult. I'm always struggling to pick the best one"). We administered the survey to over 1,700 participants in the United States and Canada who ranged in age from 16 to 81 and came from diverse ethnic backgrounds.

Different subsamples of our respondents also completed a number of other standard personality measures. Among these were the Subjective Happiness Scale (Lyubomirsky & Lepper, 1999; $n = 1627$); the Beck Depression Inventory (BDI; Beck & Beck, 1972; $n = 1006$); a measure of dispositional optimism (Life Orientation Test; Scheier & Carver, 1985; $n = 182$); a neuroticism scale (John, Donahue, & Kentle, 1991; $n = 100$); a survey assessing subjective well-being (Satisfaction With Life Scale; Diener, Emmons, Larsen, & Griffin, 1985; $n = 100$); a self-esteem measure (Rosenberg, 1965; $n = 266$); and a subscale of the Multidimensional Perfectionism Scale (Hewitt & Flett, 1990, 1991; $n = 220$). Finally, we created a five-item scale designed to assess a tendency to experience regret (e.g., "When I think about how I'm doing in life, I often assess opportunities I have passed up") and administered it to all of our participants.

In terms of self-reported happiness, there was a clear tendency for maximizers to report being significantly less happy and optimistic than satisficers. They were also less likely to report high subjective well-being scores and were more likely to be depressed. Indeed, in one subsample, of the individuals whose BDI scores met the diagnostic criterion for mild depression, 44% also scored in the top quartile for maximization whereas only 16% scored in the bottom quartile. Maximizers also reported lower self-esteem scores and higher neuroticism scores than satisficers, although the latter relationship did not reach statistical significance in our sample, suggesting discriminant validity between the constructs of maximization and neuroticism. In addition, although we observed mildly significant correlations between maximizing and the related construct of perfectionism, the latter correlated positively with happiness in our sample, suggesting that, unlike maximizing, perfectionist tendencies are not necessarily associated with unhappiness. Finally, those who scored high on the Maximization Scale were also much more likely to report experiencing regret.

Statistical analyses showed that individuals' endorsement of the regret items appeared to at least partially mediate many of the relationships between maximizing and the other personality measures, including maximizers' tendency to be less happy and more depressed. It would seem that maximization constitutes a recipe for unhappiness, in that those individuals who search for the best possible option are more likely to regret a choice once made.

In a subsequent study (Schwartz et al., 2002, Study 4), the hypothesized tendency of maximizers to experience greater sensitivity to regret was investigated in a behavioral paradigm that made use of a version of the "ultimatum game" (Zeelenberg & Beattie, 1997). In the study, individuals had the opportunity to propose a division of funds to a second player (simulated by a computer) who could choose to accept or reject the offer. If the offer was accepted, the funds would be divided up as proposed. If the second player rejected the offer, however, neither player would receive any money. Participants played both a standard version of the game and a modified version, in which, after offering a division of funds, they got to learn the other player's "reservation price," that is, the minimal offer that the other player would have accepted. In short, this modified version created a greater potential for regret of one's offer, for it carried the possibility of learning that one would not have had to be so generous in dividing up the provided funds.

As predicted, in the modified version (i.e., when participants expected to learn the other player's reservation price) maximizers made much more modest offers to their opponents than in the condition in which a participant never had to face the knowledge that a more meager offer would have been accepted. Satisficers did not show this pattern. It would seem that maximizers' greater tendency to experience regret extends to situations involving anticipated regret as well, as their behaviors in this study appeared to be aimed at minimizing the possibility of later regret.

Maximizers were also hypothesized to engage in more social comparison than satisficers—especially upward comparison, in which an individual compares him or herself to someone who is better off, as such a person would presumably provide the best "evidence" that a maximizer has not yet achieved an optimal outcome. Such a tendency was investigated in two studies. In the first (Schwartz et al., 2002, Study 2), maximizers reported on a questionnaire measure that they were more likely to engage in social comparison—both upward and downward—than satisficers, and their greater frequency of upward comparison was associated with increased unhappiness (though their greater frequency of downward comparison did not predict enhanced happiness). The same study also probed respondents' experiences with consumer decisions and found that maximizers reported seeking more social comparison information in making purchases than did satisficers. They also reported engaging in more product comparisons and counterfactual thinking (thinking about alternatives not chosen) regarding buying decisions, along with heightened regret and diminished happiness with their purchases.

A second study (Schwartz et al., 2002, Study 3) examined social comparison tendencies in maximizers versus satisficers using a procedure developed by Lyubomirsky and Ross (1997). In the study, participants performed an anagram-solving task either much slower or much faster than a confederate posing as a fellow undergraduate. Maximizers were heavily affected by their peer's performance, especially when they were outperformed by the peer. They provided higher assessments of their ability to perform the task after working alongside a slower peer than a faster peer, and in the latter condition, their self-assessment declined and their negative affect increased significantly. Satisficers, by contrast, were barely affected by the performance of the other participant, and regardless of whether the situation provided an opportunity for downward comparison (i.e., outperforming a peer) or upward comparison (i.e., being outperformed by a peer), their assessment of their own ability and their affect level remained largely unaffected. In short, maximizers were sensitive to social comparison information and were made less happy when outperformed by a peer; satisficers showed little response to the social comparison information provided by the experimental situation, and their mood remained relatively stable throughout the study.

In a later study, Iyengar, Wells, and Schwartz (2006) tracked college seniors at 15 different colleges and universities as they looked for postgraduation jobs. The seniors had all filled out the Maximization Scale. The study found that people who scored high on the Maximization Scale got better jobs than people who scored low (measured by starting salary), but on a large battery of psychological outcome measures, they felt worse about the job they got, about the entire job search process, and about their lives in general. So being a maximizer seems to enable people to do better when they make a decision, but to feel worse about how well they did.

In sum, in both survey and experimental procedures, maximizers showed themselves to be less happy and more depressed than satisficers. They were more prone to regret, both experienced and anticipated, and they engaged in more social comparison, especially upward comparison, than satisficers. In their quest for the best option, they increased their own unhappiness and regretted their choices more than individuals who reported a willingness to settle for "good enough." For maximizers, "good enough" evidently was not, but, at least in terms of their own subjective well-being, "the best" was far from ideal.

There is a caveat to this generalization, however. In a recent study of European, North American, and Chinese adults, Roets, Schwartz, and Guan (2012) found that scores on the Maximization Scale did not differ across the different cultures, but that unlike Europeans and North Americans, Chinese participants showed no relation between maximizing score and measures of well-being. Roets et al. (2012) speculated that the Chinese participants cared about the "best" just as much as Westerners did, but that as residents of a collectivist society, the stakes involved in finding the best were lower for the Chinese than for Westerners. For the Chinese, it was suggested, the choices one made were not reflections of identity—of who one was (see Iyengar & DeVoe, 2003; Iyengar & Lepper, 1999; 2002; Markus & Kitayama, 1991; Markus & Schwartz, 2010; Savani, Markus, Naidu, Kumar, & Berlia, 2010; Schwartz, 2000, 2009, 2012; Schwartz, Markus, & Snibbe, 2006; Snibbe & Markus, 2005), whereas for Westerners, choices were a reflection of identity.

## CHOICE AND WELL-BEING: WHY PEOPLE SUFFER

I have suggested that several factors conspire to undermine the objective benefits that ought to come with increased choice. I will review them, and in each case, I'll show why the choice problem is exacerbated for maximizers (see Schwartz, 2004, for more detailed discussion).

### REGRET

As I indicated, research showed that regret mediated the relation between maximizing and various measures of life satisfaction. People with high regret scores are less happy, less satisfied with life, less optimistic, and more depressed than those with low regret scores. Studies also found that people with high regret scores tend to be maximizers. Indeed, concern about regret may be a major reason *why* individuals are maximizers. The only way to be sure that you won't regret a decision is by making the best possible decision. And the more options you have, the more likely it is that you will experience regret.

*Post-decision regret*, sometimes referred to as *buyer's remorse*, induces second thoughts that rejected alternatives were actually better than the one chosen, or that there are better alternatives out there that haven't been explored. The bitter taste of regret detracts from satisfaction, whether or not the regret is justified. *Anticipated regret* may be even more debilitating because it will produce not only dissatisfaction but also paralysis. If someone asks him- or herself how it would feel to buy this house only to discover a better one next week, the person probably won't buy this house. Both types of regret—anticipated and postdecision—will raise the emotional stakes of decisions (Bell, 1982; Loomes & Sugden, 1982). Anticipated regret will make decisions harder to make and postdecision regret will make them harder to enjoy (see Gilovich & Medvec, 1995 and Landman, 1993, for thoughtful discussions of the determinants and consequences of regret).

Two of the factors affecting regret are personal responsibility for the result and how easily an individual can imagine a counterfactual, better alternative. The availability of many options exacerbates both of these factors. When there are no options, you can experience disappointment, but not regret. When you have only a few options, you do the best you can, but the world may simply not allow you to do as well as you would like. When there are many options, the chances increase that there is a really good one out there, and you feel that you ought to be able to find it. When the option you actually settle on proves disappointing, you regret not having chosen more wisely. And as the number of options continues to proliferate, making an exhaustive investigation of the possibilities impossible, concern that there may be a better option out there may induce you to anticipate the regret you will feel later on, when that option is discovered, and thus prevent you from making a decision at all. Landman (1993) sums it up this way: "Regret may threaten decisions with multiple attractive alternatives more than decisions offering only one or a more limited set of alternatives.... Ironically, then, the greater the number of appealing choices, the greater the opportunity for regret" (p. 184).

It should be clear that the problem of regret will loom larger for maximizers than for satisficers. No matter how good something is, if a maximizer discovers something better, he or she will regret having failed to choose it in the first place. Perfection is the only weapon against regret, and endless, exhaustive, paralyzing consideration of the alternatives is the only way to achieve perfection. For a satisficer, the stakes are lower. The possibility of regret doesn't loom as large, and perfection is unnecessary.

And what makes the problem of regret much worse is that thinking is not restricted to objective reality. People can also think about states of affairs that don't exist. Studies of such counterfactual thinking have found that most individuals do not often engage in this process spontaneously. Instead, counterfactual thinking is usually triggered by the occurrence of something that itself produces a negative emotion. Counterfactual thoughts are generated in response to poor exam grades, to trouble in romantic relationships, and to the illness or death of loved ones. And when the counterfactual thoughts begin to occur, they trigger more negative emotions, like regret, which in turn trigger more counterfactual thinking, which in turn triggers more negative emotion. When they examine the actual content of counterfactual thinking, researchers find that individuals tend to focus on aspects of a situation that are under their control. The fact that counterfactual thinking seems to home in on the controllable aspects of a situation only increases the chances that the emotion a person experiences when engaging in counterfactual thinking will be regret (see Roese, 1997).

Missed Opportunities

Economists point out that the quality of any given option cannot be assessed in isolation from its alternatives. One of the "costs" of any option involves passing up the opportunities that a different option would have afforded. Every choice we make has missed opportunities associated with it.

According to standard economic assumptions, the only missed opportunities that should figure into a decision are the ones associated with the next best alternative, because you wouldn't have chosen the third, fourth, or nth best alternative in any event. This advice, however, is extremely difficult to follow. The options under consideration usually have multiple features. If people think about options in terms of their features rather than as a whole, different options may rank as second best (or even best) with respect to each individual feature. Even though there may be a single, second-best option overall, each of the options may have some very desirable feature on which it beats its competition.

If we assume that missed opportunities take away from the overall desirability of the most preferred option, and that we will feel these missed opportunities associated with many of the options we reject, then the more alternatives there are from which to choose, the greater our experience of the missed opportunities will be. And the greater our experience of the missed opportunities, the less satisfaction we will derive from our chosen alternative.

This form of dissatisfaction was confirmed by a study in which people were asked how much they would be willing to pay for a flight to a weekend getaway, or subscriptions to popular magazines, or to purchase videotapes of popular movies (Brenner,

Rottenstreich, & Sood, 1999). Some were asked about individual destinations, magazines, or videos. Others were asked about these same destinations, magazines, or videos as part of a group with other destinations, magazines, or videos. In almost every case, respondents placed a higher value on the flight, the magazine, or the video when they were evaluating it in isolation than when they were evaluating it as part of a cluster. When magazines are evaluated as part of a group, missed opportunities associated with the other options reduce the value of each of them.

EFFECTS OF ADAPTATION

As Kahneman and various collaborators have shown (e.g., Kahneman, 1999), we appear to possess hedonic "thermometers" that run from negative (unpleasant), through neutral, to positive. When we experience something good, our pleasure "temperature" goes up, and when we experience something bad, it goes down. However, our responses to hedonic stimuli are not constant; repeated exposure results in adaptation (Frederick & Loewenstein, 1999).

In what is perhaps the most famous example of hedonic adaptation, respondents were asked to rate their happiness on a 5-point scale (Brickman, Coates, & Janoff-Bulman, 1978). Some of them had won between $50,000 and $1 million in state lotteries within the past year. Others had become paraplegic or quadriplegic as a result of accidents. Not surprisingly, the lottery winners were happier than those who had become paralyzed. What is surprising, though, is that after a few months, the lottery winners were no happier than people in general. And what is even more surprising is that the accident victims, although somewhat less happy than people in general, still judged themselves to be happy.

Though hedonic adaptation is almost ubiquitous, people don't expect it (Loewenstein & Schkade, 1999; see Schwartz & Sommers, 2013, for a recent discussion). Thus, the ultimate result of adaptation to positive experiences appears to be disappointment. And faced with this inevitable disappointment, people will be driven to pursue novelty, to seek out new commodities and experiences for which the pleasure potential has not been dissipated by repeated exposure. In time, these new commodities also will lose their intensity, but people still get caught up in the chase, a process that Brickman and Campbell (1971) labeled the "hedonic treadmill." Perhaps even more insidious than the hedonic treadmill is something that Kahneman (1999) called the "satisfaction treadmill," which refers to the possibility that in addition to adapting to particular objects or experiences, people also adapt to particular levels of satisfaction.

The relevance of adaptation to the proliferation of choice is this: Imagine the search costs involved in a decision as being "amortized" over the life of a decision. They may be very high in a world of overwhelming choice (especially for a maximizer), but if the results of the choice produce a long and sustained period of substantial satisfaction, their cumulative effects will be minimized. (The costs, in money and inconvenience, of painting your house may be substantial, but if you stay there for 10 years, enjoying the benefits, those costs will dissolve into insignificance.) If, however, the satisfaction with a decision is short-lived because of adaptation (you get a job transfer and have to move 2 months after having painted your house), then the "amortization schedule" will be very much abbreviated and the initial costs will subtract much more from the total satisfaction.

SOCIAL COMPARISON

Of all the sources we rely on when we evaluate experiences, perhaps nothing is more important than comparisons to other people. In many ways, social comparison parallels the counterfactual thinking process, but there is one very important difference. In principle, people have a great deal of control both over when they will engage in counterfactual thinking and what its content will be. People have less control over social comparison. There is always information available about how others are doing.

Though social comparison information is seemingly all-pervasive, it appears that not everyone pays attention to it, or at least, not everyone is affected by it. Lyubomirsky and colleagues (e.g., Lyubomirsky & Ross, 1997, 1999; Lyubomirsky, Tucker, & Kasri, 2001) conducted a series of studies that looked for differences among individuals in their responses to social comparison information, and what they found is that social comparison information had relatively little impact on dispositionally happy people. Happy people were only minimally affected by whether the person working next to them was better or worse at an anagram task than they were. In contrast, unhappy people showed increases in assessed ability and positive feelings after working beside a slower peer, and *decreases* in assessed ability and positive feelings if they'd been working beside a faster peer.

Such results parallel the findings we reported regarding maximizers, who seem more sensitive than satisficers to the behavior of others as a gauge of their own progress in obtaining "the best." Maximizers want the best, but how do you know that you have the best, except by comparison? And to the extent that we have more options, determining the "best" can become overwhelmingly difficult. The maximizer becomes a slave in his or her judgments to the experiences and judgments of other people. Satisficers don't have this problem. Satisficers can rely on their own internal assessments to develop those standards.

### HIGH EXPECTATIONS

When people evaluate an experience, they are performing one or more of the following comparisons (see Michalos, 1980, 1986):

- Comparing the experience to what they hoped it would be.
- Comparing the experience to what they expected it to be.
- Comparing the experience to other experiences they have had in the recent past.
- Comparing the experience to experiences that others have had.

As material and social circumstances improve, standards of comparison go up. As people have contact with items of high quality, they begin to suffer from "the curse of discernment." The lower-quality items that used to be perfectly acceptable are no longer good enough. The hedonic zero-point keeps rising, and expectations and aspirations rise with it. As a result, the rising quality of experience is met with rising expectations, and people are just running in place. As long as expectations keep pace with realizations, people may live better, but they won't *feel* better about how they live.

Large choice sets can have similar effects. If there are two or three styles of jeans to choose from, one's expectations about how well a pair of jeans will fit will be modest. The chosen pair may not fit that well, but one can reasonably only expect so much with such a small choice set. However, if there are dozens of styles to choose from, it seems inevitable that expectations about quality of fit will rise. Large choice sets will indeed enable people to find better-fitting jeans than small choice sets, but if expectations have risen along with the size of the choice set, a good fit will bring no more satisfaction, and may bring less, than a mediocre fit.

## Self-Blame

There is one more effect of large choice sets on satisfaction that should be discussed. Suppose one devotes a great deal of time and energy to making a decision, and then, because of some combination of regret, missed opportunities, and high expectations, one ends up disappointed with the results. The questions this person might ask are, "Why?" or "What went wrong?" or "Whose fault is it?" And what is the likely answer to these questions? When the choice set is small, it seems natural and straightforward to blame the world for disappointing results. "They only had three styles of jeans. What could I do? I did the best I could." However, when the choice set is large, blaming the world is a much less plausible option. "With so many options available, success was out there to be had. I have only myself to blame for a disappointing result." In other words, self-blame for disappointing results becomes more likely as the choice set grows larger. And because large choice sets increase the chances of disappointing results (because of regret, missed opportunities, and raised expectations), self-blame becomes a more common occurrence.

## Learned Helplessness, Control, Depression, and Self-Blame

About 45 years ago, Seligman proposed that clinical depression may be the result of lack of control or learned helplessness (see Maier & Seligman, 1976; Overmier & Seligman, 1967; Seligman, 1975; Seligman & Maier, 1967). The theory was subsequently modified by Abramson, Seligman, and Teasdale (1978), who suggested that important psychological steps intervene between the experience of helplessness and depression. According to the new theory, when people experience a lack of control, they look for causes and display a variety of predispositions to accept certain types of causes, quite apart from what the actual cause of the failure might be. There are three key dimensions to these predispositions, based on whether people view causes as being global or specific, chronic or transient (or what was labeled "stable versus unstable") or personal or universal (or "internal versus external"). The revised theory of helplessness and depression argued that helplessness induced by failure or lack of control leads to depression if a person's causal explanations for that failure are global, chronic, and personal. It is only then that people will have good reason to expect one failure to be followed by others.

Tests of this revised theory have yielded impressive results (e.g., Peterson & Seligman, 1984). People *do* differ in the types of predispositions for causal attributions they display. People who find chronic causes for failure expect failures to persist. People who find global causes for failure expect failure to follow them into every area of life. And people who find personal causes for failure suffer large losses in self-esteem.

Owing to the explosion of choice available in modern, affluent societies, many people now experience control and personal autonomy to a degree that people living in other times and places would find unimaginable. This fact, coupled with the helplessness theory of depression, might suggest that clinical depression in the developed world should be disappearing. Instead, we see explosive *growth* in the disorder. Furthermore, depression seems to attack its victims at a younger age now than in earlier eras. Current estimates are that as many as 7.5% of Americans have an episode of clinical depression before they are 14. This is twice the rate seen in young people born only 10 years earlier (Angst, 1995; Klerman et al., 1985; Klerman & Weissman, 1989; Lane, 2000; Myers, 2000). And the most extreme manifestation of depression—suicide—is also on the rise, and it, too, is happening younger. Suicide is the second leading cause of death (after accidents) among American high school and college students. In the past 45 years, the suicide rate among American college students has tripled. Throughout the developed world, suicide among adolescents and young adults is increasing dramatically (Eckersley, 2002; Eckersley & Dear, 2002). In an era of ever greater personal autonomy and control, what could account for this degree of personal misery?

I think there are several answers to this question. First, I believe that increases in experienced control over the years have been accompanied, stride-for-stride, by increases in *expectations* about control. The more we are allowed to be the masters of our fates, the more we expect to be. Emphasis on freedom of choice, together with the proliferation of possibilities that modern life affords, have contributed to these unrealistic expectations. Along with the pervasive rise in expectations, Western culture also has become more individualistic than it was, perhaps as a by-product of the desire to have control over every aspect of life. Heightened individualism means that not only do people expect perfection in all things, but they also expect to produce this perfection themselves. When they (inevitably) fail, the culture of individualism biases people toward causal explanations that focus on personal rather than universal factors. That is, the culture has established a kind of officially acceptable style of causal explanation, and it is one that encourages the individual to blame him- or herself for failure (see Weiner, 1985).

Unrealistically high expectations coupled with a tendency to take intense personal responsibility for failure make a lethal combination. And this problem is especially acute for maximizers. As they do with missed opportunities, regret, adaptation, and social comparison, maximizers will suffer more from high expectations and self-blame than will satisficers. Maximizers will put the most work into their decisions, and have the highest expectations about the results of those decisions, and thus will be the most disappointed.

Our research suggests that maximizers are prime candidates for depression (Schwartz et al., 2002). With group after group of people, varying in age, gender, educational level, geographical location, race, and socioeconomic status, we have found a strong positive relation between maximizing and measures of depression. Among people who score highest on our Maximization Scale, scores on the standard measure of depression are in the borderline clinical range. High expectations, and personal attributions for failing to meet them, can apply to educational decisions, career decisions, and marital decisions just as they apply to decisions about what clothes to buy or where to eat dinner. And even the trivial decisions add up. If the experience of disappointment is relentless, if virtually every choice you make fails to live up to expectations and aspirations, and if you consistently take personal responsibility for the disappointments, then the trivial looms larger and larger, and the conclusion that you can't do anything right becomes devastating.

## "FREEDOM," "CHOICE," "AUTONOMY," AND THE "SELF"

Virtually all of the empirical evidence on choice overload and its effects comes from contexts in which people are choosing goods. In consumer societies, the importance of contexts like these should not be dismissed. Yet, they seem to pale to insignificance when compared with decisions involving core aspects of one's identity and mode of being in the world. "What should I buy?" doesn't amount to much when compared with "What should I do with my life?" or "Who should I be?" Moreover, it is in connection with these identity-shaping decisions that the benefits of freedom and autonomy (i.e., choice) loom largest. And there is little doubt, as I have previously argued (Schwartz, 2000, 2004), that freedom of choice in these self-defining domains has expanded along with freedom of choice in the world of goods. Young people find themselves with relatively unconstrained choices when it comes to where they live, what they study, what kind of work they do, what religion they practice and how they practice it, what kind of intimate relations they will enter into, and what kind of family commitments they will make. People are free to decide matters of identity, of who they will be in the world. They are no longer stuck with identities they inherit from family and community. And having made the decision about who they are, people are also free to change it (see Gilbert & Ebert, 2002, for evidence that reversibility of decisions decreases people's satisfaction with them).

One plausible view of the modern explosion of choice is that although it does produce the negative effects I have described in the world of goods, it also produces significant positive effects with respect to the things that really matter. No longer are people "stuck" with the identities and life paths that accidents of birth, or the views of others, have imposed on them. Self-invention and reinvention are now very real possibilities. And occasional paralysis in the cereal aisle of the supermarket is a small price to pay for this kind of liberation. As I say, this is a plausible view. Nonetheless, I think, as Durkheim (1897/1951) foresaw, it is mistaken. In the admittedly speculative discussion that follows, I will try to justify this belief.

Taylor (1989, 1992a, 1992b) points out that over the past 500 years, self-understanding has been moving in a more or less straight line from "outside-in," through participation in larger entities (the divine order, the "great chain of being," nation, community, family, etc.) to "inside-out," with purpose discovered from within each individual, and the notion of "authentic" self-expression as the supreme aspiration. We in the West have seen this evolution as progress, each step enhancing freedom. And like fish that don't know they live in water, we find it hard to imagine thinking about our lives in any other way. But Markus and collaborators (e.g., Markus & Kitayama, 1991), in research on East and South Asian versus Western cultures, has shown that this movement from "outside-in" to "inside-out" is not universal: Most East and South Asians still define themselves in terms of their relations to others (and some of Markus's most recent research suggests that this "inside-out" view may be limited to the West's educated elite; see Markus & Schwartz, 2010; Schwartz, Markus, & Snibbe, 2006; Snibbe & Markus, 2005). Further, choice does not have the same significance for East or South Asians as it seems to have for Westerners (Iyengar & Devoe, 2003; Iyengar & Lepper, 1999; Kitayama, Snibbe, Markus, & Suzuki, 2004; Savani et al., 2010; see also Markus & Schwartz, 2010). This research does not challenge the notion that within *Western* culture more freedom—more "inside-out"—is better. But the Iyengar and Lepper (2000) "jam study" and its companions suggest that perhaps more "inside-out" is not better, and that it is not all just a matter of cultural preferences. Asians may know something that Westerners have forgotten.

Consistent with this possibility, there is good evidence from recent research on well-being—again, affirming Durkheim—that the most significant determinant of our well-being is our network of close relationships with other people (e.g., Diener, 2000; Diener & Biswas-Diener, 2008; Diener, Diener, & Diener, 1995; Diener, & Suh, 2001; Diener, Suh, Lucas, & Smith, 1999; Lane, 2000; Myers, 2000). The more connected we are, the better off we are. The thing to notice about close relationships, in connection with freedom, choice, and autonomy, is that close relationships generally constrain, they do not liberate. When people have responsibilities for and concerns about other people, they often cannot just do anything they might otherwise choose to do. Until now, the thought has been that this constraint is perhaps just a price worth paying for rich social ties. What the choice overload research suggests is that in modern society, with overwhelming choice in every aspect of life, the constraints of close relationships with others may actually be part of the *benefit* of those relations rather than being a cost. And like close relationships with others, "outside-in" definitions of the self provide significant constraints on what is possible, constraints that, in modern Western societies, may be desperately needed.

What is the evidence that modern Westerners are suffering from this lack of constraint? As previously mentioned, there has been a significant rise in the incidence of clinical depression and suicide, both of which are befalling people at younger and younger ages (e.g., Angst, 1995; Eckersley, 2002; Eckersley & Dear, 2002; Klerman et al., 1985; Klerman & Weissman, 1989; Lane, 2000; Myers, 2000). Second, there is a substantial increase in the rate at which college students are flocking to counseling centers (Kadison & DiGeronimo, 2004). Third, there is a palpable unease in the reports of young college graduates, who seem to lack a clear idea of what they are meant to do in their lives (Robbins & Wilner, 2001). And finally, among upper-class adolescents whose family affluence makes anything possible, there are the same levels of drug abuse, anxiety disorder, and depression as there are in the children of the poor (Luthar & Latendresse, 2005). Further, there is reason to believe that whereas the poor take drugs "recreationally," the rich do so to self-medicate (Luthar & Latendresse, 2005).

## CONCLUSION: FREEDOM FROM AND FREEDOM TO

I have tried to argue that, whereas there is no denying that choice is good, it is not always and only good. Further, the relation between choice and freedom is complex. Though one cannot be free without choice, it is arguable that choice-induced paralysis is a sign of diminished rather than enhanced freedom.

Though public policy interventions can do a good deal to minimize the negative effects of choice overload (e.g., Thaler & Sunstein, 2008), it seems to me that the best route to eliminating some of the negative effects of choice overload without also eliminating the liberating effects of choice is not through public policy, but through a change in awareness, sensibility, and aspiration on the part of individuals. If people can come to see that sometimes unfettered choice is paralyzing, whereas constrained choice may be liberating, they may seek and embrace constraints in their own lives instead of avoiding them. I have suggested elsewhere that perhaps the best model we have for the importance of constraints for freedom comes from our understanding of human language abilities (Schwartz, 2000). The capacity to use language may be the single most liberating characteristic of human beings. It frees people up in significant ways from the temporal and material limitations that afflict other organisms. People can say anything about any thing, any time, or any place—even things, times, and places that have never existed. And they can be understood. So language is probably as vivid an embodiment of human freedom and autonomy as anything. But what decades of research on language ability have made clear is that the thing that makes the liberating features of language possible is that language is heavily constrained by rules. The reason people can say anything and be understood is that they cannot say anything *in any way they want*. It is linguistic constraint, in the form of these rules, that makes linguistic freedom possible. What I have suggested in this chapter is that exactly the same thing may be true in connection with the determination of the self. Unconstrained freedom leads to paralysis and becomes a kind of self-defeating tyranny. It is freedom of choice within significant constraints—within "rules" of some sort—that leads to well-being, to optimal functioning. And a significant task for psychology is to identify which constraints on self-determination are the crucial ones.

FUTURE RESEARCH

We have only begun to investigate in a systematic fashion the behavior of so-called maximizers versus satisficers. Future research will help determine the domain specificity of maximizing behaviors. Clearly no one pursues "the best" in every arena of life, and what distinguishes maximizers from satisficers may ultimately be the number of domains in which an individual attempts to obtain something that is optimal as opposed to merely acceptable. In addition, future studies will determine whether maximizers sometimes engage in behavior that looks similar to that of satisficers but reflects different motives. For example, if a maximizer is aware of his or her tendency to engage in an exhaustive, time-consuming, and ultimately disappointing search for the most attractive option, he or she may on occasion opt to restrict a choice set by simply selecting the first acceptable option available. In other words, there may be occasions in which maximizers "choose not to choose" rather than endure the misery and paralysis that can often follow their attempts to maximize. Such speculation, of course, implies that maximizers are aware of the negative psychological consequences that typically accompany their behavior, and that, in and of itself (i.e., whether maximizers know that there is a psychological cost to be paid for their habitual "quest for the best") is worthy of further study.

Finally, additional research should investigate the origins of a maximizing versus satisficing style of choice behavior. I have speculated on the cultural pressures in a postindustrial capitalist society that might lead to the development of maximizing tendencies, especially in times of plenty (see Schwartz, 1994; and Wieczorkowska & Burnstein, 1999, for further discussion). And although at times maximizing may produce superior material outcomes (a question worth pursuing in its own right), I believe that such a strategy leads individuals to inferior psychological outcomes. I should acknowledge, though, that the causal arrow may point in the opposite direction; that is, unhappy or depressed individuals may resort to a maximizing strategy in an attempt to improve their current psychological state. Regardless of the causal direction, however, a strategy of continually searching for the best option and then regretting one's choices does not appear to be a recipe for long-term happiness.

## SUMMARY POINTS

- Choice is good, but there can be too much of a good thing.
- Too many choices lead to paralysis and dissatisfaction, rather than liberation.
- The choice problem is especially acute for people who try to get the best—to maximize rather than satisfice.
- Maximizers may make better decisions than satisficers, but they feel worse about them.
- Among the impediments to satisfying decisions brought on by too much choice and maximizing are regret, the pain of missed opportunities, the creation of unrealistically high expectations, and self-blame for any decisions that fall short.
- The choice overload and maximizing problems may be a special affliction of people living in Western societies.
- Though policy initiatives can operate to minimize the negative effects of choice overload, they contain the danger that they will simultaneously undermine the positive effects of freedom of choice.
- A more promising approach may be to sensitize people to the costs of choice and the benefits of constraints. People who appreciate the benefits of constraints might seek and embrace the constraints that arise out of membership in a close social network.

## REFERENCES

Abramson, L. Y., Seligman, M. E. P., & Teasdale, J. D. (1978). Learned helplessness in humans: Critique and reformulation. *Journal of Abnormal Psychology, 87*, 49–74.

Angst, J. (1995). The epidemiology of depressive disorders. *European Neuropsychopharmacology, 5*, 95–98.

Beck, A. T., & Beck, R. W. (1972). Screening depressed patients in a family practice: A rapid technique. *Postgraduate Medicine, 52*, 81–85.

Bell, D. E. (1982). Regret in decision making under uncertainty. *Operations Research, 30*, 861–981.

Botti, S., & Iyengar, S. S. (2004). The psychological pleasure and pain of choosing: When people prefer choosing at the cost of subsequent outcome satisfaction. *Journal of Personality and Social Psychology, 87*, 312–326.

Botti, S., & Iyengar, S. S. (2006). The dark side of choice: When choice impairs social welfare. *Journal of Public Policy and Marketing, 25*, 24–38.

Brenner, L., Rottenstreich, Y., & Sood, S. (1999). Comparison, grouping, and preference. *Psychological Science, 10*, 225–229.

Brickman, P., & Campbell, D. T. (1971). Hedonic relativism and planning the good society. In M. H. Appley (Ed.), *Adaptation-level theory: A symposium* (pp. 287–302). New York, NY: Academic Press.

Brickman, P., Coates, D., & Janoff-Bulman, R. (1978). Lottery winners and accident victims: Is happiness relative? *Journal of Personality and Social Psychology, 36*, 917–927.

Chernev, A. (2003). Product assortment and individual decision processes. *Journal of Personality and Social Psychology, 85*, 151–162.

Deci, E. L., & Ryan, R. M. (2000). The "what" and "why" of goal pursuits: Human needs and the self-determination of behavior. *Psychological Inquiry, 11*, 227–268.

Deci, E. L., & Ryan, R. M. (Eds.) (2002). *Handbook of self-determination research*. Rochester, NY: University of Rochester Press.

Diener, E. (2000). Subjective well-being: The science of happiness and a proposal for a national index. *American Psychologist, 55*, 34–43.

Diener, E., & Biswas-Diener, R. (2008). *Happiness*. New York, NY: Blackwell.

Diener, E., Diener, M., & Diener, C. (1995). Factors predicting the subjective well-being of nations. *Journal of Personality and Social Psychology, 69*, 851–864.

Diener, E., Emmons, R. A., Larsen, R. J., & Griffin, S. (1985). The Satisfaction With Life Scale. *Journal of Personality Assessment, 49*, 71–75.

Diener, E., & Suh, E. M. (Eds.) (2001). *Subjective well-being across cultures*. Cambridge, MA: MIT Press.

Diener, E., Suh, E. M., Lucas, R. E., & Smith, H. L. (1999). Subjective well-being: Three decades of progress. *Psychological Bulletin, 125*, 276–302.

Durkheim, E. (1951). *Suicide* (J. A. Spalding & G. Simpson, Trans.). New York, NY: Free Press. (Original work published 1897)

Eckersley, R. (2002). Culture, health, and well-being. In R. Eckersley, J. Dixon, & B. Douglas (Eds.), *The social origins of health and well-being* (pp. 51–70). Cambridge, England: Cambridge University Press.

Eckersley, R., & Dear, K. (2002). Cultural correlates of youth suicide. *Social Science and Medicine, 55*, 1891–1904.

Festinger, L. (1954). A theory of social comparison processes. *Human Relations, 7*, 114–140.

Frederick, S., & Loewenstein, G. (1999). Hedonic adaptation. In D. Kahneman, E. Diener, & N. Schwarz (Eds.), *Well-being: The foundations of hedonic psychology* (pp. 302–329). New York, NY: Russell Sage Foundation.

Gilbert, D. T., & Ebert, J. E. J. (2002). Decisions and revisions: The affective forecasting of changeable outcomes. *Journal of Personality and Social Psychology, 82*, 503–514.

Gilovich, T., & Medvec, V. H. (1995). The experience of regret: What, when, and why. *Psychological Review, 102*, 379–395.

Grant, A. M., & Schwartz, B. (2011). Too much of a good thing: The challenge and opportunity of the inverted-U. *Perspectives on Psychological Science, 6*, 61–76.

Hanoch, Y., & Rice, T. (2006). Can limiting choice increase social welfare? The elderly and health insurance. *Milbank Quarterly, 84*, 37–73.

Hanoch, Y., Rice, T., Cummings, J., & Wood, S. (2009). How much choice is too much?: The case of the Medicare Prescription Drug Benefit. *Health Service Research, 44*, 1157–1168.

Hewitt, P. L., & Flett, G. L. (1990). Perfectionism and depression: A multidimensional analysis. *Journal of Social Behavior and Personality, 5*, 423–438.

Hewitt, P. L., & Flett, G. L. (1991). Perfectionism in the self and social contexts: Conceptualization, assessment, and association with psychopathology. *Journal of Personality and Social Psychology, 60*, 456–470.

Iyengar, S. S., & DeVoe, S. E. (2003). Rethinking the value of choice: Considering cultural mediators of intrinsic motivation. In V. Murphy-Berman & J. Berman (Eds.), *Cross-cultural differences in perspectives on the self* (pp. 129–174). Lincoln: University of Nebraska Press.

Iyengar, S. S., Jiang, W., & Huberman, G. (2004). How much choice is too much: Determinants of individual contributions in 401K retirement plans. In O. S. Mitchell & S. Utkus (Eds.), *Pension design and structure: New lessons from behavioral finance* (pp. 83–95). Oxford, England: Oxford University Press.

Iyengar, S. S., & Lepper, M. (1999). Rethinking the value of choice: A cultural perspective on intrinsic motivation. *Journal of Personality and Social Psychology, 76*, 349–366.

Iyengar, S., & Lepper, M. (2000). When choice is demotivating: Can one desire too much of a good thing? *Journal of Personality and Social Psychology, 79*, 995–1006.

Iyengar, S. S., & Lepper, M. R. (2002). Choice and its consequences: On the costs and benefits of self-determination. In A. Tesser (Ed.), *Self and motivation: Emerging psychological perspectives* (pp. 71–96). Washington, DC: American Psychological Association.

Iyengar, S., Wells, R. E., & Schwartz, B. (2006). Doing better but feeling worse: Looking for the "best" job undermines satisfaction. *Psychological Science, 17*, 143–150.

John, O. P., Donahue, E. M., & Kentle, R. L. (1991). *The "big five" inventory—Versions 4a and 54.* Technical report. Berkeley, CA: Institute of Personality Assessment and Research.

Kadison, R. D., & DiGeronimo, T. F. (2004). *The college of the overwhelmed: The campus mental health crisis and what to do about it.* San Francisco, CA: Jossey-Bass.

Kahneman, D. (1999). Objective happiness. In D. Kahneman, E. Diener, & N. Schwarz (Eds.), *Well-being: The foundations of hedonic psychology* (pp. 3–25). New York, NY: Russell Sage Foundation.

Kitayama, S., Snibbe, A. C., Markus, H. R., & Suzuki, T., (2004). Is there any "free" choice? Self and dissonance in two cultures. *Psychological Science, 15*, 527–533.

Klerman, G. L., Lavori, P. W., Rice, J., Reich, T., Endicott, J., Andreasen, N. C., . . . Hirschfeld, R. M. A. (1985). Birth cohort trends in rates of major depressive disorder: A study of relatives of patients with affective disorder. *Archives of General Psychiatry, 42*, 689–693.

Klerman, G. L., & Weissman, M. M. (1989). Increasing rates of depression. *Journal of the American Medical Association, 261*, 2229–2235.

Landman, J. (1993). *Regret: The persistence of the possible.* New York, NY: Oxford University Press.

Lane, R. (2000). *The loss of happiness in market democracies.* New Haven, CT: Yale University Press.

Loewenstein, G., & Schkade, D. (1999). Wouldn't it be nice? Predicting future feelings. In D. Kahneman, E. Diener, & N. Schwarz (Eds.), *Well-being: The foundations of hedonic psychology* (pp. 85–108). New York, NY: Russell Sage Foundation.

Loomes, G., & Sugden, R. (1982). Regret theory: An alternative theory of rational choice under uncertainty. *Economic Journal, 92*, 805–824.

Luthar, S. S., & Latendresse, S. J. (2005). Children of the affluent: Challenges to well-being. *Current Directions in Psychological Science, 14,* 49–52.

Lyubomirsky, S., & Lepper, H. S. (1999). A measure of subjective happiness: Preliminary reliability and construct validation. *Social Indicators Research, 46,* 137–155.

Lyubomirsky, S., & Ross, L. (1997). Hedonic consequences of social comparison: A contrast of happy and unhappy people. *Journal of Personality and Social Psychology, 73,* 1141–1157.

Lyubomirsky, S., & Ross, L. (1999). Changes in attractiveness of elected, rejected, and precluded alternatives: A comparison of happy and unhappy individuals. *Journal of Personality and Social Psychology, 76,* 988–1007.

Lyubomirsky, S., Tucker, K. L., & Kasri, F. (2001). Responses to hedonically-conflicting social comparisons: Comparing happy and unhappy people. *European Journal of Social Psychology, 31,* 1–25.

Maier, S. F., & Seligman, M. E. P. (1976). Learned helplessness: Theory and evidence. *Journal of Experimental Psychology: General, 105,* 3–46.

Markus, H. R., & Kitayama, S. (1991). Culture and the self: Implications for cognition, emotion, and motivation. *Psychological Review, 98,* 224–253.

Markus, H. R., & Schwartz, B. (2010). Does choice mean freedom and well being? *Journal of Consumer Research, 37,* 344–355.

Michalos, A. C. (1980). Satisfaction and happiness. *Social Indicators Research, 8,* 385–422.

Michalos, A. C. (1986). Job satisfaction, marital satisfaction, and the quality of life: A review and a preview. In F. M. Andrews (Ed.), *Research on the quality of life* (pp. 57–83). Ann Arbor: Institute for Social Research, University of Michigan.

Myers, D. (2000). *The American paradox.* New Haven, CT: Yale University Press.

Nenkov, G. Y., Morrin, M., Schwartz, B., Ward, A., & Hulland, J. (2008). A short form of the Maximization Scale: Factor structure, reliability and validity studies. *Judgment and Decision Making, 3,* 371–388.

Overmier, J. B., & Seligman, M. E. P. (1967). Effects of inescapable shock upon subsequent escape and avoidance behavior. *Journal of Comparative and Physiological Psychology, 63,* 23–33.

Peterson, C., & Seligman, M. E. P. (1984). Causal explanations as a risk factor for depression: Theory and evidence. *Psychological Review, 91,* 347–374.

Robbins, A., & Wilner, A. (2001). *Quarterlife crisis: The unique challenges of life in your twenties.* New York, NY: Putnam.

Roese, N. J. (1997). Counterfactual thinking. *Psychological Bulletin, 121,* 133–148.

Roets, A., Schwartz, B., & Guan, Y. (2012). The tyranny of choice: A cross-cultural investigation of maximizing-satisficing effects on well-being. *Judgment and Decision Making, 7,* 689–704.

Rosenberg, M. (1965). *Society and the adolescent self-image.* Princeton, NJ: Princeton University Press.

Ryan, R. M., & Deci, E. L. (2000). Self-determination theory and the facilitation of intrinsic motivation, social development, and well-being. *American Psychologist, 55,* 68–78.

Savani, K., Markus, H. R., Naidu, N. V. R., Kumar, S., & Berlia, N. (2010). What counts as a choice? U.S. Americans are more likely than Indians to construe actions as choices. *Psychological Science, 21,* 391–398.

Scheibehenne, B., Greifeneder, R., & Todd, P. M. (2009). What moderates the too-much-choice effect? *Psychology & Marketing, 26,* 229–253.

Scheier, M. F., & Carver, C. S. (1985). Optimism, coping, and health: Assessment and implications of generalized outcome expectations. *Health Psychology, 4,* 219–247.

Schwartz, B. (1994). *The costs of living: How market freedom erodes the best things in life.* New York, NY: Norton.

Schwartz, B. (2000). Self-determination: The tyranny of freedom. *American Psychologist, 55,* 79–88.

Schwartz, B. (2004). *The paradox of choice: Why more is less.* New York, NY: Ecco Press.

Schwartz, B. (2009). Be careful what you wish for: The dark side of freedom. In R. M. Arkin, K. C. Oleson, & P. J. Carroll (Eds.), *Handbook of the uncertain self: Perspectives from social and personality psychology* (pp. 62–77). New York, NY: Psychology Press.

Schwartz, B. (2012). Choice, freedom, and autonomy. In P. R. Shaver & M. Mikulincer (Eds.), *Meaning, mortality, and choice: The social psychology of existential concerns* (pp. 271–288). Washington, DC: APA Press.

Schwartz, B., Markus, H. R., & Snibbe, A. C. (2006, February 26). Is freedom just another word for many things to buy? *New York Times Magazine,* 14–15.

Schwartz, B., & Sommers, R. (2013). Affective forecasting and well being. In D. Reisberg (Ed.), *Oxford handbook of cognitive psychology* (pp. 704–716). New York, NY: Oxford University Press.

Schwartz, B., Ward, A., Monterosso, J., Lyubomirsky, S., White, K., & Lehman, D. R. (2002). Maximizing versus satisficing: Happiness is a matter of choice. *Journal of Personality and Social Psychology, 83,* 1178–1197.

Seligman, M. E. P. (1975). *Helplessness: On depression, development, and death.* San Francisco, CA: W. H. Freeman.

Seligman, M. E. P., & Maier, S. F. (1967). Failure to escape traumatic shock. *Journal of Experimental Psychology, 74,* 1–9.

Simon, H. A. (1955). A behavioral model of rational choice. *Quarterly Journal of Economics, 59,* 99–118.

Simon, H. A. (1956). Rational choice and the structure of the environment. *Psychological Review, 63,* 129–138.

Simon, H. A. (1957). *Models of man, social and rational: Mathematical essays on rational human behavior.* New York, NY: Wiley.

Snibbe, A. C., & Markus, H. R. (2005). You can't always get what you want: Social class, agency, and choice. *Journal of Personality and Social Psychology, 88,* 703–720.

Taylor, C. (1989). *Sources of the self.* Cambridge, MA: Harvard University Press.

Taylor, C. (1992a). *The ethics of authenticity.* Cambridge, MA: Harvard University Press.

Taylor, C. (1992b). *Multiculturalism and the "politics of recognition."* Princeton, NJ: Princeton University Press.

Thaler, R. H., & Sunstein, C. R. (2008). *Nudge.* New Haven, CT: Yale University Press.

Weiner, B. (1985). An attributional theory of achievement motivation and emotion. *Psychological Review, 92,* 548–573.

Wieczorkowska, G., & Burnstein, E. (1999). Adapting to the transition from socialism to capitalism in Poland: The role of screening strategies in social change. *Psychological Science, 10,* 98–105.

Zeelenberg, M., & Beattie, J. (1997). Consequences of regret aversion 2: Additional evidence for effects of feedback on decision making. *Organizational Behavior and Human Decision Processes, 67,* 63–78.

CHAPTER 9

# A Self-Determination Theory Perspective on Fostering Healthy Self-Regulation From Within and Without

KIRK WARREN BROWN and RICHARD M. RYAN

M ANY THEORIES VIEW motivation as a unitary phenomenon that varies only in its strength. Yet a deeper analysis readily shows that individuals vary not only in how much motivation they possess but also in the orientation or type of motivation that energizes their behavior. For example, some people go to work each day because they find their jobs interesting, meaningful, even enjoyable, whereas others may do the same thing only because financial pressures demand it. Similarly, some students study out of a deep curiosity and an inner desire to learn, whereas others study only to obtain good grades or meet requirements. In these examples, both groups may be highly motivated, but the nature and focus of the motivation—that is, the "why" of the person's behavior—clearly varies, as do the consequences. For instance, the curious student may learn more than the required material, process it more deeply, talk more with others about it, and remember it more enduringly. This difference may not show up immediately on a test score, but it may have many ramifications for the student's emotional and intellectual development.

Self-determination theory (SDT; Deci & Ryan, 1985; Ryan & Deci, 2000) argues that motivational orientations that guide behavior have important consequences for healthy behavioral regulation and psychological well-being. Self-determination theory distinguishes between various types of motivation based on the implicit or explicit reasons or goals that give impetus to behavior. Among the ways in which motivation varies, of primary consideration is the relative autonomy of an individual's activity. Autonomously motivated behavior is self-endorsed, volitional, and done willingly; that is, it is self-determined. In contrast, behavior that lacks autonomy is motivated by real or perceived controls, restrictions, and pressures, arising either from social contextual or internal forces.

The importance of the relative autonomy of motivated behavior is borne out by evidence suggesting that autonomy is endorsed as a primary need and source of satisfaction to people across diverse cultures (Sheldon, Elliot, Kim, & Kasser, 2001) and promotes positive outcomes in varied cultural contexts as well (e.g., Chirkov, Ryan, Kim, & Kaplan, 2003; Jang, Reeve, Ryan, & Kim, 2009). The fundamental nature of this motivational dimension is also seen at the level of social groups. Over the course of recorded history, autonomy and self-determination have often been rallying cries among those seeking social change in the midst of oppressive or restrictive political or economic climates. Most importantly for the present discussion, however, the relative autonomy of behavior has important consequences for the quality of experience and performance in every domain of behavior, from health care to religious practice, and from education to work. In this chapter, we discuss the nature of motivation in terms of its relative autonomy and review evidence in support of its role in positive psychological and behavioral outcomes. In accord with the theme of this volume, a central focus of this discussion is the practical implications of this work—specifically, how to foster autonomy. We begin by describing variations in the orientation of motivations as outlined within SDT. We then address factors that impact motivation at two levels:

1. How motivators and social contexts can foster or undermine autonomous motivation.
2. How individuals can best access and harness self-regulatory powers from within.

## THE NATURE OF AUTONOMOUS REGULATION

For more than three decades, scholarship in motivation has highlighted the primary distinction between intrinsic and extrinsic reasons for behavioral engagement. Intrinsic motivation represents a natural inclination toward assimilation, exploration, interesting activity, and mastery. Activities are intrinsically motivated when they are done for the interest and enjoyment they provide. In contrast, extrinsically motivated activities are those done for instrumental reasons or performed as a means to some separable end. This basic motivational distinction has important functional value, but SDT takes a more nuanced view, postulating a spectrum model of regulation, wherein behavior can be guided by intrinsic motivation and by several forms of extrinsic motivation (Ryan & Deci, 2000). These extrinsic motivations can range from those that entail mere passive compliance or external control to those that are characterized by active personal commitment and meaningfulness. That is, even extrinsic motives vary in the degree to which they are autonomous or self-determined and, therefore, according to SDT, have different consequences for well-being and the quality and persistence of action.

A subtheory within SDT, organismic integration theory (OIT), details this continuum of motivation and the contextual factors that either support or hinder internalization and integration of the regulation of behavior (Deci & Ryan, 1985; Ryan & Deci, 2000). Figure 9.1 displays the taxonomy of motivational types described by OIT, arranged from left to right according to the extent to which behavior is externally or internally regulated. At the far left of the continuum is amotivation, representing a non-self-regulated state in which behavior is performed without intent or will or is not engaged in at all. Amotivation occurs when an individual can assign no meaning or value to the behavior, feels incompetent to perform it, or does not expect a desired outcome to result from performing it. The rest of the continuum displayed in Figure 9.1 outlines five conceptually and empirically distinct types of intentional behavioral regulation. At the far right is intrinsic motivation, the doing of an activity for its inherent enjoyment and interest. Such behavior is highly autonomous and represents a gold standard against which the relative autonomy of other forms of

| Quality of Behavior | Nonautonomous ......................................................................................... Autonomous | | | | | |
|---|---|---|---|---|---|---|
| Type of Motivation | Amotivation | Extrinsic Motivation | | | | Intrinsic Motivation |
| Type of Regulation | Nonregulation | External Regulation | Introjected Regulation | Identified Regulation | Integrated Regulation | Intrinsic Regulation |
| Locus of Causality | Impersonal | External | Somewhat External | Somewhat Internal | Internal | Internal |
| Regulatory Processes | Nonintentional, Nonvaluing, Incompetence, Lack of Control | Compliance, External Rewards and Punishments | Self-Control, Ego-Involvement, Internal Rewards and Punishments | Personal Importance, Conscious Valuing | Congruence, Conscious Synthesis with Self | Interest, Enjoyment, Inherent Satisfaction |

**Figure 9.1** The autonomy continuum showing types of motivation and their corresponding regulatory styles, processes, and loci of causality.

regulation are measured. Intrinsic motivation has been associated with a number of positive outcomes, including creativity (e.g., Amabile, 1996), enhanced task performance (Grolnick & Ryan, 1989; Murayama et al., in press), and higher psychological well-being (Vansteenkiste & Ryan, 2013).

On the spectrum between amotivation and intrinsic motivation lie four types of extrinsic motivation that vary in the degree of autonomy that each affords. Least autonomous among these types of extrinsic motivation is external regulation. Externally regulated behaviors are performed in accord with some external contingency—to obtain reward or avoid punishment or to otherwise comply with a salient demand. The phenomenology of external regulation is one of feeling controlled by forces or pressures outside the self, or, in attributional terms, behavior is perceived as having an external locus of causality (DeCharms, 1968; Ryan & Deci, 2004).

Behavior arising from introjected regulation is similar to that which is externally regulated in that it is controlled, but in this second form of extrinsic motivation, behavior is performed to meet self-approval-based contingencies. Thus, when operating from introjection, a person behaves to attain ego rewards such as pride or to avoid guilt, anxiety, or disapproval from self or others. Introjection has also been described as contingent self-esteem (e.g., Deci & Ryan, 1995; Ryan & Brown, 2003). A common manifestation of introjection is ego involvement (Ryan, 1982), in which an individual is motivated to demonstrate ability to maintain a sense of self-worth. Although ego involvement can be highly motivating under particular circumstances (e.g., Ryan, Koestner, & Deci, 1991), it is associated with a number of negative consequences, including greater stress, anxiety, self-handicapping, and unstable persistence.

Identified regulation is a more autonomous form of extrinsic motivation, wherein a behavior is consciously valued and embraced as personally important. For example, a person may write daily in a journal because he or she values the self-insight and clarity of mind that come from that activity. Identification represents, in attributional terms, an internal perceived locus of causality—it feels relatively volitional or self-determined. Thus, identified motivation is associated with better persistence and performance compared to behaviors motivated by external or introjected regulations, as well as more positive affect.

Finally, the most autonomous form of extrinsic motivation is integrated regulation. Behaviors that are integrated are not only valued and meaningful but also consciously assimilated into the self and brought into alignment with other values and goals. Like behaviors that are intrinsically motivated, integrated actions have an internal locus of causality and are self-endorsed, but because they are performed to obtain a separable outcome rather than as an end in themselves, they are still regarded as extrinsic.

Self-determination theory posits that as children grow older, most socialized behavior comes to be regulated in a more autonomous fashion because there is an overarching developmental tendency to seek the integration of behavioral regulation into the self (Chandler & Connell, 1987; Ryan, 1995). But this integrative process is not inevitable, and there are many factors that can disrupt or derail this tendency. Thus, the motivational model outlined in Figure 9.1 does not propose that individuals typically progress through the various forms of extrinsic motivation on their way to integrated or intrinsic regulation. Instead, when new behaviors are undertaken, any one of these motivational starting points may be predominant as a function of the content of the goal and the presence of social and situational supports, pressures, and opportunities.

The greater internalization and integration of regulation into the self, the more self-determined behavior is felt to be. Early empirical support for this claim was obtained by Ryan and Connell (1989) in a study of achievement behaviors among elementary school children. Assessing external, introjected, identified, and intrinsic reasons for engaging in academically related behaviors (e.g., doing homework), they found that the four types of regulation were intercorrelated in a quasi-simplex or ordered pattern that lent empirical support to the theorized continuum of relative autonomy. The children's differing motivational styles for academic work were also related to their achievement-related attitudes and psychological adjustment. Students whose work was done for external reasons showed less interest and weaker effort, and they tended to blame teachers and others for negative academic outcomes. Introjected regulation was related to effort expenditure but also to higher anxiety and maladaptive coping with failure. Identified regulation was associated with more interest and enjoyment of school, greater effort, and a greater tendency to cope adaptively with stressful circumstances.

Recent research has extended these findings on motivational style and outcome, showing, for example, that more autonomous extrinsic motivation is associated with greater academic engagement and performance, lower dropout rates, higher quality learning, and greater psychological well-being across cultures (see Deci & Ryan, 2012, for review). Positive outcomes linked with higher relative autonomy have also been found in the health care and psychotherapy domains, in which greater internalization of treatment protocols has been associated with higher levels of adherence and success. In fact, a number of clinical trials in areas such as obesity, medication adherence, smoking, dental hygiene, and other areas have demonstrated efficacy for SDT techniques in enhancing behavioral and health outcomes (Ryan, Patrick, Deci, &Wiliams, 2008). A number of studies relating autonomy and autonomy support to better outcomes in treatment of psychological issues have also emerged (e.g., Zuroff et al., 2007).

In fact, autonomous regulation of behavior has been associated with positive outcomes in a wide variety of life domains, including relationships (e.g., LaGuardia & Patrick, 2008), work (e.g., Ryan, Bernstein, & Brown, 2010), religion (e.g., Baard & Aridas, 2001), virtual worlds (e.g., Rigby & Ryan, 2011), and environmental practices (Pelletier, 2002), among others. These benefits include greater persistence in, and effectiveness of, behavior and enhanced well-being.

## FACILITATING AUTONOMOUS FUNCTIONING THROUGH SOCIAL SUPPORT

Considerable research has been devoted to examining social conditions that promote autonomous regulation, including both intrinsic motivation and more autonomous forms of extrinsic motivation. Despite the fact that the human organism has evolved capacities and tendencies toward the autonomous regulation of behavior (Deci & Ryan, 2000), biological, social, and other environmental influences can facilitate or undermine those tendencies. An understanding of the nature of these influences is important because, as reviewed previously, autonomous versus heteronomous functioning has manifold personal consequences.

### Supporting Intrinsic Motivation

As already noted, intrinsic motivation represents a distinctly autonomous form of functioning, in that behavior is performed for its own sake and is wholly self-endorsed. Cognitive evaluation theory (CET), another subtheory within SDT, was proposed by Deci and Ryan (1980, 1985) to specify the social contextual features that can impact, both positively and negatively, intrinsic motivational processes. Cognitive evaluation theory began with the assumption that although intrinsic motivation is a propensity of the human organism, it will be catalyzed or facilitated in circumstances that support its expression and hindered under social circumstances that undercut it. Among its major tenets, CET specifies that intrinsic motivation depends on conditions that allow (a) an experience of autonomy or an internal perceived locus of causality, and (b) the experience of effectance or competence. Factors that undermine the experiences of either autonomy or competence, therefore, undermine intrinsic motivation.

Among the most controversial implications of CET is the proposition that contexts in which rewards are used to control behavior undermine intrinsic motivation and yield many hidden costs that were unanticipated by reward-based theories of motivation. Although much debated, the most definitive summary of that research has shown that extrinsic rewards made contingent on task performance reliably weaken intrinsic motivation (Deci, Koestner, & Ryan, 1999). Cognitive evaluation theory specifies that this occurs because contingent rewards, as typically employed, foster the recipient's perception that the cause of their behavior lies in forces external to the self. Individuals come to see themselves as performing the behavior for the reward or the rewarding agent and thus not because of their own interests, values, or motivations. Accordingly, behavior becomes reward dependent, and any intrinsic motivation that might have been manifest is undermined. However, rewards are not the only type of influence that undermines intrinsic motivation. When motivators attempt to move people through the use of threats, deadlines, demands, external evaluations, and imposed goals, intrinsic motivation is diminished (Deci & Ryan, 2000).

Evidence also highlights factors that can enhance intrinsic motivation. Laboratory and field research show that the provision of choice and opportunities for self-direction and the acknowledgment of perspectives and feelings serve to enhance intrinsic motivation through a greater felt sense of autonomy. Such factors can yield a variety of salutary consequences. For example, evidence indicates that teachers who support autonomy (see Reeve, Bolt, & Cai, 1999, for specific teacher strategies) spark curiosity, a desire for challenge, and higher levels of intrinsic motivation in their students. In contrast, a predominantly controlling teaching style leads to a loss of initiative and less effective learning, especially when that learning concerns complex material or requires conceptual, creative processing (e.g., Jang et al., 2009).

In a similar vein, children of parents who are more autonomy-supportive show a stronger mastery orientation, manifest in greater spontaneous exploration and extension of their capacities, than children of more controlling parents (Grolnick & Apostoleris, 2002).

The support of autonomy in fostering intrinsic motivation is thus very critical. Yet, although autonomy support is a central means by which intrinsic motivation is facilitated, CET specifies that supports for the other basic psychological needs proposed by SDT, namely competence and relatedness, are also important, especially when a sense of autonomy is also present. Deci and Ryan (1985) review evidence showing that providing optimal challenge, positive performance feedback, and freedom from controlling evaluations facilitate intrinsic motivation, whereas negative performance feedback undermines it. Vallerand and Reid (1984) found that these effects are mediated by the individual's own perceived competence.

Intrinsic motivation also appears to more frequently occur in relationally supportive contexts. This is so from the beginning of development. As Bowlby (1979) suggested and research has confirmed (e.g., Frodi, Bridges, & Grolnick, 1985), the intrinsic motivational tendencies evident in infants' exploratory behavior are strongest when a child is securely attached to a caregiver. Self-determination theory further argues that a sense of relatedness can facilitate intrinsic motivation in older children and adults, a claim also supported by research (e.g., Ryan, Stiller, & Lynch, 1994). Practically, when teachers, parents, managers, and other motivators convey caring and acceptance, the motivatee is freed up to invest in interests and challenges that the situation presents.

In sum, research has supported CET by demonstrating how the expression of intrinsic motivation is supported by social conditions that promote a sense of autonomy, competence, and relatedness, which together make up the triad of basic psychological needs specified within SDT (Deci & Ryan, 2000; Ryan & Deci, 2000). However, by definition, intrinsic motivation will be manifest only for activities that potentially offer inherent interest or enjoyment to the individual—for example, those that offer novelty, have aesthetic value, or produce excitement. For activities that do not carry such appeal, the principles of CET do not apply. However, the role of autonomy in positive experience is not limited to intrinsically motivated behavior, and, in fact, intrinsically motivated behavior may be comparatively rare in everyday life (Ryan & Deci, 2000). This brings us to a discussion of the wide range of behaviors that have an extrinsic motivational basis.

## Supporting More Autonomous Extrinsic Motivation

Beginning in early childhood, the ratio of intrinsic to extrinsic motivation begins to shift dramatically in the direction of extrinsic activities. Indeed, as we grow older, most of us spend less and less time simply pursuing what interests us and more and more time pursuing goals and responsibilities that the social world obliges us to perform (Ryan, 1995). Given both the prevalence of extrinsic motivation and the positive consequences that accrue from autonomous functioning, an issue of key importance is how the self-regulation of these imposed activities can be facilitated by socializing agents such as parents, teachers, physicians, bosses, coaches, or therapists. Self-determination theory frames this issue in terms of how to foster the internalization and integration of the value and regulation of extrinsically motivated behavior. As noted already, internalization refers to the adoption of a value or regulation, and integration involves the incorporation of that regulation into the sense of self, such that the behavior feels self-endorsed and volitional.

Empirical research indicates that the presence of social supports for the psychological needs of competence, relatedness, and autonomy appears to foster not only the autonomous functioning seen in intrinsically motivated behavior but also the internalization and integration of behaviors focused on extrinsic goals. For example, when individuals do not have intrinsic reasons for engaging in a particular behavior, they do so primarily because the activity is prompted, modeled, or valued by another person or a group to which the individual feels, or wants to feel, in relationship. Organismic integration theory posits that internalization is more likely to occur when supports for feelings of relatedness or connectedness are present. For example, Ryan et al. (1994) found that children who felt securely attached to their parents and teachers showed more complete internalization of the regulation of academic behaviors.

There is a very close relationship between people's sense of relatedness, or secure attachment, and autonomy support. Ryan and Lynch (1989) found that adolescents who experienced their parents as accepting and noncontrolling were those who felt securely attached. In a more recent examination of within-person, cross-relationship variations in security of attachment, La Guardia, Ryan, Couchman, and Deci (2000) found that autonomy support was crucial to feeling securely attached or intimately related. Indeed, many studies support this connection, which itself is proposed in theories of attachment. As Bretherton (1987) argues, "In the framework of attachment theory, maternal respect for the child's autonomy is an aspect of sensitivity to the infant's signals" (p. 1075). Within SDT, this connection between autonomy support and intimacy is viewed as a lifelong dynamic, one evident across diverse cultures (Lynch, LaGuardia, & Ryan, 2009).

Research also indicates that perceived competence is important to the internalization of extrinsically motivated behaviors. Individuals who feel efficacious in performing an activity are more likely to adopt it as their own, and conditions that support the development of relevant skills, by offering optimal challenges and effectance-relevant feedback, facilitate internalization (Deci & Ryan, 2000). This analysis also suggests that activities that are too difficult for an individual to perform—those that demand a level of physical or psychological maturation that a child has not reached, for example—will likely be externally regulated or introjected at best.

Internalization also depends on supports for autonomy. Contexts that use controlling strategies such as salient rewards and punishments or evaluative, self-esteem-hooking pressures are least likely to lead people to value activities as their own. This is not to say that controls don't work to produce behavior—decades of operant psychology prove that they can. It is rather that the more salient the external control over a person's behavior, the more the person is likely to be merely externally regulated or introjected in his or her actions. Consequently, the person does not develop a value or investment in the behaviors, but instead remains dependent on external controls. Thus, parents who reward, force, or cajole their child to do homework are more likely to have a child who does so only when rewarded, cajoled, or forced. The salience of external controls undermines the acquisition of self-responsibility. Alternatively, parents who supply reasons, empathize with difficulties overcoming obstacles, and use a minimum of external incentives are more likely to foster a sense of willingness and value for work in their child (Grolnick & Apostoleris, 2002).

The internalization process depicted in Figure 9.1 can end at various points, and social contexts can facilitate or undermine the relative autonomy of an individual's motivation along this continuum. For instance, a teenager might initially introject the need to act a certain way in an attempt to enhance or maintain relatedness to a parent who values it. However, depending on how controlling or autonomy-supportive the context is, that introjection might evolve upward toward greater self-acceptance or integration, or downward toward external regulation. Similarly, a person who finds a behavior valuable and important, that is, regulated by identification, may, if contexts become too demanding, begin to feel incompetent and fall into amotivation.

The more integrated an extrinsic regulation, the more a person is consciously aware of the meaning and worth inherent in the conduct of a behavior and has found congruence, or an integral "fit" between that behavior and other behaviors in his or her repertoire. Integrated regulation reflects a holistic processing of circumstance and possibilities (Kuhl & Fuhrmann, 1998; Ryan & Rigby, in press; Weinstein, Przybylski, & Ryan, 2013) and is facilitated by a perceived sense of choice, volition, and freedom from social and situational controls to think, feel, or act in a particular way. It is also facilitated by the provision of meaning for an extrinsic action—a nonarbitrary rationale for why something is important. Such supports for autonomy encourage the active endorsement of values, perceptions, and overt behaviors as the individual's own and are essential to identified or integrated behavioral regulation.

A number of laboratory and field research studies provide support for this theorizing and concrete examples of the integrative process described here. An experimental study by Deci, Eghrari, Patrick, and Leone (1994) showed that offering a meaningful rationale for an uninteresting behavior, in conjunction with supports for autonomy and relatedness, promoted internalization and integration. Grolnick and Ryan (1989) found that parents who were autonomy-supportive of their children's academic goals but also positively involved and caring fostered greater internalization of those goals and better teacher- and student-rated self-motivation. These and related findings have implications for efforts aimed at enhancing student motivation (see also Grolnick & Apostoleris, 2002; Vallerand, 1997).

The role of supportive versus undermining conditions also has practical significance in the fields of health care and psychotherapy, in which issues of compliance with and adherence to treatment are of great concern, not only to frontline care providers with a vested interest in patients' health, but also to those attentive to the financial and other consequences associated with treatment (non)compliance. For example, Williams, Rodin, Ryan, Grolnick, and Deci (1998) found that patients who were more likely to endorse statements such as "My doctor listens to how I would like to do things" showed better adherence to prescription medication regimens than patients who regarded their physicians as more controlling of their treatment plans. The patients' own autonomous motivation for medication adherence mediated the relation between perception of physician autonomy support and actual adherence.

The theoretical perspective of SDT also finds convergence with clinical practices emphasized in Miller and Rollnick's (2002) Motivational Interviewing. Several investigators have suggested that some of the demonstrated clinical efficacy of motivational interviewing reflects the importance of this strategy's synergistic emphasis on autonomy support, relatedness, and competency building (e.g., Markland, Ryan, Tobin, & Rollnick, 2005).

## FACILITATING AUTONOMOUS REGULATION FROM THE INSIDE

To date, work on the promotion of autonomous functioning has been largely devoted to an examination of social contextual factors. That is, SDT has been preoccupied with the social psychology of motivation, or how supports for autonomy, competence, and relatedness facilitate self-motivation. Of equal importance is how processes within the psyche are associated with the promotion of autonomous regulation and how these processes can be facilitated. It is clear that even when environments provide an optimal motivational climate, autonomous regulation requires both an existential commitment to act congruently, as well as the cultivation of the potential possessed by almost everyone to reflectively consider their behavior and its fit with personal values, needs, and interests (Vansteenkiste & Ryan, 2013). We next discuss recent research on the role that internal resources centered in consciousness and pertaining to awareness can play in fostering more autonomous regulation. Discussion of this new research focuses particularly on the concept of mindfulness.

A number of influential organismic and cybernetic theories of behavioral regulation place central emphasis on attention, the capacity to bring consciousness to bear on events and experience as they unfold in real time (e.g., Carver & Scheier, 1981; Deci & Ryan, 1985; Varela, Thompson, & Rosch, 1991). These perspectives agree that the power of awareness and attention lies in bringing to consciousness information and sensibilities necessary for healthy self-regulation to occur. The more fully an individual is apprised of what is occurring internally and in the environment, the more healthy, adaptive, and value-consistent his or her behavior is likely to be.

Just as social forces can both inhibit and enhance healthy behavioral regulation, so too can factors associated with the enhancement or diminishment of attention and awareness. As a regulatory tool, our usual day-to-day state of attention is limited in two important ways that have cognitive and motivational bases. First, the usual reach of attention is quite restricted. Under normal circumstances, we are consciously aware of only a small fraction of our perceptions and actions (Varela et al., 1991). Evidence for such attentional limits comes from research on automatic or implicit processes. Automatic cognitive and behavioral processes are those that are activated and guided without conscious awareness. Accumulating research shows that much of our cognitive, emotional, and overt behavioral activity is automatically driven (Bargh, 1997).

The second way in which attention is limited pertains to its motivated selectivity. Among the information that is allowed into awareness, a high priority is placed on that which is relevant to the self, with the highest priority given to information that is relevant to self-preservation, in both biological and psychological terms. In developed societies, where threats to the biological organism are not usually at the forefront of concern, self-concept preservation is a primary motivation, within which is implicated our general tendency to evaluate events and experiences as good or bad for the self (Dickerson & Kemeny, 2004; Langer, 2002). Reviewing the self-regulation literature, Baumeister, Heatherton, and Tice (1994) noted that, in general, individuals give relatively low priority to accurate self-knowledge. Instead, they pay most attention to information that enhances and validates the self-concept. The invested nature of attention can thus lead to the defensive redirection of attention away from phenomena that threaten the concept of self.

Both attentional limits and selectivity biases can have adaptive value in many circumstances, but they also can hinder optimal regulation of behavior. Information we do not want to be conscious of can be actively and conveniently displaced from focal attention and even from the wider field of awareness, in favor of other information more agreeable to the self. Attentional limits and biases provide ripe conditions for compartmentalization or fracturing of the self, wherein some aspects of self are placed on the stage of awareness and play a role in an individual's behavior, whereas others are actively kept backstage, out of the spotlight of attention. For purposes of behavioral regulation, the cost of such motivated attentional limits and biases lies in the controlled nature of behavior that can result, in which the aim is to remain responsive to internal and external forces or pressures toward ego-enhancement and preservation, rather than the sense of valuing, interest, and enjoyment that characterizes autonomous functioning. An ego-invested motivational orientation uses attention to select and shape experiences or distort them in memory in a way that defends and protects against ego-threat and clings to experiences or an interpretation of them that affirms the ego (e.g., Brown, Ryan, Creswell, & Niemiec, 2008; Hodgins & Knee, 2002). The self-centered use of attention outlined here hinders the openness to events and experience that could allow for an integration of self-aspects that could permit fuller, more authentic functioning.

MINDFULNESS AND THE ENHANCEMENT OF BEHAVIORAL REGULATION

The limits and biases of attention discussed here are not immutable. Regarding automatic processes, research has provided a detailed cognitive specification of the conditions under which behavior can be implicitly triggered (see Bargh & Ferguson, 2000). But research has also begun to show how such behavior can be modified or overridden (e.g., Dijksterhuis & van Knippenberg, 2000; Macrae & Johnston, 1998). Ample evidence indicates that the enactment of automatic, habitual behavior depends on a lack of attention to one's behavior and the cues that activate it. As Macrae and Johnston note, habitual action can unfold when the "lights are off and nobody's home." Similarly, automatic thought patterns thrive while they remain out of the field of awareness (Segal, Williams, & Teasdale, 2002).

Conversely, there is evidence to indicate that enhanced attention and awareness can interfere with the development and unfoldment of automatic, habitual responses. An early demonstration was provided by Hefferline, Keenan, and Harford (1959). Using a conditioning paradigm in which individuals were reinforced for a subtle hand movement, they demonstrated that those who were unaware that conditioning was taking place showed the fastest rates of learning. Individuals who were told in a vague way that they were being conditioned showed slower learning of the response. Those who were explicitly instructed to learn the movement response that was being reinforced displayed the slowest learning. Thus, the more conscious individuals were of the conditioning, the more difficult was the development of automatized behavior. More recently, Dijksterhuis and van Knippenberg (2000) compared the ease with which stereotypes about politicians, college professors, and soccer hooligans could be activated through priming, depending on whether subjects' attention to the prime-response situation and awareness of themselves in that situation were induced. Heightened attention and self-awareness were shown to override the behavioral effects of activation of all three stereotypes examined. Evidence also suggests that the enhancement of awareness through training can intervene between the initial activation of an implicit response and the consequences that would typically follow. For example, Gollwitzer (1999) describes research showing that individuals who were made aware of their automatic stereotypic reactions to elderly people and then trained to mentally counteract them when they arose through implementation intentions no longer showed an automatic activation of stereotypic beliefs.

Collectively, this research suggests that attention, when brought to bear on present realities, can introduce an element of self-direction in what would otherwise be nonconsciously regulated, controlled behavior. But if behavior is to be regulated in a self-directed or self-endorsed manner on an ongoing, day-to-day basis, a dispositionally elevated level of attention and awareness would seem essential. Several forms of trait self-awareness have been examined over the years, including self-consciousness (Fenigstein, Scheier, & Buss, 1975) and reflection (Trapnell & Campbell, 1999), but such "reflexive consciousness" constructs (Baumeister, 1999) reflect cognitive operation on the contents of consciousness, rather than a perceptual sensitivity to the mind's contents. Neither are they designed to tap attention to and awareness of an individual's behavior and ongoing situational circumstances.

*Mindfulness*   Deci and Ryan (1980) suggested that a quality of consciousness termed *mindfulness* can act as an ongoing conscious mediator between causal stimuli and behavioral responses to them, leading to dispositional resistance to shifts away from self-determined, autonomous functioning in the presence of salient primes and other behavioral controls. A decade ago, we began an intensive investigation of mindfulness (Brown & Ryan, 2003). Although there is no single definition of mindfulness (Anālayo, 2014), the concept commonly concerns an open or receptive awareness of and attention to what is taking place in the present moment (Brown & Ryan, 2003). It has similarly been described in classical Buddhist scholarship as "an alert but receptive equanimous observation" (Anālayo, 2003, p. 60) and as "watchfulness, the lucid awareness of each event that presents itself on the successive occasions of experience" (Bodhi, 2011, p. 21). The construct has a long pedigree, having been discussed for centuries in Buddhist philosophy and psychology and more recently in Western psychology (e.g., Kabat-Zinn, 2013; Langer, 1989; Linehan, 1993; Teasdale, Segal, & Williams, 1995). Aside from the apparent role of present attention and awareness in the "de-automatization" of behavior (Safran & Segal, 1990), Wilber (2000) notes that bringing this quality of consciousness to bear on facets of the self and its experience that have been alienated, ignored, or distorted is theorized by a number of personality traditions to convert "hidden subjects" into "conscious objects" that can be differentiated from, transcended, and integrated into the self. In this sense, the quality of consciousness that is mindfulness conduces to the view that "all the facts are friendly," which Rogers (1961, p. 25) believed necessary for "full functioning."

As a monitoring function, mindfulness creates a mental gap between the "I," or self (cf., James, 1890/1999), and the contents of consciousness (thoughts, emotions, and motives), one's behavior, and the environment. One consequence of this observant stance, we argue, is enhanced self-awareness and the provision of a window of opportunity to choose the form, direction, and other specifics of action—that is, to act in an autonomous manner.

Evidence for the role of mindfulness in the autonomous regulation of behavior comes from several studies. For example, using the Mindful Attention Awareness Scale (MAAS) to assess a basic form of "mindful presence," Brown and Ryan (2003) examined the role of mindfulness in facilitating autonomous behavior in daily life. The authors asked students and working adults to complete the MAAS and then to record the relative autonomy of their behavior (based on the conceptual model in Figure 9.1) at the receipt of a pager signal. This occurred three times a day on a quasirandom basis over a 2-week (students) or 3-week (adults) period. In both groups, higher scores on the MAAS predicted higher levels of autonomous behavior on a day-to-day basis.

This study also included a state measure of mindfulness. Participants specifically rated how attentive they were to the activities that had also been rated for their relative autonomy. Individuals who were more mindfully attentive to their activities also experienced more autonomous motivation to engage in those activities. The effects of trait and state mindfulness on autonomy were independent in this study, indicating that the regulatory benefits of mindfulness were not limited to those with a mindful disposition. The fact that state mindfulness and autonomous behavior were correlated in these samples bears some similarity to the intrinsically motivated autotelic, or "flow" experience (Csikszentmihalyi, 1997), in which awareness and action merge.

In fact, Csikszentmihalyi (1997) suggests that key to the autotelic personality is the individual's willingness to be present to his or her ongoing experience.

This view of the human capacity for autonomy stands in contrast to the position that most behavior is automatically driven and that conscious will may be illusory (e.g., Wegner, 2002). Although, as we noted, it is clear that much behavior is automatic, we believe this issue is more complex than it may appear (see Ryan, Legate, Niemiec, & Deci, 2012). Although automatic processes may activate behaviors in any given moment, we contend that mindfulness of motives and the actions that follow from them can lead to an overriding or redirection of such processes (see also Bargh, 1997; Deci, Ryan, Schultz, & Niemiec, in press).

For example, Levesque and Brown (2007) examined whether mindfulness could shape or override the behavioral effects of implicit, low levels of autonomy. As with other motivational orientations, such as achievement, intimacy, and power (McClelland, Koestner, & Weinberger, 1989), Levesque and Brown (2007) hypothesized that individuals would differ not only in self-attributed relative autonomy but also in the extent to which they implicitly or nonconsciously associate themselves with autonomy. Using the Implicit Association Test (IAT; Greenwald, McGhee, & Schwartz, 1998) to assess relative levels of implicit autonomy, Levesque and Brown (2007) found that MAAS-measured dispositional mindfulness moderated the degree to which implicit relative autonomy predicted day-to-day autonomy, as measured through experience-sampling. Specifically, among less mindful individuals, implicit-relative autonomy positively predicted day-to-day motivation for behavior. Among such persons, those who implicitly associated themselves with control and pressure manifested the same kind of behavioral motivation in daily life, whereas individuals with high levels of implicit autonomy behaved in accord with this automatic self-association. However, among more mindful individuals, the relation between the automatic motivational association and daily behavior was null. Mindfulness thus served an overriding functioning, such that it facilitated self-endorsed behavior, regardless of the type of implicit motivational tendency that individuals held.

Similarly, in a series of experimental studies, Niemiec et al. (2010) demonstrated that persons higher in mindfulness did not show the kind of defensive reactions reliably observed when people are threatened with mortality salience stimuli. Whereas less mindful individuals were ready to derogate out-group members when under threat, more mindful persons did not, in part because they more fully processed the threat experience.

In this vein, it is important to note that the effect of mindfulness lies not necessarily in creating psychological experiences, many of which are conditioned phenomena (Wegner, 2002) that arise spontaneously (Dennett, 1984), but in allowing for choicefulness in whether to endorse or veto the directives that consciousness brings to awareness, thereby permitting the direction of action toward self-endorsed ends (Libet, 1999; Ryan et al., 2012). Indeed, by definition, self-endorsement requires a consciousness of one's needs or values and the role of anticipated action in meeting or affirming them (Deci & Ryan, 1985). Relatedly, an individual may be aware of several competing motives at a given time, all of which cannot be satisfied. Mindfulness creates an opportunity for choices to be made that maximize the satisfaction of needs and desires within the parameters of the situation at hand (Deci & Ryan, 1980).

Mindfulness appears not only to foster self-endorsed activity at the level of day-to-day behavior, but also to encourage the adoption of higher order goals and values that reflect healthy regulation. Kasser and colleagues (e.g., Kasser & Ryan, 1996; Kasser, Chapter 6, this volume) have shown that intrinsic values—for personal development, affiliation, and community contribution, for example—have an inherent relationship to basic psychological need satisfaction; that is, they directly fulfill needs for autonomy, competence, and relatedness. Extrinsic values, in contrast, including aspirations for wealth, popularity, and personal image, are pursued for their instrumental value and typically fulfill basic needs only indirectly, at best. Moreover, extrinsic goals are often motivated by introjected pressures or external controls (Kasser, 2002). Accordingly, accumulating research indicates that the relative centrality of intrinsic and extrinsic values has significant consequences for subjective well-being, risk behavior, and other outcomes (see Kasser, Chapter 6, this volume). It is thus noteworthy that recent research has shown that mindfulness is associated with a stronger emphasis on intrinsic aspirations, and this values orientation is in turn related to indicators of subjective well-being and healthy lifestyle choices (Brown & Kasser, 2005). Although mindfulness directly predicts higher well-being (see Brown, Creswell, & Ryan, in press), this research also shows that its salutary effects come by facilitating self-regulation.

*Cultivating Mindfulness*  Research conducted over the past 35 years indicates that mindfulness can be enhanced through training (Brown et al., in press). In such training, individuals learn, through daily practice, to sharpen their inherent capacities to attend to and be aware of presently occurring internal, behavioral, and environmental events and experience. Mindfulness training is associated with a variety of lasting positive psychological and somatic well-being outcomes (see Grossman, Niemann, Schmidt, & Walach, 2004; Hofmann, Sawyer, Witt, & Oh, 2010). Research has begun to show that such training may conduce to more self-determined behavior. For example, Brown, Kasser, Ryan, Linley, and Orzech (2009) found that meditation training-related increases in mindfulness, as assessed by two self-report measures (including the MAAS), were related to declines in wealth-related desires. Recently, Kirk, Brown, and Downer (2014) found that individuals trained in mindfulness meditation showed neural evidence of lower susceptibility to monetary rewards. Using the Monetary Incentive Delay task (Knutson, Adams, Fong, & Hommer, 2001) while undergoing functional brain imaging, mindfulness trainees and matched controls performed equally well on the task, but the meditators showed lower neural activations in brain regions involved in reward processing—both during monetary gain and loss anticipation and receipt—indicating that the former were less susceptible to monetary incentives but without task performance costs. Such training-related reduced susceptibilities to a powerful extrinsic reward may foster enhanced behavioral regulation, a proposition to be tested in future research.

## CONCLUSION

This chapter has attempted to demonstrate that autonomous regulation of inner states and overt behavior is key to a number of positive outcomes that reflect healthy behavioral and psychological functioning. The practical value of autonomy has been demonstrated through research in a number of important life domains, including child development and education, health behavior, sport and exercise, and others. Decades of research also show that when people act autonomously, whether motivated intrinsically or extrinsically through more internalized and integrated regulation, their quality of action and sense of well-being benefits.

Judgment as to the practical utility of research on autonomy relies on evidence that this regulatory style can be promoted. We have shown here that autonomy can be facilitated both from without—through social supports—and from within, through the receptive attention and awareness to present experience that helps to characterize mindfulness. Although significant in themselves, these two sources of support are not necessarily separate and may, in fact, interact to enhance autonomous regulation. For example, an individual in a position to influence the motivation of another person or group may do so more effectively and positively when mindfulness about the effects of his or her communication style and behavior is present. Just as an individual seeking to change his or her regulatory style can benefit from greater awareness of self and attention to behavior, reason suggests that parents, teachers, supervisors, and others may draw on their own mindful capacities to facilitate the support of healthy, growth-promoting regulation in others.

Research reviewed here indicated that mindfulness can enhance self-knowledge and action that accords with the self, both of which are key to authentic action (Harter, 2002). Enhanced attention and awareness also appear to undermine the effects of past and present conditioning and the external control of behavior that it may entail. It might then be possible that a greater dose of mindfulness helps to inoculate individuals against social and cultural forces acting to inhibit or undermine choicefulness and the self-endorsement of values, goals, and behaviors. In fact, it may be difficult in today's society to live autonomously without mindfulness, considering the multitude of forces, internal and external, that often pull us in one direction or another. In a world where commercial, political, economic, and other messages seeking to capture attention, allegiance, and wallets have become ubiquitous, mindful reflection on the ways in which we wish to expend the limited resource of life energy that all of us are given seems more important than ever.

## SUMMARY POINTS

- Motivation varies according to the reasons or goals that energize behavior, and this "why" of behavior has significant emotional and intellectual consequences.
- Autonomously motivated or self-determined behavior is self-endorsed and done willingly, and promotes a variety of positive intrapersonal, interpersonal, and performance outcomes.
- Social supports for autonomy, both alone and when paired with relatedness (caring and acceptance) and the support of competence (e.g., providing optimal challenge), reliably foster autonomous behavior.
- Social supports for autonomy, competence, and relatedness also encourage the internalization and integration of behavior, thereby shifting it toward being autonomously regulated.
- Healthy behavior regulation is also facilitated by internal psychological supports, notably mindfulness.
- Mindfulness, a receptive attention to and awareness of ongoing events and experiences, can foster autonomously regulated behavior and self-endorsed, or intrinsic, goals and values.
- Training in mindfulness is associated with reduced susceptibility to extrinsic rewards that can undermine autonomy, and such training may thereby promote self-determined behavior and the manifold positive outcomes that attend it.

## REFERENCES

Amabile, T. M. (1996). *Creativity in context.* New York, NY: Westview Press.

Anālayo, B. (2003). *Satipatthāna: The direct path to realization.* Birmingham, England: Windhorse.

Anālayo, B. (2014). *Mindfulness in early Buddhism.* Unpublished manuscript, University of Hamburg, Hamburg, Germany.

Baard, P. P., & Aridas, C. (2001). *Motivating your church: How any leader can ignite intrinsic motivation and growth.* New York, NY: Crossroad.

Bargh, J. A. (1997). Automaticity in social psychology. In E. T. Higgins & A. W. Kruglanski (Eds.), *Social psychology: Handbook of basic principles* (pp. 169–183). New York, NY: Guilford Press.

Bargh, J. A., & Ferguson, M. J. (2000). Beyond behaviorism: On the automaticity of higher mental processes. *Psychological Bulletin, 126,* 925–945.

Baumeister, R. F. (1999). The nature and structure of the self: An overview. In R. F. Baumeister (Ed.), *The self in social psychology* (pp.1–20). Philadelphia, PA: Psychology Press.

Baumeister, R. F., Heatherton, T. F., & Tice, D. M. (1994). *Losing control: How and why people fail at self-regulation.* San Diego, CA: Academic Press.

Bodhi, B. (2011). What does mindfulness really mean? A canonical perspective. *Contemporary Buddhism, 12*(1), 19–39.

Bowlby, J. (1979). *The making and breaking of affectional bonds.* London, England: Tavistock.

Bretherton, I. (1987). New perspectives on attachment relations: Security, communication and internal working models. In J. Osofsky (Ed.), *Handbook of infant development* (pp. 1061–1100). New York, NY: Wiley.

Brown, K. W., Creswell, J. D., & Ryan, R. M. (Eds.). (in press). *Handbook of mindfulness: Theory and research.* New York, NY: Guilford Press.

Brown, K. W., & Kasser, T. (2005). Are psychological and ecological well-being compatible? The role of values, mindfulness, and lifestyle. *Social Indicators Research, 74,* 349–368.

Brown, K. W., Kasser, T., Ryan, R. M., Linley, P. A., & Orzech, K. (2009). When what one has is enough: Mindfulness, desire discrepancies, and subjective well-being. *Journal of Research in Personality, 43,* 727–736.

Brown, K. W., & Ryan, R. M. (2003). The benefits of being present: Mindfulness and its role in psychological well-being. *Journal of Personality and Social Psychology, 84,* 822–848.

Brown, K. W., Ryan, R. M., Creswell, J. D., & Niemiec, C. P. (2008). Beyond me: Mindful responses to social threat. In H. A. Wayment & J. J. Bauer (Eds.), *Transcending self-interest: Psychological explorations of the quiet ego* (pp. 75–84). Washington, DC: American Psychological Association.

Carver, C. S., & Scheier, M. F. (1981). *Attention and self-regulation: A control theory approach to human behavior.* New York, NY: Springer-Verlag.

Chandler, C. L., & Connell, J. P. (1987). Children's intrinsic, extrinsic and internalized motivation: A developmental study of children's reasons for liked and disliked behaviors. *British Journal of Developmental Psychology, 5,* 357–365.

Chirkov, V., Ryan, R. M., Kim, Y., & Kaplan, U. (2003). Differentiating autonomy from individualism and independence: A self-determination theory perspective on internalization of cultural orientations and well-being. *Journal of Personality and Social Psychology, 84,* 97–109.

Csikszentmihalyi, M. (1997). *Finding flow: The psychology of engagement with everyday life.* New York, NY: Basic Books.

DeCharms, R. (1968). *Personal causation.* New York, NY: Academic Press.

Deci, E. L., Eghrari, H., Patrick, B. C., & Leone, D. R. (1994). Facilitating internalization: The self-determination theory perspective. *Journal of Personality, 62,* 119–142.

Deci, E. L., Koestner, R., & Ryan, R. M. (1999). A meta-analytic review of experiments examining the effects of extrinsic rewards on intrinsic motivation. *Psychological Bulletin, 125,* 627–668.

Deci, E. L., & Ryan, R. M. (1980). Self-determination theory: When mind mediates behavior. *Journal of Mind and Behavior, 1,* 33–43.

Deci, E. L., & Ryan, R. M. (1985). *Intrinsic motivation and self-determination in human behavior.* New York, NY: Plenum Press.

Deci, E. L., & Ryan, R. M. (1995). Human autonomy: The basis for true self-esteem. In M. Kernis (Ed.), *Efficacy, agency, and self-esteem* (pp. 31–49). New York, NY: Plenum Press.

Deci, E. L., & Ryan, R. M. (2000). The "what" and "why" of goal pursuits: Human needs and the self-determination of behavior. *Psychological Inquiry, 11,* 227–268.

Deci, E. L., & Ryan, R. M. (2012). Motivation, personality, and development within embedded social contexts: An overview of self-determination theory. In R. M. Ryan (Ed.), *Oxford handbook of human motivation* (pp. 85–107). Oxford, England: Oxford University Press.

Deci, E. L., Ryan, R. M., Schultz, P. P., & Niemiec, C. P. (in press). Being aware and functioning fully: Mindfulness and interest-taking within self-determination theory. In K. W. Brown, J. D. Creswell, & R. M. Ryan (Eds.), *Handbook of mindfulness.* New York, NY: Guilford Press.

Dennett, D. (1984). *Elbow room: The varieties of free will worth wanting.* Oxford, England: Clarendon Press.

Dickerson, S. S., & Kemeny, M. E. (2004). Acute stressors and cortisol responses: A theoretical integration and synthesis of laboratory research. *Psychological Bulletin, 130,* 355–391.

Dijksterhuis, A. P., & van Knippenberg, A. D. (2000). Behavioral indecision: Effects of self-focus on automatic behavior. *Social Cognition, 18,* 55–74.

Fenigstein, A., Scheier, M. F., & Buss, A. H. (1975). Public and private self-consciousness: Assessment and theory. *Journal of Consulting and Clinical Psychology, 43,* 522–527.

Frodi, A., Bridges, L., & Grolnick, W. S. (1985). Correlates of mastery-related behavior: A short-term longitudinal study of infants in their second year. *Child Development, 56,* 1291–1298.

Gollwitzer, P. M. (1999). Implementation intentions: Strong effects of simple plans. *American Psychologist, 54,* 493–503.

Greenwald, A. G., McGhee, D. E., & Schwartz, J. L. K. (1998). Measuring individual differences in implicit cognition: The Implicit Association Test. *Journal of Personality and Social Psychology, 74,* 1464–1480.

Grolnick, W. S., & Apostoleris, N. H. (2002). What makes parents controlling. In E. L. Deci & R. M. Ryan (Eds.), *Handbook of self-determination research* (pp. 161–181). Rochester, NY: University of Rochester Press.

Grolnick, W. S., & Ryan, R. M. (1989). Parent styles associated with children's self-regulation and competence in school. *Journal of Educational Psychology, 81,* 143–154.

Grossman, P., Niemann, L., Schmidt, S., & Walach, H. (2004). Mindfulness-based stress reduction and health benefits. A meta-analysis. *Journal of Psychosomatic Research, 57*(1), 35–43.

Harter, S. (2002). Authenticity. In C. R. Snyder & S. J. Lopez (Eds.), *Handbook of positive psychology* (pp. 382–394). New York, NY: Oxford University Press.

Hefferline, R. F., Keenan, B., & Harford, R. A. (1959). Escape and avoidance conditioning in human subjects without their observation of the response. *Science, 130,* 1338–1339.

Hodgins, H. S., & Knee, C. R. (2002). The integrating self and conscious experience. In E. L. Deci & R. M. Ryan (Eds.), *Handbook of self-determination research* (pp. 87–100). Rochester, NY: University of Rochester Press.

Hofmann, S. G., Sawyer, A. T., Witt, A. A., & Oh, D. (2010). The effect of mindfulness-based therapy on anxiety and depression: A meta-analytic review. *Journal of Consulting and Clinical Psychology, 78,* 169–183.

James, W. (1890/1999). The self. In R. F. Baumeister (Ed.), *The self in social psychology* (pp. 9–77). Philadelphia, PA: Psychology Press.

Jang, H., Reeve, J., Ryan, R. M., & Kim, A. (2009). Can self-determination theory explain what underlies the productive, satisfying learning experiences of collectivistically oriented Korean students? *Journal of Educational Psychology, 101,* 644–661.

Kabat-Zinn, J. (2013). *Full catastrophe living: Using the wisdom of your body and mind to face stress, pain and illness* (Rev. ed.). New York, NY: Bantam.

Kasser, T. (2002). Sketches for a self-determination theory of values. In E. L. Deci & R. M. Ryan (Eds.), *Handbook of self-determination research* (pp. 123–140). Rochester, NY: University of Rochester Press.

Kasser, T., & Ryan, R. M. (1996). Further examining the American dream: Differential correlates of intrinsic and extrinsic goals. *Personality and Social Psychology Bulletin, 22*, 280–287.

Kirk, U., Brown, K. W., & Downer, J. (2014). *Mindfulness practitioners show attenuated neural activation to incentive delay: Evidence from brain imaging.* Manuscript submitted for publication.

Knutson, B., Adams, C. M., Fong, G. W., & Hommer, D. (2001). Anticipation of increasing monetary reward selectively recruits nucleus accembens. *Journal of Neuroscience, 21*, RC159.

Kuhl, J., & Fuhrmann, A. (1998). Decomposing self-regulation and self-control. In I. Heckhausen & C. Dweck (Eds.), *Motivation and self-regulation across the life span* (pp. 15–49). New York, NY: Cambridge University Press.

La Guardia, J. G., & Patrick, H. (2008). Self-determination theory as a fundamental theory of close relationships. *Canadian Psychology, 49*, 201–209.

La Guardia, J. G., Ryan, R. M., Couchman, C. E., & Deci, E. L. (2000). Within-person variation in security of attachment: A self-determination theory perspective on attachment, need fulfillment, and well-being. *Journal of Personality and Social Psychology, 79*, 367–384.

Langer, E. (1989). *Mindfulness.* Reading, MA: Addison-Wesley.

Langer, E. (2002). Well-being: Mindfulness versus positive evaluation. In C. R. Snyder & S. J. Lopez (Eds.), *Handbook of positive psychology* (pp. 214–230). New York, NY: Oxford University Press.

Levesque, C. S., & Brown, K. W. (2007). Overriding motivational automaticity: Mindfulness as a moderator of the influence of implicit motivation on day-to-day behavior. *Motivation and Emotion, 31*, 284–299.

Libet, B. (1999). Do we have free will? *Journal of Consciousness Studies, 6*, 47–57.

Linehan, M. M. (1993). *Cognitive-behavioral treatment of borderline personality disorder.* New York, NY: Guilford Press.

Lynch, M. F., La Guardia, J. G., & Ryan, R. M. (2009). On being yourself in different cultures: Ideal and actual self-concept, autonomy support, and well-being in China, Russia, and the United States. *Journal of Positive Psychology, 4*, 290–304.

Macrae, C. N., & Johnston, L. (1998). Help, I need somebody: Automatic action and inaction. *Social Cognition, 16*, 400–417.

Markland, D., Ryan, R. M., Tobin, V., & Rollnick, S. (2005). Motivational interviewing and Self-Determination Theory. *Journal of Social and Clinical Psychology, 24*, 811–831.

McClelland, D. C., Koestner, R., & Weinberger, J. (1989). How do self-attributed and implicit motives differ? *Psychological Review, 96*, 690–702.

Miller, W. R., & Rollnick, S. (2002). *Motivational interviewing: Preparing people to change* (2nd ed.). New York, NY: Guilford Press.

Murayama, K., Matsumoto, M., Izuma, K., Sugiura, A., Ryan, R. M., Deci, E. L. & Matsumoto, K. (in press). How self-determined choice facilitates performance: A key role of the ventromedial prefrontal cortex. *Cerebral Cortex.* doi:10.1093/cercor/bht317

Niemiec, C. P., Brown, K. W., Kashdan, T. B., Cozzolino, P. J., Breen, W. E., Levesque-Bristol, C., & Ryan, R. M. (2010). Being present in the face of existential threat: The role of trait mindfulness in reducing defensive responses to mortality salience. *Journal of Personality and Social Psychology, 99*, 344–365. doi:10.1037/a0019388

Pelletier, L. G. (2002). A motivational analysis of self-determination for pro-environmental behaviors. In E. L. Deci & R. M. Ryan (Eds.), *Handbook of self-determination research* (pp. 205–232). Rochester, NY: University of Rochester Press.

Reeve, J., Bolt, E., & Cai, Y. (1999). Autonomy-supportive teachers: How they teach and motivate students. *Journal of Educational Psychology, 91*, 537–548.

Rigby, C. S., & Ryan, R. M. (2011). *Glued to games: The attractions, promise and perils of video games and virtual worlds*. New York, NY: Praeger.

Rogers, C. R. (1961). *On becoming a person*. Boston, MA: Houghton Mifflin.

Ryan, R. M. (1982). Control and information in the intrapersonal sphere: An extension of cognitive evaluation theory. *Journal of Personality and Social Psychology, 43*, 450–461.

Ryan, R. M. (1995). Psychological needs and the facilitation of integrative processes. *Journal of Personality, 63*, 397–427.

Ryan, R. M., Bernstein, J. H., & Brown, K. W. (2010). Weekends, work, and wellbeing: Psychological need satisfactions and day of the week effects on mood, vitality, and physical symptoms. *Journal of Social and Clinical Psychology, 29*, 95–122. doi:10.1521/jscp.2010.29.1.95

Ryan, R. M., & Brown, K. W. (2003). Why we don't need self-esteem: On fundamental needs, contingent love, and mindfulness. *Psychological Inquiry, 14*, 71–76.

Ryan, R. M., & Connell, J. (1989). Perceived locus of causality and internalization: Examining reasons for acting in two domains. *Journal of Personality and Social Psychology, 57*, 749–761.

Ryan, R. M., & Deci, E. L. (2000). Self-determination theory and the facilitation of intrinsic, motivation, social development, and well-being. *American Psychologist, 55*, 68–78.

Ryan, R. M., & Deci, E. L. (2004). Autonomy is no illusion: Self-determination theory and the empirical study of authenticity, awareness, and will. In J. Greenberg, S. Koole, & T. Pyszczynski (Eds.), *Handbook of experimental existential psychology* (pp. 449–479). New York, NY: Guilford Press.

Ryan, R. M., Koestner, R., & Deci, E. L. (1991). Ego-involved persistence: When free-choice behavior is not intrinsically motivated. *Motivation and Emotion, 15*, 185–205.

Ryan, R. M., Legate, N., Niemiec, C. P., & Deci, E. L. (2012). Beyond illusions and defense: Exploring the possibilities and limits of human autonomy and responsibility through self-determination theory. In P. R. Shaver & M. Mikulincer (Eds.), *Meaning, mortality, and choice: The social psychology of existential concerns* (pp. 215–233). Washington, DC: American Psychological Association.

Ryan, R. M., & Lynch, J. (1989). Emotional autonomy versus detachment: Revisiting the vicissitudes of adolescence and young adulthood. *Child Development, 60*, 340–356.

Ryan, R. M., Patrick, H., Deci, E. L. & Williams, G. C. (2008). Facilitating health behaviour change and its maintenance: Interventions based on Self-Determination Theory. *European Health Psychologist, 10*, 1–4.

Ryan, R. M., & Rigby, C. S. (in press). Did the Buddha have a self? No-self, self and mindfulness in Buddhist thought and western psychologies. In K. W. Brown, J. D. Creswell, & R. M. Ryan (Eds.), *Handbook of mindfulness: Theory and research*. New York, NY: Guilford Press.

Ryan, R. M., Stiller, J., & Lynch, J. H. (1994). Representations of relationships to teachers, parents, and friends as predictors of academic motivation and self-esteem. *Journal of Early Adolescence, 14*, 226–249.

Safran, J. D., & Segal, Z. V. (1990). *Interpersonal process in cognitive therapy*. New York, NY: Basic Books.

Segal, Z., Williams, J. M. G., & Teasdale, J. D. (2002). *Mindfulness-based cognitive therapy for depression: A new approach to preventing relapse*. New York, NY: Guilford Press.

Sheldon, K. M., Elliot, A. J., Kim, Y., & Kasser, T. (2001). What is satisfying about satisfying events? Testing 10 candidate psychological needs. *Journal of Personality and Social Psychology, 80*, 325–339.

Teasdale, J. D., Segal, Z., & Williams, J. M. G. (1995). How does cognitive therapy prevent depressive relapse and why should attentional control (mindfulness) training help? *Behavior Research and Therapy, 33*, 25–39.

Trapnell, P. D., & Campbell, J. (1999). Private self-consciousness and the five factor model of personality: Distinguishing rumination from reflection. *Journal of Personality and Social Psychology, 76*, 284–304.

Vallerand, R. J. (1997). Toward a hierarchical model of intrinsic and extrinsic motivation. In M. P. Zanna (Ed.), *Advances in experimental social psychology* (Vol. 29, pp. 271–360). San Diego, CA: Academic Press.

Vallerand, R. J., & Reid, G. (1984). On the causal effects of perceived competence on intrinsic motivation: A test of cognitive evaluation theory. *Journal of Sport Psychology, 6,* 94–102.

Vansteenkiste, M., & Ryan, R. M. (2013). On psychological growth and vulnerability: Basic psychological need satisfaction and need frustration as a unifying principle. *Journal of Psychotherapy Integration.* doi:10.1037/a0032359

Varela, F. J., Thompson, E., & Rosch, E. (1991). *The embodied mind: Cognitive science and human experience.* Cambridge, MA: MIT Press.

Wegner, D. M. (2002). *The illusion of conscious will.* Cambridge, MA: MIT Press.

Weinstein, N., Przybylski, A. K., & Ryan, R. M. (2013). The integrative process: New research and future directions. *Current Directions in Psychological Science, 22,* 69–74.

Wilber, K. (2000). *Integral psychology: Consciousness, spirit, psychology, therapy.* Boston, MA: Shambhala.

Williams, G. C., Rodin, G. C., Ryan, R. M., Grolnick, W. S., & Deci, E. L. (1998). Autonomous regulation and long-term medication adherence in adult outpatients. *Health Psychology, 17,* 269–276.

Zuroff, D. C., Koestner, R., Moskowitz, D. S., McBride, C., Marshall, M., & Bagby, M. (2007). Autonomous motivation for therapy: A new common factor in brief treatments for depression. *Psychotherapy Research, 17,* 137–147.

# CHAPTER 10

# The Complementary Roles of Eudaimonia and Hedonia and How They Can Be Pursued in Practice

VERONIKA HUTA

MANY OF US HAVE asked ourselves: What is a good life? What makes a life worth living? These are a couple of the great existential questions. The answers we develop shape our priorities, choices, and goals, and the very way we decide what is desirable. In conceptions of a good life, the two perspectives that have figured most prominently are the hedonic view and the eudaimonic view (Ryan & Deci, 2001). Briefly, a hedonic orientation involves seeking happiness, positive affect, life satisfaction, and reduced negative affect; a eudaimonic orientation includes seeking authenticity, meaning, excellence, and personal growth (Huta & Waterman, 2013). These two perspectives have been discussed for over 2,000 years by philosophers, including Aristotle and Aristippus in ancient Greece, and more recently by early psychologists and psychiatrists, such as Maslow, Jung, and Freud. Much of the current psychology research on well-being similarly addresses hedonia and/or eudaimonia, making the hedonic–eudaimonic distinction a central concept in positive psychology, as evidenced by its frequent appearance in the first edition of this volume. It is time for us to consider more systematically how these concepts might be applied in practice.

First, I discuss existing definitions and research. I then venture into more uncharted territory. I pull together a characterization of the complementary natures of hedonia and eudaimonia to clarify why the two concepts are so central to discussions of well-being, and then I propose specific strategies for pursuing hedonia and eudaimonia in practice.

## DIFFERENT CATEGORIES OF DEFINITIONS AND COMMON ELEMENTS ACROSS DEFINITIONS

Following this section, I use one specific approach to defining hedonia and eudaimonia, but before I do, I would like to outline the full range of approaches.

In a systematic review of psychology definitions of eudaimonia and hedonia (Huta & Waterman, 2013), we found that the definitions fall into four different *categories of analysis.* The categories are orientations, behaviors, experiences, and functioning, as detailed below.

Definitions of eudaimonia have been as follows:

1. *Orientations*: Orientations, values, motives, and goals, that is, the "why" of behavior—for example, valuing growth; seeking challenge; seeking personal excellence; wanting to serve a higher and meaningful purpose; having autonomous motivation and intrinsic goals; having goals that are valuable in themselves and part of one's identity (Bauer, McAdams, & Sakaeda, 2005; Delle Fave, Massimini, & Bassi, 2011; Fowers, Mollica, & Procacci, 2010; Huta & Ryan, 2010; Peterson, Park, & Seligman, 2005; Ryan, Huta, & Deci, 2008; Vittersø, Oelmann, & Wang, 2009).
2. *Behaviors*: Behavioral content and activity characteristics, that is, the "what" of behavior—for example, volunteering; giving money to those in need; expressing gratitude; mindfulness; engaging in challenging activities to which one brings commensurate skill (Delle Fave & Massimini, 1988; Ryan et al., 2008; Steger, Kashdan, & Oishi, 2007).
3. *Experiences*: Subjective experiences, emotions, and cognitive appraisals—for example, feelings of meaning and value; personal expressiveness; interest and engagement (Delle Fave, Brdar, Freire, Vella-Brodrick, & Wissing, 2011; Vittersø, Dyrdal, Røysamb, 2005; Waterman, 1993).
4. *Functioning*: Indices of a person's overall positive psychological functioning, mental health, and flourishing, that is, how well a person is doing—for example, autonomy; competence; relatedness; purpose in life; personal growth; self-acceptance; social well-being; self-discovery; self-actualization; development of one's best potentials; habitual intense involvement and effort (Keyes, 2002; Ryan et al., 2008; Ryff, 1989; Waterman, 1993).

Definitions of hedonia have fallen into three of the categories of analysis:

1. *Orientations*: For example, seeking pleasure, enjoyment, comfort, or relaxation, whether or not these aims are achieved; seeking homeostasis; having a mindset in which one evaluates things as good and bad (Huta & Ryan, 2010; Peterson et al., 2005; Vittersø, Søholt, Hetland, Thoresen, & Røysamb, 2010).
2. *Behaviors*: For example, going to a big party; attending a sporting event or concert; going on a long walk; listening to music (Steger et al., 2007).
3. *Experiences*: For example, positive affect; life satisfaction; happiness; low negative affect; low depression (Bauer, McAdams, & Pals, 2008; Delle Fave, Brdar, et al., 2011; Fowers et al., 2010; Keyes, 2002; Ryan et al., 2008; Ryff, 1989; Vittersø et al., 2005; Waterman, 1993).

Although there are certainly differences between the definitions that various psychologists have used, I will not dwell on the differences here. Instead, I will distill the concepts that emerge most consistently across definitions, regardless of the category of analysis, to anchor the reader's understanding of hedonia and eudaimonia. (See also Huta, 2013b, for an earlier summary of common elements across eudaimonia definitions.)

As shown in Huta and Waterman (2013), there is clear agreement that hedonia involves pleasure, enjoyment, and satisfaction, whether it is construed as the experience of these variables or as an orientation or behavior aimed at seeking these experiences. The majority of researchers have also associated hedonia with an absence of distress (which can be rephrased as a presence of comfort), or with an affective balance such that positive experiences outweigh negative experiences. In this chapter, I will assume that hedonia does include the concept of reduced distress. (See Vitterso, 2013, for an additional discussion of hedonia.)

Conceptions of eudaimonia have varied more widely than those of hedonia. Nevertheless, Huta and Waterman (2013) found that four core definitional elements appeared across most or all definitions: (1) *authenticity*: clarifying one's true self and deep values, staying connected with them, and acting in accord with them; (2) *meaning*: understanding a bigger picture, relating to it, and contributing to it (the bigger picture may include broader aspects of your own life or identity, a purpose, the long term, your community, society, the ecosystem, or even a conception of how the entire world works or is meant to work); (3) *excellence*: striving for higher quality and higher standards in one's behavior, performance, accomplishments, and ethics; and (4) *growth*: actualizing what one feels is right for oneself, fulfilling one's potential, and pursuing personal goals; personal growth, learning, improving, and seeking challenges; and maturing as a human being.

Although hedonia and eudaimonia are distinct concepts, both theoretically and empirically (e.g., Huta & Ryan, 2010; Peterson et al., 2005), I should add that they are by no means mutually exclusive, and that they often co-occur. Indeed, some of the most fulfilling pursuits are the ones in which eudaimonia and hedonia are so seamlessly blended that they become one.

## HEDONIC AND EUDAIMONIC ORIENTATIONS— THE CATEGORY OF ANALYSIS FOCUSED ON HERE

The study of all four categories of analysis—orientations, behaviors, experiences, and functioning—can give us a well-rounded understanding of the whole process of eudaimonia or hedonia. However, I would argue that one category is most directly at the heart of what is meant by eudaimonia and hedonia: orientations. I believe that Aristotle was mainly talking about orientations, and that it *is* primarily about orientations—the attitudes, values, motives, and goals a person can choose. All we have control over in life is our choices and aims; we cannot ensure the success of our aims (i.e., functioning, experiences) or the feelings of well-being that may result (i.e., experiences). Thus, choices are more fruitful targets for intervention than are outcomes. It also seems most fair to describe the nature of a person's life in terms of their efforts rather than their successes. And a conceptualization in terms of choices brings the focus of eudaimonia and hedonia inward rather than outward to external criteria and on the process of life rather than the outcomes—a focus that seems more intrinsic, more engaged, and richer. Even when choosing among orientations and behaviors, I would treat orientations as more fundamental, since two people can engage in the same surface behavior for very different reasons (Huta, 2013a; Huta & Ryan, 2010).

Thus, I would conclude that eudaimonia and hedonia are most fundamentally orientations. For the remainder of this chapter, this is the category of analysis that I will focus on, and the review of research findings in the next section will focus on the measures that clearly assess both eudaimonia and hedonia as orientations—the Hedonic and Eudaimonic Motives for Activities (HEMA) scale that I developed (Huta & Ryan, 2010) and the Orientations to Happiness Questionnaire (OTHQ) based on Seligman's conceptualization (Peterson et al., 2005).

The HEMA scale inquires, "To what degree [do you typically approach your activities]/[did you approach your activities today/this week/etc.] with each of the following intentions, whether or not you actually [achieve]/[achieved] your aim?" The eudaimonic motives are "Seeking to pursue excellence or a personal ideal," "Seeking to use the best in yourself," "Seeking to develop a skill, learn, or gain insight into something," and "Seeking to do what you believe in." The hedonic motives are "Seeking enjoyment," "Seeking pleasure," "Seeking fun," "Seeking relaxation," and "Seeking to take it easy." Participants give ratings of 1 (not at all) to 7 (very much). The OTHQ states, "Please indicate the degree to which each of the following statements applies to you from 1 (very much unlike me) to 5 (very much like me)." Sample items assessing eudaimonia (which Seligman, 2002, calls the life of meaning) are "My life serves a higher purpose," and "I have a responsibility to make the world a better place." Sample hedonic items (the life of pleasure) are "Life is too short to postpone the pleasures it can provide," and "In choosing what to do, I always take into account whether it will be pleasurable." Overall, the HEMA focuses on the excellence, authenticity, and growth elements of eudaimonia and the pleasure and comfort elements of hedonia; the OTHQ focuses on the meaning element of eudaimonia and the pleasure element of hedonia. Nevertheless, I have found (in unpublished data) that the subscales of the HEMA and OTHQ show convergent and discriminant validity. Furthermore, the research reviewed in the next section has often produced similar patterns of results for the two scales.

## EMPIRICAL FINDINGS

Next, I summarize research on hedonic and eudaimonic orientations to give the reader a sense of how hedonia and eudaimonia differ and how they behave in combination. Where I say "hedonia relates more," I imply a comparison with eudaimonia, and vice versa. Results refer to the trait level unless otherwise specified; the trait level focuses on a person's life as a whole, linking his or her typical or average degree of eudaimonia or hedonia with his or her typical or average score on another variable; the state level, by contrast, focuses on a given moment or time period, linking a person's hedonia or eudaimonia at that time with another variable at that time.

Hedonia and eudaimonia relate to somewhat different experiences, so that people who pursue both hedonia and eudaimonia have a *more well-rounded* picture of well-being than people who pursue only one or the other; hedonia relates more to carefreeness (at trait and state levels), positive affect (only at the state level), and low negative affect (only at the state level), whereas eudaimonia relates more to meaning (at trait and state levels), elevation (at the trait level), self-connectedness (at trait and state levels), work satisfaction, and low depression (Huta, 2013a; Huta & Ryan, 2010; Proyer, Annen, Eggimann, Schneider, & Ruch, 2012; Schueller & Seligman, 2010).

Hedonia and eudaimonia relate equally to vitality (at both trait and state levels) (Huta, 2013a; Huta & Ryan, 2010). Hedonia and eudaimonia relate equally to life satisfaction in studies with the HEMA scale (Huta, 2013a; Huta & Ryan, 2010) and some studies with the OTHQ (Chan, 2009; Chen, 2010; Peterson, Ruch, Beerman, Park, & Seligman, 2007; Proyer et al., 2012; Ruch, Harzer, Proyer, Park, & Peterson, 2010), but eudaimonia relates more to life satisfaction (and to happiness) in other studies with the OTHQ (Anić & Tončić, 2013; Kumano, 2011; Park, Peterson, & Ruch, 2009; Peterson et al., 2005, 2007; Schueller & Seligman, 2010; Vella-Brodrick, Park, & Peterson, 2009).

With the HEMA scale, hedonia and eudaimonia relate equally to positive affect (Huta, 2013a; Huta & Ryan, 2010), but with the OTHQ, eudaimonia relates more to positive affect (Anić & Tončić, 2013; Chan, 2009; Park et al., 2009; Peterson et al., 2005; Schueller & Seligman, 2010; Vella-Brodrick et al., 2009).

People who pursue both hedonia and eudaimonia have *higher degrees* of various well-being outcomes than people who pursue only one or the other (Anić & Tončić, 2013; Huta & Ryan, 2010; Peterson et al., 2005).

Hedonic activity may be associated with greater *immediate well-being*, whereas eudaimonic activity may be associated with greater *long-term well-being* (Huta, 2013a; Huta & Ryan, 2010).

Eudaimonic pursuits are associated with a more positive impact on the surrounding world, including close friends and relatives (Huta, 2012; Huta, Pelletier, Baxter, & Thompson, 2012), the broader community (Huta, 2013a; Huta, Pearce, & Voloaca, 2013), and the environment (Huta et al., 2013); generally, eudaimonia is more related to indices of long-term perspective, caring about the bigger picture, and abstract rather than concrete thinking (Huta et al., 2013).

Hedonically oriented and eudaimonically oriented individuals have somewhat *different profiles* on other individual differences, giving us a sense of how their natures differ: Of the Values in Action character strengths and virtues (Peterson & Seligman, 2004), hedonia relates more to playfulness, whereas eudaimonia relates more to judgment, wisdom, and religiousness; hedonia relates negatively to humility (Buschor, Proyer, & Ruch, 2013; Huta, 2013a; Peterson et al., 2007; Ruch, Proyer, & Weber, 2010a). Hedonia relates more to the excitement-seeking and gregariousness components of extraversion, whereas eudaimonia relates more to characteristics reflecting introversion, including introspectiveness, subjectivity/nonconformism, enjoyment of solitude, enjoyment of peace and quiet, and a focus on thoughts and ideas (Huta, 2013a). Eudaimonia relates more to integrated motivation and to a composite of intrinsic goals, whereas hedonia relates more to a composite of extrinsic goals (Anić & Tončić, 2013; Huta, 2013a). In terms of demographics, hedonia decreases with age, education, skill required in one's profession, religiousness, and being married, and eudaimonia increases with skill required in one's profession and religiousness (Peterson et al., 2005; Ruch et al., 2010; Schueller & Seligman, 2010). Additional findings show that eudaimonia relates more to self-control (Anić & Tončić, 2013), vocational identity achievement (Hirschi, 2011), and career success (Proyer et al., 2012), whereas hedonia relates more to materialism (Huta, 2013a).

Research on predictors of eudaimonia and hedonia shows the role of several parenting variables: Parental demandingness (expecting maturity, setting limits, providing challenges and enrichment) and parental responsiveness (being nurturing, taking the time to explain, listening, encouraging self-expression) both relate to the adult child's eudaimonia but not his or her hedonia, suggesting that rearing a child to be eudaimonic requires greater investment (Huta, 2012). Adult children pursue eudaimonia (or hedonia) whether their parents merely verbally endorsed eudaimonia (or hedonia) or actually role-modeled it; adult children also derive increased well-being from eudaimonia (or hedonia) if their parents role-modeled it, but derive little or no well-being if their parents only verbally endorsed eudaimonia (or hedonia) (Huta, 2012).

## THE COMPLEMENTARY NATURES OF HEDONIA AND EUDAIMONIA

The previous review of definitions and findings gives us an outline of what is meant by hedonia and eudaimonia. I would like, now, to go even deeper, toward the very heart of the hedonic–eudaimonic distinction. I do not think the distinction is some artifact of a tradition hailing from ancient Greece. I think it speaks to two very real psychological functions.

There are certainly concepts other than hedonia and eudaimonia (as I define them) that have been associated with a good life, including relationships, engagement, accomplishment, harmony, physical health, and attitudes like optimism; extrinsic values such as material wealth, image, status, power, and popularity; and basic circumstances such as safety, health, freedom, and essential material resources (Delle Fave, Brdar, et al., 2011; Grouzet et al., 2005; Kasser & Ryan, 1993; Schwartz & Bilsky, 1987; Seligman, 2011; Tafarodi et al., 2012). Eudaimonia and hedonia are not sufficient for an optimal existence, and some of the above variables are needed as well (including relationships, which play a major role in well-being; Diener & Seligman, 2002).

Yet there is something fundamental about the distinction between eudaimonia and hedonia: They play *major complementary roles* in life. Clarifying these roles can help us to explain why the hedonic–eudaimonic distinction so often appears center stage and to appreciate the importance of having a balance of *both* pursuits.

Next, I outline several complementary functions. They are not clear-cut, because hedonia includes eudaimonic functions to some degree, and vice versa. And they are rough generalizations that sometimes oversimplify the picture. Nevertheless, they are useful for developing a deeper feel for hedonia and eudaimonia, especially when pursuing them in practice.

*Hedonia is about taking something for me, now; eudaimonia is about building something broader for the long term.* This is perhaps the most fundamental distinction. Hedonia is a self-nourishing and self-care function—taking care of one's own needs and desires, typically in the present or near future; reaching personal release and peace to replenish, heal, and find a fresh perspective; and "drinking in" nutriments of energy and joy. Eudaimonia is a cultivating function—giving of oneself and investing in a larger aspect of the self, a long-term project, or the surrounding world. Thus, it is roughly about *taking versus giving, narrow versus broad perspective*, and *short-term versus long-term perspective*. The mindsets associated with these orientations might be summarized as *desire versus care*. Hedonic desire need not be seen as vulgar; I am referring to that healthy ability to feel and flow with what one needs and wants and relishes. The prerequisite for eudaimonia is caring in a very general sense, such as thoughtfulness, and caring about quality, rightness, context, or the welfare of others. Deeper still, hedonia and eudaimonia are based on distinct assumptions about oneself: that one has *rights versus responsibilities*. If one does not feel entitled to happiness, self-nourishment, and taking up space, it is difficult to pursue hedonia in the first place. Eudaimonia, on the other hand, begins when a person takes some responsibility for his or her life and for the implications of his or her actions (Frankl, 1946/1997).

*Hedonia is the pursuit of what feels good; eudaimonia is the pursuit of what one believes to be right.* Implied in the previous sentence are several distinctions (see also Steger & Shin, 2012, for similar distinctions). First, there is the *affective and biological versus cognitive* distinction—the desirability of pursuits is gauged in terms of more emotional and physical experiences in hedonia, but in terms of more abstract values and ideals in eudaimonia. We might approximate this by speaking of *pleasure versus value*. There is an *automatic versus effortful* distinction. Hedonia proceeds more directly and automatically from our hard wiring. Eudaimonia is a natural inclination as well (Maslow, 1968)—it is fulfilling to use what we have and become all that we can be. However, eudaimonic ideals must first be developed and then actively kept in mind to some degree if they are to be pursued; as such, eudaimonia is more effortful and more easily disrupted (Huta, 2013b). To some degree, there is also a *subjective versus objective* distinction (Diener, Sapyta, & Suh, 1998). Hedonia aims at activities that are pleasant for the individual in question. Eudaimonia is also largely guided by subjective inner processes and gut feelings, but some eudaimonic aims, such as ethical behavior and maturity, are informed by conceptions of what is universally of high quality in all human beings.

*Overall, hedonia is more fundamental, whereas eudaimonia is more elevated.* We cannot consider one pursuit "better" than the other; each is important in its own way. Hedonia is more fundamental in the sense that it often takes care of immediate needs and desires and is based on older brain systems that we share with other species. Eudaimonia is a "higher pleasure" (Seligman, 2002) in the sense that it allows people to develop their potential, and it exercises the higher cognitive capacities that are particularly well-developed in humans, such as values, morality, and vision (Huta 2013b; Steger & Shin, 2012). The actual proportions of hedonia and eudaimonia that best suit a person probably vary widely from individual to individual. But if a person does not have at least some hedonia and some eudaimonia, he or she may feel flat and unfulfilled, be more vulnerable to unhappiness, or develop psychopathology. To achieve optimal well-being, we need to have some degree of both complementary functions, and they probably keep each other in check.

## STEPS TOWARD EUDAIMONIA AND HEDONIA

The definitions, findings, and complementary functions previously discussed clearly indicate the importance of pursuing both hedonia and eudaimonia. This, of course, raises the question of how exactly a person goes about pursuing these. I dedicate the remainder of this chapter to a description of what eudaimonia and hedonia might look like in practice.

I first note, however, that hedonia and eudaimonia are present in various interventions already. For example, prescribing psychotropic medication is a hedonic intervention to the degree that it is treated as a means to alleviate suffering. Cognitive-behavioral therapy (Beck, 2011) includes the hedonic aim of relieving distress and the eudaimonic aim of reducing dysfunction. More strongly in the eudaimonic direction, we find therapies that also aim to reduce distress but place more emphasis on taking suffering as a flag, even an opportunity, indicating the need to move toward greater authenticity, meaning, excellence, or growth. Examples of such interventions are humanistic therapies (e.g., Frankl, 1946/1997; Maslow, 1968; Rogers, 1961), acceptance commitment therapy (Hayes, Luoma, Bond, Masuda, & Lillis, 2006), and well-being therapy (Fava & Tomba, 2009). Some interventions explicitly target the enhancement of both hedonia and eudaimonia, such as quality of life therapy and coaching (Frisch, in press). And a variety of positive psychology interventions are aimed less at alleviating suffering and more at enhancing hedonic and/or eudaimonic aspects of life (Sin & Lyubomirsky, 2009).

My aim here is to bring together some key concepts in the pursuit of hedonia and eudaimonia (which will be italicized) that could form the basis of interventions, and of research on those interventions. (The Appendix also lists some measures that could be used by researchers and practitioners.) Applied settings might include coaching, education, organizations, clinical practice, and self-help. In writing this chapter, I sacrificed much depth, illustration, and nuance for the sake of at least touching on many concepts and authors that are relevant; the topic could easily fill a book of its own. I will also say that I consider the following proposal to be a draft that will undoubtedly be revised and expanded as our field gains insight into well-being.

From here on, I use more colloquial language and speak to the reader as "you." This is in the spirit of more direct and intimate communication because I will be addressing the reader as someone who may be personally interested in the pursuit of hedonia or eudaimonia.

## STEPS TOWARD EUDAIMONIA

The four common elements across most definitions of eudaimonia—authenticity, meaning, excellence, and growth (Huta & Waterman, 2013)—form an excellent framework for the pursuit of eudaimonia. These terms therefore make up the headings of the outline below. The elements are intertwined to some degree, and what I say about one may also apply to others.

Do you have to do all of the things listed here? Certainly not. Only one or two ideas may connect with a need or interest that you currently have.

### AUTHENTICITY

As noted earlier, authenticity involves clarifying your true self and deep values, staying connected with them, and acting in accord with them. Authenticity can be very personally fulfilling and is experienced as meaningful (Schlegel, Hicks, King, & Arndt, 2011). At the same time, like the other elements of eudaimonia, it is largely pursued for a subtler reason—as an end in itself, something that simply feels right. The concept of authenticity is directly embedded in the term "eudaimonia" from ancient Greece; the term is made up of two words: "eu," meaning good or healthy, and "daimon," meaning the spirit or true self (Norton, 1976).

Facing yourself, warts and all, takes a good dose of humility. Soul-searching to establish, reevaluate, and evolve your identity brings uncertainty and may be a time of crisis (Marcia, 1967). And it is not always easy to make your persona, profession, and relationships congruent with your true self; it may take courage, there may be limitations, and you may have to compromise. Yet finding paths toward authenticity is liberating, brings clarity, makes life feel more real, and sets a firmer foundation to build upon.

Moving toward a clearer *identity* involves a dialogue between life *experiences* and the inner self (Waterman & Schwartz, 2013). You can cultivate a habit of noticing moments when something captures your interest, imagination, or *curiosity* (Kashdan & Silvia, 2009). Trust that there is a voice inside you, however vague at first, that can sort out what is "you." Humanistic psychologists called this voice the *organismic valuing process* (Rogers, 1964), and much of positive psychology implicitly assumes that we all have this ability (Joseph & Linley, 2004). You can learn to hear this inner voice and to gauge when your mind is speaking authentically and when it is biased. One trick to bypass your biases is to ask yourself, "What would someone who knows me well have to say?"

An important part of who you are is your *character strengths*. To identify these, you can take the Values in Action (VIA) Inventory of Strengths (Peterson & Seligman, 2004). The VIA includes strengths of the head (love of learning, curiosity, good judgment, creativity, appreciation of beauty) and strengths of the heart (fairness, forgiveness, gratitude, honesty, hope, humor, kindness, leadership, love, modesty, persistence, prudence, spirituality, teamwork, zest, bravery, perspective, self-regulation, social intelligence) (Park & Peterson, 2010).

More generally, you might write an essay or have a discussion (Staudinger, 2001) on questions such as: How do I act when I'm allowed to be vulnerable? Who inspires me? What did I love as a child? If money or time were not an issue, what would I do? What do I believe in? To move toward generalizations, you can start with something specific (e.g., I love cooking, I love sitting by rivers) and apply a *downward arrow technique* (Szymanska, 2008), which is a chain of "why" questions for reaching deeper into yourself, for example, "What is my reason for liking it? Why does that reason fit with me? What does my last answer say about me in general?"

Perhaps most importantly, take the time to mull things over. Instead of escaping into a TV show or videogame or Facebook, try shifting some time toward *being with yourself* or having a meaningful conversation. The human mind naturally reviews the past, highlights what was meaningful, brings up what was discrepant, and connects the dots, if we just give it the time.

To stay connected with that inner "pilot light" at any given time, it helps to practice *mindfulness*—focusing on your experiences in the present and clearing away judgments and reactions in an effort to see the experiences for what they are (Baer, Smith, Hopkins, Krietemeyer, & Tonry, 2006).

Regular *meditation* is also very helpful. It need not take long, follow someone else's prescribed technique, or be in a physically uncomfortable position. It is a regular time for encountering yourself, possibly celebrating what you are grateful for, reciting a self-made summary of what you stand for, setting the tone for the upcoming day, or anything else that helps keep you grounded.

And when you surround yourself with *things that resonate with you*—such as pictures, plants, music, or memorabilia—they provide daily reminders of your spirit. You could make some of them yourself or personalize them by building stories around them. It's about breathing your own spirit into your world.

Finally, aligning your lived life with your true self partly involves shaping your *activities* and partly involves shaping your psychological approach. Despite the constraints of life, there is usually something you can do to feel that life is more on your terms. You might live your passion through a hobby, show more of your character in your persona, steer conversations to meaningful topics, or incorporate signature strengths into your work (Seligman, 2002). Sometimes, you may do major housecleaning, such as ending a meaningless relationship or switching your work toward more of a *calling* (Wrzesniewski, McCaulay, Rozin, & Schwartz, 1997). It isn't easy, but it helps to think of how much the change will energize you and how much less energy will be leeched out of you in the form of frustration.

To shift psychologically toward taking the helm, much can be learned from research on self-determination theory, which points to the following *autonomy-supportive* principles (Deci & Ryan, 1987). Listen to your *own perspective*, and seek out others who respect your perspective. Use *noncoercive language* with yourself—consider replacing "should," "ought to," and "have to," with phrases like "it makes sense to," "now is a good time to," or "let's go for it." It is liberating to give yourself the *freedom to choose* how you will act (the core aim of existential interventions; Warnock, 1970). And think through the *rationale* for an activity to see whether and how it aligns with your interests, values, and meaning framework, even if it means lumping it in with daily unexciting chores you graciously accept as a normal part of life. Perhaps find someone who embraces the activity and ask them how they see it—their perspective can often be boiled down to a single effective phrase (consider Nike's brilliant "Just do it!").

## MEANING

Meaning involves understanding a bigger picture, relating to it, and contributing to it; the bigger picture may include broader aspects of your life or identity, a purpose, the long term, your community, society, the ecosystem, or even a conception of how the entire world works or is meant to work. There is more to the concept of meaning (Wong & Fry, 2012), but the self-transcendent aspect is especially relevant to eudaimonia.

Developing an understanding of the bigger picture may involve perplexing existential questions, and contributing to the surrounding world may involve personal sacrifice. Yet relating to a broader context gives a role to your actions and an opportunity to make a difference (Huta & Zuroff, 2007).

Seeking to understand a bigger framework means being guided by *big questions*: How does this bigger picture operate? What is its purpose? What matters in this bigger context? Such questions raise the likelihood of doubting our existing worldview, sometimes threatening our sense of stability. I therefore believe in *"nibbling"* at them, tackling only as much as you are ready for. I also believe in being comfortable with *half-baked hypotheses*—it's a life-long process and nobody has the final answers. You can be somewhat systematic in building your understanding by labeling your hypotheses; for example, "half-baked hypothesis," "quarter-baked hypothesis," or "no hypothesis but interesting question!" Just assigning such labels directs your unconscious toward seeking answers.

We often develop our life philosophies through exposure to others' theories—through our parents and local culture, religion, travel, philosophical texts, discussions with friends, immersion in biography or fiction. But it is not enough to gather material from others. You need to attend to your own experiences and then process it all—through partly unconscious mulling, through intentional use of metaphor or *narrative* (McAdams, 1993), or through an intuitive process in which you align yourself with a bigger picture "simply by doing." Meaning is based on connections, contrasts, and hierarchies—you need to *connect the dots* somehow, otherwise you simply have a pile of ideas. Perhaps that is why Aristotle placed *contemplation* as the highest of the virtues (Aristotle, 2001).

Contributions to a bigger picture have value in some broader, deeper, or longer-term sense. People can contribute in many different ways, such as *random acts of kindness* (Otake, Shimai, Tanaka-Matsumi, Otsui, & Fredrickson, 2006), service, building, creating, activism, teaching, childrearing, guiding the next generation, or investing in a worthwhile personal goal. Much of what is meant by a broader contribution is captured by the concept of *generativity*, identified by Erikson (1950) as the central task of adulthood (McAdams & de St. Aubin, 1998). Contributing also includes *refraining from harm*, which is a large part of activities like proenvironmental behavior (Kasser, 2011; Pelletier, Baxter, & Huta, 2011).

EXCELLENCE

Excellence involves striving for higher quality and higher standards in your behavior, performance, accomplishments, and ethics. I would add that the standards need to fit with your true self, your means, and your stage in life. And it's about the effort and process, whether or not the goal is achieved.

Excellence takes work, long-term commitment, and sometimes risk. Yet it can be deeply gratifying to know that you have done your best, done the right thing, or done a good job. It fills you and simultaneously brings a feeling of release, like something has culminated because you've given it your all. It builds feelings of quality and healthy pride. You appreciate things more profoundly, knowing how much work it takes to earn them. And it elevates you, inspires you, and brings you to a higher level of functioning.

To differentiate up from down in the pursuit of excellence, you need some conception of when a choice is good, right, of higher quality, true, noble, sacred, or beautiful.

We absorb such conceptions from our parents and culture, and sometimes from *character education* in school (Berkowitz & Bier, 2004). You can build a *vision* of your standard or ideal by imagining how you would behave and feel, and what you would be capable of, perhaps by writing an essay on your *best possible self* (King, 2001). You can look to *role models*, people who inspire you. It's worth learning about them in detail, to immerse yourself in their way of thinking and behaving, and to get a realistic sense of the time invested in their excellence, the costs, and how much of their life is quite ordinary. All that being said, the development of judgment and ideals needs to be balanced by tolerance, lest it turn into being judgmental toward others or yourself.

Various concepts in psychology fall under the umbrella of excellence. For example, Seligman (2002) speaks of regularly exercising your five greatest *signature strengths* and serving a *higher purpose*. He also describes how you can turn many jobs into *callings*, going beyond what is asked of you to create something special (see also Duffy & Sedlacek, 2007; Wrzesniewski et al., 1997). Wong (2010) speaks of *responsible action*—finding the right solution and doing what is morally right. Kohlberg (1984) developed a theory of *moral development*, identifying reasoning that ranged from entirely selfish and short-sighted to prosocial, universally valid, and based on a personal ability to judge what is appropriate. Orlick (1990) speaks of achieving a high level of *excellence* in the performance of your specific profession or sport. In pursuing excellence, try not to compare yourself with others unless it inspires you or teaches you something you need. That is, adopt a *mastery orientation* (focusing on the learning and improvement itself, and using your past self as a reference point) rather than a *performance orientation* (wanting to appear competent compared to others) (Dweck & Leggett, 1988). Eudaimonia is first and foremost a private dialogue—it's about your relationship with yourself.

## GROWTH

Growth involves actualizing what you feel is right for you, fulfilling your potential, and pursuing personal goals; personal growth, learning, improving, and seeking challenges; and maturing as a human being.

Like excellence, growth requires commitment and effort, and brings the uncertainty and instability of change. Yet people naturally seek out activities slightly beyond their current ability (e.g., Abuhamdeh & Csikszentmihalyi, 2012; Deci, 1971). Advertisers do us a disservice by implying that we want everything to be easy. Growth builds feelings of progress, accomplishment, and competence, and the fulfillment of bringing a personal project to fruition.

Some theories of growth have proposed universal milestones, whereas others have focused on person-specific aims (Waterman & Schwartz, 2013). Maturity is more aimed at universal goals, actualization is more person-specific, and personal growth is somewhere in between.

Several theories are relevant to the concept of maturity. Erikson (1950) stated that we pass through *stages of psychosocial development*, the sequence in adulthood being: identity—determining your true character; intimacy—connecting deeply with others; generativity—making a difference; and ego integrity—coming to terms with life. Loevinger (1966) proposed *stages of ego development*, such that people are initially conformist, then a blend of conscientious and conformist, then conscientious (rules are internalized), individualistic (autonomy of self and others is respected), autonomous (multiple facets are integrated and limitations are tolerated), and, finally, integrated (inner conflicts are reconciled). Maslow (1964) described highly *self-actualized people* as having realism, tolerance, a nonhostile sense of humor, autonomy, spontaneity, comfort with solitude, strong ethics and responsibility, a sense of fellowship with the human condition, purpose, profound relationships, continual fresh appreciation, and peak experiences.

Personal growth includes processes such as learning information and skills, gaining experience, improving, deepening insight, overcoming obstacles, transcending suffering, and setting challenges for yourself. The mind, like any muscle, wants to be used and developed.

To be open to growth, it is important to believe that it is possible and that success is based on learning and hard work (a *growth mindset*), rather than believing that people cannot change and that success depends on innate ability (a *fixed mindset*) (Dweck, 2006).

The somewhat mysterious process of inner transformation will not take place if you are not *engaged*, truly interacting with life, as flow theory shows. *Flow* is that state of immersion during an activity that you can't yet do automatically, but that you find challenging and are able to face with just enough skill to meet the challenge (too little skill leads to anxiety, too much skill leads to boredom) (Csikszentmihalyi, 2000). People seem wired to seek flow (Csikszentimihalyi & Nakamura, 2010), and since flow activities extend our abilities, they lead to personal growth (Csikszentmihalyi & Massimini, 1985). Personal growth is further facilitated by *openness to experience* and by *curiosity* (Vittersø, 2004; Vittersø, Overwien, & Martinsen, 2009).

Actualization involves developing what you feel you are meant to do, what fits with you, perhaps even what feels like a *personal destiny* (Norton, 1976). It need not look prestigious, it need not be understood by others. It's about coming into your own. People I have met who lived their passion range from a visionary department head, to a memorable grocery store employee who just shone with a zest for helping people, to a retiree who created a giant spreadsheet of historical milestones simply for personal interest.

*Follow your passion first*, without worrying about where it will take you, whether it will succeed, whether it will make money. The logistics come later. Yes, you may need to adjust your vision in the face of limiting circumstances, but you'll be further along than if you never started, and you will keep the flame alive. It's like art—the primary mindset needs to be *experiential*, to feel your way through an idea, while practical and analytical considerations play an essential but supporting role. Interestingly, things then start to fall into place, as Joseph Campbell describes:

> Follow your bliss. If you do follow your bliss, you put yourself on a kind of track that has been there all the while waiting for you, and the life you ought to be living is the one you are living. . . . If you follow your bliss, doors will open for you that wouldn't have opened for anyone else. (Campbell & Moyers, 1988, p. 120)

Finally, growth requires some self-management. It helps to be aware of your *stage of change* with respect to a project, and to only move forward when you are ready. When you rush into a project and have to back out later, it's discouraging and makes it harder to try again. Prochaska and Velicer (1997) identified the following stages of change:

- Precontemplation: You are not ready and may not be aware of the importance of the goal.
- Contemplation: You are considering the advantages and disadvantages.
- Preparation: You are ready and planning your goals.

- Action: You begin.
- Maintenance: You continue.
- Termination: The pursuit has become a part of you and there is little temptation to drop it.

The preparation stage is aided by *implementation intentions*—very specific plans for intermediate steps (Gollwitzer, 1999). Maintenance is aided by *grit*, including sustained interest, resistance to distraction, perseverance through setbacks, and simply sticking with it. Grit is partly based on the understanding that frustration, confusion, and some failure are normal parts of learning, and they do not mean that you should quit (Duckworth, Peterson, Matthews, & Kelly, 2007). Maintenance is also based on *self-regulation*—controlling your feelings, thoughts, and behaviors through clear standards, self-monitoring, and willpower. Self-regulation is a better predictor of reaching your potential than is your intelligence (Duckworth & Seligman, 2005; Maddux, 2009). When you encounter fatigue or amotivation, it helps to remind yourself of the *value* of your goal; thinking of values is a more cognitive process and achievable even when your feelings are down. I have observed that accomplished individuals often have a means of *periodically organizing their thoughts* and gaining perspective on their goals, be it a diary, pensive walks, or discussions with a confidant. Overall, the stages from contemplation onward are fueled by that remarkable class of human abilities that might be called *faith*—believing in something even before it has happened—such as *self-efficacy* or believing you can do it, *hope, optimism*, trust in the process, and positive vision (Carver & Scheier, 2002; Prochaska & DiClemente, 1984; Snyder, 1995). With such tools in hand, you can see the possibilities and run with the gifts.

## STEPS TOWARD HEDONIA

Through hedonic pursuits, we seek to experience pleasure and enjoyment, relieve distress and strain, and reach satisfaction. Hedonic pursuits cover the full range from physical to emotional, from crude to sublime, from transient to profound. Each part of these ranges can be beneficial if done in the right context and in the right way.

Hedonia can have undesirable consequences when taken to excess or when not balanced by eudaimonia—for example, destructive impulsivity, chronic escapism, addiction, selfishness, antisocial behavior, greed, and unbridled consumerism. (Eudaimonia can certainly be excessive as well.) But when pursued in a healthy way, hedonia not only leads to joy and comfort, but also "fills your tank" and fuels motivation, inspiration, broadened attention, and a desire to build (Fredrickson, 2004). It also gives you a break so you can find a fresh perspective.

Below, I focus only on healthful approaches to hedonia. In its optimal form, hedonia brings out those beautiful primal, sensual, and creature-comfort parts of ourselves that emerge spontaneously when we are fulfilled to our heart's content, well-rested, and free of preoccupations.

It is worth looking at Fordyce's (1983) 14 fundamentals of happiness, which he tested in several interventions. They provide some good advice for pursuing hedonia (*focusing on the present, not expecting too much, making happiness a high priority, not worrying needlessly, taking care of yourself*), as well as more eudaimonic recommendations (*meaningful work, authenticity, planning and organizing, solving rather than ignoring problems*), and principles relevant to both eudaimonia and hedonia (*engagement, relatedness, positive and optimistic thinking*). More recently, Lyubomirsky (2008) identified a partly overlapping list of validated positive psychology interventions: *savoring, caring for your body, gratitude, optimism, engagement, avoiding overthinking and comparing yourself with others, relationships, kindness, forgiveness, good coping strategies, goal commitment,* and *religion and spirituality.*

Let me add some comments to these recommendations. So much of well-being is in your *perspective*, and adopting a positive perspective is something you can learn (Seligman, 1998). It truly is about seeing the cup as half full rather than half empty. You can practice *selective attention*, focusing on what you have rather than what you don't—there is usually enough bad material in life to justify misery and enough good material to justify happiness, so you can make choices about your focus (Mather & Carstensen, 2003). Be wary of setting *expectations* too high (or having expectations at all), as it undermines enjoyment (Mauss, Tamir, Anderson, & Savino, 2011; Schooler, Ariely, & Loewenstein, 2003). If you have the attitude that nothing is ever good enough, nothing ever will be. Appreciate how much luckier you are than some people, an attitude called *downward social comparison* (Wills, 1981). And when things are difficult, balance entitlement with grace, acceptance, and *equanimity* (processes aided by eudaimonia, to be sure).

*Engagement* is critical (Seligman, 2011). Get immersed in what you do rather than having an evaluative mindset. *Evaluation* is useful when change is desired, but otherwise, when you're judging from "outside" yourself, it blocks personal enjoyment (Vittersø et al., 2009)—imagine someone constantly asking "Am I happy yet?" Also, *intentional activities* (e.g., exercise, hobbies, quality time with family and friends) account for much more of your happiness than *circumstances* (e.g., getting a raise, getting married, moving to California); intentional activities are sustained and provide *variety*, and thus counteract *hedonic adaptation*, the process of getting used to your situation and reverting to previous levels of happiness (Lyubomirsky, Sheldon, & Schkade, 2005). Easiness is not always a gauge of whether a hedonic activity is worthwhile—sometimes activities are more hedonically satisfying when they require *effort*, be it physical activity or emotional or cognitive investment (sometimes). Furthermore, seeing an activity as just a vehicle to happiness, rather than truly engaging in the activity itself, is an *extrinsic* mindset (Schooler et al., 2003). Extrinsic motives reduce the genuine connection with an activity that is needed for enjoyment (Deci & Ryan, 2000). Though I've been speaking of hedonia as the "pursuit" of happiness, it's important to interpret this phrase correctly. Happiness cannot be directly commanded or bought. Hedonia is about engaging in joyful and relaxing activities and attitudes, and then somehow *happiness comes in its own due time* (Martin, 2008). To quote Eleanor Roosevelt, "Happiness is not a goal . . . it's a by-product of a life well-lived."

Although happiness cannot be guaranteed, there is nevertheless a way to very much enhance the likelihood of hedonic experience: *savoring*. It's the process of actively opening your senses, emotions, and cognitive appreciation to indulge in something longer and more fully. Even the little things, especially the little things, can be relished—a great tune, a friend's laughter, or the smell of the flowers. People can savor the present moment or the past by reminiscing and reliving, or the future by anticipating and imagining (Bryant & Veroff, 2007). Savoring processes include physically luxuriating, marveling, basking and self-congratulation, and gratitude (Bryant & Veroff, 2007). *Gratitude* is a particularly powerful predictor of well-being (Emmons & McCullough, 2003), and it is worth making a habit of celebrating your blessings, perhaps as part of a daily meditation (Seligman, Steen, Park, & Peterson, 2005; Seligman, Rashid, & Parks, 2006). There is also an interpersonal form of savoring—sharing a positive event with others who then engage in *active-constructive responding*, that is, showing genuine excitement and capitalizing on the event by discussing it further, celebrating, telling others, and so on (Gable, Reis, Impett, & Asher, 2004).

In order to *take care of yourself*, you need to *take the time*. Don't hold back on vacations (they are crucial for eudaimonic development, too), and take breaks the rest of the year as well. Wells (2012) proposes a 1-3-2 principle, arguing that people need to rest, take personal time, and completely unplug from work at least 1 hour a day, 3 days a month, and 2 weeks a year. That's probably a bare minimum. Furthermore, different people find different activities fulfilling (Lyubomirsky et al., 2005), and thus it's important to *listen to yourself*. Pay attention to your (positive) fantasies, wishes, and impulses, and follow through when you can, at least in some small way. You may have gotten into the habit of ignoring these, but they do resurface here and there, and you can build on them. Also, take note of how different activities actually make you feel—we are not always good at predicting what will make us happy (Gilbert & Wilson, 2007).

Finally, I will say that hedonia need not always be a "pursuit." Sometimes it's good to just be. On a cool day in the height of summer, with the cicadas going and the sound of wind in the trees, who needs anything more than to simply sit? I truly believe, on an existential level, that we are "meant to" enjoy and just be as much as we are "meant to" pursue eudaimonia.

## CONCLUSION

The long-standing theoretical literature on eudaimonia and hedonia, the empirical findings, and the clarification of complementarities all point to the importance of having both pursuits in life. Much research is still needed regarding the outcomes, correlates, and predictors of these pursuits. Nevertheless, we do have enough of a grounding to think about applications. For one thing, discussions of how a person goes about pursuing hedonia and eudaimonia will deepen our understanding of these concepts and help with theoretical integration in more basic research. It will generate hypotheses for research on interventions; there is adequate empirical support for some of the individual elements in my proposal, but research has yet to be conducted on other elements or on combinations of elements. Most importantly, I hope that this chapter will serve as a springboard for discussions of how the vital concepts of eudaimonia and hedonia can concretely be applied to improve peoples' lives. When hedonia and eudaimonia are pursued wisely, with a feel for their deeper natures and intricacies, they can make life full and beautiful.

## SUMMARY POINTS

- Psychology definitions of eudaimonia and/or hedonia fall into different categories of analysis: orientations, behaviors, experiences, or functioning.
- There is good reason to consider the orientations category—the "why" of behavior—to be the most fundamental (though the other categories provide valuable information as well).
- The concepts appearing in most definitions of hedonia are pleasure/enjoyment and low distress; the concepts in most definitions of eudaimonia are authenticity, meaning, excellence, and growth. These sets of concepts can be operationalized as orientations and can be used to anchor and organize well-being interventions.
- Underlying the difference between the two sets of concepts is a distinction between major complementary functions in life, roughly summarized as "taking for me, now" versus "investing in something broader for the longer term."
- Research on hedonic and eudaimonic orientations shows, among other things, that they relate to somewhat different aspects of personal well-being (e.g., carefreeness versus meaning), and that they together relate to greater well-being than either pursuit alone.

- Finally, the second half of the chapter identifies specific activities and practices that a person can adopt to bring more hedonia and eudaimonia into his or her life. I have tried to provide enough examples, caveats, and principles to give the reader a feel for what these pursuits entail and when they are truly fulfilling, so that you can craft your own path to fulfillment.

## APPENDIX: MEASURES FOR ASSESSING THE OUTCOMES OF PRACTICING EUDAIMONIA OR HEDONIA

Here I suggest some measures that might be used by researchers or practitioners when they need to assess the outcomes of practicing eudaimonia or hedonia. The measures can also sometimes be useful self-assessments in our private lives. We may choose to evaluate ourselves when we experience a lack of well-being or feel that a question needs to be answered. But, as discussed earlier, excessive self-assessment can unnecessarily detract attention from engaging with life, make us feel that the glass is half empty rather than half full, and create an evaluative mindset that interferes with the experience of well-being. It's a balance.

| Scale | Author(s) | Sample Items |
|---|---|---|
| **Authenticity, Identity, Reflections of Fit Between True Self and Activity** | | |
| Dispositional Authenticity | Wood, Linley, Maltby, Baliousis, and Joseph, 2008 | "I am in touch with 'the real me,'" "I am true to myself in most situations," "I always feel I need to do what others expect me to do (R)" |
| Self-Connectedness | Huta, 2012 | "Connected with myself," "Aware of what matters to me," "Aware of how I feel" |
| Questionnaire for Eudaimonic Well-Being | Waterman et al., 2010 | "I believe I know what I was meant to do in life," "I believe I know what my best potentials are and I try to develop them whenever possible," "It is more important that I really enjoy what I do than that other people are impressed by it" |
| Personal Expressiveness | Waterman, 1993 | "This activity gives me my strongest feelings that this is who I really am," "When I engage in this activity I feel that this is what I was meant to do," "I feel a special fit or meshing when engaging in this activity" |
| Interest | Vittersø, Overwien, and Martinsen, 2009 | "Interested," "Engaged," "Immersed" |
| Autonomous Motivation, Controlled Motivation | Sheldon and Elliot, 1999 | "I pursue this activity because of the fun and enjoyment it provides me," "I pursue this activity because I really believe it's an important goal to have," "I pursue this activity because I would feel ashamed, guilty, or anxious if I did not," "I pursue this activity because somebody else wants me to" |
| Subjective Vitality | Ryan and Frederick, 1997 | "I feel energized," "I feel alive and vital," "I have energy and spirit" |

| Scale | Author(s) | Sample items |
|---|---|---|
| **Meaning** | | |
| Framework | Battista and Almond, 1973 | "I have really come to terms with what's important for me in my life," "I have a system or framework that allows me to truly understand my being alive," "I have a clear idea of what I'd like to do with my life" |
| Presence of Meaning | Steger, Frazier, Oishi, and Kaler, 2006 | "I understand my life's meaning," "I have a good sense of what makes my life meaningful," "I have discovered a satisfying life purpose" |
| Meaning Experience | Huta and Ryan, 2010 | "My activities and experiences are meaningful," "My activities and experiences are valuable," "My activities and experiences play an important role in some broader picture" |
| Purpose in Life | Ryff, 1989 | "I sometimes feel as if I've done all there is to do in life (R)," "Some people wander aimlessly through life, but I am not one of them," "I live life one day at a time and don't really think about the future (R)" |
| **Excellence** | | |
| Authentic Pride | Tracy and Robins, 2007 | "Honor," "Confidence," "Achieving" |
| Elevation | Huta and Ryan, 2010 | "Enriched," "Morally elevated," "Part of something greater than myself" |
| **Growth, Actualization, Maturity** | | |
| Personal Growth | Ryff, 1989 | "For me, life has been a continuous process of learning, changing, and growth," "I think it is important to have new experiences that challenge how you think about yourself and the world," "I gave up trying to make big improvements or changes in my life a long time ago (R)" |
| Self-Actualization | Jones and Crandall, 1986 | "I don't accept my own weaknesses (R)," "I have no mission in life to which I feel especially dedicated (R)," "I can express my feelings even when they may result in undesirable consequences" |
| Sentence Completion Test of Ego Development | Loevinger, 1979 | "The thing I like about myself is _____," "My main problem is _____," "If I can't get what I want _____" (RESPONSES NEED TO BE CODED) |

| Scale | Author(s) | Sample items |
|---|---|---|
| **Hedonia** | | |
| Positive Affect | Emmons and Diener, 1985 | "Happy," "Pleased," "Enjoyment/fun" |
| Negative Affect | Emmons and Diener, 1985 | "Unhappy," "Frustrated," "Worried/anxious" |
| Life Satisfaction | Diener, Emmons, Larsen, and Griffin, 1985 | "I am satisfied with my life," "So far I have gotten the important things I want in life," "In most ways, my life is close to my ideal" |
| Happiness | Lyubomirsky and Lepper, 1999 | "In general, I consider myself: 1—not a very happy person . . . 7—a very happy person," "Compared to most of my peers, I consider myself: 1—less happy . . . 7—more happy" |
| Carefreeness | Huta and Ryan, 2010 | "Carefree," "Easygoing," "Lighthearted" |
| Subjective Vitality | Ryan and Frederick, 1997 | "I feel energized," "I feel alive and vital," "I have energy and spirit" |

R = reverse coded.

## REFERENCES

Abuhamdeh, S., & Csikszentmihalyi, M. (2012). The importance of challenge for the enjoyment of intrinsically motivated, goal-directed activities. *Personality and Social Psychology Bulletin, 38*, 317–330. doi:10.1177/0146167211427147

Anić, P., & Tončić, M. (2013). Orientations to happiness, subjective well-being and life goals. *Psihologijske teme, 22*, 135–153.

Aristotle. (2001). Nichomachean ethics. In R. McKeon (Ed.), *The basic works of Aristotle* (pp. 928–1112). New York, NY: Modern Library. (Original work published 350 B.C.E., Oxford translation 1912–1954)

Baer, R. A., Smith, G. T., Hopkins, J., Krietemeyer, J., & Tonry, L. (2006). Using self-report assessment methods to explore facets of mindfulness. *Assessment, 13*, 27–45. doi:10.1177/1073191105283504

Battista, J., & Almond, R. (1973). The development of meaning in life. *Psychiatry, 36*, 409–427.

Bauer, J. J., McAdams, D. P., & Pals, J. L. (2008). Narrative identity and eudaimonic well-being. *Journal of Happiness, 9*, 81–104. doi:10.1007/s10902-006-9021-6

Bauer, J. J., McAdams, D. P., & Sakaeda, A. R. (2005). Interpreting the good life: Growth memories in the lives of mature, happy people. *Journal of Personality and Social Psychology, 88*, 203–217. doi:10.1037/0022-3514.88.1.203

Beck, J. S. (2011). *Cognitive behavior therapy: Basics and beyond* (2nd ed.). New York, NY: Guilford Press.

Berkowitz, M. W., & Bier, M. C. (2004). Research-based character education. *Annals of the American Academy of Political and Social Science, 591*, 72–85.

Bernard, M. E., Ellis, A., & Terjesen, M. (2006). *Rational-emotive behavioral approaches to childhood disorders: History, theory, practice and research.* New York, NY: Spring Science.

Bryant, F. B., & Veroff, J. (2007). *Savoring: A new model of positive experience.* Mahwah, NJ: Erlbaum.

Buschor, C., Proyer, R. T., & Ruch, W. (2013). Self- and peer-rated character strengths: How do they relate to satisfaction with life and orientations to happiness? *Journal of Positive Psychology, 8*, 116–127. doi:10.1080/17439760.2012.758305

Campbell, J., & Moyers, B. D. (1988). *The power of myth*. New York, NY: Doubleday.

Carver, C. S., & Scheier, M. F. (2002). Optimism. In C. R. Snyder, & S. J. Lopez (Eds.), *Handbook of positive psychology* (pp. 231–243). New York, NY: Oxford University Press.

Chan, D. W. (2009). Orientations to happiness and subjective well-being among Chinese prospective and in-service teachers in Hong Kong. *Educational Psychology, 29,* 139–151. doi:10.1080/01443410802570907

Chen, G. (2010). Validating the orientations to happiness scale in a Chinese sample of university students. *Social Indicators Research, 99,* 431–442. doi:10.1007/s11205-010-9590-y

Csikszentmihalyi, M. (2000). *Beyond boredom and anxiety*. San Francisco, CA: Jossey-Bass.

Csikszentmihalyi, M., & Massimini, F. (1985). On the psychological selection of bio-cultural information. *New Ideas in Psychology, 3,* 115–138.

Csikszentmihalyi, M., & Nakamura, J. (2010). Effortless attention in everyday life: A systematic phenomenology. In B. Bruya (Ed.), *Effortless attention: A new perspective in the cognitive science of attention and action* (pp. 179–189). Cambridge, MA: MIT Press.

Deci, E. L. (1971). Effects of externally mediated rewards on intrinsic motivation. *Journal of Personality and Social Psychology, 18,* 105–115.

Deci, E. L., & Ryan, R. M. (1987). The support of autonomy and the control of behavior. *Journal of Personality and Social Psychology, 53,* 1024–1037.

Deci, E. L., & Ryan, R. M. (2000). The "what" and "why" of goal pursuits: Human needs and the self-determination of behavior. *Psychological Inquiry, 11,* 227–268.

Delle Fave, A., Brdar, I., Freire, T., Vella-Brodrick, D., & Wissing, M. (2011). The eudaimonic and hedonic components of happiness: Qualitative and quantitative findings. *Social Indicators Research, 100,* 185–207. doi:10.1007/s11205-010-9632-5

Delle Fave A., & Massimini F. (1988). Modernization and the changing contexts of flow in work and leisure. In M. Csikszentmihalyi & I. Csikszentmihalyi (Eds.), *Optimal experience. Psychological studies of flow in consciousness* (pp. 193–213). New York, NY: Cambridge University Press.

Delle Fave, A., Massimini, F., & Bassi, M. (2011). *Psychological selection and optimal experience across cultures: Social empowerment through personal growth*. New York, NY: Springer.

Diener, E. D., Emmons, R. A., Larsen, R. J., & Griffin, S. (1985). The Satisfaction with Life Scale. *Journal of Personality Assessment, 49,* 71–75.

Diener, E., Sapyta, J. J., & Suh, E. (1998). Subjective well-being is essential to well-being. *Psychological Inquiry, 9,* 33–37.

Diener, E. D., & Seligman, M. E. P. (2002). Very happy people. *Psychological Science, 13,* 81–84.

Duckworth, A. L., Peterson, C., Matthews, M. D., & Kelly, D. R. (2007). Grit: Perseverance and passion for long-term goals. *Journal of Personality and Social Psychology, 92,* 1087–1101. doi:10.1037/0022-3514.92.6.1087

Duckworth, A. L., & Seligman, M. E. P. (2005). Self-discipline outdoes IQ in predicting academic performance of adolescents. *Psychological Science, 16,* 939–944.

Duffy, R. D., & Sedlacek, W. E. (2007). The presence of and search for a calling: Connections to career development. *Journal of Vocational Behaviour, 70,* 590–601. doi:10.1016/j.jvb. 2007.03.007

Dweck, C. S. (2006). *Mindset: The new psychology of success*. New York, NY: Random House.

Dweck, C. S., & Leggett, E. L. (1988). A social-cognitive approach to motivation and personality. *Psychological Review, 95,* 256–273.

Emmons, R. A., & Diener, E. D. (1985). Personality correlates of subjective well-being. *Personality and Social Psychology Bulletin, 11,* 89–97.

Emmons, R. A., & McCullough, M. E. (2003). Counting blessings versus burdens: An experimental investigation of gratitude and subjective well-being in daily life. *Journal of Personality and Social Psychology, 84,* 377–389. doi:10.1037/0022-3514.84.2.377

Erikson, E. H. (1950). *Childhood and society*. New York, NY: Norton.

Fava, G. A., & Tomba, E. (2009). Increasing psychological well-being and resilience by psychotherapeutic methods. *Journal of Personality, 77*, 1903–1934. doi. 1111/j.1467-6494.2009.00604.x

Fordyce, M. W. (1983). A program to increase happiness: Further studies. *Journal of Counselling Psychology, 30*, 483–498.

Fowers, B. J., Mollica, C. O., & Procacci, E. N. (2010). Constitutive and instrumental goal orientations and their relations with eudaimonic and hedonic well-being. *Journal of Positive Psychology, 5*, 139–153. doi:10.1080/17439761003630045

Frankl, V. E. (1997). *Man's search for meaning: An introduction to logotherapy.* New York, NY: Beacon Press.

Fredrickson, B. L. (2004). The broaden-and-build theory of positive emotions. *The Royal Society, 359*, 1367–1377. doi:10.1098/rstb.2004.1512

Frisch, M. B. (in press). Evidence-based well-being/positive psychology assessment and intervention with quality of life therapy and coaching and the quality of life inventory (QOLI). *Social Indicators Research.* doi:10.1007/s11205-012-0140-7

Gable, S. L., Reis, H. T., Impett, E. A., & Asher, E. R. (2004). What do you do when things go right? The intrapersonal and interpersonal benefits of sharing positive events. *Journal of Personality and Social Psychology, 87*, 228–245. doi:10.1037/0022-3514.87.2.228

Gilbert, D. T., & Wilson, T. D. (2007). Prospection: Experiencing the future. *Science, 317*, 1351–1354.

Gollwitzer, P. M. (1999). Implementation intentions: Strong effects of simple plans. *American Psychologist, 54*, 493–503.

Grouzet, F. M. E., Kasser, T., Ahuvia, A., Dols, J. M. F., Kim, Y., Lau, S., . . . Sheldon, K. M. (2005). The structure of goal contents across 15 cultures. *Journal of Personality and Social Psychology, 89*, 800–816. doi:10.1037/0022-3514.89.5.800

Hayes, S. C., Luoma, J. B., Bond, F. W., Masuda, A., & Lillis, J. (2006). Acceptance and commitment therapy: Model, processes and outcomes. *Behaviour Research and Therapy, 44*, 1–25. doi:10.1016/j.brat.2005.06.006 DOI:10.1016%2Fj.brat.2005.06.006

Hirschi, A. (2011). Effects of orientations to happiness on vocational identity achievement. *Career Development Quarterly, 59*, 367–378.

Huta, V. (2012). Linking peoples' pursuit of eudaimonia and hedonia with characteristics of their parents: Parenting styles, verbally endorsed values, and role modeling. *Journal of Happiness Studies, 13*, 47–61. doi:10.1007/s10902-011-9249-7

Huta, V. (2013a). Pursuing eudaimonia versus hedonia: Distinctions, similarities, and relationships. In A. Waterman (Ed.), *The best within us: Positive psychology perspectives on eudaimonic functioning* (pp. 139–158). Washington, DC: APA Books.

Huta, V. (2013b). Eudaimonia. In S. David, I. Boniwell, & A. C. Ayers (Eds.), *Oxford handbook of happiness* (pp. 201–213). Oxford, England: Oxford University Press.

Huta, V., Pearce, K., & Voloaca, M. (May, 2013). *How your style of pursuing personal well-being relates to how you impact the world around you.* Symposium presented at the Psychology Outside The Box Conference, Ottawa, Ontario.

Huta, V., Pelletier, L., Baxter, D., & Thompson, A. (2012). How eudaimonic and hedonic motives relate to the well-being of close others. *Journal of Positive Psychology, 7*, 399–404.

Huta, V., & Ryan, R. M. (2010). Pursuing pleasure or virtue: The differential and overlapping well-being benefits of hedonic and eudaimonic motives. *Journal of Happiness Studies, 11*, 735–762. doi:10.1007/s10902-009-9171-4

Huta, V., & Waterman A. S. (2013). Eudaimonia and its distinction from hedonia: Developing a classification and terminology for understanding conceptual and operational definitions. *Journal of Happiness Studies.* doi:10.1007/s10902-013-9485-0

Huta, V., & Zuroff, D. C. (2007). Examining mediators of the link between generativity and well-being. *Journal of Adult Development, 14*, 47–52. doi:10.1007/s10804-007-9030-7

Jones, A., & Crandall, R. (1986). Validation of a short index of self-actualization. *Personality and Social Psychology Bulletin, 12,* 63–73.

Joseph, S., & Linley, P. A. (2004). Positive therapy: A positive psychological theory of thera-peutic practice. In P. A. Linley & S. Joseph (Eds.), *Positive psychology in practice* (1st ed., pp. 354–371). Hoboken, NJ: Wiley.

Kashdan, T. B., & Silvia, P. (2009). Curiosity and interest: The benefits of thriving on novelty and challenge. In S. J. Lopez (Eds.), *Handbook of positive psychology* (2nd ed., pp. 367–375). Oxford, England: Oxford University Press.

Kasser, T. (2011). Ecological challenges, materialistic values, and social change. In R. Biswas-Diener (Ed.), *Positive psychology as social change* (pp. 89–108). Dordrecht, The Netherlands: Springer. doi:10.1007/978-90-481-9938-9_6

Kasser, T., & Ryan, R. M. (1993). A dark side of the American dream: Correlates of financial success as a central life aspiration. *Journal of Personality and Social Psychology, 65,* 410–422.

Keyes, C. L. M. (2002). The mental health continuum: From languishing to flourishing in life. *Journal of Health and Social Research, 43,* 207–222.

King, L. (2001). The health benefits of writing about life goals. *Personality and Social Psychology Bulletin, 27,* 798–807.

Kohlberg, L. (1984). *The psychology of moral development: The nature and validity of moral stages* (1st ed.). San Francisco, CA: Harper & Row.

Kumano, M. (2011). Orientations to happiness in Japanese people: Pleasure, meaning, and engagement. *Japanese Journal of Psychology, 81,* 619–624.

Loevinger, J. (1966). The meaning and measurement of ego development. *American Psychologist, 21,* 195–206.

Loevinger, J. (1979). Construct validity of the sentence completion test of ego development. *Applied Psychological Measurement, 3,* 281–311.

Lyubomirsky, S. (2008). *The how of happiness: A scientific approach to getting the life you want.* New York, NY: Penguin Press.

Lyubomirsky, S., & Lepper, H. S. (1999). A measure of subjective happiness: Preliminary relia-bility and construct validation. *Social Indicators Research, 46,* 137–155.

Lyubomirsky, S., Sheldon, K. M., & Schkade, D. (2005). Pursuing happiness: The architecture of sustainable change. *Review of General Psychology, 9,* 111–131. doi:10.1037/1089-2680.9.2.111

Maddux, J. E. (2009). Self-regulation. In S. Lopez (Ed.), *The encyclopedia of positive psychology* (pp. 874–880). Chichester, England: Blackwell.

Marcia, J. E. (1967). Ego identity status: Relationship to change in self-esteem, "general malad-justment," and authoritarianism. *Journal of Personality, 35,* 118–133.

Martin, M. W. (2008). Paradoxes of happiness. *Journal of Happiness Studies, 9,* 171–184.

Maslow, A. (1964). *Religion, values and peak experiences.* New York, NY: Viking.

Maslow, A. H. (1968). *Towards a psychology of being* (2nd ed.). New York, NY: Van Nostrand Reinhold.

Mather, M., & Carstensen, L. L. (2003). Aging and attentional biases for emotional faces. *Psy-chological Science, 14,* 409–415.

Mauss, I. B., Tamir, M., Anderson, C. L., & Savino, N. (2011). Can seeking happiness make people unhappy? Paradoxical effects of valuing happiness. *Emotion, 11,* 807–815.

McAdams, D. P. (1993). *The stories we live by: Personal myths and the making of the self.* New York, NY: Morrow.

McAdams, D. P., & de St. Aubin, E. (1998). *How and why we care for the next generation.* Washing-ton, DC: American Psychological Association.

Norton, D. L. (1976). *Personal destinies: A philosophy of ethical individualism.* Princeton, NJ: Prince-ton University Press.

Orlick, T. (1990). *In pursuit of excellence: How to win in sport and life through mental training* (2nd ed.). Champaign, IL: Leisure Press.

Otake, K., Shimai, S., Tanaka-Matsumi, J., Otsui, K., & Fredrickson, B. L. (2006). Happy people become happier through kindness: A counting kindnesses intervention. *Journal of Happiness Studies, 7*, 361–375.

Park, N., & Peterson, C. (2010). Does it matter where we live?: The urban psychology of character strengths. *American Psychologist, 65*, 535–547. doi:10.1037/a0019621

Park, N., Peterson, C., & Ruch, W. (2009). Orientations to happiness and life satisfaction in twenty-seven nations. *Journal of Positive Psychology, 4*, 273–279. doi:10.1080/17439760902933690

Pelletier, L. G., Baxter, D., & Huta, V. (2011). Personal autonomy and environmental sustainability. In V. I. Chirkov, R. M. Ryan, & K. M. Sheldon (Eds.), *Human autonomy in cross-cultural context* (pp. 257–277). Dorcrecht, The Netherlands: Springer. doi:10.1007/978-90-481-9938-9_6

Peterson, C., Park, N., & Seligman, M. E. P. (2005). Orientations to happiness and life satisfaction: The full life versus the empty life. *Journal of Happiness Studies, 6*, 25–41. doi:10.1007/s10902-004-1278-z

Peterson, C., Ruch, W., Beermann, U., Park, N., & Seligman, M. E. P. (2007). Strengths of character, orientations to happiness and life satisfaction. *Journal of Positive Psychology, 2*, 149–156. doi:10.1080/17439760701228938

Peterson, C., & Seligman, M. E. P. (2004). *Character strengths and virtues: A handbook and classification*. New York, NY: Oxford University Press.

Prochaska, J. O., & DiClemente, C. C. (1984). *The transtheoretical approach: Towards a systematic eclectic framework*. Homewood, IL: Dow Jones Irwin.

Prochaska, J. O., & Velicer, W. F. (1997). The transtheoretical model of health behavior change. *American Journal of Health Promotion, 12*, 38–48.

Proyer, R. T., Annen, H., Eggimann, N., Schneider, A., & Ruch, W. (2012). Assessing the "good life" in a military context: How does life and work satisfaction relate to orientations to happiness and career-success among Swiss professional officers. *Social Indicators Research, 106*, 577–590. doi:10.1007/s11205-011-9823-8

Rogers, C. R. (1961). *On becoming a person: A therapist's view of psychotherapy*. Boston, MA: Houghton Mifflin.

Rogers, C. R. (1964). Toward a modern approach to values: The valuing process in the mature person. *Journal of Abnormal and Social Psychology, 68*, 160–167.

Ruch, W., Harzer, C., Proyer, R. T., Park, N., & Peterson, C. (2010). Ways to happiness in German-speaking countries: The adaptation of the German version of the Orientations to Happiness Questionnaire in paper-pencil and internet samples. *European Journal of Psychological Assessment, 26*, 227–234. doi:10.1027/1015-5759/a000030

Ruch, W., Proyer, R. T., & Weber, M. (2010). Humor as a character strength among the elderly: Empirical findings on age-related changes and its contribution to satisfaction with life. *Zeitschrift für Gerontologie und Geriatrie, 1*, 13–18. doi:10.1007/s00391-009-0090-0

Ryan, R. M., & Deci, E. L. (2001). On happiness and human potentials: A review of research on hedonic and eudaimonic well-being. *Annual Review of Psychology, 52*, 141–166.

Ryan, R. M., & Frederick, C. (1997). On energy, personality, and health: Subjective vitality as a dynamic reflection of well-being. *Journal of Personality, 65*, 529–565.

Ryan, R. M., Huta, V., & Deci, E. L. (2008). Living well: A self-determination theory perspective on eudaimonia. *Journal of Happiness Studies, 9*, 139–170. doi:10.1007/s10902-006-9023-4

Ryff, C. D. (1989). Happiness is everything, or is it? Explorations on the meaning of psychological well-being. *Journal of Personality and Social Psychology, 57*, 1069–1081.

Schlegel, R. J., Hicks, J. A., King, L. A., & Arndt, J. (2011). Feeling like you know who you are: Perceived true self-knowledge and meaning in life. *Personality and Social Psychology Bulletin, 37*, 745–756. doi:10.1177/0146167211400424

Schooler, J. W., Ariely, D., & Loewenstein, G. (2003). The pursuit and assessment of happiness may be self-defeating. In J. Carrillo & I. Brocas (Eds.), *Psychology and economics* (pp. 41–70). Oxford, England: Oxford University Press.

Schueller, S. M., & Seligman, M. E. P. (2010). Pursuit of pleasure, engagement and meaning: Relationships to subjective and objective measures of well-being. *Journal of Positive Psychology, 5*, 253–263. doi:10.1080/17439761003794130

Schwartz, S. H., & Bilsky, W. (1987). Toward a universal psychological structure of human values. *Journal of Personality and Social Psychology, 53*, 550–562.

Seligman, M. E. P. (1998). *Learned optimism.* New York, NY: Pocket Books.

Seligman, M. E. P. (2002). *Authentic happiness: Using the new positive psychology to realize your potential for lasting fulfillment.* New York, NY: Free Press.

Seligman, M. E. P. (2011). *Flourish: A visionary new understanding of happiness and well-being.* New York, NY: Free Press.

Seligman, M. E. P., Rashid, T., & Parks, A. C. (2006). Positive psychotherapy. *American Psychologist, 61*, 774–788.

Seligman, M. E. P., Steen, T. A., Park, N., & Peterson, C. (2005). Positive psychology progress: Empirical validation of interventions. *American Psychologist, 60*, 410–421. doi:10.1037/0003-066X.60.5.410

Sheldon, K. M., & Elliot, A. J. (1999). Goal striving, need-satisfaction, and longitudinal well-being: The self-concordance model. *Journal of Personality and Social Psychology, 76*, 482–497.

Sin, N. L., & Lyubomirsky, S. (2009). Enhancing well-being and alleviating depressive symptoms with positive psychology interventions: A practice-friendly meta-analysis. *Journal of Clinical Psychology, 65*, 467–487. doi:10.1002/jclp.20593

Snyder, C. R. (1995). Conceptualizing, measuring, and nurturing hope. *Journal of Counseling and Development, 73*, 355–360.

Staudinger, U. M. (2001). Life reflection: A social-cognitive analysis of life review. *Review of General Psychology, 5*, 148–160.

Steger, M. F., Frazier, P., Oishi, S., & Kaler, M. (2006). The Meaning in Life Questionnaire: Assessing the presence of and search for meaning in life. *Journal of Counseling Psychology, 53*, 80–93.

Steger, M. F., Kashdan, T. B., & Oishi, S. (2007). Being good by doing good: Daily eudaimonic activity and well-being. *Journal of Research in Personality, 42*, 22–42. doi:10.1016/j.jrp.2007.03.004

Steger, M. F., & Shin, J. Y. (2012). Happiness and meaning in a technological world. In P. Brey, A. Briggle, & E. Spence (Eds.), *The good life in a technological age* (pp. 92–108). New York, NY: Routledge.

Szymanska, K. (2008). The downward arrow technique. *The Coaching Psychologist, 4*, 85–86.

Tafarodi, R. W., Bonn, G., Liang, H., Takai, J., Moriizumi, S., Belhekar, V., & Padhye, A. (2012). What makes for a good life? A four-nation study. *Journal of Happiness Studies, 13*, 783–800. doi:10.1007/s10902-011-9290-6

Tracy, J. L., & Robins, R. W. (2007). The psychological structure of pride: A tale of two facets. *Journal of Personality and Social Psychology, 92*, 506–525. doi:10.1037/0022-3514.92.3.506

Vella-Brodrick, D. A., Park, N., & Peterson, C. (2009). Three ways to be happy: Pleasure, engagement, and meaning-findings from Australian and US samples. *Social Indicators Research, 90*, 165–179. doi:10.1007/s11205-008-9251-6

Vittersø, J. (2004). Subjective well-being versus self-actualization: Using the flow-simplex to promote a conceptual clarification of subjective quality of life. *Social Indicators Research, 65*, 299–331.

Vittersø, J. (2013). Feelings, meanings, and optimal functioning: Some distinctions between hedonic and eudaimonic well-being. In A. S. Waterman (Ed.), *The best within us: Positive psychology perspectives on eudaimonia* (pp. 39–55). Washington, DC: APA Books.

Vittersø, J., Dyrdal, G. M., & Røysamb, E. (2005, June). *Utilities and capabilities: A psychological account of the two concepts and their relations to the idea of a good life.* Paper presented at the 2nd Workshop on Capabilities and Happiness, University of Milano, Bicocca, Italy.

Vittersø, J., Oelmann, H. I., & Wang, A. L. (2009). Life satisfaction is not a balanced estimator of the good life: Evidence from reaction time measures and self-reported emotions. *Journal of Happiness Studies, 10*, 1–17. doi:10.1007/s10902-007-9058-1

Vittersø, J., Overwien, P., & Martinsen, E. (2009). Pleasure and interest are differentially affected by replaying versus analyzing a happy life moment. *Journal of Positive Psychology, 4*, 14–20. doi:10.1080/17439760802060602

Vittersø, J., Søholt, Y., Hetland, A., Thoresen, I. A., & Røysamb, E. (2010). Was Hercules happy? Some answers from a functional model of human well-being. *Social Indicators Research, 95*, 1–18. doi:10.1007/s11205-009-9447-4

Warnock, M. (1970). *Existentialism* (Rev. ed.). Oxford, England: Oxford University Press.

Waterman, A. S. (1993). Two conceptions of happiness: Contrasts of perspective expressiveness (eudaimonia) and hedonic enjoyment. *Journal of Personality and Social Psychology, 64*, 678–691.

Waterman, A. S., & Schwartz, S. J. (2013). Eudaimonic identity theory. In A. Waterman (Ed.), *The best within us: Positive psychology perspectives on eudaimonic functioning* (pp. 99–118). Washington, DC: APA Books.

Waterman, A. S., Schwartz, S. J., Zamboanga, B. L., Ravert, R. D., Williams, M. K., Agocha, V. B., . . . Donnellan, M. B. (2010). The Questionnaire for Eudaimonic Well-Being: Psychometric properties, demographic comparisons, and evidence of validity. *The Journal of Positive Psychology, 5*, 41–61. doi:10.1080/1743976090343520

Wells, G. (2012). *Superbodies: How the science behind world-class athletes can transform your body and health*. New York, NY: HarperCollins.

Wills, T. A. (1981). Downward social comparison principles in social psychology. *Psychological Bulletin, 90*, 245–271.

Wong, P. T. P. (2010). Meaning therapy: An integrative and positive existential psychotherapy. *Journal of Contemporary Psychotherapy, 40*, 85–99.

Wong, P. T. P., & Fry, P. S. (Eds.). (2012). *The human quest for meaning* (2nd ed.). Mahwah, NJ: Erlbaum.

Wood, A. M., Linley, P. A., Maltby, J., Baliousis, M., & Joseph, S. (2008). The authentic personality: A theoretical and empirical conceptualization and the development of the authenticity scale. *Journal of Counseling Psychology, 55*, 385–399. doi:10.1037/0022-0167.55.3.385

Wrzesniewski, A., McCauley, C. R., Rozin, P., & Schwartz, B. (1997). Jobs, careers, and callings: People's relations to their work. *Journal of Research in Personality, 31*, 21–33.

# PART III

# PRACTICES FOR HEALTH AND WELL-BEING

# CHAPTER 11

# The Prospects, Practices, and Prescriptions for the Pursuit of Happiness

KRISTIN LAYOUS, KENNON M. SHELDON, and SONJA LYUBOMIRSKY

HAPPINESS IS A CENTRAL criterion of mental health (Keyes, 2005; Taylor & Brown, 1988) and has been found to be associated with numerous tangible benefits, such as enhanced physical health, reduced psychopathology, greater productivity, more fulfilling relationships, and even longer life (see Lyubomirsky, King, & Diener, 2005, for a review). Thus, an important goal for psychology is advancing knowledge about how to help people increase their levels of happiness, positive mental health, and personal thriving. During the last decade, researchers have made a great deal of progress investigating intentional ways to increase happiness—yielding both theory (Lyubomirsky, Sheldon, & Schkade, 2005) and empirical evidence (see Sin & Lyubomirsky, 2009, for a meta-analysis) supporting the notion that happiness levels can be increased. Furthermore, growing research is pointing to the optimal conditions under which happiness-enhancing activities work to increase well-being, as well as the processes underlying these strategies' success (Lyubomirsky & Layous, 2013). Finally, preliminary studies suggest that increasing happiness through positive activities may lead to multiple favorable downstream effects on people's health, work, and relationships (e.g., Fredrickson, Cohn, Coffey, Pek, & Finkel, 2008).

Although the concept of happiness is widely understood by laypeople, it is important to define it scientifically. Our definition corresponds to the growing consensus that happiness (or subjective well-being) comprises a global feeling that life is going well (i.e., general satisfaction with life), as well as the frequent experience of positive emotions and infrequent experience of negative emotions (Diener, Suh, Lucas, & Smith, 1999). Notably, although our definition of happiness does not explicitly include meaning and purpose in life (concepts that laypeople typically associate with overall well-being), research has shown that satisfaction with life, positive emotions, and fewer negative emotions are highly correlated with these constructs (Ryff, 1989).

Despite the growing body of evidence supporting the notion that happiness can be improved, some contemporary theories indicate that trying to increase one's happiness levels is futile—an endeavor doomed from the start. This pessimism is rooted in several assumptions about the nature of well-being, including the influence of genetics on happiness, the concept of hedonic adaptation, and the finding that well-being-related personality traits exhibit a great deal of longitudinal stability. All of these views imply that, although people might become happier or more satisfied in the short-term, they are destined to return to their original level in the long-term. However, evidence suggesting that researchers should be pessimistic about the intentional pursuit of happiness is countervailed by equally convincing evidence signaling optimism, leaving the possibility of sustainably increasing happiness open to scientific debate and inquiry. Below, we briefly outline the evidence both for and against the "intentional happiness" proposition.

## PESSIMISM (AND OPTIMISM) REGARDING THE INTENTIONAL PURSUIT OF HAPPINESS

Considerable behavioral-genetic research indicates that permanently changing one's happiness levels is very difficult, if not impossible. For example, evidence from a sample of monozygotic and dizygotic twins suggests that the heritability of well-being may be as high as 80% (Lykken & Tellegen, 1996), although a more widely accepted figure is 50% (Braungart, Plomin, DeFries, & Fulker, 1992; Røysamb, Harris, Magnus, Vittersø, & Tambs, 2002; Tellegen et al., 1988; cf. Diener et al., 1999). This suggests that each person has a built-in "attractor" for happiness, which he or she can orbit around, but never leave behind (Vallacher & Nowak, 2002). In other words, a person may have a "set range" that includes the most likely or expected value in his or her temporal distribution of happiness across the life span (see Headey, 2010). Consistent with this idea, Headey and Wearing (1989) found, in a four-wave panel study, that participants tended to keep returning to their own baselines over time (see also Suh, Diener, & Fujita, 1996).

A related source of pessimism comes from research on personality traits. Traits are cognitive, affective, and behavioral complexes that are, by definition, consistent across situations and across the life span (Allport, 1955). Therefore, they may account for part of the stability of well-being. For example, neuroticism and extraversion, the two "Big Five" traits most closely related to well-being, have shown impressive long-term stability (McCrae & Costa, 1990). For example, teacher ratings of students' adaptability predict adult cheerfulness 40 years later (Nave, Sherman, Funder, Hampson, & Goldberg, 2010). Given the relation of extraversion and neuroticism to happiness, these data suggest that people would also maintain the same relative level of happiness over time (see also Costa, McCrae, & Zonderman, 1987; Diener & Lucas, 1999).

Despite research suggesting that happiness is biologically influenced and consistent across the life span, convincing evidence also suggests that genes and personality are only part of the happiness puzzle. First, recent work from behavioral genetics indicates that the degree to which happiness can be explained by genetics may not be as high as originally thought (Stubbe, Posthuma, Boomsma, & de Geus, 2005). Second, genes influence happiness only indirectly—that is, by shaping the kinds of experiences and environments one has or seeks to have. Thus, unwanted effects of genes could be minimized by active efforts to steer oneself away from problematic situations or to avoid maladaptive behaviors (Lykken, 2000). Furthermore, genetic and environmental factors interact with one another in a dynamic process such that environmental factors can shape gene expression (Plomin, 2004). Lastly, it is worth noting that heritability coefficients describe individual differences within a population, not mean levels. Thus, even a high heritability coefficient for a particular trait (such as happiness) does not rule out the possibility that the mean level of that trait for a specific population can be elevated. Under the right conditions, everyone might become happier than they were before, even if their rank ordering relative to others remains stable.

Another source of pessimism arises from the concept of hedonic adaptation (Frederick & Loewenstein, 1999; Lyubomirsky, 2011) or the hedonic treadmill (Brickman & Campbell, 1971). These concepts state that humans have a remarkable ability to adapt to changes, positive and negative (Boswell, Boudreau, & Tichy, 2005; Fredrick & Loewenstein, 1999; Lucas, Clark, Georgellis, & Diener, 2003; Luhmann, Hofmann, Eid, & Lucas, 2012; Lyubomirsky, 2011). Thus, although new circumstances may temporarily cause people to become happier or sadder, the effect of these new circumstances on happiness diminishes quickly or even disappears entirely, once people habituate to it, suggesting that "what goes up must come down." In support of this idea, a longitudinal study showed that newlyweds experience increases in life satisfaction preceding their marriage, and then gradually return to their previous levels within an average of 2 years (Clark, Diener, Georgellis, & Lucas, 2008; Lucas et al., 2003; but see Zimmermann & Easterlin, 2006). Employees who received a voluntary promotion showed the same pattern as the newlyweds, gaining in job satisfaction immediately after the promotion, and then dipping back to baseline levels within a year (Boswell et al., 2005). The notion of adaptation brings to mind the image of a person walking up a descending escalator; although the improving circumstances of her life may propel her upward toward greater happiness, the process of adaptation eventually forces her back to her initial state.

Although studies show that, on average, people adapt to positive experiences, researchers have noted that adaptation is not inevitable (Diener, Lucas, & Scollon, 2006). Specifically, people who experience unemployment (Clark et al., 2008; Lucas, Clark, Georgellis, & Diener, 2004; but see Luhmann et al., 2012) or become disabled (Lucas, 2007) do not, on average, return to their pre-event levels of well-being. Furthermore, within studies, considerable variation is evident in individual patterns of adaptation (Diener et al., 2006). That is, some people adapt more rapidly than average, some people adapt more slowly than average, and still others do not adapt at all. Indeed, in the study of newlyweds, some participants experienced lasting increases in life satisfaction and some experienced lasting decreases, thus making the "average" effect potentially misleading (Lucas et al., 2003; Lucas, Dyrenforth, & Diener, 2008).

Theory and empirical evidence suggest that people can slow their adaptation to positive experiences if they continue to generate potentially novel, varied, and surprising experiences from an initial positive change (e.g., taking new and beautiful routes while they engage in their new running hobby or buying new flavors of coffee to make in their Keurig; Lyubomirsky, 2011; Sheldon & Lyubomirsky, 2012). For example, participants randomly assigned to receive unexpected feedback about their biggest personal strengths showed slower adaptation to the positive news than participants who received unsurprising feedback or no feedback (Jacobs Bao, Boehm, & Lyubomirsky, 2013), thus supporting the role of surprise in forestalling adaptation to positive experiences. In addition, people can thwart adaptation by fostering appreciation of the initial positive experience and the subsequent positive changes that occurred as a result of it (Lyubomirsky, 2011; Sheldon & Lyubomirsky, 2012).

For example, consciously thinking about what you appreciate about your life partner might help you to continue to obtain positive emotional boosts from your marriage long after the 2-year average adaptation period is over. So, although research suggests that people adapt to positive experiences more quickly and more frequently than to negative experiences, hedonic adaptation to positive changes is not inevitable. Indeed, several strategies are available to help individuals garner pleasant emotions from positive life changes (Lyubomirsky, 2011; Sheldon & Lyubomirsky, 2012).

## PUTTING THE EVIDENCE TOGETHER:
## HAPPINESS CAN BE INCREASED

Which arguments regarding the feasibility of increasing happiness are more compelling? Are sustainable gains in well-being possible or are they impossible? We believe that recent theory and research both persuasively suggest that increasing happiness is possible through intentional positive activities.

### THEORETICAL PERSPECTIVES

When we discuss meaningful increases in happiness, we are referring to a person's characteristic level of happiness during a particular period in his or her life, which we term the *current happiness level*. We define happiness this way because we wish to identify a quantity that is more enduring than momentary or daily happiness, but that is also somewhat malleable over time, and thus amenable to meaningful pursuit. Operationally, one might define a person's current happiness level in terms of his or her retrospective summary judgments regarding some recent period (such as the past 2, 6, or 12 months), or as the average of momentary judgments of happiness generated at multiple times during that period.

To consider whether happiness can be increased, we must first identify what influences it. As discussed earlier, genetics influence about 50% of individual differences in people's happiness levels (Røysamb et al., 2002), although not as deterministically as some interpretations suggest. In addition, in part because people show a tendency to adapt to their life circumstances (Lyubomirsky, 2011), such circumstances explain only about 10% of individual differences in happiness (Diener et al., 1999). Notably, however, after accounting for the genetic and circumstantial influences on people's happiness, a large proportion of people's happiness remains unexplained. Lyubomirsky, Sheldon, et al. (2005) reasoned that this remaining portion of happiness can be accounted for by the behaviors people choose to engage in and how they decide to respond to and interpret the experiences in their lives—that is, by people's intentional activities.

Happiness-increasing intentional activities may be cognitive (i.e., one regularly adopts an optimistic or positive attitude) or behavioral (i.e., one is regularly kind to others or habitually engages in physical exercise). Common to all of these practices is the notion of intentional effort and commitment in service of particular desired objectives or experiences. Because of their intentional character, activities are more resistant to the effects of adaptation than are life changes involving new circumstances or possessions. In other words, one can deliberately vary one's activities such that they continually provide new experiences and results. Indeed, some intentional activities (such as meditation or pausing to count one's blessings) can serve to directly counteract adaptation. Furthermore, intentional activities can create a self-sustaining cycle of positive change in which invested effort leads the person to further opportunities for satisfying actions and accomplishments. Of course, one can also perform an activity robotically, without variation, or can fail to sensitively apply or enact the strategy. In such cases (described in more detail later), the benefits of the activity are likely to fade over time, just as the impact of positive circumstantial changes dampens. Still, activities have the potential to create sustained positive change because of their relatively more dynamic and varying nature and because of their capacity to produce a steady stream of positive and rich experiences.

Of course, the boundary between activity changes and circumstantial changes is somewhat fuzzy. For example, bringing about many circumstantial changes (e.g., moving to a new job or city) undoubtedly takes intentional effort, and, conversely, circumstantial changes may enable or afford new types of activity. Furthermore, some kinds of circumstances (i.e., one's marital status) doubtless involve activity (i.e., one acts within the marital relationship). Nevertheless, the data we describe below suggest that the basic distinction between the two types of factors is meaningful and important.

*Circumstances Versus Intentional Activities*   Sheldon and Lyubomirsky (2006a) conducted a three-wave longitudinal study of 666 undergraduates. Students rated their well-being at the beginning of an academic semester using a variety of standard measures. Midway through the semester, they rated the extent to which they had experienced both positive activity and positive circumstantial changes since the beginning of the semester, and they also rated their well-being again. They then rated their well-being a final time at the end of the semester. Sheldon and Lyubomirsky (2006a) predicted that both positive activity changes and positive circumstantial changes would predict enhanced well-being from Time 1 to Time 2, but that only activity changes would predict maintained gains at Time 3.

The activity and circumstance measures each consisted of a single item, with which participants rated their agreement. The circumstances item read:

Please rate the extent to which there has been some significant positive change in the circumstances of your life since the beginning of the semester, which has given you a boost since it occurred. "Circumstances" means "facts" about your life, such as living arrangement, monetary situation, or course load. For example, you may have moved to a better dorm or better roommate, received an increase in financial support so you can have more fun, or dropped a course that you were really going to have trouble with.

The activity item read:

Please rate the extent you have adopted some significant positive new *goal or activity* since the beginning of the semester, which has given you a boost since it occurred. "Goal/activity" means something you chose to do or get involved in, which takes effort on your part. For example, you may have joined a rewarding new group, club, or sports team, decided on a major or career direction which makes it clear what to focus on, or taken on some other important new project or goal in your life.

As expected, both positive activity and circumstantial changes predicted increased happiness at Time 2. However, only activity changes predicted happiness at Time 3, indicating that the earlier activity-based gains had been maintained, whereas the earlier circumstance-based gains had been attenuated. Parenthetically, the two change variables correlated .34 with each other, suggesting that some overlap does indeed exist between the two categories. Again, however, only the activity change variable accounted for maintained change in well-being. These results suggest that, at least in the short term, it is possible to increase one's well-being above the set point and then to maintain it there.

Two other findings from this research program deserve mention. First, Sheldon and Lyubomirsky (2006a) found, in a separate study using the same two change measures, that activity changes are associated with more varied experiences and less of a sense of "getting used to" (i.e., adapting to) the change, compared to circumstantial changes. This finding supports an important premise of our longitudinal model—namely, that activity changes induce more varied experiences and less hedonic adaptation, relative to circumstantial changes. Again, we believe these characteristics of activity help account for its potential long-term effect on happiness.

Second, Sheldon and Lyubomirsky (2006a) found, in the longitudinal study, that competence and related need satisfaction (Deci & Ryan, 2000; Sheldon, Elliot, Kim, & Kasser, 2001) mediated the sustained activity effects. In other words, the reason newly adopted activities at Time 1 produced sustained gains in well-being at Time 3 is that participants felt more competent in their daily lives during the semester and felt more related to others during the semester. In contrast, circumstantial changes tend to be more superficial and bring less opportunity to fulfill deeper psychological needs. To illustrate, consider some typical circumstantial changes people listed: "I learned that I won't have to be in a lottery in order to get in my Broadcast 1 class (which is required)," "My roommate at the beginning of the semester was a cocaine addict. She is no longer my roommate," and "I was recently initiated into my fraternity. The stress level of my life has now decreased because I no longer have to worry about initiation requirements." In short, the limited relevance of circumstantial changes for psychological need satisfaction may be another reason such changes have limited influence on well-being, in addition to the reason that people more quickly habituate to altered circumstances.

In a subsequent study, Sheldon and colleagues (2010) randomly assigned participants to focus on making a positive circumstantial change in their lives or to intentionally focus on increasing their levels of need satisfaction (either autonomy, competence, or relatedness). As predicted, people who focused on increasing their levels of need satisfaction showed sustained increases in happiness relative to people who focused on changing their circumstances, thus again suggesting that intentional positive activities are a fruitful path to sustained increases in well-being.

*Intentional Positive Activities*    Sheldon et al. (2010) did not give participants exact instructions for how to increase their need satisfaction, but, on average, participants successfully did so. What if, however, particular defined activities existed that could satisfy needs and increase well-being? Indeed, many behaviors are associated with greater happiness. For example, happier people tend to be more grateful (McCullough, Emmons, & Tsang, 2002), optimistic (Scheier & Carver, 1993), and prosocial (Krueger, Hicks, & McGue, 2001) than their less happy peers. If individuals who wanted to become happier were encouraged to think more gratefully and optimistically and to behave more prosocially, could they also increase their levels of well-being? Substantial research has now been conducted to suggest that they can (Sin & Lyubomirsky, 2009). Specifically, if people intentionally engage in the thoughts and behaviors associated with dispositionally happy people (e.g., expressing gratitude, thinking positively about their future, or doing kind acts for others)—we call them "positive activities"—they can increase their happiness.

Positive activities can take many different forms. They include (but are not limited to) activities such as writing letters of gratitude (Boehm, Lyubomirsky, & Sheldon,

2011; Layous, Lee, Choi, & Lyubomirsky, in press; Lyubomirsky, Dickerhoof, Boehm, & Sheldon, 2011; Seligman, Steen, Park, & Peterson, 2005), counting one's blessings (Chancellor, Layous, & Lyubomirsky, 2012; Emmons & McCullough, 2003; Froh, Sefick, & Emmons, 2008; Lyubomirsky, Sheldon, et al., 2005; Seligman et al., 2005), practicing optimism (Boehm et al., 2011; King, 2001; Layous, Nelson, & Lyubomirsky, 2012; Lyubomirsky et al., 2011; Sheldon & Lyubomirsky, 2006b), performing acts of kindness (Chancellor, Jacobs Bao, & Lyubomirsky, 2013; Della Porta, Jacobs Bao, & Lyubomirsky, 2012; Dunn, Aknin, & Norton, 2008; Layous, Nelson, Oberle, Schonert-Reichl, & Lyubomirsky, 2012; Sheldon, Boehm, & Lyubomirsky, 2012, Study 2), using one's strengths in a new way (Seligman et al., 2005), affirming one's most important values (Nelson, Fuller, Choi, & Lyubomirsky, 2013), and meditating on positive feelings toward self and others (Fredrickson et al., 2008).

Importantly, positive activities may not only increase well-being but also alleviate symptoms of depression (Sin & Lyubomirsky, 2009). A natural question might be, how do positive activities compare to "treatment-as-usual" (i.e., talk therapy)? In contrast to traditional psychotherapy approaches, these activities are all relatively brief, self-administered, and nonstigmatizing actions that promote positive affect, positive thoughts, and positive behaviors, rather than directly aiming to address negative affect, negative thoughts, or negative behaviors. For example, in one positive activity, people are instructed to do kind acts for others during one particular day each week. The person for whom the kind act is being done can be aware of the act or the act can be kept anonymous. This simple focus on prosocial behavior has been shown to increase well-being in adults (Lyubomirsky, Sheldon, et al., 2005) and to promote liking among classmates in a middle school–based study (Layous, Nelson, Oberle, et al., 2012).

A recent meta-analysis by Sin and Lyubomirsky (2009) showed that positive interventions yielded impressive (medium-sized) effects for improvement of well-being and alleviation of depressive symptoms—effect sizes nearly identical to the classic Smith and Glass (1977) meta-analysis of the effect of psychotherapy. In further support of the comparability of positive activities to more traditional, cognitive-behavioral therapy (CBT) techniques, people who identified as being dissatisfied with their bodies showed as much improvement in body satisfaction in a gratitude diary condition (positive activity approach) as they did in a thought monitoring and restructuring condition (CBT approach; Geraghty, Wood, & Hyland, 2010). Interestingly, people in the gratitude diary condition showed half the dropout rate of people in the CBT-based condition.

In a different study, moderately depressed college freshmen were randomly assigned to read *The How of Happiness* (a book describing the empirical basis of positive activities; Lyubomirsky, 2008), *Control Your Depression* (a book describing CBT approaches to alleviating depression; Lewinsohn, Muñoz, Youngren, & Zeiss, 1992), or a waitlist control group (Parks & Szanto, 2009). Students assigned to bibliotherapy showed similar decreases in depression at post-test, but those assigned to read about positive activities showed larger increases in life satisfaction at a 6-month follow-up than those assigned to read about CBT. Also, participants reported finding the activities in *The How of Happiness* to be more meaningful and enjoyable, and they engaged in them more frequently. We are not suggesting that positive interventions should replace more tried and true techniques for improving people's lives, but, potentially, positive activities could serve as a complement to traditional approaches or as a supplement if the traditional drug and talk therapies fail to show improvements for particular individuals (Layous, Chancellor, Lyubomirsky, Wang, & Doraiswamy, 2011).

## OPTIMAL CONDITIONS FOR POSITIVE ACTIVITY SUCCESS

Empirical research over the past decade has not only shown that positive activities can increase well-being but has suggested the conditions under which they are optimally effective (Layous & Lyubomirsky, in press; Lyubomirsky & Layous, 2013). Specifically, features of the positive activity itself (e.g., exactly how one goes about expressing gratitude or practicing meditation), features of the person or happiness seeker, and, perhaps most important, the match between the person and activity all need to be considered when making recommendations for successful positive activity practice. Figure 11.1 illustrates the factors contributing to the success of positive activities and the mechanisms by which they work to increase well-being. In the following sections, we highlight a few of these factors in greater detail.

CHOOSING AN ACTIVITY: THE ROLE OF PERSON–ACTIVITY FIT

Not all activities will help a particular person become happier. People have enduring strengths, interests, values, and inclinations that predispose them to benefit more from some activities than others. This general "matching" hypothesis (Harackiewicz & Sansone, 1991; Snyder & Cantor, 1998) is supported by much work showing that the positive effects of goal attainment on subjective well-being are moderated by goal–person fit (Brunstein, Schultheiss, & Grassmann, 1998; Diener & Fujita, 1995;

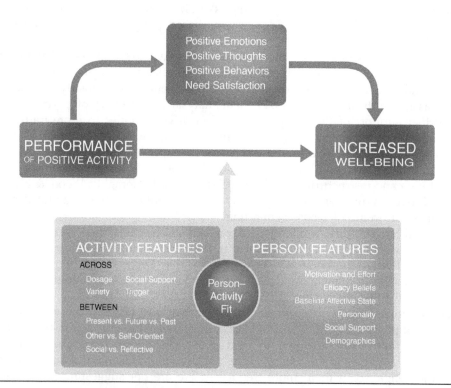

**Figure 11.1** Model of psychological mediators and moderators underlying the efficacy of positive activity interventions. Regarding "Activity Features," items under "Across" concern all potential positive activities, and items under "Between" differentiate positive activities from one another. *Source*: Reprinted from "How Do Simple Positive Activities Increase Well-Being?" by S. Lyubomirsky and K. Layous, 2013, *Current Directions in Psychological Science*, 22, p. 58.

Sheldon & Elliot, 1999; Sheldon & Kasser, 1998). It is also supported by past well-being intervention research. For example, in several studies that instructed participants to apply 14 different techniques to raise their personal happiness, the most effective happiness-increasing strategies varied greatly from one individual to another and appeared to be determined by each participant's needs and specific areas of weakness (Fordyce, 1977, 1983).

Indeed, people who report that performing a particular positive activity feels natural and enjoyable to them are relatively more likely to continue engaging in it after a prescribed intervention period and show larger increases in well-being (Dickerhoof, 2007). Similarly, in a 1-week positive intervention, people who reported that their positive activities were relatively simple, seemingly beneficial, and enjoyable adhered to practicing such activities at a higher rate and reported bigger improvements in well-being (Schueller, 2010).

Research also suggests that what types of positive activities will work for what types of individuals might be predictable. For example, if a person prefers present-oriented positive activities (e.g., appreciating the moment), he or she will likely prefer and potentially benefit from other present-oriented positive activities (e.g., performing kind acts for others) more than past-oriented (e.g., reflecting on a positive experience) or future-oriented (e.g., visualizing his or her best possible self) ones (Schueller, 2010). Indeed, when people were assigned to perform a positive activity similar to one for which they had previously indicated a preference, they showed marginally larger increases in well-being than those assigned to perform an activity dissimilar to their previous preference (Schueller, 2011).

PERSON FEATURE: MOTIVATION AND EFFORT

We assume that performing an activity requires the motivation to initiate the activity and the effort to actually carry it out and maintain it. Motivation refers to the difficulty of "overcoming inertia" or "getting over the hump," such that one starts doing an activity. For example, meditating in the morning, making time to work on at least one important project during the day, or dropping by the gym at the end of the day can have significant benefits, but only if one can remember to do them and overcome any obstacles to initiating them.

In addition, even a positive activity that has been shown to increase well-being in the average person will not work for an individual if he or she fails to put sufficient effort into performing it. In a test of the motivation and effort hypotheses, one 8-week positive intervention study recruited participants by advertising itself as either involving cognitive exercises or activities designed to make people happier (Lyubomirsky et al., 2011). Participants who signed up for the ostensible happiness-increasing activities were considered "motivated" relative to those who signed up for the cognitive exercises. As predicted, the relatively more motivated participants reported the greatest increases in well-being from performing positive activities. Furthermore, those who exhibited the highest amount of effort (as rated by independent coders) reaped the greatest well-being benefits. Further supporting the importance of motivation when engaging in happiness-increasing activities, across 51 studies, participants who self-selected into positive interventions were found to show greater gains in well-being than those who had not self-selected themselves (Sin & Lyubomirsky, 2009).

Of course, some activities will be intrinsically more appealing and will be easier to jump-start; indeed, this is undoubtedly one advantage of selecting an activity that fits one's personality. For example, rather than jogging around the block, a fitness-seeking wilderness-lover might instead choose to run on a trail through the woods, thereby feeling much less initial resistance to beginning the activity. Rather than expressing one's gratitude and appreciation in a diary, a visually oriented individual might instead choose to express herself through painting and a musical individual might instead choose to write a song. Such choices would enhance the intrinsic appeal of sitting down to engage in the activity. As these examples illustrate, finding intrinsically motivated activities may be crucial not only for one's ability to initiate the activity, but also, for one's ability to keep doing the activity in the long term. If the activity becomes boring, then the person may stop doing it.

PERSON FEATURE: CULTURE

Another potential moderator of activity effects on happiness may be the norms and traditions of the culture in which the individual resides. There is little doubt that the "pursuit of happiness" is an important and well-supported element of U.S. culture. However, in cultural settings that deemphasize individual happiness or striving, or perhaps actively disapprove of them, it may be more difficult to take action to increase one's happiness level. For example, in one experiment, European Americans and foreign-born Asian Americans were assigned to practice a positive activity or a control activity. Although all participants who engaged in positive activities showed gains in well-being, these gains were significantly larger for European Americans than for Asian Americans (Boehm et al., 2011).

Another potential source of cross-cultural differences is that, in collectivist cultures, happiness-relevant activities may merely require a somewhat different focus. In these settings, for example, it may be more effective to act in service of others rather than acting in service of personal achievements and goals. In a recent cross-cultural study, participants from the United States increased in well-being the most when they started a 6-week intervention by writing gratitude letters, whereas participants from South Korea benefited more when they started by performing acts of kindness (Layous et al., in press). The researchers speculated that, given the tendency of Asians to feel uncomfortable seeking social support (Kim, Sherman, Ko, & Taylor, 2006), the gratitude exercise may have made South Koreans feel guilty or uncomfortable. Future research should focus on which positive activities work best in certain cultures, as well as on whether certain positive activities could prove detrimental to people from certain cultures.

PERSON AND ACTIVITY FEATURE: SOCIAL SUPPORT

Social support is believed to be another important factor in enacting happiness changes. Following through on one's volitional intentions can be tough, but the task can be made easier if others are "in the same boat." Indeed, many groups and organizations, such as Alcoholics Anonymous or Weight Watchers, emphasize the import of having "teammates" during one's abstinence attempts. Thus, we assume that interpersonal support can aid an individual both in initiating a potential happiness-increasing activity and in maintaining it. In addition, because social support is an important correlate of well-being in its own right (e.g., Baldassare, Rosenfield, & Rook, 1984; Henderson & Brown, 1988), performing an intentional activity as a group or with the support of close others is likely to promote greater and more sustained happiness change than "bowling alone" (Putnam, 2000).

Although, to our knowledge, no research has yet investigated the effect of individuals' preexisting social support networks on their abilities to benefit from the practice of a positive activity, researchers have experimentally manipulated the amount of support provided within a particular positive activity. In one study, college students were randomly assigned to write about their best possible future selves or to engage in a neutral writing task (Layous, Nelson, & Lyubomirsky, 2012). Students writing about their best possible selves were either provided with weekly testimonials from ostensible peers, providing encouragement and advice about how to reach their goals, or with neutral information about campus resources. Participants who received supportive information from their peers showed larger increases in positive affect than those who received neutral information or those in the control condition. In another study, participants who received autonomy-supportive messages while they performed a positive activity (e.g., "the way you complete this activity is entirely up to you") increased in perceived autonomy or choice to a greater degree than participants who did not receive the supportive messages (Della Porta et al., 2012). The increase in perceived choice, in turn, predicted relatively greater increases in well-being.

ACTIVITY FEATURE: VARIETY

Another important factor influencing positive activities' effects on happiness likely concerns how one varies such activities. For example, by shifting attention among several projects at work, by meeting new people, or by focusing one's gratitude on different aspects of one's life, a person's activities should remain intrinsically enjoyable and conducive to many rewarding "flow" experiences (Csikszentmihalyi, 1990). Indeed, participants who were asked to vary the acts of kindness they performed from week to week during a 10-week intervention showed larger gains in well-being than those who were asked to perform the very same acts each week (Sheldon et al., 2012). Possibly, varying the acts of kindness helped keep the activity fresh and meaningful over the course of the intervention. Also highlighting the importance of variety, people who reported that a recent positive life change was associated with variable and surprising experiences showed greater sustained increases in well-being than people who reported that their positive life change was static (Sheldon & Lyubomirsky, 2012).

ACTIVITY FEATURE: DOSAGE/TIMING

Another critical factor may be the dosage or timing of an activity; if one does the activity too often, or not often enough, or at the wrong times, then it may lose its efficacy. For example, people who performed five acts of kindness all during one day of the week gained in well-being more than those who spread their five kind acts throughout the week (Lyubomirsky, Sheldon, et al., 2005), indicating that there might be an optimal packaging of positive activities to make them most effective. In a different study, students who counted their blessings once per week over 6 weeks showed larger increases in well-being than those who counted their blessings three times per week (Lyubomirsky, Sheldon, et al., 2005). This suggests that the activity may have become burdensome or ineffective when performed too frequently.

Some research indicates, however, that when people choose their own happiness-increasing activities (i.e., outside of the confines of an experiment), they perform these activities quite often—namely, several times per week for about an hour each time (Parks, Della Porta, Pierce, Zilca, & Lyubomirsky, 2012, Study 2). Similarly, participants who logged in more frequently to an iPhone application that allowed them to try various positive activities showed larger increases in well-being than those who logged in less frequently (Parks et al., 2012, Study 3). This recent evidence suggests that the optimum timing and dosage may vary depending on whether people are intrinsically motivated to engage in specific happiness-enhancing activities (i.e., if an ideal person–activity fit exists).

### OTHER FACTORS INFLUENCING THE SUCCESS OF POSITIVE ACTIVITIES

As we mentioned, there are several specific features of positive activities and features of the person that may influence the extent to which the pursuit of happiness is successful. In this section, we consider some potentially important research methods that may influence the results of happiness-increasing interventions.

One consideration is how to properly test the happiness-inducing potential of a particular program or intervention. Ideally, double-blind procedures should be used, in which neither the participant nor the experimenter is aware of the "treatment" being given, and in which the participant is unaware of the experimental hypothesis. But is this reasonable or desirable, when the intervention concerns encouraging people to take intentional action that may enhance their personal well-being? Perhaps such interventions can only work if the participant is fully aware of what the research is about. Although this possibility raises potential methodological problems concerning placebo and demand effects, such problems may be surmounted with appropriate control groups. In addition, the issue of person–activity fit suggests that some studies should allow participants to choose what intervention to enact, rather than always randomly assigning them to specific positive activities. Such self-selection procedures may challenge conventional methodological standards, but again, the problem may perhaps be offset by careful experimental design. A related issue is how happiness-enhancing programs or practices should be labeled. Should their potential relation to happiness be acknowledged directly, or should they simply be introduced as "positive life practices" involving "kindness," "gratitude," "physical exercise," and so on? The latter content-based approach may be preferable, for several reasons. First, as discussed earlier, using explicit happiness labels may create demand effects that obscure whatever real changes are occurring for participants. Second, inducements like "Do you want to be happy?" may not appeal to a segment of potential participants who might object to associations with self-help gurus and popular psychology "how-to" books, or for whom the term "happiness" denotes unrealistic and wrongheaded positivity and optimism. Third, content-based (rather than happiness-based) labeling may sidestep another possible barrier to intervention efficacy—namely, that active and conscious attempts to increase happiness might backfire altogether if the person becomes too focused on this goal and monitors his or her progress too frequently (e.g., "Am I happy yet? Am I happy yet?"; Ford & Mauss, in press; Mauss, Tamir, Anderson, & Savino, 2011; Schooler, Ariely, & Loewenstein, 2003; but see Ferguson & Sheldon, 2013). In other words, it is probably better to be fully engaged in the activities of one's life without frequently pausing to dwell on when one's long-desired happiness will finally be achieved. In this case, happiness may come as a natural by-product of a life well-lived.

## POSITIVE ACTIVITIES AND HEALTH

Positive activities designed to increase people's happiness might also have favorable downstream consequences on numerous other aspects of people's lives. Indeed, both overall happiness and positive affect in particular have been associated with positive health outcomes (e.g., stronger immune system, lower risk of mortality, etc.; Howell, Kern, & Lyubomirsky, 2007; Pressman & Cohen, 2005). Positive affect is not only associated with a reduction in the likelihood of catching the common cold (Cohen, Alper, Doyle, Treanor, & Turner, 2006; Cohen, Doyle, Turner, Alper, & Skoner, 2003), but has also been identified as an important ingredient for coping with chronic illness (Folkman & Moskowitz, 2000) and has predicted lower risk of mortality for people suffering from AIDS (Moskowitz, 2003) and diabetes (Moskowitz, Epel, & Acree, 2008). Notably, even experimental inductions of positive affect have shown significant improvement in short-term health outcomes and marginally significant improvement in long-term health outcomes (Howell et al., 2007), thus suggesting the potential of positive activities to promote better health via increased positive affect.

Growing evidence in the positive intervention literature supports the notion that positive activities can improve physical health outcomes. For example, participants randomly assigned to express gratitude reported fewer physical symptoms of illness and more hours of exercise than participants who recounted daily hassles or reported neutral life events (Emmons & McCullough, 2003). Similarly, chronic pain patients randomly assigned to engage in loving-kindness meditation (a meditative practice focused on promoting positive feelings toward self and others) reported less pain, anger, and psychological distress than patients receiving standard care (Carson et al., 2005). In a subsequent investigation of the effects of loving-kindness meditation, relatively healthy adults who engaged in the activity (versus a waitlist control group) experienced more positive emotions over time, which, in turn, predicted fewer general symptoms of illness (e.g., headaches, congestion, weakness; Fredrickson et al., 2008). In sum, intentional improvements in people's mental health predict positive physical health outcomes. Because the positive activities described in this chapter are brief, easily implemented, and effective in increasing happiness, health care organizations (including the doctors, nurses, and other practitioners that staff them) might consider providing information to patients about these practices. At the same time, future research would do well to continue exploring the effect of positive activities on physical health outcomes, adherence to medical treatment, and risk of mortality.

## POSITIVE ACTIVITIES AND WORK

Employee well-being should be a practical concern for organizations, as happiness at work predicts better supervisor evaluations (Cropanzano & Wright, 1999) and lower absenteeism (Pelled & Xin, 1999) and is associated with better job performance (DeLuga & Mason, 2000; Wright, 2010; Wright & Cropanzano, 2000), better organizational citizenship (Donovan, 2000), and less turnover intention (Donovan, 2000; Wright, 2010). One possible mechanism for these associations between happiness and positive work outcomes is through greater job satisfaction. A recent meta-analysis showed a medium to large positive correlation between life satisfaction and job satisfaction and, through cross-lagged regression analyses of longitudinal data, revealed that life satisfaction was more predictive of job satisfaction than vice versa (Bowling, Eschleman, & Wang, 2010). These findings indicate that improving happiness among employees could help them become more satisfied with their jobs.

Fortunately, research suggests that simple, brief positive activities conducted at work can effectively increase employee happiness. In a 6-week study, employees at a Japanese engineering firm were randomly assigned to report three positive events that occurred each week at work (the positive activity condition) or to list three tasks they had completed each week (the comparison group; Chancellor et al., 2012). Relative to controls, employees who recounted positive work events increased in happiness over time, showed more energy upon arriving to work, and engaged in less office chitchat.

In another study, employees at the Spanish headquarters of a multinational beverage company were randomly assigned to perform kind acts ("Givers"), to receive kind acts ("Receivers"), or to simply fill out measures online ("Controls") for 4 weeks (Chancellor et al., 2013). Relative to Controls, Givers showed fewer depressive symptoms and more flow at post-test and maintained this advantage at 1- and 3-month follow-ups. Receivers showed more immediate boosts in well-being than Givers, reporting higher weekly positive affect and life satisfaction than Controls merely 2 weeks into the intervention and at post-test. In addition, social network analyses revealed that Controls who interacted with Givers and Receivers also reported doing more positive acts of their own, perhaps from having been inspired by the kind acts they witnessed (Chancellor et al., 2013). In sum, preliminary evidence suggests that simple positive activities can improve well-being and positive behaviors at work. Because of their accessibility and minimal cost, positive activities could be offered by employers from a variety of organizations as part of a menu of options for their employees to partake in during work time. The research suggests that rather than being a distraction from task-related duties, such activities represent time well-spent, leading to less absenteeism, less turnover, better job performance, and a more positive work environment. Future research would do well to focus on how increasing employee well-being might also improve an organization's bottom line (e.g., through lower health-care costs, better performance, lower turnover).

## POSITIVE ACTIVITIES AND RELATIONSHIPS

Happiness is associated with current satisfaction with friends (Cooper, Okamura & Gurka, 1992; Diener & Seligman, 2002), marital partners (Headey, Veenhoven, & Wearing, 1991), and social activities (Cooper et al., 1992) and is also predictive of marital satisfaction (Harker & Keltner, 2001) and overall relationship closeness (Neyer & Asendorpf, 2001) years later. If happiness is related to and predictive of healthy relationships, practicing positive activities should have positive effects on people's relationships. Indeed, compelling evidence supports the role of positive activities in improving relationships. For example, participants in a loving-kindness meditation study saw overall increases in positive emotions, yet, interestingly, these increases were most prominent while they were engaging with other people, suggesting that the mediation practice helped them extract positivity from their daily social interactions (Fredrickson et al., 2008). In addition, increases in positive emotions throughout the intervention period were also predictive of increases in perceived social support and positive relationships with others, demonstrating that boosts in positive emotions can cause a cascade of positive relational outcomes (Fredrickson et al., 2008).

In another example, a sample of women suffering from metastatic breast cancer were prompted to recall what others had done for them during the past month. Those who expressed gratitude for the instances of help reported greater perceived social support 3 months later (Algoe & Stanton, 2012). Lastly, in a 6-week intervention, expressing gratitude or optimism predicted increases in feelings of relatedness (Boehm, Lyubomirsky, & Sheldon, 2012), thus further bolstering our prediction that positive activities can make people feel more connected to others. More research is needed to explore how positive activities might be able to improve a variety of types of relationships (e.g., marital, friendship, familial, work) and possibly how positive activities might help forestall adaptation to a positive relationship event such as marriage (see Lucas et al., 2003).

## CONCLUSION

More than two centuries ago, the U.S. Declaration of Independence proclaimed "the pursuit of happiness" as an unalienable right. Today, after decades of scientific research into subjective well-being, we finally have empirically based suggestions for how to increase happiness. What are the general recommendations for increasing happiness suggested by the latest research? Simply, that happiness seekers might be advised to find novel activities to become engaged in—preferably intrinsic activities that feel natural and enjoyable to them. Furthermore, people might be advised to avoid basing their happiness on the acquisition of particular circumstances or objects (e.g., buying a luxury car, arranging for cosmetic surgery, or moving to California), because they will tend to habituate to such stable factors. However, if one can remember to appreciate or actively engage with the object or circumstance (i.e., pause to savor one's new Mercedes or take advantage of the California weather), then stable objects and circumstances may not be stable after all, from a phenomenological perspective. Finally, by practicing the thoughts and behaviors of naturally happy people, happiness seekers can improve their own well-being. Such improvements will be most likely if people perform their positive activities with the optimum dosage and timing, ensure that the activities are variable, put effort into them, and infuse them with social support.

Given the breadth of beneficial effects that follow from subjective well-being, for both the individual and those around him or her (Lyubomirsky, King, et al., 2005), it seems vital to continue to investigate the conditions under which positive activities successfully increase well-being. Fortunately, there are emerging reasons to believe that "the pursuit of happiness" is indeed a practical and attainable goal. In this chapter, we have described these reasons and reviewed theoretical and empirical evidence to suggest how individuals can optimally increase their happiness. We hope these ideas will stimulate people to make positive changes in their daily lives and ultimately experience greater happiness, flourishing, and growth.

## SUMMARY POINTS

- Both theory and extensive empirical evidence demonstrate that happiness can be increased through the intentional practice of positive activities.
- Positive activities are simple, brief, intentional activities meant to mimic the myriad positive habits of naturally happy people (e.g., thinking gratefully and optimistically, behaving prosocially).
- Positive activities can be self-administered through the use of simple instructions or included as part of group or individual therapy.
- Because positive emotions predict positive health outcomes (e.g., longevity and stronger immune systems), positive activities could become an important component of integrative medicine practices.
- Similarly, because happiness has been linked to various positive work outcomes (e.g., organizational citizenship, job satisfaction), positive activities could contribute to employee-oriented mental and physical health programming in the workplace.
- Lastly, many positive activities, such as expressing gratitude and performing kind acts, promote positive relationships with others and increase the need-satisfying feeling of relatedness. Therefore, positive activities are a valuable tool to strengthen relationships and increase social support in people's lives.

# REFERENCES

Algoe, S. B., & Stanton, A. L. (2012). Gratitude when it is needed most: Social functions of gratitude in women with metastatic breast cancer. *Emotion, 12,* 163–168.

Allport, G. W. (1955). *Becoming: Basic considerations for a psychology of personality.* New Haven, CT: Yale University Press.

Baldassare, M., Rosenfield, S., & Rook, K. S. (1984). The types of social relations predicting elderly well-being. *Research on Aging, 6,* 549–559.

Boehm, J. K., Lyubomirsky, S., & Sheldon, K. M. (2011). A longitudinal experimental study comparing the effectiveness of happiness-enhancing strategies in Anglo Americans and Asian Americans. *Cognition & Emotion, 25,* 1263–1272.

Boehm, J. K., Lyubomirsky, S., & Sheldon, K. M. (2012). *The role of need satisfying emotions in a positive activity intervention.* Unpublished raw data.

Boswell, W. R., Boudreau, J. W., & Tichy, J. (2005). The relationship between employee job change and job satisfaction: The honeymoon-hangover effect. *Journal of Applied Psychology, 90,* 882–892.

Bowling, N. A., Eschleman, K. J., & Wang, Q. (2010). A meta-analytic examination of the relationship between job satisfaction and subjective well-being. *Journal of Occupational and Organizational Psychology, 83,* 915–934.

Braungart, J. M., Plomin, R., DeFries, J. C., & Fulker, D. W. (1992). Genetic influence on tester-rated infant temperament as assessed by Bayley's Infant Behavior Record: Nonadoptive and adoptive siblings and twins. *Developmental Psychology, 28,* 40–47.

Brickman, P., & Campbell, D. T. (1971). Hedonic relativism and planning the good society. In M. H. Appley (Ed.), *Adaptation-level theory: A symposium.* New York, NY: Academic Press.

Brunstein, J. C., Schultheiss, O. C., & Grassmann, R. (1998). Personal goals and emotional well-being: The moderating role of motive dispositions. *Journal of Personality and Social Psychology, 75,* 494–508.

Carson, J. W., Keefe, F. J., Lynch, T. R., Carson, K. M., Goli, V., Fras, A. M., & Thorp, S. R. (2005). Loving-kindness meditation for chronic low back pain: Results from a pilot trial. *Journal of Holistic Nursing, 23,* 287–304.

Chancellor, J., Jacobs Bao, K., & Lyubomirsky, S. (2013). *Ripples of generosity in the workplace: The benefits of giving, getting, and glimpsing.* Manuscript submitted for publication.

Chancellor, J., Layous, K., & Lyubomirsky, S. (2012). *Recalling positive events at work makes employees feel happier, move more, and chat less: A 6-week randomized controlled intervention at a Japanese workplace.* Manuscript submitted for publication.

Clark, A. E., Diener, E., Georgellis, Y., & Lucas, R. E. (2008). Lags and leads in life satisfaction: A test of the baseline hypothesis. *Economic Journal, 118,* 222–243.

Cohen, S., Alper, C. M., Doyle, W. J., Treanor, J. J., & Turner, R. B. (2006). Positive emotional style predicts resistance to illness after experimental exposure to rhinovirus or influenza A virus. *Psychosomatic Medicine, 68,* 809–815.

Cohen, S., Doyle, W. J., Turner, R. B., Alper, C. M., & Skoner, D. P. (2003). Emotional style and susceptibility to the common cold. *Psychosomatic Medicine, 65,* 652–657.

Cooper, H., Okamura, L., & Gurka, V. (1992). Social activity and subjective well-being. *Personality and Individual Differences, 13,* 573–583.

Costa, P. T., McCrae, R. R., & Zonderman, A. B. (1987). Environmental and dispositional influences on well-being: Longitudinal follow-up of an American national sample. *British Journal of Psychology, 78,* 299–306.

Cropanzano, R., & Wright, T. A. (1999). A 5-year study of change in the relationship between well being and job performance. *Consulting Psychology Journal: Practice and Research, 51,* 252–265.

Csikszentmihalyi, M. (1990). *Flow: The psychology of optimal experience.* New York, NY: Harper & Row.

Deci, E. L., & Ryan, R. M. (2000). The "what" and "why" of goal pursuits: Human needs and the self-determination of behavior. *Psychological Inquiry, 4,* 227–268.

Della Porta, M. D., Jacobs Bao, K., & Lyubomirsky, S. (2012). *Does supporting autonomy facilitate the pursuit of happiness? Results from an experimental longitudinal well-being intervention.* Manuscript submitted for publication.

DeLuga, R. J., & Mason, S. (2000). Relationship of resident assistant conscientiousness, extraversion, and positive affect with rated performance. *Journal of Research in Personality, 34,* 225–235.

Dickerhoof, R. M. (2007). Expressing optimism and gratitude: A longitudinal investigation of cognitive strategies to increase well-being. *Dissertation Abstracts International, 68,* 4174. (UMI No. 3270426).

Diener, E., & Fujita, F. (1995). Resources, personal strivings, and subjective well-being: A nomothetic and idiographic approach. *Journal of Personality and Social Psychology, 68,* 926–935.

Diener, E., & Lucas, R. E. (1999). Personality and subjective well-being. In D. Kahneman, E. Diener, & N. Schwartz (Eds.), *Well-being: The foundations of hedonic psychology* (pp. 213–229). New York, NY: Russell Sage Foundation.

Diener, E., Lucas, R. E., & Scollon, C. N. (2006). Beyond the hedonic treadmill: Revising the adaptation theory of well-being. *American Psychologist, 61,* 305–314.

Diener, E., & Seligman, M. E. P. (2002). Very happy people. *Psychological Science, 13,* 81–84.

Diener, E., Suh, E. M., Lucas, R. E., & Smith, H. L. (1999). Subjective well-being: Three decades of progress. *Psychological Bulletin, 125,* 276–302.

Donovan, M. A. (2000). Cognitive, affective, and satisfaction variables as predictors of organizational behaviors: A structural equation modeling examination of alternative models. *Dissertation Abstracts International, 60*(9-B), 4943. (UMI No. AAI9944835)

Dunn, E. W., Aknin, L. B., & Norton, M. I. (2008). Spending money on others promotes happiness. *Science, 319,* 1687–1688.

Emmons, R. A., & McCullough, M. E. (2003). Counting blessings versus burdens: An experimental investigation of gratitude and subjective well-being in daily life. *Journal of Personality and Social Psychology, 84,* 377–389.

Ferguson, Y., & Sheldon, K. M. (2013). Trying to be happier really can work: Two experimental studies. *Journal of Positive Psychology, 8,* 23–33.

Folkman, S., & Moskowitz, J. T. (2000). Stress, positive emotion, and coping. *Current Directions in Psychological Science, 9,* 115–118.

Ford, B. Q., & Mauss, I. B. (in press). The paradoxical effects of pursuing happiness and how they can be avoided: When and why wanting to feel happy backfires. In J. Gruber & J. Moskowitz (Eds.), *The light and dark side of positive emotion.* Oxford, England: Oxford University Press.

Fordyce, M. W. (1977). Development of a program to increase happiness. *Journal of Counseling Psychology, 24,* 511–521.

Fordyce, M. W. (1983). A program to increase happiness: Further studies. *Journal of Counseling Psychology, 30,* 483–498.

Frederick, S., & Loewenstein, G. (1999). Hedonic adaptation. In D. Kahneman, E. Diener, & N. Schwarz (Eds.), *Well-being: The foundations of hedonic psychology* (pp. 302–329). New York, NY: Russell Sage Foundation.

Fredrickson, B. L., Cohn, M. A., Coffey, K. A., Pek, J., & Finkel, S. M. (2008). Open hearts build lives: Positive emotions, induced through loving-kindness meditation, build consequential personal resources. *Journal of Personality and Social Psychology, 95,* 1045–1062.

Froh, J. J., Sefick, W. J., & Emmons, R. A. (2008). Counting blessings in early adolescents: An experimental study of gratitude and subjective well-being. *Journal of School Psychology, 46,* 213–233.

Geraghty, A. W., Wood, A. M., & Hyland, M. E. (2010). Attrition from self-directed interventions: Investigating the relationship between psychological predictors, intervention content and dropout from a body dissatisfaction intervention. *Social Science & Medicine, 71*, 30–37.

Harackiewicz, J. M., & Sansone, C. (1991). Goals and intrinsic motivation: You can get there from here. In M. L. Maehr & P. R. Pintrich (Eds.), *Advances in motivation and achievement* (Vol. 7, pp. 21–49). Greenwich, CT: JAI Press.

Harker, L., & Keltner, D. (2001). Expressions of positive emotions in women's college yearbook pictures and their relationship to personality and life outcomes across adulthood. *Journal of Personality and Social Psychology, 80*, 112–124.

Headey, B. (2010). The set point theory of well-being has serious flaws: On the eve of a scientific revolution? *Social Indicators Research, 97*, 7–21.

Headey, B., Veenhoven, R., & Wearing, A. (1991). Top-down versus bottom-up theories of subjective well-being. *Social Indicators Research, 24*, 81–100.

Headey, B., & Wearing, A. (1989). Personality, life events, and subjective well-being: Toward a dynamic equilibrium model. *Journal of Personality and Social Psychology, 57*, 731–739.

Henderson, A. S., & Brown, G. W. (1988). Social support: The hypothesis and the evidence. In A. S. Henderson & G. D. Burrows (Eds.), *Handbook of social psychiatry* (pp. 73–85). Amsterdam, The Netherlands: Elsevier.

Howell, R. T., Kern, M. L., & Lyubomirsky, S. (2007). Health benefits: Meta-analytically determining the impact of well-being on objective health outcomes. *Health Psychology Review, 1*, 83–136.

Jacobs Bao, K., Boehm, J. K., & Lyubomirsky, S. (2013). *Using surprise to stay happier: Thwarting hedonic adaptation to positive life events.* Manuscript submitted for publication.

Keyes, C. L. (2005). Mental illness and/or mental health? Investigating axioms of the complete state model of health. *Journal of Consulting and Clinical Psychology, 73*, 539.

Kim, H. S., Sherman, D. K., Ko, D., & Taylor, S. E. (2006). Pursuit of comfort and pursuit of harmony: Culture, relationships, and social support seeking. *Personality and Social Psychology Bulletin, 32*, 1595–1607.

King, L. A. (2001). The health benefits of writing about life goals. *Personality and Social Psychology Bulletin, 27*, 798–807.

Krueger, R. F., Hicks, B. M., & McGue, M. (2001). Altruism and antisocial behavior: Independent tendencies, unique personality correlates, distinct etiologies. *Psychological Science, 12*, 397–402.

Layous, K., Chancellor, J., Lyubomirsky, S., Wang, L., & Doraiswamy, P. M. (2011). Delivering happiness: Translating positive psychology intervention research for treating major and minor depressive disorders. *Journal of Alternative and Complementary Medicine, 17*, 1–9.

Layous, K., Lee., H. C., Choi, I., & Lyubomirsky, S. (in press). Culture matters when designing a successful positive activity: A comparison of the United States and South Korea. *Journal of Cross-Cultural Psychology.*

Layous, K., & Lyubomirsky, S. (in press). The how, who, what, when, and why of happiness: Mechanisms underlying the success of positive interventions. In J. Gruber & J. Moskowitz (Eds.), *The light and dark side of positive emotion.* Oxford, England: Oxford University Press.

Layous, K., Nelson, S. K., & Lyubomirsky, S. (2012). What is the optimal way to deliver a positive activity intervention? The case of writing about one's best possible selves. *Journal of Happiness Studies.* Advance online publication. doi:10.1007/s10902-012-9346-2

Layous, K., Nelson, S. K., Oberle, E., Schonert-Reichl, K. A., & Lyubomirsky, S. (2012). Kindness counts: Prompting prosocial behavior in preadolescents boosts peer acceptance and well-being. *PLoS ONE, 7*, e51380. doi:10.1371/journal.pone.0051380

Lewinsohn, P. M., Muñoz, R. F., Youngren, M. A., & Zeiss, A. M. (1992). *Control your depression.* New York, NY: Fireside.

Lucas, R. E. (2007). Long-term disability is associated with lasting changes in subjective well-being: Evidence from two nationally representative longitudinal studies. *Journal of Personality and Social Psychology, 92*, 717–730.

Lucas, R. E., Clark, A. E., Georgellis, Y., & Diener, E. (2003). Reexamining adaptation and the set point model of happiness: Reactions to changes in marital status. *Journal of Personality and Social Psychology, 84*, 527–539.

Lucas, R. E., Clark, A. E., Georgellis, Y., & Diener, E. (2004). Unemployment alters the set-point for life satisfaction. *Psychological Science, 15*, 8–13.

Lucas, R. E., Dyrenforth, P. S., & Diener, E. (2008). Four myths about subjective well-being. *Social and Personality Compass, 2*, 2001–2015.

Luhmann, M., Hofmann, W., Eid, M., & Lucas, R. E. (2012). Subjective well-being and adaptation to life events: A meta-analysis. *Journal of Personality and Social Psychology, 102*, 592–615.

Lykken, D. (2000). *Happiness: The nature and nurture of joy and contentment.* New York, NY: St. Martin's Griffin.

Lykken, D., & Tellegen, A. (1996). Happiness is a stochastic phenomenon. *Psychological Science, 7*, 186–189.

Lyubomirsky, S. (2008). *The how of happiness: A scientific approach to getting the life you want.* New York, NY: Penguin Press.

Lyubomirsky, S. (2011). Hedonic adaptation to positive and negative experiences. In S. Folkman (Ed.), *Oxford handbook of stress, health, and coping* (pp. 200–224). New York, NY: Oxford University Press.

Lyubomirsky, S., Dickerhoof, R., Boehm, J. K., & Sheldon, K. M. (2011). Becoming happier takes both a will and a proper way: An experimental longitudinal intervention to boost well-being. *Emotion, 11*, 391–402.

Lyubomirsky, S., King, L., & Diener, E. (2005). The benefits of frequent positive affect: Does happiness lead to success? *Psychological Bulletin, 131*, 803–855.

Lyubomirsky, S., & Layous, K. (2013). How do simple positive activities increase well-being? *Current Directions in Psychological Science, 22*, 57–62.

Lyubomirsky, S., Sheldon, K. M., & Schkade, D. (2005). Pursuing happiness: The architecture of sustainable change. *Review of General Psychology, 9*, 111–131.

Mauss, I. B., Tamir, M., Anderson, C. L., & Savino, N. S. (2011). Can seeking happiness make people unhappy? Paradoxical effects of valuing happiness. *Emotion, 11*, 807–815.

McCrae, R. R., & Costa, P. T. (1990). *Personality in adulthood.* New York, NY: Guilford Press.

McCullough, M. E., Emmons, R. A., & Tsang, J. (2002). The grateful disposition: A conceptual and empirical topography. *Journal of Personality and Social Psychology, 82*, 112–127.

Moskowitz, J. T. (2003). Positive affect predicts lower risk of AIDS mortality. *Psychosomatic Medicine, 65*, 620–626.

Moskowitz, J. T., Epel, E. S., & Acree, M. (2008). Positive affect uniquely predicts lower risk of mortality in people with diabetes. *Health Psychology, 27*, S73–S82.

Nave, C. S., Sherman, R. A., Funder, D. C., Hampson, S. E., & Goldberg, L. R. (2010). On the contextual independence of personality: Teachers' assessments predict directly observed behavior after four decades. *Social Psychological and Personality Science, 1*, 327–334.

Nelson, S. K., Fuller, J. A. K., Choi, I., & Lyubomirsky, S. (2013). *Beyond self-protection: Self-affirmation boosts well-being.* Manuscript submitted for publication.

Neyer, F. J., & Asendorpf, J. B. (2001). Personality–relationship transaction in young adulthood. *Journal of Personality and Social Psychology, 81*, 1190–1204.

Parks, A., Della Porta, M., Pierce, R. S., Zilca, R., & Lyubomirsky, S. (2012). Pursuing happiness in everyday life: The characteristics and behaviors of online happiness seekers. *Emotion.* Advance online publication. doi:10.1037/a0028587

Parks, A. C., & Szanto, R. K. (2013). Assessing the efficacy and effectiveness of a positive psychology based self-help book. *Terapia Psicológica, 31*, 141–149.

Pelled, L. H., & Xin, K. R. (1999). Down and out: An investigation of the relationship between mood and employee withdrawal behavior. *Journal of Management, 25,* 875–895.

Plomin, R. (2004). Genetics and developmental psychology. *Merrill-Palmer Quarterly, 50,* 341–352.

Pressman, S. D., & Cohen, S. (2005). Does positive affect influence health? *Psychological Bulletin, 131,* 925–971.

Putnam, R. D. (2000). *Bowling alone: The collapse and revival of American community.* New York, NY: Simon & Schuster.

Røysamb, E., Harris, J. R., Magnus, P., Vittersø, J., & Tambs, K. (2002). Subjective well-being. Sex-specific effects of genetic and environmental factors. *Personality and Individual Differences, 32,* 211–233.

Ryff, C. D. (1989). Happiness is everything, or is it? Explorations on the meaning of psychological well-being. *Journal of Personality and Social Psychology, 57,* 1069–1081.

Scheier, M. F., & Carver, C. S. (1993). On the power of positive thinking: The benefits of being optimistic. *Current Directions in Psychological Science, 2,* 26–30.

Schooler, J. W., Ariely, D., & Loewenstein, G. (2003). The explicit pursuit and assessment of happiness can be self-defeating. In J. Carrillo & I. Brocas (Eds.), *Psychology and economics* (pp. 41–70). Oxford, England: Oxford University Press.

Schueller, S. M. (2010). Preferences for positive psychology exercises. *Journal of Positive Psychology, 5,* 192–203.

Schueller, S. M. (2011). To each his own well-being boosting intervention: Using preference to guide selection. *The Journal of Positive Psychology, 6,* 300–313.

Seligman, M. E. P., Steen, T. A., Park, N., & Peterson, C. (2005). Positive psychology progress: Empirical validation of interventions. *American Psychologist, 60,* 410–421.

Sheldon, K. M., Abad, N., Ferguson, Y., Gunz, A., Houser-Marko, L., Nichols, C. P., & Lyubomirsky, S. (2010). Persistent pursuit of need satisfying goals leads to increased happiness: A 6-month experimental longitudinal study. *Motivation & Emotion, 34,* 39–48.

Sheldon, K. M., Boehm, J. K., & Lyubomirsky, S. (2012). Variety is the spice of happiness: The hedonic adaptation prevention (HAP) model. In I. Boniwell & S. David (Eds.), *Oxford handbook of happiness* (pp. 901–914). Oxford, England: Oxford University Press.

Sheldon, K. M., & Elliot, A. J. (1999). Goal striving, need-satisfaction, and longitudinal well-being: The Self-Concordance Model. *Journal of Personality and Social Psychology, 76,* 482–497.

Sheldon, K. M., Elliot, A. J., Kim, Y., & Kasser, T. (2001). What is satisfying about satisfying events? Testing 10 candidate psychological needs. *Journal of Personality and Social Psychology, 80,* 325–339.

Sheldon, K. M., & Kasser, T. (1998). Pursuing personal goals: Skills enable progress but not all progress is beneficial. *Personality and Social Psychology Bulletin, 24,* 1319–1331.

Sheldon, K. M., & Lyubomirsky, S. (2006a). Achieving sustainable increases in happiness: Change your actions, not your circumstances. *Journal of Happiness Studies, 7,* 55–86.

Sheldon, K. M., & Lyubomirsky, S. (2006b). How to increase and sustain positive emotions: The effect of expressing gratitude and visualizing best possible selves. *Journal of Positive Psychology, 1,* 73–82.

Sheldon, K. M., & Lyubomirsky, S. (2012). The challenge of staying happier: Testing the Hedonic Adaptation Prevention (HAP) model. *Personality and Social Psychology Bulletin, 38,* 670–680.

Sin, N. L., & Lyubomirsky, S. (2009). Enhancing well-being and alleviating depressive symptoms with positive psychology Interventions: A practice friendly meta-analysis. *Journal of Clinical Psychology, 65,* 467–487.

Smith, M. L., & Glass, G. V. (1977). Meta-analysis of psychotherapy outcome studies. *American Psychologist, 32,* 752–760.

Snyder, M., & Cantor, N. (1998). Understanding personality and social behavior: A functionalist strategy. In D. T. Gilbert & S. T. Fiske (Eds.), *The handbook of social psychology* (Vol. 1, 4th ed., pp. 635–679). New York, NY: McGraw-Hill.

Stubbe, J. H., Posthuma, D., Boomsma, D. I., & de Geus, E. J. C. (2005). Heritability of life satisfaction in adults: A twin-family study. *Psychological Medicine, 35*, 1581–1588.

Suh, E. M., Diener, E., & Fujita, F. (1996). Events and subjective well-being: Only recent events matter. *Journal of Personality and Social Psychology, 70*, 1091–1102.

Taylor, S. E., & Brown, J. D. (1988). Illusion and well-being: A social psychological perspective on mental health. *Psychological Bulletin, 103*, 193–210.

Tellegen, A., Lykken, D. T., Bouchard, T. J., Wilcox, K. J., Segal, N. L., & Rich, S. (1988). Personality similarity in twins reared apart and together. *Journal of Personality and Social Psychology, 54*, 1031–1039.

Vallacher, R. R., & Nowak, A. (2002). The dynamical perspective in personality and social psychology. *Personality and Social Psychology Review, 6*, 264–273.

Wright, T. A. (2010). Much more than meets the eye: The role of psychological well-being in job performance, employee retention and cardiovascular health. *Organizational Dynamics, 39*, 13–23.

Wright, T. A., & Cropanzano, R. (2000). Psychological well-being and job satisfaction as predictors of job performance. *Journal of Occupational Health Psychology, 5*, 84–94.

Zimmermann, A. C., & Easterlin, R. A. (2006). Happily ever after? Cohabitation, marriage, divorce, and happiness in Germany. *Population & Development Review, 32*, 51.

# CHAPTER 12

# Putting Positive Psychology Into Motion Through Physical Activity

GUY FAULKNER, KATE HEFFERON, and NANETTE MUTRIE

S ELIGMAN (2002) SUGGESTED THAT the goal of positive psychology is to "learn how to build the qualities that help individuals and communities not just endure and survive but also flourish" (p. 8). We believe that physical activity is one behavior that will help both individuals and communities survive and flourish. At an individual level, we will show that physical activity has the capacity to prevent mental illness, to foster positive emotions, to buffer individuals against the stresses of life, and to facilitate thriving after adversity. At a community level, we suggest that a community in which physical activity is seen as the social norm may be healthier and have greater social capital. Indeed, we would argue that physical activity is a "stellar" positive psychological intervention (PPI; Hefferon & Mutrie, 2012) as it helps to produce positive emotions, engagement, and accomplishment, as well as preventing and reducing more negative experiences and states (e.g., stress, depression).

We use *physical activity* (PA) as a term that refers to any movement of the body that results in energy expenditure above that of resting level (Caspersen, Powell, & Christenson, 1985). *Exercise* is often (incorrectly) used interchangeably with PA, but this term refers to a subset of PA in which the activity is structured, often supervised, and undertaken with the aim of maintaining or improving physical fitness or health. Examples of exercise include going to the gym, jogging, taking an aerobics class, or taking part in recreational sport for fitness.

In the field of physical activity for health, a landmark moment occurred in 2010 with the launch of The Toronto Charter for Physical Activity by the Global Advocacy Council for Physical Activity (see www.globalpa.org.uk). This document is a call for action and an advocacy tool; its aim is to create sustainable opportunities for physically active lifestyles for everyone. This advocacy resulted in the World Health Organization (2010) issuing global recommendations on physical activity for health based on a consensus process and using the most up to date epidemiological data. These recommendations include the guidance that children aged 5 to 17 years should accumulate 60 minutes of moderate- to vigorous-intensity activity on a daily basis. For adults, the guidance suggests that a minimum of 150 minutes of moderate intensity activity should be accumulated over the course of the week in bouts of no less than 10 minutes. Adults are also encouraged to take part in activities that promote muscle strengthening at least twice per week. Adults over age 65 were recommended to undertake the same level and types of activity as younger adults but it was also noted that balance training might be beneficial for some and that older adults should be as active as their own abilities allow. These guidelines are consistent with most national guidelines for physical activity.

Unfortunately, the majority of children, youth, and adults are not meeting such guidelines (Hallal et al., 2012). If we take an evolutionary look at our beginnings, we see a life in which high levels of physical activity were required for survival. As recently as one century ago, most people needed to be physically active to work, to travel, and to take care of homes and families. Our modern world has engineered such activity out of our lives. There are fewer manual jobs, we do not need to travel on foot, we do not need to hunt and harvest for our food, and many domestic chores have been mechanized. Although these changes have created many benefits for our longevity and quality of life as the centuries have passed, they have also created many problems. It has recently been estimated that across the globe, physical inactivity causes 6% of the burden of disease from coronary heart disease, 7% of type 2 diabetes, and 10% of breast cancer and colon cancer (Lee et al., 2012). Table 12.1 shows the long (and growing) list of conditions for which there is good evidence that increased physical activity can have a beneficial effect.

We cannot and would not want to return to the lifestyles of our ancestors, but we do need to take a positive approach to creating lifestyles that include physical activity. The aim of this chapter is to provide an overview of what is known about the effects of physical activity on psychological function and to raise awareness of this knowledge among psychologists. This chapter develops the principle that the body is important to how we think, feel, and behave. The principles of psychosomatic medicine have clearly established the idea that how we think and feel will affect the functioning of the body. However, our task in this chapter is to show that the reverse is also true—that there is a somatopsychic principle (Harris, 1973), which is very much in line with the principles of positive psychology. The somatopsychic principle is neatly displayed in the well-known phrase "mens sana in corpore sano" ("a healthy mind in a healthy body") (see Hefferon, 2013).

Seligman (2002) talks of building strength as one of the key principles of positive psychology. If we examine physical strength as part of this concept, we can begin to see the somatopsychic principles working. Gaining physical strength or capacity allows us to feel more confident in our ability to do everyday tasks, perhaps provides us with a more positive perception of our physical selves, and thus can influence our

**Table 12.1**
Health Benefits of Physical Activity

| Strong evidence of reduced rates of | Strong evidence of |
| --- | --- |
| All-cause mortality | Increased cardiorespiratory and muscular fitness |
| Coronary heart disease | Healthier body mass and composition |
| High blood pressure | Improved bone health |
| Metabolic syndrome | Increased functional health |
| Type 2 diabetes | Improved cognitive function |
| Breast cancer | |
| Colon cancer | |
| Depression | |
| Falling | |

*Source*: Adapted from data in Lee et al. (2012).

self-esteem. Seligman (2002) further argues that building strength should be at the forefront of treating mental illness, and we will show that this building of physical strength has a somatopsychic impact on those people who are suffering from poor mental health. Although the tides may be turning from positive psychology's predominantly cognitive approach to a more embodied approach to well-being (Hefferon, 2013; Hefferon, Chapter 45, this volume), the discipline retains somewhat of a "neck-up" focus on flourishing (Peterson, 2013; Seligman, 2011). Ultimately, we will present the evidence that shows the positive link between psychological well-being and regular physical activity, moving toward a more holistic discipline in its scope and applications.

## PHYSICAL ACTIVITY AND MENTAL HEALTH

In the past 10 years there has been tremendous growth in the study of physical activity and mental health. A new journal, *Mental Health and Physical Activity*, is devoted to the topic, and there have been numerous textbooks examining the relationship (e.g., Carless & Douglas, 2010; Clow & Edmunds, 2013; Faulkner & Taylor, 2005; Leith, 2010). Recently, the most comprehensive edited collection to date was published (see Ekkekakis, 2013). The result of this cumulative research is that we now have a convincing evidence base that supports the existence of a strong relationship between physical activity and a number of dimensions of psychological well-being. This relationship may be critical. The literature indicates that mental health outcomes motivate people to persist in physical activity while also having the potentially positive impact on well-being (Biddle & Mutrie, 2008). Without regular participation, both mental and physical benefits will not accrue.

The existing evidence can be broadly categorized in terms of four main functions of physical activity for impacting mental health. First, physical activity may prevent mental health problems. Second, exercise has been examined as a treatment or therapy for existing mental illness. Third, physical activity may improve the quality of life for people with chronic physical and mental health problems. The final function concerns the role of physical activity in improving the psychological well-being of the general public. All four of these functions have elements of positive psychology in that there is a clear preventative function; a clear function for enhancing positive emotions, mood, and affect, even for those with existing mental illness; and a clear role in a positive approach to treating mental illness. We now briefly examine each of these functions.

### THE PREVENTATIVE FUNCTION

In terms of preventing poor mental health, the strongest evidence supporting the role of physical activity comes in the area of depression. In a recent systematic review, Mammen and Faulkner (2013) reviewed studies with a prospective-based, longitudinal design examining relations between physical activity and depression over at least two time intervals. A total of 25 of the 30 studies found a significant, inverse relationship between baseline physical activity and follow-up depression, suggesting that physical activity is preventative in the onset of depression. Given the heterogeneity in physical measurement in the reviewed studies, a clear dose–response relationship between physical activity and reduced depression was not readily apparent. However, there is promising evidence that any level of physical activity, including low levels, can prevent future depression.

Such studies involve large numbers of people and measure physical activity status prior to the incidence of depression. In one of the most well-cited examples, Camacho,

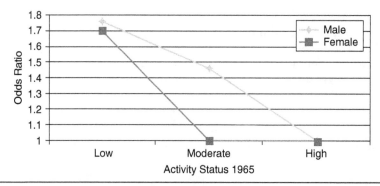

**Figure 12.1**   The odds ratios for developing depression at follow-up (1974) from different levels of baseline physical activity (1965). *Source:* Adapted from "Physical Activity and Depression: Evidence from the Alameda County Study," by T. C. Camacho, R. E. Roberts, N. B. Lazarus, G. Kaplan, and R. D. Cohen, 1991, *American Journal of Epidemiology, 134,* pp. 220–231.

Roberts, Lazarus, Kaplan, and Cohen (1991) found an association between inactivity and incidence of depression in a large population from Alameda County in California who provided baseline data in 1965 and were followed up in 1974 and 1983. Physical activity was categorized as low, medium, or high. In the first wave of follow-up (1974) the odds ratios (OR) of developing depression were significantly greater for both men and women who were low active in 1965 (OR = 1.8 for men, 1.7 for women) compared to those who were high active (see Figure 12.1).

There could be alternative explanations of the positive findings such as bias, confounding factors, or chance. Bias is unlikely in these former large studies, and careful checks of nonrespondents are made to ensure they do not differ from the responders. All of the positive studies take account of a wide range of possible confounding factors, such as disability, body mass index, smoking, alcohol, and social status; and in the statistical modeling, the relationship between physical activity and a decreased risk of depression remains. Despite consistency in the literature regarding a protective function of physical activity, some caution is required given that there may be a number of covariates, such as genetic variations (De Moor, Boomsma, Stubbe, Willemsen, & De Geus, 2008), that predict both physical activity and depression and may not have been fully accounted for in the reviewed studies.

The evidence for a preventative role for physical activity in other mental illnesses is not convincing at this point. If we accept that one of the key principles in positive psychology is to identify preventative strategies, then, at least for depression, enabling individuals to be physically active is a central target.

THE THERAPY FUNCTION

The possibility that physical activity could be used as a treatment in mental illness has long been recognized, but it was not well-researched until more recent times. For example, physical activity was seen as a popular and effective treatment for alcoholism as far back as the 19th century, as the following quotation from Cowles (1898) illustrates:

> The benefits accruing to the patients from the well-directed use of exercise and baths is indicated by the following observed symptoms: increase in weight, greater firmness of muscles, better colour of skin, larger lung capacity, more

regular and stronger action of the heart, clearer action of the mind, brighter and more expressive eye, improved carriage, quicker responses of nerves, and through them of muscle and limb to stimuli. All this has become so evident to them that only a very few are unwilling to attend the classes and many speak freely of the great benefits derived. (p. 108)

As with the preventative function, the most compelling evidence comes from studies in the area of clinical depression. The most recent review on the topic of exercise as a treatment for depression was published by The Cochrane Library and was conducted by Cooney and colleagues (2013), who found 39 studies that met their inclusion criteria. Reviews published in The Cochrane Library must have followed the standards of systematic reviewing that have been established by the Cochrane Collaboration, and so we can be confident in the manner in which this review was conducted. The meta-analysis showed a moderate effect size of −0.62 (95% confidence interval [CI] −0.81 to −0.42), for exercise versus no-treatment control conditions. For the six trials considered to be at low risk of bias (adequate allocation concealment, intention-to-treat analyses, and blinded outcome assessment), a further analysis showed a small clinical effect in favor of exercise that did not reach statistical significance. Finally, the authors compared the exercise effects to those of cognitive-behavioral therapy for the seven trials that had these comparisons and found no significant difference. Similarly, four trials compared exercise with antidepressant medication and no significant difference was found.

This suggests that exercise has a similar effect size to other recognized therapies for depression, including medication. One large study has shown that exercise equaled the effect found from a standard antidepressant drug after 16 weeks (Blumenthal et al., 1999), and after 6 months there were some indications that those who had continued to exercise had additional benefits in comparison (Babyak et al., 2000; see Figure 12.2). Cooney and colleagues (2013) concluded that exercise appears to be no more effective than psychological or pharmacological therapies. A more appropriate interpretation might be that exercise may be as beneficial as other common treatments—not necessarily better. Compared to earlier meta-analyses examining

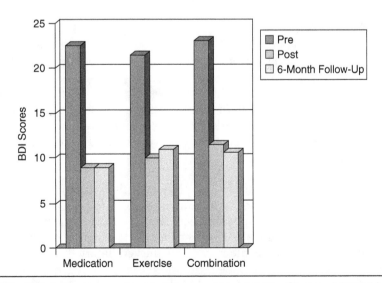

**Figure 12.2** BDI scores pre- and post- 16 weeks of treatment. *Source:* Adapted from Blumenthal et al., 1999 (pretreatment) and Babyak et al., 2000 (6-month follow-up).

exercise and depression, we are tending to see reduced effect sizes because exercise is being compared to other active treatments such as psychotherapy and medication.

There are many unanswered questions, such as the exact dosage and mode of activity that might work best. One team of systematic reviewers has examined the physical activity mode of walking (Robertson, Robertson, Jepson, & Maxwell, 2012). They found eight trials that met their inclusion criteria and an effect size of 0.86 (CI = 1.12, −0.61). The authors concluded that "Walking has a statistically significant, large effect on the symptoms of depression in some populations but the current evidence base from randomized, controlled trials is limited" (p. 73). In terms of policy and practice, the National Institute for Health and Clinical Excellence (2009) reviewed the evidence and recommended structured, supervised exercise programs three times a week (45 minutes to 1 hour) over 10 to 14 weeks as an intervention for mild to moderate depression.

### THE QUALITY OF LIFE FUNCTION

For people with chronic mental and/or physical health problems, improvement in quality of life tends to enhance the individual's ability to cope with and manage his or her disorder. Preliminary evidence suggests that regular physical activity can improve positive aspects of mental health (such as psychological quality of life and emotional well-being) in people with mental disorders and those coping with a chronic disease.

For example, improved quality of life is particularly important for individuals with severe and enduring mental health problems, such as schizophrenia, when complete remission may be unrealistic (Faulkner & Sparkes, 1999). A Cochrane review of the evidence concerning schizophrenia reported that exercise programs are possible in this population and that they can have modest effects on both the physical and mental health and well-being of individuals with schizophrenia (Gorczynski & Faulkner, 2010). An emerging evidence base concerns physical activity and quality of life among individuals with multiple sclerosis. Meta-analytic evidence suggests that exercise training is associated with a small improvement in quality of life (Motl & Gosney, 2008). Larger randomized studies are required in both cases before any definitive conclusions can be drawn.

### THE "FEEL GOOD" FUNCTION

Often when we ask someone why they exercise, they respond that it makes them "feel good." Current consensus clearly supports an association between physical activity and numerous domains of psychological well-being in the general population. This has largely been addressed through studies assessing the impact of physical activity on many variables such as quality of life, self-esteem and self-perceptions, and cognitive functioning (see Ekkekakis, 2013). We briefly review research looking at affect, stress, and anxiety, and a more recent body of work looking at physical activity and posttraumatic growth.

*Affect*   Feeling good during and/or after physical activity is motivational, serves as an important health outcome in itself, and contributes to quality of life. To a certain extent, the acute effects of physical activity have received increasing attention given its presumed motivational properties. It is certainly now reliably established that moderate levels of exercise intensity below the ventilatory threshold (the point at which relatively more carbon dioxide is produced than the oxygen that is consumed) is associated with "feeling better" (see Ekkekakis, Parfitt, & Petruzello, 2011, for a comprehensive overview of this field of research). At this level of activity you can easily talk to someone beside you. Beyond the ventilatory threshold, it becomes more difficult to do so.

Positive activated affect is described as a subjective mental state of positive energy and engagement. In two well-cited meta-analyses, both acute (Reed & Ones, 2006) and regular aerobic physical activity (Reed & Buck, 2009) increase self-reported positive activated affect by approximately one half a standard deviation in experimental participants compared to control. Alternatively, these findings suggest that "a randomly selected person who just completed aerobic activity would be about 65 to 70 per cent more likely to report higher positive activated affect than a randomly selected sedentary person" (Reed, 2013, p. 417). Simply, exercise can help people feel good, and this induction of positive emotions is a vital component for overall flourishing (Seligman, 2011).

*Coping With Stress*   Stress is a common feature of life for many of us. Often of a subclinical nature, it can have a negative impact on quality of life and health and is a major source of sickness-related absence from work. Stress can manifest itself in emotional states, such as anxiety, that reflect negative cognitive appraisal and physiological responses such as increased blood pressure.

Cross-sectional and prospective surveys in the United States and Canada (Iwasaki, Zuzanek, & Mannell, 2001; Stephens, 1988), Finland (Hassmen, Koivula, & Uutela, 2000), and the United Kingdom (Steptoe & Butler, 1996) indicate that more active individuals self-report fewer symptoms of anxiety or emotional distress. Several meta-analyses demonstrate medium effect sizes for physical activity interventions in the reduction of anxiety (Conn, 2010; Wipfli, Rethorst, & Landers, 2008).

Another focus for research concerns the effectiveness of fitness and/or regular physical activity on the mental and physical ability to cope with stress. Taylor (2000) reviewed 14 experimental studies and concluded that single sessions of moderate exercise can reduce short-term physiological reactivity to and enhance recovery from brief psychosocial stressors. An earlier meta-analysis found an overall effect size of 0.48 for reduced reactivity to stressors (Crews & Landers, 1987). Specifically, reduced reactivity to stressors (e.g., systolic and diastolic blood pressure, skin conductivity, muscle tension, self-reported psychological symptoms) or a faster recovery following a stressor were generally found for those who were fitter or improved their fitness with training, or who had undertaken a single exercise session, compared with baseline measures or a control group. Overall, exercise may act as a buffer or coping strategy for stress.

*Physical Activity: Beyond Building Resilience*   Researchers have linked participation in sports and group-based structured exercise programs, following trauma, with the facilitation of posttraumatic growth (PTG; Hefferon, Grealy, & Mutrie, 2008, 2010). PTG is the phenomenon in which, following adversity, individuals surpass previous levels of functioning than those that existed before the event occurred. Hefferon et al. (2008, 2010) found that women who had undergone a 3-month structured physical activity intervention during breast cancer treatment utilized the activity to facilitate PTG as well as considered this engagement with exercise as a positive outcome in itself. More specifically, the women perceived the exercise classes to be a "safe environment," offering a positive support system and the opportunity to transfer new learned skills (e.g., confidence) to their everyday lives. Furthermore, the women reported a heightened awareness of their health and an increase in positive health behaviors (e.g., change in diet, increased exercise) and the cessation of detrimental health behaviors (e.g., smoking). A 5-year follow-up study with the same population (Mutrie et al., 2012) reported serendipitous accounts of PTG (24%) (Hefferon, 2012),

70% of whom were part of the original intervention group. Thus, these findings suggest that there may be opportune time points during the cancer process (e.g., immediately after diagnosis and through treatment) in which engagement in physical activity can help reconnect cancer patients to their bodies, thereby helping them to grow, as well as perceiving the engagement as a positive from the trauma in itself.

Several other clinical populations have also utilized physical activity for the facilitation of PTG and considered the heightened awareness of health and engagement in activity as a positive outcome following their trauma (Hefferon, Grealy, & Mutrie, 2009). For example, Hefferon, Mallery, Gay, and Elliott (2012) found that engagement in a 6-week Boxercise class for individuals with mental health difficulties facilitated elements of PTG, including enhanced psychological well-being, sense of personal strength, and increased self-regulation over emotions and physical self. Furthermore, the participants demonstrated a progressive somatopsychic experience, attributing the sense of feeling stronger in the body (via the exercise) to becoming stronger in the mind. In summary, although the current research into the links between physical activity and growth are qualitative and exploratory, there appears to be an interesting dynamic between the utilization of exercise during trauma and PTG. Future mixed-methods research is needed to understand the complex relation between the two areas because, to date, activity and PTG research has only been studied within group environments.

## MECHANISMS: A PROCESS ORIENTATION

There is considerable agreement that the underlying mechanisms that relate to the positive effects from exercise on mental health are not yet known. Several possible mechanisms, including biochemical changes as a result of exercise, such as increased levels of neurotransmitters (such as endorphins or serotonin; see Dishman & O'Connor, 2009), physiological changes such as improved cardiovascular function or thermogenesis, and psychological changes such as an increased sense of mastery, have been proposed. From a positive psychology perspective, physical activity may foster the six main elements of Ryff and Singer's (1996, 2006) model: enhancing self-acceptance (e.g., self-esteem), offering autonomy (e.g., choice of program), gaining environmental mastery (e.g., learning a new and transferable skill), fostering positive relationships (e.g., group-based interventions), giving new purpose in life (e.g., increased importance of health), and overall personal growth for both normal and clinical populations (Hefferon & Mutrie, 2012).

This model reflects a *process* orientation for understanding the benefits of physical activity. In acknowledging the huge diversity of potential triggers (such as exercise type, environment, social context) and individual circumstances (such as state of mental health, needs, preferences, and personal background), Fox (1999) suggests that several mechanisms most likely operate in concert, with the precise combination being highly individual-specific. Studying the process of mental health change as a result of physical activity participation must therefore allow for the diverse range of factors that influence an individual's sense of psychological well-being. The isolation of a specific mechanism cannot realistically address the large number of potential psychological influences that may be experienced through physical activity. It is more realistic for a process-oriented approach to allow for the broad range of potential influences and therefore provide a more complete explanation of the causes of psychological change (Faulkner & Carless, 2006).

For example, Deci and Ryan (1985) have proposed that the basic needs for competence, autonomy, and relatedness must be satisfied across the life span for an individual to experience an ongoing sense of integrity and well-being (see also Ryan & Deci, 2000; Brown & Ryan, Chapter 9, this volume). These three basic needs are commonly reported outcomes of physical activity interventions. Existing research suggests that physical competence and self-perceptions can be improved through physical activity and that this can have a positive mental health effect (Fox, 1997). Exercise self-efficacy can be increased through interventions and is associated with positive exercise emotion (Biddle & Mutrie, 2008). Autonomy, or perceptions of personal control, is reported to be frequently lacking among people with depression, where feelings of powerlessness and helplessness are common (Seligman, 1975). Physical activity offers a potential avenue through which meaningful control can be gradually taken as the individual assumes responsibility for the organization of his or her exercise schedule or feels in control of how his or her body looks or performs. When we make progress in our physical capacity, it is hard for even the most pessimistic to attribute this progress to anything but their own efforts and abilities. It might be that autonomy gained through exercise generalizes to other areas of life through feelings of empowerment (Fox, 1997). Finally, the provision of physical activity in a supportive group environment represents one approach to providing opportunity for positive social interaction that may be valuable.

No single theory is likely to adequately explain the mental health benefits of physical activity. Process theories, such as self-determination theory (Deci & Ryan, 1985), allow for a broader theoretical stance in understanding the mechanisms underpinning the physical activity and psychological well-being relation and also suggest how motivation to be active can be facilitated (Faulkner & Carless, 2006). Specifically, we would argue that structuring the physical activity experience to support feelings of autonomy, competence, and social relatedness is a good basis for promoting adherence to exercise and enhancing psychological well-being.

## HOW CAN PEOPLE GET MORE ACTIVE?

A sedentary lifestyle is now the normal lifestyle of many of the populations in developed countries, and inactivity is a growing population health concern in developing countries. It has been estimated that over 30% of the world's population is inactive, with the percentage ranging from low levels of inactivity in Southeast Asia (17%) to high levels of inactivity in the Americas and eastern Mediterranean (43%). There is a global trend for inactivity to increase with age and for women to be less active than men. Across the world, only 20% of 13- to 15-year-olds meet the recommendation of being active for 60 minutes each day (Hallal et al., 2012). Major reported barriers to exercise participation include: *psychological barriers* (e.g., lack of motivation, perceived lack of time); *physical barriers* (e.g., weight, injury); and *contextual and environmental barriers* (e.g., employment, proximity/access to facilities, seasonal weather) (Hefferon, Murphy, McLeod, Mutrie, & Campbell, 2013).

Leading academics and practitioners from around the world reviewed evidence for interventions that were effective in increasing physical activity levels. This review led to the production of a companion document to the Toronto charter, which includes "Seven Best Investments for Physical Activity" (http://www.globalpa.org.uk/investments). These seven approaches are:

1. School programs in which children are encouraged to be active on the journey to and from school, during school break times, after school, and via quality physical education programs at all ages.

2. Transport policies and systems that prioritize walking, cycling, and public transport.
3. Urban design regulations and infrastructure that provide for equitable and safe access to recreational physical activity, and recreational and transport-related walking and cycling across the life course.
4. Physical activity and noncommunicable disease prevention integrated into primary health care systems.
5. Public education, including mass media to raise awareness and change social norms on physical activity.
6. Community-wide programs involving multiple settings and sectors and that mobilize and integrate community engagement and resources.
7. Sports systems and programs that promote "sport for all" and encourage participation across the life span.

Psychologists reading this list can see that their role may be one of advocacy in ensuring local opportunities exist for children and adults to be active. But in more individual settings, counseling people to be more active for health and well-being now has some established guidelines. An example is provided by Kirk, Barnett, and Mutrie (2007). Although originally developed for people with type 2 diabetes, these guidelines are applicable to many different populations.

## Is There an Exercise Dosage for Psychological Well-Being?

Identifying a dose–response relationship between physical activity and mental health is still not possible. Effects are likely to be highly individualized and depend on preferences, experiences, and setting, and vary in terms of the dimensions of well-being, interest, and whether we are interested in the acute or long-term effects of physical activity. In the absence of a single definitive dosage for psychological well-being, standard adult physical activity guidelines of accumulating 150 minutes of moderate to vigorous physical activity each week should apply equally to mental health promotion. In terms of acute effects, short bouts (10–15 minutes) of moderate walking have been shown to induce significant affective changes in experimental studies (Ekkekakis, Hall, VanLanduyt, & Petruzzello, 2000). The most effective dose is likely the one that individuals enjoy and can sustain. Critically, a range of exercise modes and intensities should be recommended based on the participant's previous exercise experiences, personal preferences, strengths, and goals.

The challenge of research is to establish an evidence base that demonstrates the efficacy of a dose of physical activity that can be translated into interventions acceptable to participants and feasible to deliver. An example can be seen in the work examining the role of short bouts of physical activity, such as walking at a brisk pace for 10 minutes, in alleviating cigarette cravings and withdrawal symptoms in abstinent smokers (Haasova et al., 2013).

An emerging focus for research is the impact of sedentary behavior on mental health. Sedentary behavior can be defined as any waking behavior characterized by a low energy expenditure (i.e., ≤ 1.5 resting metabolic equivalents) while in a sitting or reclining posture (see the Sedentary Behaviour Research Network website: http://www.sedentarybehaviour.org/what-is-sedentary-behaviour/). Although this field is still in its infancy, research demonstrates emerging evidence of at least an association between time engaged in sedentary behavior and mental health (Faulkner &

Biddle, 2013). In the future, intervention doses may consist of shorter bouts of low to moderate intensity physical activity to break up sedentary time in contrast to, or complementing, traditional doses of exercise.

## ACTIVE COMMUNITIES

Although definitions vary, social capital is fundamentally about how people interact with one another (Dekker & Uslaner, 2001). Evidence consistently suggests that communities with high levels of physical activity participation also have high levels of social capital. Studies using social trust as an indicator of social capital have shown that high compared to low levels of trust are associated with a reduction in the risk of physical inactivity. In a large cross-sectional study using data from the 2003 Health Survey for England, Poortinga (2006) found that individuals who experience some lack or a severe lack of social support were 20% and 24% less likely to do at least one walk of 30 minutes per week. A high level of trust, a medium level of civic participation, and a high level of civic participation increased the likelihood of doing at least one walk of 30 minutes per week by 20%, 14%, and 53%, respectively. Similarly, a large Canadian cross-sectional study showed that individuals who did not participate in any formal groups or associations were more likely to be physically inactive compared to those with high participation (Legh-Jones & Moore, 2012).

Much research has also focused on the physical aspects of social capital in terms of the built environment. For example, systematic reviews have shown that mixed land use, increased housing density, compact development patterns, and levels of open space are associated with increased levels of physical activity, primarily walking (Durand, Andalib, Dunton, Wolch, & Pentz, 2011). Such characteristics are likely to reflect greater walkability—the extent to which a particular built environment is friendly to the presence of people living, shopping, visiting, enjoying, or spending time in an area (Coyle, 2011).

Neighborhood crime and safety have also been found to be negatively associated with physical activity. Data from a population-based survey of adults in the United Kingdom found that people who felt safe in their neighborhood were more likely to be physically active (Harrison, Gemmell, & Heller, 2007). Such associations also have implications for children. Children are more physically active when they have greater independent mobility (a child's freedom to travel around their own neighborhood or to public places without adult supervision) (Mitra, Faulkner, Buliung, & Stone, in press). In a study in Toronto, Canada, Mitra et al. (in press) found that children had significantly less independent mobility when their parents were worried about strangers or thought their neighborhood was unsafe. Attractiveness of neighborhood streets and the presence of other people "talking and doing things together" were also associated with greater independent mobility among children.

Most of the evidence concerning physical activity and aspects of social capital is cross-sectional in nature. Accordingly, causality cannot be inferred. Future research should examine these relationships experimentally and explore the impact of physical activity interventions on such social outcomes, and on whether enhancing such outcomes has an impact on physical activity. At the least, we can say that where one lives is associated with how physically active one is. Urban planning and public health initiatives should focus on interventions that enable the production and maintenance of social capital among neighbors, address safety concerns, and create communities where being physically active is the easiest option.

## CONCLUSION

In conclusion, there is compelling evidence as to the positive relation between physical activity and mental health in clinical and nonclinical populations. Although methodological concerns do exist, we would contend that the potential of psychological benefits accruing through exercise far outweighs the potential risk that no effect will occur. Because physical activity is an effective method for improving important aspects of physical health, such as obesity, cardiovascular fitness, and hypertension (see Lee et al., 2012), the promotion of physical activity for psychological well-being can be seen as a "win-win" situation with both mental and physical health benefits accruing (Mutrie & Faulkner, 2003).

## SUMMARY POINTS

- There is a convincing evidence base that supports the existence of a strong relationship between physical activity and a number of dimensions of psychological well-being.
- The promotion of physical activity for psychological well-being can be seen as a "win-win" situation with both mental and physical health benefits accruing.
- Existing evidence suggests physical activity may perform a preventative function, a treatment function, and a clear function for enhancing positive emotions, mood, and affect, even for those with existing mental or physical illness.
- The challenge remains how to help people initiate physical activity and maintain participation. Professional psychologists have an important role to play in legitimizing physical activity as positive psychology in motion and in helping individuals develop the self-regulatory skills to initiate and maintain physical activity (e.g., self-monitoring, goal-setting, action planning).
- The most effective dose of physical activity is likely the one that individuals enjoy and find pleasant. A range of physical activity modes and intensities should be recommended based on the participant's previous experiences, preferences, strengths, and goals.
- Future research should examine why physical activity enhances well-being in some people but not others, adopt a process approach in exploring potential mechanisms explaining the psychological benefits of physical activity, and develop a new agenda exploring sedentary behavior and psychological well-being.

## REFERENCES

Babyak, M., Blumenthal, J. A., Herman, S., Khatri, P., Doraiswamy, M., Moore, K., . . . Krishnan, K. R. (2000). Exercise treatment for major depression: Maintenance of therapeutic benefit at 10 months. *Psychosomatic Medicine, 62,* 633–638.

Biddle, S. J. H., & Mutrie, N. (2008). *Psychology of physical activity: Determinants, well-being, and interventions* (2nd ed.). London, England: Routledge.

Blumenthal, J. A., Babyak, M. A., Moore, K. A., Craighead, E., Herman, S., Khatri, P., . . . Krishnan, K. R. (1999). Effects of exercise training on older patients with major depression. *Archives of Internal Medicine, 159,* 2349–2356.

Camacho, T. C., Roberts, R. E., Lazarus, N. B., Kaplan, G. A., & Cohen, R. D. (1991). Physical activity and depression: Evidence from the Alameda county study. *American Journal of Epidemiology, 134,* 220–231.

Carless, D., & Douglas, K. (2010). *Sport and physical activity for mental health.* Oxford, England: Wiley-Blackwell.

Caspersen, C. J., Powell, K. E., & Christenson, G. M. (1985). Physical activity, exercise and physical fitness: Definitions and distinctions for health-related research. *Public Health Reports, 100,*
126–131.

Clow, A., & Edmunds, S. (Eds.). (2013). *Physical activity and mental health.* Champaign, IL:
Human Kinetics.

Conn, V. S. (2010). Anxiety outcomes after physical activity interventions: Meta-analysis findings. *Nursing Research, 59,* 224–231.

Cooney, G. M., Dwan, K., Greig, C. A., Lawlor, D. A., Rimer, J., Waugh, F. R., . . . Mead, G. E.
(2013). Exercise for depression. *Cochrane Database of Systematic Reviews, 2013*(9), CD004366.

Cowles, E. (1898). Gymnastics in the treatment of inebriety. *American Physical Education Review,
3,* 107–110.

Coyle, S. (2011). *Sustainable and resilient communities: A comprehensive action plan for towns, cities,
and regions.* Hoboken, NJ: Wiley.

Crews, D. J., & Landers, D. M. (1987). A meta-analytic review of aerobic fitness and reactivity
to psychosocial stressors. *Medicine and Science in Sports and Exercise, 19* (Suppl.), S114–S120.

Deci, E. L., & Ryan, R. M. (1985). *Intrinsic motivation and self-determination in human behavior.*
New York, NY: Plenum Press.

Dekker, P., & Uslaner, E. M. (2001). Introduction. In E. M. Uslaner (Ed.), *Social capital and participation in everyday life.* London, England: Routledge.

De Moor, M. M., Boomsma, D. I., Stubbe, J. H., Willemsen, G., & De Geus, E. C. (2008). Testing
causality in the association between regular exercise and symptoms of anxiety and depression. *Archives of General Psychiatry, 65,* 897–905.

Dishman, R. K., & O'Connor, P. J. (2009). Lessons in exercise neurobiology: The case of endorphins. *Mental Health & Physical Activity, 2,* 4–9.

Durand, C. P., Andalib, M., Dunton, G. F., Wolch, J., & Pentz, M. A. (2011). A systematic review
of built environment factors related to physical activity and obesity risk: Implications for
smart growth urban planning. *Obesity Review, 12,* 173–182.

Ekkekakis, P. (2013). *Routledge handbook of physical activity and mental health.* Abingdon, England:
Routledge.

Ekkekakis, P., Hall, E. E., VanLanduyt, L. M., & Petruzzello, S. J. (2000). Walking in (affective)
circles: Can short walks enhance affect? *Journal of Behavioral Medicine, 23,* 245–275.

Ekkekakis, P., Parfitt, G., & Petruzzello, S. J. (2011). The pleasure and displeasure people feel
when they exercise at different intensities: Decennial update and progress towards a tripartite rationale for exercise intensity prescription. *Sports Medicine, 41,* 641–671.

Faulkner, G., & Biddle, S. J. H. (2013). Standing on top of the world: Is sedentary behavior
associated with mental health? *Mental Health and Physical Activity, 6,* 1–2.

Faulkner, G., & Carless, D. (2006). Physical activity and the process of psychiatric rehabilitation:
Theoretical and methodological issues. *Psychiatric Rehabilitation Journal, 29,* 258–266.

Faulkner, G., & Sparkes, A. (1999). Exercise as therapy for schizophrenia: An ethnographic
study. *Journal of Sport and Exercise Psychology, 21,* 52–69.

Faulkner, G., & Taylor, A. (Eds.). (2005). *Exercise, health and mental health: Emerging relationships
between physical activity and psychological well-being.* London, England: Routledge.

Fox, K. R. (1997). The physical self and processes in self-esteem development. In K. R. Fox (Ed.),
*The physical self: From motivation to well-being* (pp. 111–140). Champaign, IL: Human Kinetics.

Fox, K. R. (1999). The influence of physical activity on mental well-being. *Public Health Nutrition,
2,* 411–418.

Gorczynski, P., & Faulkner, G. (2010). Exercise therapy for schizophrenia. *Cochrane Database of
Systematic Reviews, 2010*(5), CD004412.

Haasova, M., Warren, F. C., Ussher, M., Van Rensburg, K. J., Faulkner, G., Cropley,
M., . . . Taylor, A. H. (2013). The acute effects of physical activity on cigarette cravings: Systematic review and meta-analysis with individual participant data. *Addiction, 108,* 26–37.

Hallal, P. C., Andersen, L. B., Bull, F. C., Guthold, R., Haskell, W., Ekelund, U., & Lancet Physical Activity Series Working Group. (2012). Global physical activity levels: Surveillance progress, pitfalls, and prospects. *Lancet, 380,* 247–257.

Harris, D. V. (1973). *Involvement in sport: A somatopsychic rationale.* Philadelphia, PA: Lea & Febiger.

Harrison, R. A., Gemmell, I., & Heller, R. F. (2007). The population effect of crime and neighbourhood on physical activity: An analysis of 15 461 adults. *Journal of Epidemiology and Community Health, 61,* 34–39.

Hassmen, P., Koivula, N., & Uutela, A. (2000). Physical exercise and psychological well-being: A population study in Finland. *Preventive Medicine, 30,* 17–25.

Hefferon, K. (2012). Bringing back the body into positive psychology: The theory of corporeal posttraumatic growth in breast cancer. *Psychology, 3,* 1238–1242.

Hefferon, K. (2013). *Positive psychology and the body: The somatopsychic side to flourishing.* Berkshire, England: McGraw-Hill.

Hefferon, K., Grealy, M., & Mutrie, N. (2008). The perceived influence of an exercise class intervention on the process and outcomes of post-traumatic growth. *Mental Health and Physical Activity, 1,* 32–39.

Hefferon, K., Grealy, M., & Mutrie, N. (2009). Posttraumatic growth and life threatening physical illness: A systematic review of the qualitative literature. *British Journal of Health Psychology, 14,* 343–378.

Hefferon, K., Grealy, M., & Mutrie, N. (2010). Transforming from cocoon to butterfly: The potential role of the body in the process of posttraumatic growth. *Journal of Humanistic Psychology, 50,* 224–247.

Hefferon, K., Mallery, R., Gay, C., & Elliott, S. (2012). "Leave all the troubles of the outside world": A qualitative study on the binary benefits of "Boxercise" for individuals with mental health difficulties. *Qualitative Research in Sport, Exercise and Health, 5,* 80–102.

Hefferon, K., Murphy, H., McLeod, J., Mutrie, N., & Campbell, A. (2013). Understanding barriers to exercise implementation 5-years post breast cancer diagnosis: A large-scale qualitative study. *Health Education Research, 28,* 843–856.

Hefferon, K., & Mutrie, N. (2012). Physical activity as a "stellar" positive psychology intervention. In E. O. Acevedo (Ed.), *The Oxford handbook of exercise psychology* (pp. 117–130). Oxford, England: Oxford University Press.

Iwasaki, Y., Zuzanek, J., & Mannell, R. C. (2001). The effects of physically active leisure on stress-health relationships. *Canadian Journal of Public Health, 92,* 214–218.

Kirk, A. F., Barnett, J., & Mutrie, N. (2007). Physical activity consultation for people with type 2 diabetes: Evidence and guidelines. *Diabetic Medicine, 24,* 809–816.

Lee, I. M., Shiroma, E. J., Lobelo, F., Puska, P., Blair, S. N., Katzmarzyk, P. T., & Lancet Physical Activity Series Working Group. (2012). Effect of physical inactivity on major non-communicable diseases worldwide: An analysis of burden of disease and life expectancy. *Lancet, 380,* 219–229.

Legh-Jones, H., & Moore, S. (2012). Network social capital, social participation, and physical inactivity in an urban adult population. *Social Science Medicine, 74,* 1362–1367.

Leith, L. (2010). *Foundations of exercise and mental health.* Morgantown, WV: Fitness Information Technology.

Mammen, G., & Faulkner, G. (2013). Physical activity and the prevention of depression: A systematic review of prospective studies. *American Journal of Preventive Medicine, 45,* 649–657.

Mitra, R., Faulkner, G. E. J., Buliung, R. N., & Stone, M. R. (in press). Does the neighbourhood environment influence children's independent mobility? Evidence from Toronto, Canada. *Urban Studies.*

Motl, R. W., & Gosney, J. L. (2008). Effect of exercise training on quality of life in multiple sclerosis: A meta-analysis. *Multiple Sclerosis, 14,* 129–135.

Mutrie, N., Campbell, A., Barry, S., Hefferon, K., McConnachie, A., Ritchie, D., & Tovey, S. (2012). Five-year follow-up of participants in a randomised controlled trial showing benefits from exercise for breast cancer survivors during adjuvant treatment. Are there lasting effects? *Journal of Cancer Survivorship, 6*, 420–430.

Mutrie, N., & Faulkner, G. (2003). Physical activity and mental health. In T. Everett, M. Donaghy, & S. Fever (Eds.), *Physiotherapy and occupational therapy in mental health: An evidence based approach* (pp. 82–97). Oxford, England: Butterworth Heinemann.

National Institute for Health and Clinical Excellence. (2009) *Depression: The treatment and management of depression in adults (updated edition).* National Clinical Practice Guideline No. 90. London, England: British Psychological Society and Royal College of Psychiatrists.

Peterson, C. (2013). *Pursuing the good life: 100 reflections on positive psychology.* New York, NY: Oxford University Press.

Poortinga, W. (2006). Perceptions of the environment, physical activity, and obesity. *Social Science Medicine, 63*, 2835–2846.

Reed, J. (2013). Effect of acute and regular aerobic physical activity on positive activated affect. In P. Ekkekakis (Ed.), *Routledge handbook of physical activity and mental health* (pp. 413–421). Abingdon, England: Routledge.

Reed, J., & Buck, S. (2009). The effect of regular aerobic exercise on positive activated affect: A meta-analysis. *Psychology of Sport and Exercise, 10*, 581–594.

Reed, J., & Ones, D. (2006). The effect of acute aerobic exercise on positive activated affect: A meta-analysis. *Psychology of Sport and Exercise, 7*, 477–514.

Robertson, R., Robertson, A., Jepson, R., & Maxwell, M. (2012). Walking for depression or depressive symptoms: A systematic review and meta-analysis. *Mental Health and Physical Activity, 5*, 66–75.

Ryan, R. M., & Deci, E. L. (2000). Self-determination theory and the facilitation of intrinsic motivation, social development and well-being. *American Psychologist, 55*, 68–78.

Ryff, C., & Singer, B. (1998). The contours of positive human health. *Psychological Inquiry, 9*, 1–28.

Ryff, C. D., & Singer, B. (2006). Best news yet for the six-factor model of psychological wellbeing. *Social Science Research, 35*, 1103–1119.

Seligman, M. E. P. (1975). *Helplessness: On depression, development, and death.* New York, NY: W. H. Freeman.

Seligman, M. E. P. (2002). Positive psychology, positive prevention and positive therapy. In C. R. Snyder & S. J. Lopez (Eds.), *Handbook of positive psychology* (pp. 3–9). New York, NY: Oxford University Press.

Seligman, M. E. P. (2011). *Flourish: A visionary new understanding of happiness and well-being.* New York, NY: Free Press.

Stephens, T. (1988). Physical activity and mental health in the United States and Canada: Evidence from four population surveys. *Preventive Medicine, 17*, 35–47.

Steptoe, A., & Butler, N. (1996). Sports participation and emotional wellbeing in adolescents. *The Lancet, 347*, 1789–1792.

Taylor, A. H. (2000). Physical activity, anxiety, and stress. In S. J. H. Biddle, K. R. Fox, & S. H. Boutcher (Eds.), *Physical activity and psychological well-being* (pp. 10–45). London, England: Routledge.

Wipfli, B. M., Rethorst, C. D., & Landers, D. M. (2008). The anxiolytic effects of exercise: A meta-analysis of randomized trials and dose-response analysis. *Journal of Sport and Exercise Psychology, 30*, 392–410.

World Health Organization. (2010). *Global recommendations on physical activity for health.* Geneva, Switzerland: Author.

CHAPTER 13

# Balancing Time Perspective in Pursuit of Optimal Functioning

ILONA BONIWELL and PHILIP G. ZIMBARDO

CENTRAL TO THE DISCIPLINE of positive psychology (Seligman & Csikszentmihalyi, 2000) is the answer to the question of what makes life worth living, or simply: What is a good life? What constitutes a good life is a multifaceted issue that positive psychology sets out to study across three levels: positive subjective experience, positive individual characteristics, and qualities that contribute to a good society (Seligman, 1999). One key to learning how to live a fulfilling life is discovering how to achieve a balanced temporal perspective (Boniwell & Zimbardo, 2003).

The construct of a balanced time perspective provides a unique way of linking positive psychology's three levels of research. The study of time perspective investigates how the flow of human experience is parceled into temporal categories, or time frames, usually of past, present, and future. The relative emphasis or habitual focus on any of these frames is often biased toward overusing some of them while underusing others. These learned temporal biases are influenced by culture, education, religion, social class, and other conditions. A balanced time perspective is the state and the ongoing process of being able to switch flexibly among these time frames as most appropriate to the demands of the current behavioral setting (Zimbardo & Boyd, 1999). Time perspective is a basic aspect of individual subjective experience. It also influences individual choices and actions and can become a dispositional characteristic when an individual's biased time perspective becomes a dominant way of responding. At positive psychology's third level (the good society), time perspective is both influenced by cultural values and processes and can have a major impact on social behavior as well as on cultural discourses in society. Learning to overcome our temporal biases that limit optimal, healthy functioning and discovering how to achieve a balanced time perspective should be a mandate for all of us. We believe it should be a central component in the agenda of positive psychology.

Dealing with time is a fundamental feature of the human experience, both objective, or so-called clock time, and subjective, personal constructions of time. The invention of huge clocks on impressive towers in most European town squares was a great feat of human creativity. They served to coordinate many community activities—religious, agricultural, business, and social commerce—in the many years before individual timepieces became commonplace. At first, time was controlled locally, but that meant there were almost as many time systems as there were communities (Lofy, 2000). It was only relatively recently, at the end of 19th century, that time became coordinated across geographical regions following the necessity to establish railway timetables. The impact of quantifying and standardizing time cannot be underestimated. The development of mechanical devices for measuring time changed the dominant representation of time in the West from cyclical to linear, from never-ending to irreplaceable. The unification and coordination of time, essential and beneficial for the development of economies, became a regulating structure of much human behavior.

Time not only underlies and regulates our social behavior but also penetrates the very fabric of our consciousness. The theme of time permeates poetry, songs, proverbs, homilies, metaphors, and even childhood fairytales. An image of Cinderella, having to win over a prince's heart within very tight temporal constraints, and mindful that present pleasures are transient, is likely to be embedded in the consciousness of many Western children. Similarly, the moral of the tale of The Three Little Pigs is not lost on most children, who recognize that the lazy pig who builds his house quickly of straw is not the match for the fearsome wolf as is his future-oriented brother pig, who takes the time and effort to build his fortress of bricks. In some cultural constructions, time translates into a concept like rubber that can be stretched to fit human affairs, whereas in other more industrialized societies, human affairs are subordinated to temporal demands. In idiomatic use, time has become a commodity that can be saved, spent, used, found, lost, wasted, or maximized.

It is surprising to us that in spite of the obvious importance of temporal processes in our lives, their systematic exploration has received relatively little attention from psychology and the social sciences. The psychological study of subjective time has focused on time estimation, perceived duration of experiences, perceived rate of change, pace of life, and reaction time (RT). The use of RT as a major dependent variable in experimental and cognitive psychology blends objective recording of clock time and subjective responding. Time has also been conceived of as a key methodological factor that needs to be accounted for in study designs and measurement techniques or in assessing an experiment's validity (McGrath, 1988).

The focus of this chapter is the construct of time perspective (TP), which is viewed as an integral part of the subjective or personal experience of "lived time" (Gorman & Wessman, 1977). Time perspective represents an individual's way of relating to the psychological concepts of past, present, and future. Time and its dimensions are not viewed as objective stimuli that exist independently of the person, but as psychological concepts constructed and reconstructed by the individual (Block, 1990).

One of the broadest definitions of time orientation, given by Hornik and Zakay (1996), is the "relative dominance of past, present, or future in a person's thought" (p. 385). Lennings (1996) gives a somewhat more specific definition of TP as "a cognitive operation that implies both an emotional reaction to imagined time zones (such as future, present, or past) and a preference for locating action in some temporal zone" (p. 72).

One literature review identifies up to 211 different ways of approaching the concept of TP (McGrath & Kelly, 1986). Such a multiplicity of approaches has resulted in various definitions and numerous methods of assessing dimensions of time orientation. Thus, we can find some researchers focusing on emotional valence of the past or the future, others on time dominance or dwelling on the past or the future, and some dealing with continuities among the past, present, and future, time relatedness, and many other facets of temporal perspective.

Time perspective is considered to have cognitive, emotional, and social components. The formation of TP is influenced by a host of factors, some learned in the process of socialization, such as an individual's cultural values and dominant religious orientation, kind and extent of education, socioeconomic status, and family modeling. But TP can also be influenced throughout a person's life-course development by the nature of his or her career, economic or political instability, personal experiences with mind-altering substances, traumatic events, or personal successes. Further, TP is regarded as an expression of a person's own system of meanings that allows him or her to develop a coherent framework for living (Lennings, 1998). This central aspect of human nature can be shown to affect attention, perception, decision making, and a variety of mundane and significant personal actions. Time perspective is one of the most powerful influences on virtually all aspects of human behavior. It can shape the quality of life of individuals and even the destinies of nations, such as when a majority of individuals adopt a biased temporal orientation that overly promotes a focus on the past, the future, or the present.

Gorman and Wessman (1977) suggest that it is possible to regard temporal orientation, attitudes, and experiences as persisting personality traits. Zimbardo and Boyd (1999) further agree that although TP may be affected by situational forces, such as inflation, being on vacation, or being under survival stresses, it can also become a relatively stable dispositional characteristic when a particular temporal bias comes to predominate a person's outlook and response hierarchy.

The study of TP has often focused on one temporal zone, usually that of the future or the present. Limited examples of research focus on the combination of the three dominant time zones (Rappaport, 1990). Furthermore, the majority of studies have failed to provide a multidimensional picture of TP, focusing on either time orientation as a preferred temporal region or time extension—the length of time projected into the past or the future. The few earlier empirical studies that investigated all three time zones in the same group of subjects produced scarce and inconsistent findings (Carr, 1985).

## MEASUREMENT OF TIME PERSPECTIVE

There have been several attempts to develop a measuring instrument of TP on the basis of combination of past, present, and future orientations. These endeavors have included, among others, the Circles Test (Cottle, 1976), Time Structure Questionnaire (Bond & Feather, 1988), and Time Lines (Rappaport, 1990). However, the majority of these instruments exhibited low reliability and scoring difficulties and measured only one or two temporal regions, with the past TP being largely ignored (Kazakina, 1999). The Stanford Time Perspective Inventory (STPI), developed by Zimbardo (1992), included five predominant orientations: past regret orientation future achievement orientation, two types of present orientation—hedonistic and fatalistic—and time press factor. However, this factor structure proved to be relatively unstable with subsequent factor analyses yielding four, five, or seven factors (Lennings, 2000a, 2000b).

The Zimbardo Time Perspective Inventory (ZTPI) is the latest modification of the STPI, which has addressed the shortcomings of the previous scales (Zimbardo & Boyd, 1999). This single, integrated scale for measuring TP has suitable psychometric properties and is reliable, valid, and easy to use. Five main factors underlie this empirically derived factor structure: Future, Past-Positive, Past-Negative, Present-Hedonistic, and Present-Fatalistic. These factors were derived from an extensive series of exploratory studies (including interviews, focus groups, feedback from participants, theoretical consideration, and others) and have been continuously empirically refined for more than a decade (Gonzalez & Zimbardo, 1985; Zimbardo & Boyd, 1999; Zimbardo & Gonzalez, 1984). Essentially, the scale provides a profile of relative values on each of these five factors for individuals or, when aggregated, for groups. The same factor structure has emerged from recent translations and replications with French, German, and Turkish samples. In practice, researchers typically highlight and compare individuals whose TP biases mark them as very high on one of these factors and low on others.

The ZTPI consists of 56 items that are assessed on a 5-point Likert scale ranging from very uncharacteristic (1) to very characteristic (5) of the respondent. A consistent 5-factor structure was revealed through exploratory principal component factor analysis and further supported by confirmatory factor analysis. Thirty-six percent of the total variance is explained by these factors. The ZTPI was demonstrated to have high test-retest reliability, ranging from 0.70 to 0.80 for the different factors (Zimbardo & Boyd, 1999). The convergent and discriminant validity of the instrument was established through predicted correlational patterns of each of the five factors with measures of aggression, depression, conscientiousness, ego-control, impulse control, state-trait anxiety, self-esteem, preference for consistency, reward dependence, sensation seeking, novelty seeking, and consideration of future consequences. The results confirmed associations between individual factors of the ZTPI and predicted scales in combination with low associations with inappropriate scale constructs. For example, the Present-Hedonistic factor was found to be associated with a lack of consideration of future consequences, a low preference for consistency, low ego, or impulse control, but very high interest in novelty and sensation seeking, as well as not correlating with any past- or future-oriented constructs. To ensure that ZTPI items are not reflecting the same underlying dimensions as the preceding psychological constructs, Zimbardo and Boyd (1999) carried out further tests of discriminant validity by examining robust correlations between depression and conscientiousness with Past-Negative and Future ZTPI factors. It was concluded that despite significant correlations between these two pairs of constructs, they remain distinct and not entirely overlapping.

## TIME PERSPECTIVE PROFILES AND FINDINGS FROM TIME PERSPECTIVE RESEARCH

A brief overview of features found to be characteristic of individuals who reveal a dominant bias on each of the five TP factors may help put substance on these conceptual bones. It should be clear that each of these factors may have some personal value to given individuals in particular contexts, but when they come to be an excessive orientation that excludes or minimizes the others, they may become dysfunctional.

Items on the Future TP scale include, among others: "I am able to resist temptations when I know that there is work to be done" and "When I want to achieve something, I set goals and consider specific means for reaching those goals." The future-oriented person always has an eye toward consequences, contingencies, and probable outcomes of present decisions and actions. He or she is dedicated to working for future goals and their attendant rewards, often at the expense of present enjoyment, delaying gratification, and avoiding time-wasting temptations. Such individuals live in a world of cognitive abstraction, suppressing the reality of the present for the imagined reality of an idealized future world. At micro levels of behavior, they differ from those in other TP categories by being more likely to floss their teeth, eat healthful foods regardless of flavor, get medical checkups regularly, and solve puzzles well. They tend to be more successful than others, both academically and in their careers. The third little pig who built his house from bricks, estimating the possible dangers and uncertainties of a wolf-filled future instead of partying with his quick-and-easy, straw-house-building brother, was surely a future-oriented pig. The downside of excessive future orientation is minimizing the need for social connections, not taking time for occasional self-indulgence, and not being grounded in a sense of community and cultural traditions.

The Past TP is associated with focus on family, tradition, continuity of self over time, and a focus on history. This can be either positive or negative. The Past-Positive TP reflects a warm, pleasurable, often sentimental and nostalgic view of the person's past with emphasis on maintaining relationships with family and friends. These individuals have the highest sense of self-esteem and happiness of those dominant on the other factors. The Past-Positive scale contains items such as: "It gives me pleasure to think about my past" and "I get nostalgic about my childhood." The Past-Negative TP is characterized by items such as: "I often think of what I should have done differently in my life" and is associated with focusing on personal experiences that were aversive or noxious. In general, a past orientation has the downside of being excessively conservative, cautious, avoiding change and openness to new experiences and cultures, and sustaining the status quo even when it is not in the person's best interest.

A body of research marks present-oriented individuals living in Western societies as at risk for failure of all kinds. The ZTPI distinguishes between two very different ways of being focused on the present. The Present-Hedonistic person lives in the moment, values hedonistic pleasures, enjoys high-intensity activities, seeks thrills and new sensations, and is open to friendships and sexual adventures. He or she would score highly on items such as: "It is important to put excitement in my life." That kind of person acts with little concern for the consequences of his or her actions by avoiding cost-benefit analyses and contingency planning. Indeed, all of us were such creatures as infants and children, who are essentially biologically driven, their behavior determined by physical needs, emotions, strong situational stimuli, and social input. Life is about seeking pleasure and avoiding pain. The downside of this orientation is that behavior does have consequences, as behaviorist B. F. Skinner taught us so well. Present-Hedonists are at risk for succumbing to the temptations leading to virtually all addictions, for accidents and injuries, and for academic and career failure.

The Present-Fatalistic TP, on the other hand, is associated with hopelessness and immutable beliefs that outside forces control the person's life, such as spiritual or governmental forces. It may be a rather realistic orientation for those living in poverty in ghettoes or refugee camps. It is not uncommon for the parents of poor children—living the hedonistic life—to become fatalistically resigned to be helpless in changing or improving the quality of their life. This TP orientation is expressed by statements such as: "Because whatever will be will be, it doesn't really matter what I do" and "My life path is controlled by forces I cannot influence."

Zimbardo and Boyd (1999) demonstrate that both Past-Negative and Present-Fatalistic perspectives are associated with strong feelings of depression, anxiety, anger, and aggression. Such temporal perspectives create a negative self-image that handicaps attempts at constructive actions. Even though they may be reality-based in their origin, it is their maintenance and elevation to dominance in an individual's temporal hierarchy that makes them dysfunctional and nonadaptive among middle-class high school and college students functioning in schools in the United States.

The TP construct has been found to be related to many attitudes, values, and status variables, such as educational achievement, health, sleep and dreaming patterns, and romantic partner choices. It is also predictive for a wide range of behaviors, including risky driving and other forms of risk taking, delinquency, and sexual behaviors (Zimbardo, Keough, & Boyd, 1997), as well as abuse of alcohol and drugs (Keough, Zimbardo, & Boyd, 1999). Furthermore, it appears that scores on the ZTPI factors are indicative of choice of food, health choices, parental marital state, desire to spend time with friends, and perceived time pressure, among other factors. For a full depiction of the role of TP in health and risk taking, see Boyd and Zimbardo (in press). It even predicts the extent to which unemployed people living in shelters use their time constructively to seek jobs (future-oriented) or waste time watching TV and engaging in other noninstrumental activities and avoidant coping strategies (present-oriented; Epel, Bandura, & Zimbardo, 1999).

Extension of such research data on individuals to the role of TP among nations and cultures is obviously more sociological, historical, and epidemiological, but they reveal some fascinating patterns. Protestant nations tend to be more future-oriented than Catholic nations (due to the enduring legacy of the Calvinistic focus on earthly success as an indicator of being chosen for heavenly rewards). In turn, the gross national product indexes are higher among Protestant than Catholic nations. Within countries, those living in southern sections tend to be more present-oriented than those in northern regions above the equator. Cultures with more individualistic focus tend to be more future-oriented than those emphasizing collectivism. Western ways of life have become predominantly goal-focused and future-oriented in the service of capitalist values. The new trend toward globalization implicitly promotes a future-oriented market economy of the major industrial nations on developing nations that have been more present- or past-oriented.

However, an excessive emphasis on any given TP type at the expense of the other orientations leads to an imbalance that may not be optimal for individuals nor ideal in the long run for nations. There are costs and sacrifices associated with valuing achievement-oriented, workaholic, future TP traits over and above personal indulgences and civic and social engagement. Westerners are now spending less time on the following vital activities: family, friends, churchgoing, recreation, hobbies, and even household chores (Myers, 2000; see also, Myers, Chapter 41, this volume).

It looks as though Puritan values, recapitulated in "Waste of time is the first and in principle the deadliest of sins" (Weber, 1930/1992, p. 157), have finally won the game of modern life—with a minor drawback of God heading the list of time-wasters. The rituals and narratives essential to a sense of family, community, and nation are endangered and undermined, together with a sense of personal identity, by those living such totally work-focused lives.

## BALANCED TIME PERSPECTIVE

The ideal of a balanced time perspective comes into play as a more positive alternative to living life as a slave to any particular temporal bias. A blend of temporal orientations can be considered as the most adaptive, depending on external circumstances and optimal in terms of psychological and physiological health. The construct of Balanced Time Perspective (BTP) was initially proposed by Zimbardo and Boyd (1999) at the time of the introduction of the final version of Zimbardo Time Perspective Inventory (ZTPI). "In an optimally balanced time perspective, the past, present, and future components blend and flexibly engage, depending on a situation's demands and our needs and values" (Zimbardo, 2002, p. 62).

People with a balanced TP are capable of operating in a temporal mode appropriate to the situation in which they find themselves. When they spend time with their families and friends, they are fully with them and value the opportunity to share a common past. When they take a day off work, they get involved in recreation rather than feel guilty about the work they haven't done. However, when working and studying, they may well put on their more appropriate future TP hat and work more productively. Indeed, when work is to be done and valued, the balanced TP person may get into the flow of enjoying being productive and creative—a present-hedonistic state for a future-focused activity. That is when work becomes play as the worker becomes engaged with the process of the activity and not only with a focus on the product of his or her labors.

Flexibility and "switch-ability" are essential components of a balanced TP, in our view. "The optimal time perspective depends upon the demands of the situation and its task and reward structure" (Epel et al., 1999, p. 590). These researchers found that among the unemployed living in homeless shelters and experiencing pressure to find other affordable accommodations, it may be better to be present-oriented when dealing with an acute crisis. Whereas future TP allows a greater degree of self-efficacy and fosters optimism for future gains, present orientation may be more effective in allowing one to be open to finding immediate solutions to current challenges. This is just one of the examples to show that temporal flexibility is important for dealing with extreme circumstances, but there is also emerging evidence to demonstrate how such flexibility may be important in dealing with the hassles of everyday life.

Although Zimbardo and Boyd (2008) did not develop any direct indicator of BTP, they proposed an interesting starting point for its empirical operationalizations by formulating a description of an optimal mix of time perspectives. The authors proposed that the optimal TP profile consists of:

- High on Past-Positive TP
- Moderately high on Future TP
- Moderately high on Present-Hedonistic TP
- Low on Past-Negative TP
- Low on Present-Fatalistic TP

Based on these theoretical foundations, several attempts have been made to operationalize the BTP construct. Current literature distinguishes between four different approaches to measuring balanced time perspective: The 33rd percentile cut-off approach (Drake, Duncan, Sutherland, Abernethy, & Henry, 2008), resulting in selecting about 5% of respondents with a BTP; cluster analysis approach (Boniwell, Osin, Linley, & Ivanchenko, 2010), resulting in a larger proportion of respondents selected as BTP (10% to 23%); the Deviation from Balanced Time Perspective method (Stolarski, Bitner, & Zimbardo, 2011; Zhang, Howell, & Stolarski, 2013), resulting in a linear and normally distributed variable; and a combined approach proposed by Wiberg, Sircova, Wiberg and Carelli (2012), also confirming the BTP as a normally distributed trait. A first qualitative in-depth study of the BTP individuals using interpretative phenomenological analysis showed that these individuals have a substantial consciousness of the "now" or the present moment, and they see both the past and the present, as well as the present and the future, as synchronously integrated (Wiberg, Wiberg, Carelli, & Sircova, 2012).

The results of the proposed operationalizations are that there are both strong sides and drawbacks of each approach and that the BTP construct is not yet totally explored and clarified. A great amount of work has to be done in the future, including additional exploratory case studies to get a clearer and more complete picture of the BTP construct from empirical studies in order to fully understand this optimal time-perspective profile.

## TIME PERSPECTIVE AND WELL-BEING

Over the years, there have been various attempts to establish a relationship between TP and well-being. However, taking into account the variety and complexity of measures of both TP and well-being, it is hardly surprising that early findings were inconsistent and often contradictory. A number of scholars hypothesized that a time orientation with a focus on the present is a necessary prerequisite for well-being. Among them are Csikszentmihalyi (1992), Maslow (1971), and Schopenhauer (1851), with their emphasis on the value of here-and-now experiences (see Boyd-Wilson, Walkey, & McClure, 2002).

### Past TP and Well-Being

Recent research shows that, across time (Zimbardo & Boyd, 1999, Zhang, Karabenick, Maruno, & Lauermann, 2011) and cultures (Russian, British, American), people who are largely negative about the past are also unhappy and dissatisfied with life compared to their less negative counterparts. People who tend to dwell on the negative events in their past are likely to experience more negative affect ($r$ between .38 and .56) and less positive affect ($r$ between $-.21$ and $-.11$) than people who do not dwell on the past (Zhang et al., 2011). Likewise, Past-Negative people enjoy less happiness ($r = -.45$; Boniwell et al., 2010) and satisfaction with life ($r = -.42$ to $-.59$; Zhang et al., 2011).

It is the past-temporal orientation that shows the positive associations with well-being measures. Already in a sample of older adults, Kazakina (1999) has established a positive relationship between the Past-Positive orientation and life satisfaction. Recent research confirms that people who look fondly on the past report greater satisfaction with life (SWL) ($r = .21$, Boniwell et al., 2010), and psychological need fulfillment (Zhang et al., 2011). Perhaps somewhat surprisingly, correlations between the two past time dimensions are around .30. Hence, there appears to be a substantial number of people who spend relatively more time than others ruminating on the past, pondering both the good and the bad.

### Present TP and Well-Being

Not surprisingly, fatalists tend to be unhappy ($r = -.18$ to $-.23$; Zhang et al., 2011), less satisfied with life ($r = -.16$ to $-.39$; Zhang et al., 2011), less optimistic ($r = -.27$; Boniwell et al., 2010), and have less energy ($r = -.21$; Zimbardo & Boyd, 1999) and vitality ($r = -.22$; Zhang et al., 2011) than nonfatalists. Early research has identified relations between present orientation and various measures of well-being, including general happiness (Kammann & Flett, 1983) and life satisfaction (Diener, Emmons, Larsen, & Griffin, 1985). Current research confirms that subjective happiness and SWL are consistently related with present hedonism ($r$ between .09 and .23). Hedonists report experiencing more positive affect ($r =$ from .14 to .27), being more energetic ($r = .27$; Zimbardo & Boyd, 1999) and optimistic ($r = .20$, Boniwell et al., 2010), and feeling more vitality ($r = .31$; Zhang et al., 2011). However, people who are more hedonistic also appear to be more aggressive and prone to depression ($r = .29$ and .20; Zimbardo & Boyd, 1999), indicating that too much present orientation may not be all that good.

### Future TP and Well-Being

Most of the previous literature highlighted positive connections between various future-orientation measures and well-being. Some authors argued that a focus on futurity is fundamental to well-being and positive functioning (Kazakina, 1999). Wessman and Ricks (1966) found that happy male college students were significantly more likely to be future-oriented than less happy peers. The density of the future zone, usually measured by the number of plans, commitments, and anticipated experiences, was also found to be positively correlated with well-being (Kahana & Kahana, 1983). A positive future orientation is often viewed as the essence of personal optimism, which is conceptualized as the anticipation of positive changes in the future (Kazakina, 1999). Yet, of the five ZTPI time dimensions, the Future time dimension is perhaps the least consistently associated with well-being measures, perhaps because the future orientation leads people to forego immediate pleasures. People who have a strong tendency to use the present moment to prepare for and ponder the future do not generally report being substantially happier than their less future-oriented peers ($r = .09$, ns; Boniwell et al., 2010). However, they do tend to experience somewhat more global satisfaction with life ($r = .14$ in Boniwell et al.'s [2010] Russian sample and $r = .15$ for Zhang & Howell's [2011] largely American sample).

BALANCED TP AND WELL-BEING

It should not be surprising that various unrelated studies point to positive patterns of association between virtually all temporal zones and differing aspects of well-being—precisely because all three general factors of a balanced TP are important for different aspects of positive functioning. Operating in Past-Positive and Present-Hedonistic modes enhances individuals' chances of developing happy personal relationships, which is a key factor in enhancing their well-being, according to research on exceptionally happy people (Diener & Seligman, 2002). Also, future TP shows some positive associations with life satisfaction, as well as optimism, hope, and internal locus of control.

Given the duality of findings concerning the obviously "positive" orientations (specifically Present-Hedonistic and Future), we can hypothesize that it is the balanced TP itself that would allow people to move into the future having reconciled with their past experiences while staying grounded in the system of meanings derived from the present.

Indeed, a small number of studies have looked at the relations between various measures of a generalized balanced TP and measures related to subjective well-being. Zhang et al. (2011) demonstrated that having a BTP, however measured, is related to substantially improved well-being. Maintaining a healthy balance (e.g., low scores on past negative and present fatalistic and moderate to high scores on Past-Positive, Present-Hedonism) among the five time perspectives predicts more psychological need satisfaction, vitality, satisfaction with life, subjective happiness, and positive affect, while also predicting less negative affect (Zhang et al., 2011).

## APPLICATIONS OF TIME PERSPECTIVE RESEARCH

Despite being conceived primarily at a theoretical level, the constructs of TP and a balanced TP offer considerable potential for practical interventions in clinical and occupational psychology. However, such implementations are conspicuous by their absence. Possible avenues of practical implementations can range from time-based clinical interventions with depressed patients to rehabilitation programs with disabled persons to time management counseling with elderly clients, to time-perspective based coaching.

Consider the development of clinical interventions designed for people with cognitive distortions associated with recurrent depression. Often, these clients are negatively past-focused, with global attributions, which taken together render them vulnerable to depressive ruminative cycles. An intervention program would focus on teaching them how to reconstruct past negative experiences by either neutralizing them or discovering some hidden positive elements in them. Clients could be given a slideshow metaphor training in which they learn to switch away from replaying the old slides of past negative experiences by inserting new slides into their tray and then viewing these encouraging perspectives of current positive experiences and imagined slides of a better future.

Persons suffering from disabilities typically must undergo long periods of physical rehabilitation that is effortful and painful. Many discontinue this critical treatment before it has had a chance to improve their condition precisely because of these aversive aspects of the retraining. We believe that time therapy focused on building an enriched future orientation while minimizing the present would benefit such clients. It is only with a sense of hope of improvement, of belief that present suffering will pay off in the future, that anyone can continue in rehabilitation programs that have few immediate rewards and much pain (see Zimbardo, in press).

Knowledge and understanding of TP can be a useful tool in psychological counseling. An insight into how clients think and feel about past, present, and future experiences and about their connectedness and disconnections serves as a starting point for therapeutic explorations. Extending the ideas we have championed throughout this chapter, we believe that a strong, narrowly selective temporal bias in a client should alert a counselor or therapist of a fundamental platform on which many presenting problems are erected. Seemingly disparate problems may then be seen as symptomatic of a common underlying temporal misbalance, thus the need for temporal adjustment and rebalancing (see Kazakina, 1999).

There are some rare examples of qualitative investigations of people's psychological attitudes and perception of time that reveal how discussions about time have had unexpectedly positive therapeutic effects (Elliot, 1999; Rappaport, 1990). An exploration of an individual's relationship with time has the potential to direct awareness toward fuller evaluations of his or her life, toward finding the links and connections between past and present events. Doing so helps to develop a sense of continuity between temporal zones and facilitates the process of finding deeper meaning in his or her existence. Such potential can be invaluable in working with specific categories of clients in clinical psychology, including the elderly and terminally ill. It is plausible that achieving a temporal balance can facilitate the sense of fuller involvement with life, which some believe to be paramount for successful aging (Kazakina, 1999).

Time perspective coaching is gaining in prominence both as applied to executive and life coaching domains (Boniwell, 2005). To give a taste of this process, how can the concept of TP be consciously and usefully applied in the consulting room? The first step, of course, is suggesting to the client to explore the concept together, if the coach feels it may be of relevance. Assuming the client is interested, the coach can invite him or her to discover what their time perspective profile may look like using ZTPI, which is available for free on the Time Paradox website (http://www.thetimeparadox.com/). With the exception of individuals who have had prior psychometric training, the role of the coach thereafter is not so much to communicate and explain the ZTPI results to the client, but rather to accompany the client in trying to make sense of their own results, using emerging reactions as triggers for deepening the coaching conversation. The identification of the client's TP profile could initiate further coaching work around specific issues associated with the client's time-perspective profile, using both appropriate questions and relevant evidence-based interventions (Boniwell and Osin, in press). Thus, for example, clients with a prominent Past-Negative TP may find it useful to undergo a process of creating a personal *positive portfolio*, derived from their previous personal experience of positive emotions (Fredrickson, 2009). Those interested in developing a stronger Past-Positive TP may be encouraged to create a *family tree* or a *birthdays calendar* (people low on the Past-Positive TP are usually the ones that forget everyone's birthdays), as well as participating in *community projects or events*. Development of a Present-Hedonistic TP may be facilitated by savoring and mindfulness (Bryant & Veroff, 2007), while fostering the Future TP can be achieved through the *future best self* process or *best possible selves diary* (Lyubomirsky, 2008). Needless to say, different methods would apply to coaching work aimed at minimizing excessive "positive" orientations, be it the Present-Hedonistic or Future TP.

The concept of balanced TP can also be fruitfully implemented in an organizational context. It is our belief that the current pressures being experienced by workers in offices and factories around the world will not be resolved by more time-management techniques. Normative experience is that within about 6 months following a time-management training program, participants revert to their own practices of time management. We believe this happens for two reasons. First, these programs are promoted by management and essentially are designed to make workers more future-oriented, more productive, and less wasteful of company time. But much of the sense of time press and work urgency comes from workers who are already overly future-oriented. They need very different time training. Secondly, most time-management techniques are not tied to the actual psychology of people's understanding of time. The construct of TP has a potential to provide a theoretical underpinning for time management interventions. The focus of time-management techniques can shift from advocating generalized time-management strategies—such as taking time off or putting more focus on their work—to developing interventions based on an understanding of workers' TP profiles. Doing so would help in recognizing the associated internal states and TP cognitive biases that unconsciously dominate workers. Such techniques can be useful in reducing and, ideally, preventing occupational stress. They can also be invaluable in solving the eternal dilemma of balancing the dialectic of work and play/leisure or of work as a source of personal engagement versus a source of job burnout (Maslach & Leiter, 1997).

There are sufficient theoretical grounds to assume that personalizing TP interventions to the client's existing profile would help to address their issues with time-management behaviors; however, further research would be needed to make this assumption a certainty. In the meantime, we believe that taking even baby steps toward developing a more balanced TP is already a valuable goal in itself.

## CONCLUSION

Working hard when it's time to work, playing intensively when it's time to play, enjoying listening to grandma's old stories while she is still alive, meaningfully connecting with your friends, viewing children through the eyes of wonder with which they see the world, laughing at jokes and life's absurdities, indulging in desire and passions, saving for a rainy day and spending it when it's sunny, recognizing the social and sexual animal in each of us, taking fuller control of your life—these are all part of the benefits of learning to achieve a balanced-time perspective. They are the keys to unlocking personal happiness and finding more meaning in life despite the relentless, indifferent movement of life's time clock toward its final ticking for each of us. The value of the concept of a balanced time perspective is that it both suggests novel approaches to a wide range of psychological interventions while offering yet another answer to positive psychology's enduring question—What is a good life, and how can we pursue it?

## SUMMARY POINTS

- Time perspective is a preferential direction of an individual's thoughts toward the past, present, or future that exerts a dynamic influence on their experience, motivation, thinking, and several aspects of behavior.
- ZTPI, the primary measure of time perspective, distinguishes between five time perspective profiles: Past-Negative, Past-Positive, Present-Fatalistic, Present-Hedonistic, and Future.
- The idea of a balanced time perspective emerges as an alternative to any particular temporal bias. In an optimally balanced time perspective, the past, present, and future components engage flexibly in response to individuals' values and preferences, while taking into account a situation's context and demands at the same time.
- Across the numerous studies, we have seen that each of the time perspectives, as well as composite measures of a balanced time perspective have a role to play influencing people's happiness.
- Another needed venue for researchers and practitioners is the development of intervention strategies that empower individuals to overcome the limitations of their learned, narrow temporal biases and to acquire a balanced temporal orientation.

## REFERENCES

Block, R. A. (1990). Introduction. In R. A. Block (Ed.), *Cognitive models of psychological time* (pp. xiii–xix). Hillsdale, NJ: Erlbaum.

Bond, M., & Feather, N. (1988). Some correlates of structure and purpose in the use of time. *Journal of Personality and Social Psychology, 55,* 321–329.

Boniwell, I. (2005). Beyond time management: How the latest research on time perspective and perceived time use can assist clients with time-related concerns. *International Journal of Evidence Based Coaching and Mentoring, 3*(2), 61–74.

Boniwell, I., & Osin, E. (in press). Time perspective coaching. In M. J. Stolarski, W. van Beek, & N. Fieulaine (Eds.), *The handbook of time perspective.* New York, NY: Springer.

Boniwell, I., Osin, E., Linley, P. A., & Ivanchenko, G. (2010). A question of balance: Examining relationships between time perspective and measures of well-being in the British and Russian student samples. *Journal of Positive Psychology, 5*(1), 24–40.

Boniwell, I., & Zimbardo, P. G. (2003). Time to find the right balance. *The Psychologist, 16,* 129–131.

Boyd, J. N., & Zimbardo, P. G. (2005). Time perspective, health, and risk taking. In A. Strathman & J. Joireman (Eds.), *Understanding behavior in the context of time* (pp. 85–107). Mahwah, NJ: Erlbaum.

Boyd-Wilson, B. M., Walkey, F. H., & McClure, J. (2002). Present and correct: We kid ourselves less when we live in the moment. *Personality and Individual Differences, 33,* 691–702.

Bryant, F. B., & Veroff, J. (2007). *Savouring: A new model of positive experiences.* Mahwah, NJ: Erlbaum.

Carr, M. A. (1985). *The effects of aging and depression on time perspective in women* (Unpublished doctoral dissertation). Teachers College, Columbia University, New York, NY.

Cottle, T. J. (1976). *Perceiving time.* New York, NY: Wiley.

Csikszentmihalyi, M. (1992). *Flow: The psychology of happiness.* London, England: Rider.

Diener, E., Emmons, R. A., Larsen, R. J., & Griffin, S. (1985). The Satisfaction With Life Scale. *Journal of Personality Assessment, 49*, 71–75.

Diener, E., & Seligman, M. E. P. (2002). Very happy people. *Psychological Science, 13*, 81–84.

Drake, L., Duncan, E., Sutherland, F., Abernethy, C., & Henry, C. (2008). Time perspective and correlates of wellbeing. *Time & Society, 17*, 47–61.

Elliot, M. K. (1999). *Time, work, and meaning* (Unpublished doctoral dissertation). Pacifica Graduate Institute, Carpinteria, California.

Epel, E., Bandura, A., & Zimbardo, P. G. (1999). Escaping homelessness: The influences of self-efficacy and time perspective on coping with homelessness. *Journal of Applied Social Psychology, 29*, 575–596.

Fredrickson, B. L. (2009). *Positivity*. New York, NY: Crown.

Gonzalez, A., & Zimbardo, P. G. (1985). Time in perspective: A Psychology Today survey report. *Psychology Today, 19*, 21–26.

Gorman, B. S., & Wessman, A. E. (1977). Images, values, and concepts of time in psychological research. In B. S. Gorman & A. E. Wessman (Eds.), *The personal experience of time* (pp. 218–264). New York, NY: Plenum Press.

Hornik, J., & Zakay, D. (1996). Psychological time: The case of time and consumer behavior. *Time and Society, 5*, 385–397.

Kahana, E., & Kahana, B. (1983). Environmental continuity, futurity, and adaptation of the aged. In G. D. Rowles & R. J. Ohta (Eds.), *Aging and milieu* (pp. 205–228). New York, NY: Haworth Press.

Kammann, R., & Flett, R. (1983). Affectometer 2: A scale to measure current level of general happiness. *Australian Journal of Psychology, 35*, 259–265.

Kazakina, E. (1999). *Time perspective of older adults: Relationships to attachment style, psychological well-being and psychological distress* (Unpublished doctoral dissertation). Columbia University, New York, NY.

Keough, K. A., Zimbardo, P. G., & Boyd, J. N. (1999). Who's smoking, drinking, and using drugs? Time perspective as a predictor of substance use. *Basic and Applied Social Psychology, 21*, 149–164.

Lennings, C. J. (1996). Self-efficacy and temporal orientation as predictors of treatment outcome in severely dependent alcoholics. *Alcoholism Treatment Quarterly, 14*, 71–79.

Lennings, C. J. (1998). Profiles of time perspective and personality: Developmental considerations. *Journal of Psychology, 132*, 629–642.

Lennings, C. J. (2000a). Optimism, satisfaction and time perspective in the elderly. *International Journal of Aging and Human Development, 51*, 168–181.

Lennings, C. J. (2000b). The Stanford Time Perspective Inventory: An analysis of temporal orientation for research in health psychology. *Journal of Applied Health Behavior, 2*, 40–45.

Lofy, M. M. (2000). *A matter of time: Power, control, and meaning in people's everyday experience of time* (Unpublished doctoral dissertation). The Fielding Institute, Santa Barbara, CA.

Lyubomirsky, S. (2008). *The how of happiness: A practical guide to getting the life you want*. London, England: Sphere.

Maslach, C., & Leiter, M. (1997). *The truth about burnout: How organizations cause personal stress and what to do about it*. San Francisco, CA: Jossey-Bass.

Maslow, A. H. (1971). *Farther reaches of human nature*. New York, NY: Viking Penguin.

McGrath, J. E. (Ed.). (1988). *The social psychology of time: New perspectives* (Vol. 1). New York, NY: Sage.

McGrath, J. E., & Kelly, J. (1986). *Time and human interaction: Toward a social psychology of time*. New York, NY: Guilford Press.

Myers, D. G. (2000). *The American paradox: Spiritual hunger in an age of plenty*. New Haven, CT: Yale University Press.

Rappaport, H. (1990). *Making time*. New York, NY: Simon & Schuster.

Schopenhauer, A. (1851). *The wisdom of life* [English translation, 1890]. London, England: Swan Sonnenschein.

Seligman, M. E. P. (1999). *Mission statement and conclusion of Akumal 1*. Retrieved from http://psych.upenn.edu/seligman/pospsy.htm

Seligman, M. E. P., & Csikszentmihalyi, M. (2000). Positive psychology: An introduction. *American Psychologist, 55*, 5–14.

Stolarski, M., Bitner, J., & Zimbardo, P. G. (2011). Time perspective, emotional intelligence and discounting of delayed awards. *Time & Society, 20*(3), 346–363.

Weber, M. (1992). *The Protestant ethic and the spirit of capitalism*. London, England: Routledge. (Original work published 1930)

Wessman, A. E., & Ricks, D. F. (1966). *Mood and personality*. New York, NY: Holt, Rinehart and Winston.

Wiberg, M., Sircova, A., Wiberg, B., & Carelli, M. G. (2012). Operationalizing balanced time perspective in a Swedish sample. *International Journal of Educational and Psychological Assessment, 12*(1), 95–107.

Wiberg, B., Wiberg, M., Carelli, M. G., & Sircova, A. (2012). *A qualitative and quantitative study of seven persons with balanced time perspective (BTP) according to S-ZTPI*. Poster presented at the First International Conference on Time Perspective and Research: Converging Paths in Psychology Time Theory and Research, Coimbra, Portugal.

Zhang, L., Karabenick, S. A., Maruno, S., & Lauermann, F. (2011). Academic delay of gratification and children's study time allocation as a function of proximity to consequential academic goals. *Learning and Instruction, 21*(1), 77–94.

Zhang, J. W., & Howell, R. T. (2011). Do time perspectives predict unique variance in life satisfaction beyond personality traits? *Personality and Individual Differences, 50*(8), 1261–1266.

Zhang, J. W., Howell, R. T., & Stolarski, M. (2013). Comparing three methods to measure a balanced time perspective: The relationship between a balanced time perspective and subjective well-being. *Journal of Happiness Studies, 14*(1), 169–184.

Zimbardo, P. G. (1992). *Draft Manual, Stanford Time Perspective Inventory*. Stanford, CA: Stanford University.

Zimbardo, P. G. (2002). Just think about it: Time to take our time. *Psychology Today, 35*, 62.

Zimbardo, P. G. (in press). Enriching psychological research on disability. In D. F. Thomas & F. E. Menz (Eds.), *Bridging gaps: Refining the disability research agenda for rehabilitation and the social sciences—Conference proceedings*. Menomonie: University of Wisconsin-Stout, Stout Vocational Rehabilitation Institute, Research and Training Center.

Zimbardo, P. G., & Boyd, J. N. (1999). Putting time in perspective: A valid, reliable individual-differences metric. *Journal of Personality and Social Psychology, 77*, 1271–1288.

Zimbardo, P., & Boyd, J. (2008). *The time paradox: The new psychology of time that will change your life*. New York, NY: Simon & Schuster.

Zimbardo, P. G., & Gonzalez, A. (1984). A Psychology Today reader survey. *Psychology Today, 18*, 53–54.

Zimbardo, P. G., Keough, K. A., & Boyd, J. N. (1997). Present time perspective as a predictor of risky driving. *Personality and Individual Differences, 23*, 1007–1023.

# CHAPTER 14

# Putting Positive Psychology Into Practice via Self-Help

### ACACIA C. PARKS

T HE EFFICACY OF PSYCHOLOGICAL interventions for increasing happiness is well established, but many of these interventions are only beginning to be available to the general public. The purpose of this chapter is to provide a guide to readers interested in selecting a science-based self-help tool that targets happiness—be it for one's own personal use, for one's client, or for use in research. First, the chapter provides an overview of the rationale for disseminating positive psychological interventions (PPIs) via self-help. Second, the reader is provided with some caveats and recommendations to consider when evaluating and selecting self-help PPIs. Third, several examples of publicly available self-help PPIs are described, cutting across three modalities: books, the web, and smartphones. Lastly, future directions for research and practice using self-help PPIs are discussed.

Elsewhere in this volume, Layous, Sheldon, and Lyubomirsky (Chapter 11) provide an overview of research on intentional activities that promote happiness, known in recent literature as *positive psychological interventions* (PPIs; Parks & Schueller, 2014). Dozens of studies have contributed to the general conclusion that PPIs are, on the whole, efficacious—that is, they reliably increase happiness and decrease depressive symptoms (see Sin & Lyubomirsky, 2009). Most PPI studies have been conducted in lab settings, which are designed to maximize experimental control and to reduce noise (see Parks, 2014, for an in-depth discussion). The real-world dissemination of PPIs, therefore, is still somewhat in its infancy, and the question remains open: What is the best vehicle by which to disseminate them?

In clinical psychology, interventions that are studied in research are then typically disseminated via therapy. Indeed, there has been work disseminating PPIs to a variety of clinical populations, including mild to moderately depressed young adults (Seligman, Rashid, & Parks, 2006), sufferers of schizophrenia (Meyer, Johnson, Parks, Iwanski, & Penn, 2012), individuals trying to quit smoking (Kahler et al., 2013), and suicidal inpatients (Huffman et al., 2014). However, although there is certainly a precedent for applying PPIs in therapy (e.g., Magyar-Moe, 2009), there is also the equally important task of getting PPIs to the general public—people who are not clinically depressed,

---

*Note.* Author serves as scientific advisor for Happify.com but owns no part of the company.

but who could stand to improve their happiness. Self-help methods seem to be ideal for nonclinical populations. First of all, there is significant demand for self-help, as is evidenced by the multimillion-dollar market for self-help books, products, and web-sites. Furthermore, self-help approaches have the potential to reach a much broader audience than does therapy by virtue of their being more affordable and potentially easier to access. Lastly, self-help approaches seem to be the way that PPI research is headed; whereas research used to take place in the lab, more and more, studies are starting to use real-world settings as their backdrop. It is relevant, therefore, to look at self-help modalities as a means of delivering PPIs.

The goal of the present chapter, then, is to discuss the ways in which PPIs have been and could be delivered to the general public in self-administered formats. An overarching goal is to provide a guide to readers who may want to select a self-help tool for their own personal use, for the use of a client, or for use in a research study.

## TRANSLATING PPIs FOR USE IN THE REAL WORLD: SOME CAVEATS

PPIs are, by nature, self-administered, even in research studies—they are typically delivered by giving participants a set of instructions for an activity and asking them to follow those instructions. Thus, at first blush, it is not so difficult to imagine the tran-sition from research to implementation in self-help contexts; the instructions come from a book or a website instead of an experimenter, and otherwise, the process is quite similar. However, recent research suggests that some ways that PPI usage is standardized in research are not ideal for real-world practice. Although a detailed discussion of these factors is beyond the scope of this chapter (see Parks, 2014), I will give a brief overview below, along with some recommendations for how practitioners might use this information to help clients.

First, in many studies, participants are given no choice about which activity or activities they use. Limiting participant choice is important to experimental design, as it standardizes the experience across participants, making it easier to draw infer-ences about how well the intervention works. However, research by Lyubomirsky, Dickerhoof, Boehm, and Sheldon (2011) finds that people benefit more when they have chosen to do a PPI rather than having been assigned one. Furthermore, when given free rein, participants choose to practice PPIs quite differently from how they are asked to practice them in the lab. For example, lab studies tend to ask partici-pants to use a single activity, or to use one activity and then to move on to the next activity. On average, however, happiness seekers use many different activities in a given week (Parks, Della Porta, Pierce, Zilca, & Lyubomirsky, 2012, Study 2). In one study, using a wider variety of activities predicted greater improvements in happiness than did spending the same amount of effort on a smaller number of activities (Parks et al., 2012, Study 3), suggesting that instructions to do otherwise might undermine effectiveness.

In addition, studies tend to ask participants to follow the same set of instructions for an activity over a fixed period of time (using the same example as before: a gratitude journal once a week for 6 weeks), but naturalistic data on happiness seekers suggests that they tend to gravitate toward "mixing up" their practice, trying different variations of activities from week to week in order to avoid adapt-ing to their gains (Parks et al., 2012, Study 2). Lastly, many studies emphasize making interventions as brief and simple as possible with the idea that a brief intervention will be more appealing to participants. However, happiness seekers, on average, choose to spend about an hour a day actively working on their happiness

(Parks et al., 2012, Study 2), suggesting that when left to their own devices, happiness seekers want to work hard on their happiness and are capable of working harder than traditional study designs allow.

Therefore, *when recommending self-help PPIs to clients, practitioners should not necessarily encourage clients to adhere exactly to the instructions from the published research*; with few exceptions,[1] these instructions are the way they are not because they maximize efficacy, but because the researchers had to choose some fixed duration to standardize participants' experiences.

Second, people who participate in research on PPIs may not necessarily be the same as the people who will choose to use them in real-world practice. One study found that the average level of depressive symptoms in a sample of happiness seekers on the Internet was substantially higher than the average college student, and college students are participants in many PPI studies (Parks et al., 2012; Study 1). Therefore, research done in college students may or may not be generalizable to the average client in real-world practice. Furthermore, there is some new evidence that PPIs work wonderfully for some, and not at all for others (Sergeant & Mongrain, 2011). Growing evidence suggests that person–activity fit plays an important role in PPI effectiveness (Schueller, 2014). Therefore, any findings of PPIs' efficacy must be taken with a grain of salt. *Practitioners who choose to recommend self-help PPIs should work with clients to carefully evaluate whether the intervention is working for them.*

Lastly, much PPI research leaves out social support and social networking, again trying to make sure that the experience is as similar as possible across users; introducing a social network adds noise to the data, which is not ideal for research purposes. However, social support can be a very helpful tool when instituting behavioral change, particularly when doing it outside of a formal context like therapy. Some of the interventions discussed here have social support built in, but others (especially book-based interventions) do not. Many commercial products contain social networking features by default, not necessarily to improve the efficacy of the intervention, but to improve *adherence*, which is notoriously a problem in Internet interventions (see Eysenbach, 2005). Therefore, when recommending self-help interventions, *practitioners would be well-advised to encourage clients to engage with some kind of social support*, be it through the PPI itself (if included, say, on a commercial website) or through a book club, Facebook group, or other source of accountability. As with other variables discussed in this section, these types of social features are left out of online PPI research for reasons of experimental control, not because they are considered to be unnecessary or unhelpful.

## EXAMPLES OF EXISTING SELF-HELP PPIs

In the following section, I provide examples of the different types of existing self-help PPIs. This section is not meant to be exhaustive, but rather, illustrative of the types of resources that are available to practitioners hoping to make recommendations to clients and to researchers looking for a tool to use in a study. In selecting interventions to be discussed here, I chose only those that were accessible to the general public—some for free, some for an up-front purchase price or for a subscription fee.

---

[1] In one study by Lyubomirsky, Sheldon, and Schkade (2005), dosage was varied in order to find an optimal frequency. This is the only study, to my knowledge, that has done this; otherwise, dosages are somewhat arbitrary.

Book-Based PPIs

Self-help books have been around for decades, and a subset of self-help books are based on research-validated interventions. Cognitive-behavioral therapy (CBT) lends itself particularly well to translation into a self-help book, because it centers around patients' willingness to independently practice skills via homework. Books such as *Control Your Depression* (Lewinsohn, Muñoz, Youngren, & Zeiss, 1992) and *Feeling Good* (Burns, 2008) provide many of the key components of CBT: a rationale for the cognitive model, tools for self-tracking, and a series of concrete skills for readers to practice. Numerous studies have demonstrated the efficacy of CBT-based self-help books, particularly for reducing depressive symptoms; that is, psychological interventions translated into book form can lead to significant and long-lasting improvement for depression (for a meta-analysis, see Gregory, Schwer Canning, Lee, & Wise, 2004). In some cases, bibliotherapy for depression has even been shown to be comparable to in-person therapy (Cuijpers, Donker, van Straten, Li, & Anderson, 2010).

The success of self-help books for depression lends confidence to the proposition of self-help books for increasing happiness; if CBT skills can successfully bear the transition to self-help, why not PPIs? Many science-based self-help books about happiness exist; some of the most popular include *Authentic Happiness* (Seligman, 2002), *The Happiness Hypothesis* (Haidt, 2005), *Curious?* (Kashdan, 2009), and *Thanks!* (Emmons, 2007). However, many of these books focus primarily on information and self-understanding rather than providing readers with concrete techniques. *The How of Happiness* (*HoH*; Lyubomirsky, 2008) is unique in that it more closely follows the format of other bibliotherapy volumes, with over half of the book dedicated to providing research-based happiness skills and directions for practicing them. The skills focus of *HoH* makes it an ideal choice for research examining the benefits of positive bibliotherapy. To date, only one published study has examined *HoH*'s efficacy, but the findings are positive; Parks and Szanto (2013) compared *HoH* with *Control Your Depression* and with a no-intervention control and found that *HoH* led to higher levels of life satisfaction compared to both other groups at long-term follow-up. Other more recent books, such as *Gratitude Works!* (Emmons, 2013), are similarly structured, but have not yet been studied.

Compared with clinical psychology, there has been surprisingly little work looking at the efficacy of book-based approaches in positive psychology. This is, in part, because of the great potential for technology to take what is helpful about a book and bolster it with interactive features, social networking, and greater accessibility via the Internet. Cognitive-behavioral bibliotherapy research began decades ago, when the Internet was not as widely accessible, whereas PPIs came about much later. Indeed, much recent work in the area of PPIs has focused on translating PPIs to technology-based formats with the idea that a web-based intervention can include everything a book-based intervention does, and more. Below is an overview of this work.

Web-Based PPIs

Whereas early PPI research was conducted in-person (e.g., Emmons & McCullough, 2003), a substantial number of PPIs tested in the past decade have taken place online (for a comprehensive review, see Bolier & Abello, 2014). Indeed, one of earliest studies to use the term "positive psychological intervention" was conducted online, examining the efficacy of individual happiness activities (Seligman, Steen, Park, & Peterson, 2005). Participants were given written instructions for a single activity, then they were told to practice that activity over the course of a week and report back for assessment.

Mitchell, Stanimirovic, Klein, and Vella-Brodrick (2009) examined a single happiness activity—building strengths—over the web. Unlike Seligman et al. (2005), Mitchell et al.'s (2009) activity was completed over several sessions: First, users identified their strengths, then they generated ideas for how to use those strengths more in their everyday lives, implemented those ideas, and finally, reflected on their experience. Building on these two previous studies, Schueller and Parks (2012) tested a 6-week PPI containing six different activities spread out over 6 weeks. Participants received instructions for one activity, practiced that activity independently over the course of a week, then returned the site for the next activity.

In all of these cases, activities were completely user-driven; participants were given instructions and then told to go follow those instructions in everyday life. This type of experimental design is ideal for research settings, in which it is desirable to have a standardized user experience. However, PPIs like those described in these studies are not freely available to the general public; they were used by research participants only. Furthermore, although ideal in some ways for research purposes, the above-described designs are not very realistic. In general, widely available web-based PPIs are designed more like commercial products; in this context, customization and flexibility are desirable, and self-help websites typically contain numerous "whistles and bells" in order to keep users interested and engaged. Several of those are described below.

*Simple Web-Based Interventions*    As was the case in PPI research, some web-based PPIs are comprised of a single activity; Gratitude Bucket by Zach Prager, for example, is a free website that asks users to pick someone they are grateful to, then create a "bucket," or a page where gratitude for that person can be expressed. Anyone can go to the page and add grateful comments at any time. This website is devoted entirely to the practice of one positive activity—gratitude—in one particular way. It doesn't provide much in the way of guidelines for how often to use it and in what way to use it in order to achieve maximal well-being; it's just a tool for consumers to use as they like. Thnx4.org, designed by the Greater Good Foundation, has the same idea but a bit more structure. The site helps users to keep track of and to express their gratitude using an interactive online journal. It starts with a "2-week gratitude challenge," after which users can elect to keep going as they see fit.[2] Like Gratitude Bucket, Thnx4.org is also free and available to the general public.

*Multifaceted Web-Based Interventions*    Next, I discuss three existing, publicly available interventions that contain multiple positive psychology–inspired activities designed to increase well-being.

Daily Challenge is an eclectic self-help website created by MeYou Health. Each day, it provides users with a simple self-help technique, with the target of the technique ranging from physical health to psychological health and a mixture between the two. Upon initial sign-up, users are assigned to a track that contains very quick and easy activities that only lightly address physical and psychological well-being; with further use of the website, however, users can unlock "tracks" that allow them to specialize their goals and focus on possibilities such as finding fulfillment, living mindfully, and deepening close relationships (though there are also more practical or physical-health focused activities like building physical flexibility, decluttering, and eating healthier snacks). Sample challenges from the "living mindfully" track include

---

[2]Thnx4.org is unique in that it offers itself as a tool to be used by researchers who may want to collaborate to collect data.

watching a 5-minute video of someone performing your favorite song, or starting the day with a single yoga pose. Sample challenges from the "finding fulfillment" track include writing down three words that describe an ideal future version of yourself, or finding something you haven't used in months or years to donate. To maximize user engagement, each activity on Daily Challenge earns the user points that help to unlock additional features of the site and to raise the user's rank, which is visible to other users. Users also receive reminder emails.

A study evaluating the efficacy of Daily Challenge was recently published by Cobb and Poirier (2014) and suggests that users who participated in the website fared better than an information-only control group on measures of "overall well-being," which includes health behaviors, physical health, and access to care (physical factors) as well as emotional health, work satisfaction, and general life evaluation (psychological factors; Cobb & Poirier, 2014). However, in an effort to maximize retention and compliance by making activities as brief as possible, Daily Challenge may be a less powerful intervention than some of the other available sites, which involve more in-depth activities (see below). Unfortunately, Cobb and Poirier (2014) do not include effect sizes, nor do they provide the information needed to calculate effect sizes—the authors only say that users improve by 2 points on a 0–100 scale—so it is difficult to infer whether the changes observed were clinically significant.

Daily Challenge is available to the general public at no cost, and it may be useful for people who may want to work casually on their health. For individuals whose goal is specifically to improve happiness and who are aiming to effect a relatively substantial change in their happiness, a site that specializes in happiness and that asks users to practice activities in somewhat more depth is preferable. Below, I describe two such interventions.

Psyfit is a web-based PPI created by Trimbos Institute in the Netherlands to target "mental fitness." Although the site is in Dutch, it is possible to translate aspects of the site into other languages, and so it is usable by a broad audience. The intervention contains activities that draw from literature on PPIs, as well as mindfulness and CBT to help with goal-setting, creating positive emotion, developing more positive relationships, cultivating mindfulness, and optimism (Bolier et al., 2013). Each of these topics is presented in a series of four lessons that, like Mitchell et al. (2009), walk the user through the steps of the activity in a way that is somewhat more interactive than simple written instructions. Users track their progress using self-monitoring tools and receive reminder emails.

The efficacy of Psyfit was evaluated in a recent paper by Bolier and colleagues (2013), in which the PPI was compared with a no-intervention group, and Psyfit led to significant increases in well-being through 2-month follow-up, but not through 6-month follow-up (Bolier et al., 2013). They did, however, observe lasting effects on depressive and anxious symptoms at 6 months. Although they report that the intervention group outperformed a control condition, Bolier et al. (2013) acknowledge that Psyfit lacks interactivity, social networking, and other features that could potentially increase user engagement and retention and possibly also extend long-term benefits. Psyfit is available to the general public by yearly subscription.

Happify, developed by Happify Inc., guides users through activities in five major categories: savoring, gratitude, hope/goal-setting, prosocial behavior, and empathy (Leidner, Ben-Kiki, & Parks, 2013). The user follows one of several "tracks" that help him or her use these five skills to effect a desired change in his or her life. All skills featured on the site are based directly off of PPIs from the literature; the tracks, then, suggest particular contexts in which variations of the activities can be applied toward a specific goal. For example, Seligman et al. (2005) had participants write down three good things that happened in their day; on Happify, a user might join a track about enjoying their kids more and then they would keep a "three good things" journal that centers around their family. A user on a track that focuses on getting more engaged at work might emphasize recording positive events related to his or her work environment instead. Regardless of track, the activity being offered is the same as the one tested in the research; it's just modified to be specifically relevant to the user's goals. Like Daily Challenge, Happify still generally follows the same model as previous online PPIs in that it relies on users to read instructions and do activities on their own. It also contains elements of gamification—mini-games, quizzes, and so on—as well as on-site social networking features and interactivity with Facebook.

Data on Happify's efficacy have not been published previously, but preliminary data are summarized below, based on Leidner et al. (2013). In a sample of beta users of Happify, users were split into quartiles based on their usage as follows: low-usage users ($N$ = 676; more than 5.20 days between visits) and moderately low-usage users ($N$ = 549; 3.20–5.20 days between visits) were compared with moderately high-usage users ($N$ = 576; 2.10–3.20 days between visits) and heavy-usage users ($N$ = 362; 2.10 days or fewer between visits) on their improvements in well-being over time. Well-being was evaluated using a scale designed by Happify, which contains items that tap both emotional and cognitive well-being, and which yields a score on a scale of 0–100 (Leidner et al., 2013). All users experienced change over time that was significantly greater than zero ($p < .0001$ in all cases), but those users who exhibited heavy or moderately high usage showed significantly more improvement in happiness (1.75 points per week and 1.64 points per week, respectively) than did users who used Happify with moderately low (1.17 points per week) or low (.75 points per week) frequency. Users who used the site often or moderately often did not differ from each other, however. Although these initial data do not include a control group, they do preliminarily suggest that the benefits of Happify are more than just a placebo effect or regression to the mean; low usage of Happify is arguably a better comparison group than a no-intervention group, which is often used in online PPI research. However, it is worth acknowledging that this comparison group is self-selected by their own choice not to participate, which is less than ideal.

The basic features of Happify—which include one activity per day—are available to the public and free. Premium content (i.e., additional tracks) are available with a subscription. Happify is also currently in the process of conducting a randomized, controlled trial to more rigorously evaluate its efficacy. Practitioners wishing to refer their clients to participate in the trial—which includes free access to Happify (though that access is delayed for control participants)—can contact the author by email for more information.

SMARTPHONE-BASED PPIs

Another natural extension of the self-help book is the self-help app. A plethora of self-help apps have cropped up in recent years, though a smaller subset are explicitly research-based, and an even smaller subset are based on PPI research. Some apps focus on a single PPI—for example, Gratitude Journal by Happy Tapper (free for the iPhone), asks users to enter five things they are grateful for each day, and then keeps track of these so that the user can review them later. However, given work by Lyubomirsky, Sheldon, and Schkade (2005) suggesting that it is possible to "overdose" on gratitude,[3] practitioners are advised to recommend a more open-ended gratitude app such as Gratitude Tree by Stacey Bobby (also free for the iPhone) in which users are given an empty tree graphic each month and each grateful thing they record becomes a leaf on the tree. This allows users to determine their own dosage of gratitude.

Other apps include multiple happiness activities together. LiveHappy, developed by Signal Patterns and available on the iPhone for 99 cents, gives users a choice of several different types of happiness activities, which they then practice at their leisure and log their progress into their phone. Like Happify, LiveHappy contains activities that are directly based on research. Specifically, the activities are based on the content of Lyubomirsky's *The How of Happiness*. It covers eight domains: savoring, positive memories, acts of kindness, strengthening social relationships, goal-setting, contemplating gratitude, expressing gratitude, and thinking optimistically (Parks et al., 2012; Study 3). Users can freely move between these activities and use them with any frequency. One study found that users of the app did generally benefit (Parks et al., 2012; Study 3), and that greater usage led to greater benefit; however, like the pilot study of Happify previously described, this study lacks a control group and, although potentially promising, begs for additional research to follow it up.

It is worth noting that standalone smartphone apps—particularly those with no social networking component—are prone to user dropoff. This makes sense; with no accountability, one must be self-driven to continue visiting the app. It may be, therefore, that although standalone apps can be suitable vehicles for conveying PPIs, they may not be as ideal as web-based PPIs for user retention. The optimal balance, then, would be happiness-based smartphone apps as a supplement to happiness-based websites to extend website reach and accessibility without the limitations of being a standalone app. For example, both Happify and Daily Challenge have companion apps for the iPhone. These apps contain much of the content of the parent site, but the parent site also contains social networking components and assessments that are more optimally completed at a computer, so the two platforms work in concert to make a multimodal intervention.

## CHALLENGES OF USING PPIs IN THE REAL WORLD

In this chapter, I have provided an overview of the current market of self-help interventions that target happiness. Next, I note several important issues that must be addressed in future research and practice related to self-help PPIs.

### EMPIRICAL VALIDATION

Two things should separate positive psychology–based self-help from other self-help approaches: (1) a conceptual basis in science, and (2) demonstrated efficacy through rigorous, controlled research trials. The problem is that, for the reasons previously discussed, self-help research—if it is to be at all realistic—is quite messy. For example, naturalistic intervention research is rife with dropouts, which compromises the researcher's ability to do airtight data analysis (see Allison, 2001). However, there is no getting around the fact that in the real world, people have the autonomy to start

---

[3]They found that a keeping a gratitude journal once a week was effective, but journaling three times per week was not; it seems that participants in the three-times-per-week condition "overdid" it. Thus, it seems to me that an app asking people to journal daily is potentially ill-advised, though it may be helpful for some clients.

Pharow, P., Blobel, B., Ruotsalainen, P., Petersen, F., & Hovsto, A. (2009). Portable devices, sensors and networks: Wireless personalized eHealth services. *Studies in Health and Technology Informatics, 150,* 1012–1016.

Schueller, S. M. (2014). Person-activity fit in positive psychology interventions. In A. C. Parks and S. M. Schueller (Eds.), *The Wiley-Blackwell handbook of positive psychological interventions* (pp. 385–402). Oxford, England: Wiley-Blackwell.

Schueller, S. M. & Parks, A. C. (2012). Disseminating self-help: Positive psychology exercises in an open online trial. *Journal of Medical Internet Research, 14,* e63.

Seligman, M. E. P. (2002). *Authentic happiness: Using the new positive psychology to realize your potential for lasting fulfillment.* New York, NY: Free Press.

Seligman, M. E. P., Rashid, T., & Parks, A. C. (2006). Positive psychotherapy. *American Psychologist, 61,* 774–788.

Seligman, M. E. P., Steen, T. A., Park, N., & Peterson, C. (2005). Positive psychology progress: Empirical validation of interventions. *American Psychologist, 60,* 410–421.

Sergeant, S., & Mongrain, M. (2011). Are positive psychology exercises helpful for people with depressive personality styles? *Journal of Positive Psychology, 6*(4), 260–272.

Sin, N. L., & Lyubomirsky, S. (2009). Enhancing well-being and alleviating depressive symptoms with positive psychological interventions: A practice-friendly metaanalysis. *Journal of Clinical Psychology, 65,* 467–487.

and stop things, and in the absence of compensation from researchers, they don't always have the motivation to provide complete data.

Naturalistic research is also uncontrolled; users do whatever they want at whatever pace they prefer, resulting in massive variability in the amount of time spent using an intervention, as well as the qualitative nature of the intervention experience. As a result, people get widely varied dosages in widely varying time frames. In a multifaceted intervention like LiveHappy or Happify, one user may choose to use gratitude activities and ignore relationships, whereas another user may do the opposite; they still technically received the same "intervention," but there was no overlap in the activities they use. It becomes difficult, then, to combine users together for the purposes of analysis, and even more difficult to subclassify them with an almost infinite number of permutations in user experience.

In short, studying self-help interventions naturalistically is quite a challenge. However, it is worthwhile to see how interventions validated in the lab play out in the real world. A pill that cures heart disease when used perfectly is of no use if patients cannot or do not take it as instructed; similarly, a PPI that works only when instructions are followed exactly has little utility in the real world, where users are not as restricted as are research participants. For a PPI to really "work," it must hold up to the challenges of being exported into real-world practice, and research must demonstrate that it can do so. This is not to say that there is no place for clean, simple PPIs tested in the lab; rather, I argue that rigorous, controlled research must be paired with PPI research in naturalistic settings in order to reach a general conclusion that a particular intervention is efficacious.

## THE POTENTIAL OF EMERGING TECHNOLOGY

The existing self-help PPIs are only the beginning of what is possible with new and emerging technology. Smartphones contain tremendous untapped potential to provide customized psychological interventions to individuals (Pharow, Blobel, Ruotsalainen, Petersen, & Hovsto, 2009). Specifically, one aspect of smartphone technology that has not yet received attention in the PPI literature is "context sensing"—where information about an individual's situation (i.e., location and time of day) as well as his or her phone behavior (i.e., calls and text messages) can be combined with self-report data (i.e., mood and stress levels) to decide when certain activities would be maximally useful (e.g., Burns et al., 2011). Context sensing could be rendered even richer by providing physiological data about the user using external hardware that can be linked to the phone, such as the Fitbit or Jawbone's UP24, both of which monitor activity levels and even sleep patterns. Having objective data about activity levels can help to increase accountability with goal-setting (say, a person sets a goal to be more physically active) and to help users see how behavioral choices (such as not sleeping enough) impact their mood. More advanced (and more costly) hardware, such as the Zephyr HxM, which can measure heart rate variability, or Affectiva's Q Sensor, which can measure skin conductance, have the potential to provide objective data about the stress levels and real-time coping experienced by the user, further enabling customization.

## ETHICAL CONSIDERATIONS

As promising as self-help PPIs may be, it is important also to remember that some problems are beyond the scope of a self-help intervention. This early in the life of self-help PPIs, it is impossible to know where exactly to draw that line. Careful, systematic work is necessary to determine whether PPIs' clinical utility (see previous discussion) generalizes when translated to a self-administered format. In the meantime, readers thinking of recommending a self-help PPI should be clear that PPIs in any format are not yet (and possibly will never be) considered a standalone treatment for psychological disorder. Many self-help resources will repeat this message, but it's a message worth repeating.

## CONCLUSION

Feasible dissemination of interventions to the general public is a quintessential quandary in clinical psychology, a field that is far more established than is positive psychology; dissemination is a major undertaking! Thus, even though positive psychology is a young field, it behooves PPI researchers and practitioners to think about how PPIs can be most optimally disseminated to the general public. Self-help modalities are very promising vehicles for achieving that goal; no doubt, the next decade holds many exciting possibilities for advancements in the development of PPI self-help tools and for advancements in the research methodology that we use to test them.

## SUMMARY POINTS

- Self-help is an ideal way to get PPIs to the general public.
- When using any self-help tool, guidelines such as frequency of usage and number of activities practiced should be determined based on what works for the individual, *not* on what has been done in previous research.
- There are three main types of self-help interventions: books, websites, and smartphone apps.
- There exist several science-based self-help tools that target happiness and that are publicly available.
- The above-mentioned self-help tools are all in various stages of development and evaluation; none is considered fully "validated" yet.
- The most promising self-help PPIs seem to be multimodal, consisting of instructive text (like a book) as well as interactive web tools and a supplementary smartphone app.
- Real-world PPI research using self-help interventions is challenging, but worth doing more of.

## REFERENCES

Allison, P. D. (2001). *Missing data.* Thousand Oaks, CA: Sage.

Bolier, L., & Abello, K. M. (2014). Online positive psychological interventions: State of the art and future directions. In A. C. Parks and S. M. Schueller (Eds.), *The Wiley-Blackwell handbook of positive psychological interventions* (pp. 286–309). Oxford, England: Wiley-Blackwell.

Bolier, L., Haverman, M., Kramer, J., Westerhof, G. J., Riper, H., Walburg, J. A., . . . Bohlmeijer, E. (2013). An Internet-based intervention to promote mental fitness for mildly depressed adults: Randomized controlled trial. *Journal of Medical Internet Research, 15*, e200.

Burns, D. *Feeling good: The new mood therapy.* New York, NY: Harper.

Burns, M. N., Begale, M., Duffecy, J., Gergle, D., Karr, C. J., Giangrande, E., & Mohr, D. C. (2011). Harnessing context sensing to develop a mobile intervention for depression. *Journal of Medical Internet Research, 13*, e55.

Cobb, N. K., & Poirier, J. (2013). Effectiveness of a multimodal online well-being intervention: A randomized controlled trial. *American Journal of Preventive Medicine, 46*, 41–48.

Cuijpers, P., Donker, T., van Straten, A., Li, J., & Anderson, G. (2010). Is guided self-help as eftive as face-to-face psychotherapy for depression and anxiety disorders? A systematic rev and meta-analysis of comparative outcome studies. *Psychological Medicine, 40*, 1943–195

Emmons, R. A. (2007). *Thanks! How the new science of gratitude can make you happier.* Boston, N Houghton-Mifflin.

Emmons, R. A. (2013). *Gratitude works!: A 21-day program for creating emotional prosperity.* Francisco, CA: Jossey-Bass.

Emmons, R. A., & McCullough, M. E. (2003). Counting blessings versus burdens: An expmental investigation of gratitude and subjective well-being in daily life. *Journal of Persona and Social Psychology, 84*, 377–389.

Eysenbach, G. (2005). The law of attrition. *Journal of Medical Internet Research, 7*, e11.

Gregory, R. J., Schwer Canning, S., Lee, T. W., & Wise, J. C. (2004). Cognitive bibliotherapy depression: A meta-analysis. *Professional Psychology: Research and Practice, 35*, 275–280.

Haidt, J. (2005). *The happiness hypothesis: Finding modern truth in ancient wisdom.* New York, N Basic Books.

Huffman, J. C., DuBois, C. M., Healy, B. C., Boehm, J. K., Kashdan, T. B., Celano, C. M., . Lyubomirsky, S. (2014). Feasibility and utility of positive psychology exercises for suicic inpatients. *General Hospital Psychiatry, 36*, 88–94.

Kahler, C. W., Spillane, N. S., Day, A., Clerkin, E., Parks, A., Leventhal, A. M., & Brown, R. (2013). Positive psychotherapy for smoking cessation: Treatment development, feasibili and preliminary results. *Journal of Positive Psychology, 9*, 19–29.

Kashdan, T. (2009). *Curious?* New York, NY: Morrow.

Leidner, O., Ben-Kiki, T., & Parks, A. C. (2013, June). *Happify: Bringing the science of happine to the masses.* Talk presented at the World Congress of the International Positive Psycholog Association, Los Angeles, CA.

Lewinsohn, P. M., Muñoz, R. F., Youngren, M. A., & Zeiss, A. M. (1992). *Control your depressio* New York, NY: Fireside.

Lyubomirsky, S. (2008). *The how of happiness: A scientific approach to getting the life you want.* Ne York, NY: Penguin Press.

Lyubomirsky, S., Dickerhoof, R., Boehm, J. K., & Sheldon, K. M. (2011). Becoming happier take both a will and a proper way: An experimental longitudinal intervention to boost well-being Emotion, 11, 391–402.

Lyubomirsky, S., Sheldon, K. M., & Schkade, D. (2005). Pursuing happiness: The architectur of sustainable change. *Review of General Psychology, 9*, 111–131.

Magyar-Moe, J. L. (2009). *Therapist's guide to positive psychological interventions.* New York, NY Academic Press.

Meyer, P., Johnson, D., Parks, A. C., Iwanski, C., & Penn, D. L. (2012). Positive living: A pilot study of group positive psychotherapy for people with severe mental illness. *Journal of Positive Psychology, 7*, 239–248.

Mitchell, J., Stanimirovic, R., Knein, B., & Vella-Brodrick, D. (2009). A randomized controlled trial of a self-guided internet intervention promoting well-being. *Computers in Human Behavior, 25*, 749–760.

Parks, A. C. (in press). A case for the improvement of online positive psychological intervention research. *Journal of Positive Psychology.*

Parks, A. C., Della Porta, M. D., Pierce, R. S., Zilca, R., & Lyubomirsky, S. (2012). Pursuing happiness in everyday life: A naturalistic investigation of online happiness seekers. *Emotion, 12*, 1222–1234.

Parks, A. C., & Schueller, S. M. (2014). *The Wiley-Blackwell handbook of positive psychological interventions.* Oxford, England: Wiley-Blackwell.

Parks, A. C., & Szanto, R. K. (2013). Assessing the efficacy and effectiveness of a positive psychology-based self-help book. *Terapia Psicologica, 31*, 141–149.

CHAPTER 15

# Positive Psychology
# and Life Coaching

MARGARITA TARRAGONA

L
IFE COACHING IS a rapidly growing field that has sometimes been described as a
practice in search of a theory. This chapter proposes that positive psychology
can offer a solid theoretical and research-based framework for life coaching,
which in turn can be a "natural habitat" for applied positive psychology. This paper
defines life coaching and what sets it apart from executive coaching and from psychotherapy. It briefly describes the development of life coaching and discusses the
common factors that may account for what works in different coaching models, and
it offers an overview of the existing research about the effectiveness of coaching, as
well as the evidence for the effects of positive psychology interventions. In the final
section, I discuss a conceptual framework based on the PERMA model of well-being
and propose four ways in which life coaches can incorporate positive psychology in
their work.

## WHAT IS LIFE COACHING?

There is no single definition of life coaching, but most conceptualizations of it refer to
a process that helps a person (client or coachee) clarify and achieve goals and improve
his or her well-being, in the context of a relationship with a practitioner (coach). The
Institute of Coaching defines life coaching as "a change process that mobilizes the
strengths and realizes the potential of an individual or an organization" (Institute of
Coaching, 2013). The International Coach Federation describes it as "partnering with
clients in a thought-provoking and creative process that inspires them to maximize
their personal and professional potential" (International Coach Federation, n.d.).

Coaching is an interdisciplinary field that draws from multiple knowledge
domains: philosophy, psychology, adult learning and personal development, specific
professional contexts, and dialogical practices (Stelter, 2014).

Executive coaching, according to Grant and Cavanagh (2010), helps people with
managerial responsibilities in organizations to achieve goals that improve their work
performance and the effectiveness of the organization. Workplace coaching is very
similar, but it is done with nonexecutive employees to improve productivity and skills
in work settings.

*Life coaching* generally refers to coaching clients about aspects of their lives that are outside of work, encompass more than work, or are not defined by roles in an organization. Some of the most frequent issues people want to address in life coaching include handling of finances, relationships, stress management, work–life balance, and in general a desire to have a fuller, more purposeful life (Grant & Cavanagh, 2010).

Executive and workplace coaching are usually done in the place where clients work and are paid for by the organization that employs them (which is a stakeholder in the success of the coaching process). Life coaching is usually paid for by the client and it is frequently done over the telephone.

### LIFE COACHING, PSYCHOTHERAPY, AND COUNSELING

Although it would be hard to confuse therapy with executive coaching (say, working with a CEO on improving his or her leadership skills), life coaching and therapy/counseling can be less clearly differentiated and may sometimes overlap (for example, working with a person who wants to rejoin the workforce after a painful divorce). Many authors emphasize the differences between coaching and therapy/counseling and the importance of making this distinction clear to the clients (Auerbach, 2001; Orlinsky, 2007; Whitworth, Kimsey-House, Kimsey-House, & Sandahl, 2007). One of the main differences is that therapy and counseling usually center on solving problems, alleviating pain, or healing psychological distress, whereas coaching focuses on optimizing functioning that is already good, refining skills, and achieving goals. Kauffman (2006) offers a helpful metaphor when she says that clinicians are trained to "follow a trail of tears," whereas coaches follow a "trail of dreams."

Grant and Cavanagh (2010) describe a life coach as primarily a facilitator of change whose work is based on these assumptions:

- People have a significant latent potential.
- People can change in significant ways.
- Change can happen in a short period of time.
- Clients are resourceful.
- Clients want to change and are willing to work for it.
- Coaching clients do not have serious mental health problems[1] and life coaching is not focused on repairing psychopathologies.
- Life coaching is goal-focused.

### DEVELOPMENT OF LIFE COACHING

Although there are precursors of coaching dating to the 1960s, most authors locate its emergence in the United States in the 1970s and in Europe in the 1980s (Grant & Cavanagh, 2010; Stelter, 2014) and agree on two important historical roots of coaching: sports psychology and the human potential movement. Sports psychology had a focus on goals and peak performance, whereas the human potential movement, inspired by humanistic and existential psychology, promoted self-realization (see Robbins, Chapter 3, this volume).

In its short history, coaching has grown tremendously and has evolved conceptually and in terms of its practices. Some authors talk about different "generations"

---

[1]This assumption about the absence of mental health issues among coaching clients has been challenged by research that has found that between one-quarter and one-half of clients who were studied presented some mental health problems (Grant & Cavanagh, 2010).

of coaching: Kauffman (2006) describes a first generation of practitioners who established the profession and the basic models of coaching, some of whom were "gurus" with extraordinary communication skills, and a second generation (in the mid 2000s) of coaches who work with more complex interventions and are building a more solid theoretical framework and research foundation for the field. The "second generation" described by Kauffman (2006) is more egalitarian and collaborative than the first one (which was highly influenced by the medical model), promoting the idea that coach and coachee can work as coresearchers.

Stelter (2014) also talks about generations in coaching. He sees a progression from a problem-focused way of working, to a solution-focused approach, to a reflection-focused coaching. First-generation coaches were very goal-oriented in order to help a person achieve a particular objective; second-generation coaches assumed that the clients knew how to deal with challenges; and a third generation has a less goal-oriented agenda and a focus on the co-creation of meaning in conversation in a process characterized by a symmetrical relationship between coach and coachee.

Stober and Grant (2006a) talk about the place of expert knowledge in coaching and describe a continuum that goes from giving advice (a la sports coach) to asking questions. Similarly, Kaufman and Scoular (2004; see also Kauffman, Joseph, & Scoular, Chapter 23, this volume) talk about how coaching has evolved from early approaches that were influenced by a medical model, in which the client was seen as a "high level patient," to strengths-based and positive psychology models in which the client is a coactive, equal partner.

Coaches can position themselves and move along a continuum of "intervention." Some work in highly structured ways and use strategies and techniques with a very specific objective in mind, as described by Cox, Bachkirova, and Clutterbuck (2010):

> Coaching could be seen as a human development process that involves structured, focused interaction, and the use of appropriate **strategies, tools, and techniques** to promote desirable and sustainable change for the benefit of the coachee and potentially for other stakeholders. (emphasis added)

Some coaches see themselves as co-creators of new meanings and emerging stories through dialogues:

> Coaching is described as a developmental **conversation and dialogue**, a co-creative process between coach and coachee with the purpose of giving (especially) the coachee a space and an opportunity for **immersing him/herself in reflection on and new understandings** of (1) his or her own experiences in the specific context and (2) his or her own interactions, relations and negotiations with others in specific contexts and situations. The coaching conversation should enable new possible ways of acting in the contexts that are the topic of the conversation. (emphasis added; Stelter, 2014)

However, I believe that these different approaches or focuses are not "stages" that supersede one another like steps on a staircase, but more like branches on a tree, which, although still connected, grow in different directions.

## DIFFERENT APPROACHES IN LIFE COACHING

In their *Complete Handbook of Coaching*, Cox et al. (2010) offer an overview of different approaches in coaching. It is interesting how much the list of coaching models looks like a list of schools of psychotherapy: There is psychodynamic coaching, cognitive-behavioral and solution-centered coaching, person-centered and Gestalt, existential coaching, narrative coaching, transpersonal, transactional analysis, NLP (neurolinguistic programming), in addition to ontological and positive psychology coaching.

In the field of therapy, there have been important efforts to look at what the different therapeutic models have in common, and these have identified the "active ingredients" that explain change beyond the specific schools, such as Orlinsky and Howard's (1987) Generic Model of Psychotherapy and the Common Factors proposed by Hubble, Duncan, and Miller (1999) and Messer and Wampold (2002). Given the broad spectrum of approaches to coaching, there are similar attempts to distill the commonalities of the various coaching models.

## A META-THEORY FOR LIFE COACHING

Stober and Grant (2006b) acknowledge how each of the many approaches in coaching provides its own articulate framework for practice, and they offer a "meta-theory" or explanation that accounts for the coaching process in a way that is broader than the specifics of each model. Based on Messer and Wampold's (2002) contextual model of psychotherapy, Stober and Grant (2006a) offer a contextual model that includes the elements or factors that all coaching processes have in common. These are:

- An explicit outcome or goal.
- A sensible rationale about why coaching fits the client's needs or situation.
- A procedure, something the coach does or the coach and coachee do together.
- A meaningful relationship.
- A collaborative working alliance.
- The client's ability and readiness to change.
- The coach's ability and readiness to help the client change.

Stober and Grant's (2006a) contextual model also includes seven key principles of human change processes:

1. Collaboration
2. Accountability
3. Awareness
4. Responsibility
5. Commitment
6. Action
7. Results

## RESEARCH ON LIFE COACHING

The Global Coaching Conference (GCC) Working Group (2008) reported that although the volume of research about coaching has increased, the quality of the studies is very uneven. Grant (2008) has conducted some of the most important research in coaching and carefully followed the development of research in the field. Grant and Cavanagh (2011) report that they located 81 outcome studies of the effectiveness of coaching since 1980, but that only 15 of these are between-subjects studies and 11 are randomized controlled studies. These few rigorously designed studies indicate that coaching can improve performance in different ways.

Despite the growth in research on coaching in general, there is still very little research specifically about life coaching. The four outcome studies about life coaching reviewed by Grant and Cavanagh (2011) have indicated that coaching can improve goal attainment, enhance psychological and subjective well-being as well as resilience, and that coaching can reduce depression, stress, and anxiety.

Kauffman, Boniwell, and Silberman (2010) mention that even though there is no research about the coaching relationship, what we know from psychotherapy research suggests that the relationship is the key ingredient in successful coaching outcomes.

Although most of the literature in the field supports the importance of doing solid research about coaching, there are different opinions about what can be considered evidence and how practitioners and researchers can best generate knowledge about coaching. Grant and Cavanagh (2010) point out that coaches can use knowledge that is relevant, up to date, empirically valid, and conceptually coherent, which can come from different fields, such as behavioral science, adult education, business, and philosophy. For them, a coach can be a "scholar practitioner," well-versed in areas such as counseling, human development, and positive psychology (more on this later).

Stober and Grant (2006a) argue for "a broad definition of applicable evidence and sources of knowledge" in coaching. Stelter (2014) says that there is no doubt about the importance of research in the development of the field and the assurance of quality in coaching, but he warns that a method for which evidence is derived from a certain context may not be effective in a different situation. He believes that in professions that are highly context-dependent (such as education, social work, and coaching), there is a risk of blocking creative and situationally adapted solutions when we adopt an excessively positivistic view of evidence. Stelter (2014) calls for more qualitative and action research and proposes that there can be "evidence-based practice" and "practice-based evidence."

## POSITIVE PSYCHOLOGY AND LIFE COACHING: MADE FOR EACH OTHER

Christopher Peterson (2009) used to recount that when the founders of positive psychology were discussing its prospective areas of application, they thought that coaching would be a "natural habitat" for positive psychology.

Positive psychology studies what works well in people's lives. It fits right in with the basic assumptions of coaching, for example, that the client is "naturally creative, resourceful, and whole" (Whitworth et al., 2007, p. 3). Grant and Cavanagh (2010) also list other assumptions, such as the belief that people have an important latent potential, that clients are willing to work for change, and that the process of coaching is not about repairing psychopathologies, and they state that positive psychology is one of the four main theoretical traditions on which these assumptions are based (the other three are cognitive-behavioral, solution-focused, and humanistic psychology).

The meeting of coaching and positive psychology is a fortunate one. Seligman once described coaching as "a practice in search of a backbone, two backbones actually: a scientific, evidence-based backbone and a theoretical backbone" (2007, p. 266). Several authors agree that coaching once lacked a solid conceptual foundation (Biswas-Diener, 2007; Kauffman, 2006). They also agree that positive psychology can provide a coherent theoretical framework and a body of scientific evidence that greatly enhances coaching. In Kauffman's (2006) words, "positive psychology can provide the legs on which coaching can stand."

Most coaching clients want to be happy and to have fuller, more meaningful lives. Positive psychology has much to offer toward this goal (Diener & Biswas-Diener, 2008; Lyubomirsky, 2007, 2013). People who look for coaching are doing well, but they want to do better—they want to flourish. Life coaching focuses on people's strengths, on their goals, hopes, and dreams. All of these are areas of research within positive psychology: prospection (Seligman, Railton, Baumeister, & Sripada, 2013), goal setting and achievement (Locke & Latham, 2002), hope (Lopez, 2013), character strengths (Peterson & Seligman, 2004), meaning and purpose (Steger, 2009), and human flourishing (Seligman, 2011).

Seligman (2011) says that positive psychology is about what we choose for its own sake. Life coaching works with clients' self-agency and intentionality, with their ability to choose, which is at the core of positive psychology's conception of human beings.

## POSITIVE PSYCHOLOGY COACHING

As we discuss in the following sections, positive psychology can be incorporated into different styles and models of life coaching. Additionally, there is an emerging way of working called Positive Psychology Coaching that, although still in development, is explicitly built on positive psychology concepts and research findings. Kauffman, Boniwell, and Silberman (2010) describe this nicely when they say that "positive psychology coaches attempt to weave the 'straw' of research into the 'gold' of artful coaching." For these authors, the goals of Positive Psychology Coaching include promoting positive affect and directing purposeful change. They focus on strengths rather than on weaknesses and use a variety of assessment tools to explore character strengths, life satisfaction, and potential routes to peak performance. Positive Psychology Coaches use positive interventions, or intentional activities that have been empirically proven to enhance well-being (more on these in the next section).

Biswas-Diener (2010) emphasizes that coaches who use positive psychology need to understand its technical aspects and its scientific foundation. Coaches need to be able to critically consume research literature and keep abreast of the new developments in the field, because science changes. Biswas-Diener (2010) describes his work as such:

> I am explicitly informed in my coaching work by the science and theory of positive psychology. This means I have a tendency to look for solutions rather than explore obstacles, that I use a codified vocabulary for strengths, that I draw upon empirically supported interventions and assessments, and that I attend heavily to the role of positive and negative emotions when I interact with my clients.

## POSITIVE INTERVENTIONS/ACTIVITIES

Pawelski (2011) defines positive interventions as "evidence-based, intentional acts meant to increase well-being in non-clinical populations" (p. 643). Sin and Lyubomirsky (2009) described them as "treatment methods or intentional activities aimed at cultivating positive feelings, positive behaviors, or positive cognitions" (p. 467). More recently, Lyubomirsky and her collaborators, as well as other researchers, are using the terms "positive activities" (Layous, Chancellor, & Lyubomirsky, 2013), "positive activity interventions" (Layous & Lyubomirsky, in press), and "positive psychology exercises" (Huffman et al., 2013), referring to the same kind of activities.

Positive psychology stresses the importance of choice and intentional activity. Layous et al. (2013) point out that a large part of people's happiness can be explained by how they choose to spend their time and to respond to situations in their lives. Layous and Lyubomirsky (in press) explain that positive activity interventions (PAIs) are strategies that mirror what naturally happy people think and do and improve the happiness of the person who practices them. They are usually brief, self-administered activities that cost no money, and they all promote positive feelings, thoughts, and behaviors. Some of the best-known positive exercises include keeping a gratitude journal, doing a gratitude visit, and using a character strength in a novel way (a more complete list follows in the next section).

One of the reasons why positive activity exercises are so appropriate for coaching is that, as Layous and Lyubomirsky (in press) explain, they are focused on increasing the positive and do not aim at fixing negative feelings, thoughts, or behaviors.

### Research on Positive Interventions

The effectiveness of positive interventions in increasing subjective well-being is solidly established. Huffman et al. (2013) state that there have been over 50 studies in which more than 4,000 people have used positive psychology exercises with good results in nonclinical populations. Today there is an increasing number of studies documenting the usefulness of positive psychology exercises in clinical populations as well (Huffman et al., 2013), particularly for people who are struggling with depression.

Layous and Lyubomirsky (in press) state that strategies to increase happiness clearly work. Among the positive exercises that have been proven to increase well-being, Layous and Lyubomirsky (in press) and Lyubomirsky and Layous (2013) cite:

- Writing letters of gratitude
- Counting one's blessings
- Practicing optimism
- Performing acts of kindness
- Using one's strengths in new ways
- Affirming one's most important values
- Meditating on positive feelings toward self and others
- Visualizing ideal future selves

For Layous and Lyubomirsky (in press), it is important to move forward from assessing whether positive activity interventions work (there is solid evidence that they do; see also Layous, Sheldon, & Lyubomirsky, Chapter 11, this volume) to understanding how they work. They point out that there are moderating variables that influence the effectiveness of positive activities, for example, the duration and format of the intervention and the characteristics of the person who is doing the positive exercise. They also talk about importance of a right "fit" between the person and the activity.

Lyubomirsky and Layous (2013) propose a positive activity model: Positive activities increase positive emotions, positive thoughts, and positive behaviors, all of which increase well-being. Positive activities can also satisfy the three psychological needs posited in self-determination theory: autonomy, competence, and connection.

The authors state that positive activities also increase the chance of engaging in other positive behaviors, even if they are unrelated to the positive activity exercise. There are characteristics of the activity and of the person that influence or mediate the impact of the positive exercise. Among the features of the activity there is dosage, variety, trigger, and social support, whereas some of the relevant characteristics of the person include motivation and effort, efficacy beliefs, baseline affective state, personality, social support, and demographic characteristics.

Here are some examples of these mediating variables as described by Lyubomirsky and Layous (2013): Dosage, the intensity and frequency of an activity, has an impact on its effectiveness. Doing five acts of kindness on the same day had a greater impact than doing five acts of kindness over a week. In one study, counting one's blessings once a week was more effective than doing it three times a week. These illustrate how activities can be "watered down" or "overdone" and the "ideal" dose probably varies depending on the person and the activity.

Variety plays an important role in positive activities. Several studies, naturalistic and experimental, have shown that doing a number of different activities concurrently brings the greatest benefits. Social support, virtual and in person, has been shown to increase the effectiveness of positive activities too.

Lyubomirsky and Layous (2013) think that variety and social support probably are advantageous in any positive activity, whereas other features of positive exercises vary between activities. For example, a positive activity can be self-oriented and work better for an individualist person, and a different activity can be oriented toward others and be a better fit for a collectivist person. Individual characteristics that influence the impact of positive exercises include motivation, willingness, and the belief that they will work. The emotional state of the participants in positive activities is also important: It has been shown that people who start out with low positive affect or moderate depression may benefit the most from these activities. These authors also state that research shows that older people tend to benefit more than younger people and that Western participants tend to benefit more than people from Eastern cultures.

Another variable that affects outcome is whether the person enjoys the activity, which speaks to the importance of "fit" between person and activity. Layous et al. (2013) highlight the importance of matching people's interests and values with their activities.

As we can see, research on positive activities is growing and becoming more nuanced, so coaches and clients can have more information when they chose to recommend or to try a positive psychology exercise. Biswas-Diener (2010) says that positive psychology interventions can be the "corpus of a scientific toolbox" that coaches can add to their practices. Csikszentmihalyi and Nakamura (2011) point out a potential problem we should be aware of:

> When a person charges for a specific service, he or she can not be as critical of it, lest the clients begin to suspect that the goods provided are not as advertised. So life coaches need theories of happiness, and interventions that produce them, that are beyond change and improvement. Whether they can resist this pressure or not remains to be seen.

As life coaches grounded in positive psychology research, we need to remind ourselves (and our clients sometimes) that the knowledge we have is always developing and changing.

# AN INTEGRATIVE FRAMEWORK FOR POSITIVE PSYCHOLOGY AND LIFE COACHING

There are four basic ways that positive psychology can be incorporated into life coaching (Tarragona, 2010, 2012):

1. As a perspective or general orientation in our work.
2. As a source of information to bring into the coaching conversation.
3. As positive interventions or positive activities.
4. As accompanied self-help.

## Positive Psychology as an Orientation

This is apparently the simplest, but in my opinion the most important, feature of any practice that is informed by positive psychology. It is not a technique or a strategy, but a perspective—a way of looking at people and of creating relationships with them. For me this is expressed in Csikszentmihalyi's description of positive psychology as "a metaphysical orientation toward the good" (cited in Pawelski, 2008). This orientation toward the good translates in life coaching as a curiosity to explore what works well in our clients' lives, what they do well, what they enjoy, what values are most important to them, what their greatest strengths are, which are their most meaningful relationships, what helps them overcome hurdles, and what gives them hope.

This of course coincides with the basic orientation of most life coaching models. I think what positive psychology can add is a coherent and systematic framework to guide our exploration. Seligman's (2011) PERMA model of well-being can be a very useful map. PERMA is the acronym for the five components of well-being: positivity, engagement, relationships, meaning, and achievement (Seligman, 2011).

*Positivity* refers to positive emotions. *Engagement* is about experiencing flow, focusing completely on tasks in which we use our skills to face challenges. *Relationships* is about the quality of our connections and interactions with others. *Meaning* has to do with having purpose and making sense of our experiences in a way that makes our life feel worth living. *Achievement* refers to reaching goals and having a sense of accomplishment.

Positive psychologists study topics such as happiness, positive emotions, flow experiences, optimism, goal attainment, character strengths, resilience, and loving relationships, often using experimental or quasiexperimental methods. The coach, however, can be an ethnographer of sorts, doing "micro-research" or qualitative exploration with clients into the phenomena of their lives. This kind of inquiry does not require special techniques other than good conversational and relational skills and a sensitivity and curiosity about what works well and what is most meaningful for the client: What makes you happy? What brings you most satisfaction in life? What has allowed you to go on despite the setbacks you have faced? When are you in your best mood? Who helps you pursue your goals? How do the best conversations take place in your life? When are you closer to being your "best self"? (Tarragona, 2010, 2013).

A life coaching process that is informed by positive psychology does not mean that the client can only talk about what works well and never discuss failures, difficulties, or painful experiences, nor that the coach only inquires about successes and high points. Clients should be free to talk about whatever is important to them and relevant for their goals. But it is different to talk about difficulties against a background of strengths, skills, and hopes that put current obstacles in a broader context.

White (2007) discusses maps as constructions that can guide our explorations, offer routes we might have not imagined, and show us that there are many ways to get to a destination. If we have a general "map" of the different areas of well-being, we can visit those territories when they become relevant in our coaching conversations (Tarragona, 2013). For example, I had a young client, a university student, who spontaneously said in a session that he felt he took for granted much of what he had and that he focused on what was missing in his life. This made me think of the research on gratitude and I asked him some questions about his experiences of gratitude. We talked about one area that, according to positive psychology, is related to well-being. It was not a "strategy"; I was not trying to get him to be more grateful at the moment, but wanted to find out about his experiences of gratitude and what gratitude meant for him.

Conversation itself can bring about change. As Anderson (1997) says, language and dialogue can be generative. We remember things, feel emotions, and can create new meanings that emerge when we talk together. In sum, the first way in which we can use positive psychology in life coaching is as a positioning or stance that is sensitive to what clients say and is related to the elements of well-being. Positive psychology can be a "lens" that zooms into positive emotions, flow experiences, purpose and meaning in life, positive relationships, achievements, and character strengths.

POSITIVE PSYCHOLOGY AS A SOURCE OF INFORMATION

Another way of bringing positive psychology into our work as life coaches is to offer ideas and information that come from research about well-being. Positive psychology has produced a robust body of findings about happiness, life satisfaction, and human flourishing, and we can put this knowledge at the service of our clients. We can do this in different ways, depending on our coaching style.

We can take a psychoeducational stance and "instruct" our clients about topics that are relevant to their situation, comment on evidence, share findings, or recommend a book or a video by an expert on the topic we are discussing. We might create our own handouts for clients or have a website or blog with information that is based on positive psychology.

Because I am partial to collaborative practices, I like Anderson's (1997) notion of "food for thought and dialogue," which means that the ideas that the coach brings to the conversation may not necessarily need to be presented as privileged information or *the* way to do things, but rather as material that can stimulate productive conversations.

For example, if something that a client is telling me reminds me of a research paper I have read from positive psychology, I can mention it and ask if he or she would be interested in hearing more about this topic. If the client agrees, I can put the information on the table and explore how it can connect or be useful with his or her current situation. For example, I had a client that was changing careers and was telling me about some of the regrets that she had and how she felt it was hard to let go of some goals even though she knew she had to in order to pursue her new path. This reminded me of the work on "lost possible selves" (and "found possible selves") done by King and Raspin (Raspin, 2004). I told her that what she was sharing reminded me of something that had actually been studied and I wondered if she would like to hear a little about the notion of "lost possible self." She did, and after hearing about it we had a conversation that was very meaningful to her and she said she wanted to think of ways of saying good-bye to her "lost selves." The next time we met, she said thinking about this had been very helpful and she was feeling more excited about the next stage in her life.

I often tell clients that most of the results from quantitative research describe means, trends, and statistical probabilities, but they cannot predict anything about a particular person. So I share the evidence as interesting information that may help them understand and improve their situation, but together we try to see to what extent it is applicable in their case.

There is so much evidence about what contributes to well-being that it would be impossible to try to list it in this chapter. Just to mention some examples, there are findings on savoring, positive emotions, passions, character strengths, flow experiences, creativity, gratitude, curiosity, elevation, positive relationships, happy marriages and families, goal setting and achievement, optimism, grit and perseverance, resilience, meaning and purpose in life, the effects of meditation, the benefits of physical exercise, life satisfaction and well-being among nations, and positive psychology and its contributions to public policy and social change. There is a treasure trove of information that life coaches can draw on to enrich their work and that can have a positive impact on clients' lives.

### Positive Interventions and Activities

The third way to integrate positive psychology in life coaching is using "positive interventions" (Pawelski, 2011; Seligman, Steen, Park, & Peterson, 2005; Sin & Lyubomirsky, 2009), "positive activities" (Layous et al., 2013), or "positive psychology exercises" (Huffman et al., 2013). The nomenclature seems to be changing recently, moving from the term *intervention* to *activities* or *exercises*, but the various terms refer to the same thing: Activities or exercises that are based on positive psychology, the effectiveness of which has been proven through rigorous scientific research.

I think that when most people think of "applied positive psychology," what immediately comes to mind are positive interventions: Specific, deliberate activities that a professional recommends to clients to increase their well-being.

If you recall, Lyubomirsky and Layous (in press, 2013) state that the following positive exercises have been proven to increase well-being.

*Writing Letters of Gratitude*   Lyubomirsky, Dickerhoof, Boehm, and Sheldon (2011) have studied writing letters of gratitude. People were instructed to spend 15 minutes, once a week, remembering times when they had felt grateful for something another person did. Then they were instructed to write a letter to that person, explaining in detail the specific thing this person did, how it affected their lives, and how frequently they remember that person's contribution. The letters were not meant to be sent.

*Counting One's Blessings*   This exercise is also known as the gratitude journal: Every night, before going to bed, the person has to write three things that he or she is grateful for that day. There are different variations of this exercise. Authors with a cogntive-behavioral slant, such as Seligman and his collaborators (Seligman, Steen, Park, & Peterson, 2005) call it the "Three Good Things" exercise and ask people to write down three good things that happened that day and why they think they happened, so they realize that they have an influence on their environment. Pawelski (2008) suggests reviewing the journal after a few days to see if any patterns emerge in the lists of good things and reasons for their occurence.

Other authors, such as Emmons (2008), who I think has a more spiritual perspective, do not ask for that analysis, but suggest that there are things that simply happen, or "gifts" we receive, without our having done anything to deserve them.

Lyubomirsky (2007) says that it is important for the journal not become routine, that for many people doing it once a week seems best, but that each person has to find the right "dose" and way of doing it.

A variation of the exercise is the "gratitude visit" (Pawelski, 2008; Seligman et al., 2005). In this case, people not only write the letter, but reach out to the person to whom they wrote it and invite that person to meet with them. They do not tell the recipient of the letter what the purpose of the meeting is. When they get together, the person who wrote the letter reads it out loud to the recipient.

*Performing Acts of Kindness*   The person is asked to perform acts of kindness. These can be either five acts of kindness over the course of 6 weeks, or all five in one day. Research shows that doing all of the kind acts in one day yields a greater increase in happiness (Layous & Lyubomirsky, in press).

*Using One's Strengths in New Ways*   For this exercise, participants have to identify their top character strengths (one way to do it is through the VIA inventory) and then choose one of their highest strengths, think about how they normally use it, and use it differently every day for a week. This has been shown to be one of the most lasting positive psychology interventions, the effect of which was evident up to 6 months after the exercise was practiced (Seligman et al., 2005).

*Affirming One's Most Important Values*   In this exercise, people choose one or two of their most important values and write about them for 15 minutes.

*Meditating on Positive Feelings Toward Self and Others*   People are taught to practice "loving kindness" meditation, also known as metta meditation. In this kind of meditation, the person evokes warm compassionate feelings, first for him- or herself. Then he or she expands those warm compassionate feelings to loved ones and progressively extends those wishes to familiar strangers, strangers, and the whole world.

Research by Fredrickson (2009) has shown that people who learn this meditation and practice it for as little as 8 weeks show increases in their levels of happiness.

*Visualizing Ideal Future Selves and Practicing Optimism*   The "best possible self" exercise devised by King (2001) asks people to write 20 minutes a day during 4 consecutive days, following these instructions:

> Think about your life in the future. Imagine that everything has gone as well as it possibly could. You have worked hard and succeeded at accomplishing all of your life goals. Think of this as the realization of all of your life dreams. Now, write about what you imagined. (King, 2001, p. 801)

Doing this exercise is also a way to practice optimism (Lyubomirsky et al., 2011). Layous and Lyubomirksy (in press) point out that specific recommendations for the promotion of well-being have better results than general suggestions.

POSITIVE PSYCHOLOGY AS ACCOMPANIED SELF-HELP

The fourth way in which positive psychology can enrich life coaching is as a complement or supplement to coaching sessions. Several outstanding positive psychology researchers and practitioners are making their findings available to the general public in highly readable books with a solid foundation (see Parks, Chapter 14, this volume).

We can use these books in different ways: to reinforce or expand on what we discussed in a session, or as a project that clients can take on (such as workbooks), and they can share their progress and reflections with us. We can also use the countless resources online or new apps that are designed to increase well-being.

## CONCLUSION

Life coaching is about the construction of identities (Stelter, 2014), the pursuit of life purposes, and the promotion of well-being (Grant & Cavanagh, 2010). By incorporating positive psychology into their practice, coaches are better equipped to work beside their clients as they strive to flourish and be the persons they want to be.

## SUMMARY POINTS

- Life coaching works with clients on aspects of their lives that are outside of work or encompass more than work.
- Life coaching differs from therapy in that its aim is not to alleviate psychological pain, but to optimize functioning that is already good and to help clients achieve their goals.
- Metatheoretical models can account for the factors that all different types of coaching processes have in common.
- Research shows that coaching can improve performance in different ways, but there are still very few studies that specifically evaluate life coaching.
- Life coaching can be the "natural habitat" for positive psychology, and positive psychology can provide life coaching with a solid theoretical and research foundation.
- Life coaches can incorporate positive psychology into their practice as a general orientation or as a source of information, and they can implement purposeful specific interventions and research-based self-help.
- Life coaching can help clients realign their lives with their goals, values, and preferred identities.

## REFERENCES

Anderson, H. (1997). *Conversation, language, and possibilities: A postmodern approach to therapy.* New York, NY: Basic Books.

Auerbach, J. (2001). *Personal and executive coaching: The complete guide for mental health professionals.* Ventura, CA: Executive College Press.

Biswas-Diener, R. (2007). *Positive psychology coaching: Putting the science of happiness to work for your clients.* Hoboken, NJ: Wiley.

Biswas-Diener, R. (2010). *Practicing positive psychology coaching: Assessment, activities, and strategies for success* [Kindle edition]. Hoboken, NJ: Wiley.

Cox, E., Bachkirova, T., & Clutterbuck, D. (2010). *The complete handbook of coaching* [Kindle edition]. Los Angeles, CA: Sage.

Csikszentmihalyi, M., & Nakamura, J. (2011). Positive psychology: Where did it come from, where is it going? In K. Sheldon, T. Kashdan, & M. Steger (Eds), *Designing positive psychology: Taking stock and moving forward* [Kindle edition]. New York, NY: Oxford University Press.

Diener, E., & Biswas-Diener, R. (2008). *Happiness: Unlocking the mysteries of psychological wealth.* Malden, MA: Blackwell.

Emmons, R. (2007). *Thanks!: How the new science of gratitude can make you happier.* Boston, MA: Houghton Mifflin.

Fredrickson, B. (2009). *Positivity: Groundbreaking research reveals how to embrace the hidden strength of positive emotions, overcome negativity, and thrive.* New York, NY: Crown.

GCC Working Group. (2008). *White paper of the Working Group on the Research Agenda for Development of the Field.* Retrieved from http://www.instituteofcoaching.org/images/pdfs/State-of-Coaching-Research.pdf

Grant, A. (2008). *Workplace, executive and life coaching: An annotated bibliography from the behavioural science literature.* Sydney, Australia: Coaching Psychology Unit, University of Sydney.

Grant, A., & Cavanagh, M. (2010). Life coaching. In E. Cox, T. Bachkirova, & D. Clutterbuck (Eds.), *The complete handbook of coaching.* London, England: Sage.

Grant, A., & Cavanagh, M. (2011). Coaching and positive psychology. In K. Sheldon, T. Kashdan, & M. Steger (Eds.), *Designing positive psychology: Taking stock and moving forward* (pp. 293–309). Oxford, England: Oxford University Press.

Hubble, M., Duncan, B., & Miller, S. (1999). *The heart and soul of change: What works in therapy.* Washington, DC: American Psychological Association.

Huffman, J., Dubois, C., Healy, B., Boehm, J., Kashdan, T., Celano, C., . . . Lyubormirsky, S. (2013). Feasibility and utility of positive psychology exercises for suicidal inpatients. *General Hospital Psychiatry, 36,* 88–94. doi:10.1016/j.genhosppsych.2013.10.006

Institute of Coaching. (2013). *What is coaching?* Retrieved from http://www.instituteofcoaching.org/index.cfm?page=visitorscenter

International Coach Federation. (n.d.). *How does ICF define coaching?* Retrieved from http://www.coachfederation.org/about/landing.cfm?ItemNumber=844&navItemNumber=617

Kauffman, C. (2006). Positive psychology: The science at the heart of coaching. In D. Stober & A. Grant (Eds.), *Evidence-based coaching: Putting best practices to work for your clients* [Kindle edition]. Hoboken, NJ: Wiley.

Kauffman, C., Boniwell, I., & Silberman, J. (2010). The positive psychology approach to coaching. In E. Cox, T. Bachkirova, & D. Clutterbuck (Eds.), *The complete handbook of coaching.* London, England: Sage.

Kauffman, C., & Scoular, A. (2004). Toward a positive psychology of executive coaching. In P. A. Linley & S. Joseph (Eds.), *Positive psychology in practice* (pp. 287–302). Hoboken, NJ: Wiley.

King, L. (2001). The health benefits of writing about life goals. *Personality and Social Psychology Bulletin, 27,* 798–807.

King, L., & Raspin, C. (2004). Lost and found possible selves, subjective well-being, and ego development in divorced women. *Journal of Personality, 72,* 603–632.

Layous, K., Chancellor, J., & Lyubomirsky, S. (2013). Positive activities as protective factors against mental health conditions. *Journal of Abnormal Psychology, 123,* 3–12. doi:10.1037/a0034709

Layous, K., & Lyubomirsky, S. (in press). The how, why, what, when, and who of happiness: Mechanisms underlying the success of positive activity interventions. In J. Gruber & J. Moskowitz (Eds.), *The light and dark side of positive emotion.* Oxford, England: Oxford University Press.

Locke, E. A., & Latham, G. P. (2002). Building a practically useful theory of goal setting and task motivation: A 35-year odyssey. *American Psychologist, 57,* 705–717.

Lopez, S. (2013). *Making hope happen: Create the future you want in business and life.* New York, NY: Free Press.

Lyubomirsky, S. (2007). *The how of happiness: A scientific approach to getting the life you want.* New York, NY: Penguin Press.

Lyubomirsky, S. (2013). *The myths of happiness: What should make you happy but doesn't, what shouldn't make you happy but does.* New York, NY: Penguin Press.

Lyubomirsky, S., Dickerhoof, R., Boehm, J., & Sheldon, K. (2011). Becoming happier takes both a will and a proper way: An experimental longitudinal intervention to boost well-being. *Emotion, 11,* 391–402.

Lyubomirsky, S., & Layous, K. (2013). How do simple positive activities increase well-being? *Current Directions in Psychological Science, 22,* 57–62.

Messer, S., & Wampold, B. (2002). Let's face facts: Common factors are more potent than specific therapy ingredients. *Clinical Psychology: Science and Practice, 9*(1), 21–25.

Orlinsky, D. (2007, November). *Collaborative research: How different are coaches and therapists?* Paper presented at 11th Annual International Coach Federation Conference, Long Beach, CA.

Orlinsky, D., & Howard, K. (1987). A generic model of psychotherapy. *Journal of Integrative & Eclectic Psychotherapy, 6,* 6–27.

Pawelski, J. (2008, November 25). *Una (muy) breve introducción a la psicología positiva* [A (very) brief introduction to positive psychology]. Mexico City, Mexico: Universidad Iberoamericana.

Pawelski, J. (2011). Questions conceptuelles en psychologie positive. In C. Martin-Krumm, & C. Tarquinio (Eds.), *Traité de psychologie positive* (pp. 643–657). Brussels, Belgium: De Boeck.

Peterson, C. (2009, April 18). Lecture at Diploma Program in Positive Psychology. Universidad Iberoamericana, Mexico City.

Peterson, C., & Seligman, M. E. (2004). *Character strengths and virtues. A handbook and classification.* Washington, DC: American Psychological Association.

Seligman, M. (2007). Coaching and positive psychology. *Australian Psychologist, 42,* 266–267.

Seligman, M., Railton, P., Baumeister, R., & Sripada, C. (2013). Navigating into the future or driven by the past. *Perspectives on Psychological Science, 8,* 119–141.

Seligman, M. E. (2011). *Flourish: A visionary new understanding of happiness and well-being.* New York, NY: Free Press.

Seligman, M. E., Steen, T., Park, N., & Peterson, C. (2005). Positive psychology progress: Empirical validation of interventions. *American Psychologist, 60,* 410–421.

Sin, N., & Lyubomirsky, S. (2009). Enhancing well-being and alleviating depressive symptoms with positive psychology interventions: A practice-friendly meta-analysis. *Journal of Clinical Psychology, 65,* 467–487.

Steger, M. (2009). Meaning in life. In S. Lopez, & C. Snyder (Eds.), *Oxford handbook of positive psychology* (2nd ed., pp. 679–687). New York, NY: Oxford University Press.

Stelter, R. (2014). *A guide to third generation coaching: Narrative-collaborative theory and practice* [Kindle edition]. Dordrecht, Netherlands: Springer.

Stober, D., & Grant, A. (2006a). Toward a contextual approach to coaching models. In A. Grant & D. Stober (Eds.), *Evidence-based coaching handbook: Putting best practices to work for your clients.* Hoboken, NJ: Wiley.

Stober, D., & Grant, A. (2006b). *Evidence-based coaching handbook: Putting best practices to work for your clients* [Kindle edition]. Hoboken, NJ: Wiley.

Tarragona, M. (2010). Psicología positiva y psicoterapia. In A. Castro Solano (Ed.), *Fundamentos de psicología positiva* (pp. 183–206). Buenos Aires, Argentina: Paidós.

Tarragona, M. (2012). Therapy for human flourishing: A botanical metaphor. *IPPA Newsletter, 5,* 3.

Tarragona, M. (2013) Psicología positiva y terapias constructivas: Una propuesta integradora. *Terapia Psicológica, 31,* 115–125.

White, M. (2007). *Maps of narrative practice.* New York, NY: Norton.

Whitworth, L., Kimsey-House, K., Kimsey-House, H., & Sandahl, P. (2007). *Co-active coaching: New skills for coaching people toward success in work and life* (2nd ed.). Ventura, CA: Davies-Black.

# PART IV

# METHODS AND PROCESSES OF TEACHING AND LEARNING

# CHAPTER 16

# Different Approaches to Teaching Positive Psychology

AMY C. FINEBURG and ANDREW MONK

FROM THE BEGINNING of the movement, education has been one of the main pillars of positive psychology (Seligman, 1998) and has become regarded as one of the most appropriate forms for its effectiveness (Burns, Andrews, & Szabo, 2002). Education as an institution is a natural fit into the positive psychology realm in that its entire goal is to enact positive change in individuals through learning. The institution of education also works to provide a positive outcome for communities by producing informed citizens who can interact knowledgably with society. Positive psychologists concern themselves with research and practice into what aspects of school assist students' learning and well-being, while also investigating how people within the educational system can enhance and be enhanced by their experiences in school. Researchers have examined the roles of strengths (Hodges & Clifton, 2004; Lopez & Louis, 2009), hope (Lopez, Rose, Robinson, Marques, & Pais-Reibero, 2009; Snyder et al., 2002; Worrell & Hale, 2001), gratitude (Bono, Froh, & Emmons, 2012), self-regulation (Duckworth, Grant, Loew, Oettingen, & Gollwitzer, 2011), grit (Duckworth & Seligman, 2005; Duckworth, 2013), and resilience (Gillham et al., 2007) in how well students perform in schools. This research has translated into lessons and strategies that teachers use in their classrooms either to teach the academic content of positive psychology or to teach the hidden curriculum of soft skills inherent in positive psychology interventions.

In the first edition of *Positive Psychology in Practice* (Linley & Joseph, 2004), this chapter focused on the teaching of positive psychology to the introductory psychology student. A decade ago, positive psychology was a relatively new movement, and the emphasis at that time was to introduce positive psychology to students as early as possible. The positive psychology unit plan (Fineburg, 2001) for high school classrooms was published by Teachers of Psychology in Secondary Schools (TOPSS), the high school teacher affiliate group of the American Psychological Association (APA). Authors (i.e., Blair-Broeker & Ernst, 2003; Myers, 2014) were beginning to put positive psychology concepts into their textbooks. The implications and possibilities of teaching positive psychology to students, regardless of age level, were just beginning to be explored. The need for a discussion of how positive psychology might best be introduced to students provided the impetus for the chapter in the first edition.

Since then, the theory of positive psychology has quickly been taken up by the education sector with vigor. Positive psychology now bridges into a plethora of areas related to education. This chapter broadly aims to present an overview of where positive psychology within education has progressed. More specifically, it is useful to hear of the types of approaches schools have taken to place positive psychology into their existing frameworks, the depth of their intervention, and how they have utilized this information to ameliorate positive psychology in all education circles.

The inclusion of positive psychology into a school's curriculum depends on the comfort level of the faculty and staff and the needs of the students. Three levels of implementation seem to emerge from the literature and practice. The first level is the shallowest level of implementation as individual instructors incorporate positive psychology–themed lessons into existing courses or programs. The second level goes a little deeper as instructors teach courses specifically in positive psychology. The third and final level is the deepest level of implementation. With this level, school-wide positive psychology instruction and interventions are implemented. Often, community outreach is included in this level of implementation. We see these three levels of implementation as akin to learning how to swim—some people begin to learn by dipping their toes into the water, testing it out to see if it is too hot or cold. Others wade in, gradually getting used to the water and testing their own abilities for swimming. Yet others jump right in, eager to swim on their own in the quickest way possible. The three levels can also be considered as a sequential pathway for schools to guide themselves to effectively implement organizational change or curriculum development. Each method has its advantages and disadvantages, and we will discuss each level in more detail throughout this chapter.

## APPROACHES TO TEACHING POSITIVE PSYCHOLOGY

The early approach to teaching positive psychology took two main forms (Seligman, 1998)—dedicated instruction in positive psychology principles and infusing positive psychology into existing courses. Positive psychologists worked early on to "build the fifth pillar" of the discipline (Seligman, 1998) by developing specific teaching materials on positive psychology for teachers to use. Although the original goal was to produce two unit plans for high school teachers, only one was written and eventually disseminated by the American Psychological Association (Fineburg, 2001). Since that unit plan's publication, other resources have emerged, most recently with the publication of an activities handbook for positive psychology (Froh & Parks, 2012) and a sequential set of well-being lessons for secondary school students based upon principles and findings of positive psychology (Boniwell & Ryan, 2012). Using these resources, instructors can incorporate as much positive psychology as they feel comfortable with, fulfilling the first two levels of implementation described in this chapter. In doing so, instructors should also pay attention to the importance of school settings to not only be a place to teach students tools for a successful life but also to teach fulfillment and well-being (Seligman, 2009), which can also be successfully achieved with the understanding of positive psychology principles such as character strengths. Beyond this, positive psychologists envisioned teachers emphasizing positive traits and helping students focus on participating in activities of which to be proud, such as service learning projects. This approach most closely mirrors the deepest level of implementation, in which school-wide and community efforts are used. With each level of implementation, the goals of positive psychologists to get educators and schools to teach positive psychology are in the process of being fulfilled.

TESTING THE WATERS

Because the intersection of positive psychology and education is easily drawn, educators seem naturally interested in lessons that introduce or apply positive psychology principles. As psychologists and educators discover positive psychology, they may seek out specific activities to teach positive psychology concepts in their existing courses. Although this conservative approach is slow and steady, it allows for a degree of exploration and flexibility within the comfort zone of students and staff. Justifying the introduction of applied positive psychology into a school setting may be based upon the grounds of building student knowledge, seeking evidence-based outcomes for student well-being, or applying positive psychology concepts to a context relevant to the students' lives (i.e., sport, academic achievement, building relationships in the school environment, overcoming obstacles such as social and emotional challenges). Regardless of the type of introduction, the promotion of teaching principles and concepts of positive psychology seems to be a fulfillment of positive psychology as a discipline.

These concepts are most easily integrated into the introductory psychology course, which is typically a course providing an overview of the discipline as a whole. Some positive psychology concepts have been included in traditional introductory psychology textbooks for a long while (i.e., love and attraction, prosocial behavior), whereas others have only been included in recent years (i.e., flow, optimism, hope). The gradual yet steady inclusion of positive psychology concepts into introductory psychology texts shows that the discipline has been accepted into the mainstream of psychology as a whole.

Not all psychologists and educators readily embrace positive psychology. Several detailed critiques of positive psychology have surfaced throughout the last 20 years. Some propose that positive psychology is merely a repackaging of other schools or movements, such as humanistic psychology or positive thinking (Ehrenreich, 2009; Lazarus, 2003; Schneider, 2011). This criticism may contribute to some educators and psychologists being hesitant to teach a full course in positive psychology at their institution. Budget constraints or limited time in a school's schedule also prevent schools from fully embracing positive psychology. So instead of courting criticism or altering a school's schedule or course offerings, teachers teach individual lessons or units on positive psychology topics. Data on the number of lessons in positive psychology that are taught or on the number of instructors who use this level of implementation for teaching positive psychology have not ever been collected in a formal way. However, in Australia there is anecdotal support to indicate the number of schools implementing some form of educational approach based upon the concepts of positive psychology may be in the region of 40–50 schools as of 2012. Considering there were reportedly 9,427 schools located in Australia in 2012 (Australian Bureau of Statistics, 2013), at most 50 schools who are implementing an explicit approach in school represents about 0.5%, an extremely small percentage.

According to the Positive Psychology Center at the University of Pennsylvania, 65 psychologists have identified themselves as positive psychologists. These instructors likely incorporate teaching positive psychology in their courses in a tangible way, but they do not seem to have other colleagues at their institutions that also self-identify as positive psychologists or with positive psychology in general. Since its publication in 2001, over 300 instructors worldwide have requested the 7-day unit plan on positive psychology published by the American Psychological Association, which gives some indication of how widespread the interest in teaching positive psychology is on the most basic level (A. Fineburg, personal communication, August 25, 2013).

Another approach for a school to teach positive psychology has been to build both the students' and the teachers' understanding of the most contemporary findings of positive psychology by infusing concepts into existing psychology curricula. This approach has been well-received in the past (Fineburg, 2004). An alternative integration method applies the principles of positive psychology to build levels of well-being and fulfillment as an evidence-based outcome approach. This form can have more of an active or experiential approach rather than an explicit curriculum-based approach, which may be easier for younger children and adolescents to grasp. These experiential lessons can be one-off lessons or delivered as part of an existing well-being or pastoral care program within the school; however, the level of successful integration needs to be thought through prior to implementation. Educators need to be mindful of the learning environment and learning capacities of the students in regard to the complexity of the concept being taught and the outcomes desired.

Although the effects of a single lesson or activity may be difficult to gauge, it is known that reduced levels of subjective well-being in children through negative affect is linked with decreased academic performance, whereas interventions that increase the frequency of positive emotions enhance learning (Seligman, Ernst, Gillham, Reivich, & Linkins, 2009). In addition, high levels of school satisfaction in children via greater frequency of positive affect were associated with school-based benefits such as higher GPAs, a greater sense of agency, fewer adolescent problems, and student engagement (Huebner, Gilman, Reschly, & Hall, 2009). Achieving a greater level of school satisfaction may be found in schools that contribute to social acceptance, peer support, appropriate praise, "flow," a focus on strengths rather than deficits, and promotion of autonomy and choice (Huebner, Gilman, Reschly, & Hall, 2009). It seems that simply teaching positive psychology and providing a school environment that reflects positive psychology concepts may improve school satisfaction and the learning capacity of the students.

Testing the waters of positive psychology in schools can begin with a subject-centered approach in which existing psychology curricula are enhanced or as a student-centered approach in which existing pastoral, well-being, or social-emotional learning curricula are reinforced with identified concepts and theory. Underlying this low-level approach is fidelity to the concepts taught and an exploration of the impacts of the learning and experience on student health and well-being.

## WADING IN

A second way to introduce positive psychology into a school is for instructors to complete courses in positive psychology. This secondary stage of implementation extends self-interest for an individual or organization to a point where formal education can be undertaken and then applied in personal and professional environments. Course options range from overview courses such as Introduction to Positive Psychology, to concept-specific courses such as Well-Being and the Practice of Law (offered by Dan Bowling in 2012 at Duke University), Psychology of Happiness (offered by Jamie Burk in 2006 at the University of Virginia), and Psychology of Leadership (offered by Tal Ben-Shachar in 2006 at Harvard University). According to the Positive Psychology Center's website, 36 colleges and universities have two or more faculty that identify with positive psychology, either as positive psychologists or as actively interested in topics within the positive psychology domain. At institutions with multiple faculty members who identify with positive psychology, specific courses in positive psychology are likely taught.

Educators can also wade into positive psychology by implementing programs that address specific student issues or outcomes. Programs that address so-called "noncognitive" skills that fall comfortably within the realm of positive psychology can help students build positive skill sets and tackle negative student behavior. The movement of positive psychology into the education sector has highlighted the importance of schools in the development of social, emotional, and psychological well-being of children for their lives and for academic learning. Many schools in Australia have taken on positive psychology–based interventions such as using character strengths; however, concepts such as building resilience have been instilled into education programming in Australia for some time. Programs such as Bounceback! (Noble & McGrath, 2013), Resourceful Adolescent Program (RAP; Queensland University of Technology, 2013), MoodGYM (Australian National University, 2013), and Mindmatters (Mindmatters, 2013) have been developed to assist in the development of individuals' well-being. On a much larger scale, a major step in incorporating the philosophy of positive psychology is the Australian Curriculum and Assessment Authority (ACARA). ACARA has been in a process of developing a national curriculum, and under the subject of health and physical education, a focus has been proposed to take on a strengths-based approach in ACARA's commitment to promote psychological well-being and prosocial behavior (ACARA, 2013). This level of governance demonstrates the steady progress being made to expand the horizons of education beyond the traditional academic means.

In the United States, comprehensive programs that look beyond the academic elements of school have developed alongside programs that have specific positive psychology roots. One such program is the Whole-Child Initiative, developed by the Association for Supervision and Curriculum Development (ASCD). Since its launch in 2007, this initiative has been supporting educators, parents, communities, and policymakers to change their perspective of education from one based primarily on academic achievement to one that encompasses long-term development and success of the child. This approach underscores the change occurring in education and the need to ensure each child is healthy, safe, engaged, supported, and challenged (ASCD, 2013). Such support is assisting in guiding individuals, groups, and communities to enact positive change in learning at any level of positive psychology implementation.

Diving In

A few schools and departments around the world have implemented a comprehensive approach to teaching positive psychology. This approach not only offers direct instruction in positive psychology concepts and principles, but also implements school-wide and community interventions that apply positive psychology. One institution has embraced positive psychology more fully than others. The University of Pennsylvania, the home institution of Martin Seligman, the founder of positive psychology, also houses the Positive Psychology Center (PPC), a comprehensive research program responsible for implementing programs in neuroscience, resilience training, and well-being. The University of Pennsylvania is one of only two institutions offering a degree-granting program in positive psychology, and the PPC provides support and research opportunities for undergraduate students. Undertaking such a degree enforces rigor in the teachings of positive psychology beyond simply learning about positive psychology into a domain supported with the most up-to-date findings and access to global researchers teaching about their findings. Another university that has undertaken the challenge to offer a positive psychology degree is the University of Melbourne, Australia. Akin to the Master of Applied Positive Psychology degree at the University of Pennsylvania, the University of Melbourne launched a Master of Applied Positive Psychology, and in 2013, it hosted its first course to equip its students with positive psychology principles for application in their professional and personal lives (Melbourne Graduate School of Education, 2013). Issues with the comprehensive teaching of positive psychology principles are the level of pedagogical skill of the teacher (Seligman et al., 2009), the teaching methods used, and level of training the teacher has had (Hale, Coleman, & Layard, 2011). Undertaking explicit training at a recognized postsecondary level is an important step in committing to a sustainable and effective implementation of positive psychology in schools. The degree programs offered in applied positive psychology can help build the skills of teachers in the classroom and provide resources for choosing appropriate activities and teaching methods.

Another project that teaches positive psychology in a comprehensive way is the Penn Resiliency Program (PRP). This longitudinal program, lead by Jane Gillham and Karen Reivich, trains teachers to implement lessons in schools that teach students how to be resilient. The lessons are designed for elementary and middle-school students and last 60 to 90 minutes, depending on the format chosen. The PRP is what's commonly known as a "pull-out program," where students leave their traditional classrooms and engage in the lessons in a separate environment. Trained facilitators (who can be teachers at the school or researchers with the program) teach the lessons on resilience using techniques derived from cognitive psychology. The lessons use active learning strategies and assign students homework through which they implement the skills learned in the lessons into their daily lives. The students who are involved in this program are identified as at-risk for depression. Extensive research conducted on this program has shown that the PRP is successful in helping students avoid depression later in high school (see Brunwasser, Gillham, & Kim, 2009, for a recent review of the program).

Positive psychology in schools has been particularly popular in Australia. In 2008, Seligman, Gillham, Reivich, and their team partnered with Geelong Grammar School outside of Melbourne to institute a school-wide program implementing positive psychology. Geelong Grammar is a comprehensive day and boarding school serving students from preschool to year 12. The school consists of five campuses serving different populations of students. Students in year 9 attend the Timbertop campus as full boarding students. Students spend the year learning independence, teamwork, and leadership in a natural, rustic setting. The initial partnership between Geelong and the Positive Psychology Center consisted of two phases. The first trained teachers in research and practical applications of positive psychology. Then, scholars and practitioners worked in residence at Geelong during the school year to dialogue and implement practical strategies for incorporating positive psychology principles into the daily lives of students. The program has worked to teach specific lessons in positive psychology within the traditional curriculum and infuse a focus on mental health and well-being into the daily lives of students. The partnership has developed a comprehensive definition of positive education that has identified six domains that promote flourishing in students: relationships, emotion, engagement, accomplishment, health, and purpose (Geelong Grammar School, 2013). Through this partnership, the school has implemented positive psychology instruction, mental health protocols, and positive psychology–based experiences for students; a positive leadership program for teachers and nonteaching staff; and a positive psychology retreat for parents. The school has been at the forefront of developing a truly comprehensive positive psychology emphasis in a school community.

Other schools in Australia have followed Geelong's lead in adopting positive education. There are too many to describe in detail; however, some of the more progressive institutions and their approaches are summarized. Notably these schools reflect the three ways of implementation discussed throughout this chapter and demonstrate a clear dedication in translating research into lessons and strategies that are used in explicit classroom lessons or taught in a way that may be experientially based and considered as an implicit intervention. It is encouraging to see a common theme in that schools appear to be seeking to make positive change in individuals, groups, or communities through the use of the research findings of positive psychology. Although the vision is not a written plea shared among these schools, it seems that educating students in human flourishing, well-being, social-emotional education, or positive psychology itself is an evolutionary change in education that is for the betterment of humankind.

Scotch College Adelaide is a coeducational day and boarding school that has successfully adopted a positive education program throughout the school since 2010. The school accommodates nearly 1,000 children from ages 3 to 18 and, importantly, made a strategic decision to embed a philosophy of whole-child education in which the social-emotional learning is as important as the academic learning of the student. Explicitly, it has embedded the use of character strengths across subject areas to enhance learning and, similarly to Geelong Grammar School, extended Seligman's PERMA theory and created its own positive education model based upon six domains: Meaning and Purpose, Engagement, The World and Environment, Resilience, Positive Relationships, and Physical Health (Scotch College Adelaide, 2013). The school is also building upon research in the field of teaching gratitude, and by incorporating such interventions it will promote positive emotions, increase life-satisfaction, and build upon positive relationships, while also assisting in academic motivation (Bono, Froh, & Forrett, 2014). The school also explicitly measures student well-being through the use of the Middle Years Development Instrument (MDI; Department of Education South Australia, 2013) and the Australian Early Development Index (AEDI; Australian Government, 2013). The commitment to this approach has been extended recently to a point where the timetable has been adapted to accommodate over 250 explicit classroom Well-Being and Values Education (WAVE) lessons, which include an evidence-based set of personal well-being lessons (Boniwell & Ryan, 2012). The implementation of Educational Coaching (Monk & Kemp, 2013) at Scotch Adelaide School is promoting an engaging and learning culture for both staff and students and facilitates their model of positive education. This is manifest in courses for students and staff and leadership programs, in the hope of enhancing well-being across the school, and in doing so to apply the findings of evidence-based research (Grant, Green, & Rynsaardt, 2010; Knight, 2012).

Knox Grammar School, in Sydney, is an independent boys school of over 2,000 students ranging from kindergarten (age 5) to year 12 (age 18). The school reflects a multilevel, strategic approach to creating a positive school climate that supports academic performance, mental fitness, resilience, and well-being of staff and students. This has been achieved through the application of organizational psychology, appreciative inquiry, and evidence-based coaching (Knox Grammar School, 2013). St Peter's School in Adelaide is an Anglican boys' school that has largely contributed to the broader South Australian education community in partnering with the Adelaide Thinkers in Residence Program and was visited by Martin Seligman in 2012 and 2013 (St. Peter's College, 2013). The school invested in building human resources by training all of their staff in positive psychology through the University of Pennsylvania's PPC. Their dedication was promoted beyond the physical space of the school and facilitated greater awareness in the importance of positive psychology and its value in education for the public. Specifically, the school has introduced the teaching of both explicit and implicit lessons for their boys in their Early Learning Centre to year 10 of secondary school. The programs chosen include evidence-based psychological approaches and teaching strategies such as the Penn Resiliency Program (PRP) and the Strath Haven Program. In the government sector of education, Mount Barker High School, set in the Adelaide Hills of South Australia, has also spent time working with Martin Seligman and incorporated his PERMA theory into its curriculum. This high school has been pioneering in that it garners the support of people in and outside of the school and aims to develop a "whole of community" approach to enhance the well-being of the students in their locality (Mount Barker High School, 2013). Another government-funded school that has adopted positive education is Tully State High School in Queensland, Australia. The positive education program is designed under the guidance of psychologist Suzy Green (The Positivity Institute, 2013) and specifically aims to promote resilience and positive thinking following natural disasters. Importantly, this unique program identified the needs of the school and based its approach upon evidence-based positive psychology principles such as journal writing, random acts of kindness, gratitude, and optimistic thinking (Keegan, 2013).

These particular schools all follow the notion that applying explicit lessons based upon principles of positive psychology is an integral first step for students to fully grasp the experience of a particular concept and sustain confidence in developing their social-emotional learning pathway. If individuals, groups, and communities are going to flourish through the promotion of positive psychology interventions in education, and hopefully attempt to reduce the disharmony mental illness can bring, then there needs to be a commitment to transform a school and its community so they can fulfill their obligation in raising the whole child. The schools aforementioned are well on their way to achieving this outcome.

## FUTURE DIRECTIONS

Positive psychology in education has already yielded exciting outcomes for students, teachers, and schools. Research has demonstrated that schools that incorporate positive psychology through pull-out programs or as a comprehensive school approach produce significant mental health benefits for students. As these programs are implemented in other settings, more research is needed to ensure that the programs remain effective with growth.

Research is needed to see if less-comprehensive approaches to positive education are effective in any way. Little, if any, research has been done to see how widespread positive psychology instruction is in high schools or universities. Although instructors have self-identified as positive psychologists or report that they teach positive psychology in some way, no formal research has been done to measure the quantity or quality of this instruction. In addition, research that examines whether more light-handed positive psychology interventions have any affect on student behavior or performance is scant. It is not known whether learning about positive psychology in general or participating in positive psychology lessons or activities has any effect on a student's well-being in the short or long term. Such research would be important for creating lessons and activities that not only teach the concepts of the discipline but also enhance the well-being of students learning about them.

Another area of potential for positive education is the study of qualities that enhance student learning. Educational psychologists have long been interested in student, teacher, and school qualities that enhance learning. Positive psychology has much to offer in this area. The Penn Resiliency Program has demonstrated that interventions originally targeted toward clinical psychology can be adapted for work with students at risk for doing poorly in school. As schools struggle with rising dropout rates and greater scrutiny for producing successful students, it seems as though interventions from positive psychology, with its more proactive approach to health and well-being, may offer avenues to addressing student and school failures. The Whole Child Initiative (ASCD, 2013), Duckworth's (2013) work on grit, and Dweck's (2006) work on growth mindset have all contributed to the discussion of "noncognitive" or nonacademic factors that can determine a student or school's success. These areas point to the need for more interaction between educational and positive psychology to address some of society's greatest concerns about educational systems.

Overall, there seems to be an abundance of examples in which schools have made a starting point of implementing positive psychology, which reflects the three levels of implementation. These starting points do have their weaknesses, and many future failures can be thought of, such as biased interest and enthusiasm from particular individual school members, selected positive psychology concepts failing to stand up to public scrutiny or promise too much but deliver very little, and the proponents of the implementation being self-serving and using the ideas for their own personal advantage (Csikszentmihalyi & Nakamura, 2011). There is an opportunity here to create guiding principles for schools to implement different levels and types of positive psychology approaches and for differing reasons. The challenge may be to create a set of globally agreed-upon standards to guide schools in teaching positive psychology concepts before interventions can be achieved. This would transform educational circles by reducing negative outcome repetitiveness, encouraging collaboration, and providing at least some framework for schools to have a confident starting point. Education may take a journey similar to Huppert and So (2011), whose 10 features of flourishing were identified as the opposites to diagnostic criteria for depression and anxiety. This created a starting framework of flourishing to compare, measure, and possibly better equip researchers in developing well-being on large scales, such as through national interventions (Huppert & So, 2011).

Although we may hope that many schools will begin their journey to implement positive psychology sometime in the future, we can be confident education has made significant progress so far. We are at a point where the term *positive education* is commonly viewed in schools today and a more all-encompassing education is deemed to be vital for future thriving in our students. Research is needed into the degrees of implementing positive education programs and how they are actively enhancing the well-being of the children into their adulthood.

Many positive psychology interventions for adolescents have successfully demonstrated the reduction of mental illness, such as the PRP and the RAP; however, there are opportunities for schools to investigate alternative measures of well-being, such as Keyes' two continua model (Westerhof & Keyes, 2010), which considers mental illness and mental health as interrelating dimensions and considers flourishing as a state of high subjective well-being and optimal psychological and social functioning. This would provide schools with an avenue to focus on becoming proactive with prevention of mental illness, such as depression and anxiety, while also enabling a co-focus on the measures of mental health. There is potential for research to measure and identify the symptoms of positive optimal functioning in terms of flourishing students, teachers, parents, and entire communities for the purpose of teaching skills and concepts that explicitly aim to enhance such optimal functioning. Finally, there is opportunity to discover where the correlation of positive psychology implementation with these measurements of flourishing can be demonstrated in a school environment.

## CONCLUSION

This chapter has described the three suggested levels of implementation a school can take to teach positive psychology to students. Positive psychology has certainly evolved and is becoming more popular for preparing youth for their future and facilitating schools to better address the need of whole-child education (social, emotional, physical, psychological, and cognitive well-being). In summary, one of the main pillars of positive psychology has been the field of education, and it is unquestionable that schools have successfully begun to implement explicit and implicit interventions.

## SUMMARY POINTS

- There are three main levels of intervention for a school to take on; we have affectionately termed these *testing the waters, wading in*, and *diving in*.
- Interventions in education can be based upon building knowledge of positive psychology in current psychology classes.
- Interventions may take on an evidence-based approach and attempt to build students' levels of resilience, optimism, gratitude, character strengths, and self-regulation, to name a few.
- Schools may invest in human resources and support teachers in completing a formal degree in positive psychology.
- National or international standards to assist schools in implementing evidence-based programs are a recommended area for development.

## REFERENCES

ABS. (2013). *4221.0—Schools, Australia, 2012.* Retrieved from www.abs.gov.au/AUSSTATS /abs@.nsf/Latestproducts/4221.0%20Features202012

ACARA. (2013). *Health and physical education.* Retrieved from www.acara.edu.au/verve/ _resources/Revised_HPE_curriculum_for_publication_on_ACARA_website_-_FINAL.pdf

ASCD. (2013). *The whole child.* Retrieved from www.wholechildeducation.org

Australian Government. (2013). *Australian Early Development Index.* Retrieved from www.rch .org.au/aedi

Australian National University. (2013). *The MoodGYM.* Retrieved from https://www .moodgym.anu.edu.au/welcome

Blair-Broeker, C. T., & Ernst, R. E. (2013). *Thinking about psychology.* New York, NY: Worth.

Boniwell, I., & Ryan, L. (2012). *Personal well-being lessons for secondary schools.* Berkshire, England: Open University Press.

Bono, G., Froh, J. J., & Emmons, R. A. (2012). Searching for the developmental role of gratitude: A 4-year longitudinal analysis. In J. Froh (chair), *Helping youth thrive: Making the case that gratitude matters.* Symposium conducted at the meeting of the American Psychological Association, Orlando, Florida.

Bono, G., Froh, J. J., & Forrett, R. (2014). Gratitude in school: Benefits to students and schools. In M. Furlong, R. Gilman, & E. S. Huebner (Eds.), *Handbook of positive psychology in schools* (2nd ed., pp. 67–81). New York, NY: Routledge.

Brunwasser, S. M., Gillham, J. E., & Kim, E. S. (2009). A meta-analytic review of the Penn resiliency program's effect on depressive symptoms. *Journal of Consulting and Clinical Psychology, 77,* 1042–1054.

Burns, J. M., Andrews, G., & Szabo, M. (2002). Depression in young people: What causes it and can we prevent it? *MJA, 177,* S93–S96.

Csikszentmihalyi, M., & Nakamura, J. (2011). Positive psychology: Where did it come from, where is it going? In K. M. Sheldon, T. B. Kashdan, & M. F. Steger (Eds.), *Designing positive psychology: Taking stock and moving forward* (pp. 3–21). New York, NY: Oxford University Press.

Department of Education South Australia. (2013). *Middle Years Development Instrument*. Retrieved from www.mdi.sa.edu.au

Duckworth, A. L. (2013). True grit. *The Observer, 26*(4), 1–3.

Duckworth, A. L., Grant, H., Loew, B., Oettingen, G., & Gollwitzer, P. M. (2011). Self-regulation strategies improve self-discipline in adolescents: Benefits of mental contrasting and implementation intentions. *Educational Psychology, 31*(1), 17–26.

Duckworth, A. L., & Seligman, M. E. P. (2005). Self-discipline outdoes IQ in predicting academic performance of adolescents. *Psychological Science, 16*, 939–944.

Dweck, C. S. (2006). *Mindset: The new psychology of success*. New York, NY: Random House.

Ehrenreich, B. (2009). *Bright-sided: How the relentless promotion of positive thinking has undermined America*. New York, NY: Metropolitan Books.

Fineburg, A. (2004). Introducing positive psychology to the introductory psychology student. In P. A. Linley & S. Joseph, *Positive psychology in practice* (pp. 197–209). Hoboken, NJ: Wiley.

Fineburg, A. C. (2001). *Positive psychology: A seven-day unit plan for teachers*. Washington, DC: American Psychological Association.

Froh, J. J., & Parks, A. C. (2012). *Activities for teaching positive psychology: A guide for instructors*. Washington, DC: American Psychological Association.

Geelong Grammar School. (2013). *Model of positive education*. Retrieved from http://www.ggs.vic.edu.au/PosEd/Model-of-Positive-Education.aspx

Gillham, J. E., Reivich, K. J., Freres, D. R., Chaplin, T. M., Shatte, A. J., Samuels, B., . . . Seligman, M. E. P. (2007). School-based prevention of depressive symptoms: A randomized controlled study of the effectiveness and specificity of the Penn Resiliency Program. *Journal of Consulting and Clinical Psychology, 75*, 9–19.

Grant, A. M., Green, L. S., & Rynsaardt, J. (2010). Developmental coaching for high school teachers: Executive coaching goes to school. *Coaching Psychology Journal: Practice and Research, 62*(3), 151–168.

Hale, D., Coleman, J., & Layard, R. (2011). *A model for the delivery of evidence-based PSHE (personal wellbeing) in secondary schools*. London, England: Centre for Economic Performance.

Hodges, T. D., & Clifton, D. O. (2004). Strengths-based development in practice. In P. A. Linley & S. Joseph (Eds.), *Handbook of positive psychology in practice*. Hoboken, NJ: Wiley.

Huebner, E. S., Gilman, R., Reschly, A. L., & Hall, R. (2009). Positive schools. In S. J. Lopez, & C. R. Snyder, *The Oxford handbook of positive psychology* (pp. 561–568). New York, NY: Oxford University Press.

Huppert, F. A., & So, T. T. (2011). Flourishing across Europe: Application of a new conceptual framework for defining well-being. *Social Indicators Research, 110*, 837–861. doi:10.1007/s11205-011-9966-7

Keegan, B. (2013, February 1). Students go back to school for lessons in resilience. *Cairns Post*.

Knight, J. (2012). Coaching to improve teaching: Using the instructional coaching model. In C. van Nieuwerburgh (Ed.), *Coaching in Education* (pp. 93–113). London, England: Karnac Books.

Knox Grammar School. (2013). *Positive education*. Retrieved from www.knox.nsw.edu.au/positive-education

Lazarus, R. S. (2003) Does the positive psychology movement have legs? *Psychological Inquiry, 14*, 93–109.

Linley, P. A., & Joseph, S. (Eds.). (2004). *Positive psychology in practice* (pp. 197–209). Hoboken, NJ: Wiley.

Lopez, S. J., & Louis, M. C. (2009). The principles of strengths-based education. *The Journal of College and Character, 10*(4), 1940–1639.

Lopez, S. J., Rose, S., Robinson, C., Marques, S. C., & Pais-Reibero, J. (2009). Measuring and promoting hope in schoolchildren. In R. Gilman, E. S. Huebner, & M. J. Furlong (Eds.), *Promoting wellness in children and youth: Handbook of positive psychology in the schools* (pp. 37–51). New York, NY: Routledge.

Melbourne Graduate School of Education. (2013). *Master of applied positive psychology.* Retrieved from http://education.unimelb.edu.au/study_with_us/professional_development/course_list/the_melbourne_master_of_applied_positive_psychology

Mindmatters. (2013). *About Mindmatters.* Retrieved from www.mindmatters.edu.au/about-mindmatters/what-is-mindmatters

Monk, A., & Kemp, T. (2013). *Educational coaching.* Adelaide, SA, Australia: The Educational Coaching Framework.

Mount Barker High School. (2013). *Positive education.* Retrieved from mtbhs.sa.edu.au/positive_education.htm

Myers, D. G. (2014). *Psychology for AP^{TM}* (2nd ed.). New York, NY: Worth.

Noble, T., & McGrath, H. (2013). *Bounceback!* Retrieved from www.bounceback.com.au/bounce-back

The Positivity Institute. (2013). *The Positivity Institute.* Retrieved from www.thepositivityinstitute.com.au

Queensland University of Technology. (2013). *Resourceful Adolescent Program.* Retrieved from www.rap.qut.edu.au

Schneider, K. (2011). Toward a humanistic positive psychology: Existential analysis. *Journal of the Society for Existential Analysis, 22,* 32–38.

Scotch College Adelaide. (2013). *Wellbeing and positive education.* Retrieved from www.scotch.sa.edu.au/wellbeing---positive-education.html

Seligman, M. E. (2009). Foreword. In S. J. Lopez (Ed.), *The encyclopedia of positive psychology* (pp. xviii–xix). Chichester, England: Wiley.

Seligman, M. E., Ernst, R. M., Gillham, J., Reivich, K., & Linkins, M. (2009). Positive education: Positive psychology and classroom interventions. *Oxford Review of Education, 35,* 293–311.

Seligman, M. E. P. (1998). *Positive psychology network concept paper.* Retrieved from http://www.ppc.sas.upenn.edu/ppgrant.htm

Snyder, C. R., Shorey, H. S., Cheavens, J., Pulvers, K. M., Adams, V. H., & Wiklund, C. (2002). Hope and academic success in college. *Journal of Educational Psychology, 94,* 820–826.

St. Peter's College. (2013). *Partnerships.* Retrieved from www.stpeters.sa.edu.au/wellbeing/partnerships

Westerhof, G. J., & Keyes, C. L. (2010). Mental illness and mental health: The two continua model across the lifespan. *Journal of Adult Development, 17,* 110–119.

Worrell, F. C., & Hale, R. L. (2001). The relationship of hope in the future of perceived school climate to school completion. *School Psychology Quarterly, 16,* 370–388.

# CHAPTER 17

# Positively Transforming Classroom Practice Through Dialogic Teaching

ALINA REZNITSKAYA and IAN A. G. WILKINSON

I N THIS CHAPTER, we discuss the challenges and possibilities of helping elementary school teachers engage in dialogic teaching, a pedagogical approach that capitalizes on the power of talk to foster students' thinking, understanding, and learning. We start by reviewing theory and research on dialogic teaching, demonstrating both the educational potential of this approach and the near absence of its use by practitioners. To help bridge the gap between theory and practice, we describe a professional development program in dialogic teaching designed to support teacher use of new discourse practices and their eventual transition to a more dialogic interaction with students.

There is now little, if any, disagreement about the importance of teaching students how to think through complex problems in a deliberate, informed, and rational manner. Numerous scholarly publications and major policy documents call on educators to help their students develop the ability to make better, more reasonable judgments (e.g., Kuhn, 1992; Lipman, 2003; National Governors Association Center for Best Practices & The Council of Chief State School Officers, 2010; Partnership for 21st Century Skills, 2012; Wegerif, 2010). In his book *The End of Education: Redefining the Value of School*, Postman (1995) made a convincing case for teaching students "how to argue, and to help them discover what questions are worth arguing about, and, of course, to make sure they know what happens when arguments cease" (pp. 73–74). Embracing these ideas, the latest Common Core State Standards Initiative (National Governors Association Center for Best Practices & The Council of Chief State School Officers, 2010) in the United States has placed a special emphasis on argument literacy, considering it to be a fundamental life skill that is "broadly important for the literate, educated person living in the diverse, information-rich environment of the twenty-first century" (p. 25).

Yet, despite the emerging consensus on the value of argument skills, we do not know enough about how these skills develop, nor how best to prepare today's practitioners to teach these skills in a classroom. In this chapter, we discuss dialogic

*Authors' Note.* This research was supported in part by the grant from the Institute of Educational Sciences, U.S. Department of Education. Grant # R305A120634.

teaching, a pedagogical approach that has the potential to promote the development of argumentation. In dialogic teaching, students take on roles and responsibilities that have been traditionally reserved for the teachers: They "make substantial and significant contributions . . . [as they] articulate, reflect upon, and modify their own understandings" (Mercer & Littleton, 2007, p. 41). We believe that dialogic teaching will be of interest to positive psychologists because it redefines the teacher–student relationship and supports educational experiences that are intellectually stimulating and personally meaningful. Further, an important outcome of dialogic teaching—the ability to think about complex, contestable issues in a systematic and comprehensive manner—has the potential to empower students to lead more examined and fulfilling lives.

In a chapter written for the previous edition of this volume (Reznitskaya & Sternberg, 2004), we suggested that in order to make sound judgments, students need to learn how to think dialogically. Further, we proposed that dialogic thinking develops as students take part in educational settings that are, themselves, dialogic. Over the last several years, we continued to explore the notions of dialogic teaching and learning. We refined relevant definitions and identified key features of more dialogic classrooms. We also developed a comprehensive theory of learning through dialogue and proposed the underlying epistemological assumptions, cognitive and social processes, and student outcomes. Drawing on theory and research, as well as established pedagogical frameworks that center around dialogue, we worked on translating our theory into specific instructional principles and activities to be used with elementary students in language arts classrooms. We aligned our curriculum to the institutional demands and policies of the educational establishment in the United States, and designed a professional development program for practicing teachers.

In the rest of the chapter, we define and illustrate dialogic teaching, review key theoretical propositions and relevant empirical research, and describe our first trial of a professional development program for practitioners. We discuss the general principles and goals of the program, as well as the discoveries we made as we designed and implemented our program in collaboration with language arts teachers in elementary school classrooms.

## DIALOGIC TEACHING: DEFINITIONS, THEORY, AND EVIDENCE

Following Alexander (2008), we define *dialogic teaching* as a general pedagogy that capitalizes on the power of talk to foster students' thinking, understanding, and learning. Central to this pedagogy, we believe, is the teacher's capacity to draw from a repertoire of communicative approaches that further students' development, while privileging the use of inquiry dialogue to promote rational thinking and deep understanding of a subject. We chose the term *inquiry dialogue* (Walton & Macagno, 2007) to denote that the purpose of the engagement is to collectively think about complex problems and to formulate more reasonable judgments in relation to these problems, not to win over opponents. During inquiry dialogue, participants do not simply try to convince each other by justifying their positions with reasons and evidence; they also actively seek alternative propositions and are willing to change their views in light of the new arguments considered by the group.

### TEACHING THROUGH DIALOGUE

Inquiry dialogue is initiated by an open, *big question* about a contestable issue that is relevant to students' lives. The purpose of big questions is neither to test students nor to simply lead them to a narrow range of answers deemed acceptable by the teacher. Rather, these questions invite students to take part in a disciplined inquiry—a higher pedagogical goal. They "problematize, or transform commonly accepted facts or answers into problems to be explored, thereby opening knowledge to thinking" (Lefstein, 2010, p. 176). During inquiry dialogue, students are given considerable control over the flow of discourse: They ask questions, participate in turn management, and evaluate each other's answers. Together, discussion participants search for the most reasonable solution to the contestable question, and if agreement is not possible, they work on clarifying the basis and criteria for their disagreement. The teacher's role is to support collaborative inquiry around contestable questions. During the discussion, teachers "treat students as potential sources of knowledge and opinion, and in so doing complicate expert–novice hierarchies" (Nystrand, Wu, Gamoran, Zeiser, & Long, 2003, p. 140). Importantly, such a view of teacher–student relations does not dismiss the authority of a teacher as a more knowledgeable partner in a discussion. Burbules (1993) has argued that acknowledging authority based on one's expertise or experience does not necessarily threaten the egalitarian nature of interactions and, instead, helps to enhance the intellectual rigor of inquiry.

Below we illustrate the use of inquiry dialogue in a language arts classroom. This excerpt is taken from a recent study that examined teaching practices of elementary school teachers (Reznitskaya, Glina, Carolan, et al., 2012, p. 299). The discussion is based on the story about an unusual giraffe who learns to speak human language and has to decide whether to live with humans or other "regular" giraffes in the zoo (Lipman, 1996). The story prompted students to question what makes one eligible to vote on important decisions.

| | |
|---|---|
| Cindy: | For the voting, I would think you shouldn't have to be any age, but, like, 8 or something because you could learn politics. Like Tom said. And you can learn who it is and what they want for our country. |
| Teacher: | So, as long as you know those things? |
| Cindy: | Yeah, as long as you know . . . Jennifer. |
| Jennifer: | I disagree. I think that you should be 18, because 18 is considered an adult, probably because if you get into a college or something, that's when you will be going to college, when you're 18, and also mature enough to vote for presidents and things like that . . . Anthony. |
| Anthony: | I agree, but when you're 18, most of the time you're mature by then, but sometimes you're just, you're not mature. But you can't make exceptions for the few people that aren't. So, it would be easier to make everyone at 18 vote. |
| Teacher: | Even if they're not, even if they're not mature by then? |
| Anthony: | Yeah, because it would be hard to, like, exclude them from everybody else, and it wouldn't be fair to them. |
| Teacher: | Hmmm. . . . Okay. So we, we choose an age just to be fair then? |
| Anthony: | [nods yes] . . . Ann. |
| Ann: | I don't think it's just to be fair. I mean, I think that they expect people to be mature, but really, there are kids at 18 who *die* from doing stupid stuff. Like, how are they going to tell us what's good for the country and stuff, if they're doing stupid stuff? Like, you got to be pretty dumb to do some stuff that kids do. |
| Teacher: | Well, and isn't the alternative true? Aren't there, say, 16-year-olds that maybe have had to work after school or help making big decisions in their family because, just because of circumstances? Wouldn't we say that they are, kind of, more mature than some 18-year-olds? |

Ann:        Yeah . . . Tom.

Tom:        With what Anthony said, like, "it's just to be fair," and it isn't fair for *us* then. Kids our age got to vote, and if, if voting for presidents is too major for us, then we should be able to vote for something else then, something for our school.

Note that in this excerpt students and the teacher share control over classroom discourse. The students take over two functions typically performed by the teachers: nominating to speak and, to an extent, questioning. There are exchanges with consecutive student turns without teacher interruption, which demonstrate that students are successfully contributing to the management of turn-taking. The discussion is centered around a big question that is inherently contestable and does not have a clear right answer. As students discuss their positions on the issue of voting, they provide elaborated explanations of reasoning behind their views. The teacher does not dominate the discussion, speaking less than students. He also works to raise the quality of discussion beyond simple sharing of opinions. The teacher's deliberately chosen questions serve to advance the inquiry further, by prompting students to clarify their thinking (i.e., "So, we choose the age to be fair, then?") or introducing a new perspective, overlooked by the group (i.e., " . . . and isn't the alternative true?"). Student responses are marked by a high level of collaboration; they agree and disagree with each other's viewpoints, thus developing a more complete and personally meaningful understanding of the issues involved in formulating the required qualifications for voting.

By contrast, very different patterns of engagement can be seen in an excerpt from another classroom. Students in this classroom discuss a Native American tale about a young man who showed kindness to two eagles (Rosebud Yellow Robe, 2001). In return, the eagles saved the man's life by carrying him to safety.

Teacher:    Okay. So now he got stuck on the cliff. So now what? That's a big problem. . . . But, first of all, why did he want to reach the eagles? Gabriel?

Gabriel:    Because he wanted to bring them back to his tribe so that everyone would have, like, a feather for everybody.

Teacher:    Okay. He didn't want to bring the eagles back. He wanted to bring what back, Trisha?

Trisha:     The feathers.

Teacher:    The feathers. For what? What's it called? For what headgear? Who's that person? What are they called? Andrew?

Andrew:     The chief.

Teacher:    The chief. The . . . ? Starts with a W.

Jack:       Warriors.

Teacher:    Warriors. For the warriors' headgear. And what problem did he reach, when he was trying to reach the eagles again? He got what, Marla?

Marla:      The rope, it was broke.

Teacher:    It broke.

Marla:      And he fell down.

Teacher:    Okay. And he got stuck. So he wants to reach the eaglets. The nest is very high up on the mountain top. And what does he use to lower himself? What was the resource that he used?

Jeff:       A ladder.

Teacher:    Made out of what? Donna?

Donna:      Buffalo skin.

Note that in this excerpt the teacher is clearly the sole authority in the classroom. She controls both the content and the form of the discourse, calling on students to respond, evaluating their answers, and initiating topical shifts with new questions. Her questions largely prompt students to recall the facts from the story. The teacher already knows the correct answers and is the ultimate source of expertise when evaluating students' responses. Her feedback to students represents simple positive reinforcement and the repetition of correct responses. The teacher does not prompt students to support their positions with reasons, to consider alternatives, or to question assumptions and implications. Instead, she moves rapidly from student to student, sacrificing deep intellectual engagement for broad but superficial participation. Students in this classroom do not explain their thinking in depth; their answers are brief, often consisting of only one or two words. They do not collaborate with each other; instead, they direct all their answers to the teacher, rather than peers.

The previous excerpt demonstrates the traditional sequence of (1) teacher question/nomination, (2) student answer, and (3) teacher evaluation, which is often characterized as a "recitation" script. This script is rather common in contemporary classrooms (Applebee, Langer, Nystrand, & Gamoran, 2003; Nystrand, 1997). In a recent observational study of 64 middle- and high-school English classrooms in five states, Applebee et al. (2003) found that the amount of time spent on open discussions averaged only 68 seconds per class. Similar practices have been documented in a large study of teaching practices in the United Kingdom, where the authors routinely observed "the rapid pace of teachers' questioning and the predictable sequence of teacher-led recitation" (Smith, Hardman, Wall, & Mroz, 2004, p. 408). Moreover, recitation script has been shown to be highly resistant to change, even when teachers have progressive notions about the value of dialogue in teaching (Alexander, 2005; Alvermann, O'Brien, & Dillon, 1990). Thus, intensive and sustained professional development is needed to help teachers effectively implement dialogic teaching in their classrooms. We will return to this topic in the second part of the chapter, "Professional Development in Dialogic Teaching."

Thus far, we explained the concept of dialogic teaching and related terms and used two excerpts to illustrate the key differences between more monologic and more dialogic discussions. However, the picture is more nuanced than these excerpts suggest. Although we privilege inquiry dialogue as the central feature of dialogic teaching, we also recognize the need for other instructional strategies that can be used to support the goals of rational thinking and deeper learning. Alexander (2008) has criticized the use of artificial dichotomies in educational discourse that imply, for example, that teaching students how to think is incongruous with helping them acquire basic knowledge. He explained that teachers should be able to flexibly choose from a broad repertoire of pedagogical approaches, including more traditional methods such as recitation and exposition. For instance, teachers in a more dialogic classroom might, at times, ask students to recall simple facts (i.e., Is there the right to travel in the U.S. Constitution? What does the text say about the safety of self-driving cars?). However, they would do so in the service of promoting well-informed inquiry, rather than simply to have students memorize isolated bits of information. As with any other method, the use of dialogic teaching should not become dogmatic or restrictive. Instead, teachers need to be strategic and flexible in choosing instructional interventions that are consistent with their pedagogical goals, as well as with their assumptions about knowledge, teaching, and learning.

## EPISTEMOLOGY AND THEORY UNDERLYING DIALOGIC TEACHING

We propose that effective use of dialogic teaching requires that teachers develop underlying epistemic and pedagogical frameworks that are aligned with this approach (cf. Kuhn & Udell, 2003; Windschitl, 2002). Models of epistemological development suggest that people progress from a simple view of knowledge as static and known by authorities to a more nuanced understanding of knowledge as socially constructed through the use of reasoning (for review, see Hofer, 2001). Kuhn (1991) offers a useful classification of individual theories of knowledge, proposing three stages of development: absolutist, multiplist, and evaluatist. *Absolutists* view knowledge as fixed, certain, and existing independently of human cognition. *Multiplists* see knowledge as entirely subjective, denying the role of reason and expertise and considering all opinions to be equally valid. At the most advanced stage, *evaluatists* accept the subjective nature of knowledge, while also recognizing that we can engage in a rational evaluation of different viewpoints and, as a result, consider some judgments to be more reasonable than others.

Absolutist and multiplist epistemologies are incompatible with dialogic teaching. Teachers at the absolutist level believe that only authority figures have legitimate knowledge, so there is no need to involve students in knowledge co-construction, critique, and evaluation. Teachers with multiplist views fail to appreciate the value of dialogue because they see knowledge as entirely relative and idiosyncratic, discounting the use of reasoning to support and justify claims. By contrast, teachers who subscribe to an evaluatist epistemology are more likely to successfully implement dialogic teaching because they view knowledge as "the product of a continuing process of examination, comparison, evaluation, and judgment of different, sometimes competing, explanations and perspectives" (Kuhn, 1991, p. 202).

In addition to evaluatist epistemology, dialogic teaching reflects a *social-constructivist perspective* on learning (e.g., Piaget & Inhelder, 1969; Vygotsky, 1968). According to this perspective, students are active meaning-makers who learn through constructing and negotiating new understandings in interaction-rich communities of practice. Language is viewed as not only a medium for communicating ideas, but also as a primary tool for forming new ways of thinking and knowing (Vygotsky, 1968). Following Vygotsky, we believe that argument skills are developed, at least in part, through participation in a collective activity, such as a discussion about a contestable question during which students experience novel language and thought practices. Although each discussion is different, participants engage with common "cultural tools" (Vygotsky, 1981) characteristic of argumentation, including taking a public position on an issue, supporting it with reasons and evidence, challenging other participants, and responding to counterarguments with rebuttals. Over time, these processes, which are made "visible" in a group's argumentation, become part of an individual's repertoire of thinking strategies. Thus, collaborative engagement in inquiry dialogue represents a useful model and a training ground for the development of argument skills. As participants in discussions collectively formulate, defend, and scrutinize each other's viewpoints, they begin to internalize general intellectual dispositions, skills, and knowledge of reasoned argumentation.

To further define the learning outcomes resulting from student engagement in inquiry dialogue, we rely on constructivist approaches, in particular schema theory (e.g., Anderson, 1977; Rumelhart & Ortony, 1977). Schema theory proposes that knowledge can be represented as organized mental structures, or *schemas*. Learning involves generation and modification of these schemas, and successful transfer entails accessing and using relevant abstract structures (Gick & Holyoak, 1987; Reed, 1993). Applying schema theory to argumentation development, we propose that, through consistent engagement in inquiry dialogue, students come to recognize important commonalities in their experiences and, as a result, develop an internal abstract knowledge structure we call an *argument schema* (Reznitskaya et al., 2008). In order to specify the elements of an argument schema, we draw upon the normative models proposed by argumentation scholars (e.g., Toulmin, 1958; Walton, 1996). Specifically, we suggest that a well-developed argument schema includes such elements as position, reason, evidence, warrant, counterargument, and rebuttal. It contains the knowledge about the criteria for argument evaluation (i.e., validity of inferences, acceptability of premises), as well as the informal heuristics of reasoning. This knowledge supports comprehension, construction, and evaluation of arguments in new contexts. Importantly, different components of an argument schema are linked through a higher-order mental structure that "glues together" pieces of information that otherwise would remain unrelated or acausal (Mishra & Brewer, 2003). Following Kuhn (1999), a developed argument schema is supported by epistemic beliefs that recognize the function and value of a rational argument as a means for choosing among alternative propositions or actions, or an *evaluatist epistemology*.

To recap, in a more dialogic classroom, students experience new ways of formulating and expressing their viewpoints. As students discuss big, contestable questions with their peers, they observe, practice, and eventually internalize the skills of argumentation into individual mental structures, or *argument schemas*. Students can then use their argument schemas in other contexts, such as when discussing a new issue or when reading and writing arguments. Supporting and informing the entire process of argumentation development is a progressive shift in teachers' and, eventually, their students' epistemologies from an absolutist or multiplist view of knowledge to an evaluatist view. Teachers and students who subscribe to an evaluatist epistemology are more likely to view and use inquiry dialogue as a means of forming and evaluating different points of view. In a similar way, Kuhn (1999) suggests that advanced levels of epistemology are essential for engagement in argumentation, as they provide reasons for actually using the skills of argument when solving ill-structured problems. Consequently, evaluatist epistemology is both the necessary context for dialogic teaching and an important learning outcome for the students.

## EMPIRICAL RESEARCH ON DIALOGIC TEACHING

When examining research studies on dialogic teaching (e.g., Alexander, 2003; Applebee et al., 2003; Billings & Fitzgerald, 2002; Mercer & Littleton, 2007; Soter et al., 2008), we can see considerable consensus as to what constitutes typical features of more dialogic classrooms. Supporting the theoretical propositions outlined earlier, research reveals that dialogic classrooms have more egalitarian social organization, with authority over the content and form of discourse shared among discussion participants. Student learning is supported by open, cognitively challenging questions that engage students in critical evaluation and analysis. During the discussions, teachers play an important role by facilitating focused and rigorous inquiry: They build upon student answers, ask for clarification, prompt for alternative perspectives, and encourage students to relate their ideas to those of their peers in the discussion. As a result, students in more dialogic classrooms have new opportunities to engage in collaborative construction of knowledge, because they listen to and react to each other's positions and justifications.

We now turn to studies that examined the learning processes and outcomes in a more dialogic classroom. Although such research is still tentative, studies have generally documented that, following engagement in discussions, students show gains in reasoning in new contexts, argumentative writing, inferential comprehension of text, as well as deeper conceptual understanding of disciplinary concepts and principles

(Asterhan & Schwarz, 2007; Dong, Anderson, Li, & Kim, 2008; Kuhn & Crowell, 2011; Mercer, Wegerif, & Dawes, 1999; Reznitskaya et al., 2001). For example, students' ability to generate arguments that contained more than one perspective improved as a result of their participation in dialogic inquiry (Kuhn & Crowell, 2011). Similarly, in a review of several quasi-experimental studies on dialogic teaching (Reznitskaya et al., 2009), the authors concluded that students who participated in discussions about their readings consistently wrote essays that contained a greater number of argument components, including supporting reasons, counterarguments, and rebuttals, compared to their peers from control classrooms. The authors suggested that the experience of engaging in inquiry dialogue with peers allowed students to internalize important knowledge of argumentation. For example, it helped students to consider and integrate alternative positions in their compositions, thus supporting an important shift from monologic to dialogic thinking.

There is also emerging evidence regarding the influential role of personal epistemologies in teaching and learning. Studies of teacher epistemology have shown that beliefs about knowledge and knowing are often consistent with observed classroom practices (e.g., Schraw & Olafson, 2002; Sinatra & Kardash, 2004; Stipek, Givvin, Salmon, & MacGyvers, 2001). For example, in a study by Johnston, Woodside-Jiron, and Day (2001), researchers found that teachers' epistemologies were directly aligned with their instruction, influencing the power relations between teachers and students and their interactional patterns, including the type of questions discussed and the feedback given to students. However, the relationship between teacher beliefs and practice is not simple. Subscribing to more sophisticated ideas about knowledge and knowing might not always translate into the use of inquiry dialogue in a classroom (Alvermann et al., 1990; Schraw & Olafson, 2002), especially when teachers are in the processes of changing their beliefs, with "changes in beliefs preceding changes in practice" (Richardson, Anders, Tidwell, & Lloyd, 1991, p. 579).

Research on learner epistemologies has revealed that students at more advanced stages are more likely to better comprehend texts, to develop a deeper conceptual understanding of a given subject, to identify informal reasoning fallacies, and to construct arguments of higher quality (e.g., Mason & Scirica, 2006; Qian & Alvermann, 2000; Stromso & Braten, 2009; Weinstock, 2006; Weinstock, Neuman, & Tabak, 2004). These findings are consistent with the theoretical claims outlined earlier in this chapter, indicating that epistemological beliefs may act as general filters that direct one's engagement with argumentation.

In sum, argumentation skills are considered to be of vital importance for living a productive and meaningful life in a postindustrial globalized world of the 21st century. According to contemporary theory and research, these skills can be developed through dialogic teaching—a pedagogy that strategically uses classroom talk to promote students' thinking. Yet, studies continue to document that dialogic practices are rare in today's classrooms (Alexander, 2005; Mehan, 1998; Nystrand et al., 2003; Smith et al., 2004). Considering the consistent findings from research on classroom discourse, it is possible to imagine that many students go through schooling without ever experiencing a genuine discussion during which they are invited to collaboratively reason through a complex question in a systematic and rigorous way.

In an effort to address the apparent disparity between the higher educational goal of teaching argumentation and the reality of typical classroom practices, we have begun to design a comprehensive professional development program in dialogic teaching. This program targets elementary school teachers in language arts classrooms. We now turn to the discussion of the development and implementation of our program.

## PROFESSIONAL DEVELOPMENT IN DIALOGIC TEACHING

We are currently working on a 3-year project to design and evaluate a comprehensive professional development program in dialogic teaching.

OVERVIEW OF THE PROFESSIONAL DEVELOPMENT PROGRAM

In each year, we are trialing a version of the program and collecting data from teachers and students to assess program effectiveness and inform its revisions. In other words, each year comprises a new iteration of the program. The program has the following goals:

- To help teachers develop the pedagogical and epistemic views that are aligned with dialogic teaching.
- To sensitize teachers to the nature of talk and inquiry dialogue.
- To help teachers understand argumentation and criteria for evaluating arguments (i.e., develop their argument schemas).
- To provide teachers with a repertoire of moves to facilitate inquiry dialogue.

At the time of writing, we have completed the first year of the project. We conducted the project as a design study (Collins, Joseph, & Bielaczyc, 2004), during which we worked collaboratively with teachers throughout the year to identify and organize instructional activities that support teachers' knowledge and use of dialogic teaching to promote argumentation.

PARTICIPANTS

In year 1, we worked with 10 grade 5 teachers and their students. Study participants came from school districts in two states, Ohio and New Jersey. There were six teachers at the Ohio site and four teachers at the New Jersey site, with teaching experience ranging from 2 to 22 years.

PROCEDURE

The project in year 1 was conducted in three stages: pretesting, implementation of the professional development program, and posttesting. All project activities were similar at both sites, but with some variations to test the viability and effects of different instructional approaches or sequences of approaches. During pretesting stage (September), we video-recorded two discussions in each classroom in order to collect baseline information about typical teacher practices. We also interviewed teachers about their background and experience, as well as assessed their epistemological beliefs using the interview measure developed and validated by King and Kitchener (1994).

Starting in October, we began the implementation of the professional development program. We asked teachers to conduct discussions with their students at least once per month during their language arts lessons, and we video-recorded these discussions. We also met with teachers every 2 weeks in teacher study groups. Study groups lasted for about 1.5–2 hours, totaling approximately 30 hours per year at each site. During these study-group meetings, participating teachers engaged in mini-lessons, group activities, collaborative analysis of videos of classroom discussions, and exercises on topics related to dialogic teaching, inquiry dialogue, and argumentation. In addition, teachers read and discussed articles and chapters on these topics (e.g., Govier, 2010; Michaels, O'Connor, & Resnick, 2008; Waggoner, Chinn, Yi, & Anderson, 1995). After every four study group meetings (i.e., approximately every 2 months), we conducted focus-group interviews with teachers in each study group. The purpose of these focus-group interviews was to identify what teachers found valuable (or not) in learning about dialogic teaching and argumentation. Teachers also received individual coaching in how to conduct discussions to promote argumentation. During these sessions, teachers viewed and critiqued their own classroom interactions with the help of an experienced discourse coach, who supported the teachers' ongoing development and reflection. All study group meetings, focus-group interviews, and coaching sessions were audio-recorded.

Throughout the implementation of the program, teachers also practiced using three existing classroom observation tools to assess talk in their video-recorded discussions: the Instructional Quality Assessment Tool (Junker et al., 2006), the Talk Assessment Tool for Teachers (Wilkinson, Reninger, & Soter, 2010), and the Dialogic Inquiry Tool (Reznitskaya, Glina, & Oyler, 2012). Finally, teachers routinely documented reflections about their learning by posting to a discussion board on a program website.

During the posttesting stage (May), we again interviewed teachers about their epistemological beliefs. We also piloted student measures designed to assess argument skills when speaking, reading, and writing. These measures will be used to evaluate program effectiveness in years 2 and 3.

## CURRICULUM MATERIALS AND DATA SOURCES

At the end of year 1, we developed initial materials for the program, including Power-Point slides, instructional activities, videos for illustrating inquiry dialogue, and readings for teachers and students. We also collected data from multiple sources, including study-group meetings, focus-group interviews, coaching sessions, and teacher postings to a course website. We are conducting content analysis of the data to inform the revisions of the professional development program. In the next section, we discuss lessons learned as a result of year 1 implementation.

## LESSONS LEARNED

The design of our program was informed by the principles of effective professional development described in previous studies (e.g., Dole, 2003; Elmore, 2002; Hawley & Valli, 1999; Wei, Darling-Hammond, Andree, Richardson, & Orphanos, 2009; Yoon, Duncan, Lee, Scarloss, & Shapley, 2007). These principles include: the involvement of teachers in planning and undertaking professional development, the collective participation of groups of teachers, intensive and sustained support, and the integration of professional development into the daily lives of teachers. In year 1, we were able to translate these design principles into specific instructional activities. To address the need for collegial and ongoing engagement that is relevant to classroom practice, we structured our program as a series of 12 biweekly study-group meetings, followed up by in-class video-recording and individual coaching. During the study group meetings, teachers collaborated with each other and the researchers to learn about dialogic teaching, inquiry dialogue, and argumentation.

One helpful activity that emerged from the study-group meetings was coplanning. During coplanning, teachers or researchers brought examples of children's stories and articles to the meetings. Next, we selected a text for discussion and identified important themes from this text. For instance, an article about a boy that was paralyzed after getting a concussion during a football game brought up such themes as sports violence, the role of society in encouraging aggressive behaviors, the differences in responsibilities of adults versus children, groups versus individuals, and so on. These themes were then turned into big questions that served to launch the discussion. Next, study-group participants practiced engaging in inquiry dialogue around a contestable question (e.g., Who was responsible for the boy's injury?). The discourse coach acted as a discussion facilitator, modeling good practice for the teachers. After spending time on deliberating the big question, teachers evaluated the quality of their own discussion by reflecting on helpful discourse moves that supported argumentation.

From observations and teacher feedback, we learned that coplanning and engaging in inquiry dialogue provided a useful means for learning about various aspects of inquiry dialogue, including: (a) identifying contestable issues in children's literature, (b) launching the inquiry with a big question, (c) supporting argumentation development during the discussion with strategic facilitation moves, and (d) evaluating the processes and products of the discussion. As teachers discussed contestable questions with others, they were able to personally experience the possibilities and challenges of being a participant in an inquiry dialogue: They tried out new participation structures, developed and clarified their thinking on a big question, and had their ideas challenged by peers. We believe that these experiences helped teachers to acquire procedural knowledge about facilitating inquiry dialogue and to connect it to conceptual knowledge about the role of language in student learning. Coplanning and engaging in inquiry dialogue also offered teachers a shared experience that they were able to take back to the classroom, thus grounding their learning in practice.

In addition, teachers received ongoing support and targeted feedback about their implementation of dialogic teaching through individual coaching. During the coaching sessions, a teacher and a coach watched a recording of a recent discussion and engaged in collaborative problem solving and reflection. Teachers' reactions to coaching were uniformly positive, as illustrated by the comments below:

- "The one-on-one coaching I found to be, I think, the most helpful only because it's so hyperspecific."
- "I thought [the coaching] to be the most helpful because it was even better than just watching the video . . . it was watching it with purpose."
- "The coaching has been phenomenal. Watching the video with a coach and getting feedback on how I could have made a different move has helped me transfer that right into my teaching. It has also helped when I would watch by myself and feel like something had gone wrong, but didn't know what to do in the moment. Then I would show that to the coach and they would help me figure out what to do next time."
- "A couple of things [the coach] brought up that I just simply had never even considered . . . that he called out and said, 'You maybe could have done this here.'"

It appears that teachers appreciated having an opportunity to experiment with new dialogic practices in their classrooms, to reflect on the quality of their talk, and to evaluate their progress with an expert colleague in a systematic and supportive manner.

Another principle from research on professional development highlights the importance of having practitioners develop coherent pedagogical frameworks that integrate both theoretical and practical knowledge (e.g., Elmore, 2002). Real transformation in teaching happens only when teachers

> think differently about what is going on in their classrooms, and are provided with the practices that match the different ways of thinking. The provision of practices without theory may lead to misimplementation or no implementation at all. . . . [C]hanging beliefs without proposing practices that embody those theories may lead to frustration. (Richardson et al., 1991, p. 579)

One of our challenges in year 1 was to find the right balance between theoretical and practical knowledge germane to dialogic teaching and to develop productive ways of teaching both. For example, our model of dialogic teaching assumes that evaluatist epistemology is a normative framework for effective facilitation of inquiry dialogue. In other words, teachers need to develop underlying assumptions about the nature of knowledge and the process of knowing that are aligned with dialogic teaching.

Unfortunately, there are very few studies that have examined pedagogical interventions that can bring about changes in epistemological beliefs of teachers (Brownlee, Purdie, & Boulton-Lewis, 2001; Hill, 2000). This is especially problematic, considering that college education, including teacher preparation programs, is not successful at helping learners advance their epistemologies to the evaluatist level (Brownlee et al., 2001; Schraw & Olafson, 2002). Hofer (2001) has concluded her review of research on personal epistemologies by lamenting that "our 'educated citizenry' may in fact be largely composed of individuals who view the world from a position of absolutism, or who simply accept a multiplicity of opinions about complex issues, seeing no need to support positions with evidence" (p. 369). Our own findings in year 1 confirm Hofer's assessment. Using epistemology interviews developed by King and Kitchener (1994), we found that none of the teachers started the program at the evaluatist level.

One potentially effective way to support teacher epistemological development that emerged from year 1 implementation is to involve teachers in inquiry dialogue about knowledge construction itself. For example, during one study-group meeting, teachers collaboratively deliberated about the question "What makes for a better answer during any group discussion?" We observed the teachers struggling with identifying the criteria for "a better answer," often asserting that "everyone is entitled to their own opinion." Although we hoped teachers would be able to move beyond this multiplist position, we also realized that a group inquiry into the questions of knowledge and knowing was highly effective for uncovering teachers' views and unexamined assumptions, thus making them available for analysis and reflection. We plan to expand on the idea of using collaborative discussions about epistemology during year 2 implementation, as it has also been shown to be effective in prior research (e.g., Hill, 2000).

In addition to identifying ways to address core theoretical issues, we also struggled with helping teachers understand how abstract theoretical principles of dialogic teaching can be transformed into specific classroom practices. As mentioned earlier, there is considerable consensus about what is involved in conducting productive discussions about text (e.g., Wilkinson, Soter, & Murphy, 2010). Yet, learning to implement such practices presents a serious challenge for teachers (Juzwik, Sherry, Caughlan, Heintz, & Borsheim-Black, 2012). Both novice and experienced teachers have difficulties facilitating classroom discussions in a way that supports argumentation development (e.g., Alvermann & Hayes, 1989; Caughlan, 2003; Chinn, Anderson, &

Waggoner, 2001). We believe that one reason for these difficulties has to do with insufficient opportunities teachers have to learn about the structure and the criteria for evaluating arguments. As a result, teachers may not be able to identify faulty reasoning, spot contradictions in students' claims, or hear unwarranted conclusions. Consequently, teachers might miss opportunities to make effective facilitation moves. In the absence of teacher intervention, the discussion is likely to disintegrate into simple sharing of opinions, which remain disconnected and unexamined.

We discovered that an effective approach to introducing teachers to the essentials of argument and argumentation is to situate this learning in the context of a classroom discussion. For example, during study-group meetings, we used videos and transcripts of classroom discussions to have teachers practice tracking and evaluating group arguments. As teachers watched the video or read a transcript of a group discussion, they worked on: (a) identifying key elements of an argument (i.e., positions, reasons, evidence, warrants, etc.), (b) reflecting on the quality of argumentation, and (c) suggesting effective facilitation moves to improve students' reasoning. For instance, when student arguments lacked clarity, a teacher might intervene with clarifying, summarizing, or revoicing moves, such as "What do you mean by . . . ? So, are you saying that . . . ? How are you using the word . . . ?" Similarly, to test the validity of inferences in an argument, the teacher might ask questions such as: "Does it follow? Is that the only explanation? How is this relevant?" We have learned that teaching about arguments needs to be connected to facilitation moves. There seems to be little sense in describing teachers' moves in isolation from student arguments during the discussion, and vice versa.

## CONCLUSION

In this chapter, we discussed the challenges and possibilities of helping elementary school teachers to engage in dialogic teaching in order to support the development of students' argument skills. We began by defining dialogic teaching and inquiry dialogue, illustrating their use in a discussion, and contrasting inquiry dialogue with the recitation script traditionally observed in classrooms. We then described epistemological commitments that are assumed to be aligned with the use of inquiry dialogue, and we outlined social and cognitive constructivist theoretical explanations for why inquiry dialogue might foster the development of independent and rational thinking. We next reviewed empirical research on dialogic teaching, demonstrating both the pedagogical potential of this approach and its limited use by practitioners.

In the latter part of the chapter, we described our attempt to design a professional development program in dialogic teaching to help teachers support their students in acquiring and refining their argument skills. Informed by principles of effective professional development, we worked collaboratively with 10 fifth-grade teachers over a school year to identify and organize instructional activities that might support teachers' knowledge and use of dialogic teaching. We noted that we varied the professional development activities within and between two sites to refine the program, and we collected data from multiple sources to identify what was working and what was not working to support teacher learning. The data included transcripts of study-group meetings, focus-group interviews, coaching sessions, and teacher online postings about their learning. We also analyzed video-recorded discussions at the beginning and end of the year.

The theoretical and practical outcomes of this work are a set of design principles for professional development in dialogic teaching, which we will use to guide the next iteration of the professional development program. Many of these principles parallel those derived from reflections on excellent practice in other teacher education and professional development contexts (cf., Anderson & Armbruster, 1990). They include:

- The need to situate instruction in authentic activity (e.g., actual classroom discussion).
- An orientation toward teachers' immediate needs and the contexts in which they work (e.g., coplanning a discussion).
- The use of individualized feedback (i.e., coaching).
- The importance of fostering connections between argument analysis and teacher facilitation of inquiry dialogue.
- The necessity to engage teachers in inquiry dialogue and to model effective facilitation.
- Opportunities for reflection on both theoretical and practical aspects of dialogic teaching.

In a discussion of successful efforts to improve classroom instruction, Elmore (2002) convincingly argued that "few people willfully engage in practices that they know to be ineffective; most educators have good reasons to think that they are doing the best work they can" (p. 19). Hence, practitioners need opportunities to reexamine their own teaching through systematic and critical study of their classroom communication (Walsh, 2002). Guided by our emerging principles, we hope to design a program that can support teacher adoption of new discourse practices and, eventually, enable them to effectively use classroom language to promote the development of argumentation skills in their students.

## SUMMARY POINTS

- Dialogic teaching is a pedagogical approach that capitalizes on the power of talk to offer students opportunities for making and negotiating their own understandings.
- Although dialogic teaching relies on a variety of instructional methods, in our view, it privileges the use of inquiry dialogue to promote the development of students' independent and rational thinking.
- Based on contemporary theory and emerging research, engagement in inquiry dialogue has the potential to help students develop argumentation skills.
- Inquiry dialogue is rarely present in today's classrooms.
- Learning to effectively facilitate inquiry dialogue presents a serious challenge for teachers.
- Teachers need extended professional development opportunities in dialogic teaching that allow them to try out and evaluate new approaches and to continually question their conceptions of knowing, teaching, and learning.
- Professional development programs in dialogic teaching should provide ongoing classroom-based support to practitioners; be situated in authentic educational contexts; be responsive to teachers' individual needs; offer teachers opportunities to observe and practice inquiry dialogue; and allow for systematic and supportive reflection on teachers' own practices.

## REFERENCES

Alexander, R. J. (2003). *Talk for learning: The first year*. Northallerton, England: North Yorkshire County Council.

Alexander, R. J. (2005, July). *Culture, dialogue and learning: Notes on an emerging pedagogy.* Paper presented at the Conference of the International Association for Cognitive Education and Psychology, University of Durham, UK.

Alexander, R. J. (2008). *Essays on pedagogy.* New York, NY: Routledge.

Alvermann, D. E., & Hayes, D. A. (1989). Classroom discussion of content area reading assignments: An intervention study. *Reading Research Quarterly, 24,* 305–335.

Alvermann, D. E., O'Brien, D. G., & Dillon, D. R. (1990). What teachers do when they say they're having discussions of content area reading assignments: A qualitative analysis. *Reading Research Quarterly, 25,* 297–322.

Anderson, R. C. (1977). The notion of schemata and the educational enterprise. In R. C. Anderson, R. J. Spiro, & W. E. Montague (Eds.), *Schooling and the acquisition of knowledge* (pp. 415–431). Hillsdale, NJ: Erlbaum.

Anderson, R. C., & Armbruster, B. B. (1990). *Some maxims for learning and instruction* (Technical Report No. 491). Center for the Study of Reading, University of Illinois at Urbana-Champaign.

Applebee, A. N., Langer, J. A., Nystrand, M., & Gamoran, A. (2003). Discussion-based approaches to developing understanding: Classroom instruction and student performance in middle and high school English. *American Educational Research Journal, 40*(3), 685–730. doi:10.3102/00028312040003685

Asterhan, C. S. C., & Schwarz, B. B. (2007). The effects of monological and dialogical argumentation on concept learning in evolutionary theory. *Journal of Educational Psychology, 99*(3), 626–639. doi:10.1037/0022-0663.99.3.626

Billings, L., & Fitzgerald, J. (2002). Dialogic discussion and the Paideia seminar. *American Educational Research Journal, 39*(4), 907–941. doi:10.3102/00028312039004905

Brownlee, J., Purdie, N., & Boulton-Lewis, G. (2001). Changing epistemological beliefs in pre-service teacher education students. *Teaching in Higher Education, 6*(2), 247–268. doi:10.1080/13562510120045221

Burbules, N. (1993). *Dialogue in teaching: Theory and practice.* New York, NY: Teachers College Press.

Caughlan, S. (2003). Exploring the gap between espoused and enacted cultural models of literature discussion. *National Reading Conference Yearbook, 52,* 150–161.

Chinn, C. A., Anderson, R. C., & Waggoner, M. A. (2001). Patterns of discourse in two kinds of literature discussion. *Reading Research Quarterly, 36*(4), 378–411. doi:10.1598/RRQ.36.4.3

Collins, A., Joseph, D., & Bielaczyc, K. (2004). Design research: Theoretical and methodological issues. *Journal of the Learning Sciences, 13,* 15–42.

Dole, J. A. (2003). Professional development in reading comprehension instruction. In A. P. Sweet & C. E. Snow (Eds.), *Rethinking reading comprehension* (pp. 176–206). New York, NY: Guilford Press.

Dong, T., Anderson, R. C., Li, Y., & Kim, I. (2008). Collaborative reasoning in China and Korea. *Reading Research Quarterly, 43,* 400–424. doi:10.1598/RRQ.43.4.5

Elmore, R. F. (2002). *Bridging the gap between standards and achievement: The imperative for professional development in education.* Washington, DC: Albert Shanker Institute.

Gick, M. L., & Holyoak, K. J. (1987). The cognitive basis of knowledge transfer. In S. M. Cormier (Ed.), *Transfer of learning* (pp. 9–47). San Diego, CA: Academic Press.

Govier, T. (2010). *A practical study of argument* (7th ed.). Belmont, CA: Wadsworth.

Hawley, W. D., & Valli, L. E. (1999). The essentials of effective professional development: A new consensus. In L. Darling-Hammond & G. Sykes (Eds.), *Teaching as the learning profession: Handbook for policy and practice* (pp. 127–150). San Francisco, CA: Jossey-Bass.

Hill, L. (2000). What does it take to change minds? Intellectual development of preservice teachers. *Journal of Teacher Education, 51*(1), 50–62. doi:10.1177/002248710005100106

Hofer, B. K. (2001). Personal epistemology research: Implications for learning and teaching. *Educational Psychology Review, 13*(4), 353–383. doi:10.1023/A:1011965830686

Johnston, P., Woodside-Jiron, H., & Day, J. (2001). Teaching and learning literate epistemologies. *Journal of Educational Psychology, 93*(1), 223–233. doi:10.1037/0022-0663.93.1.223

Junker, B. W., Wiesberg, J., Matsumura, L. C., Crosson, A., Wolf, M. K., Levison, A., & Resnick, L. (2006). *Overview of the Instructional Quality Assessment.* Los Angeles: University of California, National Center for Research on Evaluation, Standards, and Student Testing.

Juzwik, M. M., Sherry, M. B., Caughlan, S., Heintz, A., & Borsheim-Black, C. (2012). Supporting dialogically organized instruction in an English teacher preparation program: Video-based, web 2.0-mediated response and revision pedagogy. *Teachers College Record, 114*(3).

King, P. M., & Kitchener, K. S. (1994). *Developing reflective judgment: Understanding and promoting intellectual growth and critical thinking in adolescents and adults.* San Francisco, CA: Jossey-Bass.

Kuhn, D. (1991). *The skills of argument.* Cambridge, England: Cambridge University Press.

Kuhn, D. (1992). Thinking as argument. *Harvard Educational Review, 62*(2), 155–177.

Kuhn, D. (1999). A developmental model of critical thinking. *Educational Researcher, 28*(2), 16–46. doi:10.3102/0013189X028002016

Kuhn, D., & Crowell, A. (2011). Dialogic argumentation as a vehicle for developing young adolescents' thinking. *Psychological Science, 22*, 545–552. doi:10.1177/0956797611402512

Kuhn, D., & Udell, W. (2003). The development of argument skills. *Child development, 74*(5), 1245–1260. doi:10.1111/1467-8624.00605

Lefstein, A. (2010). More helpful as problem than solution: Some implications of situated dialogue in classrooms. In C. Littleton & C. Howe (Eds.), *Educational dialogues: Understanding and promoting productive interaction* (pp. 170–191). London, England: Routledge.

Lipman, M. (1996). *Nous.* Montclair, NJ: The Institute for Advancement of Philosophy for Children.

Lipman, M. (2003). *Thinking in education.* New York, NY: Cambridge University Press.

Mason, L., & Scirica, F. (2006). Prediction of students' argumentation skills about controversial topics by epistemological understanding. *Learning and Instruction, 16*(5), 492–509. doi:10.1016/j.learninstruc.2006.09.007

Mehan, H. (1998). The study of social interaction in educational settings: Accomplishments and unresolved issues. *Human Development, 41*(4), 245–269. doi:10.1159/000022586

Mercer, N., & Littleton, K. (2007). *Dialogue and the development of children's thinking: A socio-cultural approach.* London, England: Routledge.

Mercer, N., Wegerif, R., & Dawes, L. (1999). Children's talk and the development of reasoning in the classroom. *British Educational Research Journal, 25*(1), 95–111.

Michaels, S., O'Connor, C., & Resnick, L. B. (2008). Deliberative discourse idealized and realized: Accountable talk in the classroom and in civic life. *Studies in Philosophy and Education, 27*(4), 283–297.

Mishra, P., & Brewer, W. F. (2003). Theories as a form of mental representation and their role in the recall of text information. *Contemporary Educational Psychology, 28*, 277–303. doi:10.1016/S0361-476X(02)00040-1

National Governors Association Center for Best Practices & The Council of Chief State School Officers. (2010). *Common Core State Standards.* Available at www.corestandards.org

Nystrand, M. (1997). *Opening dialogue: Understanding dynamics of language and learning in the English classroom.* New York, NY: Teacher College Press.

Nystrand, M., Wu, L., Gamoran, A., Zeiser, S., & Long, D. A. (2003). Questions in time: Investigating the structure and dynamics of unfolding classroom discourse. *Discourse Processes, 35*(2), 135–200.

Partnership for 21st Century Skills. (2012). *A framework for 21st century learning.* Retrieved from http://www.p21.org/index.php

Piaget, J., & Inhelder, B. (1969). *The psychology of the child.* New York, NY: Basic Books.

Postman, N. (1995). *The end of education: Redefining the value of school*. New York, NY: Knopf.

Qian, Z., & Alvermann, D. E. (2000). Relationship between epistemological beliefs and conceptual change learning. *Reading & Writing Quarterly, 16*, 59–74. doi:10.1080/105735600278060

Reed, S. K. (1993). A schema-based theory of transfer. In D. K. Detterman & R. J. Sternberg (Eds.), *Transfer on trial: Intelligence, cognition, and instruction* (pp. 39–67). Norwood, NJ: Ablex.

Reznitskaya, A., Anderson, R. C., Dong, T., Li, Y., Kim, I., & Kim, S. (2008). Learning to think well: Application of Argument Schema Theory. In C. C. Block & S. Parris (Eds.), *Comprehension instruction: Research-based best practices* (pp. 196–213). New York, NY: Guilford Press.

Reznitskaya, A., Anderson, R. C., McNurlen, B., Nguyen-Jahiel, K., Archodidou, A., & Kim, S. (2001). Influence of oral discussion on written argument. *Discourse Processes, 32*(2 & 3), 155–175. doi:10.1207/S15326950DP3202&3_04

Reznitskaya, A., Glina, M., Carolan, B., Michaud, O., Rogers, J., & Sequeira, L. (2012). Examining transfer effects from dialogic discussions to new tasks and contexts. *Contemporary Educational Psychology, 37*, 288–306. doi:10.1016/j.cedpsych.2012.02.003

Reznitskaya, A., Glina, M., & Oyler, J. (2012). *Dialogic inquiry tool*. Montclair, NJ: The Institute for the Advancement of Philosophy for Children.

Reznitskaya, A., Kuo, L., Clark, A., Miller, B., Jadallah, M., Anderson, R. C., & Nguyen-Jahiel, K. (2009). Collaborative reasoning: A dialogic approach to group discussions. *Cambridge Journal of Education, 39*(1), 29–48. doi:10.1080/03057640802701952

Reznitskaya, A., & Sternberg, R. J. (2004). In P. A. Linley & S. Joseph (Eds.), *Positive psychology in practice* (pp. 181–196). Hoboken, NJ: Wiley.

Richardson, V., Anders, P., Tidwell, D., & Lloyd, C. (1991). The relationship between teachers' beliefs and practices in reading comprehension instruction. *American Educational Research Journal, 28*(3), 559–586.

Rosebud Yellow Robe. (2001). Tonweya and the Eagles. In J. Flood, J. E. Hasbrouck, J. V. Hoffman, D. Lapp, A. S. Medearis, S. Paris ... K. D. Wood (Eds.), *McGraw-Hill reading* (pp. 557–577). New York, NY: McGraw-Hill School Division.

Rumelhart, D. E., & Ortony, A. (1977). The representation of knowledge in memory. In R. C. Anderson, R. J. Spiro & W. E. Montague (Eds.), *Schooling and the acquisition of knowledge* (pp. 99–136). Hillsdale, NJ: Erlbaum.

Schraw, G., & Olafson, L. (2002). Teachers' epistemological world views and educational practice. *Issues in Education, 8*(2), 99–149.

Sinatra, G. M., & Kardash, C. M. (2004). Teacher candidates' epistemological beliefs, dispositions, and views on teaching as persuasion. *Contemporary Educational Psychology, 29*(4), 483–498. doi:10.1016/j.cedpsych.2004.03.001

Smith, F., Hardman, F., Wall, K., & Mroz, M. (2004). Interactive whole class teaching in the national literacy and numeracy strategies. *British Educational Research Journal, 30*(3), 395–411. doi:10.1080/01411920410001689706

Soter, A., Wilkinson, I. A. G., Murphy, P. K., Rudge, L., Reninger, K., & Edwards, M. (2008). What the discourse tells us: Talk and indicators of high-level comprehension. *International Journal of Educational Research, 47*, 372–391. doi:10.1016/j.ijer.2009.01.001

Stipek, D. J., Givvin, K. B., Salmon, J. M., & MacGyvers, V. L. (2001). Teachers' beliefs and practices related to mathematics instruction. *Teaching and Teacher Education, 17*(2), 213–226. doi:10.1016/S0742-051X(00)00052-4

Stromso, H. I., & Braten, I. (2009). Beliefs about knowledge and knowing and multiple-text comprehension among upper secondary students. *Educational Psychology, 29*(4), 425–445. doi:10.1080/01443410903046864

Toulmin, S. E. (1958). *The uses of argument*. Cambridge, England: Cambridge University Press.

Vygotsky, L. S. (1968). *Thought and language (newly revised, translated, and edited by Alex Kozulin)*. Cambridge, MA: MIT Press.

Vygotsky, L. S. (1981). The genesis of higher-order mental functions. In J. V. Wertsch (Ed.), *The concept of activity in Soviet psychology* (pp. 144–188). Armonk, NY: Sharpe.

Waggoner, M., Chinn, C. A., Yi, H., & Anderson, R. C. (1995). Collaborative reasoning about stories. *Language Arts, 72,* 582–589.

Walsh, S. (2002). Construction or obstruction: Teacher talk and learner involvement in the EFL classroom. *Language Teaching Research, 6*(1), 3–23. doi:10.1191/1362168802lr095oa

Walton, D. (1996). *Argument structure: A pragmatic theory.* Toronto, Canada: University of Toronto Press.

Walton, D., & Macagno, F. (2007). Types of dialogue, dialectical relevance and textual congruity. *Anthropology & Philosophy: International Multidisciplinary Journal, 8,* 101–119.

Wegerif, R. (2010). *Mind expanding: Teaching for thinking and creativity in primary education.* Buckingham, England: Open University Press.

Wei, R. C., Darling-Hammond, L., Andree, A., Richardson, N., & Orphanos, S. (2009). *Professional learning in the learning profession: A status report on teacher development in the United States and abroad.* Dallas, TX: National Staff Development Council.

Weinstock, M. P. (2006). Psychological research and the epistemological approach to argumentation. *Informal Logic, 26*(1), 103–120.

Weinstock, M. P., Neuman, Y., & Tabak, I. (2004). Missing the point or missing the norms? Epistemological norms as predictors of students' ability to identify fallacious arguments. *Contemporary Educational Psychology, 29*(1), 77–94. doi:10.1016/S0361-476X(03)00024-9

Wilkinson, I. A. G., Reninger, K. B., & Soter, A. (2010). Developing a professional development tool for assessing quality talk about text. In R. T. Jimenez, V. J. Risko, D. W. Rowe, & M. Hundley (Eds.), *59th yearbook of the National Reading Conference* (pp. 142–159). Oak Creek, WI: National Reading Conference.

Wilkinson, I. A. G., Soter, A., & Murphy, P. K. (2010). Developing a model of Quality Talk about literary text. In M. G. McKeown & L. Kucan (Eds.), *Bringing reading research to life* (pp. 142–169). New York, NY: Guilford Press.

Windschitl, M. (2002). Framing constructivism in practice as the negotiation of dilemmas: An analysis of the conceptual, pedagogical, cultural, and political challenges facing teachers. *Review of Educational Research, 72*(2), 131–175. doi:10.3102/00346543072002131

Yoon, K. S., Duncan, T., Lee, S. W.-Y., Scarloss, B., & Shapley, K. (2007). Reviewing the evidence on how teacher professional development affects student achievement. *Issues & Answers Report, 33.*

CHAPTER 18

# Teaching Well-Being and Resilience in Primary and Secondary School

CHIEKO KIBE and ILONA BONIWELL

The true measure of a nation's standing is how well it attends to its children—their health and safety, their material security, their education and socialization, and their sense of being loved, valued, and included in the families into which they are born.

UNICEF, 2007

CONTRARY TO SOCIETAL GROWTH, the wealth of countries in the 21st century appears to provide relatively little protection for their youth. Recent international data on children's well-being reveals a worrisome picture. The 2007 UNICEF report, which presents an overview of child well-being in developed countries, ranked the United States and the United Kingdom as the bottom two countries of a list of 21 industrialized countries (UNICEF, 2007). In the same report, children of Japan were reported to be the most deprived of educational and cultural resources out of 24 listed countries, with 30% of young people in Japan agreeing with the negative statement "I feel lonely." This number exceeds the second-highest-scoring country by nearly 3 times (UNICEF, 2007). As members of the global society, as educators and parents, the authors have long believed in innate human potential for positive development—Chieko Kibe, as a mother of two children, who had multicultural experiences while raising her children and has now taken her passion for positive education further into a PhD in child resilience, and Ilona Boniwell, as a mother and stepmother of five children, who had developed and evaluated multiple educational curricula aimed at enhancing well-being and resilience in secondary school pupils.

Acknowledging this controversial reality, this chapter attempts to illustrate how *positive education* can contribute to the well-being of youth and ultimately strengthen our future society. First, the what and why of positive education are briefly described. Second, a historical overview of positive education with particular focus on the concepts of well-being and resilience is offered to the reader. Third, the chapter presents some current practices of well-being and resilience education, backing them with relevant evidence. Then, fourth, some suggestions for future practice are put forward.

## WHAT IS POSITIVE EDUCATION?

Positive education concerns forms of education that teach schoolchildren both conventional skills and skills to enhance well-being (Seligman, Ernst, Gillham, Reivich, & Linkins, 2009). In other words, in addition to teaching traditional skills, such as math or languages, positive education aims to enhance young people's well-being by ameliorating mental health problems, buffering the detrimental effects of life stressors, and, more importantly, promoting their psychological health. However, it does not blindly encourage students to have "feel-good" experiences; rather, the significance of positive education is underpinned by the principles of psychological science. To be more precise, it is based on recent advances in positive psychological findings. This is what differentiates positive education as a psychological science from other self-help–based educational initiatives.

### WHY POSITIVE EDUCATION?

Data suggest that Western countries are facing an unprecedented increase in childhood and adolescent depression. At any point in time, approximately 2% of children aged 11–15 and 11% of youth aged 16–24 in the United Kingdom are suffering from major depressive disorder (Green, McGinnity, Meltzer, Ford, & Goodman, 2005). Anxiety disorders, which often precede and co-occur with depression, are found in approximately 3% of children aged 5–15 and 15% of youth aged 16–24 (Green et al., 2005). In the United States, approximately 1 in 5 adolescents has a major depressive episode by the end of high school (Lewinsohn, Hops, Roberts, & Seeley, 1993), and a similar trend has been observed in Australia (Noble & McGrath, 2005).

Children and adolescents who suffer from persistent depressive symptoms or depressive disorders are more likely to experience academic and interpersonal difficulties. They are additionally more likely to smoke, use drugs and alcohol, and attempt suicide (Covey, Glassman, & Stetner, 1998; Garrison, Schluchter, Schoenbach, & Kaplan, 1989). Further, these youth mental health problems affect societal expenditure through treatment costs, productivity decreases, and premature death of the affected people. In the United States, the annual expense resulting from depression is estimated at about $43 billion (Hirschfeld et al., 1997).

As we can see, these worrisome statistics point to an urgent need to tackle depression, to prevent further detriment of the situation, and to enhance youth mental health instead. Ample anecdotes and research findings suggest that after family, education plays the most crucial role in fostering child development. Indeed, the importance of student well-being has long been advocated by educators and school psychologists (Clonan, Chafouleas, McDougal, & Riley-Tillman, 2004). Good practitioners know from experience that emphasizing and nurturing students' strengths, rather than remedying their deficiencies, promotes their well-being and academic performance more effectively. Unfortunately, such wisdom has not been reflected in educational policy.

However, recent advances in the science of well-being offer substantial evidence to support the advantages of well-being, resulting in acceleration of change in the political agenda. For instance, the primary objective of the UK government's Every Child Matters initiative, underpinned by the Children's Act, 2004, was to "safeguard children and young people, improve their life outcomes and general well-being" (Department for Education and Skills, 2007, p. 35). As such, once implicit in the education of children, well-being has now become an overt objective. In this sense, the first decade of the 21st century might be viewed by historians of the future as a landmark decade for the explicit development of children's well-being.

When talking about positive education, we would like to position it in the context of the multiple risk factors children face and interventions provided by societal institutions to mitigate such risks. Wright and Masten (2006) assert that it is critical to investigate cumulative risk factors to accurately predict developmental outcomes.

In addition to identifying risk factors, schools can provide effective interventions for those who have already developed difficulties or who have been identified at high risk. These interventions are generally categorized in a hierarchical order. Tertiary interventions are at the top of the pyramid, targeting individuals whose symptoms or/and challenges persist and who therefore require intensive interventions. Secondary preventive interventions are in the middle of the pyramid, aimed for selected individuals or small groups of pupils who are identified at a higher than average risk. The last or the bottom layer of the pyramid is reserved to universal interventions, known as *primary prevention*, which aims to provide benefits for all, rather than for select students (Fox, Carta, Strain, Dunlap, & Hemmeter, 2009; O'Connell, Boat, & Warner, 2009). To us, the positive educational approach lies in this bottom layer for the purpose of prevention and promotion of psychological health by fortifying resilience and enhancing well-being.

We see this hierarchical positioning and separation of functions as particularly valuable, because while targeting *all* students, positive education aims both to *prevent* psychological distress through building of resilience and also to *promote* thriving (as generally defined) through cultivating positive climates within classroom and school cultures and developing well-being.

## POSITIVE EDUCATION FROM A HISTORICAL PERSPECTIVE

Educators have long struggled with the profound conflicts between their occupational purpose and its consequences for their learners. Traditionally, educators were expected to teach concepts based on academic subject groups. Nevertheless, educators' concerns about the neglect of students' emotional health prompted school administrators to reshape curricula to address such deficiencies. Hence, new programs were developed that focused on the development of socioemotional skills. Consequently, schools started to incorporate work on social and emotional issues into the curriculum, helping students appreciate the value of such skills. In this section, a brief historical overview of the main developments within what we now call *positive education* is offered to the reader.

The social and emotional lives of school-aged young people first became a focus in education in the 1970s with the emergence of the self-esteem movement. This movement was derived from the core principles of humanistic psychology, and it began to impact teachers' practices in the classroom and parents' childrearing practices. Classroom self-esteem programs typically focused on the importance of helping children gain a sense of achievement in a relatively noncompetitive and failure-free learning environment and engage in self-expression. Children were encouraged by both teachers and parents to see themselves as special and unique. "Low self-esteem" was widely regarded as an explanation for many social "ills" such as juvenile crime, teenage pregnancy, substance abuse, and low academic achievement. However, various reviews of the self-esteem literature have found little evidence that developing young people's self-esteem makes a significant difference in students' academic achievement, mental health, or societal problems, thus exposing self-esteem education as inefficacious overall (e.g., Baumeister, Campbell, Krueger, & Vohs, 2003; Emler, 2001; Kahne, 1996). In fact, Twenge (2009) documents increases in anxiety among young people since the 1970s that she links with systematic techniques used in schools to "boost" self-esteem.

The second wave in positive education, the social and emotional learning (SEL) movement, arose in the mid-1990s and was gradually integrated into educational systems from kindergarten to high school. Built upon Gardner's (1983, 1999) multiple intelligence model and Salovey and Mayer's (1990) emotional intelligence concept, Goleman (1996) made this notion known worldwide. Building upon the theoretical foundations from Goleman's emotional intelligence framework, the Collaborative for Academic, Social, and Emotional Learning (CASEL) was established at the University of Illinois in 1994. CASEL was actively engaged in the process of implementing various SEL programs, offering strong academic and scientific collaboration opportunities to participating schools (Noble & McGrath, 2013). SEL programs prepared children to be good students, citizens, and workers with social and emotional competencies by establishing "social and emotional learning as an essential part of education" (CASEL, 2004). A meta-review of school-based interventions reported SEL to be one of the most effective interventions for school-aged young people (Durlak, Weissberg, Dymnicki, Taylor, & Schellinger, 2011).

Although not explicitly articulated, several components of well-being education were integrated into the SEL paradigm (e.g., creating a committed and supportive environment, focusing on one's emotions, working to realize one's full potential, finding meaning in one's experience). As such, we view SEL as the first successful positive education approach that gradually established a powerful presence within school curricula across the board (e.g., Humphrey et al., 2008; Roffey, 2011; Sugai & Horner, 2002).

## Positive Education as Prevention: Interest in Resilience

Resilience, as a psychological concept, was conceived about 40 years ago when researchers started studying children who demonstrated positive adaptation despite the presence of high-risk circumstances (Garmezy & Nuechterlein, 1972; Rutter, Cox, Tupling, Berger, & Yule, 1975). This indicated a positive divergence from the typical pathological models (Masten, 2001). The initial impetus for the study was "the developmental and situational mechanisms involved in protective processes" (Rutter, 1987, cited in Goldstein & Brooks, 2006, p. 3) demonstrated in a high-risk population that exhibited an ability to overcome mental, developmental, economic, and environmental challenges. However, little scientific research at the time was devoted to this phenomenon and the field of study remained fairly small for a number of years (Goldstein & Brooks, 2006). Nonetheless, investigation of resilience has expanded considerably in the past 20 years, and a recent review revealed that the usage of the term "resilience" in scholarly literature increased eightfold in the past two decades (Ager, 2013; see also Yates, Tyrell, & Masten, Chapter 44, this volume).

The rise in attention toward the concept of resilience has also received increased attention in public policy, including child welfare (Administration for Children and Families, 2012), social and national security (Homeland Security Advisory Council, 2011), humanitarian development (Department for International Development, 2011), and international development (World Bank, 2011). The conceptual framework of resilience was deemed by education professionals as particularly important for young people. Additionally, the skill of resilience had begun to be perceived as a source of "psychological capital" (Luthans, Youssef, & Avolio, 2007) indispensable for adults and children alike who are continually exposed to considerable stress in the modern society.

However, despite its pervasiveness, there appears to be a need for consensus on a conceptual definition for resilience. According to Masten and Obradovic (2006), age-salient healthy growth can be conceptually categorized as "competent" (good adaptation and low history of adversity), while adequate development despite exposure to adverse life events can be categorized as "resilient" (good adaptation and high adversity). Still, the latter notion of developmental quality (i.e., resilient) indicates two aspects of child resilience: the phenomenological aspect and the attributional aspect. From the phenomenological perspective, resilience refers to the process of one's positive adaptation, characterized by good coping and outcomes, despite adverse experiences (Luthar, Cicchetti, & Becker, 2000; Masten, 2001; Rutter, 2006). Conversely, from the attributional viewpoint, resilience refers to an individual predisposition that functions as a protective factor in the face of adversity (e.g., Block, & Block, 1980; Rothbart, 1989; Wachs, 2006). The distinctive difference between these two concepts is noteworthy: Resilience as a dynamic adaptation process presupposes exposure to substantial risk, whereas a resilience factor does not (Luthar et al., 2000).

In the context of education, employing the latter definition of resilience (protective assets) to facilitate an environment where children develop and learn to utilize resilience factors (e.g., strength, personality) prior to encountering adverse life events would be more feasible. Schools can offer a strong foundation to cultivate resilience, and provide students with opportunities to challenge and expand their boundaries in a relatively safe environment. Notably, as Noble and McGrath (2013) suggest, schools may provide vital scaffolding for the enhancement of resilience, especially for students who lack adequate family support. Such programs emerged in the 1990s and have received growing attention since.

## CURRENT POSITIVE EDUCATION INITIATIVES IN PRIMARY AND SECONDARY SCHOOLS

These positive educational approaches (i.e., prevention and promotion) previously reviewed have been accentuated by the arrival of the positive psychology movement in the dawn of the new millennium (Seligman & Csikszenmihalyi, 2000). As the name implies, positive psychology holds that human positivity is a robust driving force that can facilitate a thriving life. Hence, research in this field is focused on the effects of a range of factors that may contribute to optimal functioning, such as engagement and flow (Csikszenmihalyi, 2002), optimism (Seligman, Reivich, Jaycox, & Gillham, 1995), personal character strengths (Peterson & Seligman, 2004), positive emotions (Frederickson, 2001), and resilience (Masten, 2001). A substantial number of initiatives have since been developed; next we introduce these together, presenting empirical findings around their differences.

### Positive Education as Promotion: Recent Well-Being Education Initiatives

Well-being in children is often seen to include the variables of happiness, health, and success. However, life circumstances are not always consistent with one's expectations. For example, maltreatment, poverty, educational inequity, bullying, and unemployment are sadly prevalent. Thus, it appears to us that the goal should be to teach children to live well irrespective of circumstances.

So what do we mean by well-being education and what should be included in it? Since the extensive discussion by Greek philosophers, many theories have been established around the "pursuit of a good life." Although the concept of well-being involves multifaceted dimensions, these theories grapple with and broadly conceptualize well-being from two perspectives: (1) hedonia and (2) eudaimonia (e.g., Huta, Chapter 10, this volume; Keyes & Magyar-Moe, 2003; Niemiec & Ryan, 2013). The first perspective conceptualizes well-being as subjective well-being that includes life satisfaction (or a cognitive evaluation of one's life) and positive emotion (e.g., Diener, Lucas, & Oishi, 2005; Salovey, Caruso, & Mayer, 2004; Salovey, Rothman, Detweiler, & Steward, 2000). The second perspective concerns well-being as positive functioning, including aspects of growth and meaning-making (e.g., Ryan & Deci, 2001; Ryff & Keyes, 1995). These two perspectives may provide a helpful platform for school-based initiatives that are explicitly designed to enhance student well-being. We suggest that it is beneficial to promote both the subjective well-being of students through seeing the glass as half-full and learning to experience more positive emotions (e.g., joy, gratitude) as well as helping them to build pathways to positive functioning (e.g., through meaning-making) by carefully designing programs to accommodate these multiple aspects.

Well-being–focused education is becoming more and more prevalent nowadays. A younger sibling of SEL, the primary SEAL (social and emotional aspects of learning) program is a government-led whole-school initiative for students in the United Kingdom. Approximately 90% of primary schools and 70% of secondary schools have implemented SEAL as a universal approach (Humphrey, Lendrum, & Wigelsworth, 2010). This comprehensive approach includes early interventions with small learning groups that serve to provide extra support and subsequent individual interventions for students who did not appear to have benefited from either the whole-class program or the early interventions. The extensive evaluation was made to report its positive impact on school climate, students' autonomy and influence, learning and attainment, and reduction of exclusion (Humphrey et al., 2008, 2010). Although the program documented these positive results, the results indicated that the "will and skill" of the facilitators (teachers) largely affect program effectiveness, as do time and resource allocation for pragmatic aspects.

Another example is KidsMatter, an Australian primary schools mental health initiative. This program is supported by a partnership between the Commonwealth Department of Health and Ageing, Beyond Blue: The National Depression Initiative, the Australian Psychological Society and Principals Australia, and Australian Rotary Health. One hundred schools implemented social and emotional learning programs of their choice from a program booklet that evaluated all potential programs according to CASEL criteria. The evaluation result of this initiative indicated prominent and positive changes in the schools over the 2-year trial. Research also reported that it provided common language within the school community to address and work on students' mental health issues. Parental response indicated that the school became more capable of catering to children's needs (Slee et al., 2009). The effectiveness of the program was particularly evident in students who were initially evaluated as having more extensive mental health problems (Slee et al., 2009).

In addition to the large-scale initiatives, there are several institution-wide initiatives, such as at Geelong Grammar School in Australia and Wellington College and Haberdasher's Academies in the United Kingdom (Morris, 2013; White, 2013). For example, the Well-Being Curriculum is a joint project of a partnership between the Haberdashers' Aske's Academies Federation and the University of East London (UEL). It is based on the principles and findings of positive psychology and taught weekly to students from year 1 to year 13. The curriculum targets every known major predictor and correlate of well-being using individually tested interventions to enhance learning. The emphasis of the curriculum in years 1 to 9 is on positive interventions, targeting areas that have a substantial evidence base such as happiness, positive emotions, flow, resilience, achievement, positive relationships, and meaning. The emphasis in years 10 to 13 is on positive education, enabling young people to reflect upon and make choices about their well-being and development. This four-part curriculum spans 4 years, focusing on the areas of self, being, doing, and relationships. Pilot evaluation of the program showed increases in various aspects of well-being (i.e., positive affect, satisfaction with friends, and satisfaction with self) consistent with the areas targeted (Boniwell & Ryan, 2012).

Finally, literature identifies many discrete well-being programs, building on the concepts that have been found to lead to well-being. Such attempts are briefly summarized in Table 18.1. Although it is beyond the scope of this chapter to list all available programs, the table briefly exemplifies the width of applications. All listed approaches are research-based initiatives.

POSITIVE EDUCATION AS PREVENTION: CURRENT RESILIENCE EDUCATION INITIATIVES

As previously demonstrated, ample efforts to enhance children's socioemotional development have been exerted, suggesting promising advancement of children's well-being in the school environment. Yet, the concern remains that children are presently enduring stress and pressure levels far greater than that of previous generations. Recent resilience studies have indicated that in addition to social support and nurturing environment, there are some qualities that contribute to personal resilience, for example, emotional competencies, self-control, social-competencies, self-efficacy, and optimism (Gillham et al., 2013). Therefore, in addition to elucidating the underlying mechanism of psychopathology, it is necessary to develop ways to effectively deploy these empirical findings. One of the prominent approaches to build personal resilience is the Penn Resiliency Program (PRP). Through the application of cognitive-behavior therapy (CBT), it aims to promote optimism, adaptive coping skills, and effective problem-solving skills. PRP is a school-based intervention; typical curricula consist of 12 90-minute lessons or 18 to 24 60-minute lessons. It encourages young people to challenge a habitual pessimistic explanatory style by realistically examining the evidence while avoiding unrealistic optimism. PRP was developed and researched for nearly 20 years and is consequently supported by a solid empirical base (Seligman, 2002, 2007; Reivich & Shatté, 2003). Evidence suggests that it confers lasting preventive effects against depression and anxiety. It has been shown to reduce the incidence of depression and anxiety by 50% at a 3-year follow-up period (Gillham, Reivich, & Freres, 2007). As such, CBT was found to equip young people with tangible, effective techniques. Another example is Bounce Back! (McGrath & Noble, 2003). It provides nine core curriculum units, with three levels of developmentally appropriate resources for children aged 5 to 14. It is presently delivered in primary and secondary schools in Australia and Scotland. Evidence thus far suggests the program enhances resilience in students and teachers (Axford, Blythe, & Schepens, 2010). Specifically, the program has been demonstrated to reduce depression, improve teacher resilience, and improve student resilience (McGrath & Noble, 2003).

**Table 18.1**

Discrete Well-Being Programs

| Concept | Program | Aim | Target Age | Feature | Reference |
|---------|---------|-----|------------|---------|-----------|
| Wisdom | Wisdom Curriculum | Intellectual and moral development | Middle school | 16 pedagogical principles and 6 procedures through mainstream subjects (e.g., history) | Sternberg, 2001; Reznitskaya and Sternberg, 2004 |
| Hope | Making Hope Happen | Accentuating hope, goal-setting, and acting out for purpose | Elementary school; middle school | 8 weekly 30-min sessions; 5 weekly 45-min sessions | McDermott and Hastings, 2000; Lopez et al., 2004 |
| Emotional intelligence | Self Science; The South Africa Emotional Intelligence Curriculum | Developing social and emotional competencies | Elementary school | 54 lessons for 10 goals; 58 activities focused on feelings | McCown, Jensen, Freedman, and Rideout, 1998; Salovey, Caruso, and Mayer, 2004 |
| Character strengths | Celebrating Strengths; Strengths Gym | Building strengths, emotional competencies, and resilience | Primary school; secondary school | Oral storytelling and regular community celebration; student booklets for individual or classroom exercises | Fox Eades, 2008; Linley and Govindji, 2008; Proctor and Fox Eades, 2009 |
| Mindfulness | MindUp | Enhancing perspective taking, empathy, and kindness; fostering complex problem-solving skills | Elementary school; middle school | 15 lessons based in neuroscience to learn self-regulation, mindful engagement | Schonert-Reichl, and Lawlor, 2010 |

In light of cultivating personal resilience, findings from relevant research areas may benefit comprehensive educational programs as well. Research found three prominent psychological responses in the face of adversity: (1) Succumb to the stressor (e.g., posttraumatic stress disorder; PTSD); (2) resilience or recovery; (3) posttraumatic growth (PTG; Heffron & Boniwell, 2011). The SPARK Resilience Programme involves empirical findings from such relevant research fields (Boniwell & Ryan, 2009). A typical program consists of 12 60-minute lessons for children aged 11 and above. Analysis of pre- and postassessment data showed significantly higher resilience, self-esteem, and self-efficacy scores in students who completed the SPARK program. A marginally significant decrease was observed in depression symptoms (Pluess, Boniwell, Hefferon, & Tunariu, in press). It is now being implemented in non-English-speaking cultures (e.g., France, Japan) to determine the cross-cultural validity of the program.

These CBT-based resilience programs have provided valuable evidence that the teaching of social competence, optimism, and resilience skills can offer significant benefits. The lasting decrease in depression and anxiety in children and adolescents conferred by these programs is an invaluable achievement that cannot be understated. The effectiveness of these programs in teaching children to maintain psychological health amid adverse life events by utilizing individual capacities is encouraging and corroborates the value of well-being and resilience education.

## TOWARD OPTIMIZATION OF POSITIVE EDUCATIONAL INITIATIVES

The field of education is embracing a rich development of curricula under the positive educational umbrella. It is likely that additional programs will soon be developed and applied to more diverse populations and cultures. Thus, it is necessary to establish a robust framework within the paradigm to ensure educators and practitioners apply the concepts appropriately. Several considerations are highlighted next to suggest some guidance around the optimization of positive educational initiatives.

### NEED FOR A PRACTICAL FRAMEWORK

For better understanding, clarification, and utilization of positive educational practices, Noble and McGrath (2008) proposed the Positive Educational Practices (PEPs) Framework. The PEPs specify five foundations of well-being, which were derived from research in positive psychology and other related psychological and educational areas: (1) social and emotional competency, (2) positive emotions, (3) positive relationships, (4) engagement through strengths, and (5) a sense of meaning and purpose. The first foundation further includes three components: resilience skills, emotional literacy skills, and personal achievement skills. The second foundation contains five subcategories of positive emotions: feelings of belonging, feelings of safety, feelings of satisfaction and pride, feelings of excitement and enjoyment, and feelings of optimism. The authors suggested the PEPs Framework should be used to supplement traditional educational psychologists' work, aiming to "shift the direction and mind-set of both educational systems and school personnel from a deficit model of pupil learning and behavioural difficulties to a preventative well-being model" (Noble & McGrath, 2008, p. 130). Ultimately, the PEPs Framework is intended to assist students in finding a sense of meaning and purpose at school and in life. Future practice may substantially benefit from incorporating such a practical framework for optimal implementation.

NEED FOR EFFECTIVE UTILIZATION

When applying positive educational programs, care should be taken to ensure that cognitively weighted interventions are developmentally appropriate to meet the target population's developmental phase. Especially for young children, a more comprehensive approach would be to incorporate well-being education, which focuses on well-being and emotions, with resilience education. This approach would benefit fortifying resilience in children because the major components of well-being are suggested to contribute comprehensively to the formation of resilience qualities (Richardson, 2002).

In addition to programs that target the development of specific skills, evidence suggests school-wide programs (involving all staff and pupils) that promote psychological well-being are more likely to be effective than class-based interventions (Wells, Barlow, & Stewart-Brown, 2003). A positive climate in the school as a whole is associated with teacher and student satisfaction, lower stress levels, and better academic results (Sangsue & Vorpe, 2004). Although it is difficult to define the factors that comprise a good school, researchers agree that a high-quality school encourages students to be engaged with and enthusiastic about learning. Common features of such schools include a safe environment, an articulated and shared vision of the school's purpose, explicit goals for students, emphasis on the individual student, and rewarding student effort or improvement (Peterson, 2006). Satisfaction with the school and feelings of security and belonging heavily influence students' commitment to learning and achievement (Brand, Felner, Shim, Seitsinger, & Dumas, 2003).

NEED FOR QUALITATIVE EVALUATION

Regarding program development, application, and delivery, the relevant professionals ought to be mindful that there exists no one-fits-all theoretical or pragmatic formula. Although positive education aims to approach all students as a primary intervention, to which extent the same program is effective or not inevitably varies depending on each individual. Schools in our contemporary society often contain very diverse populations (e.g., genetic composition, upbringing, educational background, personal values, familial cultures, neighborhood, and wider community), but should nonetheless provide abundant opportunities for the nurturing of individual well-being and resilience and the cultivation of strengths.

With regards to the individual differences, genetic predisposition is reported to account for approximately 50% of individual personality (Plomin, DeFries, McClearn, & McGuffin, 2008), but environmental and psychological processes also play a crucial role in shaping children's development. For example, growing evidence from differential susceptibility studies demonstrated that children with high susceptibility are prone to respond negatively to an adverse environment (hence being perceived as less resilient) but to respond more positively to high-quality environment than their counterparts (i.e., less susceptible individuals; e.g. Ellis & Boyce, 2011; Ellis, Boyce, Belsky, Bakermans-Kranenburg, & van IJzendoorn, 2011; Pluess & Belsky, 2009; 2010). Thus, the literature consequently implies the complexity and importance of gene–environment interactions (G × E), as goodness-of-fit critically predicts an outcome that may thwart or enhance human development (Caspi et al., 2002; Pluess & Belsky, 2009; Rutter, 2006). Indeed this finding indicates children's unique potential for resilience plasticity through the specification of context-endogenous characteristic interactions. Educators therefore should appreciate information provided by a qualitative evaluation within this paradigm. Given the nature of education and child development, the myopic quantitative approach may fail to identify meaningful implications regarding the psychological process of children.

NEED FOR CONTINUING EMPIRICAL VALIDATION

The need for adequate empirical validation designates positive educational initiatives as robust scientific endeavors. Such study requires painstaking effort and negotiation with the research resources available; however, such rigorous criteria will ultimately result in the refinement of the theoretical foundation and methodological advancement of the field.

According to the American Psychological Association Division 12 (clinical psychology) Task Force Criteria, psychological treatment (e.g., therapy, intervention) must meet a number of standards of scientific inquiry as follows in order to claim its efficacy: (a) The experimental treatment must have a control group, (b) studies must involve random assignment of participants, (c) the intervention must be delivered using a treatment manual, (d) the population must be clearly defined, (e) the outcome measures must be reliable and valid, and (f) the data analysis must be conducted in an appropriate and valid manner (see Chambless & Ollendick, 2001). As such, maintenance of rigorous standards is necessary to confirm the value of positive educational initiatives.

Nevertheless, compromise may occasionally be inevitable for pragmatic reasons, as conforming to the full criteria previously described necessitates considerable constraints. Therefore, evidence-based practice would be more feasible with respect to positive educational applications. In other words, it refers to "conscientious, explicit, and judicious use of current best evidence in making decisions" (Sackett, Rosenberg, Gray, Haynes, & Richardson, 1996, p. 71) for the best interest of the target population, and the critical evaluation and analysis for outcome dissemination to shareholders for continuous evaluation and quality improvement (Kerig, Ludlow, & Wenar, 2012).

## CONCLUSION

This chapter introduced the notion of positive education and explored how it has been applied in the forms of well-being and resilience education, including some considerations for future developments. Given the active global interest in children's well-being, we believe that positive education is primed for a positive future. We envisage that children, parents, teachers, and communities across the globe will benefit from this approach in the years to come. The availability of research and science in positive psychology and the multitude of initiatives will provide the bases for future developments. Nevertheless, it is important to recognize that we are still at the very beginning of the journey. The success of these programs and interventions will depend on the active collaboration among transdisciplinary professionals, because this is what can yield the essential information on the appropriate cultivation of the innate human potential during the early stages of life.

## SUMMARY POINTS

- Positive education functions as a universal (i.e., primary) preventative and promotional intervention.
- Positive education is more efficacious when implemented as a whole-school approach with a practical application framework.

- Multilayered, long-term programs appear to be more effective than single and short-term focused approaches.
- The comprehensive positive education incorporates both experiential and conceptual aspects of well-being.
- Techniques derived from cognitive-behavioral therapy often underlie the most effective intervention programs aimed at resilience enhancement.
- The teachers' skill and will account for a substantial proportion of an intervention program success.
- Novel scientific findings and empirical validation strengthen further development of positive education.

## REFERENCES

Administration for Children and Families. (2012). *Parental resilience*. Retrieved from https://www.childwelfare.gov/can/factors/resilience.cfm

Ager, A. (2013). Annual research review: Resilience and child well-being—public policy implications. *Journal of Child Psychology and Psychiatry, 54*, 488–500.

Axford, S., Blythe, K., & Schepens, R. (2010). Can we help children learn coping skills for life? A study of the impact of the Bounce Back Programme on resilience, connectedness and wellbeing of children and teachers in 16 primary schools in Perth and Kinross, Scotland, *Educational Psychology in Scotland, 12*, 2–5.

Baumeister, R. F., Campbell, J. D., Krueger, J. I., & Vohs, K. D. (2003). Does high self-esteem cause better performance, interpersonal success, happiness, or healthier lifestyles? *Psychological Science in the Public Interest, 4*, 1–44.

Block, J. H., & Block, J. (1980). The role of ego-control and ego resiliency in the organization of behavior. *Minnesota Symposium on Child Psychology, 13*, 39–101.

Boniwell, I., & Ryan, L. (2009). *SPARK resilience: A teacher's guide*. London, England: University of East London.

Boniwell, I., & Ryan, L. (2012). *Personal well-being lessons for secondary schools*. Maidenhead, England: Open University Press.

Brand, S., Felner, R., Shim, M., Seitsinger, A., & Dumas, T. (2003). Middle school improvement and reform: Development and validation of a school-level assessment of climate, cultural pluralism, and school safety. *Journal of Educational Psychology, 95*, 570–588.

Caspi, A., McClay, J., Moffitt, T. E., Mill, J., Martin, J., Craig, I. W., . . . Poulton, R. (2002). Role of genotype in the cycle of violence in maltreated children. *Science, 297*, 851–854.

Chambless, D. L., & Ollendick, T. H. (2001). Empirically supported psychological interventions: Controversies and evidence. *Annual Review of Psychology, 52*, 685–716.

Clonan, S. M., Chafouleas, S. M., McDougal, J. L., & Riley-Tillman, T. C. (2004). Positive psychology goes to school: Are we there yet? *Psychology in the Schools, 4*, 101–110.

Collaborative for Academic, Social, and Emotional Learning. (2004). *CASEL: The first ten years 1994-2004: Building a foundation for the future*. Retrieved from http://casel.org/wp-content/uploads/10YEARSMALL.pdf

Covey, L. S., Glassman, A. H., & Stetner, F. (1998). Cigarette smoking and major depression. *Journal of Addictive Diseases, 17*, 35–46.

Csikszentmihalyi, M. (2002). *Flow: The classic work on how to achieve happiness*. London, England: Rider.

Department for International Development. (2011). *Saving lives, preventing suffering and building resilience: The UK government's humanitarian policy*. Retrieved from http://www.dfid.gov.uk/Documents/publications1/1/The%20UK%20Government's%20Humanitarian%20Policy%20-%20September%202011%20-%20Final.pdf

Department for Education and Skills. (2007). *Social and emotional aspects of learning for secondary schools (SEAL): Guidance booklet*. London, England: Department for Children, Schools and Families, United Kingdom.

Diener, E., Lucas, R. E., & Oishi, S. (2005). Subjective well-being: The science of happiness and life satisfaction. In C. R. Snyder & S. J. Lopez (Eds.), *Handbook of positive psychology* (pp. 63–73). New York, NY: Oxford University Press.

Durlak, J. A., Weissberg, R. P., Dymnicki, A. B., Taylor, R. D., & Schellinger, K. B. (2011). The impact of enhancing students' social and emotional learning: A meta-analysis of school-based universal interventions. *Child Development, 82*, 405–432.

Ellis, B. J., & Boyce, W. T. (2011). Differential susceptibility to the environment: Toward an understanding of sensitivity to developmental experiences and context. *Development and psychopathology, 23*, 1–5.

Ellis, B. J., Boyce, W. T., Belsky, J., Bakermans-Kranenburg, M. J., & Van IJzendoorn, M. H. (2011). Differential susceptibility to the environment: An evolutionary–neurodevelopmental theory. *Development and Psychopathology, 23*, 7–28.

Emler, N. (2001). *Self-esteem: The costs and consequences of low self-worth*. York, England: York Publishing.

Faull, C., Swearer, S. M., Jimerson, S. R., Espelage, D. L., & Ng, R. (2008). *Promoting positive peer relationships: Middle school bullying prevention program-Classroom resource*. Adelaide, Australia: Readymade Production.

Fox, L., Carta, J., Strain, P., Dunlap, G., & Hemmeter, M. L. (2009). *Response to intervention and the pyramid model*. Tampa: University of South Florida, Technical Assistance Center on Social Emotional Intervention for Young Children.

Fox Eades, J. M. (2008). *Celebrating strength: Building strengths-based schools*. Coventry, England: CAPP Press.

Frederickson, B. L. (2001). The role of positive emotions in positive psychology: The broaden-and-build theory of positive emotions. *American Psychologist, 56*, 218–226.

Gardner, H. (1983). *Frames of mind: The theory of multiple intelligence*. New York, NY: Basic Books.

Gardner, H. (1999). *Intelligence reframed: Multiple intelligences for the 21st century*. New York, NY: Basic Books.

Garmezy, N., & Nuechterlein, K. (1972). Invulnerable children: The fact and fiction of competence and disadvantage. *American Journal of Orthopsychiatry, 42*, 328–329.

Garrison, C. Z., Schluchter, M. D., Schoenbach, V. J., & Kaplan, B. K. (1989). Epidemiology of depressive symptoms in young adolescents. *Journal of the American Academy of Child & Adolescent Psychiatry, 28*, 343–351.

Gillham, J. E., Abenavoli, R. M., Brunwasser, S. M., Linkins, M., Reivich, K. J., & Seligman, M. E. P. (2013). Resilience education. In S. A. David, I. Boniwell, & A. C. Ayers (Eds.), *The Oxford handbook of happiness* (pp. 609–630). Oxford, England: Oxford University Press.

Gillham, J. E., Reivich, K. J., & Freres, D. R. (2007). School based prevention of depressive symptoms: A randomized controlled study of the effectiveness and specificity of the Penn Resiliency Program. *Journal of Consulting and Clinical Psychology, 75*, 9–19.

Goldstein, S., & Brooks, R. B. (2006). Why study resilience? In S. Goldstein & R. B. Brooks (Eds.), *Handbook of resilience in children* (pp. 3–15). New York, NY: Springer.

Goleman, D. (1996). *Emotional intelligence: Why it can matter more than IQ*. New York, NY: Bantam Books.

Green, H., McGinnity, A., Meltzer, H., Ford, T., & Goodman, R. (2005). *Mental health of children and young people in Great Britain 2004*. New York, NY: Palgrave Macmillan.

Heffron, K., & Boniwell, I. (2011). *Positive psychology: Theory, research and applications*. Berkshire, England: McGraw-Hill.

Hirschfeld, R., Keller, M., Panico, S., Arons, B., Barlow, D., Davidoff, F., . . . Wyatt, R. J. (1997). The National Depressive and Manic-Depressive Association consensus statement on the undertreatment of depression. *Journal of the American Medical Association, 277*, 333–340.

Homeland Security Advisory Council. (2011). *Community resilience task force recommendations.* Retrieved from http://www.dhs.gov/xlibrary/assets/hsac-community-resilience-task -force-recommendations-072011.pdf

Humphrey, A., Kalambouka, A., Bolton, J., Lendrum, A., Wigelsworth, M., Lennie, C., & Farrell, P. (2008). *Primary social and emotional aspects of learning (SEAL): Evaluation of small group work.* Retrieved from http://www.dcsf.gov.uk/research/data/uploadfiles/DCSF -RB064.pdf

Humphrey, A., Lendrum, A., & Wigelsworth, M. (2010). *Social and emotional aspects of learning (SEAL) programme in secondary schools: National evaluation.* Retrieved from https://www.gov .uk/government/uploads/system/uploads/attachment_data/file/181718/DFE-RR049 .pdf

Huta, V. (2013). Eudaimonia. In S. A. David, I. Boniwell, & A. C. Ayers (Eds.), *The Oxford handbook of happiness* (pp. 201–213). Oxford, England: Oxford University Press.

Jimerson, S. R., Morrison, G. M., Pletcher, S. W., & Furlong, M. J. (2006). Youth engaged in antisocial and aggressive behaviors: Who are they? In S. R. Jimerson & M. J. Furlong (Eds.), *Handbook of school violence and school safety: From research to practice* (pp. 3–19). New York, NY: Routledge.

Kahne, J. (1996). The politics of self-esteem. *American Educational Research Journal, 33,* 3–22.

Kerig, P. K., Ludlow, A., & Wenar, C. (2012). Intervention and prevention. In P. K. Kerig, A. Ludlow, & C. Wenar (Eds.), *Developmental psychopathology* (6th ed, pp. 617–653). London, England: McGraw-Hill.

Keyes, C. L. M., & Magyar-Moe, J. L. (2003). The measuring and utility of adult subjective well-being. In S. J. Lopez & C. R. Snyder (Eds.), *Positive psychological assessment: A handbook of models and measures* (pp. 411–425). Washington, DC: American Psychological Association.

Lewinsohn, P. M., Hops, H., Roberts, R., & Seeley, J. (1993). Adolescent psychopathology: I. Prevalence and incidence of depression and other DSM-III-R disorders in high school students. *Journal of Abnormal Psychology, 102,* 110–120.

Linley, P. A., & Govindji, R. (2008). *An evaluation of celebrating strengths.* Unpublished manuscript.

Lopez, S. J., Snyder, C. R., Magyar-Moe, J. L., Edwards, L. M., Pedrotti, J. T., Janowksi, K., . . . Pressgrove, C. (2004). Strategies for accentuating hope. In P. A. Linley & S. Joseph (Eds.), *Positive psychology in practice* (pp. 388–403). Hoboken, NJ: Wiley.

Luthans, F., Youssef, C. M., & Avolio, B. J. (2007). *Psychological capital: Developing the human competitive edge.* New York, NY: Oxford University Press.

Luthar, S. S., Cicchetti, D., & Becker, B. (2000). The construct of resilience: A critical evaluation and guidelines for future work. *Child Development, 71,* 543–562.

Masten, A. S. (2001). Ordinary magic: Resilience process in development. *American Psychologist, 56,* 227–238.

Masten, A. S., & Obradovic, A. J. (2006). Competence and resilience in development. *Annals of the New York Academy of Science, 1094,* 13–27.

McCown, K. S., Jensen, A. L., Freedman, J. M., & Rideout, M. C. (1998). *Self-science: The emotional intelligence curriculum.* San Maeto, CA: Six Seconds.

McDermott, D., & Hastings, S. (2000). Children: Raising future hopes. In C. R. Snyder (Ed.), *Handbook of hope: Theory, measures, and applications* (pp. 185–199). San Diego, CA: Academia Press.

McGrath, H., & Noble, T. (2003). *Bounce Back! Teacher's handbook.* Sydney, Australia: Pearson Education.

Morris, I. (2013). Going beyond the accidental: Happiness, education, and the Wellington College experience. In S. A. David, I. Boniwell, & A. C. Ayers (Eds.), *The Oxford handbook of happiness* (pp. 644–656). Oxford, England: Oxford University Press.

Niemiec, C. P., & Ryan, R. M. (2013). What makes for a life well lived? Autonomy and its relation to full functioning and organismic wellness. In S. A. David, I. Boniwell, & A. C. Ayers (Eds.), *The Oxford handbook of happiness* (pp. 214–226). Oxford, England: Oxford University Press.

Noble, T., & McGrath, H. (2005). Emotional growth: Helping children and families "bounce back." *Australian Family Physician, 34,* 749–752.

Noble, T., & McGrath, H. (2008). The positive educational practices framework: A tool for facilitating the work of educational psychologists in promoting pupil wellbeing. *Educational and Child Psychology, 25,* 119–134.

Noble, T., & McGrath, H. (2013). Well-being and resilience in education. In S. A. David, I. Boniwell, & A. C. Ayers (Eds.), *The Oxford handbook of happiness* (pp. 563–578). Oxford, England: Oxford University Press.

O'Connell, M. E., Boat, T., & Warner, K. E. (2009). *Preventing mental, emotional, and behavioural disorders among young people: Progress and possibilities.* National Research Council and Institute of Medicine of the National Academies. Washington, DC: National Academies Press.

Peterson, C. (2006). *A primer in positive psychology.* New York, NY: Oxford University Press.

Peterson, C., & Seligman, M. E. P. (2004). *Character strengths and virtues: A handbook and classification.* Oxford, England: Oxford University Press.

Plomin, R., DeFries, J. C., McClearn, G. E., & McGuffin, P. (2008). *Behavioral genetics.* New York, NY: Worth.

Pluess, M., & Belsky, J. (2009). Differential susceptibility to rearing experience: The case of child-care. *Journal of Child Psychology and Psychiatry, 50,* 396–404.

Pluess, M., & Belsky, J. (2010). Differential susceptibility to parenting and quality child care. *Developmental Psychology, 46,* 379–390.

Pluess, M., Boniwell, I., Hefferon, K., & Tunariu, A. (in press). *Validation of SPARK resilience curriculum for Y7 and Y8 students.*

Proctor, C., & Fox Eades, J. (2009). *Strengths gym.* St. Peter Port, England: Positive Psychology Research Centre.

Reivich, K., & Shatté, A. (2003). *The resilience factor: 7 keys to finding your inner strength and overcoming life's hurdles.* New York, NY: Broadway Books.

Renshaw, T. L., & Jimerson, S. R. (2012). Enhancing student attitudes via a brief, universal-level bullying prevention curriculum. *School Mental Health, 4,* 115–128.

Reznitskaya, A., & Sternberg, R. J. (2004). Teaching students to make wise judgements: The "Teaching for Wisdom" program. In P. A. Linley & S. Joseph (Eds.), *Positive psychology in practice* (pp. 181–196). Hoboken, NJ: Wiley.

Richardson, G. E. (2002). The metatheory of resilience and resiliency. *Journal of Clinical Psychology, 58,* 307–321.

Roffey, S. (2011). Enhancing connectedness in Australian children and young people. *Asian Journal of Counselling, 18,* 15–39.

Rothbart, M. (1989). Biological processes in temperament. In G. Kohnstamm, J. Bates, & M. Rothbart (Eds.), *Temperament in childhood* (pp. 77–110). New York, NY: Wiley.

Rutter, M. (1987). *Psychological resilience and protective mechanisms.* New York, NY: Irvington.

Rutter, M. (2006). Implications of resilience concepts for scientific understanding developmental psychopathology. *Annals of the New York Academy of Science, 1094,* 1–12.

Rutter, M., Cox, A., Tupling, C., Berger, M., & Yule, W. (1975). Attainment and adjustment in two geographical areas. I: The prevalence of psychiatric disorder. *British Journal of Psychiatry, 126,* 493–509.

Ryan, R. M., & Deci, E. L. (2001). On happiness and human potentials: A review of research on hedonic and eudaimonic well-being. *Annual Review of Psychology, 52,* 141–166.

Ryff, C. D., & Keyes, C. L. (1995). The structure of psychological well-being revisited. *Journal of Personality and Social Psychology, 69,* 719–727.

Sackett, D. L., Rosenberg, W. M. C., Gray, J. A. M., Haynes, R. B., & Richardson, W. S. (1996). Evidence-based medicine: What it is and what it isn't. *British Medical Journal, 312,* 71–72.

Salovey, P., Caruso, D., & Mayer, J. D. (2004). Emotional intelligence in practice. In P. A. Linley & S. Joseph (Eds.), *Positive psychology in practice* (pp. 447–463). Hoboken, NJ: Wiley.

Salovey, P., & Mayer, J. D. (1990). Emotional intelligence. *Imagination, Cognition, and Personality, 9,* 185–211.

Salovey, P., Rothman, A. J., Detweiler, J. B., & Steward, W. T. (2000). Emotional states and physical health. *American Psychologist, 55,* 110–121.

Sangsue, J., & Vorpe, G. (2004). Professional and personal influences on school climate in teachers and pupils. *Psychologie du Travail et des Organisations, 10,* 341–354.

Schonert-Reichl, K. A., & Lawlor, M. S. (2010). The effects of a mindfulness-based education program on pre- and early adolescents' well-being and social and emotional competence. *Mindfulness, 1,* 137–151.

Seligman, M. E. P. (2002). *Authentic happiness.* London, England: Nicolas Brealey.

Seligman, M. E. P. (2007). Coaching and positive psychology. *Australian Psychologist, 42,* 266–267.

Seligman, M. E. P., & Csikszentmihalyi, M. (2000). Positive psychology. An introduction. *American Psychologist, 55,* 5–14.

Seligman, M. E. P., Ernst, R. M., Gillham, J., Reivich, K., & Linkins, M. (2009). Positive psychology and classroom interventions. *Oxford Review of Education, 35,* 293–311.

Seligman, M. E. P., Reivich, K., Jaycox, L., & Gillham, J. (1995). *The optimistic child.* New York, NY: Houghton Mifflin.

Slee, P. T., Lawson, M. J., Russell, A., Askell-Williams, H., Dix, K. L., Owens, L., . . . Spears, B. (2009). *KidsMatter evaluation final report executivesSummary.* Retrieved from https://www.bspg.com.au/dam/bsg/product?client=BEYONDBLUE&prodid=BL/0718&type=file

Sternberg, R. J. (2001). Why schools should teach for wisdom: The balance theory of wisdom in educational settings. *Educational Psychologist, 36,* 227–245.

Sugai, G., & Horner, R. H. (2002). The evolution of discipline practices: School-wide positive behavior supports. *Child and Family Behavior Therapy, 24,* 23–50.

Twenge, J. M. (2009). Generational changes and their impact in the classroom: Teaching generation me. *Medical Education, 43,* 398–405.

UNICEF Innocenti Research Centre. (2007). *Child poverty in perspective: An overview of child well-being in rich countries.* Retrieved from http://www.unicef-irc.org/publications/pdf/rc7_eng.pdf

Wachs, T. D. (2006). Contributions of temperament to buffering and sensitization processes in children's development. *Annals of the New York Academy of Sciences, 1094,* 28–39.

Wells, J., Barlow, J., & Stewart-Brown, S. (2003). A systematic review of the universal approaches to mental health promotion in schools. *Health Education, 103,* 197–220.

White, M. A. (2013). Positive education at Geelong Grammar School. In S. A. David, I. Boniwell, & A. C. Ayers (Eds.), *The Oxford handbook of happiness* (pp. 657–668). Oxford, England: Oxford University Press.

World Bank. (2011). *Social resilience and climate change.* Retrieved from http://web.worldbank.org/WBSITE/EXTERNAL/TOPICS/EXTSOCIALDEVELOPMENT/0,,contentMDK:22115092~pagePK:210058~piPK:210062~theSitePK:244363,00.html

Wright, M. O. D., & Masten, A. S. (2006). Resilience processes in development. In S. Goldstein & R. B. Brooks (Eds.), *Handbook of resilience in children* (pp. 17–37). New York, NY: Springer.

# CHAPTER 19

# Cultivating Adolescents' Motivation

REED W. LARSON and NICKKI PEARCE DAWES

O RGANIZED YOUTH PROGRAMS—INCLUDING arts, civic, technology, and leadership programs—occupy a unique place in the lives of American adolescents. They provide a valuable alternative to the educational model in schools, an alternative that is more consistent with positive psychology. In most U.S. secondary schools, learning is controlled by adults, students are positioned as recipients of knowledge, and grades given to individuals provide a principal incentive for motivating learning. In contrast, many youth programs are based on a philosophy of youth-driven learning. Participation is voluntary, youth often work together, and program staff encourage youth to exercise active control over learning activities. The learning objectives often go beyond youth's acquisition of content knowledge and include development of more holistic competencies emphasized by positive psychology, such as character and life skills (Roth & Brooks Gunn, 2003). Central to this philosophy is the belief that youth's learning can be enjoyable, engaging, and self-motivating.

This idea that learning—and human development—can be self-motivating has been advocated by a long line of progressive educators and positive psychologists, including Dewey, Montessori, Piaget, Bruner, and Csikszentmihalyi. They argued that young people do not have to be forced to learn and grow, it is a natural process—learning can be "intrinsically motivating." Indeed, research shows that when youth experience learning in a given topic area to be intrinsically motivating they, first, want to learn more on that topic, and second, their learning occurs at deeper levels—young people gain more knowledge, not just of facts, but of underlying concepts and thought processes associated with that topic area (Ryan & Deci, 2000; Shernoff, 2013). Intrinsic motivation can be a powerful "engine of learning and development" (Larson & Rusk, 2011, p. 91).

Research also confirms that this powerful alternate model of learning is experienced by many or most youth in organized programs. In time-sampling studies, adolescents report much higher average levels of intrinsic motivation as well as comparable or higher levels of challenge and cognitive engagement when participating in organized programs than during school classes (Larson, 2000; Vandell

*Authors' Note.* We would like to thank the many youth and leaders who contributed to this research, as well as the William T. Grant Foundation for its support of the work. Additional funding was provided by the USDA National Institute of Food and Agriculture, Hatch project ILLU-793-314, awarded to R. Larson.

313

et al., 2006). Diverse findings suggest that youth's experience of this motivated engagement is associated with deeper learning experiences and positive developmental outcomes (Hansen & Larson, 2007; Mahoney, Parente, & Lord, 2007; Shernoff, 2013). For example, youth in arts, leadership, and other types of programs report developing deeper process skills, including techniques of the activity and skills for managing emotions, strategic thinking, responsibility, and teamwork (Halpern, 2009; Larson, 2011).

The question of this chapter is: How do professional staff who run programs support this intrinsically motivated learning? That is, what strategies do these program leaders employ that facilitate and sustain youth's intrinsic motivation in learning tasks? The findings, we believe, have relevance to teachers, coaches, and other youth professionals who aim to support positive development.

We must note at the outset that young people's intrinsic motivation in learning tasks is not always automatic, and the efforts of youth professionals to cultivate and sustain it can meet obstacles. Many motivational theorists (and motivational speakers) would have us believe that motivation is simple. But attempts to motivate young people can backfire (Ryan & Deci, 2003). Intrinsic motivation is shaped by many factors (Eccles & Roeser, 2009) and is subject to ups and downs, as these factors change from day to day (Ryan & Deci, 2000; Urdan, 2003). Even in effective organized programs, the leaders report times when individual youth or the group are unmotivated and difficult to motivate (Larson & Walker, 2010). Very little research has been done on how program leaders—or other educators—facilitate young people's motivation; but preliminary evidence suggests that, to be effective, their motivational strategies must be adapted to the broad social-psycho-ecological context, including the immediate circumstances of the situation (Kaplan, Katz, & Flum, 2012; Turner, Warzon, & Christensen, 2011).

In this chapter, we analyze the expertise that experienced professional leaders employ to facilitate youth's intrinsically motivated learning. Our objective is to understand the motivational strategies used by these leaders, the situations in which they are used, and the underlying reasoning that makes these strategies effective. Because our focus is on facilitating and sustaining youth's self-motivation, our research draws on both leaders' and youth's accounts of their ongoing experiences in programs.

## UNDERSTANDING PROGRAM LEADERS' MOTIVATIONAL STRATEGIES IN CONTEXT

Given the importance of understanding motivation in relation to social-psycho-ecological contexts, let us first provide more background about the institutional context of youth programs and what is known about the factors that influence young people's ongoing intrinsic motivation.

### THE INSTITUTIONAL CONTEXT

American youth programs have a number of advantages over schools in the conditions they can provide for youth to be intrinsically motivated. Unlike with school, most teens in urban and suburban areas can choose from a wide selection of programs that interest them (run by public, nonprofit, for-profit, and religious organizations). In addition, programs are comparatively free of the kinds of government mandates and strictures that dictate what happens in school classrooms. As a result, programs can be more nimble in creating activities tailored to the interests of the group of youth they attract. They are able to provide the kinds of hands-on and personally meaningful real-world activities that even research in schools shows are intrinsically motivating (Faircloth, 2009).

Most programs for high school–aged youth involve projects such as arts, engineering, science, or community projects. In one of the art programs in our study, the leader had arranged for youth to paint murals that were mounted at a metro stop. In other programs, youth created videos, planned events for children, and lobbied the school board. Coaches of youth sports teams often encourage individual athletes and the team to think about the season as a project aimed at achieving defined goals. This "project method" of learning, first championed by John Dewey, aims to motivate youth to devote a cumulative effort working toward defined short- or long-term goals. It allows youth to learn from experiencing the authentic real-world consequences of their work (Heath, 1999). In Dewey's words, youth "learn from doing." They learn from deliberate trial and error.

Projects and real-world experiences generally elicit high motivation, and youth often become highly invested in their work (Dawes & Larson, 2011; Hidi & Renninger, 2006). But they can also present hazards for sustaining youth's motivation. In contrast to carefully controlled school assignments, projects are more open-ended and can career in unexpected directions. The literature documents numerous instances when, for example, youth became bored with the drudgery of real-world tasks; the murals youth mounted on the metro stop were vandalized, making youth angry and bitter (Larson & Walker, 2006); and the direction of youth's work crossed unstated boundaries and upset adult authorities, who then shut it down (Ozer et al., 2008). An educational model aimed at giving youth real-world experiences and allowing them to "learn from doing" demands flexibility from youth professionals. They need to be prepared to respond to diverse situations and motivational scenarios.

### Factors That Influence Motivation

To understand the challenges that professionals face in facilitating youth's motivation, it is also helpful to know what basic motivational research says about the factors that influence it. An important conclusion of motivational researchers in recent years is that intrinsic motivation is influenced by a wide array of factors at many levels of analysis (Eccles & Roeser, 2009; Shernoff & Bempechat, in press). To illustrate this diversity, we review factors at four levels, giving special attention to some of the factors that will be relevant later in the chapter.

One important level is *a person's immediate experience in an activity*. Csikszentmihalyi's (1984; Csikszentmihalyi & Larson, 1990) theory of "flow" identifies factors in a person's immediate interactions that influence intrinsic motivation. These include experiencing clear goals in the activity, challenges that are matched to your skills, and accurate feedback on your progress toward those goals. When people experience these elements, they are more likely to experience a state of intrinsic motivation that Csikszentmihalyi calls "flow."

At another level, psychological research identifies *individual dispositions* that influence intrinsic motivation. Ryan and Deci's (2000) self-determination theory posits that humans share three basic psychological needs (autonomy, relatedness, and competence) and that people are most motivated when an activity serves one or more of these needs. Additional disposition-like factors that contribute to motivation include a person's sense of efficacy in the activity (Bandura, 1997) and whether the activity is congruent with the person's values, expectations, and goals (Eccles & Roesner, 2009).

At another level, people's *interpersonal experiences* in the setting are critical to motivation (Shernoff, 2013). Do youth feel like they belong? Do they feel the people can be trusted and care about them? Intrinsic motivation is shaped by ongoing relationship, including the relationships that develop in working together on an activity in the setting (Meyer & Smithenry, 2014). Research also indicates that *culture* influences motivation: Many of the factors just mentioned—such as needs, expectations, goals, and the dynamics of relationships—are mediated by cultural norms and ways of thinking (Markus & Kitayama, 2003).

Together, these, and additional levels and factors, form a complex puzzle. To make things more complicated, these factors may change from day to day (for example, as a function of how well a youth's project is going). Furthermore, the set of factors that are most influential may differ from one youth to another.

How Youth Professionals Facilitate Youth's Motivation

All of these different influences on motivation are a lot for program leaders to think about! This research suggests they need to consider the full puzzle—ranging from a youth's immediate experience in a specific situation, to their needs and goals, to interpersonal and cultural processes. How do experienced leaders navigate this social-psycho-ecological complexity?

Our approach to this question has entailed identifying effective professional program leaders and learning from them. What motivational strategies do they use and find useful in the daily situations of practice? Research in other professions substantiates that over time most practitioners learn a lot about how to do their jobs effectively. They develop strategies for dealing with the most salient and frequent challenges they face in their work (Kahneman & Klein, 2009). Of course, there is not a perfect correlation between years of experience and effectiveness. We did not expect this approach would identify the full variety of effective motivational strategies, nor that it would provide conclusive evidence on what works best in every situation. Nonetheless, tapping into the experiences of professionals judged to have expertise is a good place to start in understanding a profession, especially how it is practiced in context, in relationship to day-to-day situations.

## METHODS USED FOR STUDYING PRACTICE

We selected eight high-quality programs with experienced leaders. These were programs that were identified as high quality by other youth professionals and in which we observed that youth were generally quite motivated. They included arts, technology, and leadership programs for high-school–aged youth. All of the 14 leaders in the eight programs were paid professionals with at least 2 years of experience. The sample of 80 ethnically diverse young people included 8 to 12 representative members from each program.[1]

Because our goal was to obtain accounts grounded in the daily experience of youth's changing motivation, we conducted multiple interviews (plus observations) over the natural course of the programs. In the interviews, we asked the leaders

---

[1] All these programs had a youth-centered philosophy. Six of the programs were urban and two rural. Data came from a total of 468 interviews with 80 youth (31 European American, 16 African American, 27 Latino American, 2 Asian American, 4 biracial), 110 interviews with 14 program advisors, and 136 site observations (Dawes, 2008). The text includes a few additional illustrations from a prior case study we wrote on one of the programs (Pearce [Dawes] & Larson, 2006), and from two additional programs that were in the full study (Dawes & Larson, 2011).

about their role in facilitating youth's motivation, encouraging them to provide specific examples. We asked youth open-ended questions about changes in their motivation and what influence the leaders had in those changes.

The objective of our analysis was to identify and understand the most salient motivational strategies used by the leaders. We employed systematic methods of grounded theory analysis (Strauss & Corbin, 1998). Nickki Dawes first coded the youth's reports on how leaders supported their motivation. She then analyzed the leaders' interviews and found their reports to be remarkably consistent (Dawes, 2008). For this chapter, we conducted an additional step of theoretical analysis aimed at more fully situating the leaders' implementation of these motivational strategies within their social-psycho-ecological context. This step drew on broader sources of knowledge, including other published analyses from the same data set and other research on organized programs.

NURTURING YOUTH'S EXPERIENCE OF AGENCY AND OWNERSHIP: "YOU'RE NEVER TRULY FORCED"

Western culture is individualistic and its members see self-motivation as linked to the experience of personal freedom and agency (Markus & Kitayama, 2003). In order to be genuinely engaged, people must experience themselves to be the "origins" or agents of their actions (Deci, 1975). It is not surprising, then, that the first motivational strategy that we identified relates directly to this: Leaders supported youth's experience of agency in their activities.

When describing how leaders contributed their motivation, youth frequently identified *freedom and choice* as a primary factor. For example, one youth, Chris, said that when he joined Media Masters,[2] he had low expectations because he thought they would be doing "routine work." But his motivation climbed dramatically after the first few weeks because the leaders gave him "freedom to choose whatever I feel like doing . . . and that's what's getting me into it." Some youth made this point by making a contrast to school. Carlos said he became highly motivated in the program Art First because, "they let you do whatever you want, like everything." He then described how "My photography teacher at school, he just gives us the work, he never really motivates us; like: 'You have to do this and do that.'" Lori said she was motivated because "you're never truly forced to do something." This freedom appeared to be a remarkable new experience in a learning context, one that that really helped youth get engaged.

But it was not just the freedom. Youth reported that it was also the opportunity freedom provided for them to *choose activities that were personally meaningful*. Ernesto said the leader "encourages us to do whatever you feel you're passionate about." Leaders frequently repeated the same theme. In an agricultural program, leaders said they encouraged youth to explore different activities to find one fit to their interests. In other programs, leaders reported counseling youth to make choices that allowed them to "find their motivation," develop their own artistic style, or express their interests. The Media Masters leaders emphasized to youth that "This is not school: You should allow your own ideas to shape your project, not what you think adults want."

A key concept the leaders used to describe this motivational strategy was *youth ownership*. Across programs, it was used like a mantra. Starting from the first day, leaders would tell youth "It is your program" and "It is your project." A leader overseeing youth's creation of a video at the program Harambee said he helped motivate

---

[2]All names of youth and programs are pseudonyms.

them by making sure they had input at every step in the production process. Leaders reported that they encouraged youth to express their ideas and provide input. In some programs youth had primary responsibility for their work from beginning to end (Larson, Walker, & Pearce, 2005).

This strategy of supporting youth's agency is congruent with motivational research and theory. Ryan and Deci (2000) have identified autonomy—which they define as experience of agency and ownership—as a universal psychological need and a primary contributor to intrinsic motivation (although, as noted above, individual agency is more highly valued in Western culture; Markus & Kitayama, 2003). In Ryan and Deci's (2000) motivational theory, what these leaders were doing was providing youth with "autonomy support."

In our concluding theoretical analysis, it was apparent that use of this strategy required a great deal of judgment and skill from leaders. They were *not* simply turning things over to youth with a hope and a prayer that that would make them motivated. They were active in nurturing youth's experiences of agency. First, in all programs, *leaders provided some degree of initial structure* for youth's projects—general goals, models of how the work might unfold, and sometimes deadlines—so there was a track for youth to follow. This kind of "appropriate structure" is important to motivation in many theories; in situations without any structure, motivation is often short-lived (Eccles & Gootman, 2002).

Second, as youth's work progressed, the *leaders provided judicious input on youth's work*. Youth reported drawing on leaders for advice on their work, and leaders sometimes offered advice or direction without being asked. Leaders tried to allow youth wide latitude for agency and for learning from experience. But they interjected input for a consistent set of reasons: Youth got in over their heads, got stuck, lost motivation, or were headed in a direction that was unlikely to succeed. Leaders' input helped youth get back on track, move forward, and get remotivated (Larson & Angus, 2011a, 2011b). Across the programs we studied, this input improved youth's motivation because it helped them regain a sense of agency and control over their work (Larson & Angus, 2011a).

In sum, this motivational strategy was clearly not one of giving youth total freedom. It rather was nurturing youth's *experience of* agency at a level the youth could manage and that kept projects moving forward.[3] This strategy of nurturing youth's agency involved a challenging *balancing act* in which leaders supported youth's decision making, but at the same time provided initial structures for youth's work, then monitored and provided advice when needed to keep youth on track. This requires leaders to make ongoing decisions about whether, when, and how they should provide input that sustains the forward motion of youth's work without compromising their experience of ownership (Larson & Angus, 2011a, 2011b).

## SUPPORTING YOUTH'S SENSE OF INDIVIDUAL AND COLLECTIVE EFFICACY: ADDRESSING DOUBT

Carrying out a project often involves going into the unknown: Youth are trying things they have not done before—a large work of art, taking on a bigger role, speaking up in meetings with youth or adults whom they don't know. Research shows that exploring

---

[3]From the perspective of flow theory, they were helping youth stay or get back into a "flow channel" where they experienced challenges that were matched to their skills (Larson & Walker, 2006).

things that are novel can be intrinsically motivating (Csikszentmihalyi, 1990). Yet it comes with risks—including the vertigo of self-doubt. Bandura (1997) and others have consistently found that having a sense of individual or collective efficacy ("I can do it," "We can do it") is important to sustained motivation. Supporting and stabilizing youth's sense of efficacy was the second salient motivational strategy used by the leaders in our study.

Youth reported multiple experiences of self-doubt. With each turn of events, their expectations for the success of their projects could swing from the grandiose to the catastrophic. Doubt could cascade across all the unknowns in their plans, leading to their questioning the whole enterprise. Youth reported that leaders facilitated their motivation by providing encouragement, especially at low points. They said leaders believed in them. Alan in the agricultural program said "they're always there to fire you up when you're down." Paula at The Studio described how she got despondent when she compared her skills to her peers. But the leader's repeated encouragements ("See, you can do it!") bucked up her sense of efficacy: "I was very proud of my little ideas. As little as they may be, she supported me." Research on mastery substantiates that this is an important motivational strategy of effective teachers: to shift a student's focus of attention from comparing him- or herself to others to moving upward from his or her own current level of skills (Dweck, 1999). Whereas the leaders' first strategy, providing autonomy support, entailed managing the challenges in youth's work, this set of strategies supported youth's perceptions of their skills for meeting these challenges.

A notable finding was that this strategy sometimes entailed helping youth envision where their work was headed. Camille, at *Les Misérables*, reported being energized and motivated to keep working because the leaders "very much encourage us to look to the future and think about, like, 'This is where we are now, but tomorrow night we're gonna work really hard and we're gonna try to get this to this point.'" Youth's confidence was greater when they had a tangible vision of the path ahead. One Media Masters leader said youth's motivation depended on "those things that make them feel they are doing good; that they are getting it; the vision in their heads. What they created from words is now coming to life." Bandura (2006) describes how forethought is crucial to both guiding and motivating effective work toward difficult goals. Knowing where one is going and envisioning how to reach it reduces uncertainty and increases sense of efficacy.

Theory suggests, however, that implementing this strategy in context presents challenges. The danger of supporting youth's sense of efficacy is making sure that it does not inflate youth's expectations. Critics argue that a whole generation of American youth has been made insecure and risk-averse by a post-Spock culture of indiscriminate praise and support for their self-esteem (e.g., Dweck, 1999). But these experienced leaders used encouragement and praise selectively to try to reinforce effort and help youth get through bad spots (Larson & Angus, 2011b). Helping youth envision the trajectory of their work is an adroit way to reduce uncertainty and thus support youth's sense of efficacy.

In a new study, Griffith, Larson, Johnson, and Silver (2013) found that experienced program leaders provided encouragement balanced with realism and honest feedback. The youth in that study reported that they valued straightforward feedback—and that it *increased* their motivation—because it helped them learn and do better in their projects. As with the other motivational strategies we describe, executing this strategy required leaders' discrimination and balancing of competing considerations.

## SUPPORTING RELATIONSHIPS: FACILITATING BELONGING, CAMARADERIE, AND COLLECTIVE FLOW

The third leader motivational strategy that we identified was cultivating positive relationships. Research on school motivation has often concluded, put comically: "It's the relationships, stupid!" School motivation is influenced by students' experiences of interpersonal safety, belonging, and emotional closeness to teachers and peers (Wentzel, 2009). Likewise, research in programs shows that positive relationships are important to youth's engagement (Hirsch, 2005).

Many youth described their relationships with the leaders as important to their motivation because leaders cared about them as people. Angela in the program El Concilio recounted a time when she was going through a rough patch in her life: "Robin like called me and she was just wondering how I was doing. And when I saw her concern, it motivated me, like, 'Okay, I see somebody does care.'" Similarly, Susana at Art First described the leaders' attentiveness as a critical factor in her motivation in program activities: "She's a very kind person who's showed so much interest in all of us, and she makes us feel very much appreciated, which is something that doesn't always happen with teachers at school."

Leaders also cultivated positive relationships *among* program members. At the beginning of the year, they created icebreaking activities and asked veteran youth to be welcoming to new members. As the year went on, youth said leaders encouraged them to help each other, work together, and see themselves as part of a team. Leaders described actively encouraging peer collaboration and camaraderie. Indeed, many youth reported being motivated because they experienced a collective connection to their projects (Dawes & Larson, 2011; Pearce [Dawes] & Larson, 2006). Theory and research on intrinsic motivation often focus on the individual as the unit of analysis, yet motivation can be a group experience (Markus & Kitayama, 2003). Working together toward a shared goal, youth often appeared to have collective flow experiences.

Humans are social creatures, so it makes sense that leaders' cultivation of positive relationships contributes to youth's motivation. In Ryan and Deci's (2000) self-determination theory, "relatedness" is a basic psychological need that contributes to intrinsic motivation. Collaborative work is found to promote learning, partly because it increases motivation (Rogoff, 1998).

Yet implementing this strategy of cultivating positive relationships can be challenging. Because of the importance of adolescent autonomy in American culture, many youth view adults with suspicion (Jarrett, Sullivan, & Watkins, 2005). Many leaders overcame this distrust by relating to youth as friends; but this created the challenge of navigating the tension between being a friend *and* being the adult who has ultimate responsibility in the setting. They had to balance relating to youth in personal ways that contributed to youth's motivation yet maintain needed professional boundaries (Walker, 2011; Walker & Larson, 2006). In cultivating positive peer–peer relationships, leaders navigated a murky boundary between facilitating peer interactions that helped engage youth in the work while dampening peer dynamics that distracted youth from it (Larson & Angus, 2011b; Pearce [Dawes] & Larson, 2006).

Although cultivating good relationships may seem obvious as a way to motivate youth, adults' navigation of the dynamics of these relationships can present complex challenges (Camino, 2005; Pace & Hemmings, 2007). Effective youth practitioners have skills to develop healthy relationships with youth that recognize boundaries while providing support for youth to grow as persons.

BALANCING SERIOUS WORK WITH FUN: NOT PUSHING TOO HARD

The fourth motivational strategy we identified was balancing serious work with fun. Fun is a powerful word in American adolescents' vocabulary (Csikszentmihalyi & Larson, 1984). If an activity gets too serious, it can become associated with the dull and dubious world of adults. Youth programs are a relatively rare context in which youth typically enjoy getting immersed in serious challenging activities.

Many youth attributed their motivation to leaders' efforts to make the program lighthearted, pleasant, and fun. For example, Tanya described how her motivation at Art First could wane: "Sometimes I get really discouraged or lazy, because we have to write so much, and since I write so much in school already. . . . But Rebecca tries to move away from that and make it fun."

Similarly, Krista, in the production of *Les Misérables*, described how the director, Ann, was successful in balancing serious work with fun by modeling an attitude:

> She's very into it. . . . She becomes one of us. . . . It makes the productions more enjoyable. And it makes you feel more at home, it makes you feel like this is a place where you can maybe not forget your obligations, but it's a place where you can put your homework on hold and enjoy yourself.

Our observers also reported that Ann cultivated humor and playfulness in rehearsal: Mistakes were met with laugher and gentle banter, followed by Ann gently turning youth back into working on a song. Note that both Tanya and Krista contrasted this approach to school. Youth felt that leaders' attention to keeping it fun (as compared to their more serious and dreary experiences in school) was important to supporting their motivation.

The leaders also described this strategy of balancing seriousness and fun. They were intentional in the selection, presentation, and monitoring of program elements to keep the light side in and avoid getting too serious. One Media Masters leader, Janna, said that her motivation role included "to make them laugh, to make them enjoy it." When nerves got frayed, the agricultural program leader suggested a break to play basketball. Neisha, a leader at The Studio, described trying to keep the youth "upbeat" in their projects: "It's hard work and it's a lot to take in. So I just try to keep making it fun . . . instead of like, 'Oh we gotta do all this work.'" Again, it appeared that judgment and skill were required to implement this strategy.

THE ART OF CULTIVATING INTRINSIC MOTIVATION

Intrinsic motivation is a powerful engine of learning and positive human development. When youth are self-motivated—when they are "psyched," "in love with," or "turned on"—by an activity, their attention is more deeply engaged in learning. But, whether you are a teacher, coach, program leader, or other youth professional, cultivating motivation in young people can be challenging. Intrinsic motivation can be fragile or fade. Youth professionals can inadvertently undercut intrinsic motivation by monopolizing conversation, giving students answers without giving them a chance to determine answers for themselves, using "should" too often, or having a temper tantrum that undermines their relationships with youth (Dworkin & Larson, 2006; Ryan & Deci, 2008).

In the programs we studied, the *structured but open-ended* nature of youth's projects appeared to provide a key affordance for the experience of intrinsic motivation. Leaders created structures for youth's projects (e.g., schedules, standards, examples of good work) that imposed parameters, constraints, and direction on youth's activities, and they simultaneously provided opportunities for youth's experiences of the agency, competency, and positive relationships that are important to this motivation. In a media arts program, for example, the leaders structured a sequence of assignments that each required use of different software to create a product. Within each project there were specific points at which youth obtained leader and peer feedback on their work. But youth had latitude for artistic expression within each assignment and they experienced competency in creating the product, aided in part by the feedback. Furthermore, the leaders fostered a program culture that emphasized mutual respect and assistance (Larson, 2007). This culture helped youth feel safe in forming positive collaborative relationships, which created conditions for youth to experience collective intrinsic motivation.

These leaders understood factors, such as sense of agency, clear feedback, and positive relationships, that research has identified as important influences on youth's motivation. They are central to the leaders' motivational strategies. Being an effective leader, however, involves more than knowing these factors, it involves translating and implementing them in complex and dynamic situations. The leaders in our research often had to *balance* these principles with psychological, social, pragmatic, and other situational contingencies. When and how long do you let youth continue with a project that is exciting to them but unlikely to succeed? Where do you draw the line between being a friend to youth and being firm in maintaining a safe and structured environment? How do you sustain the different factors that support intrinsic motivation without youth perceiving you as manipulative?

The leaders we studied were skilled in performing these balancing acts. Our analyses, based on youth's and leaders' accounts, identified frequent strategies that these leaders employed that involved balancing the motivational factors with situational considerations:

- They used "youth ownership" as a mantra to help youth experience freedom, agency, and meaning in their work, which fueled their motivation, but they also provided input and advice as needed to help keep youth's projects on course.
- They supported youth's sense of individual and collective efficacy as youth went through the ups and downs in the work, but they tried to keep youth grounded in a realistic vision of where their work was headed.
- They balanced relating to youth in personal ways that created conditions of social connection, trust, and friendship—which is important to intrinsic motivation (Ryan & Deci, 2000)—while also maintaining professional boundaries that allowed them to exercise authority.
- They encouraged peer camaraderie, yet sometimes had to address peer dynamics that distracted youth from their work.
- They encouraged youth's engagement with serious real-world challenges (e.g., lobbying the school board, bringing the musical *Les Misérables* to life), but they also maintained a sense of fun and good humor.

These were the most frequent strategies that we found, but this is by no means a complete list. Furthermore, in addition to being attuned to youth's motivation, these leaders were also balancing other important professional mandates of their job including keeping youth safe, teaching subject matter skills, enforcing rules, and keeping their funders happy (Larson & Walker, 2010). Leaders often mixed and matched different strategies, depending on the circumstances.

In sum, the leaders were adept at juggling multiple professional goals and applying them to varied situations. Future research is needed to further understand the guidelines and mental models that experienced leaders use to navigate different motivational scenarios (e.g., youth are overwhelmed by choices, bored with tedious work, frustrated by hitting dead ends, burned out because they set expectations too high for themselves). Research is also needed to understand how youth learn to manage these different scenarios on their own, and how youth professionals help facilitate this learning. In educational research, Hidi and Renninger (2006) identified stages in students' development of interest in a topic area, stages that are accompanied by increasing skills for self-regulation of motivation, and they observed that educators adapted their motivational strategies to students at each stage. The applicability of this model across different youth development settings also needs to be investigated.

## CONCLUSION

This ability to balance and adapt to the different goals and considerations of daily practice, we suggest, is a critical component of youth professionals' expertise. Research across diverse fields of practice—including education, health professions, and engineering—shows that skills to identify and balance multiple considerations are a consistent characteristic of practitioner expertise (Fook, Ryan, & Hawkins, 2000; Ross, Shafer, & Klein, 2006; Weiss, Kreider, Lopez, & Chatman, 2005). In preliminary research, Walker and Larson (2012) replicated this important finding with leaders of youth programs. They compared how novices and experts appraised and formulated responses to vignettes of prototypical situations in youth practice. They found that the experts identified significantly more considerations in situations and formulated responses that addressed a wider array of these considerations. The experts' responses were often multipronged: They did not just "balance" different considerations—in the sense of counterweighing trade-offs; instead, they often found win-win solutions that seemingly addressed competing considerations simultaneously. The experts' responses also included more "if/thens" that involved shaping the response to situational contingencies.

We believe that preparatory and in-service training for youth professionals should be aimed at helping them develop skills for appraising the complex, multileveled situations of youth practice and developing their repertoire of nuanced strategies for responding to these situations. Researchers can contribute by continuing to learn from experienced youth professionals and from studying how developmental and motivational theory might be pertinent to understanding the complex, dynamic situations they navigate in daily practice.

## SUMMARY POINTS

- Intrinsic motivation can be a powerful "engine" of learning and positive development. It is associated both with sustained participation and deeper engagement.
- However, young people's intrinsic motivation in learning tasks is not automatic, and cultivating it is not always easy. Motivation is influenced by many factors at multiple levels, including in the activity, in relationships, and in the dispositions and goals that youth bring to a setting.
- The ability of professionals to cultivate young people's motivation depends on their development of knowledge and skills for appraising situations and executing strategies at these multiple levels.

- Our research identified four frequent strategies that were effective in cultivating motivation in ways that were adapted to specific youth and situations: (1) nurturing youth's experience of agency and ownership; (2) supporting youth's sense of individual and collective efficacy, including by helping them envision where their work is headed; (3) supporting positive and caring youth–adult and youth–youth relationships; and (4) balancing serious work with fun.

## REFERENCES

Bandura, A. (1997). *Self-efficacy: The exercise of control*. New York, NY: Freeman.

Bandura, A. (2006). Toward a psychology of human agency. *Perspectives on Psychological Science, 1*, 164–180.

Camino, L. (2005). Pitfalls and promising practices of youth-adult partnerships: An evaluator's reflections. *Journal of Community Psychology, 33*, 75–85.

Csikszentmihalyi, M. (1990). *Flow: The psychology of optimal experience*. New York, NY: HarperCollins.

Csikszentmihalyi, M., & Larson, R. (1984). *Being adolescent*. New York, NY: Basic Books.

Dawes, N. P. (2008). *Engaging adolescents in organized youth programs: An analysis of individual and contextual factors* (Unpublished doctoral dissertation). University of Illinois at Urbana-Champaign, Champaign, IL.

Dawes, N. P., & Larson, R. W. (2011). How youth get engaged: Grounded-theory research on motivational development in organized youth programs. *Developmental Psychology, 47*, 259–269.

Deci, E. L. (1975). *Intrinsic motivation*. New York, NY: Plenum Press.

Dweck, C. S. (1999). *Self-theories: Their role in motivation, personality, and development*. Philadelphia, PA: Psychology Press.

Dworkin, J., & Larson, R. (2006). Adolescents' negative experiences in organized youth activities. *Journal of Youth Development, 1*(3), 1–19.

Eccles, J. S., & Gootman, J. A. (Eds.). (2002). *Community programs to promote youth development. Committee on community-level programs for youth*. Washington, DC: National Academy Press.

Eccles, J. S., & Roeser, R. W. (2009). Schools, academic motivation, and stage-environment fit. In R. M. Lerner & L. Steinberg (Eds.), *Handbook of adolescent psychology* (3rd ed, Vol. 1, pp. 404–434). Hoboken, NJ: Wiley.

Faircloth, B. S. (2009). Making the most of adolescence: Harnessing the search for identity to understand classroom belonging. *Journal of Adolescent Research, 24*, 321–348.

Fook, J., Ryan, M., & Hawkins, L. (2000) *Professional expertise: Practice, theory and education for working in uncertainty*. London, England: Whiting and Birch.

Griffith, A., Larson, R. W., Johnson, H., & Silver, N. (2013). *Why participants of youth programs are motivated by constructive feedback*. Unpublished paper, University of Illinois at Urbana-Champaign, Champaign, IL.

Halpern, R. (2009). *The means to grow up: Reinventing apprenticeship as a developmental support in adolescence*. Chicago, IL: Routledge.

Hansen, D., & Larson, R. (2007). Amplifiers of developmental and negative experiences in organized activities: Dosage, motivation, lead roles, and adult-youth ratios. *Journal of Applied Developmental Psychology, 28*, 360–374.

Heath, S. B. (1999). Dimensions of language development: Lessons from older children. In A. S. Masten (Ed.), *Cultural processes in child development: The Minnesota symposium on child psychology* (Vol. 29, pp. 59–75). Mahwah, NJ: Erlbaum.

Hidi, S., & Renninger, A. (2006). The four-phase model of interest development. *Educational Psychologist, 41*, 111–127.

Hirsch, B. J. (2005). *A place to call home*. New York, NY: Teachers College Press.

Jarrett, R. L., Sullivan, P. J., & Watkins, N. D. (2005). Developing social capital through participation in organized youth programs. *Journal of Community Psychology, 33,* 41–55.

Kahneman, D., & Klein, G. (2009). Conditions for intuitive expertise: A failure to disagree. *American Psychologist, 64*(6), 515–526. doi:10.1037/a0016755

Kaplan, A., Katz, I., & Flum, H. (2012). Motivation theory in educational practice. Knowledge claims, challenges, and future directions. In T. Urdan (Ed.), *APA educational psychology handbook: Vol. 2. Individual differences, cultural considerations, and contextual factors in educational psychology* (pp. 165–194). Washington, DC: American Psychological Association.

Larson, R. (2000). Towards a psychology of positive youth development. *American Psychologist, 55*(1), 170–183.

Larson, R. (2007). From "I" to "we": Development of the capacity for teamwork in youth programs. In R. Silbereisen & R. Lerner (Eds.), *Approaches to positive youth development* (pp. 277–292). Thousand Oaks, CA: Sage.

Larson, R., & Walker, K. (2006). Learning about the "real world" in an urban arts program. *Journal of Adolescent Research, 21,* 244–268.

Larson, R., Walker, K., & Pearce, N. (2005). A comparison of youth-driven and adult-driven youth programs: Balancing inputs from youth and adults. *Journal of Community Psychology, 33,* 75–74.

Larson, R. W. (2011). Positive development in a disorderly world. *Journal of Research on Adolescence, 22,* 317–334.

Larson, R. W., & Angus, R. M. (2011a). Adolescents' development of skills for agency in youth programs: Learning to think strategically. *Child Development, 82,* 277–294.

Larson, R. W., & Angus, R. (2011b). Pursuing paradox: The role of adults in creating empowering settings for youth. In M. Aber, K. Maton, & E. Seidman (Eds.), *Empowering settings and voices for social change* (pp. 65–93). New York, NY: Oxford University Press.

Larson, R. W., & Rusk, N. (2011). Intrinsic motivation and positive development. In R. M. Lerner, J. V. Lerner, & J. B. Benson (Eds.), *Advances in child development and behavior: Positive youth development* (Vol. 41, pp. 89–130). Oxford, England: Elsevier.

Larson, R. W., & Walker, K. C. (2010). Dilemmas of practice: Challenges to program quality encountered by youth program leaders. *American Journal of Community Psychology, 45,* 338–349.

Mahoney, J. L., Parente, M. E., & Lord, H. (2007). After-school program engagement: Links to child competence and program quality and content. *Elementary School Journal, 107*(4), 385–404.

Markus, H. R., & Kitayama, S. (2003). Models of agency: Sociocultural diversity in the construction of action. *Nebraska Symposium on Motivation, #49*. Lincoln: University of Nebraska Press.

Meyer, D. K., & Smithenry, D. W. (2014). Scaffolding collective engagement. In D. J. Shernoff & J. Bempechat (Eds.), Engaging youth in schools: Evidence-based models to guide future innovation. *National Society for the Study of Education Yearbook, Teachers College Record, 113*(1), 124–145.

Ozer, E. J., Cantor, J. P., Cruz, G. W., Fox, B., Hubbard, E., & Moret, L. (2008). The diffusion of youth-led participatory research in urban schools: The role of the prevention support system in implementation and sustainability. *American Journal of Community Psychology, 41,* 278–289.

Pace, J. L., & Hemmings, A. (2007). Understanding authority in classrooms: A review of theory, ideology, and research. *Review of Educational Research, 77,* 4–27.

Pearce [Dawes], N. & Larson, R. (2006). The process of motivational change in a civic activism organization. *Applied Developmental Science, 10,* 121–131.

Rogoff, B. (1998). Cognition as a collaborative process. In W. Damon (Series Ed.) & D. Kuhn & R. Siegler (Vol. Eds.), *Handbook of child psychology* (5th ed., Vol. 2, pp. 679–744). New York, NY: Wiley.

Ross, K., Shafer, J. L., & Klein, G. (2006). Professional judgments and "naturalistic decision making." In K. A. Ericsson, N. Charness, P. J. Feltovich, & R. R. Hoffman (Eds.), *Cambridge handbook of expertise and expert performance* (pp. 403–419). Cambridge, England: Cambridge University Press.

Roth, J., & Brooks-Gunn, J. (2003). Youth development programs: Risk, prevention and policy. *Journal of Adolescent Health, 32*, 170–182.

Ryan, R. M., & Deci, E. L. (2000). Self-determination theory and the facilitation of intrinsic motivation, social development, and well-being. *American Psychologist, 55*, 68–78.

Ryan, R. M., & Deci, E. L. (2003). On assimilating identities to the self: A self-determination theory perspective on internalization and integrity within cultures. In M. R. Leary & J. P. Tangney (Eds.), *Handbook of self and identity* (pp. 255–273). New York, NY: Guilford Press.

Ryan, R. M., & Deci, E. L. (2008). Self-determination theory and the role of basic psychological needs in personality and the organization of behavior. In O. P. John, R. W. Robbins, & L. A. Pervin (Eds.), *Handbook of personality: Theory and research* (pp. 654–678). New York, NY: Guilford Press.

Shernoff, D. J. (2013). *Optimal learning environments to promote student engagement.* New York, NY: Springer.

Shernoff, D. J., & Bempechat, J. (Eds.). (2014). Engaging youth in schools: Evidence-based models to guide future innovations. *National Society for the Study of Education Yearbook, Teachers College Record, 113*(1).

Strauss, A., & Corbin, J. (1998). *Basics of qualitative research: Techniques and procedures for developing grounded theory* (2nd ed.). Thousand Oaks, CA: Sage.

Turner, J. C., Warzon, K. B., & Christensen A. (2011). "They have no motivation": Changes in teachers' practices and beliefs during a nine-month collaboration on motivation in mathematics. *American Educational Research Journal, 48*, 718–762.

Urdan, T. (2003). Intrinsic motivation, extrinsic rewards, and divergent views of reality. *Educational Psychology Review, 15*, 311–325.

Vandell, D. L., Reisner, E. R., Pierce, K. M., Brown, B. B., Lee, D., Bolt, D., & Pechman, E. M. (2006). *The study of promising after-school programs: Examination of longer term outcomes after two years of program experiences.* Madison: Wisconsin Center for Education Research. Retrieved from http://www.wcer.wisc.edu/childcare/statements.html

Walker, K. C. (2011). The multiple roles that youth development program leaders adopt with youth. *Youth and Society, 43*, 635–655.

Walker, K. C., & Larson, R. W. (2006). Balancing the professional and the personal. In D. A. Blyth & J. A. Walker (Eds.), *Exceptional learning experiences for the middle years: Where high quality programs meet basic youth needs. New directions for youth development* (Vol. 112, pp. 109–118). San Francisco, CA: Jossey-Bass.

Walker, K. C., & Larson, R. (2012). Youth worker reasoning about dilemmas encountered in practice: Expert-novice differences. *Journal of Youth Development, 7*(1), 5–23.

Weiss, H. B., Kreider, H., Lopez, M. E., & Chatman, C. M. (Eds.) (2005). *Preparing educators to involve families: From theory to practice.* Thousand Oaks, CA: Sage.

Wentzel, K. R. (2009). Students' relationships with teacher as a motivational context. In K. R. Wentzel & A. Wigfield (Eds.), *Handbook of motivation at school* (pp. 301–322). New York, NY: Guilford Press.

# PART V

# POSITIVE PSYCHOLOGY AT WORK

# Bringing Positive Psychology to Organizational Psychology

SARAH LEWIS

I N 2012, BURNES AND COOKE questioned the relevance of organizational development (OD) and, by implication, much of organizational psychology, to organizations in the 21st century. In this chapter, I argue that expanding the field of organizational psychology to incorporate key aspects of positive psychology creates good grounds for suggesting that organizational psychology is still relevant to the big questions of organizations and the people within them.

To support my argument, I suggest that bringing positive psychology, with its emphasis on individual well-being as well as organizational flourishing, to the fore in organizational psychology may help us refute the accusation that OD is merely "a vehicle for managerialist co-optation" (Burnes & Cooke, 2012, p. 1416). I also suggest that it may help us rise to the challenge of addressing the big issues of human welfare through the medium of the working organization. In considering why OD may be under pressure and how positive psychology can help, I consider some of the current challenges experienced by organizations and identify how positive psychology, combined with the best of OD, offers a way forward relevant to these challenges.

Cheung-Judge and Holbeche suggest that "the main causes of change failure are usually found in the way the change process itself is managed" (2011, p. 199). In explaining the problems that change processes can cause, they make reference to the "scar tissue" that organizations can develop after repeated organizational change initiatives, becoming full of resentful, cynical, and disengaged survivors (Cheung-Judge & Holbeche, 2011). The cost of disengagement at work was calculated by Gallup to have been £64.7bn in the United Kingdom in 2008 (Cheung-Judge & Holbeche, 2011, p. 291), while failed change initiatives cost UK businesses £1.7bn (Economist Intelligence Unit, 2008). Organizational change is clearly an expensive business with no guarantee of success.

Appreciative inquiry (AI) is a whole-systems OD approach that works through the medium of conversation or dialogue to achieve system-wide motivation for positive change (Cooperrider & Whitney, 2001; Lewis, Passmore, & Cantore, 2007). It is often characterized as a strengths-based approach due to its focus on identifying the root causes of success from which, it is argued, further success can be built. This stands in contrast to most change approaches that focus on identifying the root causes of failure so they can be corrected or avoided. AI is a psychology-based approach that recognizes group diversity as a strength, emotional states as energizing, partial knowledge as a valuable contribution, dialogue as generative, and aspirations as motivating. It helps the group work together in a way that illuminates the roots of success, identifies areas of commonality, and creates shared aspirations for the future.

Seligman coined the term "positive psychology" in his inaugural address as president of the American Psychological Association in 1999. From the beginning, he suggested that it should be a field of study covering three areas: positive emotions, positive traits, and positive institutions (Seligman, 2003). Since then, interest in the field has grown, attracting scholars from related disciplines, including organizational psychology. It is to be hoped that the application of these approaches will reduce the amount of scar tissue created in organizations through change processes. In this chapter, I outline some of these challenges and consider what positive organizational psychology (POP) has to offer.

## POSITIVE ORGANIZATIONAL PSYCHOLOGY

This section explores the relevance of positive psychology to some current organizational challenges.

### THE CHALLENGE OF MOTIVATION AND THE PSYCHOLOGICAL STATE OF FLOW

Motivation is a recurring challenge in organizations, particularly during times of change and disruption. Deci and Ryan (1985) distinguished between self, or intrinsic, motivation and external, or extrinsic, motivation. People tend to find things that are intrinsically motivating more satisfying and therefore have less need for external monitoring or incentivizing to pursue them. In general terms, it is better, both from a personal and an organizational perspective, for people to work from a basis of self-motivation (see also Brown & Ryan, Chapter 9, this volume). Therefore, a challenge for organizations is to switch from providing external motivators to promoting internal motivation.

Csikszentmihalyi (2002) showed that people are likely to be self-motivated when they are in a "flow" state. They experience a flow state when they pitch their abilities against a challenge that interests them and the balance of skill and challenge is close to even. He discovered that people find the state of flow highly rewarding and will make considerable efforts to create opportunities to experience it. In this way it is self-motivating. People can experience flow states in their work as well as in leisure activities. It is an important possible source of motivation, one that draws energy, commitment, and investment out of people rather than trying to force it in. From this perspective, increasing workplace motivation is less about exhortation and incentives and more about creating inherently interesting and challenging work for people.

### THE CHALLENGE OF PERFORMANCE AND THE CONTRIBUTION OF STRENGTHS

Ensuring maximal individual contribution is a perennial organizational challenge. Positive psychology has identified personal strengths as a source of performance excellence from the very beginning (Seligman, 2003). The field has generated a lot of interest and there continues to be academic debate about the exact nature of strengths. In essence, strengths are a product of genes and experience that mean for each individual some abilities or human capacities are inherently easy and enjoyable to exercise. In this sense, they are distinct from skills (which may be well-honed but not actually enjoyable to use) and personality, which is a more holistic concept than strengths.

From an organizational perspective, strengths are key to productivity. Helping people identify and utilize their strengths can act both to increase production and to reduce cost (Stairs & Gilpin, 2010). There are various ways individuals and organizations can identify their unique and particular strengths (Lewis, 2012). For individuals they range from questions such as "What energizes me?" to sophisticated psychometric measures such as Strengthscope and Strengthsfinder. Appreciative inquiry offers organizations a strengths-based approach to organizational change and development that identifies strengths at the organizational level.

Several studies have shown that facilitating employee strengths produces benefits in terms of reduced turnover and increased productivity. Working with a hospital with a high turnover rate of 35%, Black (2001) showed that introducing a strengths-based development process that used structured talent inventory interviews and built teams using this data reduced turnover by 50%. In another study, Connelly (2002) found that strengths-based team interventions increased the per person productivity rates by up to 9%. Similar results have been reported by others (Harter, Schmidt, & Hayes, 2002). These strengths-based interventions appear to have produced additional benefits. For example, in the Black (2001) study, it is noted that there was a positive and recordable impact on employee engagement over a 2-year period as the organization moved up the Gallup ratings on their measure of employee strengths from the bottom to the top quartile. Similar benefits of introducing strengths-based interventions were reported by Clifton and Harter (2003), who found improved employee engagement across 65 organizations, and by Ko and Donaldson (2011) who report benefits in terms of increased hope, subjective well-being, and self-efficacy.

## THE CHALLENGE OF PERFORMANCE AND THE BENEFITS OF POSITIVITY

Positivity as a term is shorthand for the ratio of positive to negative emotions experienced in a particular situation. An increasing body of work suggests that a positive mood state aids performance in many different domains (Achor, 2011). Research suggests that a positivity ratio of 3:1 or higher is required for the benefits to become evident, either for individuals or for groups (Gottman, 1994; Losada & Heaphy, 2004). Recently, however, the statistical analysis on which this assertion is made has been questioned (Brown, Sokal, & Friedman, 2013), and the debate rages as to the status of the finding. Fortunately, there is other research that demonstrates that, when in positive mood states we are more likely to seek out others, be able to deal with complexity, grasp new concepts, and be innovative (Isen, 2005). It is also becoming increasingly evident that positive mood states positively affect well-being (Hefferon, 2013; Lewis, 2014). Feeling good, in other words, is good for us and in many contexts will also aid performance.

## ORGANIZATIONAL RESILIENCE AND THE BENEFITS OF VIRTUOUS BEHAVIOR

Organizational resilience is a topic of increasing interest as organizations are buffeted by turbulent economic times. Some fascinating research undertaken by Gittell, Cameron, and Lim (2006) on the effects on the aircraft industry of the assault on the Twin Towers in New York in 2001, throws some interesting light on the relation between individual airlines' responses to the immediate negative impact on their cash flow and the speed of their financial recovery.

An immediate consequence of this tragedy was that all planes were grounded for a period after the event. A longer-term effect for the airlines was that even once flights were resumed, traffic dropped below the level necessary for profitability, from 97% occupancy to near 80%. They became unprofitable and their share price dropped. The airlines took immediate action, slashing staff numbers by 16% on average; cutting flights by 20% on average; and introducing new working practices.

However, there were variations within this overall action: One of the 10 airlines studied cut their staff by 24%, while two made no layoffs at all. Of those that did lay off staff, some did so with a distinct lack of good faith: They invoked "force majeure" or "act of god" exemption clauses that allowed them to make workers redundant without regard to any severance pay. They enthusiastically seized the opportunity to push through unpopular changes to working practice. Some airlines still laid people off but with an expressed reluctance, and they honored severance and layoff agreements, even though to do so caused them to make late payments to bond holders (i.e., clearly caused them financial pain).

At the other extreme, a few airlines chose to absorb the shock and the cost, at least in the short term, and worked to find other solutions to the challenge. As others cut their routes, these airlines benefited by maintaining a presence and indeed expanding their services. This was only possible because they took the counterintuitive decision to not lay off staff. One might think that the quickest recovery would accrue to the airlines that took the quickest and most draconian measures to return to profitability. However Gittell et al.'s (2006) analysis shows that the airlines that suffered the least damage to their share price, and whose share price recovered most quickly, were those that made every effort to keep their people despite hemorrhaging money. They also were the quickest to return to profitability.

The recovery of the stock price was significantly and negatively related to the extent of the layoffs at the time of the crisis, the strength of the relationship averaging $R = -0.688$ for the 4-year period of 2001–2004 where the closer $R$ is to –1, the more heavily the stock price appears to be influenced by the extent of the layoffs. The researchers are clear that the mediating factor between response and recovery is the effect of the behavior on what they call *relational reserves*, by which they mean the goodwill of the company toward its owners. They note that "layoffs deplete relational reserves, and relational reserves allow firms to bounce back from crises, maintain desirable functions, and adjust positively to unexpected aberrations" (Gittell et al., 2006, p. 17). This research acts as a support to Cameron and Mora's research (2008) on flourishing organizations.

Cameron and Mora (2008) were interested to discover what distinguishes the best organizations (as in those that are a great place to work and doing well financially) from the rest. They found that the best organizations exhibit three key features. First, they demonstrate an affirmative bias, meaning they look for things to appreciate, praise, and affirm. Second, they demonstrate an unusual or exceptional interest in positive deviance, that is, in understanding why things sometimes turn out exceptionally well or exceptionally badly. And finally, they are exceptionally nice places to work because there is an abundance of *virtuous practices*. By this term, Cameron and Mora mean such things as helpfulness, patience, support, encouragement, forgiveness, and humility. Gittell and colleagues (2006) also identify the practices of the fastest recovering airlines as virtuous practices. They note that the way staff were treated seems to relate directly to how quickly the organization could "bounce back" from the setback of 9/11—in other words, how resilient they were.

THE CHALLENGE OF FAST, EFFECTIVE LOCAL DECISION MAKING AND RELATIONSHIPS

As the world gets faster and faster, the advantages that accrue to organizations that can make quick, effective, low-level adjustment and readjustment to changing circumstances becomes more apparent. There is a growing interest in how the quality of connection and relationship makes a difference in organizational performance. Sometimes in organizations, people have long-term ongoing relationships with their colleagues. Sometimes they may only have to interact with someone very occasionally or even once. The quality of both of these types of interaction can make a difference. Baker and Dutton (2009) characterize high-quality connections as those that add value to organizations, suggesting that even short interactions can add to organizational capacity and capability by effectively solving problems or generating new ideas and creative energy in a very short time frame. Such interactions may be short but they are highly life-affirming and energizing, with both parties coming away infused with hope and possibility.

In addition, an organization may have some more durable positive energy networks. These are networks of people that create a mutually reinforcing experience of motivating and energized interactions. Typically there are some individuals who are particularly likely to be at the center of any such network. Positive individuals have the effect of giving almost everyone they meet a sense of lift. People come away from an interaction with them feeling better than when they arrived: more energized, generating ideas, or relieved of a burden. What has recently become apparent, particularly in more straitened times, is the value they add to organizations as magnets who draw together diverse groups of people who may not have a natural affinity for working together. Given that performance in organizations is increasingly about diversely talented individuals finding ways of cooperating to solve problems and generate new profitable initiatives, this is an invaluable organizational asset or talent that is not always recognized in its own right (Baker, Cross, & Wooton, 2003).

So what happens when you bring these elements together? What does positive organizational psychology look like in practice? The following two case examples illustrate POP and show how leaders make a difference. In the first example, the leader takes an appreciative inquiry–informed approach to rebuilding an organization devastated by tragic events, and the second looks at how hope and improvement can be built by focusing on what does work in situations of hopelessness. Be warned, the first case study contains some distressing information.

*Childcare in New Jersey*   In 2003, a child living in the city of Newark, New Jersey, in the United States, was found dead and stuffed in a trunk in a locked room in the basement of his aunt's home. In the same locked room, under a cot, his brother was found severely malnourished, traumatized, and just barely alive. Later that same year, five brothers from Collingswood, New Jersey, were found in a severely emaciated state. Early in 2004, Jim Davy stepped into the role of Commissioner for the New Jersey Department of Human Services. Shortly after assuming leadership of the department, Davy attended a meeting that the director of the Division of Youth and Family Services (DYFS) had called with 40 of his district office managers. The director's purpose was to conduct an in-depth review of five cases identified as the most extreme examples of "horrendous" casework, including the Newark and Collingswood cases. For nearly 2 hours, the director stood before the 40 managers, who were seated in classroom-style rows, and "picked apart" each case. He exposed what the caseworkers, casework supervisors, and district office managers had done wrong. It was a brutal meeting—the director magnified every weakness, gap, problem, and deficit in the five cases. Davy sat and observed for the full 2 hours and felt drained just listening to the all of the negativity. At the end of his 2-hour case review, the director looked up at his audience and asked for suggestions about how to "fix things." No one offered any suggestions. As Davy reflected on this meeting, he realized that everyone learned about the deficits and problems, but that there was not one iota of conversation about the kind of casework that there *should* be.

This is not an uncommon consequence of the standard "fix the problem" approach. Although clearly the situation needed to improve, such an exclusive concentration on what had gone wrong induced low mood states and raised defensive barriers. In a negative mood state, people are less likely to want to help others (or, in this case, offer suggestions to the director) or to be at their most creative. And as Davy observed, a lot might be learned about what went wrong in the past, but little is learned about what there is to build on to improve things.

Jim decided that a more appreciative approach might help with improving things in the future. He began visiting all of the local DYFS offices around the state. At each office he met with all of the DYFS workers and answered their questions about the child welfare reform planning effort that was underway. No topic was off limits. This is a good example of authentic and positive leadership, showing clearly that taking a positive approach is different from "positive thinking" where difficult things can't be discussed. Davy stayed for as long as it took to answer all their questions. In addition to the Q&A, Davy asked the people in the room to share with him a story about a time when they provided "wow" type case work—a time when they served a child and/or family in a significant, meaningful, and perhaps life-changing way. So while Davy was very willing to engage with uncertainty and concerns about plans for the future, he also created opportunities to talk about the good and about what was working. The stories began to flow like the bursting of a dam. Incredible stories emerged about unbelievable and courageous casework. Rowland and Higgs's (2008) research into successful change revealed the importance of leaders delivering the difficult messages while also creating a "magnetic pull" toward the future. This is the behavior we see demonstrated in this case study.

What Davy noticed immediately was a change in energy. Whereas the people in the director's meeting were exhausted and drained from his deficit-based case review, the caseworkers in Davy's meetings were energized by his "wow" question and elec-trified in sharing stories of successful case practice. He also found that the stories were often told by caseworkers about other caseworkers. Even in an environment characterized by tragedy and failure, people noticed and were affected by stories of overwhelming dedication, caring, promise, and positive impact.

One story was told by a colleague of caseworker named Evelyn. The coworker related how Evelyn, a petite 5-foot Latina, walked into a dangerous crack house to remove two boys, ages 2 and 3, for whom she had case responsibility. Evelyn had spent days searching for them after their aunt, who had been fostering them, died unexpectedly. Evelyn found them with a cousin who was living in a crack house in a crime-ridden part of the city. Without thinking about the danger to herself, and amid taunts and threats from the people inside, Evelyn went into the house, scooped up the two boys, and left. Davy turned to her upon hearing the story and said, "You must have been frightened out of your mind." Evelyn responded: "Commissioner, I wasn't frightened; I was just doing my job." Then she paused a moment and said, "No, it was not my job. It's my calling." Almost without fail, appreciative inquiry positive-discovery processes produce powerful stories that have an immediate impact on the group dynamic, usually boosting motivation, morale, pride, and a sense of hope.

What Davy realized was that these child-welfare workers, who had been demonized by politicians, the press, and child-welfare advocates, were really people who cared deeply about the important work they performed on behalf of children and families. What appreciative inquiry enabled him to do was create a safe environment for the caseworkers to speak freely and openly about the incredibly demanding work they performed and to celebrate their success stories.

There were direct impacts from the appreciative leadership Davy demonstrated in DYFS. From the child-welfare meetings he convened and the stories he heard about highly successful casework, Davy began to note patterns in key elements that contributed to the successes. In this way, he was analyzing the root causes of success. He used those ideas in the system-reform process to inform the development of a new case practice model based on best practices and success. This story illustrates the use of an appreciative approach to solving a problem. By focusing on strengths, recognizing achievements, creating a positive environment, and picking up on stories of positive deviance, Jim Davy was able to transform a poor-performing organization into a strengths-based one (Davy & Weiss, 2011).

*Farmers in Malwa, India*   Another example, also illustrating the power of focusing on the positive exceptions to the norm (positive deviance), but this time on a community scale, is some work undertaken with the cotton farmers of the Malwa belt of the Punjab. Prior to 2003, the cotton yield in this area was extremely low. Suicide among farmers was increasing; businesses were becoming nonviable. There was a danger the farmers would shift to rice cultivation that would be environmentally depleting for the area. The incidence of cancer was rising due to heavy use of pesticides, and the social fabric of the area was under threat.

Whereas most experts were investigating the problem, Shri Paul Oswal, chairman of Vardhman Textiles, took a different approach. He asked about any farmers who, in the midst of mass crop failure, were still reporting decent yields; that is, he sought out examples of positive deviance, where people in the same situation as everyone else had found a way to be successful. He found a few success stories and used them to help reframe the situation from a "problem" situation into one of promise and possibility. Positive deviance is about seeking out, amplifying, and broadcasting stories of "people like you"—that is, not "experts"—who are achieving exceptional results. This can be very inspiring. In his attempt to improve the situation, he was always asking, "So what are we doing right and what can be done better?"

However, it is how the answers are heard, in what context, and by whom, that is at the heart of the change potential they contain. This is not about outside experts taking the stories, tidying them up, and presenting the findings. Rather, the stories need to be told by their owners. Oswal understood this and set up farmers' field schools in villages where his local role models shared their success stories, showing that profitable and sustainable cotton farming was possible. He also imparted scientific knowledge about crop growth and management. The power lies in the combination. Scientific knowledge alone can easily be dismissed as "won't work here."

The stories from local people of how they engaged with this and received benefit helps create the link between the "knowledge" and the motivation to try something new. Oswal brought in many other local partnership agencies, such as local universities and schools. This is an example of actively connecting different areas of strength. It started with just one village and 121 farmers, and by 2008–2009, having touched 23,000 farmers in 251 villages, it had helped create economic and social stability in the area (Verma, 2011). This is an example of actively seeking out "what works" even in a "failing situation" and using local people with contextualized knowledge of what works to inspire others to believe in the possibility of success and to be motivated to make the changes to achieve it.

These case examples illustrate how positive psychology has great potential for organizations and communities. Positive psychology can be applied in both step-change and transformational ways.

## APPLYING POSITIVE PSYCHOLOGY TO ORGANIZATIONS

Various organizations are applying positive psychology in a step-change way. For example, many individual leaders or managers within organizations have embraced the concepts of strengths and are working to improve their performance and appraisal processes by including best-self feedback and feed-forward interviews (Bouskila-Yam & Kluger, 2011) or strengths psychometrics (Brewerton & Brook, 2010). Some organizations are adopting a positive-based approach to audit and evaluation work (Dinsen, 2009; Van de Wetering, 2010). They are redesigning the process to incorporate a greater emphasis on identifying the current strengths of the process and the people as a basis for changes to improve performance. In addition, this process builds motivation to make changes and a commitment to excellence. In other places, managers are working to increase the positivity ratio in their organizations, making concerted efforts to identify, broadcast, and celebrate success. One example is adopting the practice of instituting "good news" rounds at the start of difficult meetings. Some people, however, are taking the possibilities even further. Although there are benefits to taking a step-change approach, it is the transformational potential that is really exciting.

Around 2005, the company leader of Cougar Automations in the United Kingdom, C. H., stumbled upon *First Break All the Rules* (Buckingham & Coffman, 2001), a book about strengths. He followed his nose introducing the book, ideas, and concepts into the organization and seeing where it took them. Five years on, the company was transformed. The amount of cost that can be taken out when people are working toward shared goals and playing to their strengths in a highly self-organizing way and in a high-trust environment is truly transforming. The boost to motivation and the high levels of trust mean that less management energy has to go into "getting work done" and many costly "checking" processes can be removed. Last time I heard the company leader talk about his organization, he explained how expenses claims were taken on trust and people worked together to set salaries for themselves and their managers from an understood central pot of money in any local office. Productivity and profitability have taken off exponentially.

A few principles have emerged through trial and error. Some key learning has been to recruit for strengths, attitude, and general ethos fit. Skills can be taught but attitude and strengths can't, and they make a huge difference. Another has been to give people the tools to be positive. For example, C. H. introduced the concept of "diamond feedback" to help managers feel comfortable giving positive feedback. These days, an understanding of strengths and positivity permeates all aspects of the organization's life.

Cougar Automation has transformed itself from a conventional organization where the owner-director was working himself into an early grave to one that almost runs itself—the cost base is much reduced and the profits much increased. It is a small company, only about 80 people. The big question is how transferable this experience is to larger organizations. One way to approach this challenge would be to make the mental shift from thinking of our organizations as a set of roles and responsibilities to understanding them as an economy of strengths (Cooperrider, 2008).

## ORGANIZATIONS AS ECONOMIES OF STRENGTHS

How would we organize ourselves differently if we understood the organization to be a place where the values lie in the strengths of individuals and how they were combined? How might we barter and bargain internally and externally to produce the most value? How can the modern phenomena of instant interconnectivity extend our individual resourcefulness by the factor of our network? A model of the organization as an economy of strengths may offer a better fit with the 21st century organizational context than that of the organizations as role-bound bureaucracies. Bringing organizational psychology and positive psychology together maybe a way to actively engage with these questions and to deliver the implied benefits. However, we need to be aware of the many dangers that exist between aspiration and application if we are to ensure a successful, fruitful liaison.

There is a danger at the heart of the promise of positive psychology, which is that *doing* more *with* less becomes *getting* more *from* less. Doing more with less is about people spending less time doing what they don't like doing and do badly and spending more time doing what they like doing and do well. It's about the natural incidental benefits that flow from people using their strengths, feeling engaged, and experiencing flow. It is about positive environments being more productive, with people taking less marginal sick leave and contributing value-adding citizen behaviors. In essence, doing more with less is about helping people use their strengths and creating positive environments. An organization that can offer both of these things is likely to be experienced as personally beneficial and empowering. Productivity is likely to improve as capability is enhanced and capacity increases, without additional headcount.

However, the moment this is framed as *getting* more *from* less, it starts to connect with a power-based management agenda that is less about empowerment of and benefit to the individual, and more about the power of and benefit to the shareholders. The distinction is subtle but highly significant and is easily and quickly detected by people as they try to make sense of organizational changes. When new initiatives are introduced into an organization, people try to make sense of why this is happening. If they believe that it is being done as a part of a "getting more from less of us" agenda, then the initiatives will be interpreted as exploitative not empowering. Such beliefs lead to first skepticism, then cynicism. And the growth of cynicism in an organization can undermine almost any improvement initiative.

## LEADERSHIP AND ETHICS

Positive psychology interventions lie in an ethical and moral space. They are not "quick fix" tools that can be applied in any situation to get the same results. Their effectiveness is context-bound, history-influenced, and sense-making dependent. The quality of the human relations in an organization is at the heart of positive psychology practice. As we have seen, Cameron and colleagues (Cameron, Bright, & Caza, 2004) refer to relational reserves and social capital when considering why some organizations are more resilient to shocks, such as redundancies, than others. Similarly, his work on flourishing organizations highlighted the importance of virtuous practices to productive organizational behavior (Cameron & Mora, 2008). Common to both of these areas of research are the concepts of trust and authenticity, both of which are understood to develop over time through a history of interactions. Both are strongly influenced by leadership behavior.

In the wake of various institutional scandals in which the moral compasses of individuals or a group of individuals seem to have been misplaced, questions have been asked about how such things can happen. Although answers offered may veer from the few bad apples school of thought to that of the rotten system, at some point the question of leadership is raised. Did the leaders know what was going on? Did they condone it, or just turn a convenient blind eye? Did they positively encourage such behavior, guided by the light of money? Each time one of these disasters unfolds, adversely affecting both individuals and the fabric of society, the world pays the price for the hubris of such leaders. At such times, the value of leaders with clear ethical and moral frameworks who can see beyond the profit principle becomes apparent. Offering authentic leadership with integrity is not easy because different currents and incentives pull leaders in different directions, but it is possible, and we know what makes it so.

Avolio, Griffith, Wernsing, and Walumbwa (2010) investigated the nature of authentic leadership, and leadership in general. They found that most people can learn to become good leaders. They found that valued and trusted leaders displayed four characteristics: They had a clear moral compass; they took a balanced approach to processing information, for instance taking long-term as well as short-term effects into account; they were authentic as people; and they were good at learning productively from experience. With such leaders, and with the insights offered by positive psychology to inspire the workhorse of organizational psychology, what can we not achieve in our organizations for the good of people, planet, and profit?

## CONCLUSION

Positive psychology offers organizational approaches and processes for building positive, productive, and sustainable organizational environments. It offers guidance on how to bring out the best in people in a way that will benefit them and the organization. Positive psychology has the research, the theory, and the tools to support those who want to create workplaces where people thrive. Combined with the practical experience embodied in organizational psychology, a new strand of practice may emerge that is better-suited to the work conditions of the 21st century: a potentially fruitful liaison indeed.

## SUMMARY POINTS

- The relevance of organizational psychology and its practical application through organizational development to organizations in the 21st century has recently been called into question.
- Positive psychology, with its emphasis on human and organizational flourishing, may offer a way to increase the relevance of organizational psychology to the challenges of today.
- Many key positive psychology concepts, such as flow, strengths, positivity, and high-quality relationships, offer new approaches to organizational challenges such as motivation, performance, and decision making.
- Many positive organizational psychology resources now exist, such as appreciative inquiry and strengths psychometrics.

- Thinking of organizations more as economies of strengths and less as fixed-role hierarchies may help us release the potential of positive psychology in organizations.
- Leadership is an activity that takes place in a moral and ethical space and therefore must be given special attention if the true potential of positive psychology for the workplace is to be realized.

## REFERENCES

Achor, S. (2011). *The happiness advantage: The seven principles that fuel success at work*. London, England: Virgin Books.

Avolio, B., Griffith, J., Wernsing, T. S., & Walumbwa, F. O. (2010). What is authentic leadership development? In P. A. Linley, A. S. Harrington, & N. Garcea (Eds.), *The Oxford handbook of positive psychology and work* (pp. 39–52). Oxford, England: Oxford University Press.

Baker, W., Cross, R., & Wooten, M. (2003). Positive organisational network analysis and energizing relationships. In K. Cameron, J. Dutton, & R. Quinn (Eds.), *Positive organizational scholarship* (pp. 328–342). San Francisco, CA: Berrett Koehler.

Baker, W., & Dutton, J. (2009). Enabling positive social capital in organizations. In J. E. Dutton & B. R. Ragins (Eds.), *Exploring positive relationships at work* (pp. 325–347). New York, NY: Psychology Press.

Black, B. (2001). The road to recovery. *Gallup Management Journal, 1*, 10–12.

Bouskila-Yam, O., & Kluger, A. N. (2011). Strength based performance appraisal and goal setting. *Human Resources Management Review, 21*, 137–147.

Brewerton, P., & Brook, J. (2010). *Strengths for success: Your pathway to peak performance*. London, England: Strengths Partnership Press.

Brown, N. J. L., Sokal, A. D., & Friedman, H. L. (2013). The complex dynamics of wishful thinking: The critical positivity ratio. *American Psychologist*. Advance online publication. doi:10.1037/a0032850

Buckingham, M., & Coffman, C. (2001). *First break all the rules*. London, England: Simon & Schuster.

Burnes, B., & Cooke, B. (2012). Review article: The past, present and future of organizational development: Taking the long view. *Human Relations, 65*, 1395–1429.

Cameron, K., Bright, D., & Caza, A. (2004). Exploring the relationships between organizational virtuousness and performance. *American Behavioural Scientist, 47*, 766–790.

Cameron, K., & Mora, C. (2008). *Positive practices and organizational performances* (Working paper). Ross School of Business, University of Michigan, Ann Arbor, MI.

Cheung-Judge, M., & Holbeche, L. (2011). *Organizational development: A practitioner's guide for OD and HR*. London, England: Kogan Page.

Clifton, D. O., & Harter, J. K. (2003). Investing in strengths. In K. Cameron, J. Dutton, & R. Quinn (Eds.), *Positive organizational scholarship* (pp. 111–121). San Francisco, CA: Berrett Koehler.

Connelly, J. (2002). Altogether now. *Gallup Management Journal, 2*, 13–18.

Cooperrider, D. (2008, November). The 3-circles of the strengths revolution, foreword to the AI practitioner's special issue on strengths-based organisations. *AI Practitioner*. Retrieved from www.aipractitioner.com

Cooperrider, D., & Whitney, D. (2001). A positive revolution in change: Appreciative inquiry. In D. Cooperrider, P. F. Sorensen, Jr., T. F. Yaeger, & D. Whitney (Eds.), *Appreciative inquiry: An emerging direction for organisational development*. Champaign, IL: Stipes.

Csikszentmihalyi, M. (2002). *Flow: The classic work on how to achieve happiness*. London, England: Rider.

Davy, J., & Weiss, L. (2011, February). Appreciative leadership in the face of tragedy. *AI Practitioner*. Retrieved from www.aipractitioner.com

Deci, E. L., & Ryan, R. M. (1985). *Intrinsic motivation and self-determination in human behavior.* New York, NY: Plenum Press.

Dinsen, M. S. (2009, August). Systemic appreciative evaluation: Developing quality instead of just measuring it. *AI Practitioner.* Retrieved from www.aipractitioner.com

Economist Intelligence Unit. (2008). *Securing the value of business process change.* A study commissioned by Logica Management Consulting, London.

Gittell, J., Cameron, K., & Lim, S. (2006). Relationships, layoffs and organizational resilience: Airline industry responses to September 11th. *Journal of Applied Behavioral Science, 42,* 300–329.

Gottman, J. M. (1994). *What predicts divorce? The relationship between marital processes and marital outcomes.* Hillsdale, NJ: Erlbaum.

Harter, J., Schmidt, F., & Hayes, T. (2002). Business unit level relationship between employee satisfaction, employee engagement and business outcomes: A meta-analysis. *Journal of Applied Psychology, 87,* 268–279.

Hefferon, K. (2013). *Positive psychology and the body: The somatopsychic side to flourishing.* Oxford, England: McGraw-Hill.

Isen, A. (2005). A role for neuropsychology in understanding the facilitating influence of positive affect on social behaviour and cognitive affect. In C. R. Snyder & S. J. Lopez (Eds.), *Handbook of positive psychology* (pp. 528–540). Oxford, England: Oxford University Press.

Ko, I., & Donaldson, S. I. (2011). Applied positive organisational psychology: The state of science and practice. In S. I. Donaldson, M. Csikszentmihalyi, & J. Nakamura (Eds.), *Applied positive psychology* (pp. 137–154). New York, NY: Routledge.

Lewis, S. (2012). Have we reached the tipping point for strength-based approaches to organisational challenges? *Assessment and Development Matters, 4,* 10–13.

Lewis, S. (2014). How positive psychology and appreciative inquiry can help leaders create healthy workplaces. In C. Biron, R. Burke, & C. Cooper (Eds.), *Creating healthy workplaces.* Farnham, England: Gower.

Lewis, S., Passmore, J., & Cantore, S. (2007). *Appreciative inquiry for change management: Using AI to facilitate organisational development.* London, England: Kogan Page.

Losada, M., & Heaphy, E. (2004). The role of positivity and connectivity in the performance of business teams: A nonlinear model. *American Behavioral Scientist, 47,* 740–765.

Rowland, R., & Higgs, M. (2008). *Sustaining change: Leadership that works.* West Sussex, England: Jossey-Bass.

Seligman, M. (1999, August). Presidential address, delivered in Boston at American Psychological Association's 107th Annual Convention. In J. Gillham (Ed.), *The science of optimism and hope* (pp. 415–431). Philadelphia, PA: Templeton Foundation Press.

Seligman, M. (2003). *Authentic happiness: Using the new positive psychology realise your potential for lasting fulfillment.* London, England: Nicholas Brealey.

Stairs, M., & Gilpin, M. (2010). Positive engagement: From employee engagement to work place. In P. A. Linley, A. S. Harrington, & N. Garcea (Eds.), *The Oxford handbook of positive psychology and work* (pp. 155–174). Oxford, England: Oxford University Press.

Van de Wetering, A. (2010). Appreciative auditing. *AI Practitioner, 12*(3), 25–31. Retrieved from www.aipractitioner.com

Verma, N. (2011, February). *Appreciative leadership for sustainable development in India. AI Practitioner.* Retrieved from www.aipractitioner.com

CHAPTER 21

# Improving Follower Well-Being With Transformational Leadership

HEATHER M. CLARKE, KARA A. ARNOLD, and CATHERINE E. CONNELLY

D UE TO THE CRITICAL importance of leaders in organizations, an extensive body of research has emerged that examines the effectiveness of different leadership styles. The most commonly studied of these styles is transformational leadership. Indeed, it has been suggested that this positive form of leadership has many benefits for individuals and organizations. For example, transformational leadership leads to increases in individual, team, and organizational performance (e.g., Wang, Oh, Courtright, & Colbert, 2011), safety behaviors (e.g., Clarke, 2013), organizational citizenship behaviors (Huang, 2013), and job satisfaction (e.g., Hobman, Jackson, Jimmieson, & Martin, 2011).

Researchers have also posited that transformational leadership leads to improved employee well-being. Sivanathan, Arnold, Turner, and Barling (2004) examined this relationship in their chapter in the first edition of *Positive Psychology in Practice*, "Leading Well: Transformational Leadership and Well-Being." They drew attention to the absence from the leadership literature at that time of a clear understanding of the benefits of transformational leadership for follower well-being. In particular, there was a dearth of research into the underlying process through which transformational leaders influence the well-being of their followers. With a view to addressing this gap, Sivanathan and colleagues (2004) proposed that transformational leadership impacted follower well-being indirectly through increasing followers' self-efficacy, trust in management, perception of their work as meaningful, and their identification with their organization or occupation.

Over the past decade, a significant body of research investigating the impact of transformational leadership on well-being has emerged. Leadership is now considered to be one of the most important workplace factors influencing employee well-being (Kelloway & Barling, 2010). Numerous studies also suggest that, of the various leadership styles, transformational leadership has the strongest relation with follower well-being (e.g., De Hoogh & Den Hartog, 2009; Gill, Flaschner, & Shachar, 2006; Kanste, Kyngäs, & Nikkilä, 2007). What remains unclear, however, is how this relation occurs. Does transformational leadership have a direct effect on follower well-being, or does it exert its influence indirectly through the mediators of self-efficacy, trust, meaningful work, and identification, as posited by Sivanathan and colleagues (2004)?

We address this question within this chapter. Our first objective is to review the literature on the relation between transformational leadership and follower well-being that has accumulated over the past 10 years, and to distill from this review what advances have been made in terms of developing "a body of knowledge about positive leadership" (Sivanathan et al., 2004, p. 241). Second, we hope to contribute to current knowledge in this area through proposing the theory of conservation of resources as an overarching framework to explain the process through which transformational leadership influences follower well-being. Finally, we aim, through our review of the literature, to examine how the positive psychology perspective has advanced our understanding of transformational leadership and its effects.

We begin by briefly defining transformational leadership and well-being. Next we review the research that has accumulated since Sivanathan et al. (2004) to assess whether this research supports their proposed mediated relationships. We then discuss conservation of resources theory and explicate how this theory provides a framework that aids our understanding of the effects of transformational leadership on follower well-being. We conclude with directions for future research and implications for practice.

## TRANSFORMATIONAL LEADERSHIP

A transformational leader is one who exemplifies the four behaviors of idealized influence, inspirational motivation, intellectual stimulation, and individualized consideration (Bass, 1985, 1998). *Idealized influence* refers to behaving in an ethical and moral manner, thereby earning the respect of followers. By serving as a role model, leaders who engage in idealized influence are able to elicit desirable behaviors from their followers. Leaders who inspirationally motivate their followers formulate a vision, set clear and challenging goals, and give followers the confidence to achieve those goals. Intellectual stimulation involves encouraging followers to think for themselves and problem solve, engendering creativity and innovation. Finally, leaders who display individualized consideration are supportive and show concern for their followers. They coach and mentor according to the individual needs of those they lead.

## WELL-BEING

There have been two predominant approaches to defining well-being: hedonic and eudaimonic (Ryan & Deci, 2001; Huta, Chapter 10, this volume). Hedonic well-being, or happiness, is usually measured with assessments of subjective well-being (Diener & Lucas, 1999). Subjective well-being is typically comprised of life satisfaction, the presence of positive affect, and the absence of negative affect (Ryan & Deci, 2001). Eudaimonic well-being, or human potential, is often operationalized as psychological well-being. Psychological well-being has six factors representing six aspects of human potential or actualization: autonomy, personal growth, self-acceptance, life purpose, mastery, and positive relatedness (Ryff & Keyes, 1995).

Although well-being has been conceptualized as something more than simply the absence of ill-health, it is not always operationalized in a manner that is consistent with this positive conceptualization. In transformational leadership research, measures of ill-health such as stress (e.g., Gill et al., 2006), burnout (e.g., Kanste et al., 2007), or depressive symptoms (Munir, Nielsen, & Carneiro, 2010) are frequently used to assess well-being. Knowledge of transformational leadership's effects on these outcomes is valuable in both research and practice. Such an approach, however, does not allow for the maximization of follower well-being and potential offered by a positive psychology perspective.

Within studies of the association between leadership and well-being there appears to be a growing use of measures of well-being that represent subjective or psychological well-being or their components. With respect to subjective well-being, for instance, studies have utilized scales of positive and negative affect (e.g., McMurray, Pirola-Merlo, Sarros, & Islam, 2010), positive affective well-being (e.g., Arnold, Turner, Barling, Kelloway, & McKee, 2007; Tafvelin, Armelius, & Westerberg, 2011), and positive state of mind (e.g., Munir, Nielsen, Garde, Albertsen, & Carneiro, 2012). Measures of psychological well-being appear to be employed less frequently, but examples include scales representing vitality (e.g., Nielsen & Daniels, 2012), spiritual well-being (e.g., McKee, Driscoll, Kelloway, & Kelley, 2011), and social functioning (e.g., Arnold et al., 2007).

Ryan and Deci (2001) note that the concepts of hedonic and eudaimonic well-being are overlapping but distinct, and that optimal well-being likely comprises aspects of both. Similarly Keyes, Shmotkin, and Ryff (2002) state that optimal well-being is characterized by high levels of both subjective and psychological well-being. We adopt this conceptualization of well-being herein. Therefore, when we use the term *well-being*, we refer not to the absence of mental illness but to "optimal psychological functioning and experience" (Ryan & Deci, 2001, p. 142).

## MEDIATORS OF THE EFFECTS OF TRANSFORMATIONAL LEADERSHIP ON FOLLOWER WELL-BEING

Sivanathan et al. (2004) delineated several mediators that they proposed as mechanisms through which transformational leadership exerted its positive influence on employee well-being. These mediators were self-efficacy, meaningful work, trust in management, and organizational and occupational identity. Next, we review literature from the past decade related to the model proposed in 2004.

### SELF-EFFICACY

Self-efficacy is an individual's belief in his or her ability to accomplish tasks or attain goals (Bandura, 1997). According to Bandura (1997), self-efficacy can be increased through mastery experiences, vicarious experiences, and verbal persuasion. Based on this, Sivanathan and colleagues (2004) proposed that transformational leaders would positively affect follower self-efficacy through helping them successfully accomplish tasks, modeling high self-efficacy, and encouraging them to approach challenges with a positive mind-set. Increased self-efficacy would in turn contribute to improved follower well-being. A few studies have investigated self-efficacy as a mediator in this context.

Based on social learning theory (Bandura, 1997), Liu, Siu, and Shi (2010) predicted that transformational leadership would be positively related to self-efficacy. Self-efficacy would in turn improve well-being through the increased ability to engage in problem-focused coping (Jex, Bliese, Buzzell, & Primeau, 2001; Semmer, 2003). Data were collected via survey from 745 corporate employees from various industries in the public and private sectors. Liu and colleagues found that self-efficacy, along with leader trust (discussed later in this chapter) fully mediated the negative relation between transformational leadership and perceived work stress and stress symptoms.

To examine the psychological mechanisms through which transformational leadership influences employee health and well-being, Nielsen, Yarker, Randall, and Munir (2009) completed a survey study of employees at two elder care centers in Denmark. Nielsen and colleagues (2009) hypothesized that transformational leadership would lead to high self-efficacy and team efficacy, which would increase employees' positive state of mind. Structural equation modeling revealed that there was no direct relation between transformational leadership and well-being because it was mediated by both team and self-efficacy. Nielsen and Munir (2009) analyzed data collected from health-care workers via questionnaire at two points in time. They found a direct relation between transformational leadership and well-being (i.e., positive state of mind) cross-sectionally but not over time because the relation appeared to be mediated by self-efficacy.

Overall, there is some empirical support for the proposition that self-efficacy mediates the effects of transformational leadership on follower well-being. Further, the influence of transformational leadership on self-efficacy is conceptually intuitive. For example, self-efficacy can be increased through attempting and successfully completing tasks (i.e., mastery experiences; Bandura, 1997). As such, leaders who engage in intellectual stimulation, who encourage followers to think for themselves and problem solve, are most likely to engender self-efficacy in their followers. Followers of intellectually stimulating leaders will question assumptions, trust their intuition, and pursue novel ideas. Such individuals will more frequently attempt and successfully accomplish tasks and goals, building their sense of self-efficacy.

What is less clear is how self-efficacy contributes to overall well-being, because theoretical explanations are generally not provided. In addition, self-efficacy has been positioned as a moderator in other research on employee well-being. It is generally understood that self-efficacy can buffer the negative effect of work stressors on psychological well-being (e.g., Jex & Bliese, 1999). It has been proposed that self-efficacy acts in this moderating role because those high in self-efficacy are more apt to focus on solving their problems rather than worrying about them (Kinicki & Latack, 1990). Clarification of self-efficacy's role as mediator or moderator in this context is still needed.

MEANINGFUL WORK

Finding meaning in work has been defined as "finding a purpose in work that is greater than the extrinsic outcomes of the work" (Arnold et al., 2007, p. 195). It has been proposed that meaningful work acts as a mediator between transformational leadership and follower well-being because transformational leaders instill a higher purpose in followers vis-à-vis their work, leading to improved well-being (Sivanathan et al., 2004). The limited research in this area over the past 10 years provides some support for this proposition.

Arnold et al. (2007) examined the relation between transformational leadership, the meaning that individuals ascribe to their work, and their psychological well-being. They suggested that transformational leaders would communicate to workers the importance and purpose of their work. Those workers, finding meaning in their work, would report higher levels of well-being. Their results, across two studies, suggested that meaningful work partially mediated the effects of transformational leadership on subjective well-being (i.e., positive affective well-being) and fully mediated its influence on psychological well-being (i.e., social functioning).

Nielsen, Yarker, Brenner, Randall, and Borg (2008) found that transformational leadership was associated with subjective well-being (positive state of mind) both directly and through meaningfulness. Although the cross-sectional design of this study did not provide strong support for mediation, Nielsen, Randall, Yarker, and Brenner (2008) examined the same relation longitudinally and found support for followers' perceptions of work characteristics, including meaningfulness, mediating the effects of transformational leadership on positive state of mind. They found that perceived work characteristics fully mediated the influence of transformational leadership at Time 1 on follower well-being at Time 2.

These studies provide some support for meaningful work as a mediator of the effects of transformational leadership on well-being. Further support can be found, however, from research specifically examining the ability of transformational leaders to create meaningfulness for their followers. Korek, Felfe, and Zaepernick-Rothe (2010) found that both group-level transformational leadership (the average of individual group members' perceptions of transformational leadership) and consensus (variance among group members' perceptions of transformational leadership) were positively related to followers' perceptions of meaningful task content. Indeed, it has been proposed that transformational leaders influence followers through "managing meaning" at work (e.g., Piccolo & Colquitt, 2006).

There is additional evidence indicating that meaningful work leads to improved well-being. Eakman and Eklund's (2012) survey study revealed that perceiving one's occupation as meaningful was positively related to subjective well-being (life satisfaction) and psychological well-being (meaning in life). They further demonstrated that meaningful occupation was more strongly associated with well-being than personality.

Overall, the research in this area does suggest that transformational leadership can affect follower well-being through influencing followers' perceptions of the meaningfulness of their work. We posit that this is due to the inspirational motivation dimension. Leaders who inspirationally motivate their followers give them confidence to attain challenging goals and infuse their work with a sense of meaning and purpose. Inspirationally motivating leaders, then, enhance their followers' well-being through giving their followers a sense of meaningfulness.

### TRUST IN MANAGEMENT

Briefly stated, trust is the "the willingness of a party to be vulnerable to the actions of another party" (Mayer, Davis, & Schoorman, 1995, p. 712). A substantial body of empirical work exists that supports the relation between transformational leadership and trust in management (see Dirks & Ferrin, 2002, for a meta-analysis of the transformational leadership–trust literature), but only two studies have examined whether the effects of transformational leadership on trust leads to follower well-being.

In their cross-sectional survey study of 745 Chinese employees, Liu, Siu, and colleagues (2010) found that trust in a leader, along with self-efficacy, fully mediated the negative relation between transformational leadership and perceived work stress and stress symptoms. Kelloway, Turner, Barling, and Loughlin (2012) investigated the relation between employees' perceptions of their managers' leadership style and employees' psychological well-being with a two-study research design. Their findings indicated that trust mediated the positive effects of transformational leadership and the negative effects of transactional leadership on affective well-being.

In summary, there is preliminary support for trust in management or leader trust as a mediator of the transformational leadership–well-being relationship. We note that trust has been found to mediate the effects of transformational leadership on other follower outcomes including commitment, job performance, organizational citizenship behavior, and safety-related voice behaviors (Conchie, Taylor, & Donald, 2012; Zhu, Newman, Miao, & Hooke, 2013).

We propose that the individualized consideration dimension of transformational leadership builds trust in followers. Leaders who display individualized consideration are supportive and show concern for their followers. They treat their followers as individuals and are interested in their well-being and development. Followers who believe that their leader has their best interests at heart will be more willing to be vulnerable vis-à-vis their leader. Having trust in their leader leads to more positive relationships and experiences at work, contributing to improved overall well-being.

## IDENTIFICATION

According to social identity theory (Tajfel & Turner, 1979), individuals define themselves, at least partly, in terms of their relationships with other individuals or groups. Sivanathan and colleagues (2004) proposed that transformational leaders would enhance their followers' identification with both their organization and their occupation, leading to improved well-being.

Although we were unable to find any research testing this proposition, there is empirical support for several types of identification as mediators of transformational leadership on job-related attitudes and behaviors. Leader identification has been found to mediate transformational leadership's effects on individual performance, empowerment, job satisfaction, commitment, and turnover intentions (Miao, Newman, & Lamb, 2012; Wang & Howell, 2012). Identification with one's group or work unit mediates the influence of transformational leadership on job performance, job satisfaction, and collective efficacy (Hobman et al., 2011; Walumbwa, Avolio, & Zhu, 2008; Wang & Howell, 2012). Research has also demonstrated that transformational leadership can increase employee voice behavior through fostering identification with the organization (Liu, Zhu, & Yang, 2010).

There has also been further empirical investigation into the effects of identification on well-being. For example, organizational identification is associated with fewer health complaints and lower levels of burnout (Wegge, van Dick, Fisher, Wecking, & Moltzen, 2006), as well as higher levels of elements of both subjective and psychological well-being (Knight & Haslam, 2010). At least one study, however, suggests that identification can impair well-being if it leads to workaholism. Avanzi, van Dick, Fraccaroli, and Sarchielli (2012) found a curvilinear relation between organizational identification and workaholism where workaholism initially decreased with growing identification but then increased with high levels of identification. Workaholism then mediated the relation between identification and employee well-being.

We believe that leaders who portray idealized influence will be the most likely to foster identification among their followers. Leaders who are high in idealized influence are perceived as charismatic and ethical, fostering loyalty and devotion from followers. Because they are both influential and positive role models, their followers identify with them (and their organization) and internalize their goals and values. This positive sense of relatedness contributes to followers' overall sense of well-being.

## ONE DECADE LATER: WHAT HAVE WE LEARNED?

Overall, the literature that has accumulated over the past decade provides preliminary support for the proposition that the relation between transformational leadership and follower well-being is mediated by self-efficacy, meaningful work, trust in management, and identification. However, our review of the literature suggests that this support is tentative in various aspects. First, these four mediators are very similar to various aspects of psychological well-being previously discussed (Ryff & Keyes, 1995). Self-efficacy is a concept that is similar to mastery, meaningfulness may be an element of personal growth or life purpose, trust may be a form of positive relatedness, and identification may be an aspect of life purpose or positive relatedness. From this perspective, one could reasonably argue that the four proposed mediators are in fact themselves components of psychological well-being. With this in mind, we take the position that, pursuant to conservation of resources theory, these four suggested mediators are personal and social resources that contribute to optimal well-being. Utilizing this theoretical explication of the mediator–well-being relations will allow greater specificity in identifying the mechanisms that account for the relation between transformational leadership and employee well-being.

A second concern is that there have been some conflicting findings with respect to the direction of causality within the proposed relations. For example, Strausser, Lustig, and Çiftçi (2008) posited that well-being predicts identification with one's vocation. Similarly, Nielsen and Munir (2009) found that transformational leadership at time one predicted self-efficacy at Time 2 but also that self-efficacy at Time 1 influenced ratings of transformational leadership at Time 2, suggesting a reciprocal relationship. This is consistent with previous research suggesting that follower characteristics influence leadership style (e.g., Dvir & Shamir, 2003) or ratings of leader effectiveness (Bono & Ilies, 2006).

Finally, research on transformational leadership and follower well-being completed over the past decade suggests roles for other mediators as well, including climate for innovation (Tafvelin et al., 2011), sense of community (McKee et al., 2011), and work–life conflict (Munir et al., 2012). Although it is clear that transformational leadership impacts follower well-being, this proliferation of mediators, and the issues discussed earlier, further research in this area would benefit from a stronger theoretical basis. We propose that conservation of resources theory (Hobfoll, 1989) can be applied to this literature as an overarching framework that helps to address these concerns.

## CONSERVATION OF RESOURCES THEORY

According to conservation of resources theory, individuals strive to acquire and maintain resources (Hobfoll, 1989, 2001). Resources are "objects, personal characteristics, conditions, or energies that are valued in their own right, or that are valued because they act as conduits to the achievement or protection of valued resources" (Hobfoll, 2001, p. 339). There are various types of resources identified under conservation of resources theory (e.g., see Hobfoll, 2001). Personal resources include personality traits and psychological states such as optimism and mastery. Other resources are social or relational in nature, including social support and positive intimate relationships (Hobfoll, 1989, 2001).

According to conservation of resources theory, individuals can build resilience to the negative effects of stressors (Hobfoll, 1989). That is, when resources are preserved and maintained, they can prevent individuals from perceiving events or conditions as stressors or buffer the negative impact of stressors on well-being. For example, the resources of self-esteem and employability are negative predictors of burnout (De Cuyper, Sabine, Van der Heijden, & Wittekind, 2012). Conscientiousness, another personal resource, has been found to buffer the impact of engagement on work–family interference (Halbesleben, Harvey, & Bolino, 2009). Other research suggests that resource gains buffer the effects of resource losses (e.g., Chen, Westman, & Eden, 2009; Wells, Hobfoll, & Lavin, 1999).

Although tests of conservation of resources theory have largely examined how resource losses affect well-being or how resource gains can buffer the effects of losses, resource gains may also contribute to improved psychological well-being, health, and functioning (Gorgievski & Hobfoll, 2009; Hobfoll, 2011). There is an opportunity to take a positive psychology approach using this theoretical basis. For instance, Diener and Fujita (1995) demonstrated that resources are positive predictors of satisfaction and positive mood (i.e., subjective well-being). More recently, resource gains have been found to predict higher role and emotional functioning (i.e., psychological well-being), defined as the ability to handle demands and responsibilities and make decisions (Hobfoll, Vinokur, Pierce, & Lewandowski-Romps, 2012).

Conservation of resource theory explains how individuals can acquire and build a bank of resources that contribute not only to guard against ill health but also to improve overall well-being. Because resources can aggregate or become linked to other resources, possessing resources begets further resources (Hobfoll, 2001). When one is high in resources, one is less susceptible to resource loss and in a better position to invest in further resources. However, when one is low in resources, energy is expended on defending them rather than on gaining new ones. Resource losses and gains therefore occur in spirals, where defending against losses consumes existing resources and resource investment leads to further gains. We suggest that transformational leadership acts to increase employees' personal and social resources, introducing a positive spiral that can lead to improved overall well-being.

We conceptualize the mediators proposed by Sivanathan and colleagues (2004) as resources under conservation of resources (COR) theory. Self-efficacy is akin to other personal resources such as "feeling that I am successful" (Hobfoll, 2001, p. 342). Additionally, Hobfoll (2001) identified "feeling that my life is meaningful" as a personal resource (p. 342). In the same vein, we view meaningful work as a personal resource under conservation of resources theory. Although trust has not been previously conceptualized as a resource under COR theory, it is congruent with other social resources such as coworker support and understanding from one's employer or boss (Hobfoll, 2001). Given that Hobfoll (2001) lists "involvement in organizations with others who have similar interests" as a resource (p. 342), we posit that identification is a social resource. Whether the identification is with the occupation, organization, leader, or group, it provides a sense of belonging and involvement. We propose, therefore, that transformational leaders enhance their followers' overall well-being through helping them to gain these resources.

Conservation of resources theory can also help explain the ambiguity regarding the direction of the relations between transformational leadership, proposed mediators, and well-being. Although it is rarely discussed in the literature, a reciprocal relation may exist between transformational leadership and follower well-being. It is not unreasonable to assume that follower well-being influences follower perceptions of their supervisor's transformational leadership behaviors.

This reciprocity is consistent with conservation of resources theory's concepts of resource gain spirals or caravans. Individuals can acquire and aggregate resources into constellations or groups of resources (Hobfoll, 2001). In this way, possessing resources enables further resource acquisition. When one is high in resources, one is less susceptible to resource loss and in a better position to invest in further resources. However, when one is low in resources, energy is expended on defending those resources rather than gaining new ones. De Cuyper, Mäkikangas, Kinnunen, Mauno, and De Witte (2012) demonstrated this empirically. De Cuyper et al. (2012) employed

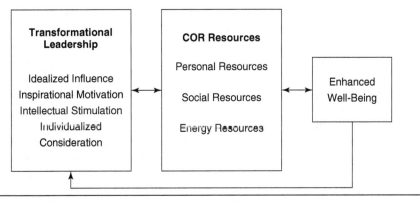

**Figure 21.1** Visual representation of proposed relationships.

COR theory to examine cross-lagged associations among perceived external employability (PEE). PEE was conceptualized as a personal resource that would protect against the resource loss of job insecurity, thereby preventing exhaustion. They found a reciprocal negative relation between PEE and job insecurity. They also found a reciprocal positive relationship between job insecurity and exhaustion.

Similarly, having a leader who engages in transformational leadership behaviors will lead to resource acquisition for followers. However, followers who are higher in resources may be better able to perceive and benefit from their leader's transformational leadership behaviors than those who are low in resources. In this manner, resource acquisition contributes to improved overall well-being, which in turn leads to more resource acquisition, and also likely increases the ability to perceive and benefit from transformational leadership behaviors.

Finally, we noted that research over the past decade has suggested roles for other mediators aside from the four originally proposed by Sivanathan and colleagues (2004). This is consistent with our conservation of resources approach because these constructs have either been identified as resources or are analogous to variables suggested to be resources, such as sense of community (McKee et al., 2011), positive affect or emotions (Bono, Foldes, Vinson, & Muros, 2007; Bono & Ilies, 2006), and sleep quality (Munir & Nielsen, 2009). These variables can be viewed as social, personal, and energy resources, respectively. Again, transformational leaders enable their followers to acquire and maintain these resources, which in turn contribute to followers' overall well-being, enabling them not only to defend against resource loss, but also to invest in further resources, leading to enhanced overall well-being. We believe that this approach is consistent with a positive psychology perspective and is a more fruitful approach than continuing to research and amass a list of mediators viewed in isolation. See Figure 21.1 for a visual representation of our proposed relationships.

## DIRECTIONS FOR FUTURE RESEARCH

Through our review of the literature on the effects of transformational leadership on follower well-being, we have identified several areas that would benefit from further research. First, surprisingly little research has examined the effects of transformational leadership on leaders themselves. A few studies have found that engaging in transformational leadership behaviors is negatively associated with self-reports of burnout (Corrigan, Diwan, Campion, & Rashid, 2002; Zopiatis & Constanti, 2009).

The results of a more recent study, however, suggest that the relation between transformational leadership and leader burnout may not be so straightforward. Arnold, Connelly, and Martin-Ginis (2013) hypothesized that transformational leadership would be positively related to deep acting and negatively related to surface acting. Individuals engage in surface acting when they are required to display emotions that are not felt or are contrary to those they are experiencing at the time. Deep acting, on the other hand, involves changing one's inner feeling state to be consistent with emotions one is required to display (Martinez-Inigo, Totterdell, Alcover, & Holman, 2007). Arnold et al. (2013) further predicted that deep acting would be negatively related and surface acting would be positively related to burnout. However, contrary to their first prediction, Arnold et al. (2013) found that transformational leadership was positively related to both surface and deep acting, and as expected, surface acting was positively associated with burnout.

It is interesting to us that Hobfoll (2001) identified having a leadership role as being a resource. We believe that one could similarly conceptualize that, above and beyond leadership itself, successfully engaging in intellectual stimulation, individualized consideration, inspirational motivation, or idealized influence may be resources that lead to enhanced well-being for the transformational leader. On the other hand, does the extra effort taken to inspirationally motivate, intellectually stimulate, ideally influence, and be individually considerate deplete one's resources and impair leader well-being? Further research on leader well-being employing conservation of resources theory is needed before we can answer such questions.

In addition to further empirical study of leader well-being, we also feel that there are specific areas where research on transformational leadership and follower well-being would benefit from further investigation. First, additional research is needed to examine the effects of individual dimensions of transformational leadership on follower well-being. A transformational leader is one who exemplifies the four behaviors of idealized influence, inspirational motivation, intellectual stimulation, and individualized consideration (Bass, 1985, 1998). In van Knippenberg and Sitkin's (2013) critique of the study of transformational leadership, one of their concerns was that "current perspectives fail to specify how each dimension has a distinct influence on mediating processes and outcomes, and distinct contingencies" (p. 2). In light of this, we attempted to identify in our literature review which dimension would theoretically be most influential in predicting each of the four mediators. We posited that intellectual stimulation would lead to self-efficacy, inspirational motivation would engender meaningfulness, individualized consideration would build trust, and idealized influence would elicit identification. Future empirical work could test these propositions.

Further research is also needed to examine whether the transformational leadership–mediator relations themselves are direct. For instance, Walumbwa and Hartnell (2011) found that relational identification, "the extent to which one defines oneself in terms of a given role-relationship" (Sluss & Ashforth, 2007, p. 11), fully mediated the positive impact of transformational leadership on self-efficacy. Other research suggests that satisfaction of the follower's basic need for competence mediated the relation between transformational leadership and occupational self-efficacy (Kovjanic, Schuh, Jonas, van Quaquebeke, & van Dick, 2012). In a similar vein Zhu, Sosik, Riggio, and Yang (2012) demonstrated that the process through which transformational leadership influences follower organizational identification was partially mediated by psychological empowerment, whereas Schaubroeck, Peng, and Hannah's (2013) longitudinal study suggested that leader trust influences organizational identification.

Finally, as Arnold and Connelly (2013) point out, much of the research examining the relation between transformational leadership and well-being has been "survey-based, used cross-sectional research designs, and been subject to monomethod, monosource bias" (p. 184). We have proposed that the relations among transformational leadership, resources, and well-being are reciprocal. In order to isolate these types of reciprocal relations, longitudinal and experimental designs are necessary.

## IMPLICATIONS FOR PRACTICE

Transformational leadership does appear to have a positive influence on employee well-being. Although more research is needed to identify the exact mechanisms explaining this relation, there is significant evidence to suggest that honing transformational leadership skills will result in positive outcomes for employees. We would encourage individuals and organizations to continue to provide training and development for leaders focusing on transformational leadership behaviors. Improving well-being for individuals within the organization should lead to a more positive working environment, contributing to a positive resource spiral. This is the type of healthy workplace where employees can thrive.

Research identifying specific mechanisms through which these leadership behaviors affect employee well-being can be utilized to focus management training and development activities. Identification, for example, of meaning as a key mediator might suggest that training focus on ways that leadership can communicate the meaning of work in ways that engage employees. In addition, work focused on how leadership behavior affects not only employee well-being but also leader well-being could also provide some clues as to how to design effective interventions to create vitality in the workplace for all organizational members.

## CONCLUSION

In 2004, Sivanathan et al. proposed that transformational leadership would positively influence follower well-being through the mediators of self-efficacy, meaningful work, trust in management, and identification. Our review of the past decade's work into this area largely supports an indirect relation through these mediators, among others. We have suggested conservation of resources theory to explain the underlying mechanism through which these relationships occur. Different dimensions of transformational leadership engender different follower resources, and these resources in turn promote enhanced overall follower well-being. Heaphy and Dutton (2008) noted the health-depleting nature of negative interactions in the workplace and called attention to the need to create opportunities for positive interactions and relationships that are health-promoting. A decade of research suggests that the transformational leadership style is one avenue to accomplishing this.

## SUMMARY POINTS

- The relationship between transformational leadership and follower well-being can be explained by conservation of resources theory.
- Transformational leaders engender personal and social resources, such as self-efficacy, meaningfulness, trust, and identification, in their followers.
- Different dimensions of transformational leadership are plausibly linked with different resources.

- Possessing these resources enables followers not only to guard against resource loss but also to gain further resources.
- Acquiring personal and social resources enhances overall well-being.

## REFERENCES

Arnold, K. A., & Connelly, C. E. (2013). Transformational leadership and psychological well-being: Effects on followers and leaders. In H. S. Leonard, R. Lewis, A. M. Freedman, & J. Passmore (Eds.), *The Wiley-Blackwell handbook of the psychology of leadership, change and organizational development* (pp. 175–194). Hoboken, NJ: Wiley.

Arnold, K. A., Connelly, C. E., & Martin-Ginis, K. (2013, April). *Transformational leadership and leader stress: The mediating effect of emotional labor.* Paper accepted for presentation as part of a symposium on leadership and emotion regulation at the Society for Industrial and Organizational Psychology, Houston, TX.

Arnold, K. A., Turner, N., Barling, J., Kelloway, E. K., & McKee, M. C. (2007). Transformational leadership and psychological well-being: The mediating role of meaningful work. *Journal of Occupational Health Psychology, 12*, 193–203.

Avanzi, L., van Dick, R., Fraccaroli, F., & Sarchielli, G. (2012). The downside of organizational identification: Relations between identification, workaholism and well-being. *Work & Stress, 26*, 289–307.

Bandura, A. (1997). *Self-efficacy: The exercise of control.* New York, NY: Freeman.

Bass, B. M. (1985). *Leadership and performance beyond expectations.* New York, NY: Free Press.

Bass, B. M. (1998). *Transformational leadership: Industrial, military, and educational impact.* Mahwah, NJ: Erlbaum.

Bono, J. E., Foldes, H. J., Vinson, G., & Muros, J. P. (2007). Workplace emotions: The role of supervision and leadership. *Journal of Applied Psychology, 92*, 1357–1367.

Bono, J. E., & Ilies, R. (2006). Charisma, positive emotions and mood contagion. *Leadership Quarterly, 17*, 317–334.

Chen, S., Westman, M., & Eden, D. (2009). Impact of enhanced resources on anticipatory stress and adjustment to new information technology: A field-experimental test of conservation of resources theory. *Journal of Occupational Health Psychology, 14*, 219–230.

Clarke, S. (2013). Safety leadership: A meta-analytic review of transformational and transactional leadership styles as antecedents of safety behaviours. *Journal of Occupational and Organizational Psychology, 86*, 22–49.

Conchie, S. M., Taylor, P. J., & Donald, I. J. (2012). Promoting safety voice with safety-specific transformational leadership: The mediating role of two dimensions of trust. *Journal of Occupational Health Psychology, 17*, 105–115.

Corrigan, P. W., Diwan, S., Campion, J., & Rashid, F. (2002). Transformational leadership and the mental health team. *Administration and Policy in Mental Health, 30*, 97–108.

De Cuyper, N., Mäkikangas, A., Kinnunen, U., Mauno, S., & De Witte, H. (2012). Cross-lagged associations between perceived external employability, job insecurity, and exhaustion: Testing gain and loss spirals according to the Conservation of Resources Theory. *Journal of Organizational Behavior, 33*, 770–788.

De Cuyper, N., Sabine, R., Van der Heijden, B. I. J. M., & Wittekind, A. (2012). The association between workers' employability and burnout in a reorganization context: Longitudinal evidence building upon the conservation of resources theory. *Journal of Occupational Health Psychology, 17*, 162–174.

De Hoogh, A. H. B., & Den Hartog, D. N. (2009). Neuroticism and locus of control as moderators of the relationships of charismatic and autocratic leadership with burnout. *Journal of Applied Psychology, 94*, 1058–1067.

Diener, E., & Fujita, F. (1995). Resources, personal strivings, and subjective well-being: A nomothetic and ideographic approach. *Journal of Personality and Social Psychology, 68,* 926–935.

Diener, E., & Lucas, R. E. (1999). Personality and subjective well-being. In D. Kahneman, E. Diener, & N. Schwarz (Eds.), *Well-being: The foundations of hedonic psychology* (pp. 213–229). New York, NY: Russell Sage Foundation.

Dirks, K. T., & Ferrin, D. L. (2002). Trust in leadership: Meta-analytic findings and implications for research and practice. *Journal of Applied Psychology, 87,* 611–628.

Dvir, T., & Shamir, B. (2003). Follower developmental characteristics as predicting transformational leadership: A longitudinal field study. *Leadership Quarterly, 14,* 327–344.

Eakman, A. M., & Eklund, M. (2012). The relative impact of personality traits, meaningful occupational value on meaning in life and life satisfaction. *Journal of Occupational Science, 19,* 165–177.

Gill, A. S., Flaschner, A. B., & Shachar, M. (2006). Mitigating stress and burnout by implementing transformational-leadership. *International Journal of Contemporary Hospitality Management, 18,* 469–481.

Gorgievski, M. J., & Hobfoll, S. E. (2009). Work can burn us out or fire us up: Conservation of resources in burnout and engagement. In J. R. B. Halbesleben (Ed.), *Handbook of stress and burnout in healthcare.* Hauppauge, NY: Nova Science.

Halbesleben, J. R. B., Harvey, J., & Bolino, M. C. (2009). Too engaged? A conservation of resources view of the relationship between work engagement and work interference with family. *Journal of Applied Psychology, 94,* 1452–1465.

Heaphy, E. D., & Dutton, J. E. (2008). Positive social interactions and the human body at work: Linking organizations and physiology. *Academy of Management Review, 33,* 137–162.

Hobfoll, S. E. (1989). Conservation of resources: A new attempt at conceptualizing stress. *American Psychologist, 44,* 513–524.

Hobfoll, S. E. (2001). The influence of culture, community, and the nested-self in the stress process: Advancing conservation of resources theory. *Applied Psychology: An International Review, 50,* 337–370.

Hobfoll, S. E. (2011). Conservation of resource caravans and engaged settings. *Journal of Occupational and Organizational Psychology, 84,* 116–122.

Hobfoll, S. E., Vinokur, A. D., Pierce, P. F., & Lewandowski-Romps, L. (2012). The combined stress of family life, work, and war in Air Force men and women: A test of Conservation of Resources Theory. *International Journal of Stress Management, 19,* 217–237.

Hobman, E. V., Jackson, C. J., Jimmieson, N. L., & Martin, R. (2011). The effects of transformational leadership behaviours on follower outcomes: An identity-based analysis. *European Journal of Work and Organizational Psychology, 20,* 553–580.

Huang, J.-W. (2013). The effects of transformational leadership on the distinct aspects development of social identity. *Group Processes & Intergroup Relations, 16,* 87–104.

Jex, S. M., & Bliese, P. D. (1999). Efficacy beliefs as moderator of the impact of work-related stressors: A multilevel study. *Journal of Applied Psychology, 86,* 349–361.

Jex, S. M., Bliese, P. D., Buzzell, S., & Primeau, J. (2001). The impact of self-efficacy on stressor-strain relations: Coping style as an explanatory mechanism. *Journal of Applied Psychology, 86,* 401–409.

Kanste, O., Kyngäs, H., & Nikkilä, J. (2007). The relationship between multidimensional leadership and burnout among nursing staff. *Journal of Nursing Management, 15,* 731–739.

Kelloway, E. K., & Barling, J. (2010). Leadership development as an intervention in occupational health psychology. *Work & Stress, 24,* 260–279.

Kelloway, E. K., Turner, N., Barling, J., & Loughlin, C. (2012). Transformational leadership and employee psychological well-being: The mediating role of employee trust in leadership. *Work & Stress, 26,* 39–55.

Keyes, C. L. M., Shmotkin, D., & Ryff, C. D. (2002). Optimizing well-being: The empirical encounter of two traditions. *Journal of Personality and Social Psychology, 82,* 1007–1022.

Kinicki, A. J., & Latack, J. C. (1990). Explication of the construct of coping with involuntary job loss. *Journal of Vocational Behavior, 36,* 339–360.

Knight, C., & Haslam, S. A. (2010). Your place or mine? Organizational identification and comfort as mediators of relationships between the managerial control of workspace and employees' satisfaction and well-being. *British Journal of Management, 21,* 717–735.

Korek, S., Felfe, J., & Zaepernick-Rothe, U. (2010). Transformational leadership and commitment: A multilevel analysis of group-level influences and mediating processes. *European Journal of Work and Organizational Psychology, 19,* 364–387.

Kovjanic, S., Schuh, S. C., Jonas, K., van Quaquebeke, N., & van Dick, R. (2012). How do transformational leaders foster positive employee outcomes? A self-determination-based analysis of employees' needs as mediating links. *Journal of Organizational Behavior, 13,* 1031–1052.

Liu, J., Siu, O.-L., & Shi, K. (2010). Transformational leadership and employee well-being: The mediating role of trust in the leader and self-efficacy. *Applied Psychology: An International Review, 59,* 454–479.

Liu, W., Zhu, R., & Yang, Y. (2010). I warn you because I like you: Voice behavior, employee identifications, and transformational leadership. *Leadership Quarterly, 21,* 189–202.

Martinez-Inigo, D., Totterdell, P., Alcover, C. M., & Holman, D. (2007). Emotional labor and emotional exhaustion: Interpersonal and intrapersonal mechanisms. *Work & Stress, 21,* 30–47.

Mayer, R. C., Davis, J. H., & Schoorman, F. D. (1995). An integrative model of organizational trust. *Academy of Management Review, 20,* 709–734.

McKee, M. C., Driscoll, C., Kelloway, E. K., & Kelley, E. (2011). Exploring linkages among transformational leadership, workplace spirituality and well-being in health care workers. *Journal of Management, Spirituality & Religion, 8,* 233–255.

McMurray, A. J., Pirola-Merlo, A., Sarros, J. C., & Islam, M. M. (2010). Leadership, climate, psychological capital, commitment, and well-being in a non-profit organization. *Leadership & Organization Development Journal, 31,* 436–457.

Miao, Q., Newman, A., & Lamb, P. (2012). Transformational leadership and the work outcomes of Chinese migrant workers: The mediating effects of identification with leader. *Leadership, 8,* 377–395.

Munir, F., & Nielsen, K. (2009). Does self-efficacy mediate the relationship between transformational leadership behaviours and healthcare workers' sleep quality? A longitudinal study. *Journal of Advanced Nursing, 65,* 1833–1843.

Munir, F., Nielsen, K., & Carneiro, I. G. (2010). Transformational leadership and depressive symptoms: A prospective study. *Journal of Affective Disorders, 120,* 235–239.

Munir, F., Nielsen, K., Garde, A. H., Albertsen, K., & Carneiro, I. G. (2012). Mediating the effects of work-life conflict between transformational leadership and health-care workers' job satisfaction and psychological wellbeing. *Journal of Nursing Management, 20,* 512–521.

Nielsen, K., & Daniels, K. (2012). Does shared and differentiated transformational leadership predict followers' working conditions and well-being? *Leadership Quarterly, 23,* 383–397.

Nielsen, K., & Munir, F. (2009). How do transformational leaders influence followers' affective well-being? Exploring the mediating role of self-efficacy. *Work & Stress, 23,* 313–329.

Nielsen, K., Randall, R., Yarker, J., & Brenner, S.-O. (2008). The effects of transformational leadership on followers' perceived work characteristics and psychological well-being: A longitudinal study. *Work & Stress, 22,* 16–32.

Nielsen, K., Yarker, J., Brenner, S.-O., Randall, R., & Borg, V. (2008). The importance of transformational leadership style for the well-being of employees working with older people. *Journal of Advanced Nursing, 63,* 465–475.

Nielsen, K., Yarker, J., Randall, R., & Munir, F. (2009). The mediating effects of team and self-efficacy on the relationship between transformational leadership, and job satisfaction and psychological well-being in healthcare professionals: A cross-sectional questionnaire survey. *International Journal of Nursing Studies, 46,* 1236–1244.

Piccolo, R. F., & Colquitt, J. A. (2006). Transformational leadership and job behaviours: The mediating role of core job characteristics. *Academy of Management Journal, 49,* 327–340.

Ryan, R. M., & Deci, E. L. (2001). On happiness and human potentials: A review of research on hedonic and eudaimonic well-being. *Annual Review of Psychology, 52,* 141–166.

Ryff, C. D., & Keyes, C. L. M. (1995). The structure of psychological well-being revisited. *Journal of Personality and Social Psychology, 69,* 719–727.

Schaubroeck, J. M., Peng, A. C., & Hannah, S. T. (2013). Developing trust with peers and leaders: Impacts on organizational identification and performance during entry. *Academy of Management Journal, 56,* 1148–1168.

Semmer, N. (2003). Individual differences, work stress and health. In M. J. Schabracq, J. A. M. Winnubst, & C. L. Cooper (Eds.), *Handbook of work and health psychology* (2nd ed., pp. 83–120). Chichester, England: Wiley.

Sivanathan, N., Arnold, K. A., Turner, N., & Barling, J. (2004). Leading well: Transformational leadership and well-being. In P. A. Linley & S. Joseph (Eds.), *Positive psychology in practice* (pp. 241–255). Hoboken, NJ: Wiley.

Sluss, D. M., & Ashforth, B. E. (2007). Relational identity and identification: Defining ourselves through work relationships. *Academy of Management Review, 32,* 9–32.

Strausser, D. R., Lustig, D. C., & Çiftçi, A. (2008). Psychological well-being: Its relation to work personality, vocational identity, and career thoughts. *Journal of Psychology, 142,* 21–35.

Tafvelin, S., Armelius, K., & Westerberg, K. (2011). Toward understanding the direct and indirect effects of transformational leadership on well-being: A longitudinal study. *Journal of Leadership & Organizational Studies, 18,* 480–492.

Tajfel, H., & Turner, J. C. (1979). An integrative theory of inter-group conflict. In W. G. Austin & S. Worchel (Eds.), *The social psychology of inter-group relations* (pp. 33–47). Monterey, CA: Brooks/Cole.

van Knippenberg, D., & Sitkin, S. B. (2013). A critical assessment of charismatic-transformational leadership research: Back to the drawing board? *Academy of Management Annals, 7,* 1–60.

Walumbwa, F. O., Avolio, B. J., & Zhu, W. (2008). How transformational leadership eaves its influence on individual job performance: The role of identification and efficacy beliefs. *Personnel Psychology, 61,* 793–825.

Walumbwa, F. O., & Hartnell, C. A. (2011). Understanding transformational leadership-employee performance links: The role of relationship identification and self-efficacy. *Journal of Occupational and Organizational Psychology, 84,* 153–172.

Wang, G., Oh, I.-S., Courtright, S. H., & Colbert, A. E. (2011). Transformational leadership and performance across criteria and levels: A meta-analytic review of 25 years of research. *Group & Organization Management, 36,* 223–270.

Wang, X.-H., & Howell, J. M. (2012). A multilevel study of transformational leadership, identification, and follower outcomes. *Leadership Quarterly, 23,* 775–790.

Wegge, J., van Dick, R., Fisher, G. K., Wecking, C., & Moltzen, K. (2006). Work motivation, organizational identification, and well-being in call centre work. *Work & Stress, 20,* 60–83.

Wells, J. D., Hobfoll, S. E., & Lavin, J. (1999). When it rains it pours: The greater impact of resource loss compared to gain on psychological distress. *Personality and Social Psychology Bulletin, 25*, 1172–1182.

Zhu, W., Newman, A., Miao, Q., & Hooke, A. (2013). Revisiting the mediating role of trust in transformational leadership effect: Do different types of trust make a difference? *Leadership Quarterly, 24*, 94–105.

Zhu, W., Sosik, J. J., Riggio, R. E., & Yang, B. (2012). Relationships between transformational and active transactional leadership and followers' organizational identification: The role of psychological empowerment. *Journal of Behavioral & Applied Management, 13*, 186–212.

Zopiatis, A., & Constanti, P. (2009). Leadership styles and burnout: Is there an association? *International Journal of Contemporary Hospitality Management, 22*, 300–320.

# CHAPTER 22

# Applications of Positive Approaches in Organizations

JANE HENRY

T HIS CHAPTER OUTLINES the application of positive approaches in organizational
practice. It discusses work and well-being and some of the main strategies used
in attempts to develop and sustain a positive and healthy organization. These
address motivation, professional development, team building, and participatory
working practices, as well as positive approaches to organizational development,
such as appreciative enquiry, solutions-focused approaches, positive psychology,
and their organizational parallels—positive organizational behavior and scholarship.

The chapter notes that although certain organizational interventions can be seen
as positive, aspects of professional development go beyond either a purely negative or positive orientation. It concludes that work is important for well-being, and
that certain organizational practices can enhance satisfaction and aid performance,
while noting that different practices may be needed for different personalities, sectors,
and cultures.

## WELL-BEING AT WORK

The full-time employed spend at least half their waking hours working, so it is a
very important avenue for well-being. Happiness at work has been examined through
job satisfaction, work engagement, positive affect, and climate. In addition, there is
increasing concern with corporate social responsibility, business ethics, and corporate
citizenship.

Studies of life satisfaction generally show higher levels of *satisfaction* and happiness among the employed than the unemployed (Dolan, Peasgood, & White, 2008).
For example, in their survey of UK satisfaction levels, the Office of National Statistics
(2012) found twice as many of the unemployed as the employed reporting their life
satisfaction as less than 7 out of 10. Exceptions to this rule include the healthy voluntarily early-retired with ample finances (Haworth, 1997). In the UK, the United States,
and various other countries, high unemployment has been found to have a negative
association with well-being (Frey & Stutzer, 2002).

The centrality of work to well-being is not surprising when you think of the number of benefits it offers: an identity, opportunities for social interaction and support,

purpose, time filling, engaging challenges, and possibilities for status, apart from the provision of income. Jahoda (1982) went further and argued that it is mainly work that supplies time structure, social contact, collective purpose, social identity and status, and regular activity—five factors whose presence she found to be central to a sense of well-being.

Part of the benefit gained from work may be attributed to its social opportunities. The social importance of work is highlighted by Hartner, Schmidt, and Keyes (2003), who found having a best friend at work predicts well-being.

Work also provides opportunities for experiencing flow—the psychological state of absorption that entails the exercise of challenging skills (Csikszentmihalyi & Csikszentmihalyi, 1988). Haworth (1997) found flow was more common in work than leisure, though Delle-Fave (2001) reported finding flow less commonly at work among white-collar staff than professionals such as doctors and teachers.

Work challenges such as high workload and complex tasks are generally positively related to job satisfaction, and hindrance stress factors such as an unclear role and inadequate resources are negatively related (Podsakoff, LePine, & LePine, 2007). Increasing job intensity can lead to problems with work–life balance. Schwartz and Ward (2004) distinguish between satisficing and maximizing. Maximizers tend to be perfectionists who try to ensure everything is right before they are willing to submit work, for example. Satisficers are more inclined to do a good enough job, balancing the amount of energy they put in with the importance of the tasks. It is satisficers who tend to be happier with their lot in life.

Warr (1987) and his colleagues have investigated well-being at work in a range of settings. Warr (1999) concludes that a combination of personal and environmental influences act to facilitate or constrain individual well-being. The environmental influences center on opportunity for control (Warr, 1990), environmental clarity (including feedback and predictability), opportunity for skill use, externally generated goals, variety, opportunity for interpersonal contact, valued social position, availability of money, and physical security. The influence of these variables is not linear, as the effect of some varies according to the degree to which they are present. For example, whereas some opportunity for control and skill use generally improves well-being, too much can be experienced as coercion with a corresponding decline in the sense of well-being (Warr, 2006). Equally, a job that has little or no challenge is also often experienced as unsatisfying. (See Warr, 2007, for amplification of his approach.)

Job-related well-being interrelates with general life satisfaction (Judge & Watanabe, 1993). Like well-being more generally, work satisfaction appears to be affected by dispositional variables. Extraversion is positively related and neuroticism negatively related to job satisfaction (Judge, Heller, & Mount, 2002). In a study using longitudinal data, Straw, Bell, and Clausen (1986) found that affective disposition in junior high school was a fair predictor of attitudes to work in middle life (40–60 years) with a correlation of around .30 to .40.

The perceived meaningfulness of work has been related to well-being and work engagement (May, Gilson, & Hartner, 2004). Work resources such as support and information have been shown to influence work engagement, for example, the dedication, energy, and absorption of teachers (Bakker, Hakanen, Demerouti, & Xanthopoulou, 2007).

Given that people spend so much of their time at work ostensibly to earn *income*, it is worth noting that in affluent countries the relation between income and well-being is not as strong as most people expect. In Western societies, the correlation is around .13 (Diener, Sandvik, Seidlitz, & Diener, 1993). Surprisingly, though GDP has gone up threefold and working conditions have improved markedly since World War II in the United States, life satisfaction ratings in the United States and United Kingdom have shown relatively little change over that period (Myers, 2000). If we compare the percentage of people who are satisfied with their lives with the average income for different countries, we find that the proportion of people who rate themselves happy rises up to a point. But for countries with an average income above about £20,000, the percentage of people who are happy varies relatively little as income rises further. This does not mean there is no relationship between income and happiness, because a greater proportion of the bottom 30% of earners are more dissatisfied than the top 30% (Myers & Deiner, 1995). The New Economics Foundation argues that people at a level of income above minimum might be happier if they took productivity gains as time off, rather than seeking further remuneration, to allow more time for interaction with friends and family (Marks, 2011).

This idea that, above a certain basic minimum level of comfort, it is other factors that account for high levels of satisfaction is now generating interest among economists and in political circles (Layard, 2005). Key factors that are important for happiness include the level of control individuals have over their life, the amount of coherence among their values, goals, and activities; and the quality of their social relationships (see Kasser, Chapter 6, this volume; Sagiv, Roccas, & Oppenheim, Chapter 7, this volume). Among work characteristics, autonomy appears to be particularly important for happiness at work (Karasek, 1979).

Comparison with others can also affect how an individual rates his or her well-being. Perceptions of fair treatment at work are associated with well-being and job engagement (e.g., Lawson, Noblet, & Rodwell, 2009). The physical environment at work can also have an effect. For example, the majority of workers in windowless offices report feeling dissatisfied with their work environment (Kaplan & Kaplan, 1989).

Job Satisfaction and Performance

Organizations have a long history of attempting to make the workplace a more efficient and pleasant environment in which to work. These attempts range from enhanced remuneration, rewards or promotion through increasing status, job variety, and enriching jobs, to aligning motivation, use of positive recognition, increased participation, and professional development (Henry, 2005). There had been a trend toward interventions involving participatory practices, such as team empowerment, open cultures, supportive supervision, and looser organizational structures, that seem to accord with the ethos of positive psychology. However, more recently, increased surveillance, work intensification, and casual contracts present more of a challenge to worker well-being and work–life balance.

Among the practices that have been employed to enhance well-being at work at the individual level are attempts to enrich jobs (for example, to offer more variety or engaging work), offer feedback, improve and align motivation, increase responsibility, and offer professional development.

Some interventions, such as job redesign, aim to improve performance directly. Others seek to improve working conditions and satisfaction at work and indirectly improve performance. Hertzberg (1966) and the human relations school stressed the idea that the happy worker was an efficient one, though the degree to which satisfaction enhances performance has been contested. Judge, Thorson, Bono, and Patten's (2001) meta-analysis of more than 300 groups covering approximately 55,000 people estimated the correlation between job satisfaction and performance to be around 0.3. They also found that global measures of job satisfaction produced a higher correlation than facet measures. The level of significance varies with profession and motivation; for example, the level of satisfaction with work appears to be much more significant for creative people (Marks, 2011).

Early attempts at enhancing individual well-being at work focused on *enhancing job variety and challenge* (Hackman & Oldham, 1980). For example, Volvo, the Swedish car manufacturer, restructured two factories to enhance job variety for the factory workers. Instead of working on one stage of the production process, workers worked in self-governing teams that could follow the cars they worked on through different production processes (Pettinger, 1996). Cell manufacturing, where groups of multiskilled workers take responsibility for sequences of production on a particular product or product group, are now commonplace.

Early attempts at enhancing *motivation* at work often focused on external rewards, ranging from recognition for good work in the form of an award or financial recompense for productive innovations to bonuses when the firm did well. Subsequently, more attention has been paid to the role of *intrinsic* motivation. Recognizing that intrinsic motivation is a key factor in job satisfaction and performance among creative scientists, some organizations have a policy of granting scientists free time and in some cases genesis grants to work on pet projects. For example, 3M has allowed scientists up to 15% of working time to work on such projects (Mitchell, 1991); Google has allowed 20%. Such practices are not just a matter of company largesse: Mayer (2009) calculated that half of Google's new launches (such as Gmail) derived from free-time projects. The ubiquitous Post-it notes, the semisticky notepads currently found on most office desks, emerged from such projects, as did superconductive materials (Mayer, 2009; Nayak & Ketteringham, 1991).

Oldham (1996) argues that a high degree of *control* over the work an individual does, and feedback on performance, enhance motivation for the job. Empowering staff to increase the amount of control they have over their working lives is likely to enhance their well-being because people with more control over their lives are generally happier than those without (Ryan & Deci, 2008). So managers are generally well-advised to grant their staff as much freedom and flexibility as possible over what work they do and how they do it. Letting staff have some choice as to which tasks they take on and some control as to how they tackle them is more likely to produce a better outcome, particularly if the job is in an area of interest to them. For many people, the most enjoyable tasks draw upon skills they have but are slightly challenging. Where the skill and challenge level is appropriately matched to the person, they are more likely to enter a state of flow where they are contentedly absorbed in the activity (Csikszentmihalyi & Csikszentmihalyi, 1988).

## PROFESSIONAL DEVELOPMENT

In organizations there is a general appreciation of the centrality of people, even in technical spheres. Perhaps this is one reason why much of the training offered to managers and professionals is concerned with psychologically oriented *personal, interpersonal, and group skills* such as listening, communication, leadership, and group process skills (see also Kauffman, Joseph, & Scoular, Chapter 23, this volume). Most managers in large organizations complete personality inventories designed to analyze their leadership, decision making, and learning styles, for example, and take part in role plays designed to help them relate to staff more sensitively and effectively.

The importance of an element of individualized personal and professional development is also now institutionalized in kitemarks such as Investors in People (IIP). Among others things, IIP ensures that attention is given to employees' personal and professional development needs by requiring that these needs be specified through an individual development plan, normally now included in the annual staff appraisal. This can sometimes turn an appraisal into more of a coaching session, in which the employee has a chance to voice his or her own development needs. An element of continuous professional development is now compulsory for most professionals in Western nations. This may involve, for example, the commitment of 5 days a year to training and updating. As part of a process of building trust, some companies have given employees money to undertake any training course they wish.

Currently training is often built around the notion of *competencies*. Competencies derive from a model of education that presumes skills can be acquired and transferred to other settings by inputting knowledge in which the individual is deficient. The use of a competency-based approach, though endorsed by governments and taken up by most management organizations, is not without its critics, including human resource professionals. One critique is that knowledge and skill are situated and do not transfer readily to other situations, so the idea of generalized competencies transferring to new settings is suspect (see Sparrow, 2002, for a review).

However, it would be a mistake to think that organizational development is entirely oriented to fixing the negative. Organizations tend to be quick to take up new approaches, such as *emotional intelligence* (Caruso, Salovey, Brackett, & Mayer, Chapter 32, this volume; Salovey & Mayer, 1990), psychological capital (Luthans, Youssef, & Avolio, 2007), and building on *strengths* (Kauffman, Joseph, & Scoular, Chapter 23, this volume). In discussing emotional intelligence, Goleman (1995) highlights the importance of self-awareness, self-regulation, motivation, empathy, and social skill in management capability. As it is taught in organizations, emotional intelligence typically reframes material once presented as social skills. Nevertheless, it serves to highlight strengths as well as weaknesses and to draw attention to noncognitive aspects of interpersonal relating.

## PSYCHOLOGICAL CAPITAL

Luthans (2002; Luthans et al., 2007) has promoted positive organizational behavior and the notion of psychological capital. The term *psychological capital* covers a positive psychological orientation found in hope, efficacy, resilience, optimism, creativity, wisdom, focused absorption, humor, forgiveness, and authenticity. Luthans and Youssef (2004) identified self-efficacy, resilience, hope, and optimism as four key elements of psychological capital. These states show some parallels with Warr's (1987) definition of mental health as positive self-regard, competence, directed aspiration, autonomous action, and integrated and balanced functioning. Psychological capital has been found to add value independent of personality and demographic variables (Avey, Luthans, & Youssef, 2010; Avey, Reichard, Luthans, & Mhatre, 2011). Luthans et al. (2007) have shown psychological capital links to happiness, which in turn predicates motivation, commitment, and retention intention. The states associated with psychological capital tend to be more malleable than personality traits such as the Big Five or self-evaluations such as self-esteem or locus of control. Straw and Barsade (1993) argue that enhanced social capital improves decision making.

Bandura (1982) has conducted many studies showing the importance of confidence or *self-efficacy*—how able individuals believe themselves to be to perform a particular task or group of tasks. *Confidence* in one's ability to do tasks tends to aid performance on that task and has been shown to positively affect goal aspiration (Bandura, 2000). Self-efficacy is a strong predictor of performance at work. Indeed, Stajkovic and Luthans (1998) found a stronger relationship between self-efficacy and work-related performance than many other variables including goal setting, feedback, job satisfaction, and conscientiousness.

Bandura (2000) has also shown how *confidence* can be developed in the workplace through mastery experiences, modeling, positive feedback on progress, and arousal. Many management-training techniques include elements that aim to reframe negative experiences as learning and/or positive experiences. For example, to overcome the limitations of negative mindsets, the "yes and" technique encourages people to accept difficulties and see how they can work toward a goal despite the difficulties.

Work can be very stressful. The ability to bounce back from adversity is an obvious trait to investigate in terms of how people cope with pressures at work (Coutu, 2002). Some evidence suggests that the *hopeful* fair better in stressful occupations than the less hopeful (Kirk & Koesk, 1995; Taylor & Brown, 1988; see also Magyar-Moe & Lopez, Chapter 29, this volume, for strategies to accentuate hope).

Another variable positive psychologists have begun to examine is *forgiveness* (McCullough & Witvliet, 2002; Fincham, Chapter 38, this volume). Blame cultures are recognized as inhibiting to creativity and innovation at work. Innovative experimentation entails the risk of failure, so it is important that managers encourage a climate where practice can be challenged and mistakes forgiven if the organization wants to encourage creativity at work (Handy, 1993). In reality, forgiving errors can be hard and managers do not always manage to "walk the talk"; nevertheless, people in many organizations appreciate the need to do so.

Similarly, it is rarely easy to be kind, considerate, and relate skillfully with everyone we meet, whether in or out of work. The emphasis on personal development and interpersonal skills in most organizations suggests a certain psychological maturity that aims to help individuals to deal with each other in a healthier manner than they might otherwise have done. This is more likely if management sets a good example in this respect.

## Strengths and Style

As in clinical settings, until recently organizations tended to give relatively little overt attention to the idea of building on an individual's *strengths*. However, considerable attention was given to correcting any perceived deficiencies through training and the notion of organizational fit, that is, fitting someone with the appropriate abilities, style, experience, and inclination to the position concerned.

Aiming for work that complements the individual's natural talents and developing areas that exploit these talents has found a ready audience in organizations. The Gallup organization has been championing the idea of building on strengths for many years and lists 34 talents, grouped under four themes (Coffman & Gonzalez-Molina, 2002):

1. Relating (e.g., communication, empathy)
2. Thinking (e.g., analytical, strategic)
3. Striving (e.g., adaptability, focus)
4. Impact (e.g., positivity, command)

Current strengths-based tools include Strengthsscope (www.strengthscope.com) and Realise2 (www.cappeau.com/Realise2.aspx). The appeal is not so much the specified talents, which are similar to the traits and capabilities that managers are familiar with, but the idea of building on and developing an individual's strengths.

The strengths rhetoric also helps organizations to legitimize a more overtly positive approach to staff selection and development.

To date, positive psychology has tended to stress the benefits of apparent virtues, but has given less attention to any downside of such traits. For example, a playful colleague may be entertaining, but this same trait can also get people into trouble.

A good deal of personal development education goes beyond focusing on the need to make good deficiencies or drawing on the merits of innate virtues and talents. Rather, it teaches the *meta-perspective* that there is a positive and negative to all things. The constructive response takes account of the situation and participants' world-views. Going beyond a purely positive or a negative orientation in this way offers a mature approach to personal development in that it can lead to increased tolerance, acceptance, and balance.

For example, most training programs include work on self and other awareness. Typically managers are given personality inventories such as the Big Five (Costa & McCrae, 1992), the Myers-Briggs Type Indicator (MBTI; Myers & MacCauley, 1989), the Kirton Adaption Innovation Inventory (KAI; Kirton, 1987), and the Learning Styles Inventory (LSI; Honey & Mumford, 1985). The great merit of many of these instruments is that they are concerned with cognitive *style* or preference, not ability. This teaches people to appreciate strengths and weaknesses, opportunities and threats that are inherent in any style or situation.

The most widely used organizational inventory in the world has been the MBTI (Myers & MacCauley, 1989). The MBTI employs four bipolar dimensions: extraversion-introversion, sensing-intuiting, thinking-feeling, and judging-perceiving. These correlate with their respective Big Five dimensions as follows: extraversion .7, openness .7, agreeableness .5, and conscientiousness .5 (Bayne, 1994). However, unlike the Big Five, which are normally presented as traits, neither pole within any of the MBTI dimensions is favored over the other. For example, MBTI judgers (high conscientiousness on the Big Five) may be focused and well-organized, and therefore good at meeting deadlines, but adaptability may be more of a weakness. In contrast, on the MBTI, perceivers (low conscientiousness on the Big Five) may maintain a number of diverse interests and be late handing over material as a consequence, but they are usually good at adapting to change (Hirsch, 1985). The key message is that people are different, with tendencies to attend to different aspects of the environment and to excel in different areas, and that groups in organizations are more productive if they harness a variety of styles.

The popular *360 degree* training also offers people the chance to assess themselves and compare their own self-assessment to appraisals of the same areas completed by one or more peers, superiors, and sometimes junior staff. This type of training offers important feedback on the accuracy of self-perception and the impact of self-presentation.

A lot of personal and professional development and training offers practices that encourage staff to treat one another with respect and integrity. Such training emphasizes understanding yourself, realizing that others are different, appreciating that all have a role to play, and encouraging ways of relating to people that make it more likely that they will be heard. This approach can be seen as one that teaches the rudiments of *wisdom*. One characteristic of wisdom is relativistic thinking, the ability to see a situation from the other's point of view and to see ramifications for different parties (see Kunzmann & Thomas, Chapter 34, this volume). Personal and professional development practices can help to facilitate *relativistic* thinking and the outcome of associated management training can enhance tolerance, acceptance, and respect for self and others.

## TEAMWORK

Team membership can provide social support and satisfy a need to belong. Various studies suggest that working in a team leads to improved well-being for its members (Sonnentag, 1996). On the basis of a series of studies with health workers, Carter and West (1999) found that employees in well-defined teams reported better psychological health than those working in ambiguously defined teams and those who worked alone.

Groups are central to most organizations' endeavors and are increasingly important as organizations decentralize and push responsibility down to multidisciplinary project teams. Perhaps for this reason there is an appreciation that many organizational problems are *people* problems and that group dynamics are important.

Most managers are familiar with the idea that new groups may be expected to go through stages, colorfully known, for example, as forming, storming, norming, and performing (Tuckman, 1965). Because teams normally need time to coalesce into a working unit, it has been common for new project teams to go off-site for a team-building exercise to aid the process, an event that may involve leisure rather than work-related activities. Such activities afford time for the development of interpersonal relationships, the goal being to build the individuals' commitment to one another and to the team. Commitment to the group and participation in decision making have been found to enhance innovation (West, 2000; West & Anderson, 1996). For example, adventure training takes managers off-site and presents teams with various physical challenges such as abseiling, crossing cold streams, and engaging in outdoor games. Proponents argue that team spirit ensures participants will help one another complete the various challenges and that the increased confidence from completing tasks that they previously found fearful, or deemed beyond their competence, has a positive payoff in workplace activities.

Some of the personal, interpersonal, and group skills that are accepted as helping organizational groups to function well include listening to others, acknowledging others' positions, affording recognition for good work, adopting a win-win attitude to negotiation, applying principles of conflict resolution where parties disagree, and affirming positive qualities.

Like personal and professional development, group process training shows a certain psychological maturity in its emphasis on valuing and working with *diversity*. The emphasis on valuing diversity is partly due to the successful popularization of empirical work, which showed that successful work groups were more likely to contain a mix of personality types, and that groups containing too many of one particular personality type, for example shapers (task leaders), could flounder (Belbin, 1981; Margerison and McCann, 1990). The use of personality and team-role inventories (Belbin, 1981) in work settings can lead group members to a better appreciation of the consequences of cognitive style and personality type for ways of working, and of the importance of differing roles. This, in turn, tends to lead to greater respect for and tolerance of others. Diversity of perspectives within a group is known to be important for successful creativity and innovation in organizations.

Most organizations utilize some form of small group–focused enquiry. Whereas many organizational enquiry processes start from the problem and work forward to a solution, positively based processes are increasingly used with individuals and groups.

A well-known affirmative approach used in organizations is the strengths-based *appreciative inquiry*. This was developed in the 1980s (Cooperrider & Whitney, 2005). Appreciative inquiry aims to inspire and implement change by focusing on the positive, asking questions, positively reframing, and building a positive image of the future through a four-stage positive process that builds on what is working well. This approach is used by individuals, pairs, and small and large groups.

One begins with a positively framed topic such as having excellent working relationships or being a good communicator.

Discovery—You ask positive questions about the past and what is working well in the present, such as: "Recall a time when everything was going well. Describe your role and how you felt. What are your best qualities? How does your work help the organization succeed?"

Dream—You are then asked to imagine what might be—a desired future when things are working well, noticing what is different from the present or how you could reinforce the positive, for example, how you have changed and key things that needed to happen to realize these changes.

Design—The next stage focuses on the practicalities of how to get to this desired future by attending to the positive changes in more detail: how your behavior has changed, anything you are doing differently, what others are saying and doing, and what systems, processes, and strategies are needed to realize the dream.

Delivery—The last stage involves preparation for the implementation of the work needed to make the dream reality.

The idea is that by focusing on the positive, people are more motivated to take action to bring their dreams into reality (Cooperrider & Witney, 2005).

Various positively oriented, solutions-focused approaches, mostly derived from psychotherapy, are now used in organizations with individuals and groups. For example, Jackson and McKergrow's (2007) solutions focus approach is based on various positively framed tools, including:

Platform—Considering how participants would like the situation to be different.

Future perfect—Using pictures, models, creative writing, or performance to describe the desired future.

Scale—Estimating on a numerical scale how far they are toward reaching the goal.

Counters—Describing what has moved them up the scale toward the goal.

Small steps—Describing what could move them further up the scale.

Affirming—Typically the facilitator encourages group members to affirm each other through compliments and exercises.

## POSITIVE ORGANIZATIONAL PRACTICES

Much of the organizational framework within which organizational practices are considered tends to orient toward *fixing the negative*. For example, managers solve problems and troubleshoot, training is dominated by a competency framework that aims to input the skills in which staff are deficient, and stress is perceived as a major problem. Researchers investigate burnout and glass ceilings. Until recently, organizational science has been very largely directed at negative aspects of the working environment, such as the effects of downsizing, job insecurity, problems with stress and burnout, and lack of career development in a world with less full-time employment.

In contrast, organizational development has not had quite the same negative bias found in much of caring and adult developmental psychology prior to the positive psychology movement. Indeed, many organizational interventions of the late 20th century had a *positive orientation*. Popular organizational literature is dominated by tales of the practices of *successful* people and organizations. For example, Covey

(1990) talks of the seven habits of highly effective people. (He argues that these are proactivity, beginning with the end in mind, putting first things first, thinking win-win, seeking to understand before being understood, synergizing, and balanced self-renewal.)

Equally, much managerial practice is positively oriented. Managers are encouraged to be proactive rather than reactive and to take time to gain buy-in and commitment up front, rather than try to mop up resistance to change after the event. Organizations have visions and mission statements that define where they would like to see themselves going and the values they espouse en route. Positive behavior such as recognizing and praising staff for good work is normal practice and an open climate in which mistakes are forgiven are encouraged. Commentators such as Handy (2001) have argued that the best staff prefer to gravitate to organizations that share their values, rather than opting to work for organizations with better pay and prospects who do not share their values.

There has also been a long history of work on *flourishing* in organizations, addressing quality of life, job satisfaction, intrinsic motivation, commitment, and engagement, for example. Much of this work is now being drawn together and taken forward under two banners: positive organizational scholarship (Cameron & Spreitzer, 2011), which focuses on positive characteristics, processes, outcomes, and flourishing in organizations; and positive organizational behavior (Luthans, 2002), which addresses various aspects of psychological capital. Positive organizational behavior and positive organizational scholarship aim to reorient organizations to focusing on positive qualities such as psychological capital, prosocial motivation, work engagement, positive emotions, engagement, creativity, and trust (Cameron & Spreitzer, 2011; Luthans, 2002; Luthans et al., 2007). Critics such as Hackman (2009) argue against a purely positive focus in organizations. Organizational science also has a long tradition of learning from failure—searching for and rectifying faults in systems. Both learning from failure and advancing from the positive seem necessary. For example, Ellis, Mendel, and Nir's (2006) simulations suggest analyzing failure is an important part of task learning. Fredrickson (2009) also found that subgroups examining systems failure did better on a subsequent simulation than those that had looked at success and a control group.

## PARTICIPATORY WORKING

One variable that has long been associated with well-being is control over one's own life. Control over one's activities is generally associated with higher levels of well-being. Lack of control over one's activities in work and elsewhere is generally associated with higher levels of stress and lower levels of satisfaction. Traditional organizational structures seem to offer staff very little control indeed. Bureaucracies tend to have rigid organizational hierarchies that place the manager as captain, deciding what the workers will do and when they will do it, with the power to check that orders have been carried out and to implement sanctions if they have not.

As far back as 1957, Argyris noted the incongruity between the demands of the traditional "command and control" organization and the needs of the individual (Argyris, 1957). Features such as task specification, chains of command, and lack of delegated authority promote passivity and dependence, in effect assuming that workers are in a state of immaturity and treating them like children who need to be told what to do (Semler, 1994). This form of organization does not appear at face value to offer much scope for well-being at work because it offers workers little control and autonomy over their working lives.

However, over the past 50 years, organizational practices have been radically transformed, largely in response to increasing competition. Organizations now need to respond more quickly to shorter product life cycles and compete with ever more cost-efficient organizations on a global scale. Bureaucratic chains of command have proven too slow and expensive, and many organizations have introduced more participatory working practices, pushing responsibility down to multidisciplinary teams. Pressure to reduce costs has led to lean, downsized organizations in which the remaining staff usually have to do more with fewer resources.

In many areas, this has led to a long-term trend away from hierarchically organized bureaucratic structures and toward more *decentralized structures* in which front-line staff have more control. Organizing companies in divisions based around product groupings is common, though certain functions need to be centralized to ensure compatibility across different product types (Ashkenas, Ulrich, Jick, & Kerr, 1995). Project-based management, in which multidisciplinary teams come together to work on particular projects, is the rule in sectors such as filmmaking and construction, which are organized around temporary project groupings (DeFillippi & Arthur, 1998). In contrast, sectors such as call centers have seen increasing IT and video-based surveillance and constraints on worker opportunities for autonomy through the introduction of standardized scripts, for example.

Many manufacturing companies have shifted to cell manufacturing, in which *multidisciplinary teams* are responsible for particular product types. Such teams may have representatives from sales and marketing as well as design and engineering. Data from Japan and elsewhere suggest that production organized in this way is more efficient in the long run. Although such groups may take longer to agree on a way to proceed, the agreed-on plans are executed more quickly so the process is more efficient in the long run (Clark & Fujimoto, 1991). However, working with people from different disciplines with their different approaches does not necessarily make life easy. There may be more conflict than before and greater challenges as a result. Whether the greater responsibility in these decentralized structures is perceived as beneficial depends partly on the personality of the workers and their commitment to the job (Henry, Gardiner, Grugulis, & Mayle, 2002).

The changes to practice have so transformed many organizations that the manager is now more commonly pictured as the *conductor,* drawing out the best in his or her staff, coordinating as much as controlling workplace activities. In some organizations, a more participatory ethos grants staff considerable responsibility for deciding when and how they set about work goals. Many staff now benefit from flex-time—flexible working hours—and in certain sectors, an increasing number of white-collar staff opt to telecommute for a portion of the working week, keeping in touch with work via email, the Internet, and video-conferencing. Such practices seem to allow for more mature adult behavior, and the individuals are trusted to be active and independent, making their own decisions and being treated as equals in terms of the value placed on ideas and opinions they might offer.

Given this move toward more *participatory working practices* that seem to afford staff more control over their actions at work, one might expect job satisfaction to have increased. However, recent measures of satisfaction at work seem to have shown a decline (Heathfield, 2010), thought to be because of increased pressures at work. The switch to more participatory practices has often been accompanied by increasing workload, which has led to greater stress for many workers. The demise of layers of middle management has led to fewer opportunities for promotion in some areas, and the perceived increase in project-based and temporary working has led to a decline in perceived job security. The move to formalized quality control systems has brought in a form of employee scrutiny that can lead to a climate of distrust (White, 2001). Taken together, these factors seem to go a long way toward accounting for the decline in satisfaction levels at work (Taylor, 2002).

However, research on positive practices has shown that positive cycles of development are possible. Cameron and colleagues have studied virtuous practices in organizations that encompass caring, support, forgiveness, inspiration, meaningful work, and respect for others (Cameron & Caza, 2013). In financial organizations, the presence of these virtuous behaviors appeared to predict employee retention and positive ratings for the organizational climate a year later. In health organizations, virtuous behaviors were linked to subsequent patient and employee satisfaction, retention, and external evaluations of the standard of care. Being treated decently by colleagues generally enhances employees' commitment to and engagement with the organization. Virtuousness also appears to enhance resilience, for example, leaving people better placed to absorb work-related stress (Cohen, 2003). Some evidence exists that leaders who express more positive emotion elicit the same from their followers (Bono & Ilies, 2006). Cameron and Caza (2013) offer a review of virtuousness as a source of happiness in organizations.

A number of companies believe that enhancing the amenities in the work environment and providing social opportunities enhance employee well-being and improve performance. Most organizations arrange social events for their staff and some provide gyms. Google and Apple provide free pastries. T-mobile found that sick leave reduced 50% and customer satisfaction increased at their call center in Wales after the introduction of a work choir (Philpot, 2012). Northumbrian Water offered access to physiotherapists, confidential counseling, and telephone support for their aging workforce. They also encouraged staff to volunteer and join an annual walk. Within a year of offering these services, they found absence was down 3% and staff turnover 3.5% less than the industry average (Business in the Community, 2012).

Perhaps another measure of a healthy organization is the extent to which they engage with their community. Organizations such as BodyShop, Whitbread, and GE Plastics have programs that involve staff in some form of community action—teaching the underprivileged, renovating buildings, or helping in some other way. Companies who have adopted this kind of scheme claim such opportunities are valued by staff, enhance motivation, act as good development training, and are excellent vehicles for team-building (Henry, 2001b). In addition, there is increasing interest in socially responsible organizational practice and notions of transparency within organizations, for example, increasing use of independent social and environmental audits that report on surveys of the opinions of the organization's stakeholders, including employees, customers, suppliers, shareholders, and community representatives (Henry, 2001b).

## ORGANIZATIONAL DEVELOPMENT

Organizations are continually on the lookout for practices that can improve performance. However, empirical work suggests organizational development is typically a difficult, lengthy, and time-consuming process. Nevertheless, managers—at least those in Anglo-Saxon countries such as the United States and the UK—have tended to maintain a remarkable faith in the possibility of a quick fix for their organizational ills.

Indeed, the past 50 years of organizational development have been characterized by a succession of so-called management fads, such as management by objectives, continuous improvement, quality, reengineering, the learning organization, empowerment, and knowledge management (Mintzberg, 1983; Pascale, 1990). Many of these organizational interventions derive initially not from academic research but from practices perceived to have been effective in other organizations.

One popular approach is *benchmarking,* which aims to compare the processes and practices of one's own organization with those in successful competitor organizations (Zairi, 1996). Sober examination after the event shows that companies lauded for good practice and exceptional performance at one point in time have not necessarily looked so rosy when examined 10 or even 5 years down the road. A classic example is the downfall of a number of the companies identified as excellent in Peters and Waterman's (1982) classic text.

Indeed, in their haste to take up the latest "good practices" and management fads, organizations can be faulted for an overly naive acceptance of the positive and a failure to appreciate that what works in one situation may not transplant to another so happily. Further, other unwanted effects may occur because the ramifications of any organizational development intervention tend to be considerable. Pascale (1999) argues that 80% of organizational change efforts fail. Nadler (1988) suggests organizational change efforts are more likely to succeed if they involve key players, get participation in the process, and build in feedback. Robertson, Roberts, and Porras's (1992) meta-analysis found that multipronged organizational change that sought to change a number of different subsystems had a better chance of success.

Perhaps the main shift in organizational practice over the past century has been the change in culture. In Anglo-Saxon countries such as the United States and the UK, the go-ahead organization seeks a culture where *trust* is sufficient for employees to feel able to challenge established practices and to innovate. Managers are urged to forgive mistakes and walk the talk, though reality does not always match the rhetoric. Various studies have shown that in sectors such as information technology, innovative companies that had *open cultures* have fared well (Jelinek & Schoonhaven, 1991). However, such cultures are not without cost, because they typically involve staff in many meetings and a good deal of confrontation.

Many organizations have gone to great lengths to try to change their culture from a more conservative to a more open one, a process that normally takes many years. The Norwegian-based Karmoy provides an example. Karmoy, which manufactures aluminum, used a gardening metaphor (which they hoped staff would easily identify with) to visualize the past, present, and desired future state of the company. A series of group meetings were held, in which they gave all staff a chance to voice their aspirations for the company. Subsequent to this intervention, the company found that health improved, absenteeism reduced, and the number of employee suggestions for organizational improvement substantially increased, all measures of an improved climate (Parker, 1990). However, in such culture change programs, middle managers often end up with less power than previously. This loss of power is not to everyone's taste and many culture change programs find they lose a portion of staff who are unable or unwilling to adapt to the new approach (Henry, 1994).

Great claims have been made for organizational culture change as a means of improving organizational performance and climate, but some high-profile culture change efforts have failed over the medium term. Legge's (1994) review questions whether the benefits of moves to more enterprising cultures have been as substantial as generally claimed.

There is some evidence that different personality types and different departments favor different organizational cultures. Ekvall (1997) found that production staff preferred a climate in which rules are clear and people work in tried and tested ways. In contrast, people in research departments tended to favor a more open, easy-going climate where staff were freer to pursue what they perceived as important.

A consequence of more participatory working practices in many organizations is that the worker is *empowered* to a greater degree than before. However, in some cases, the empowerment offered is a travesty of the term, as in McDonald's workers being allowed to modify the standard customer greeting.

At the other end of the spectrum, some companies have empowered their staff to the point where they *self-organize* and have an unusual amount of autonomy at work. Dutton, a small-scale engineering works in the United Kingdom, and Semco, a medium-sized pump-manufacturing concern in Brazil, are two examples. Dutton's self-managed teams deal directly with the customer, handle design and costs, and set delivery dates (Lewis & Lytton, 1995). In short, these organizations abolish most of the red tape traditionally associated with organizations and treat their staff like adults able to organize their own lives.

Semco employees set their own hours, get their own parts, have control of their expenses, and in some cases decide on their share of the profits. The company has abolished many standard corporate departments such as quality and personnel, and allows staff to hire employees for their area directly. They also have a policy of limiting all memos to one page. Semco uses upward appraisal where staff use a simple satisfaction measure to appraise their bosses every 6 months (Semler, 1994). Often such companies also practice open accounting where detailed information about company finances is available to employees.

Staff who work in these firms become very committed to the company, very few if any abuses of the system are reported, and levels of satisfaction and performance are high (Semler, 1994; www.semco.com). However, self-organizing companies tend to be small or medium. Such practices are more difficult to incorporate in large multinationals, where a need for coordination across departments usually necessitates some red tape.

In addition, though participatory working practices accord with individualistic Western values, we can question to what extent such practices are suited to more hierarchical cultures such as those found in South India and Malaysia and much of Africa, where high power-distance between subordinates and superiors is the norm (Hofstede, 1984).

As the boundaries between companies become more fluid, interorganizational interventions become more common, for example, partnerships across the supply chain. Typically, large private companies form long-term relationships with suppliers rather than accepting the lowest tender each year. This enables the suppliers to build a relationship with the companies they are supplying. Nissan sends engineers to help underperforming suppliers improve, rather than changing suppliers, for example. Though these partnership networks give greater prominence to trust and a committed relationship than solely to cost, they perform well compared to traditional tendering systems when all costs are taken into account (Henry et al., 2002).

There is also the question of how to measure cultural improvement in an organization over time. Most organizations rely on employees subjective ratings of how satisfied they are and how they view the organization, its prospects and management or performance, and efficiency measures such as the number of new products and time and cost of production. Karmoy used an interesting index based on the number of staff suggestions, level of absenteeism, and accident rate (Henry, 2001a).

## CONCLUSION

Most people spend much of their life at work in organizations, and a major source of well-being typically comes from work. Sustaining a sense of the good life can sometimes be more difficult in large organizations than small ones, but certain participatory organizational practices can help.

The increase in participation, moves toward more open cultures, and emphasis placed on personal development suggest that organizations have become more positive places over the past 30 years. However, satisfaction measures suggest that this is not universally so. It is thought that increasing workloads, increasing stress, the increased policing inherent in many quality-control and surveillance schemes, and uncertainty over future employment opportunities plus less faith in fair treatment may account for this decline in satisfaction, despite the enhanced autonomy and control afforded through practices such as empowerment and multidisciplinary teamwork.

In terms of much of their day-to-day practice, many mainstream organizations seem to operate from a negative orientation, that is, bureaucratic control procedures, a problem-solving orientation, and a competency framework for development. However, much personal, group, and organizational development has been framed more positively with the accent on success, good practice, intrinsic motivation, recognition, learning from mistakes, the need for a vision, empowerment, and respectful relations. Positive approaches based on strengths and appreciation have caught on in executive coaching and professional development. Positive organizational scholarship and positive organizational behavior are acting as stimuli to further work on positive approaches and flourishing in organizations.

Some management training adopts a meta-perspective that recognizes that strengths and weaknesses are inherent in any style or situation, even apparently positive ones. Positive organizations encourage respectful and supportive relationships and a positive approach to learning about self and others; these approaches can lead to enhanced respect, acceptance, and tolerance for others, as well as satisfaction at work, and they afford a basis for wise organization.

## SUMMARY POINTS

- Work is a major source of well-being, providing social engagement, time structure, identity, and in many cases meaning, with the employed generally rating themselves as happier than the unemployed.
- Happiness at work is affected by a nonlinear combination of personal and environmental factors, including disposition.
- Attempts to enhance happiness at work include job enhancement, aligning intrinsic motivation, flexible working conditions, increasing social opportunities, positive recognition, and increased participation.
- There has been a long-term trend to more participatory and transparent working practices, which might be expected to make work-based well-being more likely.
- Job satisfaction levels are declining in some Western countries, a factor largely attributed to work intensification, perceived loss of job security and prospects, and increased surveillance.
- There is evidence that psychological capital (hope, optimism resilience, efficacy) aids happiness and work performance and that openness and forgiveness aid organizational creativity.
- Both positive (e.g., solutions focused approaches) and negative approaches (e.g., learning from failure) seem necessary for work-based learning.
- Appreciative and strengths-based interventions are increasingly influential approaches in organizations.

## REFERENCES

Argyris, C. (1957). *On personality and learning.* New York, NY: Harper & Row.

Ashkenas, R., Ulrich, D., Jick, T., & Kerr, S. (1995). *The boundary-less organization: Breaking the chains of organizational structure.* San Francisco, CA: Jossey-Bass.

Avey, J. B., Luthans, F., & Youseff, C. M. (2010). The additive value of positive psychological capital: Predicting positive and negative behaviours, work attitudes and behaviours. *Journal of Management, 36,* 430–452.

Avey, J. B., Reichard, R., Luthans, F., & Mhatre, K. (2011). Meta-analysis of the impact of positive psychological capital on employee attitudes, behaviors, and performance. *Human Resource Development Quarterly, 22,* 127–152.

Bakker, A. B., Hakanen, J. J., Demerouti, E., & Xanthopoulou, D. (2007). Job resources boost work engagement, particularly when job demands are high. *Journal of Educational Psychology, 99,* 274–284.

Bandura, A. (1982). Self-efficacy mechanism in human agency. *American Psychologist, 37,* 122–147.

Bandura, A. (2000). Cultivate self-efficacy for personal and organizational effectiveness. In E. A. Locke (Ed.), *Blackwell handbook of principles of organizational behaviour* (pp. 120–136). Oxford, England: Blackwell.

Bayne, R. (1994). The Big Five versus the Myers-Briggs. *The Psychologist, 7,* 14–16.

Belbin, R. M. (1981). *Management teams: Why they succeed or fail.* Oxford, England: Heinemann.

Business in the Community. (2012). *Northumbrian Water Group, wellbeing in water—winner 2012.* Retrieved from http://www.bitc.org.uk/resources/case_studies/afe3172.html

Bono, J. E., & Ilies, R. (2006). Charisma, positive emotion and mood contagion. *Leadership Quaterly, 17,* 317–334.

Cameron, K., & Spreitzer, G. (2011). *The Oxford book of positive organizational scholarship.* Oxford, England: Oxford University Press.

Cameron, K. S., & Caza, A. (2013). Virtuousness as a source of happiness in organisations. In S. A. David, I. Boniwell, & A. Conley-Ayers (Eds.), *The Oxford handbook of happiness* (pp. 676–692). Oxford, England: Oxford University Press.

Carter, A. J., & West, M. A. (1999). Sharing the burden: Teamwork in health-care settings. In R. L. Payne & J. Firth-Cozens (Eds.), *Stress in health care professionals* (pp. 191–202). Chichester, England: Wiley.

Clark, K., & Fujimoto, T. (1991). Reducing time to market: The case of the world auto industry. In J. Henry & D. Walker (Eds.), *Managing innovation* (pp. 106–117). London, England: Sage.

Coffman, C., & Gonzalez-Molina, G. (2002). *Follow this path: How the world's greatest organizations drive growth by unleashing human potential.* New York, NY: Warner.

Cohen, S. (2003, September). *The social environment and susceptibility to infectious disease.* Conference on The Role of Environmental Influences on Health and Performance: From Organism to Organization, Ann Arbor: University of Michigan.

Cooperrider, D. L., & Whitney, D. (2005). *Appreciative inquiry: A positive revolution in change.* San Francisco, CA: Berrett-Koehler.

Costa, P. T., & McCrae, R. (1992). Normal personality assessment in clinical practice: The NEO Personality Inventory. *Psychological Assessement, 4,* 5–13, 20–22.

Coutu, D. L. (2002, May). How resilience works. *Harvard Business Review,* 46–55.

Covey, S. R. (1990). *The seven habits of highly effective people.* New York, NY: Fireside.

Csikszentmihalyi, M., & Csikszentmihalyi, I. S. (Eds.). (1988). *Optimal experience: Psychological studies of flow in consciousness.* New York, NY: Cambridge University Press.

DeFillippi, R. J., & Arthur, M. B. (1998, Winter). Paradox in project based enterprise: The case of film-making. *California Management Review, 10,* 2.

Delle Fave, A. (2001, December). *Flow and optimal experience*. Paper presented to ESRC individual and situational determinants of well-being, Seminar 3: Work, employment and well-being, Manchester Metropolitan University, Manchester, UK.

Diener, D., Sandvik, E., Seidlitz, L., & Diener, M. (1993). The relationship between income and subjective well-being. *Social Indicators Research, 28*, 195–223.

Dolan, P., Peasgood, T., & White, M. (2008). Do we really know what makes us happy? A review of the economic literature on the factors associated with subjective wellbeing. *Journal of Economic Psychology, 29*, 94–112.

Ekvall, G. (1997). Organizational conditions and level of creativity. *Creativity and Innovation Management, 6*, 195–205.

Ellis, S., Mendel, R., & Nir, M. (2006). Learning from successful and failed experience: The moderating effect of the kind of after-event review. *Journal of Applied Psychology, 91*, 669–680.

Fredrickson, B. L. (2009). *Positivity*. New York, NY: Crown Books.

Frey, B. S., & Stutzer, A. (2002) What can economists learn from the happiness literature. *Journal of Economic Literature, 40*, 402–435.

Goleman, D. (1995). *Emotional intelligence*. New York, NY: Bantam.

Hackman, J. R. (2009). The perils of positivity. *Journal of Organisational Behavior, 30*, 309–319.

Hackham, J. R., & Oldham, G. R. (1980). *Work redesign*. Reading, MA: Addison-Wesley.

Handy, C. (1993). *Understanding organizations* (4th ed.). Harmondsworth, UK: Penguin.

Handy, C. (2001). The citizen company. In J. Henry (Ed.), *Creative management* (2nd ed., pp. 240–251). London, England: Sage.

Hartner, J. K., Schmidt, F. L., & Keyes, C. L. M. (2003). Wellbeing in the workplace and its relationship to business outcomes: A review of the Gallup studies. In C. L. M. Keyes & J. Haidt (Eds.), *Flourishing: Positive psychology and the life well-lived* (pp. 205–224). Washington, DC: American Psychological Association.

Haworth, J. (1997). *Work, leisure and well-being*, London, England: Routledge.

Heathfield, S. (2010). *Keys to employee satisfaction*. Retrieved from http://humanresources .about.com/od/employeesatisfaction/a/employee_satisfaction.htm

Henry, J. (1994). *Creative management media book*. Milton Keynes, England: Open University Press.

Henry, J. (2001a). *Creativity and perception in management*. London, England: Sage.

Henry, J. (2001b). Social responsibility. In J. Henry (Ed.), *Creativity and perception in management*. London, England: Sage.

Henry, J. (2005). The healthy organisation. In A. G. Antoniou & C. L. Cooper (Eds.), *Research companion to organizational health psychology* (pp. 382–393). Cheltenham, England: Edward Elgar.

Henry, J., Gardiner, P., Grugulis, I. & Mayle, D. (2002). *Organising for innovation*. Milton Keynes, England: Open University.

Hertzberg, F. (1966). *Work and the nature of man*. Chicago, IL: World.

Hirsch, S. K. (1985). *Using the Myers-Briggs Type Indicator in organizations*. Oxford, England: Oxford Psychologists Press.

Hofstede, G. (1984). *Culture's consequences: International differences in work-related values*. Beverly Hills, CA: Sage.

Honey, P., & Mumford, A. (1985). *The manual of learning styles*. Maidenhead, England: Peter Honey.

Jackson, P. Z., & McKergrow, M. (2007). *The solutions focus*. London, England: Nicholas Brealey.

Jahoda, M. (1982). *Employment and unemployment: A social psychological analysis*. Cambridge, England: Cambridge University Press.

Jelinek, M., & Schoonhaven, C. B. (1991). Strong culture and its consequences. In J. Henry & D. Walker (Eds.), *Managing innovation* (pp. 80–89). London, England: Sage.

Judge, T. A., Heller, D., & Mount, M. K. (2002). Five-factor model of personality and job satisfaction: A meta-analysis. *Journal of Applied Psychology, 87,* 530–541.

Judge, T. A., Thorsen, C. J., Bono, J. E., & Patton, G. K. (2001). The job satisfaction–job performance relationship: A qualitative and quantitative review. *Psychological Bulletin, 127,* 376–407.

Judge, T. A., & Watanbe, S. (1993). Another look at the job-satisfaction life satisfaction relationship. *Journal of Applied Psychology, 78,* 939–948.

Kaplan, R., & Kaplan, S. (1989) *The experience of nature: A psychological perspective.* New York, NY: Cambridge University Press.

Karasek, R. A. (1979). Job demands, job decision latitude and mental strain: Implications for job re-design. *Administrative Science Quarterly, 24,* 285–308.

Kirk, S., & Koesk, G. (1995). The fate of optimism: A longitudinal study of managers' hopefulness and subsequent morale. *Research in Social Work Practice, 86,* 80–92.

Kirton, M. J. (1987). *Adaption-innovation inventory (KAI) manual* (2nd ed.). Hatfield, England: Occupational Research Centre.

Lawson, K. J., Noblet, A. J., & Rodwell, J. J. (2009). Promoting health in the public sector: The relevance of organisational justice. *Health Promotion International, 24*(3), 223–233.

Layard, R. (2005). *Happiness: Lessons from a new science,* New York, NY: Penguin.

Legge, K. (1994). Managing culture: Fact or fiction? In K. Sisson (Ed.), *Personnel management* (pp. 397–433). Oxford, England: Blackwell.

Lewis, K., & Lytton, S. (1995). *How to transform your company and enjoy it.* Oxford, England: Management Books.

Luthans, F. (2002). The need for and meaning of organizational behaviour. *Journal of Organizational Behaviour, 23,* 695–706.

Luthans, F., & Youseff, C. M. (2004). Human, social and now positive psychological capital management: Investing in people for competitive advantage. *Organizational Dynamics, 33,* 143–160.

Luthans, F., Youssef, C. M., & Avolio, B. J. (2007). *Psychological capital.* Oxford, England: Oxford University Press.

Margerison, C., & McCann, D. (1990). *Team management.* London, England: Mercury.

Marks, N. (2011, September). *Think before you think: Measuring progress in a complex world.* Presentation to 2011 CEP Conference, Oxford University, Oxford, United Kingdom.

May, D. R., Gilson, L., & Harter, L. M. (2004). The psychological conditions of meaningfulness and availability and the engagement of the human spirit at work. *Journal of Occupational and Organisational Psychology, 77,* 11–37.

Mayer, M. (2009). *Creativity at Google.* Retrieved from http://ecorner.stanford.edu/author MaterialInfo.html?mid=1554

McCullough, M. E., & Witvliet, C. V. (2002). The psychology of forgiveness. In C. R. Snyder & S. J. Lopez (Eds.), *Handbook of positive psychology* (pp. 446–458). Oxford, England: Oxford University Press.

Mintzberg, H. (1983). *Structure in fives: Designing effective organizations.* Englewood Cliffs, NJ: Prentice Hall.

Mitchell, R. (1991). Masters of innovation: How 3M keeps its products coming. In J. Henry & D. Walker (Eds.), *Managing innovation* (pp. 171–181). London, England: Sage.

Myers, D. G. (2000). The funds, friends and faith of happy people. *American Psychologist, 55,* 56–67.

Myers, I. B., & McCauley, M. H. (1989). *Manual: A guide to the development and use of the Myers-Briggs Type Indicator.* Palo Alto, CA: Consulting Psychologists Press.

Myers, D. G., & Deiner, E. (1995) Who is happy? *Psychological Science, 6,* 10–19.

Nadler, D. A. (1988). Concepts for the management of organizational change. In M. L. Tushman & W. L. Moore (Eds.), *Readings in the management of innovation* (pp. 718–732). London, England: Harper Business.

Nayak, R. M., & Ketteringham, J. (1991). 3M's little yellow post-it pads: Never mind I'll do it myself. In J. Henry & D. Walker (Eds.), *Managing innovation* (pp. 215–223). London, England: Sage.

Office of National Statistics. (2012). *Measuring national wellbeing in the UK*. London, England: Author.

Oldham, G. R. (1996). Job design. In C. Cooper & I. T. Robertson (Eds.), *International review of industrial and organizational psychology* (Vol. 11, pp. 33–60). Chichester, England: Wiley.

Parker, M. (1990). *Creating shared vision*. Clarendon Hills, IL: Dialog.

Pascale, R. (1990). *Managing on the edge*. London, England: Penguin Press.

Pascale, R. (1999). *From complexity and the unconscious: Creativity, innovation and change*. Milton Keynes, England: Open University.

Peters, T., & Waterman, R. H. (1982). *In search of excellence*. London, England: Harper and Row.

Pettinger, R. (1996). *Introduction to organisational behaviour*. London, England: MacMillan.

Philpot, A. (2012). *Reward strategies for employee well-being*. Retrieved from http://www.2012 performance.co.uk/blog/reward-strategies-for-employee-wellbeing-why-creativity-and-happiness-matter

Podsakoff, N. P., LePine, J. A., & LePine, M. A. (2007). Extending the challenge stressor–hindrance stressor framework: A meta-analytic test of differential relationships with job attitudes and retention criteria. *Journal of Applied Psychology, 92*, 438–454.

Robertson, P. J., Roberts, D. R., & Porras, J. I. (1992). An evaluation of a model of planned organizational change: Evidence from a meta-analysis. In R. W. Woodman & W. A. Pasmore (Eds.), *Research in organizational change and development* (Vol. 7). Greenwich, CT: JAI Press.

Ryan, R. M., & Deci, E. L. (2008) A self-determination theory approach to psychotherapy: The motivation basis for effective change, *Canadian Psychology, 49*, 3, 186–193.

Salovey, P., & Mayer, J. D. (1990). Emotional intelligence. *Imagination, Cognition and Personality, 9*, 185–211.

Schwartz, B., & Ward, A. (2004) Doing better and feeling worse. In P. A. Linley & S. Joseph (Eds.), *Positive psychology in practice* (pp. 86–104). Hoboken, NJ: Wiley.

Semler, R. (1994). *Maverick*. London, England: Arrow.

Sonnentag, S. (1996). Work group factors and individual well-being. In M. A. West (Ed.), *The handbook of work-group psychology* (pp. 346–367). Chichester, England: Wiley.

Sparrow, P. (2002). To use competencies or not to use competencies, that is the question. In M. Pearn (Ed.), *Individual differences and development in organisation* (pp. 107–130). Chichester, England: Wiley.

Stajkovic, A. D., & Luthans, F. (1998). Self-efficacy and work-related performance: A meta-analysis. *Psychological Bulletin, 124*, 240–261.

Straw, B. M., & Barsade, S. G. (1993) Affect and managerial performance: A test of the sadder but wiser versus happier but smarter hypothesis. *Administrative Science Quarterly, 38*, 304–331.

Straw, B. M., Bell, N. E., & Clausen, J. A. (1986, March). The dispositional approach to job satisfaction. *Administrative Science Quarterly*, 40–53.

Taylor, R. (2002). *The future of work-life balance*. London, England: ESRC.

Taylor, S., & Brown, J. D. (1988). Illusion and well-being. *Psychological Bulletin, 103*, 193–210.

Tuckman, B. W. (1965). Developmental sequences in small groups. *Psychological Bulletin, 6*, 384–399.

Warr, P. B. (1987). *Work, unemployment and mental health*. Oxford, England: Clarendon Press.

Warr, P. B. (1990). Decision latitude, job demands and employee well-being. *Work and Stress, 4*, 285–294.

Warr, P. B. (1999). Well-being and the workplace. In D. Kahneman, E. Diener, & N. Schwarz (Eds.), *Wellbeing: The foundations of hedonic psychology* (pp. 393–412). New York, NY: Russell Sage Foundation.

Warr, P. B. (2006). Differential activation of judgments in employee well-being. *Journal of Occupational and Organizational Psychology, 79,* 225–244.

Warr, P. B. (2007). *Work, happiness and unhappiness.* Mahwah, NJ: Erlbaum.

West, M. (2000). Creativity and innovation at work. *The Psychologist, 13,* 460–464.

West, M. A., & Anderson, N. (1996). Innovation in top management teams. *Journal of Applied Psychology, 81,* 680–693.

White, M. (2001, December 18). *Conditions for well-being in working life: Evidence from Working in Britain 2000 survey.* Paper presented at the ESRC Social and Individual Determinants of Well-Being, Seminar 2: Work, Employment and Well-Being, Manchester Metropolitan University, Manchester, United Kingdom.

Zairi, M. (1996). *Benchmarking for best practice.* Oxford, England: Butterworth Heinemann.

# CHAPTER 23

# Leadership Coaching and Positive Psychology

CAROL KAUFFMAN, STEPHEN JOSEPH, and ANNE SCOULAR

E XACTLY 10 YEARS AGO, we outlined how the then relatively new field of positive psychology could add new impetus to leadership coaching, and we sketched out some of the research that would be needed to bring that to fruition. A great deal has happened since. Positive psychology is now a primary body of theory and research that informs the practice of leadership and executive coaching and can be integrated into other coaching approaches. In this chapter, we describe some of the theoretical orientations of coaching and examine how these might be related to applications of positive psychology. We then make more explicit what a positive psychology model of coaching might entail. In addition, we explore how the field of coaching can be enriched by drawing upon the rigorous research and theoretical solidity provided by the traditions of scientific inquiry.

## EXECUTIVE COACHING: A GENERATION CHANGE

After 30 years of executive coaching in both the United States and the United Kingdom, we believe we are now moving from what we call "first-generation" to "second-generation" coaching. The first generation of coaches established the existence of the profession, brought it to the attention of the business world, and established basic models of application. Those who did this best brought enthusiasm, inspiration, and the ability to bring fresh new skills to jaded executives. This first generation is the guru generation, which often has exceptional command and communication skills (see Buckingham & Clifton, 2001) but on occasion has created closed systems in which their own talents and experience are the sine qua non of their approach. As such, they are ultimately limited (Storr, 1996).

The second generation faced different challenges as interventions became more complex and clients became more sophisticated in their expectations of what executive coaching can offer. The field needed to become an open system based on explicit theoretical principles, including those from psychology, and built on the foundation of solid empirical research, not based on the personal strengths of a few visionaries.

In general, executive coaching is an egalitarian relationship with the goal of empowering the coachee to increase self-awareness and self-responsibility

(Whitmore, 1996). Through this process, the leader being coached can widen his or her repertoire of leadership behaviors, attitudes, and mindsets. This is done via a co-created, designed relationship (Kimsey-House, Kimsey-House, & Sandahl, 2011) that is implicitly or explicitly based on a strengths orientation that helps the client learn rather than having a hierarchical advising stance. Unlike life coaching (see Tarragona, Chapter 15, this volume), the leadership coach needs a good knowledge-base of the field of leadership, organizational behavior, dynamics, and systems, as well as solid overviews of challenges facing corporations and nonprofit institutions.

In addition, leadership coaches may often have a point of view to share, but do so in a way in which their insights are not mandates or advice but are offerings of different perspectives. The coach then continues by asking questions through which the leader can evaluate the relevance of the information.

The structure of an executive coaching engagement usually takes the form of regularly scheduled one-on-one meetings. The number of sessions can vary from one session to many. For example, a one-time consultation for a particular task, a few sessions focusing on specific performance-enhancement issues, or open-ended "developmental" contracts where the coaching team helps the organization move through a series of transitions. Individual coaching engages the coachee, the coachee's line manager, and the coachee's human resources partner; and the coach artfully navigates the system to retain client confidentiality while at the same time aligning the coaching goals to the needs of the organization as well as the individual. Frequently "360-degree" feedback is used, where the leader's line managers, peers, subordinates, and other stakeholders are interviewed. The coach then integrates this information and has development feedback sessions with the coachee. For less senior leaders, there are numerous electronic 360-degree surveys.

## What Are Typical Reasons to Engage a Coach?

In a survey of 140 senior leadership coaches (Kauffman & Coutu, 2009), the three most frequent reasons behind coaching assignments were: to develop the capabilities of a senior or a high-potential executive; to facilitate a transition, such as moving to a larger role; and to provide a sounding board on organizational dynamics and to enhance the interactions of a team. This shift is not new to researchers, as Kiel, Rimmer, Williams, and Doyle (1996) note that only one-fourth of executive coaching clients are in need of "remedial" assistance to improve performance. Three-fourths are doing well and request coaching to help negotiate increases in responsibility as they are moving up the organizational ladder, often quite quickly. Wasylyshyn (2003) also found that a vast majority of executive coaching clients want to focus on their career success. These bright, accomplished individuals don't want diagnoses or proclamations; they want data about themselves and their subordinates that they can use as feedback. In addition, they value and benefit from having an independent sounding board to help them develop, challenge, and enhance their strengths (Coutu & Kauffman, 2009). Positive psychology–based leadership coaching also paradoxically assists leaders to grapple with the inevitable negative, toxic, or near-impossible demands of business life. Just having space to think and vent can restore equilibrium. Once back on an even keel, the executive can consider challenging issues more dispassionately.

## Who Provides Executive Coaching Services?

Ten years ago, the field of coaching was without regulation, professional standards, required certification, practice benchmarks, or safety procedures (Grant, 2001;

Scoular, 2001). Since then, as academically more rigorous coaching training programs have emerged globally, the second generation of coaches has become much more proficient and able to put their knowledge into action in leadership coaching. Resources for these populations have also increased with education and research offerings such as the Institute of Coaching (www.instituteofcoaching.org) and the International Positive Psychology Association (www.ippanetwork.org) and a veritable cascade of theory-based books and a few peer-reviewed journals dedicated to coaching. Coaches from psychology backgrounds as well as business are increasingly interested in current research (Doggett & Kauffman, 2013). Attempts to establish standards have intensified, but the credentialing subfield remains fragmented. (For full list and further details, see Scoular, 2001.)

## TOWARD A NEW SYNTHESIS: POSITIVE PSYCHOLOGY AND COACHING

Executive coaching and positive psychology are highly aligned. The goal of coaching has always been to maximize the potential of the client by building his or her strengths and skills and applying these to the professional challenges being faced by the leader. Positive psychology coaching focuses on identifying and building the strengths and positive vision of the leader.

### CORE ASSUMPTION

The core assumption in coaching is that the client has the resources necessary to address the challenge. This orientation is illustrated in Kimsey-House et al.'s (2011) *Co-Active Coaching*, a training manual that is built on the cornerstone that the client is naturally creative, resourceful, and whole. At the beginning of the engagement, the work is for coach and client to codesign a mutually optimal relationship. The leader creates a clear of vision of what she wants to achieve and who she wants to be.

This core assumption of course dates back to the work of Rogers (1963), whose main theoretical principle was the notion of an actualizing tendency. The metaphor used to describe this is that of an acorn, which contains within it all the potential to be a magnificent oak tree. As an acorn requires nourishment to release the "oaktreeness" that is already within, human beings require the support of their basic needs if they are to realize their potential. Rogers (1963) originally used the term "nondirectivity" to make the point that the direction of the sessions did not come from the therapist. But he did not mean that the sessions were directionless, simply that the direction comes instead from the client. The therapist is nondirective, providing an authentic, empathic, and accepting relationship in the understanding that this will satisfy the client's needs so that self-determination may be realized. Rogers referred to this as the *person-centered approach*.

The person-centered notion of the actualizing tendency and its practice implication of going with the client's direction, is, in some form or another, at the core of many approaches to coaching (Whitmore, 1996) and it is what sets coaching apart from the medical ideology (Joseph, 2006). It is in this sense that coaching is not a remedial intervention but a developmental one, in which the coach uses his or her knowledge and skills in such a way as to meet the needs of the coachee.

The evidence base for the person-centered approach is impressive, particularly when one considers the more recent and theoretically compatible work of Deci and Ryan (2008) and their colleagues on self-determination theory (SDT; see also Brown & Ryan, Chapter 9, this volume; and Patterson & Joseph, 2007, and Sheldon, 2013, for reviews of the similarities between person-centered psychology and SDT).

SDT describes three basic psychological needs of autonomy, relatedness, and competence. When these basic needs are satisfied, people's intrinsic motivation toward growth and positive change is promoted. Often the core of coaching is discerning the leader's intrinsic motivations so as to counteract his or her extrinsic motivations. These are explored in the light of the leader's career trajectory to align his vision to his "real" self. Consistent with this philosophy, there is a shift from the "socialized self" to the "self-authored" way of navigating life and work (Kegan, 2008).

## AUTHENTIC LEADERSHIP COACHING

One strengths-based approach that is becoming more widespread is leadership development programs based on George, McLean, and Craig's (2008) work on authentic leadership. This leadership model is based on the concept of authenticity, which refers to the leader developing a deep self-awareness, and tying her life experiences together in a way that allows her to respond in an agile way to leadership challenges. Typically this model will include the leader reflecting on significant experiences for leadership lessons and sense of meaning. Part of the process is developing clarity on values, which are identified and translated into observable action steps. The leader synthesizes this information in order to identify his or her core purpose, and then harnesses this knowledge and energy into optimizing individual, team, and organization dynamics, and ultimately, personal and business performance (George et al., 2008).

Authentic leadership is similar to Collins's (2001) description of shifting from a charismatic leader to one who is both determined and humble. It also can be aligned with Kegan's (2008) perspective of moving from "self-authored" to "self-transforming" approach to leadership.

## FLOW STATES AND OPTIMAL PERFORMANCE

A related area of positive psychology, Csikszentmihalyi's (1991) study of the ultra-high-performance state ("flow") has enormous potential for use by executive coaches. The benefits of being fully engaged and experiencing flow have been examined in many studies (e.g., Csikszentmihalyi, 1997). Csikszentmihalyi (1997) elaborated "nine conditions of flow," including the optimal balance between challenge and skill, immediate feedback, and a task being autotelic, that is, inherently satisfying. Scoular (2011) breaks the nine conditions down for leadership coaches. The crucial ones for coaching, she argues, are the first four, which she calls the "preconditions" of flow, that is, the things that need to be in place before flow is likely to happen. Coaches and clients can take each in turn to identify blocks to attaining the flow state.

A positive psychology theoretical base does not assume that clients are paragons of virtue or that everything goes smoothly. Some leaders are dominating. Clear feedback and confrontation based on who they could be (but aren't) is often necessary. Others hold back or have an inner sabotaging voice that can undermine their leadership journey. At these times, the coach actively listens and uses curiosity to draw on his or her learning and experience to find the powerful questions that will help the client to reaccess her strengths, deepen her learning, and move toward fulfillment. Often this includes a "360," where those "all around" the leader give anonymous feedback that is harnessed to discover blind spots, leadership impact, and help create a leadership development agenda.

In addition to the skills discussed above, executive coaches will also use various techniques derived from other more traditional approaches.

## SOME TECHNIQUES USED BY COACHES

The following list is not meant to be exhaustive, but to point to some of the techniques that coaches may use.

### BEHAVIORAL AND COGNITIVE TECHNIQUES

The techniques that executive and life coaches have pulled from behavior psychology include relaxation techniques, methods developed from systematic desensitization, and stress-management interventions. These interventions have been modified for high-performance athletes and executives needing to operate successfully despite stressful circumstances. The foundations of learning theory, however, were originally based on observation and study of normal behavior, and it has enormous potential for the field of positive psychology. Learning to enhance relaxation responses in the face of stress is an extraordinarily useful skill that top-level executives can tap into, as are diaphragmatic breathing and mindfulness meditation. A behavioral approach also suggests we look at the behavior of the leader, what supports it, and how it trickles or cascades down through an organization. Behavior analysis looks at each step of the chain of behaviors, identifies what reinforces these, and where in that process is most amenable to an intervention.

Cognitive therapy–based coaching takes techniques proven useful with anxious and depressed clients and applies them to those seeking self and performance enhancement. The literature is new, and there is emerging support for its effectiveness (Dendato & Diener, 1986; McCombs, 1988; Zimmerman & Paulson, 1995). The kinds of interventions used with high performers include cognitive restructuring (Davis, 1991), attribution training, and visualization. However, cognitive-behavioral *coaching* moves beyond the therapy model and focuses on optimal ways of thinking. For example, a visionary leader needs big picture, future-focused thinking. After launch, however, the same leader needs to narrow focus to identify obstacles, long-term strategic thinking, and capacity to engage in strategic deep dives where problems may exist. Cognitive coaching language moves beyond the idea of cognitive distortions and more to developing agile, lean, and synthetic thinking that can help leaders navigate complexity and rapid change.

### MULTIMODAL THERAPY

The coaching potential of the Lazarus (1976, 1997) multimodal therapy has been discussed by Richard (1999), who suggests that executive coaching should be integrative and holistic in approach. To achieve this, the coach evaluates seven dimensions of the client's life in terms of his or her BASIC ID: behavior, affect, sensation, imagery, cognition, interpersonal relationships, and drug/biology modality. Although opening up various modalities for coaching skills is useful, the tone of Richard's work is extremely medical and has a remedial focus.

In building a positive psychology approach, it is possible to use these dimensions as potential reservoirs of strength or as seven "intelligences." Kauffman (2010) has expanded and applied this model to coaching with her PERFECT perspective. When making split-second decisions, how can we scan through all we have learned and apply it to our client's challenge? One way of scanning is to think of P—What might be going on *physically* with the client. Is there a medical or neuropsychological force behind how they are managing? E—What is going on in the *environment*. This includes cultural issues, organizational dynamics, and shifts in organizational structure (mergers and acquisitions, shifting to a matrix or performance culture).

R is for interpersonal *relationships*—exploring and adjusting how we relate to peers, bosses, and direct reports. F addresses *feelings*—including emotional intelligence, core emotional style, and pace. E is for *effective thinking*—working toward the ideal match between cognitive style and specific challenge. C is the exploration of *continuity* of past, present, and future. The coachee examines lessons from the past, drawing on current resources and experience and developing an ideal relationship with and vision of the future. Finally, T speaks to *transcendence*—a mind-set of rising above ego, pulling on values, understanding personal and organizational purpose, and shifting to a strong ethical moral stance when navigating business development and decisions.

## Systems Theory

Systems theory is another theoretical reservoir that has been used by coaching psychologists. Laske (1999) harnesses insights from family systems theory and constructive-developmental psychology in working with executives. Kilburg (1996) has developed a highly complex model of executive coaching based on systems theory, psychodynamic theory, and models of change that include elements of applications from chaos theory. While his work is complex, with a 17-dimensional model, his extensive experience and integrative approach have been used to train many American executive coaches. In Britain, systems theory is more commonly brought into coaching directly from management writers such as Senge (1990). Pascale and Miller (1999) use both systems theory and emergent change/complexity work to help people articulate bigger possibilities than previously thought and to identify steps toward achieving them. In essence, like any ecological niche, changes in one area affect the whole environment and the reverse. The systems coach explores these overview dynamics and is alert to the law of unintended consequences that arise from these interventions.

## Emotional Intelligence

Although not a psychological school of thought in itself, Goleman's (1995, 1998) work on emotional intelligence (see also Caruso, Salovey, Brackett, & Mayer, Chapter 32, this volume) has had a significant impact on executive coaching. His five areas of emotional and social intelligence include self-awareness, self-regulation, motivation, empathy, and social skills. In theory, Goleman's orientation, which builds also on Gardner's (1983) classic *Frames of Mind*, is compatible with positive psychology's emphasis on multiple and diverse intelligences and strengths.

## Transtheoretical Model of Change

The Transtheoretical Model of Change, developed by Prochaska, Norcross, and DiClemente (1994) is a theory used by many executive and life coaches. It is highly relevant to individual and organizational change processes. Prochaska et al. (1994) suggest six stages of change: precontemplation, contemplation, preparation, action, maintenance, and termination. Clients are not expected to move through these in a linear fashion. The normal course of change is described as a repeated spiral through the early stages until the client can enter into an action mode, eventually achieving maintenance of the targeted skill set, and finally moving through termination and pursuit of a new goal area. It is crucial, as Dean (2004) emphasizes, to create stage-matched interventions rather than to assume that all clients are ready to move into action. For example, the measure of success with someone in the contemplation stage would be shifts in his or her thinking, not completion of action steps. Prochaska, Prochaska, and Levesque (2001) examine in more detail how to apply the stages of change to development within organizations, in order to reduce resistance to change and to synthesize models of change. This is a useful model because the coachee's goals often shift over the course of coaching (Kauffman & Coutu, 2009).

## PSYCHOMETRIC ASSESSMENT

As part of coaching, various assessment tools are often used to help the coach and the coachee to identify areas of challenge and development. Specific measures that are commonly used in executive coaching are described next.

### The Myers-Briggs Type Indicator (MBTI)

The Myers-Briggs Type Indicator (MBTI) is an application of Jungian theory widely used by leadership coaches. Much of its powerful draw stems from its inherent positive psychological premise—*all healthy personality profiles have different but equal contributions to make*—and an assumption that anyone can learn to recognize and develop their preferred strengths. Like other strengths approaches, it emphasizes that no single pattern is inherently good or bad; organizations need all types if they are to function at their best. Businesspeople find this valuable because it accords with their reality for numerous reasons (flawed selection processes, restructuring/change, the need for entrepreneurs to take on radically different tasks as their organizations grow). The MBTI is useful in understanding how individuals respond to stress (Scoular, 2011).

### Strengths Finder

The strengths-building perspectives (Buckingham & Clifton, 2001) suggest that coaches should focus on strengths and values, rather than weaknesses. Several tools can be used to assess strengths. The Gallup Organization's StrengthsFinder identifies 34 strengths, such as harmony, focus, input, strategic, and winning over others (WOO; persuasion). Gallup is used by many Fortune 500 companies and is nearly always part of an extensive, companywide program requiring large numbers (typically 1,000) to participate. The Gallup emphasis is on identifying and using one's talents.

### Values in Action

The Values in Action (VIA) instrument (Peterson & Seligman, 2004) describes 24 strengths that are divided into 6 categories: cognitive, humanity, community, courage, temperance, and transcendence. The VIA is available free (www.viacharacter.org). Taking one's top five strengths is seen as a "strengths signature," which is as unique as one's signature. The VIA Strengths Survey is used often in life coaching and has been somewhat adapted to an executive population (www.viacharacter.org). Clients can take the VIA and learn their top strengths and virtues, then brainstorm with their coach for ways to "recraft" their jobs to "deploy their strengths and virtues every day" (Seligman, 2002, p. 166). Preliminary research suggests that using these strengths at work increases emotional well-being and job satisfaction.

The VIA approach suggests we negotiate our challenges by using our top strengths. For example, someone afraid of conflict can use their love of learning (and teaching) to shift from feeling they need to ramp up assertiveness and bravery to considering how to turn the encounter into a teaching rather than fighting model.

REALISE

The Realise2 was based originally on the VIA's UK data subset but has been further developed to assess three dimensions: natural strength, usage, and energy (Linley, Willars, & Biswas-Diener, 2010). As such, clients' use of strengths can be described one of four ways: (1) "realized strengths" (natural, frequently used, and energizing); (2) "learned behaviors" (which become useful with practice but otherwise don't come naturally, and therefore drain energy); (3) "weaknesses" (things we are not good at, typically don't use, and drain energy if we do); and (4) "unrealized strengths" (which are natural strengths that energize us when using them, but that for some reason we seldom currently use).

Such assessment tools as those described here (see also Rashid, Chapter 31, this volume, on strengths-based assessment) may yield "aha" moments for the coachee. Leaders may be surprised to see their signature strengths, or to discover unrealized strengths, quickly providing new impetus for change. In addition, positive psychology offers many other instruments, such as those measuring optimism (Seligman, 2002), positive and negative affect (Watson, Clark, & Tellegen, 1988), psychological well-being (Ryff & Keyes, 1995), satisfaction with life (Diener, Emmons, Larsen, & Griffin, 1985), subjective happiness (Lyubomirsky & Lepper, 1999), mental well-being (Tennant et al., 2007), or authenticity (Wood, Linley, Maltby, Baliousis, & Joseph, 2008), which can also be used in practice and research.

## STATE OF COACHING RESEARCH

When surveying the emerging body of coaching research, Stern and Stout-Rostron (2013a) identified 263 peer-reviewed research articles on coaching from 2008 to 2013. Their overview identified the gaps where new research is strongly needed. They organized their work by categorizing Kauffman, Russell, and Bush's (2008) 100 coaching-research proposals created by a diverse body of coaching researchers at the first International Coaching Research Forum in 2008 into 16 thematic areas. Stern and Stout-Rostron (2013b) then tracked research studies from 2008 to 2012 to determine where the field is strongest and to identify gaps. Their overview suggested that coaching research, although still in its infancy, has developed from the more generic "Does coaching work?" to very specific and focused research questions. Of the 263 articles, 88 focused on coaching process, 46 on outcomes, 22 on coaching in organizations, 16 on coaches, 15 on coaching versus other forms of helping, and 11–12 each on training, the business of coaching, coachee readiness, and the coaching relationship. There were 8 or fewer studies in other areas of interest. Theeboom, Beersma, and van Vianen's (2014) meta-analysis on the effects of coaching on individual outcomes in an organizational context showed a significant positive effect for coaching. They examined outcomes of 18 studies finding that coaching interventions had significant impacts in five categories. The strongest impact was found in the area of goal-directed self-regulation followed by work attitudes, coping, well-being, and improvements in performance and skills. This study looked at the impact on individuals, and more research is needed to see how this translates into wider impact in an organization.

Research points to common factors that underlie effectiveness. These are: the nature of the coaching relationship and the reflective space it offers, setting intrinsic goals and working toward them in a way that increases self efficacy, and systematically engaging in a solution versus problem mind-set that can also build resilience and self-regulation.

## FUTURE RESEARCH DIRECTIONS

Turning to possible future directions for research, given the newness of the field and marked paucity of existing data, there are several research opportunities for psychologists and business researchers. The field is open to many levels of research, from demographic and descriptive data collection to qualitative studies and experimental and quasi-experimental research.

### What Works?

The most pertinent question for most coaches is what works most effectively for whom. There is evidence on effectiveness of matching methods that promote well-being with individual characteristics (Lyubomirsky, Dickerhoof, Sheldon, & Boehm, 2011; see also Layous, Sheldon, & Lyubomirsky, Chapter 9, this volume), but we know very little about the techniques and tools that are most helpful in the executive coaching relationship (Kauffman & Bachkirova, 2009). In part this is because executive coaching is often associated with helping the client reach specific goals as opposed to promoting well-being. However, this is not always the case, and executive coaching can fulfill a variety of functions (David, Clutterbuck, & Megginson, 2013). For example, some forms of executive coaching are more open-ended, directed toward the leadership identity and development of the client. Others are more specific and solution-focused. Randomized controlled studies measuring outcome of coaching interviews are ideal to answer this question. Such trials are expensive and difficult to run. At this early stage of development, however, even small-scale studies remain useful for hypothesis generation and for building pilot data to support the argument for a more sophisticated trial. In addition to establishing that coaching works, we also need to understand why it works.

### Understanding the Process of Change

Qualitative studies can be useful to develop our understanding of why coaching is helpful. There have been few thematic analyses of coaching sessions, exploring just what is being talked about and how. Similarly, there are few studies in which researchers observed live or recorded sessions. Such studies provide rich data from which to build new hypotheses about how coaching may work and what in-session factors may be influential. Quantitative studies can then be used to further investigate the statistical association between within-session factors and outcome measures.

Bennett (2006) reviewed coaching research and found six themes. These can both organize our thinking and provide a roadmap for developing specific research questions. How do the coach, the coachee, and the relationship impact effectiveness? Do theoretical orientations and tools make a difference? Finally, what about the culture, environment, or organizational context for coaching? The following are six areas for research that we hope will stimulate reflective practice.

1. *The coach.* What aspects of the coach might impact the nature and effectiveness of coaching? How important are background, business experience, or specific

coaching competencies? Do more effective coaches have a higher commit-ment to learning, academic training, a growth mind-set, or cognitive agility? Although intuition is lauded, it's not well understood. It would also be useful to study and reflect on intangible qualities of who the coach "is" rather than what he or she "does," for example, level of confidence, sense of purpose, ethical maturity, joy, or resilience.

2. *The client.* Intuitively it seems obvious that a client who has greater readiness, capacity to relate, and is interested in coaching should get more out of the experience. However, these are assumptions that anecdotal experience does not always support. Reluctant coachees can become avid supporters of coaching. What does make for a "great" client, or someone who absorbs coaching? The factors mentioned above referring to the qualities of the coach would be relevant for the client as well.

3. *The relationship.* In psychotherapy research, the quality of the relationship is seen as the key predictor of successful outcome (Orlinsky & Rønnestad, 2005). Are "hierarchical" coaching relationships less successful than egalitarian relationships? How much time do coaches mentor and advise, and is this related to outcome? We need new research that explores the range of coaching relationships and how these vary according to what the leader requires for development. Some engagements are nondirective, delicate, iterative interac-tions, whereas others are directive and confrontational. Are there situations in which the latter is preferable to the former?

4. *Coaching tools, techniques, and theory.* What processes matter the most in coach-ing? Are lengthy initial assessments helpful or is it more effective to begin coach-ing immediately? Do we know how coaches decide to match a particular part of their toolbox to a particular client? Does it matter how techniques are intro-duced into the session and whether they arise from the coach or the coachee's frame of reference? Do those emphasizing strengths and positive psychology fare better than coaches using more traditional approaches?

5. *Coaching outcomes.* What is our understanding of what makes coaching effective? What is under the surface—what are the mechanisms of coaching? These could be the reflective space, increased self-efficacy, locating blind spots, or increasing awareness. It could be, for example, the reflective space, increased self-efficacy, locating blind spots, increasing awareness, focus on strengths, or building hope. How long do the effects last? There are few longitudinal studies of coaching. Such studies are critical to judge the lasting effects of coaching efficacy. How far do they generalize? Does quality of life improve outside of the work setting? Are those who are coached more resilient than those who are not coached? Finally, what are guidelines that contraindicate coaching?

6. *Organizational context.* In leadership coaching, an additional challenge is, what is the goodness of fit between the leader and the organization? Do the values, purpose, and style align enough for a good partnership? Is the coach clear about how to handle confidentiality? There is wide interest in global and cross-cultural coaching. How important is this expertise? It is now common for organizations to shift drastically in the face of changing, discontinuous markets. How well does a coach manage sudden shifts in corporate culture?

## CONCLUSION

The development of coaching, like the development of leaders, is an exciting ven-ture as best practices become more evidence-based and sophisticated. Why are more organizations seeing coaching as a strategic advantage? Coaching is an iterative process that is quickly responsive to the needs of an individual or an organization. This is similar to the mind-set shift required for corporations or governments to be successful in today's complex, shifting marketplace and society. There is a need to explore aspects of leadership coaching and how evolving complexity in the corporate space requires new stances on coaching.

## SUMMARY POINTS

- We looked at basic definitions of coaching, structure of coaching sessions, and how coaching is a developmental intervention rather than a remedial intervention.
- There are many theories that can be utilized in coaching interventions. We examine issues in coaching research, future directions for study, and the state of current research.
- The greatest challenge is translation from research and theory to practice.
- Coaching invites you to view the client as capable of learning and developing. Do you fundamentally believe this? How do you work when someone does not seem to meet that requirement?

## REFERENCES

Bennett, J. L. (2006). An agenda for coaching-related research: A challenge for researcher: *Consulting Psychology Journal: Practice and Research, 58*, 240–249.

Buckingham, M., & Clifton, D. O. (2001). *Now, discover your strengths*. New York, NY: Free Press.

Collins, J. (2001). *Good to great: Why some companies make the leap . . . and others don't*. New York, NY: HarperCollins.

Coutu, D., & Kauffman, C. (2009). What can coaches do for you? *Harvard Business Review Research Report, 81*, 91–97.

Csikszentmihalyi, M. (1991). *Flow: The psychology of optimal experience*. New York, NY: HarperCollins.

Csikszentmihalyi, M. (1997). *Finding flow: The psychology of engagement with everyday life*. New York, NY: Basic Books.

David, S., Clutterbuck, D., & Megginson, D. (Eds.). (2013). *Beyond goals: Effective strategies for coaching and mentoring*. Aldershot, England: Gower.

Davis, K. (1991). Performance enhancement program for a college tennis player. *International Journal of Sport Psychology, 22*, 140–153.

Dean, B. (2004). *The mentorcoach training program foundations manual*. Bethesda, MD: Mentor-Coach.

Deci, E., & Ryan, R. M. (2008). Self-determination theory: A macrotheory of human motivation, development and health. *Canadian Psychology, 49*, 182–185.

Dendato, K. M., & Diener, D. (1986). Effectiveness of cognitive/relaxation therapy and study-skills training in reducing self-reported anxiety and improving the academic performance of test-anxious students. *Journal of Counseling Psychology, 33*, 131–135.

Diener, E., Emmons, R. A., Larsen, R. J., & Griffin, S. (1985). The satisfaction with life scale. *Journal of Personality Assessment, 49*, 71–75.

Doggett, L., & Kauffman, C. (2013). *Survey of priorities and interest*. Unpublished manuscript, McLean Hospital Institute of Coaching, Harvard Medical School, Boston, MA.

Gardner, H. (1983). *Frames of mind*. New York, NY: Basic Books.

George, B., McLean, A., & Craig, N. (2008). *Finding your true north: A personal guide*. San Francisco, CA: Jossey Bass.

Goleman, D. (1995). *Emotional intelligence*. New York, NY: Bantam Books.

Goleman, D. (1998). *Working with emotional intelligence*. New York, NY: Bantam Books.

Grant, A. M. (2001). *Toward a psychology of coaching*. Unpublished manuscript, Coaching Psychology Unit, University of Sydney, Australia. Retrieved from http://www.psychcoach.org

Joseph, S. (2006). Person-centred coaching psychology: A meta-theoretical perspective. *International Coaching Psychology Review, 1*, 47–55.

Kauffman, C. (2010). The last word: How to move from good to great coaching by drawing on the full range of what you know. *Coaching: An International Journal of Theory, Research & Practice, 3*, 87–98.

Kauffman, C., & Bachkirova, T. (2009). Spinning order from chaos: How do we know *what* to study in coaching research and use it for self-reflective practice? [Editorial.] *Coaching: An International Journal of Theory, Research & Practice, 2*, 1–9.

Kauffman, C., & Coutu, D. (2009). The realities of executive coaching. *Harvard Business Review: HBR Research Report*, 1–25.

Kauffman, C., Russell G., & Bush, M. W. (Eds.). (2008). *100 coaching research abstracts*. Cambridge, MA: International Coaching Research Forum. Retrieved from www.institute ofcoaching.org

Kegan, R. (2008). What "form" transforms? In J. Mezirow & Associates (Eds.), *Learning as transformation: Critical perspectives on a theory in progress* (pp. 35–69). San Francisco, CA: Jossey-Bass.

Kiel, F., Rimmer, E., Williams, K., & Doyle, M. (1996). Coaching at the top. *Consulting Psychology Journal: Practice and Research, 48*, 67–77.

Kilburg, R. (1996). Toward a conceptual understanding and definition of executive coaching. *Consulting Psychology Journal: Practice and Research, 48*, 134–144.

Kimsey-House, H., Kimsey-House, K., & Sandahl, P. (2011). *Co-active coaching: Changing business, transforming lives* (3rd ed.). London, England: Nicholas Brealey.

Laske, O. E. (1999). An integrated model of developmental coaching. *Consulting Psychology Journal: Practice and Research, 51*, 139–159.

Lazarus, A. (1976). *Multimodal behavior therapy*. New York, NY: Springer.

Lazarus, A. (1997). *Brief but comprehensive psychotherapy: The multimodal way*. New York, NY: Springer.

Linley, P. A., Willars, J., & Biswas-Diener, R. (2010). *The strengths book: Be confident, be successful, and enjoy better relationships by realising the best of you*. Coventry, England: CAPP Press.

Lyubomirsky, S., Dickerhoof, R., Sheldon, K., & Boehm, J. (2011). Becoming happier takes both a will and a proper way: An experimental longitudinal intervention to boost well-being. *Emotion, 11*, 391–402.

Lyubomirsky, S., & Lepper, H. (1999). A measure of subjective happiness: Preliminary reliability and construct validation. *Social Indicators Research, 46*, 137–155.

McCombs, B. L. (1988). Motivational skills training: Combining metacognitive, cognitive, and affective learning strategies. In C. E. Weinstein, E. T. Goetz, & P. A. Alexander (Eds.), *Learning and study strategies: Issues in assessment, instruction and evaluation* (pp. 141–169). San Diego, CA: Academic Press.

Orlinsky, D. E., & Rønnestad, M. H. (2005). *How psychotherapists develop: A study of therapeutic work and professional growth*. Washington, DC: American Psychological Association.

Pascale, R. T., & Miller, A. H. (1999, October). The action lab: Creating a greenhouse for organizational change. *Strategy and Business*, 64–72.

Patterson, T., & Joseph, S. (2007). Person-centered personality theory: Support from self-determination theory and positive psychology. *Journal of Humanistic Psychology, 47*, 117–139.

Peterson, C., & Seligman, M. E. (2004). *Character strengths and virtues: A handbook and classification*. New York, NY: Oxford University Press.

Prochaska, J. M., Prochaska, J. O., & Levesque, D. A. (2001). A transtheoretical approach to changing organizations. *Administration and Policy in Mental Health, 28,* 247–260.

Prochaska, J. O., Norcross, J. C., & DiClemente, C. C. (1994). *Changing for good.* New York, NY: Morrow.

Richard, J. (1999). Multimodal therapy: A useful model for the executive coach. *Consulting Psychology Journal: Practice and Research, 51,* 24–30.

Rogers, C. R. (1963). The actualizing tendency in relation to "motives" and to consciousness. In M. R. Jones (Ed.), *Nebraska symposium on motivation* (Vol. 11, pp. 1–24). Lincoln: University of Nebraska Press.

Ryff, C. D., & Keyes, C. L. (1995). The structure of psychological well-being revisited. *Journal of Personality and Social Psychology, 69,* 719–727.

Scoular, P. A. (2001). *Is U.K. business coaching based on testable psychological theory?* (Unpublished master's dissertation). Guildhall University, London, England.

Scoular, P. A. (2011). *The Financial Times guide to business coaching.* London, England: FT/Pearson Hall.

Seligman, M. E. P. (2002). *Authentic happiness: Using the new positive psychology to realize your potential for lasting fulfillment.* New York, NY: Free Press.

Senge, P. M. (1990). *The fifth discipline: The art and practice of the learning organization.* London, England: Century Business.

Sheldon, K. (2013). Self-determination theory, person-centered approaches, and personal goals: Exploring the links. In J. H. D. Cornelius-White, R. Motschnig-Pitrik., & M. Lux (Eds.), *Interdisciplinary handbook of the person-centered approach: Research and theory* (pp. 227–244). New York, NY: Springer.

Stern, L., & Stout-Rostron, S. (2013a). *Bibliography of coaching research: List of journal articles by focus area, date and author.* Retrieved from www.instituteofcoaching.org

Stern, L., & Stout-Rostron, S. (2013b). What progress has been made in coaching research in relation to 16 ICRF focus areas from 2008 to 2012? *Coaching: An International Journal of Theory, Research and Practice, 6,* 72–96.

Storr, A. (1996). *Feet of clay: A study of gurus.* London, England: HarperCollins.

Tennant, R., Hiller, L., Fishwick, R., Platt, S., Joseph, S., Weich, S., . . . Stewart-Brown, S. (2007). The Warwick-Edinburgh Mental Well Being Scale (WEMWBS): Development and UK validation. *Health and Quality of Life Outcomes, 5,* 63.

Theeboom, T., Beersma, B., & van Vianen, A. E. M. (2014). Does coaching work? A meta-analysis on the effects of coaching on individual level outcomes in an organizational context. *Journal of Positive Psychology, 9,* 1–18.

Wasylyshyn, K. (2003). Executive coaching: An outcome study. *Consulting Psychology Journal: Practice and Research, 55,* 94–106.

Watson, D., Clark, L. A., & Tellegen, A. (1988). Development and validation of brief measures of positive and negative affect: The PANAS scales. *Journal of Personality and Social Psychology, 54,* 1063–1070.

Whitmore, J. (1996). *Coaching for performance* (2nd ed.). London, England: Nicholas Brearley.

Wood, A. M., Linley, P. A., Maltby, J., Baliousis, M., & Joseph, S. (2008). The authentic personality: A theoretical and empirical conceptualization and the development of the authenticity scale. *Journal of Counselling Psychology, 55,* 385–399.

Zimmerman, B. J., & Paulson, A. S. (1995). Self-monitoring during collegiate studying: An invaluable tool for academic self-regulation. In P. Pintrich (Ed.), *New directions for teaching and learning* (Vol. 63, pp. 13–27). San Francisco, CA: Jossey-Bass.

# PART VI

# HEALTH, CLINICAL, COUNSELING, AND REHABILITATION

# CHAPTER 24

# Complementary Strengths of Health Psychology and Positive Psychology

JOHN M. SALSMAN and JUDITH T. MOSKOWITZ

T HE PREVALENCE OF SERIOUS chronic illnesses that can be attributed largely to behavioral factors (e.g., type-2 diabetes, cardiovascular disease, and certain types of cancer) has continued to increase over the past decade. One commonly cited estimate is that by 2020, 157 million Americans, approximately 45% of the total U.S. population, will be living with at least one chronic illness (Wu & Green, 2000). Given that chronic illness affects not only patients but also their families, friends, and caregivers, it is clear that health psychologists will be increasingly challenged to address the needs of all the individuals who are affected by the stress of chronic illness.

Over the past decade, the science of positive psychology has seen a burgeoning growth as researchers have explored components of well-being and factors predictive of resilience and human flourishing. Advances in management of the negative impact of acute and chronic health conditions have led to improved symptom management and quality of life, but similar advances in the utility of positive traits and processes for supporting healthy adaptation have lagged behind. Although health psychologists have benefited from the contributions of positive psychology, there is a need for greater collaboration between these subfields of psychology.

The purpose of this chapter is to describe areas of potential synergy between health psychology and positive psychology and the collective contributions these disciplines can provide for promoting health and well-being. We will describe these two subfields of psychology and summarize the relationship of common positive psychology constructs and health outcomes. We will then turn to two areas we see as critical to the optimal growth of the field of positive health psychology: interventions that specifically target positive constructs and better measurement of positive outcomes. After reviewing emerging intervention results and highlighting critical measures and measurement issues, we will conclude with recommendations for future research.

*Authors' Note.* Dr. Salsman's effort on this publication was supported in part by the National Cancer Institute of the National Institutes of Health under award number K07CA158008. Dr. Moskowitz's effort was supported in part by K24MH093225. The content is solely the responsibility of the authors and does not necessarily represent the official views of the NIH.

## HEALTH PSYCHOLOGY AND POSITIVE PSYCHOLOGY

Health psychology is the scientific study of the relations of psychological factors, behavior, and the social environment with physical health and illness. Accordingly, health psychologists often adhere to a biopsychosocial model of health to understand the multifactorial contributions of biological, psychological, and social factors to health and well-being. This "mind–body" model recognizes the dynamic impact on health from various biological (e.g., a tumor, virus), psychological (e.g., perceived stress, attitudes, behaviors), and social influences (e.g., socioeconomic status, culture, ethnicity; Ogden, 2012).

Much of the focus of health psychology is on the reciprocal association between stress and health. Health psychologists study both the impact of psychological stress on physical health and the extent to which living with a health condition is stressful. Given the central role that stress has within health psychology, it is important to first describe what we mean by *stress* and then highlight a number of the physical health sequelae of chronic stress. Stress is "a relationship between the person and the environment that is appraised by the person as taxing or exceeding his or her resources and endangering his or her well-being" (Lazarus & Folkman, 1984, p. 19). The physiological response to perceived stress (i.e., "fight or flight") is adaptive and accompanied by the release of epinephrine and norepinephrine, which increases cardiovascular responses (heart rate and blood pressure), respiration, perspiration, blood flow to active muscles, muscle strength, and mental activity. Perceptions of stress also activate cortisol release, which triggers protein and fat mobilization, increases access to energy storage, and decreases inflammation (Selye, 1956). Although this acute stress response serves important adaptive functions, chronic stress can result in negative physical effects and can negatively impact every major system in the body.

In response to the compelling evidence of the deleterious effects of stress on health, health psychologists have focused primarily on reducing negative affect and stress. However, there has been a shift from this negative-affect-only focus toward the potential unique effects of positive psychological states and traits. Although a number of researchers were doing significant work in positive domains prior to this (e.g., Isen & Shalker, 1982; Lazarus, Kanner, & Folkman, 1980; Ryff, 1989), in 2000, Seligman and Csikszentmihalyi raised the profile of the subfield by naming and drawing attention to what they called "positive psychology." In their influential *American Psychologist* article, the authors noted:

> Psychologists know very little about how normal people flourish under more benign conditions. Psychology has, since World War II, become a science largely about healing. It concentrates on repairing damage within a disease model of human functioning. This almost exclusive attention to pathology neglects the fulfilled individual and the thriving community. The aim of positive psychology is to begin to catalyze a change in the focus of psychology from preoccupation only with repairing the worst things in life to also building positive qualities. (Seligman & Csikszentmihalyi, 2000, p. 5)

In the past decade, there has been an exponential increase in studies of positive psychology that include specific focus on constructs like positive affect, life satisfaction, meaning and purpose, self-efficacy, and optimism, among others. Seligman and Csikszentmihalyi (2000) were emphasizing a need to look at flourishing under normal conditions. In the present chapter, we focus on the ways in which positive psychological constructs may play an adaptive role for people who are experiencing chronic disease or other forms of chronic life stress—an area of particular interest to health psychologists.

Two theories are particularly relevant to the role of positive psychological constructs in the context of chronic illness: Revised Stress and Coping Theory (Folkman, 1997) and the Broaden-and-Build theory of positive emotion (Fredrickson, 1998). Both theories are specific to positive affect but likely also apply to other related positive psychological constructs.

Folkman (1997) proposed a revision to Stress and Coping Theory that explicitly posits a role for positive affect in the coping process. According to the original theory (Lazarus & Folkman, 1984), the coping process begins when an event is appraised as threatening, harmful, or challenging. These appraisals are associated with affect (negative affect in response to threat or harm, a mix of positive and negative in response to challenge) and prompt coping. If the event is resolved favorably, a positive affective state is the result. If the event is resolved unfavorably or if it is unresolved, a negative affective state results and the coping process continues through reappraisal and another round of coping. The revised model suggests that the negative affect associated with unfavorable resolution motivates coping processes that draw on important goals and values, including positive reappraisal and goal-directed, problem-focused coping. These coping processes result in positive affect, which is hypothesized to serve important coping functions: For example, positive affect may provide a psychological "time-out" from the distress associated with chronic stress and help motivate and sustain ongoing efforts to cope with the situation (Lazarus et al., 1980). In the context of serious life stress such as living with a chronic illness, positive affect may facilitate adaptive coping and foster challenge appraisals that lead to more proactive and adaptive coping efforts.

Fredrickson (1998) proposed the "Broaden-and-Build" model of the function of positive emotion that complements Revised Stress and Coping Theory. In this model, the "broadening" function of positive affect enables the individual to see beyond the immediate stressor and possibly come up with creative alternative solutions to problems. The "building" function helps to rebuild resources (such as self-esteem and social support) depleted by enduring stressful conditions. In contrast to the narrowing of attention and specific action tendencies associated with negative affect, positive affect broadens the individual's attentional focus and behavioral repertoire. Repeated experiences of positive affect are inherently reinforcing, and build social, intellectual and physical resources. Although the Broaden-and-Build model was not developed specifically to address positive affect in the context of stress, under stressful conditions the functions of positive affect suggested by the model become especially important. In the context of stress, positive affect may prevent the individual from feeling overwhelmed, lead to more flexibility in coping efforts, and, ultimately, help build resilience to the stress.

## POSITIVE PSYCHOLOGY AND HEALTH OUTCOMES

Several of the constructs within the positive psychology framework have shown significant positive relationships with health outcomes, independent of the effects of negative affective constructs such as depression and anxiety. Positive affect, mastery and control, and meaning and purpose are among those with particular relevance to health and well-being. We will briefly describe some of the notable findings in each of these subdomains and highlight potential mechanisms of action, where applicable.

## Positive Affect

The relationship between positive affect and health is well-documented (Pressman & Cohen, 2005), and in the past decade, convincing empirical evidence has emerged suggesting that positive affect may be an important target for stress-reduction interventions given its relationship with health outcomes. Most striking, positive affect is associated with lower risk of morbidity and mortality in a number of healthy and chronically ill samples, independent of the effects of negative affect (Chida & Steptoe, 2008).

However, the mechanisms by which positive affect impacts health remain unclear. Positive affect may serve a Broaden-and-Build function in individuals as described above, and it may have both direct and stress-buffering effects on health outcomes. In a direct effect model, physiological states associated with positive affect (e.g., sympathetic/parasympathetic and brain activation patterns) are directly associated with health outcomes; in the stress-buffering model, positive affect moderates relationships between stress and poor health outcomes.

Pressman and Cohen (2005) further hypothesized that positive affect is most beneficial among those diseases in which health behaviors may have an impact, and less beneficial (or perhaps even detrimental) in diseases in which short-term mortality is high. Research conducted since publication of Pressman and Cohen (2005) has further supported the hypothesis that positive affect predicts better health behaviors. A recent study demonstrated that the association between positive affect and lower risk of mortality among cardiac patients was mediated by increased exercise (Hoogwegt et al., 2013). Positive affect also prospectively predicts greater likelihood of engagement in medical care and better medication adherence, independent of the effects of negative affect (Carrico & Moskowitz, in press).

## Mastery and Control

The main subdomains of mastery and control include autonomy and independence, self-efficacy, and problem-solving and adaptation. These are often key components of multiple theories of health behavior change. Besides experiences of independence, the concept of autonomy includes the ability to regulate one's behavior and to maintain an internal locus of control (Ryff, 1989). In Bandura's social-cognitive theory, the related concept of self-efficacy has been defined as beliefs about the ability to perform instrumental activities and to be influential in one's own life. Bandura (1991) posited that compared to those with low self-efficacy, individuals who possess a high degree of self-efficacy are better able to manage potential challenges or stressors. Problem-solving abilities imply creativity, flexibility, open-mindedness, originality, and adaptation to a changing environment (Duckworth, Steen, & Seligman, 2005).

Autonomy and self-determination have been associated with increases in healthy behaviors over the life span, including late life (Ozaki, Uchiyama, Tagaya, Ohida, & Ogihara, 2007). Self-efficacy has been related to improved outcomes in rheumatoid arthritis (Rahman, Reed, Underwood, Shipley, & Omar, 2008), cardiac complaints (Schwerdtfeger, Konermann, & Schönhofen, 2008), and stroke (Jones, Partridge, & Reid, 2008). An individual's coping self-efficacy, or confidence in coping, has been associated with a number of important health outcomes, such as successful weight control (Linde, Rothman, Baldwin, & Jeffery, 2006; Meredith, Strong, & Feeney, 2006) and more successful disease adjustment (Beckham, Burker, Lytle, Feldman, & Costakis, 1997), as well as fewer episodes of psychological distress (Bandura, 1997).

MEANING AND PURPOSE

Meaning and purpose in life may be reflected in such subdomains as self-actualization and altruism. Self-actualization has been characterized as the desire for self-fulfillment, personal growth, and the achievement of one's full potential (Jahoda, 1958). It often includes a future orientation, a sense of directedness and intentionality, and a capacity for hope. The idea of altruism reflects a selfless focus on the needs of others (Compton, 2001). This includes a focus on family, community, and other affiliations as sources of meaning (Lee Duckworth et al., 2005). Values, religious beliefs, and spirituality have also been associated with sustaining a sense of meaning (Zika & Chamberlain, 1992). Data from a nationwide survey of older people in the United States demonstrated that those with a higher sense of meaning derived from important life roles enjoyed better health than those lower in meaning in life (Krause & Shaw, 2003); further, a higher sense of meaning predicted lower subsequent mortality (Krause, 2009).

Having a strong sense of meaning in life may influence health and well-being through both direct and indirect pathways. For example, in experimental research, higher levels of meaning in life were related to better autonomic nervous system functioning (Ishida & Okada, 2006), lower mean heart rate, and decreased heart rate reactivity (Edmondson et al., 2005). In addition, meaning in life was associated with lower aortic calcification in a community sample of middle-aged women (Matthews, Owens, Edmundowicz, Lee, & Kuller, 2006) and lower blood pressure in a representative sample of people in Chicago (Buck, Williams, Musick, & Sternthal, 2009). A sense of life meaning can lead to clearer guidelines for living and continued motivation to strive toward one's goals and take care of oneself (Klinger, 2012).

SUMMARY

The literature consisting of observational studies that demonstrate unique associations of positive psychological constructs with better health outcomes has reached a critical mass. We have touched on some of the constructs that have the most supportive evidence, but there are a number of others that show promise as well (e.g., posttraumatic growth, Barskova & Oesterreich, 2009; or dispositional mindfulness, Bränström, Duncan, & Moskowitz, 2011) and merit further attention. Given the now substantial body of observational research linking positive psychological constructs with physical health, health psychologists have begun to explore the possibility of experimentally increasing positive psychological constructs with the ultimate goal of integrating these interventions into clinical care, particularly for individuals coping with the stress of chronic illness.

## POSITIVE PSYCHOLOGY INTERVENTIONS

In this section, we briefly review the positive psychology interventions that have some evidence for efficacy in people coping with significant chronic conditions or illnesses. In addition, we focus on interventions that may be more appropriate for application within clinical health psychology settings. (For a broader review of positive interventions in a range of samples, see Moskowitz, 2010; Saslow, Cohn, & Moskowitz, in press.) Although there are therapies that target other positive psychological constructs, such as meaning or optimism (e.g., Bach & Hayes, 2002; Lee, Robin Cohen, Edgar, Laizner, & Gagnon, 2006; Singer, Singer, & Berry, 2013), the bulk of the experimental or clinical trials thus far have positive affect as the primary target of the intervention.

POSITIVE REAPPRAISAL

According to Stress and Coping Theory (Lazarus & Folkman, 1984) the extent to which an event is experienced as stressful depends on the individual's appraisal—the interpretation of the significance of the event for the individual. Positive reappraisal is a form of coping in which the significance of the event is reinterpreted in a more positive way. Positive reappraisal is similar to cognitive restructuring or reframing, which is a standard part of many forms of cognitive-behavioral therapy and is included in several interventions for people coping with serious health concerns or other types of life stress. The reappraisals in these interventions, however, usually concern replacing negative thoughts with more rational ones, and do not explicitly focus on possible positive aspects of the situation.

In one study that explicitly tested a positive reappraisal intervention, 55 women undergoing fertility treatment were assigned to either a positive reappraisal condition or a positive self-statement condition (Lancastle & Boivin, 2008). Participants were given a card with 10 statements and asked to repeat the statements at least twice per day during the period between embryo implantation and pregnancy test. Positive reappraisal statements began with the stem, "During this experience, I will:" and included "Focus on the positive aspects of the situation" and "See things positively." The self-affirmation/positive-mood statements began with the stem, "During this experience, I feel that:" and included "I really do feel positive," "I'm creative," and "I feel happy." The positive reappraisal group reported fewer harm emotions and significantly more positive challenge emotions than the positive self-statements group (Lancastle & Boivin, 2007). In addition, the positive reappraisal group evaluated the intervention as more beneficial and felt that it would help them to "carry on or keep going" during the waiting period. Although preliminary, the fact that the positive self-statements were not associated with increased positive affect supports the idea that simply telling oneself to feel positive ("I feel happy") may not result in an actual experience of that positive affect or other subsequent benefits associated with positive affect.

GRATITUDE INTERVENTIONS

Gratitude is defined as a feeling of thankfulness and appreciation expressed toward other people, nature, or God. Gratitude interventions are easily implemented in a clinical setting, and the association between intentionally noting things for which one is grateful and increased well-being is well-supported empirically (Emmons, 2007). Emmons and McCullough (2003) tested a gratitude intervention in 65 adults with neuromuscular disease. Participants in the gratitude condition were asked to complete daily gratitude lists—"things in your life that you are grateful or thankful for"—for 21 days. Control participants were asked to report affect, well-being, and global appraisals only. Results indicated that participants in the gratitude condition not only had higher positive affect and lower negative affect, but they also had improved sleep amount and quality. There were no effects on pain, however (Emmons & McCullough, 2003).

ACTS OF KINDNESS

A third type of positive psychology intervention that could be easily implemented in clinical health psychology for patients with few functional limitations is acts of kindness. Volunteerism, acts of kindness, and other altruistic behaviors are associated in observational studies with better psychological well-being (Post, 2005), lower risk of mortality (Musick & Wilson, 2003; Oman, Thoresen, & McMahon, 1999), and lower risk of serious illness (Moen, Dempster-McCain, & Williams, 1993). Experiencing a major life event, such as a diagnosis with a serious illness, can leave an individual feeling helpless and hopeless. In this context, doing something for someone else may be particularly empowering, helping the individual realize that he or she does have something to offer, leading to more positive affect and more adaptive coping behaviors. To our knowledge, acts of kindness interventions have not been tested in samples of people living with chronic illness. However, there have been a number of studies in more general population samples. For example, Dunn, Aknin, and Norton (2008) randomly assigned participants to receive either $5 or $20 and to spend the money that day on themselves or someone else. At the end of the day, participants who spent the money on someone else were higher on self-rated happiness than those who spent it on themselves, regardless of whether they had received $5 or $20.

MULTIPLE-COMPONENT INTERVENTIONS

In clinical settings, researchers are unlikely to rely on a single component intervention such as gratitude or positive reappraisal on its own. Instead, most offer a package of multiple components to increase the odds that at least one of the components will be effective for the patient. For example, Zautra and colleagues (2008) tested a multiple-component positive intervention designed specifically for people living with rheumatoid arthritis. The intervention covered a variety of skills and included (a) mindfulness, particularly awareness and acceptance of the full range of negative and positive emotions; (b) noticing and enhancing positive emotions by scheduling and enjoying positive events; and (c) learning to improve and better enjoy social relationships. The control groups were cognitive-behavioral therapy for pain (covering relaxation training and ways to manage pain) or an education-only attention placebo control group. Results indicated that participants in either the mindfulness or cognitive-behavioral groups had a statistically significant increase in positive affect over time compared to the education-only control condition. Participants with a history of recurrent depression from the mindfulness and emotion-regulation group appeared to benefit most, as compared with the other two groups.

Lyubomirsky and colleagues tested a telemedicine multicomponent positive psychology intervention for patients hospitalized for acute coronary syndrome or heart failure (Huffman et al., 2011). The skills involved included two forms of gratitude practice, best-possible-self exercises, and acts of kindness. In the control conditions, participants were taught relaxation exercises or were asked to report their daily events. Although none of the differences was statistically significant, pre- and posttreatment effects showed that individuals in the positive psychology program had increases on some, but not all, of the measures of positive affect compared to the other two groups.

Several recent papers examined the effects of a patient education intervention enhanced with a positive affect induction and self-affirmation (Mancuso et al., 2012; Ogedegbe et al., 2012; Peterson et al., 2012; Peterson et al., 2013). Across studies, participants in the positive affect group received patient education information as well as a positive affect induction (small gifts were mailed to the participants) and telephone calls and information to help them foster their feelings of positive affect and self-affirmation. The intervention increased physical activity among patients who had undergone percutaneous coronary intervention (Peterson et al., 2012) and improved medication adherence among patients with hypertension (Ogedegbe et al., 2012) but was not successful in significantly increasing physical activity among asthma patients (Mancuso et al., 2012). In a fourth paper that combined the results from the three individual studies, the researchers report that across intervention and control groups, those participants who reported at least a 1-standard-deviation decline in positive affect from baseline to 12 months were less likely to maintain their behavior change. This suggests that positive affect may play an important role in adherence to medical recommendations. However, the research did not directly report on whether the positive affect and self-affirmation intervention was more effective at increasing positive affect, the hypothesized mediator of the beneficial effects of the intervention on health behaviors (Peterson et al., 2013).

Moskowitz and colleagues (Caponigro, Moran, Kring, & Moskowitz, 2014; Dowling et al., in press; Moskowitz et al., 2012) have developed a multicomponent intervention that consists of eight behavioral and cognitive components hypothesized to increase positive affect: (1) noting daily positive events, (2) capitalizing on or savoring positive events, (3) gratitude, (4) mindfulness, (5) positive reappraisal, (6) focusing on personal strengths, (7) setting and working toward attainable goals, and (8) acts of kindness. The intervention has been pilot-tested in a number of samples coping with significant life stress and is showing good preliminary efficacy for increasing positive affect both immediately after the approximately 6-week intervention and at a 1-month follow up (Saslow et al., in press). Larger trials of this intervention are underway in people coping with significant health-related stress such as type-2 diabetes, HIV, and metastatic breast cancer.

### Beyond Positive Affect as a Target

Most of the interventions we review here explicitly aimed to increase positive affect, and it may well be that positive affect is a core component of positive psychological constructs and serves as the underlying driver of their beneficial effects. The literature is not at a point, however, where we can make this determination. In fact, there is significant evidence that positive affect can be harmful under some conditions (Gruber & Moskowitz, 2014). For example, there is growing evidence of a paradox in which the more someone pursues happiness, the less likely he or she is to experience positive outcomes such as happiness and psychological well-being (Ford & Mauss, in press). Thus, a key area for future work is in targeting a broader range of positive psychological constructs and teasing out, where possible, unique effects associated with individual constructs.

One significant problem with the rapidly expanding literature on positive interventions is that our measurement frequently does not capture the construct as well as we would hope. This problem is not unique to positive health psychology, but if we are to grow as a discipline and make a significant impact on quality of life in people coping with chronic illness, we need to evaluate the interventions with the best outcome measures possible. Next, we go into some detail on approaches to measurement of positive constructs and make some suggestions for measurement tools that may better capture the effects of positive interventions.

## ASSESSMENT OF POSITIVE CONSTRUCTS IN HEALTH SETTINGS

Two complementary yet distinct approaches to conceptualization and measurement of positive constructs exist. Many researchers and theorists distinguish between: (1) "experienced" or hedonic well-being, typically captured by measures of positive affect, serenity, and happiness, and their converse, negative affect, despair, or distress, and (2) "evaluative" or global well-being, typically assessed through judgments of overall life satisfaction or of fulfillment on distinct domains of personal functioning, such as autonomy, personal growth, or meaning and purpose in life.

Recently, the National Institutes of Health (NIH) has made a concerted effort to improve measurement of neurological and behavioral function and this effort includes a focus on psychological well-being. The NIH Toolbox was one of the initiatives of the NIH Blueprint for Neuroscience Research (Gershon et al., 2010) and was designed to identify, create, and validate brief comprehensive assessment tools to measure outcomes in longitudinal, epidemiological, and intervention studies across the life span from ages 3 to 85 years. By providing a standard set of measures for cognition, emotion, motor, and sensory function across diverse study designs and populations, the goal was to maximize yield from large, expensive studies with minimal increment in subject burden and cost.

The NIH Toolbox made use of two approaches to significantly strengthen the measurement of positive psychological constructs: Item-response theory (IRT) and computerized adaptive testing (CAT). IRT is an alternate approach to classical test theory but unlike classical test theory, which describes scores relative to group-specific norms, IRT models the probability of a particular item response to the respondent's position on the underlying construct in question (Anastasi & Urbina, 1997; Lord, 1980; Richardson, 1936; Streiner & Norman, 1995). An IRT approach can be useful for providing item-level properties of an instrument across the full range of the construct.

CAT assessments are emerging options in the context of medical settings and/or clinical trials and offer a number of advantages. CAT exams are, on average, half as long as paper-and-pencil measures with equal or better precision (Embretson, 2006; Embretson & Reise, 2000; Weiss, 2004). Thus, such an application may allow for briefer, more efficient, more flexible, and more precise assessments, providing an opportunity to assess more domains of interest without adversely affecting respondent burden. This approach can yield a more robust and informative assessment battery.

Within the emotion domain of the NIH Toolbox, the mandate was to develop assessments with a broad focus, incorporating healthy emotional functioning. For the assessment of psychological well-being in adults ages 18 and older, item banks and short forms were created for three content areas: positive affect, life satisfaction, and meaning and purpose (Salsman et al., 2013). Although most measures of positive affect assess activated emotion (Cohen & Pressman, 2006), the Toolbox positive affect bank assesses both high-arousal (e.g., excitement, joy) and low-arousal (e.g., contentment, peace) positive affect. The activating nature of an emotion and not just its valence may be an important distinction for improving our understanding about the relation between psychological well-being and physical health.

The NIH Toolbox Life Satisfaction item bank assesses global or general satisfaction with life as captured by multiple items from the Satisfaction with Life Scale (Diener, Emmons, Larsen, & Griffin, 1985) and the Students' Life Satisfaction Scale (Huebner, 1991). The NIH Toolbox Meaning and Purpose item bank was created using items from a number of different sources, including the Meaning-in-Life Questionnaire (MLQ; Steger, Frazier, Oishi, & Kaler, 2006), the Life Engagement Test (Scheier et al., 2006), the Functional Assessment of Chronic Illness Therapy–Spiritual Well-Being Scale (Peterman, Fitchett, Brady, Hernandez, & Cella, 2002). All item banks can be administered as static short forms or as CAT assessments, providing the opportunity for optimal flexible, efficient, and precise assessment of these important dimensions of psychological well-being.

The field of health psychology is increasingly taking advantage of more fine-grained assessment approaches, such as the Day Reconstruction Method

(Kahneman, Krueger, Schkade, Schwarz, & Stone, 2004) and applications of Ecological Momentary Assessment (EMA; Shiffman, Stone, & Hufford, 2008). Both methods could be adapted to be compatible with CAT approaches. EMA assesses phenomena at the moment they occur and in the subjects' natural environment, is dependent upon careful timing of assessments, and involves a substantial number of repeated observations (Shiffman et al., 2008). EMA uses real-time data capture, which enhances compliance, minimizes recall bias, and can capture diurnal rhythms, but it can miss important events and be burdensome and expensive (Stone, Shiffman, Atienza, & Nebling, 2007). An alternative approach to EMA is the Day Reconstruction Method (Kahneman et al., 2004), which involves a reconstruction of the recall period to assess affect, activities, and time use in everyday life. This process involves responding to standard life-satisfaction questions; segmenting the preceding day into episodes, like scenes in a movie; and asking detailed questions about the setting of each episode and participants' feelings. The Day Reconstruction Method allows for relatively rapid assessment of emotions and can be associated with time usage, but requires skilled interviewers and is costly. Notably, a comparison of ratings of experienced well-being obtained with EMA and the Day Reconstruction Method have found that the Day Reconstruction Method provides reasonably reliable estimates of the intensity of affect as well as variations in affect over the day, thus supporting its use as a viable methodology for assessing experienced well-being (Dockray et al., 2010).

Even though positive psychological constructs have been the focus of research for many years, there has been scant attention paid to optimal assessment of these constructs. The NIH Toolbox initiative and newer approaches, such as the Day Reconstruction Method, promise to enhance our understanding of positive psychology and its role in health and well-being.

## FUTURE DIRECTIONS

As we have reviewed here, the science of health psychology and positive psychology holds significant promise for improving the lives of those affected by chronic illnesses and emerging research highlights the benefit of these subfields for enhancing adaptive health outcomes. Clearly, however, there is still some distance to cover before we declare positive health psychology a success. In particular, we suggest three areas for attention: (1) consideration of a wider array of positive constructs, both as targets for intervention and as independent variables in observational research; (2) attention to optimal measurement of these and other health-related constructs; and (3) designs that will allow the determination of which positive interventions work and for whom.

Health psychologists should expand the focus of observational and interventional studies to include a broader array of positive psychological constructs. In the present chapter, we discuss positive affect, optimism, meaning/purpose, and mastery/control in some depth and mention stress-related growth and mindfulness, but there are a number of other positive constructs that may prove to be important in terms of their role in health. Curiosity (Swan & Carmelli, 1996), humor (Martin, 2001, 2002; Martin & Lefcourt, 1983), grit (Duckworth, Peterson, Matthews, & Kelly, 2007), and self-compassion (Neff, 2003; Neff, Rude, & Kirkpatrick, 2007) are just a few examples of constructs that are garnering significant interest within the field. Rather than having each researcher pick a single construct on which to build a program, to the extent possible, studies should include multiple positive constructs in order to determine shared variance within the same study population. In this way, we will be able to move forward on the question of whether a given positive construct is uniquely important or if it is simply reflecting a common underlying construct of positivity.

In terms of measurement, the array of new options for measuring positive psychology constructs is very promising. Health psychologists should carefully consider the measures they select with an eye toward measures that are valid and reliable, certainly, but also as brief as possible and easy to fill out for patients coping with significant illness or life stress. Initiatives such as the NIH Toolbox are likely to clarify the options and allow researchers and clinicians to select the best outcome measures for their patient population. In addition to different approaches to measurement, such as CAT, we should also consider different ways to analyze the data we do collect. For example, Mroczek and colleagues (in press) recently demonstrated that level of positive and negative affect over the course of an 8-day diary study were not associated with 10-year mortality. However, the extent to which positive affect was reactive to daily stressful events did predict mortality, such that the more positive affect dropped in response to stress, the higher the likelihood of mortality over the course of the study period. Negative affect reactivity was not predictive. If the researchers had simply looked at level of positive and negative and not considered going a step further to consider the data in another way, the unique importance of emotional reactivity and mortality would likely have been lost.

As with the discussion of expanding our focus to include a broader array of positive constructs, an important next step is to begin to differentiate among the various positive constructs to determine whether there are significant differential effects or, instead, a core latent component that drives the benefits regardless of which positive construct is considered. Applications of IRT and CAT are particularly helpful in this regard, because they allow for a greater ability to assess more domains of interest with minimal respondent burden. Multiple positive domains could then be analyzed using a bifactor analysis in which the scales together load on a common factor but have separate factor loadings of their own. This could be a particularly illuminating approach to understanding the degree to which multiple positive constructs contribute to a global "positivity" factor and to help delineate to what extent the global versus the individual positive psychology component parts contribute to better health outcomes.

Information on which constructs are most effective and under what circumstances will help to tailor future interventions to specifically target the constructs that will most likely have the strongest beneficial effects. This is critically important because to optimize the strengths of positive health psychology, we need to determine what works and for whom. One potential determinant of intervention effectiveness may be the extent to which a disease has controllable aspects. Pressman and Cohen (2005) noted that positive affect seemed to have a bigger effect in illnesses that had some element of control, where behavioral strategies can have an impact, for example. If we extend these findings to positive interventions, we might hypothesize that for diseases where the individual's behavior can significantly influence outcomes (e.g., type-2 diabetes, cardiovascular disease) an intervention that specifically targets positive affect may be most effective, whereas for diseases or conditions in which there is less control (e.g., metastatic cancer) an intervention that targets meaning and purpose might be more applicable. Multicomponent interventions offer unique opportunities to examine the effects of a variety of skills and techniques for individuals with chronic health conditions but it is not always easy to identify what approaches work best and for which group of people from these intervention designs. A compelling and emerging strategy is the use of adaptive randomized controlled trials. Adaptive randomized controlled trials are flexible and efficient approaches to data collection because they increase the probability that a participant will be assigned to the best treatment (Chow & Chang, 2008; Coffey et al., 2012). These, and similar approaches, may prove particularly helpful in accelerating our understanding of the "active ingredients" of interventions and the mechanisms through which positive psychology impacts health. Ultimately, this will lead to better-designed interventions and individualized treatment plans, resulting in more patient-centered care and optimal health outcomes throughout the illness and health continuum.

## CONCLUSION

Health psychologists who incorporate positive psychology into their practices are well-poised to address the needs of the growing population of patients, caregivers, and family members coping with the stress of chronic illness. Positive psychology holds promise for improving the lives of people living with chronic illness, and health psychologists are at the forefront of the observational and interventional research that will advance the field. However, as the field of positive health psychology matures, there is a danger of the pendulum swinging too far in the direction of overemphasis on positive constructs, while neglecting the importance and adaptational significance of negative affective constructs. A myopic focus on the positive runs the risk of ignoring the potential downsides that may be associated with positive affect (e.g., Gruber & Moskowitz, 2014). Furthermore, exclusive focus on the positive runs the risk of blaming the patient for not thinking the right positive thoughts that will improve his or her health or save his or her life. This focus is unfair and minimizes the very real stress and distress that often accompany chronic illness. Instead, we envision a positive health psychology that understands and values these very real and understandable negative emotions while making space alongside for the positive constructs.

## SUMMARY POINTS

- Health psychology is the scientific study of the relations of psychological factors, behavior, and the social environment with physical health and illness.
- The aim of positive psychology is to catalyze a change in the focus of psychology from preoccupation only with repairing the worst things in life to also building positive qualities.
- The Revised Stress and Coping and Broaden-and-Build theories are particularly relevant to the role of positive psychological constructs in the context of chronic illness.
- Positive psychology constructs (e.g., positive affect, self-efficacy, optimism, meaning and purpose in life) are uniquely related to beneficial health outcomes.
- Positive interventions (e.g., positive reappraisal, gratitude, acts of kindness) are demonstrating efficacy in people coping with chronic illness.
- New measurement approaches, such as the NIH Toolbox Psychological Well-Being item banks, have the potential to better capture the effects of these interventions.
- Measurement modalities such as the Day Reconstruction Method or applications of Ecological Momentary Assessment may provide innovative opportunities to assess and better understand the variable nature of some positive psychology constructs.
- Future work should consider a wider array of positive constructs both as targets for intervention and as independent variables in observational research. Future research should also attend to optimal measurement approaches of these and other health-related constructs and utilize research designs that allow the determination of which positive interventions work and for whom.

# REFERENCES

Anastasi, A., & Urbina, S. (1997). *Psychological testing*. Upper Saddle River, NJ: Prentice Hall.

Bach, P., & Hayes, S. C. (2002). The use of acceptance and commitment therapy to prevent the rehospitalization of psychotic patients: A randomized controlled trial. *Journal of Consulting and Clinical Psychology, 70*(5), 1129.

Bandura, A. (1991). Self-efficacy mechanism in physiological activation and health-promoting behavior. In J. Madden (Ed.), *Neurobiology of learning, emotion and affect*. New York, NY: Raven Press.

Bandura, A. (1997). *Self-efficacy: The exercise of control*. New York, NY: W. H. Freeman.

Barskova, T., & Oesterreich, R. (2009). Post-traumatic growth in people living with a serious medical condition and its relations to physical and mental health: A systematic review. *Disability and Rehabilitation, 31*(21), 1709–1733.

Beckham, J. C., Burker, E. J., Lytle, B. L., Feldman, M. E., & Costakis, M. J. (1997). Self-efficacy and adjustment in cancer patients: A preliminary report. *Journal of Behavioral Medicine, 23*(3), 138–142.

Bränström, R., Duncan, L. G., & Moskowitz, J. T. (2011). The association between dispositional mindfulness, psychological well-being, and perceived health in a Swedish population-based sample. *British Journal of Health Psychology, 16*(2), 300–316. doi:10.1348/135910710x501683

Buck, A. C., Williams, D. R., Musick, M. A., & Sternthal, M. J. (2009). An examination of the relationship between multiple dimensions of religiosity, blood pressure, and hypertension. *Social Science and Medicine, 68*(2), 314–322. doi:10.1016/j.socscimed.2008.10.010

Caponigro, J. M., Moran, E. K., Kring, A. M., & Moskowitz, J. T. (2014). Awareness and coping with emotion in schizophrenia: Acceptability, feasibility and case illustrations. *Clinical Psychology & Psychotherapy, 21*(4), 371–380.

Carrico, A. W., & Moskowitz, J. T. (in press). Positive affect promotes engagement in care following HIV diagnosis. *Health Psychology*.

Chida, Y., & Steptoe, A. (2008). Positive psychological well-being and mortality: A quantitative review of prospective observational studies. *Psychosomatic Medicine, 70*(7), 741–756. doi: 10.1097/PSY.0b013e31818105ba

Chow, S.-C., & Chang, M. (2008). Adaptive design methods in clinical trials—A review. *Orphanet Journal of Rare Diseases, 3*(11).

Coffey, C. S., Levin, B., Clark, C., Timmerman, C., Wittes, J., Gilbert, P., & Harris, S. (2012). Overview, hurdles, and future work in adaptive designs: Perspectives from a National Institutes of Health-funded workshop. *Clinical Trials, 9*(6), 671–680.

Cohen, S., & Pressman, S. D. (2006). Positive affect and health. *Current Directions in Psychological Science 15*(3), 122–125. doi:10.1111/j.0963-7214.2006.00420.x

Compton, W. C. (2001). Toward a tripartite factor structure of mental health: Subjective well-being, personal growth, and religiosity. *Journal of Psychology, 135*(5), 486–500.

Diener, E., Emmons, R. A., Larsen, R. J., & Griffin, S. (1985). The Satisfaction with Life Scale. *Journal of Personality Assessment, 49*(1), 71–75. doi:10.1207/s15327752jpa4901_13

Dockray, S., Grant, N., Stone, A. A., Kahneman, D., Wardle, J., & Steptoe, A. (2010). A comparison of affect ratings obtained with Ecological Momentary Assessment and the Day Reconstruction Method. *Social Indicators Research, 99*(2), 269–283.

Dowling, G. A., Merrilees, J., Mastick, J., Chang, V. Y., Hubbard, E., & Moskowitz, J. T. (in press). Life enhancing activities for family caregivers of people with frontotemporal dementia. *Alzheimer's Disease and Associated Disorders*.

Duckworth, A. L., Peterson, C., Matthews, M. D., & Kelly, D. R. (2007). Grit: Perseverance and passion for long-term goals. *Journal of Personality and Social Psychology, 92*(6), 1087.

Duckworth, A. L., Steen, T. A., & Seligman, M. E. (2005). Positive psychology in clinical practice. *Annual Review of Clinical Psychology, 1*, 629–651.

Dunn, E. W., Aknin, L. B., & Norton, M. I. (2008). Spending money on others promotes happiness. *Science, 319*(5870), 1687–1688.

Edmondson, K., Lawler, K., Jobe, R., Younger, J., Piferi, R., & Jones, W. (2005). Spirituality predicts health and cardiovascular responses to stress in young adult women. *Journal of Religion and Health, 44*(2), 161–171. doi:10.1007/s10943-005-2774-0

Embretson, S. E. (2006). The continued search for nonarbitrary metrics in psychology. *American Psychologist American Psychologist, 61*(1), 50–55.

Embretson, S. E., & Reise, S. P. (2000). *Item response theory for psychologists.* Mahwah, NJ: Erlbaum.

Emmons, R. A. (2007). *Thanks!: How the new science of gratitude can make you happier.* New York, NY: Houghton Mifflin.

Emmons, R. A., & McCullough, M. E. (2003). Counting blessings versus burdens: An experimental investigation of gratitude and subjective well-being in daily life. *Journal of Personality and Social Psychology, 84,* 377–389.

Folkman, S. (1997). Positive psychological states and coping with severe stress. *Social Science and Medicine, 45,* 1207–1221.

Ford, B. Q., & Mauss, I. B. (in press). The paradoxical effects of pursuing positive emotion: When and why wanting to feel happy backfires. In J. M. Gruber, J. T. Moskowitz (Ed.), *The dark and light sides of positive emotion.* New York, NY: Oxford University Press.

Fredrickson, B. L. (1998). What good are positive emotions? *Review of General Psychology, 2,* 300–319.

Gershon, R. C., Cella, D., Fox, N. A., Havlik, R. J., Hendrie, H. C., & Wagster, M. V. (2010). Assessment of neurological and behavioural function: The NIH Toolbox. *Lancet Neurology, 9*(2), 138–139. doi:S1474-4422(09)70335-7 [pii] 10.1016/S1474-4422(09)70335-7

Gruber, J., & Moskowitz, J. T. (Eds.). (2014). *The dark and light sides of positive emotion.* New York, NY: Oxford University Press.

Hoogwegt, M. T., Versteeg, H., Hansen, T. B., Thygesen, L. C., Pedersen, S. S., & Zwisler, A.-D. (2013). Exercise mediates the association between positive affect and 5-year mortality in patients with ischemic heart disease. *Circulation: Cardiovascular Quality and Outcomes.* doi:10.1161/circoutcomes.113.000158

Huebner, E. S. (1991). Initial development of the Student's Life Satisfaction Scale. *School Psychology International, 12*(3), 231–240. doi:10.1177/0143034391123010

Huffman, J. C., Mastromauro, C. A., Boehm, J. K., Seabrook, R., Fricchione, G. L., Denninger, J. W., & Lyubomirsky, S. (2011). Development of a positive psychology intervention for patients with acute cardiovascular disease. *Heart International, 6*(2), e14.

Isen, A. M., & Shalker, T. E. (1982). The effect of feeling state on evaluation of positive, neutral, and negative stimulie: When you "accentuate the positive," do you "eliminate the negative"? *Social Psychology Quarterly, 45,* 58–63.

Ishida, R., & Okada, M. (2006). Effects of a firm purpose in life on anxiety and sympathetic nervous activity caused by emotional stress: Assessment by psycho-physiological method. *Stress and Health, 22*(4), 275–281. doi:10.1002/smi.1095

Jahoda, M. (1958). *Current concepts of positive mental health.* New York, NY: Basic Books.

Jones, F., Partridge, C., & Reid, F. (2008). The Stroke Self-Efficacy Questionnaire: Measuring individual confidence in functional performance after stroke. *Journal of Clinical Nursing, 17*(7b), 244–252.

Kahneman, D., Krueger, A. B., Schkade, D. A., Schwarz, N., & Stone, A. A. (2004). A survey method for characterizing daily life experience: The Day Reconstruction Method. *Science, 306*(5702), 1776–1780. doi:10.1126/science.1103572

Klinger, E. (2012). The search for meaning in evolutionary perspective and its clinical implications. In P. T. P. Wong & P. S. Fry (Eds.), *The human quest for meaning: A handbook of psychological research and clinical applications* (2nd ed., pp. 23–56). Mahwah, NJ: Erlbaum.

Krause, N. (2009). Meaning in life and mortality. *Journals of Gerontology. Series B, Psychological Sciences and Social Sciences, 64B*(4), 517–527. doi:10.1093/geronb/gbp047

Krause, N., & Shaw, B. A. (2003). Role-specific control, personal meaning, and health in late life. *Research on Aging, 25*(6), 559–586. doi:10.1177/0164027503256695

Lancastle, D., & Boivin, J. (2007, December). *Feasibility, acceptability and usefulness of a self-administered positive reappraisal coping intervention (PRCI) card for stressful medical situations.* Paper presented at the 3rd Annual Meeting of the United Kingdom Society for Behavioural Medicine, Warwick, England.

Lancastle, D., & Boivin, J. (2008). A feasibility study of a brief coping intervention (PRCI) for the waiting period before a pregnancy test during fertility treatment. *Human Reproduction, 23,* 2299–2307.

Lazarus, R. S., & Folkman, S. (1984). *Stress, appraisal, and coping.* New York, NY: Springer.

Lazarus, R. S., Kanner, A. D., & Folkman, S. (1980). Emotions: A cognitive-phenomenological analysis. In R. Plutchik & H. Kellerman (Eds.), *Theories of emotion* (pp. 189–217). New York, NY: Academic Press.

Lee, V., Robin Cohen, S., Edgar, L., Laizner, A. M., & Gagnon, A. J. (2006). Meaning-making intervention during breast or colorectal cancer treatment improves self-esteem, optimism, and self-efficacy. *Social Science and Medicine, 62*(12), 3133–3145.

Linde, J. A., Rothman, A. J., Baldwin, A. S., & Jeffery, R. W. (2006). The impact of self-efficacy on behavior change and weight change among overweight participants in a weight loss trial. *Health Psychology, 25*(3), 282–291. doi:10.1037/0278-6133.25.3.282

Lord, F. M. (1980). *Applications of item response theory to practical testing problems.* Hillsdale, NJ: Erlbaum.

Mancuso, C. A., Choi, T. N., Westermann, H., Wenderoth, S., Hollenberg, J. P., Wells, M. T., ... Charlson, M. E. (2012). Increasing physical activity in patients with asthma through positive affect and self-affirmation: A randomized trial. *Archives of Internal Medicine, 172,* 337–343. doi:10.1001/archinternmed.2011.1316

Martin, R. A. (2001). Humor, laughter, and physical health: Methodological issues and research findings. *Psychological Bulletin, 127*(4), 504–519.

Martin, R. A. (2002). Is laughter the best medicine? Humor, laughter, and physical health. *Current Directions in Psychological Science, 11*(6), 216–220.

Martin, R. A., & Lefcourt, H. M. (1983). Sense of humor as a moderator of the relation between stressors and moods. *Journal of Personality & Social Psychology, 45*(6), 1313–1324.

Matthews, K. A., Owens, J. F., Edmundowicz, D., Lee, L., & Kuller, L. H. (2006). Positive and negative attributes and risk for coronary and aortic calcification in healthy women. *Psychosomatic Medicine, 68*(3), 355–361. doi:10.1097/01.psy.0000221274.21709.d0

Meredith, P., Strong, J., & Feeney, J. A. (2006). Adult attachment, anxiety, and pain self-efficacy as predictors of pain intensity and disability. *Pain, 123*(1–2), 146–154. doi:10.1016/j.pain.2006.02.025

Moen, P., Dempster-McCain, D., & Williams, R. M. (1993). Successful aging. *American Journal of Sociology, 97,* 1612–1632.

Moskowitz, J. T. (2010). Coping interventions and the regulation of positive affect. In S. Folkman (Ed.), *The Oxford handbook of stress, health, and coping* (pp. 407–427). Oxford, England: Oxford University Press.

Moskowitz, J. T., Hult, J. R., Duncan, L. G., Cohn, M. A., Maurer, S. A., Bussolari, C., & Acree, M. (2012). A positive affect intervention for people experiencing health-related stress: Development and non-randomized pilot test. *Journal of Health Psychology, 17*(5), 677–693. doi:10.1177/1359105311425275

Mroczek, D. K., Stawski, R. S., Turiano, N. A., Chan, W., Almeida, D. M., Neupert, S. D., & Spiro, A. (in press). Emotional reactivity and mortality: Longitudinal findings from the VA Normative Aging Study. *Journals of Gerontology: Psychological Sciences.*

Musick, M. A., & Wilson, J. (2003). Volunteering and depression: The role of psychological and social resources in different age groups. *Social Science & Medicine, 56*, 259–269.

Neff, K. (2003). Self-compassion: An alternative conceptualization of a healthy attitude toward oneself. *Self and Identity, 2*(2), 85–101.

Neff, K. D., Rude, S. S., & Kirkpatrick, K. L. (2007). An examination of self-compassion in relation to positive psychological functioning and personality traits. *Journal of Research in Personality, 41*(4), 908–916.

Ogden, J. (2012). *Health psychology: A textbook* (5th ed.). Maidenhead, England: Open University Press.

Ogedegbe, G. O., Boutin-Foster, C., Wells, M. T., Allegrante, J. P., Isen, A. M., Jobe, J. B., & Charlson, M. E. (2012). A randomized controlled trial of positive-affect intervention and medication adherence in hypertensive African Americans. *Archives of Internal Medicine, 172*(4), 322.

Oman, D., Thoresen, C. E., & McMahon, K. (1999). Volunteerism and mortality among the community-dwelling elderly. *Journal of Health Psychology, 4*, 301–316.

Ozaki, A., Uchiyama, M., Tagaya, H., Ohida, T., & Ogihara, R. (2007). The Japanese Centenarian Study: Autonomy was associated with health practices as well as physical status. *Journal of the American Geriatrics Society, 55*(1), 95–101.

Peterman, A. H., Fitchett, G., Brady, M. J., Hernandez, L., & Cella, D. (2002). Measuring spiritual well-being in people with cancer: The Functional Assessment of Chronic Illness Therapy-Spiritual Well-being Scale (FACIT-Sp). *Annals of Behavioral Medicine, 24*(1), 49–58.

Peterson, J. C., Charlson, M. E., Hoffman, Z., Wells, M. T., Wong, S.-C., Hollenberg, J. P., . . . Allegrante, J. P. (2012). Randomized controlled trial of positive affect induction to promote physical activity after percutaneous coronary intervention. *Archives of Internal Medicine, 172*, 329–336. doi:10.1001/archinternmed.2011.1311

Peterson, J. C., Czajkowski, S., Charlson, M. E., Link, A. R., Wells, M. T., Isen, A. M., . . . Ogedegbe, G. (2013). Translating basic behavioral and social science research to clinical application: The EVOLVE mixed methods approach. *Journal of Consulting and Clinical Psychology, 81*(2), 217.

Post, S. G. (2005). Altruism, happiness, and health: It's good to be good. *International Journal of Behavioral Medicine, 12*, 66–77.

Pressman, S. D., & Cohen, S. (2005). Does positive affect influence health? *Psychological Bulletin, 131*(6), 925–971. doi:10.1037/0033-2909.131.6.925

Rahman, A., Reed, E., Underwood, M., Shipley, M. E., & Omar, R. Z. (2008). Factors affecting self-efficacy and pain intensity in patients with chronic musculoskeletal pain seen in a specialist rheumatology pain clinic. *Rheumatology, 47*(12), 1803–1808. doi:10.1093/rheumatology/ken377

Richardson, M. (1936). The relation between the difficulty and the differential validity of a test. *Psychometrika, 1*(2), 33–49. doi:10.1007/BF02288003

Ryff, C. D. (1989). Happiness is everything, or is it? Exploration on the meaning of psychological well-being. *Journal of Personality and Social Psychology, 57*(6), 1069–1081.

Salsman, J., Lai, J.-S., Hendrie, H., Butt, Z., Zill, N., Pilkonis, P., . . . Cella, D. (2013). Assessing psychological well-being: Self-report instruments for the NIH Toolbox. *Quality of Life Research, 23*(1), 205–215. doi:10.1007/s11136-013-0452-3

Saslow, L. R., Cohn, M., & Moskowitz, J. T. (in press). Positive affect interventions to reduce stress: Harnessing the benefit while avoiding the Pollyanna. In J. Gruber & J. T. Moskowitz (Eds.), *The dark and light sides of positive emotion*. New York, NY: Oxford University Press.

Scheier, M., Wrosch, C., Baum, A., Cohen, S., Martire, L., Matthews, K., . . . Zdaniuk, B. (2006). The Life Engagement Test: Assessing purpose in life. *Journal of Behavioral Medicine, 29*(3), 291–298.

Schwerdtfeger, A., Konermann, L., & Schönhofen, K. (2008). Self-efficacy as a health-protective resource in teachers? A biopsychological approach. *Health Psychology, 27*(3), 358–368.

Seligman, M. E. P., & Csikszentmihalyi, M. (2000). Positive psychology: An introduction. *American Psychologist, 55*(1), 5. doi:10.1037/0003-066X.55.1.5

Selye, H. (1956). *The stress of life*. New York, NY: McGraw-Hill.

Shiffman, S., Stone, A. A., & Hufford, M. R. (2008). Ecological Momentary Assessment. *Annual Review of Clinical Psychology, 4*(1), 1–32. doi:10.1146/annurev.clinpsy.3.022806.091415

Singer, J. A., Singer, B. F., & Berry, M. (2013). A meaning-based intervention for addiction: Using narrative therapy and mindfulness. In J. A. Hicks & C. Routledge (Eds.), *The experience of meaning in life: Classical perspectives, emerging themes, and controversies* (pp. 379–392). Dordrecht, The Netherlands: Springer.

Steger, M. F., Frazier, P., Oishi, S., & Kaler, M. (2006). The Meaning in Life Questionnaire: Assessing the presence of and search for meaning in life. *Journal of Counseling Psychology, 53*(1), 80–93. doi:10.1037/0022-0167.53.1.80

Stone, A. A., Shiffman, S., Atienza, A., & Nebling, L. (2007). *The science of real-time data capture: Self-reports in health research*. New York, NY: Oxford University Press.

Streiner, D. L., & Norman, G. R. (1995). *Health measurement scales: A practical guide to their development and use*. Oxford, England: Oxford University Press.

Swan, G. E., & Carmelli, D. (1996). Curiosity and mortality in aging adults: A 5-year follow-up of the Western Collaborative Group Study. *Psychology and Aging, 11*(3), 449.

Weiss, D. J. (2004). Computerized adaptive testing for effective and efficient measurement in counseling and education. *Measurement and Evaluation in Counseling and Development, 37*(2), 70–84.

Wu, S., & Green, A. (2000). *Projection of chronic illness prevalence and cost inflation*. Washington, DC: RAND Health.

Zautra, A. J., Davis, M. C., Reich, J. W., Nicassario, P., Tennen, H., Finan, P., . . . Irwin, M. R. (2008). Comparison of cognitive behavioral and mindfulness meditation interventions on adaptation to rheumatoid arthritis for patients with and without history of recurrent depression. *Journal of Consulting and Clinical Psychology, 76*(3), 408–421.

Zika, S., & Chamberlain, K. (1992). On the relation between meaning in life and psychological well-being. *British Journal of Psychology, 83*(Pt. 1), 133–145.

CHAPTER 25

# Deconstructing the Illness Ideology and Constructing an Ideology of Human Strengths and Potential in Clinical Psychology

JAMES E. MADDUX and SHANE J. LOPEZ

T HIS CHAPTER IS CONCERNED with the ways that clinical psychologists think about or *conceive* psychological illness and wellness, and especially how they conceive the *difference* between psychological wellness and illness. More specifically, it is concerned with how clinical psychologists traditionally *have conceived* the difference between psychological illness and wellness and how positive psychology suggests they *should conceive* this difference. Thus, the major purpose of this chapter is to challenge traditional conceptions of psychological wellness and illness and to offer a new conception based on positive psychology and a corresponding new *vision* of and *mission* for clinical psychology.

A *conception* of the difference between wellness and illness is not a *theory* of either wellness or illness (Wakefield, 1992). A conception of the difference between wellness and illness attempts to define these terms—to delineate which human experiences are to be considered "well" or "ill." More specifically, a conception of "psychopathology" does not try to explain the psychological phenomena that are considered pathological, but instead tells us what psychological phenomena are considered pathological and thus need to be explained. A *theory* of psychopathology, however, is an attempt to explain those psychological phenomena and experiences that have been identified by the conception as pathological (see also Maddux, Gosselin, & Winstead, 2012).

Conceptions are important for a number of reasons. As medical philosopher Lawrie Reznek (1987) has said, "Concepts carry consequences—classifying things one way rather than another has important implications for the way we behave towards such things" (p. 1). In speaking of the importance of the conception of *disease*, Reznek (1987) wrote:

The classification of a condition as a disease carries many important consequences. We inform medical scientists that they should try to discover a cure for the condition. We inform benefactors that they should support such research.

We direct medical care towards the condition, making it appropriate to treat the condition by medical means such as drug therapy, surgery, and so on. We inform our courts that it is inappropriate to hold people responsible for the manifestations of the condition. We set up early warning detection services aimed at detecting the condition in its early stages when it is still amenable to successful treatment. We serve notice to health insurance companies and national health services that they are liable to pay for the treatment of such a condition. Classifying a condition as a disease is no idle matter. (p. 1)

To label is to classify. If we substitute the labels *psychopathology* or *mental disorder* for the label *disease* in this paragraph, Reznek's message still holds true. How we conceive psychological illness and wellness has wide-ranging implications for individuals, medical and mental health professionals, government agencies and programs, and society at large. It determines what behaviors we consider it necessary to explain with our theories, thus determining the direction and scope of our research efforts. It also determines how we conceive the subject matter of clinical psychology, the roles and functions of clinical psychologists, and the people with whom they work.

Unlike theories of psychological wellness and illness, conceptions of psychological wellness and illness cannot be subjected to empirical validation. One cannot conduct research on the validity of conceptions of psychological wellness and illness because they are social constructions grounded in values, not science, and socially constructed values cannot be proven true or false. (We will return to this issue later in this chapter.) Because this chapter deals with socially constructed conceptions, it offers no new facts or research findings intended to persuade the reader of the greater value of one conception of psychological wellness and illness over another. Instead, this chapter offers a different perspective based on a different set of values. More than anything else, as stated previously, it offers a vision and a mission statement.

## THE ILLNESS IDEOLOGY AND CLINICAL PSYCHOLOGY

Words can exert a powerful influence over thought. Long after the ancient roots of the term *clinical psychology* have been forgotten, they continue to influence our thinking about the discipline. *Clinical* derives from the Greek *klinike* or "medical practice at the sickbed," and *psychology* derives from *psyche*, meaning "soul" or "mind." Although few clinical psychologists today literally practice at people's bedsides, many practitioners and most of the public still view clinical psychology as a kind of medical practice for people with "sick souls" or "sick minds." The discipline is still steeped not only in an illness metaphor but also an illness ideology—as evidenced by the fact that the language of clinical psychology remains the language of medicine and pathology. Terms such as *symptom, disorder, pathology, illness, diagnosis, treatment, doctor, patient, clinic, clinical,* and *clinician* are all consistent with the ancient assumptions captured in the term *clinical psychology* and with both a metaphor and an ideology of illness and disease (Maddux, 2002, 2008). Although the illness metaphor (also referred to as the *medical model*) prescribes a certain way of thinking about psychological problems (e.g., a psychological problem is *like* a biological disease), the illness ideology goes beyond this and tells us to what aspects of human behavior we should pay attention. Specifically, it dictates that the focus of our attention should be disorder, dysfunction, and disease rather than health. Thus, it narrows our focus on what is weak and defective about people to the exclusion of what is strong and healthy.

This illness ideology emphasizes abnormality over normality, poor adjustment over healthy adjustment, and sickness over health. It promotes dichotomies between normal and abnormal behaviors, between clinical and nonclinical problems, and between clinical and nonclinical populations. It locates human adjustment and maladjustment inside the person rather than in the person's interactions with the environment and encounters with sociocultural values and societal institutions. Finally, this ideology and its language portray people who seek help for problems in living as passive victims of intrapsychic and biological forces beyond their direct control. As a result, they are relegated to the role of passive recipient of an expert's care as opposed to an active participant in solving their own problems and taking control over their own lives.

Clinical psychology's deeply entrenched association with the illness ideology has gone on far too long. We believe that it is time for a change in the way that clinical psychology views itself and the way it is viewed by the public. We believe that the illness ideology has outlived its usefulness for clinical psychology. Decades ago, the field of medicine began to shift its emphasis from the treatment of illness to the prevention of illness and then moved from the prevention of illness to the enhancement of health (Snyder, Feldman, Taylor, Schroeder, & Adams, 2000). Furthermore, more than three decades ago, the field of health psychology acknowledged the need to emphasize illness prevention and health promotion. Unless clinical psychology embraces a similar change in emphasis, it will struggle for identity and purpose in much the same manner as psychiatry has for the last several decades (Frances, 2013; Wilson, 1993). For example, over half a century ago, clinical psychologists overtook psychiatrists as the major providers of psychotherapy. Now, social workers are overtaking clinical psychologists in the provision of these same services. Clinical psychology needs to redefine itself as a science and a profession and expand its roles and opportunities in order to survive and thrive in the rapidly changing market of mental health services. The best way to do this is to abandon the illness ideology and replace it with a positive clinical psychology grounded in positive psychology's ideologies of health, happiness, and human strengths.

## HISTORICAL ROOTS OF THE ILLNESS IDEOLOGY IN CLINICAL PSYCHOLOGY

Despite the illness ideology's current hold on clinical psychology, the discipline was not steeped in the illness ideology at its start. Some historians of psychology trace the beginning of the profession of clinical psychology in the United States back to the 1886 founding of the first "psychological clinic" in the United States by Lightner Witmer at the University of Pennsylvania (Reisman, 1991). Witmer and the other early clinical psychologists worked primarily with children who had learning or school problems, not with "patients" with "mental disorders" (Reisman, 1991; Routh, 2000). Thus, they were more influenced by psychometric theory and its emphasis on careful measurement than by psychoanalytic theory and its emphasis on psychopathology and illness. Following Freud's 1909 visit to Clark University, however, psychoanalysis and its derivatives dominated both psychiatry and clinical psychology (Barone, Maddux, & Snyder, 1997; Korchin, 1976). Psychoanalytic theory, with its emphasis on hidden intrapsychic processes and sexual and aggressive urges, provided a fertile soil into which the illness ideology deeply sank its roots.

Several other factors encouraged clinical psychologists to devote their attention to psychopathology and thereby strengthened the hold of the illness ideology on the field. First, although clinical psychologists were trained academically in universities, their practitioner training occurred primarily in psychiatric hospitals and clinics (Morrow, 1946). In these settings, clinical psychologists worked primarily as psychodiagnosticians under the direction of psychiatrists trained in medicine and psychoanalysis. Second, after World War II, the United States Veterans Administration was founded and soon joined the American Psychological Association in developing training centers and standards for clinical psychologists. Because these early training centers were in Veterans Administration hospitals, the training of clinical psychologists continued to occur primarily in psychiatric settings, which were steeped in both biological models and psychoanalytic models. Third, the United States National Institute of Mental Health was founded in 1947. Given the direction that the NIMH took from the beginning, perhaps it should have been named the National Institute for Mental *Illness*. Regardless of the name, very soon "thousands of psychologists found out that they could make a living treating mental illness" (Seligman & Csikszentmihalyi, 2000, p. 6). By the 1950s, clinical psychologists in the United States had come "to see themselves as part of a mere subfield of the health professions" (Seligman & Csikszentmihalyi, 2000, p. 6), and the practice of clinical psychology was grounded firmly in the illness ideology and was characterized by four basic assumptions about its scope and nature of psychological adjustment and maladjustment (Barone et al., 1997).

First, clinical psychology is concerned with *psychopathology*—deviant, abnormal, and maladaptive behavioral and emotional conditions. Thus, its focus is not on facilitating mental health but on alleviating mental "illness," and not on the everyday problems in living experienced by millions, but on severe conditions experienced by a relatively small number of people. Common problems in living became the purview of counseling psychology, social work, and child guidance. Counseling psychology, in fact, because of its concern with everyday problems in living, gradually shifted away from an intrapsychic illness approach and toward interpersonal theories (Tyler, 1972), thus making counseling psychologists less enamored with the illness ideology and with formal psychiatric diagnoses such as those described in the *DSM*.

Second, psychopathology, clinical problems, and clinical populations differ in kind, not just in degree, from normal problems in living, nonclinical problems, and nonclinical populations. Psychopathologies are *disorders*, not merely extreme variants of common problems in living and expected human difficulties and imperfections. As such, understanding psychopathology requires theories different from those theories that explain normal problems in living and effective psychological functioning. This separation became concretely evident in 1965 when the *Journal of Abnormal and Social Psychology* was split into the *Journal of Abnormal Psychology* and the *Journal of Personality and Social Psychology*.

Third, psychological disorders are analogous to biological or medical diseases in that they reflect distinct conditions *inside* the individual; moreover, these internal conditions cause people to think, feel, and behave maladaptively. This illness analogy does not hold that psychological disorders are necessarily directly caused by biological dysfunction. Instead, it holds that the causes of emotional and behavioral problems are located inside the person, rather than in the person's interactions with his or her environment (including his or her relationships with other people and society at large). Thus, to understand psychological problems, it is more important to understand and measure the fixed properties of people (e.g., personality traits) than to understand and assess the complex interactions between the person and the wide range of his or her life situations.

Fourth, following from the illness analogy, the psychological clinician's task, similar to the medical clinician's task, is to identify (diagnose) the disorder (disease) inside the person (patient) and to prescribe an intervention (treatment) for eliminating (curing) the internal disorder (disease). This treatment consists of alleviating conditions, either biological or psychological, that reside inside the person and that are believed to be responsible for the symptoms. Even if the attempt to alleviate the problem is a purely verbal attempt to educate or persuade, it is still referred to as *treatment* or *therapy*, unlike often equally beneficial attempts to educate or persuade on the part of teachers, ministers, friends, and family (see also Szasz, 1978). In addition, these psychotherapeutic interactions between clinicians and their patients differ in quality from helpful and distress-reducing interactions between the patient and other people in his or her life, and understanding these psychotherapeutic interactions requires special theories (see also Maddux, 2010).

Once clinical psychology became pathologized, there was no turning back. Albee (2000) suggests that "the uncritical acceptance of the medical model, the organic explanation of mental disorders, with psychiatric hegemony, medical concepts, and language" (p. 247) was the "fatal flaw" of the standards for clinical psychology training in the United States. These standards were established in 1950 by the American Psychological Association at a conference in Boulder, Colorado. At this same conference, the "scientist-practitioner" model of clinical psychology training was established. Albee (2000) argues that this fatal flaw "has distorted and damaged the development of clinical psychology ever since" (p. 247).

Little has changed since 1950. The basic assumptions of the illness ideology continue as implicit guides to clinical psychologists' activities, and they permeate the view of clinical psychology held by the public and policy makers. In fact, the influence of the illness ideology has increased over the past three decades as clinical psychologists have fallen more and more deeply under the spell of the American Psychiatric Association (APA)'s *Diagnostic and Statistical Manual of Mental Disorders* (*DSM*; APA, 2013). First published in the early 1950s, the *DSM* (APA, 1952) is now in its fifth edition (actually the seventh, if one counts as "editions" the "text revisions" of the third and fourth editions, in 1987 and 2000, respectively), and its size and influence have increased with each revision. The influence of the first two editions (1952 and 1968) on research, practice, and clinical training was negligible, but its influence increased exponentially after the publication of the greatly expanded third edition in 1980.

The influence of the *DSM* has increased with the increasing size and scope of the subsequent revisions. The first edition (including all appendices) ran 130 pages; the fifth edition is just over 900 pages. The number of official mental disorders recognized by the American Psychiatric Association has increased from six in the mid-19th century to close to 300 in the *DSM-5* (Frances & Widiger, 2012). The *DSM* continues to provide the organizational structure for almost all textbooks and courses on abnormal psychology and psychopathology, as well as almost all books on the assessment and treatment of psychological problems for practicing clinical psychologists. The growth in the role of third-party funding for mental health services in the United States during this same period fueled the growth of the influence of the *DSM* as these third parties began requiring a *DSM* diagnostic label as a condition for payment or reimbursement for mental health services. Nowhere is the power of the illness ideology over clinical psychology more evident than in the dominance of the *DSM*. (Although we acknowledge the international importance and influence of the World Health Organization's *International Classification of Disease* [*ICD-10*; WHO, 1992], it has not generated the heated ideological and professional controversies that have been sparked by the *DSM*.)

Although most of the previously noted assumptions of the illness ideology are disavowed in the *DSM-5* introduction (APA, 2013), most of the manual is nonetheless

inconsistent with this disavowal. For example, still included in the revised definition of *mental disorder* is the notion that a mental disorder is "a dysfunction in the
individual" (p. 20). Numerous common problems in living are viewed as mental disorders (Frances, 2013), and several others are listed as "conditions for further study"
(e.g., persistent complex bereavement disorder, caffeine use disorder, Internet gaming
disorder), and therefore are likely to find their way into *DSM-6*.

In addition, "diagnostic fads" are sparked by each new edition. Allen Frances,
responsible for the fourth edition, notes four "epidemics" that were sparked by
changes from *DSM-III* to *DSM-IV*: autism, attention deficit/hyperactivity disorder,
childhood bipolar disorder, and paraphilia not otherwise specified (Frances, 2013).
He also warns that *DSM-5* threatens to provoke new epidemics of at least four
new disorders that emerged in *DSM-5*: disruptive mood dysregulation disorder,
binge-eating disorder, mild neurocognitive disorders, and "behavioral addictions"
(Frances, 2013; see also Paris, 2013).

We acknowledge that *DSM-5* is an improvement over *DSM-IV* in its greater attention to alternative dimensional models for conceptualizing psychological problems
and its greater attention to the importance of cultural considerations in determining
whether a problematic pattern should be viewed as a "mental disorder." Yet it remains
steeped in the illness ideology for most of its 900 pages.

So closely aligned are the illness ideology and the *DSM*, and so powerful is the
influence of the *DSM* over clinical psychology (at least in the United States), that
clinical psychology's rejection of the illness ideology must go hand in hand with its
rejection of *DSM* as the best way to conceive of psychological difficulties.

## THE SOCIAL CONSTRUCTION OF PSYCHOLOGICAL WELLNESS AND ILLNESS

Positive clinical psychology rejects the illness ideology as the most accurate or effective approach for conceiving of the psychologically problematic aspects of human
life. As such, positive clinical psychology refutes the illness ideology's premise that
normal problems in living are symptoms of psychopathologies—that is, psychological illnesses, diseases, or disorders—and that giving a person a formal diagnosis for
a problem in living adds any additional understanding to that person and his or her
problem (see also Williams, 2012, for a discussion of mental disorder theory versus
psychosocial problem theory). This refutation is based on the assumption that the illness perspective is not a scientific theory or set of facts but rather a *socially constructed
ideology*. The process of social constructionism involves "elucidating the process by
which people come to describe, explain, or otherwise account for the world in which
they live" (Gergen, 1985, pp. 3–4; see also Gergen, 1999). Social constructionism is
concerned with

> examining ways in which people understand the world, the social and political
> processes that influence how people define words and explain events, and the
> implications of these definitions and explanations—who benefits and who loses
> because of how we describe and understand the world. (Muehlenhard & Kimes,
> 1999, p. 234)

From this perspective, our ways of thinking about human behavior and our explanations for human problems in living "are products of particular historical and cultural understandings rather than . . . universal and immutable categories of human

experience" (Bohan, 1996, p. xvi). Because the prevailing views depend on who has the power to determine them, universal or "true" conceptions and perspectives do not exist. The people who are privileged to define such views usually are people with power, and their conceptions reflect and promote their interests and values (Muehlenhard & Kimes, 1999). Therefore, "When less powerful people attempt to challenge existing power relationships and to promote social change, an initial battleground is often the words used to discuss these problems" (Muehlenhard & Kimes, 1999, p. 234). Because the interests of people and institutions arc based on their values, debates over the definition of concepts often become clashes between deeply and implicitly held beliefs about the way people should live their lives and about differences between right and wrong.

The social constructionist perspective can be contrasted with the *essentialist* perspective that is inherent in the illness ideology. Essentialism assumes that there are natural categories and that all members of a given category share important characteristics (Rosenblum & Travis, 1996). For example, the essentialist perspective views our categories of race, sexual orientation, and social class as objective categories that are independent of social or cultural processes. It views these categories as representing "empirically verifiable similarities among and differences between people" (Rosenblum & Travis, 1996, p. 2). In the social constructionist view, however, "reality cannot be separated from the way that a culture makes sense of it" (Rosenblum & Travis, 1996, p. 3). In social constructionism, such categories represent not what people *are* but rather the ways that people think about and attempt to make sense of differences among themselves. Social processes also determine what differences among people are more important than other differences (Rosenblum & Travis, 1996).

Thus, from the essentialist perspective, the distinctions between psychological wellness and illness and among various so-called psychopathologies and mental disorders are natural distinctions that can be discovered and described. From the social constructionist perspective, however, these distinctions are abstract ideas that are defined by people and thus reflect cultural, professional, and personal values. The social constructionist view of the illness ideology and its various presumed psychopathologies and mental disorders is that they are not scientifically verifiable "facts" or even scientifically testable theories. Instead, they are abstract ideas that have been constructed by people with particular personal, professional, and cultural values. The meanings of these and other concepts are not *revealed* by the methods of science but are *negotiated* among the people and institutions of society who have an interest in their definitions. What people often call "facts" are not truths but reflect reality negotiations (or social constructions) by those people who have an interest in using "the facts" (see Snyder & Higgins, 1997).

Not surprisingly, we typically refer to psychological concepts as *constructs* because their meanings are constructed and negotiated rather than discovered or revealed (Maddux, 1999). The ways in which conceptions of basic psychological constructs such as the "self" (Baumeister, 1987) and "self-esteem" (Hewitt, 2002) have changed over time and the different ways they are conceived by different cultures (e.g., Cross & Markus, 1999; Cushman, 1995; Hewitt, 2002) illustrate this process. Thus, in social constructionism, "all categories of disorder, even physical disorder categories convincingly explored scientifically, are the product of human beings constructing meaningful systems for understanding their world" (Raskin & Lewandowski, 2000, p. 21).

Therefore, our basic thesis is that conceptions of psychological normality and abnormality, along with our specific diagnostic labels and categories, are not facts about people but social constructions—abstract concepts reflecting shared world views that were developed and agreed upon collaboratively over time by the members of society, including theorists, researchers, professionals, their clients, the media, and the culture in which all are embedded. For this reason, the illness ideology, its conception of "mental disorder," and the various specific categories of mental disorders found in traditional psychiatric diagnostic schemes (such as the *DSM* and *ICD*) are not psychological facts about people, nor are they testable scientific theories. Instead, they are social artifacts that serve the same sociocultural goals as do our constructions of race, gender, social class, and sexual orientation—maintaining and expanding the power of certain individuals and institutions, as well as maintaining social order as defined by those in power (Beall, 1993; Becker, 1963; Parker, Georgaca, Harper, McLaughlin, & Stowell-Smith, 1995; Rosenblum & Travis, 1996). As are these other social constructions, our concepts of psychological normality and abnormality are tied ultimately to social values—in particular, the values of society's most powerful individuals, groups, and institutions—and the contextual rules for behavior derived from these values (Becker, 1963; Parker et al., 1995; Rosenblum & Travis, 1996).

Reznek (1987) has demonstrated that even our definition of physical disease "is a normative or evaluative concept" (p. 211) because to call a condition a disease "is to judge that the person with that condition is less able to lead a good or worthwhile life" (p. 211) as defined by the person's society and culture. If this is true of physical disease, it certainly is true of psychological "disease." Because our notions of psychological normality–abnormality and health–illness are social constructions that serve sociocultural goals and values, they are linked to our assumptions about how people should live their lives and what makes life worth living.

The socially constructed illness ideology and associated traditional psychiatric diagnostics schemes, also socially constructed, have led to the proliferation of "mental illnesses" and to the pathologization of human existence (e.g., Frances, 2013). Given these precursors, it comes as no surprise that a highly *negative* clinical psychology evolved during the 20th century. The increasing heft and weight of the *DSM*, which has been accompanied by its increasing influence over clinical psychology, provides evidence for this. As the socially constructed boundaries of "mental disorder" have expanded with each *DSM* revision, more relatively mundane human behaviors have become pathologized; as a result, the number of people with diagnosable "mental disorders" has continued to grow. This growth has occurred largely because mental health professionals have not been content to label only the obviously and blatantly dysfunctional patterns of behaving, thinking, and feeling as "mental disorders." Instead, they (actually, *we*) have gradually pathologized almost every conceivable human problem in living. As a result of the growing dominance of the illness ideology among both professionals and the public, eventually everything that human beings think, feel, do, and desire that is not perfectly logical, adaptive, efficient, or "creates trouble in human life" (Paris, 2013, p. 43) will become a "mental disorder" (Frances, 2013; Paris, 2013). This is not surprising, given that Frances notes that in his more than two decades of working on three *DSM*s, "never once did he recall an expert make a suggestion that would reduce the boundary of his pet disorder" (Frances & Widiger, 2012, p. 118). *DSM-5* has made normality "an endangered species" partly because we live in a society that is "perfectionistic in its expectations and intolerant of what were previously considered to be normal and expectable distress and individual differences" (Frances & Widiger, 2012, p. 116), but also partly because pharmaceutical companies are constantly trying to increase the market for their drugs by encouraging the loosening and expanding of the boundaries of mental disorders described in the *DSM* (Frances, 2013; Paris, 2013). Essentially, *DSM-5* "just continues a long-term trend of expansion into the realm of normality" (Paris, 2013,

p. 183). As it does, "with ever-widening criteria for diagnosis, more and more people will fall within its net [and] many will receive medications they do not need" (Paris, 2013, p. 38).

The powerful sociocultural, political, professional, and economic forces that constructed the illness ideology now continue to sustain it. In this ongoing saga, however, the debate over the conception of psychological wellness and illness is not a search for "truth." Rather, it is a struggle over the definition of a socially constructed abstraction and over the personal, political, and economic benefits that flow from determining what and whom society views as normal and abnormal. The most vivid and powerful embodiment of the illness ideology is the *DSM*, and the struggle is played out in the continual debates involved in its revision (Frances, 2013; Kirk & Kutchins, 1992; Kutchins & Kirk, 1997).

These debates and struggles are described in detail by Horwitz (2002):

> The emergence and persistence of an overly expansive disease model of mental illness was not accidental or arbitrary. The widespread creation of distinct mental diseases developed in specific historical circumstances and because of the interests of specific social groups. . . . By the time the *DSM-III* was developed in 1980, thinking of mental illnesses as discrete disease entities . . . offered mental health professionals many social, economic, and political advantages. In addition, applying disease frameworks to a wide variety of behaviors and to a large number of people benefited a number of specific social groups including not only clinicians but also research scientists, advocacy groups, and pharmaceutical companies, among others. The disease entities of diagnostic psychiatry arose because they were useful for the social practices of various groups, not because they provided a more accurate way of viewing mental disorders. (p. 16)

Wilson (1993) offered a similar view. He argued that a noncategorical dimensional/continuity view of psychological wellness and illness posed a basic problem for psychiatry because it "did not demarcate clearly the well from the sick" (p. 402). He also argued that psychosocial modes of psychological difficulties posed a problem for psychiatry because "if conceived of psychosocially, psychiatric illness is not the province of medicine, because psychiatric problems are not truly medical but social, political, and legal" (p. 402; see also Szasz, 1974). According to Wilson (1993), the *DSM-III* gave psychiatry a means for marking its professional territory. Kirk and Kutchins (1992; Kutchins & Kirk, 1997) reached the same conclusion from their review of the papers, letters, and memos of the various *DSM* working groups—namely, that many of the most important decisions made about the inclusion or exclusion of certain "disorders" or certain "symptoms" were political decisions arrived at through negotiation and compromise rather than through an objective analysis of scientific facts (see also Frances, 2013, for a similar discussion). Of course, once a condition finds itself called a "disorder" in a diagnostic manual, it becomes *reified* and treated as if it were a natural entity existing apart from judgments and evaluations of human beings (Hyman, 2010).

## THE ILLNESS IDEOLOGY AND THE CATEGORIES VERSUS DIMENSIONS DEBATE

Embedded in the illness ideology's conception of psychological wellness and illness is a *categorical model* in which individuals are determined to either have or not have a disorder—that is, to be either psychologically well or psychologically ill—and, if they do have a disorder, that it is a specific type of disorder. An alternative model is the *dimensional model*, which assumes that normality and abnormality, wellness and illness, and effective and ineffective psychological functioning lie along a continuum. In this dimensional approach, so-called psychological disorders are simply extreme variants of normal psychological phenomena and ordinary problems in living (Keyes & Lopez, 2002; Widiger, 2012). The dimensional model is concerned not with classifying people or disorders but with identifying and measuring individual differences in psychological phenomena such as emotion, mood, intelligence, and personal styles (e.g., Lubinski, 2000; Williams, 2012). Great differences among individuals on the dimensions of interest are expected, such as the differences we find on formal tests of intelligence. As with intelligence, divisions made between normality and abnormality may be demarcated for convenience or efficiency, but they are *not* to be viewed as reflecting a true discontinuity among types of phenomena or types of people.

Empirical evidence for the validity of a dimensional approach to psychological adjustment can be found in research on personality disorders (Coker & Widiger, 2012; Costello, 1996; Maddux & Mundell, 2004; Trull & Durrett, 2005), the variations in normal emotional experiences (e.g., Oatley & Jenkins, 1992), adult attachment patterns in relationships (Fraley & Waller, 1998), self-defeating behaviors (Baumeister & Scher, 1988), children's reading problems or dyslexia (Shaywitz, Escobar, Shaywitz, Fletcher, & Makuch, 1992), attention deficit/hyperactivity disorder (Barkeley, 1997), posttraumatic stress disorder (Anthony, Lonigan, & Hecht, 1999), depression (Costello, 1993a), somatoform disorders (or somatic symptom disorders) (Eifert, McCormack, & Zvolensky, 2012), anxiety disorders (Williams, 2012), sexual dysfunctions and disorders (Gosselin, 2012), and schizophrenia (Claridge, 1995; Costello, 1993b). Even the inventor of the term *schizophrenia*, Eugen Bleuler, viewed so-called pathological conditions as being continuous with so-called normal conditions, and he noted the occurrence of schizophrenic symptoms among normal individuals (Gilman, 1988). In fact, Bleuler referred to the major symptom of schizophrenia, thought disorder, as simply "ungewohnlich," which in German means "unusual," not "bizarre," as it was translated in the first English version of Bleuler's classic monograph (Gilman, 1988).

Understanding the research supporting the dimensional approach is important because the vast majority of this research undermines the illness ideology's assumption that we can make clear, scientifically based distinctions between the psychologically well or healthy and the psychologically ill or disordered. Inherent in the dimensional view is the assumption that these distinctions are not natural demarcations that can be discovered; instead, they are created or constructed "by accretion and practical necessity, not because they [meet] some independent set of abstract and operationalized definitional criteria" (Frances & Widiger, 2012, p. 111).

## SOCIAL CONSTRUCTIONISM AND SCIENCE IN CLINICAL PSYCHOLOGY

A social constructionist perspective is not anti-science. To say that conceptions of psychological wellness and illness are socially constructed rather than scientifically constructed is not to say that human psychological distress and suffering are not real. Nor is it to say that the patterns of thinking, feeling, and behaving that society decides to label as "ill"—including their causes and treatments—cannot be studied objectively and scientifically. Instead, it is to acknowledge that science can no more determine the proper or correct conceptions of psychological wellness and illness than it can deter-mine the proper and correct conceptions of other social constructions such as beauty, justice, race, and social class. We nonetheless can use science to study the psycholog-ical phenomena that our culture refers to as "well" or "ill." We can use the methods of science to understand a culture's conception of psychological wellness and illness, how this conception has evolved, and how it affects individuals and society. We also can use the methods of science to understand the origins of the patterns of thinking, feeling, and behaving that a culture considers psychopathological and to develop and test ways of modifying those patterns.

The science of medicine is not diminished by acknowledging that the notions of *health* and *illness* are socially constructed (Reznek, 1987), nor is the science of economics diminished by acknowledging that the notions of *poverty* and *wealth* are socially constructed. Likewise, the science of clinical psychology will not be dimin-ished by acknowledging that its basic concepts are socially and not scientifically constructed. We agree with Lilienfeld and Marino (1995) that it is important to "make the value judgments underlying these decisions more explicit and open to criticism" (p. 418). We also agree that

> heated disputes would almost surely arise concerning which conditions are deserving of attention from mental health professionals. Such disputes, however, would at least be settled on the legitimate basis of social values and exigencies, rather than on the basis of ill-defined criteria of doubtful scientific status. (Lilienfeld & Marino, 1995, pp. 418–419)

## BEYOND THE ILLNESS IDEOLOGY: POSITIVE CLINICAL PSYCHOLOGY

The solution to this problem is not to move even closer to pathology-focused psychi-atry. Instead, the viability and survival of clinical psychology depends on our ability to build a *positive clinical psychology* that breaks with its pathological past. Heretofore, clinical psychologists always have been "more heavily invested in intricate theories of failure than in theories of success" (Bandura, 1998, p. 3). If we are to change our paradigm, we need to acknowledge that "much of the best work that [we] already do in the counseling room is to amplify strengths rather than repair the weaknesses of [our] clients" (Seligman & Csikszentmihalyi, 2000, p. 8). The illness ideology and its medicalizing and pathologizing language are inconsistent with positive psychol-ogy's view that "Psychology is not just a branch of medicine concerned with illness or health; it is much larger. It is about work, education, insight, love, growth, and play" (Seligman & Csikszentmihalyi, 2000, p. 7).

In building a positive clinical psychology, we must adopt not only a new ideology, but also a new language for talking about human behavior. In this new language, ineffective patterns of behaviors, cognitions, and emotions are construed as problems in living, not as disorders or diseases. Likewise, these problems in living are con-strued not as located inside individuals but in the interactions between the individual and other people that are embedded in situations that include rules for behavior that are, in turn, embedded in the larger culture. Also, those who seek assistance in enhancing the quality of their lives are clients or students, not patients. The profes-sionals who specialize in facilitating psychological health are teachers, counselors, consultants, coaches, or even social activists, not clinicians or doctors. Strategies and techniques for enhancing the quality of lives are educational, relational, social, and political interventions, not medical treatments (see also Tarragona, Chapter 15, this volume; Vossler, Steffen, & Joseph, Chapter 26, this volume). Finally, the facilities to which people will go for assistance with problems in living are centers, schools, or resorts, not clinics or hospitals. Such assistance might even take place in community centers, public and private schools, churches, and people's homes rather than in specialized facilities.

The positive psychology ideology emphasizes goals, well-being, satisfaction, happiness, interpersonal skills, perseverance, talent, wisdom, and personal responsibility. It is concerned with understanding what makes life worth living, with helping people become more self-organizing and self-directed, and with recognizing that "people and experiences are embedded in a social context" (Seligman & Csikszentmihalyi, 2000, p. 8; see also Duckworth, Steen, & Seligman, 2005).

These principles offer a conception of psychological functioning that gives at least as much emphasis to mental health as to mental illness and that gives at least as much emphasis to identifying and understanding human strengths and assets as to human weaknesses and deficits (see Lopez & Snyder, 2003). More specifically, a positive clinical psychology is as much concerned with understanding and enhancing subjective well-being and effective functioning as it is with alleviating subjective distress and maladaptive functioning. This does not entail a shift away from a focus on relieving suffering to a focus on enhancing positive emotions and positive functioning but rather "an integrated and equally weighted focus on both positive and negative functioning in all areas of research and practice" (Wood & Tarrier, 2010, p. 819).

A shift to a greater emphasis on the positive and healthy aspects of functioning also has great practical value. Research suggests that

> Positive characteristics (a) can predict disorder above and beyond the predictive power of the presence of negative characteristics; (b) buffer the impact of negative life events on distress, potentially preventing the development of a disorder, (c) can be promoted in nonclinical population to promote resilience, (d) can be fostered to treat clinical disorders, (e) offer opportunity for clinical psychologists to use their unique skills in new domains of life, and (f) have the potential to rapidly expand the knowledge base of clinical psychology. (Wood & Tarrier, 2010, p. 820)

Consistent with our social constructionist perspective, we are not arguing that the positive psychology ideology is more "true" than the illness ideology. Both ideologies are socially constructed views of the world, not scientific theories or bodies of facts. We argue, however, that positive psychology offers an ideology that is more useful to clinical psychology than the obsolete illness ideology. As Bandura (1978) has observed:

> Relatively few people seek cures for neuroses, but vast numbers of them are desirous of psychological services that can help them function more effectively in their everyday lives. . . . We have the knowledge and the means to bring benefit to many. We have the experimental methodology with which to advance psychological knowledge and practice. But to accomplish this calls for a broader vision of how psychology can serve people, and a fundamental change in the uses to which our knowledge is put. (p. 99–100)

## CONCLUSION

As we indicated at the beginning, this chapter has presented no new facts or research findings intended to persuade the reader of the greater the efficacy of clinical psychological interventions grounded in positive psychology over those grounded in the illness ideology. Conceptions themselves do not offer new facts and findings instead, they are concerned with what one views as facts and as findings, how one organizes existing facts and findings, and, perhaps most important, what questions one considers worthy of attention. The illness ideology is more concerned with telling us what should be changed than with how it should be changed. The same is true of positive psychology. The greater utility of the positive psychology ideology for clinical psychology is found in its expanded view of what is important about human behavior and what we need to understand about human behavior to enhance people's quality of life, which results in an expanded view of what clinical psychology has to offer society (see also Duckworth et al., 2005).

Unlike a traditional negative clinical psychology based on the illness ideology, a positive clinical psychology is concerned not only just with identifying weaknesses and treating or preventing disorders, but also with identifying human strengths and promoting mental health (see also Maddux, Feldman, & Snyder, in press.) It is concerned not just with alleviating or preventing "suffering, death, pain, disability, or an important loss of freedom" (APA, 2000, p. xxxi), but also with promoting health, happiness, physical fitness, pleasure, and personal fulfillment through the free pursuit of chosen and valued goals.

A clinical psychology that is grounded not in the illness ideology but in a positive psychology ideology rejects (a) the categorization and pathologization of humans and human experience; (b) the assumption that so-called mental disorders exist in individuals rather than in the relationships between the individual and other individuals and the culture at large; and (c) the notion that understanding what is worst and weakest about us is more important than understanding what is best and bravest. Rejecting these notions paves the way for a new mission for clinical psychology and new roles of functions for clinical psychologists that go beyond those to which the science and profession have traditionally limited themselves.

Positive psychological *assessments* will emphasize the evaluations of people's strengths and assets along with their weaknesses and deficiencies (Joseph & Wood, 2010; Keyes & Lopez, 2002; Lopez, Snyder, & Rasmussen, 2003; Wood & Tarrier, 2010; Wright & Lopez, 2002). More often than not, strategies and tactics for assessing strengths and assets will borrow from the strategies and tactics that have proven useful in assessing human weaknesses and deficiencies (Lopez et al., 2003; Wood & Tarrier, 2010). Positive psychological *interventions* will emphasize the enhancement of people's strengths and assets in addition to, and at times instead of, the amelioration of their weaknesses and deficiencies, secure in the belief that strengthening the strengths will weaken the weaknesses. The interventions often will derive their strategies and tactics from traditional treatments of traditional psychological disorders (Wood & Tarrier, 2010). The efficacy of this new focus in improving the human condition remains to be examined. The major change for clinical psychology, however, is not a matter of strategy and tactics, but a matter of vision and mission.

## SUMMARY POINTS

- The roles and functions of clinical psychologists (and other mental health professionals) are determined not so much by *theories* of psychological wellness and illness but of *conceptions* of psychological wellness and illness that determine which human conditions are considered healthy or well and which are considered unhealthy or ill.

- Conceptions of psychological wellness and illness cannot be subjected to tests of empirical evaluation because they are not scientific terms but *social constructions* determined by social and cultural values, norms, and rules of behavior that themselves cannot be proven true or false by the methods of science.
- For most of its 100+-year history, the field of clinical psychology has been dominated by conceptions of wellness and illness that not only braces a medical model that places the cause of psychological problems inside the person, but also an illness ideology that dictates that the focus of our attention should be on what is weak and ineffective about people rather than on what is strong and healthy.
- This illness ideology has greatly limited the roles and functions of clinical psychology to the detriment of the profession and the people it serves and needs to be replaced by a positive psychology ideology that emphasizes health, happiness, and human strengths in addition to the traditional emphasis on dysfunction and disorder.
- The rejection of the illness ideology and the transition to a positive psychology ideology will be facilitated by clinical psychology's rejection of categorical schemes of psychological problems (such as the *DSM* and the *ICD*) that artificially divide illness from wellness, artificially divide psychological problems into distinct disorders or diseases, and continually expand the number of expected problems in living and the expected range of human diversity that are classified as illnesses.
- A vast and growing body of research supports replacing the categorical approach with a dimensional approach that rejects the assumption that we can clearly demarcate between psychological illness and wellness and between types of psychological illness and embraces the assumption that such categories are not scientifically constructed but socially constructed.
- A dimensional view that rejects the distinction between illness and wellness provides an intellectual foundation for integrating positive psychology's focus on health and human strengths with clinical psychology's traditional focus on disorder, disease, and psychological pathology.
- Research indicates that adding an emphasis on positive functioning to clinical psychology's traditional emphasis on negative functioning will enhance the effectiveness of clinical psychological assessment and interventions.

## REFERENCES

Albee, G. W. (2000). The Boulder model's fatal flaw. *American Psychologist, 55,* 247–248.

American Psychiatric Association. (1952). *Diagnostic and statistical manual of mental disorders.* Washington, DC: Author.

American Psychiatric Association. (1968). *Diagnostic and statistical manual of mental disorders* (2nd ed.). Washington, DC: Author.

American Psychiatric Association. (1980). *Diagnostic and statistical manual of mental disorders* (3rd ed.). Washington, DC: Author.

American Psychiatric Association. (1987). *Diagnostic and statistical manual of mental disorders* (3rd ed., rev.). Washington, DC: Author.

American Psychiatric Association. (1994). *Diagnostic and statistical manual of mental disorders* (4th ed.). Washington, DC: Author.

American Psychiatric Association. (2000). *Diagnostic and statistical manual of mental disorders* (4th ed., text rev.). Washington, DC: Author.

American Psychiatric Association. (2013). *Diagnostic and statistical manual of mental disorders* (5th ed.). Washington, DC: Author.

Anthony, J. L., Lonigan, C. J., & Hecht, S. A. (1999). Dimensionality of post-traumatic stress disorder symptoms in children exposed to disaster: Results from a confirmatory factor analysis. *Journal of Abnormal Psychology, 108*, 315–325.

Bandura, A. (1978). On paradigms and recycled ideologies. *Cognitive Therapy and Research, 2*, 79–103.

Bandura, A. (1998, August). *Swimming against the mainstream: Accenting the positive aspects of humanity*. Invited address presented at the Annual Meeting of the American Psychological Association, San Francisco, CA.

Barkeley, R. A. (1997). *ADHD and the nature of self-control*. New York, NY: Guilford Press.

Barone, D. F., Maddux, J. E., & Snyder, C. R. (1997). *Social cognitive psychology: History and current domains*. New York, NY: Plenum Press.

Baumeister, R. F. (1987). How the self became a problem: A psychological review of historical research. *Journal of Personality and Social Psychology, 52*, 163–176.

Baumeister, R. F., & Scher, S. J. (1988). Self-defeating behavior patterns among normal individuals: Review and analysis of common self-destructive tendencies. *Psychological Bulletin, 104*, 3–22.

Beall, A. E. (1993). A social constructionist view of gender. In A. E. Beall & R. J. Sternberg (Eds.), *The psychology of gender* (pp. 127–147). New York, NY: Guilford Press.

Becker, H. S. (1963). *Outsiders*. New York, NY: Free Press.

Bohan, J. (1996). *The psychology of sexual orientation: Coming to terms*. New York, NY: Routledge.

Claridge, G. (1995). *Origins of mental illness*. Cambridge, MA: Malor Books/ISHK.

Coker, L. A., & Widiger, T. A. (2012). Personality disorders. In J. E. Maddux & B. A. Winstead (Eds), *Psychopathology: Foundations for a contemporary understanding* (3rd ed.). New York, NY: Routledge.

Costello, C. G. (1993a). *Symptoms of depression*. New York, NY: Wiley.

Costello, C. G. (1993b). *Symptoms of schizophrenia*. New York, NY: Wiley.

Costello, C. G. (1996). *Personality characteristics of the personality disordered*. New York, NY: Wiley.

Cross, S. E., & Markus, H. R. (1999). The cultural constitution of personality. In L. A. Pervin & O. P. John (Eds.), *Handbook of personality: Theory and research* (2nd ed., pp. 378–396). New York, NY: Guilford Press.

Cushman, P. (1995). *Constructing the self, constructing America*. New York, NY: Addison-Wesley.

Duckworth, A. L., Steen, T. A., & Seligman, M. E. P. (2005). Positive psychology in clinical practice. *Annual Review of Clinical Psychology, 1*, 229–651.

Eifert, G. H., McCormack, E., & Zvolensky, M. J. (2012). Somatoform and dissociative disorders. In J. E. Maddux & B. A. Winstead (Eds.), *Psychopathology: Foundations for a contemporary understanding* (3rd ed., pp. 347–371). New York, NY: Routledge.

Fraley, R. C., & Waller, N. G. (1998). Adult attachment patterns: A test of the typological model. In J. A. Simpson & W. S. Rholes (Eds.), *Attachment theory and close relationships* (pp. 77–114). New York, NY: Guilford Press.

Frances, A. (2013). *Saving normal: An insider's revolt against out-of-control psychiatric diagnosis, DSM-5, big pharma, and the medicalization of everyday life*. New York, NY: HarperCollins.

Frances, A. J., & Widiger, T. (2012). Psychiatric diagnosis: Lessons from the DSM-IV past and cautions for the DSM-5 future. *Annual Review of Clinical Psychology, 8*, 109–130.

Gergen, K. J. (1985). The social constructionist movement in modern psychology. *American Psychologist, 40*, 266–275.

Gergen, K. J. (1999). *An invitation to social construction*. Thousand Oaks, CA: Sage.

Gilman, S. L. (1988). *Disease and representation: Images of illness from madness to AIDS*. Ithaca, NY: Cornell University Press.

Gosselin, J. T. (2012). Sexual dysfunctions and disorders. In J. E. Maddux & B. A. Winstead (Eds.), *Psychopathology: Foundations for a contemporary understanding* (3rd ed., pp. 307–345). New York, NY: Routledge.

Hewitt, J. P. (2002). The social construction of self-esteem. In C. R. Snyder & S. J. Lopez (Eds.), *Handbook of positive psychology* (pp. 135–147). New York, NY: Oxford University Press.

Horwitz, A. V. (2002). *Creating mental illness*. Chicago, IL: University of Chicago Press.

Hyman, S. E. (2010). The diagnosis of mental disorders: The problem of reification. *Annual Review of Clinical Psychology, 6*, 155–179.

Joseph, S., & Wood., A. (2010). Assessment of positive functioning in clinical psychology: Theoretical and practical issues. *Clinical Psychology Review, 30*, 830–838.

Keyes, C. L., & Lopez, S. J. (2002). Toward a science of mental health: Positive directions in diagnosis and interventions. In C. R. Snyder & S. J. Lopez (Eds.), *Handbook of positive psychology* (pp. 45–59). New York, NY: Oxford University Press.

Kirk, S. A., & Kutchins, H. (1992). *The selling of DSM: The rhetoric of science in psychiatry*. New York, NY: Aldine de Gruyter.

Korchin, S. J. (1976). *Modern clinical psychology*. New York, NY: Basic Books.

Kutchins, H., & Kirk, S. A. (1997). *Making us crazy: DSM: The psychiatric bible and the creation of mental disorder*. New York, NY: Free Press.

Lilienfeld, S. O., & Marino, L. (1995). Mental disorder as a Roschian concept: A critique of Wakefield's "harmful dysfunction" analysis. *Journal of Abnormal Psychology, 104*, 411–420.

Lopez, S. J., & Snyder, C. R. (Eds.). (2003). *Positive psychological assessment: A handbook of models and measures*. Washington, DC: American Psychological Association.

Lopez, S. J., Snyder, C. R., & Rasmussen, H. N. (2003). Striking a vital balance: Developing a complementary focus on human weakness and strength through positive psychological treatment. In S. J. Lopez & C. R. Snyder (Eds.), *Positive psychological assessment: A handbook of models and measures* (pp. 3–20). Washington, DC: American Psychological Association.

Lubinski, D. (2000). Scientific and social significance of assessing individual differences: "Sinking shafts at a few critical points." *Annual Review of Psychology, 51*, 405–444.

Maddux, J. E. (1999). The collective construction of collective efficacy: Comment on Paskevich, Brawley, Dorsch, and Widmeyer (1999). *Group Dynamics: Theory, Research, and Practice, 3*, 1–4.

Maddux, J. E. (2002). Stopping the madness: Positive psychology and the deconstruction of the illness ideology and the *DSM*. In C. R. Snyder & S. J. Lopez (Eds.), *Handbook of positive psychology* (pp. 13–25). New York, NY: Oxford University Press.

Maddux, J. E. (2008). Positive psychology and the illness ideology: Toward a positive clinical psychology. *Applied Psychology: An International Review, 57*, 54–70.

Maddux, J. E. (2010). Social psychological foundations of clinical psychology: An overview of basic principles. In J. E. Maddux & J. P. Tangney (Eds.), *Social psychological foundations of clinical psychology*. New York, NY: Guilford Press.

Maddux, J. E., Feldman, D. B., & Snyder, C. R. (in press). Mental health: General guidelines. In T. Gullotta & M. Bloom (Eds), *Encyclopedia of primary prevention and health promotion* (2nd ed.). New York, NY: Kluwer/Plenum.

Maddux, J. E., Gosselin, J. T., & Winstead, B. A. (2012). Conceptions of psychopathology: A social constructionist perspective. In J. E. Maddux & B. A. Winstead (Eds), *Psychopathology: Foundations for a contemporary understanding* (3rd ed., pp. 3–21). New York, NY: Routledge.

Maddux, J. E., & Mundell, C. E. (2004). Disorders of personality: Diseases or individual differences? In V. J. Derlega, B. A. Winstead, & W. H. Jones (Eds.), *Personality: Contemporary theory and research* (2nd ed., pp. 541–571). Chicago, IL: Nelson-Hall.

Morrow, W. R. (1946). The development of psychological internship training. *Journal of Consulting Psychology, 10*, 165–183.

Muehlenhard, C. L., & Kimes, L. A. (1999). The social construction of violence: The case of sexual and domestic violence. *Personality and Social Psychology Review, 3*, 234–245.

Oatley, K., & Jenkins, J. M. (1992). Human emotions: Function and dysfunction. *Annual Review of Psychology, 43*, 55–85.

Paris, J. (2013). *The intelligent clinician's guide to the DSM-5.* New York, NY: Oxford University Press.

Parker, I., Georgaca, E., Harper, D., McLaughlin, T., & Stowell-Smith, M. (1995). *Deconstructing psychopathology.* London, England: Sage.

Raskin, J. D., & Lewandowski, A. M. (2000). The construction of disorder as human enterprise. In R. A. Neimeyer & J. D. Raskin (Eds.), *Constructions of disorder: Meaning-making frameworks for psychotherapy* (pp. 15–40). Washington, DC: American Psychological Association.

Reisman, J. M. (1991). *A history of clinical psychology.* New York, NY: Hemisphere.

Reznek, L. (1987). *The nature of disease.* London, England: Routledge & Kegan Paul.

Rosenblum, K. E., & Travis, T. C. (1996). Constructing categories of difference: Framework essay. In K. E. Rosenblum & T. C. Travis (Eds.), *The meaning of difference: American constructions of race, sex and gender, social class, and sexual orientation* (pp. 1–34). New York, NY: McGraw-Hill.

Routh, D. K. (2000): Clinical psychology training: A history of ideas and practices prior to 1946. *American Psychologist, 55*, 236–240.

Seligman, M. E. P., & Csikszentmihalyi, M. (2000). Positive psychology: An introduction. *American Psychologist, 55*, 5–14.

Shaywitz, S. E., Escobar, M. D., Shaywitz, B. A., Fletcher, J. M., & Makuch, R. (1992). Evidence that dyslexia may represent the lower tail of a normal distribution of reading ability. *New England Journal of Medicine, 326*, 145–150.

Snyder, C. R., Feldman, D. B., Taylor, J. D., Schroeder, L. L., & Adams, V., III. (2000). The roles of hopeful thinking in preventing problems and enhancing strengths. *Applied and Preventive Psychology, 15*, 262–295.

Snyder, C. R., & Higgins, R. L. (1997). Reality negotiation: Governing oneself and being governed by others. *General Psychology Review, 4*, 336–350.

Szasz, T. (1974). *The myth of mental illness* (Rev. ed.). New York, NY: Harper & Row.

Szasz, T. (1978). *The myth of psychotherapy mental healing as religion, rhetoric, and repression.* Garden City, NY: Anchor Press/Doubleday.

Trull, T. J., & Durrett, C. A. (2005). Categorical and dimensional models of personality disorders. *Annual Review of Clinical Psychology, 1*, 355–380.

Tyler, L. (1972). Reflecting on counseling psychology. *The Counseling Psychologist, 3*, 6–11.

Wakefield, J. C. (1992). The concept of mental disorder: On the boundary between biological facts and social values. *American Psychologist, 47*, 373–388.

Widiger, T. A. (2012). Classification and diagnosis: Historical development and contemporary issues. In J. E. Maddux & B. A. Winstead (Eds.), *Psychopathology: Foundations for a contemporary understanding* (3rd ed., pp. 101–120). New York, NY: Routledge.

Williams, S. L. (2012). Anxiety disorders. In J. E. Maddux & B. A. Winstead (Eds.), *Psychopathology: Foundations for a contemporary understanding* (3rd ed., pp. 163–194). New York, NY: Routledge.

Wilson, M. (1993). DSM-III and the transformation of American psychiatry: A history. *American Journal of Psychiatry, 150*, 399–410.

Wood, A. M., & Tarrier, N. (2010). Positive clinical psychology: A new vision and strategy for integrated research and practice. *Clinical Psychology Review, 30*, 819–829.

World Health Organization. (1992). *The ICD-10 classification of mental and behavioural disorders: Clinical descriptions and diagnostic guidelines.* Geneva, Switzerland: Author.

Wright, B. A., & Lopez, S. J. (2002). Widening the diagnostic focus: A case for including human strengths and environmental resources. In C. R. Snyder & S. J. Lopez (Eds.), *Handbook of positive psychology* (pp. 26–44). New York, NY: Oxford University Press.

CHAPTER 26

# The Relationship Between Counseling Psychology and Positive Psychology

ANDREAS VOSSLER, EDITH STEFFEN, and STEPHEN JOSEPH

THE AIM OF THIS chapter is to explore the relation between the professional specialty of counseling psychology and positive psychology. Following a brief historical overview of counseling psychology, we explore its theoretical convergence with positive psychology and examine how the ideas from positive psychology have been received by counseling psychologists. We argue that although counseling psychology has its roots in ideas that are consistent with positive psychology, the profession has developed a broad practice range in recent decades accommodating a diversity of ways of working, many of which prioritize working with distress and its origins over seeking to enhance and build on existing strengths.

As such, the positive psychology movement can offer a new impetus for the profession of counseling psychology to reexamine its fundamental assumptions and reflect on its training curriculum. Based on this overview, we conclude that further bridges need to be built between positive psychology and counseling psychology. Our goal is to encourage counseling psychologists to engage more fully with the ideas and research of positive psychology.

## DEVELOPMENT AND IDENTITY OF COUNSELING PSYCHOLOGY

Counseling psychology first emerged as a separate professional discipline in the United States, where it is the domain of Division 17 of the American Psychological Association (APA). Originally formed in 1946 as the Division of Personnel and Guidance Psychologists, it was renamed not long after as the Division of Counseling and Guidance before it became the Division of Counseling Psychology in 1955 and more recently, in 2003, the Society of Counseling Psychology. The earlier names give an indication of the discipline's roots in vocational guidance (Meara & Myers, 1999).

However, practitioners found that the scope of their work went beyond a strictly vocational focus and included the facilitation of general life planning, which involved "encouraging the client to talk about values, beliefs, misgivings, and wishes and by reflecting back to him or her the pattern that can be detected in the combination of feelings revealed" (Tyler, 1992, p. 344). As such, the professional specialty that evolved was concerned with the process of making choices and the facilitation of optimal lifelong development, including building on strengths and developing new skills, and thus had a decidedly preventative rather than curative function.

The profession tended to deal with the general nonclinical population and had an early established concern with individuals in their environmental contexts. This helped prepare the discipline to adopt a commitment to diversity as early as 1974 when, against the background of the Civil Rights Movement, the Vietnam War, and the rise of feminism, training needs with regard to diversity and cultural identities were identified (Orlans & Van Scoyoc, 2009). Embracing a philosophy of multiculturalism in combination with the emphasis on prevention meant that counseling psychology was also able to widen its focus beyond the individual to include a social justice approach as part of its fundamental concerns (Hage, 2003). Both the educational-preventative core and the emphasis on diversity and multiculturalism have remained central within counseling psychology.

Today, counseling psychology in the United States is defined as:

A psychological specialty [that] facilitates personal and interpersonal functioning across the lifespan with a focus on emotional, social, vocational, educational, health-related, developmental, and organizational concerns. Through the integration of theory, research, and practice, and with a sensitivity to multicultural issues, this specialty encompasses a broad range of practices that help people improve their well-being, alleviate distress and maladjustment, resolve crises, and increase their ability to live more highly functioning lives. (APA, 2013a, p. 2)

As Sharon Bowman, the current president of the Society of Counseling Psychology, states, "Our philosophy emphasizes developmental, strength-based, multicultural, and social justice principles, as well as positive psychology and international perspectives" (APA, 2013b).

Being a much younger discipline than its American counterpart, the beginnings of counseling psychology in the United Kingdom can be traced to the 1970s, when an increasing number of psychology graduates with additional training in counseling or psychotherapy were seeking a professional home, leading to the establishment of a Section of Counselling Psychology within the British Psychological Society (BPS) in 1982, which eventually became the professional Division of Counselling Psychology in 1994 (see Orlans & Van Scoyoc, 2009).

The UK Division of Counselling Psychology has defined counseling psychology as:

A branch of professional psychological practice strongly influenced by human science research as well as the principal psychotherapeutic traditions [that] draws upon and seeks to develop phenomenological models of practice and enquiry in addition to that of traditional scientific psychology. It continues to develop models of practice and research which marry the scientific demand for rigorous empirical enquiry with a firm value base grounded in the primacy of the counselling or psychotherapeutic relationship. (British Psychological Society, 2005, p. 1)

Counseling psychology in the United Kingdom has a strong phenomenological tradition, and in recent years, a pluralistic stance has been put forward (e.g., McAteer, 2010). Central to pluralistic thinking is the notion that there are many factors contributing to clients' problems, and many different possible ways to help clients and facilitate change (and not a one-size-fits-all approach; Cooper & McLeod, 2011).

Examining the identity of counseling psychology in the United States and United Kingdom, as well as in other countries, shows the diversity of counseling psychology cross-nationally, which is at least partly due to the different stages in the development of the profession toward a fully established discipline (Orlans & Van Scoyoc, 2009). It is therefore not easy to strike a balance between local specifics and an overarching understanding of the profession. Although there are exceptions to every broad generalization, some of the philosophical underpinnings that appear to be shared across different strands of counseling psychology could be summarized as taking a holistic perspective on human beings, which includes valuing and respecting subjective—and intersubjective—experience and understanding people as situated within a context. This contextualized view of the person is seen to have historical, developmental, and sociocultural dimensions and includes particular attention to diversity as well as to formulating issues in a developmental and nonpathologizing way, thus focusing on people's strengths, adaptations, and potentialities rather than on deficiencies alone. Furthermore, this includes a commitment to equality and empowerment, for example, because it is embedded in the U.S. emphasis on social justice work at group and systems levels and in the UK emphasis on antidiscriminatory practice and pluralism.

Having thus arrived at a broader description of counseling psychology, it is now possible to look in more detail at the discipline's relationship with positive psychology in theory and practice.

## COUNSELING PSYCHOLOGY AND POSITIVE PSYCHOLOGY: A FRUITFUL DIALOGUE?

The previous section has already pointed out some of the overlaps between counseling psychology and positive psychology, particularly as the discipline of counseling psychology has developed in the United States. Indeed, Division 17 even has a section solely dedicated to positive psychology, and there is an abundance of scholarly output that supports the connection between positive psychology and counseling psychology. It has been observed that positive psychology has not adequately acknowledged counseling psychology for its particular role in "embracing a strength-based perspective" (Mollen, Ethington, & Ridley, 2006, p. 305) or its focus on positive adaptation and optimal human functioning (Frazier, Lee, & Steger, 2006), and it was pointed out that positive psychology presented itself as a newcomer in the 1990s when, in fact, it had a history in counseling psychology research and practice (Mollen et al., 2006).

Indeed, there had been an emphasis on developing personal and social resources from the very beginnings of the discipline of counseling psychology in the early 20th century. Key figures and milestones to mention are Frank Parson's focus on strengths and healthy functioning in educational and vocational counseling from 1908 onward; the development of goal-oriented student counseling by F. G. Williamson in the 1930s; and most notably, the humanistic approach to psychology and the work of Rogers (1951). In recognizing the humanistic roots of counseling psychology, it is of note that the origins of positive psychology can also be seen in humanistic psychology (see Robbins, Chapter 3, this volume). Shlien (1956/2003) said:

> In the past, mental health has been a "residual" concept—the absence of disease. We need to do more than describe improvement in terms of, say, "anxiety reduction." We need to say what the person can *do* as health is achieved. As the emphasis on pathology lessons, there have been a few recent efforts toward positive conceptualizations of mental health. Notable among these are Carl Rogers's "Fully Functioning Person," A. Maslow's "Self-Realizing Persons." (p. 17)

As such, the notions of well-being, flourishing, and attending to what people can do are not new ideas that originated with the positive psychology movement of the past decade, but date back to the same roots as counseling psychology itself.

In 2006, *The Counseling Psychologist* dedicated a major contribution to counseling psychology's emphasis on the positive, and the leading article by Lopez et al. (2006) charted this focus in the discipline's scholarship through the decades by means of a content analysis.

The content analysis by Lopez et al. (2006) revealed that 29% of scholarship in counseling psychology journals had a positive focus, with the most frequent themes concerning values or ethics, followed by self-efficacy, adjustment, coping, and empathy. It was noteworthy that the most commonly researched positive processes and constructs concerned either practitioner characteristics and attitudes, positive client resources to draw on in therapeutic practice, or positive outcomes such as achievement, adjustment, and actualization. The authors observed that despite the positive focus present in this subsection of the discipline's output, positive psychological constructs and processes, as highlighted in the works of Seligman and Csikszentmihalyi (2000), for example, had received less attention.

Furthermore, Lopez et al. (2006) observed that only a handful of articles had focused on themes such as hope, optimism, and positive emotion or love, and character strengths such as gratitude or wisdom were missing altogether. However, as Linley (2006) pointed out, building a classification of strengths and virtues was an early agenda of the positive psychology movement that may not have had a great deal of practical utility, and counseling psychologists may have been best placed to further positive psychology scholarship in more applicable ways. Furthermore, cross-cultural differences in what may count as a strength or a weakness "present a dilemma for proposed universal explanations of happiness and well-being" (Linley, 2006, p. 316). Thus, there has been a call for the integration of cross-cultural concerns into counseling psychology's positive psychology focus. For example, Constantine and Sue (2006) argue for a recognition of cultural assets as pertaining to people of color in the United States, which could include research into collectivistic values such as interdependence, collective self-esteem, community respect, and group harmony, a research focus that may require the employment of (qualitative) methodologies that are able to address limitations of traditional methodologies with regard to cross-cultural validity (Gerstein, 2006).

As such, it is possible to see how counseling psychology has similar roots to positive psychology and had an initial focus on well-being and growth, which involved adopting a nonpathologizing and developmental stance to clients. However, the practice range of counseling psychology has widened in recent decades to include a range of clients and therapeutic approaches drawn from psychodynamic, cognitive-behavioral, and the humanistic traditions. As a consequence, there has been a move toward a focus on "disease and distress rather than health and well-being"

(Hage, 2003, p. 555). Hence, it seems, as Gelso and Woodhouse (2003) said, "despite counseling psychology's long history of attention to human strengths and positive development, the empirical study of therapies that focus on the positive, as well as positive aspects of traditional therapies, have been sadly neglected" (pp. 195–196).

Also commenting on counseling psychology's stance toward positive psychology, Robitschek and Spering (2013) conclude that the discipline does perhaps "not embrace positive psychology as clearly as we profess" (p. 339). As such, it seems clear that counseling psychology has always had a positive focus but needs to reaffirm its identity (e.g., Mollen et al., 2006; Robitschek & Woodson, 2006), which, it is suggested, has been watered down by an increased focus on deficits and allegiance to the medical model. Although the closer alignment with the medical model brought with it greater prestige (Tyler, 1992) and employment opportunities (Meara & Myers, 1999), it has also had implications for the identity of the profession and led to a situation where it has become so focused on working with distress that it has at least partly lost sight of its traditional growth orientation.

It is counseling psychology scholars in the United States who have mostly been at the forefront of this debate, and, as we have already seen, embrace positive psychology to a greater extent than their UK counterparts. This is illustrated by several practice-relevant publications by U.S. counseling psychologists in recent years (e.g., Conoley & Conoley, 2009; Magyar-Moe, 2009; Owens & Patterson, 2013). In the United Kingdom, the impact of positive psychology on counseling psychologists has been minimal. With few exceptions (e.g., Hutchinson & Lema, 2009; Nelson, 2009), there has been a dearth of articles published in national counseling psychology publications that have embraced a positive psychology agenda. As such, counseling psychology practitioners remain relatively unaware of the positive psychology movement and other international developments.

There are also cautious or even critical voices within counseling psychology that question the general value of positive psychology and how its ideas and concepts could be utilized. In her book *Psychotherapy and the Quest for Happiness*, van Deurzen (2009) raises some reservations about the positive psychology agenda. She argues against the view that counselors and psychotherapists should help their clients with "quick fix" interventions to strive for happiness and eradicate negative emotions at all costs. From her point of view, the therapeutic task is rather to equip clients to cope with the misery and suffering they will inevitably face in their lives, without being afraid of negative emotions.

Similarly, Lambert and Erekson (2008) suggest that positive psychology interventions may be "most appropriate for persons who are not in psychotherapy" (p. 225), echoing van Deurzen's (2009) critique. Although we would agree that many of the interventions in positive psychology are no substitute for psychotherapy, we would argue that van Deurzen's critique of positive psychology seems to ignore the fact that there are many scholars and researchers within positive psychology who adopt the view that therapy needs to help clients cope with negative emotions. Indeed, we would draw attention to client-centered psychotherapy and counseling, which is a good example of an established, widely practiced form of therapy that has the ideology of positive psychology at its core and is increasingly recognized as a positive therapy (Joseph & Linley, 2006). Another increasingly popular model that has come to counseling psychologists' attention in recent years is acceptance and commitment therapy (ACT), a mindfulness-based third-wave CBT approach that seeks to enhance people's resilience to suffering through opening up to experience and acceptance while helping clients move in the direction of living a life in accordance with their values (Hayes, Luoma, Bond, Masuda, & Lillis, 2006; Hayes, Strosahl, & Wilson,

2011). It thus includes a strong positive focus; in fact, the paradoxically positive act of embracing negative emotions rather than trying to get rid of them is seen to lead to positive outcomes for clients.

Apart from reservations as expressed in van Deurzen's (2009) critique, it is possible to speculate about the reasons for the relative absence of positive psychology in counseling psychologists' output; the potential reasons are not exclusive to the United Kingdom, but could be seen as latently present elsewhere. These are particularly related to counseling psychology's rootedness in and continued connectedness with humanistic psychology. Although positive psychology now regards humanistic psychology as one of its historical foundations (Waterman, 2013), there was once much conflict between the two fields. For example, in its early years, positive psychology sought to present generalized understandings of positive attributes and virtues using a positivist framework. This was seen as conflicting with an emphasis on subjectivity and individual understandings and experiences around "the good life," truth, and personal fulfillment, a focus that counseling psychology shares with humanistic psychology.

Positive psychology was also criticized for being less contextualized and reductionistic in contrast with humanistic psychology's holism (Friedman, 2008; Friedman & Robbins, 2012), for taking a narrow-minded view of its subject matter and ignoring important scholarly fields altogether (Tennen & Affleck, 2003), and for oversimplifying the roles of emotions (Lazarus, 2003), human flourishing, and adaptiveness (Schneider, 2011).

A different strand of critique, as voiced by Rennie (2012), has suggested that positive psychology is not really a separate discipline but could be seen as part of humanistic psychology. He observes that positive psychology has sought to dissociate itself from humanistic psychology mainly for methodological reasons, which he suggests are ill-founded due to the strong empirical traditions within humanistic psychology that may have been overlooked. A reason for this could be that much high-quality research done within humanistic psychology is published in journals not connected with the movement, similar to counseling psychologists in the United Kingdom who often publish their work in journals relating to their field of research rather than to their professional discipline, which makes it more difficult to trace back their output.

However, now that the humanistic background to positive psychology is increasingly recognized and positive psychology has matured, these criticisms are not as pertinent as they once were. Although an extended discussion with regard to these issues has not taken place within the discipline of counseling psychology, it is argued here that it is important to reopen this debate and to address these criticisms in order to advance a fruitful collaboration between the two fields and to build bridges of understanding (Joseph & Murphy, 2013).

It is also suggested that counseling psychology has a contribution to make to positive psychology and psychology as a whole through "a positive psychology that matters" by furthering "socially significant strength-based research and practice" (Lopez & Magyar-Moe, 2006, p. 323) and by making its presence felt beyond the confines of the discipline. Similarly, Linley (2006) suggests that counseling psychologists "might contribute much in terms of the important questions to ask and how to ask them" (p. 315), particularly due to being situated "at the interface of individual strengths and environmental factors" (p. 319). Positive psychology can learn from counseling psychologists' focus on person–environment fit rather than on changing people's personality structures in order to fit them to a particular environment and its contextualized view of the person and commitment to social justice.

## POSITIVE PSYCHOLOGY IN COUNSELING
## PSYCHOLOGY PRACTICE

The previous section focused on theoretical overlap between counseling psychology and positive psychology. In this section, we focus on how ideas and concepts from positive psychology have impacted counseling psychology practice and what the possibilities and limitations are for positive counseling psychology.

As previously discussed, counseling psychology and positive psychology have shared roots in the humanistic paradigm. As such, it would not be realistic to expect that ideas and concepts from positive psychology have triggered a radical paradigm shift in the practice of counseling psychology (Gerstein, 2006), but positive psychology can help to refocus the profession of counseling psychology onto its roots in the humanistic paradigm and its self-understanding that it is traditionally a discipline concerned with the promotion of fully functioning behavior and the cultivation of strengths rather than the cure of deficits.

As described earlier, the identity of counseling psychology as a discipline has been formed over the past five decades and is grounded in a value base shaped by influential political and social movements and developments in psychology and psychotherapy during that time. Although positive psychology has been identified as one of the influential and defining factors for counseling psychology, it is still a relatively new movement with a short research history. Hence, more time and effort on both sides are needed to establish a productive exchange and a stronger and flourishing relationship between these two traditions. However, what can be found in the current practice of counseling psychology are examples for areas where interventions grounded in positive psychology theory and research have been developed and practiced. Next, we give four examples of areas in which positive psychology research is burgeoning and taking hold within counseling psychology.

First, one of these areas is the clinical work inspired by the concept of *posttraumatic growth*, a term coined by Tedeschi and Calhoun (1996) to refer to positive changes in individuals that occur as the result of attempts to cope in the aftermath of a traumatic life event (see Tedeschi, Calhoun, & Groleau, Chapter 30, this volume). The concept of posttraumatic growth, and related positive psychology research, has been employed and integrated into counseling psychology practice. Hutchinson and Lema (2009), for example, discuss the dominant negative and pathological narratives of the effects of trauma (with labels like "victims" and "damaged"). They describe how drawing on a positive psychology framework in their work with trauma can enable counselors and psychotherapists to focus on strength and competencies and develop rich meaningful alternative stories together with their clients. Steffen and Coyle (2011) have explored posttraumatic growth processes as a consequence of spiritual and religious meaning-making following sense-of-presence experiences in bereavement, an experience that has traditionally been pathologized in bereavement scholarship and in clinically oriented psychology and grief therapy approaches. Drawing on positive psychology theory and research and his clinical experience in working with trauma, Joseph (2011) provides comprehensive practical information on how to aid and nurture posttraumatic growth in a therapeutic setting.

Second, a further area is the promotion and cultivation of resilience in counseling psychology practice by increasing the likelihood for positive emotions such as humor, serenity, trust, and compassion. Experiencing these kinds of positive emotions is assumed to help "people cope with adversity and improve the possibility of emotional well-being and coping better in the future" (Fredrickson, 2005, p. 22). Hutchinson and Pretelt (2010), for example, present their preventative work with children in the context of a primary school–based group work program. Based on Fredrickson's (2003, 2005) "broaden-and-build" theory, the aim of this group work is to create opportunities for positive emotions to occur, ideally leading to a reflexive "upward spiral": Positive emotional experiences can lead to increased personal resources, which in turn increase the opportunities for the experience of positive emotions, and so on (Kok, Catalino & Fredrickson, 2008).

Third, counseling psychologists can begin to emphasize the notion of "build what's strong" as a supplement to the traditional "fix what's wrong" approach (Nelson, 2009, p. 46)—a view that is also supported by research findings. Based on their investigation of mainstream therapies, Scheel, Klentz Davis, and Henderson (2012) point to the importance of giving equal attention to both problems and strengths. The therapists involved in their research "saw problems and strengths as comprising two different continuums, making it possible to simultaneously concentrate on the client's problems and his or her strengths" (p. 423). Gassman and Grawe (2006) found that "successful therapists" tend to focus first on resources and strengths before working with the presented problem, thus broadening their clients' perspectives of themselves as well-functioning individuals. In contrast, "unsuccessful therapists" work with their clients' strengths either too late in the session or not at all.

Fourth, gratitude is one of the positive emotions conceptualized and investigated within the positive psychology paradigm that has received attention within the field of counseling psychology. It can be conceptualized in different ways, from a momentary feeling of appreciation and recognition of benefits to a long-term disposition (see Bono, Krakauer, & Froh, Chapter 33, this volume). People with grateful dispositions are characterized by an appreciation of smaller pleasures, the contribution of others, and a sense of abundance (Watkins, Woodward, Stone, & Kolts, 2003). Positive psychology research into the nature and importance of gratitude has indicated two possible ways in which a grateful mood can promote well-being, either directly via a causal link or indirectly as a buffer against negative states and emotions (Emmons & McCullough, 2003; Watkins et al., 2003). Nelson (2009) has reviewed the concept of gratitude and the research findings on the impact of this positive emotion on individual well-being, with a specific focus on the potential therapeutic value of this concept and implications for the practice of counseling psychology. The conclusion she draws from the gratitude research is that counseling psychologists should not exclusively focus on elevating negative states and emotions but equally use interventions with the aim to foster and encourage positive emotional experiences, such as gratitude. However, studies to evaluate direct gratitude inventions in counseling psychology practice are lacking, and Nelson (2009) seems to question the compatibility of these programs with the more traditional person-centered approach often employed by counseling psychologists when working, for example, with bereavement and crisis.

Despite these four examples of how ideas and concepts from positive psychology have been applied in counseling psychology practice, the positive psychological perspective hasn't been truly and comprehensively embraced and integrated in counseling psychology practice so far. There is still a gap between the original strength- and growth-oriented philosophy of counseling psychology and the deficit-focused reality of counseling psychology and training as it has subsequently evolved (Hage, 2003; Meara & Myers, 1999). Many counseling psychologists in the Western world work in medicalized settings dominated by an "illness ideology" (see Maddux & Lopez, Chapter 25, this volume) in which deficit models of behavior and intervention are an integral part of the organizational culture. Insurance-based health systems, such as those in the United States and Australia, favor a focus on pathology and dysfunctional behavior with their reimbursement policies (Gerstein, 2006). Similarly, counseling psychologists working in the United Kingdom's National Health System (NHS) are expected to think in pathological categories and submit diagnostic codes for payment (Pilgrim, 2010).

The medical dominance is certainly hampering the possibilities of integrating positive psychological thinking into counseling psychology practice, and it also has an impact on training provision in counseling psychology. As we have already mentioned, main psychotherapeutic approaches now taught in counseling psychology training programs, such as psychodynamic and cognitive-behavioral therapy, are rather deficit-oriented, and it has become one of the core aspects of counseling psychology training and practice to try to manage the difficult balance of working in a medicalized setting while holding on to a humanistic value base. One consequence of this balancing act is that many training programs are no longer able to educate counseling psychology trainees in specific strength-based ways of working that can be applied to deficit-centered practice settings. As such, practitioners and trainees "lack the specific behavioral skills to effectively display a strength-based, developmental paradigm of conceptualization and action" (Gerstein, 2006, p. 278; see also, Bedi, Klubben, & Barker, 2012).

A reorientation of counseling psychology toward its original roots can help the profession deal with these internal and external obstacles. Our view is that counseling psychology needs to reevaluate ideas and concepts developed in positive psychology for counseling psychology practice, and particularly to make clearer what distinguishes it from clinical psychology now that this profession too has begun to question the dominance of the illness ideology and to embrace concepts from positive psychology (e.g., Wood & Tarrier, 2010).

A first step toward a more balanced and strength-oriented way of working in counseling psychology would be a stronger emphasis on and recognition of positive elements inherent in traditional therapeutic approaches. Using and building on client strengths is, at least to some extent, common across all major therapy theories (Scheel et al., 2012). Gelso and Woodhouse (2003) have identified strength-oriented processes in cognitive-behavioral therapy (reinforcement and support) and humanistic-experimental approaches (working toward self-actualization, congruence, and self-acceptance), and they see the promotion of insight as the primary positive process in psychoanalytic-psychodynamic approaches to therapy (albeit this approach seems generally rather focused on pathology). In solution-focused therapy, the positive methods to bypass problems in favor of solutions (e.g., miracle question, exception finding; de Shazer, 2005) have the potential to amplify strengths and construct new goals and meanings (Vossler, 2012). Similar positive processes are employed in systemic family therapy, in which therapists use techniques such as reframing to develop new and positive meanings for problematic emotions or behaviors (by describing them in a fundamentally different and positive frame; Vossler, 2010). This technique can be utilized as a form of gratitude intervention, for example, in trauma therapy when discussing the potential positive changes and ways of functioning in the aftermath of trauma (Nolen-Hoeksema & Davis, 2005). A lot of the work that experienced counseling psychologists do with their clients is about building strengths rather than exploring weaknesses and developing the positive potential of their clients. However, this brief overview also illustrates how counseling psychology is in danger of losing sight of its traditional focus on strengths and resources. Engaging more with positive psychology offers the chance for the profession to reflect on its meta-theoretical assumptions (Joseph & Linley, 2006).

A second step toward a more positive counseling psychology practice would be a stronger focus on strengths and optimal human functioning in counseling psychology training curricula. As already noted, this would involve an assessment and revision of the underlying philosophy and educational strategies for training programs (Gerstein, 2006). Ideas and interventions based on positive psychological theory and research, such as the philosophically oriented concept of "the good life," could be integrated into teaching on life-span development. Existing modules on psychopathology, mental illness, or human distress could be reformulated to include material on strength-oriented interventions, and trainees could be provided with guidance on assessments and interventions to employ when conducting therapy from a positive psychological perspective (see, e.g., Joseph & Worsley, 2005; Magyar-Moe, 2009).

These two steps could provide a better balance to the increased focus on the pathology and disease model that has crept into counseling psychology training and practice, and could help the discipline recommit to a more growth-oriented model. Accomplishing these steps, together with more research and examination of strength-oriented therapeutic practice (Scheel et al., 2012), can lead the way to the development of a more coherent framework for a positive counseling psychology. The work on such a framework can benefit from groundwork that has been laid by the discussions around positive psychological approaches to therapy (e.g., Hubble & Miller, 2004; Joseph & Linley, 2006).

## CONCLUSION

Positive psychology and counseling psychology can stimulate each other to further develop their fields "guided by their shared philosophy of human strengths and optimal functioning" (Gerstein, 2006, p. 289). Specifically, positive psychology can serve as a reminder to counseling psychology about its roots in humanistic psychology and that a focus on positive development has been a defining feature of the discipline. The framework of positive psychology poses a challenge for counseling psychology "to transcend our rhetoric and integrate into practice a model of thinking and intervention consistent with the basic tenets of counseling psychology" (Gerstein, 2006, p. 278). However, to fully embrace a positive perspective in counseling psychology, it will be necessary to overcome the powerful obstacles mentioned in the previous sections, which have led to an increasing allegiance to medical and deficit approaches by counseling psychologists. As such, we propose that there is a need for counseling psychologists to reflect on their fundamental theoretical assumptions and for training programs to integrate a more positive perspective of human behavior. Simultaneously, it is important for positive psychologists to recognize that there is a long tradition in counseling psychology of a growth-oriented approach. Hence, a more extensive exchange between both fields could be stimulation for the future development of positive psychology.

## SUMMARY POINTS

- Counseling psychology traditionally emphasizes the facilitation of optimal life-long development, including building on strengths and developing new skills, and originally it had a decidedly preventative rather than curative function.
- Recent decades have seen a shift in counseling psychology practice toward a focus on disease and distress rather than health and well-being.
- Both counseling psychology and positive psychology have shared roots in the humanistic approach.

- Counseling psychology could develop a more balanced and strength-oriented way of working, with a stronger emphasis on and recognition of positive elements inherent in traditional therapeutic approaches.
- A stronger focus on strengths and optimal human functioning in counseling psychology training curricula is recommended.
- New areas of positive psychology research, such as hope, gratitude, strengths, and posttraumatic growth, offer new ways of working that will be of interest to counseling psychologists.
- In engaging with the positive psychological framework, counseling psychology has the chance to reflect on its fundamental assumptions and move the balance toward a more growth-oriented rather than deficit-oriented discipline.

## REFERENCES

American Psychological Association. (2013a). *Society of counseling psychology: What is counseling psychology?* Retrieved from http://www.div17.org/wp-content/uploads/WhatIs CounselingPsychology-Brochure-10-02-2012.pdf

American Psychological Association. (2013b). *Society of counseling psychology: President's welcome.* Retrieved from http://www.div17.org/about/presidents-welcome

Bedi, R. P., Klubben, L. M., & Barker, G. T. (2012). Counselling vs. clinical: A comparison of psychological doctoral programs in Canada. *Canadian Psychology, 53,* 228–253.

British Psychological Society. (2005). *Division of counselling psychology: Professional practice guidelines.* Leicester, England: Author.

Conoley, C. W., & Conoley, J. C. (2009). *Positive psychology and family therapy: Creative techniques and practical tools for guiding change and enhancing growth.* Hoboken, NJ: Wiley.

Constantine, M. G., & Sue, D. W. (2006). Factors contributing to optimal human functioning in people of color in the United States. *The Counseling Psychologist, 34,* 228–244.

Cooper, M., & McLeod, J. (2011). *Pluralistic counselling and psychotherapy.* London, England: Sage.

de Shazer, S. (2005). *More than miracles: The state of the art of solution-focused therapy.* Binghamton, NY: Haworth Press.

Emmons, R. A., & McCullough, M. E. (2003). Counting blessings versus burdens: An experimental investigation of gratitude and subjective well-being in daily life. *Journal of Personality and Social Psychology, 84(2),* 377–389.

Frazier, P. A., Lee, R. M., & Steger, M. F. (2006). What can counseling psychology contribute to the study of optimal human functioning? *The Counseling Psychologist, 34,* 293–303.

Fredrickson, B. L. (2003). The value of positive emotions. *American Scientist, 91,* 330–335.

Fredrickson, B. L. (2005). Positive emotions. In C. R. Snyder & S. J. Lopez, *Handbook of positive psychology.* New York, NY: Oxford University Press.

Friedman, H. L. (2008). Humanistic and positive psychology: The methodological and epistemological divide. *Humanistic Psychologist, 36,* 113–126.

Friedman, H. L., & Robbins, B. D. (2012). The negative shadow cast by positive psychology: Contrasting views and implications of humanistic and positive psychology on resiliency. *Humanistic Psychologist, 40,* 87–112.

Gassman, D., & Grawe, K. (2006). General change mechanisms: The relation between problem activation and resource activation in successful and unsuccessful therapeutic interactions. *Clinical Psychology and Psychotherapy, 13,* 1–11.

Gelso, C. J., & Woodhouse, S. (2003). Toward a positive psychotherapy: Focus on human strength. In B. W. Walsh (Ed.), *Counseling psychology and optimal human functioning* (pp. 171–197). Mahwah, NJ: Erlbaum.

Gerstein, L. H. (2006). Counseling psychology's commitment to strengths: Rhetoric or reality? *The Counseling Psychologist, 34*, 276–292.

Hage, S. M. (2003). Reaffirming the unique identity of counseling psychology: Opting for the "road less traveled by." *The Counseling Psychologist, 31*, 555–563.

Hayes, S. C., Luoma, J. B., Bond, F. W., Masuda, A., & Lillis, J. (2006). Acceptance and commitment therapy: Model, processes and outcomes. *Behaviour Research and Therapy, 44*, 1–25.

Hayes, S. C., Strosahl, K. D., & Wilson, K. G. (2011). *Acceptance and commitment therapy: The process of mindful change* (2nd ed.). New York, NY: Guilford Press.

Hubble, M. A., & Miller, S. D. (2004). The client: Psychotherapy's missing link for promoting a positive psychology. In P. A. Linley & S. Joseph (Eds.), *Positive psychology in practice* (pp. 335–353). Hoboken, NJ: Wiley.

Hutchinson, J., & Lema, J. C. (2009). Ordinary and extraordinary narratives of heroism and resistence: Uncovering resilience, competence and growth. *Counselling Psychology Review, 24*, 9–15.

Hutchinson, J., & Pretelt, V. (2010). Building resources and resilience: Why we should think about positive emotions when working with children, their families and their schools. *Counselling Psychology Review, 24*(1), 20–27.

Joseph, S. (2011). *What doesn't kill us: The new psychology of posttraumatic growth.* New York, NY: Basic Books.

Joseph, S., & Linley, P. A. (2006). *Positive therapy: A meta-theoretical approach to positive psychological practice.* London, England: Routledge.

Joseph, S., & Murphy, D. (2013). Person-centered approach, positive psychology and relational helping: Building bridges. *Journal of Humanistic Psychology, 53*, 26–51.

Joseph, S., & Worsley, R. (Eds.). (2005). *Person-centred psychopathology: A positive psychology of mental health.* Ross-on-Wye, England: PCCS Books.

Kok, B. E., Catalino, L. I., & Fredrickson, B. L. (2008). The broadening, building, buffering effects of positive emotions. In S. J. Lopez (Ed.), *Positive psychology: Exploring the best of people: Vol. 3. Capitalizing on emotional experiences* (pp. 1–19). Westport, CT: Greenwood.

Lambert, M. J., & Erekson, D. M. (2008). Positive psychology and the humanistic tradition. *Journal of Psychotherapy Integration, 18*, 222–232.

Lazarus, R. S. (2003). Does the positive psychology movement have legs? *Psychological Inquiry, 14*, 93–100.

Linley, P. A. (2006). Counseling psychology's positive psychological agenda: A model for integration and inspiration. *The Counseling Psychologist, 34*, 313–322.

Lopez, S. J., & Magyar-Moe, J. L. (2006). A positive psychology that matters. *The Counseling Psychologist, 34*, 323–330.

Lopez, S. J., Magyar-Moe, J. L, Petersen, S. E., Ryder, J. A., Krieshok, T. S., O'Byrne, K. K., . . . Fry, N. A. (2006). Counseling psychology's focus on positive aspects of human functioning. *The Counseling Psychologist, 34*, 205–227.

Magyar-Moe, J. (2009). *Therapist's guide to positive psychological interventions (Practical resources for the mental health professional).* Burlington, MA: Academic Press.

McAteer, D. (2010). Philosophical pluralism: Navigating the sea of diversity in psychotherapeutic and counselling psychology practice. In M. Milton (Ed.), *Therapy and beyond: Counselling psychology contributions to therapeutic and social issues* (pp. 5–19). Chichester, England: Wiley.

Meara, N. M., & Myers, R. A. (1999). A history of Division 17 (Counseling Psychology): Establishing stability amid change. In D. A. Dewsbury (Ed.), *Unification through division: Histories of the divisions of the American Psychology Association* (Vol. 3, pp. 9–41). Washington, DC: American Psychological Association.

Mollen, D., Ethington, L. L., & Ridley, C. R. (2006). Positive psychology: Considerations and implications for counseling psychology. *The Counseling Psychologist, 34*, 304–312.

Nelson, C. (2009). Appreciating gratitude: Can gratitude be used as a psychological intervention to improve individual well-being? *Counselling Psychology Review, 24*(1), 38–50.

Nolen-Hoeksema, S., & Davis, C. G. (2005). Positive responses to loss: Perceiving benefits and growth. In C. R. Snyder & S. J. Lopez (Eds.), *The handbook of positive psychology* (pp. 598–607). New York, NY: Oxford University Press.

Orlans, V., & Van Scoyoc, S. (2009). *A short introduction to counselling psychology*. London, England: Sage.

Owens, R. L., & Patterson, M. M. (2013). Positive psychological interventions for children: A comparison of gratitude and best possible selves approaches. *Journal of Genetic Psychology: Research and Theory on Human Development, 174*, 403–428.

Pilgrim, D. (2010). The diagnosis of mental health problems. In M. Barker, A. Vossler, & D. Langdridge (Eds.), *Understanding counselling and psychotherapy* (pp. 21–43). London, England: Sage.

Rennie, D. L. (2012). Occluded humanistic qualitative research: Implications for positive psychology. *The Humanistic Psychologist, 40*, 166–178.

Robitschek, C., & Spering, C. (2013). A critical review of positive psychology theory and research. In N. A. Fouad (Ed.-in-Chief), *APA handbook of counseling psychology: Vol. 1. Theories, research, and methods* (pp. 329–344). Washington, DC: American Psychological Association.

Robitschek, C., & Woodson, S. J. (2006). Vocational psychology: Using one of counseling psychology's strengths to foster human strength. *The Counseling Psychologist, 34*, 260–275.

Rogers, C. R. (1951). *Client-centered therapy: Its current practice, implication and theory*. Boston, MA: Houghton Mifflin.

Scheel, M. J., Klentz Davis, C., & Henderson, J. D. (2012). Therapist use of client strengths: A qualitative study of positive processes. *The Counseling Psychologist, 41*, 392–427.

Schneider, K. (2011). Toward a humanistic positive psychology: Why can't we just get along? *Existential Analysis, 22*(1), 32–38.

Seligman, M. E. P., & Csikszentmihalyi, M. (2000). Positive psychology: An introduction. *American Psychologist, 55*(1), 5–14.

Shlien, J. M. (2003). A criterion of psychological health. In P. Sanders (Ed.), *To lead an honourable life: Invitations to think about client-centered therapy and the person-centered approach* (pp. 15–18). Ross-on-Wye, England: PCCS Books.

Steffen, E., & Coyle, A. (2011). Sense of presence experiences and meaning-making in bereavement: A qualitative analysis. *Death Studies, 35*, 579–609.

Tedeschi, R. G., & Calhoun, L. G. (1996). The posttraumatic growth inventory: Measuring the positive legacy of trauma. *Journal of Traumatic Stress, 9*, 455–471.

Tennen, H., & Affleck, G. (2003). While accentuating the positive, don't eliminate the negative or Mr. In-Between. *Psychological Inquiry, 14*, 163–169.

Tyler, L. E. (1992). Counseling psychology—Why? *Professional Psychology: Research and Practice, 23*, 342–344.

van Deurzen, E. (2009). *Psychotherapy and the quest for happiness*. London, England: Sage.

Vossler, A. (2010). Systemic approaches. In M. Barker, A. Vossler, & D. Langdridge (Eds.), *Understanding counselling and psychotherapy* (pp. 191–210). London, England: Sage.

Vossler, A. (2012). Salutogenesis and the sense of coherence: Promoting health and resilience in counselling and psychotherapy. *Counselling Psychology Review, 27*(3), 68–78.

Waterman, A. S. (2013). The humanistic psychology-positive psychology divide: Contrasts in philosophical foundations. *American Psychologist, 68*, 124–133.

Watkins, P. C., Woodward, K., Stone, T., & Kolts, R. L. (2003). Gratitude and happiness: Development of a measure of gratitude and relationships with subjective well-being. *Social Behavior and Personality, 31*(5), 431–452.

Wood, A. M., & Tarrier, N. (2010). Positive clinical psychology: A new vision and strategy for integrated research and practice. *Clinical Psychology Review, 30*, 819–829.

CHAPTER 27

# Positive Psychology in Rehabilitation Psychology Research and Practice

CLAUDIO PETER, SZILVIA GEYH, DAWN M. EHDE,
RACHEL MÜLLER, and MARK P. JENSEN

I N THIS CHAPTER, we first provide an introduction to rehabilitation psychology as a field concerned with disability. We then discuss how rehabilitation psychology is related to positive psychology and the "good life," and summarize the current state of rehabilitation research with respect to positive psychology. Next, we describe common psychosocial rehabilitation interventions and examine the extent to which positive psychology interventions have been applied in rehabilitation practice. Finally, we discuss and suggest future directions contributing to the integration of positive psychology and rehabilitation psychology research and practice.

The term *rehabilitation* stems from the medieval Latin word *rehabilitationem* ("restoration") from *rehabilitare*, composed of *re-* ("again") and *habitare* ("make fit"), and from the Latin *habilis* ("easily managed, fit") (Harper, 2013). Rehabilitation has been defined as "a set of measures that assist individuals who experience, or are likely to experience, disability to achieve and maintain optimal functioning in interaction with their environments" (World Health Organization & World Bank, 2011, p. 96).

Disability has traditionally been understood from a biomedical perspective as a decrease or interference in functioning resulting from disease or trauma, caused and fully determined by the pathogenic process (Boorse, 1977). Today, the World Health Organization's *International Classification of Functioning, Disability and Health (ICF)* provides a widely accepted conceptual framework that expands simple biomedical thinking into a comprehensive biopsychosocial formulation of human functioning (World Health Organization, 2001). According to the *ICF*'s biopsychosocial framework, the *health condition* (e.g., disease or trauma) of an individual interacts with *environmental* (e.g., physical and social barriers and facilitators) and *personal factors* (e.g., age, gender, but also coping strategies or lifestyle), and thus gives rise to the phenomenon of functioning and its opposite: disability. *Disability* is defined as impairments in bodily *functions and structures*, limitations in individual *activities*, and restrictions in social *participation*.

Disability is on the rise worldwide and represents a universal challenge that many people share. This is partly due to the aging of individuals across societies due to advances in medical technology. The World Health Organization has estimated the prevalence of moderate to severe disability worldwide as 15% of the population (World Health Organization & The World Bank, 2011).

Rehabilitation psychology is an applied discipline rooted in the scientific foundations of psychology and strongly relying on a research-practitioner model. The American Psychological Association (APA) defines rehabilitation psychology as:

> A specialty area within psychology that focuses on the study and application of psychological knowledge and skills on behalf of individuals with disabilities and chronic health conditions in order to maximize health and welfare, independence and choice, functional abilities, and social role participation across the lifespan. Rehabilitation psychologists are uniquely trained and specialized to engage in a broad range of activities including clinical practice, consultation, program development, service provision, research, teaching and education, training, administration, development of public policy and advocacy related to persons with disability and chronic health conditions. (American Psychological Association Division 22: Rehabilitation Psychology, 2014)

Clinical rehabilitation psychologists work in interdisciplinary rehabilitation settings. They provide information and education, support and counseling, training and therapy for individuals with disabilities. They use diagnostic, preventive, and curative strategies. Their clients are not only the affected individuals, but also the partners and relatives of those individuals and the entire rehabilitation team (American Psychological Association Division 22: Rehabilitation Psychology, 2014; Gordon, 2000). Rehabilitation psychology is related to and draws on the expertise of other psychological fields, such as clinical psychology and psychotherapy, medical and health psychology, and neuropsychology. Although rehabilitation psychology lacks institutionalization in some countries, in all countries there are academic and clinical research and clinical practices that *qualify* as rehabilitation psychology.

## HOW IS REHABILITATION PSYCHOLOGY RELATED TO POSITIVE PSYCHOLOGY AND "THE GOOD LIFE"?

Positive psychology and its study of "the good life" aims to counterbalance the overemphasis on pathology in psychological research and practice and turns instead to human potential and those "positive features that make life worth living" (Seligman & Csikszentmihalyi, 2000, p. 5). Positive psychology focuses on what is best in people and has been defined as "the scientific study of optimal human functioning" (Linley, Joseph, Harrington & Wood, 2006, p. 8). Positive psychology has sought to update and integrate hedonic as well as eudaimonic conceptualizations of well-being, happiness, and "the good life"—crudely put, to reconcile pleasure with excellence. In this section, we identify three commonalities between rehabilitation psychology and positive psychology: (1) positive principles, (2) a focus on individual strengths and resources, and (3) well-being, participation, and growth as key outcomes.

### Positive Principles

Both rehabilitation psychology and positive psychology have followed positive principles from the beginning of each discipline. But just as the disease model dominated psychology until the 1980s, when positive psychology gained momentum (Seligman & Csikszentmihalyi, 2000), rehabilitation research was traditionally dominated by the biomedical deficit model of disability (Dunn & Brody, 2008; Ehde, 2010), although this model has always been rejected by prominent scholars within the field of rehabilitation psychology and disability advocacy (Wright, 1972, 1983).

For example, in 1972, Wright formulated 20 "value-laden" guiding principles that underlie rehabilitation psychology (Wright, 1972, 1983). These principles continue to have a strong influence on the field. She stressed the dignity and rights of persons with disabilities, the relevance of psychological factors throughout the rehabilitation process, the importance of considering the embeddedness of the persons with disabilities in immediate and larger social and physical environments, and the importance of involving and empowering the affected persons themselves in shaping rehabilitation, community, and policy processes. She stated that "it is essential that society as a whole continuously and persistently strives to provide the basic means toward the fulfillment of the lives of all its inhabitants, including those with disabilities" (Wright, 1983, p. xv). Wright further emphasized that "the assets of the person must receive considerable attention in the rehabilitation effort" (Wright, 1983, p. xii).

Rehabilitation psychology does not solely focus on deficits, but considers the whole-life situation of the person from physical, psychological, and social perspectives, adhering to the dictum of Lewin that behavior is influenced by both personal and environmental factors, $B = f(P,E)$ (Larson & Sachs, 2000; Lewin, 1936). It considers the physical and social environment of individuals with disabilities ranging from assistive devices, architectonical barriers, family caregivers, societal attitudes, or the availability and affordability of support services. Rehabilitation psychology examines what still works and strives for constructive and creative solutions in the interaction of person, body, psyche, and physical and social environment (Dunn & Dougherty, 2005). Positive psychology, in contrast, pays less attention to environmental factors, with the exception of social resources (Ehde, 2010). Research indicates that a full 10% of the variation in well-being is dependent on environmental circumstances (Lyubomirsky, 2007). Given these findings, it seems important to take person–environment interactions into account when developing models of well-being (see also Layous, Sheldon & Lyubomirsky, Chapter 11, this volume).

### FOCUS ON INDIVIDUAL STRENGTHS AND RESOURCES

Both rehabilitation psychology and positive psychology view personal strengths and psychological resources as foundational elements that contribute to well-being and flourishing. Dunn and Dougherty (2005) state: "The presence of disability does not negate an individual's existing assets, nor does it preclude the acquisition of new ones" (p. 306). In rehabilitation psychology, disability is seen as "only one aspect—and not a defining characteristic—of an individual's identity" (Dunn & Dougherty, 2005, p. 306). People with disabilities, like all individuals, possess a range of strengths, resources, assets, and abilities that exist despite disability and chronic disease. In individuals with disabilities, the optimal use of strengths and a resource-based approach is essential, because they will not necessarily "heal," but will need to manage and thrive despite persistent impairments and limitations.

Dunn and Dougherty (2005) suggest that rehabilitation psychologists "identify, enhance, and encourage reliance on each consumer's strengths, thereby maximizing mental and physical recovery" (p. 306). The perspective taken by positive psychology is similar: Knowing, using, and developing one's own strengths is a key issue in what Seligman calls the "engaged life" in authentic happiness theory (Seligman, 2011). Accordingly, positive psychology proponents developed a systematic classification of 24 character strengths that are structured according to six major virtues:

wisdom, courage, humanity, justice, temperance, and transcendence. They can be measured, for example, with the Values in Action–Inventory of Strengths (VIA-IS; Peterson & Seligman, 2004).

Although rehabilitation psychology and positive psychology share a focus on strengths and resources, their operationalization of these concepts differ. Rehabilitation psychology research often addresses single resources such as self-efficacy or self-esteem. Positive psychology usually considers a broad range of character strengths simultaneously (e.g., self-regulation, persistence, or social intelligence). Hope, optimism, and purpose in life are considered in both disciplines. Overall, whether addressing character strengths in the tradition of positive psychology can be relevant and helpful for individuals with disabilities needs to be determined through thorough testing in future research.

## Well-Being, Participation, and Growth as Key Outcomes

Both rehabilitation psychology and positive psychology share the common goals to enhance well-being, participation, and growth. Historically, however, their perspectives and their conceptualizations of these key outcomes have differed to some extent.

*Well-Being*   The notion of "well-being" is central to positive psychology and has been increasingly recognized in rehabilitation psychology research. The related concept of quality of life, however, is far more salient (Fuhrer, 2000; Tulsky & Rosenthal, 2003). How quality of life is understood in rehabilitation contexts has changed during the past decades.

Initially, quality of life was primarily conceptualized from a negative or deficit perspective in the health and rehabilitation context. So-called health-related quality of life questionnaires, such as the Medical Outcomes Study Short-Form Health Survey (SF-36; Ware, Snow, Kosinski, & Gandek, 1993), have been used to assess disease symptoms, functional disability, and/or psychiatric and psychological dysfunction.

More recently, positive accounts of quality of life have been recognized in rehabilitation contexts. One example is Diener's influential conceptualization of subjective well-being (Diener, Suh, Lucas, & Smith, 1999). Subjective well-being is a multidimensional construct consisting of a cognitive component, including general life satisfaction and satisfaction with specific life domains, and an emotional component, including positive and negative affect as independent dimensions. Accordingly, frequently used questionnaires in rehabilitation ask for satisfaction/dissatisfaction with life as a whole and various life domains, including self-care, work, finances, leisure, relationships or sexuality; some examples include the Life Satisfaction Questionnaire (LISAT; Fugl-Meyer, Bränholm, & Fugl-Meyer, 1991) or the Quality of Life Index (QLI; Ferrans & Powers, 1985).

Satisfaction questionnaires cover the hedonic aspect of well-being. However, a conceptualization of well-being in the sense of flourishing or "the full life," which stresses an eudaimonic approach without neglecting the hedonic, has not yet arrived in rehabilitation. The full life is characterized as not only leading a "pleasant life" of positive experiences (positive emotions, pleasures, and gratifications), but also an "engaged life" (exercising and developing one's own strengths and virtues) and a "meaningful life" (an experience of being part of and serving a larger good; Seligman, 2011). The Orientations to Happiness Scale (OTH) is one example of an instrument assessing three aspects of the full life: pleasure, engagement, and meaning (Peterson, Park, & Seligman, 2005).

More recently, Seligman (2011) suggests an understanding of well-being as a latent construct, operationalized and measureable through five distinct elements: *Positive* experience or positive emotion, *Engagement* and flow, positive *Relationships* with others, *Meaning* and purpose, and *Accomplishment/achievement* (PERMA). The PERMA model states that through these five elements individuals can flourish. Overall, rehabilitation psychology research and practice have only started to recognize these eudaimonic conceptual models and to explore their potential to enhance theory, research, and practice (Chou, Lee, Catalano, Ditchman, & Wilson, 2009; Dunn & Brody, 2008; Dunn & Dougherty, 2005).

*Social Participation*   A second key outcome, which is common to positive psychology as well as rehabilitation psychology, is social participation. Rehabilitation psychology aims for the full inclusion of people with disabilities in society and to "maximize health and welfare, independence and choice, functional abilities, and social role participation" (American Psychological Association Division 22: Rehabilitation Psychology, 2014). According to the *ICF*, areas of social participation include, among others: interpersonal relationships, socializing, and assisting others; work and education; exercise and creativity; community and political life, citizenship, and human rights. These are the same life areas in which, according to positive psychology, an engaged and meaningful life can be fulfilled and in which the PERMA elements (positivity, engagement, relationships, meaning, and achievement) can be realized.

However, rehabilitation psychology research has more often had a negative than a positive approach toward the study of participation. Participation is typically operationalized and measured referring to difficulties in life areas rather than referring to life fulfilment (Magasi & Post, 2010). A similar focus on the negative can be found in questionnaire items assessing participation in the areas of social relationships, engagement, or work. Research often refers to the need for or the amount of support received by a person with a disability. However, little research has examined the beneficial effects of active social support on the well-being of individuals with disabilities (Brown, Nesse, Vinokur, & Smith, 2003). Likewise, low employment rates of individuals with disabilities and the achievement of returning to work are a major concern (Blessing, Golden, Pi, Bruyere, & Van Looy, 2012), and positive work experience, including the experiences of flow, meaning, or purpose, has not yet been considered in rehabilitation psychology research (Warr, 1999).

*Growth*   Both positive psychology and rehabilitation psychology acknowledge the potential for growth and positive changes following the onset of a disability. Posttraumatic growth as a conceptualization of eudaimonic well-being is one of the most salient concepts referring to these positive changes (Tedeschi & Calhoun, 2004; see also Tedeschi, Calhoun, & Groleau, Chapter 30, this volume). Common synonyms are adversarial growth, thriving, finding benefits, or stress-related growth (Zoellner & Maercker, 2006). Posttraumatic growth is different from "recovery" because the individual does not merely return to pretraumatic levels of functioning. Rather, the concept involves an experience of additional and higher states of functioning than existed before the trauma or disability onset—something has changed for the better.

Accounts of posttraumatic growth have been observed in about 30% to 70% of individuals affected by trauma (Joseph, 2013), including individuals with a history of cancer, heart attack, multiple sclerosis, or HIV (Helgeson, Reynolds, & Tomich, 2006). Similarly, in spite of the serious bodily, social, and psychological consequences associated with spinal cord injury (SCI), individuals with SCI may experience positive changes following the injury, such as an increased appreciation of life with changing values and life perspectives, enhanced relationships, or a feeling of more personal strength (McMillen & Cook, 2003).

To summarize, positive psychology and rehabilitation psychology share positive principles and the emphasis on well-being, social participation, and growth as key outcomes. Rehabilitation psychology research and practice could benefit from positive psychology's comprehensive and systematic approach toward the strengths and resources of individuals as well as from a stronger consideration of the eudaimonic aspects of "the good life" (e.g., meaning and purpose) in relation to participation of persons with disabilities. On the other hand, positive psychology could benefit from a stronger consideration of person–environment interactions.

## CURRENT STATE OF RESEARCH
## IN REHABILITATION PSYCHOLOGY

Empirical scientific research on psychological issues in individuals with disabilities has been guided by the main aims of rehabilitation: to ameliorate the negative impact of disability, optimize functioning, support reintegration, and increase quality of life and well-being of individuals with disabilities. Rehabilitation psychologists search for answers to questions such as: How do persons respond to the onset of disability? What are the challenges and obstacles individuals with disabilities might face? Which potentially malleable factors could be targeted in interventions to support and empower individuals with disabilities?

Disability onset can affect well-being and cause stress, anxiety, depression, or other disorders calling for psychological intervention, as it has been shown in individuals with coronary heart disease, cancer, diabetes, osteoporosis, rheumatoid arthritis, epilepsy, multiple sclerosis, brain injury, or SCI (e.g., Craig, Tran, & Middleton, 2009; Glassman & Shapiro, 1998; Hoppe & Elger, 2011; Kubzansky & Kawachi, 2000). Although disability can have a negative impact on well-being, not all persons are equally affected. Indeed, it is more common for individuals with a disability to be resilient rather than to suffer from elevated levels of distress (Bonanno, Westphal, & Mancini, 2011).

Differences in how well individuals function after the onset of a disability are determined by a multifactorial process. Sociodemographic factors such as gender, ethnicity, or current age can act as predictors or moderators of response to disability (Stanton, Revenson, & Tennen, 2007). Similarly, health condition–related factors such as age at disability onset, disability severity, or time since disability onset (or diagnosis) can influence physical and psychological functioning in individuals with disabilities. Findings, however, are mixed and partly health condition–specific (Livneh & Martz, 2012).

Coping and appraisal processes are extensively studied in rehabilitation psychology research. The findings suggest that the use of engagement-type (active) coping, such as planning, is generally associated with better outcomes, whereas the use of deengagement-type coping, such as avoidance, is associated with poorer outcomes. Illness-related appraisals, such as persons' perceptions regarding the controllability, cause, and consequences of disability, have also been identified as key predictors of functioning (Dennison, Moss-Morris, & Chalder, 2009; Galvin & Godfrey, 2001; Livneh & Martz, 2012; Stanton et al., 2007). Likewise, a number of psychosocial factors consistently demonstrate associations with better well-being and positive mental health in individuals with a disability. Among these are self-efficacy and (internal) locus of control, self-esteem, purpose in life and optimism, social support, spirituality, and positive affect (Livneh & Martz, 2012; Luszczynska, Pawlowska, Cieslak, Knoll, & Scholz, 2013; Peter, Müller, Cieza, & Geyh, 2012).

To what extent have positive psychology and related concepts been considered and investigated in individuals with disabilities? To get a more systematic answer to this question, we analyzed the titles and abstracts of articles published in the journal *Rehabilitation Psychology*, other rehabilitation journals, and selected health condition–specific journals since 2000. The analysis shows that positive psychology concepts such as character strengths and virtues have received very little attention in rehabilitation research. More emphasis has been placed on quality of life and mental health variables, as well as concepts such as self-efficacy or purpose in life (see Table 27.1), which are viewed as contemporary examples of positive psychology, although their conceptualization and examination preceded positive psychology by

**Table 27.1**
Selected Positive Psychology, Well-Being, Mental Health Resources and Strengths Mentioned in Title or Abstract of Articles Published in *Rehabilitation Psychology* and Other Rehabilitation and Health Condition–Specific Journals Since 2000

|  | Rehabilitation Psychology | Rehabilitation Journals[a] | Health Condition– Specific Journals[b] |
|---|---|---|---|
| Anxiety | 29 | 225 | 763 |
| Bravery | 0 | 0 | 0 |
| Character strength | 0 | 0 | 0 |
| Creativity | 0 | 2 | 1 |
| Curiosity | 0 | 1 | 2 |
| Depression | 122 | 536 | 883 |
| Forgiveness | 1 | 2 | 1 |
| Gratitude | 1 | 2 | 3 |
| Happiness | 0 | 9 | 11 |
| Hope | 8 | 22 | 121 |
| Humor | 1 | 4 | 16 |
| Life satisfaction | 20 | 99 | 60 |
| Locus of control | 1 | 18 | 29 |
| Mastery | 5 | 14 | 11 |
| Mental health | 33 | 180 | 166 |
| Motivation | 10 | 87 | 59 |
| Optimism | 8 | 15 | 83 |
| Persistence | 4 | 24 | 20 |
| Personality | 16 | 44 | 61 |
| Positive affect | 7 | 10 | 20 |
| Positive psychology | 5 | 1 | 2 |
| Posttraumatic growth | 3 | 6 | 37 |
| Posttraumatic stress | 25 | 24 | 31 |
| Purpose in life | 17 | 4 | 12 |
| Quality of life | 42 | 780 | 1475 |
| Resilience | 9 | 6 | 30 |
| Self-efficacy | 32 | 166 | 114 |
| Self-esteem | 13 | 42 | 62 |
| Sense of coherence | 2 | 16 | 25 |
| Spirituality | 8 | 14 | 70 |
| Well-being | 27 | 217 | 414 |
| Wisdom | 0 | 2 | 8 |

[a]PubMed search considering the following journals: *Archives of Physical Medicine and Rehabilitation, Clinical Rehabilitation, European Journal of Physical and Rehabilitation Medicine, Disability and Rehabilitation, Disability and Health Journal,* and *Neurorehabilitation.*
[b]PubMed search considering the following journals: *Nature Reviews Cancer, Lancet Oncology, Supportive Care in Cancer, European Journal of Cancer Care, Psycho-Oncology, Multiple Sclerosis International, The Journal of Spinal Cord Medicine, Spinal Cord, Topics in Spinal Cord Injury Rehabilitation, Topics in Stroke Rehabilitation,* and *Stroke Research and Treatment.*

**Table 27.2**

Selected Chronic Health Conditions and Diseases Mentioned in Title or Abstract of Articles Published in Positive Psychology Journals

|  | Hits in the *Journal of Positive Psychology* and the *Journal of Happiness Studies* |
|---|:---:|
| Amputation | 1 |
| Brain injury | 0 |
| Cancer | 2 |
| Cardiovascular | 1 |
| Chronic pain | 1 |
| Congenital condition | 0 |
| Hearing disorder | 0 |
| Hearing loss | 0 |
| HIV | 2 |
| Multiple sclerosis | 2 |
| Spinal cord injury | 0 |
| Stroke | 0 |
| Vision disorder | 0 |
| Vision loss | 0 |
| Rehabilitation | 1 |
| Rehabilitation psychology | 0 |

decades (Duckworth, Steen, & Seligman, 2005). The fact that positive psychology journals have published very few studies with individuals with disabilities reinforces the impression that efforts toward an application of positive psychology in rehabilitation practice could be intensified (see Table 27.2). Do we observe a similar picture when we move our focus from observational to interventional research and practice?

## HOW IS POSITIVE PSYCHOLOGY APPLIED IN REHABILITATION PRACTICE?

Today, psychological and psychosocial interventions are an integral part of interdisciplinary inpatient treatment as well as community-based rehabilitation of individuals with disabilities. Rehabilitation psychology practice is strongly rooted in a behavioral or cognitive-behavioral approach and applies person-centered and supportive counseling. Which psychosocial interventions are typically applied in rehabilitation practice? To what extent do these focus on positive aspects of the human experience after disability? And to what extent have positive psychotherapy interventions been conducted and examined in individuals with disabilities?

### Psychosocial Interventions in Individuals With Disabilities

The evidence on the beneficial effects of cognitive-behavioral and psychosocial interventions on emotional distress and mental health in individuals with disabilities is rich and robust, for example, in cancer, cardiovascular diseases, fibromyalgia, spinal cord injury, multiple sclerosis, stroke, arthritis, and traumatic brain injury (e.g., Osborn, Demoncada, & Feuerstein, 2006; Thomas, Thomas, Hillier, Galvin, & Baker, 2006; Whalley et al., 2011). In individuals with disabilities, depression, anxiety, and pain can be effectively reduced, and coping and quality of life can be enhanced by psychosocial interventions.

The typical repertoire of rehabilitation psychology interventions includes coping-skills development, stress management, relaxation training, pain management, problem-solving training, self-management interventions, social and communication skills training, social support interventions, contingency management, and patient education, often in the form of "packaged" interventions labeled cognitive-behavioral psychotherapy (Ayers et al., 2007; Frank & Elliott, 2000; Wilson et al., 2009).

*Coping-skills training*, for example, according to Sharoff (2004), facilitates the development of self-esteem, tolerance, and accommodation skills after the onset of chronic illness and treats irrational responses to suffering, guilt, or bitterness, primarily by using cognitive restructuring. *Stress-management interventions* assist people in dealing with stressors, negative emotions, physiological arousal, and negative health consequences of distress (Kenny, 2007). They can include a variety of specific strategies, such as cognitive restructuring, relaxation techniques, development of coping and problem-solving skills, anger management, social-skills training, and lifestyle education, all of which can be applied in individual or group settings. *Relaxation techniques*, including mindfulness-based approaches (Grossman, Niemann, Schmidt, & Walach, 2004; Stahl & Goldstein, 2010), progressive muscle relaxation (Jacobsen, 1929), autogenic training (Stetter & Kupper, 2002), guided imagery, hypnotherapeutic techniques (Robertson, 2013), and biofeedback can have beneficial effects on pain, fatigue, medication use, and health-related quality of life in individuals with osteoarthritis, multiple sclerosis, SCI, fibromyalgia, or cancer (e.g., Dimeo, Thomas, Raabe-Menssen, Pröpper, & Mathias, 2004; Jensen et al., 2009). Within *multimodal pain management*, psychological interventions emphasize the mutual influences between psychological states and the experience of pain and use educational components, cognitive restructuring, attention management, relaxation, hypnosis, and biofeedback to ameliorate the experience of pain, increase pain coping skills, and increase meaningful activity (e.g., Jensen et al., 2009; Thieme, Flor, & Turk, 2006). *Problem-solving training* typically includes a series of steps, from recognizing and defining the problem, to collecting strategies to fix the problem, identifying the best way(s) to deal with the problem, planning concrete actions, realizing the actions in everyday life, and finally evaluating the solution (Hopko et al., 2011). *Self-management interventions* teach participants and their significant others the skills necessary for the everyday management of "symptoms, disability, emotional impact, complex medication regimens, and difficult lifestyle adjustments and obtaining helpful health care" (Redman, 2004, p. 4). *Social support interventions* may also be provided for individuals with disabilities in rehabilitation settings, and these can include involvement of significant others in individual therapy, professional-led support groups, peer support or self-help groups, and assertiveness and social-skills training.

POSITIVE ASPECTS INTEGRATED IN PSYCHOSOCIAL INTERVENTIONS
FOR INDIVIDUALS WITH DISABILITIES

Many of the previously mentioned rehabilitation psychology interventions focus on reducing negative outcomes as opposed to increasing positive ones. Nevertheless, several positive aspects are embedded in these interventions. Their primary aim is to enhance quality of life and well-being of individuals with disabilities. Several of these interventions focus on strengths and elicit positive emotional states. For example, they strengthen psychosocial resources of the individuals when targeting and building self-efficacy, assertiveness, and adaptive skills. Pain management directs the attention toward positive emotional states and meaningful activity despite the experience of pain. Relaxation techniques and hypnoses are used to induce positive experiences, and support groups imply not only receiving support but also giving support to others.

## OUTLOOK AND FUTURE DIRECTIONS

Newly developed positive psychology intervention programs are currently not part of typical rehabilitation psychology practice. These programs have not yet been applied to individuals with disabilities and have not been empirically tested in the rehabilitation context. *Positive psychotherapy* interventions build on individuals' strengths and virtues (e.g., using one's signature strengths) and include a broad range of exercises that promote positive activities, cognitions, and feelings (Sin & Lyubomirsky, 2009). *Well-being therapy* (Fava, Rafanelli, Cazzaro, Conti, & Grandi, 1998) targets the six dimensions autonomy, personal growth, environmental mastery, purpose in life, positive relations, and self-acceptance (Ryff & Singer, 1998; see also Ruini & Fava, Chapter 28, this volume). *Quality of life therapy* (Frisch, 2006) aims to enhance satisfaction in 16 life domains (e.g., work, play, or relationships) and integrates positive psychology with cognitive-behavioral therapy.

Positive psychology exercises, which have been examined in randomized controlled trials, include writing letters of gratitude, counting one's blessings, practicing optimism, performing acts of kindness, meditating on positive feelings toward others, and using one's signature strengths (Seligman, Steen, Park, & Peterson, 2005). Results of two meta-analyses of positive psychology-based interventions revealed that they can significantly increase well-being (mean effect size ranging from 0.20 to 0.34) and decrease depressive symptoms (mean effect size ranging from 0.23 to 0.31; Bolier et al., 2013; Sin & Lyubomirsky, 2009) even in the long term (Seligman et al., 2005). For comparison, a meta-analysis of 375 psychotherapy studies in the general population found that psychotherapy demonstrated an average effect size of 0.32 for outcomes such as self-esteem and psychosocial functioning (Smith & Glass, 1977).

Positive psychology interventions have a number of advantages. Consisting of brief, simple, and self-administered positive activities, they are less expensive and time consuming to administer compared with psychotherapy. They promise to yield rapid improvements of mood symptoms, show long-lasting effects, hold little to no stigma, and carry no negative side effects (Lyubomirsky, Dickerhoof, Boehm, & Sheldon, 2011; Seligman et al., 2005). Overall, applied to individuals with disabilities, they could add to and improve, broaden, and diversify current rehabilitation psychology practices.

### REHABILITATION PSYCHOLOGY PRACTICE

Rehabilitation psychologists such as Dunn (Dunn & Brody, 2008; Dunn & Dougherty, 2005), Ehde (2010), and Elliott (Elliott, Kurylo, & Rivera, 2005) have started to promote a connection of their discipline with positive psychology. Whereas the programmatic principles by Wright (1983) contain a strong positive core, rehabilitation psychology practice still works only to a limited extent applying explicit positive strategies. Positive psychology interventions, techniques, or exercises that directly address the experience of positive emotion, cultivate clients' strengths and resources, enhance meaning and purpose in life, and promote citizenship and client's contributions to community and social life could supplement the typical repertoire of rehabilitation psychology interventions. Future rehabilitation psychology practice could incorporate elements from well-being therapy and quality of life therapy. Intervention programs and manuals could be developed to explicitly include positive psychology elements and modules. Rehabilitation psychologists could guide and encourage individuals with disabilities to participate in positive psychology–based activities such as counting blessings, appreciation of life circumstances, and gratitude toward persons; writing about best possible future selves (optimism); doing good deeds for others (engagement, meaning, and purpose in life); strengthening and enjoying relationships by creating a routine to get together and reunite (socializing); or striving for states of intense and complete absorption (flow).

Within comprehensive multidisciplinary rehabilitation practice, disciplines closely related to rehabilitation psychology, such as art or music therapy, can also promote the tenets of positive psychology. These therapies have been proposed as a way to find and make meaning; to induce flow experience; to use personal signature strengths, such as creativity; and to generate positive emotions (Croom, 2012; Wilkinson & Chilton, 2013).

Overall, via a connection with positive psychology, rehabilitation psychologists could move toward a truly integrated and balanced perspective in their everyday practice by following the goals of promoting growth, well-being, and meaningful participation in individuals with disabilities. Although the connection of rehabilitation psychology with approaches toward "the good life" seems to be a promising avenue for further development, the proposed applications and potential benefits need to be put through rigorous scientific testing.

### REHABILITATION PSYCHOLOGY RESEARCH

Although rehabilitation psychology has gathered considerable evidence in relation to individuals' well-being and response to disability onset, several content-related and methodological gaps have been identified (Dennison et al., 2009; Livneh & Martz, 2012; Ownsworth, Hawkes, Steginga, Walker, & Shum, 2009; Stanton et al., 2007). Research efforts in rehabilitation psychology should be directed toward:

- An intensified focus on the influence of environmental factors, such as access to quality health care, and on indicators of well-being and mental health.
- The examination of multidimensional models, including mediating and moderating processes, to better understand the mechanism underlying processes following disability onset.
- The use of prospective, possibly intensive longitudinal study designs and appropriate statistical methodologies to help disentangle cause from effect.
- A consistent use of specific measurement instruments to allow for a population comparison both within and between specific disability populations.
- The disentanglement of the conceptual overlap between psychosocial factors, appraisals, coping, and rehabilitation outcomes.
- The translation from current knowledge to interventions.

Positive psychology can contribute to these future endeavors from both conceptual/theoretical and applied research perspectives. Rehabilitation psychology research suffers from ambiguity and overlap of concepts (e.g., mastery, self-efficacy, control) as well as the lack of an agreed overarching framework or meta-theory (Chou et al., 2009; Rath & Elliott, 2012). Positive psychology could bring new dynamics and fresh input into rehabilitation psychology theory when researchers consider and discuss their concepts and models in connection and in comparison across the disciplines. Because incorporating and considering these concepts might also carry the risk of adding further ambiguity, we emphasize the need for clear definitions and conceptual differentiation.

Future basic research aimed at understanding the factors that contribute to well-being following disability onset could not only help clarify the factors that buffer the effects of disability on negative outcomes, but could also help clarify the factors that contribute to positive outcomes. Research should target not only disability, but also positive functioning; not only emotional distress, but also well-being; not only impairments, difficulties, and barriers to activity and participation, but also facilitators, strengths, and resources. There is also a need for greater preventive focus in rehabilitation psychology research that would help us understand how positive characteristics, positive activities, and positive relationships can lower the risk for secondary health conditions or further deterioration and enhance physical health in individuals with disabilities. There is a need to apply, validate, and, if indicated, modify positive psychology measurement instruments for individuals with disabilities.

Future intervention research is needed to determine whether positive psychology interventions are transferable to populations of individuals with disabilities. Which techniques work in individuals with disabilities and which do not? Are certain positive psychology exercises more effective than others? Do positive psychology exercises work better, as well, or less effectively than problem-based "traditional" approaches in the rehabilitation of individuals with disabilities? How can positive interventions be tailored to specific disability groups and individual characteristics?

## CONCLUSION

In this chapter, our aim was to build a bridge between rehabilitation psychology and positive psychology. Rehabilitation psychology is on its way toward a fuller consideration of "the good life" for individuals with disabilities. Positive psychology as a research stream examining "the good life" has the potential of contributing to the future pathways of rehabilitation psychology. It can give input on conceptual, basic, and applied research levels. At the same time, positive psychology could also benefit from rehabilitation psychology and its focus on person–environment interactions.

However, rehabilitation psychology still needs to be aware of some cautionary notes regarding positive psychology. The danger of one-sidedness is to be avoided: Negative reductionism should not be replaced by positive reductionism. Positive reductionism could lead to romanticizing disability and chronic disease and neglecting the full realities of an individual's experience. It could also put additional pressure on individuals with disabilities and their families by "blaming the victim" or creating a "tyranny" or "prison of positive thinking" through a prescriptive or perfectionistic tone. We strongly assert the need to advance rehabilitation psychology research and practice according to the notions of "the good life" while following an integrated and balanced perspective that acknowledges both the positive as well as the negative.

## SUMMARY POINTS

- Rehabilitation psychology is the application of psychological knowledge and understanding on behalf of individuals with disabilities and includes activities such as research, clinical practice, teaching, public education, and development of social policy and advocacy.

- The main aims of rehabilitation encompass ameliorating the negative impact of disability, optimizing functioning, supporting reintegration, and increasing quality of life and well-being of individuals with disabilities.
- Disability onset can have a negative impact on well-being; however, it is more common for individuals with a disability to be resilient rather than to suffer from a psychological dysfunction.
- Differences in how persons respond to the onset of a disability result from a multifactorial process involving sociodemographic and health condition–related variables, appraisals, coping, and other psychosocial, biological, and environmental factors.
- Rehabilitation psychology and positive psychology share three key commonalities: (1) positive principles; (2) focus on individual strengths and resources; and (3) well-being, participation, and growth as key outcomes.
- The evidence on the beneficial effects of cognitive-behavioral and psychosocial interventions on psychological functioning in individuals with a disability is rich and robust.
- Positive psychology interventions have rarely been applied to individuals with disabilities, have not been empirically tested in rehabilitation contexts, and are currently not part of typical rehabilitation psychology practices.
- Future intervention research needs to determine whether positive psychology interventions are transferable to populations of individuals with disabilities.
- While integrating positive psychology and rehabilitation psychology, a balanced perspective acknowledging both the positive as well as the negative is essential.

## REFERENCES

American Psychological Association Division 22: Rehabilitation Psychology. (2014). *What is rehabilitation psychology?* Retrieved from http://www.apadivisions.org/division-22/about/rehabilitation-psychology/index.aspx?item=4

Ayers, S., Baum, A., McManus, C., Newman, S., Wallston, K., Weinman, J., & West, R. (2007). *Cambridge handbook of psychology, health and medicine* (2nd ed.). Cambridge, England: Cambridge University Press.

Blessing, C., Golden, T. P., Pi, S., Bruyere, S. M., & Van Looy, S. (2012). Vocational rehabilitation, inclusion, and social integration. In P. Kennedy (Ed.), *The Oxford handbook of rehabilitation psychology* (pp. 453–473). Oxford, England: Oxford University Press.

Bolier, L., Haverman, M., Westerhof, G. J., Riper, H., Smit, F., & Bohlmeijer, E. (2013). Positive psychology interventions: A meta-analysis of randomized controlled studies. *BMC Public Health, 13*, 119.

Bonanno, G. A., Westphal, M., & Mancini, A. D. (2011). Resilience to loss and potential trauma. *Annual Review of Clinical Psychology, 7*, 511–535.

Boorse, C. (1977). Health as a theoretical concept. *Philosophy of Science, 44*, 542–573.

Brown, S. L., Nesse, R. M., Vinokur, A. D., & Smith, D. M. (2003). Providing social support may be more beneficial than receiving it: Results from a prospective study of mortality. *Psychological Science, 14*, 320–327.

Chou, C. C., Lee, E., Catalano, D., Ditchman, N., & Wilson, L. M. (2009). Positive psychology and psychosocial adjustment to chronic illness and disability. In F. Chan, E. da Silva Cardoso, & J. A. Chronister (Eds.), *Understanding psychosocial adjustment to chronic illness and disability: A handbook for evidence-based practitioners in rehabilitation* (pp. 207–242). New York, NY: Springer.

Craig, A., Tran, Y., & Middleton, J. (2009). Psychological morbidity and spinal cord injury: A systematic review. *Spinal Cord, 47*, 108–114.

Croom, A. M. (2012). Music, neuroscience, and the psychology of well-being: A précis. *Frontiers in Psychology, 2*, 393.

Dennison, L., Moss-Morris, R., & Chalder, T. (2009). A review of psychological correlates of adjustment in patients with multiple sclerosis. *Clinical Psychology Review, 29*, 141–153.

Diener, E., Suh, E. M., Lucas, R. E., & Smith, H. L. (1999). Subjective well-being: Three decades of progress. *Psychological Bulletin, 125*, 276–302.

Dimeo, F. C., Thomas, F., Raabe-Menssen, C., Pröpper, F., & Mathias, M. (2004). Effect of aerobic exercise and relaxation training on fatigue and physical performance of cancer patients after surgery: A randomised controlled trial. *Supportive Care in Cancer, 12*, 774–779.

Duckworth, A. L., Steen, T. A., & Seligman, M. E. P. (2005). Positive psychology in clinical practice. *Annual Review of Clinical Psychology, 1*, 629–651.

Dunn, D. S., & Brody, C. (2008). Defining the good life following acquired physical disability. *Rehabilitation Psychology, 53*, 413–425.

Dunn, D. S., & Dougherty, S. B. (2005). Prospects for a positive psychology of rehabilitation. *Rehabilitation Psychology, 50*, 305–311.

Ehde, D. M. (2010). Application of positive psychology to rehabilitation psychology. In R. G. Frank, M. Rosenthal, & B. Caplan (Eds.), *Handbook of rehabilitation psychology* (2nd ed., pp. 417–424). Washington, DC: American Psychological Association.

Elliott, T. R., Kurylo, M., & Rivera, P. (2005). Positive growth following acquired physical disability. In C. R. Snyder & S. J. Lopez (Eds.), *Handbook of positive psychology* (pp. 687–699). New York, NY: Oxford University Press.

Fava, G. A., Rafanelli, C., Cazzaro, M., Conti, S., & Grandi, S. (1998). Well-being therapy: A novel psychotherapeutic approach for residual symptoms of affective disorders. *Psychological Medicine, 28*, 475–480.

Ferrans, C., & Powers, M. (1985). Quality of Life Index: Development and psychometric properties. *Advances in Nursing Science, 8*, 15–24.

Frank, R. G., & Elliott, T. R. (2000). *Handbook of rehabilitation psychology.* Washington, DC: American Psychological Association.

Frisch, M. B. (2006). *Quality of Life Therapy: Applying a life satisfaction approach to positive psychology and cognitive therapy.* Hoboken, NJ: Wiley.

Fugl-Meyer, A. R., Bränholm, I.-B., & Fugl-Meyer, K. S. (1991). Happiness and domain-specific life satisfaction in adult northern Swedes. *Clinical Rehabilitation, 5*, 25–33.

Fuhrer, M. J. (2000). Subjectifying quality of life as a medical rehabilitation outcome. *Disability and Rehabilitation, 22*, 481–489.

Galvin, L. R., & Godfrey, H. P. (2001). The impact of coping on emotional adjustment to spinal cord injury (SCI): Review of the literature and application of a stress appraisal and coping formulation. *Spinal Cord, 39*, 615–627.

Glassman, A. H., & Shapiro, P. A. (1998). Depression and the course of coronary artery disease. *American Journal of Psychiatry, 155*, 4–11.

Gordon, W. A. (2000). Rehabilitation psychology. In A. E. Kadzin (Ed.), *Encyclopedia of psychology* (Vol. 7, pp. 24–27). Washington, DC: American Psychological Association.

Grossman, P., Niemann, L., Schmidt, S., & Walach, H. (2004). Mindfulness-based stress reduction and health benefits: A meta-analysis. *Journal of Psychosomatic Research, 57*, 35–43.

Harper, D. (2013). *Online etymology dictionary.* Retrieved from http://www.etymonline.com

Helgeson, V. S., Reynolds, K. A., & Tomich, P. L. (2006). A meta-analytic review of benefit finding and growth. *Journal of Consulting and Clinical Psychology, 74*, 797–816.

Hopko, D. R., Armento, M. E., Robertson, S. M., Ryba, M. M., Carvalho, J. P., Colman, L. K., . . . Lejuez, C. W. (2011). Brief behavioral activation and problem-solving therapy for depressed breast cancer patients: Randomized trial. *Journal of Consulting and Clinical Psychology, 79*, 834–849.

Hoppe, C., & Elger, C. E. (2011). Depression in epilepsy: A critical review from a clinical perspective. *Nature Reviews. Neurology, 7,* 462–472.

Jacobsen, E. (1929). *Progressive relaxation.* Oxford, England: University of Chicago Press.

Jensen, M. P., Barber, J., Romano, J. M., Hanley, M. A., Raichle, K. A., Molton, I. R., . . . Patterson, D. R. (2009). Effects of self-hypnosis training and EMG biofeedback relaxation training on chronic pain in persons with spinal-cord injury. *International Journal of Clinical and Experimental Hypnosis, 57,* 239–268.

Joseph, S. (2013). *What doesn't kill us: The new psychology of posttraumatic growth.* New York, NY: Basic Books.

Kenny, D. (2007). Stress management. In S. Ayers, A. Baum, C. McManus, S. Newman, K. Wallston, J. Weinman, & R. West (Eds.), *Cambridge handbook of psychology, health and medicine* (2nd ed., pp. 403–406). Cambridge, England: Cambridge University Press.

Kubzansky, L. D., & Kawachi, I. (2000). Going to the heart of the matter: Do negative emotions cause coronary heart disease? *Journal of Psychosomatic Research, 48,* 323–337.

Larson, P. C., & Sachs, P. R. (2000). A history of Division 22 (Rehabilitation Psychology). In D. A. Dewsbury (Ed.), *Unification through division: Histories of the divisions of the American Psychological Association* (Vol. 5, pp. 33–58). Washington, DC: American Psychological Association.

Lewin, K. (1936). *Principles of topological psychology.* New York, NY: McGraw-Hill.

Linley, P. A., Joseph, S., Harrington, S., & Wood, A. M. (2006). Positive psychology: Past, present, and (possible) future. *Journal of Positive Psychology, 1,* 3–16.

Livneh, H., & Martz, E. (2012). Adjustment to chronic illness and disability: Theoretical perspectives, empirical findings, and unresolved issues. In P. Kennedy (Ed.), *The Oxford handbook of rehabilitation psychology* (pp. 47–87). New York, NY: Oxford University Press.

Luszczynska, A., Pawlowska, I., Cieslak, R., Knoll, N., & Scholz, U. (2013). Social support and quality of life among lung cancer patients: A systematic review. *Psychooncology, 22,* 2160–2168.

Lyubomirsky, S. (2007). *The how of happiness: A new approach to getting the life you want.* New York, NY: Penguin Press.

Lyubomirsky, S., Dickerhoof, R., Boehm, J. K., & Sheldon, K. M. (2011). Becoming happier takes both a will and a proper way: An experimental longitudinal intervention to boost well-being. *Emotion, 11,* 391–402.

Magasi, S., & Post, M. W. (2010). A comparative review of contemporary participation measures' psychometric properties and content coverage. *Archives of Physical Medicine and Rehabilitation, 91,* S17–S28.

McMillen, J. C., & Cook, C. L. (2003). The positive by-products of spinal cord injury and their correlates. *Rehabilitation Psychology, 48,* 77–85.

Osborn, R. L., Demoncada, A. C., & Feuerstein, M. (2006). Psychosocial interventions for depression, anxiety, and quality of life in cancer survivors: Meta-analyses. *International Journal of Psychiatry in Medicine, 36,* 13–34.

Ownsworth, T., Hawkes, A., Steginga, S., Walker, D., & Shum, D. (2009). A biopsychosocial perspective on adjustment and quality of life following brain tumor: A systematic evaluation of the literature. *Disability and Rehabilitation, 31,* 1038–1055.

Peter, C., Müller, R., Cieza, A., & Geyh, S. (2012). Psychological resources in spinal cord injury: A systematic literature review. *Spinal Cord, 50,* 188–201.

Peterson, C., Park, N., & Seligman, E. (2005). Orientations to happiness and life satisfaction: The full life versus the empty life. *Journal of Happiness Studies, 6,* 25–41.

Peterson, C., & Seligman, M. E. (2004). *Character strengths and virtues: A handbook and classification.* Washington, DC: APA Press.

Rath, J. F., & Elliott, T. R. (2012). Psychological models in rehabilitation psychology. In P. Kennedy (Ed.), *The Oxford handbook of rehabilitation psychology* (pp. 32–46). Oxford, England: Oxford University Press.

Redman, B. K. (2004). *Patient self-management of chronic disease. The health care provider's challange*. Sudbury, MA: Jones & Bartlett.

Robertson, D. (2013). *The practice of cognitive-behavioural hypnotherapy: A manual for evidence-based clinical hypnosis*. London, England: Karnac.

Ryff, C. D., & Singer, B. (1998). The contours of positive human health. *Psychological Inquiry, 9*, 1–28.

Seligman, M. E. (2011). *Flourish: A visionary new understanding of happiness and well-being*. New York, NY: Free Press.

Seligman, M. E., & Csikszentmihalyi, M. (2000). Positive psychology: An introduction. *American Psychologist, 55*, 5–14.

Seligman, M. E., Steen, T. A., Park, N., & Peterson, C. (2005). Positive psychology progress: Empirical validation of interventions. *American Psychologist, 60*, 410–421.

Sharoff, K. (2004). *Coping skills manual for treating chronic and terminal illness*. New York, NY: Springer.

Sin, N. L., & Lyubomirsky, S. (2009). Enhancing well-being and alleviating depressive symptoms with positive psychology interventions: A practice-friendly meta-analysis. *Journal of clinical psychology, 65*, 467–487.

Smith, M. L., & Glass, G. V. (1977). Meta-analysis of psychotherapy outcome studies. *American Psychologist, 32*, 752–760.

Stahl, B., & Goldstein, E. (2010). *A mindfulness-based stress reduction workbook*. Oakland, CA: New Harbinger.

Stanton, A. L., Revenson, T. A. & Tennen, H. (2007). Health psychology: Psychological adjustment to chronic disease. *Annual Review of Psychology, 58*, 565–592.

Stetter, F., & Kupper, S. (2002). Autogenic training: A meta-analysis of clinical outcome studies. *Applied Psychophysiology and Biofeedback, 27*, 45–98.

Tedeschi, R. G., & Calhoun, L. G. (2004). Posttraumatic growth: Conceptual foundations and empirical evidence. *Psychological Inquiry, 15*, 1–18.

Thieme, K., Flor, H., & Turk, D. C. (2006). Psychological pain treatment in fibromyalgia syndrome: Efficacy of operant behavioural and cognitive behavioural treatments. *Arthritis Research & Therapy, 8*, R121.

Thomas, P. W., Thomas, S., Hillier, C., Galvin, K., & Baker, R. (2006). Psychological interventions for multiple sclerosis. *Cochrane Database of Systematic Reviews, 2006*(1), CD004431.

Tulsky, D. S., & Rosenthal, M. (2003). Measurement of quality of life in rehabilitation medicine: Emerging issues. *Archives of Physical Medicine and Rehabilitation, 84*, S1–S2.

Ware, J. E., Snow, K. K., Kosinski, M., & Gandek, B. (1993). *SF-36 Health Survey: Manual and interpretation guide*. Boston, MA: The Health Institute, New England Medical Center.

Warr, P. (1999). Well-being and the workplace. In D. Kahneman, E. Diener, & N. Schwarz (Eds.), *Well-being: The foundations of hedonic psychology* (pp. 392–412). New York, NY: Russell Sage Foundation.

Whalley, B., Rees, K., Davies, P., Bennett, P., Ebrahim, S., Liu, Z., . . . Taylor, R. S. (2011). Psychological interventions for coronary heart disease. *Cochrane Database of Systematic Reviews, 2011*(8), CD002902.

Wilkinson, R. A., & Chilton, G. (2013). Positive art therapy: Linking positive psychology to art therapy theory, practice, and research. *Art Therapy: Journal of the American Art Therapy Association, 30*, 4–11.

Wilson, C., Huston, T., Koval, J., Gordon, S. A., Schwebel, A., & Gassaway, J. (2009). Classification of SCI rehabilitation treatments. SCIRehab project series: The psychology taxonomy. *Journal of Spinal Cord Medicine, 32*, 319–328.

World Health Organization. (2001). *International classification of functioning, disability and health: ICF*. Geneva, Switzerland: Author.

World Health Organization & The World Bank. (2011). *World report on disability*. Geneva, Switzerland: World Health Organization.

Wright, B. A. (1972). Value-laden beliefs and principles for rehabilitation psychology. *Rehabilitation Psychology, 19*, 38–45.

Wright, B. A. (1983). *Physical disability: A psychosocial approach*. New York, NY: Harper & Row.

Zoellner, T., & Maercker, A. (2006). Posttraumatic growth in clinical psychology: A critical review and introduction of a two component model. *Clinical Psychology Review, 26*, 626–653.

# PART VII

# CONTEXTS OF CLINICAL PRACTICE

# CHAPTER 28

# Clinical Applications of Well-Being Therapy

## CHIARA RUINI and GIOVANNI A. FAVA

THE CONCEPT OF PSYCHOLOGICAL well-being has received increasing attention in clinical psychology. Recent investigations have documented the complex relationship between well-being, distress, and personality traits, both in clinical (Fava, Rafanelli, et al., 2001) and nonclinical populations (Ruini et al., 2003). The findings show that psychological well-being could not be equated with the absence of symptomatology, nor with personality traits. It is thus particularly important to analyze the concept of well-being in clinical settings with emphasis on changes in well-being occurring during psychotherapy.

A relevant methodological issue is the broad definition of psychological well-being and optimal functioning. A review by Ryan and Deci (2001) has shown that research on well-being has followed two main directions: (1) happiness and hedonic well-being and (2) development of human potential (eudaimonic well-being). In the first realm all studies dealing with concepts of subjective well-being (Diener, Suh, Lucas, & Smith, 1999), life satisfaction (Neugarten, Havighurst, & Tobin, 1961), and positive emotions (Fredrickson, 2002) can be included. The concept of well-being here is equated with a cognitive process of evaluation of an individual's life, or with the experience of positive emotions.

According to the eudaimonic perspective, happiness consists of fulfilling one's potential in a process of self-realization. Under this umbrella some researchers describe concepts such as the fully functioning person, meaningfulness, self-actualization, and vitality. In particular, Ryff's (1989) model of psychological well-being—encompassing autonomy, personal growth, environmental mastery, purpose in life, positive relations, and self-acceptance—has been found to be particularly useful in clinical psychology and psychotherapy (Fava, Rafanelli, et al., 2001; Rafanelli et al., 2000; Rafanelli et al., 2002; Ruini et al., 2002; Ryff & Singer, 1996). Importantly, in describing optimal human functioning, Ryff and Singer (2008) emphasize Aristotle's admonishment to seek "that which is intermediate," avoiding excess and extremes. The pursuit of well-being may in fact be so solipsistic and individualistic to leave no room for human connection and the social good; or it could be so focused on responsibilities and duties outside the self that personal talents and capacities are neither recognized or developed (Ryff & Singer, 2008).

These two approaches have led to different areas of research, but they complement each other in defining the construct of well-being (Ryan & Deci, 2001). Some
authors have also suggested that they can compensate each other; thus individuals
may have profiles of high eudaimonic well-being and low hedonic well-being, or vice
versa. These profiles are also associated with sociodemographic variables, such as
age, years of education, and employment (Keyes, Shmotkin, & Ryff, 2002). However,
in this investigation, the authors underlined the fact that only a small proportion of
individuals present with optimal well-being, that is, high hedonic and eudemonic
well-being, paving the way for possible psychosocial interventions.

In clinical settings, however, early contributions to well-being research were formulated by authors such as Maslow (1968), Rogers (1961), Allport (1961), and Jung
(1933), describing concepts such as self-actualization, fully functioning, maturity,
and individuation. In 1958 Jahoda outlined positive criteria for defining mental
health, but all these aspects of psychological well-being were neglected for a long
time because the development of psychotherapeutic strategies that led to symptom
reduction was the main focus of research. Such developments have been particularly
impressive for cognitive behavioral therapies (CBTs; Fava, 2000). Even though
Parloff, Kelman, and Frank suggested as early as 1954 that the goals of psychotherapy were increased personal comfort and effectiveness, these latter achievements
were viewed only as by-products of the reduction of symptoms or as a luxury that
clinical investigators could not afford. Four converging developments have modified
this stance.

1. Relapse and recurrence in mood and anxiety disorders.
   There has been increasing awareness of the bleak long-term outcome of
   mood and anxiety disorders (Fava, 1996; Fava, Tomba, & Grandi, 2007), and
   particularly in unipolar major depression (Fava, 1999a). Various follow-up
   studies, in fact, have documented relapses and recurrence in affective disorders
   (Ramana et al., 1995). As a result, the challenge of treatment of depression today
   appears to be the prevention of relapse more than the attainment of recovery.
   Thunedborg, Black, and Bech (1995) found that quality of life measurement,
   and not symptomatic ratings, could predict recurrence of depression. An
   increase in psychological well-being may thus protect against relapse and
   recurrence (Fava, 1999b; Wood & Joseph, 2010). Therefore, an intervention that
   targets the positive may address an aspect of functioning and health that is
   typically left unaddressed in conventional treatments.
2. Clinical response mistaken as recovery.
   There is increasing awareness that clinicians and researchers in clinical psychiatry confound response to treatment with full recovery (Fava, 1996). A substantial residual symptomatology (anxiety, irritability, interpersonal problems)
   was found to characterize the majority of patients who were judged to be remitted according to *Diagnostic and Statistical Manual of Mental Disorders* (DSM) criteria and no longer in need of active treatment. Further, psychological well-being
   needs to be incorporated in the definition of recovery (Fava, 1996). Ryff and
   Singer (1996) have suggested that the absence of well-being creates conditions
   of vulnerability to possible future adversities and that the route to enduring
   recovery lies not exclusively in alleviating the negative, but in engendering the
   positive. Interventions that bring the person out of the negative functioning
   (e.g., exposure treatment in panic disorder with agoraphobia) are one form of
   success, but facilitating progression toward the restoration of positive is quite
   another (Ryff & Singer, 1996).

3. Quality of life and positive health.

There has been an upsurge of interest in quality of life assessment in health care (Fava & Sonino, 2010; Frisch, 2006) and in the concept of positive health (Ryff & Singer, 2000). Clinical researchers have turned their attention to quality-of-life assessment as a means of broadening the evaluation of treatment outcome encompassing satisfaction, functioning, and objective life circumstances (Gladis, Gosch, Dishuk, & Crits-Cristoph, 1999). The benefits of well-being are now well documented in cross-sectional and longitudinal research and include a better physical health (Chida & Steptoe, 2008; Fava & Sonino, 2010; Howell, Kern, & Lyubomirsky, 2007), improved productivity at work, having more meaningful relationships, and social functioning (Seeman, Singer, Ryff, Dienberg Love, & Levy-Storms, 2002). In the same line, research has indeed suggested the important role of positive affectivity (Fredrickson & Joiner, 2002) in promoting resilience and growth. Such directions in health care call for strategies to enhance the well-being that underlies these constructs.

4. The growth of positive psychology.

Issues such as the building of human strength in different psychotherapeutic strategies and the characteristics of subjective well-being have become increasingly important in psychological research (Diener et al., 1999; Gillham & Seligman, 1999). A growing number of investigations on positive emotions (Fredrickson & Joiner, 2002), subjective well-being (Diener, 2000; Diener et al., 1999), human strengths (Park, Peterson, & Seligman, 2004), and other positive personality characteristics such as compassion, hope, and altruism (Park et al., 2004) paved the way for developing "positive interventions" (Magayar-Moe, 2009; Seligman, Steen, Park, & Peterson, 2005; Sin & Lyubomirsky, 2009) such as the positive psychotherapy (Seligman, Rashid, & Parks, 2006); wisdom psychotherapy (Linden, Baumann, Lieberei, Lorenz, & Rotter, 2011); gratitude interventions (Wood, Maltby, Gillett, Linley, & Joseph, 2008); positive coaching (Biswas-Diener, 2010); strengths-based approaches (Biswas-Diener, Kashdan, & Minhas, 2011; Govindji & Linley, 2007; Linley & Burns, 2010); hope therapy (Geraghty, Wood, & Hyland, 2010; Snyder, Ilardi, Michael, Yamhure, & Sympson, 2000); and forgiveness therapy (Lamb, 2005).

In a recent meta-analysis, Bolier et al. (2013) showed that these positive psychology interventions significantly enhance subjective and psychological well-being and reduce depressive symptoms, even though effect sizes were in the small to moderate range. The main aim of all these positive interventions, in fact, is the promotion of happiness, positive emotions, and positivity in general. However, excessively elevated levels of positive emotions can become detrimental and are more connected with mental disorders and impaired functioning (Fredrickson & Losada, 2005). The issues of positivity and well-being, thus, need to be approached considering the complexity of phenomena in clinical settings, and the balance between positivity and distress (Rafanelli et al., 2000; Ruini & Fava, 2012).

## THE COMPLEXITY OF WELL-BEING IN CLINICAL SETTINGS

Early pioneer works to enhance well-being include Ellis and Becker's (1982) guide to personal happiness, Fordyce's (1983) program to increase happiness, Padesky's (1994) work on schema change processes, Frisch's (2006) quality of life therapy, and Horowitz and Kaltreider's (1979) work on positive states of mind. However, these approaches had only a limited effect in clinical practice.

In a naive conceptualization, yet the one implicitly endorsed by *DSM*, well-being and distress are seen as mutually exclusive (i.e., well-being is lack of distress). According to this model, well-being should result from removal of distress. Yet, there is evidence both in psychiatric (Rafanelli et al., 2000) and psychosomatic (Fava, Mangelli, & Ruini, 2001) research to question such views. In order to justify therapeutic efforts aimed at increasing psychological well-being, we should demonstrate impaired levels of psychological well-being in a clinical population. This was achieved by using an instrument, the Psychological Well-Being Scales (PWB) developed by Ryff (1989). In a controlled investigation (Rafanelli et al., 2000), 20 remitted patients with mood or anxiety disorders displayed significantly lower levels in all six dimensions of well-being according to the PWB compared to healthy control subjects matched for sociodemographic variables. It is obvious, however, that the quality and degree of impairment may vary from patient to patient and within the same patient, according to clinical status. Further, Fava, Ranfanelli, et al. (2001) administered the PWB to 30 remitted patients with panic disorder and 30 matched controls and found impairments in some specific areas, but not in others. The model described by Ryff (1989) and Ryff and Keyes (1995) was thus found to satisfactorily describe the variations in psychological well-being that may occur in a clinical setting.

In 1991 Garamoni et al. suggested that healthy functioning is characterized by an optimal balance of positive and negative cognitions and affects, and that psychopathology is marked by deviations from the optimal balance. More recently, Larsen and Prizmic (2008) argued that the balance of positive to negative affect (i.e., the positivity ratio) is a key factor in well-being and in defining whether a person flourishes. Several authors (Fredrickson & Losada, 2005; Larsen & Prizmic, 2008; Schwartz, 1997; Schwartz et al., 2002) suggest that, to maintain an optimal level of emotional well-being and positive mental health, individuals need to experience approximately three times more positive than negative affect. Fredrickson and Losada (2005), in fact, have found that above this ratio, there is an excessively high positivity that becomes detrimental to functioning. Grant and Schwartz (2011) suggest that all positive traits, states, and experiences have costs that, at high levels, may begin to outweigh their benefits, creating the non-monotonicity of an inverted U. For this reason, traditional clinical psychology has a crucial role in planning and implementing interventions for enhancing positive affect. Positive interventions, thus, should not be simply aimed to increase happiness and well-being, but should consider the complex balance between psychological well-being and distress (MacLeod & Moore, 2000) and be targeted to specific and individualized needs.

These clinical and conceptual frameworks were thus instrumental in developing a well-being enhancing psychotherapeutic strategy, defined as well-being therapy (Fava, 1999b; Fava, Rafanelli, Cazzaro, Conti, & Grandi, 1998; Fava & Ruini, 2003; Ruini & Fava, 2012).

## PROTOCOL OF WELL-BEING THERAPY

Well-being therapy is a short-term psychotherapeutic strategy that extends over eight sessions, which may take place every week or every other week. The duration of each session may range from 30 to 50 minutes. It is a technique that emphasizes self-observation (Emmelkamp, 1974), with the use of a structured diary, and interaction between patients and therapists. Well-being therapy is based on Ryff's cognitive model of psychological well-being (Ryff, 1989). This model was selected on the basis of its easy applicability to clinical populations (Fava, Rafanelli, et al., 2001; Rafanelli et al., 2000). Well-being therapy is structured, directive, problem-oriented, and based on an educational model. The development of sessions is described in the following sections.

## INITIAL SESSIONS

These sessions are simply concerned with identifying episodes of well-being and setting them into a situational context, no matter how short-lived they were. Patients are asked to report in a structured diary the circumstances surrounding their episodes of well-being, rated on a 0 to 100 scale, with 0 being absence of well-being and 100 the most intense well-being that could be experienced. When patients are assigned this homework, they often object that they will bring a blank diary, because they never feel well. It is helpful to reply that these moments do exist but tend to pass unnoticed. Patients should therefore monitor them anyway.

Meehl (1975) described

> how people with low hedonic capacity should pay greater attention to the "hedonic book keeping" of their activities than would be necessary for people located midway or high on the hedonic capacity continuum. That is, it matters more to someone cursed with an inborn hedonic defect whether he is efficient and sagacious in selecting friends, jobs, cities, tasks, hobbies, and activities in general. (p. 305)

Patients are particularly encouraged to search for well-being moments, not only in special hedonic-stimulating situations, but also during their daily activities. Several studies have shown that individuals preferentially invest their attention and psychic resources in activities associated with rewarding and challenging states of consciousness, in particular with optimal experience (Csikszentmihalyi, 1990; Delle Fave & Massimini, 2003). Patients are thus asked to report when they feel optimal experiences in their daily life and are invited to list the associated activities or situations.

This initial phase generally extends over a couple of sessions. Yet its duration depends on the factors that affect any homework assignment, such as resistance and compliance.

## INTERMEDIATE SESSIONS

Once the instances of well-being are properly recognized, the patient is encouraged to identify thoughts and beliefs leading to premature interruption of well-being. The similarities with the search for irrational, tension-evoking thoughts in Ellis and Becker's rational-emotive therapy (1982) and automatic thoughts in cognitive therapy (Beck, Rush, Shaw, & Emery, 1979) are obvious. The trigger for self-observation is, however, different, being based on well-being instead of distress.

This phase is crucial, since it allows the therapist to identify which areas of psychological well-being are unaffected by irrational or automatic thoughts and which are saturated with them. The therapist may challenge these thoughts with appropriate questions, such as "What is the evidence for or against this idea?" or "Are you thinking in all-or-none terms?" (Beck et al., 1979). The therapist may also reinforce and encourage activities that are likely to elicit well-being (for instance, assigning the task of undertaking particular pleasurable activities for a certain time each day). Such reinforcement may also result in graded task assignments (Beck et al., 1979), with special reference to exposure to feared or challenging situations, which the patient is likely to avoid. Over time patients may develop ambivalent attitudes toward well-being.

468    Contexts of Clinical Practice

They complain of having lost it, or they long for it, but at the same time they are scared when positive moments actually happen in their lives. These moments trigger specific negative automatic thoughts, usually concerning the fact that they will not last (i.e., it's too good to be true) or that they are not deserved by patients, or that they are attainable only by overcoming difficulties and distress. Encouraging patients in searching and engaging in optimal experiences and pleasant activities is therefore crucial at this stage of well-being therapy (WBT).

This intermediate phase may extend over two or three sessions, depending on the patient's motivation and ability, and it paves the way for the specific well-being enhancing strategies.

### Final Sessions

The monitoring of the course of episodes of well-being allows the therapist to realize specific impairments in well-being dimensions according to Ryff's conceptual framework. An additional source of information may be provided by Ryff's PWB, an 84-item self-rating inventory (Ryff, 1989). In the original validation study of well-being therapy (Fava, Rafanelli, Cazzaro, et al., 1998), however, PWB results were not available to the therapist, who just worked from the patient's diary. Ryff's six dimensions of psychological well-being are progressively introduced to the patients, as long as the material that is recorded lends itself to it. For example, the therapist could explain that autonomy consists of possessing an internal locus of control, independence, and self-determination; or that personal growth consists of being open to new experiences and considering self as expanding over time, if the patient's attitudes show impairments in these specific areas. Errors in thinking and alternative interpretations are then discussed. At this point in time the patient is expected to be able to readily identify moments of well-being, be aware of interruptions to well-being feelings (cognitions), utilize cognitive behavioral techniques to address these interruptions, and pursue optimal experiences. Meeting the challenge that optimal experiences may entail is emphasized, because it is through this challenge that growth and improvement of self can take place.

## CONCEPTUAL FRAMEWORK OF WELL-BEING THERAPY

Cognitive restructuring in WBT follows Ryff's conceptual framework (Ryff & Singer, 1996). The goal of the therapist is to lead the patient from an impaired level to an optimal level in the six dimensions of psychological well-being. This means that patients are not simply encouraged to pursue the highest possible levels in psychological well-being, in all dimensions, but to obtain a balanced functioning. This optimal-balanced well-being could be different from patient to patient, according to factors such as personality traits, social roles, and cultural and social contexts (Ruini & Fava, 2012; Ruini et al., 2003)

The various dimensions of positive functioning can compensate each other (some being more interpersonally oriented, some more personal/cognitive), and the aim of WBT, such as other positive interventions, should be the promotion of an optimal-balanced functioning between these dimensions, in order to facilitate individual flourishing (Keyes, 2002). This means that sometimes patients should be encouraged to decrease their level of positive functioning in certain domains. Without this clinical framework, the risk is to lead patients to having too high levels of self-confidence, with unrealistic expectations that may become dysfunctional and/or stressful to individuals (see Table 28.1).

**Table 28.1**
Modifications of Well-Being Following WBT

| Ryff Psychological Well-Being Dimensions and Related Dimensions | Low Level | Balanced-Functional Level | High Level |
|---|---|---|---|
| Environmental mastery, Wisdom, Self-determination, Optimal experience, Passion | The person has or feels difficulties in managing everyday affairs; feels unable to change or improve surrounding context; is unaware of surrounding opportunities; lacks sense of control over external world. | The person has a sense of mastery and competence in managing the environment; controls external activities; makes effective use of surrounding opportunities; able to create or choose contexts suitable to personal needs and values. | The person is unable to savor positive emotions and hedonic pleasure. He or she is unable to relax and gets easily bored. |
| Personal growth, Meaning, Post-traumatic growth, Benefit finding, Intrinsic motivation | The person has a sense of personal stagnation; lacks sense of improvement or expansion over time; feels bored and uninterested with life; feels unable to develop new attitudes or behaviors. | The person has a feeling of continued development; sees self as growing and expanding; is open to new experiences; has sense of realizing own potential; sees improvement in self and behavior over time. | The person is unable to process negativity; forgets or does not give enough emphasis to past negative experiences; cultivates benign illusions that do not fit with reality; sets unrealistic standards for overcoming adversities |
| Purpose in life, Goals, Hope, Passion | The person lacks a sense of meaning in life; has few goals or aims, lacks sense of direction, does not see purpose in past life; has no outlooks or beliefs that give life meaning. | The person has goals in life and a sense of directedness; feels there is meaning to present and past life; holds beliefs that give life purpose; has aims and objectives for living, despite adversities. | The person has obsessional passions and is unable to admit failures. He or she manifests persistence and rigidity and is unable to change perspective and goals. Excessive hope is paralyzing and hampers facing negativity and failures. |
| Autonomy, Leadership, Locus of controls, Self-determination, Bravery | The person is overconcerned with the expectations and evaluation of others; relies on judgment of others to make important decisions; conforms to social pressures to think or act in certain ways. | The person is self-determining and independent; able to resist to social pressures; regulates behavior from within; evaluates self by personal standards. | The person is unable to get along with other people, to work in team, to learn from others. He or she spends time and energy for fighting for his or her opinions and rights. This person relies only on himself or herself for solving problems, and is unable to ask for advice or help. |

ENVIRONMENTAL MASTERY

This is the most frequent impairment that emerges, which is felt by patients as a lack of sense of control. This leads the patients to miss surrounding opportunities, with the possibility of subsequent regret over them. On the other hand, sometimes patients may require help because they are unable to enjoy and savor daily life, as they are too engaged in work or family activities. Their ability to plan and solve problems may lead others to constantly ask for their help, with the resulting feeling of being exploited and overwhelmed by requests. These extremely high levels of environmental mastery thus become a source of stress and allostatic load to the individual. Environmental mastery can be considered a key mediator or moderator of stressful life experiences (Fava, Guidi, Semprini, Tomba, & Sonino, 2010). A positive characterization of protective factors converges with efforts to portray the individual as a psychological activist, capable of proactive and effective problem solving, rather than passively buffeted by external forces (Ryff & Singer, 1998), but also capable of finding time for rest and relaxing in daily life.

PERSONAL GROWTH

Patients often tend to emphasize their distance from expected goals much more than the progress that has been made toward goal achievement. A basic impairment that emerges is the inability to identify the similarities between events and situations that were handled successfully in the past and those that are about to come (transfer of experiences). On the other hand, people with levels of personal growth that are too high tend to forget or do not give enough emphasis to past experiences because they are exclusively future oriented. Negative or traumatic experiences could particularly be underestimated, as a sort of extreme defense mechanism (denial), that is, "I just need to get over this situation and go on with my life" (Held, 2002; Norem & Chang, 2002). Dysfunctional high personal growth is similar to a cognitive benign illusion, or wishful thinking, which hinders the integration of past (negative) experiences and their related learning process.

PURPOSE IN LIFE

Patients may perceive a lack of sense of direction and may devalue their function in life. This particularly occurs when environmental mastery and sense of personal growth are impaired. On the other hand, many other conditions worthy of clinical attention may arise from too high levels of purpose in life. First of all, individuals with a strong determination in realizing one (or more) life goal(s) could dedicate themselves fully to their activity, thereby allowing them to persist, even in the face of obstacles, and to eventually reach excellence. This again could have a cost in terms of stress. Further, Vallerand et al. (2003) have proposed the concept of obsessive passion for describing an activity or goal that becomes a central feature of one's identity and serves to define the person. Individuals with an obsessive passion come to develop ego-invested self-structures (Hodgins & Knee, 2002) and, eventually, display a rigid persistence toward the activity, thereby leading to less than optimal functioning. Such persistence is rigid because it not only occurs in the absence of positive emotions and sometimes of positive feedbacks, but even in the face of important personal costs such as damaged relationships, failed commitments, and conflicts with other activities in the person's life (Vallerand et al., 2007). The individual engagement for a certain goal could thus become a form of psychological inflexibility (Kashdan & Rottenberg, 2010) that is more connected with psychopathology than well-being.

Some individuals, in fact, remains attached to their goals even when these seem to be unattainable, and keep believing that they would be happy pending the achievement of these goals. These mechanisms are associated with hopelessness (Hadley & MacLeod, 2010; MacLeod & Conway, 2007) and parasuicidal behaviors (Vincent, Boddana, & MacLeod, 2004). Further, this confirms the idea that hope, another future-oriented positive emotion, can become paralyzing and hampers facing and accepting negativity and failures (Bohart, 2002; Geraghty et al., 2010).

## Autonomy

It is a frequent clinical observation that patients may exhibit a pattern whereby a perceived lack of self-worth leads to unassertive behavior. For instance, patients may hide their opinions or preferences, go along with a situation that is not in their best interests, or consistently put their needs behind the needs of others. This pattern undermines environmental mastery and purpose in life and these, in turn, may affect autonomy, since these dimensions are highly correlated in clinical populations. Such attitudes may not be obvious to the patients, who hide their considerable need for social approval. A patient who tries to please everyone is likely to fail to achieve this goal and the unavoidable conflicts may result in chronic dissatisfaction and frustration. On the other hand, in Western countries particularly, individuals are culturally encouraged to be autonomous and independent. Certain individuals develop the idea that they should rely only on themselves for solving problems and difficulties, and are thus unable to ask for advice or help. Also in this case, an unbalanced high autonomy can become detrimental for social/interpersonal functioning (Seeman et al., 2002). Some patients complain they are not able to get along with other people, or work in teams, or maintain intimate relationships, because they are constantly fighting for their opinions and independence.

## Self-Acceptance

Patients may maintain unrealistically high standards and expectations, driven by perfectionistic attitudes (that reflect lack of self-acceptance) and/or endorsement of external instead of personal standards (that reflect lack of autonomy). As a result, any instance of well-being is neutralized by a chronic dissatisfaction with oneself. A person may set unrealistic standards for her performance. On the other hand, an inflated self-esteem may be a source of distress and clash with reality, as was found to be the case in cyclothymia and bipolar disorder (Fava, Rafanelli, Tomba, Guidi, & Grandi, 2011; Garland et al., 2010).

## Positive Relations With Others

Interpersonal relationships may be influenced by strongly held attitudes of perfectionism that the patient may be unaware of and that may be dysfunctional. Impairments in self-acceptance (with the resulting belief of being rejectable and unlovable, or others being inferior and unlovable) may also undermine positive relations with others. There is a large body of literature (Uchino, Cacioppo, & Kiecolt-Glaser, 1996) on the buffering effects of social integration, social network properties, and perceived support. On the other hand, little research has been done on the possible negative consequences of an exaggerated social functioning. Characteristics such as empathy, altruism, and generosity are usually considered universally positive. However, in clinical practice, patients often report a sense of guilt for not being able to help someone, or to forgive an offense. An individual with a strong pro-social attitude can sacrifice his or her needs and well-being for those of others, and this in the long run becomes detrimental and sometimes disappointing. This individual can also become overconcerned and overwhelmed by others' problems and distress and be at risk for burn-out syndrome. Finally, a generalized tendency to forgive others and be grateful toward benefactors could mask low self-esteem and low sense of personal worth.

## VALIDATION STUDIES

Well-being therapy has been employed in several clinical studies. Other studies are currently in progress.

### Residual Phase of Affective Disorders

The effectiveness of well-being therapy in the residual phase of affective disorders was first tested in a small controlled investigation (Fava, Rafanelli, Cazzaro, et al., 1998). Twenty patients with affective disorders who had been successfully treated by behavioral (anxiety disorders) or pharmacological (mood disorders) methods were randomly assigned to either a WBT or CBT of residual symptoms. Both well-being and cognitive behavioral therapies were associated with a significant reduction of residual symptoms, as measured by the Clinical Interview for Depression (CID; Guidi, Fava, Bech, & Paykel, 2011; Paykel, 1985), and in PWB well-being. However, when the residual symptoms of the two groups were compared after treatment, a significant advantage of well-being therapy over cognitive behavioral strategies was observed with the CID. Well-being therapy was associated also with a significant increase in PWB well-being, particularly in the Personal Growth scale.

The improvement in residual symptoms was explained on the basis of the balance between positive and negative affect (Fava, Rafanelli, Cazzaro, et al., 1998). If treatment of psychiatric symptoms induces improvement of well-being, and indeed subscales describing well-being are more sensitive to drug effects than subscales describing symptoms (Kellner, 1987; Rafanelli & Ruini, 2012), it is conceivable that changes in well-being may affect the balance of positive and negative affect. In this sense, the higher degree of symptomatic improvement that was observed with well-being therapy in this study is not surprising: In the acute phase of affective illness, removal of symptoms may yield the most substantial changes, but the reverse may be true in its residual phase.

### Prevention of Recurrent Depression

Well-being therapy was a specific and innovative part of a cognitive behavioral package that was applied to recurrent depression (Fava, Rafanelli, Grandi, Conti, & Belluardo, 1998). This package included also CBT of residual symptoms and lifestyle modification. Forty patients with recurrent major depression, who had been successfully treated with antidepressant drugs, were randomly assigned to either this cognitive behavioral package including well-being therapy or clinical management. In both groups, antidepressant drugs were tapered and discontinued. The group that received CBT-WBT had a significantly lower level of residual symptoms after drug discontinuation in comparison with the clinical management group. CBT-WBT also resulted in a significantly lower relapse rate (25%) at a 2-year follow-up than did clinical management (80%). At a 6-year follow-up (Fava et al., 2004) the relapse rate was 40% in the former group and 90% in the latter. Further, the group treated with CBT-WBT had a significantly lower number of recurrences when multiple relapses were taken into account (Fava et al., 2004).

These promising results have been recently replicated by a group of German investigators (Stangier et al., 2013) who applied WBT together with CBT and mindfulness as a maintenance therapy for patients with recurrent depression. One hundred and eighty patients with three or more previous major depressive episodes were randomly assigned to 16 sessions of either CBT or manualized psychoeducation over 8 months and then followed up for 12 months. Even though time to relapse or recurrence of major depression did not differ significantly between treatment conditions, a significant interaction was observed between treatment condition and number of previous episodes (five or more). Within the subsample of patients with five or more previous episodes, CBT was significantly superior to manualized psychoeducation.

## Loss of Clinical Effect During Drug Treatment

The return of depressive symptoms during maintenance antidepressant treatment is a common and vexing clinical phenomenon (Fava & Offidani, 2011). Ten patients with recurrent depression who relapsed while taking antidepressant drugs were randomly assigned to dose increase or to a sequential combination of cognitive-behavior and well-being therapy (Fava, Ruini, Rafanelli, & Grandi, 2002). Four out of five patients responded to a larger dose, but all relapsed again on that dose by 1 year follow-up. Four out of the 5 patients responded to psychotherapy and only one relapsed. The data suggest that application of well-being therapy may counteract loss of clinical effect during long-term antidepressant treatment.

## Treatment of Generalized Anxiety Disorder

Well-being therapy has been applied for the treatment of generalized anxiety disorder (GAD; Fava et al., 2005; Ruini & Fava, 2009). Twenty patients with *DSM-IV* GAD were randomly assigned to eight sessions of CBT or the sequential administration of four sessions of CBT followed by four other sessions of WBT. Both treatments were associated with a significant reduction of anxiety. However, significant advantages of the WBT-CBT sequential combination over CBT were observed, both in terms of symptom reduction and psychological well-being improvement. These preliminary results suggest the feasibility and clinical advantages of adding WBT to the treatment of GAD. A possible explanation for these findings is that self-monitoring of episodes of well-being may lead to a more comprehensive identification of automatic thoughts than that entailed by the customary monitoring of episodes of distress in cognitive therapy (Ruini & Fava, 2009).

## Cyclothymic Disorder

Well-being therapy was recently applied (Fava et al., 2011) in sequential combination with CBT for the treatment of cyclothymic disorder, which involves mild or moderate fluctuations of mood, thought, and behavior without meeting formal diagnostic criteria for either major depressive disorder or mania (Baldessarini, Vázquez, & Tondo, 2011). Sixty-two patients with *DSM-IV* cyclothymic disorder were randomly assigned to CBT-WBT ($n = 31$) or clinical management (CM; $n = 31$). An independent blind evaluator assessed the patients before treatment, after therapy, and at 1- and 2-year follow-ups. At post-treatment, significant differences were found in all outcome measures, with greater improvements after treatment in the CBT-WBT group compared to the CM group. Therapeutic gains were maintained at 1- and 2-year follow-ups. The results of this investigation suggest that a sequential combination of CBT and WBT, which addresses both polarities of mood swings and comorbid anxiety, was found to yield significant and persistent benefits in cyclothymic disorder.

## Posttraumatic Stress Disorder

The use of WBT for the treatment of traumatized patients has not been tested in controlled investigations yet. However, two cases were reported (Belaise, Fava, & Marks, 2005) in which patients improved with WBT, even though their central trauma was discussed only in the initial history-taking session. The findings from these two cases should of course be interpreted with caution (the patients may have remitted spontaneously), but they are of interest because they indicate an alternative route to overcoming trauma and developing resilience and warrant further investigation (Fava & Tomba, 2009).

## Child Well-Being Therapy

Well-being therapy has been recently modified to be applied with children and adolescents, both in clinical and educative settings. In clinical setting, it was applied to a child population of patients with mood, anxiety, and conduct disorders, with the aim of testing its effects in reducing symptoms and in improving new skills and competencies in children (Albieri, Visani, Offidani, Ottolini, & Ruini, 2009). Four children with different diagnoses according to *DSM-IV* criteria (one oppositional-defiant disorder; one attention-deficit/hyperactivity disorder [ADHD]; one major depressive disorder; and one GAD) underwent this new treatment protocol. None of these children were receiving pharmacological treatment, but two of them had a special tutor for helping them in school activities. WBT intervention consisted of eight 1-hour sessions, once a week, and was conducted using games and role-playing. It involved the use of a diary during each session with specific homework assignments. Positive and negative emotions were discussed with patients from the beginning of the protocol, but in the first four sessions more emphasis was upon negative emotions, whereas in the last three sessions the focus was upon the enhancement of psychological well-being according to a sequential strategy. Two additional sessions were addressed to parents' training. Child WBT was associated in all patients with a decrease in symptomatology (particularly anxiety and somatization) and an improvement in psychological well-being (particularly autonomy and interpersonal functioning). In two of our four patients, WBT was associated also with improvements in school performance.

The innovative ingredient of child WBT is the focus on promoting psychological well-being and optimal functioning in children (Caffo, Belaise, & Forresi, 2008). Further, WBT strategies were feasible for different sets of symptoms (anxious, depressive, behavioral). These results are promising, but further research with controlled design is needed.

In school settings, the protocol of WBT was modified for a group setting and for students aged 11 to 18. In three controlled investigations (Ruini, Belaise, Brombin, Caffo, & Fava, 2006; Ruini et al., 2009; Tomba et al., 2010) school WBT was compared to CBT school protocol or placebo and resulted to be associated with a decrease in anxiety and somatization, and an increase in psychological well-being. School-based WBT could have important clinical implications in view of the documented high prevalence of somatic symptoms in children and adolescents (Ginsburg, Riddle, & Davies, 2006; Muris, Vermeer, & Horselenberg, 2008). With young populations, promoting positive functioning and building individual strengths could also be more beneficial in the long term than simply addressing depressive or anxious symptoms.

## POTENTIAL MECHANISMS OF ACTION AND CASE STUDIES

Well-being therapy's effectiveness may be based on two distinct yet ostensibly related clinical phenomena. The first has to do with the fact that an increase in psychological well-being may have a protective effect in terms of vulnerability to chronic and acute life stresses (Ryff & Singer, 1998, 2000). The second has to do with the complex balance of positive and negative affects. There is extensive research—reviewed in detail elsewhere (Rafanelli et al., 2000; Ruini et al., 2003)—that indicates a certain degree of inverse correlation between positive and negative affects. As a result, changes in well-being may induce a decrease in distress, and vice versa. In the acute phase of illness, removal of symptoms may yield the most substantial changes, but the reverse may be true in its residual phase. An increase in psychological well-being may decrease residual symptoms that direct strategies (whether cognitive behavioral or pharmacological) would be unlikely to affect.

Further, it has been suggested that cognitive behavioral psychotherapy may work at the molecular level to alter stress-related gene expression and protein synthesis or influence mechanisms implicated in learning and memory acquisition in neuronal structures (Goddard & Charney, 1997). For instance, in one study sadness and happiness affected different brain regions: Sadness activated limbic and paralimbic structures, whereas happiness was associated with temporal parietal decreases in cortical activity (George et al., 1995). Such effects were not merely opposite activity in identical brain regions. The pathophysiological substrates of well-being therapy may thus be different compared to symptom-oriented cognitive behavioral strategies, to the same extent that well-being and distress are not merely opposites (Rafanelli et al., 2000).

By a psychotherapeutic viewpoint, the techniques that are used in WBT derived from traditional CBT packaging—which may also involve positive thinking (MacLeod & Moore, 2000)—may include cognitive restructuring (modification of automatic or irrational thoughts), scheduling of activities (mastery, pleasure, and graded task assignments), assertiveness training, and problem solving (Beck et al., 1979; Ellis & Becker, 1982; Pava, Fava, & Levenson, 1994; Weissman & Markowitz, 1994). What differentiates well-being therapy from standard cognitive therapies is the *focus* (which in well-being therapy is on instances of emotional well-being, whereas in cognitive therapy it is on psychological distress). A second important distinction is that in cognitive therapy the *goal* is abatement of distress through automatic thought control or contrast, whereas in well-being therapy the goal is promotion of optimal functioning, along Ryff's (1989) dimensions, as illustrated by the following two clinical cases. The first one provides an example of how obsessions and negative thoughts are triggered by initial instances of well-being. The second one provides an example of cognitive restructuring performed according to well-being concepts and how this yielded to behavioral modifications.

### Case Study A

Tom is a 23-year-old philosophy student with a severe obsessive illness, fulfilling the *DSM-IV* criteria, and refractory to drug treatment (fluvoxamine up to 200 mg per day and clomipramine 150 mg per day) and cognitive behavioral therapy (he dropped out of treatment after six sessions). He is treated by the second author with well-being therapy. After the first two sessions he is able to identify that obsessions start when

**Table 28.2**
Prevention of Obsessive Thoughts by Cognitive Restructuring

| Situation | Feeling of Well-Being | Interrupting Thoughts | Observer's Interpretation |
|---|---|---|---|
| Lunch with family | Maybe I am getting better and my life will change. | A terrible crisis is on its way. I feel it . . . | To acknowledge some progress does not mean asking for trouble. The problem is that you do not believe you can feel well. You are afraid of being well, because you do not think it is possible. |

well-being ensues. Adding an observer's interpretation column makes the patient realize that an effective contrast of pre-obsessive thoughts triggered by well-being may prevent obsessions and ruminations (Table 28.2). As long as therapy goes on (one session every other week), the intensity and perceived importance of obsessions decrease. After eight sessions, the patient no longer meets *DSM-IV* criteria for obsessive-compulsive disorder and feels much better. He is able to finish his studies. He no longer reports obsessive-compulsive disturbances at a 4-year follow-up.

CASE STUDY B

A middle-aged male patient with recurrent major depression (third episode) may learn how his lack of autonomy leads his workmates to consistently take advantage of him. This situation results in a work load that, because of its diverse nature, undermines his environmental mastery and constitutes a significant stress, also in terms of working hours. The situation is accepted in virtue of a low degree of self-acceptance: The patient claims that this is the way he is, but at the same time he is dissatisfied with himself and chronically irritable. When he learns to say no to his colleagues (assertive training) and consistently endorses this attitude, a significant degree of distress ensues, linked to perceived disapproval by others. However, as time goes by, his tolerance for self-disapproval gradually increases and in the last session he is able to make the following remark: "Now my workmates say that I am changed and have become a bastard. In a way I am sorry, since I always tried to be helpful and kind to people. But in another way I am happy, because this means that—for the first time in my life—I have been able to protect myself." The patient had no further relapse at a 6-year follow-up, while being medication free.

This clinical picture illustrates how an initial feeling of well-being (being helpful to others) that was identified in the diary was likely to lead to an overwhelming distress. Its appraisal and the resulting change in behavior initially led to more distress, but then yielded a lasting remission. The example clarifies that a similar behavioral change might have been achieved by distress-oriented psychotherapeutic strategies (indeed, the approach that was used to tackle this specific problem was no different). However, these changes would not have been supported by specific modifications of well-being dimensions.

## CONCLUSION

WBT has been originally developed as a strategy for promoting psychological well-being that was still impaired after standard pharmacological or psychotherapeutic treatments. It was based on the assumption that these impairments may vary from one illness to another, from patient to patient, and even from one episode to another of the same illness in the same patient. These impairments represent a vulnerability factor for adversities and relapses (Fava & Tomba, 2009; Ryff & Singer, 1996; Wood & Joseph, 2010). WBT, thus, can be considered a therapeutic positive intervention developed in clinical psychology, which takes into consideration both well-being and distress in predicting patients' clinical outcomes (Rafanelli & Ruini, 2012). This individualized approach characterizes the treatment protocol, which requires careful self-monitoring before any cognitive restructuring takes place. WBT develops on the basis of findings from self-observation in the diary. In some cases some psychological dimensions need reinforcement and growth. In other cases excessive or distorted levels of certain dimensions need to be adjusted because they may become dysfunctional and impede flourishing.

As a result, WBT may be used to address specific areas of concern in the course of treatment, in sequential combination with other approaches of pharmacological and psychological nature. The model is realistic, instead of idealistic, but more in line with the emerging evidence on the unsatisfactory degree of remission that one course of treatment entails (Fava et al., 2007). Unlike standard cognitive therapy, which is based on rigid specific assumptions (e.g., the cognitive triad in depression), WBT is characterized by flexibility (Kashdan & Rottenberg, 2010) and by an individualized approach for addressing psychological issues that other therapies have left unexplored, such as the promotion of eudaimonic well-being and optimal human functioning.

## SUMMARY POINTS

- Impairments in well-being are observable in patients successfully treated for anxiety and mood disorders.
- These impairments create conditions of vulnerabilities to stress and relapses.
- A specific psychotherapeutic strategy aimed at improving patients' well-being has been created and validated in a number of investigations (well-being therapy, or WBT).
- WBT has been found to be effective in promoting optimal functioning in patients with mood and anxiety disorders, such as depression, bipolar disorders, generalized anxiety disorder, and posttraumatic stress disorder.
- A modified version of WBT protocol, adapted for younger population, has been validated in school settings and with children with anxiety and behavioral disorders.
- WBT provides an individualized approach for addressing psychological issues that other therapies have left unexplored, such as the promotion of eudaimonic well-being and optimal human functioning.

## REFERENCES

Albieri, E. Visani, D., Offidani, E., Ottolini, F., & Ruini, C. (2009). Well-being therapy in children with emotional and behavioral disturbances: A pilot investigation. *Psychotherapy and Psychosomatics, 78*, 387–390.

Allport, G. W. (1961). *Pattern and growth in personality*. New York, NY: Holt, Reinhart & Winston.

Baldessarini, R. J., Vázquez, G., & Tondo, L. (2011). Treatment of cyclothymic disorder: Commentary. *Psychotherapy and Psychosomatics, 80*, 131–135.

Beck, A. T., Rush, A. J., Shaw, B. F., & Emery, G. (1979). *Cognitive therapy of depression*. New York, NY: Guilford Press.

Belaise, C., Fava, G. A. & Marks, I. M. (2005). Alternatives to debriefing and modifications to cognitive behavior therapy for posttraumatic stress disorder. *Psychotherapy and Psychosomatics, 74,* 212–217.

Biswas-Diener, R. (2010). A positive way of addressing negatives: Using strengths-based interventions in coaching and therapy. In G. W. Burns (Ed.), *Happiness, healing and enhancement: Your casebook collection for applying positive psychology in therapy* (pp. 291–302). Hoboken, NJ: Wiley.

Biswas-Diener, R., Kashdan, T. B., & Minhas, G. (2011). A dynamic approach to psychological strength development and intervention. *Journal of Positive Psychology, 6,* 106–118.

Bohart, A. C. (2002). Focusing on the positive, focusing on the negative: Implications for psychotherapy. *Journal of Clinical Psychology, 58,* 1037–1043.

Bolier, L., Haverman, M., Westerhof, G. J., Riper, H., Smit, F., & Bohlmeijer, E. (2013). Positive psychology interventions: a meta-analysis of randomized controlled studies. *BMC Public Health, 13,* 19–139.

Caffo, E., Belaise, C., & Forresi, B. (2008). Promoting resilience and psychological well-being in vulnerable life stages. *Psychotherapèy and Psychosomatics, 77,* 331–336.

Chida, Y., & Steptoe, A. (2008). Positive psychological well-being and mortality: A quantitative review of prospective observational studies. *Psychosomatic Medicine, 70,* 741–756.

Csikszentmihalyi, M. (1990). *Flow: The psychology of optimal experience.* New York, NY: Harper & Row.

Delle Fave, A. & Massimini F. (2003). Optimal experience in work and leisure among teachers and physicians. *Leisure Studies, 22,* 323–342.

Diener, E. (2000). Subjective well-being: The science of happiness, and a proposal for a national index. *American Psychologist, 55,* 34–43.

Diener, E., Suh, E. M., Lucas, R. E., & Smith, H. L. (1999). Subjective well-being: Three decades of progress. *Psychological Bulletin, 125,* 276–302.

Ellis, A., & Becker, I. (1982). *A guide to personal happiness.* Hollywood, CA: Melvin Powers Wilshire Book Company.

Emmelkamp, P. M. G. (1974). Self-observation versus flooding in the treatment of agoraphobia. *Behaviour Research and Therapy, 12,* 229–237.

Fava, G. A. (1996). The concept of recovery in affective disorders. *Psychotherapy and Psychosomatics, 65,* 2–13.

Fava, G. A. (1999a). Subclinical symptoms in mood disorders: Pathophysiological and therapeutic implications. *Psychological Medicine, 29,* 47–61.

Fava, G. A. (1999b). Well-being therapy. *Psychotherapy and Psychosomatics, 68,* 171–178.

Fava, G. A. (2000). Cognitive behavioral therapy. In M. Fink (Ed.), *Encyclopedia of stress* (pp. 484–497). San Diego, CA: Academic Press.

Fava, G. A., Guidi, J., Semprini, F., Tomba, E., & Sonino, N. (2010). Clinical assessment of allostatic load and clinimetric criteria. *Psychotherapy and Psychosomatics, 79,* 280–284.

Fava, G. A., Mangelli, L., & Ruini, C. (2001). Assessment of psychological distress in the setting of medical disease. *Psychotherapy and Psychosomatics, 70,* 171–179.

Fava, G. A., & Offidani, E. (2011). The mechanisms of tolerance in antidepressant action. *Progress in Neuro-psychopharmacology & Biological Psychiatry, 35,* 1593–1602.

Fava, G. A., Rafanelli, C., Cazzaro, M., Conti S. & Grandi, S. (1998). Well-being therapy. A novel psychotherapeutic approach for residual symptoms of affective disorders. *Psychological Medicine, 28,* 475–480.

Fava, G. A., Rafanelli, C., Grandi, S., Conti, S., & Belluardo, P. (1998). Prevention of recurrent depression with cognitive behavioral therapy. *Archives of General Psychiatry, 55,* 816–820.

Fava, G. A., Rafanelli, C., Ottolini, F., Ruini, C., Cazzaro, M., & Grandi, S. (2001). Psychological well-being and residual symptoms in remitted patients with panic disorder and agoraphobia. *Journal of Affective Disorders, 31,* 899–905.

Fava, G. A., Rafanelli, C., Tomba, E., Guidi, J., & Grandi, S. (2011). The sequential combination of cognitive behavioral treatment and well-being therapy in cyclothymic disorder. *Psychotherapy and Psychosomatics, 80,* 136–143.

Fava, G. A., & Ruini, C. (2003). Development and characteristics of a well-being enhancing psychotherapeutic strategy: Well-being therapy. *Journal of Behavior Therapy and Experimental Psychiatry, 34,* 45–63.

Fava, G. A, Ruini, C., Rafanelli, C., Finos, L., Conti, S., & Grandi, S. (2004). Six year outcome of cognitive behavior therapy for prevention of recurrent depression. *American Journal of Psychiatry, 161,* 1872–1876.

Fava, G. A., Ruini, C., Rafanelli, C., Finos, L., Salmaso, L., Mangelli, L., & Sirigatti, S. (2005). Well-being therapy of generalized anxiety disorder. *Psychotherapy and Psychosomatics, 74,* 26–30.

Fava, G. A., Ruini, C., Rafanelli, C., & Grandi, S. (2002). Cognitive behavior approach to loss of clinical effect during long-term antidepressant treatment. *American Journal of Psychiatry, 159,* 2094–2095.

Fava, G. A., & Sonino, N. (2010). Psychosomatic medicine. *International Journal of Clinical Practice, 64,* 1155–1161.

Fava, G. A., & Tomba, E. (2009). Increasing psychological well-being and resilience by psychotherapeutic methods. *Journal of Personality, 77,* 1903–1934.

Fava, G. A., Tomba, E., & Grandi, S. (2007). The road to recovery from depression. *Psychotherapy and Psychosomatics, 76,* 260–265.

Fordyce, M. W. (1983). A program to increase happiness. *Journal of Counseling Psychology, 30,* 483–498.

Fredrickson, B. L. (2002). Positive emotions. In C. R. Snyder & S. J. Lopez (Eds.), *Handbook of positive psychology* (pp. 120–134). New York, NY: Oxford University Press.

Fredrickson, B. L., & Joiner, T. (2002). Positive emotions trigger upward spirals toward emotional well-being. *Psychological Science, 13,* 172–175.

Fredrickson, B. L., & Losada, M. F. (2005). Positive affect and the complex dynamics of human flourishing. *American Psychologist, 60,* 678–686.

Frisch, M. B. (2006). *Quality of life therapy: Applying a life satisfaction approach to positive psychology and cognitive therapy.* Hoboken, NJ: Wiley.

Garamoni, G. L., Reynolds, C. F., Thase, M. E., Frank, E., Berman, S-R., & Fasiczska A. L. (1991). The balance of positive and negative affects in major depression. *Psychiatry Research, 39,* 99–108.

Garland, E. L., Fredrickson, B., Kring, A. M., Johnson, D., Meyer, P. S., & Penn, D. L. (2010). Upward spirals of positive emotions counter downspirals of negativity: Insights from the broaden-and-built theory and affective neurosciense on the treatment of emotion dysfunction and deficits in psychopathology. *Clinical Psychology Review, 30,* 849–864.

George, M. S., Ketter, T. A., Parekh, P. I., Horowitz, B., Herscovitch, P., & Post, R. M. (1995). Brain activity during transient sadness and happiness in healthy women. *American Journal of Psychiatry, 152,* 341–351.

Geraghty, A. W. A., Wood, A. M., & Hyland, M. E. (2010). Dissociating the facets of hope: Agency and pathways predict dropout from unguided self-help therapy in opposite directions. *Journal of Research in Personality, 44,* 155–158.

Gillham, J. E., & Seligman, M. E. P. (1999). Footstep on the road to a positive psychology. *Behaviour Research and Therapy, 37,* 5163–5173.

Ginsburg, G. S., Riddle, M. A., & Davies, M. (2006). Somatic symptoms in children and adolescents with anxiety disorders. *Journal of the American Academy of Child & Adolescent Psychiatry, 45,* 1179–1187.

Gladis, M. M., Gosh, E. A., Dishuk, N. M., & Crits-Cristoph, P. (1999). Quality of life: Expanding the scope of clinical significance. *Journal of Consulting and Clinical Psychology, 67,* 320–331.

Goddard, A. W., & Charney, D. S. (1997). Toward an integrated neurobiology of panic disorder. *Journal of Clinical Psychiatry, 58*(Suppl. 2), 4–11.

Govindji, R., & Linley, P. A. (2007). Strengths use, self-concordance and well-being: Implications for strengths coaching and coaching psychologists. *International Coaching Psychology Review, 2*, 143–153.

Grant, A. M., & Schwartz, B. (2011). Too much of a good thing: The challenge and opportunity of the inverted U. *Perspectives on Psychological Science, 6*, 61–76.

Guidi, J., Fava, G. A., Bech, P., & Paykel, E. S. (2011). The Clinical Interview for Depression. *Psychotherapy and Psychosomatics, 80*, 10–27.

Hadley, S., & MacLeod, A. K. (2010). Conditional goal-setting, personal goals and hopelessness about the future. *Cognition and Emotion, 24*, 1191–1198.

Held, B. S. (2002). The tyranny of positive attitude in America: Observation and speculation. *Journal of Clinical Psychology, 58*, 965–992.

Hodgins, H. S., & Knee, R. (2002). The integrating self and conscious experience. In E. L. Deci & R. M. Ryan (Eds.), *Handbook of self-determination research* (pp. 87–100). Rochester, NY: University of Rochester Press.

Horowitz, M. J., & Kaltreider, N. B. (1979). Brief therapy of the stress response syndrome. *Psychiatric Clinics of North America, 2*, 365–377.

Howell, R. T., Kern M. L., & Lyubomirsky, S. (2007). Health benefits: Meta-analytically determining the impact of well-being on objective health outcomes. *Health Psychological Review, 1*, 83–136.

Jahoda, M. (1958). *Current concept of positive mental health.* New York, NY: Basic Books.

Jung, C. G. (1933). *Modern man in search of a soul.* New York, NY: Harcourt, Brace and World.

Kashdan, T. B., & Rottenberg, J. (2010). Psychological flexibility as a fundamental aspect of health. *Clinical Psychology Review, 30*, 865–878.

Kellner, R. (1987). A symptom questionnaire. *Journal of Clinical Psychiatry, 48*, 269–274.

Keyes, C. L. (2002). The mental health continuum: From languishing to flourishing in life. *Journal of Health and Social Behavior, 43*, 207–222.

Keyes, C. L. M., Shmotkin, D., & Ryff, C. D. (2002). Optimizing well-being: The empirical encounter of two traditions. *Journal of Personality and Social Psychology, 82*, 1007–1022.

Lamb, S. (2005). Forgiveness therapy: The context and conflict. *Journal of Theoretical and Philosophical Psychology, 25*, 61–80.

Larsen, R. J., & Prizmic, Z. (2008). Regulation of emotional well-being: Overcoming the hedonic treadmill. In M. Eid & R. J. Larsen (Eds.), *The science of subjective well-being* (pp. 259–289). New York, NY: Guilford Press.

Linden, M., Baumann, K., Lieberei, B., Lorenz, C., & Rotter, M. (2011). Treatment of posttraumatic embitterment disorder with cognitive behaviour therapy based on wisdom psychology and hedonia strategies. *Psychotherapy and Psychosomatics, 80*, 199–205.

Linley, P. A., & Burns, G. W. (2010). Strengthspotting: Finding and developing client resources in the management of intense anger. In G. W. Burns (Ed.), *Happiness, healing and enhancement: Your casebook collection for applying positive psychology in therapy* (pp. 3–14). Hoboken, NJ: Wiley.

MacLeod, A. K., & Conway, C. (2007). Well-being and the anticipation of future positive experiences: The role of income, social networks and planning ability. *Cognition and Emotion, 18*, 357–374.

MacLeod, A. K., & Moore, R. (2000). Positive thinking revisited: Positive cognitions, well-being and mental health. *Clinical Psychology and Psychotherapy, 7*, 1–10.

Magayar-Moe, J. (2009). *Therapist's guide to positive psychological interventions.* New York, NY: Academic Press.

Maslow, A. H. (1968). *Toward a psychology of being* (2nd ed.). New York, NY: Van Nostrand.

Meehl, P. E. (1975). Hedonic capacity: Some conjectures. *Bulletin of Menninger Clinic, 39,* 295–307.

Muris, P., Vermeer, E., & Horselenberg, R. (2008). Cognitive development and the interpretation of anxiety-related physical symptoms in 4–13-year-old non-clinical children. *Journal of Behavior Therapy and Experimental Psychiatry 39,* 73–86.

Neugarten, B. L., Havighurst, R., & Tobin, S. (1961). The measurement of life satisfaction. *Journal of Gerontology, 16,* 134–143.

Norem, J. K., & Chang, E. C. (2002). The positive psychology of negative thinking. *Journal of Clinical Psychology, 58,* 993–1001.

Padesky, C. A. (1994). Schema change processes in cognitive therapy. *Clinical Psychology and Psychotherapy, 1,* 267–278.

Park, N., Peterson, C., & Seligman, M. E. P. (2004). Strengths of character and well-being. *Journal of Social and Clinical Psychology, 23,* 603–619.

Parloff, M. B., Kelman, H. C., & Frank, J. D. (1954). Comfort, effectiveness, and self-awareness as criteria of improvement in psychotherapy. *American Journal of Psychiatry, 11,* 343–351.

Pava, J. A., Fava, M., & Levenson, J. A. (1994). Integrating cognitive therapy and pharmacotherapy in the treatment and prophylaxis of depression. *Psychotherapy and Psychosomatics, 61,* 211–219.

Paykel, E. S. (1985). The Clinical Interview for Depression. *Journal of Affective Disorders, 9,* 85–96.

Rafanelli, C., Conti, S., Mangelli, L., Ruini, C., Ottolini, F., Fabbri, S., . . . Fava, G. A. (2002). Psychological well-being and residual symptoms in patients with affective disorders. II. *Rivista di Psichiatria, 37,* 179–183.

Rafanelli, C., Park, S. K., Ruini, C., Ottolini, F., Cazzaro, M., & Fava, G. A. (2000). Rating well-being and distress. *Stress Medicine, 16,* 55–61.

Rafanelli, C., & Ruini, C. (2012). The assessment of psychological well-being in psychosomatic medicine. *Advances in Psychosomatic Medicine, 32,* 182–202.

Ramana, R., Paykel, E. S., Cooper, Z., Hayburst, H., Saxty, M., & Surtees, P. G. (1995). Remission and relapse in major depression. *Psychological Medicine, 25,* 1161–1170.

Rogers, C. R. (1961). *On becoming a person.* Boston, MA: Houghton Mifflin.

Ruini, C., Belaise, C., Brombin, C., Caffo, E. & Fava, G. A. (2006). Well-being therapy in school settings: a pilot study. *Psychotherapy and Psychosomatics 75,* 331–336.

Ruini, C., & Fava, G. A. (2009). Well-being therapy for generalized anxiety disorder. *Journal of Clinical Psychology, 65,* 510–519.

Ruini, C., & Fava, G. A. (2012). Role of well-being therapy in achieving a balanced and individualized path to optimal functioning. *Clinical Psychology and Psychotherapy, 19,* 291–304.

Ruini, C., Ottolini, F., Rafanelli, C., Tossani, E., Ryff, C. D., & Fava, G. A. (2003). The relationship of psychological well-being to distress and personality. *Psychotherapy and Psychosomatics, 72,* 268–275.

Ruini, C., Ottolini, F., Tomba, E., Belaise, C., Albieri, E., Visani, D., . . . Fava G. A. (2009). School intervention for promoting psychological well-being in adolescence. *Journal of Behavior Therapy and Experimental Psychiatry, 40,* 522–532.

Ruini, C., Rafanelli, C., Conti, S., Ottolini, F., Fabbri, S., Tossani, E., . . . Fava, G. A. (2002). Psychological well-being and residual symptoms in patients with affective disorders. I. *Rivista di Psichiatria, 37,* 171–178.

Ryan, R. M., & Deci, E. L. (2001). On happiness and human potential: A review of research on hedonic and eudaimonic well-being. *Annual Review of Psychology, 52,* 141–166.

Ryff, C. D. (1989). Happiness is everything, or is it? Explorations on the meaning of psychological well-being. *Journal of Personality and Social Psychology, 6,* 1069–1081.

Ryff, C. D., & Keyes, C. L. M. (1995). The structure of psychological well-being revisited. *Journal of Personality and Social Psychology, 69,* 719–727.

Ryff, C. D., & Singer, B. H. (1996). Psychological well-being: Meaning, measurement, and implications for psychotherapy research. *Psychotherapy and Psychosomatics, 65*, 14–23.

Ryff, C. D., & Singer, B. H. (1998). The contours of positive human health. *Psychological Inquiry, 9*, 1–28.

Ryff, C. D., & Singer, B. H. (2000). Biopsychosocial challenges of the new millennium. *Psychotherapy and Psychosomatics, 69*, 170–177.

Ryff, C. D., & Singer, B. H. (2008). Know thyself and become what you are: A eudaimonic approach to psychological well-being. *Journal of Happiness Studies, 9*, 13–39.

Schwartz, R. M. (1997). Consider the simple screw: Cognitive science, quality improvement, and psychotherapy. *Journal of Consulting and Clinical Psychology, 65*, 970–983.

Schwartz, R. M., Reynolds, C. F., Thase, M. E., Frank, E., Fasiczka, A. L., & Haaga, D. (2002). Optimal and normal affect balance in psychotherapy of major depression: Evaluation of the balanced states of mind model. *Behavioral and Cognitive Psychotherapy, 30*, 439–450.

Seeman, T. E., Singer, B. H., Ryff, C. D., Dienberg Love, G., & Levy-Storms L. (2002). Social relationships, gender, and allostatic load across two age cohorts. *Psychosomatic Medicine, 64*, 395–406.

Seligman, M. E. P., Rashid, T., & Parks, A. C. (2006). Positive psychotherapy. *American Psychologist, 61*, 774–788.

Seligman, M. E. P., Steen, T. A., Park, N., & Peterson, C. (2005). Positive psychology progress: Empirical validation of interventions. *American Psychologist, 60*, 410–421.

Sin, N. L., & Lyubomirsky, S. (2009). Enhancing well-being and alleviating depressive symptoms with positive psychology interventions: A practice-friendly meta-analysis. *Journal of Clinical Psychology, 65*, 467–487.

Snyder, C. R., Ilardi, S., Michael, S. T., Yamhure, L., & Sympson, S. (2000). The role of hope in cognitive behavior therapies. *Cognitive Therapy and Research, 24*, 747–762.

Stangier, U., Hilling, C., Heidenreich, T., Risch, A. K., Barocka, A., Schlösser, R., . . . Hautzinger, M. (2013). Maintenance cognitive-behavioral therapy and manualized psychoeducation in the treatment of recurrent depression: A multicenter prospective randomized controlled trial. *American Journal of Psychiatry, 1*, 170, 624–632.

Thunedborg, K., Black, C. H., & Bech, P. (1995). Beyond the Hamilton depression scores in long-term treatment of manic-melancholic patients: Prediction of recurrence of depression by quality of life measurements. *Psychotherapy and Psychosomatics, 64*, 131–140.

Tomba, E., Belaise, C., Ottolini, F., Ruini, C., Bravi, A., Albieri, E., . . . Fava, G. A. (2010). Differential effects of well-being promoting and anxiety management strategies in a non-clinical school setting. *Journal of Anxiety Disorders, 24*, 326–333.

Uchino, B. N., Cacioppo, J. T., & Kiecolt-Glaser, J. K. (1996). The relationship between social support and physiological processes. *Psychological Bulletin, 119*, 488–531.

Vallerand, R. J., Blanchard, C. M., Mageau, G. A., Koestner, R., Ratelle, C., Leonard, M., . . . Marsolais, J. (2003). Les passions de l'ame: On obsessive and harmonious passion. *Journal of Personality and Social Psychology, 85*, 756–767.

Vallerand, R. J., Salvy, S. J., Mageau, G. A., Elliot, A. J., Denis, P. L., Grouzet, F. M. E., & Blanchard, C. (2007). On the role of passion in performance. *Journal of Personality, 75*, 505–534.

Vincent, P. J., Boddana, P., & MacLeod, A. K. (2004). Positive life goals and plans in parasuicide. *Clinical Psychology and Psychotherapy, 11*, 90–99.

Weissman, M. M., & Markowitz, J. C. (1994). Interpersonal psychotherapy. *Archives of General Psychiatry; 51*, 599–606.

Wood, A. M., & Joseph, S. (2010). The absence of positive psychological (eudemonic) well-being as a risk factor for depression: A ten year cohort study. *Journal of Affective Disorders, 122*, 213–217.

Wood, A. M., Maltby, J., Gillett, R., Linley, P. A., & Joseph, S. (2008). The role of gratitude in the development of social support, stress, and depression: Two longitudinal studies. *Journal of Research in Personality, 42*, 854–871.

CHAPTER 29

# Strategies for Accentuating Hope

JEANA L. MAGYAR-MOE and SHANE J. LOPEZ

P
EOPLE SOMEHOW SUMMON enough mental energy to set the goal of seeking a therapist or other healer. Likewise, they identify pathways to the desired helper and
muster the requisite energy to build a working alliance with their newfound
agent of change. In essence, self-referred clients already have demonstrated hope
in their pursuit of therapeutic support by the time they reach their therapists.
In turn, therapists can help clients to name and to nurture the hope that they
already possess.

In this chapter, we identify formal strategies for accentuating the hope that people possess. We discuss the effectiveness data, where available, associated with these
strategies. Given that most therapists are eclectic, we also describe informal strategies that could be implemented within any therapeutic framework; moreover, we
address common strategies that can be assigned to clients as homework. We begin
by outlining hope theory and discuss hope's role as an active ingredient in psychological change.

## HOPE THEORY

According to hope theory, hope reflects individuals' perceptions of their capacities
to (a) clearly conceptualize goals; (b) develop the specific strategies to reach those
goals (pathways thinking); and (c) initiate and sustain the motivation for using those
strategies (agency thinking).

The pathways and agency components are both necessary, but neither by itself is
sufficient to sustain successful goal pursuits. As such, pathways and agency thoughts
are additive, reciprocal, and positively related, but they are not synonymous (Snyder,
1989, 1994, 2000a, 2000b, 2002; Snyder et al., 1991). According to hope theory, a goal
can be anything that an individual desires to experience, create, get, do, or become. As
such, a goal may be a significant, lifelong pursuit (e.g., developing a comprehensive
theory of human motivation), or it may be mundane and brief (e.g., getting a ride to
school). Goals also may vary in terms of having perceived probabilities of attainment
that vary from very low to very high. On this point, high-hope individuals prefer
stretch goals that are slightly more difficult than previously attained goals.

Whereas other positive psychology concepts such as goal theory (Covington, 2000; see also Dweck, 1999), optimism (Scheier & Carver, 1985), self-efficacy (Bandura, 1982), and problem solving (Heppner & Petersen, 1982) give differentially weighted emphases to the goal itself or to the future-oriented agency- or pathways-related processes, hope theory equally emphasizes all of these goal-pursuit components (Snyder, 1994). For detailed comparisons of the similarities and differences between hope theory and other theories (e.g., achievement motivation, flow, goal setting, mindfulness, optimism, optimistic explanatory style, problem solving, resiliency, self-efficacy, self-esteem, Type A behavior pattern), see Magaletta and Oliver (1999), Peterson (2000), Snyder (1994, 2002), and Snyder, Rand, and Sigmon (2002).

## HOPE AS AN AGENT OF CHANGE

The power of hope as a motivating force has been discussed throughout modern time and, for the past century, has been examined by medical and psychological scholars. Over the past 40 years, Jerome Frank's (1968, 1975) work has conceptualized hope as a process that is common to all psychotherapy approaches. Karl Menninger (1959), in his academic lecture on hope when he was president of the American Psychiatric Association, issued a call for more rigorous examination of the role of hope in change. As a response to Menninger's request, Snyder's operationalization of this robust construct has facilitated, over the past three decades, the scholarly inquiry into hope as a change agent. Indeed, whatever the system of psychotherapy, beneficial change may be attributable, in part, to hope. According to Snyder, Ilardi, Cheavens, et al. (2000), change occurs because people learn more effective agentic and pathways goal-directed thinking. In particular, the agency component is reflected in the placebo effect (i.e., the natural mental energies for change that clients bring to psychotherapy). The particular psychotherapy approaches that are used to provide the client with a route or process for moving forward to attain positive therapeutic goals reflect the pathways component. Furthermore, Snyder and his colleagues (Snyder, Ilardi, Cheavens, et al., 2000; Snyder, Ilardi, Michael, & Cheavens, 2000) have offered detailed hypotheses about how hope, and agency and pathways in particular, might help to explain the role of common and specific treatment factors in psychotherapy. Before any specific treatment strategies are applied, the primary source of change is the client's expectancy that therapy will make a positive difference in his or her life. These initial improvements are analogous to increases in the agency component of hope—determination that an individual can make improvements in his or her life. Therefore, it is believed that increases in agency, as opposed to increases in pathways thinking, are related to positive change in the first stages of therapy. The positive changes that occur in these early stages of therapy have been described elsewhere as "remoralization" (Howard, Krause, Saunders, & Koptka, 1997), and they are characterized by enhanced subjective well-being. More specifically, clients begin to experience relief from distress and have renewed hope that their situation can and will improve. Increased well-being even may take place before the client steps into the therapy room; that is, an initial phone call to set up the appointment may engender feelings of relief from distress.

From this perspective on hope, it is conceivable that hope is malleable and that it can be the spark for and pathway to change. Likewise, beneficial change may lead to more hope for creating a good life. Because most people have the capacity to hope (they possess the basic components of the cognitive skills needed to generate a hopeful line of thought), accentuating this change agent requires naming and nurturing this personal strength in the context of supportive helping relationships.

We propose that hope finding, bonding, enhancing, and reminding are the essential strategies for accentuating hope and taken together form the foundation of hope therapy. Therapists who practice hope therapy help clients to conceptualize clearer goals, to learn how to produce multiple pathways to reach goals, and to generate the mental energy needed to sustain goal pursuits in order to positively change client self-perceptions regarding their abilities to engage in goal-directed and agentic thinking (Lopez, Floyd, Ulven, & Snyder, 2000). Hope therapy is designed to be a brief, semistructured form of therapy in which the primary focus is upon current goals with emphasis upon exploration of possibilities and past successes rather than on problems or past failures (Lopez, Floyd, et al., 2000).

During hope therapy, hope finding is enacted in order to strengthen clients' expectations that the therapists can and will help them. Bolstering clients' expectations for assistance simultaneously may instill hope for change and enhance the therapeutic bond between client and therapist. Hope bonding entails the formation of a sound hopeful therapeutic alliance; it grounds the client in a hopeful therapeutic context. Therapists possessing high levels of hope may be most facile at meeting the important therapeutic goal of establishing an emotionally charged connection. They also may be best at collaborating on mutually agreed-on goals by engaging in productive tasks. Hope-enhancing strategies typically involve enlisting clients in tasks that are designed to

- Conceptualize reasonable goals more clearly
- Produce numerous pathways to attainment
- Summon the energy to maintain pursuit
- Reframe obstacles as challenges to be overcome

Hope reminding is the promotion of effortful daily use of hopeful cognitions. Goal thoughts and barrier thoughts are identified as cognitive cues that stimulate the client to incorporate therapeutic techniques that have previously enhanced hopeful thought.

In the following sections, we identify formal and informal strategies for accentuating hope via finding, bonding, enhancing, and reminding.

## HOPE FINDING

Hope can exist as a relatively stable personality disposition (i.e., a trait) or as a more temporary frame of mind (i.e., a state). Similarly, hopeful thought can occur at various levels of abstraction. For example, individuals can be hopeful about achieving

- Goals in general (i.e., a trait)
- Goals in a certain life arena (i.e., domain specific)
- One goal in particular (i.e., goal specific)

Finding the hope that each person possesses is essential to building personal resources in preparation for the therapeutic change process. Naming and measuring the type of hope most relevant to a client's goal pursuit can be achieved via formal and informal means.

### FORMAL HOPE-FINDING STRATEGIES

Brief, valid measures of hope can be used during initial phases of therapy to assess an individual's level of hope. Snyder et al. (1997) developed the Children's Hope

Scale (CHS) as a trait hope measure for children ages 7 through 14 years (see Exhibit 29.1). The CHS is composed of three agency and three pathways items, and it has demonstrated satisfactory psychometric properties: (a) internal consistency reliabilities (overall alphas from 0.72 to 0.86); (b) test–retest reliabilities of 0.71 to 0.73 over 1 month; and (c) convergent and discriminant validities. Furthermore, this scale has been used with physically and psychologically healthy children from public schools, boys diagnosed with attention-deficit/hyperactivity disorder, children with various medical problems, children under treatment for cancer or asthma, child burn victims, adolescents with sickle-cell disease, and early adolescents exposed to violence (Snyder et al., 1997).

To measure the trait aspect of hope in adolescents and adults, ages 15 and higher, Snyder et al. (1991) developed the Adult Dispositional Hope Scale (see Exhibit 29.2). This scale consists of four items measuring agency, four items measuring pathways, and four distracter items. Having been used with a wide range of samples, the Adult Dispositional Hope Scale has exhibited acceptable reliability and validity: (a) internal consistency reliabilities (overall alphas from 0.74 to 0.88, agency alphas of 0.70 to 0.84, and pathways alphas of 0.63 to 0.86); (b) test–retest reliabilities ranging from 0.85 for 3 weeks to 0.82 for 10 weeks; and (c) concurrent and discriminant validity (Snyder et al., 1991). (Lopez, Ciarlelli, Coffman, Stone, and Wyatt [2000] provide an in-depth coverage of these formal measures, including the development and validation of additional self-report, observational, and narrative measures of hope. In addition, a number of translations of Snyder's hope scales have been developed and validated for use with those who speak Slovak [Halama, 1999], Japanese [Kato & Snyder, 2005], Arabic [Abdel-Khalek & Snyder, 2007], French (Gana, Daigre, & Ledrich, 2013), and Portuguese [Marques, Pais-Ribeiro, & Lopez, 2009]).

## EXHIBIT 29.1

### Children's Hope Scale

Directions: Read each item carefully. Using the scale shown below, please select the number that best describes YOU and put that number in the blank provided.

| 1 | 2 | 3 | 4 | 5 | 6 |
|---|---|---|---|---|---|
| None of the time | A little of the time | Some of the time | A lot of the time | Most of the time | All of the time |

_____ 1. I think I am doing pretty well.

_____ 2. I can think of many ways to get the things in life that are most important to me.

_____ 3. I am doing just as well as other kids my age.

_____ 4. When I have a problem, I can come up with lots of ways to solve it.

_____ 5. I think the things I have done in the past will help me in the future.

_____ 6. Even when others want to quit, I know that I can find ways to solve the problem.

*Source*: From "The Development and Validation of the Children's Hope Scale," by C. R. Snyder, B. Hoza, W. E. Pelham, M. Rapoff, L. Ware, M. Danovsky, . . . K. J. Stahl, 1997, *Journal of Pediatric Psychology*, 22, pp. 399–421. Reprinted with permission.

## EXHIBIT 29.2

### Adult Dispositional Hope Scale

Directions: Read each item carefully. Using the scale shown below, please select the number that best describes YOU and put that number in the blank provided.

1 = Definitely False    2 = Mostly False    3 = Mostly True    4 = Definitely True

_____ 1. I can think of many ways to get out of a jam.

_____ 2. I energetically pursue my goals.

_____ 3. I feel tired most of the time.

_____ 4. There are lots of ways around any problem.

_____ 5. I am easily downed in an argument.

_____ 6. I can think of many ways to get the things in life that are most important to me.

_____ 7. I worry about my health.

_____ 8. Even when others get discouraged, I know I can find a way to solve the problem.

_____ 9. My past experiences have prepared me well for my future.

_____ 10. I've been pretty successful in life.

_____ 11. I usually find myself worrying about something.

_____ 12. I meet the goals that I set for myself.

*Notes.* When we administer this scale, we call it the Goals Scale rather than the Hope Scale because on some initial occasions when giving the scale, people became interested in the fact that hope could be measured and wanted to discuss this issue rather than take the scale. No such problems have been encountered with the rather mundane Goals Scale. Items 3, 5, 7, and 11 are distracters and are not used for scoring. The pathways subscale score is the sum of items 1, 4, 6, and 8; the agency subscale is the sum of items 2, 9, 10, and 12. Hope is the sum of the four pathways and four agency items. In our original studies, we used a 4-point response continuum, but to encourage more diversity in scores in our more recent studies, we have used the 8-point scale:

| | | | |
|---|---|---|---|
| 1 = Definitely False | 2 = Mostly False | 3 = Somewhat False | 4 = Slightly False |
| 5 = Slightly True | 6 = Somewhat True | 7 = Mostly True | 8 = Definitely True |

Scores using the 4-point continuum can range from a low of 8 to a high of 32. For the 8-point continuum, scores can range from a low of 8 to a high of 64.

*Source:* From "The Will and the Ways: Development and Validation of an Individual Differences Measure of Hope," by C. R. Snyder, C. Harris, J. R. Anderson, S. A. Holleran, L. M. Irving, S. T. Sigmon, . . . P. Harney, 1991, *Journal of Personality and Social Psychology, 60*, pp. 570–585. The scale can be used for research or clinical purposes without contacting the author. Reprinted with permission of the American Psychological Association and the senior author of the scale.

INFORMAL HOPE-FINDING STRATEGIES

Narrative approaches often have been used to illustrate the theory of hope to children, adolescents, and adults in individual therapy and psychoeducational programs. By telling stories of fictitious and real characters, therapists engage clients in thinking about goals, agency, and pathways. Furthermore, with time, clients tell stories about their goal pursuits, thereby making hope more personally relevant. Hope-related themes are captured when clinicians explore the following 14 aspects of clients' stories:

1. How did the client generate goals?
2. What was the motivation?
3. How attainable or realistic were the goals?
4. How were the goals perceived?
5. What was the client's mood/attitude during the process?
6. How was movement toward goals initiated?
7. How was movement maintained?
8. What were the biggest barriers to reaching the goals?
9. What emotions did these barriers elicit?
10. How were barriers overcome, and what steps were taken to reach the goals?
11. Were the goals attained?
12. How does the client feel about the outcome?
13. If the client were to attempt the same goal today, what would he or she do differently?
14. Can the client recast the experience in more hopeful terms (i.e., by identifying lessons learned that can facilitate future efforts)?

It may be necessary to offer some suggestions to direct the client's attention to hopeful elements in their stories. These narratives should support a sense of movement rather than stagnant rumination. The benefits of narrative techniques come from the integration of these cognitive and emotional elements of the client's stories.

Another informal strategy, hope profiling, is a semistructured intervention in which the therapist requests that the client write (or audiotape) brief stories about past and current goal pursuits to uncover the hope that is part of a person's psychological makeup. Typically, five stories (two to five pages) detailing goal pursuits in various life domains reveal the requisite pathways and agency involved in hopeful pursuits. Review of these stories in the therapeutic context can help clients to realize that they have the resources necessary to make positive changes. In addition, clients learn the language of hope by identifying the goal thoughts, pathway thinking, and agency sources referred to in their narrative.

## HOPE BONDING

Bordin (1979) defined the working alliance as the collaboration between the therapist and client that is based on their agreement on the goals and tasks of counseling and on the development of a personal attachment bond. As described previously, Snyder's (1994) conceptualization of hope suggests a model composed of three cognitive components: goals, agency, and pathways. Goals are considered the targets or endpoints of mental action sequences and, as such, form the anchor of hope theory (Snyder, Ilardi, Michael, et al., 2000). Pathways, which are the routes toward desired goals, are necessary to attain goals and navigate around obstacles. Finally, agency taps the motivation that is necessary to begin and sustain movement toward goals. Given these definitions, it seems plausible that working alliance goals coincide with hope goal thoughts, tasks coincide with pathways, and the bond translates to agency (Lopez, Floyd, et al., 2000). Indeed, empirical research has supported this theoretical relationship between the working alliance and hope and their components (i.e., tasks and pathways, bond and agency; Magyar-Moe, Edwards, & Lopez, 2001). Although the causality cannot be determined through correlational data, the large amount of shared variance ($r = 0.48$) between these two models suggests that increasing an individual's level of hope also may increase working alliance ratings and vice versa. Thus, working to build hopeful alliances seems appropriate, given the many positive correlations among the working alliance, hope, and various positive outcomes (Horvath & Greenberg, 1994; Martin, Garske, & Davis, 2000; Snyder, 2000b).

FORMAL HOPE-BONDING STRATEGIES

Working alliance and hope researchers have outlined what it takes to form a productive therapeutic relationship and have described how a sound relationship is associated with beneficial change. Indeed, Bordin (1994) stated that negotiation between the client and therapist about the change goal that is most relevant to the client's struggle is essential. Such negotiation depends largely on the bonding component, defined as the positive personal attachment between the client and the therapist that results from working together on a shared activity. Bonding in therapy usually is expressed in terms of liking, trusting, and respecting one another, in addition to a feeling of mutual commitment and understanding in the activity (Bordin, 1994). Such a relationship mirrors that required for begetting hope. According to Snyder et al. (1997), hope flourishes when people develop a strong bond to one or more caregivers, allowing the person to perceive himself or herself as having some sense of control in the world. "As social creatures, we need to confide in someone about our dreams and goals" (Rodriguez-Hanley & Snyder, 2000, p. 46). Thus, it seems that for both the therapeutic alliance and for hope to develop, a supportive environment is needed in which people receive basic instruction in goal pursuits from a positive model (Snyder, 2000b).

Taken together, the working alliance and hope literature suggests that building a hopeful alliance involves

- Respectfully negotiating flexible therapeutic goals.
- Generating numerous and varied pathways to goal attainment.
- Translating the sense of connectedness between therapist and client into the mental energy necessary to sustain pursuit toward therapeutic goals.

INFORMAL HOPE-BONDING STRATEGIES

Based on the assumption that hope begets more hope, hopeful familial relationships and friendships could serve as hope-enhancing agents. Clients could benefit from evaluating their relationships and determining which generate mental energy that facilitates coping and those that drain this energy. Though data about hope in friendships, siblingships, and marriages have not been collected, the infectious nature of hope in such contexts has been assumed (Snyder, 1994). Therefore, therapists should encourage the development of new relationships that increase the hope in an individual's life. Associating with individuals who are supportive of goal pursuits, who challenge their peers to pursue stretch goals, and who encourage those peers to overcome barriers may help people crystallize their hopeful thought.

## HOPE ENHANCING

All individuals inherently possess hope (Snyder et al., 1991; Snyder et al., 1997), however, there is much variability in terms of individual's levels of hope and the outcomes experienced based upon those levels. Indeed, research has shown that children, adolescents, and adults with higher levels of hope do better in school and athletics, have better health, have better problem-solving skills, and are more adjusted psychologically (Snyder, 2002; Snyder, Cheavens, & Michael, 1999) than their counterparts who score lower on measures of hope. Such research suggests that hope enhancement can help people at all stages of development to achieve a wide array of better life outcomes and that such hope enhancement can occur within a variety of settings. Indeed, formal strategies for enhancing hope have been examined in a variety of contexts, including therapeutic and educational settings with both adult and youth populations.

## FORMAL HOPE-ENHANCING STRATEGIES WITH YOUTH

One of the first interventions aimed at increasing hope in children was developed by McDermott and Hastings (2000). This program involved eight weekly sessions with first- through sixth-grade students at a culturally diverse elementary school. During each week of this program, students were presented with information about hope- and goal-setting, as well as stories about high-hope children. Through hearing and discussing these stories each week for 30 minutes, children had the opportunity to identify goals in the lives of protagonists, as well as to apply the hope concepts to their own lives. Evaluation of the program was conducted through comparing pre- and posttest hope scores for the intervention group to a control group of students, and results demonstrated that there were modest gains. Furthermore, teacher ratings of students' levels of hope were significantly higher at posttest, suggesting that they perceived increases in their students' levels of hopeful thinking. McDermott and Hastings concluded that an 8-week session was not sufficient time to instill high hope, but they considered their results promising.

Another elementary school intervention, Making Hope Happen for Kids (Edwards & Lopez, 2000), was developed to enhance hope in fourth-grade students. This five-session program, based on the general format of the junior high school program (described subsequently), involves age-appropriate activities and lessons related to learning about hope and applying this construct to children's lives. During this five-session program, which was conducted in several classrooms, two graduate student cofacilitators led groups of 7 to 10 students in various activities and lessons.

The first week of the program involved learning about the hope model and acting out the parts of the model with laminated props. Students pretended to be goals, obstacles, pathways, and willpower (i.e., agency) in a brief psychodrama depicting meaningful goal pursuits. In the second week, children were introduced to a story that described a young girl navigating obstacles as she worked toward the goal of learning lines for her school play. The third week of the program involved the Hope Game (a board game depicting multiple goal pursuits), during which children identified obstacles, pathways, and agency thoughts as they worked in teams to accomplish a shared goal. During the fourth week, children designed hope cartoons, emphasizing hopeful language. Finally, during the last week of the program, children were asked to write hope stories describing the goals on which they had been working and then share their stories with one another; they then enjoyed snacks to celebrate the end of the program.

Evaluation of the program was conducted at the end of the first and second years. The Children's Hope Scale (Snyder et al., 1997) was administered before and after delivery of the intervention with all children. While the evaluation of this program did not include a control group, comparisons of means at pre- and posttest demonstrated significant gains in hope scores in the fourth-grade students. Thus, hope was enhanced in these young children.

Pedrotti, Lopez, and Krieshok (2000) developed a program for seventh graders designed to enhance hope through five weekly 45-minute sessions. Assistance from classroom teachers allowed this version of the Making Hope Happen program to be integrated into the regular school day as a part of a family consumer sciences course. Groups consisting of 8 to 12 students were formed, and each was facilitated by two graduate student leaders. The program was designed to enhance the hope inherent in these youth by teaching them about the hope model.

The five sessions were developed to take these adolescents through the hope model step by step. During the first session, students were taught about the hope model in general, through the use of posters and cartoons. Pictorial representations were used to exemplify the different components to help students to commit these to memory. In addition, in this first session, two narratives depicting characters with high levels of hope were read. Group discussions followed in which the children delineated the behaviors that the characters had exhibited that corresponded to these hope components. Students also were placed in partnerships called Hope Buddies on this first day. These pairs were designed to help students to work with a peer to talk about their goals for the future. Finally, participants formed their own goals on which to work for the coming weeks. Goals varied from student to student, with some being very long term ("I want to graduate from an Ivy League college"), and others more short term ("I will keep my locker clean for five weeks"). All goals were treated as equal in terms of importance, and an emphasis was placed on the process as opposed to the actual achievement of the goal.

In Week 2, the tenets learned during the first week were reemphasized through the use of more narratives and exercises. Youth were taught about G-POWER this week as well. Each letter of this acronym was used to remind students of the various components of the hope model and to emphasize the goal-seeking process. Each letter was accompanied by a question designed to assist participants as they talked through this process (see the following list).

### G-POWER
G  What is the character's Goal?
P  Which Pathways does the character identify to use to move toward his or her stated goal?
O  What Obstacles lay in the character's pathway?
W  What source of Willpower is keeping the character energized in this process?
E  Which pathway did the character Elect to follow?
R  Rethink the process—would you have made the same decisions and choices?

During the third week, the components of the hope model were reinforced through other forms of media—including the use of a board game (the Hope Game) developed specifically for use in the program. Differing forms of media were used throughout the program to tap into the many different learning styles. In Week 4, the group moved to a more individual focus to work more closely on goals relevant for each student. During this week, the concept of Hope Talk was introduced in which group leaders explained that the statements we tell ourselves about our goals often influence our goal pursuit process in general. Participants were then asked to determine if particular statements made by historical figures, book characters, and sports stars were of a hopeful or unhopeful nature. Individual worksheets emphasizing hopeful language were also completed during this portion of the program.

In the last activity of the fourth session, the students began to write their personal hope stories. From the goals formed during the first session, the students were asked to think about each of the components in the hope model. Separate paragraphs were written for each session, and the finished product was a short essay that told the story of students' progress and listed their future steps toward this goal. Each student read his or her hope story to the group during the fifth and final session.

As to program evaluation, before the first session, all participants were administered the CHS (Snyder et al., 1997). At the conclusion of the program, the CHS again was administered to the junior high students. Scores were then compared to those found on the CHS given to a group who had not participated in the program. When analyzed statistically, the participants in the program had significantly higher levels of hope in comparison to their counterparts who did not participate in the program. As such, the program appeared to enhance the hope in these children. In a follow-up study, the higher hope levels were maintained after 6 months, pointing to the robustness of the intervention results even after the program was completed. Therefore, apparently, the participants continued to use the tools taught to them during the Making Hope Happen program.

A similar psychoeducational intervention program was developed and tested with sixth-grade students in Portugal (Marques, Lopez, & Pais-Ribeiro, 2009). The intervention occurred in a group format over the course of 5 weeks and was designed to target the enhancement of hope, life satisfaction, self-worth, mental health, and academic achievement.

Participants were introduced to hope theory and the connections between hope, change, and positive outcomes in the first session. The following sessions were focused upon structuring hope, creating positive and specific goals, practicing hope, and review and applications of hope for the future. Each session started with a 10-minute segment dedicated to modeling and developing enthusiasm for the program and to reinforcing ideas learned in the previous session. Compared to previous hope intervention studies with children, Marques, Lopez, et al. (2009) included an intervention component focused upon the key social networks in the lives of the student participants, namely, parents, guardians, and teachers. Parents and teachers were included because past research suggests that children develop hope through learning to trust in the predictability of cause and effect interactions with parents and caregivers, as does building hope through learning to trust in the ordered predictability and consistency of their interactions with their teachers. Moreover, multiple factors are involved in the positive thinking of children and adolescents, and research clearly demonstrates the importance of ecological factors (Huebner, 2004) embedded in an interpersonal, social-familial, and institutional context (Gordon & Crabtree, 2006; Sarason, 1997). Such findings are inconsistent with programs that focus exclusively on changing individuals rather than environments. Hence, a 1-hour informational session with teachers and guardians of the students of the intervention group was conducted during the 1st week of the students' intervention. In addition, these adults were given hope manuals designed to (a) increase parents/teacher awareness of the principles of hope and enhance their goal-setting behavior; and (b) promote goal-setting behavior in their children or students.

Results indicated higher hope and greater levels of life satisfaction and self-worth for those in the intervention group following the 5-week intervention and being maintained at 6-month and 18-month follow-ups. The results did not support any significant changes in mental-health or academic achievement as a result of the intervention. The researchers conclude that the

> findings of this study are consistent with previous interventions to enhance goal-directed thinking and strongly support the application of group-based approaches for raising the hopeful thinking of all students (e.g., the curriculum and school environment for students could be arranged and improved in the direction of supporting hopeful thinking). (Marques, Lopez, et al., 2009, p. 150)

## FORMAL HOPE-ENHANCING STRATEGIES WITH ADULTS

A number of group and individual hope enhancement strategies for adults have also been developed and evaluated. For example, Klausner et al. (1998) demonstrated that depressed older adults benefited from group therapy focused on goal setting and increasing the production of pathways and agency through actual work on reasonable goals, discussion of the process, and weekly homework assignments. Hopelessness and anxiety lessened significantly, whereas state hope increased reliably. Moreover, in comparison to members of a reminiscence therapy group, members of the hope-focused group experienced a more substantial decrease in depressive symptomatology. Irving et al. (2004) demonstrated that a 5-week pretreatment orientation group focusing on hope had benefits for a group of incoming clients who were in need of assistance. Those lower in hope reported greater responsiveness (as suggested by scores on measures of well-being, level of functioning, coping, and symptomatology) to the hope-focused orientation.

Cheavens and colleagues (2006) developed a treatment manual for an 8-week hope therapy group intervention that they tested on a community sample. Each 2-hour group therapy session was divided into four segments consisting of (1) review of the previous week and progress on homework assignments; (2) psychoeducation in which new hope-related skills were taught; (3) discussion of ways of applying hope skills to participants' lives and using hope skills in problem solving; and (4) introduction of homework for the upcoming week focused upon application of hope skills in daily living. Each participant selected a specific goal to work on over the course of the group sessions and was asked to apply the skills taught at each session to that specific goal. Results showed that participants experienced increased agency thinking, life meaning, and self-esteem and decreases in symptoms of anxiety and depression in comparison to a wait-list control group. In addition, increases in Adult Dispositional Hope Scale scores were related to reductions in posttreatment anxiety and depression scores, even after accounting for the variance associated with the respective pretreatment scores. The researchers conclude that such findings are very promising, for they suggest that there is indeed value in therapies designed around hope and other strength-based constructs.

> The significant changes in agency scores, meaning, and self-esteem suggest that interventions designed to increase client strengths (in this case, hope), influence other psychological constructs. This fits with the premise that in addition to targeting symptom reduction, effective treatments also should bolster and augment other areas of strength and resiliency. (Cheavens et al., 2006, p. 75)

Feldman and Dreher (2011) tested a single-session, 90-minute intervention designed to increase college students' hopeful goal-directed thinking. The researchers note that such an intervention is highly relevant to college students, given the reported increases in psychological distress and lack of perceived control for this population (Lewinsohn, Rohde, Seeley, & Fischer, 1993; Twenge, Zhang, & Im, 2004). Participants were assigned to one of three conditions, namely, hope intervention, progressive muscle relaxation, or no intervention. Assessments were conducted at intervention pretest, at posttest, and at 1-month follow-up.

The hope intervention used consisted of a single, 90-minute session in which participants choose a personal goal that would like to accomplish within the next 6 months, received psychoeducation about hope theory, completed a hope-based goal mapping activity, and participated in a hope visualization exercise. More specifically, the goal mapping activity consisted of completion of a worksheet designed to foster hope-based planning via putting their goals to paper, writing three steps that they could take along their pathways to achieving their goals, and writing an obstacle that possibly could hamper their pathways as well as an alternative route around the obstacle. The workshop also contained prompts for participants to write how they could maintain their agency throughout the goal pursuit process. The goal mapping worksheet then served as the foundation for the hope visualization exercise that followed. The researchers note than a crucial component of this exercise is its realism; therefore, participants were instructed to make the visualization as vivid as possible. At the end of the exercise, participants were guided to see themselves accomplishing their goals and feeling the positive emotions and increased agency that result.

Participants in the hope intervention showed greater increases from pre- to posttest on both agency and pathways hope scores as well as in sense of life purpose and vocational calling. These increases were not maintained at 1-month follow-up; however, at follow-up those who received the hope intervention reported making significantly more progress on their goals in comparison with those in both the no-treatment control condition and the relaxation condition. The researchers conclude that this result is particularly meaningful given the extremely brief duration of the intervention. Finally, hope scores regarding the goals that participants' chose to work toward during the intervention predicted goal progress at 1-month follow-up. This finding supports a central tenet of hope theory (Snyder, 1994), namely, that hope is a strong predictor of goal attainment. Overall, this study offers some evidence that a single-session intervention can increase hope in the short term as well as lead to greater levels of goal progress as much as a month later. The researchers note that "from a more pragmatic standpoint, it offers hope that even a brief intervention can help a stressed generation of college students find greater direction" (Feldman & Dreher, 2011, p. 756).

Another single-session workshop intervention program featuring hope theory (Davidson, Feldman, & Margalit, 2012) was designed for use with 1st-year college students based on the same principles as the study by Feldman and Dreher (2011) previously reported. The workshop offered in this study consisted of segments featuring hope theory (emphasizing future goal-directed expectations through applying mental-rehearsal strategies focused on agency and pathways; Snyder, 2002), sense of coherence (emphasizing current experiences of comprehensibility, manageability, and meaningfulness; Antonovsky, 1987), and self-efficacy (focused verbal persuasion; Bandura, 1997). The combination of constructs targeted in this intervention was hypothesized to work together in increasing first-year college student academic achievement via hope serving to get students focused on achieving future goals, sense of coherence helping them to experience more confidence in themselves within their environment, and self-efficacy-enhancing beliefs in their ability to perform well while confronted with demanding tasks. Results showed that students who achieved higher levels of hope following the workshop got higher grades in the semester following the intervention. Sense of coherence and self-efficacy scores were significantly related to levels of hope at 1-month follow-up and to mean grades.

Hope interventions have also been tested within the context of adult relationship enrichment (Worthington et al., 1997). This type of intervention focuses on a mutual goal as defined by the presenting couple and enhances the relationship via growth, communication, and a mutual level of commitment to the identified goal. Reported outcomes of this program included increased partner satisfaction and quality of couple skills with higher satisfaction being maintained at a 3-week posttest. An additional follow-up study (Ripley & Worthington, 2002) indicated that the hope-focused intervention was particularly effective in increasing the ratio of positive to negative communications between couples.

INFORMAL HOPE-ENHANCEMENT STRATEGIES

It is probable that many clinicians already have incorporated hope theory tenets into their interventions. Hence, we encourage clinicians to reflect on their practice and identify those strategies that work to enhance hopeful thinking. Sharing a list with other clinicians can serve to improve one's strategies and generate more resources.

Snyder, McDermott, Cook, and Rapoff's (2002) *Hope for the Journey: Helping Children Through Good Times and Bad* and McDermott and Snyder's *Making Hope Happen: A Workbook for Turning Possibilities Into Realities* (1999) and *The Great Big Book of Hope: Help Your Children Achieve Their Dreams* (2000) provide well-conceptualized examples of how to engage clients and students in a therapeutic process focused on hope. For convenience, we have summarized the basic principles and steps of an informal approach to enhancing hope in the therapeutic context in Exhibit 29.3. *The Psychology of Hope*, Snyder's (1994) first book on the topic, provides numerous recommendations for enhancing hope that a clinician can share with a client. This information is summarized in Exhibit 29.4.

EXHIBIT 29.3

Steps to Enhancing Hope in Adult Clients

---

I. Administration of the Adult Dispositional Hope Scale (trait)
The first step in this process is the completion of the Adult Dispositional Hope Scale. The therapist then tallies the total score and computes subscale scores for both pathway and agency.

II. Learning About Hope
Once a baseline hope score is determined, the therapist can then discuss hope theory with the client and its relevance to the therapy process and to positive outcomes.

III. Structuring Hope for the Client
In this step, the client creates a list of important life components, determines which areas are most important, and discusses the level of satisfaction within those areas.

IV. Creating Positive and Specific Goals
Using the important life components identified earlier, the client and therapist work together to create workable goals that are both positive and specific. These goals should be salient to the client and attainable. Additionally, the client develops multiple pathways for each goal and identifies agency thoughts for each goal.

V. Practice Makes Perfect
Once the client and therapist have agreed on these goals, clients should visualize and verbalize the steps to reach their goals. With this practice, the client and therapist can collaborate on the most effective pathways and the agency behind the goals.

VI. Checking In

Clients incorporate these goals, pathways, and agency into their lives and report back to the therapist on the process of goal attainment. Again, collaboration can occur to adjust or modify any disparities in actions or thinking that may hinder the successful achievement of their desired goals.

This process is cyclical and requires continual assessment by both the client and the therapist. Once clients have grasped the concepts of hope theory, however, they can then assume the bulk of responsibility in the implementation of hope theory to their unique experiences.

---

EXHIBIT 29.4

Checklist for Enhancing Pathways and Agency in Adults

---

**Pathways**

**Do**

Break a long-range goal into steps or subgoals.

Begin your pursuit of a distant goal by concentrating on the first subgoal.

Practice making different routes to your goals and select the best one.

Mentally rehearse scripts for what you would do should you encounter a blockage.

Learn a new skill if you need it to reach your goal.

Cultivate two-way friendships where you can give and get advice.

**Don't**

Think you can reach your big goals all at once.

Be too hurried in producing routes to your goals.

Be rushed to select the best or first route to your goal.

Overthink with the idea of finding one perfect route to your goal.

Conclude you are lacking in talent or are no good when an initial strategy fails.

Get into friendships where you are praised for not coming up with solutions to your problems.

**Agency**

**Do**

Tell yourself that you have chosen the goal, so it is your job to go after it.

Learn to talk to yourself in positive voices (e.g., I can do this!).

Recall your previous successful goal pursuits, particularly when you are in a jam.

Be able to laugh at yourself, especially if you encounter some impediment to your goal pursuits.

Find a substitute goal when the original goal is blocked solidly.

Enjoy the process of getting to your goals and do not focus only on the final attainment.

**Don't**

Allow yourself to be surprised repeatedly by roadblocks that appear in your life.

Try to squelch totally any internal put-down thoughts because this may only make them stronger.

Get impatient if your willful thinking doesn't increase quickly.

Conclude that things never will change, especially if you are down.

Engage in self-pity when faced with adversity.

Stick to a blocked goal when it is truly blocked.

Constantly ask yourself how you are doing to evaluate your progress toward a goal.

---

## HOPE REMINDING

Hope reminding could be thought of as a feedback loop for the therapeutic process. It is this strategy that encourages clients to become their own hope-enhancing agents. Over the course of therapy or psychoeducational sessions, clients become facile at finding hope through narratives and assessment, at bonding with their therapists and others who generate hopeful thoughts, and at enhancing their levels of hope through narrative, solution-focused, and cognitive-behavioral techniques. With the use of hope-reminding strategies, effortful daily use of hopeful cognitions is promoted.

### FORMAL HOPE-REMINDING STRATEGIES

Being able to identify goal thoughts as well as barrier thoughts is a key element of the hope-reminding process. These thoughts serve as cues for the client to initiate the cognitive feedback loop. Self-monitoring techniques can be used to respond to these cues and for facilitating hopeful reminding. When the client has become adept at identifying cognitive cues of goal and barrier thoughts (this may occur early in treatment, or it may be a treatment goal that is difficult to attain), the therapist should encourage the client to use mini-interventions in sessions and outside of sessions. These mini-interventions should be selected by the therapist and the client on the basis of what has worked for the client in the past. Examples of mini-interventions include

- Reviewing a favorite hope narrative
- Constructing and completing a brief automatic thought record that refines goals and confronts barrier thoughts
- Reviewing personal hope statements
- Bonding with a hopeful person and meeting to discuss current goals and barriers

Clients can use these interventions on a daily basis each time they become aware of a significant goal thought or barrier thought.

### INFORMAL HOPE-REMINDING STRATEGIES

Increasing clients' cognizance of goal and barrier thoughts, effectively modeling full-scale versions of interventions during sessions, and helping clients choose and refine mini-interventions are the therapists' how-tos of hope reminding. Clients make effortful daily use of hopeful cognitions by responding to cognitive cues with hope-assessing and hope-enhancing interventions. (See Tennen and Affleck [1999] for a discussion of benefit-finding and reminding, processes that influenced the development of the hope-reminding strategy.)

## CULTURAL CONSIDERATIONS WHEN IMPLEMENTING HOPE STRATEGIES

As with all positive psychological interventions, it is important for therapists to be sensitive to the cultural contexts in which clients exist when implementing strategies for accentuating hope. Although there is evidence that hope is prevalent across cultures and ethnic groups (Chang & Banks, 2007), it has also been reported that barriers arise more often in the goal pursuits for some members of minority groups (Lopez, Floyd, et al., 2000). Indeed, all people come across obstacles in the process of working toward their life goals and those who are high in hope are able to perceive these obstacles as challenges to be overcome. However, members of non-privileged religious backgrounds, ethnic and racial groups, immigrants, and gender and sexual minority groups are prone to experiencing larger impediments to their goals on a more frequent basis due to such factors as prejudice, racism, sexism, stereotyping, poverty, acculturation stress, language barriers, lack of privilege, and more. These obstacles exist on various levels, including the interpersonal, societal, and institutional (Lopez, Floyd, et al., 2000).

Practitioners who want to be sure that they conduct hope therapy in a culturally appropriate manner are advised to be aware of the fact that various obstacles are more likely to be encountered by members of diverse groups, but to also realize that some marginalized racial or ethnic minority groups within the United States have shown equal and higher hope levels than European Americans (Chang & Banks, 2007). Indeed, it appears that early experiences or expectancies of goal-related obstacles for some minorities may serve as opportunities for developing higher levels of hope and greater pathways of thinking later in life. This research suggests that helping clients to develop goals within the context of their cultural frameworks and examining factors that are likely to make goals more or less available or attainable is key. Finally, providing culture-specific examples of hope during the narrative work of the hope-finding phase of hope therapy is recommended (Lopez, Floyd, et al., 2000).

Hope therapy practitioners should also be aware of the findings of Chang and Banks (2007), which indicate that although hope is a universally valid positive expectancy variable that functions similarly across different racial/ethnic groups, cultivation of hope appears to differ based upon one's cultural makeup. More specifically, being satisfied with one's life served as a source of agentic hope thinking for European Americans, Latinos, and African Americans but not for Asian Americans. Positive affect was found to be predictive of pathways hope thinking for European, African, and Asian Americans but not for Latinos. Based upon these findings, Chang and Banks (2007) suggest that fostering hope in European Americans may be best achieved via using interventions that target the promotion of greater life satisfaction and positive affect in this group. For African Americans, lack of a negative problem orientation was the best predictor of agentic thinking, whereas positive problem orientation was the strongest predictor of pathways thinking. Therefore, increasing hope for African Americans might best be achieved through interventions that aim to reduce negative problem orientation and aim to increase positive problem orientation. For Latinos, rational problem solving was found to be the strongest predictor of agentic thinking, and life satisfaction was found to be the only predictor of pathways thinking. Increasing hope for Latinos, therefore, might be best achieved through interventions that promote greater rational problem solving and life satisfaction. Finally, for Asian Americans, positive affect was the strongest predictor of agentic thinking, and positive problem orientation was the best predictor of pathways thinking. Higher hope levels with Asian Americans might therefore be accomplished through interventions that target the promotion of positive affect and positive problem orientation.

## CONCLUDING COMMENTS AND RECOMMENDATIONS

Strategies for accentuating hope have been incorporated into a clinical approach called hope therapy (Lopez, Floyd, et al., 2000). Hope therapy was developed in response to a call by clinicians for a systematic application of hope theory principles in a therapeutic context. Though it may be considered a manualized intervention, it is undergirded by the assumption that common factors account for psychological change (see, e.g., Luborsky et al., 2002). Despite the existence of dozens of strategies for accentuating hope, the development of hope therapy, and 20 years of scientific examination of hope theory and its application, many clinical needs and questions are yet to be rigorously considered.

## SUMMARY POINTS

Our recommendations for future work in the area are arranged according to the categories of strategies: finding, bonding, enhancing, and reminding.

### Hope Finding
- Develop and validate a children's version of the state hope scale to account for static changes in hopeful thinking and to round out the selection of hope measures.
- Identify novel methods of detecting hope during clinical intake and orientation procedures.

### Hope Bonding
- Examine the possible cause–effect relationship associated with high-hope therapists sharing agency with low-hope clients.
- Determine if a hope contagion exists among high-hope groups of friends.

### Hope Enhancing
- Refine techniques to orient clients to the hopeful pursuit of therapeutic goals via low-cost, brief video, CD-ROM, or web-based psychoeducation that could be administered before the first therapy session.
- Examine the effectiveness of hope therapy as a specific clinical approach.
- Examine the role of greater attention to and inclusion of client social networks, environmental contexts, and cultural contexts in development, and delivery of hope interventions.

### Hope Reminding
- Develop and examine hope booster sessions that could be facilitated during a brief office visit or over the telephone or other media.
- Identify effective hope-reminding procedures that clients have developed over the 6-month course following the termination of therapy.

Continued focus on hope as a change agent and the effectiveness of hope-accentuating strategies is needed. Hope is a human strength that fuels our pursuit of the good life. The more we understand about hope, the closer we get to a good life for all.

## REFERENCES

Abdel-Khalek, A., & Snyder, C. R. (2007). Correlates and predictors of an Arabic translation of the Snyder Hope Scale. *Journal of Positive Psychology, 2*, 228–235.

Antonovsky, A. (1987). *Unraveling the mystery of health.* San Francisco, CA: Jossey-Bass.

Bandura, A. (1982). Self-efficacy mechanism in human agency. *American Psychologist, 37*, 122–147.

Bandura, A. (1997). *Self-efficacy: The exercise of control.* New York, NY: Freeman.

Bordin, E. S. (1979). The generalizability of the psychoanalytic concept of the working alliance. *Psychotherapy: Theory, Research, and Practice, 16*, 252–260.

Bordin, E. S. (1994). Theory and research on the therapeutic working alliance: New directions. In A. O. Horvath & L. S. Greenberg (Eds.), *The working alliance: Theory, research, and practice* (pp. 13–37). New York, NY: Wiley.

Chang, E. C., & Banks, K. H. (2007). The color and texture of hope: Some preliminary findings and implications for hope theory and counseling among diverse racial/ethnic groups. *Cultural Diversity and Ethnic Minority Psychology, 13*(2), 94–103.

Cheavens, J., Gum, A., Feldman, D. B., Gum, A., Michael, S. T., & Snyder, C. R. (2006). Hope therapy in a community sample: A pilot investigation. *Social Indicators Research, 77*, 61–78.

Covington, M. V. (2000). Goal theory, motivation, and school achievement: An integrative review. *Annual Review of Psychology, 51*, 171–200.

Davidson, O. B., Feldman, D. B., & Margalit, M. (2012). A focused intervention for 1st-year college students: Promoting hope, sense of coherence, and self-efficacy. *Journal of Psychology: Interdisciplinary and Applied, 146*(3), 333–352.

Dweck, C. S. (1999). *Self-theories: Their role in motivation, personality, and development.* Philadelphia, PA: Psychology Press.

Edwards, L. M., & Lopez, S. J. (2000). *Making hope happen for kids.* Unpublished protocol, University of Kansas, Lawrence.

Feldman, D. B., & Dreher, D. E. (2011). Can hope be changed in 90 minutes? Testing the efficacy of a single-session goal-pursuit intervention for college students. *Journal of Happiness Studies, 13*(4), 745–759.

Frank, J. D. (1968). The role of hope in psychotherapy. *International Journal of Psychiatry, 5*, 383–395.

Frank, J. D. (1975). The faith that heals. *Johns Hopkins Medical Journal, 137*, 127–131.

Gana, K., Daigre, S., & Ledrich, J. (2013). Psychometric properties of the French version of the Adult Dispositional Hope Scale. *Assessment, 20*(1), 114–118.

Gordon, G., & Crabtree, S. (2006). *Building engaged schools.* New York, NY: Gallup.

Halama, P. (1999). Snyder's Hope Scale. *Studia Psychologica, 41*(4), 329–332.

Heppner, P. P., & Petersen, C. H. (1982). The development and implications of a personal problem-solving inventory. *Journal of Counseling Psychology, 29*, 66–75.

Horvath, A. O., & Greenberg, L. S. (Eds.). (1994). *The working alliance: Theory, research, and practice.* New York, NY: Wiley.

Howard, K. I., Krause, M. S., Saunders, S. M., & Koptka, S. M. (1997). Trials and tribulations in the meta-analysis of treatment differences: Comment on Wampold et al. (1997). *Psychological Bulletin, 122*, 221–225.

Huebner, E. S. (2004). Research on assessment of life satisfaction of children and adolescents. *Social Indicators Research, 66*, 3–33.

Irving, L. M., Cheavens, J., Snyder, C. R., Gravel, L., Hanke, J., Hilberg, P., & Nelson, N. (2004). The relationships between hope and outcomes at pretreatment, beginning, and later phases of psychotherapy. *Journal of Psychotherapy Integration, 44*(4), 419–443.

Kato, T., & Snyder, C. R. (2005). The relationship between hope and subjective well-being: Reliability and validity of the Dispositional Hope Scale, Japanese version. *Japanese Journal of Psychology, 76,* 227–234.

Klausner, E. J., Clarkin, J. F., Spielman, L., Pupo, C., Abrams, R., & Alexopoulos, G. S. (1998). Late-life depression and functional disability: The role of goal-focused group psychotherapy. *International Journal of Geriatric Psychiatry, 13,* 707–716.

Lewinsohn, P. M., Rohde, P., Seeley, J. R., & Fischer, S. A. (1993). Age-cohort changes in the lifetime occurrence of depression and other mental disorders. *Journal of Abnormal Psychology, 102,* 110–120.

Lopez, S. J., Ciarlelli, R., Coffman, L., Stone, M., & Wyatt, L. (2000). Diagnosing for strengths: On measuring hope building blocks. In C. R. Snyder (Ed.), *Handbook of hope: Theory, measures, and interventions* (pp. 57–85). San Diego, CA: Academic Press.

Lopez, S. J., Floyd, R. K., Ulven, J. C., & Snyder, C. R. (2000). Hope therapy: Helping clients build a house of hope. In C. R. Snyder (Ed.), *Handbook of hope: Theory, measures, and applications* (pp. 123–166). San Diego, CA: Academic Press.

Luborsky, L., Rosenthal, R., Diguer, L., Andrusnya, T. P., Berman, J. S., Levitt, J. T., . . . Krause, E. D. (2002). The Dodo verdict is alive and well—mostly. *Clinical Psychology: Science and Practice, 9,* 2–12.

Magaletta, P. R., & Oliver, J. M. (1999). The hope construct, will, and ways: Their relations with self-efficacy, optimism, and general well-being. *Journal of Clinical Psychology, 55,* 539–551.

Magyar-Moe, J. L., Edwards, L. M., & Lopez, S. J. (2001, March). *A new look at the working alliance: Is there a connection with hope?* Paper presented at the Division 17 National Counseling Psychology Conference, Houston, TX.

Martin, D. J., Garske, J. P., & Davis, M. K. (2000). Relation of the therapeutic alliance with outcome and other variables: A meta-analytic review. *Journal of Consulting and Clinical Psychology, 68,* 438–450.

Marques, S. C., Lopez, S. J., & Pais-Ribeiro, J. L. (2009). "Building hope for the future": A program to foster strengths in middle-school students. *Journal of Happiness Studies, 12*(1), 139–152.

Marques, S. C., Pais-Ribeiro, J. L., & Lopez, S. J. (2009). Validation of a Portuguese version of the Children's Hope Scale. *School Psychology International, 30,* 538–551.

McDermott, D., & Hastings, S. (2000). Children: Raising future hopes. In C. R. Snyder (Ed.), *Handbook of hope: Theory, measures, and interventions* (pp. 185–199). San Diego, CA: Academic Press.

McDermott, D., & Snyder, C. R. (1999). *Making hope happen: A workbook for turning possibilities into realities.* Oakland, CA: New Harbinger.

McDermott, D., & Snyder, C. R. (2000). *The great big book of hope: Help your children achieve their dreams.* Oakland, CA: New Harbinger.

Menninger, K. (1959). The academic lecture on hope. *American Journal of Psychiatry, 190,* 481–491.

Pedrotti, J. T., Lopez, S. J., & Krieshok, T. (2000). *Making hope happen: A program for fostering strengths in adolescents.* Manuscript submitted for publication.

Peterson, C. (2000). The future of optimism. *American Psychologist, 55,* 44–55.

Ripley, J. S., & Worthington, E. L. (2002). Hope-focused and forgiveness-based group interventions to promote marital enrichment. *Journal of Counseling and Development, 80,* 452–463.

Rodriguez-Hanley, A., & Snyder, C. R. (2000). The demise of hope: On losing positive thinking. In C. R. Snyder (Ed.), *Handbook of hope: Theory, measures, and applications* (pp. 39–56). San Diego, CA: Academic Press.

Sarason, S. B. (1997). *How schools might be governed and why.* New York, NY: Teachers College Press.

Scheier, M. F., & Carver, C. S. (1985). Optimism, coping, and health: Assessment and implications of generalized outcome expectancies. *Health Psychology, 4,* 219–247.

Snyder, C. R. (1989). Reality negotiation: From excuses to hope and beyond. *Journal of Social and Clinical Psychology, 8,* 130–157.

Snyder, C. R. (1994). *The psychology of hope: You can get there from here.* New York, NY: Free Press.

Snyder, C. R. (Ed.). (2000a). *Handbook of hope: Theory, measures, and applications.* San Diego, CA: Academic Press.

Snyder, C. R. (2000b). The past and possible futures of hope. *Journal of Social and Clinical Psychology, 19,* 11–28.

Snyder, C. R. (2002). Hope theory: Rainbows in the mind. *Psychological Inquiry, 13,* 249–275.

Snyder, C. R., Cheavens, J., & Michael, S. T. (1999). Hoping. In C. R. Snyder (Ed.), *Coping: The psychology of what works* (pp. 205–231). New York, NY: Oxford University Press.

Snyder, C. R., Harris, C., Anderson, J. R., Holleran, S. A., Irving, L. M., Sigmon, S. T., . . . Harney, P. (1991). The will and the ways: Development and validation of an individual-differences measure of hope. *Journal of Personality and Social Psychology, 60,* 570–585.

Snyder, C. R., Hoza, B., Pelham, W. E., Rapoff, M., Ware, L., Danovsky, M., . . . Stahl, K. J. (1997). The development and validation of the Children's Hope Scale. *Journal of Pediatric Psychology, 22,* 399–421.

Snyder, C. R., Ilardi, S., Cheavens, J., Michael, S. T., Yamhure, L., & Sympson, S. (2000). The role of hope in cognitive behavior therapies. *Cognitive Therapy and Research, 24,* 747–762.

Snyder, C. R., Ilardi, S., Michael, S. T., & Cheavens, J. (2000). Hope theory: Updating a common process for psychological change. In C. R. Snyder & R. E. Ingram (Eds.), *Handbook of psychological change: Psychotherapy processes and practices for the 21st century* (pp. 128–153). New York, NY: Wiley.

Snyder, C. R., McDermott, D., Cook, W., & Rapoff, M. (2002). *Hope for the journey: Helping children through good times and bad* (Rev. ed.). Clinton Corners, NY: Percheron Press.

Snyder, C. R., Rand, K. L., & Sigmon, D. R. (2002). Hope theory: A member of the positive psychology family. In C. R. Snyder & S. J. Lopez (Eds.), *Handbook of positive psychology* (pp. 257–266). New York, NY: Oxford University Press.

Tennen, H., & Affleck, G. (1999). Finding benefits in adversity. In C. R. Snyder (Ed.), *Coping: The psychology of what works* (pp. 279–304). New York, NY: Oxford University Press.

Twenge, J. M., Zhang, L., & Im, C. (2004). It's beyond my control: A cross-temporal meta-analysis of increasing externality in locus of control, 1960–2002. *Personality and Social Psychology Review, 8,* 308–319.

Worthington, E. L., Jr., Hight, T. L., Ripley, J. S., Perrone, K. M., Kurusu, T. A., & Jones, D. R. (1997). Strategic hope-focused relationship-enrichment counseling with individual couples. *Journal of Counseling Psychology, 44,* 381–389.

CHAPTER 30

# Clinical Applications of Posttraumatic Growth

RICHARD G. TEDESCHI, LAWRENCE G. CALHOUN, and JESSICA M. GROLEAU

FOR ALMOST 30 YEARS, we have been examining a phenomenon that has been recognized since ancient times, that suffering sometimes yields strengthening and growth (Tedeschi & Calhoun, 1995). It is a theme found in literature, both ancient and modern, in religion and philosophy, and more recently it has been reported in the social and behavioral science literature. Pioneering thinkers such as Caplan (1964) and Frankl (1963) recognized the possibility that positive psychological change could occur in the context of highly stressful circumstances. In earlier empirical reports, growth associated with attempts to adapt to highly challenging events was examined as a peripheral factor (e.g., Andreasen & Norris, 1972; Lopata, 1973). More recently, we have considered how this process occurs in attempts to cope with bereavement (Calhoun & Tedeschi, 1989–1990; Calhoun, Tedeschi, Fulmer, & Harlan, 2000; Taku, Calhoun, Cann, & Tedeschi, 2008; Tedeschi & Calhoun, 2003; Tedeschi & Calhoun, 2007; Tedeschi, Calhoun, Morrell, & Johnson, 1984), physical disability (Tedeschi & Calhoun, 1988), and war (Powell, Rosner, Butollo, Tedeschi, & Calhoun, 2003; Tedeschi, Calhoun, & Engdahl, 2001; Tedeschi, 2011; Tedeschi & McNally, 2011), and looked at how this process may affect entire societies (Tedeschi, 1999). The available data suggest that at least a significant minority of individuals facing a wide array of traumas, including loss of a home in a fire, divorce, the birth of a medically vulnerable child, sexual assault, bone marrow transplantation, military combat and captivity, diagnosis with HIV, and others, report some aspect of personal growth, and we have reviewed these reports in other places (Calhoun & Tedeschi, 1999, 2006, 2013; Tedeschi & Calhoun, 1995, 2004; Tedeschi, Park, & Calhoun, 1998; see also Joseph, 2011, and Linley & Joseph, 2004).

In this chapter we briefly review the literature that shows that growth occurs in the aftermath of a variety of life crises, and summarize ways of understanding how this growth occurs. We then explore how the therapeutic relationship can be a vehicle for recognizing growth at a time of vulnerability. Finally, we encourage clinicians to utilize an existential-narrative-cognitive framework for approaching growth in clients.

## THE CONCEPT OF POSTTRAUMATIC GROWTH

We coined the term *posttraumatic growth* (Calhoun & Tedeschi, 1999; Tedeschi & Calhoun, 1996) to describe the experience of positive changes that occur as the result of the struggle with major life crises. Other terms have been used for the phenomenon of posttraumatic growth, including *stren conversion* (Finkel, 1974, 1975), *positive psychological changes* (Yalom & Lieberman, 1991), *perceived benefits* or *construing benefits* (Calhoun & Tedeschi, 1991; McMillen, Zuravin, & Rideout, 1995; Tennen, Affleck, Urrows, Higgins, & Mendola, 1992), *stress-related growth* (Park, Cohen, & Murch, 1996), *discovery of meaning* (Bower, Kemeny, Taylor, & Fahey, 1998), *positive emotions* (Folkman & Moskovitz, 2000), *flourishing* (Ryff & Singer, 1998), *thriving* (O'Leary & Ickovics, 1995), and *adversarial growth* (Linley & Joseph, 2004). Taylor and Brown (1988) have labeled similar outcomes *positive illusions*. Coping mechanisms of positive reinterpretation (Scheier, Weintraub, & Carver, 1986), *drawing strength from adversity* (McCrae, 1984), and *transformational coping* (Aldwin, 1994; Pargament, 1996) have also been described. The term *posttraumatic growth* appears to capture the essentials of this phenomenon better than others since (a) it occurs most distinctively in conditions of severe crisis rather than lower-level stress; (b) it is often accompanied by transformative life changes that appear to go beyond illusion; (c) it therefore is experienced as an outcome rather than a coping mechanism; and (d) it often requires a challenging of basic assumptions about one's life that thriving or flourishing does not imply.

Our conceptualization of posttraumatic growth and of the inclusion of these elements into psychological intervention relies on two elements: the growing literature on this phenomenon and our combined clinical experiences as practicing clinical psychologists. The empirical literature focused specifically on posttraumatic growth is rather recent and still limited in some ways. And, when one relies on clinical experience, the possibility of inadvertent bias always exists. However, since our conceptualizations of posttraumatic growth have data to support them, this way of thinking appears to offer a helpful expansion of the way psychological interventions are done with persons struggling with trauma and its aftermath.

## THE PARADOXICAL CHANGES OF POSTTRAUMATIC GROWTH

The kinds of positive changes people experience in their struggle with major stressors are reflected in the Posttraumatic Growth Inventory (Tedeschi & Calhoun, 1996): improved relationships, new possibilities for one's life, a greater appreciation for life, a greater sense of personal strength, and spiritual development. There appears to be a basic paradox that is apprehended by trauma survivors who report these aspects of posttraumatic growth, that *their losses have produced gains.*

We also find other paradoxes. For example, "I am more vulnerable, yet stronger." Individuals who experience negative life events not surprisingly tend to report an increased sense of vulnerability, congruent with the fact that they have suffered in ways they may not have been able to control or prevent (Janoff-Bulman, 1992). However, a common theme in the experience of persons who have faced major life challenges *is an increased sense of their own capacities to survive and prevail* (Calhoun & Tedeschi, 1999).

Another paradox often reported is that in the midst of suffering through the worst times in life, trauma survivors discover both the worst and best in others. People talk about finding out "who their real friends are" or "who you can really count on." People often find themselves disappointed in the responses of some of those persons with whom they may have been close, but on the other hand, pleasantly surprised by the helpfulness of others they may not have been particularly close to. A need to talk about the traumatic events sets in motion tests of interpersonal relationships—some pass, others fail. Another aspect of this self-disclosure is that trauma survivors find themselves becoming *more comfortable with intimacy*. A further component of the interpersonal elements of posttraumatic growth is the experience of *greater sense of compassion* for others who experience life difficulties. Although this increased sense of compassion may extend to other persons generally, it seems to be particularly the case for others who experience similar life difficulties.

People who face traumatic events, particularly those that make human mortality salient, may be more likely to become cognitively engaged with fundamental existential questions about death and the purpose of life. A commonly reported change is for the individual to *value the smaller things in life more*, and the apparently more important things less. For example, one's family, friends and small daily pleasures can be viewed as more important than before, and perhaps are now seen as more important than others, such as working long hours at one's occupation.

Facing mortality can produce important changes in the *religious, spiritual, and existential* components of philosophies of life. The specific content varies, of course, contingent on the individual's initial belief system and the cultural contexts within which the struggle with a life crises occurs. A common theme, however, is that after a period of spiritual or existential quest, individuals often report that *their philosophies of life are more fully developed, satisfying, and meaningful* to them. It appears that for many trauma survivors, a period of questioning their beliefs is ushered in because existential or spiritual issues have become more salient and less abstract. Although firm answers to the questions raised by trauma—why do traumatic events happen, what is the point to my life now that this trauma has occurred, why should I continue to struggle—are not necessarily found, grappling with these issues often produces a satisfaction in trauma survivors that they are experiencing life at a deeper level of awareness. This may be part of a developing life wisdom (see Linley, 2003), particularly in terms of the "fundamental pragmatics of life" (Baltes & Freund, 2003; Baltes & Smith, 1990) and the further development of the individual's own life narrative (McAdams, 1993; Tedeschi & Calhoun, 1995). It should be clear by now that the reflections on one's traumas and their aftermath are often unpleasant, although necessary in reconstructing the life narrative and establishing a wiser perspective on living that accommodates these difficult circumstances. Therefore, posttraumatic growth does not *necessarily* yield less emotional distress.

POSTTRAUMATIC GROWTH, PSYCHOLOGICAL COMFORT, AND SELF-ENHANCEMENT

One of the areas in which there is some inconsistency in the empirical data is on the relationship between posttraumatic growth and the sense of psychological comfort (Park, 1998). Although some studies find some relationship between measures of distress and measures of growth, others do not. It appears that the experience of posttraumatic growth, and psychological distress and comfort, may be essentially separate dimensions. This is relevant to the clinical context, because *people who experience significant levels of posttraumatic growth will not necessarily experience a commensurate decrease in their levels of distress nor an increase in their levels of happiness.* Furthermore, the maintenance of the growth experienced may require periodic cognitive reminders, which are not pleasant, of what has been lost, so that in an apparently paradoxical way, what has been gained remains in focus as well. Posttraumatic growth may lead to a more fulfilling and meaningful life, but it seems not to be the same as simply being carefree, being happy, or feeling good. Living a life at a deeper level of personal, interpersonal, and spiritual awareness is not necessarily the same as feeling good.

Given that survivors of major life crises may reflect on any of these aspects of post-traumatic growth, clinicians need to be prepared to grapple together with their clients as they address these issues. Clinicians need to appreciate paradox and ambiguity, the usefulness of thinking dialectically, and the patience necessary to process these concerns. Clinicians may also recognize some elements of self-enhancing bias at work in the experience of posttraumatic growth (McFarland & Alvaro, 2000). Our view, however, is that the clinician should approach such experiences on the part of their patients by accepting the reality of the experience for the individual. In addition, the available empirical evidence suggests that the self-ratings of growth on the part of individuals facing significant life challenges tend to be correlated with the ratings given to them by others (Moore et al., 2011; Park et al., 1996; Shakespeare-Finch & Enders, 2008; Weiss, 2002), indicating that the experience of posttraumatic growth is more than the mere manifestation of a self-enhancing cognitive bias.

*A Clarification About Viewing Trauma as Beneficial*   We interrupt our discussion with a perhaps unnecessary reminder that these traumatic events tend to produce a variety of distressing responses in the persons who experience them. These responses are almost always unpleasant, sometimes long lasting, and for some people the traumatic sets of circumstances may lead to the development of identifiable psychiatric disorders. It would be a misunderstanding to think that trauma is good—*we most certainly are not saying that.* What we are saying is that despite these distressing experiences people often report positive transformations, what we have called posttraumatic growth. An important way to think about this, which has implications for clinical practice, is that the traumatic events set in motion attempts to cope and that *the struggle in the aftermath of the crisis, not the event itself,* produces the posttraumatic growth. We also wish to make clear that the empirical evidence indicates that *posttraumatic growth is common but certainly not universal,* and as clinicians, we should never have the expectation that every survivor will experience growth, or that it is a necessary outcome for full trauma recovery.

## THE PROCESS OF POSTTRAUMATIC GROWTH

A central theme of the life challenges that are the focus here is their *seismic* nature (Calhoun & Tedeschi, 1998). Much like earthquakes can impact the physical environment, the events that represent major life crises are those that severely shake, challenge, or sometimes shatter the individual's way of understanding the world and her place in it (Janoff-Bulman, 1992). These seismic circumstances, characterized by their unusual, uncontrollable, potentially irreversible and threatening qualities, can produce a severe upheaval in the individuals' major assumptions about the world, their place in it, and how they make sense of their daily lives. When this shaking of the foundations of the individual's assumptive world (Parkes, 1970) reaches a sufficient catastrophic threshold, then the individual can be thought of as experiencing a traumatic event. In our model of posttraumatic growth (Calhoun, Cann, & Tedeschi, 2010; Calhoun & Tedeschi, 1998; Tedeschi & Calhoun, 1995), we emphasize that events must be of great enough impact to force individuals to reconsider the basic assumptions about who they are, what people around them are like, what kind of world they live in, or what the future may hold. In this reconsideration, there are the seeds for new perspectives on all these matters, and a sense that valuable, though painful, lessons have been learned. From a narrative perspective, the story of one's life has been divided into before and after the traumatic event, and the person after is quite different from the person before (McAdams, 1993; Tedeschi & Calhoun, 1995). This is particularly so when trauma has produced a very strong challenge to, or has invalidated, higher order goals or schemas (Carver, 1998).

COGNITIVE ENGAGEMENT AND COGNITIVE PROCESSING

Challenged or shattered assumptive worlds, or schemas, must be revised or reconstructed. The necessity of rebuilding a more resilient set of schemas leads people who have experienced trauma to think repeatedly about their circumstances, a form of cognitive processing that is characterized by "making sense, problem solving, reminiscence, and anticipation" (Martin & Tesser, 1996, p. 192). In the encounter with a traumatic event, the individual's *cognitive engagement*, recurring ruminative thought, tends to reflect the lack of fit between what has happened and the individual's reaction on the one hand, and the organizing schemas, beliefs, and life goals, on the other hand. This repeated cognitive engagement with the elements that have been made salient by the crisis, can lead to the recognition that certain life goals are no longer attainable, that certain schemas no longer accurately reflect what is, and that certain beliefs (e.g., *my world is safe*) are no longer valid.

As the person comes to recognize some goals as no longer attainable and that some components of the assumptive world cannot assimilate the reality of the aftermath of the trauma, then it is possible for the individual to begin to formulate new goals and to revise major components of the assumptive world in ways that acknowledge his changed life circumstances. To the extent that cognitive engagement produces these kinds of changes, and the individual begins to experience a movement toward the achievement of new life goals, then increased life satisfaction might be expected as a result (Little, 1998).

People who face major stressors often experience high levels of emotional distress that, for some persons, can be debilitating. Our assumption is that for many persons the level of emotional distress, which tends to be higher in the time following a traumatic event, tends also to be accompanied by cognitive engagement that may be more automatic than deliberate. These are automatic processes of coping with negative emotional states that at the earlier stages are more likely to include intrusive thoughts and intrusive images. As the individual's adaptive mechanisms become more effective at managing the high levels of emotional distress, eventually the reduction of distress and the process of ongoing cognitive engagement with trauma can lead to the adaptive disengagement from the goals and fundamental beliefs and assumptions that are no longer tenable. It is important, however, to keep in mind that for some persons this process will take a long time, perhaps months or years. And it is also possible that for some persons the attempt at adaptation to loss or trauma will never achieve a fully satisfactory psychological outcome (Wortman & Silver, 2001).

For many people faced with major crises and losses, their circumstances tend to lead them to become cognitively engaged in two general domains: making sense out of the immediate circumstances and making sense of the more fundamental elements of significance raised by the circumstances (Calhoun, Selby, & Selby, 1982; Davis, Nolen-Hoeksema, & Larson, 1998). The first domain reflects the process of attempting to understand the particular sequence of events that produced the set of circumstances with which the person must now cope. For example, what led a loved one to commit suicide, or what sequence of events produced a transportation accident? The second general domain reflects broader and more abstract concerns, often existential or spiritual in nature, about the fundamental meaning of circumstances of one's life as it exists in the aftermath of a trauma. These two domains of making sense of trauma are interwoven to some degree, although the dealing successfully with the first probably allows the trauma survivor to focus more on the second. Cognitive processing of trauma is not a neat process that can be easily reduced to a formula. There are many recursive and iterative aspects to it.

We are following the model of Martin and Tesser (1996), who describe this cognitive processing as conscious, which is easily cued, but also as occurring without direct cueing and involving attempts to make sense, problem solve, reminisce, or anticipate. There is some empirical suggestion that this kind of cognitive processing can be related to higher levels of posttraumatic growth. In one study, for example, young adults who had experienced major life stressors tended to report greater levels of posttraumatic growth when also reporting higher levels of cognitive engagement and processing recalled as occurring soon after crisis events (Calhoun, Cann, Tedeschi, & McMillan, 2000). In a study of the effects of journaling (Ullrich & Lutgendorf, 2002), university students who had been instructed to cognitively process their emotional responses, as compared to those instructed to focus on the facts or the associated emotions alone, reported higher levels of posttraumatic growth after four weeks. As such, cognitive engagement has become an integral component of the posttraumatic growth model (Calhoun et al., 2010; Calhoun & Tedeschi, 2013).

We have made a distinction in our model between the cognitive engagement of "deliberate rumination" and intrusive or automatic rumination. This distinction has also been described as reflective rumination versus brooding (Treynor, Gonzalez, & Nolen-Hoeksema, 2003). It appears that deliberate rumination about changes in core beliefs may be a strong predictor of posttraumatic growth (Triplett, Tedeschi, Cann, Calhoun, & Reeve, 2012).

## Disclosure, Support, and Narrative

The individual's cognitive engagement with, and cognitive processing of, crisis events may be assisted by the disclosure of that internal process to others in socially supportive environments. The available evidence suggests that such disclosure, in the form of written communications, can have useful health benefits (Pennebaker, 1997). Written disclosure of trauma-related material can also have an impact on the extent of posttraumatic growth experienced (Slavin-Spenny, Cohen, Oberleitner, & Lumley, 2011; Smyth, Hockemeyer, & Tulloch, 2008; Ullrich & Lutgendorf, 2002), particularly when the focus is on the processing of cognitive and emotional elements. The degree to which individuals perceive their social contexts to either encouraging and accepting, or inhibiting and sanctioning, their disclosure of trauma-related thoughts and feelings may play an important role in the process of posttraumatic growth. When people affected by trauma perceive their significant others as not wanting to hear about their difficulties, cognitive processing may be inhibited. And, to the extent that cognitive engagement with crisis related material is limited, it might be expected that crisis related growth is less likely (Cordova, Cunningham, Carlson, & Andrykowski, 2001).

The experience of social constraints that inhibit the disclosure of trauma-related thoughts, particularly those thoughts that are troubling and intrusive, produces a reliable relationship between the occurrence of those thoughts and depression (Lepore & Helgeson, 1998; Lepore, Silver, Wortman, & Wayment, 1996). Persons who are engaging in significant levels of trauma-related cognitive processing, but who experience social constraints limiting or prohibiting such disclosure, appear to be at higher risk for dysphoric emotions in the aftermath of a major life crisis. Conversely, trauma survivors who are supported when they engage in the disclosure of their cognitive processing may not only be less likely to experience depression, but may experience somewhat higher levels of posttraumatic growth as well (Nolen-Hoeksema & Larson, 1999). This assumption has also been empirically confirmed in a sample of cancer survivors who had undergone hematopoietic stem cell transplant. The results of this study indicate that social support is positively associated with self-reported posttraumatic growth (Nenova, DuHamel, Zemon, Rini, & Redd, 2013). In addition, it may be the case that *the presence of a social environment that explicitly addresses and encourages growth* may be an important factor in promoting posttraumatic growth. The availability of examples of growth narratives in the immediate social environment, perhaps in stories about how others have been changed positively by their encounters with trauma, or by exposure to others who have experienced similar difficulties and exhibit or describe ways in which their struggles have changed them, may enhance the likelihood that the individual will experience posttraumatic growth (Calhoun & Tedeschi, 2000).

## COGNITIVE PROCESSING, THE LIFE NARRATIVE, AND WISDOM

As individuals weave the experience of posttraumatic growth into the fabric of their life narratives (McAdams, 1993), the way they understand themselves and their lives can change. Trauma can become incorporated in the individual's own life story as a "reckoning time" that sets the stage for some fundamental changes in outlook (Tedeschi & Calhoun, 1995) or at least as "redemption sequences" (McAdams, Reynolds, Lewis, Patten, & Bowman, 2001) that are incorporated into life narratives. At some point, trauma survivors may be able to engage in a sort of metacognition or reflection on their own processing of their life events, seeing themselves as having spent time making a major alteration of their understanding of themselves and their lives. This becomes part of the life narrative and includes an appreciation for new, more sophisticated ways of grappling with life events. This is part of how posttraumatic growth develops dynamically over time, and the processes that lead to its maintenance—and, for some, perhaps its abatement over time—are dynamic also.

## WAYS CLINICIANS CAN FACILITATE THE PROCESS OF POSTTRAUMATIC GROWTH

With a basic understanding of the variables involved in the process of posttraumatic growth, we can consider how a clinician can affect this process in useful ways. We have talked about clinicians playing roles as facilitators of this process, because posttraumatic growth is likely to be inhibited by heavy-handed attempts to move trauma survivors toward understandings they have not yet directly experienced (Calhoun & Tedeschi, 1999, 2013). The changes that life crises produce are experiential, not merely intellectual, and that is what can make them so powerful. This is the same for posttraumatic growth—there is a compelling affective or experiential flavor to it that is important for the clinician to honor. Therefore, we see the clinician's role as often subtle in this facilitation. The clinician must be well attuned to the client when the client may be in the process of reconstructing schemas, thinking dialectically, recognizing paradox, and generating a revised life narrative. What follows here are some general guidelines to follow in this process. We refer the reader to Calhoun and Tedeschi (2013) for more extensive discussion and case examples.

We also wish to emphasize that the clinical activity we recommend does not constitute a technique to be employed, nor is this a proposal for a new therapy school.

The recommendation is that clinicians broaden their clinical perspectives so that elements of posttraumatic growth, and the possibility of helping clients further develop it, are part of the general clinical perspective they employ when trying to understand and assist persons who have been psychologically affected by a variety of events that might be considered traumatic for particular clients. Attention to elements of posttraumatic growth is compatible with a wide variety of the approaches that are currently utilized to provide help to persons dealing with trauma. Initially, clinicians should address high levels of emotional distress, providing the kind of support that can help make this manageable (Tedeschi & Calhoun, 1995). Allowing a distressed client to regain the ability to cognitively engage the aftermath of the trauma in a rather deliberate fashion will promote the possibility for posttraumatic growth. Then, it is likely that the domain the clinician may find to be the most productive for a possible focus on elements of posttraumatic growth is the process of cognitive engagement, cognitive processing, and cognitive change, including narrative reconstruction.

## THE EXPERT COMPANION

When working with people who come to us for assistance in coping with trauma and its aftermath, we refer to the stance we take as professionals as *expert companionship* (Calhoun & Tedeschi, 2013; Tedeschi & Calhoun, 2006). This term emphasizes the view that both professional expertise as well as human companionship are crucial for the people seeking our help. We chose these words carefully; we view ourselves as *facilitators* rather than creators of growth, and *companions* who offer some *expertise* in nurturing naturally occurring processes of healing and growth. Just as many of the procedures that physicians perform on the body facilitate a healing process that the body must ultimately do for itself, we see ourselves as likewise facilitating the natural process of psychological healing, which may not be able to function smoothly on its own in the aftermath of trauma. In the remainder of this chapter, we will review various aspects of the facilitation that the expert companion provides. We will also describe the kind of companionship we seek to give to trauma survivors, and the various aspects of expertise that are necessary to address the tasks that appear to be important in moving toward a growth outcome.

*General Considerations in Facilitating Posttraumatic Growth*   Particularly when working with survivors of traumatic events, who may be very distressed and vulnerable, it is important to utilize the best clinical practices. We also believe that these practices are critical to the facilitation of posttraumatic growth. We will highlight the relationship between these practices and how the clinician can act as a facilitator.

*The Framework of the Trauma Survivor*   Although for most clinicians the reminder is unnecessary, it is probably useful to repeat a general recommendation to make a good effort to understand the client's way of thinking about the situation. We emphasize three aspects of the client's perspective that need to concern clinicians. First, it is imperative that *clinicians listen carefully to the language of crisis and psychological response that clients use, and that they judiciously join clients in this form of communication.* Second, it is useful for clinicians to feel comfortable and willing to help their clients process their cognitive engagement with existential or spiritual matters. It is important *for clinicians to respect and work within the existential framework that clients have developed or are trying to rebuild in the aftermath of a trauma.* Another way in which the clinician should respect the client's framework, particularly when issues of posttraumatic growth are the focus, regards the acceptance of what the clinician may view as positive illusions (Taylor & Brown, 1988). Human beings generally tend to operate with certain benign cognitive distortions and persons facing major crises are probably not an exception. When working with clients dealing with traumatic circumstances, *clinicians may need to have some degree of tolerance and respect for the use of some benign cognitive biases*. Although the evidence tends to support the veracity of reports of posttraumatic growth, some clinicians may still be somewhat skeptical about the realistic foundations of the client's experience of growth. Although there certainly can be exceptions, our assumption is that clinical attempts to directly modify cognitions so that the benign illusory elements are corrected are likely to do psychological harm rather than to produce psychological benefit.

*The Value of Effective Listening*    As we have suggested, individuals in the aftermath of trauma exhibit a high level of cognitive engagement with and cognitive processing of their life situation. Such cognitive processes can lay the foundation for the development of the elements of posttraumatic growth. The availability of a skilled listener, who can encourage the individual to disclose the cognitive processing related to the crisis event, can encourage the kinds of cognitive changes that not only enhance coping generally, but also may promote posttraumatic growth. Although individual clients may need additional specific interventions designed to alleviate crisis related psychological symptoms, we think that the clinical guideline of *listen without necessarily trying to solve* (Calhoun & Tedeschi, 1999, 2013) can be a helpful one. One way of ensuring that clinicians practice this approach is to relate to survivors in such a way that their story affects the clinician personally. Being open to the possibility of being changed oneself, as a result of listening to the story of the trauma and its aftermath, communicates the highest degree of respect for clients, and encourages them to see the value in their own experience. This acknowledged value is a short step away from posttraumatic growth.

People who have been exposed to trauma may find it useful to tell their story repeatedly, and the clinician may need to listen patiently as the client repeats the story of what has happened. The individual's repetition of the account of the difficult experience can serve a safe exposure function when the difficulty is associated with an identifiable stimulus array, and this alone can have therapeutic value. The retelling of the account can also help the person engage in the kinds of cognitive activity that can help the individual accommodate cognitive structure to the undeniable events, and in this process the possibility of discovering posttraumatic growth exists.

Although we are encouraging what may seem to be a rather passive clinical stance, the way the clinician listens and what the clinician listens and attends to can have significant therapeutic consequences. As is apparent, our assumption is that clinicians will need to be skilled at deciding the types of responses to make and what to encourage the client to say and do. For example, in listening to the repeated telling of stories, clinicians may highlight the subtle changes in the tellings—details never included before, differences in the descriptors used, changes in the perspective taken, shifts in the affect displayed. Any such elements can be pointed out, especially when there is a hint of an emerging aspect of posttraumatic growth. Although compared to more structured approaches, what is suggested here does lack a certain degree of prescriptiveness, this general framework can certainly be woven into even rather prescriptive, manual driven psychological interventions designed to help persons coping with the aftermath of trauma.

*Listen for and Label Posttraumatic Growth*    Clients will routinely and spontaneously articulate ways in which their struggle has produced highly meaningful changes in them, without clinicians prompting them. However, our experience has been that only rarely will clients actually identify such changes as a representation of posttraumatic growth. A small but very useful change that clinicians can make in their work with persons who are dealing trauma, then, is simply to *listen for themes of posttraumatic growth* in what their clients say. When clinicians notice and label as positive the positive changes that clients relate, this can be a therapeutic cognitive experience for the client. The clinician must have good knowledge of the domains and elements of posttraumatic growth, listen for and attend to the client's account of the experience of growth, and label the experience in a way that makes the growth experience cognitively salient for the client. However, *the clinician must guard against the mechanistic offering of empty platitudes* that tell the client, for example, what wonderful opportunities for growth are offered by the experience of trauma. If the clinician has listened well to the client's account of the circumstances and of the client's personal reactions, including affective, cognitive, and behavioral components, the insensitive and inappropriate offering of platitudes becomes extremely unlikely. What we are suggesting is that the clinician should respond in ways that reflect discoveries that their clients themselves are making. As we have implied, however, the way in which the client has cognitively constructed the posttraumatic experience may only implicitly reflect the experience of growth, and the clinician can highlight these statements that imply growth.

*How and When a Clinician Chooses to Highlight*   The posttraumatic growth that is emerging in a client is an important consideration. Just as a clinician could make insensitive remarks that come across as platitudes, getting the timing of posttraumatic growth remarks wrong can also have a counterproductive effect. Our experience suggests to us that *very early in the posttrauma process is usually not a good time* for attention to be directed toward the possibility of posttraumatic growth. The immediate aftermath of tragedy is a time during which clinicians must be particularly sensitive to the psychological needs of the patient, and never engage in the insensitive introduction of didactic information or trite comments about growth coming from suffering. This is not to say that systematic treatment programs designed for trauma survivors should not include growth-related components, since these may indeed by helpful (Antoni et al., 2001). But we tend to think that even as part of a systematic intervention program, matters related to growth are best addressed only after the client has had a sufficient time to achieve at least some degree of equilibrium.

*Focus on the Struggle, Rather Than the Event*   For some trauma survivors, what has happened to them may have been so horrible, and the aftermath may be so devastating, that the very concept of posttraumatic growth may be repellent. Clinicians should respect that perspective. The available data, however, indicate that some people coping with even the most horrible events can experience some degree of posttraumatic growth (Tedeschi & Calhoun, 1995). The clinician who is interested in the encouragement of growth that some clients may experience, then, must perform what on the surface may be a paradoxical task—to acknowledge the reality that for some persons the very discussion of growth coming from the struggle may be unacceptable given the horrific nature of what they have undergone, but at the same time the clinician should be open to the possibility that clients themselves may experience growth from their struggle with even the most tragic and traumatic sets of circumstances. To try to address this issue, a clinician may say, "You may have heard people say that they have found some benefit in their struggle with trauma. Given what has happened to you, do you think that is possible?" Also notice that in this question, the clinician makes a clear distinction between the events that have happened and the individual's *struggle* to survive psychologically and adapt to their painful circumstances. A useful way to speak of the possibility of growth is to use words that indicate that the experience of growth the patient may have undergone is a result *of the struggle* to adapt to the trauma and not to the situation itself.

Clinicians who work with survivors of highly stressful events often find them selves using metaphors in their conversations with clients, because description of the traumatic events and their effects may be difficult to achieve in more straight-forward language. Listening for metaphors a client uses, or introducing metaphors that might be particularly salient for an individual, allows for discussions of posttraumatic growth in these more indirect ways, allowing trauma survivors to acknowledge things that otherwise would be difficult. For example, we have described a case where a photographer whose son died could recognize changes in himself as photos emerging from developing fluid (Calhoun & Tedeschi, 1999, 2013).

*Exposure to Models of Posttraumatic Growth*    Trauma survivors may be better able to develop an ability to recognize, or even aspire to, posttraumatic growth if they are exposed to other survivors who have responded in this way. For this reason we have favored the use of group treatments for many trauma survivors (Tedeschi & Calhoun, 1995, 2003), with the expectation that the mutual help exchanged in such groups may also give trauma survivors an opportunity to experience the power of their own gifts of empathy and compassion, learned from their trauma. We also have recommended a number of books and other resources that include growth themes in trauma survival (Calhoun & Tedeschi, 1999, 2013; Tedeschi & Calhoun, 1995, 2003).

*A Little Push Toward Growth*    Without announcing to clients that we have any expectations for them to experience posttraumatic growth, we sometimes offer assignments that may allow them to begin to notice aspects of growth in their struggles. Writing assignments that encourage narrative development are often useful for trauma survivors (Resick & Calhoun, 2001), and in these narratives growth can emerge. We also have suggestions for assignments that involve self-monitoring of changing beliefs in the aftermath of trauma (Calhoun & Tedeschi, 1999). Focus on these assignments in subsequent therapy sessions can allow clinicians an opportunity to highlight emerging growth perspectives.

## UTILIZING A MODEL OF POSTTRAUMATIC GROWTH INTEGRATED WITH TRAUMA TREATMENT

Effective clinicians treating trauma survivors should maintain a focus on the possibility of posttraumatic growth from the start of treatment as they use empirically supported trauma treatment approaches together with empirically based growth facilitation. Calhoun and Tedeschi (2013) offer a description of five elements of growth-oriented trauma therapy that expert companions can use: a psychoeducational component that emphasizes normal trauma responses that act as precursors to growth; the development of emotion-regulation strategies to allow for effective deliberate rumination; methods of constructive self-disclosure within relationships; the creation of a new life narrative with posttraumatic growth elements; and the development of life principles and core beliefs that are robust to future traumas and promote resilience.

CAVEATS AND REMINDERS

Posttraumatic growth occurs in the context of suffering and significant psychological struggle, and a focus on growth should not come at the expense of empathy for the pain and suffering of trauma survivors. For most, posttraumatic growth and distress will coexist. It is also important to remember that trauma is not necessary for growth. People can mature and develop in meaningful ways without experiencing tragedy or trauma. In no way are we suggesting that trauma is good. We regard life crises, loss, and trauma as undesirable, and our wish would be that nobody would have to experience such life events. We regard traumatic events as indeed negative, but the evidence suggests that those who are forced to struggle with them can experience highly meaningful personal changes. To repeat what we have previously said—posttraumatic growth is neither universal nor inevitable. Although a majority of people experiencing a wide array of highly of challenging life circumstances experience posttraumatic growth, there are also a significant number of persons who experience little or no growth in their struggle with trauma. This sort of outcome is quite acceptable; we are not raising the bar on trauma survivors—they should not be expected to show posttraumatic growth before being considered recovered.

## THE CLINICIAN'S GAIN

Work with survivors of traumatic events from the growth perspective we have outlined can be highly rewarding for clinicians. In listening to clients with respect for their strength and ability to change, we find ourselves changed for the better. We learn lessons along with our clients and find that many of our colleagues can also identify this vicarious posttraumatic growth (Arnold, Calhoun, Tedeschi, & Cann, 2000; Horrell, Holohan, Didion, & Vance, 2011; Linley, Joseph, & Loumidis, 2005; Profitt, Calhoun, Tedeschi, & Cann, 2002). The model we have outlined allows us to share both the suffering and the possibilities with those who are being tempered by the fire.

## SUMMARY POINTS

- Be aware of the possibility of posttraumatic growth (PTG) from the beginning of trauma treatment.
- Highlight and explore PTG indications when they begin to appear in the client's story.
- PTG is not a way to eliminate the distress of trauma.
- A focus primarily of symptom reduction will tend to retard the process of growth.
- To be an expert companion for trauma survivors, focus on learning from them and let this be the conversation you have, rather than being intent on changing them.

## REFERENCES

Aldwin, C. M. (1994). *Stress, coping, and development*. New York, NY: Guilford Press.

Andreasen, N. L., & Norris, A. S. (1972). Long-term adjustment and adaptation mechanisms in severely burned adults. *Journal of Nervous and Mental Disease, 154*, 352–362.

Antoni, M. H., Lehman, J. M., Kilbourn, K. M., Boyers, A. E., Yount, S. E., Culver, J. L., . . . Carver, C. S. (2001). Cognitive-behavioral stress management intervention decreases the prevalence of depression and enhances the sense of benefit among women under treatment for early-stage breast cancer. *Health Psychology, 20*, 20–32.

Arnold, D., Calhoun, L. G., Tedeschi, R. G., & Cann, A. (2000, August). *Vicarious transformation in psychotherapy with trauma survivors.* Poster presented at the Annual Convention of the American Psychological Association, Washington, DC.

Baltes, P. B., & Freund, A. M. (2003). Human strengths as the orchestration of wisdom and selective optimization with compensation. In L. G. Aspinwall & U. M. Staudinger (Eds.), *A psychology of human strengths* (pp. 23–35). Washington, DC: American Psychological Association.

Baltes, P. B., & Smith, J. (1990). Toward a psychology of wisdom and its ontogenesis. In R. J. Sternberg (Ed.), *Wisdom: Its nature, origins, and development* (pp. 87–120). New York, NY: Cambridge University Press.

Bower, J. E., Kemeny, M. E., Taylor, S. E., & Fahey, J. L. (1998). Cognitive processing, discovery of meaning, CD 4 decline, and AIDS-related mortality among bereaved HIV-seropositive men. *Journal of Consulting and Clinical Psychology, 66,* 979–986.

Calhoun, L. G., Cann, A., & Tedeschi, R. G. (2010). The posttraumatic growth model: Sociocultural considerations. In T. Weiss & R. Berger (Eds.), *Posttraumatic growth and culturally competent practice* (pp. 1–14). Hoboken, NJ: Wiley.

Calhoun, L. G., Cann, A., Tedeschi, R. G., & McMillan, J. (2000). A correlational test of the relationship between posttraumatic growth, religion, and cognitive processing. *Journal of Traumatic Stress, 13,* 521–527.

Calhoun, L. G., Selby, J. W., & Selby, L. E. (1982). The psychological aftermath of suicide: An analysis of current evidence. *Clinical Psychology Review, 2,* 409–420.

Calhoun, L. G., & Tedeschi, R. G. (1989–1990). Positive aspects of critical life problems: Recollections of grief. *Omega, 20,* 265–272.

Calhoun, L. G., & Tedeschi, R. G. (1991). Perceiving benefits in traumatic events: Some issues for practicing psychologists. *Journal of Training & Practice in Professional Psychology, 5,* 45–52.

Calhoun, L. G., & Tedeschi, R. G. (1998). Posttraumatic growth: Future directions. In R. G. Tedeschi, C. L. Park, & L. G. Calhoun, (Eds.), *Posttraumatic growth: Positive change in the aftermath of crisis* (pp. 215–238). Mahwah, NJ: Erlbaum.

Calhoun, L. G., & Tedeschi, R. G. (1999). *Facilitating posttraumatic growth: A clinician's guide.* Mahwah, NJ: Erlbaum.

Calhoun, L. G., & Tedeschi, R. G. (2000). Early posttraumatic interventions: Facilitating possibilities for growth. In J. M. Volanti, D. Paton, & C. Dunning (Eds.), *Posttraumatic stress intervention: Challenges, issues and perspectives* (pp. 135–152). Springfield, IL: Charles C. Thomas.

Calhoun, L. G., & Tedeschi, R. G. (2006). *Handbook of posttraumatic growth.* Mahwah, NJ: Erlbaum.

Calhoun, L. G., & Tedeschi, R. G. (2013). *Posttraumatic growth in clinical practice.* New York, NY: Routledge.

Calhoun, L. G., Tedeschi, R. G., Fulmer, D., & Harlan, D. (2000, August). *Parental grief: The relation of rumination, distress, and posttraumatic growth.* Poster presented at the Annual Convention of the American Psychological Association, Washington, DC.

Caplan, G. (1964). *Principles of preventive psychiatry.* New York, NY: Basic Books.

Carver, C. S. (1998). Resilience and thriving: Issues, models, and linkages. *Journal of Social Issues, 54,* 245–266.

Cordova, M. J., Cunningham, L. L. C., Carlson, C. R., & Andrykowski, M. A. (2001). Posttraumatic growth following breast cancer: A controlled comparison study. *Health Psychology, 20,* 176–185.

Davis, C. G., Nolen-Hoeksema, S., & Larson, J. (1998). Making sense of loss and benefiting from the experience: Two construals of meaning. *Journal of Personality and Social Psychology, 75,* 561–574.

Finkel, N. J. (1974). Strens and traumas: An attempt at categorization. *American Journal of Community Psychology, 2,* 265–273.

Finkel, N. J. (1975). Strens, traumas and trauma resolution. *American Journal of Community Psychology, 3*, 173–178.

Folkman, S., & Moskowitz, J. T. (2000). Stress, positive emotion, and coping. *Current Directions in Psychological Science, 9*, 115–118.

Frankl, V. E. (1963). *Man's search for meaning.* New York, NY: Pocket Books.

Horrell, S. C. V., Holohan, D. R., Didion, L. M., & Vance, G. T. (2011). Treating traumatized OEF/OIF veterans: How does trauma treatment affect the clinician? *Professional Psychology: Research and Practice, 42*, 79–86.

Janoff-Bulman, R. (1992). *Shattered assumptions.* New York, NY: The Free Press.

Joseph, S. (2011). *What doesn't kill us: The new psychology of posttraumatic growth.* New York, NY: Basic Books.

Lepore, S. J., & Helgeson, V. S. (1998). Social constraints, intrusive thoughts, and mental health after prostate cancer. *Journal of Social and Clinical Psychology, 17*, 89–106.

Lepore, S. J., Silver, R. C., Wortman, C. B., & Waymant, H. A. (1996). Social constraints, intrusive thoughts, and depressive symptoms among bereaved mothers. *Journal of Personality and Social Psychology, 70*, 271–282.

Linley, P. A. (2003). Positive adaptation to trauma: Wisdom as both process and outcome. *Journal of Traumatic Stress, 16*(6), 601–610.

Linley, P. A., & Joseph, S. (2004). Positive change following trauma and adversity: A review. *Journal of Traumatic Stress, 17*(1), 11–21.

Linley, P. A., Joseph, S., & Loumidis, K. (2005). Trauma work, sense of coherence, and positive and negative changes in therapists. *Psychotherapy and Psychosomatics, 74*(3), 185–188.

Little, B. R. (1998). Personal project pursuit: Dimensions and dynamics of personal meaning. In P. T. P. Wong & P. S. Fry (Eds.), *The human quest for meaning: A handbook of psychological research and clinical applications* (pp. 193–212). Mahwah, NJ: Erlbaum.

Lopata, H. Z. (1973). Self-identity in marriage and widowhood. *Sociological Quarterly, 14*, 407–418.

Martin, L. L., & Tesser, A. (1996). Clarifying our thoughts. In R. S. Wyer (Ed.), *Advances in social cognition: Vol. 9. Ruminative thoughts* (pp. 189–209). Mahwah, NJ: Erlbaum.

McAdams, D. P. (1993). *The stories we live by: Personal myths and the making of the self.* New York, NY: Morrow.

McAdams, D. P., Reynolds, J., Lewis, M., Patten, A. H., & Bowman, P. J. (2001). When bad things turn good and good things turn bad: Sequences of redemption and contamination in life narrative and their relations to psychosocial adaptation in midlife adults and in students. *Personality and Social Psychology Bulletin, 27*, 474–485.

McCrae, R. R. (1984). Situational determinants of coping responses: Loss, threat, and challenge. *Journal of Personality and Social Psychology, 46*, 919–928.

McFarland, C., & Alvaro, C. (2000). The impact of motivation on temporal comparisons: Coping with traumatic events by perceiving personal growth. *Journal of Personality and Social Psychology, 79*, 327–343.

McMillen, C., Zuravin, S., & Rideout, G. (1995). Perceived benefits from child sexual abuse. *Journal of Consulting and Clinical Psychology, 63*, 1037–1043.

Moore, A. M., Gamblin, T., Geller, D. A., Youssef, M. N., Hoffman, K. E., Gemmell, L., . . . Steel, J. L. (2011). A prospective study of posttraumatic growth as assessed by self report and family caregiver in the context of advanced cancer. *Psycho-Oncology, 20*(5), 479–487. doi: 10.1002/pon.1746

Nenova, M., DuHamel, K., Zemon, V., Rini, C., & Redd, W. H. (2013). Posttraumatic growth, social support, and social constraint in hematopoietic stem cell transplant survivors. *Psycho-Oncology, 22*(1), 195–202. doi: 10.1002/pon.2073

Nolen-Hoeksema, S., & Larson, J. (1999). *Coping with loss.* Mahwah, NJ: Erlbaum.

O'Leary, V. E., & Ickovics, J. R. (1995). Resilience and thriving in response to challenge: An opportunity for a paradigm shift in women's health. *Women's Health: Research on Gender, Behavior, and Policy, 1*, 121–142.

Pargament, K. I. (1996). Religious methods of coping: Resources for the conservation and trans-formation of significance. In E. P. Shafranske (Ed.), *Religion and the clinical practice of psychology* (pp. 215–240). Washington, DC: American Psychological Association.

Park, C. L. (1998). Implications of posttraumatic growth for individuals. In R. G. Tedeschi, C. L. Park, & L. G. Calhoun (Eds.), *Posttraumatic growth: Positive change in the aftermath of crisis* (pp. 153–177). Mahwah, NJ: Erlbaum.

Park, C. L., Cohen, L., & Murch, R. (1996). Assessment and prediction of stress-related growth. *Journal of Personality, 64*, 71–105.

Parkes, C. M. (1970). Psycho-social transitions: A field for study. *Social Science and Medicine, 5*, 101–115.

Pennebaker, J. W. (1997). *Opening up: The healing power of expressing emotions.* New York, NY: Guilford Press.

Powell. S., Rosner, R., Butollo, W., Tedeschi, R. G., & Calhoun, L. G. (2003). Posttraumatic growth after war: A study with former refugees and displaced people in Sarajevo. *Journal of Clinical Psychology, 59*, 71–83.

Profitt, D. H., Calhoun, L. G., Tedeschi, R. G., & Cann, A. (2002, August). *Clergy and crisis: Cor-relates of posttraumatic growth and well-being.* Poster presented at the Annual Convention of the American Psychological Association, Chicago, IL.

Resick, P. A., & Calhoun, K. S. (2001). Posttraumatic stress disorder. In D. H. Barlow (Ed.), *Clinical handbook of psychological disorders* (3rd ed., pp. 60–113). New York, NY: Guilford Press.

Ryff, C. D., & Singer, B. S. (1998). The role of purpose in life and personal growth in positive human health. In P. T. P. Wong & P. S. Fry (Eds.), *The human quest for meaning: A handbook of psychological research and clinical applications* (pp. 213–235). Mahwah, NJ: Erlbaum.

Scheier, M. F., Weintraub, J. K., & Carver, C. S. (1986). Coping with stress: Divergent strategies of optimists and pessimists. *Journal of Personality and Social Psychology, 51*, 1257–1264.

Shakespeare-Finch, J., & Enders, T. (2008). Corroborating evidence of posttraumatic growth. *Journal of Traumatic Stress, 21*, 421–424.

Slavin-Spenny, O. M., Cohen, J. L., Oberleitner, L. M., & Lumley, M. A. (2011). The effects of different methods of emotional disclosure: Differentiating post-traumatic growth from stress symptoms. *Journal of Clinical Psychology, 67*, 993–1007.

Smyth, J. M., Hockemeyer, J. R., & Tulloch, H. (2008). Expressive writing and post-traumatic stress disorder: Effects on trauma symptoms, mood states, and cortisol reactivity. *British Jour-nal of Health Psychology, 13*, 85–93.

Taku, K., Calhoun, L. G., Cann, A., & Tedeschi, R. G. (2008). The role of rumination in the coexistence of distress and posttraumatic growth among bereaved Japanese university stu-dents. *Death Studies, 32*(5), 428–444.

Taylor, S. E., & Brown, J. D. (1988). Illusion and well-being: A social psychological perspective on mental health. *Psychological Bulletin, 103*, 193–210.

Tedeschi, R. G. (1999). Violence transformed: Posttraumatic growth in survivors and their soci-eties. *Aggression and Violent Behavior, 4*, 319–341.

Tedeschi, R. G. (2011). Posttraumatic growth in combat veterans. *Journal of Clinical Psychology in Medical Settings, 18*(2), 137–144.

Tedeschi, R. G., & Calhoun, L. G. (1988, August). *Perceived benefits in coping with physical hand-icaps.* Paper presented at the annual meeting of the American Psychological Association, Atlanta, GA.

Tedeschi, R. G., & Calhoun, L. G. (1995). *Trauma and transformation: Growing in the aftermath of suffering.* Thousand Oaks, CA: Sage.

Tedeschi, R. G., & Calhoun, L. G. (1996). The Posttraumatic Growth Inventory: Measuring the positive legacy of trauma. *Journal of Traumatic Stress, 9,* 455–471.

Tedeschi, R. G., & Calhoun, L. G. (2003). *Helping the bereaved parent: A clinician's guide.* New York, NY: Brunner-Routledge.

Tedeschi, R. G. & Calhoun, L. G. (2004). Posttraumatic growth: Conceptual foundations and empirical evidence. *Psychological Inquiry, 15*(1), 1–18.

Tedeschi, R. G., & Calhoun, L. G. (2006). Expert Companion: Posttraumatic growth in clinical practice. In L. G. Calhoun & R. G. Tedeschi (Eds.), *Handbook of posttraumatic growth: Research and practice* (pp. 291–310). Mahwah, NJ: Erlbaum.

Tedeschi, R. G., & Calhoun, L. G. (2007). Beyond the concept of recovery: Growth and the experience of loss. *Death Studies, 32*(1), 27–39.

Tedeschi, R. G., Calhoun, L. G., & Engdahl, B. E. (2001). Opportunities for growth in survivors of trauma. *National Center for PTSD Clinical Quarterly, 10,* 23–25.

Tedeschi, R. G., Calhoun, L. G., Morrell, R. W., & Johnson, K. A. (1984, August). *Bereavement: From grief to psychological development.* Paper presented at the annual meeting of the American Psychological Association, Toronto, ON.

Tedeschi, R. G., & McNally, R. J. (2011). Can we facilitate posttraumatic growth in combat veterans? *American Psychologist, 66*(1), 19.

Tedeschi, R. G., Park, C. L., & Calhoun, L. G. (Eds.). (1998). *Posttraumatic growth: Positive change in the aftermath of crisis.* Mahwah, NJ: Erlbaum.

Tennen, H., Affleck, G., Urrows, S., Higgins, P., & Mendola, R. (1992). Perceiving control, construing benefits, and daily processes in rheumatoid arthritis. *Canadian Journal of Behavioral Science, 24,* 186–203.

Treynor, W., Gonzalez, R., & Nolen-Hoeksema, S. (2003). Rumination reconsidered: A psychometric analysis. *Cognitive Therapy and Research, 27,* 247–259.

Triplett, K. N., Tedeschi, R. G., Cann, A., Calhoun, L. G., & Reeve, C. L. (2012). Posttraumatic growth, meaning in life, and life satisfaction in response to trauma. *Psychological Trauma: Theory, Research, Practice, and Policy, 4,* 400–410.

Ullrich, P. M., & Lutgendorf, A. K. (2002). Journaling about stressful events: Effects of cognitive processing and emotional expression. *Annals of Behavioral Medicine, 24,* 244–250.

Weiss, T. (2002). Posttraumatic growth in women with breast cancer and their husbands: An intersubjective validation study. *Journal of Psychosocial Oncology, 20,* 65–80.

Wortman, C. B., & Silver, R. C. (2001). The myths of coping with loss revisited. In M. S. Stroebe, R. O. Hansson, W. Stroebe, & H. Schut (Eds.), *Handbook of bereavement research: Consequences, coping and care* (pp. 405–429). Washington, DC: American Psychological Association.

Yalom, I. D., & Lieberman, M. A. (1991). Bereavement and heightened existential awareness. *Psychiatry, 54,* 334–345.

# CHAPTER 31

# Strength-Based Assessment

TAYYAB RASHID

A SSESSMENT, WHETHER FORMAL or informal, objective or projective, psycho-emotional or sociocultural, intrapersonal or interpersonal, is an inherent part of good clinical practice (Butcher, 2006). Traditionally, clinical assessment has explored underpinning of deficits, disorders, symptoms, syndrome, weaknesses, and vulnerabilities. Expanding the scope of clinical assessment, the chapter describes a strength-based approach within the clinical context. First, the chapter discusses the limitations of deficit-oriented assessment. Second, it defines and describes, with illustrations, a strengths-based clinical assessment and proposes a theoretical framework to understand clinical concerns not only as the presence of symptoms but also as a lack or excess of strengths. Third, the chapter ends with concrete suggestions about incorporating strengths into clinical practice.

A strength-based assessment (SBA) explores a rich diversity of attributes, experiences, and processes that are positive and adaptive within their context. SBA explores psychological abilities, assets, and strategies that can further be nurtured in order to encounter and potentially buffer against psychological disorders. SBA, despite its name and explicit emphasis on strengths, is not only about strengths. By giving equal attention and importance to strengths, SBA integrates symptoms and skills, risk and resource, and vulnerability and resilience to yield complex yet realistic portrayals of clients, thereby offering multiple routes toward obtaining and sustaining healthy psychological functioning.

Clinical assessment has almost exclusively focused on deficits for plausible reasons. Negatives are far more pervasive and more potent than positives. By one estimate, for one positive emotional term there are 10 negatives (Nesse, 1991). Their potency and prevalence forms the undercurrent of negativity bias, which has influenced literary, religious, and cultural sources, as well as psychological domains including learning, attention, impression formation, contagion, moral judgment, development, and memory. Negativity bias has a number of clinical implications, including (a) negatives stand out in clients' experiences of equal valence; (b) negative experiences are approached more rapidly in time and space in clinical settings than are positive ones; (c) while weighing the combination of negative and positive experiences, negative experiences tend to dominate clients' emotions; and (d) compared to positive, negative experiences may invite more complex and deeper clinical discourse—for clients and clinicians. Therefore, it is not surprising that clients seeking clinical services easily recall negative events, setbacks, and failures and clinicians readily assess, elaborate, and interpret stories of conflict, ambivalence, deceit, personal, or interpersonal deficits. Because of their apparent greater informational value, clinicians pay greater attention to negatives and engage in complex cognitive processing (e.g., Peeters & Czapinski, 1990). Thus, clinical assessment is typically conducted to explore presence or absence of disorder.

Deficit-based clinical assessment has helped to decipher both the global and granular aspects of psychopathology. A number of personality and behavioral measures have been widely researched and have substantially helped psychotherapy through the mechanism of feedback to be more effective (Lambert, 2007). Yet, clinical assessment has three serious shortcomings.

First, it assumes that only symptoms are valid and central ingredients that ought to be assessed carefully, whereas positives are by-products of symptomatic relief lying on clinical peripheries that do not need to be assessed. So entrenched is this assumption that traditionally positive attributes are considered defenses. For example, anxiety has been theorized as a driving force behind a work ethic that characterized the Reformation (Weber, 2002). Depression has been theorized as process that dealt by feeling guilty, and out of this guilt comes compassion (McWilliams, 1994). By contrast, in SBA, strengths are as real as human weaknesses, as old as time, and valued in every culture (Peterson & Seligman, 2004). In clinical assessment and treatment, strengths are as critical in evaluating and treating psychopathology as are symptoms. Strengths are not considered defenses, by-products, or compensations. They are valued in their own right and weighed independent of weaknesses in the assessment procedure.

Second, deficit-oriented assessment reduces clients and may compartmentalize them into synthetic labels carefully ascertained within the synthetic categories of the *Diagnostic and Statistical Manual of Mental Disorders*, fifth edition (*DSM-V*; American Psychiatric Association, 2013). The use of these labels is so widespread that some clients, courtesy of a Google search, seek clinical services with expectations of fitting themselves in these categories. A psychiatric diagnosis, otherwise a careful and discerning process, frequently becomes an exercise in confirming or ruling out a diagnostic label. Labeling, itself, is not undesirable. Labels categorize and organize the world, but reducing or objectifying clients to labels of psychopathology may strip clients of their rich complexity (Szasz, 1961). In turn, clients may think of themselves as deeply disturbed, anxious, or depressed—the content of these labels. Thus, labels describe but also restrict clinical experience.

Finally, a deficit-based assessment inadvertently exposes clinicians to disproportionately more negatives. Eliciting, discussing, and interpreting nuances of traumas, hurts, resentments, deceits, and disappointments likely leads to emotional exhaustion, depersonalization, and a lessened sense of personal accomplishment (Jenaro, Flores, & Arias, 2007). Idiosyncratic details of negatives may trigger, among some clinicians, recall of their personal trauma, or they may experience negative reactions toward some clients (Pope & Tabachinick, 1994).

Deficit-based assessment paints an incomplete and skewed portrayal of clients, with reduced clarity, lacking important information that could be critical in treatment planning. Clinical assessment ought be a hybrid process that explores strengths as well as weaknesses. The focus of assessment should be collecting not only stories of unmet needs but also tales of fulfillment. Assessment should explore not just conflicts but also compromises, transgressions as well as acts of compassion, selfishness of others but also genuine actions of sharing, grudges as well as expressions of gratitude, and episodes of vengeance as well instances of forgiveness. It is about exploring in an authentic way hubris as well as humility, haste as well as self-restraint, hate as well as love, pain of trauma as well as growth from it. SBA is not about dismissing negatives. It is about fine tuning of clinical assessment toward balance.

## STRENGTH-BASED ASSESSMENT

Emphasis on SBA is consistent with the contemporary thrust in positive psychology, which studies conditions and processes that enable individuals, communities, and institutions to flourish. Positive psychology explores *what works, what is right, and what can be nurtured* (Rashid, Summers, & Seligman, in press). Although strengths are not a standard feature of a typical clinical assessment, they are not alien to humanistic, educational, solution-focused, and family-based approaches (e.g., Epstein & Sharma, 1998; Friedman & MacDonald, 2006; Iveson, 1994; Saleebey, 1996). Unfortunately, because of political and economic factors, and the uncritical embrace of medical models by clinical psychology, the assessment and treatment of deficits has traditionally been the primary function of clinical practice (Maddux, 2002). Career-driven pragmatic specializations and tightening of disciplinary boundaries further phased strengths (as well as ethics) out from the social and clinical realms into philosophical discourse (Sloan, 1980). Following the psychiatric instructional model, training of clinicians, especially in hospitals, medical clinics, and community health centers—which operate on the deficit model—further entrenched deficit-oriented assessment in clinical practice.

Current clinical assessment is largely geared toward uncovering childhood traumas, evaluating distorted thoughts, and assessing interpersonal difficulties. People avoid seeking clinical services because they fear being stigmatized if their challenges are formulated into a psychiatric diagnosis (Corrigan, 2004). Portrayal of individuals with mental health illnesses in the popular media, using diagnostic labels such as paranoid schizophrenia, borderline personality disorder, obsessive-compulsive disorder, psychopath, and antisocial personality disorder, maintain the stigma against mental health. Moreover, increasingly diverse and cosmopolitan patrons do not readily subscribe with Eurocentric diagnostic labels.

Assessing strengths can provide the clinician with a powerful tool to understand a client's intact repertoires, which can be effectively utilized in treatment planning, enabling clients and clinicians to intervene and evaluate treatment through multiple avenues (reduction in symptoms, increase in positive emotions, improved social relationships, better work–life balance, etc.). Considering what strengths a client brings to effectively deal with troubles stimulates a very different discussion and therapeutic relationship from a deficit-oriented inquiry probing, "What weaknesses have led to your symptoms?"

Strength-based assessment offers distinct advantages. Assessing strengths changes the orientation of clinical services from remediation to nurturance of resilience and well-being. Knowledge of strengths offers clients an additional but important strategy to solve their problems, which likely increases their self-efficacy. Assessment and deployment of strengths such as optimism, hope, zest, curiosity, creativity, social intelligence, and gratitude cultivates positive emotions.

Strength awareness also builds a cumulative advantage. Evidence shows that people who are aware of their strengths can build self-confidence at a young age and tend to reap a "cumulative advantage" that continues to grow over a lifetime (Judge & Hurst, 2008). The broaden-and-build theory of positive emotions (Fredrickson, 2001) applied to clinical practice argues that strengths broaden the repertoire of action potentials in the present and build resources in the future. A strength- and not deficit-based assessment approach is more likely to meet contemporary needs. By refocusing and incorporating strengths, clinical assessment becomes more inclusive, innovative, open-minded, and adaptable to contemporary real-time digital zeitgeist.

## Theoretical Threads

Theoretical underpinnings of strengths, although sparingly, have been discussed in the psychological literature (e.g., Cawley, Martin, & Johnson, 2000; Jahoda, 1958; Maslow, 1959; Rokeach, 1973; Ryff & Singer, 1996). But these notions have not evolved in an organized system of clinical assessment and intervention. The emergence of positive psychology since 2000, as a movement to refocus and redirect psychological attention and efforts to positives as well as negatives, has sparked interest in SBA. However, the notions have been echoed previously. Evans (1993), more than two decades ago, postulated negative behaviors or symptoms have alternative positive forms. To some extent, this reciprocity is a matter of semantics. Symptoms are defined in everyday language that can always be translated into their simple opposites, although not all symptoms or disorders lend themselves naturally to this reciprocity. For example, courage could be conceptualized as the antithesis of anxiety, yet not all anxious individuals lack courage. Evans (1993) has argued that most constructs in psychopathology could be scaled into two parallel dimensions:

1. Pathological or undesirable attribute moving from severe deviance through some neutral point to its positive nonoccurrence
2. The antithetical attribute, moving from nonoccurrence through some neutral point to its desirable form

Peterson and Seligman's (2004) Classification of Virtues and Strengths (CVS) spearheaded the first comprehensive, coherent, and systematic effort in psychology to classify 24 core human strengths. The definitions of these core strengths, subsumed under six broader categories called virtues, are listed in Table 31.1.

According to Peterson and Seligman (2004), character strengths are ubiquitous traits that are valued in their own right and not necessarily tied to tangible outcomes. Character strengths, for the most part, do not diminish others; rather, they elevate those who witness the strength, producing admiration rather than jealousy. There are tremendous individual variations in the patterns of strengths that individuals possess. Societal institutions, through rituals, attempt to cultivate these character strengths. However, the CVS classification is descriptive rather than prescriptive, and character strengths can be studied like other behavioral variables. Character strengths are expressed in combinations (rather than singularly) and viewed within the context in which they are used. For example, strengths such as kindness and forgiveness can cement social bonds, but if used in excess, these strengths can be taken for granted. In this classification scheme, character strengths (e.g., kindness, teamwork, zest) are distinct from talents and abilities. Athletic prowess, photographic memory, perfect pitch, manual dexterity, and physical agility are examples of talents and abilities. Strengths have moral features, whereas talents and abilities do not.

Consistent with Evans's notion of parallel dimensions, Peterson (2006) has proposed a model for evaluating psychopathology along the spectrum of strengths, instead of symptoms. Peterson proposes that psychological disorders could be considered as an absence of strength—a state or trait that signifies its opposite or a state or trait that displays its exaggeration. A disorder may result from the absence

**Table 31.1**
Classification of Virtues and Character Strengths (Peterson & Seligman, 2004)

**The VIA Classification of Character Strengths**

1. *Wisdom and Knowledge*—cognitive strengths that entail the acquisition and use of knowledge
   - Creativity [originality, ingenuity]: Thinking of novel and productive ways to conceptualize and do things; includes artistic achievement but is not limited to it
   - Curiosity [interest, novelty-seeking, openness to experience]: Taking an interest in ongoing experience for its own sake; finding subjects and topics fascinating; exploring and discovering
   - Judgment [open-mindedness; critical thinking]: Thinking things through and examining them from all sides; not jumping to conclusions; being able to change one's mind in light of evidence; weighing all evidence fairly
   - Love of Learning: Mastering new skills, topics, and bodies of knowledge, whether on one's own or formally; related to the strength of curiosity but goes beyond it to describe the tendency to add systematically to what one knows
   - Perspective [wisdom]: Being able to provide wise counsel to others; having ways of looking at the world that make sense to oneself/others

2. *Courage*—emotional strengths that involve the exercise of will to accomplish goals in the face of opposition, external or internal
   - **Bravery** [valor]: Not shrinking from threat, challenge, difficulty, or pain; speaking up for what's right even if there's opposition; acting on convictions even if unpopular; includes physical bravery but is not limited to it
   - **Perseverance** [persistence, industriousness]: Finishing what one starts; persevering in a course of action in spite of obstacles; "getting it out the door"; taking pleasure in completing tasks
   - **Honesty** [authenticity, integrity]: Speaking the truth but more broadly presenting oneself in a genuine way and acting in a sincere way; being without pretense; taking responsibility for one's feelings and actions
   - **Zest** [vitality, enthusiasm, vigor, energy]: Approaching life with excitement and energy; not doing things halfway or halfheartedly; living life as an adventure; feeling alive and activated

3. *Humanity*—interpersonal strengths that involve tending and befriending others
   - **Love** [capacity to love and be loved]: Valuing close relations with others, in particular those in which sharing and caring are reciprocated; being close to people
   - **Kindness** [generosity, nurturance, care, compassion, altruistic love, "niceness"]: Doing favors and good deeds for others; helping them; taking care of them
   - **Social Intelligence** [emotional intelligence, personal intelligence]: Being aware of the motives/feelings of others and oneself; knowing what to do to fit into different social situations; knowing what makes other people tick

4. *Justice*—civic strengths that underlie healthy community life
   - **Teamwork** [citizenship, social responsibility, loyalty]: Working well as a member of a group or team; being loyal to the group; doing one's share
   - **Fairness**: Treating all people the same according to notions of fairness and justice; not letting feelings bias decisions about others; giving everyone a fair chance
   - **Leadership**: Encouraging a group of which one is a member to get things done and at the same time maintain good relations within the group; organizing group activities and seeing that they happen

*(continued)*

**Table 31.1**

*(Continued)*

---

1. *Temperance*—strengths that protect against excess
   - **Forgiveness** [mercy]: Forgiving those who have done wrong; accepting others' shortcomings; giving people a second chance; not being vengeful
   - **Humility** [modesty]: Letting one's accomplishments speak for themselves; not regarding oneself as more special than one is
   - **Prudence**: Being careful about one's choices; not taking undue risks; not saying or doing things that might later be regretted
   - **Self-Regulation** [self-control]: Regulating what one feels and does; being disciplined; controlling one's appetites and emotions
2. *Transcendence*—strengths that forge connections to the universe and provide meaning
   - **Appreciation of Beauty and Excellence** [awe, wonder, elevation]: Noticing and appreciating beauty, excellence, and/or skilled performance in various domains of life, from nature to art to mathematics to science to everyday experience
   - **Gratitude**: Being aware of and thankful for the good things that happen; taking time to express thanks
   - **Hope** [optimism, future-mindedness, future orientation]: Expecting the best in the future and working to achieve it; believing that a good future is something that can be brought about
   - **Humor** [playfulness]: Liking to laugh and tease; bringing smiles to other people; seeing the light side; making (not necessarily telling) jokes
   - **Spirituality** [religiousness, faith, purpose]: Having coherent beliefs about the higher purpose and meaning of the universe; knowing where one fits within the larger scheme; having beliefs about the meaning of life that shape conduct and provide comfort

---

of a given character strength, but it can also result from its presence in extreme forms. Peterson (2006) argues absence of character strengths is hallmark of real psychopathology. Like Evans, Peterson acknowledges that absence of character strengths may not necessarily apply to disorders such as schizophrenia and bipolar disorder, which have clear biological markers. However, many psychologically based disorders (e.g., depression, anxiety, attention and conduct problems, and personality disorders) may be more holistically understood in terms of presence of symptoms as well as the absence character strengths. It is also important to note that the presence of specific strengths, categorically or dimensionally, doesn't guarantee optimal functioning. Extrapolating from a 24 strengths scores (based on CVS model of strengths) of 83,576 adults, McGrath, Rashid, Park, and Peterson (2010) found that no matter how data is analyzed, no matter what strengths are considered, the results unanimously support a dimensional structure than a categorical view of character strengths. Therefore, it is important to keep in mind that much like diagnostic categories aren't sufficient to characterize an individual as completely insane, strengths should not be used to exemplify an individual as completely sane. In short, a dimensional approach, although less conducive to convenience of categorizing individuals based on scores, could more effective.

Joseph and Wood (2010) have articulated a somewhat similar dimensional approach. Illustrating two widely assessed affective states in clinical practice, depression and anxiety, Joseph and Wood posit that even widely used measures of depression (Center for Epidemiologic Studies Depression Scale—Revised [CES-D]; Radloff, 1977) and anxiety (Spielberger State-Trait Anxiety Inventory [STAI];

Spielberger, Gorsuch, Lushene, Vagg, & Jacobs, 1983)—both of which consist of equal balance of positively and negatively worded items—could be adopted toward a dimensional approach, such as depression to happiness and anxiety to relaxation. Instead of focusing on evaluating negative categories—the usual focus of clinical assessment—it could evolve into a more informative, inclusive, and balanced process by adopting a dimensional approach suggested by independent but converging lines, parallel dimensions (Evans, 1993), and strength continuum including absence, opposite, or excess (AOE) of strengths (Peterson, 2006), or a continuum approach (Joseph & Wood, 2010).

Extending these arguments, I have listed symptoms of major psychological disorders in terms of lack or excess of strengths (Table 31.2). For example, depression can result, in part, because of lack of hope, optimism, and zest, among other variables; likewise, a lack of grit and patience can explain some aspects of anxiety and a lack of fairness, equity, and justice might underscore conduct disorders. The notion of lack of character strengths as a plausible cause of psychopathology is gathering empirical support. In a longitudinal study of 5,500 people, individuals low on positive characteristics such as self-acceptance, autonomy, purpose in life, positive relationships with others, environmental mastery, and personal growth were up to 7 times more likely to experience depressive symptoms in the clinical range (Wood & Joseph, 2010), the cluster of interpersonal strengths (e.g., social intelligence, love, kindness, citizenship) that play a key role in mortality. Holt-Lunstad, Smith, and Layton, (2010) in their meta-analysis of 148 studies (308,849 participants) have found a 50% increased likelihood for participants with stronger social relationships. Similarly, Wood and Joseph (2010) have found that absence of positive characteristics independently forms a risk factor for disorder above the presence of numerous negative aspects, including current and previous depression, neuroticism, and physical ill-health. Moreover, not only more negative life events but also low or lack of positive attributions are associated with increased risk of suicide (Johnson, Gooding, Wood, & Tarrier, 2010).

While negative attributes are causally linked with psychopathology, not only does a lack of positive characteristics independently predict psychological disorder, but their presence also facilitates in recovery. Huta & Hawley (2010) have found that character strengths such as optimism, appreciation of beauty, and spirituality facilitates recovery from depression. Summarizing more than a decade of research and practice of character strengths, Niemiec (2013) has found that presence of character strengths is strongly linked with well-being and inversely linked—both correlationally as well as causally—with psychological distress. Therefore, clinical assessment devoid of positive characteristics yields a narrow and primarily negative picture of clients, with limited treatment options.

EMPIRICAL EVIDENCE

Assessment of strengths, especially within the burgeoning field of positive psychology, has attracted both empirical and clinical attention. A systematic review of SBA by Bird et al. (2012) identified 12 strengths assessments (five quantitative, seven qualitative). These assessments varied as to whether they focused primarily on strengths, for example, Value in Action Inventory of Strengths (VIA-IS; Peterson & Seligman, 2004), or a combination of strengths and challenges, for example, Strengths Assessment Worksheet (SAW; Rapp & Goscha, 2006) or the four-front model (Lopez & Snyder, 2003). The systematic review identified a total of 39 themes to operationalize strengths across assessments. The most common themes were personal attributes, interpersonal

**Table 31.2**

Major Psychology Disorder and Dysregulation of Strengths

Lack = diminished capacity to exercise/use a character strength
Excess = excess of strength, not to be considered as excess of symptoms

| Presence of Symptoms | Dysregulation of Strengths Lack or Excess |
|---|---|
| *Major Depressive Disorder* | |
| Depressed mood, feeling sad, hopeless (observed by others; e.g., appears tearful), helpless, slow, fidgety, bored | Lack of joy, delight, hope and optimism, playfulness, spontaneity, goal orientation |
| | Excess: prudence, modesty |
| Diminished pleasure | Lack of savoring, zest, curiosity |
| | Excess: self-regulation, contentment |
| Fatigued, slow | Lack of zest, alertness |
| | Excess: relaxation, slacking |
| Diminished ability to think or concentrate and indecisiveness, brooding | Lack of determination and resolution winnowing, divergent thinking, |
| | Excess: being overanalytical |
| Suicidal Ideation/plan | Lack of meaning, hope, social connectivity, resolution and winnowing, divergent thinking, resourcefulness |
| | Excess: carefreeness (defensive pessimism) |
| *Disruptive Mood Dysregulation Disorder* | |
| Severe temper outbursts (verbal and physical) | Lack of self-regulation, prudence |
| Persistent irritability and anger | Excess: enthusiasm |
| *Unspecified Depressive Disorder With Anxious Distress* | |
| Feeling keyed up or tense, feeling unusually restless | Lack of contentment (distress tolerance), gratitude, relaxation, prudence |
| | Lack of openness to new and novel ideas (curiosity) |
| | Excess: zest, gusto, eagerness |
| Bipolar Disorder | |
| Elevated, expensive, irritable mood | Lack of equanimity, even-temperedness and level-headedness |
| | Excess: composure, passion |
| Inflated self-esteem or grandiosity | Lack of humility, self and social intelligence |
| | Excess: willpower, introspection |
| More talkative than usual | Lack of reflection and contemplation |
| | Excess: zest, passion |
| Excessive involvement in pleasurable activities (e.g., unrestrained buying sprees, sexual indiscretions, thoughtless business/career choices) | Lack of moderation, prudence, simplicity |
| | Excess: passion (obsession), self-indulgence |
| Excessive involvement in activities that have a high potential for painful consequences (e.g., engaging in unrestrained buying sprees, sexual indiscretions, or foolish business investments) | Lack of self-regulation, perspective, balance, humility, emotional regulation |
| | Excess: self-care (self-indulgence), zeal, gratification |

Table 31.2
(*Continued*)

| Presence of Symptoms | Dysregulation of Strengths<br>Lack or Excess |
|---|---|
| *Generalized Anxiety Disorder* | |
| Worrying excessively about real or perceived danger | Lack of perspective, wisdom, critical thinking<br>Excess: caution, attentiveness |
| Feeling restless, fatigued, fidgety, jittery, edgy, difficulty concentrating and sleeping | Lack of equanimity, mindfulness, spontaneity<br>Excess: farsightedness, composure |
| *Separation Anxiety Disorder* | |
| Persistent and excessive worry about losing major attachment figures | Lack of capacity to love and be loved, social trust, optimism, bonding<br>Excess: affection, self-regulation |
| *Selective Mutism* | |
| Failure to speak in specific social situations in which there is an expectation to speak | Lack of initiative, personal and social intelligence, social skills<br>Excess: prudence, self-scrutiny |
| *Specific Phobia* | |
| Marked anxiety about a specific object or situation | Lack of courage, creativity<br>Excess: sensitivity, cautious reactivity |
| Active avoidance or endured with intense fear or anxiety;<br>out-of-proportion fear | Lack of relaxation, mindfulness, courage to withstand social judgment, rational self-talk (reflection and introspection)<br>Excess: observance, awareness, caution |
| Feeling restless, fidgety, jittery, edgy | Lack of equanimity, self-intelligence, self-evaluation, monitoring, relaxation, mindfulness, level-headedness, self-composure<br>Excess: caution, sensitivity, reactivity, critical evaluation |
| *Social Phobia* | |
| Fear of social or performance situation | Lack of courage, extemporaneity, trust in others<br>Excess: social intelligence (self seen as audience, rather than part of the social picture), critical appraisal and evaluation |
| *Agoraphobia* | |
| Marked fear or anxiety using public transportation, parking lots, bridges, shops, theaters, standing or being in a crowd<br>Being outside of the home alone | Lack of courage, extemporaneity, open-mindedness, flexibility<br>Excess: sensitivity, caution about a situation |
| *Panic Disorder* | |
| Intense fear of "going crazy" marked by heart pounding, feeling dizzy, unsteady, or light-headed<br>Derealization and depersonalization<br>Persistence concern about additional attacks | Lack of composure, social and personal intelligence, creativity and curiosity to explore the environment/situation beyond the surface, optimism (expecting unexpected adverse outcomes)<br>Excess: sensitivity, reactivity to environmental cues, awareness |

(*continued*)

**Table 31.2**
*(Continued)*

| Presence of Symptoms | Dysregulation of Strengths Lack or Excess |
| --- | --- |
| *Obsessive-Compulsive Disorder* | |
| Recurrent, persistent, intrusive, unwanted thoughts, urges, or images | Lack of mindfulness and letting go, curiosity, perspective |
| | Excess: reflection and introspection, morality or fairness, |
| Repetitive behaviors or mental acts individual feels compelled to do to prevent anxiety | Lack of contentment with less than perfect objects and performance, creativity, flexibility, ability to restrain |
| | Excess: reflection and introspection, planning |
| *Body Dysmorphic Disorder* | |
| Preoccupation with perceived defects in physical appearance that are not observable to others | Lack of contentment with less than perfect self-image, acknowledgment of personal character strengths, modesty |
| | Excess: personal intelligence, self-care, self-worth |
| *Hoarding Disorders* | |
| Persistent difficulty discarding or parting with possessions, regardless of actual values | Lack of perspective of what is important and meaningful, distinct self-image (identity melded with objects), relationship more with object and artifacts than with people and experiences, inability to override one's perceived needs (lack of compassion) |
| | Excess: optimism, caution |
| *Posttraumatic Stress Disorder* | |
| Recurrent, involuntary, and intrusive distressing memories of a traumatic event | Lack of resilience, ability to bounce back, lack of personal intelligence to process emotions or to seek support to process emotions, lack of ability to take risks/creativity to explore various coping mechanisms, lack of persistence, optimism, hope, lacking social support |
| | Lack of the ability to make meaning of the traumatic event or putting things in perspective |
| | Excess: reflection (rumination), viewing or perceiving the event only through negative lens or perspective, adherence (to the traumatic experience) |
| Intense or prolonged psychological distress and fear of external cues that symbolize the traumatic event | Lack of ability to self-soothe or relax, or regain composure, creativity and courage to experience the distressing objection or situation in a different or adaptive manner, self-determination |
| | Excess: composure, caution, keeping the status quo |

**Table 31.2**
*(Continued)*

| Presence of Symptoms | Dysregulation of Strengths Lack or Excess |
|---|---|
| Avoidance of distressing memories (people, places, conversational activities, objects, situations) | Lack of resolve to handle distressing memories head-on (emotional bravery) Excess: self-preservation at the cost of not yielding to spontaneous experiences, or taking necessary risks |
| *Attention-Deficit/Hyperactivity Disorder* | |
| Failing to give close attention to details, not seeming to listen when spoken to directly | Lack of vigilance, social intelligence Excess: excessive watchfulness |
| Difficulty organizing tasks and activities | Lack of discipline, managing Excess: gusto, eagerness |
| Avoiding or disliking tasks requiring sustained attention or mental effort | Lack of grit and patience Excess: hedonic pleasures |
| Excessive fidgeting, motor activity, running, pacing | Lack of calmness, composure Excess: agility, fervor |
| Talking excessively, interrupting or intruding others, difficulty awaiting turn | Lack of social intelligence, self-awareness Excess: zest, initiative, curiosity |
| *Oppositional Defiant Disorder* | |
| Annoying people deliberately | Lack of kindness, empathy, fairness Excess: clemency |
| Often being angry, resentful, spiteful, or vindictive | Lack of forgiveness, gratitude, level-headedness Excess: fairness, equality |
| *Disruptive, Impulse-Control, and Conduct Disorder and Antisocial Personality Disorder* | |
| Bullying, threatening, intimidating others | Lack of kindness and citizenship Excess: leadership, control, governance |
| Stealing, destroying other's property | Lack of honesty, fairness, justice Excess: courage, fairness |
| **Personality Disorders** | |
| *Paranoid Personality Disorder* Suspicion without sufficient basis that others are exploiting, harming, or deceiving | Lack of social intelligence, trust in others, open-mindedness, curiosity Excess: caution, diligence |
| Doubts loyalty or trustworthiness of others, reluctant to confide in others, reading hidden demeaning or threatening meaning into benign remarks or events | Lack of personal intelligence, giving or receiving love, deep and secure attachment Excess: social intelligence, open-mindedness |
| *Borderline Personality Disorder* | |
| Pervasive relationship instability, imagined or real abandonment | Lack of capacity to love and be loved in deep and sustained one-to-one relationships, lack of secure attachment, emotional intimacy and reciprocity in relationships, relational prudence and kindness, empathy |

*(continued)*

Table 31.2
(*Continued*)

| Presence of Symptoms | Dysregulation of Strengths Lack or Excess |
|---|---|
| | Excess: curiosity and zest that phase out quickly, excess of attachment, emotional intelligence |
| Idealization and devaluation | Lack of authenticity and trust in close relationships, moderation, prudence and open-mindedness (swaying by a single event), reality orientation, perspective |
| | Excess: judgment, spontaneity |
| Self-damaging impulsivity (e.g., spending, reckless driving, binge eating) and anger outburst | Lack of self-regulation (tolerance), moderation, prudence |
| | Excess: bravery without prudence (actions without prudence), risk taking |
| Narcissistic Personality Disorder | |
| Pattern of grandiosity, arrogance, need for admiration, sense of self-importance | Lack of authenticity, humility |
| | Excess: self-deprecation, criticism |
| Lack of empathy | Lack of social intelligence and kindness (being genuinely interested in others) |
| | Excess: personal intelligence (personal needs or wants are prioritized) |
| Fantasies of unlimited success, power, brilliance, beauty, or ideal love | Lack of humility, perspective, personal intelligence |
| | Excess: creativity (fantasizing), rationalizing, intellectualizing, |
| Sense of entitlement, expectations of unreasonably favorable treatment, requires excessive admiration | Lack of humility, citizenship and fairness |
| | Excess: leadership, need for appreciation |
| Interpersonal exploitation | Lack of fairness, equity and justice |
| | Excess: righteousness, despotism, bossiness |
| Envious of others | Lack of generosity and appreciation |
| | Excess: self-preservation |
| *Histrionic Personality Disorder* | |
| Excessive emotionality and attention seeking | Lack of equanimity and modesty |
| | Excess: personal and emotional intelligence |
| Easily suggestible (i.e., easily influenced by others or circumstances) | Lack of persistence, determination, goal orientation |
| | Excess: efficiency of concentration |
| Inappropriate sexual seduction, overemphasis on physical appearance | Lack of discretion and self-regulation |
| | Excess: emotional disinhibition |
| Shallow and hasty emotional expression | Lack of mindfulness and social intelligence |
| | Excess: spontaneity |
| Self-dramatization, theatricality, and exaggerated and shallow expression of emotion | Lack of authenticity, lack of authentically expressing one's needs, emotions, and interests, moderation, mindfulness |
| | Excess: emotional intelligence, enthusiasm |

**Table 31.2**

*(Continued)*

| Presence of Symptoms | Dysregulation of Strengths Lack or Excess |
| --- | --- |
| Overvaluing relationships | Lack of social intelligence |
| | Excess: tending and betriending |

*Obsessive Compulsive Disorder*

| | |
| --- | --- |
| Preoccupation with details, orderliness and perfectionism | Lack of perspective as to what is more important, lack of spontaneity |
| | Excess: persistence, orderliness |
| Interpersonal control at the expense of flexibility, openness, and efficiency | Lack of kindness, empathy, ability to follow |
| | Excess: submission, leniency |
| Preoccupation with details, rules, lists, organizations, or schedules to the extent that primary aim of the activity is overshadowed | Lack of flexibility, creativity in thinking of novel and productive ways to do things |
| | Excess: perfection, organization |
| Excessively devoted to work at the expense of leisure and friendships | Lack of balance, savoring, appreciation for relationships |
| | Excess: self-indulgence |
| Rigidity and stubbornness | Lack of adaptability, flexibility, creative problem-solving |
| | Excess: discipline, prudence |
| Overconscientious, scrupulous, and inflexible about morality, ethics, or values | Lack of perspective, consideration of implication of decision, adaptability, flexibility, creative problem-solving |
| | Excess: self-righteousness |

*Avoidant Personality Disorder*

| | |
| --- | --- |
| Avoiding activities with others due to fear of criticism, disapproval, or rejection | Lack of interpersonal courage to take risks, lack of critical reasoning to put criticism or disapproval of others in perspective, courage |
| | Excess: self-awareness, caution |
| Social isolation, avoiding people, inhibition in new interpersonal situation because of feelings of inadequacy | Lack of interpersonal strengths, melding one's identity with others/group |
| | Excess: prudence, critical thinking |
| Views self as socially inept, personally unappealing, and inferior to others | Lack of self-assurance, self-efficacy, hope and optimism |
| | Excess: humility, authenticity |
| Reluctance to take risks to engage in any new activities | Lack of bravery and curiosity |
| | Excess: self-regulation, compliance |

*Dependent Personality Disorder*

| | |
| --- | --- |
| Excessive need to be taken care of, fear of being left alone | Lack of independence, initiative and leadership |
| | Excess: seclusion |
| Difficulty making everyday decisions, lack of perspective | Lack of determination and perspective |
| | Excess: critical analysis, focusing on details |

*(continued)*

### Table 31.2
*(Continued)*

| Presence of Symptoms | Dysregulation of Strengths Lack or Excess |
|---|---|
| Difficulty expressing disagreements with others | Lack of bravery, not being able to speak up for what is right, lack of judgment |
| | Excess: uncompromising |
| Difficulty initiating | Lack of self-efficacy, optimism, curiosity |
| | Excess: organization, autonomy |
| *Anti-Social Personality Disorder* | |
| Failure to conform to social norms or laws | Lack of citizenship, lack of communal purpose, lack of respect for authority, kindness, mercy, forgiveness, less giving but demanding more |
| | Excess: courage (risk taking), vitality |
| Deceitfulness, repeated lying, conning others for personal profits | Lack of honesty, integrity, fairness, moral compass, empathy |
| | Excess: self-centered personal intelligence |
| Irritability, impulsivity, aggressiveness as indicated by physical fights or assaults | Lack of equanimity, mindfulness, tolerance, kindness and consideration, knowledge of others, self-control, perspective (inability to anticipate consequences) |
| | Excess: mental and physical vigor, passion, ambition, courage, too ready to go out of zone of comfort |

*Note.* Italic entries represent virtues, while character strengths are listed alphabetically within each virtue.

relationships, skills, talents, capabilities, resilience and coping, and community and social supports. These themes could be organized into three categories; individual, interpersonal, and environmental. Bird et al.'s (2012) review also found 10 evaluations of SBA including three randomized controlled trials (RCT), four quasi-experimental studies, and three nonexperimental designs providing supportive evidence for the effectiveness of SBA, although it was stressed that further rigorous studies are needed.

By adopting a dimensional approach, SBA offers the option that psychological interventions that are effective in reducing symptoms could also be adapted to include cultivation of well-being. Connectedness, hope and optimism, identity, meaning and purpose, and empowerment have been identified as five key processes underlying the recovery process (Leamy, Bird, Le Boutillier, Williams, & Slade, 2011). Within the core category of empowerment, "focusing on strengths" is considered vital to individual's personal recovery. A strength-based approach to case management (SBCM) has been devised and empirically evaluated (Rapp & Goscha, 2006). SBCM focuses on the relationships between staff and consumers and prioritizes strengths over deficits. Studies of SBCM including a limited number of RCTs and quasi-experimental designs have reported a range of positive outcomes including reduced hospitalization and increased social support. A growing number of studies, including RCTs, have shown that interventions that incorporate strengths, along with other active therapeutic exercises, are effective in clinical settings, reducing symptoms of psychiatric distress and increasing well-being (e.g., Flückiger, Caspar, Grosse, & Willutzki, 2009; Goodwin, 2010; Kahler et al., 2014; Seligman, Rashid, & Parks, 2006).

## ILLUSTRATIONS OF STRENGTH-BASED ASSESSMENT IN CLINICAL SETTINGS

Strengths in clinical practice are mostly assessed through quantitative, self-report measures such as VIA-IS (Peterson & Seligman, 2004), Realise2 (Linley, Willars, & Biswas-Diener, 2010), and Adult Needs and Strengths Assessment (Nelson & Johnston, 2008), and Quality of Life Inventory (QOLI; Frisch, 2013). Typically a straightforward strategy of "identity and use and your strengths" is used, and the top five scores are regarded as signature strengths. Clients are then asked to find new ways to use their signature strengths. This approach, although useful and effective in nonclinical setting, may not meet critical clinical needs. For example, exclusive focus on top-ranked strength scores could give an inadvertent message to clients that their top five strengths carry more therapeutic potential when it may not be the case for every client, as illustrated in case scenarios later in this chapter. The most critical aspect of a strength-based therapeutic approach is contextualized use of strengths, keeping presenting problems (symptoms) front and center.

The clinical setting may require a more nuanced and theoretically driven approach (Biswas-Diener, Kashdan, & Minhas, 2011) of using strengths. To overcome this shortcoming, a comprehensive strength assessment approach is suggested (Rashid & Seligman, 2013; see Table 31.3). In this approach, the clients are first provided a sheet with brief descriptions (approximately 20 to 25 words per strength) of core strengths (based on the CVS model), and are asked to identify (not rank) up to five strengths that best illustrate their personality. Identical collateral data is collected from a friend or family member. Clients are then provided descriptions with titles to give strengths names and specific contexts. Next, clients are encouraged to share memories, experiences, real-life stories, anecdotes, accomplishments, and skills that illustrate the use of these strengths in specific situations. Clients then complete a self-report measure of strengths (e.g., VIA-IS). Collaboratively, with therapists, clients set specific, attainable, behavioral, and measurable goals that target their presenting concerns and adaptive use of their signature strengths.

It is important that goals are personally meaningful as well as adaptive in the interpersonal context of clients. For example, if the goal is that clients use their curiosity more, an optimal balance of curiosity through concrete actions is discussed so that it doesn't become intrusiveness (excess/overuse) or boredom (lack/underuse). While setting goals, clients are also taught to use their strengths in a calibrated and flexible way that could adaptively meet situational challenges (Biswas-Diener et al., 2011; Schwartz & Sharpe, 2006; see also Kauffman, Joseph, & Scoular, Chapter 23, this volume). In doing so, specific actions or habits are highlighted that may explain symptoms or troubles as either lack or excess of strengths. Some illustrations include depressed mood and feeling hopeless or slow, as lack of zest and playfulness; worrying excessively, as lack of gratitude or inability to let go; indecision, as lack of determination; repetitive, intrusive thoughts, as lack of mindfulness; narcissism, as lack of modesty; feeling inadequate, as lack of self-efficacy; or difficulty making decisions, as excess of prudence. Furthermore, therapists also discuss that sometimes clients get into trouble for overuse of love and forgiveness (being taken for granted), underuse of self-regulation in a specific domain of life (indulgence), fairness only in a few situations or teamwork only with preferred groups (bias and discrimination). Throughout the course of treatment, clients and clinicians continuously explore the nuances and subtleties of strengths, especially about encountering their challenges through strengths. The following case scenario is from a client I saw as an individual at a university counseling center, illustrating an adaptive use of strengths linked with presenting problems (Rashid & Ostermann, 2009).

**Table 31.3**
Comprehensive Strengths Process

| | Character Strength | 1<br>Self | 2<br>Family | 3<br>Friend | 4<br>SSQ-72 | 5<br>Composite | 6<br>Under/Over | 7<br>Desired |
|---|---|---|---|---|---|---|---|---|
| 1 | Appreciation of beauty and excellence | | | | | | | |
| 2 | Authenticity and honesty | | | | | | | |
| 3 | Bravery and valor | | | | | | | |
| 4 | Creativity and originality | | | | | | | |
| 5 | Curiosity, interest in the world, and openness to experience | | | | | | | |
| 6 | Fairness, equity, and justice | | | | | | | |
| 7 | Forgiveness and mercy | | | | | | | |
| 8 | Gratitude | | | | | | | |
| 9 | Hope, optimism, and future-mindedness | | | | | | | |
| 10 | Humor and playfulness | | | | | | | |
| 11 | Kindness and generosity | | | | | | | |
| 12 | Leadership | | | | | | | |
| 13 | Capacity to love and be loved | | | | | | | |
| 14 | Love of learning | | | | | | | |
| 15 | Modesty and humility | | | | | | | |
| 16 | Open-mindedness and critical thinking | | | | | | | |
| 17 | Perseverance, diligence and industry | | | | | | | |
| 18 | Perspective (wisdom) | | | | | | | |
| 19 | Prudence, caution, and discretion | | | | | | | |
| 20 | Religiousness and spirituality | | | | | | | |
| 21 | Self-regulation and self-control | | | | | | | |
| 22 | Social intelligence | | | | | | | |
| 23 | Teamwork, citizenship, and loyalty | | | | | | | |

**Table 31.3**
(*Continued*)

| | Character Strength | 1 Self | 2 Family | 3 Friend | 4 SSQ-72 | 5 Composite | 6 Under/Over | 7 Desired |
|---|---|---|---|---|---|---|---|---|
| 24 | Zest, enthusiasm, and energy | | | | | | | |
| | Strengths not listed above | | | | | | | |
| | | | | | | | | |
| | | | | | | | | |

Directions: Compile your signature strengths profile using this worksheet. Each column is independent from the other.

**Column 1 (Self):** Clients record the five positive character attributes illustrated in their strength narratives/positive introduction. Client place a check mark inside the box that correspond to the attributes that most often characterize clients.

**Column 2 (Family):** Clients record attributes, identified by a family member.

**Column 3 (Friend):** Clients record attributes, identified by a close friend.

**Column 4 (Signature Strengths Questionnaire [SSI-72;** www.tayyabrashid.com] **or VIA-IS;** www.viacharacter.org): Clients complete an online self-report measure and record their top five strengths.

**Column 5 (Composite):** Clients add the number of times that each attribute was checked in the previous four columns.

**Column 6 (Under/Overuse):** Clients identify five strengths that they feel they lack (underuse) or use in excess (overuse). They denote the strength with either X-O (Over) or X-U (under).

**Column 7 (Desired):** Clients identify five strengths that they desire to have and denote these with D

A 29-year-old, Caucasian, single female, with presenting symptoms of depression and anxiety, reported doing things halfway or halfheartedly, not feeling alive, and being unable to approach life with excitement and feeling tired. The comprehensive strength assessment process, described earlier, uncovered creativity, curiosity, love of learning, kindness, and spirituality as her signature strengths. She shared with the therapist that she used to be very good at graphic designing and, during college, worked part time for an agency that designed various brochures. Despite experiencing depressive symptoms, she kept up with nonfiction reading on her topic of interest, although with less enthusiasm. The therapeutic process focused on helping her to recall previous accomplishments, improving her self-efficacy moderately. She struggled financially. To reignite her creativity, she was encouraged to think creatively to make cost-effective, small but personally meaningful changes in her apartment. Although she has heard from others previously that she is creative, the act of naming the attribute as her signature strength changed her orientation toward her own strengths. At the same time, she started thinking of alternative ways of solving her problems. For instance, she realized that her strength of loving and being loved tended to be unconditional—often sacrificing her legitimate needs for others who had been taking her for granted. Her therapeutic goals were to set healthy boundaries through creative ways. Furthermore, she coped with her symptoms of depression and anxiety through emotional eating. A discussion on using creativity with self-regulation helped her to generate a list of adaptive and accessible activities she could engage in easily to cope with her distress.

I saw a young-adult male for crisis intervention. He has significant emotional dysregulation challenges. After four individual therapy sessions, which focused developing adaptive coping to deal with the crisis, he was transitioned into a Positive Psychotherapy (PPT; Rashid et al., 2013) group. PPT is a strength-based approach;

clients identity their strengths from multiple perspectives. Following this process, social intelligence, love, forgiveness, humility, and prudence were identified as this client's signature strengths. Reflecting and appraising the adaptive usage of these strengths, the client realized that his emotional dysregulation was closely linked with dysregulation of his strengths. For instance, he invariably used his signature strengths excessively. He loved his partner unconditionally and forgave her at repeated transgressions of the same nature. He realized that his humility and prudence prevented him from asserting himself and clearly expressing his frustrations and needs. The group discussion helped him to learn a calibrated use of strengths and incorporate strengths that, although not his signature strengths, may still facilitate his meeting his needs. For example, he opted to work on bravery from the perspective of standing up for himself. His work is still in progress, and continues to go through the ebb and flow of emotions. However, the assessment of strengths from the perspective of a lack or excess helped him to understand his challenges as well as his strengths from a more inclusive, malleable, and less stigmatizing place.

In addition to illustrations of SBA described above, there are other approaches. One such approach is the four-front assessment (Wright & Lopez, 2002; Magyar-Moe, 2009). At the core of this approach, the clinician gathers information about four fronts by asking questions: (1) What deficiencies do clients contribute to their problems? (2) What strengths do clients bring to deal effectively with their lives? (3) What environmental factors serve as impediments to healthy functioning? (4) What environmental resources accentuate positive functioning of clients? Methods include solution-focused interviews and structured tests of psychology and negative symptomatology, individual strengths positive attributions, and environment. After assessing the four fronts, results are shared with clients (as well as colleagues and others who may provide support and care to clients) and documented in progress notes and written reports with equal space, time, and emphasis placed on each of the four dimensions.

Strength-based assessment also invites interesting alternative hypotheses in clinical settings regarding the course an treatment of psychopathology. For example, assessment of depression may not just be a cluster of symptoms described in the *DSM-V*, but it could also identify a lack of positive emotions and meaning in a client's life. With a depressed client, the clinician can explore and work on strengths like perspective, zest, and gratitude. Shoring up social strengths of the client such as teamwork, social intelligence, and kindness could be a viable way of counteracting depression. Similarly, anxiety might represent excess of worrying, feeling restless, fidgety and impulsive behavior, and lacking focus, and be a lack of purposeful goals, actions, and habits that utilize the client's strengths and absorb him or her immensely. SBA approach also draws our attention that absence of weaknesses is the only clinical goal, but presence of well-being—facilitated by strengths, is equally important for treatment and further prevention of psychological disorders (Keyes, 2013). Some clinicians may concerned that assessment of strengths may either reinforce narcissistic attitudes for some clients or distract them from serious problems that need immediate attention. The goal of an SBA is neither to create Pollyannaish or Panglossian caricatures of clients, nor is it to inflate grandiose egos of clients. Of course, in assessing strengths, the goal is never to minimize or mask negative experiences such as abuse, neglect, and suffering.

Clinicians can choose validated instruments to assess specific positive constructs listed in two volumes that discuss their usage, psychometric properties, and relevant research (Lopez & Snyder, 2003; Simmons & Lehmann, 2013). In addition, Ong and Van Dulmen (2006) describe SBA issues. Also, Levak, Siegel, and Nichols (2011) offer useful insights into using one of the most widely used and validated measures of psychopathology, the Minnesota Multiphasic Personality Inventory—2 (MMPI-2; Butcher, Dahlstrom, Graham, Tellegen, & Kaemmer, 1989) within the context of SBA.

## STRENGTH-BASED ASSESSMENT: RECOMMENDATIONS FOR CLINICAL PRACTICE

The following eight concrete strategies, my own extracted clinical experience, and the experience of others can help clinicians to integrate strengths in their practice:

1. Most measures of psychopathology are expensive and require completion in clinical settings. Valid and reliable strength measures, developed by practitioners and researchers of positive psychology, are readily available online without any charge. For example, the Authentic Happiness website (www.authentichappiness .sas.upenn.edu; affiliated with the University of Pennsylvania) and the Values in Action website (www.viacharacter.org) offer these measures. Clients can complete these measures at home and can bring printouts of results to therapy. For instance, one of the most widely used measures to assess strengths is the VIA-IS (Peterson & Seligman, 2004; www.viacharacter.org). The VIA-IS is a 240-item, self-report measuring 24 character strengths. A 72-item brief version (Rashid et al., 2013) with feedback options is available (at www.tayyabrashid.com). These measures could also be used to track changes over the course of psychotherapy. All three of previously mentioned websites provide these measures without any charge and also provide instantaneous feedback about strengths and other positive attributes

2. Many existing measures of psychopathology also assess some aspects of well-being and strengths. As mentioned earlier, CES-D (depression) and STAI (anxiety) also capture elements of well-being and relaxation, respectively. Clinicians can reinterpret these existing measures to widen scope of their assessment (Joseph & Wood, 2010). Measures of reverse coding positive items could be used in two versions: with and without reverse coding. This may help clinicians to compare construct and incremental validity of two versions and may also help in examining alternative theoretical perspective regarding course and treatment of psychopathology.

3. In addition to self-report measures, interviews guided by research can also be used to assess strengths. If a clinician prefers not to use formal assessment, then he or she can use questions during intake or ongoing therapy to elicit strengths, positive emotions, and meaning. Some sample questions could be, "What gives your life a sense of meaning?" "Let's pause here and talk about what you are good at." "Tell me what you are good at." "What are your initial thoughts and feelings when you see someone doing an act of kindness or courage?" Flückiger and colleagues (2009) have used the clinical interview to elicit clients' strengths in the therapeutic process. Following are several of their resource activation questions that can be readily incorporated into a Life History Questionnaire or clinical interview in routine practice:

- What do you enjoy most? Please describe your most enjoyable experiences.
- What are you good at? Please describe experiences that brought out the best in you.
- What are your inspirations for the future?
- What makes a satisfying day for you?
- What experiences give you a sense of authenticity?
- Please describe a time when you felt "the real you."

4. Not all strengths are within the awareness of clients, and others can spot them better. Clinicians can also seek collateral information from family members,

colleagues, and friends about the strengths of their client as well as strengths of concerned individuals as they relate to the client. This is particularly helpful in assessing and identifying social and communal buffers. For example, in addition to inquiring about problems with family members, clinicians may also assess attachment, love, and nurturance from the primary support group. Instead of looking for problems related to social environment, a clinician can ask clients to describe humor and playful interactions, connectedness, and empathetic relationships at work.

5. To help clients to discern and identify their own strengths, clinicians can also use icons of certain strengths (e.g., Malala Yusuf Zai, Gandhi, Mother Theresa, Nelson Mandela, Martin Luther King Jr., Albert Einstein, Aung San Suu Kyi, Ken Saro-Wiwa) real-life narratives, and popular films (*Life of Pi*, *Hugo*, *Precious*, *Pay It Forward*, *Forrest Gump*, *My Left Foot*). By using strengths displayed by specific icons and film characters, the clinician can discuss with clients whether they partly or fully identify with these icons and characters and, if so, which conditions clients see that display these strengths maximally and what might be consequences of displaying these strengths. (For a comprehensive list of films, please see Niemiec & Wedding, 2014).

6. Assess strengths early in the therapeutic process. After establishing rapport and empathically listening to the concerns that brought the client to therapy, the clinician can mindfully explore strengths. I reckon that during the course of treatment as usual, most clinicians become aware of their clients' strengths. But it is also possible that this vital information never becomes available during a crisis, and most clients don't know how to use their strengths to cope with the challenging situation.

7. Assessment of strengths provides the clinician with a powerful mechanism with which to encourage clients to pursue absorption and deep engagement. Clients could be encouraged to pursue concrete activities that use their strengths, such as creativity, curiosity, appreciation of beauty, love of learning, and social intelligence, or they can tweak activities to experience more engagement. Engagement can be especially beneficial for clients who have concentration difficulties, boredom, and listlessness. In addition, strengths-based engaging activities are also likely to reduce brooding and rumination.

8. Clinicians who, for practical and clinical reasons, prefer not to use formal measures of strengths, can use a narrative strategy, which I have found to be very helpful in eliciting strengths. It is called *positive introduction*. In this assessment strategy, after listening to the account of troubles, the clinician encourages the client to introduce him- or herself through a real-life story (about 300 words, with a beginning, a middle, and a positive end) that shows the client at his or her best or during a peak moment of life. The clinician discusses the story with the client in detail in terms of what strengths are displayed and whether they are accurate descriptions of the client's current functioning. Clients having difficulty writing a story or identifying specific strengths may be encouraged to ask family members and friends to tell a story depicting their strengths. This strategy reveals the client's strengths to the clinician as well as to significant others.

Finally, clinicians can assess whether the client is currently able to translate the abstract strengths into concrete actions, behaviors, and habits. This assessment is important because real-life challenges rarely come in neat packages with labeled instructions such as, "When depressed, use zest and vitality." Challenges and hassles often occur amid a dizzying jumble of emotions, actions, and their effects. The role of clinician is to assess and gently guide the client to use her or his strengths to solve a problem. Strengths elicited from the positive introduction or from the VIA-IS are used to refine and reframe problems solving. This narrative becomes dynamic and can assist clients to visualize their optimal selves. For instance, a clinician may say to a client, "Let's discuss the strengths that you displayed in your positive introduction. What role might they play in this challenging situation?" This exercise provides rich data on the client's past and current strengths and weaknesses.

## CONCLUSION

When weaknesses and strengths are assessed through strength-based assessment in an authentic and integrative manner, clients are likely to find therapeutic process self-efficacious, affirming, and empowering. They are likely to view themselves as more than sum of symptoms, and clinicians can foster a healthier and egalitarian relationship, which is perhaps the bedrock of therapeutic change.

## SUMMARY POINTS

- Traditionally, assessment has been concerned with deficits and disorder, whereas SBA gives equal attention to positive attributes and processes to make clinical services more effective.
- Identifying, measuring, and further building strengths changes the scope of clinical services from remediation to nurturance of resilience and well-being.
- SBA invites clinicians to reconceptualize psychological disorders such as absence, excess, and opposites of strengths or on dimensions of a lack or excess of strengths.
- A number of approaches have been incorporated in clinical settings. These approaches often incorporate collateral data from close family and friends.
- SBA invites alternative hypothesis regarding the course and treatment of psychopathology.
- SBA does not dismiss or deny negatives. Neither is its goal is to create Pollyannaish caricatures of clients. The goal is to yield a realistic and balanced picture of clients.

## REFERENCES

American Psychiatric Association (2013). *Diagnostic and statistical manual of mental disorders* (5th ed.). Washington, DC: Author.

Bird, V. J., Le Boutillier, C., Leamy, M., Larsen, J., Oades, L. G., Williams, J., & Slade, M. (2012). Assessing the strengths of mental health consumers: A systematic review. *Psychological Assessment, 24*(4), 1024–1033. doi:10.1037/a0028983

Biswas-Diener, R., Kashdan, T. K., & Minhas, G. (2011). A dynamic approach to psychological strength development and intervention. *Journal of Positive Psychology, 6*, 106–118.

Butcher, J. N. (2006). Assessment in clinical psychology: A perspective on the past, present challenges, and future prospects. *Clinical Psychology: Science and Practice, 13*(3), 205–209. doi:10.1111/j.1468-2850.2006.00025.x

Butcher, J. N., Dahlstrom, W. G., Graham, J. R., Tellegen, A., & Kaemmer, B. (1989). *Minnesota Multiphasic Personality Inventory—2 (MMPI-2): Manual for administration and scoring*. Minneapolis: University of Minnesota Press.

Cawley, M. J., Martin, J. E., & Johnson, J. A. (2000). A virtues approach to personality. *Personality and Individual Differences, 28*, 997–1013.

Corrigan, P. (2004). How stigma interferes with mental health care. *American Psychologist, 59*, 614–625.

Epstein, M. H., & Sharma, J. M. (1998). *Behavioural and emotional rating scale: A strength-based approach to assessment*. Austin, TX: Pro-Ed.

Evans, I. M. (1993). Constructional perspectives in clinical assessment. *Psychological Assessment, 5*, 264–272. doi:10.1037/1040-3590.5.3.264

Flückiger, C., Caspar, F. H., Grosse, M., & Willutzki, U. (2009). Working with patients' strengths: A microprocess approach. *Psychotherapy Research, 19*, 213–223.

Fredrickson, B. (2001). The role of positive emotions in positive psychology: The broaden-and-build theory of positive emotions. *American Psychologist, 56*, 218–226.

Friedman, H. L., & MacDonald, D. A. (2006). Humanistic testing and assessment. *Journal of Humanistic Psychology, 46*, 510–529.

Frisch, M. B. (2013). Evidence-based well-being/positive psychology assessment and intervention with quality of life therapy and coaching and the Quality of Life Inventory (QOLI). *Social Indicators Research, 114*(2), 193–227. doi:10.1007/s11205-012-0140-7

Goodwin, E. M. (2010). Does group positive psychotherapy help improve relationship satisfaction in a stressed and/or anxious population? (Order No. 3428275, Palo Alto University). *ProQuest Dissertations and Theses, 166*.

Holt-Lunstad, J., Smith, T. B, & Layton, J. B. (2010). Social relationships and mortality risk: A meta-analytic review. *PLoS Medicine 7*(7), e1000316.

Huta, V., & Hawley, L. (2010). Psychological strengths and cognitive vulnerabilities: Are they two ends of the same continuum or do they have independent relationships with well-being and ill-being? *Journal of Happiness Studies, 11*, 71–93. doi:10.1007/s10902-008-9123-4.

Iveson, C. (1994). Solution focused brief therapy: Establishing goals and assessing competence. *The British Journal of Occupational Therapy, 57*(3), 95–98.

Jahoda, M. (1958). *Current concepts of positive mental health*. New York, NY: Basic Books.

Jenaro, C., Flores, N., & Arias, B. (2007). Burnout and coping in human service practitioners. *Professional Psychology: Research and Practice, 38*, 80–87. doi:10.1037/0735-7028.38.1.80

Johnson, J., Gooding, P. A., Wood, A. M., & Tarrier, N. (2010). Resilience as positive coping appraisals: Testing the schematic appraisals model of suicide (SAMS). *Behaviour Research and Therapy, 48*, 179–186.

Joseph, S., & Wood, A. (2010). Assessment of positive functioning in clinical psychology: Theoretical and practical issues. *Clinical Psychology Review, 30*, 830–838. doi:10.1016/j.cpr.2010.01.002

Judge, T. A., & Hurst, C. (2008). How the rich (and happy) get richer (and happier): Relationship of core self-evaluations to trajectories in attaining work success. *Journal of Applied Psychology, 93*, 849–863.

Kahler, C. W., Spillane, N. S., Day, A., Clerkin, E. M., Parks, A., Leventhal, A. M., & Brown, R. A. (2014). Positive psychotherapy for smoking cessation: Treatment development, feasibility, and preliminary results. *Journal of Positive Psychology, 9*, 19–29. doi:10.1080/17439760.2013.826716

Keyes, C. L. M. (2013). *Promotion and protection of positive mental health: Towards complete mental health in human development*. New York, NY: Oxford University Press.

Lambert, M. (2007). Presidential address: What we have learned from a decade of research aimed at improving psychotherapy outcome in routine care. *Psychotherapy Research, 17*, 1–14. doi:10.1080/10503300601032506

Leamy, M., Bird, V., Le Boutillier, C., Williams, J., & Slade, M. (2011). A conceptual framework for personal recovery in mental health: systematic review and narrative synthesis. *British Journal of Psychiatry, 199*, 445–452.

Levak, R. W., Siegel, L., & Nichols, S. N. (2011). *Therapeutic feedback with the MMPI-2: A positive psychology approach*. New York, NY: Taylor & Francis.

Linley, P. A., Willars, J., & Biswas-Diener, R. (2010). *The strengths book*. [Computer software]. CAPP Press.

Lopez, S. J., & Snyder, C. R. (2003). *Positive psychological assessment: A handbook of models and measures*. Washington, DC: American Psychological Association.

Maddux, J. E. (2002). Stopping the "madness": Positive psychology and the deconstruction of the illness ideology and the *DSM*. In C. R. Snyder & S. J. Lopez (Eds.), *Handbook of positive psychology* (pp. 13–24). New York, NY: Oxford University Press.

Magyar-Moe, J. L. (2009). Four-front assessment approach. In S. J. Lopez (Ed.), *The encyclopedia of positive psychology* (Vol. 1, pp. 410–412). Oxford, England, & Malden, MA: Wiley-Blackwell.

Maslow, A. H. (1959). Cognition of being in the peak experiences. *Journal of Genetic Psychology, 94*, 43–66.

McGrath, R. E., Rashid, T., Park, N., & Peterson, C. (2010). Is optimal functioning a distinct state? *The Humanistic Psychologist, 38*, 159–169. doi:10.1080/08873261003635781.

McWilliams, N. (1994). *Psychoanalytic diagnosis*. New York, NY: Guilford Press.

Nelson, C., & Johnston, M. (2008). Adult Needs and Strengths Assessment–Abbreviated Referral Version to specify psychiatric care needed for incoming patients: Exploratory analysis. *Psychological Reports, 102*, 131–143.

Niemiec, R. M. (2013). VIA character strengths: Research and practice (the first 10 years). In H. H. Knoop & A. Delle Fave (Eds.), *Well-being and cultures: Perspectives on positive psychology* (pp. 11–30). New York, NY: Springer.

Niemiec, R. M., & Wedding, D. (2014). *Positive psychology at the movies: Using films to build character strengths and well-being* (2nd ed.). Cambridge, MA: Hogrefe.

Nesse, R. M. (1991). What good is feeling bad? *The Sciences, 31*, 30–37.

Ong, A. D., & Van Dulmen, M. (Eds.). (2006). *The Oxford handbook of methods in positive psychology*. New York, NY: Oxford University Press.

Peeters, G., & Czapinski, J. (1990). Positive–negative asymmetry in evaluations: The distinction between affective and informational negativity effects. *European Review of Social Psychology, 1*, 33–60.

Peterson, C. (2006). The Values in Action (VIA) classification of strengths. In M. Csikszentmihalyi & I. Csikszentmihalyi (Eds.), *A life worth living: Contributions to positive psychology* (pp. 29–48). New York, NY: Oxford University Press.

Peterson, C., & Seligman, M. E. P. (2004). *Character strengths and virtues: A handbook and classification*. New York, NY: Oxford University Press/Washington, DC: American Psychological Association.

Pope, K. S., & Tabachnick, B. G. (1994). Therapists as patients: A national survey of psychologists' experiences, problems, and beliefs. *Professional Psychology: Research and Practice, 25*, 247–258. doi:10.1037/0735-7028.25.3.247.

Radloff, L. (1977). The CES-D scale: A self-report depression scale for research in the general population. *Applied Psychological Measurement, 1*, 385–401.

Rapp, C. A., & Goscha, R. J. (2006). *The strengths model: Case management with people with psychiatric disabilities* (2nd ed.). New York, NY: Oxford University Press.

Rashid, T., Anjum, A., Lennox, C., Quinlan, D., Niemiec, R., Mayerson, D., & Kazemi, F. (2013). Assessment of character strengths in children and adolescents. In C. Proctor & A. Linley (Eds.), *Research, applications, and interventions for children and adolescents: A positive psychology perspective* (pp. 81–115). New York, NY: Springer.

Rashid, T., & Ostermann, R. F. (2009). Strength-based assessment in clinical practice. *Journal of Clinical Psychology, 65*, 488–498. doi:10.1002/jclp.20595.

Rashid, T., & Seligman, M. E. P. (2013). Positive psychotherapy. In D. Wedding & R. J. Corsini (Eds.), *Current psychotherapies* (pp. 461–498). Belmont, CA: Cengage.

Rashid, T., Summers, R, & Seligman, M. E. P. (in press). Positive psychology. In A. Tasman, J. Kay, J. A. Lieberman, M. B. First, & M. Riba (Eds.), *Psychiatry* (4th ed.) Hoboken, NJ: Wiley.

Rokeach, M. (1973). *The nature of human values*. New York, NY: Free Press.

Ryff, C. D., & Singer, B. (1996). Psychological well-being: Meaning, measurement, and implications for psychotherapy research. *Psychotherapy and Psychosomatics, 65*, 14–23.

Saleebey, D. (1996). The strengths perspective in social work practice: Extensions and cautions. *Social Work, 41*, 296–305.

Schwartz, B., & Sharpe, K. E. (2006). Practical wisdom: Aristotle meets positive psychology. *Journal of Happiness Studies, 7*, 377–395.

Seligman, M. E. P., Rashid, T., & Parks, A. C. (2006). Positive psychotherapy. *American Psychologist, 61*, 774–788.

Simmons, C., & Lehmann, P. (2013). *Strength-based assessment and evaluation*. New York, NY: Springer.

Sloan, D. (1980). Teaching of ethics in the American undergraduate curriculum, 1876–1976. In D. Callahan & S. Bok (Eds.), *Ethics teaching in higher education* (p. 30). New York, NY: Plenum Press.

Spielberger, C. D., Gorsuch, R. L., Lushene, R., Vagg, P. R., & Jacobs, G. A. (1983). *Manual for the State-Trait Anxiety Inventory (Form Y)*. Palo Alto, CA: Consulting Psychologists Press.

Szasz, T. (1961). *The myth of mental illness: Foundations of a theory of personal conduct*. New York, NY: Harper & Row.

Weber, M. (2002). *The Protestant ethic and the spirit of capitalism* (P. Baehr, Ed.). New York, NY: Penguin. (Original work published 1905) doi:10.1522/cla.wem.sec

Wood, A. M., & Joseph, S. (2010). The absence of positive psychological (eudemonic) wellbeing as a risk factor for depression: A ten-year cohort study. *Journal of Affective Disorders, 122*, 213–217.

Wright, B. A., & Lopez, S. J. (2002). *Widening the diagnostic focus: A case for including human strengths and environmental resources*. New York, NY: Oxford University Press.

# PART VIII

# INNER RESOURCES AND POSITIVE DEVELOPMENT ACROSS THE LIFE SPAN

# CHAPTER 32

# The Ability Model of Emotional Intelligence

DAVID R. CARUSO, PETER SALOVEY, MARC BRACKETT, and JOHN D. MAYER

Human intelligence consists of a general factor, or *g*, which means that no matter how intelligence is defined and measured, its various components are moderately and positively correlated with one another (see, for example, Carroll, 1993). Yet, researchers have also found that underneath this general factor of intelligence, or the ability to learn and acquire knowledge, lies a number of more specific abilities or intelligences ranging from verbal to spatial intelligence. Over the decades, many specific abilities or intelligences have been proposed, including a set of intelligences sometimes referred to as "hot" intelligences. These hot intelligences operate on data that is important to us as humans, such as social relations and emotions. One of the more recently proposed hot intelligences is emotional intelligence (EI; Salovey & Mayer, 1990). Even though EI was originally defined as an intelligence, where reasoning operates on emotions and emotions constructively inform reasoning, the term has been broadened to encompass a variety of views that some have labeled as *soft skills* or even more curiously, as *noncognitive abilities*. We'll briefly explore the many meanings of EI and then focus our attention on EI as an intelligence. In this chapter we expand upon research that demonstrates the validity of EI and also incorporate research on the influence of programs to enhance EI.

The general public was made aware of the concept of EI through the publication of a book in 1995 (Goleman, 1995). EI was broadly conceived in this popular book as a set of skills, abilities, and desirable personality traits, but focused on four core abilities of self and other emotional awareness and management. As a result, EI has come to refer to traits such as optimism and assertiveness, competencies such as leadership, and emotional abilities such as accurate emotion perception (for a review, see Mayer, Roberts, & Barsade, 2008). In turn, these three approaches to EI have been operationally defined through a set of personality self-report measures, 360-degree competency assessments, and ability-based measures of emotional skills (Mayer et al., 2008). These are described in Table 32.1.

**Disclosures:** Mayer, Salovey, and Caruso receive royalties from sales of the MSCEIT assessment; Brackett and Caruso receive royalties from sales of a book used for school-based EI training; and Caruso and Salovey receive royalties from the sales of a book.

**Table 32.1**
Three Approaches to Emotional Intelligence

| Approach | Definition | Example Traits |
|---|---|---|
| Personality | Noncognitive traits | Assertiveness, optimism, happiness |
| Competency | Leadership competencies | Achievement, transparency, service orientation |
| Ability | Emotion skills | Emotion perception, emotion regulation |

Not surprisingly, the personality approach has a great deal of overlap with traditional models and measures of standard personality trait models such as the big five (Brackett & Mayer, 2003). Competency-based models are based on standard leadership competency models. Our focus in this chapter will be on the ability-based approach to EI. This integrative approach to the conceptualization of EI represents the construct as a standard intelligence. Research on this approach to EI shows that it can be reliably measured using performance tests, that it appears to have discriminant validity with regard to traditional personality models, and that it predicts a set of important outcomes.

## PRECURSORS TO A THEORY OF EMOTIONAL INTELLIGENCE

Emotions are often viewed as confusing and disruptive to cognitive processing and decision making. Yet, research on emotions demonstrates that they are adaptive. For example, for many years, Averill has argued that just as intellectual skills are learned and developed, so too can we acquire a repertoire of emotional skills that allow us to achieve, in his words, our full potential (Averill & Nunley, 1992). Likewise, in his model of multiple intelligences, Gardner (1985) described two personal intelligences: interpersonal and intrapersonal intelligence. The latter is defined as

> the core capacity at work here is *access to one's own feeling life*—one's range of affects or emotions: the capacity instantly to effect discriminations among these feelings and, eventually, to label them, to enmesh them in symbolic codes, to draw upon them as a means of understanding and guiding one's behavior. In its most primitive form, the intrapersonal intelligence amounts to little more than the capacity to distinguish a feeling of pleasure from one of pain and, on the basis of such discrimination, to become more involved in or to withdraw from a situation. At its most advanced level, intrapersonal knowledge allows one to detect and to symbolize complex and highly differentiated sets of feelings. One finds this form of intelligence developed in the novelist (like Proust) who can write introspectively about feelings. (p. 239 in paperback edition, original italics)

In the spirit of Gardner, Averill, and others (Leuner, 1966; Payne, 1986), we believe that there is an intelligence involving the processing of affectively-charged information (Salovey & Mayer, 1990). We define emotional intelligence as involving the capacity both to reason about emotions and to use emotions to assistance reasoning. Our model of EI includes the abilities to identify emotions accurately in oneself and in other people, understand emotions and emotional language, manage emotions in oneself and in other people, and use emotions to facilitate cognitive activities and motivate adaptive behavior (Mayer & Salovey, 1997).

In this chapter, we outline the four-branch model of EI and consider some issues in its assessment. Then we review research on the application of EI in various domains of life, and finally we consider the key findings, limitations, and opportunities for future research.

## A FOUR-BRANCH ABILITY MODEL OF EMOTIONAL INTELLIGENCE

We began work on a model of EI in the late 1980s by reviewing the research literature and asking what emotion-related skills and abilities modern investigators of emotion had tried—successfully or not—to operationalize over the years (reviewed in Mayer, Salovey, & Caruso, 2008). Could these skills be pulled together into a coherent whole? Four clusters or branches of EI emerged from the research (Mayer & Salovey, 1997): (1) perceiving emotions, (2) using emotions to facilitate thought, (3) understanding emotions, and (4) managing emotions in a way that enhances personal growth and social relations. We see a distinction between the second branch (using emotions) and the other three. Whereas the first, third, and fourth branches involve reasoning about emotions, the second branch uniquely involves using emotions to enhance reasoning. The four branches form a hierarchy, with identifying emotion in the self and others as the most fundamental or basic-level skill and managing emotions as the most superordinate skill. The ability to manage emotions in oneself and others is the culmination of the competencies represented by the other three branches. Individual differences in the four areas of EI have been reviewed elsewhere (e.g., Mayer, Salovey, & Caruso, 2000a, 2000b; Mayer, Salovey, et al., 2008; Salovey, Bedell, Detweiler, & Mayer, 2000; Salovey, Mayer, & Caruso, 2002); here, we provide a brief summary of the skills (see Exhibit 32.1).

### EXHIBIT 32.1

The Four-Branch Ability Model of Emotional Intelligence

---

**Branch Names and Exemplary Skills**

**Branch 1: Perceiving Emotion**

- Ability to identify emotion in one's physical and psychological states.

- Ability to identify emotion in other people.

- Ability to express emotions accurately and to express needs related to them.

- Ability to discriminate between accurate/honest and inaccurate/dishonest feelings.

**Branch 2: Using Emotions to Facilitate Thought**

- Ability to redirect and prioritize thinking on the basis of associated feelings.

- Ability to generate emotions to facilitate judgment and memory.

- Ability to capitalize on mood changes to appreciate multiple points of view.

- Ability to use emotional states to facilitate problem solving and creativity.

**Branch 3: Understanding Emotions**

- Ability to understand relationships among various emotions.

- Ability to perceive the causes and consequences of emotions.

*(Continued)*

EXHIBIT 32.1
*(Continued)*

---

- Ability to understand complex feelings, emotional blends, and contradictory states.
- Ability to understand transitions among emotions.

**Branch 4: Managing Emotions**

- Ability to be open to feelings, both pleasant and unpleasant.
- Ability to monitor and reflect on emotions.
- Ability to engage, prolong, or detach from an emotional state.
- Ability to manage emotions in oneself.
- Ability to manage emotions in others.

---

PERCEIVING EMOTIONS

Emotion perception involves registering, attending to, and deciphering emotion-laden messages as they are expressed in facial expressions, voice tone, or cultural artifacts. Individuals differ in their abilities to discern the emotional content of such stimuli. These competencies are basic information-processing skills in which the relevant information consists of feelings and mood states. For example, some individuals with *alexithymia* have difficult expressing their emotions verbally, presumably because they have difficulty identifying those feelings (Apfel & Sifneos, 1979; Bagby, Parker, & Taylor, 1994a, 1994b).

USING EMOTIONS TO FACILITATE THOUGHT

This second branch of EI focuses on how emotion affects the cognitive system and, as such, can be harnessed for more effective problem solving, reasoning, decision making, and creative endeavors. Of course, cognition can be disrupted by emotions, such as anxiety and fear, but emotions also can prioritize the cognitive system to attend to what is important (Easterbrook, 1959; Leeper, 1948; Mandler, 1975; Simon, 1982), and even to focus on what it does best in a given mood (e.g., Palfai & Salovey, 1993; Schwarz, 1990). This second ability turns on its head the notion that emotions always interfere with decision making and that we need to "check our emotions at the door," especially in the workplace.

UNDERSTANDING EMOTIONS

The most fundamental competency at this level concerns the ability to label emotions with words and to recognize the relationships among exemplars of the affective lexicon. The emotionally intelligent individual is able to recognize that the terms used to describe emotions are arranged into families and that groups of emotion terms form fuzzy sets (Ortony, Clore, & Collins, 1988). Perhaps more importantly, the relations among these terms are deduced—for example, that annoyance and irritation can lead to rage if the provocative stimulus is not eliminated. This is the branch of EI that we would expect to be most highly correlated with verbal intelligence.

MANAGING EMOTIONS

The emotionally intelligent individual can repair her negative moods and emotions and maintain positive moods and emotions when doing so is appropriate. (It is also sometimes desirable to maintain negative emotional states, such as when one antic-ipates having to be part of a debate, collect an unpaid bill, or compete in a race.) This regulatory process comprises several steps. Individuals must (a) believe that they can modify their emotions; (b) monitor their moods and emotional states accu-rately; (c) identify and discriminate those moods and emotions in need of regulation; (d) employ strategies to change these moods and emotions, most commonly, to alle-viate negative feelings or maintain positive feelings; and (e) assess the effectiveness of those strategies.

Individuals differ in the expectancy that they can alleviate negative moods. Some people believe that when they are upset they can do something that will make them feel better; others insist that nothing will improve their negative moods. Individuals who believe they can successfully repair their moods engage in active responses to stress, whereas people low in self-efficacy of regulation display avoidance responses, as well as depressive and mild somatic symptoms (Cantanzaro & Greenwood, 1994; Goldman, Kraemer, & Salovey, 1996). The ability to help others enhance their moods is also an aspect of EI, as individuals often rely on their social networks to provide not just a practical but an emotional buffer against negative life events (Stroebe & Stroebe, 1996). Moreover, individuals appear to derive a sense of efficacy and social worth from helping others feel better and by contributing to their joy.

MEASURING EMOTIONAL INTELLIGENCE

Over the years, we have developed a set of task-based measures of EI, the latest being the Mayer-Salovey-Caruso Emotional Intelligence Test (MSCEIT; Mayer, Salovey, & Caruso, 2002a). Elsewhere, we have tried to make the case that ability-based measures may be a more appropriate way to operationalize our model of EI as compared to self-report inventories (Brackett, Rivers, Shiffman, Lerner, & Salovey, 2006; Mayer, Salovey, & Caruso, 2008).

EXHIBIT 32.2

The Four-Branch Model of Emotional Intelligence as Operationalized by the
Mayer-Salovey-Caruso Emotional Intelligence Test (MSCEIT V2.0)

---

**Branch Names and Exemplary Tasks**

**Branch 1: Perceiving Emotion**

- *Faces*: Identifying emotions expressed in faces.

- *Pictures*: Identifying emotions suggested by photographs of landscapes and abstract artistic designs.

**Branch 2: Using Emotions to Facilitate Thought**

- *Sensations*: Matching tactile, taste, and color terms to specific emotions.

- *Facilitation*: Indicating how moods and emotions affect cognitive processes such as thinking, reasoning, problem solving, and creativity.

**Branch 3: Understanding Emotions**

- *Blends*: Identifying the emotions that may encompass a complex feeling state.

*(Continued)*

EXHIBIT 32.2
*(Continued)*

---

- *Changes*: Noticing how feelings and emotions progress or transition from one state to another.

**Branch 4: Managing Emotions**

- *Management*: Estimating the effectiveness of various strategies that could modify one's feelings in various situations.

- *Relations*: Estimating the consequences of various strategies for emotional reactions involving other people.

---

The MSCEIT has eight tasks, as depicted in Exhibit 32.2: Two tasks measure each of the four branches of EI. Branch 1, Perceiving Emotions, is measured through (1) Faces, for which participants are asked to accurately identify the emotions in faces, and (2) Pictures, for which participants are asked to accurately identify the emotions conveyed by landscapes and designs. Branch 2, Using Emotions to Facilitate Thought, is measured by the (3) Sensations task, for which participants compare emotions to other tactile and sensory stimuli, and, (4) Facilitation, for which participants identify which emotions would best facilitate a type of thinking (e.g., planning a birthday party). Branch 3, Understanding Emotions, is measured through (5) Changes, which tests a person's ability to know which emotion would change into another (e.g., frustration into aggression), and (6) Blends, which asks participants to identify which emotions would form a third emotion. Branch 4, Managing Emotions, is measured through (7) Emotional Management, which involves presenting participants with hypothetical scenarios and asking how they would maintain or change their feelings in them, and (8) Emotional Relations, which involves asking participants how to manage others' feelings.

The MSCEIT produces a total score, scores at two area levels, and at the four branch levels, as well as scores for the eight individual tasks. Reliabilities at the total and branch levels of the MSCEIT are adequate. We (Mayer, Salovey, Caruso, & Sitarenios, 2001, 2003) were able to establish that the MSCEIT test's overall reliability is $r = .91$ or .93 (depending upon whether expert-based or general consensus–based scoring is employed; see Mayer et al., 2002b), with branch scores (representing the four-branch model) of $r = .76$ to .91. Brackett and Mayer (2003) have reported that the MSCEIT has test–retest reliability of $r = .86$ after 1 month.

PREDICTING OUTCOMES

We have provided more substantial summaries of the relations between MSCEIT scores and important, real-life outcomes elsewhere (Brackett, Rivers, & Salovey, 2011; Mayer, Salovey, et al. 2008) and we summarize them briefly here. First, we know that EI, measured as an ability with the MSCEIT, does not overlap substantially with other psychological constructs such as the Big Five personality traits (Brackett & Mayer, 2003; Lopes, Salovey, & Straus, 2003). Self-report measures of EI, on the other hand, tend to be highly correlated with existing measures of personality. For instance, Brackett and Mayer (2003) reported a multiple $R$ between the Big Five and the Bar-On EQ-i of .75, whereas for the MSCEIT the $R$ was only .38. The MSCEIT appears to be free of the biasing influences of mood and social desirability as well (Lopes et al., 2003).

EI seems especially relevant when discussing psychological constructs related to a life well lived. People higher in EI are less likely to engage in violent behavior such as bullying and are less likely to use tobacco, drink alcohol to excess, or take illicit drugs (Brackett & Mayer, 2003; Brackett, Mayer, & Warner, 2004; Trinidad & Johnson, 2002). Individuals high in EI also report more positive interactions and relations with other people (Côté, Lopes, Salovey, & Miners, 2010).

APPLICATIONS OF EMOTIONAL INTELLIGENCE

There have been several major areas of application of EI theory and measurement—in education, human resources management (especially executive coaching), and politics—and we will look at these three domains in turn.

*Education*   In recent years, the theme of emotional intelligence has been used in a general manner to organize efforts to teach schoolchildren various kinds of skills that help to build competency in self-management and social relations. In the educational literature, this is usually called *social and emotional learning* (SEL; Elias, Hunter, & Kress, 2001; Payton et al., 2000), and programs range from the teaching of discrete skills in, for example, social problem solving (reviewed in Cohen, 2001; Elias et al., 1997) and conflict management (e.g., Lantieri & Patti, 1996), to larger curricula organized around broader issues of social development. A recent meta-analysis of a large number of eclectic approaches to SEL by the advocacy group CASEL (Collaborative for Academic, Social and Emotional Learning) showed positive effects for such programs (Durlak, Weissberg, Dymnicki, Taylor, & Schellinger, 2011).

Zins, Elias, Greenberg, and Weissberg (2000) suggest that to be successful, school-based programs should be comprehensive, multiyear, and integrated into the curriculum and extracurricular activities. They should be theoretically based, as well as developmentally and culturally appropriate. They should promote a caring, supportive, and challenging classroom and school climate; teach a broad range of skills; be undertaken by well-trained staff with adequate, ongoing support; promote school, family, and community partnerships; and be systematically monitored and evaluated. In addition, it is important to conduct randomized control studies of such programs, and to date, few have been conducted (e.g., Reyes, Brackett, Rivers, Elbertson, & Salovey, 2012).

One of the few randomized control studies has been based on the ability model of EI, which was adapted for use in primary and secondary schools for teachers, administrators, and students and their families (Brackett, Caruso, & Stern, 2013). This approach teaches the emotion skills of recognizing, understanding, labeling, expressing, and regulating emotions (a subset of the Mayer-Salovey ability model known by the acronym RULER), and the curriculum has been implemented in hundreds of schools. In one study, students in middle school classrooms using RULER for one academic year had higher end-of-year grades and higher teacher ratings of social and emotional competence compared to students in the comparison group (Brackett, Rivers, Reyes, & Salovey, 2012). A randomized control trial in 62 schools tested whether RULER improves the social and emotional climate of classrooms (Rivers, Brackett, Reyes, & Elbertson, 2012). After one academic year, schools that implemented RULER were rated by independent observers as having higher degrees of warmth and connectedness, more autonomy and leadership and less bullying among students, and teachers who focused more on students' interests and motivations, compared to non-RULER classrooms. Additional research examined whether first-year shifts in the emotional qualities of classrooms were followed by improvements in classroom organization and instruction at the end of the second year (Hagelskamp, Brackett, Rivers, & Salovey, 2013). Classrooms in RULER schools exhibited greater emotional support, better classroom organization, and more instructional support at the end of the second year of program delivery as compared to comparison classrooms. Other research shows that, consistent with RULER's implementation plan, mere delivery of RULER lessons is not enough for cultivating benefits for students. In one study, students had more positive outcomes, including higher EI, when they were in classrooms with teachers who had attended more training, taught more lessons, *and* were rated by independent observers as high-quality program implementers (Reyes et al., 2012). Thus, SEL programs such as RULER must be taught authentically, consistently, and with high quality in order to achieve intended outcomes. In addition, the dearth of randomized control studies, and the lack of multiyear longitudinal studies to demonstrate the long-term impact of SEL training, suggest a cautious, research-based approach to program development and implementation.

*Human Resources Management*    The workplace has been the most popular domain for applications of EI, in part because following Goleman's (1995) best-selling book on EI, he teamed up with Hay Group, one of the leading human resources development and consulting firms worldwide, to promote their measures of workplace competencies and the programs developed to enhance these skills among workers (Goleman, 1998; Goleman, Boyatzis, & McKee, 2002). Some of the extravagant claims about EI that can be found in this literature have been criticized quite deservedly (Dulewicz & Higgs, 2000). For example, Cooper and Sawaf (1997, p. xxvii) wrote that "if the driving force of intelligence in twentieth century business has been IQ, then . . . in the dawning twenty-first century it will be EQ" or that "use of EI for recruitment decisions leads to 90-percentile success rates" (Watkin, 2000, p. 91). This kind of hyperbole notwithstanding, there is a slowly growing literature suggesting that EI may matter in the workplace (Ashkanasy & Daus, 2002; Cherniss & Goleman, 2001; Jordan, Ashkanasy, & Härtel, 2003).

From our own work, we have seen that business students working together in task groups who scored highly on the MSCEIT are more likely to be viewed by their peers as developing well-articulated, visionary goals for the group than those students with lower MSCEIT scores (Côté et al., 2010). In a different study, business students working in teams who scored highly on the MSCEIT, especially the managing emotions branch, were more likely to have satisfying social interactions and to elicit social support from the other group members (Côté et al., 2010). In both of these studies, associations with EI and the various outcomes held even after controlling for the Big Five personality dimensions. Similarly, students with high MSCEIT scores were more likely to perform well (e.g., on examinations) in an organizational behavior and leadership course (Dasborough & Ashkanasy, 2002) and in their campus jobs (Janovics & Christiansen, 2001).

In real-world studies of organizations and leadership, there have been some hints that EI is related to more positive outcomes. In a study among employees of the finance group within a health insurance company, the understanding emotions branch and total MSCEIT scores appear to predict the size of annual salary raises, and the managing emotions branch score appears to predict total compensation. Our propensity to take risk and our willingness to make risky decisions is a function, in part, of our EI. Decision making occurs due to both our thoughts about the decision as well as our current mood state. In an ingenious set of experiments, Yip and Côté (2013) found that those low in EI, specifically their emotional understanding ability (EUA), allowed the effects of incidental anxiety to impact their willingness to make risky decisions. Those higher on EUA were not influenced by their incidental anxiety. The effect disappeared, however, when low-EUA participants were instructed on the spillover effect of anxiety onto unrelated decisions.

As we write this, only 4.2% of CEOs of Fortune 500 companies are female (catalyst.org). That number may not be surprising, as American corporations have been male-dominated since their inception. We won't go into the reasons for the lack of representation of women in positions of leadership, but we will point out differences between men and women in EI. As a group, women outperform men on our ability-based measure of EI (MSCEIT). The difference is statistically significant and the greatest difference is on the fourth branch, emotion management (Mayer, Salovey, & Caruso, 2002b). At the same time, women tend to underestimate their EI and men tend to overestimate their ability. Insofar as EI predicts important outcomes such as quality of relationships, how work is performed, and being able to generate compelling visions, it is our belief that the edge women have over men with regard to EI may begin to address these gender imbalances. And, perhaps, they will also begin to address a bias that emotions are unprofessional. Indeed, the fundamental premise of EI is that emotions contain data, that they can help us think, create empathic connections between people, and assist us in making good decisions.

*Politics* As compared to education and human resources management, applications of EI in politics are relatively recent. Based loosely on discoveries about the neurological underpinnings of the interactions between emotion and rational decision making (e.g., Adolphs & Damasio, 2001; Damasio, 1994; Jaušovec, Jaušovec, & Gerlič, 2001; LeDoux, 1996, 2000), Marcus, Neuman, and MacKuen (2000) provide a perspective on political judgment that they call *affective intelligence*. This is designed to examine how momentary psychological states, such as mood and emotion, interact with ongoing beliefs and values, such as self-interest, in determining political behavior.

Other scholars have looked especially at case examples of political leadership. In a study of all the presidents of the United States from Roosevelt to Clinton, Greenstein (2000) suggests that six qualities are needed for successful presidential leadership: (1) effectiveness as a public communicator; (2) organizational capacity; (3) political skill; (4) vision; (5) cognitive style; and (6) emotional intelligence. In considering EI, Greenstein focuses most explicitly on the fourth branch of our model, the management of emotions, and notes that the presidents differed quite a bit in this regard:

> The vesuvian LBJ was subject to mood swings of clinical proportions. Jimmy Carter's rigidity was a significant impediment to his White House performance. The defective impulse control of Bill Clinton led him into actions that led to his impeachment. Richard Nixon was the most emotionally flawed of the presidents considered here. His anger and suspiciousness were of Shakespearean proportions. He more than any other president summons up the classic notion of the tragic hero who is defeated by the very qualities that brought him success (p. 199).

In the final sentences of his fascinating analysis, Greenstein (2000, p. 200) reveals just how central he believes EI is to presidential success: "Beware the presidential contender who lacks EI. In its absence all else may turn to ashes."

CLINICAL APPLICATIONS

The ability model of EI may have applications in psychotherapy and the treatment of mental illness. An intervention program in early-course schizophrenia (Eack, Greenwald, et al., 2010) found significant increases in MSCEIT scores after a year of cognitive enhancement therapy. In a sample of patients diagnosed with schizophrenia, MSCEIT scores negatively correlated with disorganized symptoms and poorer functioning in the community (Kee et al., 2009). In addition, the managing emotions subtests of the MSCEIT have been included as a standard measure of social cognitive functioning in schizophrenia research (Eack, Greeno, et al., 2010).

It is possible that EI predicts attachment style or orientation, with secure attachment positively correlated with MSCEIT scores (Kafetsios, 2004). Similarly, some data suggest that EI predicts relationship quality. If both partners are low on EI, they tend to experience more conflict and report poorer-quality relationships. Interestingly, couples with a mismatch in EI, that is, where one partner is high and the other low, report greater satisfaction than do couples where both partners have high EI (Brackett, Warner, & Bosco, 2005).

EI also may have a protective factor, but perhaps for men only. In a series of studies, EI predicted the extent to which men engaged in "bad behavior" such as vandalism, physical fights, and illegal drug use (Brackett & Mayer, 2003; Brackett et al., 2004).

## CONCLUSION

In this chapter, we outlined various approaches to EI and then focused on the ability model of EI. EI is a form of intelligence that predicts a set of outcomes related to health and well-being as well as to longer-term relationships. Research on human intelligence is just a little over 100 years old, and research on EI began only about 20 years ago. However, there are a number of things we do know about EI and a number of questions we hope that researchers and practitioners will address in the future.

## SUMMARY POINTS

- EI is a form of standard intelligence; it is not a soft skill, nor is it a set of personality traits.
- EI can and should be measured objectively.
- EI can be differentiated from traditional personality traits such as the Big Five.
- EI predicts important life outcomes in children and adults, and does so at levels one associates with other important psychological constructs.
- The next phase of research should include the development of integrative models of EI and objective measures of a wide range of emotional abilities.
- The question as to whether, and how, EI itself can be increased needs to be addressed with experimental interventions. If the underlying aptitude cannot be raised, applied research should determine what sorts of positive impact EI training has on people's lives.

## REFERENCES

Adolphs, R., & Damasio, A. R. (2001). The interaction of affect and cognition: A neurobiological perspective. In J. P. Forgas (Ed.), *Handbook of affect and social cognition* (pp. 27–49). Mahwah, NJ: L. Erlbaum.

Apfel, R. J., & Sifneos, P. E. (1979). Alexithymia: Concept and measurement. *Psychotherapy and Psychosomatics*, 32, 180–190.

Ashkanasy, N. M., & Daus, C. S. (2002). Emotion in the workplace: The new challenge for managers. *The Academy of Management Executive*, 16, 76–86.

Averill, J. R., & Nunley, E. P. (1992). *Voyages of the heart: Living an emotionally creative life*. New York, NY: Free Press.

Bagby, R. M., Parker, J. D. A., & Taylor, G. J. (1994a). The Twenty-Item Toronto Alexithymia Scale—I. Item selection and cross-validation of the factor structure. *Journal of Psychosomatic Research, 38*, 23–32.

Bagby, R. M., Parker, J. D. A., & Taylor, G. J. (1994b). The Twenty-Item Toronto Alexithymia Scale—II. Convergent, discriminant, and concurrent validity. *Journal of Psychosomatic Research, 38*, 33–40.

Brackett, M. A., Caruso, D. R., & Stern, R. (2013). *The anchors of emotional literacy.* Port Chester, NY: Dude Press.

Brackett, M. A., & Mayer, J. D. (2003). Convergent, discriminant, and incremental validity of competing measures of emotional intelligence. *Personality and Social Psychology Bulletin, 29*, 1147–1158.

Brackett, M. A., Mayer, J. D., & Warner, R. M. (2004). Emotional intelligence and its relation to everyday behavior. *Personality and Individual Differences, 36*, 1387–1402.

Brackett, M. A., Rivers, S. E., Reyes, M. R., & Salovey, P. (2012). Enhancing academic performance and social and emotional competence with the RULER feeling words curriculum. *Learning and Individual Differences, 22*, 218–224.

Brackett, M. A., Rivers, S. E., & Salovey, P. (2011). Emotional intelligence: Implications for personal, social, academic, and workplace success. *Social and Personality Psychology Compass, 5*, 88–103.

Brackett, M. A., Rivers, S. E., Shiffman, S., Lerner, N., & Salovey, P. (2006). Relating emotional abilities to social functioning: A comparison of self-report and performance measures of emotional intelligence. *Journal of Personality and Social Psychology, 91*, 780.

Brackett, M. A., Warner, R. M., & Bosco, J. S. (2005). Emotional intelligence and relationship quality among couples. *Personal Relationships, 12*, 197–212.

Cantanzaro, S. J., & Greenwood, G. (1994). Expectancies for negative mood regulation, coping and dysphoria among college students. *Journal of Consulting Psychology, 41*, 34–44.

Carroll, J. B. (1993). *Human cognitive abilities: A survey of factor-analytic studies.* New York, NY: Cambridge University Press.

Cherniss, C., & Goleman, D. (2001). *The emotionally intelligent workplace: How to select for, measure and improve emotional intelligence in individuals, groups and organizations.* San Francisco, CA: Jossey-Bass.

Cohen, J. (2001). Social and emotional education: Core concepts and practices. In Jonathan Cohen (Ed.), *Caring classrooms/intelligent schools: The social emotional education of young children* (pp. 3–29). New York, NY: Teachers College Press.

Cooper, R. K., & Sawaf, A. (1997). Applying emotional intelligence in the workplace. *Training & Development, 51*(12), 31–38.

Côté, S., Lopes, P. N., Salovey, P., & Miners, C. T. H. (2010). Emotional intelligence and leadership emergence in small groups. *The Leadership Quarterly, 21*, 496–508.

Damasio, A. (1994). *Descartes' error: Emotion, reason and the human mind.* New York, NY: Grossett/Putnam.

Dasborough, M. T., & Ashkanasy, N. M. (2002). Emotion and attribution of intentionality in leader-member relationships. *Leadership Quarterly, 13*, 615–634.

Dulewicz, V., & Higgs, M. (2000). Emotional intelligence: A review and evaluation study. *Journal of Managerial Psychology, 15*, 341–372.

Durlak, J. A., Weissberg, R. P., Dymnicki, A. B., Taylor, R. D., & Schellinger, K. B. (2011). The impact of enhancing students' social and emotional learning: A meta-analysis of school-based universal interventions. *Child Development, 82*, 405–432.

Eack, S. M., Greeno, C. G., Pogue-Geile, M. F., Newhill, C. E., Hogarty, G. E., & Keshavan, M. S. (2010). Assessing social-cognitive deficits in schizophrenia with the Mayer-Salovey-Caruso Emotional Intelligence Test. *Schizophrenia Bulletin, 36*, 370–380.

Eack, S. M., Greenwald, D., Hogarty, S., Cooley, S., DiBarry, A. L., & Montrose, D. (2010). Cognitive enhancement therapy for early-course schizophrenia: Effects of a two-year randomized controlled trial. *Psychiatric Services, 60*, 1468–1476.

Easterbrook, J. A. (1959). The effect of emotion on cue utilization and the organization of behavior. *Psychological Review, 66*, 183.

Elias, M. J., Hunter, L., & Kress, J. S. (2001). Emotional intelligence and education. In J. Ciarrochi, J. P. Forgas, & J. D. Mayer (Eds.), *Emotional intelligence in everyday life: A scientific inquiry* (pp. 133–149). Philadelphia, PA: Psychology Press.

Elias, M. J., Zins, J. E., Weissberg, R. P., Frey, K. S., Greenberg, M. T., Hayens, N. M., & Shriver, T. P. (1997). *Promoting social and emotional learning: Guidelines for educators.* Alexandria, VA: Association for Supervision and Curriculum Development.

Gardner, H. (1985). *Frames of mind: The theory of multiple intelligences.* New York, NY: Basic Books.

Goldman, S. L., Kraemer, D. T., & Salovey, P. (1996). Beliefs about mood moderate the relationship of stress to illness and symptom reporting. *Journal of Psychosomatic Research, 41*, 115–128.

Goleman, D. (1995). *Emotional intelligence.* New York, NY: Bantam.

Goleman, D. (1998). *Working with emotional intelligence.* New York, NY: Random House.

Goleman, D., Boyatzis, R. E., & McKee, A. (2002). *The new leaders: Transforming the art of leadership into the science of results.* London, England: Little, Brown.

Greenstein, F. I. (2000). *The presidential difference: Leadership style from FDR to Clinton.* New York, NY: Free Press.

Hagelskamp, C., Brackett, M. A., Rivers, S. E., & Salovey, P. (2013). Improving classroom quality with the RULER Approach to social and emotional learning: Proximal and distal outcomes. *American Journal of Community Psychology, 51*(3–4), 530–543.

Janovics, J., & Christiansen, N. D. (2001, April). *Emotional intelligence at the workplace.* Paper presented at the 16th Annual Conference of the Social of Industrial and Organizational Psychology, San Diego, CA.

Jaušovec, N., Jaušovec, K., & Gerlič, I. (2001). Differences in event-related and induced EEG patterns in the theta and alpha frequency bands related to human emotional intelligence. *Neuroscience Letters, 311*, 93–96.

Jordan, P. J., Ashkanasy, N. M., & Härtel, C. E. (2003). The case for emotional intelligence in organizational research. *The Academy of Management Review, 28*, 195–197.

Kafetsios, K. (2004). Attachment and emotional intelligence abilities across the life course. *Personality and Individual Differences, 37*, 129–145.

Kee, K. S., Horan, W. P., Salovey, P., Kern, R. S., Sergi, M. J., Fiske, A. P., . . . Green, M. F. (2009). Emotional intelligence in schizophrenia. *Schizophrenia Research, 107*, 61–68.

Lantieri, L., & Patti, J. (1996). The road to peace in our schools. *Educational Leadership, 54*, 28–31.

LeDoux, J. E. (1996). *The emotional brain: The mysterious underpinnings of emotional life.* New York, NY: Simon & Schuster.

LeDoux, J. E. (2000). Emotion circuits in the brain. *Annual Review of Neuroscience, 23*, 155–184.

Leeper, R. W. (1948). A motivational theory of emotion to replace emotion as disorganized response. *Psychological Review, 55*, 5.

Leuner, B. (1966). Emotional intelligence and emancipation: A psychodynamic study on women. *Praxis der kinderpsychologie und kinderpsychiatri, 15*, 196.

Lopes, P. N., Salovey, P., & Straus, R. (2003). Emotional intelligence, personality, and the perceived quality of social relationships. *Personality and Individual Differences, 35*, 641–658.

Mandler, G. (1975). *Mind and emotion.* New York, NY: Wiley.

Marcus, G. E., Neuman, W. R., & MacKuen, M. (2000). *Affective intelligence and political judgment.* Chicago, IL: University of Chicago Press.

Mayer, J. D., Roberts, R. D., & Barsade, S. G. (2008). Human abilities: Emotional intelligence. *Annual Review of Psychology, 59*, 507–536.

Mayer, J. D. & Salovey, P. (1997). What is emotional intelligence? In P. Salovey & D. J. Sluyter (Eds.), *Emotional development and emotional intelligence: Educational implications* (pp. 3–34). New York, NY: Basic Books.

Mayer, J. D., Salovey, P., & Caruso, D. R. (2000a). Emotional intelligence as zeitgeist, as personality, and as a standard intelligence. In R. Bar-On & J. D. A. Parker (Eds.), *Handbooks of emotional intelligence* (pp. 92–117). San Francisco, CA: Jossey-Bass.

Mayer, J. D., Salovey, P., & Caruso, D. R. (2000b). Models of emotional intelligence. In R. J. Sternberg (Ed.), *Handbooks of intelligence* (pp. 396–420). Cambridge, England: Cambridge University Press.

Mayer, J. D., Salovey, P., & Caruso, D. R. (2002a). *The Mayer-Salovey-Caruso Emotional Intelligence Test (MSCEIT), Version 2.0*. Toronto, Canada: Multi Health Systems.

Mayer, J. D., Salovey, P., & Caruso, D. R. (2002b). *Mayer-Salovey-Caruso Emotional Intelligence Test (MSCEIT) user's manual*. Toronto, Ontario: Multi Health Systems.

Mayer, J. D., Salovey, P., & Caruso, D. R. (2008). Emotional intelligence: New ability or eclectic traits? *American Psychologist, 63*, 503–517.

Mayer, J. D., Salovey, P., Caruso, D. R., & Sitarenios, G. (2001). Emotional intelligence as a standard intelligence. *Emotion, 1*(3), 232–242.

Mayer, J. D., Salovey, P., Caruso, D. R., & Sitarenios, G. (2003). Measuring emotional intelligence with the MSCEIT V2.0. *Emotion, 3*, 97.

Ortony, A., Clore, G. L., & Collins, A. (1988). *The cognitive structure or emotions*. Cambridge, England: Cambridge University Press.

Palfai, T. P., & Salovey, P. (1993). The influence of depressed and elate mood on deductive and inductive reasoning. *Imagination, Cognition, and Personality, 13*, 57–71.

Payne, W. L. (1986). A study of emotion, developing emotional intelligence: Self-integration, relating to fear, pain, and desire. *Dissertation Abstracts International, 47*, 203A.

Payton, J. W., Wardlaw, D. M., Graczyk, P. A., Bloodworth, M. R., Tompsett, C. J., & Weissberg, R. P. (2000). Social and emotional learning: A framework for promoting mental health and reducing risk behavior in children and youth. *Journal of School Health, 70*, 179–185.

Reyes, M. R., Brackett, M. A., Rivers, S. E., Elbertson, N. A., & Salovey, P. (2012). The interaction effects of program training, dosage, and implementation quality on targeted student outcomes for the RULER Approach to social and emotional learning. *School Psychology Review, 41*, 82–99.

Rivers, S. E., Brackett, M. A., Reyes, M. R., & Elbertson, N. A. (2012). Improving the social and emotional climate of classrooms: A clustered randomized controlled trial testing the RULER Approach. *Prevention Science, 14*, 77–87.

Salovey, P., Bedell, B. T., Detweiler, J. B., & Mayer, J. D. (2000). Current directions in emotional intelligence research. *Handbook of Emotions, 2*, 504–520.

Salovey, P., & Mayer, J. D. (1990). Emotional intelligence. *Imagination, Cognition, and Personality, 9*, 185–211.

Salovey, P., & Mayer, J. D., & Caruso, D. R. (2002). The positive psychology of emotional intelligence. In C. R. Snyder & S. J. Lopez (Eds.), *The handbook of positive psychology* (pp. 159–171). New York, NY: Oxford University Press.

Schwarz, N. (1990). Feelings as information: informational and motivational functions of affective states. In E. T. Higgins & E. M. Sorrentino (Eds.): *Handbook of motivation and cognition* (Vol. 2, pp. 527–561), New York, NY: Guilford Press.

Simon, H. A. (1982). *Models of bounded rationality: Empirically grounded economic reason* (Vol. 3). Cambridge, MA: MIT Press.

Stroebe, W., & Stroebe, M. (1996). The social psychology of social support. In E. T. Higgins & A. W. Kruglanski (Eds.), *Social psychology: Handbook of basic principles* (pp. 597–621). New York, NY: Guilford Press.

Trinidad, D. R., & Johnson, C. A. (2002). The association between emotional intelligence and early adolescent tobacco and alcohol use. *Personality and Individual Differences, 32*, 95–105.

Watkin, C. (2000). Developing emotional intelligence. *International Journal of Selection and Assessment, 2*, 89–92.

Yip, J. A., & Côté, S. (2013). The emotionally intelligent decision maker: Emotion-understanding ability reduces the effect of incidental anxiety on risk taking. *Psychological Science, 24*, 48–55.

Zins, J. E., Elias, M. J., Greenberg, M. T., & Weissberg, R. P. (2000). Promoting social and emotional competence in children. In K. M. Minke & G. C. Bear (Eds.), *Preventing school problems—promoting school success: Strategies and programs that work* (pp. 71–100). Bethesda, MD: National Association of School Psychologists.

CHAPTER 33

# The Power and Practice of Gratitude

GIACOMO BONO, MIKKI KRAKAUER, and JEFFREY J. FROH

A CENTRAL TENET OF RESEARCH in positive psychology is that supportive social relationships are essential to human thriving. Gratitude is perfectly suited to this end. Gratitude is the feeling people experience when they receive a gift or benefit from another person. It can also be an attitude of appreciating life as a gift. People with a grateful disposition tend to experience it more frequently, more intensely, toward more people, and for more things in their life at any given moment (McCullough, Emmons, & Tsang, 2002). We begin this chapter with a brief review of basic research on gratitude, focusing first on adult populations and then on youth populations. We then turn to applied research pertaining to clinical purposes for adults and academic purposes for youth. Finally, we discuss how gratitude is related to the "good life" for adults and youth and close with suggestions for future research directions. It is our contention that gratitude is important for positively transforming individuals, families, and organizations.

## A BRIEF HISTORY OF RESEARCH ON GRATITUDE

Social scientists have focused on gratitude since the 1930s (Baumgarten-Tramer, 1938; Bergler, 1945, 1950; Gouldner, 1960; Heider, 1958; Schwartz, 1967; Simmel, 1950). Though it has been considered fundamental to the maintenance of reciprocity obligations between people (Gouldner, 1960; Simmel, 1950) and evolutionarily adaptive for its promotion of altruistic behavior (Trivers, 1971), the bulk of empirical research occurred over the past dozen years because psychological research was long dominated by a focus on pathology rather than flourishing (Seligman & Csikszentmihalyi, 2000). Two classic studies—showing that expressing and experiencing gratitude bring peace of mind, satisfying personal relationships, and well-being (Emmons & McCullough, 2003; McCullough et al., 2002)—catalyzed the field, and since then a wealth of research on gratitude and its applications has emerged.

## CONCEPTUALIZATIONS OF GRATITUDE AS A MORAL AFFECT

Gratitude is considered a moral affect because it results from and stimulates behavior that is motivated by a concern for other people's well-being (McCullough, Kilpatrick,

*Authors' Note.* Preparation of this chapter was supported by a generous grant from the John Templeton Foundation.

559

Emmons, & Larson, 2001). Unlike other moral emotions that operate when one falls short of important standards or obligations (i.e., guilt and shame) or when one is motivated to help another in need (i.e., sympathy and empathy), gratitude is distinctly operant when one is the *recipient* of prosocial behavior and serves to increase prosocial behavior between people.

McCullough et al. (2001) delineated three moral functions of gratitude in social life by examining the existing empirical research on gratitude and related concepts (i.e., thankfulness, appreciation). First, the emotion of gratitude serves as a moral barometer by indicating a change in one's social relationships; recipients regard benefactors as moral agents for having augmented their personal well-being and acknowledge the particular importance of relationships with them. Second, as a moral reinforcer, the expression of gratitude increases the chances that a benefactor will respond benevolently again in the future, just as the expression of ingratitude can anger benefactors and discourage them from acting benevolently again. Finally, gratitude serves as moral motive because its experience motivates recipients to then behave prosocially or inhibit destructive behavior toward a benefactor in return or toward others. However, the reciprocity motivation resulting from gratitude is distinct from those sparked by indebtedness and inequity in that it is a pleasant emotion linked to positive psychological states, much like contentment, pride, and hope. McCullough et al. (2001) found ample support in the literature for the first two functions, and subsequent experiments using behavioral measures of helping provided support for the moral motive function (Bartlett & DeSteno, 2006; Tsang, 2006).

## REVIEW OF SOCIAL SCIENTIFIC RESEARCH ON GRATITUDE

The empirical research falls into three major categories: (1) how gratitude is measured and conceptualized; (2) what kind of people tend to be grateful; and (3) how gratitude has been and can be applied to society. A growing body of research also cuts across these categories by focusing on the measurement of gratitude in youth, its benefits to development, and factors and interventions that promote gratitude development. Researchers wanting to develop practical applications of gratitude to improve human health and well-being would benefit from considering these areas of research.

It seems reasonable to conclude from the available empirical evidence that gratitude can indeed be regarded as a moral emotion. We experience gratitude when we acknowledge the gratuitous role sources of social support play in producing beneficial outcomes in our lives. Expressing gratitude to people who have been kind to us validates their efforts and reinforces such behavior in the future. And gratitude motivates us to extend kindness in response to those who have been kind to us but to others as well. Therefore, people who experience and express gratitude more tend to strengthen their existing relationships *and* form new supportive relationships. That is, the more they tune in to how others have helped them along, the more they will do the same in return; and the more frequently such exchanges occur, the more suited relationship networks become to maximizing the mutual benefits for those involved.

## GRATITUDE AS AN AFFECTIVE TRAIT: MEASURES AND CORRELATES

Researchers have derived four different facets of emotional experiences that distinguish people with a more grateful disposition from those with a less grateful disposition. Compared to less grateful individuals, highly grateful individuals feel gratitude more *intensely* for a positive event, more *frequently* or more easily throughout the day;

they have a wider *span* of benefits or life circumstances for which they are grateful at any given time (e.g., for their families, their jobs, friends, their health); and they experience gratitude with greater *density* for any given benefit (i.e., toward a more people).

RESEARCH WITH ADULTS

In four studies, McCullough et al. (2002) broadly examined the correlates of the grateful disposition and developed the GQ-6 (a six-item, self-report measure of the grateful disposition). Highly grateful people, compared to their less grateful counterparts, tend to experience positive emotions more often, enjoy greater satisfaction with life and more hope, and experience less depression, anxiety, and envy. They tend to score higher in prosociality and be more empathic, forgiving, helpful, and supportive as well as less focused on materialistic pursuits, compared to their less grateful counterparts. They replicated these findings in a large nonstudent sample and showed that the associations persisted even after controlling for social desirability (Paulhus, 1998). Among the Big Five dimensions of personality (John, Donahue, & Kentle, 1991), the grateful disposition was correlated with Agreeableness, Extraversion/positive affectivity, and Neuroticism/negative affectivity. Moreover, similar associations were obtained using both self-report and peer-report methods.

Other researchers have come to similar conclusions (Watkins, Woodward, Stone, & Kolts, 2003). Watkins and colleagues devised the Gratitude Resentment and Appreciation Test (GRAT), a self-report measure conceptualizing dispositional gratitude as a combination of four aspects: appreciating benefactors, valuing the experience and expression of gratitude, sensing more abundance than deprivation in life, and appreciating common simple pleasures more than extravagant ones. Scores on the GRAT were positively related to satisfaction with life and negatively related to depression. Two reasons gratitude is linked to reduced depression are that it helps individuals experience more positive emotions and positively reframe negative or neutral situations (Lambert, Fincham, & Stillman, 2012).

Gratitude, whether measured as a mood or trait, is also linked to lower aggression in adults. Using various methods, DeWall, Lambert, Pond, Kashdan, and Fincham (2012) found that grateful participants exhibited lower aggression daily, and after feeling hurt or insulted, they exhibited less hurt feelings in daily interactions and less aggressive personality. These researchers also found that increased empathy mediated this link, suggesting that the prosocial quality of gratitude can be used to mitigate aggression. Helping to explain such findings, evidence shows that gratitude builds trust (Dunn & Schweitzer, 2005) and that expressing gratitude increases prosocial behavior by enabling people to feel socially valued (Grant & Gino, 2010).

Finally, research shows that gratitude promotes relationship formation and maintenance. One study, examining gratitude naturally in the context of college sororities' gift-giving week (Algoe, Haidt, & Gable, 2008), found that gratitude was predicted by new members perceiving older members to be more responsive to their needs during the week and that this predicted their gratitude at the end of the week and consequently greater relationship quality between members 1 month later. Other research corroborates this relationship-building function, linking gratitude to more liking and inclusiveness (Bartlett, Condon, Cruz, Baumann, & DeSteno, 2012). Evidence also shows that gratitude boosts relationship maintenance behaviors like sensitivity and concern (Lambert & Fincham, 2011), strengthens romantic relationships by promoting commitment (Joel, Gordon, Impett, MacDonald, & Keltner, 2013) and feelings of connection and satisfaction with relationships (Algoe, Gable, & Maisel, 2010), and makes for more satisfying marital relationships (C. L. Gordon, Arnette, & Smith, 2011). Thus, gratitude appears to help individuals find, remind, and bind to attentive relationship partners (Algoe, 2012).

RESEARCH WITH YOUTH

In recent years, evidence shows that many similar psychological, physical, and relational benefits found with adults occur with youth, whether examined cross-sectionally (Froh, Emmons, Card, Bono, & Wilson, 2011) or longitudinally (Froh, Bono, & Emmons, 2010). Much of this work has focused on the effects of gratitude on youth's adjustment, social relationships, and psychological well-being, with implications for positive youth development and potential for helping to turn young people into healthy, successful adults.

In order to determine which adult measure was most appropriate in measuring gratitude in children and adults, Froh, Fan, et al. (2011) assessed the psychometric properties of the GQ-6, the Gratitude Adjective Checklist (GAC; McCullough et al., 2002), and the GRAT–short form (Thomas & Watkins, 2003) using a sample of 1,405 youth ages 10 to 19 years. Results showed that all three gratitude scales correlated positively. The GRAT–short form showed low correlations with the other two scales among younger youth (ages 10 to 13 years), suggesting that the GRAT–short form measures something different in comparison to the GAC and the GQ-6 among younger youth. The GQ-6 was found to perform better with youth only when using the first five questions (not the sixth).

In a recent longitudinal study by Bono, Froh, and Emmons (2012) 436 adolescents (11- to 14-year-olds) completed self-report questionnaires just before entering high school and then again 4 years later. Gratitude at Time 1 significantly predicted greater positive emotions, life satisfaction, and happiness and lower negative emotions and depression at Time 2. Even stronger effects were observed when examining the change in gratitude from Year 1 to Year 4. Increases in gratitude during high school predicted greater increases in positive emotions, life satisfaction, and happiness at the end of high school. Furthermore, increases in gratitude predicted less antisocial and delinquency behavior toward the end of high school (Bono et al., 2012). That is, teens who developed more gratitude during high school reported better behavior at school (e.g., not cheating on tests) and lower levels of negative behaviors toward peers (e.g., teasing, upsetting, and gossiping) when finishing high school, compared to teens who developed less gratitude during high school.

Another longitudinal study observed adolescents' level of social integration—their motivation to give back to the neighborhood and society (Froh et al., 2010). Results showed that grateful adolescents were more likely than less grateful adolescents to report increases in social integration 6 months later, and this was partially because of increases in life satisfaction and engagement in prosocial behaviors at 3 months. Gratitude and social integration also were found to mutually increase each other. Together, these findings suggest that gratitude supports well-being and prosocial development.

## INTERVENTIONS TO PROMOTE GRATITUDE

In addition to cross-sectional and longitudinal studies, intervention studies also provide evidence that gratitude has a variety of benefits for adults and youth. This research has also uncovered different strategies that are effective for promoting gratitude.

## INTERVENTIONS TO INCREASE GRATITUDE IN ADULTS

Emmons and McCullough (2003) conducted a seminal study of gratitude's effects on psychological and physical well-being using a Counting Blessings intervention. In one experiment, college students were randomly assigned to complete one of three journaling conditions weekly for 10 weeks: counting blessings, listing hassles, or describing neutral events. Participants in the gratitude condition exercised more regularly, reported fewer physical symptoms, felt better about life and more connected to others, and were more optimistic about the upcoming week than those in the hassles or control conditions. To test if the benefits resulted from gratitude rather than just feeling better off than others, a second experiment included a downward social comparisons condition (i.e., ways they had it better than others) rather than a neutral events condition and had students journal about this, blessings, or hassles daily for 2 weeks. Participants in the gratitude condition reported more positive affect, compared to the hassles condition, and reported offering others more emotional support or help with a personal problem, compared to those in the other two conditions.

Finally, in a third experiment Emmons and McCullough (2003) examined if a gratitude intervention would help adults with neuromuscular diseases. Participants assigned to describe blessings (vs. mundane experiences) daily for 3 weeks reported more positive affect and satisfaction with life than those in the control condition—effects observed through spouses' reports, too. Moreover, they reported less negative affect, feeling more connected to others, and sleeping longer and better. This study supported the notion that gratitude can improve physical and psychological well-being for a variety of populations.

The benefits of gratitude were further confirmed in a study that compared the efficacy of five different interventions hypothesized to lastingly increase happiness and decrease depression using a random-assignment placebo-controlled design (Seligman, Steen, Park, & Peterson, 2005). Participants in the Three Good Things intervention were instructed to write down three good things that had happened to them and attribute causes to these events daily for one week. Although this intervention showed no immediate benefits, individuals experienced lasting effects with an increase in happiness and decrease in depressive symptoms 6 months later. Another intervention, the Gratitude Visit, had individuals write a letter to someone they were grateful for and then deliver their letter in person. Individuals who completed this activity reported large gains in happiness and reductions in depression 1 month later. Though effects were short-lived, the magnitude of change was greatest for this intervention out of the five tested, presumably because of the hyperemotional nature of expressing meaningful thanks.

Recent gratitude interventions harness the power of thanking by incorporating a behavioral component. For instance, one experiment instructed participants to journal grateful experiences and share them with a partner biweekly for 4 weeks (control participants kept a journal of grateful experience without sharing or kept a journal of class learnings and shared them with a partner; Lambert et al., 2013). Those who shared their positive experiences had increased positive affect, happiness, and life satisfaction by the end of the intervention, compared to either of the control participants.

Lambert and Fincham (2011) found that expressing gratitude in close relationships produced higher comfort voicing concerns and more positive perceptions of partners.

INTERVENTIONS TO INCREASE GRATITUDE IN CHILDREN AND ADOLESCENTS

A pioneering intervention study attempted to see if the Counting Blessings intervention done with adults (Emmons & McCullough, 2003) could influence well-being in adolescents ages 11 to 12 (Froh, Sefick, & Emmons, 2008). Eleven classrooms ($N = 221$) were randomly assigned to one of three conditions: gratitude, hassles, or no-treatment control. Each day for 2 weeks, students in the gratitude condition were instructed to list up to five things they were grateful for in their lives. Classrooms in the hassles condition listed annoyances. Results indicated that counting blessings was related to higher life satisfaction, more optimism, fewer physical complaints, and less negative affect. Students in the gratitude group reported more school satisfaction at both the immediate posttest and at the 3-week follow-up, compared to both control groups.

Another intervention study using a similar intervention method found a link between gratitude and prosociality in adolescents (Chaplin, Rindfleisch, John, & Froh, 2013). Sixty-one adolescents (ages 11 to 17) in a summer program were randomly assigned to journal about blessings (intervention) or mundane activities (control) for 2 weeks. Everyone received 10 $1 bills for participating and had the option of keeping it for themselves or donating some or all of it to charity anonymously. Results showed that adolescents in the gratitude condition donated 60% more compared to those in the control condition ($6.81 vs. $2.43). Further, they were also more grateful and less materialistic at posttest compared to those in the control condition.

A recent study showed that the social cognitive appraisals underlying grateful thinking can be trained in children ages 8 to 11 (Froh et al., 2014). Using a quasi-experimental design, classrooms were randomly assigned to a benefit appraisal curriculum or a control condition. The benefit appraisal condition trained students to appreciate the *personal value* of kind actions or gifts, the *altruistic intention of the benefactor*, and the *cost to the benefactor* in terms of time or effort. The control condition had students focus on mundane daily events. All sessions included class discussions, writing assignments, and role-playing activities. Five curriculum sessions were delivered to six classrooms daily for 1 week in one study and to four classrooms weekly for 5 weeks in a second study. In both studies, students who received benefit appraisal training reported stronger benefit appraisals and more grateful emotion than students in the control condition. In the daily study, these students reported immediate increases in grateful thinking and mood and also wrote 80% more thank-you cards to their Parent Teacher Association compared to control students. In the weekly study, they reported more grateful thinking and grateful mood, as well as more positive affect 5 months after the intervention.

This grateful thinking curriculum is advantageous because it is easier to use with younger participants (i.e., in elementary or middle school), for whom it might not be feasible or possible to keep a gratitude journal. Another advantage is that it can be easily infused in existing reading/writing programs or used to personalize and enhance lessons focused on cooperation, helping, or giving.

## OBSTACLES TO PROMOTING GRATITUDE:
## INTERVENTION MODERATORS

Any discussion of the benefits of gratitude would be incomplete without a consideration of factors that render gratitude difficult. Moderators must be examined to design effective gratitude interventions because some individuals may be more responsive than others. Different people experience different amounts of gratitude depending on the size of the gift they are accustomed to receiving and the amount of effort benefactors invest (Wood, Brown, & Maltby, 2011). Thus, cultural and attitudinal factors likely moderate gratitude's effects on well-being. Indeed, a cross-cultural study found gratitude interventions focusing on family and others to be more effective in collectivist samples, whereas those focusing on oneself were more effective with individualistic samples (Boehm, Lyubomirsky, & Sheldon, 2011). Thus, researchers can personalize interventions with a focus on the types of benefits recipients most value (e.g., focusing on benefits that affirm, increase, or maintain harmony in relationships for interdependent selves and focusing on benefits that affirm, increase, or maintain personal autonomy and achievement for independent selves).

Research is needed to better understand how the experience, expression, and consequences of gratitude differ across cultures. People may be grateful for different reasons or because of distinct determinants; ways of expressing gratitude to others may differ; and gratitude may differentially impact mental, physical, or relational outcomes across cultures. Understanding universal versus distinctive patterns in these areas would advance basic knowledge about gratitude in society.

Scholars suggest that a number of attitudes are incompatible with gratitude, including perceptions of victimhood (Seligman, 2002), inability to admit to one's shortcomings (Solomon, 2002), envy and resentment (Etchegoyen & Nemas, 2003), and an overemphasis on materialistic values (Kasser, 2002). Interventions to cultivate gratitude cannot ignore these obstacles to gratitude, for it may be necessary to confront these on their own terms prior to initiating a gratitude focus. We may learn that individuals with such characteristics benefit more strongly from gratitude interventions.

Some of these obstacles are likely to be deeply ingrained in personality. A major personality variable that is likely to thwart gratitude is narcissism (Watkins et al., 2003). People with narcissistic tendencies erroneously believe they are deserving of special rights and privileges without assuming reciprocal responsibilities. The sense of entitlement combined with insensitivity to the needs of others engenders interpersonal exploitation. They might be reluctant to express gratitude in response to benefactors whose generosity or kindness they summarily dismiss as little more than attempts to curry favor. Farwell and Wohlwend-Lloyd (1998) found that in the context of a laboratory-based interdependence game, narcissism was inversely related to the extent to which participants experienced liking and gratitude for their partners. In short, if one feels entitled to everything, then one is thankful for nothing.

Another possible moderator of gratitude on well-being is personal responsibility. Chow and Lowery (2010) found that individuals do not experience gratitude without the belief that they are responsible for their success, even when they acknowledge that they received help. Such knowledge can be useful in improving gratitude interventions, particularly those targeting younger populations. Indeed, longitudinal evidence shows that youth who developed lots of gratitude from ages 11–14 to ages 15–18 reported more self-respect, self-control, goals/plans for the future, and self-regulation, compared to youth who developed little gratitude during this period (Froh & Bono, 2014).

Research has examined moderators for gratitude interventions among youth. In one study, children and adolescents (ages 8 to 19) were randomly assigned to either a gratitude visit condition (writing a thank-you letter to a benefactor and then reading it to the individual in person) or a control condition (describing daily events). Students in the gratitude condition who were also low in positive affect reported more gratitude and positive affect at post-treatment and more positive affect at the 2-month follow-up than youths in the control condition (Froh, Kashdan, Ozimkowski, & Miller, 2009). Therefore, youth lower in positive affect seem to benefit more from gratitude interventions.

## CREATIVE APPLICATIONS FOR GRATITUDE INTERVENTIONS

Thus far, the research studies that we have reviewed were designed to examine the effects of gratitude on well-being. It is also possible to examine changes in gratitude as a result of interventions designed for other purposes, such as to promote mindfulness (Shapiro, Schwartz, & Santerre, 2002), relaxation (Khasky & Smith, 1999), or forgiveness (Witvliet, Ludwig, & Bauer, 2002). Gratitude appears to be facilitated by meditation practice referred to as *intentional systematic mindfulness* (Shapiro et al., 2002). In another research program, progressive muscle relaxation has been shown to produce a number of positive emotional benefits, including among them increased feelings of love and thankfulness (Khasky & Smith, 1999). Lastly, Witvliet et al. (2002) found that a forgiveness intervention, such as imagining oneself being forgiven by someone, resulted in increased feelings of gratitude. These studies demonstrate that a number of innovative psychological interventions have the capacity to engender states of gratitude and its attendant benefits, though they were not designed explicitly for this purpose.

One particular type of psychotherapy originating in Japan, known as Naikan therapy, is based in Buddhist philosophy and mobilizes techniques of isolation and meditation to expand clients' awareness of their moral relationships with significant others in their lives. Currently, there are about 40 Naikan centers in Japan, as well as centers in Austria, Germany, and the United States (Krech, 2002). The overall aim of Naikan therapy is to have clients achieve interpersonal balance by realizing a deep sense of connection with the significant others in their lives and to experience a strong sense of gratitude toward people who have provided them with benefits (Hedstrom, 1994; Reynolds, 1983). It is notable that this form of therapy, based so strongly in gratitude, has been used to treat many disorders too—including anorexia nervosa (Morishita, 2000), alcoholism (Suwaki, 1985), neuroses, and personality disorders (Sakuta, Shiratsuchi, Kimura, & Abe, 1997)—and it has been applied to the rehabilitation of prisoners and counseling in school and business settings (Krech, 2002).

### USE OF GRATITUDE IN CLINICAL THERAPY

Researchers have suggested ways that gratitude interventions can be used in therapeutic settings and reasons why this would be beneficial (Bono & McCullough, 2006; Duckworth, Steen, & Seligman, 2005; Seligman, Rashid, & Parks, 2006). More studies are needed, though, comparing gratitude inductions against true neutral control conditions rather than conditions focused on hassles (Wood, Froh, & Geraghty, 2010). This will allow researchers to more accurately assess intervention effects. Wood et al. (2010) also recommend that experiments use clinical samples to examine if gratitude interventions could treat mental disorders better than other existing therapies.

Psychologists are increasingly considering the use of gratitude strategies to treat clients experiencing depression, substance abuse, or bereavement (Young & Hutchinson, 2012). Other studies have found that gratitude listing was as effective as daily automatic thought records for treating people with severe body image dissatisfaction (Geraghty, Wood, & Hyland, 2010a) or people with generalized anxiety (Geraghty, Wood, & Hyland, 2010b), compared to a waitlist control. Importantly, these researchers found that patients were 2 times more likely to remain in the gratitude treatment than in the automatic thought record treatment. Such findings corroborate earlier research showing that being more thankful in the practice of religion can protect people from both internalizing (e.g., depression and anxiety) and externalizing (e.g., substance abuse) disorders (Kendler et al., 2003).

Sergeant and Mongrain (2011) examined the use of gratitude exercises with two depressive personality types: self-critical individuals and needy individuals. Individuals were randomly assigned to one of three conditions: gratitude listing, listening to uplifting music, or writing about childhood memories (control). Participants completed these interventions daily for 1 week and follow-up assessment was conducted 1, 3, and 6 months later. Interestingly, the gratitude music exercises only benefited the self-critical individuals; they reported increases in self-esteem and decreases in physical symptoms. Needy individuals reported decreases in happiness and increases in physical symptomology as a result of the gratitude and music exercises. These findings suggest that the use of gratitude exercises in treatment with clinical populations can be detrimental to certain personality types (Sergeant & Mongrain, 2011).

## USING GRATITUDE TO IMPROVE COPING AND RESILIENCY

Gratitude can be therapeutically useful for populations without mental disorders but who may be experiencing stress, such as coping with lifelong disease or traumatic events. For example, Algoe and Stanton (2011) found that the experience and expression of gratitude may help patients with metastatic breast cancer find improved quality of life by tapping into sources of social support. Another study found that gratitude was a powerful emotion for coping with the tragic events of September 11, 2001 (Fredrickson, Tugade, Waugh, & Larkin, 2003). Such findings are consistent with the view that positive emotions broaden the scope of individuals' thoughts and generate upward spirals of improved coping and functioning (Fredrickson, 2001).

McAdams and Bauer's (2004) analyses of redemption sequences revealed that even painful experiences could become something for which people are ultimately grateful. Therefore, gratitude will likely play a valuable role in improving peoples' lives as such therapeutic applications are developed.

There is evidence that gratitude may play a significant role in coping and resiliency among youth, too. A study of newspaper accounts about what children were thankful for before and after the September 11 event found that their thankfulness for basic human needs, such as family, friends, and teachers, increased (A. K. Gordon, Musher-Eizenman, Holub, & Dalrymple, 2004). This suggests gratitude helps buffer children from adverse events as it does with adults.

Beyond solidifying social resources, gratitude may lend humans strength for other reasons. Researchers have identified sustained patterns of physiological coherence that operate during feelings of appreciation, suggesting mechanisms for such positive psychosocial outcomes. By *physiological coherence* they refer to the degree of order, stability, and efficiency generated by the body's oscillatory systems—such as heart rhythms, respiratory rhythms, blood pressure oscillations, low frequency brain rhythms, craniosacral rhythms, electrical skin potentials, and rhythms in the digestive system (McCraty, Atkinson, Tomasino, & Bradley, 2009). The more people experience sincere feelings of appreciation, the more this coherence emerges, reinforcing coherent patterns in the neural architecture as a familiar reference for the brain. Given such findings, McCraty and Childre (2004) developed techniques for focusing attention to the area around the heart (the subjective site of positive emotions) and simultaneously engaging in intentional self-inductions of positive emotional states, such as appreciation. Such techniques may be useful tools for interventions seeking to increase gratitude in individuals; that these interventions employ techniques similar to other mind–body interventions may make them particularly useful for fostering gratitude as an attitude or mind-set.

## HOW IS GRATITUDE RELATED TO THE GOOD LIFE?

When considering how gratitude is related to the good life, it is useful to bear in mind the various populations that have been shown to benefit from gratitude.

### BENEFITS TO ADULTS

We have already seen that people suffering from tragic events, deadly diseases, or serious mental illness appear to cope better as a result of gratitude. Similarly, we saw that gratitude helps individuals form and strengthen social, romantic, and marital relationships. Research has also shown that expressions of gratitude can reinforce kidney donation (Bernstein & Simmons, 1974) and volunteering behavior toward people with HIV/AIDS (Bennett, Ross, & Sunderland, 1996), and field experiments have shown that mere thank-you notes can bring increased tips from customers (Rind & Bordia, 1995), higher response rates on mail surveys (Maheux, Legault, & Lambert, 1989), and more visits from case managers in a residential treatment program (Clark, Northrop, & Barkshire, 1988).

Gratitude interventions have been effective with undergraduate students, adults with neuromuscular diseases, and clinical patients. Use of Naikan psychotherapy techniques suggest that gratitude mind-sets may help students and employees to resolve interpersonal conflicts, prisoners to rehabilitate, and people to recover from various disorders. Finally, appreciation interventions have also shown that people (of various ages and religious affiliations) in organizational, educational, and health-care settings may likewise benefit from experiences of gratitude as well (Childre & Cryer, 2000). Informally, church organizations and self-help groups for years have relied on gratitude exercises to help empower individuals.

### WHY GRATITUDE MAY BE A CRITICAL INGREDIENT IN POSITIVE YOUTH DEVELOPMENT

Positive youth development (PYD) theory emphasizes the importance of fostering young people's potential for growth by providing them with opportunities and supportive environments that help build up their strengths (Benson, Scales, Hamilton, & Semsa, 2006). The theory suggests that five strengths are essential for optimal youth development: *competence* (or a positive view of one's skills), *confidence* (or overall self-worth), *connection* (or positive bonds with people, groups, or communities), *character* (or respect for societal/cultural rules and sense of integrity and morality), and *caring* and compassion (having sympathy and empathy for others; Lerner et al., 2005). PYD theory stresses the importance of youth contributing to their own strengths and development, and, in turn, giving back to the people, groups, institutions, or communities that nurture them (Benson et al., 2006).

Whether bolstered through intervention or measured naturally, the evidence provided earlier suggests that gratitude plays a strong role in PYD. It promotes the strength of caring and compassion for all parties involved in beneficial social exchanges. It supports the strengths of connection and character by virtue of the three moral functions (motive, barometer, and reinforcer). Finally, because gratitude counters hedonic penchants associated with materialism and promotes intrinsic motivation and self-improvement, it should therefore also support the strength of competence. Recent longitudinal evidence supports the idea that gratitude development is strongly associated with PYD. Adolescents who entered high school with a moderate amount of gratitude and exhibited steady gains during high school also reported experiencing more empathy, self-awareness, self-efficacy, self-regulation, and goals for the future, and a stronger sense of identification with their community and a motivation to improve society by the end of high school (Bono, Froh, Emmons, & Card, 2013).

## GUIDELINES FOR THE EMPIRICAL STUDY OF GRATITUDE AND GRATITUDE INTERVENTIONS

To evaluate gratitude interventions and their effectiveness, researchers should adhere to several guidelines. Most importantly, if researchers wish to foster well-being by increasing people's gratitude, it is important to make sure that the intervention is actually successful in fostering gratitude. The degree of gratitude that participants experience can be measured in terms intensity, frequency, span, and density (McCullough et al., 2002). Including the GQ-6 (McCullough et al., 2002) or the GRAT (Watkins et al., 2003) in the battery of dependent variables will assist to this end. Gratitude as a component of daily emotional and mood experience can also help evaluate intervention effects in everyday life (see McCullough, Tsang, & Emmons, 2004).

Second, intervention methods matter. Diary techniques have proved useful for inducing individuals to focus on and experience gratitude (Emmons & McCullough, 2003). Having participants write about positive events and people in their lives, or even writing letters to people to whom they feel grateful, may also be useful to this end (Watkins et al., 2003). Behavioral expressions of thanks are especially potent in changing people's subjective well-being. Finally, to achieve sustainable intervention effects, researchers should ensure that methods meaningfully engage participants by having them know about, endorse, and commit to the intervention (Lyubomirsky, Dickerhoof, Boehm, & Sheldon, 2011).

Third, researchers are advised to measure dependent variables that reflect the different ways gratitude might influence participants and their relationships with others (McCullough et al., 2002). To assess individual outcomes, researchers should measure dependent variables corresponding to the different ways gratitude has been shown to benefit children, adolescents, and adults in terms of well-being (i.e., positive and negative affect, anxiety, depression, satisfaction with life, hope, etc.), prosociality (i.e., how much others help them and they help others), and their health and development. Research has just started to uncover how individuals benefit from increased gratitude. Perhaps different relationships benefit in different ways or degrees? Researchers may further assess the effects of gratitude on health and well-being by examining how gratitude buffers targets from various life stressors and bestows improved coping and decision making. The use of daily diary methods may be the best way to assess such individual, relational, and health outcomes.

## FUTURE DIRECTIONS FOR RESEARCH ON GRATITUDE AND GRATITUDE INTERVENTIONS

An important setting for adult gratitude applications is the workplace. Emmons (2003) proposed several ways gratitude can benefit organizations. Most directly, as a cognitive strategy, gratitude can improve individual well-being and lower toxic emotions in the workplace, such as resentment and envy. Moods are important determiners of efficiency, productivity, success, and employee loyalty. Evidence demonstrates that employee happiness and well-being are positively linked to performance, commitment, and morale, and negatively linked to absenteeism, burnout, and turnover (e.g., Wright & Staw, 1999). As society increasingly relies on teamwork and the harnessing of individuals' diverse strengths to achieve group and organizational goals, gratitude is an easy way to buffer individuals from stress and facilitate the mutual achievements of individuals, groups, and organizations (Emmons, 2003).

Although gratitude has been linked to positive youth development and well-being, applications in the school setting are lacking. Researchers should further investigate this population and gratitude's potential benefits for schools and other educational settings. Why wait until adulthood to begin to reap the benefits of grateful living? Gratitude leads to many positive outcomes of central importance in youth development (e.g., well-being, prosocial relationships, improved motivation, satisfaction with school, and a focus on priorities and planning for the future). Therefore, applying gratitude in schools promises to advance student learning and engagement with school. Gratitude can easily complement social emotional learning programs and may enhance bullying and character education programs, helping to improve school climate in general. Promoting gratitude early in development will undoubtedly produce many benefits for individuals and society.

## CONCLUSION

Gratitude shows surprisingly few downsides. That people typically consider gratitude a virtue and not simply a pleasure also points to the fact that it does not always come naturally or easily. Gratitude must, and can, be cultivated. And by cultivating this virtue, people not only get to experience its pleasure but all of its other attendant benefits, too, for free. As this chapter demonstrates, gratitude can produce many advantages for society.

Through gratitude individuals find coherence in life. They learn to elevate others and make a difference in the world. Like the moral memory of humankind (Simmel, 1950), gratitude reflects the story of the best that individuals and societies could be. We hope this chapter helps readers appreciate how gratitude can be used to improve ourselves and to inch us toward a better world.

## SUMMARY POINTS

- Gratitude serves as three moral functions: a moral barometer, a moral reinforcer, and a moral motive. Individuals with grateful personalities feel gratitude more intensely, more frequently, more densely (toward more people), and for a wider span of benefits.
- To test for effectiveness of interventions, researchers should consider if gratitude is increased in terms of intensity, frequency, density, and span.
- To be effective, intervention methods (i.e., diary of gratitude, behavioral expressions of thanks) should meaningfully engage participants by having them know about, endorse, and commit to the intervention.
- Researchers should measure dependent variables corresponding to the different ways gratitude has been shown to benefit children, adolescents, and adults in terms of well-being, prosociality, and their health and development.
- Cultural and attitudinal factors (e.g., materialism, resentment) likely moderate gratitude's effects on well-being. Research is needed to better understand how the experience, expression, and consequences of gratitude differ across cultures.

- Researchers can personalize interventions with a focus on the types of benefits recipients most value (e.g., focusing on benefits that affirm, increase, or maintain harmony in relationships for interdependent selves).
- Personality characteristics such as narcissism, low personal responsibility, and low positive affect (in youth populations) may prevent gratitude. Such knowledge can be useful in improving gratitude interventions in the future.
- A number of innovative psychological interventions have the capacity to engender states of gratitude and its attendant benefits, though they were not designed explicitly for this purpose (e.g., meditation practice).
- Gratitude interventions can be used in therapeutic settings. It is recommended that experiments use clinical samples to examine if gratitude interventions could treat mental disorders better than other existing therapies. Gratitude can also benefit populations who do not have mental disorders but suffer from severe stress/adversity, disease, or trauma.
- Important settings for future applications with adults include the workplace because gratitude can facilitate the mutual achievements of individuals, groups, and organizations. Similarly, researchers should investigate if gratitude applications with children have such effects on schools and other educational settings.

## REFERENCES

Algoe, S. B. (2012). Find, remind, and bind: The functions of gratitude in everyday relationships. *Social and Personality Psychology Compass, 6*, 455–469.

Algoe, S. B., Gable, S. L., & Maisel, N. (2010). It's the little things: Everyday gratitude as a booster shot for romantic relationships. *Personal Relationships, 17*, 217–233.

Algoe, S. B., Haidt, J., & Gable, S. L. (2008). Beyond reciprocity: Gratitude and relationships in everyday life. *Emotion, 8*, 425–429.

Algoe, S. B., & Stanton, A. L. (2011). Gratitude when it is needed most: Social functions of gratitude in women with metastatic breast cancer. *Emotion, 12*, 163–168. doi:10.1037/a0024024

Bartlett, M. Y., Condon, P., Cruz, J., Baumann, J., & DeSteno, D. (2012). Gratitude: Prompting behaviors that build relationships. *Cognition and Emotion, 26*, 2–13.

Bartlett, M. Y., & DeSteno, D. (2006). Gratitude and prosocial behavior: Helping when it costs you. *Psychological Science, 17*, 319–325.

Baumgarten-Tramer, F. F. (1938). "Gratefulness" in children and young people. *The Pedagogical Seminary and Journal of Genetic Psychology, 53*, 5353–5366.

Bennett, L., Ross, M. W., & Sunderland, R. (1996). The relationship between recognition, rewards, and burnout in AIDS caregiving. *AIDS Care, 8*, 145–153.

Benson, P. L., Scales, P. C., Hamilton, S. F., & Semsa, A., Jr. (2006). Positive youth development: Theory, research, and applications. In W. Damon & R. M. Lerner (Eds.-in-Chief) & R. M. Lerner (Vol. Ed.), *Handbook of child psychology: Vol. 1. Theoretical models of human development* (6th ed., pp. 894–941). Hoboken, NJ: Wiley. doi:10.1002/9780470147658.chpsy0116

Bergler, E. (1945). Psychopathology of ingratitude. *Diseases of the Nervous System, 6*, 6226–6229.

Bergler, E. (1950). Debts of gratitude paid in "guilt denomination." *Journal of Clinical Psychopathology, 11*, 57–62.

Bernstein, D. M., & Simmons, R. G. (1974). The adolescent kidney donor: The right to give. *American Journal of Psychiatry, 131*, 1338–1343.

Boehm, J. K., Lyubomirsky, S., & Sheldon, K. M. (2011). A longitudinal experimental study comparing the effectiveness of happiness-enhancing strategies in Anglo Americans and Asian Americans. *Cognition and Emotion, 25*(7), 1263–1272. doi:10.1080/02699931.2010.541227

Bono, G., Froh, J. J., & Emmons, R. A. (2012, August). *Searching for the developmental role of gratitude: A 4-year longitudinal analysis.* Paper presented at the annual meeting of the American Psychological Association, Orlando, FL.

Bono, G., Froh, J. J., Emmons, R. A., & Card, N. A. (2013, April). *The benefits of gratitude to adolescent development: Longitudinal models of gratitude, wellbeing and prosocial behavior.* Paper presented at the annual meeting of the Society for Research in Child Development, Seattle, WA.

Bono, G., & McCullough, M. E. (2006). Positive responses to benefit and harm: Bringing forgiveness and gratitude into cognitive psychotherapy. *Journal of Cognitive Psychotherapy, 20*(2), 147–158. doi:10.1891/jcop.20.2.147

Chaplin, L., Rindfleisch, A., John, D. R., & Froh, J. J. (2013). *Reducing materialism in adolescents.* Manuscript submitted for publication.

Childre, D., & Cryer, B. (2000). *From chaos to coherence: The power to change performance.* Boulder Creek, CA: Planetary.

Chow, R. M., & Lowery, B. S. (2010). Thanks, but no thanks: The role of personal responsibility in the experience of gratitude. *Journal of Experimental Social Psychology, 46,* 487–493.

Clark, H. B., Northrop, J. T., & Barkshire, C. T. (1988). The effects of contingent thank-you notes on case managers' visiting residential clients. *Education and Treatment of Children, 11,* 45–51.

DeWall, C. N., Lambert, N. M., Pond, R. S., Kashdan, T. B., & Fincham, F. D. (2012). A grateful heart is a nonviolent heart: Cross-sectional, longitudinal, experience sampling, and experimental evidence. *Social Psychological and Personality Science, 3,* 232–240.

Duckworth, A. L., Steen, T. A., & Seligman, M. E. P. (2005). Positive psychology in clinical practice. *Annual Review of Clinical Psychology, 1*(1), 629–651.

Dunn, J. R., & Schweitzer, M. E. (2005). Feeling and believing: The influence of emotion on trust. *Journal of Personality and Social Psychology, 88*(5), 736–748.

Emmons, R. A. (2003). Acts of gratitude in organizations. In K. S. Cameron, J. E. Dutton, & R. E. Quinn (Eds.), *Positive organizational scholarship* (pp. 81–93). San Francisco, CA: Berrett-Koehler.

Emmons, R. A., & McCullough, M. E. (2003). Counting blessings versus burdens: An experimental investigation of gratitude and subjective wellbeing in daily life. *Journal of Personality and Social Psychology, 84,* 377–389.

Etchegoyen, R. H., & Nemas, C. R. (2003). Salieri's dilemma: A counterpoint between envy and appreciation. *International Journal of Psychoanalysis, 84,* 45–58.

Farwell, L., & Wohlwend-Lloyd, R. (1998). Narcissistic processes: Optimistic expectations, favorable self-evaluations, and self-enhancing attributions. *Journal of Personality, 66*(1), 65–83.

Fredrickson, B. L. (2001). The role of positive emotions in positive psychology: The broaden-and-build theory of positive emotions. *American Psychologist, 56,* 218–226.

Fredrickson, B. L., Tugade, M. M., Waugh, C. E., & Larkin, G. R. (2003). What good are positive emotions in crises? A prospective study of resilience and emotions following the terrorist attacks on the United States on September 11th, 2001. *Journal of Personality & Social Psychology, 84,* 365–376.

Froh, J. J., & Bono, G. (2014). *Making grateful kids: The science of building character.* West Conshohocken, PA: Templeton Press.

Froh, J. J., Bono, G., & Emmons, R. A. (2010). Being grateful is beyond good manners: Gratitude and motivation to contribute to society among early adolescents. *Motivation & Emotion, 34,* 144–157.

Froh, J. J., Bono, G., Fan, J., Emmons, R. A., Henderson, K., Harris, C., ... Wood, A. (2014). Nice thinking! An educational intervention that teaches children how to think gratefully [Special Issue: Theoretical Frameworks in School Psychology Intervention Research: Interdisciplinary Perspectives and Future Directions]. *School Psychology Review, 43,* 132–152.

Froh, J. J., Emmons, R. A., Card, N. A., Bono, G., & Wilson, J. (2011). Gratitude and the reduced costs of materialism in adolescents. *Journal of Happiness Studies*, *12*, 289–302.

Froh, J. J., Fan, J., Emmons, R. A., Bono, G., Huebner, E. S., & Watkins, P. (2011). Measuring gratitude in youth: Assessing the psychometric properties of adult gratitude scales in children and adolescents. *Psychological Assessment*, *23*, 311–324.

Froh, J. J., Kashdan, T. B., Ozimkowski, K. M., & Miller, N. (2009). Who benefits the most from a gratitude intervention in children and adolescents? Examining positive affect as a moderator. *Journal of Positive Psychology*, *4*, 108–122.

Froh, J. J., Sefick, W. J., & Emmons, R. A. (2008). Counting blessings in early adolescents: An experimental study of gratitude and subjective wellbeing. *Journal of School Psychology*, *46*, 213–233.

Geraghty, A. W. A., Wood, A. M., & Hyland, M. E. (2010a). Attrition from self-directed interventions: Investigating the relationship between psychological predictors, technique and dropout from a body image intervention. *Social Science & Medicine*, *71*, 30–37.

Geraghty, A. W. A., Wood, A. M., & Hyland, M. E. (2010b). Dissociating the facets of hope: Agency and pathways predict dropout from unguided self-help therapy in opposite directions. *Journal of Research in Personality*, *44*(1), 155–158. doi:10.1016/j.jrp.2009.12.003

Gordon, A. K., Musher-Eizenman, D. R., Holub, S. C., & Dalrymple, J. (2004). What are children thankful for? An archival analysis of gratitude before and after the attacks of September 11. *Applied Developmental Psychology*, *25*, 541–553. doi:10.1016/j.appdev.2004.08.004

Gordon, C. L., Arnett, R. A. M., & Smith, R. E. (2011). Have you thanked your spouse today? Felt and expressed gratitude among married couples. *Personality and Individual Differences*, *50*, 339–343.

Gouldner, A. W. (1960). The norm of reciprocity: A preliminary statement. *American Sociological Review*, *25*, 161–178.

Grant, A. M., & Gino, F. (2010). A little thanks goes a long way. Explaining why gratitude expression motivate prosocial behavior. *Journal of Personality and Social Psychology*, *98*(6), 946–955.

Hedstrom, L. J. (1994). Morita and Naikan therapies: American applications. *Psychotherapy*, *31*, 154–160.

Heider, F. (1958). *The psychology of interpersonal relations*. New York, NY: Wiley.

Joel, S., Gordon, A. M., Impett, E. A., MacDonald, G., & Keltner, D. (2013). The things you do for me: Perceptions of a romantic partner's investments promote gratitude and commitment. *Personality and Social Psychology*, *39*(10), 1333–1345.

John, O. P., Donahue, E. M., & Kentle, R. L. (1991). *The Big Five Inventory—Versions 4a and 54*. Berkeley: University of California, Berkeley, Institute of Personality and Social Research.

Kasser, T. (2002). *The high price of materialism*. Cambridge, MA: MIT Press.

Kendler, K. S., Liu, X., Gardner, C. O., McCullough, M. E., Larson, D., & Prescott, C. A. (2003). Dimensions of religiosity and their relationship to lifetime psychiatric and substance use disorders. *American Journal of Psychiatry*, *160*, 496–503.

Khasky, A. D., & Smith, J. C. (1999). Stress, relaxation states and creativity. *Perceptual and Motor Skills*, *88*, 409–416.

Krech, G. (2002). *Naikan: Gratitude, grace and the Japanese art of self-reflection*. Berkeley, CA: Stone Bridge Press.

Lambert, N. M., & Fincham, F. D. (2011). Expressing gratitude to a partner leads to more relationship maintenance behavior. *Emotion*, *11*, 52–60.

Lambert, N. M., Fincham, F. D., & Stillman, T. F. (2012). Gratitude and depressive symptoms: The role of positive reframing and positive emotion. *Cognition and Emotion*, *26*, 602–614.

Lambert, N. M., Gwinn, A. M., Baumeister, R. F., Fincham, F. D., Gable, S. L., Strachman, A., & Washburn, I. J. (2013). A boost of positive affect: The perks of sharing positive experiences and grateful experiences. *Journal of Social and Personal Relationships*, *30*, 24–43.

Lerner, R. M., Lerner, J. V., Almerigi, J. B., Theokas, C., Phelps, E., Gestsdottir, S., . . . Eye, A. (2005). Positive youth development, participation in community youth development programs, and community contributions of fifth-grade adolescents: Findings from the first wave of the 4-H Study of positive youth development. *Journal of Early Adolescence, 25,* 17–71. doi:10.1177/0272431604272461

Lyubomirsky, S., Dickerhoof, R., Boehm, J. K., & Sheldon, K. M. (2011). Becoming happier takes both a will and a proper way: An experimental longitudinal intervention to boost well-being. *Emotion, 11*(2), 391–402. doi: 10.1037/a0022575

Maheux, B., Legault, C., & Lambert, J. (1989). Increasing response rates in physicians' mail surveys: An experimental study. *American Journal of Public Health, 79,* 638–639.

McAdams, D. P., & Bauer, J. J. (2004). Gratitude in modern life: Its manifestations and development. In R. A. Emmons and M. E. McCullough (Eds.), *The psychology of gratitude.* New York, NY: Oxford University Press.

McCraty, R., Atkinson, M., Tomasino, D., & Bradley, R. T. (2009). The coherent heart: Heart–brain interactions, psychophysiological coherence, and the emergence of system-wide order. *Integral Review, 5*(2), 10–114.

McCraty, R., & Childre, D. (2004). The grateful heart: The psychophysiology of appreciation. In R. A. Emmons & M. E. McCullough (Eds.), *The psychology of gratitude* (pp. 230–255). New York: Oxford University Press.

McCullough, M. E., Emmons, R. A., & Tsang, J. (2002). The grateful disposition: A conceptual and empirical topography. *Journal of Personality and Social Psychology, 82,* 112–127.

McCullough, M. E., Kilpatrick, S. D., Emmons, R. A., & Larson, D. B. (2001). Is gratitude a moral affect? *Psychological Bulletin, 127*(2), 249–266. doi:10.1037/0033-909.127.2.249

McCullough, M. E., Tsang, J., & Emmons, R. A. (2004). Gratitude in intermediate affective terrain: Links of grateful moods with individual differences and daily emotional experience. *Journal of Personality and Social Psychology, 86,* 295–309.

Morishita, S. (2000). Treatment of anorexia nervosa with Naikan therapy. *International Medical Journal, 7,* 151.

Paulhus, D. L. (1998). Interpersonal and intrapsychic adaptiveness of trait self-enhancement: A mixed blessing? *Journal of Personality and Social Psychology, 74,* 1197–1208.

Reynolds, D. K. (1983). *Naikan psychotherapy: Meditation for self-development.* Chicago, IL: University of Chicago Press.

Rind, B., & Bordia, P. (1995). Effect of server's "thank you" and personalization on restaurant tipping. *Journal of Applied Social Psychology, 25,* 745–751.

Sakuta, T., Shiratsuchi, T., Kimura, Y., & Abe, Y. (1997). Psychotherapies originated in Japan. *International Medical Journal, 4,* 229–230.

Schwartz, B. (1967). The social psychology of the gift. *American Journal of Sociology, 73,* 1–11.

Seligman, M. E. P. (2002). *Authentic happiness: Using the new positive psychology to realize your potential for lasting fulfillment.* New York, NY: Free Press.

Seligman, M. E. P., & Csikszentmihalyi, M. (2000). Positive psychology: An introduction. *American Psychologist, 55*(1), 5–14. doi:10.1037/0003-066X.55.1.5

Seligman, M. E. P., Rashid, T., & Parks, A. C. (2006). Positive psychotherapy. *American Psychologist, 61,* 774–788.

Seligman, M. E. P., Steen, T. A., Park, N., & Peterson, C. (2005). Positive psychology progress: Empirical validation of interventions. *American Psychologist, 60*(5), 410–421. doi:10.1037/0003-066X.60.5.410.

Sergeant, S., & Mongrain, M. (2011). Are positive psychology exercises helpful for people with depressive personality styles? *Journal of Positive Psychology, 6*(4), 260–272. doi:10.1080/17439760.2011.577089

Shapiro, S. L., Schwartz, G. E. R., & Santerre, C. (2002). Meditation and positive psychology. In C. R. Snyder & S. J. Lopez (Eds.), *Handbook of positive psychology* (pp. 632–645). London, England: Oxford University Press.

Simmel, G. (1950). *The sociology of Georg Simmel*. Glencoe, IL: Free Press.

Solomon, R. C. (2002). *Spirituality for the skeptic*. New York, NY: Oxford University Press.

Suwaki, H. (1985). International review series: Alcohol and alcohol problems research: II. Japan. *British Journal of Addiction, 80*, 127–132.

Thomas, M., & Watkins, P. (2003, April). *Measuring the grateful trait: Development of the revised GRAT*. Poster session presented at the Annual Convention of the Western Psychological Association, Vancouver, BC.

Trivers, R. L. (1971). The evolution of reciprocal altruism. *Quarterly Review of Biology, 46*, 35–57.

Tsang, J. (2006). Gratitude and prosocial behaviour: An experimental test of gratitude. *Cognition and Emotion, 20*, 138–148.

Watkins, P. C., Woodward, K., Stone, T., & Kolts, R. L. (2003). Gratitude and happiness: Development of a measure of gratitude, and relationships with subjective wellbeing. *Social Behavior and Personality, 31*, 431–451.

Witvliet, C. V., Ludwig, T. E., & Bauer, D. J. (2002). Please forgive me: Transgressors' emotions and physiology during imagery of seeking forgiveness and victim responses. *Journal of Psychology and Christianity, 21*, 219–233.

Wood, A. M., Brown, G. D. A., & Maltby, J. (2011). Thanks, but I'm used to better: A relative rank model of gratitude. *Emotion, 11*, 175–180.

Wood, A. M., Froh, J. J., & Geraghty, A. (2010). Gratitude and wellbeing: A review and theoretical integration [Special Issue]. *Clinical Psychology Review, 30*, 890–905.

Wright, T. A., & Staw, B. M. (1999). Affect and favorable work outcomes: Two longitudinal tests of the happy-productive worker thesis. *Journal of Organizational Behavior, 20*, 1–23.

Young, M. E., & Hutchinson, T. S. (2012). The rediscovery of gratitude: Implications for counseling practice. *Journal of Humanistic Counseling, 51*, 99–113.

# CHAPTER 34

# Wisdom-Related Knowledge Across the Life Span

UTE KUNZMANN and STEFANIE THOMAS

THE SEARCH FOR human strengths is a continuous journey with a long history. Since antiquity, one of the guideposts in this search has been the concept of wisdom (e.g., Assmann, 1994; Kekes, 1995). At the core of this concept is the notion of a perfect, perhaps utopian, integration of knowledge and character, mind and virtue.

Societal beliefs suggest that wisdom is an attribute of aging and old age (e.g., Clayton & Birren, 1980; Heckhausen, Dixon, & Baltes, 1989; Sternberg & Jordan, 2005). There are also suggestions in the literature that wisdom and old age are closely intertwined; for example, Erikson postulated in his personality theory of life-span development that generativity and wisdom constitute advanced stages in personality development (Erikson, 1959). Because wisdom has been considered an ideal end point of human development, psychological work on this concept has evolved in the context of life-span developmental psychology and the study of aging (e.g., Baltes, Smith, & Staudinger, 1992).

However, not only life-span and aging researchers value the investigation of human resources; the search for positive human functioning has also been a hallmark of positive psychology (e.g., Seligman & Csikszentmihalyi, 2000). For at least two reasons, research in this area might benefit from considering wisdom. First, wisdom identifies the highest forms of expertise that humans can acquire. Certainly only few achieve wisdom in its higher form; yet it is those few who hold the key to what humans could be at their best. Second, although it surely takes a lifetime of experience and practice and an ensemble of supportive conditions to acquire wisdom in its higher form, empirical wisdom research suggests that wisdom can be conceptualized as a more-or-less (i.e., quantitative) phenomenon, and, even more to the point, there is a growing body of evidence suggesting that even a little wisdom can make a substantial difference in our lives (e.g., Kramer, 2000). Thus, wisdom is a vital component of the three spheres of positive psychology suggested by Seligman and Csikszentmihalyi (2000). That is, wisdom can be considered a positive person characteristic; it involves valuable subjective experiences; and it is a life orientation that contributes to productivity and well-being at the individual, social group, and societal levels.

It deserves note that the acquisition of wisdom during ontogenesis most likely is incompatible with a hedonic life orientation and a predominantly pleasurable and sheltered life (Kunzmann & Baltes, 2003a, 2003b; Staudinger & Kunzmann, 2005). Given their interest in maximizing a common good, wiser people are likely to partake in behaviors that contribute to, rather than consume, resources. In addition, an interest in understanding the significance and deeper meaning of phenomena, including the blending of developmental gains and losses, most likely is linked to emotional complexity and a tolerance for negative affective experiences (Labouvie-Vief, 1990, 2003) or to what has been called "constructive melancholy" (Baltes, 1997b).

## DEFINING WISDOM

Because of its enormous cultural and historical heritage, a comprehensive psychological definition and operationalization of wisdom is extremely difficult, if not impossible. At least three types of conceptualizations of wisdom can be identified in the literature. In these conceptualizations, wisdom has been defined as a part of personality development in adulthood (e.g., Ardelt, 2003; Erikson, 1959; Wink & Helson, 1997), a form of postformal dialectic thinking (e.g., Kramer, 1990, 2000; Labouvie-Vief, 1990), and an expanded form of intelligence (e.g., Baltes & Staudinger, 2000; Sternberg, 1998).

Despite their different origins, these three types of conceptualizations share several theoretical ideas. A first is that wisdom is different from other person characteristics in that it is integrative and involves cognitive, affective, and motivational elements. Second, wisdom is an ideal: Many people may strive for wisdom but only few, if any, will ever become truly wise. Third, wisdom sets high behavioral standards; it guides a person's behavior in ways that simultaneously optimize this person's own potential and that of fellow mortals (see also Baltes & Staudinger, 2000; Sternberg, 1998). We return to these three ideas in the course of this chapter as we discuss the Berlin wisdom paradigm and the research initiated by this paradigm.

### THE BERLIN WISDOM PARADIGM

Informed by cultural-historical work, in the Berlin wisdom paradigm, wisdom has been defined as expert knowledge about fundamental questions regarding the meaning and conduct of life (e.g., Baltes & Kunzmann, 2003; Baltes & Smith, 1990; Baltes & Staudinger, 2000). Five criteria serve to describe this type of expert knowledge. The first two general, basic criteria (factual and procedural knowledge) are characteristic of all types of expertise. Applied to wisdom-related expertise, these criteria are rich factual knowledge about human nature and the life course and rich procedural knowledge about ways of dealing with fundamental questions about the meaning and conduct of life. The following three meta-criteria are considered to be specific for wisdom-related expertise: life-span contextualism, value relativism and tolerance, and an awareness and management of uncertainty. Life-span contextualism refers to a deep understanding about the many contexts of the given life problem, how these contexts are interrelated, and how they change over time. Value relativism and tolerance describes the acknowledgment of individual and cultural differences in values and life priorities. A person with high wisdom-related knowledge tolerates and even embraces the various and often opposing viewpoints on a life problem and has available heuristics on how to deal with them in a balanced fashion. Finally, the awareness and management of uncertainty refers to an understanding that life decisions, evaluations, or plans will never be free of uncertainty, but must be made as well as one can and not be avoided in a resigning manner. Expert knowledge about the meaning and conduct of life is said to approach wisdom, if it meets all five criteria.

As this definition of wisdom suggests, wisdom is neither technical nor intellectual knowledge. On the contrary, at the core of this body of knowledge is a deep understanding of human nature and the close intertwinement of the three faculties of the mind: cognition, emotion, and motivation. For example, outstanding knowledge about life's uncertainties and ways of dealing with them requires knowledge about the emotions that are associated with uncertainty. Value relativism and tolerance reflects a deep understanding about the causes and dynamics of human motives and goals. Life-span contextualism includes knowledge about normative and idiographic events that not only shape a person's future life but are also a source of deep emotional experiences (e.g., birth of a child, death of loved ones).

In the traditional empirical paradigm, participants read short vignettes about difficult life problems and think aloud about these problems. For example, a problem related to life review might be, "In reflecting over their lives, people sometimes realize that they have not achieved what they had once planned to achieve. What could they do and consider?" Another dilemma reads, "Somebody receives a phone call from a good friend. He or she says that he or she cannot go on anymore and has decided to commit suicide. What could one consider and do?" Trained raters evaluate responses to the Berlin wisdom tasks by using the five criteria that were specified as defining wisdom-related knowledge. As demonstrated in our past research, the assessment of wisdom-related knowledge on the basis of these criteria exhibits satisfactory reliability and validity (for reviews see Baltes & Kunzmann, 2003; Baltes & Staudinger, 2000; Staudinger & Glück, 2011).

## PERSONAL VERSUS GENERAL WISDOM

As a conceptual refinement, Staudinger and colleagues have recently suggested a differentiation between general wisdom (i.e., insight into life in a generalized form that transcends self-related experience and evaluation) and personal wisdom (i.e., insight into one's own life and self-related experiences; e.g., Staudinger & Glück, 2011). According to the authors, the traditional Berlin wisdom tasks that ask for knowledge about fundamental life problems in a largely decontextualized and generalized fashion are well-suited to assess general wisdom. Other expertise-based wisdom approaches such as Sternberg's balance theory of wisdom or neo-Piagetian conceptions of wisdom as postformal thought may be assigned to the approach of assessing general wisdom as well. By contrast, the idea of personal wisdom is closely linked to past approaches that have considered wisdom as a stage of personality development (e.g., Ardelt, 2003; Helson & Wink, 1987). Whereas approaches that conceptualize wisdom as part of personality have used self-report measures to assess the wise personality, Staudinger and colleagues developed a measure of personal wisdom that is in the tradition of performance-based testing (for a review of different approaches to assess wisdom, see Kunzmann & Stange, 2007). More specifically, participants are asked to think aloud about the self and the resulting think-aloud protocols are assessed on the basis of wisdom criteria that are similarly structured as the traditional Berlin wisdom criteria (e.g., Mickler & Staudinger, 2008). More specifically, two basic criteria are self-knowledge (the insight into oneself) and growth and self-regulation (heuristics to deal with challenges); three meta-criteria are interrelating the self (the insight into possible causes of one's own behavior), self-relativism (distance from the self), and tolerance of ambiguity (to recognize and manage uncertainties in one's own life).

For several reasons, personal wisdom and general wisdom do not necessarily coincide. For example, highly intellectual individuals who are interested in questions regarding human nature and the life course but who have had a difficult personal life history may be able to give valuable wise advice to others or to think about uncertain and difficult questions related to the meaning and conduct of life on a general and abstract level, but they may have a particularly hard time making sense of their own authentic experiences and feelings and, thus, gaining insight into what makes their own lives difficult. Other individuals, perhaps the majority of individuals, may have the personal requirements to acquire some wisdom as it pertains to their own life experiences and problems, but they may not be able or motivated to reflect about human nature on a more abstract level and to generalize and integrate their self-related insights what would bring them closer to wisdom in its ideal and higher form.

On a more general level, we believe that a conceptualization of wisdom as a concept that encompasses several distinct forms makes intuitive sense as soon as one considers individuals rather than cultural products as carriers of wisdom (Baltes & Kunzmann, 2004). Human beings are fallible (Baltes, 1997a), and it is impossible to nominate a truly wise individual, that is, an individual with only vices and no weaknesses. Empirical work provided by Mickler and Staudinger (2008) is consistent with this idea in that it suggests that only few individuals are high on both general wisdom and personal wisdom. These two types of wisdom are highly distinct and show only a low positive correlation.

### The Assessment of Wisdom-Related Knowledge via Real-Life Rather Than Hypothetical Problems

Another recent refinement of the traditional Berlin paradigm has been the development of new wisdom tasks that present real-life problems rather than hypothetical dilemmas (Thomas & Kunzmann, 2013). With this approach, a major goal has been to address the concern that the traditional Berlin wisdom tasks are too cognitive in that they present life dilemmas in a highly abstract and condensed fashion so that the dilemmas hardly evoke any emotions and may not even require a deep understanding of emotions in order to be dealt with wisely (e.g., Ardelt, 2004; Redzanowski & Glück, 2013).

To address this concern and develop wisdom tasks that present real-life life problems, we have produced short film clips of couples as they discuss a real, long-lasting, and serious conflict in their marriage. Participants are asked to carefully watch a film and to then think aloud about what the couple might want to think and do to go about solving their problem. The development of these film-based tasks involved a multiple-step validation procedure, ensuring that the spouses, two experts in marital interaction research, and a sample of lay people consistently rated the films as highly authentic, the problems as serious and complex, and the couples' emotional distress as extremely high (Thomas, 2012; Thomas & Kunzmann, 2013). A first study with a heterogeneous sample of almost 200 adults spanning the adult life span provided initial support for the idea that these tasks elicit greater emotional reactions than the traditional hypothetical vignettes. Interestingly, however, the new film-based tasks and the traditional vignette-based tasks did not differ in terms of the degree to which they elicited concrete and practical rather than abstract and theoretical knowledge (Thomas, 2012).

Together our findings suggest that it is worth the effort to develop wisdom tasks that present real-life life dilemmas in more context-rich and natural ways than is possible via the traditional Berlin text vignettes. Our film-based tasks appear to be particularly well suited to elicit a wide range of emotions and, thus, to investigate the dynamic between emotional and cognitive processes inherent in wisdom.

## THE DEVELOPMENT OF WISDOM-RELATED KNOWLEDGE: THEORETICAL IDEAS

The conceptualization of wisdom as expertise suggests that wisdom can only be acquired through an extended and intensive process of learning and practice. According to the Berlin wisdom model (see Figure 34.1), this process requires multiple factors that can be subsumed under (a) *facilitative experiential contexts*, as determined for example by a person's age, social context, or culture; (b) *expertise-specific factors* such as life experience, professional practice, or receiving and providing mentorship; and (c) more general *person-related factors* such a certain degree of academic intelligence, certain personality traits, emotional dispositions, and motivational orientations. These three types of resources are thought to influence the ways in which individuals actually plan, manage, and evaluate important events in life (e.g., how they deal with a particular problem and how they evaluate the costs and benefits of the different solutions to it). These organizing processes are at the core of the Berlin model and are meant to highlight that wisdom-related knowledge can only be gained though accumulated experience and dealing with important and uncertain questions regarding the meaning and conduct of life. In this sense, wisdom-related knowledge has been thought to be "own" experience based; it cannot be acquired vicariously (e.g., by reading books) or by direct instruction (see also Sternberg, 1998).

Three aspects of the model deserve special note. First, there most likely are several paths leading to wisdom rather than only one. Put differently, similar levels of wisdom may result from different combinations of facilitative resources and organizational processes. If a certain coalition of facilitative factors and processes

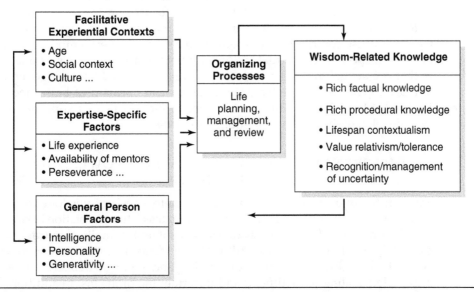

**Figure 34.1** Developmental of wisdom: Antecedents, correlates, and consequences
*Note.* The acquisition of wisdom-related knowledge is assumed to be dependent on an effective coalition of life-context, expertise-specific, and general person-related factors.

is present, some individuals continue a developmental trajectory toward higher levels of wisdom-related knowledge. Second, the facilitating factors (e.g., a certain family background, critical life events, professional practice, or societal transitions) are thought to interact in complex additive, compensatory, and time-lagged ways. Third, wisdom-related knowledge is considered an outcome and precursor of the resources and organizational processes related to the meaning and conduct of life. For example, openness to new experience and wisdom-related knowledge most likely mutually influence each other.

Recently, Glück and colleagues have presented a developmental model of personal wisdom, the so-called MORE model (e.g., Glück & Bluck, 2013). Consistent with the Berlin wisdom model, the MORE model states that wisdom can only be gained through exposure to existential challenges and crises. Of course, it is not the amount of experience with critical life events per se that is thought to lead to wise thought and action, rather the ways experiences are perceived and dealt with. The acronym MORE refers to the person-related resources that are thought to support the development of wisdom: mastery, openness to experience, reflexivity, and empathy, including emotion regulation. According to the authors, a sense of mastery helps individuals going through hard times, trusting their own abilities and strengths while recognizing that many things in life are uncertain and out of personal control. Openness to experience facilitates tolerating life's challenges and enhances the motivation to learn from them. Reflexivity helps to recognize the multiple sides and meanings of a problem, including the critical questioning of one's own preferred ways of interpreting events. Finally, the authors elaborate two emotional competences that support the complex process of wisdom attainment. Empathy facilitates attention and emotional responsiveness to others' problems and concerns, while emotion regulatory skills help the wise advice giver to not become overwhelmed by others' problems, and it supports the constructive management of own and others' emotions in the face of serious and existential problems.

The two theoretical models about the ontogenesis of wisdom reviewed earlier obviously have many ideas in common. One aspect that is distinct refers to broadness of the models. More specifically, the MORE model focuses on the person-related resources for the attainment of wisdom and is less concerned with social and contextual factors that also contribute to wisdom. In this sense, the Berlin model is more comprehensive; it specifies contextual factors on micro and macro levels as one set of factors that is essential in the development of wisdom-related knowledge. From a life-span developmental perspective, one important implication of both models is the idea that, at least during adulthood, becoming older is neither sufficient nor necessary to develop higher levels of wisdom knowledge.

## AGE DIFFERENCES IN WISDOM-RELATED KNOWLEDGE: EMPIRICAL EVIDENCE

Consistent with the two theoretical models of the ontogenesis of wisdom, in several cross-sectional studies utilizing the Berlin wisdom tasks, the association between age and wisdom-related knowledge was nonsignificant and virtually zero (reviews: Staudinger, 1999; Staudinger & Glück, 2011). This evidence is not surprising given that the way to higher wisdom is resource demanding and requires a deliberate, intensive, and extended dealing with difficult and uncertain life problems. In addition, a range of supportive person-related and contextual factors is likely involved in the development of wisdom. Some wisdom-facilitating resources have been shown to decline with age, others remain stable, and yet others increase, suggesting a zero-sum game and age-related stability in overall wisdom-related knowledge (e.g., Staudinger, 1999). As reviewed next, a differentiation between distinct forms of wisdom even suggests that there may be some facets of wisdom-related knowledge that decline with age. In addition, there is reason to believe that the development of wisdom-related knowledge may be better described as a process of sequential gain and loss rather than a process of cumulative growth.

## Personal Versus General Wisdom: Multidirectional Age Differences?

In a cross-sectional study with a sample that covered most of the adult life span, Staudinger and colleagues recently found that, consistent with past cross-sectional evidence, general wisdom remained stable across the age groups studied; however, personal wisdom, as assessed by criteria such as self-relativism and tolerance of ambiguity, declined with age (Mickler & Staudinger, 2008). The authors have argued that this age-related decline may be associated with parallel age-related declines in openness to new experience (e.g., Specht, Egloff, & Schmukle, 2011), making it increasingly unlikely that older individuals have to test previously established self-related insights against new evidence—a prerequisite to developing higher levels of personal wisdom. On a more general level, one could describe the aging process as one that involves an increase in social, cognitive, and health-related losses that ultimately makes it less and less likely that older adults come to make new experiences and question their previously proven and familiar ways of seeing the self and others. Adopting an environmental perspective, one could also argue that our society is still structured in a way that prevents older adults from making new and varied experiences with the outer world.

Before accepting this and related ideas, however, it certainly remains to be seen if the currently cross-sectional evidence for an age-related deficit in personal wisdom will be replicated in the context of longitudinal data. For example, it could well be that the decrease in personal wisdom across the age groups studied is at least partly the result of cohort rather than age effects, given that the members of earlier cohorts most likely are less used to talking and thinking about the self than later cohorts.

## The Ontogenesis of Wisdom: A Sequence of Gain and Loss?

Most people seem to be aware that not everyone develops wisdom in old age and that wisdom—in a domain-general and ideal sense—may be a rare phenomenon regardless of age. And yet, it is still possible that many adults can gain some wisdom about some problems, namely, the problems that are particularly salient in their current life (Thomas & Kunzmann, 2013). Typically, the problems an individual has a high need to deal with and solve are at least partly influenced by this individual's age (Baltes, 1987; Erikson, 1968). For example, old age has been described as a period of loss during which individuals need to let go of many goals and find meaning in their lives as lived. Eventually because of their greater exposure to the theme of loss, older adults may be more likely to gain wisdom-related knowledge about the problems and challenges that surround this theme than their younger counterparts. This does not necessarily mean, however, that older adults generally have greater wisdom-related knowledge than younger people. There may be problem areas that are more familiar to young adults than to older adults and that may elicit greater wisdom-related knowledge in the young. In a recent study, we provided the first evidence for the idea that conflict in intimate relationships may be such a domain

(Thomas & Kunzmann, 2013). In a study with 200 adults spanning the adult life span, we found that wisdom-related knowledge about marital conflict, a problem that is way more common in young adulthood than in old age (e.g., Birditt, Fingerman, & Almeida, 2005), was highest in the youngest age group studied (20 to 29 years of age) and linearly decreased across the subsequent age groups. A follow-up analysis revealed that young adults' greater exposure to serious conflicts and greater willingness to actively engage in conflicts partly accounted for the age differences in wisdom-related knowledge about marital conflict. In contrast, wisdom-related knowledge about suicide, a nonnormative life event that is not particularly likely to occur at a specific age during the adult life span, remained stable across age groups.

Taken together, this evidence is consistent with the idea that young adults can be wiser than older adults in some domains and that the development of wisdom-related knowledge may not be cumulative. Just as any type of knowledge, wisdom-related knowledge about a particular type of problem may only be available if it is regularly used (Förster, Liberman, & Higgins, 2005; Jarvis, 1987). In this sense, the development of wisdom may be described as a sequential process of gain and loss: most individuals are likely to gain a certain degree of wisdom-related knowledge about the problems that are highly salient in their current life; however, this knowledge may become less available and may even vanish if it is not adaptive anymore (i.e., if it is not used because it refers to developmental tasks and problems that are not salient anymore). Consistent evidence was reported by Glück and colleagues (Glück, Bluck, Baron, & McAdams, 2005; König & Glück, 2012). The authors asked their participants from different age groups to report situations in which they themselves thought, said, or did something wise. These situations were later classified according to the form of wisdom that they primarily require. There were systematic age differences in what people considered as instances of wisdom in their own life; and, more to the point, these age differences reflected the developmental tasks of each age group.

## SUMMARY

Taken together, past evidence from different laboratories has supported the view that wisdom does not automatically come with age. We all can learn lessons about the challenges and problems that are part of life regardless of whether we are in our 20s or 60s. Given that individuals have limited resources, however, they have to be selective and can neither acquire wisdom-related knowledge in all possible life domains nor maintain wisdom-related knowledge that they had previously acquired if this knowledge has lost its relevance. Only for very few individuals, and if a rare constellation of facilitating factors and processes is present, domain-specific wisdom-related knowledge may be a stepping-stone to wisdom-related knowledge in a more generalized sense that transcends a particular problem type. Seen in this light, the absence of a normative increase in wisdom-related knowledge with age, which the current cross-sectional evidence for a nonsignificant relationship between age and wisdom-related knowledge suggests, is not surprising. As long as wisdom-related knowledge is assessed by age-neutral and rather general life dilemmas, more domain-specific gains and losses in wisdom-related knowledge cannot be made visible. Notably, these ideas are consistent with several models of successful life-span development, particularly the model of selection, optimization, and compensation proposed by Baltes and his colleagues (Baltes & Baltes, 1990; Freund & Baltes, 2002).

## WISDOM AS THE SUCCESSFUL INTEGRATION OF COGNITION AND EMOTION

The definition of wisdom as an expert knowledge system about the meaning and conduct of life may suggest to some that the Berlin wisdom model is too cognitive and ignores emotional competencies—that are also central elements of wisdom. However, from a life-span developmental point of view, certain emotional experiences and dispositions have been considered to be fundamental to the acquisition of wisdom-related knowledge. In addition, the effectiveness of wisdom-facilitating factors that are not primarily emotional in nature (e.g., stimulating social environments or the availability of a high-quality education) not only depends on a person's intellectual functioning (e.g., ability to learn new things, abstract reasoning, or accuracy of information processing) but also on this person's social and affective competencies and dispositions (e.g., level of emotional balance, impulsivity, neuroticism, or social competence).

It is also likely that the expression of wisdom-related knowledge in a particular situation is moderated by certain emotional dispositions and competencies (e.g., Kunzmann & Baltes, 2005). An advice giver who is not able or willing to imagine how a person in need feels, for example, is not likely to make an effort and engage in wisdom-related thinking that would involve careful and detailed analysis of the advice seeker's problem, the weighting and moderation of different parts of the situation, and the consideration of multiple views. Similarly, during a mutual conflict with another person, being able to imagine how this person feels or how one would feel in the other's place may be one stepping-stone to value tolerance and a cooperative approach typical of wisdom.

At the same time, however, one can easily think of emotional reactions to difficult and potentially stressful situations that are likely to hinder a wisdom-like approach. Examples are self-centered feelings that indicate personal distress, especially if these negative feelings are intense and long lasting. Two examples: If people are not able or willing to control their feelings of anger, contempt, or jealousy, they are likely to hurt or enrage others rather than come up with a wise solution to the problem at hand. Strong and chronic feelings of anxiety might inhibit wisdom-related thinking, which requires distance from the immediate situation, balance, and elaboration. It is in this sense that cold cognition and hot emotion have been described as two forces that antagonize one another (see Keltner & Gross, 1999).

Taken together, when considering the adaptive value of (negative) emotions in the face of existential problems, it certainly is important to differentiate two dimensions referring to the self-centeredness of emotions (self-related vs. empathy-related) and the intensity of emotions (low vs. moderate vs. high).

Certainly, the links between emotion and cognition can take any direction. The idea that certain emotions hinder or facilitate the activation of wisdom-related knowledge and behavior may be less popular in the wisdom literature than the notion that it is wisdom that regulates a person's emotional experiences and reactions. In this vein, wisdom researchers have conceptualized wisdom as a resource or personal characteristic that encourages the experiencing of certain positive emotions such as sympathy and compassionate love, and decreases the experience of negative emotions (e.g., feelings of hostility, contempt, or personal distress; e.g., Ardelt, 2003). Although we are sympathetic to the idea that wisdom can involve emotional down-regulation in the face of difficult problems, in our own work we proceed from the idea that wisdom does not involve the total absence of negative emotions. Rather, in the face of a difficult and uncertain problem, it should facilitate emotional responses of moderate intensity (neither extremely high nor extremely low) through a balancing of two opposing emotion regulatory styles: emotional distancing and emotional responsiveness (for more details see later discussion).

## WISDOM AS THE SUCCESSFUL INTEGRATION OF COGNITION AND MOTIVATION

Does wisdom-related knowledge guide a person's behaviors in grappling with difficult problems and interacting with others? How do people use their wisdom-related knowledge in everyday life, and what is the motivational orientation that goes hand in hand with this type of knowledge? If wisdom-related knowledge were an end in itself and had no correspondence with what an individual wants and does in his or her life, it could hardly be considered a resource. This is at least the idea that was proposed by several modern philosophers influenced by the tradition of early Greek philosophy. This group of researchers has argued that wisdom as knowledge is closely linked to wisdom as manifested in an individual's everyday behavior. In this tradition, wisdom has been thought to be a resource facilitating behavior aimed at promoting a good life at both an individual and a societal level. For example, Ryan (1996) defined a wise person as follows: "A person S is wise if and only if (1) S is a free agent, (2) S knows how to live well, (3) S lives well, and (4) S's living well is caused by S's knowledge of how to live well" (p. 241). Kekes (1983) wrote, "Wisdom is a character trait intimately connected with self-direction. The more wisdom a person has the more likely it is he will succeed in living a good life" (p. 277).

Notably, a good life is not linked exclusively to self-realization and personal happiness but encompasses more, namely, the well-being of others. In this sense, Kekes (1995) has stressed that wisdom is knowledge about ways of developing oneself not only without violating others' rights but also with co-producing resources for others to develop. Thus, in these philosophical conceptualizations, a central characteristic of a wise person is the ability to translate knowledge into action geared toward the development of oneself and others.

Psychological wisdom researchers have begun to respond to the longstanding notion that wisdom-related knowledge requires and reflects certain motivational tendencies, which in turn shape the use of wisdom-related knowledge and guide its application in daily life (e.g., Baltes & Staudinger, 2000; Kramer, 2000; Sternberg, 1998). Notably, however, wise persons have been described as being primarily concerned with other people's well-being rather than with their own (e.g., Ardelt, 2003; Holliday & Chandler, 1986). Consistent with this view, Helson and Srivastava (2002) provided evidence that wise persons tend to be benevolent, compassionate, caring, and interested in helping others. The idea that wisdom is different from prosocial behavior in that it involves a joint consideration of self- and other-related interests, however, has rarely been tested empirically. In the following section, we will discuss empirical studies from our lab that can be considered a first step in demonstrating that wisdom is inherently of an intra- and interpersonal nature.

## EMOTIONAL-MOTIVATIONAL ELEMENTS OF WISDOM: EMPIRICAL EVIDENCE

In the following, we will review three empirical studies that examined various person characteristics as correlates of wisdom-related knowledge. By highlighting the role of wisdom-related knowledge in certain personality characteristics (e.g., openness to new experiences or psychological mindedness), affective experiences, value orientations, and preferences for certain conflict-management strategies, we aim to broaden our understanding of the concept of wisdom and the behavioral sphere in which it is embedded.

## WISDOM: INTELLIGENCE, PERSONALITY, AND SOCIAL-COGNITIVE STYLE?

To test parts of the Berlin developmental model of wisdom-related knowledge (see Figure 34.1), Staudinger, Lopez, and Baltes (1997) investigated three general person factors as correlates of wisdom-related knowledge. These factors were test intelligence, personality traits, and several facets of social-cognitive style. A central goal of this study was to empirically demonstrate that intelligence, as assessed by traditional psychometric tests, would be a relatively weak predictor of wisdom-related knowledge, whereas personality traits and especially social-cognitive style would be more important. This prediction was tested in a study with 125 adults. In a first individual interview session, wisdom-related knowledge was assessed by the traditional Berlin wisdom tasks. During a second session, the authors employed 33 measures to assess multiple indicators of intelligence (e.g., speed of information processing, logical thinking, practical knowledge), personality (e.g., neuroticism, extraversion, openness to new experiences), and social-cognitive style (e.g., social intelligence, creativity, interest in others' needs). Not all indicators were significant predictors. For example, unrelated to wisdom-related knowledge were speed of information processing and four of the five classic personality traits (i.e., neuroticism, extraversion, agreeableness, and conscientiousness); only openness to experience was positively related to wisdom-related knowledge. When analyzed separately, the significant intelligence measures accounted for 15% of the variance in wisdom-related knowledge, social-cognitive style accounted for 35% of the variance, and personality for 23%. The simultaneous analyses of all three sets of predictors in hierarchical multiple regression analyses revealed that the unique prediction of intelligence and personality was small (i.e., 2% each), whereas indicators of social-cognitive style contributed a larger share of unique variance, namely, 15%.

Together this evidence clearly supports the notion that wisdom-related knowledge, as operationalized via the Berlin wisdom tasks, is not simply a variant of intelligence. It deserves special note that neither academic intelligence nor basic personality dispositions such as neuroticism or extraversion show substantial relationships to wisdom-related knowledge. Our general life orientation, cognitive style, and social preferences—all aspects that individuals can and do shape during adult development—seem to be more closely related to wisdom-related knowledge.

## EMOTIONAL AND MOTIVATIONAL DISPOSITIONS AS CORRELATES OF WISDOM AS KNOWLEDGE

Extending the study reviewed earlier, Kunzmann and Baltes (2003b) provided further evidence for the idea that wisdom-related knowledge is associated with certain motivational and emotional dispositions. These dispositions referred to affective experiences (pleasantness, interest/involvement, and negative affect), value orientations (pleasurable life, personal growth, insight, well-being of friends, environmental protection, societal engagement), and preferred modes of conflict management (dominance, submission, avoidance, cooperation). By highlighting the relations between wisdom-related knowledge and these indicators, our aim was to broaden our understanding of the emotional-motivational side of wisdom-related knowledge.

The main predictions were based on the notion that wisdom-related knowledge requires and reflects a joint concern for developing one's own and others' potential (see also Sternberg, 1998). In contrast, a predominant search for self-centered pleasure and comfort should not be associated with wisdom. Accordingly, people high on wisdom-related knowledge should report (a) an affective structure that is positive but process- and environment-oriented rather than evaluative and self-centered; (b) a profile of values that is oriented toward personal growth, insight, and the well-being of others rather than a pleasurable and comfortable life; and (c) a cooperative approach to managing interpersonal conflicts rather than a dominant, submissive, or avoidant style.

The findings were consistent with these predictions. People with high levels of wisdom-related knowledge reported that they less frequently experience self-centered pleasant feelings (e.g., happiness, amusement) but more frequently experience process-oriented and environment-centered positive emotions (e.g., interest, inspiration). People with higher levels of wisdom-related knowledge also reported less preference for values revolving around a pleasurable and comfortable life. Instead, they reported preferring self-oriented values such as personal growth and insight as well as a preference for other-oriented values related to environmental protection, societal engagement, and the well-being of friends. Finally, people with high levels of wisdom-related knowledge showed less preference for conflict-management strategies that reflect either a one-sided concern with one's own interest (i.e., dominance), a one-sided concern with others' interests (i.e., submission), or no concern at all (i.e., avoidance). As predicted, they preferred a cooperative approach reflecting a joint concern for one's own and the opponent's interests.

Together, the evidence clearly supports the notion that wisdom-related knowledge is linked to certain motivational orientations (i.e., a joint concern for developing one's own potential and that of others) and affective dispositions (i.e., the tendency to experience positive, environment-oriented emotions rather than evaluative, self-centered feelings such as happiness or negative feelings such as anger, fear, sadness).

EMOTIONAL REACTIONS TO FUNDAMENTAL LIFE PROBLEMS: WISDOM MAKES A DIFFERENCE

A main goal of a third study that we recently completed in our laboratory was to provide evidence for the idea that wisdom-related knowledge facilitates a balanced emotion regulatory style that helps individuals at any age to react to negative emotion inducing events in a moderate fashion (Kunzmann & Thomas, in preparation). More specifically, we proceeded from the idea that individuals with high wisdom-related knowledge will neither become overwhelmed by existential problems nor will they remain emotionally unaffected because wisdom-related knowledge facilitates a balancing of two opposing emotion regulatory principles, emotional distance and emotional responsiveness.

We began to test this idea in a study with almost 200 participants spanning the adult life span. As to the procedure, our participants were first presented with a traditional wisdom task (i.e., the suicide task) and asked to think about it silently for 2 minutes. They were then instructed to report their feelings during this silent phase on an emotion adjective list covering 18 positive and negative emotions. Finally, they thought aloud about the task and their think-aloud responses were later coded according to the three Berlin wisdom meta-criteria. Given that we were the first to assess emotional reactions to a traditional wisdom task, it may be worthwhile to report that the task elicited emotional reactions of moderate intensity, especially shock, sadness, and fear. This may be surprising given that the task presents the suicide problem in a highly abstract and decontextualized way. However, most of the participants were able to relate to the problem while thinking about it. In addition, in the entire sample, the association between wisdom-related knowledge and negative emotional reactivity was nonsignificant. At first sight, this evidence speaks against the idea that wisdom-related knowledge makes a difference for an individual's emotional reactions. This conclusion may be unwarranted, however, given that the main finding of this study was that age differences in the intensity of emotional reactions were dependent on an individual's level of wisdom-related knowledge. Our follow-up analyses revealed that the emotional reactions of people with high wisdom-related knowledge were of moderate size, independent of whether they were young or old and, thus, more or less concerned with an existential life problem related to death and dying. By contrast, the emotional reactions of people with low wisdom-related knowledge were dependent on age and, thus, arguably, by the degree to which the problem at hand was self-relevant: Older adults, for whom the task was highly self-relevant, reported the highest level of negative emotional reactivity, most likely because they had difficulties contextualizing the problem and considering it on an abstract level of analyses that would have helped them down-regulate their negative feelings; younger adults, for whom the task was of little self-relevance, reported the lowest level of negative reactivity, most likely because they had difficulties understanding the significance and implications of a problem that was not particularly self-relevant (the findings are graphically depicted in Figure 34.2).

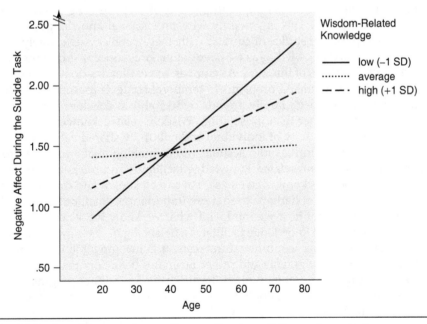

**Figure 34.2** Age differences in negative emotional reactivity are dependent on wisdom-related knowledge
*Notes.* To test our predictions regarding the effects of age and wisdom-related knowledge on negative emotional reactivity, we conducted a hierarchical multiple regression analysis. The dependent variable referred to the level of negative affect during the suicide task. As to the independent variables, in the first step, negative affect experienced during a baseline period served as a predictor. In the second step, the main effects of age and wisdom-related knowledge were entered into the regression equation. In the third step, the interaction term (i.e., age by wisdom) were tested for significance. There was a main effect of age ($\beta = 21$, $t = 2.89, p < .01$). The main effect of wisdom was nonsignificant ($\beta = -.05, t = .75$). The interaction between age and wisdom became significant ($\beta = -.16, t = -2.18, p < .05$).

Notably, the findings from this study oppose the view that individuals with high levels of wisdom-related knowledge generally are emotionally distant and detached (e.g., Erikson, 1959; Kross & Grossmann, 2012). Rather, wisdom-related knowledge appears to involve a balancing between emotional distance and emotional responsiveness, and, thus, emotional reactions of moderate intensity.

## CONCLUSION

Given the emotional and motivational benefits that come with wisdom-related knowledge, the question arises as to whether this type of knowledge can be taught in school (e.g., Sternberg, 2001) or in contexts of professional training and practice (e.g., Küpers & Pauleen, 2013). At one time or another in their career, most professionals have to struggle with one or more of the following questions: How can I coordinate my professional career and family development, balance my work load and leisure time, get along with my colleagues, identify my interests, and pursue those interests cooperatively? From a leadership perspective, one might add questions such as, How can I maximize a common good rather than optimize the interests of certain individuals or small groups of individuals, get employees involved and motivated, develop and communicate a useful and inspiring vision, and coordinate the long-term and short-term goals of my cooperation or institution?

What the problems mentioned here have in common is that they are fundamental, complex, and uncertain; they are poorly defined, have multiple yet unknown solutions, and require coordinating multiple and often conflicting interests within and among individuals. This is precisely why professional knowledge in the narrow sense is typically insufficient to deal with these problems effectively. In contrast, wisdom-related knowledge, as we have defined this concept, is designed to deal especially with problems of this kind. As emphasized earlier, wisdom-related knowledge encourages us to embed problems in temporal contexts (past, present, future) and thematic contexts (e.g., family, friends, work) and to consider problems from a broad perspective rather than in isolation. Wisdom-related knowledge also helps to acknowledge the relativity of individual and culturally shared values and to take other values and life priorities into account when thinking about possible problem solutions. Finally, wisdom-related knowledge facilitates an understanding of what one knows and does not know, as well as what can be known and cannot be known at a given time and place. Perhaps even more important, a small but growing body of evidence suggests that how we think and what we know influences how we feel and act. Wisdom-related knowledge facilitates a balancing of one's own interests and those of others, including institutional interests. It is incompatible with impulsive, mindless, or immoral judgments and rather facilitates behaviors that can maximize what has been called the common good. Participating in training programs on wisdom will surely inspire some people to deal in new and constructive ways with the difficulties of life that none of us can avoid.

## SUMMARY POINTS

- Several promising definitions of wisdom have been proposed in the psychological literature. The Berlin wisdom model focuses on one facet of wisdom, that is, knowledge. On the most general level, wisdom-related knowledge has been defined as deep and broad knowledge about difficult and uncertain problems related to the meaning and conduct of life. This type of knowledge can be specified on the basis of five wisdom criteria, including life-span contextualism, value relativism and tolerance, and uncertainty acknowledgement and management.

- The way to higher wisdom-related knowledge is resource demanding and requires a deliberate, intensive, and extended dealing with difficult and uncertain life problems. This process can be facilitated or hindered by a number of person-related and contextual factors. As a consequence, age per se is not sufficient for the acquisition and further development of wisdom-related knowledge.
- There is reason to believe that becoming older may not even be necessary for wisdom-related knowledge to develop during adulthood and old age. Some wisdom-facilitating resources have been shown to decline with age, others remain stable, and yet others increase, suggesting a zero-sum game and age-related stability in overall wisdom-related knowledge. Furthermore, a conceptualization of wisdom-related knowledge as domain-specific allows studying the idea that wisdom-related knowledge may not be constant across the adult life span, but better described as a process of sequential gain and loss. Given that all humans have limited resources, they may selectively acquire and maintain wisdom-related knowledge about only those life problems that are currently most salient. As a consequence, there may be problems that elicit greater wisdom-related knowledge in younger adults (i.e., problems that are typical and salient in young adulthood), whereas other problems elicit greater wisdom-related knowledge in older adults (i.e., problems that are more typical and salient in old age).
- Even if the way to higher wisdom is cumbersome and most adults only acquire some wisdom about some problems, it is worth the effort to strive for it. Certainly there are many competencies that people can bring to bear when dealing with life's challenges and problems—but no other capacity will be as integrative as wisdom is. Because of its integrative nature spanning cognitive, motivational, and emotional elements, wisdom can be seen as the most general framework that directs and optimizes human development.
- Proceeding from the definition of wisdom as knowledge, we have begun to explore the emotional and motivational characteristics of individuals with high wisdom-related knowledge. This endeavor can be seen as a first step in testing the idea that wisdom-related knowledge is a resource with emotional and motivational benefits. Proceeding from the general theoretical idea that wisdom involves balance, moderation, and reflectivity, we consider it likely that high wisdom-related knowledge is related to moderate affective experiences and to a balancing of opposing interests and concerns. Confirming this idea, empirical evidence suggests that individuals with higher wisdom-related knowledge report (a) higher affective involvement combined with lower negative and pleasant affect; (b) a value orientation that focuses conjointly on other-enhancing values and personal growth combined with a lesser tendency toward values revolving around a pleasurable life; (c) a preference for cooperative conflict-management strategies combined with a lower tendency to adopt submissive, avoidant, or dominant strategies; and (d) moderate emotional reactions to difficult and uncertain problems (i.e., emotional reactions that are neither extremely high nor extremely low).

## REFERENCES

Ardelt, M. (2003). Empirical assessment of a three-dimensional wisdom scale. *Research on Aging,* *25,* 275–324.

Ardelt, M. (2004). Wisdom as expert knowledge system: A critical review of a contemporary operationalization of an ancient concept. *Human Development, 47,* 257–285.

Assmann, A. (1994). Wholesome knowledge: Concepts of wisdom in a historical and cross-cultural perspective. In D. L. Featherman, R. M. Lerner, & M. Perlmutter (Eds.), *Life-span development and behavior* (Vol. 12, pp. 187–224). Hillsdale, NJ: Erlbaum.

Baltes, P. B. (1987). Theoretical propositions of life-span developmental psychology: On the dynamics between growth and decline. *Developmental Psychology, 23,* 611–626.

Baltes, P. B. (1997a). On the incomplete architecture of human ontogeny: Selection, optimization, and compensation as foundation of developmental theory. *American Psychologist, 52,* 366–380.

Baltes, P. B. (1997b). Wolfgang Edelstein: *Über ein Wissenschaftsleben in konstruktivistischer* [Wolfgang Edelstein: A scientific life in constructivist melancholy]. *Reden zur Emeritierung von Wolfgang Edelstein.* Berlin, Germany: Max Planck Institute for Human Devleopment.

Baltes, P. B., & Baltes, M. M. (1990). Psychological perspectives on successful aging: The model of selective optimization with compensation. In P. B. Baltes & M. M. Baltes (Eds.), *Successful aging: Perspectives from the behavioral sciences* (pp. 27–34). Cambridge, England: Cambridge University Press.

Baltes, P. B., & Kunzmann, U. (2003). Wisdom: The peak of human excellence in the orchestration of mind and virtue. *The Psychologist, 16,* 131–133.

Baltes, P. B., & Kunzmann, U. (2004). The two faces of wisdom: Wisdom as a general theory of knowledge and judgment about excellence in mind and virtue vs. wisdom as everyday realization in people and products. *Human Development, 47,* 290–299.

Baltes, P. B., & Smith, J. (1990). Toward a psychology of wisdom and its ontogenesis. In R. J. Sternberg (Ed.), *Wisdom: Its nature, origins, and development* (pp. 87–120). Cambridge, England: Cambridge University Press.

Baltes, P. B., Smith, J., & Staudinger, U. M. (1992). Wisdom and successful aging. In T. B. Sonderegger (Ed.), *Nebraska symposium on motivation* (Vol. 39, pp. 123–167). Lincoln: University of Nebraska Press.

Baltes, P. B., & Staudinger, U. M. (2000). Wisdom: A metaheuristic (pragmatic) to orchestrate mind and virtue toward excellence. *American Psychologist, 55,* 122–136.

Birditt, K. S., Fingerman, K. L., & Almeida, D. M. (2005). Age differences in exposure and reactions to interpersonal tensions: A daily diary study. *Psychology and Aging, 20,* 330–340.

Clayton, V., & Birren, J. E. (1980). The development of wisdom across the lifespan: A reexamination of an ancient topic. In P. B. Baltes & O. G. Brim (Eds.), *Life-span development and behavior* (Vol. 3, pp. 103–135). New York, NY: Academic Press.

Erikson, E. H. (1959). *Identity and the life cycle.* New York, NY: International University Press.

Erikson, E. H. (1968). *Identity, youth, and crisis.* New York, NY: Norton.

Freund, A. M., & Baltes, P. B. (2002). Life-management strategies of selection, optimization, and compensation: Measurement by self-report and construct validity. *Journal of Personality and Social Psychology, 82,* 642–662.

Förster, J., Liberman, N., & Higgins, E. T. (2005). Accessibility from active and fulfilled goals. *Journal of Experimental Social Psychology, 41,* 220–239.

Glück, J., & Bluck, S. (2013). The MORE life experience model: A theory of the development of personal wisdom. In M. Ferrari & N. M. Weststrate (Eds.), *The scientific study of personal wisdom: From contemplative traditions to neuroscience* (pp. 75–98). New York, NY: Springer.

Glück, J., Bluck, S., Baron, J., & McAdams, D. P. (2005). The wisdom of experience: Autobiographical narratives across adulthood. *International Journal of Behavioral Development, 29,* 197–208.

Heckhausen, J., Dixon, R. A., & Baltes, P. B. (1989). Gains and losses in development throughout adulthood as perceived by different adult age groups. *Developmental Psychology, 25,* 109–121.

Helson, R., & Srivastava, S. (2002). Creative and wise people: Similarities, differences, and how they develop. *Personality and Social Psychology Bulletin, 28,* 1430–1440.

Helson, R., & Wink, P. (1987). Two conceptions of maturity examined in the findings of a longitudinal study. *Journal of Personality and Social Psychology, 53,* 531–541.

Holliday, S. G., & Chandler, M. J. (1986). Wisdom: Explorations in adult competence. In J. A. Meacham (Ed.), *Contributions to human development* (Vol. 17, pp. 1–96). Basel, Switzerland: Karger.

Jarvis, P. (1987). Meaningful and meaningless experience: Towards an analysis of learning from life. *Adult Education Quarterly, 37,* 164–172.

Kekes, J. (1983). Wisdom. *American Philosophical Quarterly, 20,* 277–286.

Kekes, J. (1995). *Moral wisdom and good lives.* Ithaca, NY: Cornell University Press.

Keltner, D., & Gross, J. J. (1999). Functional accounts of emotions. *Cognition and Emotion, 13,* 467–480.

König, S., & Glück, J. (2012). Situations in which I was wise: Autobiographical wisdom memories of children and adolescents. *Journal of Research on Adolescence, 22,* 512–525.

Kramer, D. A. (1990). Conceptualizing wisdom: The primacy of affect–cognition relations. In R. J. Sternberg (Ed.), *Wisdom: Its nature, origins, and development* (pp. 279–313). Cambridge, England: Cambridge University Press.

Kramer, D. A. (2000). Wisdom as a classical source of human strength: Conceptualization and empirical inquiry. *Journal of Social and Clinical Psychology, 19,* 83–101.

Kross, E., & Grossmann, I. (2012). Boosting wisdom: Distance from the self enhances wise reasoning, attitudes, and behavior. *Journal of Experimental Psychology: General, 141,* 43–48.

Kunzmann, U., & Baltes, P. B. (2003a). Beyond the traditional scope of intelligence: Wisdom in action. In R. J. Sternberg, J. Lautry, & T. I. Lubart (Eds.), *Models of intelligence for the next millennium* (pp. 329–343). Washington, DC: American Psychological Association.

Kunzmann, U., & Baltes, P. B. (2003b). Wisdom-related knowledge: Affective, motivational, and interpersonal correlates. *Personality and Social Psychology Bulletin, 29,* 1104–1119.

Kunzmann, U., & Baltes, P. B. (2005). The psychology of wisdom: Theoretical and empirical challenges. In R. J. Sternberg & J. Jordan (Eds.), *A handbook of wisdom: Psychological perspectives* (pp. 110–135). New York, NY: Cambridge University Press.

Kunzmann, U., & Stange, A. (2007). Wisdom as a classical human strength: Psychological conceptualizations and empirical inquiry. In A. D. Ong & M. H. M. van Dulmen (Eds.), *Oxford handbook of methods in positive psychology* (pp. 306–322). Oxford, England: Oxford University Press.

Kunzmann, U., & Thomas, S. (in preparation). *Age differences in negative emotional reactions: Wisdom-related knowledge matters.*

Küpers, W., & Pauleen, D. (2013). *A handbook of practical wisdom leadership, organization and integral business practice.* Farnham, England: Ashgate.

Labouvie-Vief, G. (1990). Wisdom as integrated thought: Historical and developmental perspectives. In R. J. Sternberg (Ed.), *Wisdom: Its nature, origins, and development* (pp. 52–83). Cambridge, England: Cambridge University Press.

Labouvie-Vief, G. (2003). Dynamic integration: Affect, cognition, and the self in adulthood. *Current Directions in Psychological Science, 12,* 201–206.

Mickler, C., & Staudinger, U. M. (2008). Personal wisdom: Validation and age-related differences of a performance measure. *Psychology and Aging, 23,* 787–799.

Redzanowski, U., & Glück, J. (2013). Who knows who is wise? Self and peer ratings of wisdom. *Journals of Gerontology, Series B: Psychological Sciences and Social Sciences, 68,* 391–394.

Ryan, S. (1996). Wisdom. In K. Lehrer, B. J. Lum, B. A. Slichta, & N. D. Smith (Eds.), *Knowledge, teaching, and wisdom* (pp. 233–242). Dordrecht, The Netherlands: Wolters Kluwer.

Seligman, M. E. P., & Csikszentmihalyi, M. (2000). Positive psychology: An introduction. *American Psychologist, 55,* 5–14.

Specht, J., Egloff, B., & Schmukle, S. C. (2011). Stability and change of personality across the life course: The impact of age and major life events on mean-level and rank-order stability of the Big Five. *Journal of Personality and Social Psychology, 101,* 862–882.

Staudinger U. M. (1999). Older and wiser? Integrating results on the relationship between age and wisdom-related performance. *International Journal of Behavioral Development, 23,* 641–664.

Staudinger, U. M., & Glück, J. (2011). Psychological wisdom research: Commonalities and differences in a growing field. *Annual Review of Psychology, 62,* 215–241.

Staudinger, U. M., & Kunzmann, U. (2005). Positive adult personality development: Adjustment and/or growth? *European Psychologist, 10,* 320–329.

Staudinger, U. M., Lopez, D. F., & Baltes, P. B. (1997). The psychometric location of wisdom-related performance. *Personality and Social Bulletin, 23,* 1200–1214.

Sternberg, R. J. (1998). A balance theory of wisdom. *Review of General Psychology, 2,* 347–365.

Sternberg, R. J. (2001). Why schools should teach for wisdom: The balance theory of wisdom in educational settings. *Educational Psychologist, 36,* 227–245.

Sternberg, R., & Jordan, J. (2005). *A handbook of wisdom: psychological perspectives.* Cambridge, England: Cambridge University Press.

Thomas, S. (2012). *Wisdom-related knowledge about social conflict: Age differences and integration of cognition and affect* (Unpublished doctoral thesis). Institute of Psychology, University of Leipzig, Germany.

Thomas, S., & Kunzmann, U. (2013). Age differences in wisdom-related knowledge: Does the age relevance of the task matter? *Journals of Gerontology, Series B: Psychological Sciences and Social Sciences.* Advanced online publication.

Wink, P., & Helson, R. (1997). Practical and transcendent wisdom: Their nature and some longitudinal findings. *Journal of Adult Development, 4,* 1–15.

# CHAPTER 35

# Positive Aging

GEORGE E. VAILLANT

ALFRED PAINE WAS a model of the Sad-Sick. True, he did not acknowledge either his alcoholism or his depression. Like Pollyanna, Voltaire's Dr. Pangloss, and *Mad* magazine's Alfred E. Neuman, Paine was a master of denial. On pencil and paper tests of neuroticism, he scored very low on the depression subscale. On questionnaires, he described himself as close to his children and in quite good physical health. Thus, it was only by interviewing him personally, talking with his wife, examining his objective medical record, reading the disappointed questionnaires from his children—and then, finally, by reading his obituary—that Alfred Paine's misery could be fully appreciated. The uncomplaining nature of Paine's written replies did not alter the fact that his life story had always been terribly sad. Thus, one of the great lessons of the 75-year prospective study that I am about to describe is that it is what people do, not what they say in personality inventories, that predicts the future.

On the other hand, Richard Luckey was a well-loved child who took excellent care of himself, but unlike Alfred Paine, Luckey had come from more modest beginnings. None of his four grandparents had gone beyond grade school. One grandfather had been a police officer and the other a self-made owner of a large baking company. His father graduated from high school and went on to become a successful businessman so that Richard Luckey, like Alfred Paine, had gone to an excellent boarding school. After college Luckey became head of two successful businesses (one of which he created)—at the same time. Always careful to take care of himself, Luckey married well. Unlike Paine, he knew how to take care of his money, how to appreciate his wife, and how to make his own luck. More on these two characters later. But another lesson of the study is that over multiple decades it is the good things, not the bad things (e.g. poverty and parental death), that affect us at the age of 80.

As we contemplate surviving until old age, a common worry is that we will spend decades helpless and/or in pain. We forget to look at the positive. Our problem is that there have been many longitudinal studies of physical longevity (e.g., Baltes & Mayer, 1999; Dawber, 1980; Fries, 1980; Rowe & Kahn, 1999) but very few studies that have examined psychological longevity. I first wrote this chapter when the men were at least 80 and I was 68. Now the men are all 90 and I am 79 (Vaillant, 2012). In rewriting this chapter I realize that the Greek philosopher Heraclites was right: "No one steps in the same river twice; for it is not the same river; and he is not the same man." I am now able to walk the walk instead of talk the talk about positive aging, and an astonishing 30% of the College men from the study have lived to celebrate their 90th birthday.

The mission of positive aging is very clear: to add more life to years, not just more years to life. For example, we worry that impotence is an inevitable consequence of old age, but Simone de Beauvoir (1972) cheers us. She offers the hopeful example of an admittedly exceptional 88-year-old man. He reported intercourse with his 90-year-old wife one to four times a week. A member of our study took only one medicine at age 88—Viagra twice a week. True, at 75 to 80 for most surviving husbands and wives in good health, the average is more likely to be once every 10 weeks (Bortz, Wallace, & Wiley, 1999).

To begin with, it is as profoundly misleading to look at the average old person as it is to look at the average 20-year-old car. Careful driving and maintenance are everything. Often, old cars evolve into cripples not because of aging but because of poor maintenance, poor driving, and misuse. So, too, with humans. Much of what we view as the inexorable decay of aging between age 70 and 90 is a result of accident and disease. Proper maintenance is everything.

Eventually, the years take their toll, but an aging octogenarian can do almost everything a young person can do; it just takes a little longer and must begin a little earlier. Such limitations, however, did not impede Will Durant from winning the Pulitzer Prize for history at 83, or Frank Lloyd Wright from designing the Guggenheim Museum at 90, or 80-year-old expert marathoners from being able to run 26 miles faster than 99% of 20-year-olds (though, admittedly, it takes the 80-year-olds twice as long as it did in their salad days). While performing his daily routine of cello practice, the 91-year-old Pablo Casals was once asked by one of his students, "Master, why do you continue to practice?" Casals answered, "Because I am making progress" (Heimpel, 1981).

True, from age 30 on, nominal aphasia (our inability to remember names) steadily worsens, but this does not lead to Alzheimer's. Over time we also become less adept at remembering spatial cues, and so by 80 we lose our cars in parking lots. But we remain just as adept at remembering emotionally nuanced events as we did when we were much younger; and in the healthy, a majority of facets of intelligence have not declined. For example, in an unpublished study of our men now that they all have reached 90, if men who died or had dementia or MCI (minimal cognitive impairment) are excluded, then the average score of the remaining men on the 41-item TICS (Telephone Interview for Cognitive Status) had declined only 0.7 of a point between 80 and 90!

A major difficulty in studying positive aging is measurement. Good health, both psychological and physical, is a very real and very tangible boon. But the quantification of good health is by no means easy. Two men have colostomies; for one man it is only a minor inconvenience; for the other it is a devastating blow to self-image. Why? To understand positive aging we need to be able to answer this question. Most observers can agree upon illness. But as soon as positive health is raised, a multitude of voices, often quite heated voices, cry value judgment.

In this chapter I shall measure successful aging by assessing four facets of health—both physical health and psychosocial health, both subjective health and objective health. Only when all four facets of health are present will good health be declared. First, with the passage of time, progressively diminished physical reserves are an inevitable part of aging, but, of course, the rate at which these diminished reserves occur is variable. Biologically, one can be young or old for one's chronological age. Second, physical health can involve experiencing the biological ravages of age without feeling sick. Good self-care, high morale, intimate friends, mental health, and coping strategies often make the difference between being ill and feeling sick. Third, age and social class are important. To control for age, all the participants reported in this chapter have been studied for 70 years, and each participant's health was known at every age from 20 to 90. To control for social class, the health of two homogeneous cohorts at opposite ends of the social spectrum—a College cohort and an Inner-City cohort—was studied. Within-cohort differences and between-cohort similarities are emphasized. Fourth, in 1948 the founders of the World Health Organization (WHO) defined health as physical, mental, and social well-being, not merely the absence of disease or infirmity (WHO, 1952). Thus, measuring positive objective psychosocial health is more difficult than measuring physical health but an equally important task. At age 90 some people are able to endure wheelchairs in good cheer and with close friends. Others are not only active; they still climb mountains—that is even more desirable. Clearly, subjective mental health is as important to aging as are objective indicators. Healthy aging, then, is being both contented *and* vigorous as well as being not sad or sick or dead.

The College cohort included 268 Harvard University sophomores selected for physical and mental health around 1940 (Vaillant, 1977). The socially disadvantaged Inner-City cohort included 456 nondelinquent schoolboys with a mean IQ of 95 and a mean education of 10 years (Glueck & Glueck, 1950, 1968). The details of the study have been well described in previous reports (Vaillant, 1995, 2002; Vaillant, Meyer, Mukamal, & Soldz, 1998).

To increase the chances of successful contrast and to minimize value judgment, the study focused on men at the ends of the health spectrum. In each cohort I shall contrast the one fourth of the men who lived out the last decade feeling the healthiest—the Happy-Well—with the one half who spent most of the last decade either feeling both sad and sick or being dead. To reduce argument, I shall deliberately exclude the one man in four who fell somewhere in the gray zone of being either healthy or sick depending on the criteria chosen. In short, three quarters of the men will reflect black and white categories of aging—the Happy-Well, the Sad-Sick, and the Prematurely Dead—and one quarter, the intermediate group, will be excluded (Table 35.1).

Of 268 College men originally admitted to the study at about age 19 to 20, 31 men (12%) died before age 50 or withdrew from the study. This left 237 College men in Table 35.1. All men who died between 50 and 75 were classified as dead. The three quarters who survived until 75 were classified *Happy-Well*, *Intermediate*, and *Sad-Sick* (see Table 35.1).

**Table 35.1**
Definition of Positive Aging

|  | College Sample Age 80 N = 237 | | Core-City Sample Age 70 N = 332 | |
| --- | --- | --- | --- | --- |
|  | N | (%) | N | (%) |
| Happy-Well: | 62 | (26%) | 95 | (29%) |
| Intermediate: | 75 | (32%) | 114 | (34%) |
| Sad-Sick: | 40 | (17%) | 48 | (14%) |
| Prematurely Dead: | 60 | (25%) | 75 | (23%) |

*Note*: The Happy-Well, the Intermediate, and the Sad-Sick all survived until age 75 if College men and until age 65 if Core-City men. However, at the time that the data for this paper was analyzed, not all of the College men were quite 80 and not all of the Core-City sample were quite 70.

Of 456 Inner-City men originally admitted to the study at age 12 to 16, 44 (10%) died by age 50 and 80 (17.5%) withdrew. This left 332 men in the study. Although they were 10 years younger than the College men, their objectively rated health (i.e., the proportion physically well, chronically ill, disabled, or dead) at 70 was the same as that of the College men at 80. Much of this variance came from differences in education, which, in turn, predicted obesity, cigarette and alcohol abuse, diabetes, and blood pressure. The variance did not depend upon differences in parental social class per se. Part of the variance came from the fact that poor physical, and especially poor mental, health led to downward social mobility; for adults, social class is powerfully associated with physical health.

To differentiate the Happy-Well unambiguously from the Sad-Sick, I chose six contrasting dimensions of health. These measures are described in detail in Vaillant (2002) and Vaillant and Mukamal (2001).

1. Absence of Objective Physical Disability (at age 75 Harvard cohort or at age 65 Inner-City cohort). Every 5 years, the study sought from each Harvard and Inner-City man a complete physical exam, including chest X-rays, routine blood chemistries, urinalysis, and an electrocardiogram. A study internist, blind to psychosocial adjustment, then rated all of these physical examinations on a 4-point scale (Vaillant, 1979). He rated the men as 1 if they were still without any irreversible illness and 2 if they were afflicted with an irreversible illness that was neither life shortening nor disabling. Such illnesses might be mild glaucoma, treatable hypertension, or noncrippling arthritis. If in the judgment of the study internist, the College men suffered from an irreversible life-threatening illness, they were called a 3, or chronically ill. This category refers to illnesses that could be expected to be progressive and to shorten life or eventually to affect daily living, but that were not in the eyes of the study internist disabling. Examples of such illnesses are coronary thrombosis or diabetes or hypertension not fully controlled by medication.

Finally, the internist rated the men a 4 if they suffered both irreversible illness and, in his judgment, significant disability. Examples would be multiple sclerosis, chronic congestive heart failure, and disabling arthritis of the hip. Only this category 4 reflected unsuccessful aging. The men, after all, were 75 to 85 years old and could be expected to have some illnesses.

2. Subjective Physical Health at Age 75. Since human beings are remarkably adaptable and suggestible, physical disability is in part subjective. When asked to rate his health subjectively, a depressed man may whine that his health is bad even when it is quite good, and a happy stoical woman may boast that her health is excellent when in fact it is objectively poor. In public life the severely physical ill John F. Kennedy and Franklin D. Roosevelt offer such examples. Still others were rated objectively *disabled* by their physicians and denied subjective disability not from stoicism and good cheer but by dissociating themselves from reality. The most common ailments of men and women who saw themselves as *disabled* but who were called *not* disabled by study physicians were arthritis and depression. Health is anything but black or white.

The rating for this second dimension of successful aging was subjective and was based on a 15-point scale of self-reported Instrumental Activities of Daily Living (Vaillant, 2002). The scale measured whether at 75 the men believed that they could still carry out most daily tasks as before. Such men reported that they still took part in activities such as tennis singles or downhill skiing or chopping wood. They could climb two flights of stairs without resting, carry their suitcases through airports, and walk two miles with their grandchildren—albeit, they might perform all of these tasks more slowly than in the past. Finally, they could still drive, care for the yard, travel, and shop without assistance.

3. Length of Active Life. A third dimension of successful physical aging was how many years of living the men lost by subjective and/or by objective physical disability or from premature death. By definition none of the Happy-Well had spent any time prior to age 80 disabled—either objectively or subjectively. By way of contrast, prior to age 80, the Prematurely Dead (those men dying between age 50 and 75), had spent an average of 18 years either dead or disabled. Prior to age 80 the Sad-Sick had all spent at least 5 and an average of 9 years irreversibly disabled.

4. Objective Mental Health (range 9 to 23). There is not much fun in living to old age if you are unhappy. So a fourth dimension of successful aging was Objective Mental Health. At age 65 independent raters assessed the Harvard and Inner-City men's objective global mental health with good interrater agreement (Vaillant & Vaillant, 1990). Good objective mental health reflected late midlife success in four areas: work, love, play, and avoiding psychiatric care. A mentally healthy man continued to grow in and to enjoy his career until long after 50. Over the last 15 years, his marriage through his eyes and those of his wife would have been clearly happy. He had played games with friends and taken enjoyable vacations. He neither consulted psychotherapists nor took psychiatric medicines. On average he took less than 5 days of sick leave a year. A low score on any single item was still consistent with excellent mental health, but some men, often those with alcohol abuse or major depression prior to age 50, fared badly in most or all areas and so fell in the bottom quartile (range 15 to 23). By definition none of the Happy-Well and a majority of the Sad-Sick fell in the bottom quarter of mental health.

5. Objective Social Supports (range 2.5 [best] to 14.0 [worst]). Social supports are a crucial dimension of healthy aging. Good social supports were defined as being closely connected with wives, with children, with siblings, with playmates (e.g., bridge and golf), with a religious group, with social networks (e.g., clubs and civic organizations), and with confidantes. Two independent raters made these judgments by reviewing at least 10 questionnaires—including those from wives and children—and usually at least one 2-hour interview (Vaillant et al., 1998). This variable was not available for the Inner-City sample. A score of 10.5 to 14.0 reflected social supports in the worst quartile.

6. Subjective Life Satisfaction (range 10 to 40). The study developed a scale to quantify joy—a subjective life satisfaction scale to measure a sixth dimension of healthy aging: Subjective Life Satisfaction. Nine facets of life were assessed on two consecutive questionnaires. Each item was rated over the last 20 *years* as to how the men regard their marriage): *highly satisfying* (2.0 points), *generally satisfying* (1.5 points), *somewhat satisfying* (1.0 points), *not very satisfying* (0.5 points), *not at all satisfying*, or "does not apply to my life" (0 points). The same question was asked for income-producing work, children, friendships, hobbies, community service activities, religion, recreation, and other. The total score was adding the four underlined items and adding the most satisfying score from the other five. To meet criteria for being among the Happy-Well on the last two biennial questionnaires, a study member needed to regard at least *two* of the five activities selected as *highly satisfying* or have a total score of 7.0 or more.

Sometimes evidence for enjoyment of life was utterly unambiguous. For example, as a means of describing his life, an Inner-City man marked four facets as *highly satisfying*. He marked three additional facets—friendship, social contacts, and recreation/sports—*highly satisfying* with *two* checks. Among the eight facets the only exception was his marriage. Here, rather than check an answer, he wrote, "Hard to answer as I have been divorced a long time, but I have a super relationship with my ex-wife." He then ad-libbed, "I just love being with people and family and helping them when needed as well as traveling and having the health and enough money to be satisfied." Positive psychology happens.

## A RESEARCH DEFINITION OF HEALTHY AGING

Each of the six dimensions of aging was significantly associated with each other—roughly as strongly as height correlates with weight. Of the 237 Harvard men active in the study, 62 men were categorized as Happy-Well. These were men who had experienced objectively *and* subjectively, biologically *and* psychologically good health in all six dimensions. Such Happy-Well men could be defined as follows: Prior to age 80 they spent no years physically disabled—either objectively or subjectively. In addition, compared to their peers in the study, their social supports were in the top three quarters, their mental health was in the top three quarters, and their life satisfaction was in the top two thirds.

Forty of the 237 men were classified as Sad-Sick. These were men who by age 80 had experienced at least 5 years of subjective or objective physical disability. In addition, all of these 40 Sad-Sick men were classified as psychosocially unhappy in at least one of the three psychosocial dimensions: Mental Health, Social Support, or Life Satisfaction.

Sixty of the 237 men died after age 50 and before age 75. They were classified as Prematurely Dead. We often think of death, especially premature death, as an act of God; a tumor striking down the innocent in the flower of youth. (This was one reason that the 12 deaths from the College sample before 50 were excluded: six men were killed in action in World War II and the others in freak accidents or from rare genetic illnesses.) There were other early deaths even more senseless and tragic, but these deaths were the exceptions. By this I mean that prior to death the 60 College men who died prematurely (i.e., after 50 and before age 75) were almost as psychosocially impaired as the surviving Sad-Sick men. Prior to death all but 18 of these 60 men had suffered poor social supports or poor mental health or were dissatisfied with their lives.

I followed the same procedure for categorizing the health of the 332 participating Inner-City men who survived past 50 and for whom the study had complete records. In contrast to the College sample, half of the 44 early (i.e., before age 50) deaths were due to some form of self-neglect. At age 65 to 70 there were 95 Happy-Well, 114 Intermediate, 48 Sad-Sick, and 75 Prematurely Dead by age 65. Although the proportions of Inner-City men in each outcome category were almost identical to those of the Harvard men, it should be noted that the Inner-City men were 10 years younger.

## CLINICAL EXAMPLES

I hope the life stories of Alfred Paine and Richard Luckey, who introduced this chapter, will make my operational definitions of the Happy-Well and the Sad-Sick come alive, so that the concept of positive aging becomes more than mere platitude or value judgment. (Names and identifying details have been altered to protect anonymity.)

The ancestors of Alfred Paine had been successful New England clipper ship captains. All his grandparents had graduated from high school. One grandfather became a merchant banker and the other president of the New York Stock Exchange. His father had graduated from Harvard, and his mother from a fashionable boarding school. From childhood on, however, Paine was the unlucky owner of a handsome trust fund—unlucky because of how he obtained it.

When Alfred Paine was only 2 weeks old, his mother died from the complications of childbirth. When he was only 2 years old, his father died, too. So it was that the orphaned Paine became an heir. As an only child, Paine was bottle-fed by a variety of surrogates and raised by his grandmother and aunt. They were old and did not enjoy the challenge of dealing with an energetic young boy who was also a head-banger. In adolescence, Paine was a lone wolf.

In college, Alfred Paine was often in love. But it appeared to the study staff that, for Paine, being in love meant having someone to care for him. His multiple marriages were all unhappy—in part because of the alcoholism that he maintained that he did not have, and in part because he was frightened of intimacy. At 50, Paine answered "true" to the statement "Sexually most people are animals" and "I would have preferred an asexual marriage." But he did not complain. Thus, of his second marriage he could write, "I have doubts about the real value of marriage . . . the state of my own marriage, which is excellent, has nothing to do with my philosophizing." But his "excellent" marriage soon ended in divorce. Positive psychology must be assessed by what people do, not what they say. In old age, Paine's third wife was protective and loving toward him. In return, he was quite disrespectful and uncaring toward her. Before he died, I had asked how Paine and his wife collaborated, he replied, "We don't. We lead parallel lives."

At 47, Alfred Paine recalled the ages from 1 to 13 as the unhappiest in his life. At age 70 Paine changed his story and believed that the ages from 20 to 30 were the unhappiest. But there had never been a time that Paine was happy. It was only that Paine, as I have suggested, was not a complainer. He had never sought psychotherapy, and none of his doctors ever called him mentally ill. Early on, however, his wife volunteered, "I wish he'd be analyzed not only for our sex life but for his ulcer and to give me someone to talk to."

Subjectively, Paine described his own physical health as excellent; objectively, his health was anything but. In fact, by age 68 he was seriously overweight, was afflicted by hypertension and gout, and suffered from obstructive pulmonary disease—the result of lifelong smoking. On paper, he could sound assertive. For example, in 1947, he favored a preventive war with Russia—"Let's go all out and get it done"—and during the Vietnam War he was in favor of using hydrogen bombs. But his occupational life documented his real-life timidity. "Security was the brightest part of my job," he confided. "I haven't the guts to go out on my own as a man of the world."

When I interviewed Paine at 73, he appeared to me like an old man in a nursing home. Both his kidneys and his liver were failing, and he was cursed with a mild dementia, the result of a drunken automobile accident. He was at least 30 pounds overweight and looked 10 years older than his age. There was no question that he was physically disabled. He was the only College man in the study to have lost all his teeth.

Although he had made a good living in middle management over the years, Paine's handsome trust fund had evaporated, and his pension had eroded through multiple divorces and tax troubles. His house looked as if furnished from yard sales. The only exception was the elegant Cantonese porcelain umbrella stand that stood guard by the front door, in mute testimony to the fact that his New England ancestors had waxed rich in the China clipper trade. Little other than television now absorbed Paine. He rarely left his sofa. At no time in his life had he ever had hobbies or learned to play.

Alone of all the men who returned the age 75 questionnaire, Paine refused to answer the part that dealt with life enjoyment. Thus, his unacknowledged lack of joy in life could be inferred from his behavior. Over the past 20 years, there was no area of his life, other than his religious activities, in which he had expressed satisfaction.

Admittedly, in questionnaires he said nice things about his children, but during the interview when I asked him what he had learned from them, he responded irritably, "Nothing. I hardly see my children. They hardly let me see my grandchildren." Turning to questionnaires from his children, one daughter saw him only every 3 years; one daughter saw him once a year and viewed her father as having "lived an emotionally starved life," and at age 35, Alfred Paine's only son believed that he had never been close to his father.

In terms of social supports, Paine, orphaned at age 2, had no siblings and he was close to no relative. Since the age of 50, he had engaged in no pastimes with friends. When I asked him at 73 to describe his oldest friend, he growled, "I don't have any." He rarely talked to anybody on the telephone. His only confidante was, occasionally, his wife.

Only Paine's religious affiliation was strong. He was proud that he was a committed Episcopalian, and he went on religious retreats, which brought him real satisfaction. Sadly, although these retreats reflected the only social network he possessed, after age 72 he could no longer afford to go on them. Paine could not care for teeth, his money, or his soul.

At age 73, Paine could climb stairs only with difficulty. He had great difficulty walking even 100 yards; he was unable to drive at night, and he had had to give up golf because of his gout. On his last questionnaire, in a shaky hand, Paine, age 75, referred to his general health as "very good" and reported that he had no difficulty in physical activities. Both his wife and his doctor, however, saw him as seriously impaired. The very next year Paine was placed in a nursing home; a year later he died from his multiple illnesses. (For research purposes, Paine was classified with the Sad-Sick rather than with the Prematurely Dead because he survived past his 75th birthday.)

Having followed the easy path and described negative aging, let me describe positive aging. Richard Luckey tells a different story. At 70, when looked at through the eyes of their internists, Richard Luckey's objective physical health had seemed actually worse than Alfred Paine's. Luckey had high blood pressure, atrial fibrillation, a cardiac pacemaker, pancreatitis, and was "status post back surgery." He was even more overweight than Paine. On the basis of all this, the study internist classified the 70-year-old Luckey as disabled. But being ill is very different from feeling sick. Truth is revealed through follow-up.

From age 70 to 80, Paine sickened unto death, while Luckey's health only got better. Luckey not only said his health was excellent, but by age 75 his objective health could no longer be classified by the study internist as disabling. Luckey had completely recovered from his pancreatitis. His "status post back surgery"—which loomed so ominously to the study internist when Luckey was 70—turned out to have been 30 years in the past. Indeed, at age 76 Luckey spent 2 months downhill skiing in Vail. True, he still wore a pacemaker, and, true, his blood pressure remained high. But in his doctor's words—not just his own—"Mr. Luckey continues to enjoy relatively good health . . . he continues to be active physically and also mentally. He is now writing a book on the Civil War." As Luckey himself expressed it, "I have done less chain sawing, but I still split wood."

Another crucial difference between Paine and Luckey was that Luckey had friends with whom he exercised regularly. In addition, he had never smoked, and he used alcohol in moderation. But, of course, as the song suggests, it is easier to "button up your overcoat" and "take good care of yourself" if you belong to someone, and Luckey had always enjoyed social supports. At the risk of oversimplification, Richard Luckey's mother had loved him as a child, and a half century later, "Almost everything we do," he trumpeted, "is family oriented. We have practically no social calendar." His wife amplified, "We rarely go out, but we will have groups for supper such as the church fellowship group or the basketball team for a weekend of skiing, or a vestry meeting at the house." Without a social calendar, Luckey was also commodore of his distinguished West Coast yacht club. Actions speak louder than pencil and paper questionnaires—a fact that future research workers in positive psychology must learn to embrace.

In its efforts to define positive aging, the study asked each man to describe his relative satisfaction over the past 20 years with eight different facets of living. Remember, Alfred Paine had chosen to leave that part of his biennial questionnaire blank. In contrast, Richard Luckey described not only his hobbies, his religion, and his income-producing work as *highly satisfying*, but, more important, he experienced his relationships with his wife and with his children as *highly satisfying*. His wife and children's questionnaires revealed a similar satisfaction with him. Luckey's daughter had described her parents' marriage as "better than my friends"; then, for good measure she had added two pluses. Luckey's wife gave her marriage a 9 out of 9, and, clearly, the marriage had worked even better for her husband. Luckey was close to his brother, with whom he skied regularly in the winter and fished regularly in the summer. He stayed in very close touch with, and took great pleasure from, his children and his grandchildren. His recreational activities included active involvement not only with his brother and children but also with the other sailors of his yacht squadron. Subjectively, Luckey perceived himself with relatively few close friends and would have liked more. Objectively, his friendship network was very rich.

It was so easy for Luckey to take in, to metabolize, any love that he was offered. When he was 60, he wrote in the study about his father, who had died 20 years before, "I have never completely gotten over Dad's death. I will always remember him as the finest man I ever knew."

Wondering how the Luckeys still played together while the Paines led "parallel lives," I asked how his marriage had lasted for 40 years. With Churchillian simplicity, Luckey replied, "I really love Chrissie and she loves me. I really respect her, highly esteem her, and she is a real person." On her recent questionnaire Chrissie wrote the study, "My husband is my best friend; I like looking after him. We have grown closer and fonder every year." There were 50 years of stable marriage to back up their words. In 1970, Luckey and his wife had sailed by themselves from San Francisco to Bali. The trip led to many months of close cooperation and shared physical labor. On the journey Luckey illustrated his sailing journal with his own watercolors.

All during his 15 years, Luckey had loved writing and painting for fun. At 77, he had put on a solo exhibition of his marine watercolors. "With painting," he added dreamily, "you forget everything, and that is why it is so very relaxing." In church, Luckey sang both solo and in the choir. "I don't have a day when I don't have something to do that I want to do . . . creativity is absolutely necessary for someone to be healthy." Ten years before, with no more intelligence than Paine, Luckey, at age 67, told the study that he had "just finished a screen play and sent it to a literary agent." No, it was never performed, and to my knowledge his book on the Civil War is still unpublished. But as Luckey had written to the study at 70, "I am living in the present—enjoying life and good health while it lasts. I think very little about the past or future, and I don't take myself very seriously."

Ten more years of follow-up revealed that Luckey died at 83 of heart disease. As of this writing, 60% of the 40 Happy-Well at 80 are still alive and 12 have reached 93 years of age; 13% of the Sad- Sick are still alive and none have made it to 93.

## THE PREDICTORS OF HEALTHY AGING

To many it seems as if heart attacks and cancer are visitations from malicious fate and that much of the pain of old age seems in the hands of a cruel god—or at least of cruel genes. The whole process of growing old sometimes feels completely out of our control. In addition, there is much data, well represented by the Whitehall II study (Marmot et al., 1991), that emphasizes the importance of social class to successful aging. But blessed with prospectively gathered data, I was astonished that fate was relatively unimportant. Much of a septuagenarian's positive aging or lack of it is determined by factors already established prior to age 50. What seemed even more astonishing was that these factors are more or less controllable.

Ten years ago, a leading gerontologist, Paul Baltes, acknowledged that research had not yet reached a stage where there was good causal evidence for predicting healthy aging (Baltes & Baltes, 1990, p. 18). True, there have been several distinguished 10- to 20-year prospective studies of physical aging (Baltes & Mayer, 1999; Busse & Maddox, 1988; Rowe & Kahn, 1999; Shock, 1984; Thomae, 1987). All have contributed valuable understanding about the course of old age. But none of these studies have followed their subjects for more than 25 years, and few knew what their members were like before 50. In contrast, the Study of Adult Development has illuminated predictors that at 50 could foretell whether a man would be enjoying his 70th or 80th year—or 90th year (Vaillant, 2012). I shall identify these predictors one by one. But first let me note variables that, surprisingly, did not predict successful aging.

## SIX VARIABLES THAT *DID NOT* PREDICT POSITIVE AGING

### ANCESTRAL LONGEVITY

Lacking lifetime studies of humans, scientists have studied aging in fruit flies. You can breed and study many generations of fruit flies in a year, and in the longevity of fruit flies, it appears that genes are very important. Therefore, one of the first variables the study looked at was ancestral longevity. For the Harvard men, ancestral longevity was estimated by computing the age at death of the subjects' parents and their four grandparents. For the Inner-City men, only the longevity of parents could be computed with accuracy. At age 60 the longevity of the ancestors of study members who died young was significantly shorter than the ancestral longevity of those who still survived. But to my surprise, by age 75, the average life spans of the ancestors of the Happy-Well and of the Sad-Sick were identical (see Table 35.2). In a replication study on ninety 75- to 79-year-old women in the Terman study (Vaillant, 2002), ancestral longevity was only weakly correlated with vigorous late life adaptation. The longevity of the Inner-City men's parents contributed not at all to whether they were aging well or poorly at 70. The most likely explanation for the insignificant effect of ancestral longevity is the sheer number of genes involved. Obviously, specific genes are very important in predicting specific illnesses that shorten life; there may be other genes that facilitate longevity. But in a given individual there may be so many good and bad longevity genes that ancestral effects tend to average out.

### CHOLESTEROL

Next, everyone worries about cholesterol, especially in popular magazines. But, of course, these magazines would lose valuable advertising revenues if they chose to worry their readers about really significant risks to health—like smoking and alcohol abuse. It is true that *low-density* cholesterol is harmful, and that for young men or for those who have already had a heart attack, lowering total cholesterol is beneficial.

**Table 35.2**

Correlation of Uncontrollable < Age 50 Predictors With Five Outcomes of Positive Aging 15 to 25 Years Later

| Variables (Range) | Successful Aging<br><br><br>College/<br>Inner-City<br>1–4 | Physical Health | | Mental Health | |
|---|---|---|---|---|---|
| | | Mean # of Years Disabled < 80/<70<br>0–40 | Dead < 75/ Dead < 65<br>0–1 | Subjective Satisfaction College/ Inner-City 10–40 | Objective Mental Health College/ Inner-City 9–25 |
| "Fate" (Ages 10 to 49): | | | | | |
| Ancestral Longevity (40–100) | .15/n.s. | .16/.01 | −.19/−.11 | n.s./n.s. | n.s./n.s. |
| Cholesterol mg./100 ml. | n.s./n.s. | n.s./n.s. | n.s./n.s. | n.s./n.s. | n.s./n.s. |
| Parental Social Class (1–5) | n.s./n.s. | n.s./n.s. | n.s./n.s. | n.s./n.s. | n.s./n.s. |
| Warm Childhood Environment (5–25) | .18/n.s. | n.s./n.s. | n.s./n.s. | n.s./n.s. | .19/.14 |
| Stable Childhood Temperament (1–5) | n.s./n.s. | n.s./n.s. | n.s./n.s. | n.s./.18 | n.s./.20 |

For all dependent and independent variables a low score is healthy, with the exception of ancestral longevity. All values and variables (if different) for the two samples are presented as College/Core-City. $n = 237$ (College sample); $n = 332$ (Core-City sample); n.s. = not significant, otherwise all correlations $p < .05$, but $p > .01$
Spearman rho (two-tailed) used throughout

It was equally true, however, that total cholesterol levels at age 50 did not distinguish the Happy-Well from the Sad-Sick or even from the Prematurely Dead (see Table 35.2). This finding has been confirmed by much larger, more representative studies (Krumholz et al., 1994).

PARENTAL SOCIAL CLASS

Interest in the importance of social class and mental health has been fostered by many studies showing the strong cross-sectional association between job prestige and social class with physical health. But in our prospective study, parental social class was unassociated with late-life physical health. For example, at age 47, the social class of the Inner-City men (I = upper class, V = underclass; Hollingshead & Redlich, 1958) was powerfully associated with physical heath at age 70. Forty percent of the men in Classes I to III were still not dead or disabled, and 37% fell in the Happy-Well category. In contrast, only 9% of the men in Class V were not disabled and only 3% were among the Happy-Well. But the relationship was not causal. Rather both poor social class and poor health were a function of alcohol abuse, mental illness, and poor education. However, there was no significant correlation between *parental* social class of the men at 14 and their health at 70 (see Table 35.2).

WARM CHILDHOOD ENVIRONMENT

Surprisingly, by age 70, stability of parental marriage, parental death in childhood, family cohesion, and warm childhood environment—variables important to health in young adulthood—were no longer predictive of outcome (see Table 35.2).

This was true for both the Harvard and Inner-City study cohorts. For both cohorts, two research assistants, blinded to all subsequent data, rated five facets of the men's childhood environmental strengths (global impression, family cohesion, and relations with mother, father, and siblings) on a scale from 1 to 5 (range: 5 = *warmest environment*, 25 = *bleakest environment*; Vaillant, 1974, 1995).

## STABLE CHILDHOOD TEMPERAMENT

Likewise, stable childhood temperament (rated by parental report of childhood temperament: 1 = *easy baby and toddler*; 3 = *minor problems*; 5 = *phobias, shyness, tantrums, enuresis*; Vaillant, 1974, 1995) was unrelated to physical and mental health and successful aging in the Harvard men. However, it did show a small association with mental health alone in the Inner-City men (see Table 35.2).

## STRESS

Stress did not appear to be an important predictor. Many believe that stress or multiple physical symptoms secondary to stress are detrimental to health. For the psychologically minded, an attractive contrarian hypothesis is that men who hold stress in age poorly. Neither of these hypotheses was supported by the study data. The number of physical symptoms under stress before age 50 did not correlate with physical health at age 75. The number of illnesses, thought by some to be psychosomatic, such as ulcers, asthma, and colitis, that the men had endured between 20 and 65 did not affect physical health at age 75. The number of serious negative life events before 65 did not predict physical health at 75 (Cui & Vaillant, 1996). Over the short term, stress can, of course, seriously affect health, but over the long term how one deals with stress seems more important.

## SEVEN FACTORS THAT *DID* PREDICT POSITIVE AGING

Table 35.3 illustrates the factors that did predict positive aging. Five factors assessed prior to age 50 did predict healthy aging for both cohorts. A sixth protective factor, education, was important to aging well for the Inner City men but was not really applicable to the College cohort whose education was too homogeneous to be a differential predictor. A seventh independent predictor, exercise, was available for the College men but not for the Inner City men. The univariate importance of these predictors is illustrated in Table 35.3, and each variable was important to positive aging when the others were controlled (Vaillant, 2002).

## NOT BEING A SMOKER OR STOPPING SMOKING YOUNG

Smoking was calculated in pack-years (packs/day × years smoking) by age 50. In both male cohorts, not being a heavy smoker before the age of 50 was the most important single predictive factor of healthy physical aging. Among the College men, heavy smoking (more than a pack a day for 30 years) was 10 times more frequent among the Prematurely Dead than among the Happy-Well. Yet if a man had stopped smoking by about age 45, the effects of smoking (as much as one pack a day for 20 years) could no longer be discerned at 70 or 80.

## ADAPTIVE COPING STYLE (MATURE DEFENSES)

The second most powerful predictor of being among the Happy-Well was an adaptive involuntary coping style. Independent raters—blinded to the men's current physical

**Table 35.3**

Correlation of Relatively Controllable < Age 50 Predictors With Five Outcomes of Positive Aging 15 to 25 Years Later

| | Successful Aging | Physical Health | | Mental Health | |
| --- | --- | --- | --- | --- | --- |
| | College/ Inner-City 1–4 | Length of Active Life Years Disabled < 80 0–40 | Dead < 75/ Dead < 65 0–1 | Subjective Satisfaction College/ Inner-City 10–40 | Objective Mental Health College/ Inner-City 9–25 |
| **Self-Care Predictors** (Range) | | | | | |
| Pack-Years of Smoking (0–90) | **.35/.31** | −.30/−.31 | .30/.23 | n.s./n.s. | .26/.14 |
| Maturity of Defenses (1–9) | **.32/.23** | −.27/−.17 | n.s./n.s. | **.34/.28** | **.41/.46** |
| Alcohol Abuse (*DSM-III*) (1–3) | **.42/.19** | −.38/−.18 | .40/.15 | .21/n.s. | .32/.21 |
| Healthy Weight (1–2) | .14/.11 | −.14/n.s. | n.s./n.s. | n.s./n.s. | n.s./n.s. |
| Exercise (1–2) Education (6–19) | **.22/.20** | −.18/−.20 | n.s./n.s. | n.s./n.s. | **.24/.25** |
| Stable Marriage (1–2) | **.27/.22** | −.15/−.13 | n.s./.17 | **.33/.27** | **.39/.33** |

For all dependent and independent variables a low score is healthy. All values and variables (if different) for the two samples are presented as College/Inner-City.
$n = 237$ (College sample); $n = 332$ (Inner-City sample); n.s. = not significant, unbold correlations $p < .05$, bold correlations $p < .001$
Spearman rho (two-tailed) used throughout

health and, of course, ignorant of their future—had reviewed each individual's entire record to rate his defenses. An adaptive coping style is referred to as the use of *mature defenses*. For each man, the mean maturity of defensive behaviors, largely identified from the age of 47 (S.D. 2 years) interview, were scored on a 9-point scale consistent with the *DSM-IV* Defensive Functioning Scale (American Psychiatric Association, 1994) 1 = *most adaptive*, 9 = *most maladaptive*. In everyday life, the term *mature defenses* refers to our capacity to turn lemons into lemonade and not to turn molehills into mountains. Analogous to immune and clotting mechanisms, the choice of defense mechanisms is relatively involuntary. The term *mature* refers to the fact that when adults are followed over 60 years (Vaillant 1977; Vaillant & Mukamal, 2001), immature all-about-me coping styles of passive aggression, dissociation, projection, fantasy, and acting out decline, and the mature all-about-the-other coping styles of altruism, sublimation, suppression (stoicism), and humor increase. In both samples, mature defenses were common among the Happy-Well and virtually absent among the Sad-Sick. This strong association was because mature defenses at 50 predicted mental health in older age. Mature defenses did *not* predict the men's future objective physical health, but mature defenses often did keep objectively disabled men from feeling subjectively disabled.

ABSENCE OF ALCOHOL ABUSE

*DSM-III* criteria (American Psychiatric Association, 1980) were used to assess alcohol abuse (1 = *no abuse*; 2 = *alcohol abuse*, 3 = *alcohol dependence*). Absence of alcohol abuse was the only protective factor in this study that powerfully predicted both psychosocial and physical health. Alcohol abuse was defined as the evidence of multiple alcohol-related problems (with spouse, family, employer, law, and health). Until now, most major longitudinal studies of health, for example, the Framingham Study (Dawber, 1980) in Massachusetts and the Marmot et al. (1991) Whitehall English studies, have only controlled for reported alcohol *consumption*, not abuse. Unfortunately, reported alcohol consumption reflects alcohol abuse (loss of voluntary control and/or adverse consequences from alcohol abuse) almost as poorly as reported food consumption reflects obesity. Neither reported alcohol or calorie consumption is a useful predictor of poor aging, while obesity and symptomatic alcohol abuse are.

Prospective study reveals that alcohol abuse is a *cause*—not a result—of increased life stress (Cui & Vaillant, 1996), of depression (Vaillant, 1995), of divorce (Vaillant, 2012), and of downward social mobility. In addition, alcohol abuse causes death for many reasons other than liver cirrhosis and motor vehicle accidents. Alcohol abuse causes suicide, homicide, cancer, heart disease, and a depressed immune system. Indeed, alcohol abuse was almost as bad for health in nonsmokers as heavy smoking was bad for health among social drinkers (Vaillant, Schnurr, Baron, & Gerber, 1991).

## Healthy Weight

Healthy weight was measured by the body mass index (BMI) ($kg/m^2$): At age 50 men with a BMI > 28 (overweight) or a BMI < 22 (underweight) = 2; men with BMI < 29 and > 21 (healthy weight) = 1.

## Stable Marriage

Stable marriage was defined as married without divorce, separation, or serious problems until age 50 =1; otherwise = 2.

## Exercise

Exercise (recorded for College men only) was defined as exercise that burned more than 500 kilocalories/week was classified as regular exercise (Schnurr, Vaillant, & Vaillant, 1990). Less than 500 kilocalories of exercise a week was recorded as exercise absent.

## Years of Education

Years of education was a continuous variable from 6 to 19. Because the range of education for the College men was truncated, education was used as a predictor for Inner-City men only. For the Inner-City men, years of education were an important protective variable. Although length of education is often viewed as merely a manifestation of social class and intelligence, its association with healthy aging depended upon neither of these factors. The components of education that appeared to correlate with physical health in old age were self-care, future orientation, and perseverance—not IQ and paternal income. The effect of education upon health was indirect. The more education the Inner-City men obtained, the more likely they were to stop smoking, eat sensibly, and use alcohol in moderation. Thus, a major reason that the health of the Inner-City men declined so much more rapidly than the College men was that the Inner-City men were not only much less educated, but they led far less healthy lifestyles. The Inner-City men were almost twice as likely as the Harvard

**Table 35.4**

The Relation of Health at Age 70 to Years of Education

| Health | Education of Inner-City Men | | Education of College Men | |
|---|---|---|---|---|
| | < 16 yr *n* = 302 | 16 yr[a] *n* = 26[b] | 16 yr *n* = 78[c] | 17+ yr *n* = 156 |
| Excellent | 0% | **0%** | **8%** | 12% |
| Good | 7% | **23%** | **30%** | 30% |
| Chronic Illness | 20% | **42%** | **24%** | 35% |
| Disabled | 22% | **12%** | **11%** | 8% |
| Dead | 51% | **23%** | **27%** | 16% |

[a]Three men attended graduate school.
[b]Four men did not yet have health rated at age 70.
[c]Three men were excluded as they did not graduate.
*Note.* Bold numbers allow the reader to contrast the Inner-City Men and College Men with equal educations.

**Table 35.5**

Contrast of the "Social Class" of College Men and Inner-City Men With 16 Years of Education

| | Inner-City Men | College Men |
|---|---|---|
| | *n* = 30 | *n* = 78 |
| I.Q. | 104 ± 11 | 133 ± 12 |
| Height | 69.6 2.3 | 70.8 ± 2.4 |
| Parental Social Class I or II | 0% | 68% |
| Income at Age 47 | 27K ± 15 K | 63 K ± 57K |
| Social Class at Age 47 | 20% | 37% |

men to abuse alcohol and cigarettes, and they were more than 3 times as likely to be overweight. In Table 35.4 the contrast in physical health between the Inner-City men who did not attend college and the College men who attended graduate school is dramatic.

Let me add a crucial piece of evidence that supports the fact that education predicts positive aging for reasons independent of parental social class and intelligence. True, the physical health of the 70-year-old Inner-City men was as poor as that of the Harvard men at 80. But remarkably, the health of the *college-educated* Inner-City men at 70 was as good as that of the Harvard men at 70 (see Table 35.4). This was in spite of the fact that their childhood social class, their tested IQ, their income at age 47, and the prestige of their colleges and jobs were markedly inferior to those of the Harvard men (see Table 35.5). Parity of education alone was enough to produce parity in physical health.

## CONCLUSION

The protective factors in Table 35.3—a stable marriage, the ability to make lemonade from lemons, avoiding cigarettes, modest use of alcohol, regular exercise, persevering with education, and maintaining normal weight—allow us to predict positive health *30 years* in the future.

Sixty-six College men—still in good health at age 50—possessed less than four protective factors. At age 80, not one—not a single one—of these men was among the Happy-Well; and 21, or almost a third, were among the Sad-Sick and 3 times as many as expected were dead. All seven men who, like Alfred Paine, had less than two protective factors at age 50 were dead by age 80. In contrast, 44 College men had all six factors present; 25 were among the Happy-Well, and only one was among the Sad-Sick.

Although the average Inner-City man at age 50 tended to have fewer protective factors than the Harvard men, the power of these protective factors was the same. For example, there were 52 Inner-City men who at age 50 enjoyed both good health and five or more protective factors. Twenty years later, only 2% of such men were among the Sad-Sick or Prematurely Dead, and 33 were among the Happy-Well. There were 37 Inner-City men who were not disabled at age 50 but who possessed less than two protective factors. At 70, 25 were among the Sad-Sick or Prematurely Dead and only three were among the Happy-Well. In other words, positive aging to an extraordinary degree is controllable and thus teachable by positive psychology.

Of course, there are exceptions. Some people are struck by lightning; others are crippled by someone else's stupidity or die from malignant genes. But the vast majority—at least in these two White male cohorts—of septuagenarians are products of their own, often involuntary, behavior.

The good news, however, is that most of us—if we start young and try hard—can voluntarily control our weight, our exercise, and our abuse of cigarettes, at least by the time we are 50. And with hard work and with the help of able intervention, we can improve our relationships with our most significant other, achieve abstinence from alcohol, and use fewer maladaptive defenses. Indeed, the fellowship of Alcoholics Anonymous offers a valuable object lesson to positive psychology. I do not wish to blame the victim, but I do wish to accentuate the positive. Whether we live to a vigorous old age lies not so much in our stars or in our genes as in ourselves.

## SUMMARY POINTS

- The mission of positive aging is to add more life to years, not just more years to life.
- The Study of Adult Development is unique because it has followed a sample of men over a 70-year period in order to determine the predictors of positive aging.
- Results show that much of a septuagenarian's positive aging or lack of it is determined by controllable factors established before the age of 50.
- Six factors that do not predict positive aging are ancestral longevity, cholesterol, parental social class, warm childhood environment, stable childhood temperament, and stress.
- Seven factors that do predict positive aging are not being a smoker (or stopping smoking young), adaptive coping style, absence of alcohol abuse, healthy weight, stable marriage, exercise, and more years of education.

## REFERENCES

American Psychiatric Association. (1980). *Diagnostic and statistical manual of mental disorders* (3rd ed.). Washington, DC: Author.

American Psychiatric Association. (1994). *Diagnostic and statistical manual of mental disorders* (4th ed). Washington, DC: Author.

Baltes, P. B., & Baltes, M. M. (1990). *Successful aging*. Cambridge, England: Cambridge University Press.

Baltes, P. B., & Mayer, K. V. (Eds.). (1999). *The Berlin Aging Study*. Cambridge, England: Cambridge University Press.

Bortz, W. M., Wallace, D. H., & Wiley, D. (1999). Sexual function in 1,202 aging males: Differentiating aspects. *Journal of Gerontology: Medical Sciences, 54A*, M237–M241.

Busse, E. W., & Maddox, G. L. (1988). *The Duke Longitudinal Studies of Normal Aging: 1955–1980.* New York, NY: Springer.

Cui, X. J., & Vaillant, G. E. (1996). Antecedents and consequences of negative life events in adulthood: A longitudinal study. *American Journal of Psychiatry, 152*, 21–26.

Dawber, T. R. (1980). *The Framingham Study.* Cambridge, MA: Harvard University Press.

de Beauvoir, S. (1972). *The coming of age.* New York, NY: G. P. Putnam.

Fries, J. F. (1980). Aging: Natural death and the compression of morbidity. *New England Journal of Medicine, 303*, 130–135.

Glueck, S., & Glueck, E. (1950). *Unraveling juvenile delinquency.* New York, NY: Commonwealth Fund.

Glueck, S., & Glueck, E. (1968). *Delinquents and nondelinquents in perspective.* Cambridge, MA: Harvard University Press.

Heimpel, H. (1981). Schlusswort. In Max Planck Institut für Geschicte (Ed.), *Hermann Heimpel zum 80 Geburtstag* (pp. 1–20). Göttingen, Germany: Hubert.

Hollingshead, A. B., & Redlich, F. C. (1958). *Social class and mental illness.* New York, NY: Wiley.

Krumholz, H. M., Seeman, T. E., Merrill, S. S., Mendes de Leon, C. F., Vaccarino, V., Silverman, D. I., . . . Berkman, L. F. (1994). Lack of association between cholesterol and coronary heart disease mortality and morbidity and all-cause mortality in persons older than 70 years. *Journal of the American Medical Association, 272*, 1335.

Marmot, M. G., Smith, G. D., Stansfeld, S., Patel, C., North, F., Head, J., . . . Feeney, A. (1991). Health inequalities among British civil servants: The Whitehall II study. *Lancet, 337*, 1387–1393.

Rowe, J. W., & Kahn, R. L. (1999). *Successful aging.* New York, NY: Dell.

Schnurr, P. P., Vaillant, C. O., & Vaillant, G. E. (1990). Predicting exercise in late midlife from young adult personality characteristics. *International Journal Aging and Human Development, 30*, 153–161.

Shock, N. (1984). *Normal human aging.* Washington, DC: U.S. Government Printing Office.

Thomae, H. (1987). Conceptualizations of responses to stress. *European Journal of Personality, 1*, 171–191.

Vaillant, G. E. (1974). The natural history of male psychological health: II. Some antecedents of healthy adult adjustment. *Archives of General Psychiatry, 31*, 15–22.

Vaillant, G. E. (1977). *Adaptation to life.* Boston, MA: Little, Brown.

Vaillant, G. E. (1979). Natural history of male psychological health: Effects of mental health on physical health. *New England Journal of Medicine, 301*, 1249–1254.

Vaillant, G. E. (1995). *Natural history of alcoholism revisited.* Cambridge, MA: Harvard University Press.

Vaillant, G. E. (2002). *Aging well.* New York, NY: Little Brown.

Vaillant, G. E. (2012). *Triumphs of experience: The men of the Harvard Grant Study.* Cambridge, MA: Harvard University Press.

Vaillant, G. E., Meyer, S. E., Mukamal, K., & Soldz, S. (1998). Are social supports in late midlife a cause or a result of successful physical aging? *Psychological Medicine, 28*, 1159–1168.

Vaillant, G. E., & Mukamal, K. (2001). Positive aging in two male cohorts. *American Journal of Psychiatry, 158*, 839–847.

Vaillant, G. E., Schnurr, P. P., Baron, J. A., & Gerber, P. D. (1991). A prospective study of the effects of cigarette smoking and alcohol abuse on mortality. *Journal of General Internal Medicine, 6*, 299–304.

Vaillant, G. E., & Vaillant, C. O. (1990). Natural history of male psychological health: XII. A 45-year study of successful aging at age 65. *American Journal of Psychiatry, 147*, 31–37.

World Health Organization (1952). Constitution of the World Health Organization. In *World Health Organization Handbook of Basic Documents* (5th ed.). Geneva, Switzerland: Palais des Nations.

# PART IX

# BUILDING COMMUNITY THROUGH INTEGRATION AND REGENERATION

CHAPTER 36

# Psychological and Relational Resources in the Experience of Disability and Caregiving

ANTONELLA DELLE FAVE, ANDREA FIANCO, and RAFFAELA D. G. SARTORI

PHARMACOLOGICAL AND TECHNOLOGICAL advancements in the medical field and growing resource investment in social services have substantially increased life expectancy in most countries. However, one of the consequences of these changes is the so-called epidemiological paradox: The number of years that people spend living with chronic diseases and mental disorders dramatically increased as well (Keyes, 2007).

The implications for researchers and practitioners in the health domain are manifold. In particular, there is growing empirical evidence of the fact that physical health and daily life functioning are different concepts, and that subjective outlooks, beliefs, and evaluations substantially influence individual health and quality of life. The necessity of guaranteeing an adequate quality of life to people with permanent disabilities and chronic diseases and their families has become a priority for governments and institutions. At the same time, intervention programs have to take into account the subjective dimensions of well-being and health.

This chapter aims at illustrating some of the main theoretical and empirical contributions to the study and promotion of well-being among people with disabilities and their caregivers, within the bio-psycho-social perspective endorsed by the World Health Organization. The psychological and interpersonal resources that allow individuals and families to successfully cope with health challenges will be briefly outlined, and empirical evidence derived from qualitative studies will be provided.

These issues were already addressed in a chapter included in the previous edition of this book (Delle Fave & Massimini, 2004). However, it explicitly focused on the investigation of the individual resources perceived by people with sensorial and motor disabilities, which were analyzed within the specific conceptual framework of optimal experience and psychological selection. The present chapter aims at broadening and updating this perspective. It provides an overview of the most

*Authors' Note.* We are grateful to IRCCS Fondazione Don Carlo Gnocchi, Fondazione Telecom Italia, and the Italian Ministries of Health and of Education for the financial support to this work.

recent theoretical approaches and empirical works investigating the resources that people with chronic diseases, as well as their caregivers, identify in daily life. Two of these approaches—optimal experience and resilience—will be specifically explored through the illustration of findings derived from both people with chronic diseases and caregivers. Moreover, attention will be paid not only to the individual resources, but also to the assets and facilitators perceived within the family and the social context.

## THEORETICAL FRAMEWORK

In the past few decades the complex relationship between disease, well-being, and quality of life has obtained increasing attention within the biomedical and social domains. In particular, there is growing consensus among researchers and practitioners about considering quality of life as a subjective concept, involving perceived opportunities for action and skill development in the daily environment, social relations, values, personality features, and the pursuit of goals that are not necessarily dependent on physical functioning (Fitzpatrick, 2000; Skevington & McCrate, 2011; Veenhoven, 2002). Objective indicators, and in particular physical health conditions, only partially influence this evaluation.

### A Shift in Focus: From Disease to Person, from Deficits to Resources

The investigation of subjective indicators of quality of life shed light on the only apparently paradoxical evidence of the positive consequences of illness (Sodergren & Hyland, 2000). Disease can be experienced as a problem, but also as a challenge and an opportunity for action and personal growth. In line with the definition of health and functioning provided by the World Health Organization (WHO, 1946) and the bio-psycho-social model (Engel, 1977), several studies were conducted with the aim of identifying and quantifying subjective indicators of well-being. In particular, the emergence of the field of positive psychology shed light on the importance of detecting and implementing individuals' functions and abilities, instead of focusing on deficits and limitations only.

This shift from a biomedical and problem-focused view of disease to a bio-psycho-social and resource-based approach is reflected in the International Classification of Functioning, Disability and Health (ICF; WHO, 2001, 2007). ICF is the official system of classification developed by WHO in order to observe and evaluate the level of functioning, health, and quality of life of human beings. By virtue of its comprehensive structure, it can be used to assess the bio-psycho-social functioning of any individual, including persons with diseases and disabilities of different severity. In the ICF, each dimension of functioning is conceptualized as a dynamic interaction between individual features and the social and physical environment. This classification takes into account three major aspects of individual functioning: body functions, activities, and participation. It also aims at evaluating the role of contextual barriers and facilitators, represented by personal and environ-mental features that can promote or hinder functioning. The interaction between all these components contributes to define the overall health condition of the individual. This multidimensional approach calls for a closer collaboration and integration of knowledge among helping professionals, based on the assumption that biological, psychological, social, educational, and cultural aspects play a specific role in the promotion of the person's functioning. From this perspective, interventions to promote health and well-being—especially in suboptimal health conditions—cannot be confined to medical treatments, but should comprise the removal or reduction of barriers and the promotion of facilitators at multiple levels. Furthermore, by virtue of its assessment of the positive components of functioning, ICF represents an opportunity for health professionals to pay attention not merely to problems, deficits, and barriers, but also to personal and environmental resources that may enhance the individuals' level of bio-psycho-social health and functioning, as well as their social inclusion and participation.

Several factors influence the outcomes of disease and disablement. As suggested in the ICF model, both environmental and personal features can mediate the impact of health conditions on the quality of life (Dixon, Johnston, Rowley, & Pollard, 2008; Schopp et al., 2007; Seekins, Traci, Cummings, Oreskovich, & Reveslot, 2008). At the environmental level, attitudes and behavior of caregivers and family members play a primary role, together with interpersonal, educational, and organizational facilitators and barriers (Bodde & Seo, 2009). At the personal level, studies have highlighted the mediating function of psychological resources and coping style (Bauer, Koepke, Sterzinger, & Spiessl, 2012).

## Psychological and Relational Resources

Any intervention program in the health domain should aim at promoting the best attainable physical, psychological, and social well-being. As concerns the psychological realm, the identification of positive experiences under stressful circumstances can represent a good starting point to transform negative emotions and to support development and psychological adjustment (Folkman & Moskowitz, 2000). The theoretical and empirical contributions provided by positive psychology offer a useful perspective to identify individual psychological resources and to contextualize them in broader conceptualizations of well-being, such as Keyes' (2002, 2007) model of mental health as a continuum between the two poles of flourishing and languishing, and the articulation of well-being into hedonic and eudaimonic dimensions (Ryan & Deci, 2001).

This section will provide a brief overview of the main psychological resources that have been identified and investigated among people with chronic diseases or disabilities and their caregivers. In particular, from the ICF perspective family and caregivers represent important environmental resources and facilitators for persons with disabilities and chronic disease. For this reason, caregivers' psychological resources and quality of life must be explored and supported in intervention programs. However, little information is available on this topic, due to the prominent emphasis of researchers on caregiver burden, defined as a multidimensional response to the negative appraisal and perceived stress resulting from taking care of an ill person. Caregivers frequently suffer from depression, exhibit maladaptive coping strategies, report more physical and psychological symptoms, and use more frequently medications and health-care services than comparable non-caregivers (Molyneux, McCarthy, McEniff, Cryan, & Conroy, 2008; Serrano-Aguilar, Lopez-Bastida, & Yanes-Lopez, 2006). Some studies suggest that moderate to severe disability is related to high caregiver burden (Conde-Sala, Garre-Olmo, Turro-Garriga, Vilalta-Franch, & Lopez-Pousa, 2010; Rinaldi et al., 2005). However, a positive perspective may shed light on how caregivers can successfully cope with daily care activities and on which resources they can rely (Sussman & Regehr, 2009). Positive psychology offers many constructs that can allow researchers and practitioners to consider the caregiving role from a constructive perspective, highlighting protective factors through which caregivers' well-being can be supported and enhanced. A recent and unique contribution in this domain is represented by the development of the Adult Carers Quality of Life Questionnaire (AC-QoL; Joseph, Becker, Elwick, & Silburn, 2012), which quantifies both the negative and the positive aspects of caregiving. The latter comprise individual as well as contextual dimensions, such as environmental mastery, personal growth, sense of value, satisfaction, social support, and financial resources.

*Self-Efficacy*   Self-efficacy is defined as the level of competence individuals perceive in facing a specific situation (Bandura, 2004). It is based on individuals' perceived level of competence in pursuing and achieving goals in specific life domains, as well as on the perception of internal locus of control. Individuals with high self-efficacy beliefs actively face negative events, since they perceive themselves as directly responsible for these events' outcomes. For example, studies conducted among people with cardiovascular diseases showed that high self-efficacy predicted high adherence to rehabilitation treatment, functional recovery, low anxiety and depression, and low probability of being readmitted to the hospital (Arnold, Ranchor, Koëter, De Jongste, & Sanderman, 2005; Sarkar, Ali, & Whooley, 2009). Rutterford and Wood (2006) found that self-efficacy contributed to the perception of a good quality of life 10 years after brain injury.

As for caregivers, self-efficacy positively influences performance, feeling of accomplishment, and search for challenging and novel experiences. Self-efficacious caregivers of people with physical and mental disabilities more often identified positive aspects in caregiving, and managed negative emotions more effectively (Carbonneau, Caron, & Desrosiers, 2010; Semiatin & Connor, 2012). Sharing enriching events and experiences with their ill relatives reduced the negative aspects and reinforced the positive aspects of caring (Hellstrom, Nolan, & Lundh, 2007; Hwang, Rivas, Fremming, Rivas, & Crane, 2009).

*Positive Emotions*   Emotions remarkably influence selection, memorization, and cognitive evaluation of the information, driving the perception of risk, control, perceived well-being, and expectancies on the success or failure in daily situations. Positive emotions facilitate adequate risk perception (Isen & Geva, 1987), mobilize cognitive and motivational resources (Aspinwall & Brunhart, 1996), and promote adaptive coping strategies (Lazarus & Folkman, 1984) and prosocial behaviors (Isen, 1987). Fredrickson (2001) synthesized the role of positive emotions in promoting well-being and development in the broaden-and-build theory: In problem-solving situations, positive emotions expand the cognitive and behavior repertoire available to the individual (broadening). This cognitive broadening fosters the development of stable resources in the long run (building). An extensive study conducted among women with moderate to severe disabilities showed that emotional vitality—defined as a condition of high sense of personal mastery, happiness, and low depressive symptoms and anxiety—was associated with a significant decrease of the risk of incidents in performing daily activities, and with a lower risk of mortality (Pennix et al., 2001).

The influence of positive and negative emotions on caregivers' well-being was also investigated (Robertson, Zarit, Duncan, Rovine, & Femia, 2007). Four possible emotion patterns were identified: high positive and low negative affect (well-adjusted), low positive and negative affect (ambiguous), high positive and negative affect (intense), high negative and low positive affect (distressed). Well-adjusted caregivers showed the highest levels of physical health, compared with participants characterized by other emotional patterns. They also reported higher sense of competence and fewer behavior problems, showing the ability to access positive emotions and use them to adaptively cope with stressful experiences.

*Sense of Coherence*   Sense of coherence (SOC) represents a general orientation toward reality, based on the assumption that life events and situations—including the negative ones—are ultimately meaningful, comprehensible and manageable. People reporting high levels of SOC are able to find and bring order and organization in apparently ambiguous and disruptive situations (Antonovsky, 1987; see also Sagy, Eriksson, & Braun-Lewensohn, Chapter 5, this volume). Among people with disabilities, SOC was found to be strongly associated with life satisfaction (Jacobson, Westerberg, Malec, & Lexell, 2011). As for caregivers, the relation between SOC, depressive symptoms and burnout were investigated. Positive correlations were detected between high levels of stress, poor health, low SOC, and higher risk of burn-out (Oelofsen & Richardson, 2006). Research also linked caregivers' SOC with physical and psychological well-being and the use of adaptive coping strategies (Ekwall, Sivberg, & Hallberg, 2007).

*Posttraumatic Growth*   Ill people frequently report improvements in interpersonal relationships, positive personality changes, life reappraisal, and restructuring (Soder-gren & Hyland, 2000). Identifying positive consequences in disease influences health and well-being in the long term through two major processes: benefit finding (King & Miner, 2000; Tennen & Affleck, 2002) and posttraumatic growth (Joseph & Linley, 2005; Tedeschi & Calhoun, 1996). Studies conducted among people with cancer (Morris & Shakespeare-Finch, 2011; Scrignaro, Barni, & Magrin, 2009), spinal cord injuries (Pollard & Kennedy, 2007), and traumatic brain injuries (Powell, Ekin-Wood, & Collin, 2012) emphasized the positive relation between posttraumatic growth and a sense of personal meaning, life satisfaction, and social support.

Analogously, among caregivers positive relations were detected between post-traumatic growth and humor, support and spirituality (Cadell, 2007). Posttraumatic growth was positively related with life satisfaction, social support, emotional pro-cessing strategies, and problem-focused coping strategies (Mosher, Danoff-Burg, & Brunker, 2006).

*Optimal Experience*   Several studies showed that the quality of subjective experience undergoes changes in relation to the levels of perceived environmental challenges and personal skills (Massimini & Delle Fave, 2000). These changes correspond to well-defined experiential states among which a peculiarly structured and positive condition was identified: *optimal experience* or *flow* (Csikszentmihalyi, 1975/2000; Delle Fave, Massimini, & Bassi, 2011). Flow is characterized by high concentration, involvement, control of the situation, and clear goals. Its core feature is the per-ception of high environmental challenges balanced with adequate personal skills. The activities associated with optimal experience tend to be selectively replicated and cultivated in the long run, promoting the refinement of related skills and competences and shaping the lifelong process of individual psychological selection (Csikszentmihalyi & Massimini, 1985).

Optimal experience in daily life was constantly identified among people with congenital and acquired disabilities such as blindness, spinal cord injuries, dwarfism, and psychosis (Bassi, Ferrario, Ba, Delle Fave, & Viganò, 2012; Cortinovis, Luraschi, Intini, Sessa, & Delle Fave, 2011; Delle Fave, 2010; Delle Fave & Massimini, 2004, 2005a, 2005b). Physical conditions however influenced the kind of activities individu-als engaged in: For example, blind people primarily reported media-related activities and manual tasks. However, overall participants associated optimal experience with complex and demanding activities in the domains of work and leisure, and to a smaller extent family relations. Moreover, even though acquired disabilities often prevented individuals from practicing activities previously associated with optimal experience, most participants succeeded in identifying new opportunities for optimal experience, showing the ability to flexibly adapt to the new condition, and to pursue developmental goals in spite of biological limitations.

*Resilience*    Resilience is the ability to withstand and rebound from disruptive life challenges. It involves dynamic processes fostering positive adaptation within the context of significant adversity (Bonanno, 2004; Luthar, 2006), allowing the individual to mobilize psychological and social resources along a positive growth pathway.

While earlier studies focused on the individual aspects of resilience, researchers presently consider resilience as the outcome of the dynamic interplay of multiple risk factors and protective processes over time that can be identified within the individual, as well as at the interpersonal, social, and cultural levels (Garmezy & Masten, 1991; Rutter, 1987; Zautra, Stuart Hall, & Murray, 2012). Biological, psychological, and social resources are therefore involved in the resilience process. Particularly interesting to the purpose of this chapter is the contribution of Froma Walsh (2003, 2006, 2011), who formalized the concept of family resilience, considering family as a functional unit. From such a systemic perspective, resilience is one of the key processes that mediate the adaptation of all family members and their relationships (Mackay, 2003; Patterson, 2002; Simon, Murphy, & Smith, 2008). Inverting the deficit-based perspective, life adversities can become potential opportunities for redefining the meaning and quality of relationships within the family. Furthermore, since the family is not isolated from the context, environmental resources and risk factors at the community and culture levels interact with the family resilience pattern in influencing the final outcome of a problematic condition. The systemic conceptualization of resilience was also successfully adopted in studies investigating caregivers' resource mobilization and management strategies (Gerstein, Crnic, Blacher, & Baker, 2009).

## IN THEIR OWN VOICE: CHALLENGES AND RESOURCES OF CARETAKERS AND CAREGIVERS

In order to more directly investigate challenges and resources perceived by people with disabilities and their caregivers, in the following pages we will illustrate qualitative findings derived from two different studies. The first one was conducted among people with hereditary spastic paraparesis (HSP) and their caregivers. The second study involved parents of children with intellectual disabilities.

### LIVING WITH HSP: DAILY EXPERIENCES AND FUTURE EXPECTATIONS

HSP is a rare genetic neurodegenerative disease that includes a variety of clinically similar disorders. The clinical classification distinguishes between pure and complicated forms. The former are characterized by progressive weakness and increased muscle tone in the lower limbs (Fink, 2003; Fink, Heiman-Patterson, & Bird, 1996), while the latter include additional neurological impairments such as distal muscle wasting, peripheral neuropathy, and mental retardation.

Our research group recently conducted a study among Italian people with HSP and their caregivers in order to identify the activities and situations participants associated with optimal experiences, their perceived challenges in daily life, as well as their future goals.

*Sample, Instruments, and Procedure*   Participants with HSP were 22 women and 32 men, aged 46 on average, and diagnosed with a pure disease form (50%) or a complicated one (14.8%). For the remaining 35.2% a clinical diagnosis of HSP was available, while its genetic substratum had not been identified yet. This is not surprising, due to the still limited knowledge on this rare condition. Only 11.1% of the participants could walk autonomously, while 35.2% reported an altered gait, 20.4% needed crutches, and 33.3% needed a wheelchair. A mild cognitive impairment was documented in 20.4% of the interviewees. Most participants (68.5%) were entitled to a disability retirement pension, while 31.5% worked, prominently as office employees. In this group, 50% of the participants were married, 38.9% were single, and 11.1% were separated or divorced.

We also got the collaboration of 31 caregivers, 24 women and 7 men, aged 51 on average. The majority (56.7%) were spouses of the participants with HSP, 36.7% were parents, and the two remaining cases comprised a daughter and a sibling. In this group, 51.6% of the interviewees worked, prominently as employees, while 48.4% were retired or housewives.

Data were collected by two researchers through Flow Questionnaire (FQ) and Life Theme (LT) Questionnaire (Delle Fave & Massimini, 2004). The vast majority of the participants requested the researcher's presence to fill out the questionnaires. In FQ, participants were invited to read three descriptions of optimal experience, derived from interviews with lay people reporting this state of consciousness in association with various daily activities (Csikszentmihayi, 1975/2000; Delle Fave & Massimini, 2004). Participants were then asked to indicate whether they had ever felt optimal experience in their life. In case they did, they were invited to list the associated activities or situations (optimal activities). LT allowed for exploring, by means of open-ended questions, participants' life history and developmental trajectories. Among other aspects, the prominent challenges that participants perceived in the present life, and the most relevant goals they aimed at pursuing in the future, were investigated.

For the purposes of this chapter, we provide information on the optimal activities reported by the participants, their perceived challenges, and future goals. Based on the open structure of the questions, no limitations were set to the number of answers (optimal activities, challenges, and goals) that participants could provide. After data collection, answers were assigned numeric codes, and they were grouped into broad functional categories, reflecting the main daily life domains (such as productive activities, leisure, social relations, and personal care); category percentages were subsequently calculated for the two groups of participants. In order to perform between-group comparisons, the number of participants who provided at least one answer in each category was computed. Fisher's exact test was run on these frequencies to check for group differences.

*Optimal activities.* The majority of people with HSP (76%) and of their caregivers (81%) reported optimal experiences in their daily lives. Table 36.1 shows the percentage distribution of optimal activities in the two groups.

People with HSP prominently reported leisure activities, in particular painting, reading or computer-related tasks. Productive activities followed in rank, such as studying, working or performing manual tasks at a psychosocial rehabilitation center. Health care was only marginally represented, mostly referring to physiotherapy. Caregivers prominently associated optimal experience with productive activities, such as work and house chores, and passive leisure (reading, watching TV), followed by family interactions, mostly referring to caregiving. Fisher's exact test highlighted

**Table 36.1**
Percentage Distribution of the Optimal Activities Reported by People With HSP
and Caregivers

| Optimal Activities | People With HSP ($N^a$ = 41) | Caregivers ($N^a$ = 25) |
|---|---|---|
| Productive activities | 30 | 35 |
| Volunteering | 4.3 | 2.5 |
| Social relations | 2.9 | 2.5 |
| Leisure | 51.3 | 30 |
| Family interactions | 5.7 | 27.5 |
| Health/personal care | 2.9 | — |
| Religious practice | 2.9 | 2.5 |
| Number of answers | 70 | 40 |

[a] Number of participants

that a significantly higher percentage of caregivers associated optimal experience with family interactions and activities ($p < .05$).

Overall, these findings suggest that the onset and degenerative course of HSP did not hinder the occurrence of optimal experiences in participants' daily life; on the other side, the disease impacted the kind of activities associated with this experience. In particular, and in line with previous findings (Delle Fave & Massimini, 2005b), leisure tasks involving very limited body activity predominated. Optimal experience was also associated with productive activities, such as work and studying. Participants who could work described their job as an important opportunity to socialize and improve skills and capabilities.

As for caregivers, these results showed that taking care of a family member can be associated with positive and engaging experiences, promoting adequate caring performances but also personal fulfillment and positive family relations (Delle Fave & Massimini, 2004), in spite of the daily challenges and the long-term commitment entailed in this role.

*Present challenges and future goals.* Table 36.2 shows the percentage distribution of answer categories referring to the present challenges and the future goals perceived by the two groups of participants.

Participants with HSP identified health as their prominent challenge, in particular highlighting the importance of secondary prevention and the need for more frequent and intensive physiotherapy treatments in order to improve motor functionality. Family and productive activities followed, with answers emphasizing the participants' effort to provide their active contribution in these domains (such as "being a good parent" and "going back to work"). The category Personal Life included descriptions of the difficulties in coping with HSP and in pursuing autonomy despite physical constraints. The vast majority of caregivers quoted family as their present challenge, specifically referring to their commitment to provide adequate care to their ill relative. Significant group differences were detected through Fisher's exact test: Productive activities and health emerged as prominent challenges for people with HSP ($p < .05$ and $p < .001$, respectively), while a higher percentage of caregivers referred to family ($p < .001$).

As concerns future goals, people with HSP prominently referred to family and health; productive activities, leisure, and personal life followed in rank. Among caregivers family largely predominated, with answers referring to the promotion of health and autonomy of their ill relatives. Personal life and productive activities followed

**Table 36.2**

Percentage Distribution of the Challenges and Goals Perceived by People With HSP and Caregivers

| | Present Challenges | | Future Goals | |
|---|---|---|---|---|
| | People with HSP ($N^a$ = 54) | Caregivers ($N^a$ = 31) | People with HSP ($N^a$ = 54) | Caregivers ($N^a$ = 31) |
| Productive activities | 13.9 | — | 14.1 | 9.9 |
| Family | 19.5 | 78.8 | 27.1 | 57.7 |
| Standard of living | 8.3 | 6.4 | 2.4 | 1.4 |
| Social relations | 2.8 | — | 3.5 | 1.4 |
| Health care | 37.5 | 6.4 | 22.3 | 7.1 |
| Personal life | 11.1 | 4.2 | 10.6 | 11.3 |
| Leisure | — | — | 10.6 | 4.2 |
| Religion | — | — | 2.4 | 2.8 |
| Volunteering | 2.8 | 4.2 | 4.6 | 4.2 |
| Others | 4.2 | — | 2.4 | — |
| Number of answers | 72 | 47 | 85 | 71 |

[a]Number of participants

in much lower percentages. The prevalence of answers referring to family among caregivers was confirmed by Fisher's exact test, that highlighted a significant group difference in this domain ($p < .001$).

The answers provided to these two questions by the participants with HSP are consistent with previous studies (Delle Fave & Massimini, 2004) showing that, compared with individuals with congenital disabilities, people with acquired impairments more frequently reported health as a current challenge and a future goal. Acquired pathologies, especially when degenerative in nature, imply a constant commitment in order to prevent complications and to preserve a good quality of life. Family, though not representing a relevant occasion of optimal experiences, predominated among present challenges and future goals. These results can be interpreted in the light of the substantially care-recipient role played by the participants in their family, entailing the perception of a passiveness and dependence that does not allow for the emergence of optimal experiences in this domain, and that at the same time makes the family an essential component of the person's life in the long run.

As concerns caregivers, their answers suggest a pervasive commitment to the health and well-being of their ill relative, in the daily life and in future perspective. Such a substantial investment of energy and attention is, however, counterbalanced by the optimal experiences derived from caregiving. A vast amount of studies have shown that the association of optimal experiences with complex, meaningful, and socially relevant activities—such as caring—plays a crucial role in individual development, promoting eudaimonic well-being and personal growth (Delle Fave et al., 2011).

CAREGIVERS' PERCEIVED FACILITATORS AND BARRIERS

As discussed in the previous pages, the importance of considering disability from a bio-psycho-social perspective has been endorsed by WHO through the development of the ICF. Besides disease-related constraints, the environmental facilitators and barriers should be taken into account in evaluating health and well-being among people with disabilities and their families. On the other side, the psychological resources that allow people with disabilities and their caregivers to successfully adapt to the situation are specifically investigated by the research domain of positive psychology. We have combined these two approaches in designing a qualitative study conducted among caregivers of children and adolescents with psychophysical disabilities.

*Sample, Instruments, and Procedure*    A semistructured interview was administered to 196 adult participants. Among them, 105 (83 women and 22 men, with an average age of 41) were parents of children with mild disability attending a primary or secondary public school. The other 91 participants (70 women and 21 men, aged 50 on average) were caregivers of children and adolescents with severe psychophysical disabilities who attended special education courses at Don Carlo Gnocchi Foundation.

The interview questions reflected the ICF model and the construct of family resilience. They investigated the barriers and facilitators perceived by the participants as caregivers in their daily life management and organization, at the personal, family, and social levels. Like in the previous study, no limitations were set to the number of answers that participants could provide to each question. More specifically, the personal, family, and social barriers were explored through the following questions: "What are the needs and problems that you face in the daily care of your child?"; "What are the prominent difficulties for your family?"; "What are the main problems that hinder the social inclusion of your child?" As concerns the investigation of personal, family, and social resources and facilitators, participants were asked, "In your opinion, which personal skills and resources are the most important to cope with this situation?"; "What are the main resources used by your family to cope with this situation?"; "Which services, associations or institutions have been/are helpful to your family?"

The answers were grouped into categories organized according to the ICF perspective, taking into account environmental barriers and resources/facilitators, as well as the functioning level of the care recipient (in its physical, cognitive, emotional, and relational components). The caregivers' personal and family resources were grouped into categories reflecting the major psychological constructs identified by stress and coping research, and by positive psychology.

*Perceived Problems and Barriers*    As Table 36.3 shows, the main problems that caregivers in both groups perceived in their personal life were related to the child functioning levels (including mobility, autonomy level in daily activities, learning difficulties, and school performance) and to the challenges encountered in the management and organization of daily time budget. These two aspects are often intertwined, especially in situations where severe disabilities impose substantial limitations on children's autonomy and social participation. As reported by a 39-year-old mother of a child with a severe disability, "The needs mainly concern the continued assistance in all daily activities, bathing, dressing, taking him around, and assisting him in any task he wants or has to perform, continuously clashing with his stubbornness and opposition that increase with age."

As concerns the family challenges, for both groups of participants they included the daily routine management and the quality of family relationships. As highlighted in the resilience model developed by Walsh and described in the previous pages, the disability of one member influences the whole family, in terms of daily routine organization and reciprocal interactions, imposing the necessity to redefine priorities,

**Table 36.3**

Percentage Distribution of Challenges/Barriers Perceived by Caregivers of Children With Mild and Severe Disabilities at the Personal, Family, and Social Levels

| | Personal Barriers | | Family Barriers | | Social Barriers | |
|---|---|---|---|---|---|---|
| | Mild[a] ($N^c = 105$) | Severe[b] ($N^c = 91$) | Mild[a] ($N^c = 105$) | Severe[b] ($N^c = 91$) | Mild[a] ($N^c = 105$) | Severe[b] ($N^c = 91$) |
| Problem management | 25.1 | 24.3 | 19.7 | 23.6 | — | — |
| Emotions | — | — | 2.1 | 1.2 | — | — |
| Coherence and meaning | — | — | — | 3.1 | — | — |
| Resilience development | — | — | — | 4.4 | — | — |
| Child functioning level | 51.9 | 43.1 | 15.2 | 11.4 | 28.7 | 26.3 |
| Family relationships | 9.6 | 5.8 | 17.5 | 15.1 | — | — |
| Work/family balance | — | — | — | 3.8 | — | 1.2 |
| Social attitudes | 1.9 | 12.8 | 12.2 | 10.8 | 34.9 | 41.1 |
| Services and policies | 1.9 | 10.1 | 14.5 | 18.4 | 13.2 | 28.8 |
| Other | — | 3.9 | 4.3 | 4.4 | 2.3 | 2.6 |
| None | 9.6 | | 14.5 | 3.8 | 20.9 | — |
| Number of answers | 155 | 181 | 137 | 157 | 143 | 156 |

[a]Caregivers of children and adolescents with mild psychophysical disabilities
[b]Caregivers of children and adolescents with severe psychophysical disabilities
[c]Number of participants

roles, and responsibilities. These problems are reflected in the words of a 49-year-old mother:

> I think that a family living with a disease like autism is at risk for becoming autistic itself. . . .It is difficult to build meaningful relationships because everything has to be adjusted to times, rituals, stereotypes that cannot be ignored. Even for the child's brothers it is very difficult to find a balance between personal, family and social identity.

Inadequacies in health and social services that directly affected family life were more frequently identified by caregivers of children with severe disabilities, while—interestingly—child functioning was quoted in a relatively low percentage of answers by participants in both groups, suggesting that the development of family cooperation and resilience can effectively counterbalance the negative impact of disability, even in its most severe forms.

The major social barriers identified by caregivers in both groups primarily consisted in the negative social attitudes toward disability. Participants referred to problems related to ignorance, discrimination, and prejudice that can be expressed in different forms. As 43-year-old mother said, "I think that still too many people are scared of disability. In a society where only success, amusement and physical beauty matter, 'disabled' like us represent an obstacle to lightness." A 43-year-old father noted, "People's attitude of compassion. We want our son to be treated like others, no discount."

The inadequacy of health and social services ranked second for caregivers of children with severe disabilities, while the impact of child health conditions accounted for around one fourth of the answers provided by participants in both groups. It is worth noting that the identification of no problems/barriers was relatively frequent among caregivers of children with mild disabilities, ranking third in reference to the social context, and fourth in reference to family. This result attests to the potential for resilience and successful adaptation that individuals possess in facing suboptimal life conditions, especially when interacting with a supportive and facilitating context.

*Perceived Resources and Facilitators*   While caregivers' burden and stress-related problems have been often addressed by researchers and practitioners, studies investigating the personal and interpersonal resources that can be mobilized in coping with a relative's disease are still limited. We attempted to shed light on this neglected issue by asking caregivers to describe these resources. Findings are illustrated in Table 36.4.

The participants caring for children with mild disabilities quoted patience as the most important personal resource allowing them to adaptively face the situation. Problem-focused coping strategies and educational competences in interacting with their child—such as listening, talking style, and autonomy support—followed in frequency. The fourth personal resource in rank was hardiness (Maddi, 2002), which includes abilities such as courage, perseverance and commitment toward goal pursuit, and the tendency to approach problems as challenges and opportunities for growth rather than obstacles. These aspects clearly emerge from the answer of a 43-year-old father: "A lot of patience, firmness, and ability to step back in order

**Table 36.4**

Percentage Distribution of Personal, Family, and Social Resources/Facilitators Perceived by Caregivers of Children With Mild and Severe Disabilities

|  | Personal Resources | | Family Resources | | Social Resources | |
|---|---|---|---|---|---|---|
|  | Mild[a] ($N^c$ = 105) | Severe[b] ($N^c$ = 91) | Mild[a] ($N^c$ = 105) | Severe[b] ($N^c$ = 91) | Mild[a] ($N^c$ = 105) | Severe[b] ($N^c$ = 91) |
| Problem-focused coping | 18.6 | 21.9 | 4.6 | 20.8 | — | — |
| Patience | 31.9 | 17.5 | 7.9 | — | — | — |
| Hardiness | 13.3 | 19.5 | 6.6 | 6.7 | — | — |
| Resilience | 3.7 | 13.1 | 3.9 | 4.2 | — | — |
| Educational role | 18.7 | 11.7 | — | — | — | — |
| Optimism and hope | 2.2 | 3.4 | 2.9 | — | — | — |
| Emotions | — | 2.4 | — | 2.8 | — | — |
| Coherence and meaning | 1.6 | — | — | — | — | — |
| Child functioning level | — | 1.9 | — | — | 1.4 | — |
| Family relationships | — | — | 22.5 | 26.4 | — | — |
| Social relationships | 4.7 | 4.8 | — | — | — | — |
| Work/family balance | — | — | 2.3 | 4.8 | — | — |
| Services and policies | — | 2.4 | 15.8 | 20.3 | 75.4 | 74.4 |
| School | — | — | 9.2 | — | 10.9 | 6.2 |
| Associations | — | — | — | — | 5.4 | 17.3 |
| Money | — | — | 9.9 | 6.6 | — | — |
| Other | 5.3 | 1.4 | 3.9 | 7.4 | — | — |
| None | — | — | 10.5 | — | 6.9 | 2.1 |
| Number of answers | 188 | 205 | 151 | 163 | 201 | 225 |

[a]Caregivers of children and adolescents with mild psychophysical disabilities
[b]Caregivers of children and adolescents with severe psychophysical disabilities
[c]Number of participants

to make my child more autonomous." The answers provided by the caregivers of children with severe disabilities fell into the same major categories, though with a different percentage distribution. This group gave less relevance to patience and educational competences, and more importance to resilience and hardiness, highlighting the crucial role of detecting constructive and positive aspects in an objectively problematic condition in order to preserve a good quality of life. These dimensions are clearly expressed by a 61-year-old father: "Courage, faith, desire to find always new solutions to live better (even in the face of disability). Ability not to hide one's own discomfort or difficulties, avoiding seclusion within the home walls, also for the wellbeing of my child."

As reported in theoretical framework, the family is a fundamental contextual factor influencing the caregivers' functioning and well-being. At this level, the main resources perceived by the participants in both groups were relationships, in terms of family unity, solidarity, and ability to share problems and resources. Such positive relationships often represented the outcome of a challenging growth process of the family system, as a 42-year-old mother described, "After facing a long period of crisis, we are united more than before."

The support provided to the family by health and educational institutions and professionals was also identified as a prominent resource. Economic affluence and, again, patience were quoted by caregivers of children with mild disabilities. The other group instead emphasized the role of adaptive, problem-centered coping in the daily family adjustment to the situation.

Finally, the resources and facilitators perceived at the social level mainly included social services and policies for participants in both groups. In particular, their answers referred to health and school professionals, such as physicians, physiotherapists, and special education teachers. Caregivers of children with severe disabilities also highlighted the important role played by associations, which are often founded and managed by parents of persons with specific disabilities who can meet and discuss shared problems and related solutions. This aspect emerges from the words of a 52-year-old mother: "I joined an association of families that allowed me to get information and relief....We became friends and we still try to share and help each other."

## SUGGESTIONS FOR A RESOURCE-FOCUSED PRACTICE

The theoretical framework and empirical evidence provided in this chapter underscore the importance of building person-centered intervention programs that, besides personal and environmental limitations and barriers, take into account individual, family, and social resources and facilitators.

The onset of a pathology and the communication of a disease involving a child or a spouse represent traumatic experiences for individuals and families. Nevertheless, a large amount of evidence from the literature and the results presented in the previous pages highlight that people with disabilities and their caregivers can perceive a good quality of life, through the mobilization and improvement of personal resources and with the support of family and social relationships.

Optimal experiences can be retrieved even under difficult circumstances; the heavy and often long-term burden of caregiving can provide opportunities for fulfillment, enjoyment, and gratification, as well as life goals and meanings; behavioral flexibility and resilience allow individuals and families to successfully cope with the disease demands and to pursue developmental goals despite constraints in the daily routine.

At the level of practice, it is worth noting that the constructs developed or implemented in positive psychology research—from self-efficacy to resilience, from optimal experience to sense of coherence—are not just individual features that can be observed and measured, but also represent psychological potentials that can be improved and implemented. Health professionals working with people with disabilities and their caregivers can actively foster this process of resource development and mobilization through their technical competences, but also by offering their empathic support and encouraging their clients' participation in social life.

The promotion of well-being and daily functioning should be based on the evaluation of individuals' specific abilities, interests, and life expectations, with the aim of improving their quality of life through the exposure to both positive and meaningful activities and environments. The human ability to turn difficulties and problems into stimulating challenges and opportunities plays a pivotal role in these situations, and it should be substantially exploited by fostering self-efficacy, personal growth, and adaptive coping. The human tendency to give order and meaning to life events and situations should be supported by helping people with disabilities and their caregivers to identify lifelong projects and occasions of personal development within a disadvantageous situation. In this process, the analysis of the environmental facilitators and barriers could shed light on the pathways to follow in order to promote the collaboration of family members and social networks, and to allow people with disabilities to share their experiences, improve their abilities, and actively contribute to the context they live in.

Some specific hints for interventions, both at the individual and at the social levels, can be derived from the empirical studies presented in this chapter. As concerns people with neurodegenerative diseases like HSP that imply a progressive mobility impairment, at the individual level it would be important to promote the association of optimal experiences with activities fostering physical autonomy and active resource mobilization, rather than passive and purely intellectual leisure tasks. The person's active participation and responsibility in family life management should be encouraged, instead of perpetuating the negative self-representation of a passive and dependent member. At the social and policy levels, involvement in socially meaningful activities should be fostered—through job opportunities, social and cultural initiatives, advocacy campaigns conducted through associations, and local services.

As far as caregivers are concerned, at the individual level the association of optimal experiences with extra-family activities should be promoted, in order to allow them to expand their range of interests and opportunities for well-being in multiple life domains, in order to counterbalance the daily stress related to the caring role (Cramm & Nieboer, 2012). Caregivers should also be encouraged to find positive experiences within the family, beyond and besides their caregiving tasks. The active search for opportunities for diversion and relaxation, as well as a greater attention to the relationship with the other family members, should be encouraged.

Finally, families with disabilities have to deal with social barriers, whose negative impact is less evident but often more relevant than the problems derived from architectonic and physical barriers (Cortinovis et al., 2011; Delle Fave & Massimini, 2005b). The process of resilience development is based on the multiple interactions within a complex system encompassing the individual, the family, the social network, and the community as a whole. Any intervention should systematically explore all the possible actions that can be performed at the contextual level in order to promote personal well-being and/or reduce the social barriers faced by caregivers and caretakers.

## CONCLUSION

In line with the ICF model, a steadily growing research and clinical literature in the domain of chronic illness and disability suggests that resources and barriers identified at one single level—person, family, or society—have multiple repercussions on the individual functioning at all the other levels. It is therefore of paramount importance for psychologists and psychotherapists to focus on the potential for improvement and empowerment of clients' personal resources, with the aim of promoting a virtuous cycle implying, on the one side, the mobilization of family and social facilitators and, on the other side, the reduction of relational and social barriers. In this process, echoing Epictetus's famous statement, the clients should be supported in the endeavor to change what can be changed, to accept what cannot be changed, and to discriminate between the two situations.

## SUMMARY POINTS

- The worldwide increase in life expectancy entails more years spent in conditions of chronic illness and disability.
- In line with the bio-psycho-social approach endorsed by WHO's recent International Classification of Functioning, physical health and daily functioning are different concepts: Besides body functions, the latter includes psychological and social resources and barriers.
- Research in positive psychology highlights the protective role of psychological and social resources in promoting well-being in disease conditions.
- Based on the ICF model, the investigation of daily functioning, barriers, and resources should involve not only people with chronic diseases, but also their caregivers and families.
- The majority of people with chronic and degenerative diseases report opportunities for optimal experiences in daily life, at the same time expressing the need for a more active life, better job opportunities, and social participation.
- Empirical evidence suggests that family caregivers perceive their role as gratifying and enriching, though challenging.
- Besides personal resources, barriers and assets perceived within the family and social context substantially influence caregivers' and care recipients' well-being and daily functioning.
- At the practice level, the improvement and the empowerment of psychological resources can enhance a virtuous cycle promoting the mobilization of family and social resources, together with the reduction of relational and social barriers.

## REFERENCES

Antonovsky, A. (1987). *Unraveling the mystery of health: How people manage stress and stay well.* San Francisco, CA: Jossey-Bass.

Arnold, R., Ranchor, A., Koëter, G., De Jongste, M., & Sanderman, R. (2005). Consequences of chronic obstructive pulmonary disease and chronic heart failure: The relationship between objective and subjective health. *Social Science & Medicine, 61,* 2144–2154.

Aspinwall, L. G., & Brunhart, S. M. (1996). Distinguishing optimism from denial: Optimistic beliefs predict attention to health threats. *Personality and Social Psychology Bulletin, 22,* 993–1003.

Bandura, A. (2004). Health promotion by social cognitive means. *Health Education and Behavior, 31,* 143–164.

Bassi, M., Ferrario, N., Ba, G., Delle Fave, A., & Viganò, C. (2012). Quality of experience during psychosocial rehabilitation: A real-time investigation with Experience Sampling Method. *Psychiatric Rehabilitation Journal, 35,* 447–453.

Bauer, R., Koepke, F., Sterzinger, L., & Spiessl, H. (2012). Burden, rewards, and coping—the ups and downs of caregivers of people with mental illness. *Journal of Nervous and Mental Disease, 200,* 928–934.

Bodde, A. E., & Seo, D. (2009). A review of social and environmental barriers to physical activity for adults with intellectual disabilities. *Disability and Health Journal, 2,* 57–66.

Bonanno, G. A. (2004). Loss, trauma, and human resilience: Have we underestimated the human capacity to thrive after extremely aversive events? *American Psychologist, 59,* 20–28.

Cadell, S. (2007). The sun always comes out after it rains: Understanding posttraumatic growth in HIV caregivers. *Health & Social Work, 32,* 169–176.

Carbonneau, H., Caron, C., & Desrosiers, J. (2010). Development of a conceptual framework of positive aspects of caregiving in dementia. *Dementia, 9,* 327–353.

Conde-Sala, J. L., Garre-Olmo, J., Turro-Garriga, O., Vilalta-Franch, J., & Lopez-Pousa, S. (2010). Differential features of burden between spouse and adult-child caregivers of patients with Alzheimer's disease: An exploratory comparative design. *International Journal of Nursing Studies, 47,* 1262–1273.

Cortinovis., I., Luraschi, E., Intini, S., Sessa, M., & Delle Fave, A. (2011). The daily experience of people with achondroplasia. *Applied Psychology: Health and Well-Being, 3,* 207–227.

Cramm, J. M., & Nieboer, A. P. (2012). Longitudinal study of parents' impact on quality of life of children and young adults with intellectual disabilities. *Journal of Applied Research in Intellectual Disabilities, 25,* 20–28.

Csikszentmihalyi, M. (2000). *Beyond boredom and anxiety.* San Francisco, CA: Jossey-Bass. (Original work published 1975)

Csikszentmihalyi, M., & Massimini, F. (1985). On the psychological selection of bio-cultural information. *New Ideas in Psychology, 3,* 115–138.

Delle Fave, A. (2010). Development through disability: The unfolding and sharing of psychological resources. In G. W. Burns (Ed.), *Happiness, healing, enhancement: Your casebook collection for applying positive psychology in the therapy* (pp. 88–99). Hoboken, NJ: Wiley.

Delle Fave, A., & Massimini, F. (2004). Bringing subjectivity into focus: Optimal experiences, life themes, and person-centered rehabilitation. In P. A. Linley & S. Joseph (Eds.), *Positive psychology in practice* (pp. 581–597). Hoboken, NJ: Wiley.

Delle Fave, A., & Massimini, F. (2005a). The investigation of optimal experience and apathy: developmental and psychosocial implications. *European Psychologist, 10,* 264–274.

Delle Fave, A., & Massimini, F. (2005b). The relevance of subjective well-being to social policies: Optimal experience and tailored intervention. In F. Huppert, N. Baylis, & B. Keverne (Eds.), *The science of well-being* (pp. 379–402). Oxford, England: Oxford University Press.

Delle Fave, A., Massimini, F., & Bassi, M. (2011). *Psychological selection and optimal experience across cultures.* Dordrecht, The Netherlands: Springer Science.

Dixon, D., Johnston, M., Rowley, D., & Pollard, B. (2008). Using the ICF and psychological models of behavior to predict mobility limitations. *Rehabilitation Psychology, 53,* 191–200.

Ekwall, A. K., Sivberg, B, & Hallberg, I. R. (2007). Older caregivers' coping strategies and sense of coherence in relation to quality of life. *Journal of Advanced Nursing, 57,* 584–596.

Engel, G. L. (1977). The need for a new medical model: A challenge for biomedicine. *Science, 196,* 129–136.

Fink, J. K. (2003). Advances in the hereditary spastic paraplegias. *Experimental Neurology, 184,* 106–110.

Fink, J. K., Heiman-Patterson, T., & Bird, T. (1996). Hereditary spastic paraplegia: Advances in genetic research. *Neurology, 46,* 1507–1514.

Fitzpatrick, R. (2000). Measurement issues in health-related quality of life: Challenges for health psychology. *Psychology and Health, 15,* 99–108.

Folkman, S., & Moskowitz, J. T. (2000). Stress, positive emotions and coping. *Current Directions in Psychological Science, 9,* 115–118.

Fredrickson B. L. (2001). The role of positive emotions in positive psychology: The broaden-and-build theory of positive emotions. *American Psychologist, 56,* 218–226.

Garmezy, N., & Masten, A. (1991). The protective role of competence indicators in children at risk. In E. M. Cummings, A. L. Greene, & K. H. Karraker (Eds.), *Perspectives on stress and coping* (pp. 151–174). Hillsdale, NJ: Erlbaum.

Gerstein, E. D., Crnic, K. A., Blacher, J., & Baker, B. L. (2009). Resilience and the course of daily parenting stress in families of young children with intellectual disabilities. *Journal of Intellectual Disability Research, 53,* 981–997.

Hellstrom, I., Nolan, M., & Lundh, U. (2007). Sustaining "couplehood": Spouses' strategies for living positively with dementia. *Dementia, 6,* 383–409.

Hwang, J., Rivas, J., Fremming, R., Rivas, M., & Crane, K. (2009). Relationship between perceived burden of caring for a family member with Alzheimer's disease and decreased participation in meaningful activities. *Occupational Therapy in Health Care, 23,* 249–266.

Isen, A. M. (1987). Positive affect, cognitive processes and social behaviour. In L. Berkowitz (Ed.), *Advances in experimental social psychology* (pp. 203–253). New York, NY: Academic Press.

Isen, A. M., & Geva, N. (1987). The influence of positive affect on acceptable level of risk: The person with a large canoe has a large worry. *Organizational Behavior and Human Decision Processes, 39,* 145–154.

Jacobson, L. J., Westerberg, M., Malec, J. F., & Lexell, J. (2011). Sense of coherence and disability and the relationship with life satisfaction 6–15 years after traumatic brain injury in northern Sweden. *Neuropsychological Rehabilitation, 21,* 383–400.

Joseph, S., Becker, S., Elwick, H., & Silburn, R. (2012). Adult Carers Quality of Life Questionnaire (AC-QoL): Development of an evidence-based tool. *Mental Health Review Journal, 17,* 57–69.

Joseph, S., & Linley, P. A. (2005). Positive adjustment to threatening events: An organismic valuing theory of growth through adversity. *Review of General Psychology, 9,* 262–280.

Keyes, C. L. M. (2002). The mental health continuum: From languishing to flourishing in life. *Journal of Health and Social Behavior, 43,* 207–222.

Keyes, C. L. M. (2007). Promoting and protecting mental health as flourishing: A complementary strategy for improving national mental health. *American Psychologist, 62,* 95–108.

King, L., & Miner, K. (2000). Writing about the perceived benefits of traumatic life events: Implications for physical health. *Personality and Social Psychology Bulletin, 26,* 220–230.

Lazarus, R., & Folkman, S. (1984). *Stress, appraisal, and coping.* New York, NY: Springer.

Luthar, S. S. (2006). Resilience in development: A synthesis of research across five decades. In D. Cicchetti & D. J. Cohen (Eds.), *Developmental psychopathology: Risk, disorder, and adaptation* (Vol. 3, 2nd ed., pp. 739–795). Hoboken, NJ: Wiley.

Mackay, R. (2003). Family resilience and good child outcomes: An overview of the research literature. *Social Policy Journal of New Zealand, 20,* 98–118.

Maddi, S. R. (2002). The story of hardiness: Twenty years of theorizing, research, and practice. *Consulting Psychology Journal, 54,* 173–185.

Massimini, F., & Delle Fave, A. (2000). Individual development in a bio-cultural perspective. *American Psychologist, 55,* 24–33.

Molyneux, G. J., McCarthy, G. M., McEniff, S., Cryan, M., & Conroy, R. M. (2008). Prevalence and predictors of carer burden and depression in carers of patients referred to an old age psychiatric service. *International Psychogeriatrics, 20,* 1193–1202.

Morris, B. A., & Shakespeare-Finch, J. (2011). Rumination, post-traumatic growth, and distress: Structural equation modeling with cancer survivors. *Psycho-Oncology, 20,* 1176–1183.

Mosher, C. E., Danoff-Burg, S., & Brunker, B. (2006). Post-traumatic growth and psychological adjustment of daughters of breast cancer survivors. *Oncology Nursing Forum, 33,* 543–551.

Oelofsen, N., & Richardson, P. (2006). Sense of coherence and parenting stress in mothers and fathers of preschool children with developmental disability. *Journal of Intellectual & Developmental Disability, 31,* 1–12.

Patterson, J. (2002). Understanding family resilience. *Journal of Clinical Psychology, 58,* 233–246.

Pennix, B. W., Beekman, A. T., Honig, A., Deeg, D. J., Schoevers, R. A., van Eijk, J. T., & van Tilburg, W. (2001). Depression and cardiac mortality. *Archives of General Psychiatry, 58,* 221–227.

Pollard, C., & Kennedy, P. (2007). A longitudinal analysis of emotional impact, coping strategies and post-traumatic psychological growth following spinal cord injury: A 10-year review. *British Journal of Health Psychology, 12,* 347–362.

Powell, T., Ekin-Wood, A., & Collin, C. (2012). Post-traumatic growth after head injury: A long-term follow-up. *Brain Injury, 21,* 31–38.

Rinaldi, P., Spazzafumo, L., Mastriforti, R., Mattioli, P., Marvardi, M., Polidori, M. C., . . . Study Group on Brain Aging of the Italian Society of Gerontology and Geriatrics. (2005). Predictors of high level of burden and distress in caregivers of demented patients: Results of an Italian multi center study. *International Journal of Geriatric Psychiatry, 20,* 168–174.

Robertson, S. M., Zarit, S. H., Duncan, L. G., Rovine, M. J., & Femia, E. E. (2007). Family caregivers' patterns of positive and negative affect. *Family Relations, 56,* 12–23.

Rutter, M. (1987). Psychosocial resilience and protective mechanisms. *American Journal of Orthopsychiatry, 57,* 316–331.

Rutterford, N. A., & Wood, R. (2006). Evaluating a theory of stress and adjustment when predicting long-term psychosocial outcome after brain injury. *Journal of International Neuropsychological Society, 12,* 359–367.

Ryan, R. M., & Deci, E. L. (2001). On happiness and human potentials: A review of research on hedonic and eudaimonic well-being. *Annual Review of Psychology, 52,* 141–166.

Sarkar, U., Ali, S., & Whooley, M. A. (2009). Self-efficacy as a marker of cardiac function and predictor of heart failure hospitalization and mortality in patients with stable coronary heart disease: Findings from the Heart and Soul Study. *Health Psychology, 28,* 166–173.

Schopp, L. H., Clark, M. J., Hagglund, K. J., Sherman, A. K., Stout, B. J., Gray, D. B., & Boninger, M. L. (2007). Life activities among individuals with spinal cord injury living in the community: Perceived choice and perceived barriers. *Rehabilitation Psychology, 52*(1), 82–88.

Scrignaro, M., Barni, S., & Magrin, E. (2009). The combined contribution of social support and coping strategies in predicting post-traumatic growth: A longitudinal study on cancer patients. *Psycho-Oncology, 20,* 823–831.

Seekins, T., Traci, M., A., Cummings, S., Oreskovich, J., & Reveslot, C. (2008). Assessing environmental factors that affect disability: Establishing a baseline of visitability in a rural state. *Rehabilitation Psychology, 53,* 80–84.

Semiatin, A. M., & Connor, M. K. (2012). The relation between self-efficacy and positive aspects of caregiving in Alzheimer's disease caregivers. *Aging and Mental Health, 16,* 683–688.

Serrano-Aguilar, P. G., Lopez-Bastida, J., & Yanes-Lopez, V. (2006). Impact on health-related quality of life and perceived burden of informal caregivers of individuals with Alzheimer's disease. *Neuroepidemiology, 27,* 136–142.

Simon, J., Murphy, J., & Smith, S. (2008). Building resilience: Appreciate the little things in life. *British Journal of Social Work, 38,* 218–235.

Skevington, S., & McCrate, F. (2011). Expecting a good quality of life in health: Assessing people with diverse diseases and conditions using the WHOQOL-BREF. *Health Expectations, 15,* 49–62.

Sodergren, S. C., & Hyland, M. E. (2000). What are the positive consequences of illness? *Psychology and Health, 15*, 85–97.

Sussman, T., & Regehr, C. (2009). The influence of community-based services on the burden of spouses caring for their partners with dementia. *Health & Social Work, 34*, 29–39.

Tedeschi, R. G., & Calhoun, L. G. (1996). The Posttraumatic Growth Inventory: Measuring the positive legacy of trauma. *Journal of Traumatic Stress, 9*, 455–471.

Tennen, H., & Affleck, G. (2002). Benefit-finding and benefit-reminding. In C. R. Snyder & S. J. Lopez (Eds.), *Handbook of positive psychology* (1st ed., pp. 584–597). New York, NY: Oxford University Press.

Veenhoven, R. (2002). Why social policy needs subjective indicators. *Social Indicators Research, 58*, 33–45.

Walsh, F. (2003). Family resilience: A framework for clinical practice. *Family Process, 42*, 1–18.

Walsh, F. (2006). *Strengthening family resilience* (2nd ed.). New York, NY: Guilford Press.

Walsh, F. (2011). Resilience in families with serious health challenges. In M. Craft-Rosenberg & S. R. Pehler (Eds.), *Encyclopedia of family health* (pp. 895–899). Thousand Oaks, CA: Sage.

World Health Organization (1946). Preamble to the Constitution of the World Health Organization. Official records of the World Health Organization, no. 2 (p. 100).

World Health Organization. (2001). *International Classification of Functioning, Disability and Health (ICF)*. Geneva, Switzerland: Author.

Word Health Organization (2007). *International classification of functioning, disability and health for children and youth*. Geneva, Switzerland: Author.

Zautra, A. J., Stuart Hall, J., & Murray, K. E. (2012). Resilience: A new definition of health for people and communities. In J. W. Reich, A. J. Zautra, & J. Stuart Hall (Eds.), *The handbook of adult resilience* (pp. 3–29). New York, NY: Guilford Press.

# CHAPTER 37

# Good Lives and the Rehabilitation of Sex Offenders

CLARE-ANN FORTUNE, TONY WARD, and RUTH MANN

T HE TREATMENT OF SEX offenders in the past two decades has focused on reducing the psychological and social deficits associated with offending. The predominant rehabilitation model is the risk-need-responsivity (RNR) approach, which is concerned with decreasing the likelihood that offenders will engage in harmful behavior (Andrews & Bonta, 2010; Ward & Stewart, 2003a). The expectation is that by identifying and managing dynamic risk factors (e.g., antisocial attitudes and deviant sexual arousal), offending rates will be reduced. The primary goal of treatment is the reduction and management of risk rather than the enhancement of offenders' lives (Ward, 2002).

In recent years a number of clinicians and researchers (e.g., Pithers, 1990) have argued that understanding the process of relapse is central to the treatment of sexual offenders. Clear behavioral patterns translate into distinct clusters of cognitive, affective, and behavioral offense variables among sexual offenders (Ward, Louden, Hudson, & Marshall, 1995). Models of the relapse process provide a rich description of the cognitive, behavioral, motivational, and contextual risk factors associated with a sexual offense (Ward & Hudson, 2000). Theoretical approaches typically include an explicit temporal factor and focus on proximal causes or the "how" of sexual offending. The aim in treatment is therefore to ensure individuals acquire skills to cope with risk factors in a nonabusive manner. The different stages of an individual's offense process are typically linked to distinct treatment strategies.

We argue that treatment based on eliminating deficits or risk factors is unlikely to sufficiently motivate offenders in treatment and fails to account fully for the issues of psychological agency and personal identity. Rather than adopting a relapse prevention (RP) program we recommend locating or embedding it within a more constructive, strength-based capabilities approach—called the Good Lives Model of offender rehabilitation (Ward, 2002; Ward & Maruna, 2007). The Good Lives Model (GLM) views risk factors as obstacles that challenge an individual's capacity to live a more fulfilling life. Risk factors function as indicators that an individual's pursuit of primary human goods is compromised in some way. That is, the internal and external conditions necessary to achieve valued outcomes may be missing or incomplete. Therefore, the therapeutic focus should be on implementing offenders' good lives plans as well as managing risk. According to the GLM, the modification of crimino-genic needs, or dynamic risk factors, will occur as a consequence of implementing a personally meaningful good lives plan.

In this chapter we suggest the GLM rehabilitation framework has the necessary conceptual resources to provide therapists with comprehensive guidelines for treating sex offenders. The GLM is conceptually deeper than the RNR and underpins the risk management approach providing an explanation of why risk factors are problematic for the individual and society, and accounts for their interrelationships. First, we discuss the required features of a good rehabilitation theory and briefly critique the RNR approach to offender rehabilitation based on this analysis. We then outline the GLM and examine its application to the assessment and treatment of sex offenders.

## WHAT SHOULD A REHABILITATION THEORY LOOK LIKE?

A good theory of offender rehabilitation should specify the aims of therapy, provide justification of these aims in terms of the theory's core assumptions about etiology and the values underpinning the approach, and identify clinical targets. Treatment should proceed in the light of these assumptions and goals (Ward & Marshall, 2004). Etiological theories and practice models are conceptually linked by an overarching theory of rehabilitation. For example, there is a close relationship between deficit models of sexual offending and problem-based clinical practice by virtue of the RNR theory of rehabilitation and its attendant RP treatment framework. The RNR theory connects assumptions about the causes of sexual offending (i.e., psychological deficits), the type of interventions that should be used (i.e., problem reducing), and most significantly, the way these interventions should be implemented (i.e., to reduce or manage risk). In RP the focus is on moderating or reducing risk factors, not enhancing an individual's capacity to live a more fulfilling life.

A good rehabilitation model should also specify the style of treatment (e.g., skills based, structured, etc.), inform therapists about the appropriate attitudes to take toward offenders, address motivation, and clarify the role and importance of therapeutic alliance. These features of treatment are often ignored by standard RP approaches and viewed as concerns about process rather than substance or content.

We suggest that motivating offenders and creating a sound therapeutic alliance are pivotal components of effective treatment. In addition, therapists cannot quarantine ethical or moral issues from therapeutic ones when working with sex offenders (Ward, 2002). The fact an offender has harmed another human being and been punished is likely to evoke therapist beliefs about the nature of unjustified harm (i.e., evil), forgiveness, and revenge. Therapists' attitudes toward the offender are strongly influenced by their conception of the nature and value of human beings, and the extent to which engaging in harmful actions diminishes that value.

A seminal paper by Bill Marshall (1996) argues the importance of regarding sex offenders as human beings with the same intrinsic value as any other individual, irrespective of the wrongs they have committed. Therapist attitudes toward sex offenders emerge from an analysis of the relationship between the character of the offender (i.e., the source of harmful actions) and his or her criminal acts. Focusing on harmful actions means therapists are likely to form a pejorative view of the individual. In contrast, if therapists see offenders as possessing intrinsic value because of their status as human beings—based on their autonomy, potential for change, or some other quality—then respect for the person but condemnation of the offense is more likely to arise.

We suggest the position individuals take on this issue partially depends on their view of human nature; first, some will believe human beings are essentially good and only commit harmful actions if they fail to cultivate more prosocial values and the ability to achieve their goals (human goods) in adaptive and socially acceptable ways. Second, some people are fundamentally bad, born criminals and initiators of harmful acts. Third, people are equally capable of beneficial or harmful actions by virtue of their natural dispositions and characteristics.

A mixed view of human nature involving both dispositions to behave in ways that increase *and* reduce human welfare is most consistent with the scientific evidence. Individuals have tendencies to behave altruistically and aggressively toward fellow human beings. There is an asymmetrical relationship between our good-producing and evil-avoiding activities (Kekes, 1990). The latter involves making sure people do not act in certain ways, while the former involves changing the world in a way that is beneficial for a person. The former is positive and the latter negative. Clinicians should not restrict therapeutic actions simply to the production of human goods or meeting needs; they must also focus on the avoidance of harm (i.e., risk management). Giving someone capabilities to seek goods may also reduce their disposition to inflict harm. It is important to keep both goals in mind when working with sexual offenders as on their own neither is sufficient to reduce reoffending. This is a way of integrating a risk management rehabilitation perspective with a good lives approach (see later discussion).

It is crucial to distinguish between the actions of sexual offenders and the respect owed to them because of their status as human beings (Cordner, 2002). The perception of offenders as worthwhile because they are human agents or persons and thus of fundamental value should partially determine therapy.

Therapist attitudes toward offenders have two distinct, although related, foci: (1) their value and dignity as human beings and rights to live good lives and (2) as individuals who have inflicted harm on other people. Both attitudes allow space for therapeutic growth and are based on the idea that while punishment should give a moral message to the offender and confront him with the harm he has inflicted on victims, it should not involve seeking revenge.

Forgiveness is also important; the fact that someone has been punished and is in therapy to alter his sexually aggressive behavior means he is likely to have to grapple with the realization he severely harmed another human being. Once an offender takes responsibility for the harm done to his victim(s) (and secondary and tertiary victims—see later discussion), he is likely to desire some form of forgiveness. Govier (2002) argues forgiveness means a person can move on and seek to transform himself, making it a critical element in the process of behavior change.

It is not always possible to forgive the offender on behalf of his primary victim (Govier, 2002). Perhaps this is because it feels as if the victim of a sexual offense is the only person who has the right to offer forgiveness, and if we take that right away, we are acting as if the victim's rights are unimportant and exacerbating his or her previous experience of being disregarded. Therapists working with sex offenders must manage this complexity of working with one damaged person while not undermining the experience of the victim(s).

There are arguably distinct levels of victimization ranging from the primary (the direct recipient of harm), secondary (family and close friends), and finally, tertiary levels (e.g., the community as a whole). If you accept that tertiary victims can play an important role in forgiveness, and that forgiveness is often necessary for an offender to accept responsibility and to turn his life around, then it can be a critical therapeutic response. It is unclear whether it is ever appropriate for therapists to take on this role, although an argument can be made for its utility and value. The point is that it is not possible for therapists to sidestep this issue. The attitude they adopt toward the offender reflects their implicit (rarely explicit) forgiveness (or lack of forgiveness) of the individual in question and the belief that he is entitled to be treated with respect because of his value as a person.

Thus therapists' interactions with offenders are partly based on their views of the nature of person, the source of harm, forgiveness, and their implications for the worth of the offender and his right to live a different kind of life. The GLM fits in well with a constructive view of punishment as it is based on a more positive view of human nature and the intrinsic value of human beings. This point has been powerfully argued by Margalit (1996):

> Even if there are noticeable differences among people in their ability to change, they are deserving of respect for the very possibility of changing. Even the worst criminals are worthy of basic human respect for the possibility that they may radically reevaluate their past lives and, if they are given the opportunity, may live the rest of their lives in a worthy manner. (p. 70)

Offenders are viewed as individuals who have committed wrongs and who may have enduring dispositions to do so again. The aim of intervention is not to seek revenge, but rather therapists should act in a way that allows the offender to vindicate himself (Govier, 2002) by actively engaging in therapy and also by helping him live a better life. Revenge only results in the infliction of further suffering (a wrong) in response to a prior wrong and runs the risk of reinforcing offense-related risk factors such as grievance/persecution beliefs. By *revenge* we are referring to punitive actions directed toward offenders by clinicians because they are perceived to be bad people, undeserving of forgiveness or a chance at a new life. These actions may involve aggressive confrontation, a failure to reward or praise efforts at behavior change, negative interpretations of problematic group behavior or lack of progress, or simply the failure to do the best for a given individual. These observations are entirely consistent with research on the impact of therapist and process factors in treatment outcome. Marshall et al. (2003) have concluded that increasing sexual offenders' self-esteem, working collaboratively with offenders in developing treatment goals, and the cultivation of therapist features such as displays of empathy and warmth, and encouragement and rewards for progress, facilitate the change process. We suggest it is easier to achieve these things if a therapist has a positive view about sex offenders based on the preceding considerations. Therapist and process variables reflect underlying assumptions about forgiveness, intrinsic value, and the nature of unjustified harm.

The degree to which offenders perceive the therapist to be trustworthy is also likely to be a function of these basic attitudes toward the offender and other members of the group (Potter, 2002). We tend to find individuals trustworthy if they take care of things that we, and others, care about or value (e.g., feelings, hopes, and desires; Potter, 2002). Trustworthy therapists have a responsibility to communicate that they are trustworthy to offenders, to be aware of their own values and attitudes and to critically evaluate them, and to be sensitive to the offender's particular situation (Potter, 2002). Therapists should not naively believe everything the offender reports during therapy while also not being unduly suspicious and confronting; rather they should take a middle position. Trust is essential to the development of the therapeutic alliance (Ackerman & Hilsenroth, 2003).

Personal identity for offenders in the process of behavior change is also important. Maruna (2001) examined the differences between offenders who desist or persist in committing further crimes and found that effectively rehabilitated individuals established a coherent, prosocial identity. This required the construction of a narrative that made sense of their earlier crimes and experiences of adversity and created a bridge between their undesirable life and the adoption of new ways of living. The capacity of individuals to seek meaning and direct their actions in the light of reasons and values constitutes an essential aspect of human functioning according to the good lives perspective (Ward, 2002; Ward & Maruna, 2007).

An adequate theory of rehabilitation should have the conceptual resources to create a bridge between etiology and treatment; specify treatment targets; provide a rationale and theoretical basis for the importance of forming positive attitudes toward offenders and clarify the role of a therapeutic alliance; deal with agency and identity; be strength based; explain the relationship between risk and goods (adopt the twin foci of seeking to equip offenders to live good lives but also to minimize and control risk); have a rich conceptualization of human nature and the related issues of values and motivation; and provide concrete suggestions for the assessment and treatment of sex offenders.

## THE RISK-NEED-RESPONSIVITY MODEL

Here we outline the basic assumptions of this approach to rehabilitation to provide an appropriate context for the subsequent discussion of the GLM (for a comprehensive critique, see Ward & Brown, 2003; Ward & Maruna, 2007; Ward & Stewart, 2003a).

Three general principles underpin the RNR approach to the treatment of offenders (see Andrews & Bonta, 2010). First, there is the *risk principle*, which is concerned with matching level of risk and the amount of treatment received. Second, according to the *need principle*, programs should primarily target criminogenic needs, that is, dynamic risk factors associated with recidivism, which can be changed. Third, the *responsivity principle* is concerned with a program's ability to actually reach and make sense to the participants. Interventions should utilize behavioral, social learning, and cognitive behavioral approaches (Andrews & Bonta, 2010).

Treatment derived from this model is commonly relapse prevention. The goal is to help sex offenders understand their offense pattern and cope with situational and psychological factors that place them at risk for reoffending (Ward & Hudson, 2000). The best way to reduce recidivism is to identify and reduce or eliminate an individual's array of dynamic risk factors. These factors constitute clinical needs or problems that should be explicitly targeted. Therefore treatment programs for sexual offenders are typically problem focused and aim to eradicate or reduce the various psychological and behavioral difficulties associated with sexually abusive behavior. These problems include intimacy deficits, deviant sexual preferences, cognitive distortions, empathy deficits, and difficulties managing negative emotional states.

It is clear the risk management and related RP models have resulted in more effective treatment and lower recidivism rates (Hollin, 1999; Laws, Hudson, & Ward, 2000). The emphasis on empirically supported therapies and accountability is a laudable goal. However, alongside these undoubted strengths there are also some areas of weakness, particularly offender responsivity and the difficulty of motivating offenders using this approach.

We argue that as a theory of rehabilitation, RNR lacks the conceptual resources to adequately guide therapists and engage offenders (Ward & Stewart, 2003c). More specifically, it adopts a pincushion model of treatment and views offenders as disembodied bearers of risk. Second, it does not address the issue of human agency and personal identity, and so becomes a reductionist approach to human behavior. Third, it disregards the crucial importance of human needs and their influence in determining offending behavior. It also fails to explicitly focus on the establishment of a strong therapeutic relationship with the offender; it is silent on questions of therapist factors and attitude to offenders. Fourth, the risk-need model does not systematically address offender motivation and tends to lead to avoidant treatment goals. Finally, this perspective often results in a mechanistic, one-size-fits all approach to treatment and does not really deal with the critical role of contextual factors in the process of rehabilitation. Porporino (2010) has suggested it is time to look beyond the current evidence-based approaches to offender rehabilitation currently used (e.g., RNR), as he cautions that the field may have reached a point where further refinement of such programs will not produce significant improvements. Porporino argues we need to look beyond simply teaching skills to consider the offenders' broader ecological and personal contexts.

## GOOD LIVES MODEL OF OFFENDER REHABILITATION

The GLM of offender rehabilitation is a strength-based approach and seeks to give offenders the capabilities to secure primary human goods in socially acceptable and personally meaningful ways (Kekes, 1989; Rapp, 1998; Ward & Stewart, 2003a). Primary goods are actions, states of affairs, characteristics, experiences, and states of mind that are viewed as intrinsically beneficial to human beings and are sought for their own sake rather than as means to some more fundamental ends (Deci & Ryan, 2000; Emmons, 1999; Schmuck & Sheldon, 2001). In this model, humans are by nature active, goal-seeking beings who are engaged in the process of constructing a sense of purpose and meaning in their lives. This is hypothesized to emerge from the pursuit and achievement of a number of primary human goods (valued aspects of human functioning and living) that collectively allow individuals to flourish and achieve high levels of well-being. In the GLM, the identification of risk factors is a critical part of assessment as they alert clinicians to obstacles or problems in the way offenders are seeking to achieve valued or personally satisfying outcomes. For example, social isolation indicates difficulties in the way the goods of intimacy and community are sought and may indicate skill deficits and/or a lack of social opportunities and resources.

The core idea is that all meaningful human actions reflect attempts to achieve primary human goods (Emmons, 1999; Ward, 2002) irrespective of education, intelligence, or class. Primary goods are viewed as objective and are tied to certain ways of living that if pursued involve the actualization of potentialities that are distinctively human. Individuals can, therefore, be mistaken about what is really of value and what is in their best interests. Primary goods emerge out of basic needs while instrumental or secondary goods provide concrete ways of securing these goods. For example, the primary good of excellence in work that provides mastery experiences can be achieved by working as a mechanic, psychologist, or teacher. Secondary goods are available to individuals by way of the numerous models and opportunities for attaining goods in everyday life (i.e., types of relationships, work) and dictate the form these goods take in specific contexts. The choice to seek a particular cluster of secondary goods will be determined by an offender's preferences, strengths, and opportunities. One individual might realize the primary good of work and mastery (mastery experiences are components of excellence at work) working as a mechanic, while another might train as a computer operator. Secondary goods put flesh on the bones of the more abstract primary goods; when the attainment of goods is difficult the problem often resides in the type of secondary goods utilized. Thus, a person might seek the primary good of intimacy in a relationship characterized by violence, controlling behavior, and emotional distance. Such a relationship choice will clearly not realize the primary good of intimacy. The different types of goods sought by individuals are packaged together in lifestyles, reflecting the priority given to specific types of goods and also the chosen ways of realizing them. It must be noted that in the course of their development, individuals may simply be socialized into accepting specific ways of living rather than intentionally shaping their lives according to a rationally derived plan. However, in Western democratic societies the notion of free choice with respect to values and beliefs is fundamental, so it is expected that all individuals, at least in a nominal sense, have the capacity to alter their lifestyle and are held responsible for the choices they make. In a real sense, they are able to shape their lives to a significant degree, within the constraints posed by social, biological, and individual factors.

There is a consensus (in Western culture at least) regarding the lists of primary human goods noted in psychological and social science research (Cummins, 1996; Emmons, 1999), evolutionary theory (Arnhart, 1998), practical ethics (Murphy, 2001), and philosophical anthropology (Nussbaum, 2000; Rescher, 1990). Based on this literature (especially the work of Murphy, 2001), Ward and colleagues (e.g., Laws & Ward, 2011; Ward, Mann, & Gannon, 2007) have identified 11 classes of primary human goods: (1) life (including healthy living and functioning), (2) knowledge, (3) excellence in play, (4) excellence in work (including mastery experiences), (5) excellence in agency (i.e., autonomy and self-directedness), (6) inner peace (i.e., freedom from emotional turmoil and stress), (7) friendship (including intimate, romantic, and family relationships), (8) community, (9) spirituality (in the broad sense of finding meaning and purpose in life), (10) happiness, and (11) creativity (Ward & Gannon, 2006, p. 79). Each of these primary goods can be broken down into subclusters or components; in other words, the primary goods are complex and multifaceted. For example, the primary good of relatedness contains the subcluster goods of intimacy, friendship, support, caring, reliability, honesty, and so on.

The possibility of constructing and translating conceptions of good lives into actions and concrete ways of living depends crucially on the possession of *internal* (skills and capabilities) and *external* conditions (opportunities and supports). The specific form a conception takes depends on the actual abilities, interests, and opportunities of each individual and the weightings he gives to specific primary goods. The weightings or priorities allocated to specific primary goods is constitutive of an offender's *personal identity* and spells out the kind of life sought, and the kind of person he would like to be. As human beings naturally seek a range of primary goods or desired states, it is important that all classes of primary goods are addressed in a good lives plan (GLP); they should be ordered and coherently related. If an offender decides to pursue a life characterized by service to the community, a core aspect of his identity will revolve around the primary goods of relatedness and community. Their sense of mastery, meaning, and agency will all reflect the overarching goods of relatedness and community and their associated subclusters of goods (e.g., intimacy, caring, reliability, honesty). The resulting GLP should be organized in ways that ensure each primary good has a role to play and can be secured or experienced by the individual concerned. A GLP that is fragmented and lacks coherence is likely to lead to frustration and harm to the individual concerned, as well as leading to a life lacking an overall sense of purpose and meaning (Emmons, 1996). Additionally, a GLP is always *context dependent*—there is no such thing as the right kind of life for any specific person; there are always a number of feasible possibilities, although there are limits defined by circumstances, abilities, and preferences (Kekes, 1989; Ward & Maruna, 2007; Ward & Stewart, 2003b).

Psychological, social, and lifestyle problems emerge when GLPs are faulty in some way. In the case of criminal behavior, it is hypothesized there are four major types of difficulties: (1) problems with the *means* used to secure goods, (2) a lack of *scope* within a GLP, (3) the presence of *conflict* among goals (goods sought) or incoherence, or (4) a lack of the necessary *capacities* to form and adjust a GLP to changing circumstances (e.g., impulsive decision making).

Taking into account the type of GLP problem an offender has, a treatment plan should be *explicitly* constructed taking into account an offender's preferences, strengths, primary goods, and relevant environments, and specify exactly what competencies and resources are required to achieve these goods. This crucially involves identifying the internal and external conditions necessary to implement the plan and designing a rehabilitation strategy to equip the individual with these required skills, resources, and opportunities. Such an approach to offender rehabilitation is significantly contextualized, and promotes the importance of personal identity and its emergence from daily living. It is also value laden in the sense that primary human goods represent outcomes that are beneficial to human beings and their absence harmful (to the individual and to others). Therefore, rehabilitation should be tailored to the individual offender's particular GLP and only seek to install the internal and external conditions that will enable its realization. The detection of dynamic risk factors or criminogenic needs signals there are problems of scope, coherence, inappropriate means, and planning deficits. Risk analysis simply informs therapists there are problems in the way offenders seek human goods. Treatment should proceed on the assumption that effective rehabilitation requires the acquisition of competencies and external supports, and opportunities to live a different kind of life.

SUMMARY

We have briefly described the GLM of offender rehabilitation and now consider whether it meets the criteria for a good rehabilitation theory.

The GLM states human beings are naturally inclined to seek a number of basic goods that are valued states of affairs, actions, and characteristics. These goods are sought for their own sake and if secured result in high levels of well-being, and if not achieved, result in lower levels of well-being. Typically these goods are instantiated in concrete ways of living, the practices and everyday routines that constitute a life. In light of these remarks, it is not surprising the GLM is able to deepen our etiological theories by including an explicit reference to the goods sought by sexually abusive behavior and by doing so, provide clear directions for rehabilitation interventions. Any justifiable intervention should focus on installing and/or strengthening the internal and external conditions necessary for an individual to realize his particular GLP, taking into account his unique circumstances, abilities, preferences, and strengths. A strength of the model is that, by virtue of its focus on human goods, it provides an explicit avenue by which to motivate offenders. Thus, the link between etiology and treatment is clear and focuses on the notion of human goods, problems in an individual's GLP, and the role of therapy in stalling the internal and external conditions to implement a particular individual's GLP.

Aside from its ability to provide intelligible treatment targets, the GLM is also explicit about the nature and types of values associated with the rehabilitation of offenders. The importance of therapists valuing and respecting offenders as people is also clear. In a sense people are viewed as interdependent and therefore rely on the goodwill of others when attempting to implement their GLP.

The GLM supports the importance of maintaining a twin focus in treatment: promoting welfare and reducing harm. The idea that risk factors are internal or external obstacles that frustrate or block the acquisition of human goods provides a useful way of integrating the two approaches. From the GLM perspective, treatment should focus first on identifying the various obstacles preventing offenders from living a balanced and fulfilling life, and then seek to equip them with the skills, beliefs, values, and supports needed to counteract their influence.

Finally, the importance of human agency and the construction of a personal identity are key features of the GLM. The selection of an overarching set of primary goods and their related commitments results in a meaningful and rich life characterized by high levels of well-being.

## IMPLICATIONS FOR THE ASSESSMENT OF SEXUAL OFFENDERS

If the GLM is adopted as a foundation for sexual offender treatment, assessment is important—in particular, risk, treatment needs, and responsivity factors (i.e., the personal factors such as IQ, personality, and learning style that affect the way in which he will respond to treatment). A typical assessment package for sexual offenders includes structured interviews focusing on personal history, relapse knowledge (e.g., Beckett, Fisher, Mann, & Thornton, 1988) and personality (e.g., the Psychopathy Checklist–Revised; Hare, 1991); a battery of psychometric tests measuring areas related to risk of sexual recidivism such as impulsivity, offense-supportive attitudes, and socio-affective functioning; a psycho-physiological assessment such as phallometric testing (Marshall & Fernandez, 2000); IQ testing; and behavioral observation.

Assessors may be trained in the technical aspects of psychometric assessment, such as the importance of not acting in any way that could influence the client's responses. In order to adhere to these principles, the assessor often does not attempt to build a relationship with the offender, but presents assessment tasks in as neutral a way as possible. The sexual offender client often responds to this presentation with suspicion, as he has no indication the process of assessment is adapted to his personal needs or issues. In the 1980s, due to concerns sex offenders were likely to manipulate the assessment and treatment process, specialists were guided to expect "the client will have goals that the therapist does not share and the therapist is expected to override the client's wishes" (Salter, 1988, p. 87). In practice, this assumption could lead to reluctance by therapists or assessors to discuss the purpose of assessment or to invite the client's thoughts and ideas about his needs.

Such an approach to assessment is not consistent with the GLM. The GLM leads to a prediction a person will be most responsive to an intervention that is tailored to his own personal goals and needs. Sexual offender assessment should be seen as an intervention in its own right, as a process that is capable of bringing about change. For instance, a well-conducted collaborative risk and need assessment (see later discussion) can lead a client to start thinking about change or to gain insight into his problems. Assessment can also lead to change in a person's environment. For example, an assessment that concludes that a particular offender is both high risk and high need can lead to the offender being moved to more secure conditions or receiving an increased level of social punishment. Therefore, the assessment process should be treated with the same level of care as the treatment intervention. In doing so, attention should be paid to both the style and content of assessments.

## Assessing Personal Goals and Priorities

First, we will examine the content of an assessment package that would be GLM consistent. We believe risk, needs, and responsivity are three major issues to be explored through assessment. However, we also recommend a fourth area for exploration: *priorities*. RNR principles should be embedded within a good lives framework. It is essential to assess a client's own goals, life priorities, and aims for intervention in order to understand how a client prioritizes and operationalizes the primary human goods outlined earlier. If this fourth area is overlooked, sexual offender assessment concentrates only on vulnerabilities and fails to recognize the importance of understanding how an individual can become fulfilled. It is important to balance the assessment of risk and vulnerability with each individual's good life conceptualization (e.g., Laws & Ward, 2011; Yates, Prescott, & Ward, 2010).

At present there is no psychometric tool for this assessment, so a detailed clinical interview is recommended. We recommend an open ended interview where the assessor's intentions and the rationale for the interview are transparent. This allows an opportunity for self-exploration as well as identifying how offenders prioritize their primary human goods. The interview could be introduced in the following way:

> Researchers have suggested there are a number of activities and experiences that human beings need if they are to have a good (fulfilling) life. I want to talk about these things with you and find out which you feel you have achieved in your life and which you don't. We can then talk about how treatment can help you focus on the things that you don't have in your life and how you can go about building up those areas. We can also play to your strengths—the areas where you have achieved happiness or satisfaction—and build on those positives. The outcome for you from treatment should be that you feel your life to be more rewarding, satisfying and balanced. It is my hope and expectation that this would also mean that you don't experience the problems you had before when you were offending.

The interview should address these questions with respect to each human good:

- What does this mean to you?
- How important is this to you? Has your view of its importance changed over time?
- How have you gone about achieving this in your life? Which strategies have worked the best and least well?
- Would you like to have more of this in your life?
- What has prevented you from achieving this in your life?
- Where would you like to be with respect to this in one year's time? Five years' time? Ten years' time?

Such questions allow for the assessment of each individual's conception of a good life. They also facilitate an understanding of the individual's strategies for realizing primary goods. In order to make a more comprehensive assessment of each individual's potential for achieving a good life, the assessing clinician should have an understanding of the following areas, so that answers to the preceding questions can be probed in line with the theory behind the GLM. The following issues, taken from Ward and Stewart (2003b), could form the basis for a final good lives formulation.

1. Is there restricted scope? That is, are some goods focused on to the detriment of other goods, contributing to a lack of adequate balance and range of priorities? For instance, mastery is overemphasized and relationships underemphasized.
2. Are some human goods pursued through inappropriate means? That is, has the individual chosen counterproductive strategies for achieving goods? For example, pursuing the goal of intimacy by adopting extremely controlling behaviors toward partners.
3. Is there conflict among the goals articulated? For instance, does the individual state priorities that cannot coexist easily, such as wanting emotional intimacy with a romantic partner but also wanting sexual freedom and a variety of partners? Emmons (1999) has described the stress that results from a lifestyle that is inconsistent with one's most valued goods.
4. Does the person have the capacity or capabilities to enact their plan—implicit or explicit? Is the plan realistic, taking into account their abilities, likely opportunities, deep preferences, and values?

An exploration of a sexual offender's GLP can assist the clinician in formulating a treatment plan that provides the opportunity for the individual to achieve greater satisfaction and well-being. If the offender is able to see how the treatment plan will directly benefit him in terms of goods he values, he is more likely to engage enthusiastically in treatment. Men who reoffend despite receiving sex offender treatment were consciously unengaged with the treatment process (Webster, 2001), so a high perception of treatment relevance will be associated with reduced risk of further offending. Recently, there have been some promising developments with structured assessment of offenders' primary and secondary goods that may provide clinicians with more systematic ways of establishing intervention targets (see Laws & Ward, 2011; Yates et al., 2010).

ASSESSMENT STYLE

It has become fashionable to approach sexual offender assessment with a primary intention of assessing risk (Hart, Laws, & Kropp, 2003) and is the primary preoccupation for many involved professionally with the sexual offender: from the sentencing authority to the treatment provider, policy maker, and those engaged in monitoring and offense prevention. However, understanding of risk is *not* the primary preoccupation of most sexual offenders. Instead, offenders tend to be more concerned about their links with family and friends; their physical circumstances; their position within their immediate and wider community; and relief of stress and other negative personal symptoms. For instance, a survey of sex offenders who refused treatment in Her Majesty's (HM) Prison Service (Mann & Webster, 2003) established that maintaining family support was the most important priority for this group. Denial or treatment refusal were seen as necessary in order to maintain important relationships.

Given the risk assessor's priority is in conflict with the offender's during risk assessment, it is often unlikely such an assessment will uncover the full picture of a person's functioning. For instance, the offender who is not motivated to work with the risk assessor is likely to conceal or minimize areas related to risk that are unpleasant to reveal, such as deviant sexual interests. Assessment is more accurate and more productive if both parties share goals and priorities. Mann and Shingler (2002) produced guidelines for collaborative risk assessment, which attempts to reconcile the goals of clinician and offender. The collaborative approach reconceptualizes risk assessment as needs assessment, and involves the therapist and client working collaboratively to define the nature of the client's problems and agree on a process for working towards solutions. A collaborative approach to assessment is consistent with the GLM, emphasizing the fundamental autonomy and dignity of the human being, even though he has committed crimes or other harmful acts on others (Laws & Ward, 2011).

In essence, the collaborative approach involves a genuine commitment from the therapist to working transparently and respectfully, and to emphasizing that the client's best interests are to be served by the assessment process. Potential issues of risk and need are presented to the client as areas for collaborative investigation. Results of assessment procedures such as phallometric and psychometric testing are discussed and the client is invited to collaborate in drawing conclusions from them. Perhaps most relevant of all to the GLM, the client's strengths and life achievements are considered to be as important as his offense-related needs in determining his prognosis and treatment plan. Early indications are that relationships between treatment staff and clients are greatly improved when risk assessment is a collaborative process, with a subsequent positive effect on treatment motivation and retention (Mann & Shingler, 2002).

In conclusion, the GLM approach to assessing sexual offenders must be seen in both the content and style of the assessment procedure. Assessment of sexual offenders must continue to examine risk, need, and responsivity factors, but must also involve a full consideration of the individual's GLP. Assessment should be collaborative wherever possible, in order to convey the professional's commitment to respecting the client. Treatment plans arising from such assessments will be individualized, consistent with the individual's priorities, and therefore less likely to conflict with his personal goals. This sets an individual up to enter treatment believing it will be a relevant and important activity for him to engage in.

## IMPLICATIONS FOR THE TREATMENT OF SEXUAL OFFENDERS

Principles that must underlie the construction of a sex offender treatment program using the GLM are as follows:

1. Many sex offenders have experienced adversarial developmental experiences as children, and should be seen as individuals who have lacked the opportunities and support necessary to achieve a coherent GLP.
2. Consequently, sexual offenders lack many of the essential skills and capabilities necessary to achieve a fulfilling life.
3. Sexual offending represents an attempt to achieve human goods that are desired but where the skills or capabilities necessary to achieve them are not possessed. Alternatively, sexual offending can arise from an attempt to relieve the sense of incompetence, conflict, or dissatisfaction that arises from not achieving valued human goods.
4. Certain human goods seem to be more strongly associated with sexual offending: agency, inner peace, and relatedness.
5. The risk of sexual offending may be reduced by assisting offenders to develop the necessary skills and capabilities to achieve the full range of human goods through prosocial means.
6. Treatment is an activity that should *add to* a sexual offender's repertoire of personal functioning, rather than an activity that simply *removes* a problem or is devoted to *managing* problems, in order to avoid offending. Treatment should aim to return individuals to as normal a level of functioning as possible, and only place restrictions on activities highly related to the problem behavior.

We believe the GLM conceptualization of sexual offending therefore differs in several important ways from the traditional sexual offender treatment model. These differences will now be elaborated.

### AIMS OF GLM TREATMENT

The aims of GLM treatment are specified as *approach goals* (Emmons, 1996; Mann, 2000; Mann, Webster, Schofield, & Marshall, 2004) and are defined in terms of what clients will achieve and gain, rather than in terms of what they will cease to think or do. Such goals are more likely to resonate with the client's intrinsic motivation to change, in that change is more appealing if results appear obviously life enhancing. Second, goals are more likely to fit with offenders' own preoccupations following conviction. Much as we would like to think that most sexual offenders are preoccupied with avoiding future offending, the truth is they are more preoccupied with their own quality of life. An approach-goal focused program offers a better quality of life, while still focused on achieving what most programs are funded to achieve: reductions in recidivism. Third, an approach-goal focused program is pragmatically more likely to work (Cox, Klinger, & Blount, 1991). Sexual offenders undergoing an approach-focused self-management intervention showed greater compliance with treatment compared to a more traditional avoidance-focused relapse prevention program, yet they emerged with an equally clear idea of their personal risk factors and warning signs (Mann et al., 2004).

### MANUALIZED OR FORMULATION-BASED TREATMENT?

Traditionally, sexual offender treatment programs have been highly structured psychoeducational programs, where skills are taught in a series of modules such as emotion management, victim empathy, and so forth. Such programs may not be consistent with the GLM's emphasis on person-centered values (Drake & Ward, 2003). On the other hand, unstructured treatment programs have been found to have no impact on recidivism rates and therefore, presumably, are not sufficiently targeting offense-relevant areas of pathology. Drake and Ward (2003) argue for a formulation-based treatment approach, where intervention covers topics relevant to an individual formulation of the client, based on the kind of assessment procedure described earlier. It must, however, be emphasized that formulation-based interventions are not the same as unstructured programs. It is possible to manualize a formulation-based program; for example, a program run by William Marshall and colleagues in Canada (e.g., see Marshall, Anderson, & Fernandez, 1999) adopted a rolling format, where group members worked through a series of assignments at their own pace. Assignments included both offense-related topics, such as victim empathy, and topics related to achieving human goods, such as intimacy, attachment, and emotional management. Although one way to deliver such a program would be for each group member to simply complete each assignment, it is also possible to tailor the program for each individual, based on a personalized formulation. In such an approach, one group member might spend only one session examining his self-esteem, but several sessions examining the issue of other-esteem. Another group member might complete more victim empathy assignments than usual, if this was a particular area of deficit. In order to operate a manual-based program according to individual formulations, it is necessary to have considered all possible areas of need within the program, from which a selection will be drawn for each individual, and to have a careful system of recording work undertaken, so that evaluations of treatment efficacy can still be conducted. It would also be necessary to have some clear guidelines that specify conditions under which each possible area of treatment would be either offered or deemed unnecessary. Such manualized but individualized programs are rare within today's state of the art, but there is evidence of programs moving in this direction, and we encourage further consideration of such treatment design.

### Reconceptualizing Sex Offender Treatment Targets According to the GLM

Treatment involves two steps. First, the offender must construe himself as someone who can secure all the important human goods in socially acceptable and personally rewarding ways (Ward & Stewart, 2003b).

Secondly, the treatment program should endeavor to assist offenders to develop the scope, capacities, coherence, and strategies necessary for a healthy personal GLP. For sex offenders, it is suggested the personal goods that are most often corrupted or neglected are agency, relatedness, and inner peace. In order to achieve a GLM-consistent treatment approach, goals of treatment need to be considered and aligned with the GLM. In this section, we examine some of the best-established goals of sexual offender treatment, and reinterpret them in terms of the GLM. Table 37.1 displays 14 treatment need areas defined by Thornton (2002) and offers suggestions for how relevant offense-related psychological characteristics may be understood and treated within a good lives approach. The table also outlines possible links to human goods and therapy options; it is not meant to be rigidly prescriptive.

From Table 37.1, it is clear specific activities of a GLM-based treatment program for sexual offenders are not significantly different from a conventional treatment program, but the goal of each intervention component is explicitly linked to GLM theory. A more holistic treatment perspective is taken, based on the core idea that the best way to reduce risk is by helping offenders live more fulfilling lives. Therapy is tailored to each offender's GLP while still being administered in a systematic and structured way. It is envisaged offenders need only undertake treatment activities that provide the ingredients of their particular plan. The focus is on a better fit between therapy and offenders' specific issues, abilities, preferences, and contexts, and greater attention is paid to the development of a therapeutic alliance and the process of therapy. Basic respect for the offender is derived from the GLM assumptions about the value of persons and their pursuit of primary goods. Risk factors are regarded as internal and external obstacles that make it difficult for an individual to implement a GLP in a socially acceptable and personally fulfilling manner. Thus, a major focus is on the establishment of skills and competences needed to achieve a better kind of life, alongside the management of risk. This twin focus incorporates the strengths of the relapse prevention and capabilities approaches to treatment. It is easier to motivate offenders when reassured the goods they are aiming for are acceptable; the problem resides in the way they are sought. Sometimes individuals mistake the means (secondary goods) for the end (primary goods), and it may be necessary to spend quite a bit of time exploring the goods that underlie their offending behavior and the specific problems in their GLP. In the GLM approach, the goal is always to create new skills and capacities within the *context* of individuals' good lives plans and to encourage fulfilment through the achievement of human goods.

An exercise within HM Prison Service confirmed sexual offenders are more likely to respond positively to treatment targets that are formulated according to the GLM. Three focus groups of sexual offenders were convened to discuss their ideas for a

**Table 37.1**
Good Lives Model of Treatment

| Treatment Need Area | GLM Conceptualization | GLM Treatment Approach |
|---|---|---|
| 1. Sexual preoccupation | Offender is limited in alternative strategies for achieving the human goods of agency, or inner peace. Or, intimacy and sex are seen as blurred rather than independent goals. Or, offender's GLP lacks scope: too much emphasis placed on the achievement of one secondary good.<br><br>Another possibility is overvaluing goods of physical satisfaction (health/living good) and play. | Develop wider range of strategies for achieving goods of agency and inner peace.<br><br>Increase scope of offender's GLP so that secondary goods other than sexual activity increase in importance.<br><br>Seek other means of achieving physical stimulation, pleasure, and sense of adventure/play. |
| 2. Sexual preference for children | Offender has not developed alternative strategies for achieving the secondary goods of sexual satisfaction and sexual intimacy. Or, lack of scope within offender's GLP: too much emphasis placed on achieving sex/intimacy at any cost. Or, corruption of agency/mastery good: agency considered to be achieved through sexual domination of a minor. | Develop wider range of strategies for achieving secondary goods of sexual satisfaction and sexual intimacy.<br><br>Increase strategies for achieving agency and mastery in nonsexual situations. |
| 3. Sexual preference for rape | Conflict between goals of relatedness, agency, and sexual activity. A corruption of the agency good: The offender achieves a sense of autonomy by humiliating or dominating others while neglecting the secondary goods of emotional and sexual intimacy. | Increase strategies for achieving agency; realign GLP to separate agency from relatedness.<br><br>Increase importance of emotional and sexual intimacy within the good lives plan. |
| 4. Adversarial sexual attitudes | Problems in the way the good of relatedness is sought and/or frustration arising from failure to achieve this good through inappropriate means. Women are viewed as unreliable or untrustworthy. | Seek to establish appropriate means of seeking good of relatedness and managing feelings of anger and frustration (mood management skills). |

*(continued)*

**Table 37.1**
*(Continued)*

| Treatment Need Area | GLM Conceptualization | GLM Treatment Approach |
| --- | --- | --- |
| 5. Sexual entitlement | Tendency to value own needs above those of others; competence and agency linked to asserting self over others.<br><br>Lack of scope of GLP, lack of attention to establishing relationships, intimacy, good of communication and, therefore failure to appreciate needs and rights of others. | Focus on broadening scope of GLP to include goods of relatedness and community.<br><br>Learn that establishing own competence and agency through asserting own needs over others is likely to be counterproductive in the long run. |
| 6. Offense-supportive beliefs | Refers to offenders' representations of their own goals and the beliefs that support them. For example, children are sexual beings or women are unknowable.<br><br>Offense-supportive beliefs function as maps that help offenders to make sense of their life, partially confer identity, and stipulate way to achieve goals. | Clarify that primary goods are not the problem but rather the way they are sought. Therefore, focus on selecting ways of achieving human goods that take into account offenders' preferences, abilities, contexts, and values while ensuring outcome is ethically acceptable and personally satisfying. |
| 7. Beliefs that women are deceitful | This belief is likely to be related to intimacy failures and resulting emotional turbulence (failure of inner peace): anger, resentment, and so on. | Therapy to concentrate on providing greater understanding of the source of this belief and associated emotional states.<br><br>Encourage offenders to understand the relationship between this belief and frustrated pursuit of human goods in their circumstances. Then develop GLP that can rectify problems. |
| 8. Inadequacy (low self-esteem, external locus of control, loneliness) | Lack of capacity to achieve agency (autonomy, self-directedness) and mastery (excellence in work/play). | Teach skills to enhance achievement of agency and mastery (e.g., skills of self-directedness, emotional management). Assess and enhance aspects of life that result in mastery good being achieved (i.e., areas where skill, knowledge, or ability already exist or are potentially achievable). |

**Table 37.1**
(*Continued*)

| Treatment Need Area | GLM Conceptualization | GLM Treatment Approach |
|---|---|---|
| 9. Distorted intimacy balance | Goods of intimacy sought through associations with children because of lack of capacity (e.g., confidence, skill) to achieve intimacy/relatedness with adults). Or, lack of social connectedness with community and, therefore, lack of access to social opportunities. | Teach skills and increase confidence to achieve relatedness successfully with adults.<br><br>Increase access to social relationships and institutions that appeal to offenders (e.g., hobby classes, work opportunities). |
| 10. Grievance schema | Obstacles to achieving inner peace, likely to be caused by lack of access to number of other goods, especially overarching good. | Work to assist in dismantling grievance beliefs and replace with strategies to achieve inner peace.<br><br>Identify problems in implementation of GLP and seek to install internal and external conditions required to successfully implement it within offenders' unique contexts. |
| 11. Lack of emotional intimacy | Either neglect of intimacy as a human good within the individual's GLP, lack of capacity to achieve intimacy/relatedness, or problems regulating emotions (i.e., achieve inner peace). | Consider role of intimacy within GLP; teach skills to assist better achievement of relatedness.<br><br>Help to modulate and manage emotions more effectively. |
| 12. Lifestyle impulsivity | Lack of necessary capacity to form and adjust a GLP to changing circumstances.<br><br>Lack of capacity to achieve good of agency because of difficulties inhibiting desires, planning, and implementation. | Teach skills of decision making, adapting to changing circumstances, considering longer term consequences before acting.<br><br>Acquire basic self-control strategies. |
| 13. Poor problem solving | Lack of capacity to achieve agency (autonomy and self-directedness). | Teach skills of problem solving, negotiation, conflict resolution. |
| 14. Poor emotional control | Lack of capacity to achieve agency (autonomy and self-directedness) and inner peace. | Teach emotional management skills. |

*Note.* Treatment need areas adapted from *Structured Risk Assessment*, by D. Thornton, 2002, Sinclair Seminars Conference on Sex Offender Re-offense Prediction.

new booster treatment program.[1] Participants were all graduates of a conventional cognitive behavioral treatment program. All three groups stressed the focus of a booster group should be positive and future oriented. Going over the past was experienced as demoralizing. They wanted to get support and practice new skills on topics such as improving relationships and intimacy, building self-esteem, learning how to deal with emotions, practicing coping strategies, developing a support network, and considering how to disclose their offending to others. Each one of these suggestions is consistent with the GLM of sexual offender treatment, suggesting the GLM is likely to be perceived as highly relevant by offenders.

CHANGING THE LANGUAGE OF TREATMENT

A GLM reformulation of sex offender treatment probably affects the aims and principles of treatment more than it affects the content of modern programs. The language of treatment is important: Modern texts on sexual offender treatment constantly use language associated with negative evaluations, or negative expectancies (e.g., *deficit, deviance, distortion, risk,* and *prevention*). The GLM is a positive model, based on assumptions people are more likely to embrace positive change and personal development, and so the kinds of language associated with such an approach should be future oriented, optimistic, and approach-goal focused. Thus we make the following suggestions.

Language associated with avoidance goals should be changed to language associated with approach goals. Thus, *relapse prevention* could be retermed *self-management* or *change for life*; problems and deficits should be rephrased as approach goals: *intimacy building* should be used in preference to *intimacy deficits*. Program names should be changed to reflect the future-orientation of treatment; thus programs named STOP (a popular acronym) or Sex Offender Risk Management, could be renamed Healthy Sexual Functioning. The use of positive language has a compelling effect on those we treat. For example, in HM Prison Service, changing the term *dynamic risk factor* to *treatment need* has greatly facilitated collaboration in assessment and treatment (as well as being a more accurate description of the results of therapeutic assessment).

## UPDATES

The GLM has continued to attract interest internationally (see Willis, Ward, & Leveson, 2014; Willis, Yates, Gannon, & Ward, 2013).

RESEARCH

The literature on the application of the GLM framework to offender rehabilitation is expanding, although many studies have explored the GLM as an *additional* component to an existing program (e.g., Mann et al., 2004; Martin, Hernandez, Hernandez-Fernaud, Arregui, & Hernandez, 2010; Ware & Bright, 2008). Studies of the effectiveness of using the GLM include Gannon, King, Miles, Lockerbie, and Willis (2011); Harkins, Flak, Beech, and Woodhams (2012); and Simons, McCullar, and Tyler (2006) for offender rehabilitation in a range of program settings (e.g., prison, inpatient mental health and community based). Although research into the GLM is in its infancy, some concern has emerged that there is insufficient attention

---

[1]The authors wish to gratefully acknowledge the contribution of Rebecca Milner, who facilitated these focus group sessions.

paid to risk factors (Gannon et al., 2011; Harkins et al., 2012). Overall, however, the outcomes for GLM-consistent programs are producing results consistent with RNR-adherent programs, with some evidence for more positive outcomes (Simons et al., 2006) and increased participant and therapist satisfaction (Harkins et al., 2012).

## APPLICATION TO PROBATION CASE MANAGEMENT

While there is increasing interest in the GLM being applied to offender treatment programs, there has been less application to case management. Purvis, Ward, and Shaw (2013) provide guidelines to assist probation officers in applying the GLM principles to case management work. They outline the process of identifying what an offender values in his life and obstacles that may prevent them achieving these in a prosocial and personally meaningful manner. Probation workers can conceptualize obstacles (criminogenic needs) that contribute to offending occurring and use this information to develop a plan to address these through focusing on the offender acquiring the necessary skills, internal and external resources, supports, and so on, to achieving their GLP without causing harm to others. The authors suggested that using the GLM framework to approach case management will mean probation plans are individualized, guided by the individual offenders' interests, priorities, and needs. The probation officer is reminded that focusing on individual strengths or capacities and personally meaningful goals should see a corresponding increase in motivation and should be associated with long-term and positive behavior change.

## YOUTH SEX OFFENDERS

Historically the RNR model (Andrews & Bonta, 2010), which dominated correctional and forensic psychology, has also dominated the approach to rehabilitation with youth offenders. There is increasing interest in the application of strength-based approaches to youth offenders, including sexually abusive youth. The GLM is one example of this approach that has been adapted for use with youth offenders. Fortune, Ward, and Print (2014) have made suggestions on how the GLM can be adapted to better suit the developmental level of juvenile sex offenders and has much to offer how we approach the assessment and treatment of young sex offenders. The adaptions allow for simplification of the language used and are based on program developments in the United Kingdom. For example, the 11 primary goods can be presented as seven key needs using more accessible terminology and defined in ways that young people and their family/caregivers will understand. As the GLM is a rehabilitative *framework* rather than a treatment program, it can provide a structure that can inform the rehabilitative process, including assessment, treatment, and relapse prevention with juvenile sex offenders. This means that specific, empirically supported treatment techniques for juvenile sex offenders such as those used to develop empathy skills, social skills, or emotional regulation can be wrapped around a GLM-derived good lives plan to build capabilities and reduce dynamic risk factors (criminogenic needs). From a therapeutic perspective, approaching assessment, treatment, and case management plans from the viewpoint of what a young person wants and can achieve can be more motivating than simply listing situations they should avoid.

## CONCLUSION

In this chapter we have presented a new theory of offender rehabilitation and applied it to sex offenders. The good lives model is a strength-based approach and proposes that the major aim of treatment is to equip offenders with the necessary internal and external conditions required to implement a GLP in their particular set of circumstances. In the GLM, risk factors are viewed as distortions in these conditions and are not expected to provide the sole focus of rehabilitation. Instead there is a twin focus on establishing good lives and avoiding harm. In our view, this theory has the conceptual resources to provide a comprehensive guide for therapists in the difficult task of treating sex offenders and making society a safer place.

## SUMMARY POINTS

- Offenders, like all human beings, have multiple natural needs, such as needs to be loved, to be valued, to function competently, to be part of a community, and to live meaningful lives.
- To lose sight of this fact is to risk becoming simply agents of social control rather than also facilitators of hope.
- Risk management is necessary for effective change but is not sufficient.
- The best way to lower sexual offending recidivism rates is to equip offenders with the internal and external resources to live more fulfilling lives.

## REFERENCES

Ackerman, S. J., & Hilsenroth, M. J. (2003). A review of therapist characteristics and techniques positively impacting on the therapeutic alliance. *Clinical Psychology Review, 23*, 1–33.

Andrews, D. A., & Bonta, J. (2010). *The psychology of criminal conduct* (5th ed.). New Providence, NJ: Matthew Bender.

Arnhart, L. (1998). *Darwinian natural right: The biological ethics of human nature.* Albany: State University of New York Press.

Beckett, R., Fisher, D., Mann, R. E., & Thornton, D. (1998). Relapse prevention interview. In H. Eldridge, *Therapist guide to maintaining change: Relapse prevention for adult male perpetrators of child sexual abuse* (pp. 138–150). London, England: Sage.

Cordner, C. (2002). *Ethical encounter: The depth of moral meaning.* Basingstole, England: Palgrave.

Cox, M., Klinger, E., & Blount, J. P. (1991). Alcohol use and goal hierarchies: Systematic motivational counselling for alcoholics. In W. R. Miller & S. Rollnick (Eds.), *Motivational interviewing: Preparing people to change addictive behavior* (pp. 260–271). New York, NY: Guilford Press.

Cummins, R. A. (1996). The domains of life satisfaction: An attempt to order chaos. *Social Indicators Research, 38*, 303–328.

Deci, E. L., & Ryan, R. M. (2000). The "what" and "why" of goal pursuits: Human needs and the self-determination of behavior. *Psychological Inquiry, 11*, 227–268.

Drake, C. R., & Ward, T. (2003). Treatment models for sex offenders: A move toward a formulation-based approach. In T. Ward, D. R. Laws, & S. M. Hudson (Eds.), *Sexual deviance: Issues and controversies* (pp. 226–243). Thousand Oaks, CA: Sage.

Emmons, R. A. (1996). Striving and feeling: Personal goals and subjective well-being. In P. M. Gollwitzer & J. A. Bargh (Eds.), *The psychology of action: Linking cognition and motivation to behavior* (pp. 313–337). New York, NY: Guilford Press.

Emmons, R. A. (1999). *The psychology of ultimate concerns.* New York, NY: Guilford Press.

Fortune, C. A., Ward, T., & Print, B. (2014). Integrating the Good Lives Model with relapse prevention: Working with juvenile sex offenders. In D. Bromberg & W. O'Donohue (Eds.), *Toolkit for working with juvenile sex offenders* (pp. 405-426). New York, NY: Academic Press.

Gannon, T. A., King, T., Miles, H., Lockerbie, L., & Willis, G. M. (2011). Good Lives sexual offender treatment for mentally disordered offenders. *British Journal of Forensic Practice, 13*, 153–168. doi:10.1108/14636641111157805

Govier, T. (2002). *Forgiveness and revenge*. London, England: Routledge.

Hare, R. (1991). *Manual for the Hare Psychopathy Checklist-Revised*. Toronto, Ontario: Multi-Health Systems.

Harkins, L., Flak, V. E., Beech, A., & Woodhams, J. (2012). Evaluation of a community-based sex offender treatment program using a Good Lives Model approach. *Sexual Abuse: A Journal of Research and Treatment, 24*(6), 519–543. doi: 10.1177/1079063211429469

Hart, S., Laws, D. R., & Kropp, P. R. (2003). The promise and peril of sex offender risk assessment. In T. Ward, D. R. Laws, & S. M. Hudson (Eds.), *Sexual deviance: Issues and controversies* (pp. 207–225). Thousand Oaks, CA: Sage.

Hollin, C. R. (1999). Treatment programs for offenders: Meta-analysis, "what works" and beyond. *International Journal of Law and Psychiatry, 22*, 361–372. doi:10.1016/S0160-2527(99)00015-1

Kekes, J. (1989). *Moral tradition and individuality*. Princeton, NJ: Princeton University Press.

Kekes, J. (1990). *Facing evil*. Princeton, NJ: Princeton University Press.

Laws, D. R., Hudson, S. M., & Ward, T. (Eds.). (2000). *Remaking relapse prevention with sex offenders: A sourcebook*. Thousand Oaks, CA: Sage.

Laws, D. R., & Ward, T. (2011). *Desistance and sex offending: Alternatives to throwing away the keys*. New York, NY: Guilford Press.

Mann, R. E. (2000). Managing resistance and rebellion in relapse prevention. In D. R. Laws, S. M. Hudson, & T. Ward (Eds.), *Remaking relapse prevention with sex offenders*. Thousand Oaks, CA: Sage.

Mann, R. E., & Shingler, J. (2002, April). *Collaborative risk assessment*. Paper presented to Tools to Take Home conference, Cardiff, Wales.

Mann, R. E., & Webster, S. D. (2003, April). *Why do some sex offenders refuse treatment?* Workshop presented at Tools to Take Home conference, Birmingham, England. Available from the authors at Room 725 Abell House, John Islip Street, London SW1P 4LH.

Mann, R. E., Webster, S. D., Schofield, C., & Marshall, W. L. (2004). Approach versus avoidance goals in relapse prevention with sexual offenders. *Sexual Abuse: A Journal of Research and Treatment, 16*(1), 65–75. doi:10.1177/107906320401600105

Margalit, A. (1996). *The decent society*. Cambridge, MA: Harvard University Press.

Marshall, W. L. (1996). The sexual offender: Monster, victim, or everyman? *Sexual Abuse: A Journal of Research and Treatment, 8*, 317–335. doi:10.1177/107906329600800406

Marshall, W. L., Anderson, D., & Fernandez, Y. M. (1999). *Cognitive behavioral treatment of sexual offenders*. Chichester, England: Wiley.

Marshall, W. L., & Fernandez, Y. M. (2000). Phallometric testing with sexual offenders: Limits to its value. *Clinical Psychology Review, 20*, 807–822. doi: 10.1016/S0272-7358(99)00013-6

Marshall, W. L., Fernandez, Y. M., Serran, G. A., Mulloy, R., Thornton, D., Mann, R. E., & Anderson, D. (2003). Process variables in the treatment of sexual offenders: A review of the relevant literature. *Aggression and Violent Behavior, 8*(2), 205–234. doi: 10.1016/S1359-1789(01)00065-9

Martin, A. M., Hernandez, B., Hernandez-Fernaud, E., Arregui, J. L., & Hernandez, J. A. (2010). The enhancement effect of social and employment integration on the delay of recidivism of released offenders trained with the R & R programme. *Psychology, Crime & Law, 16*, 401–413. doi:10.1080/10683160902776835

Maruna, S. (2001). *Making good: How ex-convicts reform and rebuild their lives*. Washington, DC: American Psychological Association.

Murphy, M. C. (2001). *Natural law and practical rationality*. New York, NY: Cambridge University Press.

Nussbaum, M. C. (2000). *Women and human development: The capabilities approach*. New York, NY: Cambridge University Press.

Pithers, W. D. (1990). Relapse prevention with sexual aggressors: A method for maintaining therapeutic gain and enhancing external supervision. In W. L. Marshall, D. R. Laws, &

H. E. Barbaree (Eds.), *Handbook of sexual assault: Issues, theories and treatment of the offender* (pp. 346–361). New York, NY: Plenum Press.

Porporino, F. J. (2010). Brining sense and sensitivity to corrections: From programmes to "fix" offenders to services to support desistance. In J. Brayford, F. Cowe, & J. Derring (Eds.), *What else works? Creative work with offenders* (pp. 61–85). Portland, OR: Willan.

Potter, N. N. (2002). *How can I be trusted? A virtue theory of trustworthiness.* Lanham, MD: Rowman & Littlefield.

Purvis, M., Ward, T., & Shaw, S. (2013). *Applying the Good Lives Model to the case management of sexual offenders: A practical guide for probation officers, parole officers, and case workers.* Brandon, VT: Safer Society Press.

Rapp, C. A. (1998). *The strengths model: Case management with people suffering from severe and persistent mental illness.* New York, NY: Oxford University Press.

Rescher, N. (1990). *Human interests: Reflections on philosophical anthropology.* Stanford, CA: Stanford University Press.

Salter, A. C. (1988). *Treating child sex offenders and victims: A practical guide.* Newbury Park, CA: Sage.

Schmuck, P., & Sheldon, K. M. (Eds.). (2001). *Life goals and well-being.* Toronto, Ontario: Hogrefe & Huber.

Simons, D. A., McCullar, B., & Tyler, C. (2006, September). *Evaluation of the Good Lives model approach to treatment planning.* Paper presented at the 25th Annual Association for the Treatment of Sexual Abusers Research and Treatment Conference, Chicago, IL.

Thornton, D. (2002). *Structured risk assessment.* Sinclair Seminars Conference on Sex Offender Re-offense prediction, Madison, WI. Videotape available from www.sinclairseminars.com

Ward, T. (2002). Good Lives and the rehabilitation of offenders: Promises and problems. *Aggression and Violent Behavior, 7,* 513–528. doi:10.1016/S1359-1789(01)00076-3

Ward, T., & Brown, M. (2003). The risk-need model of offender rehabilitation: A critical analysis. In T. Ward, D. R. Laws, & S. M. Hudson. (Eds.), *Sexual deviance: Issues and controversies* (pp. 338–353). Thousand Oaks, CA: Sage.

Ward, T., & Gannon, T. A. (2006). Rehabilitation, etiology, and self-regulation: The comprehensive Good Lives Model of treatment for sexual offenders. *Aggression and Violent Behavior, 11*(1), 77–94. doi:10.1016/j.avb.2005.06.001

Ward, T., & Hudson, S. M. (2000). A self-regulation model of relapse prevention. In D. R. Laws, S. M. Hudson, & T. Ward (Eds.), *Remaking relapse prevention with sex offenders: A sourcebook* (pp. 79–101). Thousand Oaks, CA: Sage.

Ward, T., Louden, K., Hudson, S. M., & Marshall, W. L. (1995). A descriptive model of the offence chain in child molesters. *Journal of Interpersonal Violence, 10,* 452–472.

Ward, T., Mann, R. E., & Gannon, T. A. (2007). The Good Lives Model of offender rehabilitation: Clinical implications. *Aggression and Violent Behavior, 12*(1), 87–107. doi:10.1016/j.avb.2006.03.004

Ward, T., & Marshall, W. L. (2004). Good lives, aetiology, and the rehabilitation of sex offenders: A bridging theory. *Journal of Sexual Aggression, 10*(2), 153–169. doi:10.1080/13552600412331290102

Ward, T., & Maruna, S. (2007). *Rehabilitation: Beyond the risk assessment paradigm,* London, England: Routledge.

Ward, T., & Stewart, C. A. (2003a). Criminogenic needs and human needs: A theoretical model. *Psychological, Crime, & Law* (2), 125–143. doi:10.1080/1068316031000116247

Ward, T., & Stewart, C. A. (2003b). Good lives and the rehabilitation of sexual offenders. In T. Ward, D. R. Laws, & S. M. Hudson (Eds.), *Sexual deviance: Issues and controversies* (pp. 21–44). Thousand Oaks, CA: Sage.

Ward, T., & Stewart, C. A. (2003c). The treatment of sex offenders: Risk management and good lives. *Professional Psychology: Research and Practice, 34*(4), 353–360. doi:10.1037/0735-7028.34.4.353

Ware, J., & Bright, D. A. (2008). Evolution of a treatment programme for sex offenders: Changes to the NSW Custody-Based Intensive Treatment (CUBIT). *Psychiatry, Psychology and Law, 15,* 340–349. doi:10.1080/13218710802014543

Webster, S. D. (2001). *Pathways to sexual offence recidivism following treatment: A qualitative study.* Unpublished MSc dissertation, London School of Economics.

Willis, G., Ward, T., & Leveson, J. (2014). The Good Lives Model (GLM): An evaluation of GLM operationalization in North American treatment programs. *Sexual Abuse: A Journal of Research and Treatment, 26,* 58–81.

Willis, G., Yates, P., Gannon, T., & Ward, T. (2013). How to integrate the Good Lives Model into treatment programs for sexual offending: An introduction and overview. *Sexual Abuse: A Journal of Research and Treatment, 25,* 123–142. doi:10.1177/1079063212452618

Yates, P., Prescott, D., & Ward, T. (2010). *Applying the Good Lives Model to sex offender treatment: A practical handbook for clinicians.* Brandon, VT: Safer Society Press.

# CHAPTER 38

# Facilitating Forgiveness Using Group and Community Interventions

FRANK D. FINCHAM

EELING HURT, LET DOWN, betrayed, disappointed, or wronged by another human being is a universal experience. In the face of such injury, negative feelings (e.g., anger, resentment, disappointment) are common. Motivation to avoid the source of the harm, or even a desire to retaliate or seek revenge, is also typical. Indeed, revenge occurs across species (Aureli, Cozzolino, Cordischi, & Scucchi, 1992), and its corrosive effects are undeniable. Retaliatory impulses may motivate the victim to reciprocate the transgression in kind, but reciprocated harm is usually perceived to be greater than the original offense by the transgressor, who, in turn, may retaliate to even the score. Given such escalating cycles of vengeance, it is not surprising that revenge is implicated in many of our most ignominious acts as a species, including homicide, suicide, terrorism, and genocide (McCullough, Kurzban, & Tabak, 2010).

Limited data exist on how people manage to inhibit the tendency to respond negatively to a partner's bad behavior and respond constructively instead, a process called accommodation. Some initial data suggest that such responses are related to relationship commitment, greater interdependence between persons, and having plentiful time, rather than a limited time, to respond (e.g., Yovetich & Rusbult, 1994). Although important, such findings provide only a partial understanding of how relationships are maintained in the face of partner transgressions. Consider the case of an extramarital affair where the perceived reason for the affair is the adulterous spouse's selfish focus on his or her own immediate wishes. Assuming equal levels of commitment, what happens in one marriage that allows the betrayed partner to overcome his or her anger and resentment and behave in a conciliatory manner toward the spouse, whereas in another marriage the relationship remains tense for years? As they remain constant in this example, neither the major relationship macro-motive (commitment) nor the proximal determinant (reasons for the event) identified in research on accommodation can help in providing an answer. This example highlights the need for a new category of relationship process that may follow a transgression and the initial hurt engendered by it but that may also influence the aftermath of the event. One such process is forgiveness, a construct that has engaged the attention of social scientists and that is an important human strength with the potential to contribute to the good life and, for some, the meaningful life.

## WHAT IS FORGIVENESS?

Although it is a complex construct without a consensual definition, at the center of various approaches to forgiveness is the idea of a freely chosen motivational transformation in which the desire to seek revenge and to avoid contact with the transgressor is lessened, a process sometimes described as an altruistic gift (e.g., Enright, Freedman, & Rique, 1998; Worthington, 2001). This core feature immediately distinguishes forgiveness from constructs such as denial (unwillingness to perceive the injury), condoning (removes the offense and, hence, the need for forgiveness), pardon (granted only by a representative of society such as a judge), forgetting (removes awareness of offense from consciousness; to forgive is more than not thinking about the offense), and reconciliation (which restores a relationship and is, therefore, a dyadic process). Thus, the common phrase "forgive and forget" is misleading because forgiveness is possible only in the face of remembered wrongs or hurt.

But is this decrease in unforgiveness sufficient, especially in the context of ongoing relationships? It is a logical error to infer the presence of the positive (e.g., health, forgiveness) from the absence of the negative (e.g., illness, unforgiveness). Therefore, it bears noting that what may be equally fundamental to forgiveness is "an attitude of real goodwill towards the offender as a person" (Holmgren, 1993, p. 342). However, there is less agreement among researchers on whether forgiveness requires a benevolent or positive response (e.g., compassion, affection, approach behavior) to the offender or whether the absence of negative responses (e.g., hostility, anger, avoidance) is sufficient (Exline, Worthington, Hill, & McCullough, 2003; Fincham, 2000). Both cross-sectional and longitudinal data show that the two dimensions may function differently; spouses' retaliatory motivation following a transgression is related to partner reports of psychological aggression and, for husbands, to ineffective arguing, whereas benevolence motivation correlates with partner reports of constructive communication and, for wives, partners' reports of ineffective arguing (Fincham & Beach, 2002b; Fincham, Beach, & Davila, 2004). Also, unforgiveness, but not forgiveness, is associated with partner reports of marital satisfaction (Paleari, Regalia, & Fincham, 2009). A longitudinal study showed that in the first few weeks following a transgression, avoidance and revenge motivation decreased whereas benevolence motivation did not change (McCullough, Fincham, & Tsang, 2003).[1]

To complicate matters further, forgiveness can be conceptualized at different levels of specificity: as a trait, as a tendency toward a specific relationship partner, and as an offense-specific response. Trait forgiveness, or forgivingness, occurs across relationships, offenses, and situations, whereas the tendency to forgive a particular relationship partner, sometimes referred to as dyadic forgiveness (Fincham, Hall, & Beach, 2005), is the tendency to forgive him or her across multiple offenses. Finally, offense-specific forgiveness is defined as a single act of forgiveness for a specific offense within a particular interpersonal context. Associations among these levels of forgiveness is modest at best (e.g., Allemand, Amberg, Zimprich, & Fincham, 2007; Eaton, Struthers, & Santelli, 2006). In fact, Paleari et al. (2009) found that both positive and negative dimensions of forgiveness were more strongly related to relationship variables than to trait forgivingness, arguing that "relational characteristics may be more important in understanding forgiveness of interpersonal transgressions in close relationships than a global disposition to forgive" (Paleari et al., 2009, p. 205).

---

[1]Most studies use a single unidimensional measure of forgiveness and do not differentiate forgiveness from unforgiveness. For ease of presentation the word *forgiveness* is used in describing results from these studies.

Finally, forgiveness is sometimes even used to characterize social units (e.g., families, communities).

What is becoming clear, however, is that laypeople may use and conceptualize interpersonal forgiveness in ways that differ from researchers (see Kearns & Fincham, 2004). For example, Kantz (2000) found laypersons believe that reconciliation is a necessary part of forgiveness, an element explicitly rejected by many definitions of forgiveness used in research. In this study, subjects also endorsed the view that forgiveness could cause emotional problems, which again runs counter to the salutary effects attributed to forgiveness in most research. This finding raises the legitimate question of whether forgiveness is harmful or, as scholars have claimed, a human strength.

## IMPLICATIONS OF DEFINING FORGIVENESS FOR APPLIED WORK

Because lay conceptions appear to confuse forgiveness and related constructs, conceptual clarity is particularly important in applied work that attempts to facilitate forgiveness. For example, the lay conception that forgiveness involves reconciliation may lead some who forgive to place themselves in danger of future harm. Thus, attempts to facilitate forgiveness should include an educational component to ensure that participants understand fully what forgiveness does and does not entail. It may also be necessary to assess perceived negative consequences of forgiving before making an attempt to encourage forgiveness. Before turning to applied work, we first examine whether forgiveness is associated with positive outcomes.

## FORGIVENESS AND WELL-BEING

The presumed benefits of forgiveness for well-being have been the single most important stimulus for the upsurge of research on forgiveness in the past 25 years. In fact, there is even some fMRI evidence to show that forgiveness activates a specific region of the brain (posterior cingulated gyrus) that is distinct from that activated by empathy (Farrow et al., 2001). The potential existence of a distinct functional anatomy for forgiveness points to its evolutionary advantage (see McCullough, 2008). In fact, McCullough et al. (2010) provide evidence consistent with the view that "forgiveness systems evolved in response to selection pressures for restoring relationships that, on average, boosted lifetime reproductive fitness" (p. 231).

### PHYSICAL HEALTH

There is growing evidence from large national probability samples, as well as smaller scale studies, that forgiveness is associated with psychophysiological and psychoneuroimmunological processes, as well as self-reported measures of health (e.g., Lawler-Row, Karremans, Scott, Edlis-Matityahou, & Edwards, 2008; Worthington, Witvliet, Pietrini, & Miller, 2007). In fact, forgiveness is associated with cardiac risk in both community and patient populations (Friedberg, Suchday, & Shelov, 2007; Toussaint & Cheadle, 2009). One study has even shown that conditional forgiveness, forgiveness that depends on the post-transgression behavior of the transgressor, predicts mortality (Toussaint, Owen, & Cheadle, 2012). That is, failure to forgive unconditionally poses health risks and appears to be life threatening. Not surprisingly, forgiveness has been associated with better outcomes for medical conditions such as heart disease (Friedberg, Suchday, & Srinivas, 2009; Waltman et al. 2009) and spinal cord injuries (Webb, Touissant, Kalpakjian, & Tate, 2010).

In a similar vein, forgiveness can facilitate the repair of supportive close relationships, and such relationships are known to protect against negative health outcomes. For example, marital conflict is associated with poorer health (Burman & Margolin, 1992) and with specific illnesses, such as cancer, cardiac disease, and chronic pain (see Schmaling & Sher, 1997). Hostile behaviors during conflict relate to alterations in immunological (Kiecolt-Glaser et al., 1997), endocrine (Kiecolt-Glaser et al., 1997), and cardiovascular (Ewart, Taylor, Kraemer, & Agras, 1991) functioning. An association exists between both forgiveness and unforgiveness and marital quality (see Fincham, 2010; Fincham et al., 2005), with some indication of a more robust relationship for unforgiveness (Gordon, Hughes, Tomcik, Dixon, & Litzinger, 2009). Longitudinal evidence suggests that marital quality predicts later forgiveness and that forgiveness also predicts later marital satisfaction (Fincham & Beach, 2007; Paleari, Regalia, & Fincham, 2005). It is therefore possible that forgiveness is health protective because it helps people maintain stable, supportive relationships (see Fincham, in press). Consistent with this view, married couples report that the capacity to seek and grant forgiveness is one of the most important factors contributing to marital longevity and marital satisfaction (Fenell, 1993).

Studies on physiological reactivity provide more direct evidence on forgiveness and physical functioning. For example, Witvliet, Ludwig, and Van der Laan (2001) demonstrated that engaging in unforgiving imagery (rehearsing hurtful memories and nursing a grudge) produced more negative emotions and greater physiological stress (significantly higher EMG, skin conductance, heart rate, and blood pressure changes from baseline), which endured longer into recovery periods. On the other hand, forgiving imagery (engaging in empathic perspective taking and imagining forgiveness) produced lower physiological stress levels. In a second study, Lawler-Row, Hyatt-Edwards, Wuench, and Karremans (2011) showed that forgiveness was inversely related to self-reported health problems and that both state forgiveness and trait forgivingness were related to heart rate and heart rate reactivity in response to, and recovery from, a stressor. Berry and Worthington (2001) showed that the tendency to forgive predicted cortisol reactivity (indicating higher stress) in low-quality relationships following imagination of typical relationship events, thereby suggesting that hormonal factors may also be implicated in any link between forgiveness and health. It is not difficult to imagine how such physiological or hormonal reactivity could over time adversely influence health.

An overlooked but potentially important consideration is the motivation for forgiving. During descriptions of an offense, people who forgave out of religious obligation showed more anger-related responses (e.g., masking smiles, downcast eyes) and elevated blood pressure compared to those who forgave out of love (Huang & Enright, 2000). This suggests that what forgiveness means to a person may be critical for his or her physiological and behavioral responses. This study alerts us to the fact that only freely given forgiveness that conforms to the criteria outlined earlier is relevant to the good life. Forgiveness born of obligation, pain avoidance, manipulation, and so on is neither a strength nor virtue.

## MENTAL HEALTH

Forgiveness has been investigated in relation to numerous mental health outcomes, most frequently depressive symptoms and life satisfaction. Across 22 studies involving 4,510 participants a statistically significant inverse relationship emerged between forgiveness and depression ($r = -.26$; Riek & Mania, 2012). As might be expected, higher levels of forgiveness are related to greater life satisfaction ($r = .25$, 11 studies,

2,984 participants) and reported positive affect ($r = .32$, nine studies, 1,502 participants; Riek & Mania, 2012). In a similar vein negative associations exist between forgiveness and anxiety ($r = -.18$), perceived stress ($r = -.23$), and negative affect ($r = -.47$; Riek & Mania, 2012).

Likewise, to the extent that forgiveness helps enhance relationship quality, a possibility supported by numerous studies documenting a robust association between forgiveness and such constructs as commitment and relationship satisfaction (for reviews see Fincham, 2009, 2010), forgiveness may be associated with improved well-being because of links between overall relationship quality and mental health. For example, the link between relationship quality and numerous psychological disorders is well established (see Beach & Whisman, 2012). There is also some direct evidence that forgiveness is linked to relationship destructive factors in that lower levels of forgiving predict psychological aggression and protracted conflict in marriage (Braithwaite, Selby, & Fincham, 2011; Fincham, Beach, & Davila, 2004, 2007).

## CRITIQUE

Remarkably little attention has been given to potential adverse effects of forgiveness. This is somewhat surprising as forgiveness is a motivated behavior, and where motives exist, they can be good or bad. Thus, forgiveness can be used strategically to manipulate others, to put them down, and so on. Under such circumstances forgiveness can be quite harmful. However, if the outward expressions of forgiveness truly reflect internal motivations, it is safe to conclude that forgiveness plays an important salutary role in close relationships and that this role can promote health both directly and indirectly by repairing the relationship. However, this potential may not always be achieved. For example, McNulty's (2008) work shows that expressing forgiveness in the context of ongoing conflictual relationships predicts lower satisfaction in newlyweds over the first year of marriage and perhaps indirectly leads to poorer health. In a further study McNulty (2010) found that more forgiving spouses experienced stable or growing levels of psychological and physical aggression over the first 5 years of marriage, whereas less forgiving spouses experienced declines in partner transgression (see McNulty & Fincham, 2012, for further data and discussion). Psychological and physical aggression are linked to poorer health outcomes.

Compelling, direct evidence documenting a causal link between forgiveness and physical and mental health is lacking. Experimental or longitudinal research that might address the issue of causality is rare in the literature on forgiveness. An exception is McCullough, Bellah, Kilpatrick, and Johnson's (2001) study, which showed no relation between change in forgiveness and life satisfaction, a finding that could reflect disparity in level of measurement of the two constructs (e.g., forgiveness for a specific event versus a global measure of functioning), the existence of a causal lag that is different from the 8-week period investigated, or limited variability in life satisfaction over this short period. Data are sorely needed to demonstrate that forgiveness improves individual well-being. Nonetheless, recognition of the negative physical and mental health outcomes associated with processes that can occur in the absence of forgiving (e.g., preoccupation with blame, rumination) appears to sustain theoretical attempts to identify processes linking forgiveness and physical and mental health.

Applied studies that attempt to facilitate forgiveness currently provide the only direct evidence about the effects of forgiveness on well-being. Because such studies are often experimental in design, they are an important test of the hypothesis that facilitating forgiveness actually influences well-being rather than merely being associated with it. I, therefore, begin my discussion of applied research by reviewing the evidence it provides on the impact of forgiveness on well-being.

## APPLIED RESEARCH ON FORGIVENESS

Since Close (1970) published a case study on forgiveness in counseling, various models of forgiving have emerged in the counseling/psychotherapy literature. From the inception of forgiveness intervention research, however, model builders have skipped the task of validating their models and proceeded directly to intervention outcome research. Perhaps more importantly, the psychotherapy literature has far outstripped empirical data on forgiveness, leaving us in the awkward position of attempting to induce forgiveness without knowing how it operates in everyday life. Finally, it is important to note that the vast majority of invention studies have not been conducted with clinical populations but instead with community samples.

Regular meta-analyses have emerged beginning with Worthington, Sandage, and Berry's (2000) summary of 14 available studies (delivered to 393 participants) that showed a linear dose–effect relationship for the effect sizes they yielded. Specifically, clinically relevant interventions (defined as those of 6 or more hours' duration) produced a change in forgiveness (effect size [ES] = 0.76) that was reliably different from zero, with nonclinically relevant interventions (defined as 1 or 2 hours' duration) yielding a small but measurable change in forgiveness (ES = 0.24). These authors tentatively conclude that "amount of time thinking about forgiveness is important in the amount of forgiveness a person can experience" (p. 234). In a subsequent meta-analysis, Baskin and Enright (2004) found that 1-hour, one-time interventions were ineffective in promoting forgiveness (ES = −0.04) and may have been iatrogenic. Wade, Worthington, and Meyer's (2005) meta-analysis of 27 studies showed that although amount of time spent in the intervention predicted efficacy, intervention status (full vs. partial vs. no intervention) predicted outcome over and beyond intervention duration. Focusing on 16 studies of "process" models of forgiveness, where forgiveness is achieved only after going through several different phases or steps, Lundhal, Taylor, Stevenson, and Roberts (2008) found large effect sizes for increasing forgiveness (ES = 0.82) and positive affect (ES = 0.81). Negative affect was also decreased (ES = 0.54). Participants with elevated levels of distress benefitted more than those with lower distress levels and participants who received the intervention individually showed greater improvement than those who experienced group interventions. In contrast to individual outcomes no improvement in the relationship with the perpetrator of the transgression was found. This led to the suggestion that intervention programs may "not be consistently better than no treatment in improving relationships" (p. 474).

In light of the preceding suggestion, it is important to note the growing literature on interventions to promote forgiveness in marital and family contexts (for review see Worthington, Jennings, & DiBlasio, 2010). In this literature, there is evidence to show that forgiveness interventions have led to decreased psychological symptoms and in some studies increased relationship satisfaction. Unfortunately, this literature includes numerous studies that use small sample sizes and are therefore underpowered.

In a field in which it is difficult to do experimental research, intervention studies have the potential to provide much needed information on mechanisms involved in forgiveness. To date, however, this potential remains largely untapped because the dismantling of these multicomponent interventions to determine the active ingredients for changing forgiveness is notably absent. Also absent are data on the impact of induced forgiveness on relationship outcomes. Thus, the potential of applied research to advance understanding of forgiveness remains unrealized.

CRITIQUE

Because interventions are a relatively blunt experimental manipulation that may influence a number of variables, it will be important in future intervention studies to show that changes in forgiveness are correlated with changes in psychological well-being. Perhaps most importantly in the current context, intervention research has thus far focused on the individual experience of forgiving and not the interactions that occur around forgiveness. The result is that most intervention research tells us little about how to help people negotiate forgiveness. This is an important omission because repentance and apology (phenomena that involve interpersonal transactions) facilitate forgiveness and because, in the context of an ongoing relationship, forgiveness may involve numerous transactions.

The intervention literature demonstrates that there has been good progress in devising interventions to induce forgiveness. But this is analogous to focusing on a manipulation check in experimental research. What about the dependent variable; does inducing forgiveness produce positive psychological outcomes? Here results are more mixed. A problem with many of the available studies is that the interventions are delivered to samples that are either asymptomatic or show limited variability in mental health symptoms, making it difficult to demonstrate intervention effects on these variables. In fact, most interventions are primarily psychoeducational and not specifically designed to deal with patient populations. Because certain conditions such as depression and marital discord tend to be comorbid, it is quite possible that psychopathology may be present in distressed couples who seek such interventions. However, forgiveness intervention research and work on forgiveness more generally tends to focus on community samples and make use of dimensional measures of symptoms (e.g., anger, depression).

The limitations of the available data are more understandable when we recall that less than 25 years ago, pioneering publications did not contain reference to any published empirical research on forgiveness (e.g., Hebl & Enright, 1993; Mauger et al., 1992). Research on forgiveness is growing and steadily lending weight to the case for the importance of forgiveness in maintaining and promoting well-being. However, it is clear that attempts to promote forgiveness have been limited in conceptualization and scope. In particular, they reflect the traditional assumptions made in psychotherapy/counseling, namely, that people (patients, clients) wronged by another need to seek help from professionals (therapists/counselors) in a special environment divorced from their natural setting (the clinic). The remainder of the chapter therefore offers a much expanded view for research on facilitating forgiveness.

## TOWARD A COMPREHENSIVE, EVIDENCE-BASED MODEL FOR FACILITATING FORGIVENESS

This section begins by examining the implications of positive psychology for attempts to facilitate forgiveness; then it identifies the premises underlying the approach offered. Finally, it discusses the facilitation of forgiveness in terms of two dimensions, breadth of reach and intensity, and relates them to delivery formats.

### FORGIVENESS THROUGH THE LENS OF POSITIVE PSYCHOLOGY

Viewing forgiveness through the lens of positive psychology (e.g., McCullough, Root, Tabak, & Witvliet, 2009) has implications for a more complete understanding of the construct and for evaluating efforts to facilitate forgiveness. As a human strength, forgiveness has the potential to enhance functioning and not simply protect against dysfunction. But because measurement of forgiveness has primarily focused on its negative dimension (avoidance, retaliation), most of what has been learned about forgiveness rests on inferences made from the absence of the negative (dysfunction). Here there is the danger of falling prey to a logical error noted earlier—the absence of a negative quality (e.g., vengeance) is not equivalent to the presence of a positive quality (e.g., benevolence). Like psychology itself, forgiveness research has (unwittingly) focused on human dysfunction in opposition to which positive psychology was born. What positive emotions, strengths, and virtues (other than empathy) correlate with forgiveness? Our inability to answer this question immediately points to the need to broaden the nomological network in which forgiveness is situated to include strengths and virtues (for an analysis of the interplay between forgiveness and gratitude, see Fincham & Beach, 2013b). Similarly, attempts to facilitate forgiveness should not simply be evaluated in terms of the prevention or amelioration of dysfunction but also in terms of their ability to promote optimal functioning (Fincham & Beach, 2010). I advocate a focus on the positive in forgiveness research as a complement to, rather than a substitute for, existing work, mindful of the admonition that "a positive approach cannot ignore pathology or close its eyes to the alienation and inauthenticity prevalent in our society" (Ryan & Deci, 2000, p. 74).

Awareness of possible positive correlates of forgiveness also directs attention to the positive dimension of forgiveness, benevolence. As noted, forgiveness cannot be understood completely by studying unforgiveness, just as marital quality cannot be fully understood by the study of marital distress or optimism by the study of learned helplessness. Thus, we must remain open to the possibility that negative and positive dimensions of forgiveness may have different determinants, correlates, and consequences. For example, it can be hypothesized that negative and positive dimensions predict avoidance/revenge and conciliatory behaviors, respectively. Similarly, different intervention efforts may be needed for reducing retaliatory and avoidance motivations versus increasing benevolence.

Finally, the lens of positive psychology alerts us to different ways in which forgiveness may function in relation to optimal human experience. Thus far, I have noted that the exercise of forgiveness facilitates gratification in one of the main realms of life (the interpersonal) and thus contributes to the good life (Seligman, 2002). But forgiveness may also promote a meaningful life. All three of the major monotheistic religions emphasize forgiveness, and the practice of forgiveness in Judaism, Christianity, and Islam can easily be seen as serving something much larger than the forgiver and, therefore, contributing to the meaningful life. However, two very important caveats must be added. First, forgiveness does not necessarily contribute to a meaningful life among the faithful; it will do so only when exercised freely and not as the mindless exercise of a religious obligation (see Huang & Enright, 2000). Second, the exercise of forgiveness can also contribute to the meaningful life for nonreligious forgivers. However, to do so, it is likely to require the forgiver to be consciously motivated by a desire to create a better community or society and to view his or her action as contributing to the realization of this goal. At an applied level, the implication is that, where appropriate, efforts should be made to show the link between the individual's action and the service of something greater than the individual, such as God's will for the faithful, or for the secular, the betterment of a social unit (e.g., family, neighborhood, school) or the community as a whole (e.g., through the establishment of more humane norms). In short, the lens of positive psychology alerts us to an important but relatively unexplored issue pertaining to forgiveness, its meaning for the forgiver.

## UNDERLYING PREMISES

The approach that is now offered reflects a number of premises that shape its form, which are, therefore, briefly articulated. First, it is informed by an integrated prevention and treatment perspective. It moves beyond the positive psychology approach toward prevention, which focuses on strengths in people at risk. Laudable as such an expanded view of prevention might be, it suffers from decontextualizing risk and ignoring cultural and structural factors that maintain risk behavior. For example, facilitating forgiveness for someone who has a strong social network that encourages a hostile response may deprive the person of social support and, at worst, set him or her in conflict with support providers. Recognizing the central role of religion and religious communities in the majority of the world's population, Fincham and colleagues have investigated how prayer might be used to facilitate the use of strengths, including forgiveness (Lambert, Fincham, Stillman, Graham, & Beach, 2010); avoid risk (Fincham, Lambert, & Beach, 2010); and facilitate well-being (Fincham & Beach, 2013a).

A second premise is that persons who might benefit from forgiving may not be seeking help. This means that the traditional waiting mode familiar to psychologists needs to be replaced by the seeking mode embraced by the community mental health movement (Rappaport & Chinsky, 1974). In contrast to waiting for clients to present at the office for diagnosis and treatment, in seeking mode we move into the community taking on nontraditional roles such as developer of community programs, consultant to local groups, and evaluator of community-based intervention efforts. In the present context, this is particularly important because many potential beneficiaries of forgiveness are likely to be reached through natural community groups (e.g., religious organizations).

Third, persons who might benefit from forgiving may not have the financial resources to obtain professional help or be located in areas served by mental health care providers. Therefore, any forgiveness intervention should be designed to reach people in a variety of settings (including rural and geographically isolated settings) and be viable for use in these settings. Thus, at a minimum, the intervention should be easily implemented, reasonably brief, and economic to implement. Ideally, it should involve a familiar process that occurs naturally in the community. This means that there is likely to be a need to look to a broader range of persons (e.g., media specialists) and modes of delivery (e.g., distance learning) than is typical in traditional psychological interventions.

Finally, I operate from the premise that any attempt to facilitate forgiveness should represent best practice in terms of what is currently known scientifically about forgiveness and its facilitation. A corollary is that any intervention must lend itself to evaluation, for without evaluation no program can be assumed to be effective. The notion that "something is better than nothing" is simply misguided, no matter how well intentioned, and, as Bergin (1963) reminds us, anything that has the potential to help also has the potential to harm. We now consider forgiveness facilitation in a two-dimensional framework.

## DIMENSION 1: BREADTH OF REACH

Forgiveness interventions have been limited to those delivered by a professional to an individual or a small group of individuals. Given the observation made in the chapter opening that everyone will, at some point, feel hurt, let down, betrayed, disappointed, or wronged, these interventions are inadequate to reach everyone for whom forgiveness is relevant. Moreover, in asking about the nature of forgiveness, I noted that it can be applied to social units. By facilitating forgiveness in such units, researchers not only provide a more complete approach to facilitating forgiveness but also begin to address the problem of decontextualized interventions. Broadening our approach in this manner is clearly a radical departure from the traditional clinical model that has informed prior intervention efforts.

The importance of including community-level intervention in a comprehensive approach to facilitating forgiveness is emphasized by the observation that "a large number of people exposed to a small risk may generate more cases than a small number exposed to a high risk" (Rose, 1992, p. 87). But the inclusion of community-level intervention in our approach brings with it new challenges. It needs to be recognized, for example, that outcome for individuals is alone insufficient to evaluate such interventions because the unit of intervention and evaluation is the community or organization. A comprehensive model, therefore, needs to encompass change in collectives and not only individuals. How do we assess the community or organization environment? This is not the context in which to address such questions. These kinds of questions are being addressed in the field of public health where community-level intervention has taken root. Readers interested in these challenges are referred to analyses of methodological issues arising from community-level and community-based intervention (Sorensen, Emmons, Hunt, & Johnson, 1998; Thompson, Coronado, Snipes, & Puschel, 2003).

## DIMENSION 2: INTENSITY

It is a truism that the intensity of interventions differs, and I use this dimension to order prevention, enhancement, and remediation efforts. Prevention and enhancement are appropriate for those who are not manifesting levels of distress that impair their normal functioning, whereas remediation is targeted at those experiencing clinical levels of distress.

As to prevention, I distinguish among universal preventive measures, considered desirable for everyone in the population; selective preventive measures, considered desirable for subgroups of the population at higher than average risk; and indicated preventive measures, desirable for individuals who are known to be at high risk (Mrazek & Haggerty, 1994). In universal prevention, benefits outweigh the minimal costs and risks for everyone. In contrast, indicated interventions are not minimal in cost (e.g., time, effort). This reflects the fact that recipients of an indicated prevention may be experiencing some (subclinical) level of distress associated with the transgression.

Determining the place of enhancement on the intensity continuum is difficult. On the one hand, persons appropriate for enhancement should not be motivated by an experienced transgression but rather the desire to improve their life experience. As such, they most closely resemble recipients of universal or selective prevention. On the other hand, the minimal preventions provided in these cases do not match the motivation that prompts their involvement in intervention. As a result, I place enhancement between prevention and remediation on the intensity dimension.

Having briefly described the two dimensions integral to my approach to facilitating forgiveness, I next discuss the interventions to which they give rise.

## FACILITATING FORGIVENESS

Table 38.1 illustrates our framework for facilitating forgiveness. Reflecting the premise that intervention should reflect best practice, I derive two important

**Table 38.1**

An Expanded Framework for Facilitating Forgiveness

| | | Breadth of Reach | |
| --- | --- | --- | --- |
| Intensity of Intervention | Individual | Group | Social Unit/Institution in Community |
| Prevention | | | |
| Universal | Forgiveness information campaign | | |
| Selective | Psychoeducation | | |
| Indicated | Psychoeducation with forgiveness implementation | | |
| Enhancement | Psychoeducation with relationship skills training | | |
| Remediation | Forgiveness-focused therapeutic intervention | | |

implications from the forgiveness literature. First, interventions should include an educational component about what forgiveness does and does not entail with both appropriate and inappropriate examples of forgiveness (e.g., use of forgiveness as a means—to manipulate, assert moral superiority—rather than an end) and their consequences. This can serve both to avoid dangers likely to result from misconceptions about forgiveness (e.g., returning to a dangerous situation because reunion is confused with forgiveness) and to relieve psychological distress when individuals feel the need to forgive a transgressor but find themselves unable to do so because forgiveness is confused with something they may not want to do either consciously or, more often, unconsciously (e.g., condone transgressor's action). Second, when interventions address forgiveness of a specific transgression, they should require the participants to spend time thinking about forgiveness, which seems to be related to the occurrence of forgiveness (with the corollary that simply exposing people to the transgression they experienced without facilitating forgiveness may be iatrogenic).

The first level of intervention shown is an information campaign to promote awareness of forgiveness and describe what it does and does not involve, its correlates, and its status as a human strength. Although I advocate use of the mass media for this purpose, the campaign does not preclude some contact with professional staff (e.g., telephone information line).

I advocate use of the mass media for a forgiveness information campaign because the media has played a useful role in disseminating health information to the public. Here we can envision a cross-media promotion strategy that includes newspapers, posters, billboards, informational pamphlets, television, and the Internet. Television in particular has proved useful in modifying potentially harmful behaviors such as cigarette smoking and poor diet (Biglan, 1995; Sorensen et al., 1998), and we envision it as the core around which the campaign is organized. In particular, skilled use of infotainment (e.g., a feature story in which forgiveness themes are embedded, followed by a celebrity interviewed about overcoming a hurt in his or her life) is preferred over the more traditional public health announcement for two reasons. First, a television series, if well executed, is likely to gain greater attention. Second, such a series can become a longer-term resource that offsets campaign costs. Finally, it needs to be recognized that the success of such a campaign should not be judged in terms of its impact on forgiveness per se, but rather on its ability to raise awareness and to produce a climate in which forgiveness is supported.

At the next level of intervention is psychoeducation. What distinguishes this level from the last is that factors that facilitate forgiveness, described in generic terms, are added to the intervention. Hence, topics such as empathy and humility, which have been emphasized in existing interventions, will garner attention. In addition, recipients of the intervention will be directed to recall instances in which they were forgiven as a vehicle to draw attention to our common frailty as human beings and to elaborate on the virtue of gratitude (Fincham & Beach, 2013b). This level of intervention does not include exercises designed to bring about forgiveness of a specific transgression. Rather, its goal is to create conditions propitious to consideration of forgiveness as a possible response when a transgression is experienced. Both levels of intervention described thus far are intended to entail relatively low cost for the recipients.

Greater recipient time and effort are required for the third level of intervention, psychoeducation with forgiveness implementation. It is only at this level that response to a specific transgression in the recipient's life is addressed. An important element of this level of intervention is screening of recipients because not everyone who has experienced a transgression (and, therefore, is at risk) will be a suitable candidate. At the most fundamental level, recipients need to be screened for clinical disorder. However, even in the absence of such disorder, when the transgression occasions a traumatic response (shatters basic beliefs about the world, etc.; see Gordon, Baucom, & Snyder, 2000), this level of intervention is not appropriate, even if the response does not reach the level of diagnosable posttraumatic stress disorder. This level of intervention is most similar to the majority of extant group interventions for forgiveness. However, these interventions have yet to capitalize on a growing body of research showing that writing about past traumatic experiences has beneficial effects on mental and physical health (see Esterling, L'Abate, Murray, & Pennebaker, 1999; for a study concerning transgressions, see McCullough, Root, & Cohen, 2006). Our approach to facilitating forgiveness, therefore, makes extensive use of writing exercises. We have described this intervention in detail elsewhere (Fincham & Beach, 2002a).

The next level of intervention is enhancement. Participants in enhancement programs generally are self-selected; hence, their motivation is likely to be high. At this level, recipients learn forgiveness as a general skill without targeting a specific transgression. Ripley (1998) provides an example of such an approach. Community couples participated in this intervention with the goal of increasing intimacy and preventing future problems in their relationships. Many of the couples in Ripley's program denied having any unresolved hurts, which supports my decision not to target specific participant transgression at the level of enhancement. As an interpersonal process, forgiveness as a general skill is difficult to imagine in the absence of more general relationship skills (e.g., communication skills). Hence, intervention at the level of enhancement includes training in such relationship skills.

Finally, remedial interventions are targeted at persons whose functioning has been impaired by a transgression or series of transgressions. Little is known about interventions for severe and long-lasting harms because these have not been the subject of the group interventions that have dominated the forgiveness intervention literature. However, there are notable examples of such interventions for individuals (e.g., Coyle & Enright, 1997). Whether forgiveness in this situation simply becomes a component of a broader intervention or can be sustained as an independent self-contained intervention is open to question. The answer to this question may rest on the extent to which the transgression and the response to it are part of a chronic pattern of functioning in the person's life. It is conceivable that self-contained forgiveness interventions are viable to the extent that they deal with single, precisely defined harms (e.g., marital infidelity). Most of what is known about this level of intervention derives from clinical experience and is largely anecdotal. This has not prevented the emergence of more formal process models of forgiveness (e.g., Enright & Coyle, 1998) to inform intervention, but these models have not been subject to empirical evaluation that demonstrates forgiveness unfolds in the manner specified. Nonetheless, outcome studies based on interventions using these models (e.g., Coyle & Enright, 1997; Freedman & Enright, 1996) make useful contributions to our knowledge about the benefits of promoting forgiveness in the context of psychotherapy. Wade, Johnson, and Meyer (2008) provide a useful discussion of the concerns that arise when forgiveness is explicitly included in psychotherapy.

## DELIVERY FORMAT

Consistent with my broadened view of facilitating forgiveness, I advocate diverse delivery formats for forgiveness interventions. I have already discussed use of the mass media in a forgiveness information campaign. Use of mass media need not be limited to this level of intervention, however. Indeed, one can conceive of judicious use of this delivery format for all levels of intervention except remediation. For example, there already exists a competitive market of trade books dealing with forgiveness, some of which take the form of self-help, but, as is too often the case, this self-help domain is relatively uninformed by research on forgiveness.

Delivery of interventions via the print medium is necessarily limited as compared to audiovisual presentation. More information can be presented more vividly in a shorter time frame using the audiovisual medium. Given this advantage, as well as its ability to engage attention, I advocate the development of audiovisually based interventions. However, both of these delivery formats provide minimal control over the delivery of the intervention because readers can access pages in whatever order they choose, and viewers can fast forward videotapes at the click of a button. The issue of control becomes important where interventions include programmatic, cumulative exercises designed either to facilitate forgiveness of a specific transgression or to develop a relationship skill. Everything presented via the print or audiovisual medium can be delivered in a more controlled manner through the digital medium. Delivery of an intervention on a CD or DVD can control access to later parts of the intervention by making it contingent on performing earlier parts. Mastery of material can also be assessed once it has been accessed and immediate feedback given with further progress through the intervention dependent on a minimal level of mastery. Programs can also be written to individualize the intervention by tailoring what material is presented dependent on a participant's answers to relevant questions.

Almost anything that can be delivered via CD and DVD can also be delivered via the Internet. This latter medium of delivery is particularly exciting because of its growing penetration of households throughout the world and because it allows greater control over the delivery of the intervention (e.g., time spent on writing exercises can be monitored precisely, writing can be analyzed online, and so on). The possibility of delivering an intervention to millions of people throughout the world via the Internet makes the road ahead both an exciting and daunting path to travel.

I would be remiss if I did not comment on the face-to-face delivery format with individuals and groups. In my judgment, this medium is the sine qua non of the remedial level of intervention, though it is also an option for other levels. But even here, my vision is broader than that traditionally found. Consistent with the premises of a seeking mode of intervention and participant resources not necessarily enabling access to professionals, I see a critical role for paraprofessionals in facilitating forgiveness. Indeed, there has long been data to suggest that psychotherapy interventions delivered by professionals and paraprofessionals do not differ in effectiveness (e.g., Christensen, Miller, & Munoz, 1978). This brings me to the issue of starting points for implementing my vision of facilitating forgiveness.

## STARTING POINTS

Rather than approach the task de novo and reinvent the wheel, a useful starting point is to look for existing interventions in the community that might include forgiveness as well as those that might be enhanced by including a focus on forgiveness. I identify an example of each before highlighting limitations of the approach advocated in this chapter.

An unlikely but promising starting point is the legal system where forgiveness is gaining attention in both criminal (e.g., Nygaard, 1997) and civil contexts (e.g., Feigenson, 2000). Two entry points are particularly promising from our perspective. First is the recent emergence of problem-solving courts, particularly community courts, which use judicial authority to solve legal and nonlegal problems that arise in individual cases and consider outcomes that go beyond mere application of the law. Denckla (2000) describes the role and impact of forgiveness in problem-solving courts. Two obvious next steps might be to (1) index the degree to which forgiveness operates in particular courts and relate this to relevant outcomes (e.g., recidivism), and (2) compare jurisdictions in which such courts do and do not operate.

Perhaps more obvious as a point of entry for forgiveness research are restorative justice programs. There is a diversity of views on what is meant by *restorative justice* (Johnstone, 2002), but several themes underlie this diversity, including attention to what should be done for the victim, relating to offenders differently (not seeing them as enemies from the outside but as one of us), and the community's willingness to be involved in conflict resolution between victim and offender (Johnstone, 2002). By allowing for forgiveness, restorative justice programs empower the victim and allow the perpetrator to be affirmed both by the victim and the community as a person of worth and to regain—or for many gain for the first time—their respect and be reintegrated, or integrated, into society. Recognizing these themes does not give rise to a particular method but rather offers a set of purposes and values to guide responses to crime (Morris & Young, 2000; see also Fortune, Ward, & Mann, Chapter 37, this volume). I now briefly consider one form in which restorative justice has been implemented, victim–offender mediation (VOM), sometimes called victim–offender reconciliation programs.

VOM programs began in the 1970s in Canada, and there are now hundreds of programs throughout the world (focused largely on juvenile offenders), evaluation of which yields salutary findings, including in participant satisfaction, perceived fairness of restitution agreement, restitution completion, and recidivism (see Umbreit, 2001). Note, however, that forgiveness is not an explicit goal of such programs. Indeed, good mediators avoid use of terms such as *forgiveness* and *reconciliation* because they "pressure and prescribe behavior for victims" (p. 25). But this does not preclude forgiveness from taking place in VOM. This provides the opportunity to compare outcomes in cases where forgiveness does and does not take place. An obvious additional need is to examine the features of cases where forgiveness occurs in an attempt to identify its potential determinants.

It can be argued that forgiving subverts the course of justice and that when forgiveness occurs justice is not served. The relationship between forgiveness and justice is a complex one (Exline et al., 2003) and certainly attention to forgiveness in legal contexts is not without danger. However, a detailed analysis of the justice–forgiveness relationship adduces both logic and data to show that justice and forgiveness are positively related and that each might facilitate the other (Fincham, 2009).

Finally, I identify a widely accepted program that does not make reference to forgiveness—peer mediation in educational institutions. There is evidence that peer mediation in schools helps students resolve their conflicts constructively, which tends to result in reducing the numbers of student–student conflicts referred to teachers and administrators, which, in turn, tends to reduce suspensions (Johnson & Johnson, 1996). The outcomes of such programs might well be enhanced in educational institutions in which a forgiveness information campaign has been conducted, compared to matched institutions that have not experienced such a campaign. Alternatively, inclusion of educational material on forgiveness in such peer mediation programs themselves seems appropriate provided it does not implicitly pressure students to engage in forgiveness but only outlines forgiveness as one of many possible outcomes. Once introduced, an outcome evaluation of programs that do and do not include this enhancement would be needed. These suggestions alert one to an important consideration: the need for developmentally appropriate materials in facilitating forgiveness in people of different ages as the understanding of forgiveness changes with age.

LIMITATIONS

My suggestions exhibit the same major weakness of extant forgiveness programs: They do not speak to the issue of forgiveness transactions between people. Indeed, they do not capitalize on the fact that the transgressions often occur in ongoing relationships where the victim has direct access to the transgressor. Transgressor and victim usually engage in systematic, but differing, distortions of the original event (Stillwell & Baumeister, 1997; Kearns & Fincham, 2005), setting the stage for conflict around the issue of forgiveness. This observation draws attention to the perspective of the transgressor. Acknowledging wrongdoing and accepting forgiveness may itself be a human strength, but they have not been the topic of this chapter, which has focused instead on the granting of forgiveness. This is not to suggest that the facilitation of forgiveness is entirely independent of the transgressor. On the contrary, there is strong evidence that transgressor behavior (e.g., apology, offers of restitution) facilitates forgiveness (Fehr, Gelfand, & Nag, 2010). Thus, supplemental materials or even a set of interventions parallel to those described that emphasize the perspective of the transgressor need to be developed.

In addition, although I have incorporated social units/groups into my analysis, I have not addressed the issue of forgiveness between such units. Forgiveness at this level of analysis raises its own set of thorny problems, which are beyond the scope of this chapter (see Chapman, 2007; Hanke et al., 2013). Finally, I have outlined a systematic program for research on facilitating forgiveness in global terms, a necessary limitation given space constraints.

## CONCLUSION

In this chapter, I identified forgiveness as a human strength, analyzed evidence on the benefits of forgiving, and summarized research on forgiveness interventions. I analyzed forgiveness with a positive psychology focus and offered a much broader conception of how forgiveness might be facilitated. A next step is to develop detailed protocols for the levels of intervention identified and to investigate the efficacy of each, not only in preventing distress but also in enhancing optimal human functioning. Such a remit is clearly beyond that of a single investigator and will require our collective efforts. The enormity of the challenge is matched only by the potential payoff of work that, with the help of modern technology, has the potential to enhance the lives of millions of fellow humans.

## SUMMARY POINTS

- Forgiveness is a freely chosen motivational transformation in which desired revenge is replaced by an attitude of goodwill toward an offender.
- Better mental and physical health are related to forgiveness, but demonstration of a causal relationship is needed.
- Although forgiveness interventions are a blunt instrument for determining causality, they yield results consistent with the view that forgiveness influences health. This most likely occurs by reducing stress and/or increasing adaptive coping.
- The process of forgiveness can be taught and is frequently done in group settings. This opens up the possibility of wider dissemination by modes of delivery that can reach large numbers of people (e.g., media, Internet).
- Breadth of delivery (reach) and depth of delivery (intensity) are two dimensions used to offer a framework for facilitating forgiveness.
- According to the framework described, forgiveness interventions range from the broadest level, where a universal prevention intervention might be offered (such as a forgiveness awareness media campaign), through psychoeducation that includes instruction on how to forgive for those who have suffered a transgression to forgiveness-focused individual psychotherapy.
- There is evidence that forgiveness can in some circumstances be detrimental. This appears to be the case in ongoing conflictual relationships and is likely due to the transgressor not being held fully accountable for his or her actions.
- Much of the impact of forgiveness may be indirect and occur through change in the relationship between victim and transgressor, especially in intimate relationships. For example, in the marital literature, it is well established that the quality of the marital relationship has a strong impact on the physical and mental health of spouses, as well as their offspring.

## REFERENCES

Allemand, M., Amberg, I., Zimprich, D., & Fincham, F. D. (2007). The role of trait forgiveness and relationship satisfaction in episodic forgiveness. *Journal of Social and Clinical Psychology, 26*, 199–217.

Aureli, F., Cozzolino, R., Cordischi, C., & Scucchi, S. (1992). Kin-oriented redirection among Japanese macaques: An expression of a revenge system? *Animal Behavior, 44*, 283–291.

Baskin, T. W., & Enright, R. D. (2004). Intervention studies on forgiveness: A meta-analytic review. *Journal of Counseling and Development, 82*, 79–90.

Beach, S. R. H., & Whisman, M. (2012). *Relationship distress: Impact on mental illness, physical health, children, and family economics.* In S. R. H. Beach, R. Heyman, A. Smith Slep, & H. Foran (Eds.), *Family problems and family violence* (pp. 91–100). New York, NY: Springer.

Bergin, A. E. (1963). The effects of psychotherapy: Negative results revisited. *Journal of Counseling Psychology, 10*, 244–250.

Berry, J. W., & Worthington, E. L. (2001). Forgivingness, relationship quality, stress while imagining relationship events, and physical and mental health. *Journal of Counseling Psychology, 48*, 447–455.

Biglan, A. (1995). Translating what we know about the context of antisocial behavior into a lower prevalence of such behavior. *Journal of Applied Behavior Analysis, 28*, 479–492.

Braithwaite, S., Selby, E., & Fincham, F. D. (2011). Forgiveness and relationship satisfaction: Mediating mechanisms. *Journal of Family Psychology, 25*, 551–559.

Burman, B., & Margolin, G. (1992). Analysis of the association between marital relationships and health problems: An interactional perspective. *Psychological Bulletin, 112*, 39–63.

Chapman, A. R. (2007). Truth commissions and intergroup forgiveness: The case of the South African Truth and Reconciliation Commission. *Peace and Conflict: Journal of Peace Psychology, 13*, 51–69.

Christensen, A., Miller, W. R., & Munoz, R. F. (1978). Paraprofessionals, partners, peers, paraphernalia and print: Expanding mental health service delivery. *Professional Psychology, 9*, 249–270.

Close, H. T. (1970). Forgiveness and responsibility: A case study. *Pastoral Psychology, 21*, 19–25.

Coyle, C. T., & Enright, R. D. (1997). Forgiveness intervention with postabortion men. *Journal of Consulting and Clinical Psychology, 65*, 1042–1046.

Denckla, D. A. (2000). Forgiveness as a problem-solving tool in the courts: A brief response to the panel on forgiveness in criminal law. *Fordham Urban Law Journal, 27*, 1613–1619.

Eaton, J., Struthers, C. W., & Santelli, A. G. (2006). Dispositional and state forgiveness: The role of self-esteem, need for structure, and narcissism. *Personality and Individual Differences, 41*, 371–380.

Enright, R. D., & Coyle, C. T. (1998). Researching the process model of forgiveness within psychological interventions. In E. L. Worthington (Ed.), *Dimensions of forgiveness: Psychological research and theological perspectives* (pp. 139–161). Philadelphia, PA: Templeton Press.

Enright, R. D., Freedman, S., & Rique, J. (1998). The psychology of interpersonal forgiveness. In R. D. Enright & J. North (Eds.), *Exploring forgiveness* (pp. 46–62). Madison: University of Wisconsin Press.

Esterling, B. A., L'Abate, L., Murray, E. J., & Pennebaker, J. W. (1999). Empirical foundations for writing in prevention and psychotherapy: Mental and physical health outcomes. *Clinical Psychology Review, 19*, 79–96.

Ewart, C. K., Taylor, C. B., Kraemer, H. C., & Agras, W. S. (1991). High blood pressure and marital discord: Not being nasty matters more than being nice. *Health Psychology, 103*, 155–163.

Exline, J. J., Worthington, E. L., Hill, P., & McCullough, M. E. (2003). Forgiveness and justice: A research agenda for social and personality psychology. *Personality and Social Psychology Bulletin, 7*, 337–348.

Farrow, T. F. D., Zheng, Y., Wilkinson, I. D., Spence, S. A., Deakin, J. F. W., Tarrier, N., . . . Woodruff, P. W. (2001). Investigating the functional anatomy of empathy and forgiveness. *Neuroreport, 12*, 2433–2438.

Fehr, R., Gelfand, M. J., & Nag, M. (2010). The road to forgiveness: A meta-analytic synthesis of its situational and dispositional correlates. *Psychological Bulletin, 136*, 894–914.

Feigenson, N. R. (2000). Merciful damages: Some remarks on forgiveness, mercy and tort law. *Fordham Urban Law Journal, 27*, 1633–1649.

Fenell, D. (1993). Characteristics of long-term first marriages. *Journal of Mental Health Counseling, 15*, 446–460.

Fincham, F. D. (2000). The kiss of the porcupines: From attributing responsibility to forgiving. *Personal Relationships, 7*, 1–23.

Fincham, F. D. (2009). Forgiveness: Integral to close relationships and inimical to justice? *Virginia Journal of Social Policy and the Law, 16*, 357–384.

Fincham, F. D. (2010). Forgiveness: Integral to a science of close relationships? In M. Mikulincer & P. Shaver (Eds.), *Prosocial motives, emotions, and behavior: The better angels of our nature* (pp. 347–365). Washington, DC: American Psychological Association.

Fincham, F. D. (in press). Forgiveness, family relationships and health. In L. Toussaint, E. L. Worthington, Jr., & D. Williams (Eds.), *Forgiveness and health: Scientific evidence and theories relating forgiveness to better health*. New York, NY: Springer.

Fincham, F. D., & Beach, S. R. (2002a). Forgiveness: Toward a public health approach to intervention. In J. H. Harvey & A. E. Wenzel (Eds.), *A clinician's guide to maintaining and enhancing close relationships* (pp. 277–300). Mahwah, NJ: Erlbaum.

Fincham, F. D., & Beach, S. R. (2002b). Forgiveness in marriage: Implications for psychological aggression and constructive communication. *Personal Relationships, 9*, 239–251.

Fincham, F. D., & Beach, S. R. H. (2007). Forgiveness and marital quality: Precursor or consequence in well-established relationships. *Journal of Positive Psychology, 2*, 260–268.

Fincham, F. D., & Beach, S. R. H. (2010). Of memes and marriage: Towards a positive relationship science. *Journal of Family Theory and Review, 2*, 4–24.

Fincham, F. D., & Beach, S. R. H. (2013a). Can religion and spirituality enhance prevention programs for couples? In K. I. Pargament (Ed.), *APA handbook of psychology, religion, and spirituality* (Vol. 2, pp. 461–480). Washington, DC: American Psychological Association.

Fincham, F. D., & Beach, S. R. H. (2013b). Gratitude and forgiveness in relationships. In J. A. Simpson & L. Campbell (Eds.), *The Oxford handbook of close relationships* (pp. 638–663). Oxford, England: Oxford University Press.

Fincham, F. D., Beach, S. R. H, & Davila, J. (2004). Forgiveness and conflict resolution in marriage. *Journal of Family Psychology, 18*, 72–81.

Fincham, F. D., Beach, S. R. H., & Davila, J. (2007). Longitudinal relations between forgiveness and conflict resolution in marriage. *Journal of Family Psychology, 21*, 542–545.

Fincham, F. D., Hall, J. H., & Beach, S. R. H. (2005). 'Til lack of forgiveness doth us part: Forgiveness in marriage. In E. L. Worthington (Ed.), *Handbook of forgiveness* (pp. 207–226). New York, NY: Routledge.

Fincham, F. D., Lambert, N. M., & Beach, S. R. H. (2010). Faith and unfaithfulness: Can praying for your partner reduce infidelity? *Journal of Personality and Social Psychology, 99*, 649–659.

Freedman, S. R., & Enright, R. D. (1996). Forgiveness as an intervention goal with incest survivors. *Journal of Consulting and Clinical Psychology, 64*, 983–992.

Friedberg, J. P., Suchday, S., & Shelov, D. V. (2007). The impact of forgiveness on cardiovascular reactivity and recovery. *International Journal of Psychophysiology, 7*, 87–94.

Friedberg, J. P., Suchday, S., & Srinivas, V. S. (2009). Relationship between forgiveness and psychological indices in cardiac patients. *International Journal of Behavioral Medicine, 16*(3), 205–211.

Gordon, K. C., Baucom, D. H., & Snyder, D. K. (2000). Forgiveness in marital therapy. In M. E. McCullough, K. I. Pargament, & C. E. Thoresen (Eds.), *Forgiveness: Theory, research and practice* (pp. 203–227). New York, NY: Guilford Press.

Gordon, K. C., Hughes, F. M., Tomcik, N. D., Dixon, L. J., & Litzinger, S. C. (2009). Widening spheres of impact: The role of forgiveness in marital and family functioning. *Journal of Family Psychology, 23*, 1–13.

Hanke, K., Liu, J. H., Hilton, D. J., Bilewicz, M., Garber, I., Huang, L., . . . Wang, F. (2013). When the past haunts the present: Intergroup forgiveness and historical closure in post–World War II societies in Asia and in Europe. *International Journal of Intercultural Relations, 37*, 287–301.

Hebl, J. H., & Enright, R. D. (1993). Forgiveness as a psychotherapeutic goal with elderly females. *Psychotherapy, 30*, 658–667.

Holmgren, M. R. (1993). Forgiveness and the intrinsic value of persons. *American Philosophical Quarterly, 30*, 342–352.

Huang, S. T., & Enright, R. D. (2000). Forgiveness and anger-related emotions in Taiwan: Implications for therapy. *Psychotherapy, 37*, 71–79.

Johnson, D. W., & Johnson, R. T. (1996). Conflict resolution and peer mediation programs in elementary and secondary schools: A review of the research. *Review of Education Research, 66*, 459–506.

Johnstone, G. (2002). *Restorative justice: Ideas, values, debates.* Cullumpton, Devon, England: Willan.

Kantz, J. E. (2000). How do people conceptualize and use forgiveness? The Forgiveness Attitudes Questionnaire. *Counseling and Values, 44*, 174–186.

Kearns, J. N., & Fincham, F. D. (2004). *A prototype analysis of forgiveness: Personality and Social Psychology Bulletin, 30,* 838–855.

Kearns, J. N., & Fincham, F. D. (2005). Victim and perpetrator accounts of interpersonal transgressions: Self-serving or relationship-serving biases? *Personality and Social Psychology Bulletin, 31,* 321–333.

Kiecolt-Glaser, J. K., Glaser, R., Cacioppo, J. T., MacCullum, R. C., Snydersmith, M., Kim, C., & Malarkey, W. B. (1997). Marital conflict in older adults: Endocrine and immunological correlates. *Psychosomatic Medicine, 59,* 339–349.

Lambert, N. M., Fincham, F. D., Stillman, T. F., Graham, S. M., & Beach, S. R. M. (2010). Motivating change in relationships: Can prayer increase forgiveness? *Psychological Science, 21,* 126–132.

Lawler-Row, K. A., Hyatt-Edwards, L., Wuench, K. L., & Karremans, J. C. (2011). Forgiveness and health: The role of attachment. *Personal Relationships, 18,* 170–183.

Lawler-Row, K., Karremans, J., Scott, C., Edlis-Matityahou, M., & Edwards, L. (2008). Forgiveness, physiological reactivity and health: The role of anger. *International Journal of Psychophysiology, 68,* 51–58.

Lundahl, B. W., Taylor, J., Stevenson, R., & Roberts, K. D. (2008). Process-based forgiveness interventions: A meta-analytic review. *Research on Social Work Practice, 18,* 465–478.

Mauger, P. A., Perry, J. E., Freeman, T., Grove, D. C., McBride, A. G., & McKinney, K. E. (1992). The measurement of forgiveness: Preliminary research. *Journal of Psychology and Christianity, 11,* 170–180.

McCullough, M. E. (2008). *Beyond revenge: The evolution of the forgiveness instinct.* San Francisco, CA: Jossey-Bass.

McCullough, M. E., Bellah, C. G., Kilpatrick, S. D., & Johnson, J. L. (2001). Vengefulness: Relationships with forgiveness, rumination, well-being, and the Big Five. *Personality and Social Psychology Bulletin, 27,* 601–610.

McCullough, M. E., Fincham, F. D., & Tsang, J. (2003). Forgiveness, forbearance, and time: The temporal unfolding of transgression-related interpersonal motivations. *Journal of Personality and Social Psychology, 84,* 540–557.

McCullough, M. E., Kurzban, R., & Tabak, B. A. (2010). Evolved mechanisms for revenge and forgiveness. In P. R. Shaver & M. Mikulincer (Eds.), *Understanding and reducing aggression, violence, and their consequences* (pp. 221–239). Washington, DC: American Psychological Association.

McCullough, M. E., Root, L. M., & Cohen, A. D. (2006). Writing about the benefits of an interpersonal transgression facilitates forgiveness. *Journal of Consulting and Clinical Psychology, 74,* 887–897.

McCullough, M. E., Root, L. M., Tabak, B., & Witvliet, C. v. O. (2009). Forgiveness. In S. J. Lopez (Ed.), *Handbook of positive psychology* (2nd ed., pp. 427–435). New York, NY: Oxford University Press.

McNulty, J. K. (2008). Forgiveness in marriage: Putting the benefits into context. *Journal of Family Psychology, 22,* 171–175.

McNulty, J. K. (2010). Forgiveness increases the likelihood of subsequent partner transgressions in marriage. *Journal of Family Psychology, 24,* 787–790.

McNulty, J. K., & Fincham, F. D. (2012). Beyond positive psychology? Toward a contextual view of psychological processes and well-being. *American Psychologist, 67,* 101–110.

Morris, A., & Young, W. (2000). Reforming criminal justice: The potential for restorative justice. In H. Strang & J. Braithwaite (Eds.), *Restorative justice: Philosophy to practice* (pp. 11–31). Aldershot, England: Ashgate/Dartmouth.

Mrazek, P. J., & Haggerty, R. J. (Eds.). (1994). *Reducing risks for mental disorders: Frontiers for preventive intervention research.* Washington, DC: National Academy Press.

Nygaard, R. L. (1997). On the role of forgiveness in criminal sentencing. *Seton Hall Law Review*, 27, 980–1022.

Paleari, F. G., Regalia, C., & Fincham, F. D. (2005). Marital quality, forgiveness, empathy, and rumination: A longitudinal analysis. *Personality and Social Psychology Bulletin*, 31, 368–378.

Paleari, F. G, Regalia, C., & Fincham, F. D. (2009). Measuring offence-specific forgiveness in marriage: The Marital Offence-Specific Forgiveness Scale (MOFS). *Psychological Assessment*, 21, 194–209.

Rappaport, J., & Chinsky, J. M. (1974). Models for delivery of service from a historical and conceptual perspective. *Professional Psychology*, 5, 42–50.

Riek, B. M., & Mania, E. W. (2012). The antecedents and consequences of interpersonal forgiveness: A meta-analytic review. *Personal Relationships*, 19, 304–325.

Ripley, J. S. (1998). *The effects of marital social values on outcomes of forgiveness: Couples enrichment psychoeducational groups or communication couples enrichment psychoeducational groups* (Unpublished doctoral dissertation). Virginia Commonwealth University, Richmond.

Rose, G. (1992). *The strategy of preventive medicine*. New York, NY: Oxford University Press.

Ryan, R. M., & Deci, E. L. (2000). Self-determination theory and the facilitation of intrinsic motivation, social development, and well-being. *American Psychologist*, 55, 68–78.

Schmaling, K. B., & Sher, T. G. (1997). Physical health and relationships. In W. K. Halford & H. J. Markman (Eds.), *Clinical handbook of marriage and couples intervention* (pp. 323–345). New York, NY: Wiley.

Seligman, M. E. P. (2002). *Authentic happiness: Using the new positive psychology to realize your potential for lasting fulfillment*. New York, NY: Free Press.

Sorensen, G., Emmons, K., Hunt, M., & Johnston, D. (1998). Implications of the results of community intervention trials. *Annual Review of Public Health*, 19, 379–416.

Stillwell, A. M., & Baumeister, R. F. (1997). The construction of victim and perpetrator memories: Accuracy and distortion in role-based accounts. *Personality and Social Psychology Bulletin*, 23, 1157–1172.

Thompson, B., Coronado, G., Snipes, S. A., & Puschel, K. (2003). Methodological advances and ongoing challenges in designing community-based health promotion programs. *Annual Review of Public Health*, 24, 315–340.

Toussaint, L., & Cheadle, A. C. D. (2009). Unforgiveness and the broken heart: Unforgiving tendencies, problems due to unforgiveness, and 12-month prevalence of cardiovascular health conditions. In M. T. Evans & E. D. Walker (Eds.), *Religion and psychology* (pp. 135–170). New York, NY: Nova.

Toussaint, L. L., Owen, A. D., & Cheadle, A. C. D. (2012). Forgive to live: Forgiveness, health, and longevity. *Journal of Behavioral Medicine*, 35, 375–386.

Umbreit, M. S. (2001). *The handbook of victim offender mediation: An essential guide to practice and research*. San Francisco, CA: Jossey-Bass.

Wade, N. G., Johnson, C. V., & Meyer, J. E. (2008). Understanding concerns about interventions to promote forgiveness: A review of the literature. *Psychotherapy: Theory, Research, Practice, Training*, 45, 88–102.

Wade, N. G., Worthington, E. L., Jr., & Meyer, J. E. (2005). But do they work? A meta-analysis of group interventions to promote forgiveness. In E. L. Worthington Jr. (Ed.), *Handbook of forgiveness* (pp. 423–440). New York, NY: Routledge.

Waltman, M. A., Russell, D. C., Coyle, C. T., Enright, R. D., Holter, C., & Swoboda, C. M. (2009). The effects of a forgiveness intervention on patients with coronary artery disease. *Psychology and Health*, 24(1), 11–27.

Webb, T. R., Touissant, L., Kalpakjian, C. Z., & Tate, D. G. (2010). Forgiveness and health-related outcomes among people with spinal cord injury. *Disability and Rehabilitation*, 32(5), 360.

Witvliet, C. V., Ludwig, T. E., & Van der Laan, K. L. (2001). Granting forgiveness or harboring grudges: Implications for emotion, physiology, and health. *Psychological Science*, 121, 117–123.

Worthington, E. L. (2001). Unforgiveness, forgiveness, and reconciliation and their implications for societal interventions. In R. G. Helmick & R. L. Petersen (Eds.), *Forgiveness and reconciliation: Religion, public policy, and conflict transformation* (pp. 161–182). Philadelphia, PA: Templeton Press.

Worthington, E. L., Jennings, D. J., & DiBlasio, W. (2010). Interventions to promote forgiveness in couple and family context: Conceptualization, review, and analysis. *Journal of Psychology and Theology, 38*, 231–245.

Worthington, E. L., Sandage, S. J., & Berry, J. W. (2000). Group interventions to promote forgiveness. In M. E. McCullough, K. I. Pargament, & C. E. Thoresen (Eds.), *Forgiveness: Theory, research, and practice* (pp. 228–253). New York, NY: Guilford Press.

Worthington, E. L., & Wade, N. G. (1999). The psychology of unforgiveness and forgiveness and implications for clinical practice. *Journal of Social and Clinical Psychology, 18*, 385–418.

Worthington, E. L., Witvliet, C. V. O., Pietrini, P., & Miller, A. J. (2007). Forgiveness, health and wellbeing: A review of evidence for emotional versus decisional forgiveness, dispositional forgivingness, and reduced unforgiveness. *Journal of Behavioral Medicine, 30*, 291–302.

Yovetich, N. A., & Rusbult, C. E. (1994). Accommodative behavior in close relationships: Exploring transformation of motivation. *Journal of Experimental Social Psychology, 30*, 138–164.

# CHAPTER 39

# The Interface Between Positive Psychology and Social Work in Theory and Practice

RACHEL DEKEL and ORIT TAUBMAN–BEN-ARI

THE FIELDS OF SOCIAL WORK and psychology—each with its own unique missions and perspectives—have developed over the years as independent professions. However, with the evolvement of positive psychology on the one hand and the strength perspective in social work on the other, it seems the time has come to look at both fields together and see what they can learn from one another. The aims of the current chapter are to explore the interfaces between positive psychology and social work, to highlight common and complementary aspects of each profession, and to offer an integrative view. In the first part of the chapter, we present the basic underpinnings of positive psychology and social work and discuss the similarities between their definitions and goals; we also make note of their differences. In the second part, we focus on two major areas of intervention in social work, namely, domestic violence and mental health. Lastly, we discuss the challenges likely to arise from the integration of positive psychology principles and social work strategies into a unified new concept of positive regard for people and their environments.

## POSITIVE PSYCHOLOGY AND SOCIAL WORK— DEFINITIONS AND MISSIONS

The term *positive psychology* is a comprehensive term for the study of positive emotions, positive character traits, and enabling institutions (Seligman, Steen, Park, & Peterson, 2005). Positive psychology embodies the striving to understand individuals' positive attributes, psychological assets, and strengths (Kobau et al., 2011) and to study the conditions and processes that contribute to the flourishing or optimal functioning of people, groups, and institutions (Gable & Jonathan, 2005). Fundamentally, positive psychology sees the field of psychology as one which includes an understanding of suffering and happiness as well as the interaction between the two, and offers validated interventions that both relieve suffering and increase happiness, two separable concepts and endeavors (Seligman, 2007).

Similarly, but with a more central and fundamental emphasis on specific populations, the primary mission of the social work profession, according to the official definition of social work jointly developed by the International Federation of Social Workers (IFSW) and the International Association of Schools of Social Work, is to promote "social change, problem solving in human relationships and the empowerment and liberation of people to enhance well-being" (IFSW, 2005).

Within the broad goal of promoting well-being, social work has these specific aims: first, *relief of psychological distress and material need*, thus helping people to function effectively in their social environment, including providing for basic survival needs (adequate nutrition, shelter, and medical care) and creating opportunities that enhance social productivity; second, *social control*, thus encouraging adherence to social norms and minimizing, eliminating, or normalizing deviant behavior; and finally, *social reform*, thus altering the conditions that are related to psychological distress and material need. This goal stems from the belief that the faulty social structure—and not the unworthiness of individual persons—is responsible for social problems (Conrad & Schneider, 1992; Gambrill, 2006).

Social work by definition thus shares with positive psychology the mission of enhancing individuals' well-being. However, social work's specific target populations include those who may be in need of special attention and/or professional help, both as a result of stressful life events and/or poor living conditions. Moreover, many social workers come to the aid of clients who do not seek help voluntarily; that is, people who are legally required or mandated to receive social work services (Ivanoff, Blythe, & Tripodi, 1994).

In addition to enhancing individuals' well-being, positive psychology and social work are taking this goal a step further. According to the Council on Social Work Education (CSWE, 2008), the purpose of the social work profession is to "promote human and community well-being" (Educational Policy and Accreditation Standards [EPAS], 2008, p. 1). Furthermore, that purpose "is actualized through its quest for social and economic justice, the prevention of conditions that limit human rights, the elimination of poverty, and the enhancement of the quality of life for all persons" (EPAS, 2008, p. 1). In other words, the promotion of well-being in individuals and communities is a common mission behind both approaches.

The purpose of promoting human and community well-being is conceptualized in social work as "guided by a person and environment construct, a global perspective, respect for human diversity, and knowledge based on scientific inquiry" (EPAS, 2008, p. 1). This suggests that social workers examine individual behavior in its context, reflecting on how that behavior is a response to and, in turn, influences the individual's environment (Hepworth, Rooney, Rooney, Strom-Gottffried, & Larsen, 2010).

In accordance with this approach, any gaps in environmental resources, limitations of individuals who need or utilize these resources, or dysfunctional transactions between individuals and environmental systems threaten to block the fulfillment of human needs and lead to stress or impaired functioning. To reduce or remove this stress requires coping efforts aimed at gratifying these human needs: that is, achieving an adaptive fit between person and environment. People, however, often do not have access to adequate resources or may lack effective coping methods. Social work involves helping such people meet their needs by linking them with or developing essential resources (Hepworth et al., 2010).

Earlier writings on positive psychology focused on happiness, and positive psychology was defined as the investigation of optimal experience and the life worth living (Seligman & Csikszentmihalyi, 2000). *Happiness* in this sense was the study of positive emotion and pleasure, engagement, and meaning (Seligman, 2002, 2007). A decade later, the central goals of positive psychology have evolved, and attention has been redirected toward the broader term *well-being*, now called "flourishing" by Seligman (2011), and the ways in which individuals endeavor to increase its presence and extent in their lives.

According to Seligman (2011), well-being has five measurable elements (PERMA) that equally—and either exclusively or jointly—contribute to it: *Positive emotion* (of which happiness and life satisfaction are aspects); *Engagement*; *Relationships*; *Meaning and purpose*; and *Accomplishment.* All five elements are pursued for their own sake; they are exclusive and thus may be defined and measured independently of the other elements; and, whereas none of the elements defines well-being, each contributes to it.

So it seems there is some overlap in the aims of positive psychology and social work when it comes to promoting well-being. In positive psychology, however, a greater amount of effort has been invested in identifying and defining the core elements of this broader term. These efforts could be helpful for social work as well, in terms of determining operative aims when promoting well-being as part of intervention processes.

The framework of positive psychology provides a comprehensive scheme for describing and understanding the good life: positive subjective experiences (e.g., life satisfaction, fulfillment); positive individual traits (e.g., character, values); positive relationships (e.g., friendship, marriage, colleagueship); and positive groups and institutions (e.g., families, schools, communities). Positive groups and institutions enable the development and display of positive relationships and positive traits, which in turn enable positive subjective experiences and flourishing (Seligman, 2011). People are at their best when institutions, relationships, traits, and experiences are in alignment, and doing well in life represents a coming together of all four domains (Park & Peterson, 2008). This alignment is also in keeping with the mission of social work, in its quest to empower individuals and communities and help them to both maximize their potential and find fulfillment.

Moreover, both positive psychology and social work share a holistic outlook on the human experience: an acknowledgment of the coexistence of both the good and the bad. In response to positive psychology's many critics, experts in the field continuously stress that this positive approach neither replaces nor denies the problems in people's lives, and does not ignore distress and misery. What positive psychology has done is to divert the main focus from psychopathology to a fuller and more balanced depiction of human thriving and flourishing, and to offer a better way to integrate and complement existing knowledge about mental illness with knowledge about positive mental health (Kobau et al., 2011). Positive psychology's most basic assumption is that human goodness and excellence are as authentic as disease, disorder, and distress and therefore deserve equal attention from psychologists and other human service providers (Peterson & Park, 2003). These basic assumptions are shared by the social work field, with the key difference being that social work has not had to confront criticism on this front since its very existence emerged out of the need to help weakened populations (i.e., those individuals dealing with the greatest misery and despair). The integrative view of human experience is, however, fully acknowledged by the social work profession.

Examining these aims of both perspectives reveal several similarities. However, it seems that social work takes into account the importance of the social and cultural context in which individuals live, and tries to improve the fit between the person and the environment. Nevertheless, both social work and psychology practices have operated for many years from a problem-focused basis, and have used medical-model terms, such as diagnosis. A call for a change in such perspectives has led to a gradual switching over to a strength-based approach and practice.

## PERSONAL AND PSYCHOLOGICAL STRENGTHS IN POSITIVE PSYCHOLOGY AND THE STRENGTH PERSPECTIVE IN SOCIAL WORK

A key aspect of the positive psychology research agenda has been a focus on personal and psychological strengths, the use of which can lead to energizing experiences and elevated, sustainable well-being (Peterson & Seligman, 2004). This focus on people's strengths is also the most important aspect of social work's strength perspective.

The strength perspective emerged in the late 1980s as an alternative to the dominant deficit-oriented psychotherapeutic models in social work practice (Guo & Tsui, 2010; Saleebey, 2009); it evolved in reaction to the prior exclusive focus on problems, limitations, or diagnoses that tended to reduce a person to a problem-saturated label, a situation that is fundamentally antithetical to the values of social work (Weick, Rapp, Sullivan, & Kisthardt, 1989). A strength-based approach, rather, sees the profession of social work as geared toward respecting the dignity and worth of every human being, regardless of their current situation. It is aimed at bringing the practice of social work back to its foundation of valuing and collaborating with the client. It moved the profession away from focusing on the problems and deficits as defined by the social worker or other helping professionals, and toward identifying and focusing on the strengths, abilities, and possibilities of clients through an egalitarian, collaborative relationship (Blundo, 2001).

The strength perspective focuses on client capabilities, knowledge, abilities, motivations, experience, intelligence, and other positive qualities that can be put to use to solve problems and pursue positive changes (Blundo, 2008; CSWE, 2008; Kim, 2008; Sheafor & Horejsi, 2008). This approach emphasizes the notion that people have the ability to grow, change, and enhance their own well-being (Kirst-Ashman & Hull, 2010).

The idea that "every individual, group, family, and community has strengths" (Saleebey, 2009, p. 15), a fundamental social work claim, is also identified with the claims of positive psychology. Differences between the perspectives emerge with relation to the typology and types of strengths, the unit of observance for strength, and the way the manifestations of strengths are encouraged.

Within the social work context, various attempts have been made to identify strengths. Cowger, Anderson, and Snively (2006), for example, have come up with evaluative questions to operationalize the strength-based perspective. Others have called for a "diagnostic strengths manual" (Saleebey, 2009), a manual that would provide a list of strengths. Currently, the social work field offers a general classification of areas of strength: behaviors and accomplishments, personal qualities and characteristics, and finally, a client's material and social resources (Saleebey, 2009).

Positive psychology provides a more specific and descriptive classification. Peterson and Seligman (2004) developed a model called values in action (VIA) which includes 24 character strengths, each related to one of the following six broader virtues: (1) wisdom and knowledge (including creativity, curiosity, open-mindedness, love of learning, perspective); (2) courage (including bravery, integrity, persistence, zest); (3) humanity (including kindness, love, social intelligence); (4) justice (including fairness, leadership, teamwork); (5) temperance (including forgiveness, modesty, prudence, self-regulation); and (6) transcendence (including appreciation of beauty, gratitude, hope, humor, spirituality). In Seligman's new well-being theory, these

24 strengths underpin all five elements of PERMA: deploying one's greatest strengths leads to more positive emotion, to more meaning, to more accomplishment, and to better relationships (Seligman, 2011).

In addition to recognizing individuals' strengths and resources, the social work literature points to the importance of actually finding and realizing them. Saleebey (2009) suggests several types of questions for social workers to ask that would, for instance, try to target how their service users have managed to cope thus far and what they have learned about themselves and their world during the course of their struggles. Furthermore, these questions aim to single out those people and organizations or groups that have been especially helpful to and supportive of the individuals. In trying to focus on positive aims and using personal and individual strengths to achieve them—rather than focusing solely on reducing symptoms—the clients and the social worker together explore the hopes, visions, and aspirations of the clients.

These questions highlight additional assumptions of the strength perspective. One assumption is that the person him- or herself is an expert on his or her life. Because most of the people who come to or are sent to a social worker have lived with their problems for a long period of time, they have thought and worried about them extensively. They are thus in a position to know their problems better than anyone else does. The clients have the wisdom, knowledge, and experience that they bring with them and, in combination with the specialized skills and experience offered by the social worker, they may be able to create a valuable outcome for themselves (Pulla, 2012). Moreover, as we emphasized earlier, the social work field sees the person as a part of his or her environment, which has its own strengths and resources. These strengths and resources must also be identified and recognized.

Recent theoretical developments in positive psychology have refined the concept of strengths, and suggest that strengths are characteristics that allow people to perform well or at their personal best, and that using one's greatest strengths (e.g., physical talents, creativity, and intelligence) leads to increased well-being and superior performance (Wood, Linley, Maltby, Kashdan, & Hurling, 2011). They continue by suggesting that while it is important to possess strengths, it is even more important to use them (Wood et al., 2011). It is the unblocked *use* of the strength that would lead to the greatest benefit. In other words, people who report greater use of their strengths develop greater levels of well-being over time. In keeping with this understanding, social work defines as one of its primary goals helping clients first recognize and then use their strengths.

Having reviewed some of the similarities and differences in focus between social work's and positive psychology's approaches to the human experience, we would like to turn now to two practical examples of professional use of the previously reviewed principles in social work field practice. We will look at violence in families and rehabilitation in mental health: two representative endeavors of social workers in two of their most common working arenas.

## DOMESTIC VIOLENCE FROM A STRENGTH PERSPECTIVE

Domestic violence is defined as a pattern of behavior in a relationship in which the batterer attempts to control his or her victim by use of a variety of tactics (Barnett, Miller-Perrin, & Perrin, 1997), such as fear and intimidation, physical and/or sexual abuse, psychological and emotional abuse (Register, 1993). Social workers form a central part of the support offered to women who experience domestic violence, as they have a statutory mandate to attend to vulnerable individuals and families, which includes the safeguarding of children and their mothers (Keeling & Van Wormer,

2012). Studies have found that 15% to 32% of women on welfare, who comprise the population with whom social workers primarily work, experience domestic violence, and an additional 60% have been abused in the past (Raphael & Tolman, 1997).

For many years, people who experienced various traumatic events, including domestic violence, were called victims (Herman, 1992). In their zeal to help and advocate for battered women, practitioners and researchers in the area of domestic violence used to depict battered women as victims who were weak and without options (Black, 2003; Peled, Eisikovits, Enosh, & Winstok, 2000). In her seminal work, Walker (1979), for example, portrayed the battered woman as one who had fallen into an abyss of hopelessness, helplessness. Although this work was paramount in terms of gaining insight into battered women's lives and catapulting their situation into the public consciousness, this portrayal inadvertently focused on their weaknesses instead of on their survival skills (Peled et al., 2000; Rothenberg, 2003). Today, in keeping with a positive perspective and in line with the strength approach, they are called survivors (e.g., Profitt, 2000; Roche, 1999). This term reflects the fact that in order to survive domestic violence a woman must be active and cope well enough to keep both herself and her children alive. Whereas the woman's coping patterns may at times be perceived by others—for example, professionals, society in general—as maladaptive, she has nevertheless managed to survive the insidious and ongoing pattern of abuse (Postmus, 2000).

Additional facet of the strength perspective is the ability to listen sensitively to one's clients: that is, both to the women and to the men who have undergone domestic violence. It is imperative that these stories be told, heard, and believed, although this process is a highly complex and sensitive one (Pyles, Katie, Mariame, Suzette, & DeChiro, 2012).

In an empirical examination, Black (2003) analyzed the narratives of 20 battered women to determine whether court advocates used principles of the strength perspectives to assist the women in obtaining protective orders and devising safety plans. She found that most of the women were satisfied with the services provided by the advocates and believed that the advocates showed concern for their plights. "Taking time to listen" was cited as a major aspect of that display of concern, and it exemplifies a basic principle of conducting a strength-based assessment: giving preeminence to the client's understanding of the facts (Cowger, 1994). Advocates helped uncover women's strengths, often reinforcing steps the women had taken to effect positive change in their lives. In addition, many communities offer services to assist survivors of domestic violence in seeking safety from their abusive partners, and most communities have survivor advocates who, among other things, educate the public to understand that domestic violence is a public, not a private, issue. Some communities have established coalitions of advocates and professionals from a variety of fields, such as health care, criminal justice, law enforcement, and community social services. These coalitions strive to ensure that professionals who work with survivors are aware of and understand the issues related to domestic violence (Postmus, 2000).

However, Keeling and Van Wormer (2012) examined the narratives of seven women as they spoke in detail about their interactions with social workers following domestic violence. The researchers revealed that the participants had not felt free to disclose all the facts about the true nature of the family violence, especially with regard to their children. The women's fears—that the social worker might take action against them and remove their children from their care as a result of what they had revealed—were an indication of a serious lack of trust in the social work agency.

The perception of what defines a successful resolution of a domestic abuse situation has undergone a major change, now that women who have suffered abuse are seen as having strengths and as being experts regarding their own lives. Earlier writings and interventions were aimed at convincing women to leave their abusive partners. This goal was based on the assumption that battered women were trapped in their relationships against their better judgment or against their will (e.g., Walker, 1979). Contemporary authors, however, are pioneering in suggesting that these interventions should present staying in the relationship as a legitimate choice as well, which choice of course does not preclude the women's attempts to end the domestic abuse from within the relationship (Peled et al., 2000).

Another area of change, brought about in part by use of the strength perspective, pertains to the way the social work field now views the parenting skills of mothers who are abused by their partners. In the earlier literature on the subject, battered women were depicted as helpless victims of abuse who could not protect themselves, let alone their children (e.g., Loseke, 1992). Or they were portrayed as bad mothers who failed to protect their children by virtue of the fact that they chose to stay with the men who abused them (Roberts, 1999). These portrayals highlighted the women's deficiencies and revealed them to be failures as mothers (Semaan, Jasinski, & Bubriski-McKenzie, 2013).

Recent studies, however, highlight the role of motherhood as a source of affirmation and strength, something that in fact helped these women to survive their difficult domestic situations. In two studies many of the women reported that motherhood served as a turning point, compelling them to end their relationships with the men who abused them (Peled & Gil, 2011; Semaan et al., 2013). The battered women who had children spoke very positively about their mothering abilities, and their self-perceptions as good mothers. Moreover, all of the women felt stronger as a result of being—and empowered by their role as—mothers, a role that helped them live through a period when they were with their abusive intimate partners. The fact that they had to care for their children empowered and strengthened them.

In sum, this section demonstrates just how far we have come in the domestic violence arena, in terms of implementing a positive theoretical and practical perspective, as well as in putting an emphasis on strengths. However, it also highlights some gaps and areas of concern that warrant further examination.

## THE STRENGTH PERSPECTIVE AND RECOVERY IN MENTAL HEALTH

One group with whom social workers have applied the strength perspective is people who have psychiatric disabilities (Rapp, 1998). Social workers constitute the largest group of practitioners in the mental health field (Bentley, 2002) and are one of multiple professional groups who work in this area.

For many years, the medical model dominated the mental health field. The medical model was designed around the assumption that psychiatric disabilities were chronic, and it predicted ongoing deterioration (Kruger, 2000). The current perspective of helping people with psychiatric disabilities, however, follows the recovery model. The recovery model challenges the medical model and the assumption of chronicity. The recovery perspective is grounded in concern for the empowerment of an oppressed population, a belief in the right of all individuals to self-determination, and an understanding of the effect of the environment on the experience of people with psychiatric disabilities.

The most fundamental premise of the recovery paradigm is that people with psychiatric disabilities can and do recover. This vision presents a challenge to the establishment message that one should expect less from a life affected by mental illness

(Frese & Davis, 1997). The recovery vision suggests a positive goal in place of a negative one: Rather than attempting to reduce the risk of relapse, the individual in recovery works to achieve personal success (Sullivan, 1994). The vision describes a life beyond psychiatric diagnosis that is both vital and valuable, whether or not symptom relief—which is the main goal according to the medical model—is ever achieved (Anthony, 1993; Frese & Davis, 1997). Finally, recovery is often said to be a nonlinear process that involves making progress, losing ground, and pressing forward again (e.g., Anthony, 1993; Ralph, 2000).

Several authors suggest that social work inhabits a unique position among the mental health professions and is ideally situated both to support this vision and to develop within it. Social workers play a major role in supporting individuals as they draw on natural resources in their environments. They operate from the perspective that all people have both profound immediate worth and the potential for tremendous, self-defined growth; they advocate for meaningful system change at all levels; and they work toward the kind of community change and environmental enrichment that will facilitate the recovery of people with psychiatric disabilities. Therefore, the recovery paradigm offers social workers a perspective that upholds the profession's values and may be used as a foundation for direct practice and agency administration, a guide for policy making, and a theoretical base for mental health research (Buckles et al., 2008; Carpenter, 2002).

The recovery process is consistent with the ecological framework that guides social workers. As mentioned earlier, the ecological perspective incorporates both the individual and the environment and focuses on the relationship between the two, with an emphasis on interactions and transactions. Thus recovery can be viewed as facilitated or impeded through the dynamic interplay of forces that are complex, synergistic, and linked (Onken, Dumont, Ridgway, Dornan, & Ralph, 2002). The dynamic interaction among characteristics of the individual (such as hope), characteristics of the environment (such as opportunity), and characteristics of the exchange between the individual and the environment (such as choice), can promote or hinder recovery.

Moreover, social work professionals emphasize the social aspects of recovery (Topor, Borg, Di Girolamo, & Davidson, 2009). For the most part, existing recovery research suggests that individuals need to enter into and pursue highly individualistic journeys of healing and improvement in order to overcome the consequences of mental illnesses. However, many other factors are involved in recovery narratives, factors that lie outside of or beyond the person's own efforts or control. As such, recovery should be seen as not just an individual journey but rather as a journey composed of many social factors and structures—elements that, taken together, can either facilitate or impede an individual's inclusion in community life such as friends, family, and good material conditions, that is, proper housing, a meaningful occupation, and access to the community's cultural resources (Mezzina et al., 2006).

Strengths model case management (SMCM) denotes a specific use of the strength model to enhance recovery among people with psychiatric disabilities (Fukui et al., 2012). Full implementation of SMCM consists of structural components (low caseload sizes, low supervisor–to–case manager ratio, weekly group supervision using a structured format for case presentations, and so on) and practice components (such as use of the strengths assessment and personal recovery plan tools, use of naturally occurring resources to achieve goals, and in-person service delivery). It also requires specific supervisory behaviors to teach and reinforce practice skills of frontline staff. Studies testing the effectiveness of using SMCM to assist people with psychiatric disabilities have reported positive outcomes in the areas of hospitalization, housing, employment, symptoms, leisure time, social support, and family burden (Fukui et al., 2012).

In addition, the literature describes several standardized interventions that aim to help individuals acquire knowledge and skills to manage their illnesses effectively and achieve personal recovery goals. Interventions include psychoeducation, cognitive-behavioral approaches to medication adherence, relapse prevention, social skills training, and coping skills training (Roe, Hasson-Ohayon, Salyers, & Kravetz, 2009). Other interventions include emotion training and situation assessment (Penn, Roberts, Combs, & Sterne, 2007) and hope enhancing (Repper & Perkins, 2003).

In summary, this subchapter reflects the major changes that have taken place in the area of mental health. Moreover, it provides a good example of cooperation between the different types of professionals working in this area: psychiatrists, psychologists, social workers, occupational workers, and the affected individuals themselves.

## FUTURE DIRECTIONS

Life can be difficult, particularly for people who come from disadvantaged backgrounds and lack the resources that would help them thrive. Some live in very poor conditions and are mandated to receive social services; others have undergone destabilizing life events and need professional care and help. However, when a flourishing, strength-oriented outlook stands behind the provision of these services, no less than a comprehensive empathy for people's positive qualities and potential strengths develops, as do the individuals themselves. Therefore, in parallel with working to lower negativism, hatred, misery, and pain, practitioners—both psychologists and social workers—must also acknowledge individuals' altruism, optimism, and well-being. Looking to find the best in human existence and cultivating a positive regard for individuals, we can better understand individuals' choices and the potential they have to master even the most painful and stressful events; we can see the important roles played by interpersonal relationships and community assets. In many ways, positive psychology advocates what social workers have been striving to do for many years: promote human potential. Both fields belong to the positive social sciences and share a positive regard for human experience. Both oppose the medical model, with its emphasis on a deficit-centered pathology-focused conception of health and with its end goal of "returning to normal" (Ryff & Singer, 1998). Both positive psychology and social work share fundamental assumptions about human nature that hold that people have within them a natural tendency to want to grow and develop their potential, and when their environment supports them in doing so, they thrive (Linley & Harrington, 2005). Perhaps the time has come to abandon the old-school profession-specific differentiated definitions and work together toward developing an integrated view to understanding, caring for and nurturing human flourishing, which would not be dependent in any way on the clinician's profession. Rather, it would rely on jointly utilizing individual and environmental resources in a strength-oriented approach, with the aim of actualizing each individual's and community's best.

Practitioners of both positive psychology and the strength perspective in social work should make additional efforts to see these movements become more integrated into the broad scope of their professions, to acknowledge earlier writings on these topics, and to act as a unified entity. For example, Hung (2010), a clinical social worker, has called attention to the fact that the psychoanalyst Karen Horney's ideas actually reflect a basic assumption of the strength perspective. Horney (1950) theorized that all people naturally strive toward self-realization and have a natural propensity to grow and realize their unique potential. Efforts to enhance the integration between what seem to be diverse perspectives—but aren't—could help expand the use of the strength theory. One area in which the idea that people are striving toward growth has been developed is in the field of trauma, where it is recognized that posttraumatic growth is a common occurrence (Joseph & Murphy, 2014).

While advocating for a united comprehensive use, attention should be paid to the current limitations and criticisms of positive psychology and the strength perspective in social work, voiced by supporters and opponents alike. Pulla (2012), for instance, continues to raise the question of how we can expect to find the assets, strengths, and protective factors in human beings if we are still fundamentally and primarily trained to look for problems and deficits. In her view this tendency is so deep-rooted that much more stringent efforts would have to be made in order to see beyond the damage: fighting against ourselves, our biases, our training, and even our own culture in order to widen the perspective.

With regard to practice, Rapp, Saleebey, and Sullivan (2005) highlight the need to develop a clearer definition of strength-based practice. They want to know how and when one defines a strength-based practice as such, and which and how many elements should be included in order for a strength-based practice to meet its own definition. In addition, they suggest greater clarity about the relationship between problems and challenges on the one hand, and strength, competencies, and resources on the other.

Some critics go even farther. Murphy, Duggan, and Joseph (2013) argue that the current policy and professional context require practitioners to act instrumentally on behalf of the state in relation to the most vulnerable cases, and in these situations the service user's right to self-determination can never be unconditionally respected; theories and concepts calling for egalitarian relations must therefore be adopted. Finally, Guo and Tsui (2010) claim that the strength perspective and the encouragement of clients to discover their own strengths are not enough. According to them, if social work's mission is to emancipate, empower, and enable vulnerable people, then social workers should support the attempts of people to enhance their strength by resisting and even subverting power relations instead of forcing them to be rehabilitated according to middle-class values and behaviors.

The examples we have presented in this chapter show that the attempts to alter the language, attitude, relations, and outcomes of the strength perspective interventions have been employed in the field with a large degree of success. Moreover, in this chapter, we gave two examples of the strides that have been made. It should be stated that the application of strength-based practice in social work has also been conducted in many additional areas such as drug addiction (Okundaye, Smith, & Lawrence-Webb, 2001), adolescence (Yip, 2006), and families (Early & GlenMaye, 2000). In order to continue and find strengths in our clients, we have first to find the strengths within ourselves. The authentic belief in a client and his or her potential can only be achieved after shifting our internal perspective and becoming aware of our own strengths, our hope and positive expectations for our own lives. We as workers and educators have to go through a continuous process of reflection and discovery. Only then will we be able to use and practice the strength perspective (Pulla, 2012).

## CONCLUSION

In a symbolic and parallel manner, this chapter was written jointly by a social worker and a psychologist. The writing process, like the process being written about, enabled a mutual learning and recognition of the similarities and complementarities between our personal and professional beliefs to take place. It seems to us that those working in the fields of positive psychology and social work aim to provide a balanced understanding of the human experience—integrating both the more negative and the more positive aspects of it, and caring in a comprehensive manner for individuals. Both attempt to help individuals become their best selves, enhance their well-being, and enable them to flourish. Taken together, positive psychology principles and social work strategies ought to be synergized into a unified new concept of positive regard for people and their environments.

## SUMMARY POINTS

- During the past decade, the field of positive psychology has stimulated research aimed at addressing the science and practice imbalance between psychopathology relative to strengths and well-being.
- Social work has undergone a similar development, moving from a medical model to a healing one, embracing a strength perspective for its service users.
- Positive psychology and social work both focus on promoting well-being and identifying personal strengths. However, social work's specific target populations include those who may be in need of special attention and/or professional help. In addition, social work takes into account the importance of the social and cultural context in which individuals live, and tries to improve the fit between the person and the environment.
- Change in practice is a gradual process. Language and use of different concepts promote the change. The time has come to abandon the old-school profession-specific differentiated definitions and work together toward developing an integrated view to understanding, caring for, and nurturing human flourishing.
- By prioritizing positive psychology and strength-oriented research in clinical practice, practitioners can promote the presence of well-being, engaging one's own personal and environmental strengths, rather than simply focusing on the alleviation of disorder and deficit. It seems that in order to work from a strength-based perspective we have to find our own strengths and personal hopes.

## REFERENCES

Anthony, W. A. (1993). Recovery from mental illness: Guiding vision of mental health service system in 1990s. *Psychosocial Rehabilitation Journal, 16,* 11–23.

Barnett, O. W., Miller-Perrin, C. L., & Perrin, R. D. (1997). *Family violence across the life span: An introduction.* Thousand Oaks, CA: Sage.

Bentley, K. A. (Ed.) (2002). *Social work practice and mental health: Contemporary roles, tasks, and techniques.* Pacific Grove, CA: Wadsworth.

Black, C. J. (2003). Translating principles into practice: Implementing the feminist and strengths perspectives in work with battered women. *Affilia: Journal of Women and Social Work, 18,* 332–349.

Blundo, R. (2001). Learning strengths-based practice: Challenging our personal and professional frames. *Families in Society, 82,* 296–304.

Blundo, R. (2008). Strengths-based framework. In T. Mizrahi & L. E. Davis (Eds.), *Encyclopedia of social work* (20th ed., Vol. 4, pp. 173–177). Washington, DC: NASW Press and Oxford University Press.

Buckles, B., Brewer, E., Kerecman, J., Mildred, L., Ellis, A., & Ryan, J. (2008). Beyond stigma and discrimination: Challenges for social work practice in psychiatric rehabilitation and recovery. *Journal of Social Work in Disability & Rehabilitation, 7*, 232–283.

Carpenter, J. (2002). Mental health recovery paradigm: Implications for social work. *Health and Social Work, 27*, 86–94.

Conrad, P., & Schneider, J. W. (1992). *Deviance and medicalization: From badness to sickness.* Philadelphia, PA: Temple University Press.

Council on Social Work Education. (2008). *Educational policy and accreditation standards.* Washington, DC: Author.

Cowger, C. D. (1994). Assessing client strengths: Clinical assessment for client empowerment. *Social Work, 39*, 262–268.

Cowger, C. D., Anderson, K., & Snively, C. A. (2006). Assessing strengths: The political context of individual family and community empowerment. In D. Saleebey (Ed.), *The strengths perspective in social work practice* (4th ed., pp. 93–115). Boston, MA: Allyn & Bacon.

Early, T. J., & GlenMaye, L. F. (2000). Valuing families: Social work practice with families from a strengths perspective. *Social Work, 45*, 118–130.

Educational Policy and Accreditation Standards. (2008). *Family therapy: A feminist perspective.* Newbury Park, CA: Sage.

Frese, F. J., & Davis, W. W. (1997). The consumer-survivor movement, recovery and consumer professionals. *Professional Psychology: Research and Practice, 28*, 243–245.

Fukui, S., Goscha, R., Rapp, C., Mabry, A., Liddy, P., & Marty, D. (2012). Strengths model case management fidelity scores and client outcomes. *Psychiatric Services, 63*, 708–710.

Gable, S. F., & Jonathan, H. (2005). What (and why) is positive psychology? *Review of General Psychology, 9*, 103–110.

Gambrill, E. (2006). *Social work practice: A critical thinker's guide* (2nd ed.). Oxford, England: Oxford University Press.

Guo, W., & Tsui, M. (2010). From resilience to resistance: A reconstruction of the strengths perspective in social work practice. *International Social Work, 53*, 233–245.

Hepworth, D. H., Rooney, R. H., Rooney, G. D., Strom-Gottfried, K., & Larsen, J. (2010). *Direct social work practice: Theory and skills* (8th ed.). Belmont, CA: Brooks/Cole.

Herman, J. L. (1992). *Trauma and recovery: The aftermath of violence—from domestic to political terror.* New York, NY: Basic Books.

Horney, K. (1950). *Neurosis and human growth: The struggle toward self-realization.* New York, NY: Norton.

Hung, T. (2010). Karen Horney's contribution to the strengths perspective in clinical social work. *Voices, The Silberman Journal of Social Work.* http://silbermanvoices.com/article-4-2/

International Federation of Social Workers. (2005). *International definition of social work.* Available at http://ifsw.org/policies/global-standards/

Ivanoff, A., Blythe, B. J., & Tripodi, T. (1994). *Involuntary clients in social work practice: A research based approach.* New York, NY: Aldine de Gruyter.

Joseph, S., & Murphy, D. (2014). Trauma: A unifying concept for social work. *British Journal of Social Work, 44*, 1094–1109.

Keeling, J., & Van Wormer, K. (2012). Social worker interventions in situations of domestic violence: What we can learn from survivors' personal narratives? *British Journal of Social Work, 42*, 1354–1370.

Kim, J. S. (2008). Strengths perspective. In T. Mizrahi & L. E. Davis (Eds.), *Encyclopedia of social work* (20th ed., Vol. 4, pp. 177–181). Washington, DC: NASW Press.

Kirst-Ashman, K. K., & Hull, G. H. (2010). *Understanding generalist practice* (6th ed.). Belmont, CA: Brooks/Cole.

Kobau, R., Seligman, M. E. P., Peterson, C., Diener, E., Zack, M. M., Chapman, D., & Thompson, W. (2011). Mental health promotion in public health: Perspectives and strategies from positive psychology. *American Journal of Public Health, 101*, e1–e9.

Kruger, A. (2000). Schizophrenia: Recovery and hope. *Psychiatric Rehabilitation Journal, 24,* 29–37.

Linley, P. A., & Harrington, S. (2005). Positive psychology and coaching psychology: Perspectives on integration. *The Coaching Psychologist, 1,* 13–14.

Loseke, D. (1992). *The battered woman and shelters: The social construction of wife abuse.* Albany: State University of New York Press.

Mezzina, R., Davidson, L., Borg, M., Marin, I., Topor, A., & Sells, D. (2006). The social nature of recovery: Discussion and implications for practice. *American Journal of Psychiatric Rehabilitation, 9,* 63–80.

Murphy, D., Duggan, M., & Joseph, S. (2013). Relationship-based social work and its compatibility with the person-centered approach: Principled versus instrumental perspectives. *British Journal of Social Work, 43,* 703–719.

Okundaye, J. N., Smith, P., & Lawrence-Webb, C. (2001). Incorporating spirituality and the strengths perspective into social work practice with addicted individuals. *Journal of Social Work Practice in the Addictions, 1,* 65–82.

Onken, S. J., Dumont, J. M., Ridgway, P., Dornan, D. H., & Ralph, R. (2002). *Mental health recovery: What helps and what hinders?* A national research project for the development of recovery facilitating system performance indicators. Phase one research report: a national study of consumer perspectives on what helps and hinders recovery. Alexandria, VA: National Technical Assistance Center for State Mental Health Planning.

Park, N., & Peterson, C. (2008). Positive psychology and character strengths: Application to strengths-based school counseling. *Professional School Counseling, 12,* 85–92.

Peled, E., Eisikovits, Z., Enosh, G., & Winstok, Z. (2000). Choice and empowerment for battered women who stay: Toward a constructivist model. *Social Work, 45,* 9–25.

Peled, E., & Gil, I. B. (2011). The mothering perceptions of women abused by their partner. *Violence Against Women, 17,* 457–479.

Penn, D. L., Roberts, D. L., Combs, D., & Sterne, A. (2007). Best practice: The development of the social cognition and interaction training program for schizophrenia spectrum disorders. *Psychiatric Services, 58,* 499–451.

Peterson, C., & Park, N. (2003). Positive psychology as the evenhanded positive psychologist views it. *Psychological Inquiry, 14,* 141–146.

Peterson, C., & Seligman, M. E. P. (2004). *Character strengths and virtues: A handbook and classification.* Washington, DC: American Psychological Association.

Postmus, J. L. (2000). Analysis of the family violence option: A strengths perspective. *Affilia: Journal of Women and Social Work, 15,* 244–258.

Profitt, N. J. (2000). Survivors of woman abuse: Compassionate fires inspire collective action for social change. *Journal of Progressive Human Services, 11,* 77–102.

Pulla, V. (2012). What are strengths based practices all about? In V. Pulla, L. Chenoweth, A. Francis, & S. Bakaj, *Papers in strength based practice* (pp. 51–68). New Delhi, India: Allied.

Pyles, L., Katie, M., Mariame, B., Suzette, G., & DeChiro, J. (2012). Building bridges to safety and justice: Stories of survival and resistance. *Affilia: Journal of Women and Social Work, 27,* 84–94.

Ralph, R. (2000). *Review of recovery literature: A synthesis of a sample of recovery literature 2000.* Alexandria, VA: National Technical Assistance Center for State Mental Health Planning.

Raphael, J., & Tolman, R. M. (1997). *Trapped by poverty and trapped by abuse: New evidence documenting the relationship between domestic violence and welfare: Executive summary.* Chicago, IL: Taylor Institute.

Rapp, C. A. (1998). *The strength model: Case management with people suffering from severe and persistent mental illness.* New York, NY: Oxford University Press.

Rapp, C. A., Saleebey, D., & Sullivan, W. P. (2005). The future of the strengths perspective. *Advances in Social Work, 6,* 79–90.

Register, E. (1993). Feminism and recovering from battering: Working with the individual woman. In M. Hansen & M. Harway (Eds.), *Battering and family therapy: A feminist perspective* (pp. 93–104). Newbury Park, CA: Sage.

Repper, J., & Perkins, R. (2003). *Social inclusion and recovery: A model for mental health practice.* Edinburgh, Scotland: Balliere Tindall.

Roberts, D. E. (1999). Mothers who fail to protect their children: Accounting for private and public responsibility. In E. N. Glenn, G. Chang, & L. R. Forcey (Eds.), *Mothering: Ideology, experience, and agency* (pp. 31–49). New York, NY: Routledge.

Roche, S. F. (1999). Using a strengths perspective for social work practice with abused women. *Journal of Family Social Work, 3,* 23–37.

Roe, D., Hasson-Ohayon, I., Salyers, M. P., & Kravetz, S. (2009). A one year follow-up of illness management and recovery: Participants' accounts of its impact and uniqueness. *Psychiatric Rehabilitation Journal, 32,* 285–291.

Rothenberg, B. (2003). We don't have time for social change: Cultural compromise and the battered woman syndrome. *Gender & Society, 17,* 771–787.

Ryff, C. D., & Singer, B. H. (1998). The contours of positive human health. *Psychological Inquiry, 9,* 1–28.

Saleebey, D. (2009). *The strength perspective in social work practice* (5th ed.). Boston, MA: Allyn & Bacon.

Seligman, M. E. P. (2002). *Authentic happiness.* New York, NY: Free Press.

Seligman, M. E. P. (2007). Coaching and positive psychology. *Australian Psychologist, 42,* 266–267.

Seligman, M. E. P. (2011). *Flourish: A visionary new understanding of happiness and well-being.* New York, NY: Free Press.

Seligman, M. E. P., & Csikszentmihalyi, M. (2000). Positive psychology: An introduction. *American Psychologist, 55,* 1–20.

Seligman, M. E. P., Steen, T. A., Park, N., & Peterson, C. (2005). Positive psychology progress: Empirical validation of interventions. *American Psychologist, 60,* 410–421.

Semaan, I., Jasinski, J. L., & Bubriski-McKenzie, A. (2013). Subjection, subjectivity, and agency: The power, meaning, and practice of mothering among women experiencing intimate partner abuse. *Violence Against Women, 19,* 69–88.

Sheafor, B. W., & Horejsi, C. R. (2008). *Techniques and guidelines for social work practice* (8th ed.). Boston, MA: Allyn & Bacon.

Sullivan, W. P. (1994). A long and winding road: The process of recovery from severe mental illness. *Innovations and Research, 3,* 19–27.

Topor, A., Borg, M., Di Girolamo, S., & Davidson, L. (2009). Not just an individual journey: Social aspects of recovery. *Psychiatry International Journal of Social, 57,* 90–99.

Walker, L. E. (1979). *The battered woman.* New York, NY: Harper & Row.

Weick, A., Rapp, C., Sullivan, W. P., & Kisthardt, W. (1989). A strengths perspective for social work practice. *Social Work, 34,* 350–354.

Wood, A. M., Linley, P. A., Maltby, J., Kashdan, T. B., & Hurling, R. (2011). Using personal and psychological strengths leads to increases in well-being over time: A longitudinal study and the development of the strengths use questionnaire. *Personality and Individual Differences, 50,* 15–19.

Yip, K. S. (2006). A strengths perspective in working with an adolescent with self-cutting behaviors. *Child and Adolescent Social Work Journal, 23,* 134–146.

# CHAPTER 40

# Building Recovery-Oriented Service Systems Through Positive Psychology

SANDRA G. RESNICK and MEAGHAN A. LEDDY

POSITIVE PSYCHOLOGY IS "the study of conditions and processes that contribute to the flourishing or optimal functioning of people, groups, and institutions" (Gable & Haidt, 2005, p. 103). As a movement, it seeks to expand the science of psychology to study what is good (Gable & Haidt, 2005). It is divided into three pillars: positive emotions, consisting of the pleasant life; positive traits, such as strengths and virtues, which contribute to the engaged life; and the study and promotion of positive institutions (Seligman, 2002). Positive psychology shares much in common with the recovery movement in mental health services.

## WHAT IS RECOVERY?

The most proximal predecessor of the recovery movement is the consumer/survivor/ex-patient movement of the 1970s, a social movement that stood in opposition to the medical model of mental illness (Bassman, 2001). This antipsychiatry movement sought to give voice to former psychiatric patients who felt silenced and disenfranchised by the system intended to serve them, with the goal of liberation. Professionals, or nonpatients, were excluded, and groups such as the Insane Liberation Front formed around the goals of activism and the development of mutual-help alternatives to professional services (Chamberlin, 1990).

Recovery stemmed from these earlier movements, but diverged. Individuals in the recovery movement also sought social justice and hoped to empower individuals by rejecting the labels of mental illness that were often accompanied by poor prognoses given to them by professionals. Recovery supported the capacity of individuals to redefine their lives and find meaning regardless of the symptomatic and functional effects of mental illness. Like those in the consumer/survivor/ex-patient movements, leaders in the recovery movement used social activism and mutual-help as tools. However, instead of liberating individuals from the system, many recovery leaders sought to change the mental health system to be consistent with these values. This included those who obtained professional mental health degrees (Frese & Davis, 1997), published in academic journals to educate professionals, and collaborated with mental health professionals both for work and for their own care (Deegan,

1997; Mead & Copeland, 2000). This opened the door for well-intentioned professionals who had been previously excluded from the consumer/survivor/ex-patient reform efforts to join the cause.

Although many are still fundamentally opposed to the medical model (Braslow, 2013), today most efforts to implement recovery are either within or parallel to medical model services, rather than in replacement of them. The modern mainstream recovery movement seeks to reform the existing mental health service system to increase the focus on strengths and resilience (Anthony, 2000; Braslow, 2013; Resnick & Rosenheck, 2006). In spite of widespread acceptance of the broad goals of the recovery movement, there remains a great deal of variability about the definition of recovery itself. There is no consensus as to a singular definition of the recovery concept (Gordon, 2013; Onken, Craig, Ridgway, Ralph, & Cook, 2007).

## RECOVERY AND POSITIVE PSYCHOLOGY AS MAINSTREAM MOVEMENTS

The growth of the recovery movement from the radical movements of the 1970s is similar to the growth of positive psychology from humanistic psychology. Some point to the humanistic psychology movement of the 1950s and 1960s as the precursor to the positive psychology movement. The positive psychology movement and the humanistic psychology movements share a focus on helping individuals strive toward growth and the promotion of optimal functioning (Bohart & Greening, 2001). However, the humanistic psychology movement saw the medical model approach of labeling and categorizing mental illnesses as inconsistent with the larger goal of promoting an understanding of the whole person (Joseph & Linley, 2006). Humanistic psychologists also worked toward scientific inclusiveness, broadening the scientific methods that captured the range of human experience, including qualitative methods (Friedman, 2008; see also, Robbins, Chapter 3, this volume). Although the movements are similar in some ways, founders of the emerging positive psychology movement initially sought to differentiate it from these two fundamental humanistic elements. Although the extent of the overlap between positive psychology and humanistic psychology continues to be debated, the positive psychology movement as a whole continues to operate within the medical model (Joseph & Linley, 2006), to the disappointment of some who seek a fuller embracing of the humanistic philosophy. These positive psychologists fully reject the medical model, the notion of diagnosis, and the incorporation of psychology as part of the pathology-oriented health-care field, and instead support a wholesale change in ideology (Maddux, 2005; Maddux & Lopez, Chapter 25, this volume). Like those in the consumer/survivor/ex-patient movement, these psychologists seek a revolution. However, this continues to be a minority view. If the recovery movement is the modern mainstream adaptation of the consumer/survivor/ex-patient movement, the positive psychology movement is perhaps the modern mainstream adaptation of humanistic psychology.

For the purposes of this chapter, we remain agnostic on the fundamental issues of the dominance of the medical model, and whether these movements are sufficient for true reform (for two thoughtful discussions of recovery in this context, see Braslow, 2013, and Hopper, 2007). Instead, we acknowledge our mainstream perspective as well-intentioned professionals working with a medical model system, and seek to speculate on how some of the best of the positive psychology movement might inform the development of a mental health system consistent with the goals of the recovery movement, which, for lack of a better term, we refer to as a *recovery-oriented mental health system*.

A system is more than a group of service providers and programs. It may consist of individual programs staffed by a group of providers, but a system is more than the sum of its parts (Litaker, Tomolo, Liberatore, Stange, & Aron, 2006; Rosenblatt, 2009). From the bottom up, a system of care has at least three levels: (1) the individual client level, (2) the program, and (3) the system itself. In the first section of this chapter, we describe how recovery on the individual level, roughly equivalent to the first two pillars of positive psychology (subjective experience and positive characteristics) might benefit from positive psychology interventions. We then turn to the much less explored level of organizations and institutions, and hypothesize how the study of positive institutions and positive psychology in the workplace might foster recovery-oriented service systems. The third pillar of positive psychology, the study and development of positive institutions, may also provide useful tools for conceptualizing and developing recovery-oriented mental health systems.

Given the diversity of thought in mental health reform movements, it is no surprise that there is no singular term used to describe people who receive mental health diagnoses and/or receive services from mental health programs. In this chapter we use the simple term *individual* to refer to this group of people wherever possible, occasionally adding *in mental health systems* when necessary for clarification.

## POSITIVE INTERVENTIONS IN A RECOVERY-ORIENTED SYSTEM

Positive psychologists have developed a range of positive interventions that aim to increase pleasure, engagement, and meaning in life. Such interventions may be useful for individuals in mental health systems, though they have typically only been applied with nonclinical populations. Many, over 100 (Seligman, Steen, Park, & Peterson, 2005), such interventions have been developed. An extensive review of these interventions is outside the scope of this chapter and can be found elsewhere (e.g., Bolier et al., 2013; Seligman et al., 2005; Sin & Lyubomirsky, 2009). This section highlights three common tenets of positive interventions and recovery, and how positive interventions might inform recovery-oriented treatment.

There are at least three principles shared between positive interventions and recovery: (1) Mental illness and well-being are not mutually exclusive; (2) interventions can and should be expanded beyond the traditional scope of psychiatric care; and (3) individual differences should be important factors in treatment. By highlighting these three overlapping values we hope to support the view that positive interventions can guide treatment planning for the creation of positive, recovery-oriented therapeutic interventions.

### MENTAL ILLNESS AND WELL-BEING ARE NOT MUTUALLY EXCLUSIVE

Positive psychology research supports the dual continua model, which posits that mental illness and well-being exist on different, albeit correlated, axes (Keyes, 2005). The alleviation of psychiatric symptoms does not necessarily result in increased well-being, and an individual can simultaneously experience well-being and distress (Bergsma, ten Have, Veenhoven, & de Graaf, 2011). Similarly, champions of the recovery movement recognize the view that mental illness and wellness exist on separate continua. Recovery proponents encourage individuals to strive for a fulfilling and pleasant life in spite of mental illness and symptoms. In this vein, both fields promote the expansion of mental health care beyond its traditional scope of practice: the alleviation of psychiatric symptoms. Both positive interventions and recovery-oriented mental health care target positive aspects of individuals, and recognize that the reduction of psychiatric symptoms alone is not sufficient.

## EXPANSION BEYOND THE DEFICIT FOCUS

Given the evidence supporting the dual continua model, supporters of positive psychology and recovery have argued for expansion beyond the confines of deficit-based psychiatric care to include the enhancement of positive mental health. Positive psychologists argue that focusing solely on mental illness renders an incomplete view of a person; instead strengths, values, and talents should be investigated, encouraged, and utilized. Similarly, instead of adhering to the pessimistic notion that a mental illness has a long and debilitating course, champions of the recovery movement focus on building a life worth living. Recovery widens the scope of care to encourage individuals to participate in work, leisure, and social activities that build meaning into their lives.

## INDIVIDUAL DIFFERENCES

Positive psychology and recovery also share an emphasis on the importance of individual differences. Research suggests that individual characteristics influence the impact of positive interventions. A randomized controlled trial (Giannopoulos & Vella-Brodrick, 2011) demonstrated the importance of an individual's orientation to happiness, whether he or she primarily chooses to seek pleasure, meaning, or engagement. The study compared four positive interventions (focusing on pleasure, engagement, meaning, or a combination of these) and two control groups. Participants assigned to an intervention that matched their dominant orientation to happiness had more positive outcomes at the end of the study (though these differences were no longer significant at follow-up) than those without such a match.

In another example, Shapira and Mongrain (2009) conducted an Internet-based randomized controlled trial that compared the outcomes of self-compassion and optimism exercises. Outcomes were better for self-critical individuals if they received the optimism intervention, whereas those with more connectedness fared better after the self-compassion intervention. These findings underscore the need to offer interventions that complement the unique characteristics of each client.

The philosophy of recovery also emphasizes the need to tailor clinical interactions to individual characteristics and personal goals. An individual hoping to return to school may benefit from cognitive remediation to strengthen memory and attention, whereas an individual who prefers to reenter the workforce may benefit most from supported employment programs (Becker & Drake, 1994). A randomized controlled study of a recovery-oriented peer intervention demonstrated that outcomes were predicted by the individual's level of civic engagement, friendship, and spirituality (Kaplan, Salzer, & Brusilovskiy, 2012). This study highlights the possibility that identifying individual differences can enable providers to more accurately tailor recovery services to enhance supports specific to the domains where individuals have strengths, such as spirituality and peer support.

Recovery and positive interventions thus share similar values and can facilitate a holistic perspective of an individual to include both mental illness and mental health. Positive interventions that have been demonstrated to be effective and are compatible with a recovery orientation would be of benefit as evidence-based means by which to support individuals in reaching recovery goals.

## EVIDENCE FOR POSITIVE INTERVENTIONS

Interventions targeting hope and positive self-beliefs are likely candidates for translation to a recovery paradigm. Several studies have highlighted the important role that hope and self-esteem play in contributing to recovery outcomes. Specifically, hope and self-views influence recovery from psychosis (Hodgekins & Fowler, 2010). Low self-esteem has been associated with the development of delusions and hallucinations in individuals with psychosis (Romm et al., 2011), and less hopeful illness beliefs are associated with poorer quality of life for those with early psychosis (Theodore et al., 2012). Given that recovery outcomes may be better for those with more hope and positive self-schemas, the inclusion of positive interventions to promote hope and self-esteem in recovery-oriented treatment could improve outcomes for individuals. By boosting self-esteem and hope (i.e., the factors that mediate recovery-consistent outcomes) positive interventions may augment the improvements garnered via recovery interventions. An example of this might be incorporating hope therapy groups (e.g., Cheavens, Feldman, Gum, Michael, & Snyder, 2006) into the treatment of individuals. An 8-week hope intervention has been shown to increase hope and other psychological strengths (Cheavens et al., 2006). Hope therapy may maximize the benefits gained from other recovery-oriented programming by building and nurturing hope, which can then promote recovery.

### Multimodal Integrative Cognitive Stimulation Therapy

Despite the possibility that positive interventions may assist individuals with their recovery goals, they have only recently been implemented with this group. Multimodal integrative cognitive stimulation therapy (Ahmed & Boisvert, 2006) is one such intervention that incorporates positive and recovery aspects. This intervention combines elements of social skills training, relaxation exercise, cognitive rehabilitation, and traditional psychotherapy using visual and auditory modalities. Rather than targeting symptoms, it takes them into consideration while trying to capitalize on intact capabilities. For example, when individuals become disorganized or confused, the clinician redirects them to focus on factual discussions of other topics. By engaging with consumers through intact domains, clinicians facilitate recovery.

### Positive Living

Meyer, Johnson, Parks, Iwanski, and Penn (2012) recently investigated the applicability of positive interventions for people with schizophrenia. They provided a group positive psychotherapy intervention called Positive Living to individuals diagnosed with schizophrenia. Participants completed 10 sessions and one booster session while also completing well-known positive interventions as homework, such as using strengths, savoring, gratitude visits, developing positive goals, and practicing mindfulness. The Positive Living intervention was associated with increased hope, well-being, savoring, and recovery. The authors also reported the intervention reduced paranoia, psychosis, and depression, although this was not the target of the intervention.

### Well-Being Therapy

Well-being therapy is a third positive intervention that has been implemented in mental health systems. Whereas traditional models of cognitive therapy focus on learning to replace unhelpful or distorted thought patterns with more rational thoughts, well-being therapy is a cognitive therapy that focuses on enhancing helpful thinking and instances of emotional well-being (Fava & Tomba, 2009; see also Ruini & Fava, Chapter 28, this volume), which is crucial in attaining and maintaining recovery (Fava & Tomba, 2009; Meyer et al., 2012). Well-being therapy has been demonstrated to have enduring advantageous outcomes for individuals diagnosed with depression, obsessive-compulsive disorder, post-traumatic stress disorder, and generalized anxiety disorders (Fava & Tomba, 2009). By building strengths, resilience, and well-being (Moeenizadeh & Salagame, 2010), individuals can improve their functioning, return to the community, and pursue recovery.

The outcomes of the studies on multimodal integrative cognitive stimulation therapy, positive living, and well-being therapy for individuals with psychiatric disabilities highlight the need for recovery-oriented programs to incorporate more positive interventions into their repertoire. For example, recovery programs may benefit from moving away from traditional cognitive therapy, which targets negative, maladaptive thinking, and instead incorporate a positive psychology orientation. Rather than challenge paranoid thoughts, cognitive therapy might better serve individuals to develop adaptive beliefs (Grant, Reisweber, Luther, Brinen, & Beck, 2013). By focusing on cognitions of hope, resilience, well-being, and self-esteem, it may buffer against unhelpful thoughts and improve quality of life.

## COMBINING POSITIVE INTERVENTIONS AND RECOVERY-CONSISTENT INTERVENTIONS: POTENTIAL APPLICATIONS

Positive interventions might be incorporated into and improve existing self-management interventions, such as Wellness Recovery Action Planning (WRAP; Copeland, 1997), Wellness Self-Management (Salerno et al., 2011), and Illness Management and Recovery (Gingerich & Mueser, 2005). Although they vary in specific content, self-management interventions are designed to help individuals learn to better manage chronic disorders, including medical disorders (Barlow, Wright, Sheasby, Turner, & Hainsworth, 2002). Mental health self-management strategies employ such strategies as psychoeducation, identifying protective factors, teaching self-care skills, and detailing crisis plans, which ensure that personal choice and autonomy exist even during periods of crisis. Positive interventions may enhance self-management interventions, with the timing guided by positive psychology research. For example, it has been shown that gratitude visits have more intense, but shorter-lived positive changes (Seligman et al., 2005). As such, a gratitude visit might be most useful during periods when the individual needs a more intense burst of positive emotions. Similarly, completing acts of kindness all in one day, as opposed to over the course of several days, is associated with increased happiness levels (Lyubomirksy, Sheldon, & Schkade, 2005). These are potentially useful to either provide a boost at the beginning of treatment to increase optimism and self-esteem, or they could be implemented during more acute phases to counter negative emotions and avoid crises.

Research on positive interventions can also educate us as to *how* recovery-oriented interventions should be offered. A meta-analysis of 51 positive interventions (Sin & Lyubomirsky, 2009) suggested that intervention format influences outcomes, with the greatest effect sizes for individually administered interventions, followed by group-based interventions, and, finally, self-administered formats. The aforementioned three positive interventions that have been provided to individuals in mental health systems—multimodal integrative cognitive stimulation therapy, positive living, and well-being therapy—were offered via group format. However, the evidence from Sin and Lyubomirsky calls into question this mode of delivery. It is possible that adapting these interventions to be administered individually may elicit even greater improvements and recovery outcomes.

Individual interventions are not always feasible given staff resources. As such, maximizing the number of individuals who receive services must be considered when determining the feasibility and appropriateness of various interventions. While an individualized course of well-being therapy might be most effective, it may be more important to have a large number of people get a moderate benefit from a group treatment as opposed to a few individuals have a maximum benefit via individual therapy. As such, cost-effectiveness research would be beneficial to help inform decisions as to how resources should be allocated within positive, recovery-oriented systems.

## RECOVERY-ORIENTED MENTAL HEALTH SYSTEMS

The third pillar of positive psychology, the study and development of positive institutions, may provide useful tools for conceptualizing and developing recovery-oriented mental health systems. Like the recovery concept itself, no consensus has been reached about the key components of a recovery-oriented service system. As Braslow (2013) writes, "Though brimming with well-meaning platitudes about hope and the urgent need for 'system transformation,' the recovery literature tells us much less about how to practically construct a recovery-based system of care" (p. 801). Further, the literature on systems change in mental health ranges widely in scope, alternatively referring to the entire United States publically funded mental health system (New Freedom Commission on Mental Health, 2003), a single mental health agency (Anthony, 2000), or general principles for service delivery (Sowers, 2005). Although rarely explicitly addressed, many of these writings hint at an understanding that mental health systems have multiple inputs and levels, including policy (Jacobson & Curtis, 2000); challenges of poverty and the larger social context (Hopper, 2007); the need for coordination of services across programs (Hogan, 2008); policies, procedures, and values within agencies (Anthony, 2000); how service providers are organized, trained, and supervised, and the services that these providers deliver (Sowers, 2005).

Many mental health administrators believe that transformation is a straightforward workforce development problem, and typically provide training to service providers on the history and meaning of recovery. The expectation is that they will develop recovery attitudes and beliefs, and by so doing, create a transformed culture of recovery. Additionally, they may train providers to deliver specific interventions that they believe will help to enhance recovery-consistent outcomes. However, even if training is skillful, providers are engaged, and both attitudinal and behavior change occurs, will this result in increased recovery-consistent outcomes for individuals receiving services? Is it accurate to say that a group of providers with recovery attitudes providing recovery-consistent interventions is truly a recovery-oriented *system*?

Training providers in recovery-consistent beliefs and attitudes is a necessary but minimally effective strategy in the development of recovery-oriented systems. It is necessary because providers must understand what the system is hoping to accomplish, but it is not sufficient for at least three reasons. First, there is a preponderance of evidence that provider trainings, even those designed to develop specific skills and competencies, do not easily result in provider behavior change, and that uptake of complex behavioral interventions requires targeted trainings with follow-up consultation or supervision (Sholomskas et al., 2005). Second, the recovery literature has yet to provide convincing evidence that our current training approaches in broad recovery attitudes have successfully increased desired outcomes. Finally, the emerging field of implementation science suggests that implementation of new practices requires change on multiple levels in an organization, not just at the level of the individual provider (Proctor et al., 2009). Thus, there is room for improvement in training providers as part of a recovery-oriented system.

If a system is more than the sum of its parts, recovery must somehow become an intrinsic part of the system itself. The study of positive organizational psychology[1] may help to further inform these efforts on these two levels: on the system level, to provide practical understanding of how entire mental health systems can become positive organizations, and on the program or provider level, to provide guidelines on how best to support providers to be part of a recovery system.

POSITIVE ORGANIZATIONAL PSYCHOLOGY AND THE PROVIDER LEVEL

Recovery attitude training programs for providers focus on such strategies as increasing the provider's levels of hope about the possibility of recovery of those they serve. In contrast, the positive organizational psychology literature focuses on the employee attitudes and beliefs about their own capabilities or about the organization as a whole; for example, understanding the relationship between resilient employees and employee behaviors and performance. This is a useful paradigm for a recovery-oriented system. Increasing positive attitudes in service providers may facilitate the development of recovery attitudes toward others. It stands to reason that individuals who are not hopeful about their own abilities and futures may not easily develop hope for others. Further, there is some evidence that when service providers participate in positive interventions focused on their own flourishing, there are benefits to the service recipients.

For example, in a study of psychotherapists in training, psychotherapists were randomly assigned to one of two groups: to regularly practice Zen meditation at the workplace, or to a no-intervention control group (Grepmair et al., 2007). Individuals participating in an inpatient program who were blind to these conditions were then randomly assigned to these psychotherapists. The individuals randomly assigned to the therapists practicing Zen meditation had significantly better outcomes on a range of clinical outcomes, even though there was no difference in the treatment that they received. This is a powerful example of how institutional policies that promote positive interventions targeted at clinicians in health-care systems may ultimately, albeit indirectly, improve the care provided to service recipients (Grepmair et al., 2007). In most mental health systems, this type of positive worker intervention is labeled *self-care* and is considered to be the responsibility of the service provider, to be done outside of the workday. However, the evidence from positive organizational psychology suggests that mental health systems might benefit from developing institutional strategies to support the development of positive affectivity in service providers.

One of the most common strategies for supporting workers is the workplace wellness program. A case study of successful workplace wellness programs indicated that effective wellness programs demonstrate a return on investment through worker productivity and increased morale (Berry, Mirabito, & Baun, 2010). Berry and colleagues describe several characteristics of successful programs, including: Leadership across

---

[1]We have chosen to use the term *positive organizational psychology* as an umbrella term, rather than draw distinctions between subfields such as positive organizational behavior and positive organizational scholarship.

all levels must not only support but also personally utilize the wellness resources, the scope and quality of the programs should be worth the investment of an employee's time, services should be accessible and the message of wellness should be consistently communicated across the organization, and the wellness program should be aligned with the mission of the organization and consistent with the culture. One good wellness target for providers delivering recovery-oriented care would be the development of hope, not just for those receiving services, but in the providers themselves.

Strong evidence for the powerful impact of hope comes from a meta-analysis of 45 studies from 36 published articles across diverse work environments examining hope in the workplace. Reichard, Avey, Lopez, and Dollwet (2013) examined the relationship between the levels of hope among various types of employees and three indicators of performance, including self-rated, supervisor-rated, and objective indicators of performance. All three relationships were significant with moderate effect sizes. Although the performance of clinicians is substantively different than the performance of a factory worker or salesman, the diversity of work environments included in the studies selected for the meta-analysis suggests that the effect of hope on performance is robust enough to carry over to health care, and that active interventions designed to foster hope in service providers may have the potential to improve outcomes in service recipients.

Hope is one component of psychological capital (PsyCap), described as the shared variance between hope, efficacy, resilience, and optimism (Avey, Reichard, Luthans, & Mhatre, 2011). In a meta-analysis of PsyCap studies in the workplace, PsyCap was positively related to a number of desirable attitudes, including job satisfaction and workplace well-being, and negatively associated with undesirable attitudes, such as turnover intentions and employee stress. Importantly, PsyCap was also positively associated with desirable workplace behaviors, such organizational citizenship behaviors and a range of ratings of work performance. Another meta-analysis examining the relationship between employee engagement, described as an individual's satisfaction with and enthusiasm for work, found small but significant positive relationships between business unit employee engagement and measures of outcome such as profit, customer satisfaction, productivity, and inverse relationships with employee turnover and number of safety incidents (Harter, Schmidt, & Hayes, 2002).

If positive attitudes are positively associated with workplace performance, is it feasible to train mental health providers to have more hope, resilience, or other positive states? While this has yet to be definitively established, there is some preliminary evidence that this is possible. An intervention designed to increase PsyCap in workers called the PsyCap Intervention (PCI), shows some promise (Luthans, Avey, Avolio, Norman, & Combs, 2006). Two different types of PCIs, one in person (Luthans et al., 2006) and one delivered as an Internet-based training (Luthans, Avey, & Patera, 2008), have been developed. The authors report that both have been successful at increasing participants' self-reported levels of PsyCap, with studies underway to assess more distal performance effects (Luthans et al., 2006).

In addition to training service providers to understand and believe in recovery, a complementary strategy that focuses on developing happier and more engaged service providers may be effective in increasing recovery-consistent outcomes in individuals served by these clinicians. Further, organizational policies that clearly communicate a system-wide dedication to recovery across all levels of the organization to include provider flourishing may help to transform the entire organization from one that supports recovery to one that could be truly called a recovery-oriented system. A true recovery-oriented system has policies and procedures that embody recovery and empower individuals at all levels of the organization, including service providers. Recovery is not a zero-sum game; providers who are supported by policies and procedures that recognize the importance of their well-being might in fact be more effective in providing recovery-oriented care. Positive organizational psychology may have some helpful insights into this.

## POSITIVE ORGANIZATIONAL PSYCHOLOGY AND THE SYSTEM LEVEL

Organizational systems have structures, policies, and processes that may support or detract from a recovery-oriented system. For example, service systems do not have unlimited resources of staff or capacity. Therefore, rules for how these resources are allocated, such as intake and referral procedures, may or may not be viewed as recovery oriented, even if the service providers within the system deliver recovery-oriented care. Davidson, Tondora, and O'Connell (2007) suggest that recovery-oriented systems must include the development of local procedures that eliminate barriers to care, and Anthony (2000) proposes that service access be guided by the preferences of individuals served in the system, rather than by service providers.

Policies that support recovery-oriented systems at all levels might include those that involve providers in decision making. Economic researchers conducted a laboratory experiment in which participants were able to vote on a policy to improve cooperation in a prisoners' dilemma game. A computer either randomly allowed the majority vote, or overwrote the majority vote, notifying the participants of whether their democratically chosen policy was implemented, or whether the computer imposed a policy instead. Later cooperation among participants was higher when a policy that encouraged cooperation was selected by a majority vote of the participants (Dal Bo, Foster, & Putterman, 2010). This is consistent with research on self-determination theory, another concept under the positive psychology umbrella. Self-determination theory suggests that environments that support autonomy can also facilitate well-being (Biswas-Diener, Kashdan, & King, 2009). Although it is a leap from the laboratory to a mental health system, provider involvement is also consistent with the literature on systems change that suggests the importance of both top-down and bottom-up approaches to implementation (Proctor et al., 2009). The development of explicit procedures in which all providers are able to participate in decision making at all levels of the organization, through voting or other forms of meaningful input, would ultimately help foster recovery at an organizational level.

Another important component of a recovery-oriented system is the organizational values held by the agency providing services that guide service delivery. It is not uncommon for mental health service systems to develop value and mission statements, but it is not always clear how these written statements are then operationalized into service delivery. How, then, might a recovery-oriented system develop values on the system level?

The positive organizational psychology concept of organizational compassion may be informative. Kanov et al. (2004) discuss the importance of developing organizational compassion, identifying three subprocesses—*collective noticing*, *collective feeling*, and *collective responding*. Organizational compassion seems to fit the requirements for a recovery-oriented system, in which caring and compassion across the organization help to create a culture of healing and empowerment. Kanov and colleagues' example of noticing may be particularly relevant. They describe Cisco Systems Serious Health Notification System, a technology that was built in support of the CEO's policy in which the CEO is to be notified within 48 hours of every instance of death or serious illness among employees or immediate family members. The notification system allows for all employees to enter or receive this information.

From the top down, from policy through the development of a technological solution to facilitate communication, the leadership of the organization communicates the importance of compassion for employees during a time of need. Kanov et al. suggest that individual engagement in compassionate behavior in the workplace may ultimately result in emotional exhaustion or burnout among workers, but they speculate that the development of organizational compassion may help those individual workers be replenished through the organization. Health-care systems would do well to consciously develop such tangible and explicit systems of noticing, feeling, and responding to employee needs. Similarly, notification systems used for compassionate noticing could also be tweaked for noticing success throughout the organization, both client and provider level.

## SUGGESTIONS FOR FUTURE RESEARCH

The synergies between the positive psychology and recovery movements were first outlined in publication in 2006 (Resnick & Rosenheck, 2006). Since then, the research in both positive psychology and in recovery has multiplied, but the area of intersection between the positive psychology and recovery movements remains largely uninvestigated. Researchers who wish to pursue this area have a wide-open field. Based on the small sample of positive psychology research applied to the recovery movement outlined earlier, we recommend several broad areas of future research.

Clinical researchers might begin by testing the efficacy of positive interventions for the full range of individuals receiving services in mental health systems. Positive interventions, such as those described earlier, have predominantly been evaluated in nonclinical samples and in those with mild to moderate depressive and anxiety disorders. Likewise, researchers might investigate the feasibility and efficacy of augmenting positive interventions into existing recovery practices. One example of this would be to compare a group treatment of WRAP planning and a group treatment of WRAP augmented with positive interventions (e.g., using the gratitude visit in the WRAP plan for when a boost of positive affect is needed) to determine if that addition of positive interventions has any incremental benefit, and on what domains. These are the most obvious preliminary steps on the individual level. If these areas of investigation prove successful, research on whether positive interventions ultimately support individuals' ability to flourish in meaningful life roles, such as in relationships and employment, would be of great utility.

Research on positive organizations is an area for general expansion, not just in the overlap between positive psychology and recovery. Although there has been an increase in the number of peer-reviewed articles in positive organizational psychology in the last decade, the overall number is not great and the majority is theoretical rather than empirical (Donaldson & Ko, 2010). The application of positive organizational psychology in the development of recovery-oriented mental health systems is thus replete with opportunity. One specific target is to develop and test programs that support provider flourishing, such as those that support provider hope, compassion, and the use of the provider's own strengths. Although a truly recovery-oriented system might support provider flourishing as a worthy goal in its own right, future research might also investigate the link between provider flourishing and distal outcomes, such as improvement among those receiving services, for example, the demonstrated links between employee attitudes and performance described earlier. Finally, organizational researchers might work to understand the role and effect of organizational policies and structures, and how policies and structures can create positive organizations across organization types.

## CONCLUSION

Theoretical synergies between positive psychology and recovery have been established (Farkas, 2007; Resnick & Rosenheck, 2006; Slade, 2010), yet the work of empirically demonstrating the utility of this cross-pollination of ideas has yet to occur in any meaningful way. This chapter expands the conversation from one that focuses on theoretical parallels to one that seeks concrete applications of positive psychology at all levels of a recovery-oriented system. We strongly advocate for those in positive psychology to expand their reach to include clinical populations and health-care organizations. Both positive psychology and recovery are engaged in a search to rediscover the full humanity of psychology and our health-care system. And for this, we will need all of our finest thinkers and healers to join together.

## SUMMARY POINTS

- Positive psychology has the potential to inform the development of a recovery-oriented system on three levels: (1) clinical interventions, (2) strategies to improve provider well-being, (3) policies and structures that support the development of a positive, recovery-oriented organization.
- Positive interventions and recovery-oriented care share a conceptualization of mental illness and well-being as existing on separate dimensions, and that treatments should be focused on bolstering the positive domains that are unique to each individual.
- Positive interventions designed for nonclinical populations developed as part of positive psychology have the potential to enhance the well-being of the full range of individuals receiving mental health services.
- Future research should examine the efficacy of positive interventions in the full range of individuals receiving mental health services as stand-alone interventions, and as additions to and augmentation of existing recovery-oriented care.
- The positive organizational psychology focus on the development of resilient employees and enhancement of positive attitudes in employees should be investigated for their potential in building a recovery-oriented workforce.
- Policies and technologies that support positive organizations should be studied for the potential to develop positive organizational systems.

## REFERENCES

Ahmed, M., & Boisvert, C. M. (2006). Using positive psychology with special mental health populations. *American Psychologist, 61*, 333–335.

Anthony, W. A. (2000). A recovery-oriented service system: Setting some system level standards. *Psychiatric Rehabilitation Journal, 24*, 159–168.

Avey, J. B., Reichard, R. J., Luthans, F., & Mhatre, K. H. (2011). Meta-analysis of the impact of positive psychological capital on employee attitudes, behaviors, and performance. *Human Resource Development Quarterly, 22*, 127–152.

Barlow, J., Wright, C., Sheasby, J., Turner, A., & Hainsworth, J. (2002). Self-management approaches for people with chronic conditions: A review. *Patient Education and Counseling, 48*, 177–187.

Bassman, R. (2001). Whose reality is it anyway? Consumer/survivors/ex-patients can speak for themselves. *Journal of Humanistic Psychology, 41*, 11–35.

Becker, D. R., & Drake, R. E. (1994). Individual placement and support: A community mental health center approach to vocational rehabilitation. *Community Mental Health Journal, 30*, 193–206.

Bergsma, A., ten Have, M., Veenhoven, R., & de Graaf, R. (2011). Most people with mental disorders are happy: A 3-year follow-up in the Dutch general population. *The Journal of Positive Psychology, 6,* 253–259.

Berry, L. L., Mirabito, A. M., & Baun, W. B. (2010). What's the hard return on employee wellness programs? *Harvard Business Review, 88,* 104–112.

Biswas-Diener, R., Kashdan, T. B., & King, L. A. (2009). Two traditions of happiness research, not two distinct types of happiness. *The Journal of Positive Psychology, 4,* 208–211.

Bohart, A. C., & Greening, T. (2001). Humanistic psychology and positive psychology. *American Psychologist, 56,* 81–82.

Bolier, L., Haverman, M., Westerhof, G. J., Riper, H., Smit, F., & Bohlmeijer, E. (2013). Positive psychology interventions: A meta-analysis of randomized controlled studies. *BMC Public Health, 13,* 119–139.

Braslow, J. T. (2013). The manufacture of recovery. *Annual Review of Clinical Psychology, 9,* 781–809.

Chamberlin, J. (1990). The ex-patients' movement: Where we've been and where we're going. *The Journal of Mind and Behavior, 11,* 323–336.

Cheavens, J., Feldman, D., Gum, A., Michael, S., & Snyder, C. R. (2006). Hope therapy in a community sample: A pilot investigation. *Social Indicators Research, 77,* 61–78.

Copeland, M. E. (1997). *Wellness Recovery Action Plan.* Brattleboro, VT: Peach Press.

Dal Bo, P., Foster, A., & Putterman, L. (2010). Institutions and behavior: Experimental evidence on the effects of democracy. *American Economic Review, 100,* 2205–2229.

Davidson, L., Tondora, J., & O'Connell, M. J. (2007). Creating a recovery-oriented system of behavioral health care: Moving from concept to reality. *Psychiatric Rehabilitation Journal, 31,* 23–31.

Deegan, P. E. (1997). Recovery and empowerment for people with psychiatric disabilities. *Social Work in Health Care, 25,* 11–24.

Donaldson, S. I., & Ko, I. (2010). Positive organizational psychology, behavior, and scholarship: A review of the emerging literature and evidence base. *The Journal of Positive Psychology, 5,* 177–191.

Farkas, M. (2007). The vision of recovery today: What it is and what it means for services. *World Psychiatry, 6,* 68–74.

Fava, G. A., & Tomba, E. (2009). Increasing psychological well-being and resilience by psychotherapeutic methods. *Journal of Personality, 77,* 1903–1934.

Frese, F. J., & Davis, W. W. (1997). The consumer-survivor movement, recovery, and consumer professionals. *Professional Psychology: Research and Practice, 28,* 243–245.

Friedman, H. (2008). Humanistic and positive psychology: The methodological and epistemological divide. *The Humanistic Psychologist, 36,* 113–126.

Gable, S. L., & Haidt, J. (2005). What (and why?) is positive psychology? *Review of General Psychology, 9,* 103–110.

Giannopoulos, V., & Vella-Brodrick, D. (2011). Effects of positive interventions and orientations to happiness on subjective well-being. *The Journal of Positive Psychology, 6,* 95–105.

Gingerich, S., & Mueser, K. (2005). Illness management and recovery. In R. E. Drake, M. R. Merren, & D. W. Lynde (Eds.), *Evidence-based mental health practice: A textbook.* New York, NY: Norton.

Gordon, S. E. (2013). Recovery constructs and the continued debate that limits consumer recovery. *Psychiatric Services, 64,* 270–271.

Grant, P. M., Reisweber, J., Luther, L., Brinen, A. P., & Beck, A. T. (2013). Successfully breaking a 20-year cycle of hospitalizations with recovery-oriented cognitive therapy for schizophrenia. *Psychological Services, 11*(2), 125–133.

Grepmair, L., Mitterlehner, F., Loew, T., Bachler, E., Rother, W., & Nickel, M. (2007). Promoting mindfulness in psychotherapists in training influences the treatment results of their patients: A randomized, double-blind, controlled study. *Psychotherapy and Psychosomatics, 76*, 332–338.

Harter, J. K., Schmidt, F. L., & Hayes, T. L. (2002). Business-unit-level relationship between employee satisfaction, employee engagement, and business outcomes: A meta-analysis. *Journal of Applied Psychology, 87*, 268–279.

Hodgekins, J., & Fowler, D. (2010). CBT and recovery from psychosis in the ISREP trial: Mediating effects of hope and positive beliefs on activity. *Psychiatric Services, 61*, 321–324.

Hogan, M. F. (2008). Transforming mental health care: Realities, priorities, and prospects. *Psychiatric Clinics of North America, 31*, 1–9.

Hopper, K. (2007). Rethinking social recovery in schizophrenia: What a capabilities approach might offer. *Social Science & Medicine, 65*, 868–879.

Jacobson, N., & Curtis, L. (2000). Recovery as policy in mental health services: Strategies emerging from the states. *Psychiatric Rehabilitation Journal, 23*, 333–342.

Joseph, S., & Linley, P. A. (2006). Positive psychology versus the medical model? *American Psychologist, 61*, 332–333.

Kanov, J. M., Maitlis, S., Worline, M. C., Dutton, J. E., Frost, P. J., & Lilius, J. M. (2004). Compassion in organizational life. *American Behavioral Scientist, 47*, 808–827.

Kaplan, K., Salzer, M. S., & Brusilovskiy, E. (2012). Community participation as a predictor of recovery-oriented outcomes among emerging and mature adults with mental illnesses. *Psychiatric Rehabilitation Journal, 35*, 219–229.

Keyes, C. L. (2005). Mental illness and/or mental health? Investigating axioms of the complete state model of health. *Journal of Consulting and Clinical Psychology, 73*, 539–548.

Litaker, D., Tomolo, A., Liberatore, V., Stange, K. C., & Aron, D. (2006). Using complexity theory to build interventions that improve health care delivery in primary care. *Journal of General Internal Medicine, 21*, S30–S34.

Luthans, F., Avey, J. B., Avolio, B. J., Norman, S. M., & Combs, G. M. (2006). Psychological capital development: Toward a micro-intervention. *Journal of Organizational Behavior, 27*, 387–393.

Luthans, F., Avey, J. B., & Patera, J. L. (2008). Experimental analysis of a web-based training intervention to develop positive psychological capital. *Academy of Management Learning & Education, 7*, 209–221.

Lyubomirksy, S., Sheldon, K., & Schkade, D. (2005). Pursuing happiness: The architecture of sustainable change. *Review of General Psychology, 9*, 111–131.

Maddux, J. E. (2005). Stopping the "madness." In C. R. Snyder & S. J. Lopez (Eds.), *Handbook of positive psychology* (pp. 13–25). Cary, NC: Oxford University Press.

Mead, S., & Copeland, M. E. (2000). What recovery means to us: Consumers' perspectives. *Community Mental Health Journal, 36*, 315–328.

Meyer, P., Johnson, D., Parks, A., Iwanski, C., & Penn, D. (2012). Positive Living: A pilot study of group positive psychotherapy for people with schizophrenia. *The Journal of Positive Psychology, 7*, 239–248.

Moeenizadeh, M., & Salagame, K. (2010). Well-being therapy (WBT) for depression. *International Journal of Psychological Studies, 2*, 107–115.

New Freedom Commission on Mental Health. (2003). *Achieving the promise: Transforming mental health care in America. Final Report.* DHHS Pub. No. SMA-03-3832. Rockville, MD: Author.

Onken, S. J., Craig, C. M., Ridgway, P., Ralph, R. O., & Cook, J. A. (2007). An analysis of the definitions and elements of recovery: A review of the literature. *Psychiatric Services, 31*, 9–22.

Proctor, E. K., Landsverk, J., Aarons, G., Chambers, D., Glisson, C., & Mittman, B. (2009). Implementation research in mental health services: An emerging science with conceptual, methodological, and training challenges. *Administration and Policy in Mental Health, 36*, 24–34.

Reichard, R. J., Avey, J. B., Lopez, S., & Dollwet, M. (2013). Having the will and finding the way: A review and meta-analysis of hope at work. *The Journal of Positive Psychology, 8*, 292–304.

Resnick, S. G., & Rosenheck, R. A. (2006). Recovery and positive psychology. *Psychiatric Services, 57*(1), 120–122.

Romm, K. L., Rossberg, J. I., Hansen, C. F., Haug, E., Andreassen, O. A., & Melle, I. (2011). Self-esteem is associated with premorbid adjustment and positive psychotic symptoms in early psychosis. *BMC Psychiatry, 11*, 136–144.

Rosenblatt, A. (2009). If it walks like a duck and quacks like a duck then must it be a rabbit? Programs, systems and a cumulative science of children's mental health services. *Evaluation and Program Planning, 33*, 14–17.

Salerno, A., Margolies, P., Cleek, A., Pollack, M., Gopalan, G., & Jackson, C. (2011). Wellness self-management: An adaptation of the illness management and recovery practice in New York State. *Psychiatric Services, 62*, 456–458.

Seligman, M. E. (2002). *Authentic happiness: Using the new positive psychology to realize your potential for lasting fulfillment.* New York, NY: Simon and Schuster.

Seligman, M. E., Steen, T. A., Park, N., & Peterson, C. (2005). Positive psychology progress: Empirical validation of interventions. *American Psychologist, 60*, 410–421.

Shapira, L., & Mongrain, M. (2009). The benefits of self-compassion and optimism exercises for individuals vulnerable to depression. *The Journal of Positive Psychology, 5*, 377–389.

Sholomskas, D. E., Syracuse-Siewert, G., Rounsaville, B. J., Ball, S. A., Nuro, K. F., & Carroll, K. M. (2005). We don't train in vain: A dissemination trial of three strategies of training clinicians in cognitive-behavioral therapy. *Journal of Consulting and Clinical Psychology, 73*, 106–115.

Sin, N. L., & Lyubomirsky, S. (2009). Enhancing well-being and alleviating depressive symptoms with positive psychology interventions: A practice-friendly meta-analysis. *Journal of Clinical Psychology, 65*, 467–487.

Slade, M. (2010). Mental illness and well-being: The central importance of positive psychology and recovery approaches. *BMC Health Services Research, 10*, 26.

Sowers, W. (2005). Transforming systems of care: The American Association of Community Psychiatrists guidelines for recovery oriented services. *Community Mental Health Journal, 41*, 757–774.

Theodore, K., Johnson, S., Chalmers-Brown, A., Doherty, R., Harrop, C., & Ellett, L. (2012). Quality of life and illness beliefs in individuals with early psychosis. *Social Psychiatry and Psychiatric Epidemiology, 47*, 545–551.

# PART X

# PUBLIC POLICY AND SYSTEMS FOR RESILIENCE AND SOCIAL PLANNING

CHAPTER 41

# Balancing Individuality and Community in Public Policy

DAVID G. MYERS

W E HUMANS ARE SOCIAL ANIMALS. We come with a need to belong, to connect, to bond. When those needs are met, through intimate friendships and equitable marriages, self-reported happiness runs high and children generally thrive. This chapter describes the need to belong, documents the links between close relationships and subjective well-being, identifies some benefits and costs of modern individualism, and suggests how communitarian public policies might respect both essential liberties and communal well-being.

## WHO IS HAPPY?

Who lives with the greatest happiness and life satisfaction? The last quarter-century has offered some surprising, and some not-so-surprising, answers. Self-reported well-being is *not* much predicted from knowing a person's age or gender (Myers, 1993, 2000). Despite a smoothing of the emotional terrain as people age, and contrary to rumors of midlife crises and later-life angst, happiness is about equally available to healthy men and women of all ages. At all of life's ages and stages, there are many happy people and fewer unhappy. Moreover, despite striking gender differences in ailments such as depression (afflicting more women) and alcoholism (afflicting more men), happiness does not have a favorite gender.

So, who *are* the relatively happy people?

- As Tay and Diener (2011) indicate, some *cultures* (especially those where people enjoy political freedom with basic needs met) are conducive to increased satisfaction with life.
- Certain *traits* and temperaments appear to predispose happiness. Some of these traits, such as extraversion, are genetically influenced. That helps explain Lykken and Tellegen's (1996) finding that about 50% of the variation in current happiness is heritable. Like cholesterol levels, happiness is genetically influenced but not genetically fixed.
- National Opinion Research Center surveys of 49,941 Americans over three decades indicate that people active in *faith communities* more often report being

"very happy" (as have 48% of those attending religious services more than weekly and 26% of those never attending).

## MONEY AND HAPPINESS

Does money buy happiness? Many people presume there is *some* connection between wealth and well-being. From 1970 to 2012, the number of entering American collegians who consider it "very important or essential" that they become "very well off financially" rose from 39% to 81% (UCLA Higher Education Research Institute's annual "American Freshman" reports).

Are people in rich nations, indeed, happier? National wealth does predict national well-being up to a certain point, with diminishing returns thereafter (Myers, 2000). But national wealth rides along with confounding factors such as civil rights, literacy, and years of stable democracy.

Within any nation, are rich people happier? Yes, again, especially in poor countries where low income threatens basic human needs (Argyle, 1999; Diener, Tay, & Oishi, 2013). Nevertheless, the human capacity for adaptation has made happiness nearly equally available to the richest Americans, to lottery winners, to middle income people, and to those who have adapted to disabilities (Myers, 2000).

Does economic growth boost happiness? The happiness boost that comes with increased money has a short half-life. Over the past five decades, Americans' per person income, expressed in constant dollars, has more than doubled (thanks to increased real wages into the 1970s, the doubling of women's employment, and increasing non-wage income). Although income inequality has also increased, the rising economic tide has enabled today's Americans to own twice a many cars per person, to eat out more than twice as often, and to mostly enjoy (unlike their 1960 counterparts) dishwashers, clothes dryers, and air conditioning. So, believing that it is very important to be very well off financially and having seen their affluence ratchet upward, are Americans now happier? As Figure 41.1 indicates, their self-reports suggest not.

Economists have recently debated whether economic growth in various countries has produced *some* increase in personal or social well-being (Easterlin, 1995; Frank, 2012; Stevenson & Wolfers, 2008). It appears that absolute income has some influence on well-being, but that people also adapt to changing income and assess their relative income (which may be steady, even if everyone's income rises).

Not only does wealth but modestly boost well-being, those individuals who strive the hardest for wealth tend to have lower-than-average well-being—a finding that "comes through very strongly in every culture I've looked at," reported Richard Ryan (quoted in Kohn, 1999; see Kasser & Ryan, 1996). His collaborator, Tim Kasser, concludes from their studies that those who instead strive for "intimacy, personal growth, and contribution to the community" experience a higher quality of life (Kasser, 2000, p. 3; Kasser, Chapter 6, this volume). Ryan and Kasser's research echoes an earlier finding by H. W. Perkins: Among 800 college alumni surveyed, those with "Yuppie values"—who preferred a high income and occupational success and prestige to having very close friends and a close marriage—were twice as likely as their former classmates to describe themselves as "fairly" or "very" *unhappy* (Perkins, 1991).

We know the perils of materialism, sort of. In a nationally representative survey, Princeton sociologist Robert Wuthnow found that 89% of more than 2,000 participants felt "our society is much too materialistic." *Other* people are too materialistic, that is. For 84% also wished they had more money, and 78% said it was "very or fairly important" to have "a beautiful home, a new car and other nice things" (Wuthnow, 1994).

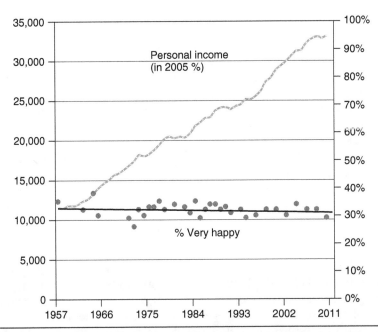

**Figure 41.1** Economic growth and human morale. *Source:* Happiness data from General Social Surveys, National Opinion Research Center (2012). Income data from Bureau of the Census (1975) and *Economic Indicators*.

One has to wonder, what's the point? What's the point of accumulating music players full of unplayed music, closets full of seldom worn clothes, garages with luxury cars? What's the point of corporate and government policies that inflate the rich while leaving the working poor to languish? What's the point of leaving huge estates for one's children, as if inherited wealth could buy them happiness, when that wealth could do so much good in a hurting world? (If self-indulgence can't buy us happiness, and cannot buy it for our kids, why not leave any significant wealth we accumulate to bettering the human condition?)

In *Happy Money: The Science of Smarter Spending*, Elizabeth Dunn and Michael Norton (2013) offer practical principles for getting more happiness out of our money. Research has shown that the most expensive forms of leisure (sitting on a yacht) often provide less flow experience than gardening, socializing, or craft work. Money buys more happiness when spent on experiences that you can look forward to, enjoy, and remember than when spent on material stuff. Money spent on a luxury car buys less happiness than money spent on an equally satisfying economy car plus a memorably happy experience. And, surprisingly to many, money given to others often returns more happiness than money spent on self.

Our human capacities for adaptation to changing circumstance and for social comparison give us pause. They imply that the quest for happiness through material achievement requires continually expanding affluence. But the good news is that adaptation to simpler lives can also happen. If we shrink our consumption by choice or by necessity, we will initially feel a pinch, but the pain likely will pass. "Weeping may tarry for the night, but joy comes with the morning," reflected the Psalmist. Indeed, thanks to our capacity to adapt and to adjust comparisons, the emotional impact of significant life events—losing a job or even a disabling accident—dissipates sooner than most people suppose.

## THE NEED TO BELONG[1]

Aristotle would not be surprised that those who value intimacy and connection are happier than those who lust for money. He called us "the social animal." Indeed, noted Baumeister and Leary (1995), we humans have a deep need to belong, to feel connected with others in enduring, close, supportive relationships. Soon after birth, we exhibit powerful attachments. We almost immediately prefer familiar faces and voices. By 8 months, we crawl after our caregivers and wail when separated from them. Reunited, we cling.

Adults, too, exhibit the power of attachment. Separated from friends or family—isolated in prison, alone at a new school, living in a foreign land—people feel their lost connections with important others. If, as Barbra Streisand sings, "people who need people are the luckiest people in the world," then most people are lucky.

### Aiding Survival

Social connections serve multiple functions. Social bonds boosted our ancestors' survival rate. By keeping children close to their caregivers, attachments served as a powerful survival impulse. As adults, those who formed attachments were more likely to come together to reproduce and to stay together to nurture their offspring to maturity. To be wretched literally means, in its Middle English origin (*wrecche*), to be without kin nearby.

Cooperation in groups also enhanced survival. In solo combat, our ancestors were not the toughest predators. But as hunters they learned that six hands were better than two. Those who foraged in groups also gained protection from predators and enemies. If those who felt a need to belong were also those who survived and reproduced most successfully, their genes would in time predominate. The inevitable result: an innately social creature. People in every society on earth belong to groups.

### Wanting to Belong

The need to belong colors our thoughts and emotions. We spend a great deal of time thinking about our actual and hoped-for relationships. When relationships form, we often feel joy. Falling in mutual love, people have been known to feel their cheeks ache from their irrepressible grins. Asked, "What is necessary for your happiness?" or "What is it that makes your life meaningful?" most people mention—before anything else—close, satisfying relationships with family, friends, or romantic partners (Berscheid, 1985). Happiness hits close to home.

One study found that *very* happy university students are not distinguished by their money but by their "rich and satisfying social relationships" (Diener & Seligman, 2002, p. 83).

The need to belong runs deeper, it seems, than any need to be rich. When our need for relatedness is satisfied in balance with two other basic psychological needs—*autonomy* (a sense of personal control) and *competence*—the result is a deep sense of well-being (Deci & Ryan, 2002, 2009; Milyavskaya et al., 2009; Sheldon & Niemiec, 2006). To feel connected, free, and capable is to enjoy a good life.

---

[1]Some of what follows is excerpted and adapted, with permission, from my *Psychology*, 10th edition (New York, NY: Worth, 2013).

## ACTING TO INCREASE SOCIAL ACCEPTANCE

When we feel included, accepted, and loved by those important to us, our self-esteem rides high. Indeed, say Leary, Haupt, Strausser, and Chokel (1998), our self-esteem is a gauge of how valued and accepted we feel. Much of our social behavior therefore aims to increase our belonging—our social acceptance and inclusion. To avoid rejection, we generally conform to group standards and seek to make favorable impressions. To win friendship and esteem, we monitor our behavior, hoping to create the right impressions. Seeking love and belonging, we spend billions on clothes, cosmetic products and surgeries, and diet and fitness aids—all motivated by our quest for acceptance.

## MAINTAINING RELATIONSHIPS

For most of us, familiarity breeds liking, not contempt. We resist breaking social bonds. Thrown together at school, at summer camp, on a vacation cruise, people resist the group's dissolution. Hoping to maintain our relationships, we promise to call, to write, to come back for reunions. Parting, we feel distress.

When something threatens or dissolves our social ties, negative emotions overwhelm us. The first weeks living on a college campus away from home distress many students. But if feelings of acceptance and connection build, so do self-esteem, positive feelings, and desires to help rather than hurt others (Buckley & Leary, 2001). When immigrants and refugees move, alone, to new places, the stress and loneliness can be depressing. After years of placing such families individually in isolated communities, today's policies encourage "chain migration" (Pipher, 2002). The second refugee Sudanese family that settles in a town generally has an easier time adjusting than the first.

For children, even a brief time-out in isolation can be an effective punishment. For adults as well as children, social ostracism can be even more painful. To be shunned—given the cold shoulder or the silent treatment, with others' eyes avoiding yours—is to have one's need to belong threatened, observes Williams (2007, 2009; Williams & Zadro, 2001). People often respond to social ostracism with depressed moods, initial efforts to restore their acceptance, and then withdrawal. "It's the meanest thing you can do to someone, especially if you know they can't fight back. I never should have been born," said Lea, a lifelong victim of the silent treatment by her mother and grandmother. "I came home every night and cried. I lost 25 pounds, had no self-esteem and felt that I wasn't worthy," reported Richard, after 2 years of silent treatment by his employer.

If rejected and unable to remedy the situation, people sometimes turn nasty. In a series of studies, Twenge and her collaborators (Baumeister, Twenge, & Nuss, 2002; Twenge, Baumeister, DeWall, Ciarocco, & Bartels, 2007; Twenge, Baumeister, Tice, & Stucke, 2001; Twenge, Catanese, & Baumeister, 2002) either told people (based on a personality test) that they would have "rewarding relationships throughout life" or that "everyone chose you as someone they'd like to work with." They told other participants that they were "the type likely to end up alone later in life" or that others whom they had met didn't want them in a group that was forming. Those excluded became much more likely to engage in self-defeating behaviors and underperform on aptitude tests. They also exhibited more antisocial behavior, such as by disparaging someone who had insulted them or aggressing (with a blast of noise) against them. "If intelligent, well-adjusted, successful university students can turn aggressive in response to a small laboratory experience of social exclusion," noted the research team, "it is disturbing to imagine the aggressive tendencies that might arise from a series of important rejections or chronic exclusion from desired groups in actual social life."

Most socially excluded teens do not commit violence, but some do. Charles "Andy" Williams, described by a classmate as someone his peers derided as "freak, dork, nerd, stuff like that," went on a shooting spree at his suburban California high school, killing two and wounding 13 (Bowles & Kasindorf, 2001).

Exile, imprisonment, and solitary confinement are progressively more severe forms of punishment. The bereaved often feel life is empty, pointless. Children reared in institutions without a sense of belonging to anyone, or locked away at home under extreme neglect, become pathetic creatures—withdrawn, frightened, speechless. Adults denied acceptance and inclusion may feel depressed. Anxiety, jealousy, loneliness, and guilt all involve threatened disruptions of our need to belong. Even when bad relationships break, people suffer. In one 16-nation survey, separated and divorced people were only half as likely as married people to say they were "very happy" (Inglehart, 1990). After such separations, feelings of loneliness and anger—and sometimes even a strange desire to be near the former partner—are commonplace.

## CLOSE RELATIONSHIPS AND HAPPINESS

So far we have seen that age, gender, and a rising economic tide are but modest predictors of happiness. Valuing intimacy and connection more than increasing material possessions *does* predict well-being. It's no wonder, given our human need to belong. So, if that need is met, are people happier? Healthier?

### FRIENDSHIPS AND WELL-BEING

Attachments with intimate friends have two effects, believed Francis Bacon (1625): "It redoubleth joys, and cutteth griefs in half." "I get by with a little help from my friends," sang John Lennon and Paul McCartney (1967). Indeed, people report happier feelings when with others (Pavot, Diener, & Fujita, 1990).

Asked by National Opinion Research Center interviewers, "How many close friends would you say you have?" (excluding family members), 26% of those reporting fewer than five friends and 38% of those reporting five or more said they were "very happy."

### MARRIAGE AND WELL-BEING

Mountains of data reveal that most people are happier attached. Compared with those who never marry, and especially compared with those who have separated or divorced, married people report greater happiness and life satisfaction. This marriage–happiness correlation extends across countries and (contrary to some pop psychology) both genders (see Figure 41.2).

Why are married people happier? Does marriage breed happiness? Or are happy people more likely to marry and stay married? The marriage–happiness traffic appears to run both ways. First, happy people, being more good-natured, outgoing, and sensitive to others, may be more appealing as marital partners. Unhappy people experience more rejection. Misery may love company, but company does not love misery. An unhappy (and therefore self-focused, irritable, and withdrawn) spouse or roommate is generally not fun to be around (Gotlib, 1992; Segrin & Dillard, 1992). For such reasons, positive, happy people more readily form happy relationships.

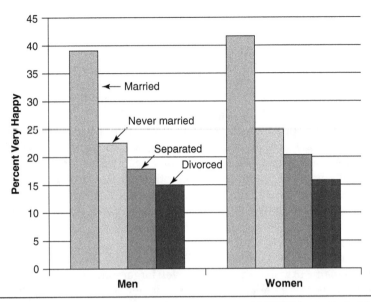

**Figure 41.2** National Opinion Research Center surveys of 35,535 ever-married Americans, 1972 to 2010.

Yet "the prevailing opinion of researchers," noted Mastekaasa (1995), is that the marriage–happiness correlation is "mainly due" to the beneficial effects of marriage. Consider: If the happiest people marry sooner and more often, then as people age (and progressively less happy people move into marriage), the average happiness of both married and never-married people should decline. (The older, less happy newlyweds would pull down the average happiness of married people, leaving the unhappiest people in the unmarried group.) However, the data refute this prediction, which suggests that marital intimacy, commitment, and support do, for most people, pay emotional dividends. Marriage offers people new roles that produce new stresses, but it also offers new rewards and sources of identity and self-esteem. When marked by intimacy, marriage (friendship sealed by commitment) reduces loneliness and offers a dependable lover and companion (Hendrick & Hendrick, 1997).

CLOSE RELATIONSHIPS AND HEALTH

Linda and Emily had much in common. When interviewed for a study conducted by UCLA psychologist Shelley Taylor (1989), both Los Angeles women had married, raised three children, suffered comparable breast tumors, and recovered from surgery and 6 months of chemotherapy. But there was a difference. Linda, a widow in her early 50s, was living alone, her children scattered in Atlanta, Boston, and Europe. "She had become odd in ways that people sometimes do when they are isolated," reported Taylor. "Having no one with whom to share her thoughts on a daily basis, she unloaded them somewhat inappropriately with strangers, including our interviewer" (Taylor, 1989, pp. 139–142).

Interviewing Emily was difficult in a different way. Phone calls interrupted. Her children, all living nearby, were in and out of the house, dropping things off with a quick kiss. Her husband called from his office for a brief chat. Two dogs roamed the house, greeting visitors enthusiastically. All in all, Emily "seemed a serene and contented person, basking in the warmth of her family" (Taylor, 1989, pp. 139–142).

Three years later, the researchers tried to reinterview the women. Linda, they learned, had died 2 years before. Emily was still lovingly supported by her family and friends and was as happy and healthy as ever. Because no two cancers are identical, we can't be certain that different social situations led to Linda's and Emily's fates. But they do illustrate a conclusion drawn from several large studies: Social support—feeling liked, affirmed, and encouraged by intimate friends and family—promotes not only happiness, but also health.

Relationships can sometimes be stressful, especially in living conditions that are crowded and lack privacy (Evans, Palsane, Lepore, & Martin, 1989). "Hell is others," wrote Jean-Paul Sartre. Warr and Payne (1982) asked a representative sample of British adults what, if anything, had emotionally strained them the day before. Their most frequent answer? Family. Even when well-meaning, family intrusions can be stressful. And stress contributes to heart disease, hypertension, and a suppressed immune system.

On balance, however, close relationships more often contribute to health and happiness (Tay, Tan, Diener, & Gonzalez, 2012). Asked what prompted yesterday's times of pleasure, the same British sample, by an even larger margin, again answered, "Family." For most of us, family relationships provide not only our greatest heartaches but also our greatest comfort and joy.

When Brigham Young University researchers combined data from 148 studies totaling more than 300,000 people worldwide, they confirmed a striking effect of social support (Holt-Lunstad, Smith, & Layton, 2010). During the studies, those with ample social connections had survival rates about 50% greater than those with meager connections. The impact of meager connections appeared roughly equal to the effect of smoking 15 cigarettes a day or being alcohol dependent, and double the effect of not exercising or being obese.

Moreover, seven massive investigations, each following thousands of people for several years, revealed that close relationships affect health. Compared with those having few social ties, people are less likely to die prematurely if supported by close relationships with friends, family, fellow workers, members of a church, or other support groups (Cohen, 1988; House, Landis, & Umberson, 1988; Nelson, 1988).

It has long been known that married people live longer, healthier lives than the unmarried. A seven-decade-long Harvard study found that a good marriage at age 50 predicts healthy aging better than does a low cholesterol level at 50 (Vaillant, 2002; see also Vaillant, Chapter 35, this volume). But why? Is it just that healthy people are more likely to marry and stay married? Two recent analyses conclude, after controlling for various possible explanations, that marriage does get under the skin. Marriage "improves survival prospects" (Murray, 2000) and "makes people" healthier and longer-lived (Wilson & Oswald, 2002). What also matters is marital functioning. Positive, happy, supportive marriages are conducive to health; conflict-laden ones are not (Kiecolt-Glaser & Newton, 2001).

There are several possible reasons for the link between social support and health (Helgeson, Cohen, & Fritz, 1998). Perhaps after symptoms appear family members who offer social support also help patients to receive medical treatment more quickly. Perhaps people eat better and exercise more because their partners guide and goad them into adhering to treatment regimens. Perhaps they smoke and drink less. One study following 50,000 young adults through time found that such unhealthy behaviors drop precipitously after marriage (Marano, 1998). Perhaps supportive relationships also help us evaluate and overcome stressful events, such as social rejection. Perhaps they help bolster our self-esteem. When we are wounded by someone's dislike or by the loss of a job, a friend's advice, assistance, and reassurance may be good medicine (Cutrona, 1986; Rook, 1987).

Environments that support our need to belong also foster stronger immune functioning. Social ties even confer resistance to cold viruses. Cohen, Doyle, Skoner, Rabin, and Gwaltney (1997) demonstrated this after putting 276 healthy volunteers in quarantine for 5 days after administering nasal drops laden with a cold virus. (The volunteers were paid $800 each to endure this experience.) The cold fact is that the effect of social ties is nothing to sneeze at. Age, race, sex, smoking, and other health habits being equal, those with the most social ties were least likely to catch a cold and they produced less mucus. More than 50 studies further reveal that social support calms the cardiovascular system, lowering blood pressure and stress hormones (Uchino, Cacioppo, & Kiecolt-Glaser, 1996; Uchino, Uno, & Holt-Lunstad, 1999).

Close relationships also provide the opportunity to *confide* painful feelings, a social support component that has now been extensively studied (Frattaroli, 2006). In one study, Pennebaker and O'Heeron (1984) contacted the surviving spouses of people who had committed suicide or died in car accidents. Those who bore their grief alone had more health problems than those who could express it openly. Talking about our troubles can be open-heart therapy. Older people, many of whom have lost a spouse and close friends, are somewhat less likely to enjoy such confiding. So, sustained emotional reactions to stressful events can be debilitating. However, the toxic impact of stressful events can be buffered by a relaxed, healthy lifestyle and by the comfort and aid provided by supportive friends and family.

## DOES RADICAL INDIVIDUALISM SUBVERT OUR NEED TO BELONG?

We humans have a deep need to belong that, if met, helps sustain our happiness and health. Yet consider some contemporary mantras of Western pop psychology:

> Do your own thing. If it feels good, do it. Shun conformity. Don't force your values on others. Assert your personal rights (to sell and buy guns, to sell and buy pornography). To love others, first love yourself. Listen to your own heart. Prefer solo spirituality to communal religion. Be self-sufficient. Expect others likewise to believe in themselves and to make it on their own.

Such sentiments define the heart of economic and social individualism, which finds its peak expression in modern America.

All post-Renaissance Western cultures to some extent express the triumph of individualism as what Fox-Genovese (1991, p. 7) calls "*the* theory of human nature and rights" (italics in original). But contemporary America is the most individualistic of cultures. One famous comparison of 116,000 IBM employees worldwide found that Americans, followed by Australians, were the most individualistic (Hofstede, 1980). We can glimpse America's individualism in its comparatively low tax rates. Taxes advance the common good through schools, roads, parks, and health, welfare, and defense programs that serve and protect all—but at a price to individuals. And in the contest among American values, individual rights trump social responsibilities.

Individualism is a two-sided coin. It supports democracy by fostering initiative, creativity, and equal rights for all individuals. But taken to an extreme it becomes egoism and narcissism—the self above others, one's own present above posterity's future. Shunning conformity, commitment, and obligation, modern individualists prefer to define their own standards and do as they please, noted Bellah, Madsen, Sullivan,

Swidler, and Tipton (1985) in their discernment of American *Habits of the Heart*. And as Robert Putnam (2000) massively documented, we have become more, not less individualistic. Compared to a half century ago, we are more often "bowling alone," and also voting, visiting, entertaining, car-pooling, trusting, joining, meeting, neighboring, and giving proportionately less. Social capital—the family and community networks that nurture civility and mutual trust—has waned.

The celebration and defense of personal liberty lies at the heart of the American dream. It drives our free market economy and underlies our respect for the rights of all. In democratic countries that guarantee basic freedoms, people live more happily than in those that don't. Migration patterns testify to this reality. Yet for today's radical individualism, we pay a price: a social recession that has imperiled children, corroded civility, and slightly diminished happiness. *When individualism is taken to an extreme, individual well-being can become its ironic casualty.*

## IS INEQUALITY SOCIALLY TOXIC?

Individualism also supports inequality, and in both developed and emerging economies inequality has grown. In the 34 Organisation for Economic Co-operation and Development (2011) countries, the richest 10% now average 9 times the income of the poorest 10%. (The gap is less in the Scandinavian countries, and substantially greater in Israel, Turkey, the United States, Mexico, and Chile.) Countries with greater inequality not only have greater health and social problems, but also higher rates of mental illness (Pickett & Wilkinson, 2011). Likewise, American states with greater inequality have higher rates of depression (Messias, Eaton, & Grooms, 2011). And over time, years with more income inequality—and associated increases in perceived unfairness and lack of trust—correlate with less happiness among those with lower incomes (Oishi, Kesebir, & Diener, 2011).

Although people often prefer the economic policies in place, a national survey found that Americans overwhelmingly preferred an income distribution that just happened to be Sweden's. Moreover, people preferred (in an ideal world) the top 20% income share ranging between 30% and 40% (rather than the actual 84%), with modest differences between Republicans and Democrats and between those making less than $50,000 and more than $100,000 (Norton & Ariely, 2011).

Even in China, income inequality has grown. This helps explain why rising affluence has not produced increased happiness—there or elsewhere. Rising income inequality, notes Michael Hagerty (2000), makes for more people who have rich neighbors. Television's modeling of the lifestyles of the wealthy also serves to accentuate feelings of "relative deprivation" and desires for more (Schor, 1998).

### A VISION OF A MORE CONNECTED FUTURE

To counter radical individualism and the other forces of cultural corrosion, one can affirm the following:

- Liberals' indictment of the demoralizing effects of poverty and conservatives' indictment of toxic media models.
- Liberals' support for family-friendly workplaces and conservatives' support for committed relationships.
- Liberals' advocacy for children in all sorts of families and conservatives' support for marriage and coparenting.

Without suppressing our differences do most people not share a vision of a better world? Is it not one that rewards initiative but restrains exploitative greed? That balances individual rights with communal well-being? That respects diversity while embracing unifying ideals? That is accepting of other cultures without being indifferent to moral issues? That protects and heals our degrading physical and social environments? In our utopian social world, adults and children will together enjoy their routines and traditions. They will have close relationships with extended family and with supportive neighbors. Children will live without fear for their safety or the breakup of their families. Fathers and mothers will jointly nurture their children; to say "He fathered the child" will parallel the meaning of "She mothered the child." Free yet responsible media will entertain us with stories and images that exemplify heroism, compassion, and committed love. Reasonable and rooted moral judgments will motivate compassionate acts and enable noble and satisfying lives.

### THE COMMUNITARIAN MOVEMENT

Supported by research on the need to belong, on the psychology of women, and on communal values in Asian and Third World cultures, many social scientists are expressing renewed appreciation for human connections. A late-20th-century communitarian movement offered a third way—an alternative to the individualistic civil libertarianism of the left and the economic libertarianism of the right. It implored us, in the words of Martin Luther King Jr., "to choose between chaos and community," to balance our needs for independence and attachment, liberty and civility, me thinking and we thinking. The communitarian platform "recognizes that the preservation of individual liberty depends on the active maintenance of the institutions of civil society."

Typically, conservatives are economic individualists and moral collectivists. Liberals are moral individualists and economic collectivists. Third-way communitarians have advocated moral and economic policies that balance rights with communal responsibility. "Democratic communitarianism is based on the value of the sacredness of the individual, which is common to most of the great religions and philosophies of the world," explained Bellah (1995/1996, pp. 4–5). But it also "affirms the central value of solidarity . . . that we become who we are through our relationships." Agreeing that "it takes a village to raise a child," communitarians remind us of what it takes to raise a village.

Listen to communitarians talk about European-style child benefits, extended parental leaves, flexible working hours, campaign finance reform, and ideas for "fostering the commons," and you'd swear they are liberals. Listen to them talk about covenant marriages, divorce reform, father care, and character education, and you'd swear they are conservatives.

Communitarians have welcomed incentives for individual initiative and appreciate why Marxist economies have crumbled. "If I were, let's say, in Albania at this moment," said Communitarian Network cofounder Etzioni (1991, p. 35), "I probably would argue that there's too much community and not enough individual rights." In communal Japan (where "the nail that sticks out gets pounded down"), Etzioni said he would sing a song of individuality. In the individualistic Western context, he has sung a song of social order, which in times of chaos (as in crime-plagued or corrupt countries) is necessary for liberty (Etzioni, 1994). Where there is chaos in a neighborhood, people may feel like prisoners in their homes.

Opposition to communitarians has come from civil libertarians of the left, economic libertarians of the right, and special interest libertarians (such as the American

National Rifle Association in the 2013 debate over gun control). Much as these organizations differ, they are branches of the same tree—all valuing individual rights in the contest with the common good. Communitarians take on all such varieties of libertarians. Unrestrained personal freedom, they say, destroys a culture's social fabric; unrestrained commercial freedom exploits workers and plunders the commons. Etzioni (1998) sums up the communitarian ideal in his *New Golden Rule*: "Respect and uphold society's moral order as you would have society respect and uphold your autonomy" (p. xviii).

To reflect on your own libertarian versus communitarian leanings, consider what restraints on liberty you support: luggage scanning at airports? Smoking bans in public places? Speed limits on highways? Sobriety checkpoints? Drug testing of pilots and rail engineers? Prohibitions on leaf burning? Restrictions on TV cigarette ads? Regulations on stereo or muffler noise? Pollution controls? Requiring seat belts and motorcycle helmets? Disclosure of sexual contacts for HIV carriers? Outlawing child pornography? Background checks before gun purchases? Banning AK-47s and other nonhunting weapons of destruction? Required school uniforms? Wire taps on suspected terrorists? Fingerprinting checks to protect welfare, unemployment, and Social Security funds from fraud?

All such restraints on individual rights, most opposed by libertarians of one sort or another, aim to enhance the public good. When New York City during the 1990s took steps to control petty deviances—the panhandlers, prostitutes, and sex shops—it made the city into a more civil place, with lessened crime and fear. "It is better to live in an orderly society than to allow people so much freedom they can become disruptive," two thirds of Canadians but only one half of Americans have agreed (Lipset & Pool, 1996, p. 42).

Libertarians often object to restraints on guns, panhandlers, pornography, drugs, or business by warning that such may plunge us down a slippery slope leading to the loss of more important liberties. If today we let them search our luggage, tomorrow they'll be invading our houses. If today we censor cigarette ads on television, tomorrow the thought police will be removing books from our libraries. If today we ban assault weapons, tomorrow's Big Brother government will take our hunting rifles. Communitarians reply that if we don't balance concern for individual rights with concern for the commons, we risk chaos and a new fascism. The true defenders of freedom, contends Etzioni, are those who seek to balance rights with responsibilities, individualism with community, and liberty with fraternity.

This broadly based social ecology movement affirms liberals' concerns about income inequality and their support for family-friendly workplaces and children in all family forms. It affirms conservatives' indictments of toxic media models and their support for marriage and coparenting. And it found encouragement in the recent subsiding of teen violence, suicide, and pregnancy.

## CONCLUSION

To sum up, humans are social animals. We flourish when connected in close, supportive relationships.

## SUMMARY POINTS

- Human happiness is not much predicted by age or gender, but it does tend to be greater among those with certain traits, those in countries where basic needs are met and people experience freedom, and those active in supportive faith communities.

- People in rich (rather than poor) countries and rich (compared to poor) individuals do report greater happiness. Yet, unlike a rising tide, economic growth over time has not substantially lifted our emotions.
- People who prioritize intimacy and connection report greater quality of life than those who prioritize wealth and material possessions.
- The human need to belong is apparent from
    - The survival value of attachments and cooperative action.
    - Our desire for close, satisfying relationships with family, friends, and romantic partners.
    - Our efforts to gain acceptance, through tactics that range from conformity to cosmetic surgery.
    - Our distress over lost relationships, ostracism, or exile.
- Close relationships, such as intimate friendship and marriage, predict health as well as happiness.
- Western individualism fosters initiative, creativity, and human rights. But taken to an extreme it can also foster egoism, erode the communal social fabric, and increase inequality.
- Economic inequality is a predictor of increased social, emotional, and health problems.
- Communitarians seek to advance human flourishing with public policies that balance individual incentives and rights with communal solidarity and well-being.

For public policy makers these are important points to ponder—perhaps especially in my country, where

- The child poverty rate has increased (from 16% to 22% between 1999 and 2011, reports Child Trends, 2012).
- The gap between rich and poor also continues to increase. Between 1970 and 2011, the richest 1% of Americans' share of the national income pie more than doubled—from 9% to 20% (Kuziemko & Stantcheva, 2013).

Bipartisan voices recognize that liberals' social risk factors (poverty, inequality, hopelessness) and conservatives' social risk factors (early sexualization, unwed parenthood, family fragmentation) all come in the same package. For example, a 2013 "Call for a New Conversation on Marriage," signed by 75 American leaders from across the political spectrum, "brings together gays and lesbians who want to strengthen marriage with straight people who want to do the same." It asks, for example, "What economic policies strengthen marriage?" and "What marriage policies create wealth?" (Institute for American Values, 2013). Recognizing our need to belong and having a vision for positive communal life, practitioners of positive psychology may wish to ponder and explore such questions, and to join the effort to promote a social ecology that nurtures happiness, health, and civility.

## REFERENCES

Argyle, M. (1999). Causes and correlates of happiness. In D. Kahneman, E. Diener, & N. Schwartz (Eds.), *Well-being: The foundations of hedonic psychology* (pp. 353–373). New York, NY: Russell Sage Foundation.

Bacon, F. (1625). Of friendship. *The essays or counsels, civil and moral*. London, England: Iohn Haviland for Hanna Barret.

Baumeister, R. F., & Leary, M. R. (1995). The need to belong: Desire for interpersonal attachment as a fundamental human motivation. *Psychological Bulletin, 117,* 497–529.

Baumeister, R. F., Twenge, J. M., & Nuss, C. K. (2002). Effects of social exclusion on cognitive processes: Anticipated aloneness reduces intelligent thought. *Journal of Personality and Social Psychology, 83,* 817–827.

Bellah, R. N. (1995/1996, Winter). Community properly understood: A defense of "democratic communitarianism." *The Responsive Community,* 49–54.

Bellah, R. N., Madsen, R., Sullivan, W. M., Swidler, A., & Tipton, S. M. (1985). *Habits of the heart: Individualism and commitment in American life.* Berkeley: University of California Press.

Berscheid, E. (1985). Interpersonal attraction. In G. Lindzey & E. Aronson (Eds.), *The handbook of social psychology* (pp. 413–484). New York, NY: Random House.

Bowles, S., & Kasindorf, M. (2001, March 6). Friends tell of picked-on but "normal" kid. *USA Today,* p. 4A.

Buckley, K. E., & Leary, M. R. (2001, February). *Perceived acceptance as a predictor of social, emotional, and academic outcomes.* Paper presented at the Society of Personality and Social Psychology annual convention, San Antonio, TX.

Bureau of the Census. (1975). *Historical abstract of the United States: Colonial times to 1970.* Washington, DC: Superintendent of Documents.

Child Trends (2012, October). *Children in poverty: Indicators on children and youth.* Retrieved from www.ChildTrendsDataBank.org

Cohen, S. (1988). Psychosocial models of the role of social support in the etiology of physical disease. *Health Psychology, 7,* 269–297.

Cohen, S., Doyle, W. J., Skoner, D. P., Rabin, B. S., & Gwaltney, J. M., Jr. (1997). Social ties and susceptibility to the common cold. *Journal of the American Medical Association, 277,* 1940–1944.

Cutrona, C. E. (1986). Behavioral manifestations of social support: A microanalytic investigation. *Journal of Personality and Social Psychology, 51,* 201–208.

Deci, E. L., & Ryan, R. M. (Eds.). (2002). *Handbook of self-determination research.* Rochester, NY: University of Rochester Press.

Deci, E. L., & Ryan, R. M. (2009). Self-determination theory: A consideration of human motivational universals. In P. J. Corr & G. Matthews (Eds.), *The Cambridge handbook of personality psychology.* New York, NY: Cambridge University Press.

Diener, E., & Seligman, M. E. P. (2002). Very happy people. *Psychological Science, 13,* 81–84.

Diener, E., Tay, L., & Oishi, S. (2013). Rising income and the subjective well-being of nations. *Journal of Personality & Social Psychology, 104*(2), 267–276.

Dunn, E., & Norton, M. (2013). *Happy money: The science of smarter spending.* New York, NY: Simon & Schuster.

Easterlin, R. (1995). Will raising the incomes of all increase the happiness of all? *Journal of Economic Behavior and Organization, 27,* 35–47.

Etzioni, A. (1991, May–June). The community in an age of individualism. Interview in *The Futurist,* 35–39.

Etzioni, A. (1994). *The spirit of community: The reinvention of American society.* New York, NY: Simon & Schuster.

Etzioni, A. (1998). *The new golden rule.* New York, NY: Basic Books.

Evans, G. W., Palsane, M. N., Lepore, S. J., & Martin, J. (1989). Residential density and psychological health: The mediating effects of social support. *Journal of Personality and Social Psychology, 57,* 994–999.

Fox-Genovese, E. (1991). *Feminism without illusions: A critique of individualism.* Chapel Hill: University of North Carolina Press.

Frank, R. H. (2012). The Easterlin paradox revisited. *Emotion, 12,* 1188–1191.

Frattaroli, J. (2006). Experimental disclosure and its moderators: A meta-analysis. *Psychological Bulletin, 132,* 823–865.

Gotlib, I. H. (1992). Interpersonal and cognitive aspects of depression. *Current Directions in Psychological Science, 1,* 149–154.

Hagerty, M. R. (2000). Social comparisons of income in one's community: Evidence from national surveys of income and happiness. *Journal of Personality and Social Psychology, 78,* 764–771.

Helgeson, V. S., Cohen, S., & Fritz, H. L. (1998). Social ties and cancer. In J. C. Holland (Ed.), *Psycho-oncology* (pp. 730–742). New York, NY: Oxford University Press.

Hendrick, S. S., & Hendrick, C. (1997). Love and satisfaction. In R. J. Sternberg & M. Hojjat (Eds.), *Satisfaction in close relationships* (pp. 56–78). New York, NY: Guilford Press.

Hofstede, G. (1980). *Culture's consequences.* Beverly Hills, CA: Sage.

Holt-Lunstad, J., Smith, T. B., & Layton, J. B. (2010). Social relationships and mortality risk: A meta-analytic review. *PLoS Medicine, 7,* e1000316.

House, J. S., Landis, K. R., & Umberson, D. (1988). Social relationships and health. *Science, 241,* 540–545.

Inglehart, R. (1990). *Culture shift in advanced industrial society.* Princeton, NJ: Princeton University Press.

Institute for American Values. (2013). *A call for a new conversation about marriage.* Retrieved from www.americanvalues.org

Kasser, T. (2000). Two versions of the American dream: Which goals and values make for a high quality of life? In E. Diener & D. R. Rahtz (Eds.), *Advances in quality of life: Theory and research* (Vol. 1, pp. 3–12). Dordrecht, The Netherlands: Kluwer.

Kasser, T., & Ryan, R. (1996). Further examining the American dream: Differential correlates of intrinsic and extrinsic goals. *Personality and Social Psychology Bulletin, 22,* 280–287.

Kiecolt-Glaser, J. K., & Newton, T. L. (2001). Marriage and health: His and hers. *Psychological Bulletin, 127,* 472–503.

Kohn, A. (1999, February 2). In pursuit of affluence, at a high price. *New York Times.* Retrieved from www.nytimes.com

Kuziemko, I., & Stantcheva, S. (2013, April 21). Our feelings about inequality: It's complicated. *New York Times.* Retrieved from www.nytimes.com

Leary, M. R., Haupt, A. L., Strausser, K. S., & Chokel, J. T. (1998). Calibrating the sociometer: The relationship between interpersonal appraisals and state self-esteem. *Journal of Personality and Social Psychology, 74,* 1290–1299.

Lennon, J., & McCartney, P. (1967). *Sgt. Pepper's lonely hearts club band* [Album].

Lipset, S. M., & Pool, A. B. (1996, Summer). Balancing the individual and the community: Canada versus the United States. *The Responsive Community,* 37–46.

Lykken, D., & Tellegen, A. (1996). Happiness is a stochastic phenomenon. *Psychological Science, 7,* 186–189.

Marano, H. E. (1998, August 4). Debunking the marriage myth: It works for women, too. *New York Times.* Retrieved from www.nytimes.com

Mastekaasa, A. (1995). Age variations in the suicide rates and self-reported subjective well-being of married and never married persons. *Journal of Community and Applied Social Psychology, 5,* 21–39.

Messias, E., Eaton, W. W., & Grooms, A. N. (2011). Income inequality and depression prevalence across the United States: An ecological study. *Psychiatric Services, 62,* 710–712.

Milyavskaya, M., Gingras, I., Mageau, G. A., Koestner, R., Gagnon, H., Fang, J., & Bolché, J. (2009). Balance across contexts: Importance of balanced need satisfaction across various life domains. *Personality and Social Psychology Bulletin, 35,* 1031–1045.

Murray, J. E. (2000). Marital protection and marital selection: Evidence from a historical-prospective sample of American men. *Demography, 37,* 511–521.

Myers, D. G. (1993). *The pursuit of happiness*. New York, NY: Avon.

Myers, D. G. (2000). The funds, friends, and faith of happy people. *American Psychologist, 55,* 56–67.

National Opinion Research Center. (2012). *General social survey data for 1972 to 2010*. Retrieved from http://sda.berkeley.edu/cgi-bin/hsda?harcsda+gss12

Nelson, N. (1988). *A meta-analysis of the life-event/health paradigm: The influence of social support* (Unpublished doctoral dissertation). Temple University, Philadelphia, PA.

Norton, M. I., & Ariely, D. (2011). Building a better America—one wealth quintile at a time. *Perspectives on Psychological Science, 6,* 9–12.

Oishi, S., Kesebir, S., & Diener, E. (2011). Income inequality and happiness. *Psychological Science, 22,* 1095–1100.

Organisation for Economic Co-operation and Development. (2011). *An overview of growing income inequalities in OECD countries: Main findings*. Paris: Author. Retrieved from http://www.oecd.org/els/soc/49499779.pdf

Pavot, W., Diener, E., & Fujita, F. (1990). Extraversion and happiness. *Personality and Individual Differences, 11,* 1299–1306.

Pennebaker, J. W., & O'Heeron, R. C. (1984). Confiding in others and illness rate among spouses of suicide and accidental death victims. *Journal of Abnormal Psychology, 93,* 473–476.

Perkins, H. W. (1991). Religious commitment, Yuppie values, and well-being in post-collegiate life. *Review of Religious Research, 32,* 244–251.

Pickett, K., & Wilkinson, R. (2011). *The spirit level: Why greater equality makes societies stronger*. New York, NY: Bloomsbury.

Pipher, M. B. (2002). *The middle of everywhere: The world's refugees come to our town*. San Diego, CA: Harcourt Brace.

Putnam, R. (2000). *Bowling alone: The collapse and revival of American community*. New York, NY: Simon & Schuster.

Rook, K. S. (1987). Social support versus companionship: Effects on life stress, loneliness, and evaluations by others. *Journal of Personality and Social Psychology, 52,* 1132–1147.

Schor, J. B. (1998). *The overworked American*. New York, NY: Basic Books.

Segrin, C., & Dillard, J. P. (1992). The interactional theory of depression: A meta-analysis of the research literature. *Journal of Social and Clinical Psychology, 11,* 43–70.

Sheldon, K. M., & Niemiec, C. P. (2006). It's not just the amount that counts: Balanced need satisfaction also affects well-being. *Journal of Personality and Social Psychology, 91,* 331–341.

Stevenson, B., & Wolfers, J. (2008). Economic growth and subject well-being: Reassessing the Easterlin paradox. *Brookings Papers on Economic Activity, 39,* 1–87.

Tay, L., & Diener, E. (2011). Needs and subjective well-being around the world. *Journal of Personality and Social Psychology, 101,* 354–365.

Tay, L., Tan, K., Diener, E., & Gonzalez, E. (2012). Social relations, health behaviors, and health outcomes: A survey and synthesis. *Applied Psychology: Health and Well-Being, 5,* 28–78.

Taylor, S. E. (1989). *Positive illusions: Creative self-deception and the healthy mind*. New York, NY: Basic Books.

Twenge, J. M., Baumeister, R. F., DeWall, C. N., Ciarocco, N. J., & Bartels, J. M. (2007). Social exclusion decreases prosocial behavior. *Journal of Personality and Social Psychology, 92,* 56–66.

Twenge, J. M., Baumeister, R. F., Tice, D. M., & Stucke, T. S. (2001). If you can't join them, beat them: Effects of social exclusion on aggressive behavior. *Journal of Personality and Social Psychology, 81,* 1058–1069.

Twenge, J. M., Catanese, K. R., & Baumeister, R. F. (2002). Social exclusion causes self-defeating behavior. *Journal of Personality and Social Psychology, 83,* 606–615.

Uchino, B. N., Cacioppo, J. T., & Kiecolt-Glaser, J. K. (1996). The relationship between social support and physiological processes: A review with emphasis on underlying mechanisms and implications for health. *Psychological Bulletin, 119,* 488–531.

Uchino, B. N., Uno, D., & Holt-Lunstad, J. (1999). Social support, physiological processes, and health. *Current Directions in Psychological Science, 8*, 145–148.

Vaillant, G. E. (2002). *Aging well: Surprising guideposts to a happier life from the landmark Harvard study of adult development*. Boston, MA: Little, Brown.

Warr, P., & Payne, R. (1982). Experiences of strain and pleasure among British adults. *Social Science and Medicine, 16*, 1691–1697.

Williams, K. D. (2007). Ostracism. *Annual Review of Psychology, 58*, 425–452.

Williams, K. D. (2009). Ostracism: A temporal need-threat model. *Advances in Experimental Social Psychology, 41*, 275–313.

Williams, K. D., & Zadro, L. (2001). Ostracism: On being ignored, excluded and rejected. In M. Leary (Ed.), *Rejection* (pp. 21–53). New New York, NY: Oxford University Press.

Wilson, C. M., & Oswald, A. J. (2002). *How does marriage affect physical and psychological health? A survey of the longitudinal evidence*. Working paper, University of York and Warwick University.

Wuthnow, R. (1994). *God and Mammon in America*. New York, NY: Free Press.

# CHAPTER 42

# Happiness as a Priority in Public Policy

RUUT VEENHOVEN

## INTRODUCTION

ATTEMPTS TO IMPROVE the human lot begin typically with treating compelling miseries, such as hunger and epidemics. When these problems are solved, attention shifts to broader and more positive goals; we can see this development in the history of social policy, the goal of which has evolved from alleviating poverty to providing a decent standard of living for everybody. The field of medicine has witnessed a similar shift from assisting people to survive to, in addition, promoting a good quality of life. This policy change has put some difficult questions back on the agenda, such as "What is a good life?" and "What good is the best?" The social sciences cannot provide good answers to these questions, since they have also focused on misery. Yet, a good answer can be found in a classic philosophy, and it is one that is worth reconsidering.

### THE GREATEST HAPPINESS PRINCIPLE

Two centuries ago Jeremy Bentham (1789) proposed a new moral principle. He wrote that the goodness of an action should not be judged by the decency of its intentions, but by the utility of its consequences. Bentham conceived final *utility* as human *happiness*. Hence, he concluded that we should aim at the greatest happiness for the greatest number. Bentham defined happiness in terms of psychological experience, as "the sum of pleasures and pains." This philosophy is known as *utilitarianism*, because of its emphasis on the utility of behavioral consequences. *Happyism* would have been a better name, since this utility is seen as contribution to happiness.

When applied at the level of individual choice, this theory runs into some difficulties. Often, we cannot foresee what the balance of effects on happiness will be. In addition the theory deems well-intended behavior to be amoral if it happens to pan out adversely. Imagine the case of a loving mother who saves the life of her sick child, a child who grows up to be a criminal; mothers can seldom foresee a child's future and can hardly be reproached for their unconditional motherly love.

The theory is better suited for judging general rules, such as the rule that mothers should care for their sick children. It is fairly evident that adherence to this rule will add to the happiness of a great number. Following such rules is then morally correct, even if consequences might be negative in a particular case. This variant is known as *rule-utilitarianism*.

Rule-utilitarianism has been seen as a moral guide for legislation and has played a role in discussions about property laws and the death penalty. The principle can also be applied to wider issues in public policy, such as the question of what degree of income inequality we should accept. The argument is that inequality is not bad in and of itself; it is only so if it reduces the happiness of the average citizen. The greatest happiness principle can also be used when making decisions about health care and therapy. Treatment strategies can be selected on the basis of their effects on the happiness of the greatest number of patients.

### Objections Against the Principle

The greatest happiness principle is well-known, and it is a standard subject in every introduction to moral philosophy. Yet the principle is seldom put into practice. Why is this? The answer to this question is also to be found in most introductory philosophy books: Utilitarianism is typically rejected on pragmatic and moral grounds.

*Pragmatic Objections* Application of the greatest happiness principle requires that we know what happiness is and that we can predict the consequences of behavioral alternatives on it. It also requires that we can check the results of applying this principle; that is, we can measure resulting gains in happiness. At a more basic level, the principle assumes that happiness can be affected by what we do. All of this is typically denied. It is claimed that happiness is an elusive concept and one that we cannot measure. As a consequence, we can only make guesses about the effects of happiness on behavioral alternatives and can never verify our suppositions. Some even see happiness as an immutable trait that cannot be influenced. Such criticism often ends with the conclusion that we would do better to stick to more palpable seasoned virtues, such as justice and equality.

*Moral Objections* Another objection is that happiness is mere pleasure or an illusionary matter and hence not very valuable in and of itself. It is, therefore, not considered as the ultimate ethical value. Another moral objection is that happiness spoils; in particular, it fosters irresponsible consumerism and makes us less sensitive to the suffering of others. Still another objection holds that the goal of advancing happiness justifies amoral means, such as genetic manipulation, mind control, and dictatorship. Much of these ethical qualms are featured in Huxley's (1932) *Brave New World*.

### Plan of This Chapter

The preceding discussion is armchair theorizing, mainly by philosophers and novelists. How do these objections stand up to empirical tests? I first introduce modern empirical research on happiness, then consider the qualms mentioned previously in the light of the findings.

## RESEARCH ON HAPPINESS

Empirical research on happiness started in the 1960s in several branches of the social sciences. In sociology, the study of happiness developed from social indicators research. In this field, *subjective* indicators were used to supplement traditional *objective* indicators, and *happiness* became a main subjective indicator of social system performance (Andrews & Withey, 1976; Campbell, 1981).

In psychology, the concept was used in the study of mental health. Jahoda (1958) saw happiness as a criterion for positive mental health, and items on happiness figured in the pioneering epidemiological surveys on mental health by Gurin, Veroff, and Feld (1960) and Bradburn and Caplovitz (1965). At that time, happiness also figured in the groundbreaking cross-national study of human concerns by Cantril (1965) and came to be used as an indicator of successful aging in gerontology (Neugarten, Havighurst, & Tobin, 1961). Twenty years later, the questionnaires on health related to quality of life, such as the much-used SF-36 (Ware, 1996). Since 2000, economists such as Frey and Stutzer (2002) have also picked up the issue and a first institute of happiness economics has been established.[1]

Most empirical studies on happiness are based on large-scale population surveys, but there are also many studies of specific groups, such as single mothers, students, or lottery winners. The bulk of these studies revolve around one-time questionnaire studies, but there are a number of follow-up studies and even some experimental studies. To date, some 7,000 research reports have been published, and the number of publications is increasing exponentially, as shown in Figure 42.1.

The study of happiness has been institutionalized rapidly over the past few years. Most investigators have joined forces and formed the International Society for Quality of Life Studies (ISQOLS).[2] The topic is central in the *Journal of Happiness Studies*[3] and in

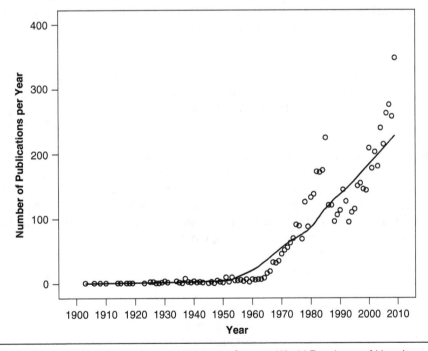

**Figure 42.1**   Rise of publications on happiness. *Source:* World Database of Happiness (Veenhoven 2013a).

[1]Erasmus Happiness Economics Research Organization, Erasmus University Rotterdam, Netherlands (www.eur.nl/ehero).

[2]International Society for Quality of Life Studies (www.isqols.org). Next to this social science association, there is a health-science oriented association, named International Society for Quality of Life Research (www.isoqol.org).

[3]*Journal of Happiness Studies* (http://www.springeronline.com/social+sciences/wellbeing/journal/10902).

the *International Journal of Happiness and Development*[4] and prominent in several other scientific journals on subjective well-being. The findings from this strand of research are gathered in the World Database of Happiness (Veenhoven, 2013a).

This collaboration has created a considerable body of knowledge, which I use in the following discussion to determine the reality value of philosophical objections against the greatest happiness principle.

## IS HAPPINESS A PRACTICABLE GOAL?

Pragmatic objections against the greatest happiness principle are many. The most basic objection is that happiness cannot be defined; therefore, all talk about happiness is mere rhetoric. The second objection is that happiness cannot be measured, so we can never establish an absolute degree and number for happiness. A third objection holds that lasting happiness of a great number is not possible; at best, we can find some relief in fleeting moments of delusion. The last claim is that we cannot bring about happiness. I next discuss these objections individually.

### CAN HAPPINESS BE DEFINED?

The word *happiness* has different meanings, and these meanings are often mixed up, which gives the concept a reputation for being elusive. Yet, a confusion of tongues about a word does not mean that no substantive meaning can be defined. Let us consider what meanings are involved and which of these is most appropriate as an end goal.

*Four Qualities of Life*   When used in a broad sense, the word *happiness* is synonymous with quality of life or well-being. In this meaning, it denotes that life is good, but does not specify what is good about life. The word is also used in more specific ways, which can be clarified with the help of the classification of qualities of life presented in Table 42.1.

This classification of meanings depends on two distinctions. Vertically there is a difference between *chances* for a good life and actual *outcomes* of life. Chances and outcomes are related, but are certainly not the same. Chances can fail to be realized, because of stupidity or bad luck. Conversely, people sometimes make much of their life in spite of poor opportunities. This distinction is common in the field of public-health research. Preconditions for good health, such as adequate nutrition and professional care, are seldom confused with health itself. Yet means and ends are less well distinguished in the discussion on happiness.

**Table 42.1**
Four Qualities of Life

|  | *External* | *Internal* |
|---|---|---|
| Life chances | Livability of environment | Life-ability of the person |
| Life results | Usefulness of life | **Satisfaction with life** |

*Source:* Veenhoven (2000).

---

[4]*International Journal of Happiness and Development* (http://www.inderscience.com/browse/index.php?journalCODE=ijhd).

Horizontally there is a distinction between *external* and *internal* qualities. In the first case the quality is in the environment; in the latter it is in the individual. Lane (2000) made this distinction clear by emphasizing "quality of persons." This distinction is also commonly made in public health. External pathogens are distinguished from inner afflictions, and researchers try to identify the mechanisms by which the former produce the latter and the conditions in which this is more or less likely. Yet again this basic insight is lacking in many discussions about happiness.

Together, these two dichotomies mark four qualities of life, all of which have been denoted by the word *happiness*.

LIVABILITY OF THE ENVIRONMENT    The top left quadrant of Table 42.1 denotes the meaning of good living conditions. Often the terms *quality of life* and *well-being* are used in this particular meaning, especially in the writings of ecologists and sociologists. Economists sometimes use the term *welfare* for this meaning. *Livability* is a better word, because it refers explicitly to a characteristic of the environment and does not carry the connotation of paradise. Politicians and social reformers typically stress this quality of life.

LIFEABILITY OF THE PERSON    The top right quadrant denotes inner life-chances, that is, how well we are equipped to cope with the problems of life. This aspect of the good life is also known by different names. Especially doctors and psychologists use the terms *quality of life* and *well-being* to denote this specific meaning. There are more names, however. In biology the phenomenon is referred to as *adaptive potential*. On other occasions it is denoted by the medical term *health*, in the medium variant of the word.[5] Sen (1993) calls this quality of life variant *capability*. I prefer the simple term *lifeability*, which contrasts elegantly with *livability*. This quality of life is central in the thinking of therapists and educators.

USEFULNESS OF LIFE    The bottom left quadrant represents the notion that a good life must be good for something more than itself. This presumes some higher value, such as ecological preservation or cultural development. In fact, there are myriad values on which the utility of life can be judged. There is no current generic for these external turnouts of life. Gerson (1976) referred to these kinds as *transcendental* conceptions of quality of life. Another appellation is *meaning of life*, which then denotes *true* significance instead of mere subjective sense of meaning. I prefer the more simple *utility of life*, admitting that this label may also give rise to misunderstanding.[6] Moral advisers, such as a pastor, emphasize this quality of life.

SATISFACTION WITH LIFE    Finally, the bottom right quadrant represents the inner outcomes of life, that is, the quality in the eye of the beholder. As we deal with conscious humans, this quality boils down to subjective appreciation of life, commonly referred to by terms such as *subjective well-being*, *life-satisfaction*, and *happiness* in a limited sense of the word.[7] Life has more of this quality, the more and the longer it is enjoyed. In fairy tales this combination of intensity and duration is denoted with the phrase

---

[5]There are three main meanings or health: The maxi variant is all the good (World Health Organization definition), the medium variant is lifeability, and the mini-variant is absence of physical defect.

[6]A problem with this name is that the utilitarians used the word *utility* for subjective appreciation of life, the sum of pleasures and pains.

[7]This quality of life is the subject of the *Journal of Happiness Studies*.

"They lived happily ever after." There is no professional interest group that stresses this meaning, and this seems to be one of the reasons for the reservations surrounding the greatest happiness principle.

Which of these four meanings of the word *happiness* is most appropriate as an end goal? I think the last one. Commonly policy aims at improving life-chances by, for example, providing better housing or education, as indicated in the upper half of Table 42.1. Yet more is not always better, and some opportunities may be more critical than others. The problem is that we need a criterion to assign priorities among the many life-chances policy makers want to improve. That criterion should be found in the outcomes of life, as shown in the lower half of Table 42.1. There, *utility* provides no workable criterion, since external effects are many and can be valued differently. *Satisfaction with life* is a better criterion, since it reflects the degree to which external living conditions fit with inner life-abilities. Satisfaction is also the subjective experience Jeremy Bentham had in mind.

*Four Kinds of Satisfaction*   This brings us to the question of what *satisfaction* is precisely. This is also a word with multiple meanings we can elucidate. Table 42.2 is based on two distinctions: The vertical distinction is between satisfaction with *parts of life* versus satisfaction with *life-as-a-whole*, the horizontal distinction between *passing* satisfaction and *enduring* satisfaction. These two bipartitions yield again a fourfold taxonomy.

PLEASURE   Passing satisfaction with a part of life is called *pleasure*. Pleasures can be sensory, such as a glass of good wine, or mental, such as the reading of this text. The idea that we should maximize such satisfactions is called *hedonism*.

PART-SATISFACTIONS   Enduring satisfaction with a part of life is referred to as *part-satisfaction*. Such satisfactions can concern a domain of life, such as working life, and aspects of life, such as its variety. Sometimes the word *happiness* is used for such part-satisfactions, in particular for satisfaction with your career.

TOP EXPERIENCE   Passing satisfaction can be about life-as-a-whole, in particular when the experience is intense and oceanic. This kind of satisfaction is usually referred to as top-experience. When poets write about happiness they usually describe an experience of this kind. Likewise, religious writings use the word *happiness* often in the sense of a mystical ecstasy. Another word for this type of satisfaction is *enlightenment*.

LIFE SATISFACTION   Enduring satisfaction with your life-as-a-whole is called *life-satisfaction* and also commonly referred to as *happiness*. This is the kind of satisfaction Bentham seems to have had in mind when he described happiness as the "sum of pleasures and pains." I have delineated this concept in more detail

**Table 42.2**
Four Kinds of Satisfaction

|  | *Passing* | *Enduring* |
|---|---|---|
| Life aspects | Pleasure | Domain satisfaction |
| Life-as-a-whole | Peak experience | **Life satisfaction** |

elsewhere, and defined it as "the overall appreciation of one's life-as-a-whole" (Veenhoven, 1984, pp. 22–23).

Life-satisfaction is most appropriate as a policy goal. Enduring satisfaction is clearly more valuable than passing satisfactions, and satisfaction with life-as-a-whole is also of more worth than mere part-satisfaction. Moreover, life-satisfaction is probably of greater significance, since it signals the degree to which human needs are being met. I return to this point later.

**In sum,** *happiness can be defined as the overall enjoyment of your life as-a-whole.*

### CAN HAPPINESS BE MEASURED?

A common objection to the greatest happiness principle is that happiness cannot be measured. This objection applies to most of the previously discussed meanings of the word, but does it apply to happiness in the sense of life-satisfaction?

Happiness in this sense is a state of mind, which cannot be assessed objectively in the same way as weight or blood pressure. Happiness cannot be measured with access to merit-goods, since the effect of such life-chances depends on life-abilities. Though there is certainly a biochemical substrate to the experience, we cannot as yet measure happiness using physical indicators. The hedometer awaits invention. Extreme states of happiness and unhappiness manifest in nonverbal behavior, such as smiling and body posture, but these indications are often not well visible. This leaves us with self-reports. The question is then whether happiness can be measured adequately in this way.

*Self-Reports*   There are many reservations about self-report measures of happiness: People might not be able to oversee their lives, self-defense might distort the judgment, and social desirability could give rise to rosy answers. Thus, early investigators experimented with indirect questioning. Happiness was measured by a clinical interview, by content analysis of diaries and using projective methods such as the Thematic Apperception Test. These methods are laborious and their validity is not beyond doubt. Hence, direct questions have also been used from the beginning. A careful comparison of these methods showed that direct questioning yields the same information at a lower cost (Wessman & Ricks, 1966).

*Direct Questionioning*   Direct questions on happiness are often framed in larger questionnaires, such as the much-used 20-item Life Satisfaction Index (LSI) of Neugarten et al. (1961). There are psychometric advantages with the use of multiple-item questionnaires, in particular a reduction of error due to difference in interpretation of key words. Yet, a disadvantage is that most of the happiness inventories involve items that do not quite fit the concept defined previously. For instance, the LSI contains a question on whether the individual has plans for the future, which is clearly something other than enjoying current life.

The use of multiple items is common in psychological testing because the object of measurement is mostly rather vague. For example, *neuroticism* cannot be sharply defined and is therefore measured with multiple questions about matters that are likely to be linked to that matter. Yet, happiness is a well-defined concept (overall enjoyment of life-as-a-whole) and can, therefore, be measured by one question. Another reason for the use of multiple items in psychological measurement is that respondents are mostly unaware of the state to be measured. For instance, most respondents do not know how neurotic they are, so neuroticism is inferred from their responses to various related matters. Yet, happiness is something of which the respondent is conscious. Hence, happiness can also be measured by single direct questions, which is common practice and one that works.

*Common Survey Questions*    Because happiness can be measured with single direct questions, it has become a common item in large-scale surveys among the general population in many countries. A common question reads:

> Taken all together, how satisfied or dissatisfied are you currently with your life as a whole?
>
> 0    1    2    3    4    5    6    7    8    9    10
>
> Dissatisfied                                        Satisfied

Many more question-and-answer formats have been used. All acceptable items are documented in full detail in the collection of happiness measures of the World Database of Happiness (Veenhoven, 2013d).

*Validity*    Though these questions are fairly clear, responses can be flawed in several ways. Responses may reflect how happy people think they should be rather than how happy they actually feel, and it is also possible that people present themselves as happier than they actually are. These suspicions have given rise to numerous validation studies. Elsewhere I have reviewed this research and concluded that there is no evidence that responses to these questions measure something other than what they are meant to measure (Veenhoven, 1984, Chapter 3; 1998). Though this is no guarantee that research will never reveal a deficiency, we can trust these measures of happiness for the time being.

*Reliability*    Research has also shown that responses are affected by minor variations in wording and ordering of questions and by situational factors, such as the race of the interviewer or the weather. As a result, the same person may score 6 in one investigation and 7 in another. This lack of precision hampers analyses at the individual level. It is less of a problem when average happiness in groups is compared, since random fluctuations tend to balance, typically the case when happiness is used in policy evaluation.

*Comparability*    The objection is made that responses on such questions are not comparable, because a score of 6 does not mean the same for everybody. A common philosophical argument for this position is that happiness depends on the realization of wants and that these wants differ across persons and cultures (Smart & Williams, 1973). Yet, it is not at all sure that happiness depends on the realization of idiosyncratic wants. The available data are more in line with the theory that it depends on the gratification of universal needs (Veenhoven, 1991, 2009). I will come back on this point in the later discussion on the signal function of happiness.

A second qualm is whether happiness is a typical Western concept that is not recognized in other cultures. Happiness appears to be a universal emotion that is recognized in facial expression all over the world (Ekman & Friesen, 1975) and for which words exist in all languages. A related objection is that happiness is a unique experience that cannot be communicated on an equivalent scale. Yet from an evolutionary point of view, it is unlikely that we differ very much. As in the case of pain, there will be a common human spectrum of experience.

Last, there is methodological reservation about possible cultural bias in the measurement of happiness, due to problems with translation of keywords and cultural variation in response tendencies. I have looked for empirical evidence for these distortions elsewhere, but did not find any (Veenhoven, 1993, Chapter 5). All these objections imply that research using these measures of happiness will fail to find any meaningful correlations. Later we see that this is not true.

**In sum,** *happiness as life-satisfaction is measurable with direct questioning and well comparable across persons and nations.* Hence, happiness of a great number can be assessed using surveys.

Is Happiness Possible?

Aiming at happiness for a great number has often been denounced as *illusionary* because long-term happiness, and certainly happiness for a great number, is a fantasy. This criticism has many fathers. In some religions the belief is that man has been expelled from Paradise: Earthly existence is not to be enjoyed; we are here to chasten our souls. Classic psychologists have advanced more profane reasons.

Freud (1929/1948) saw happiness as a short-lived orgasmic experience that comes forth from the release of primitive urges. Hence, he believed that happiness is not compatible with the demands of civilized society and that modern man is, therefore, doomed to chronic unhappiness. In the same vein, Adorno believed that happiness is a mere temporary mental escape from misery, mostly at the cost of reality control (Rath, 2002).

The psychological literature on adaptation is less pessimistic, but it, too, denies the possibility of enduring happiness for a great number. It assumes that aspirations follow achievements and, hence, concludes that happiness does not last. It is also inferred that periods of happiness and unhappiness oscillate over a lifetime, and the average level is, therefore, typically neutral. Likewise, social comparison is seen to

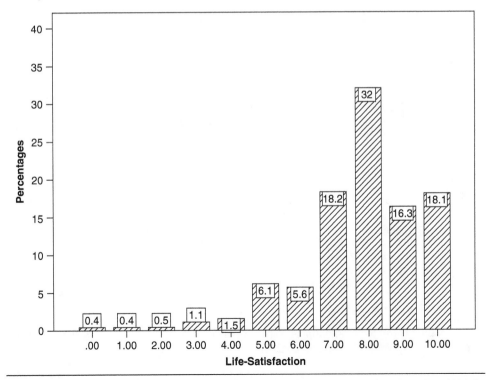

**Figure 42.2**   Life-satisfaction in the United States, 2007. *Source:* Gallup World Poll (2007).

**Table 42.3**
Life-Satisfaction in 12 Nations, 2000–2009

| Best | | Middle | | Worst | |
|------|------|--------|------|-------|------|
| Costa Rica | 8.5 | South Korea | 6.0 | Benin | 3.0 |
| Denmark | 8.3 | Estonia | 6.0 | Burundi | 2.9 |
| Iceland | 8.2 | Tunisia | 5.9 | Tanzania | 2.8 |
| Switzerland | 8.0 | Turkey | 5.7 | Togo | 2.6 |

*Note.* Average scores on a 0–10 Scale.
*Source: Happiness in Nations.* World Database of Happiness (Veenhoven, 2013c).

result in a neutral average, and enduring happiness is possible only for a "happy few" (Brickman & Campbell, 1971).

*Enduring Happiness*   Figure 42.2 presents the distribution for responses to the 0-to-10-step question on life-satisfaction in the United States. The most frequent responses are between 7 and 10 and less than 5% scores below neutral. The average is 7.85.[8] This result implies that most people must feel happy most of the time. That view has been corroborated by yearly follow-up studies over many years (Ehrhardt, Saris, & Veenhoven, 2000) and by studies that use the technique of experience sampling (Schimmack & Diener, 2003).

*Happiness of a Great Number*   The high level of happiness is not unique to the United States. Table 42.3 shows similar averages in other Western nations. In fact, average happiness tends to be above neutral in most countries of the world. So happiness for a great number is apparently possible.

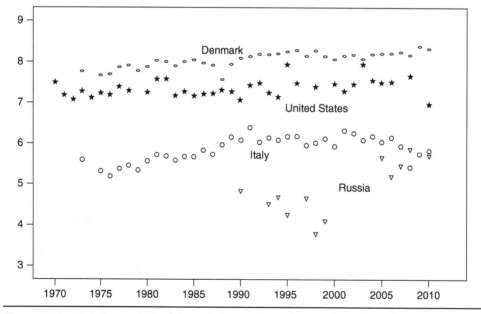

**Figure 42.3**   Trend average happiness in four nations. *Source: Happiness in Nations.* World Database of Happiness (Veenhoven, 2013c).

---

[8]The average on a similar question in 2006 was 7.02. The mean score in these two surveys is 7.4.

Table 42.3 also shows that average happiness was below neutral in several African countries. All this is in flat contradiction to Freudian theory, which predicts averages below 4 everywhere and defies adaptation theory that predicts universal averages around 5.

*Greater Happiness*   Average happiness in nations is not static, but has changed over the years, typically to the positive (see Figure 42.3). Particularly noteworthy is that average happiness has gone up in Denmark, where the level of happiness was already highest.

**In sum,** *enduring happiness for a great number of people is possible.*

## CAN HAPPINESS BE MANUFACTURED?

The observation that people *can* be happy does mean that they can be *made* happier by public policy. Like the wind, happiness could be a natural phenomenon beyond our control. Several arguments have been raised in support of this view. A common reasoning holds that happiness is too complex a thing to be controlled. In this line, it is argued that conditions for happiness differ across cultures, and the dynamics of happiness are of a chaotic nature and one that will probably never be sufficiently understood. The claim that happiness cannot be created is also argued with a reversed reasoning. We understand happiness sufficiently well to realize that it cannot be raised. One argument is that happiness depends on comparison and that any improvement is, therefore, nullified by "reference drift" (VanPraag, 1993). Another claim in this context is that happiness is a trait-like matter and hence not sensitive to improvement in living conditions (Cummins, 2010). All this boils down to the conclusion that planned control of happiness is an illusion.

### Can We Know Conditions for Happiness?

As in the case of health, conditions for happiness can be charted inductively using epidemiological research. Many such studies have been performed over the last decade. The results are documented in the earlier mentioned World Database of Happiness (Veenhoven, 2013a) and summarized in reviews by Argyle (2002); Diener, Suh, Lucas, and Smith (1999); and Veenhoven (1984, in press). What does this research teach us about conditions for happiness?

*External Conditions*   Happiness research has focused very much on social conditions for happiness. These conditions are studied at two levels: At the macro level, there are studies about the kind of society where people have the most happy lives, and at the micro level, there is much research about differences in happiness across social positions in society. As yet there is little research at the meso level. Little is known about the relation between happiness and labor organizations, for example.

*Livability of Society*   In Table 42.3, we have seen that average happiness differs greatly across nations. Table 42.4 shows that there is system in these differences. People live happier in rich nations than in poor ones, and happiness is also higher in nations characterized by rule of law, freedom, good citizenship, cultural plurality,

**Table 42.4**

Happiness and Society in 151 Nations in 2006

| Characteristics of Society | Correlation with Happiness | | N |
| --- | --- | --- | --- |
| | Zero Order | Controlled for Wealth | |
| **Affluence** | +.61 | | 136 |
| **Rule of Law** | | | |
| • Civil Rights | +.49 | +.27 | 127 |
| • Absence of corruption | +.60 | +.24 | 145 |
| • Murder rate | +.15 | + .44 | 103 |
| **Freedom** | | | |
| • Economical | +.54 | +.27 | 137 |
| • Political | +.59 | +.36 | 131 |
| • Personal | +.46 | +.12 | 82 |
| **Equality** | | | |
| • Income equality | +.10 | −.21 | 119 |
| • Gender equality | +.78 | +.61 | 96 |
| **Citizenship** | | | |
| • Participation in voluntary associations | +.17 | +.15 | 145 |
| • Preference for participative leadership | +.61 | +.47 | 49 |
| **Pluriformity** | | | |
| • Percent migrants | +.27 | −.17 | 123 |
| • Tolerance towards minorities | +.50 | +.35 | 81 |
| **Modernity** | | | |
| • Schooling | +.52 | +.24 | 145 |
| • Informatization | +.61 | +.27 | 139 |
| • Urbanization | +.59 | +.32 | 136 |
| Explained variance ($R^2$) | 84% | | |

Variables used: *Happiness:* HappinessLS10.11_2000s; *Affluence:* RGDP_2007; *Civil rights:* CivilLiberties_2004; *Absence of corruption:* Corruption3_2006; *Murder rate:* MurderRate_2004.09; *Economic freedom:* FreeEconIndex2_2007; *Political freedom:* DemocracyIndex5_2006; *Personal freedom:* PrivateFreedom_1990s; *Income equality:* IncomeInequality1_2005; *Gender equality:* GenderEqualIndex4_2007; *Participation in voluntary associations:* VolunteerActive2_2010; *Preference for participative leadership:* GoodLeaderParticip_1990s; *% migrants:* EthnicDiversity2_1955.2001; *Tolerance towards minorities:* Tolerance_1990s2; *Schooling:* EduEnrolGrossRatio_2000_04; *Informatization:* InternetUse_2005; *Urbanization*: UrbanPopulation_2005.
*Source: States of Nations.* World Database of Happiness (Veenhoven, 2013e).

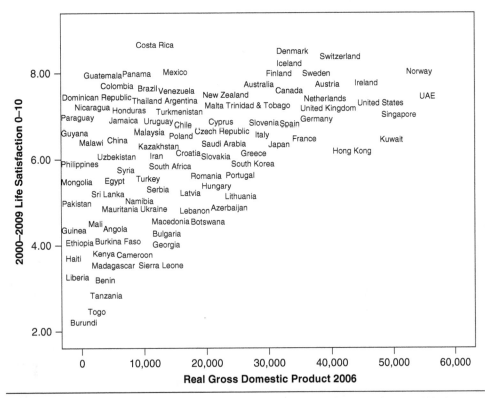

**Figure 42.4** Affluence and happiness in 123 nations in 2006. *Source: States of Nations.* World Database of Happiness (Veenhoven, 2013e). Variables: HappinessLS10.11_2000s and RGDP_2007

and modernity. Not everything deemed desirable is related, however. Income equality in nations appears to be unrelated to average happiness.[9]

There is much interrelation between the societal characteristics in Table 42.4; the most affluent nations are also the most free and modern ones. It is therefore difficult to estimate the effect of each of these variables separately. Still, it is evident that these variables together explain almost all the differences in happiness across nations; $R^2$ is .84!

The relationship between happiness and material affluence is presented in more detail in Figure 42.4. Note that the relationship is not linear, but tends to a convex pattern. This indicates that economic affluence is subject to the economic law of diminishing returns, which means that economic growth will add less to average happiness in poor nations than in rich countries.[10] This pattern of diminishing returns is not general. Figure 42.5 shows that the relationship with corruption is more linear, which suggests that happiness can be improved by combating corruption—even in the least corrupt countries.

These findings fit the theory that happiness depends very much on the degree to which living conditions fit universal human needs (livability theory). They do not fit

---

[9] The relationship between average happiness and income inequality in nations is discussed in more detail in Berg and Veenhoven (2010).

[10] Contrary to the so-called Easterlin paradox, economic growth does add to average happiness in rich nations (Veenhoven & Vergunst, in press).

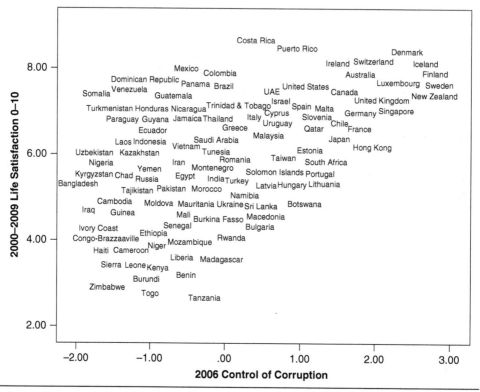

**Figure 42.5** Absence of corruption and happiness in 125 nations in 2006. *Source: States of Nations*. World Database of Happiness (Veenhoven, 2013e). Variables: HappinessLS10.11_2000s and Corruption3_2006

the theory that happiness depends on culturally variable wants (comparison theory) or that happiness is geared by culturally specific ideas about life (folklore theory). I have discussed these theoretical implications in more detail elsewhere (Veenhoven & Ehrhardt, 1995).

*Position in Society*   Many studies have considered the relationship between happiness and position in society. The main results are summarized in Table 42.5. Happiness is moderately related to social rank in Western nations, and in non-Western nations, the correlations tend to be stronger. Happiness is also related to social participation, and this relationship seems to be universal. Being embedded in primary networks appears to be crucial to happiness, in particular, being married. This relationship is also universal. Surprisingly, the presence of offspring is unrelated to happiness, at least in present-day Western nations.

These illustrative findings suggest that happiness can be improved by facilitating social participation and primary networks (see Myers, Chapter 41, this volume).

INTERNAL CONDITIONS   Happiness depends on the livability of the environment, and on the individual's ability to deal with that environment. What abilities are most crucial? Some findings are presented in Table 42.6. Research findings show that good health is an important requirement and that mental health is more critical to happiness than physical health. This pattern of correlations is universal. Intelligence appears to be unrelated to happiness, at least school intelligence as measured by common IQ

**Table 42.5**

Happiness and Position in Society

|  | Correlation<br>*within* Western nations[a] | Similarity of correlation<br>*across* all nations[b] |
|---|:---:|:---:|
| *Social rank* | | |
| Income | + | − |
| Education | ± | − |
| Occupational prestige | + | + |
| *Social participation* | | |
| Employment | ± | + |
| Participation in associations | + | + |
| *Primary network* | | |
| Spouse | ++ | + |
| Children | 0 | ? |
| Friends | + | + |

[a]++ = Strong positive; + = Positive; 0 = No relationship; − = Negative; ? = Not yet investigated; ± = varying
[b]+ = Similar; − = Different; ? = No data
*Source: Correlational Findings*. World Database of Happiness (Veenhoven, 2013b).

**Table 42.6**

Happiness and Life-Abilities

|  | Correlation<br>*within* Western nations[a] | Similarity of correlation<br>*across* all nations[b] |
|---|:---:|:---:|
| *Proficiencies* | | |
| Physical health | + | + |
| Mental health | ++ | + |
| IQ | 0 | + |
| *Personality* | | |
| Internal control | + | + |
| Extraversion | + | + |
| Conscientiousness | + | ? |
| *Art of living* | | |
| Lust acceptance | + | + |
| Sociability | ++ | + |

[a]++ = Strong positive; + = Positive; 0 = No relationship; − = Negative; ? = Not yet investigated; ± = Varying;
[b]+ = Similar; − = Different; ? = No data
*Source: Correlational Findings*. World Database of Happiness (Veenhoven, 2013b).

tests.[11] Happiness is strongly linked to psychological autonomy in Western nations. This appears in correlations with inner control, independence, and assertiveness. We lack data on this matter from non-Western nations.

Happiness has also been found to be related to moral conviction. The happy are more acceptant of pleasure than the unhappy, and they are more likely to endorse

---

[11] The relationship between happiness and IQ is discussed in more detail in Veenhoven and Choi (2012).

social values such as solidarity, tolerance, and love. Conversely, the happy tend to be less materialistic than the unhappy. It is as yet unclear whether this pattern is universal.

From an evolutionary view, it is also unlikely that happiness is a trait-like matter. If so, happiness could not be functional and neither could the affective signals on which it draws. It is more plausible that happiness is part of our adaptive equipment and that it serves as a compass in life. Mobile organisms must be able to decide whether they are in the right pond or not, and hedonic experience is a main strand of information when determining the answer. If the animal is in a biotope that does not fit its abilities, it will feel bad and move away. This seasoned orientation system still exists in humans, who, moreover, can estimate how well they feel over longer periods and reflect on the possible reasons for their feeling. In this view, happiness is an automatic signal that indicates an organism or person's thriving. In addition, it is logical that we can raise happiness by facilitating conditions in which people thrive.

**In sum,** *happiness of the great number can be raised, just like public health can be promoted.* At best, there is an upper limit to happiness, analogous to the ceiling of longevity.

## IS HAPPINESS A DESIRABLE OUTCOME?

The fact that public happiness *can* be raised does not mean that happiness *should* be raised. Several arguments have been brought against this idea. Happiness has been denounced as trivial and of less worth than other goal values. It has also been argued that happiness will spoil people and that the promotion of happiness requires objectionable means. Much of this criticism has been advanced in discussions about different concepts of happiness. The question here is whether these objections apply for happiness as life-satisfaction.

### Is Happiness Really Desirable?

In his *Brave New World*, Huxley (1932) paints a tarnished picture of mass happiness. In this imaginary model society, citizens derive their happiness from uninformed unconcern and from sensory indulgence in sex and a drug called soma. This is indeed superficial enjoyment, but is this enjoyment happiness? It is not. This kind of experience was classified as pleasures on the top left in Table 42.2 and distinguished from life-satisfaction in the bottom right. Enduring satisfaction with life-as-a-whole cannot be achieved by mere passive consumption. Research shows that it is typically a byproduct of active involvement. Likewise, Adorno depicted happiness as a temporary escape from reality and rejected it for that reason (Rath, 2002). Here, happiness is mixed up with top-experience. Life-satisfaction is typically not escapism. Research shows that it is linked with reality control.

Happiness has also been equated with social success and, on that basis, rejected as conformist rat-race behavior. This criticism may apply to satisfaction in the domain of career (top right quadrant in Table 42.2), but not to satisfaction with life-as-a-whole (bottom right quadrant). In fact, happy people tend to be independent rather than conformist and tend not to be materialistic. Happiness has also been denounced on the basis of assumptions about its determinants. As noted earlier, it is commonly assumed that happiness depends on social comparison. In this view, happiness is merely thinking oneself to be better off than the Joneses. Likewise, it is assumed that happiness depends on the meeting of culturally determined standards of success, and that the happiness of present-day Americans draws on their ability to live up to the models presented in advertisements. Both these theories see happiness as cognitive contentment and miss the point that happiness is essentially an affective phenomenon that signals how well we thrive (Veenhoven, 2009).

**In sum,** *there are no good reasons to denounce happiness as insignificant.*

## Is Happiness the Most Desirable Value?

Agreeing that happiness is desirable is one thing, but the tenet of utilitarianism is that happiness is the *most* desirable value. This claim is criticized on two grounds: First, it is objected that it does not make sense to premise one particular value, and second, there are values that rank higher than happiness. There is a longstanding philosophical discussion on these issues (Sen & Williams, 1982; Smart & Williams 1973), to which the newly gained knowledge about happiness can add the following points.

One new argument in this discussion is in the previously mentioned signal function of happiness. If happiness does indeed reflect how well we thrive, it concurs with living according to our nature. From a humanistic perspective, this is valuable.

Another novelty is in the insight that effect of external living conditions on happiness depends on inner life-abilities (Table 42.2). Democracy is generally deemed to be good, but it does not work well with anxious and uneducated voters. Likewise, conformism is generally deemed to be bad, but it can be functional in collectivist conditions. This helps us to understand that general end values cannot be found in the top quadrants. Instead, end values are to be found in the bottom quadrants, in particular, the bottom right quadrant. Happiness and longevity indicate how well a person's life-abilities fit the conditions in which that person lives, and as such, reflect more value than is found in each of the top quadrants separately. Happiness is a more inclusive merit than most other values, since it reflects an optimal combination.

A related point is that there are limits to most values, too much freedom leads into anarchy, and too much equality leads into apathy. The problem is that we do not know where the optimum level lies and how optima vary in different value combinations. Here again, happiness is a useful indicator. If most people live long and happily, the mix is apparently livable. In sum, if one opts for one particular end value, happiness is a good candidate.

## Will Promotion of Happiness Take Place at the Cost of Other Values?

Even if there is nothing wrong with happiness in itself, maximization of it could still work out negatively for other valued matters. Critics of utilitarianism claim this will happen. They foresee that greater happiness will make people less caring and responsible and fear that the premise for happiness will legitimize amoral means. This state of affairs is also described in *Brave New World*, where citizens are concerned only with petty pleasures and the government is dictatorial.

*Does Happiness Spoil?*    Over the ages, preachers of penitence have glorified suffering. This sermonizing lives on in the idea that happiness does not bring out the best of us. Happiness is said to nurture self-sufficient attitudes and to make people less sensitive to the suffering of their fellows. Happiness is also seen to lead to complacency and thereby to demean initiative and creativeness. It is also said that happiness fosters superficial hedonism and that these negative effects on individuals will harm society in the long run. Hence, promotion of happiness is seen to lead into societal decay—Nero playing happily in a decadent Rome that is burning around him.

There is some literature on the positive effects of happiness, recently in the context of positive psychology. This writing suggests that happiness is an activating force and facilitates involvement in tasks and people. Happiness is seen to open us to the world, while unhappiness invites us to retreat (Fredrickson, 2000). This view fits the theory that happiness functions as a "go" signal. Research findings support this latter view of the consequences of happiness. Happiness is strongly correlated with activity and predicts sociable behaviors, such as helping. Happiness also has a positive effect on intimate relations. There is also good evidence that happiness lengthens life (Danner, Snowdon, & Friessen, 2001). Thus, happiness is clearly good for us. All this does not deny that happiness may involve some negative effects, but apparently the positive effects dominate.

*Does a Premise for Happiness Excuse Amoral Means?*    The main objection against utilitarianism is that the greatest happiness principle justifies any way to improve happiness and hence permits morally rejectable ways, such as genetic manipulation, mind control, and political repression. It is also felt that the rights of minorities will be sacrificed on the altar of the greatest number.

The possibility of such undesirable consequences is indeed implied in the logic of radical utilitarianism, but is it likely to materialize? The available data suggest this is not true. In Table 42.4 we have seen that citizens are happiest in nations that respect human rights and allow freedom. It also appears that people are happiest in the most educated and informatized nations. Likewise, happy people tend to be active and independent. In fact, there is no empirical evidence for any real value conflict. The problem exists in theory, but not in reality.

**In sum,** *there is no ground for the fear that maximizing of happiness will lead into consequences that are morally rejectable.*

## CONCLUSION

The empirical tests falsify all the theoretical objections against the greatest happiness principle. The criterion appears practically feasible and morally sound. Hence the greatest happiness principle deserves a more prominent place in policy making.

## SUMMARY POINTS

- Happiness can be defined as subjective enjoyment of one's life as a whole.
- This happiness of great numbers of people can be measured using surveys.
- Conditions for happiness can be identified inductively.
- Effects of policies on happiness can be assessed empirically.
- Hence, evidence-based happiness policy is possible.
- Happiness is a desirable policy goal in itself.
- The pursuit of greater happiness for a greater number does not interfere with other values.

## REFERENCES

Andrews, F. M., & Withey, S. B. (1976). *Social indicators of well-being: Americans' perceptions of life quality*. New York, NY: Plenum Press.

Argyle, M. (2002). *The psychology of happiness* (3rd ed., rev.). London, England: Methuen.

Bentham, J. (1789). *Introduction to the principles of morals and legislation*. London, England: Payne.

Berg, M., & Veenhoven, R. (2010). Income inequality and happiness in 119 nations. In B. Greve (Ed.), *Social policy and happiness in Europe* (pp. 174–194). Cheltenham, England: Edward Elgar.

Bradburn, N. M., & Caplovitz, D. (1965). *Reports on happiness: A pilot study of behavior related to mental health*. Chicago, IL: Aldine.

Brickman, P., & Campbell, D. T. (1971). Hedonic relativism and planning the good society. In M. H. Appley (Ed.), *Adaptation level theory: A symposium* (pp. 287–302). London, England: Academic Press.

Campbell, A. (1981). *The sense of well-being in America*. New York, NY: McGraw-Hill.

Cantril, H. (1965). *The pattern of human concern*. New Brunswick, NJ: Rutgers University Press.

Cummins, R. A. (2010). Subjective wellbeing, homeostatically protected mood and depression: A synthesis. *Journal of Happiness Studies, 11*, 1–17.

Danner, D. D., Snowdon, D. A., & Friessen, W. V. (2001). Positive emotions in early life and longevity: Findings from the nun-study. *Journal of Personality and Social Psychology, 80*, 804–819.

Diener, E., Suh, E. M., Lucas, R. E., & Smith, H. L. (1999). Subjective well-being: Three decades of progress. *Psychological Bulletin, 125*, 276–301.

Ehrhardt, J. J., Saris, W. E., & Veenhoven, R. (2000). Stability of life-satisfaction over time: Analysis of ranks in a national population. *Journal of Happiness Studies, 1*, 177–205.

Ekman, P., & Friesen, P. W. (1975). *Unmasking the face*. Englewood Cliffs, NJ: Prentice Hall.

Fredrickson, B. L. (2000). Cultivating positive emotions to optimize health and well-being. *Prevention and Treatment, 3*, article 1a.

Freud, S. (1948). *Das Unbehagen mit der Kultur, Gesammte Werke aus den Jahren 1925–1931* [Culture and its discontents]. Frankfurt-am-Main, Germany: Fisher Verlag. (Original work published 1929)

Frey, B. S., & Stutzer, A. (2002). *Happiness and economics: How the economy and institutions affect human well-being*. Princeton, NJ: Princeton University Press.

Gallup World Poll. (2007). Retrieved from http://www.gallup.com/strategicconsulting/en-us/worldpoll.aspx

Gerson, E. M. (1976). On quality of life. *American Sociological Review, 41*, 793–806.

Gurin, G., Veroff, J., & Feld, S. (1960). *Americans view their mental health*. New York, NY: Basic Books.

Huxley, A. (1932). *Brave new world*. Stockholm, Sweden: Continental Books.

Jahoda, M. (1958). *Current concepts of positive mental health*. New York, NY: Basic Books.

Lane, R. E. (2000). *The loss of happiness in market democracies*. New Haven, CT: Yale University Press.

Neugarten, B. L., Havighurst, R. J., & Tobin, S. S. (1961). The measurement of life satisfaction. *Journal of Gerontology, 16*, 134–143.

Rath, N. (2002). The concept of happiness in Adorno's critical theory. *Journal of Happiness Studies, 3*, 1–21.

Schimmack, U., & Diener, E. (Eds.). (2003). Experience sampling methodology in happiness research [Special Issue]. *Journal of Happiness Studies, 1–4*.

Sen, A. (1993). Capability and wellbeing. In M. Nussbaum & A. Sen (Eds.), *The quality of life* (pp. 30–53). Oxford, England: Clarendon.

Sen, A., & Williams, B. (Eds.). (1982). *Utilitarianism and beyond*. Cambridge, England: Cambridge University Press.

Smart, J. J., & Williams, B. (1973). *Utilitarianism, for and against*. Cambridge, England: Cambridge University Press.

VanPraag, B. M. (1993). The relativity of welfare. In M. Nussbaum & A. Sen (Eds.), *The quality of life* (pp. 362–385). Oxford, England: Clarendon Press.

Veenhoven, R. (1984). *Conditions of happiness*. Dordrecht, The Netherlands: Kluwer Academic.

Veenhoven, R. (1991). Is happiness relative? *Social Indicators Research, 24,* 1–34.

Veenhoven, R. (1993). *Happiness in nations: Subjective appreciation of life in 56 nations 1946–1992.* Rotterdam, The Netherlands: Erasmus University Press, Center for Socio-Cultural Transformation, RISBO.

Veenhoven, R. (2000). The four qualities of life: Ordering concepts and measures of the good life. *Journal of Happiness Studies, 1,* 1–39.

Veenhoven, R. (2009). How do we assess how happy we are? In A. K. Dutt & B. Radcliff (Eds.), *Happiness, economics and politics: Towards a multi-disciplinary approach* (pp. 45–69). Cheltenham, England: Edward Elgar.

Veenhoven, R. (2013a). *Archive of research findings on subjective enjoyment of life. World Database of Happiness.* Rotterdam, The Netherlands: Erasmus University Press. Retrieved from http://worlddatabaseofhappiness.eur.nl

Veenhoven, R. (2013b). *Correlational findings.* World Database of Happiness. Retrieved from http://worlddatabaseofhappiness.eur.nl/hap_cor/cor_fp.htm

Veenhoven, R. (2013c). *Happiness in nations.* World Database of Happiness. Retrieved from http://worlddatabaseofhappiness.eur.nl/hap_nat/nat_fp.php

Veenhoven, R. (2013d). *Measures of happiness.* World Database of Happiness. Retrieved from http://worlddatabaseofhappiness.eur.nl/hap_quer/hqi_fp.htm

Veenhoven, R. (2013e). *States of nations: Data set for the cross-national analysis of happiness.* World Database of Happiness. Retrieved from http://worlddatabaseofhappiness .eur.nl//statnat/statnat_fp.htm

Veenhoven, R. (in press). Overall satisfaction with life. In W. Glatzer (Ed.), *Global handbook of quality of life.* New York, NY: Springer.

Veenhoven, R., & Choi, Y. (2012). Does intelligence boost happiness? Smartness of all pays more than being smarter. *International Journal of Happiness and Development, 1,* 5–27.

Veenhoven, R., & Ehrhardt, J. (1995). The cross-national pattern of happiness: Test of predictions implied in three theories of happiness. *Social Indicators Research, 43,* 33–86.

Veenhoven, R., & Vergunst, F. (in press). The Easterlin illusion: Economic growth does go with greater happiness. *International Journal of Happiness and Development.*

Ware, J. E., Jr. (1996). The SF-36 Health Survey. In B. Spilker (Ed.), *Quality of life and pharmaco-economics in clinical trials* (pp. 337–345). Philadelphia, PA: Lippincott-Raven.

Wessman, A. E., & Ricks, D. F. (1966). *Mood and personality.* New York, NY: Holt, Rhinehart and Winston.

# CHAPTER 43

# Positive Social Planning

NEIL THIN

SOCIAL PLANNERS AT ALL levels worldwide have been taking inspiration from both the positivity and the subjectivism of the positive psychology (PP) movement. Referred to here as *positive social planning*, this movement is emerging as a disparate set of practices sharing a common interest in the understanding and promotion of social goods, and in people's subjective experience and evaluation of them. This could be strengthened, first, by ethical recognition of the *intrinsic value of social goods*, as distinct from their instrumental value in facilitating happiness. Second, planners will need systematic description and analysis of social goods and of their interaction with mental goods: A *social well-being matrix* is recommended here as a simple tool for distinguishing core categories of social quality at all levels. Third, this chapter explores two kinds of normative implication: the importance of systematic appreciation of happiness and social goods as a route to empathy, and the translation from this into better policy and practice. Finally, the Bhutanese Gross National Happiness movement is offered as a case study in the development of these ethical, descriptive-analytical, and normative shifts.

When we ask ourselves, "What matters?" rather than the habitual "What is the matter?" our positive concern can go in two directions: inward, to inspect our mental goods and strengths, and outward, to appraise our social and physical environments and our interactions with them. As our attentions shift outward, we move from our own social mind to consider dyadic relationships, family, and neighborhood qualities; social networks; and ultimately the qualities of society in general. Increasingly, these general social qualities that we care about are transnational and global, yet we are collectively ill-equipped to analyze, discuss, and evaluate these qualities.

Most governments and many businesses worldwide have social departments, and although no doubt they do important work, they are predominantly concerned with social pathologies and compensations or repairs. It is still rare to see formal and institutionalized efforts to construct positive goals and indicators for promoting good social qualities. This very different approach to the expression of social responsibilities, which I call positive social planning (PSP), contrasts with the default minimalist social policies whose concern is to meet basic standards of decency. It also contrasts with psychological approaches that rarely pay significant heed to social quality beyond micro-levels and individual-focused perspectives.

After briefly reviewing global trends toward more explicitly positive attention to social goods in policies and appraisals, this chapter explores

Ethics: recent efforts worldwide to consider what matters in our social environment.

Descriptive and analytical capabilities: a social well-being matrix is recommended as a simple tool for distinguishing core categories of social quality at all levels, and for understanding how social quality relates to individual mental well-being; and

Normative implications: how these capabilities can and ought to be applied to promote appreciative empathy as a social good, and to improve the quality of social planning.

The Bhutanese Gross National Happiness movement is offered as a case study in the development of these ethical, descriptive-analytical, and normative shifts.

## THE GLOBAL OUTBREAK OF SOCIAL POSITIVITY

Social planning and policy evaluation are rapidly changing worldwide by taking on some of the positivity and appreciative psychosocial understanding that have been core principles of PP. This rethinking of our priorities is in large part due to a long-term global social progress: gains in productivity, security, health, education, and civility, have all permitted in most parts of the world a gradual shift of attention from survivalist minimalism to more ambitious concerns with positive personal and social flourishing (Helliwell, Layard, & Sachs, 2012, 2013; Inglehart & Welzel, 2005; Kenny, 2011; Pinker, 2011). The rethinking is also driven by new medium-term adversities: environmental harms and unsustainabilities; financial inequalities; the current global economic volatilities and recessions and the appalling governance and ethical failures that led to them; and increased awareness of various cultural and social harms in both traditional and modern societies.

Whichever of these may be the most significant underlying driver, more proximate triggers of change in trend assessments have been the PP movement, the longer term strengthening of happiness research, and the global movement toward strengthening of business ethics and reporting on corporate social responsibility, which is now also percolating into public and voluntary sector agencies. The combined insistence on both *positivity* (attending to goods, not just bads) and respect for *subjectivity* (taking an empathic interest in people's experience) prepares the way for greatly enhanced *ethical transparency* in the moral reasoning that planners apply in the analysis and evaluation of states of affairs, causes, objectives, and outcomes. Together, these constitute the core functions of the deployment of the happiness lens in social policy (Thin, 2012b). There are good prospects for synergies and collaborations between social analysts and psychologists. Although many politicians, planners, and investors worldwide are embracing the shift of attention from economic goods toward well-being and positive social goods, social scholars remain in general slow and reluctant to capture the spirit of the PP movement. It remains to be seen whether and how the identification and promotion of social goods can be improved.

Planners, managers, and evaluators at all levels from global down to local seem to be becoming more empathic and ethically transparent by taking a more systematic interest in psychological strengths and enjoyments, and by encouraging the expression of subjective experiences of clients, workers, pupils, community members, and citizens. Information on subjective valuation is being used to identify and promote convivial urban spaces (Dinnie, Brown, & Morris, 2013; Shaftoe, 2008), positive school climates (Cohen, 2013; Reasoner, 2006), great places to work (Henderson, 2013), and at higher levels community quality of life or societal quality of life (Sirgy, 2011; Sirgy, Phillips, & Rahtz, 2011), social quality (Lin, 2013; van der Maesen & Walker, 2011), or global civil society (Kaldor, 2003; Walzer, 1998). In public, voluntary, and business sectors, and in both small and large organizations, there is a new tide of enthusiasm for the idea of assessing the social value of production (Cox, Bowen, & Kempton, 2012; Jordan, 2008), although there is a bewildering diversity of interpretations of this concept.

However, before we rush to celebrate positive social entrepreneurship and public social planning, we must sharpen our collective ability to conceptualize, discuss, and assess social quality in sensible ways. Psychosocial planning needs to be appreciative (recognizing and promoting mental and social goods), but it is important that we promote intelligent appreciation rather than just naive enthusiasms. An intelligently appreciative approach will avoid on the one hand the excessive individualism and psychologism of some positive psychology, and on the other hand the excessive externalism and pathological clinicalism that have pervaded social research and social policy and planning. To be persuasive, this approach will require clear articulation of social goods that have widespread appeal worldwide, as well as clear and valid tools for promoting better understanding of interactions between mind and society.

## NATIONAL AND GLOBAL-LEVEL CONCEPTIONS OF SOCIAL PROGRESS

There have, of course, been numerous lists of social qualities advertised since before the dawn of the modern era, ranging from wildly utopian to more realistically aspirational. Most of them are somewhat ad hoc, culture bound, and too abstract to offer much guidance to planners or evaluators. More concerted efforts to forge a global consensus on social quality took off in the modern development era with the UN *Universal Declaration of Human Rights* (1948), and follow-up texts such as the 1969 UN *Declaration on Social Progress and Development*. These made frequent use of abstract and strong-sounding and appealing but analytically weak categories of social goods: equality, dignity, liberty, the rule of law, peace, religion, and education.

In parts this rhetoric also descended into utopianism, as in the 1969 declaration's call for "immediate and final elimination of all forms of inequality" and for "continuous raising of the material and spiritual standards of living of all members of society." But UN declarations also paved the way for unpacking these into more specific requirements for the good society, such as free speech and thought; security; nondiscrimination; national citizenship; marriage; access to public service; work and free choice of employment; the right to peaceful assembly and trade unions; and participation in the cultural life of the community and in scientific advancement.

Generally, the UN Department of Economic and Social Affairs (UN-DESA), its associated wings such as the Economic and Social Council and the UN Research Institute for Social Development, and its annual *Report on the World Social Situation* (e.g., UN-DESA, 2011) have defined *social progress* mainly defined in terms of poverty reduction, social sectors, and needs of vulnerable interest groups. But they have also drawn attention to the importance of social integration and inclusion; family integrity; social protection; crime and social instability; employment; economic volatility; inequality (mainly financial); and demographic trends (fertility, population expansion, ageing, dependency ratios, gender ratios). Table 43.1 summarizes a sample of recent attempts at global and national levels to articulate goals and indicators for social progress.

## POSITIVE PSYCHOLOGY AND SOCIAL QUALITY

The PP movement and associated studies and practices have already done humanity an enormously important service in promoting our understanding of mental goods and our ability and willingness to think about, debate, and promote these in rational ways. To a lesser extent, and mainly at the level of individual capabilities and dyadic or other small-scale interactions, the movement has promoted appreciation of social dimensions of psychological health (Baumeister & Leary, 1995; Berscheid, 2003; Roffey, 2012; Ryff & Singer, 2000). One of the five qualities of flourishing in Seligman's PERMA formula is positive relationships (Seligman, 2011). Similarly, the *character strengths* in the Values in Action inventory include several categories that pay strong attention to social virtues, particularly Humanity (including love, compassion, and social intelligence), Justice (citizenship, fairness, and leadership), Courage (which includes honesty), and Temperance (which includes forgiveness and humility; Peterson & Seligman, 2004). In the former case, the perspective is that of individual self-interest: A sound mind requires good relationships. In the latter there is a shift toward social virtue: A decent person shows prosocial character. Still, both schemas focus on the individual mind and associated actions.

But we can and should expand our appreciative horizon to promote clearer understanding and appreciation of *positive social qualities* with a view to promoting these more effectively and enhancing the positive synergies between mental and social dimensions of human experience and value. This is an argument in favor of social realism as much as it is an argument in favor of tactics and effectiveness: The various kinds of positivity that the PP movement promotes cannot be taken for granted as psychological valences, but must be interpreted and contested as sociocultural values. We explore here some of the ways in which this socialization of PP, and complementary positivization and mentalization of social planning, has already been happening worldwide, particularly in the past decade.

Most people with an interest in PP already hope that it leads to practices that result in social benefits—that is, benign social transformations, not just happier individual minds or individual social capabilities. Among those that argue carefully about PP in moral terms, there is often an implicit belief that social progress is driven by changes in individual minds, rather than the other way around. Indeed, Seligman's iconic popular text *Authentic Happiness* (2003) offers virtually no treatment of the social facilitation or inhibition of happiness, other than a few mentions of the importance of nice relationships. Seligman is astonishingly dogmatic and pessimistic in claiming that it is "usually impractical and expensive" to change any of your life circumstances, including your social environment (p. 50). As in the nonacademic self-help and life coaching world, the dominant emphasis in PP has been the individual mind as the locus for progressive action: If people can pursue their own happiness more authentically and intelligently, and play to their mental strengths while also exercising prosocial virtues such as kindness and gratitude, the world will surely become a better place to live.

But for most of people worldwide, the opportunities to follow the excellent advice of personal advisers, positive psychologists, life coaches, and therapists are to some extent thwarted by adversities in our social and cultural environments (for a fuller discussion of examples from around the world, see Thin, 2011). Or, viewed positively, our ability to fulfill our mental capabilities, or to choose which of our many potentials we want to fulfill, is facilitated by our culture, our relationships, and our institutions.

**Table 43.1**
Social Progress Keywords in Recent Key Texts

| Texts and Agencies | Social Goods and Harms |
| --- | --- |
| United Nations Human Development Index (HDI)/Human Development Reports; Millennium Development Goals (MDGs); and proposed post-2015 goals | HDI and MDGs both complement information on financial resources with social sector input, process, and outcome indicators, in effect using aggregate individual scores as a proxy for social quality; HD reports do sometimes offer qualitative information on social qualities: inequality, justice, social unrest. Post-2015 there are three proposed overarching categories—development; peace and security; and human rights—with perhaps five core social themes: (1) inclusion, (2) sustainability, (3) jobs/inclusive growth, (4) peace/accountability, (5) global partnership and solidarity. |
| European Thematic Network on Indicators of Social Quality, socialquality.org; Beck, van der Maesen, and Walker (1997); Beck, van der Maesen, Thomése, and Walker (2001); Lin (2013); and *International Journal of Social Quality* | Explicitly established as the first genuinely social alternative to the individual-focused quality of life approach; indicators are structured under four categories of social condition—socioeconomic security; social inclusion; social cohesion; and social empowerment—plus further efforts to link these analytically to both societal and biographical processes, and to both macro-level formal systems and institutions and less formal meso and micro-level communities and groups. |
| WikiProgress Statistics, http://stats.wikiprogress.org (see also further resources at www.wikiprogress.org) | Social and welfare (gender equality; access to services; child well-being; religion); peace. |
| Global Peace Index, economicsandpeace.org (2013); see also Coleman and Deutsch (2012); and De Rivera (2009) | Traditionally focused on negative peace so mainly measures negatives—indicators that a peace lover would want to reduce to nil or minimize. However, now includes a Positive Peace Index—eight categories of peace-promoting attitudes, structures, and institutions: equitable distribution of resources; human capital; free flow of information; control of corruption; acceptance of the rights of others; governance; good relations with neighbors. |
| Freedom in the World (since 1971) www.freedomhouse.com | Two main categories: political rights (electoral process; political pluralism and participation; governance) and civil liberties (freedom of expression and belief; associational and organizational rights; rule of law; and personal autonomy and individual rights). |
| *Report by the Commission on the Measurement of Economic Performance and Social Progress* (Stiglitz, Sen, & Fitoussi, 2009) | Mainly focused on living standards and personal capabilities and well-being, with limited consideration of social quality and collective capabilities; explicitly intended to address the social problem of the loss of public confidence in national statistics (p. 7), yet the large advisory panel was entirely composed of (mainly Western) economists. Argues for more attention to distribution of income, consumption, and wealth; to nonmarket activities; to social connections and relationships to civic and social engagement; and to social capital, trust, and isolation (pp. 13,14,15, 160, 185). |

*(continued)*

**Table 43.1**

*(Continued)*

| Texts and Agencies | Social Goods and Harms |
| --- | --- |
| Genuine Well-Being Index (Genuine Wealth Institute), www.genuinewealthinc.com; see, e.g., Anielski (2012) | Standard of living; psychological well-being; health; time use; community vitality; education; culture; environment; governance. |
| Organisation for Economic Co-operation and Development (OECD; n.d.) Better Life Index, www.oecdbetterlifeindex.org | Eleven social indicators (though some of these are personal resources and satisfactions): housing, income, jobs, community, education, environment, governance, health, life satisfaction, safety, work–life balance; recognizing cultural and personal differences in values, the online Your Better Life Index version facilitates weighting of indicators according to preferences. |
| *World Happiness Report* (Helliwell et al., 2013) | The most ambitious attempt yet to synthesize global knowledge about the global and intranational distribution of happiness and its correlations with social quality; shows that self-reported happiness correlates strongly both with income/GDP and with social factors (political freedom, job security, trust, strong social networks, controls on corruption, family stability); South Asia, so often labeled as having collectivist cultural values, scores very low on social support. |
| Legatum Prosperity Index, www.prosperity.com | Eight pillars: economy; entrepreneurship/opportunity; governance; education; health; security; personal freedom; social capital (including tolerance). |
| Weighted Index of Social Progress, since 1974 by Richard Estes (see, e.g., Estes, 2010); University of Pennsylvania's social work faculty, formerly Index of National Social Vulnerability | This remains somewhat pathological despite use of the terms *social progress* and *social well-being*; 41 indicators are nearly all about deficits, violations, and social sector activities, plus some frankly implausible indicators such as cultural diversity indicated by the percent of the population with similar racial/ethnic origins and religious beliefs. |
| Social Progress Index, www.socialprogressimperative.org (2013) | Focused entirely on noneconomic outcome indicators: basic needs; well-being (learning, health), and opportunity (rights, freedom, choice, equity, inclusion). |

So all serious PP must seek to understand synergies between mind and society, and between mental and social progress. And this requires interactive approaches, not just noticing the social environment.

In Seligman's famously problematic equation metaphor, happiness is a result of genetics plus circumstances plus voluntary effort (2003, p. 45). In Lyubomirsky's similarly simplistic pie chart metaphor, our circumstances account for just 10% of our happiness (2008, p. 20). These kinds of reductionism dumb down the science of happiness and detract from the meaning of positivity. It is vital for the PP movement to take a systematic interest in the *interactions* between our minds, our behaviors, and our circumstances. Our circumstances are not an inflexible percentage of determining factors. Particularly in the case of our sociocultural circumstances, we are co-responsible for them: We co-create our culture and our relationships and our institutions through-out our lives, while also being influenced by them as to go along.

   Prospects for the socialization of PP have already been explored in generic texts on social change (Biswas-Diener, 2011; Donaldson, 2011) and in more specific texts on family and community therapy (Conoley & Conoley, 2009; Prilleltensky & Prilleltensky, 2006), organizational development (Cameron, Dutton, & Quinn, 2003), and schooling (Gilman, Huebner, & Furlong, 2009). Here, I would like to explore some of the basic prerequisites for this to be pursued explicitly through rational planning. Many benefits may, of course, happen without or in spite of rational planning. But if we want to make good social transformations intentionally, we had better hone our ability to agree with collaborators on what kinds of social goods we want to bring about. And our social diagnoses, proposals, and indicators for assessment had better be not only clear but also informed by philosophical and psychological wisdom, spelling out the sources and processes of valuation and appreciation, and both the mental causes of social progress as well as the mental benefits of living in the improved society.

## ETHICS: ON SOCIAL VALUES AND
## THE RETHINKING OF PROSPERITY

PSP refers to any rational and collective efforts to understand and promote social goods at any level from the family to the world. Social quality matters not only *instrumentally*, by facilitating production systems and psychological well-being, but also *intrinsically* insofar as people care about social quality independently of their mental self-evaluations: As socially constituted humans, we want to live well *and* in good societies (Marangos, 2012). Though analytically separable, these desiderata are in practice so strongly interwoven that our happiness, along with the rest of our minds and our identities, is in large part constituted by social quality. (Sociocultural factors also matter *epistemologically*, by affecting how individuals think about and report their own well-being, though that important theme is not the focus of this chapter, and has been addressed by many PP scholars, usually under a culture rubric (e.g., Butler, Lee, & Gross, 2007; Diener & Suh, 2000). Evidence on the distribution of mental well-being clearly matters a great deal for the understanding of social quality, particularly social justice but also other factors such as solidarity, social participation, and security (Helliwell et al., 2012, 2013); but it does not in itself tell us all we want to know about social quality.

   In an important philosophical paper on irreducibly social goods, Charles Taylor (1990/1995) argued that due to the inseparability of culture, society, and individual well-being, there are some sociocultural goods that have intrinsic value. Taylor's writing is unhelpfully abstract and mystical, but he means by this that their importance to us is not reducible to their roles in facilitating our individual well-being. It doesn't mean that they can't also be useful, nor that their goodness is unconditional. Intrinsic goods are often useful, but they can also sometimes be harmful. For example, peace-ability is useful (it helps the economy work), but it can be dangerous (if a society is threatened by aggressors). Intrinsic value is endlessly debatable, but most people appreciate that some social qualities are good in themselves. The practical importance of this lies in the need to escape from atomistic worldviews that see society as nothing more than a heap of individuals and their interests, and from the supporting subjectivism that treats people's minds as the only ultimate source of evidence on goodness (Taylor, 1990/1995, pp. 129–130).

This underlines the importance of socializing the twin influences of positive psychology mentioned earlier (positivity and subjectivity). Aggregate measures of individually self-reported happiness do not in themselves tell us much about social quality. A society of happy pigs does not fulfill most people's vision of social goodness. Although no doubt happiness and social quality tend to be mutually supportive, you could have a society high in average self-reported happiness that was low in social qualities such as fairness or citizen engagement. If we care about these social goods, we should assess them separately from happiness. Our happiness is qualified by, and conditional on, our belonging in a social environment that is partly built on our own self-transcending social motivations and virtuous engagements. As many recent texts on the evolution of morality have insisted, we are hardwired with capabilities and motivations that transcend the satisfaction our immediate selfish desires (Pinker, 2011; Smith, 2003; Wright, 1995), even if these have to fight it out with more selfish drives relating to survival (Wilson, 2004). A great deal of empirical research on the psychological rewards of altruistic or prosocial behavior supports this (Aknin, Dunn, & Norton, 2012; Borgonovi, 2008), as does a great deal of research on deferred gratification and self-regulation (Shoda, Mischel, & Peak, 1990).

Understanding social goods and the evidence and debates relating to them will take us well beyond minimalist social responsibility approaches that simply try to minimize social harms. It will also take us beyond the basic functions and efficiencies that are lumped together under social development and human development rubrics—the medical systems, legal systems, schooling, environmental infrastructure, and financial safety nets through which citizens may or may not be enabled to live long, safe, and healthy lives. These are *instrumental* social values, the outcomes and performance indicators of the well-ordered society. This chapter focuses, instead, on the identification of those social qualities that are attributed *intrinsic* value, that are deemed good in themselves and so are worthy to serve as social goals. I propose that our ability to identify, discuss, and evaluate such goals can be significantly enhanced through closer engagements between positive psychologists, social theorists, and planners.

Both the PP and the PSP movements draw our attention to questions of value. Rhetorical use of the term *social* has in recent years often been combined with *well-being* and/or *happiness*, marking the promotion of renewed vigor in considering what really matters in life. As one recent policy research report puts it, "Local progress as a concept is often used interchangeably with concepts such as 'well-being,' 'happiness,' and 'societal progress'" (Caistor-Arendar & Mguni, 2013, p. 6; see also, e.g., Lawlor, Nicholls, & Neitzert, 2009; Wood & Leighton, 2010). As the Social Return on Investment Network's (SROI) guide puts it, "SROI is about value, rather than money" (SROI, 2012, p. 8). In other words, suspicion of monetary reductionism and so-called materialism is closely associated with an interest in elusive and hitherto unmeasured aspects of personal and social well-being. This linkage between happiness and social value has been particularly evident in the United Kingdom, where the Conservative Party announced in 2008 a strong interest in promoting both, and where the big society concept is now associated with formal requirements to promote and assess happiness, well-being, and social value at national and local levels, and at institutional levels in the public and voluntary sectors (Wood & Leighton, 2010, p. 18).

It is, however, important not to confuse skepticism about money metrics with anti-market sentiments. A first step toward strengthening the analysis of social quality must be to fight the artificial economy-versus-society opposition that distracts and misleads so much public discourse, and instead to recognize markets as absolutely central to positive social quality. Evidently, since most people in most corners of the world have become highly dependent on markets, finance, and commercial transactions, these must be regarded as part of social quality and included in our understanding of social goods and social progress, rather than glibly treated as separate from or necessarily antithetical to society, community, and culture.

Economic freedom correlates strongly with self-reported happiness worldwide (Gropper, Lawson, & Thorne, 2011), but recognizing both the intrinsic and the instrumental value of markets does not entail naive assumptions about their goodness. Indeed, it is important to recognize corporate financial recklessness, for example, not just as some de-humanized and abstracted economic failure, but as a serious social and psychological pathology that threatens even more widespread erosion of social values and democracy (Stiglitz, 2012, p. 13). Whether we see markets as amoral (as economists traditionally do) or as immoral (as social critics often do) it is quite wrong to partition the economy off from society. It makes no philosophical sense to call for "a better balance between social and economic development" (Estes, 2010, p. 364). No social goods are *necessarily* benign, not even freedom, peace, and solidarity. There is no plausible reason why rethinking prosperity critics should single out free markets and economic growth as peculiarly ethically suspect. Other social goods such as democracy, justice systems, schooling systems, medical services, and social security systems can also produce harmful effects.

Markets are, of course, mainly of interest for their instrumental rather than intrinsic value. But it is also worth pausing to consider whether some aspects of markets can be considered to have intrinsic social quality. The global movement toward well-being-focused social planning and evaluation therefore shares with PP not only a reaction against excessive pathologism, but also a concern for authenticity in the face of purportedly inauthentic valuation. In other words, there are synergies and commonalities between the pursuit of authentic happiness and genuine wealth. Economistic planning and growth obsession at national levels are portrayed as the sources of inauthenticity just as materialism and shortsighted hedonism have been the bogeymen of the PP movement at the individual level.

In addition to the false economy/society dichotomy, the other problematic opposition commonly deployed in debates about value is that between society and the individual, and consequently between social and individual well-being. In a somewhat overstated but brilliant essay on social well-being based on the phenomenological concept of *Mitsein* (conviviality, social being, or being-with-others), Stephen Webb has argued that

> The well-being of the person is fundamentally determined in its mode of being through the relationships in which it stands to other people. If this is correct then language and communication rather than mental perception is the locus of well-being. . . . The contribution of *Mitsein* to considerations of well-being is one that not only provides for a more expansive and richer social dimension but most importantly is a foundation for meaning and ethics. (Webb, 2010, pp. 971, 974)

Similarly, a collection of Amazonian ethnographic essays on conviviality has argued that for Amazonians social being (including concepts of peace, harmony, and sociability) is so paramount that Western concepts of individual well-being are inapplicable (Overing & Passes, 2000, p. xiii). Like Webb, and like many texts on Eastern, African, and Pacific collectivism—the editors exaggerate cultural differences in collectivism versus individualism. All humans are clearly social beings, and nearly all recognize this frequently and in many ways, but no anthropologist has yet produced a credible account of a society in which the individual person is not recognized as in some ways a separate agent with discrete interests. Still, in much of Western scholarly and popular psychology, and in quality of life studies in general, the intrinsic value of sociality is under-recognized, crowded out by the implicit and fallacious assumption that well-being only resides in the individual person.

## THE SOCIAL WELL-BEING MATRIX: A TOOL FOR DESCRIBING AND ANALYZING SOCIAL QUALITY

Positive psychologists and sociologists have attended to social dimensions of well-being at four levels, each of which is sometimes called social development:

1. Individual: self-transcendence, prosocial attitudes, and social intelligence.
2. Interpersonal: relational well-being, qualities of dyadic relationships and inter-actions such as friendship, romantic love, parental warmth, and acts of kindness.
3. Organization or community levels: positive qualities of social processes and institutions such as families, decent workplaces, and community vitality.
4. Societal/global: the overall state of national and global society and culture.

Though few would have any difficulty agreeing to these basic distinctions, in prac-tice social factors get discussed without specification as to which level is meant. Indi-vidual scholars and practitioners also tend to specialize in one or two of these four levels and hence are professionally or situationally inhibited from developing the abil-ity to explore relationships between the different levels at which social and cultural processes operate. In Table 43.2, the social well-being matrix is proposed as a simple tool to facilitate clearer description and analysis of how social goods manifest at these different levels.

For the sake of simplicity, just four categories of social quality are distinguished: *justice, solidarity, participation*, and *security*. Based on a global review of international, national, and local agencies promoting social change, I identified these as a mini-mal list of social processes that seemed to be universally valued in principle, even if endlessly debatable in practice (Thin, 2002). Other possibly distinct categories could include *collective capabilities* (such as the demonstrable ability to cooperate and share knowledge and resources efficiently; Evans, 2002); *freedom* (respect for cultural diver-sity and individual autonomy, choice; Sen, 1999); *cultural integrity* (transgenerational shared knowledge and beliefs; Foster, 1998); and *interest* (facilitating the creative chal-lenges and entertainments and enabling citizens to achieve flow and avoid boredom; Swedberg, 2005). Nonetheless, I see no difficulty in fitting all of these comfortably within this matrix. Freedom, for example, though featuring in some way in most visions of social progress, seems to be most effectively described and analyzed under these headings separately than it is as a generalized good: People value freedom as political rights and as freedom from want and violence (negative liberty); and as freedom to choose friends and partners, and to participate in social decision making (positive liberty).

Probably no one will ever come up with the definitive list of social goods, just as PP scholars continue to diversify the ways of classifying psychological goods. But further work on such lists, combined with analytical work exploring how the different social qualities interact with one another and with mental goods, should greatly improve the prospects for intelligently positive social planning.

Social planning, then, requires positive visions of really good social quality. It also requires recognition of social progress together with efforts to understand how this

**Table 43.2**
Social Well-Being Matrix: Intrinsically Valuable Social Qualities at Four Levels

| | Justice | Solidarity | Participation | Security |
|---|---|---|---|---|
| **Individual** (social capability) | Prosocial attitudes, sense of responsibility for fair play (Batson, Ahmad, Powell, & Stocks, 2008) | Empathic capability and scope; diversity and quality of attachments (Eisenberg & Fabes, 1990) | Active prosocial engagement, e.g., work participation, voting, volunteering, serious leisure (Stocks, Lishner, & Decker, 2009) | Social confidence and trust; sensitivity to other people's fears (Miller & Coll, 2007) |
| **Interpersonal** (relationship quality) | Equity, respect, and reciprocity within relationships (Donaghue & Fallon, 2003) | Love and warmth in couples and families, including trans-generational, transgender, and cross-cultural (Roffey, 2012) | Mutual interest and positive interaction in pairs, families, and small teams (Demir, 2013) | Mutual trust, calmness, and safety within relationships (Lakey, 2013) |
| **Organizational** (communal quality) | Fair recruitment, rewards, promotions in schools, clubs and workplaces (Prilleltensky, 2012) | Warm organizational climate; local bonding social capital; strong intra-organizational ties and affections (Fetchenhauer, Flache, Buunk, & Landenberg, 2006) | Active member engagement in goal setting, planning, and management (Jiranek, 2013) | Trust and freedom from fear within organizations; job security (Helliwell, Huang, & Putnam, 2009) |
| **Societal/ Global** (social quality) | Overall fairness in allocation of resources and opportunities worldwide and within nations (Sachs, 2013) | Global sense of common humanity; positive sense of national affiliation (Cunha & Gomes, 2012) | Economic and political freedom; active citizen engagement at national and global levels (Gropper et al., 2011; UN Volunteers, 2011) | Global and national peace, livelihood security, and freedom from avoidable vulnerability (Diener & Tov, 2007; Staub, 2010) |

happens—themes that are in short supply in social research (Best, 2001; Thin, 2002). If positivity gets short shrift among social theorists and activists, so, too, does psychology. Social planners hardly ever refer to the kinds of personal development advice offered by self-help authors and life coaches as the high road to better lives. Theories and practices aimed at becoming a better you have surprisingly rarely been linked systematically with efforts to make a better society.

Distinguishing these levels and categories of social quality does not seem particularly intellectually fraught or practically challenging. To understand why, in practice, so many scholars and agencies make such a poor job of discussing and promoting social goods, it is also necessary to appreciate that in policy discourse the term *social* carries a rich and often bewildering variety of meanings, some of which stray a long way from the commonsense understanding of social as pertaining to society (as in *social science* and *social structure*). Policy usages include

1. *Public goods (instrumentally valued)*: public as opposed to private goods (as in social marketing, social forestry, social design, social procurement, social profit, social return on investment, social economy, social value, corporate social responsibility, and social entrepreneur, and the extension of social sector to include commercial provision of schooling and medical services).

2. *Residual, neglected, or elusive and disparate factors*: nonmarket or not-for-profit rather than purely commercial transactions (as in social sectors, social infrastructure, social reporting, and social fund); elusive and intangible, nonbiophysical or nontechnical factors (as in social medicine, social town planning, social factors, and some uses of social value and social well-being); habitually neglected social factors and to the voices of ordinary people (as in social history); relatively uninstitutionalized and informal social processes (as in social movement and sociolegal studies).

3. *Problems*: pathologically and/or remedially, referring to various matters of inequity, injustice, and poverty (as in the most common uses of social impact, social indicators, and social issues), and various compensatory or remedial policies and clinical practices (e.g., social housing, social debt, social firms, social banking, social work, social policy, social administration, social service, social welfare, and some usages of social goals).

4. *Personal capabilities and character*: psychologically, as used by developmental psychologists and educators, referring to the external, relational self as opposed to the introspective self (as in the terms social intelligence, social skills, social identity, and social development).

5. *Positive social qualities (intrinsically valued)*: the desirable qualities of social processes such as the equity, kindness, and affective quality of interpersonal and intergroup relationships, institutions, trust, and citizen engagement (as in social quality and social progress, and some uses of social thought/philosophy, social well-being, social goods, social teaching/gospel/creed/ministry, and social advantage).

The first three usages are of at least passing interest to positive psychologists, both because of the insertion of well-being and happiness into the residual social category, but also to the extent that they all involve choosing social as a form of deliberate linguistic positivity in preference to the negative terminologies such as nonprofit, nonprivate, nongovernment, poverty, and disadvantage. The fourth, the social capabilities and dispositions of individuals, has always been a core concern of psychologists. In the next section we will explore the normative implications this last meaning of *positive social quality*, which in some ways overlaps with the others but which scholars and planners alike seem to find difficult to conceptualize clearly.

## LINKING SOCIAL QUALITY WITH MENTAL THRIVING

With these twin movements toward psychological and social positivity, we live in an era of unprecedented interest in synergies between social and psychological progress.

Against widespread antimodernist cultural and environmental pessimism, there is a tide of evidence-based optimism about synergies between personal happiness, virtue, and social progress. Since the PP movement has so far located positivity mainly in the individual mind, there is scope for enriching the discipline by strengthening its attention to social quality, recognizing that positivity can be a property of sociocultural environments not just of individual minds.

Though inevitably individualistic, the PP movement has from the time of its inauguration paid significant heed to social well-being. The point, its founders told us, was to "understand and build the factors that allow individuals, communities, and societies to flourish" (Seligman & Csikszentmihalyi, 2000, p. 5). Many of the strengths studied and promoted are social capabilities that require two or more minds to work in harmony (Snyder & Lopez, 2002). Much of the public policy engagement associated with PP and happiness research has been about transcending economism by looking at residual social factors that influence or constitute well-being, as is evident for example in the emphasis on noneconomic factors in Diener and Seligman's "Beyond Money" article (2004, p. 1).

Positive psychologists can therefore enrich their understanding and enhance their practical influence by expanding their attention beyond the personal level to explore interactions between people's minds and the social qualities of their environment. For their part, social planners and development activists can improve their scope and effectiveness by attending to the need to incorporate psychological experience, or 'subjectivity', into our understanding of positive social qualities. Social justice isn't simply an objectively fair set of circumstances and relationships: Citizens need to appreciate the fairness of the processes that matter to them. Security is more than just the objective lack of damaging volatilities and vulnerabilities: People must recognize that they are secure and act accordingly by showing trust in other people and in the future.

## NORMATIVE CONSIDERATIONS: WHAT CAN AND SHOULD WE DO ABOUT POSITIVE SOCIAL QUALITIES?

Normative considerations proceed from ethical debates about values and from the descriptive and analytical capabilities discussed earlier. The problem of inadequate conceptualization of social goods was recognized already in the very first edition of the *Social Indicators Research* journal as a critical factor inhibiting normative translation from values to plans, which argued that "*we have no normative models for prescribing means of enhancing social welfare.* . . . Fragmented social programs, welfare services community projects and the like, prevail" (Galnoor, 1974, pp. 28, 29; emphasis added).

Despite the massive expansion of the social indicators and social reporting industries worldwide since Galnoor wrote those words, his pessimism would be just as valid four decades later. In practice, most proponents of social goods offer no attempt at defining these. Instead, they implicitly assume an adequate degree of common understanding of what qualities we all hope to see in the good society. These assumptions are ill-founded, and this becomes particularly clear when we see how the happiness lens reveals important disjunctures between presumed social goods and the evidence of private self-reported happiness.

For example, it has become all too common for scholars and media on the beyond-GDP bandwagon to make glib claims that economic growth does not increase happiness, despite many robust examples of evidence showing correlations between growth or income and happiness (Helliwell et al., 2012). Arguably, though, it is much more interesting and disturbing that cherished public expenditures such as expensive public schooling and medical services, and even educational attainments and gender equality, do not seem to correlate with self-reported happiness (Stevenson & Wolfers, 2009; Veenhoven, 2000). This research exposes the naïveté of mistaking social expenditures for good social processes and outcomes.

Whether or not we find the term *happiness* useful in policy and practice, few would argue against the idea that development should help people to thrive, not just to survive and avoid undue discomfort. Living conditions matter, of course, but so does mental experience. It matters both for its intrinsic value and for the benign effects of well-organized minds. Indeed, you do not need to be a declinist to recognize that in some ways humanity's triumphs over material discomfort have led to setbacks in psychological functioning (Eckersley, 2000; Steedman, Atherton, & Graham, 2011) and that in some ways capitalism can lead to dismantling of social capital (Putnam, 2000) and social recession (Rutherford, 2008).

Instead of the spurious idea that there is a growing gap between economic growth and happiness, a more persuasive argument would be that many of the most important benefits of modernity are neither caused primarily by economic growth (itself a somewhat blunt and arbitrary invention of the 1930s), nor well captured in so-called economic statistics (Kenny, 2005). Economism must be offset by attention to positive subjective experiences. For example, despite economic and political gender inequalities worldwide, women tend to report themselves as happy as men or happier, and to enjoy many more happy life-years. This does not mean that gender inequality does not matter, but it does reveal complexities in gender relations that require us to recognize, celebrate and promote women's and men's positive experiences and strengths. If the PP movement could join forces with a new parallel movement focused on social goods and social progress, there would surely be important benefits both to individuals and to society.

Perhaps the most important outcome of the PP movement is that it has made it much harder for psychologists and associated professionals to avoid considering psychological goods. Sadly, pathologism and clinicalism still dominate the rest of the social sciences along with applied social policy and social work. Until very recently, social scholars and professionals have attended mainly to harms and to their mitigation or prevention, rather than looking at social goods and flourishing societies. It is still quite normal worldwide for students to complete degrees in social science, even in applied subjects like social development, social work, or social policy, without ever learning how to identify or analyze social goods or social progress, let alone assess or measure them systematically. Sociocultural anthropology is still routinely taught in ways that not only neglect but also actively discourage the moral evaluation of cultural and social phenomena, on the relativist grounds that we should not judge phenomena in one cultural context using values and concepts that are alien to that environment.

## THE INTRINSIC VALUE AND PLAUSIBILITY OF POSITIVE SOCIAL APPRECIATION

Happiness research and monitoring of positive social goods may or may not lead to improvements in services, treatments, and effectiveness, and there is no shortage of public skeptics and pessimists in this regard (Johns & Ormerod, 2007). Meanwhile, it is important to recognize and celebrate the *intrinsic* value of attending to social goods such as aggregate happiness, peace, and trust (Bruni, 2010). An organization or society that takes a systematic interest in members or citizens' psychosocial well-being and the quality of the social fabric is, other things being equal, better than one that does not. The pursuit of cross-cultural understanding and solidarity requires *appreciative* empathy (recognizing and sharing people's good experiences, not just their sufferings). As the Dalai Lama has repeatedly argued, recognition of humanity's common striving for happiness marks a crucial empathic move away from the exaggeration of cultural differences (Dalai Lama & Cutler, 1998, p. 21).

Whether we value happiness and social progress research for its intrinsic or for its instrumental value, however, it is first of all crucial to answer the skeptics by making this work scientifically robust and persuasive rather than tokenistic. Unlike a century ago, today social scientists are generally reluctant even to use the tainted term *social progress*. So the job of examining it is left to bureaucrats and planners who rarely seem prepared to articulate any vision of society that you or I would find aspirational.

The root problem seems to be that social policy evaluation is driven less by rational appraisal of what social processes matter most, than by two quite different criteria: *countability* and *clinical priority*. The (parsimonious) countability criterion persuades us to assess those kinds of social change that seem amenable to reduction into numerical form, for which statistical evidence can be affordably gathered and which can offer the public simple and memorable information. This criterion does not in itself rule out the measurement of social goods. You can count trust and call it social capital. You can count things like intercultural empathy and tolerance. But the clinical priority criterion persuades scholars, governments, and media to pay attention mainly not to social goods but to those social harms that we ought to be immediately worried about: poverty, injustice, violence, crime, and so on.

Regarding the countability criterion, in both the social quality/social audit movement and in happiness studies, there are worrying tendencies for scholars and practitioners to look beyond GDP but not beyond measurement. I have already criticized elsewhere the problem of distortive uses of pseudo-accurate and pseudo-realist measurements of happiness (Thin, 2012a; Thin, 2012b, Chapter 7). Similarly, among promoters of social audit, the worthy enthusiasm for drawing our attention to goods that have traditionally gone unmeasured seems all too easily to be distracted by an obsession with assigning numerical values to elusive and complex goods (Thin, 2012b). For example, the previously mentioned government-endorsed 108-page SROI guide offers multiple assurances about the possibility of accurate monetization of social values, despite the fact that its authors seem unable to identify clearly any of the social goods that urge us to evaluate. Texts on social audit available from sites like www.neweconomics.org, www.socialauditnetwork.org.uk, www.accountability.org, and www.philanthropycapital.org are similarly long on numerophilia and short on social or philosophical analysis.

What really matters is not that we pretend to be able to measure social goods accurately, but rather that we acknowledge their importance and sharpen our ability to observe and discuss them intelligently, in order to promote them better. If public happiness scholarship is to have intrinsic value by constituting public empathy, it has to be pursued through empathy-inducing processes, and it is hard to see how the numerical reductionism of surveys can achieve that. It is therefore imperative that future efforts to improve the evidence base for PSP diversify the methods used to generate knowledge about subjective experiences of social quality.

Our collective goal should not be to aim for accurate factual information on either happiness or social quality, but rather to foster intelligent conversations about these by improving our concepts, our analytical capabilities, and the availability of a variety of quantitative and qualitative evidence. Whereas the *positivity* of the PP movement can surely make a benign difference to social planning, there are ample signs that *positivism*, in the form of naive beliefs about pseudo-accurate measures of personal happiness and social quality, can all too easily capture the imagination of public media and planners alike and distort our conversations in unhelpful ways. The mind and social systems are complex, intertwined, emergent systems that are both understood and generated through conversations. Numbers can sometimes play a part in facilitating conversations, but most of what matters in life is very poorly represented by numbers.

## CONCLUSION: GROSS NATIONAL HAPPINESS IN BHUTAN

I have traced the logical progression from ethical discussion of values, through the process of sharpening our descriptive and analytical abilities, to normative considerations leading toward improvements in practice. It may help to conclude by exploring how these processes have unfolded in the now globally iconic example of Bhutan's promotion of the idea of Gross National Happiness (GNH) as a policy rubric. It started with an off-the-cuff remark by the new 16-year-old king to a journalist in the 1970s: "Gross National Happiness is more important than Gross National Product." This obviously echoes the earlier idea, first expressed by Francis Hutcheson during the Scottish Enlightenment in 1727, that happiness is what counts, and Sinclair's later development of the idea that it can be counted in national statistics (Thin, 2012b, Chapter 1). GNH has become a rallying cry for diverse array of not only happiness policy promoters but also anti-GDP critics, antimodernists, and advocates of cultural and environmental conservation.

The king's quip made two *ethical* claims: that economic growth is not ultimately as important as other goods, and that what ultimately matters in life is happiness. However, given the great diversity of meanings of happiness and related concepts in all cultural contexts, all it does is tell us to think about what is good—that is, that values matter. Essentially, happiness is a conversation starter but never in itself an analytical term. There followed a couple of decades during which the king's GNH slogan was echoed around the world, and meanwhile his government rapidly modernized the country with (despite the much-vaunted cultural and environmental conservationism) a surprisingly strong emphasis on economic liberalization and growth, which greatly reduced the poverty, ill health, and illiteracy of the Bhutanese population. Perhaps during this era happiness and social qualities improved, but until very recently they were not systematically monitored.

From the late 1990s, the government of Bhutan with assistance from various international agencies and scholars began trying to develop the *analytical and descriptive tools* that would give GNH some practical substance within Bhutan as well as credibility on a global stage (Ura, Alkire, Zangmo, & Wangdi, 2012). After a series of national consultations and international GNH conferences, Bhutan's Centre for Bhutan Studies began helping various government agencies to monitor a variety of goods, all subsumed under the GNH rubric. In practice, this meant expanding the concept of happiness a very long way from its normal Anglophone meaning of mental well-being. Adapted from Anielski's Genuine Well-Being Index (2012; see earlier summary), the GNH Index uses the same nine domains. Of these, three are particularly focused on positive social qualities: *governance* includes participation, freedom, and services; *community vitality* includes social support, relationships, family, and crime; and *cultural diversity* includes linguistic affiliation and collective recreational activities such as arts and crafts, festivals, drama, and music.

Doubtless many people looking at the Bhutanese list of indicators may detect hints of dogmatic conservatism and be tempted to question whether the full diversity of citizens' preferences is well represented. Indeed, before and since the 2013 change of government, the importance of GNH has been a matter for heated public debate in Bhutan (Sonam, 2013). Still, there can be little doubt that the immense effort at conceptual clarification and development of assessment tools has raised public awareness within and beyond Bhutan of the importance of discussing and promoting the goods we value. A key concept is that of sufficiency in a select set of those domains the respondents see as important: Self-reported sufficiency in 50% of the 124 variables classifies 90% of the population as happy. This provides an important *normative* restraint on the default assumption that if something is good, then more of it must be better. In this form, GNH has become sufficientarian in its recognition that people can't simultaneously pursue the full variety of goods, and that we need good enough but not maximal satisfaction in the goods that we pursue.

A key moment in the globalization of GNH came with the unanimous adoption on July 19, 2011, of the UN General Assembly's Resolution 65/309: "Happiness: Towards a Holistic Approach to Development," introduced by Bhutan's prime minister and cosponsored by 68 nations. At the time of going to press it seems highly likely that the follow-up work by a Bhutan-led international panel of experts, which is developing evidence-based analysis of the intrinsic and instrumental values of the nine GNH domains, will ensure that the UN's post-2015 development goals will pay substantial attention to happiness and to social goods (Government of Bhutan, 2013).

## SUMMARY POINTS

- Social planners at all levels and in many countries worldwide have been taking inspiration from the positivity of the PP movement, and from its emphasis on the importance of subjective experience. The new rubric of *positive social planning* is recommended as a way of drawing these disparate processes together.
- It is important for PSP to be based on philosophic recognition of the *intrinsic value of social goods*, and not just on their instrumental value in facilitating happiness. Our happiness is constituted, in part, by the knowledge that we live in a good society.
- *Social quality* is an important concept that neither social planners nor the PP movement have yet used systematically. Further work is needed on social quality for it to become a sure basis for positive social planning: Key categories of social goods need to be spelled out, and it needs to be rescued from the diverse other uses of social in research and public planning, which tend to be too general, residualist, and pathological.
- *There is intrinsic value in public happiness and social quality research and evaluation*, since a society that takes systematic interest in well-being and in social goods is better than one that does not. This value can be strengthened by shifting emphasis from reductionist survey-based measurements toward more empathic qualitative methods.
- It is essential that further analytical work is done by psychologists, sociologists, and planners together to *map out the interactions between social and psychological goods and harms*, exploring both universal generic interactions and the ways in which these operate differently in various cultural and socioeconomic settings.

## REFERENCES

Aknin, L. B., Dunn, E.W., & Norton, M. I. (2012). Happiness runs in a circular motion: Evidence for a positive feedback loop between prosocial spending and happiness. *Journal of Happiness Studies*, 13(2), 347–355.

Anielski, M. (2012). *Building flourishing economies of wellbeing: A strategic white paper*. Retrieved from http://www.genuinewealthinc.com/download/whitepapers/Building%20Economies%20of%20Wellbeing.pdf

Batson, C. D., Ahmad, N., Powell, A. A., & Stocks, E. L. (2008). Prosocial motivation. In J. Y. Shah & W. L. Gardner (Eds.), *Handbook of motivation science* (pp. 135–149). New York, NY: Guilford Press.

Baumeister, R. F., & Leary, M. R. (1995). The need to belong: Desire for interpersonal attachments as a fundamental human motivation. *Psychological Bulletin, 117*, 497–529.

Beck, W., van der Maesen, L. J. G., Thomése, F., & Walker, A. C. (Eds.). (2001). *Social quality: A vision for Europe*. The Hague, the Netherlands: Kluwer.

Beck, W., van der Maesen, L. J. G., & Walker, A. (1997). *The social quality of Europe*. Bristol, England: Policy Press.

Berscheid, E. (2003). The human's greatest strength: Other humans. In L. G. Aspinwall & U. M. Staudinger (Eds.), *A psychology of human strengths* (pp. 37–47). Washington, DC: American Psychological Association.

Best, J. (2001). Social progress and social problems: Toward a sociology of gloom. *The Sociological Quarterly, 42*(1), 1–12.

Biswas-Diener, R. (Ed.). (2011). *Positive psychology as social change*. Dordrecht, The Netherlands: Springer.

Borgonovi, F. (2008). Doing well by doing good: The relationship between formal volunteering and self-reported health and happiness. *Social Science & Medicine, 66*, 2321–2334.

Bruni, L. (2010). The happiness of sociality: Economics and eudaimonia: A necessary encounter. *Rationality and Society, 22*(4), 383–406.

Butler, E. A., Lee, T. L., & Gross, J. J. (2007). Emotion regulation and culture: Are the social consequences of emotion suppression culture-specific? *Emotion, 7*(1), 57–67.

Caistor-Arendar, L., & Mguni, N. (2013). *Beyond GDP: Report on conceptual framework to measure social progress at the local level and case studies*. Retrieved from http://youngfoundation.org

Cameron, K. S., Dutton, J. E., & Quinn, R. E. (2003). *Positive organizational scholarship: Foundations of a new discipline*. San Francisco, CA: Berrett-Koehler.

Cohen, J. (2013). Creating a positive school climate: A foundation for resilience. In S. Goldstein & R. B. Brooks (Eds.), *Handbook of resilience in children* (2nd ed., pp. 411–426). Dordrecht, The Netherlands: Springer.

Coleman, P. T., & Deutsch, M. (2012). *Psychological components of sustainable peace*. Dordrecht, The Netherlands: Springer.

Conoley, C. W., & Conoley, J. C. (2009). *Positive psychology and family therapy: Creative techniques and practical tools for guiding change and enhancing growth*. Chichester, England: Wiley.

Cox, J., Bowen, M., & Kempton, O. (2012). *Social value: Understanding the wider value of public policy interventions*. Manchester, England: New Economy Working Papers. Retrieved from neweconomymanchester.com/stories/843-new_economy_working_papers

Cunha, T., & Gomes, R. (2012). Intercultural education: Learning empathy to transgress. In Y. Ohana & H. Otten (Eds.), *Where do you stand?* (pp. 91–107). Dordrecht, The Netherlands: Springer.

Dalai Lama, & Cutler, H. (1998). *The art of happiness: A handbook for living*. New York, NY: Doubleday.

Demir, M. (Ed.). (2013). Relationships and happiness. In S. David, I. Boniwell, & C. Ayers (Eds.), *Oxford handbook of happiness* (pp. 817–872). Oxford, England: Oxford University Press.

De Rivera, J. (Ed.). (2009). *Handbook on building cultures of peace*. Dordrecht, The Netherlands: Springer.

Diener, E., & Seligman, M. (2004). Beyond money: Toward an economy of well-being. *Psychological Science in the Public Interest, 5*(1), 1–31.

Diener, E., & Suh, E. M. (Eds.). (2000). *Culture and subjective well-being*. Cambridge, MA: MIT Press.

Diener, E., & Tov, W. (2007). Subjective well-being and peace. *Journal of Social Issues, 63*, 421–440.

Dinnie, E., Brown, K. M., & Morris, S. (2013). Community, cooperation and conflict: Negotiating the social well-being benefits of urban greenspace experiences. *Landscape and Urban Planning, 112*, 1–9.

Donaghue, N., & Fallon, B. J. (2003). Gender-role self-stereotyping and the relationship between equity and satisfaction in close relationships. *Sex Roles, 48*(5–6), 217–230.

Donaldson, S. (Ed.). (2011). *Applied positive psychology: Improving everyday life, schools, work, health, and society*. Hove, England: Psychology Press.

Eckersley, R. (2000). The mixed blessings of material progress: Diminishing returns in the pursuit of happiness. *Journal of Happiness Studies, 1*(3), 267–292.

Eisenberg, N., & Fabes, R. A. (1990). Empathy: Conceptualization, measurement, and relation to prosocial behavior. *Motivation and Emotion, 14*(2), 131–149.

Estes, R. (2010). The world social situation: Development challenges at the outset of a new century. *Social Indicators Research, 989*(3), 363–402.

Evans, P. B. (2002). Collective capabilities, culture, and Amartya Sen's *Development as Freedom*. *Studies in Comparative International Development, 37*, 54–60.

Fetchenhauer, D., Flache, A., Buunk, A., & Landenberg, S. (Eds.). (2006). *Solidarity and prosocial behavior: An integration of sociological and psychological perspectives*. Dordrecht, The Netherlands: Springer.

Foster, J. M. (1998). *The communitarian organization: Preserving cultural integrity in the transnational economy*. New York, NY: Garland.

Galnoor, I. (1974). Social indicators for social planning: The case of Israel. *Social Indicators Research, 1*(1), 27–57.

Gilman, R., Huebner, E. S., & Furlong, M. J. (Eds.). (2009). *Handbook of positive psychology in schools*. London, England: Routledge.

Government of Bhutan. (2013). New Development Paradigm website. Retrieved from http://www.newdevelopmentparadigm.bt

Gropper, D. M., Lawson, R. A., & Thorne, J. T. (2011). Economic freedom and happiness. *Cato Journal, 31*(2), 237–256.

Helliwell, J., Layard, R., & Sachs, J. (Eds.). (2012). *World happiness report*. New York, NY: Columbia University Earth Institute.

Helliwell, J., Layard, R., & Sachs, J. (Eds.). (2013). *World happiness report*. New York, NY: United Nations Sustainable Development Solutions Network. Retrieved from www.unsdsn.org

Helliwell, J. F., Huang, H., & Putnam, R. D. (2009). How's the job? Are trust and social capital neglected workplace investments? In V. Bartkus & J. Davis (Eds.), *Social capital: Reaching out, reaching in*. Cheltenham, England: Edward Elgar.

Henderson, M. E. (2013). *Identifying great places to work: A systems framework*. Proceedings of the 56th Annual Meeting of the ISSS, 2012, San Jose, CA. Retrieved from http://journals.isss.org/index.php/proceedings56th/article/view/1858

Inglehart, R., & Welzel, C. (2005). *Modernization, cultural change, and democracy: The human development sequence*. Cambridge, England: Cambridge University Press.

Jiranek, P. (2013). Volunteering as a means to an equal end? The impact of a social justice function on intention to volunteer. *Journal of Social Psychology, 153*(5), 520–541.

Johns, H., & Ormerod, P. (2007). *Happiness, economics and public policy*. London, England: Institute of Economic Affairs.

Jordan, B. (2008). *Welfare and well-being: Social value in public policy*. Bristol, England: Policy Press.

Kaldor, M. (2003). *Global civil society: An answer to war*. Cambridge, England: Polity Press.

Kenny, C. (2005). Does development make you happy? Subjective wellbeing and economic growth in developing countries. *Social Indicators Research, 73*(2), 199–219.

Kenny, C. (2011). *Getting better: Why global development is succeeding—and how we can improve the world*. New York, NY: Basic Books.

Lakey, B. (2013). Perceived social support and happiness: The role of personality an relational processes. In S. David, I. Boniwell, & C. Ayers (Eds.), *Oxford handbook of happiness* (pp. 847–859). Oxford, England: Oxford University Press.

Lawlor, E., Nicholls, J., & Neitzert, E. (2009). *Seven principles for measuring what matters: A guide to effective public policy-making*. London, England: New Economics Foundation. Retrieved from http://www.neweconomics.org/publications/seven-principles-measuring-what-matters

Lin, K. (2013). A methodological exploration of social quality research: A comparative evaluation of the quality of life and social quality approaches. *International Sociology, 28*(3), 316–334.

Lyubomirsky, S. (2008). *The how of happiness: A practical guide to getting the life you want*. New York, NY: Penguin Press.

Marangos, J. (Ed.). (2012). *Alternative perspectives of a good society*. Houndmills, England: Palgrave Macmillan.

Miller, S. R., & Coll, E. (2007). From social withdrawal to social confidence: Evidence for possible pathways. *Current Psychology, 26*(2), 86.

Organisation for Economic Co-operation and Development. (n.d.). *Better Life Index*. Retrieved from www.oecdbetterlifeindex.org

Overing, J., & Passes, A. (Eds.). (2000). *The anthropology of love and anger: The aesthetics of conviviality in native Amazonia*. London, England: Routledge.

Peterson, C., & Seligman, M. (Eds.). (2004). *Character strengths and virtues: A handbook and classification*. New York, NY: Oxford University Press.

Pinker, S. (2011). *The better angels of our nature: Why violence has declined*. Harmondsworth, England: Penguin Press.

Prilleltensky, I. (2012). Wellness as fairness. *American Journal of Community Psychology, 49*, 1–21.

Prilleltensky, I., & Prilleltensky, O. (2006). *Promoting well-being: Linking personal, organizational, and community change*. Chichester, England: Wiley.

Putnam, R. J. (2000). *Bowling alone: The collapse and revival of American community*. New York, NY: Simon & Schuster.

Reasoner, R. W. (2006). Can the use of self-esteem programs in schools actually reduce problem behaviors and create more positive school climates? *International Council for Self-Esteem*. Retrieved from http://www.politicsoftrust.net

Roffey, S. (Ed.). (2012). *Positive relationships: Evidence based practice across the world*. Dordrecht, The Netherlands: Springer.

Rutherford, J. (2008). *Capitalism and social recession*. London, England: Compass Thinkpiece. Retrieved from http://compassonline.org.uk/publications/thinkpieces/item.asp?d=399

Ryff, C. D., & Singer, B. (2000). Interpersonal flourishing: A positive health agenda for the new millennium. *Personality and Social Psychology Review, 4*(1), 30–44.

Sachs, J. D. (2013). Restoring virtue ethics in the quest for happiness. In J. Helliwell, R. Layard, & J. Sachs (Eds.), *World happiness report* (pp. 80–97). New York, NY: United Nations Sustainable Development Solutions Network (www.unsdsn.org).

Seligman, M. E. P. (2003). *Authentic happiness: Using the new positive psychology to realize your potential for lasting fulfillment*. London, England: Nicholas Brealey.

Seligman, M. E. P. (2011). *Flourish: A visionary new understanding of happiness and well-being*. New York, NY: Free Press.

Seligman, M. E. P., & Csikszentmihalyi, M. (2000). Positive psychology: An introduction. *American Psychologist, 55*(1), 5–14.

Sen, A. (1999). *Development as freedom*. Oxford, England: Oxford University Press.

Shaftoe, H. (2008). *Convivial urban spaces: Creating effective public spaces*. London, England: Earthscan.

Shoda, Y., Mischel, W., & Peak, P. K. (1990). Predicting adolescent cognitive and self-regulatory competencies from preschool delay of gratification: Identifying diagnostic conditions. *Developmental Psychology, 26*(6), 978–986.

Sirgy, M. J. (2011). Societal QOL is more than the sum of QOL of individuals: The whole is greater than the sum of the parts. *Applied Research in Quality of Life, 6*, 329–334.

Sirgy, M. J., Phillips, R., & Rahtz, D. (Eds.). (2011). *Community quality-of-life indicators: Best cases* (Vol. 5). Dordrecht, The Netherlands: Springer.

Smith, C. (2003). *Moral, believing animals: Human personhood and culture.* Oxford, England: Oxford University Press.

Snyder, C. R., & Lopez, S. J. (2002). The future of positive psychology: A declaration of independence. In C. R. Snyder & S. J. Lopez (Eds.), *Handbook of positive psychology* (pp. 751–767). New York, NY: Oxford University Press.

Social Return on Investment Network. (2012). *A guide to social return on investment.* Retrieved from http://www.thesroinetwork.org/publications/publications/cat_view/29-the-sroi-guide/223-the-guide-in-english-2012-edition

Sonam, P. (2013, August 17). Bhutan, not government, will spearhead GNH. *Kuensel Online* [Bhutan]. Retrieved from www.kuenselonline.com

Staub, E. (2010). A world without genocide: Prevention, reconciliation, and the creation of peaceful societies. *Journal of Social Issues, 69*(1), 180–199.

Steedman, I., Atherton, J. R., & Graham, E. (Eds.). (2011). *The practices of happiness: Political economy, religion and wellbeing.* London, England: Routledge.

Stevenson, B., & Wolfers, J. (2009). The paradox of declining female happiness. NBER Working Paper No. 14969.

Stiglitz, J. E. (2012). *The price of inequality.* New York, NY: Norton.

Stiglitz, J. E., Sen, A., & Fitoussi, J. E. (2009). *Report by the Commission on the Measurement of Economic Performance and Social Progress.* Paris, France: OECD.

Stocks, E. L., Lishner, D. A., & Decker, S. K. (2009). Altruism or psychological escape: Why does empathy promote prosocial behavior? *European Journal of Social Psychology, 39*, 649–665.

Swedberg, R. (2005). *Interest.* Maidenhead, England: Open University Press.

Taylor, C. (1995). Irreducibly social goods. In C. Taylor, *Philosophical arguments* (pp. 45–63). Cambridge, MA: Harvard University Press. (Original work published 1990)

Thin, N. (2002). *Social progress and sustainable development.* London, England: ITDG, and Bloomfield, CT: Kumarian Press.

Thin, N. (2011). Socially responsible cheermongery: On the sociocultural contexts and levels of social happiness policies. In R. Biswas-Diener (Ed.), *Positive psychology as social change* (pp. 33–52). Dordrecht, the Netherlands: Springer.

Thin, N. (2012a). Counting and recounting happiness and culture: On happiness surveys and prudential ethnobiography. *International Journal of Wellbeing, 2*(4), 313–332.

Thin, N. (2012b). *Social happiness: Research into policy and practice.* Bristol, England: Policy Press.

United Nations. (1948). *Universal declaration of human rights.* New York, NY: United Nations. Retrieved from www.un.org/en/documents/udhr/

United Nations. (1969). *Declaration on social progress and development,* G.A. res. 2542 (XXIV). New York, NY: Author.

United Nations Department of Economic and Social Affairs. (2011). *The report on the world social situation 2011: The global social crisis.* New York, NY: Author.

UN Volunteers. (2011). *State of the world's volunteerism report 2011: Universal values for global well-being.* Retrieved from http://www.unv.org/swvr2011

Ura, K., Alkire, S., Zangmo, T., & Wangdi, K. (2012). *A short guide to Gross National Happiness Index.* Thimphu, Bhutan: Centre for Bhutan Studies. Retrieved from www.grossnationalhappiness.com

van der Maesen, L. J. G., & Walker, A. (Eds.). (2011). *Social quality: From theory to indicators.* Houndmills, England: Palgrave Macmillan.

Veenhoven, R. (2000). Well-being in the welfare state: Level not higher, distribution not more equitable. *Journal of Comparative Policy Analysis, 2,* 91–125.

Walzer, M. (Ed.). (1998). *Toward a global civil society.* Oxford, England: Berghahn.

Webb, S. (2010). Theorizing social wellbeing: Subjective mental states, preference satisfaction or Mitsein? In T. Lovat, R. Toomey, & N. Clement (Eds.), *International research handbook on values education and student wellbeing* (pp. 959–976). Dordrecht, The Netherlands: Springer.

Wilson, C. (2004). *Moral animals: Ideals and constraints in moral theory.* Oxford, England: Oxford University Press.

Wood, C., & Leighton, D. (2010). *Measuring social value: The gap between policy and practice.* London, England: DEMOS. Retrieved from http://www.demos.co.uk/files/Measuring_social_value_-_web.pdf

Wright, R. (1995). *The moral animal.* New York, NY: Vintage.

# CHAPTER 44

# Resilience Theory and the Practice of Positive Psychology From Individuals to Societies

TUPPETT M. YATES, FANITA A. TYRELL, and ANN S. MASTEN

ESILIENCE SCIENCE EMERGED more than half a century ago when trailblazers in psychology, psychiatry, and pediatrics searching for clues to the origins and treatment of problems in child development observed the striking variation in outcomes among children at risk due to disadvantage and adversity. From the outset, resilience research pioneers, such as Norman Garmezy, Lois Murphy, Michael Rutter, and Emmy Werner, sought to inform practice by understanding the processes that explained how some individuals fared well in the face of adversity while others floundered (Masten, 2013). Their compelling ideas and research propagated the field of resilience science, which has transformed frameworks for practice in multiple disciplines by shifting the emphasis away from deficit-focused orientations toward models centered on positive aims, promotive and protective factors, and adaptive capacities (Masten, 2011).

With its emphasis on competence despite exposure to adversity, the concept of resilience has long been attractive to applied practitioners seeking to promote strength in vulnerable individuals, groups, and societies. A wealth of research has documented processes by which individuals achieve positive developmental outcomes despite exposure to known threats to adaptation (Cicchetti, 2010; Goldstein & Brooks, 2013; Luthar, 2006; Masten, 2013, 2014; Panter-Brick & Leckman, 2013; Rutter, 2012). More recently, researchers have examined resilience processes at broader levels of development, including families (Becvar, 2013; Walsh, 2006), schools (Doll, 2013; Gettinger & Stoiber, 2009), communities (Davis, Cook, & Cohen, 2005; Norris, Stevens, Pfefferbaum, Wyche, & Pfefferbaum, 2008; Zautra, Hall, & Murray, 2008), and societies (Allenby & Fink, 2005; Birkmann, 2006).

Preparation of this chapter was supported in part by a grants from the National Science Foundation (NSF) Developmental and Learning Sciences (ID 0951775) and William T. Grant Foundation to the first author, and to the University of Minnesota (Ann S. Masten, Stephanie M. Carlson, and David Philip Zelazo, Co-PIs) from the Institute of Education Sciences (IES), U.S. Department of Education (R305A110528). The opinions expressed are those of the authors and do not represent the views of NSF, the William T. Grant Foundation, IES, the U.S. Department of Education, or other funders.

Drawing on empirical studies and theoretical models of resilience, researchers have articulated frameworks for translating resilience research into applied efforts to foster positive development (Masten & Powell, 2003; Wyman, Sandler, Wolchik, & Nelson, 2000). Amidst vociferous calls for research-informed practice, however, there emerged a growing appreciation for the need and opportunity for reciprocal translation to practice-informed research on resilience (Masten, 2011; Yates & Masten, 2004). In this chapter, we take stock of recent advances in resilience-based practice with a particular focus on expanding our scope beyond the individual level, and lament the still untapped wealth of practical information that awaits reciprocal translation to resilience research.

We begin with a review of key concepts and models of resilience as translated to the design and implementation of applied efforts to promote positive development. We emphasize the need for resilience-guided practice that accommodates the dynamic nature of human development at multiple levels of analysis within and across individuals, families, institutions, communities, and nations. We also encourage greater recognition of resilience-based practice as an underutilized resource for testing core tenets of resilience theory and broadening bidirectional paths from science-based practice to practice-based science.

## RESILIENCE AND RELATED CONCEPTS

Resilience is most appropriately conceptualized as a developmental process or a dynamic capacity rather than as a static outcome or trait. Applicable to a broad range of systems ranging from children and families to institutions and societies, resilience encompasses *the capacity of a dynamic system to adapt successfully to disturbances that threaten system function, viability, or development* (Masten, 2014). In the context of applied science, resilience also carries a connotation of positive or typical developmental adaptations despite exposure to clear threat or adversity. Thus, identifying processes of resilience requires clear operational definitions of both adversity and positive adaptation or competence. Moreover, contemporary models of resilience explicitly recognize that adversity and competence, as well as the processes that underlie them, may vary across levels of analysis within and across cultures.

### Characterizing Resilience: Adversity and Competence

*Adversity* refers to negative contexts and experiences that have the potential to disrupt or challenge adaptive functioning and development (Obradović, Shaffer, & Masten, 2012). Adversities may be chronic (e.g., poverty, racism) or acute (e.g., sudden loss of a loved one, victim of an armed robbery). They may affect systems within the individual (e.g., a virus that attacks the immune system) or multiple levels and settings simultaneously (e.g., a natural disaster that affects individual systems of stress, beliefs, and behaviors, as well as broader systems of family, school, health care, agriculture, etc.).

Adverse effects on development may result from experiences that block, exhaust, or compromise/distort the function of adaptive systems that usually foster and protect development. For example, political violence may influence human development in multiple ways: It may traumatize the whole community, harm parents or parenting, destroy health-care systems and homes, disrupt educational and occupational activities, and in many additional ways generate stress, erode resources, and stymie protective processes in development. Core adaptive processes, such as the natural predilection to seek protection and comfort from more powerful others in contexts of danger, may be co-opted in these contexts. For example, young people seeking safety, companionship, or opportunities for agency may be recruited into dangerous political activities (Barber, 2009). At multiple levels of function, and through varied mechanisms of process, adversity threatens the viability, stability, or development of adaptive systems and undermines positive adaptation. Nonetheless, capacities for competence may persist, which, when expressed in contexts of adversity, characterize resilience.

*Competence* refers to the capacity to adapt successfully and meet contextual, developmental, and cultural expectations for a particular individual, group, or social structure (Havighurst, 1972; Masten, Burt, & Coatsworth, 2006). Competence is enabled by the integrated organization and function of an adaptive system in context. Until recently, competence was typically indicated by observable evidence of effective performance in developmental tasks that were defined by Western European ideals. However, a growing global and multicultural body of work has begun to highlight cultural and contextual differences in the definition of what it means to be "doing okay" in a particular period of development, historical context, and cultural setting (Masten, 2014; Ungar, Ghazinour, & Richter, 2013).

In addition, research on manifest indicators of positive adaptation at individual levels of analysis has been supplemented by growing consideration of multilevel definitions of competence. For example, with respect to individual adaptation, contemporary notions of competence include indicators of positive *internal* adaptation, such as health, well-being, happiness, or a cohesive sense of self, along with external indices of competence, such as work or school achievement, quality of relationships, and law-abiding conduct (Brody et al., 2013; Luthar, 2006; Yates & Grey, 2012). Although specific phenotypes indicative of resilience may vary by level of analysis, historical time, or cultural context, all entail the situated expression of competence despite prior or ongoing adversity.

### Risks, Resources, and Processes Underlying Resilience

Whereas *risk factors* are broadly associated with negative or undesirable outcomes in a given population, *resource factors* (also known as assets or promotive factors) generally support positive or desirable development across individuals. Risks and resources are population-level constructs that are associated with negative or positive effects on development. However, at the level of individual members of a population (e.g., a person, school, or neighborhood), the significance of any particular factor for development may be influenced by the broader context of risks and resources that surrounds the system, as well as by specific vulnerabilities of the system. For example, a parent's serious illness will increase family strain, but this effect will be magnified in contexts where the parent is the sole provider for the family, and/or if there is a specific vulnerability, such as limited access to health-care. Thus, the adaptive significance of a particular risk or resource for a given individual in a population may be influenced by other factors.

Risk factors tend to aggregate and pile up in the lives of individuals, in families, and in communities (Masten & Wright, 1998; Obradović et al., 2012; Seifer & Sameroff, 1987). Unemployment of a parent, for example, may precipitate a decline in the family's financial security that disrupts housing stability, increases stress, renders family members more vulnerable to illness, and strains social support networks (Masten & Monn, in press). Likewise, at a more macro level, political violence may threaten the integrity of religious and educational institutions, disrupt patterns of food distribution and access, and threaten environmental health and safety. In a remarkable longitudinal study of cascading effects from the macro to the individual level, Boxer and colleagues (2013) found that interethnic political violence in the social ecology spread over time into proximal systems that youth interact with at the community, school, and family levels, resulting in higher levels of individual youth aggression.

Risks and resources, by definition, contribute directly to adaptation (i.e., main effects). However, their effects can be influenced by other factors or by interactions among risks and resources in combination (i.e., moderated effects). *Vulnerability* factors refer to moderators that increase the negative effects of risks, as in the aforementioned case where lack of health-care is a vulnerability that exacerbates the negative effect of illness or injury. *Protective* factors mitigate risk effects, taking on greater salience in adverse contexts as when positive teacher–student relationships disproportionately support academic and behavioral competence among disadvantaged students (Pianta, 1999).

Over the past decade, researchers have identified a third kind of moderating effect, which has been termed *differential susceptibility* (Belsky, Bakermans-Kranenburg, & van IJzendoorn, 2007; Ellis & Boyce, 2011) or *sensitivity to context* (Boyce & Ellis, 2005). In these instances, the same characteristic may serve protective and vulnerability functions depending on the context. For example, some individuals appear to be more reactive to experience, which can be good in positive situations and negative in risky contexts (Obradović, Bush, Stamperdahl, Adler, & Boyce, 2010). Importantly, individual differences of this kind may confer vulnerability in contexts of adversity, but also heightened responsiveness to positive experiences, including interventions.

RESILIENCE IN DYNAMIC SYSTEMS

Contemporary resilience science extends across the life span; considers multiple levels of analysis, from molecular to cultural; and examines multiple systems, from families and schools to neighborhoods and nations (e.g., Cicchetti, 2013; Kim-Cohen & Turkewitz, 2012; Masten, 2013, 2014; Panter-Brick & Leckman, 2013; Reich, Zautra, & Hall, 2010; Russo, Murrough, Han, Charney, & Nestler, 2012). These studies converge on a model of resilience that is grounded in relational developmental systems theory (Lerner & Overton, 2008; Overton, 2013), which holds that the capacity for competence at any given time reflects the possibilities that arise from many interacting systems, both within the individual and in the contexts that surround the individual at the time. These interactions between an individual system (e.g., a person, a school, or a country) and the surrounding context of risks and resources contribute to nuanced processes of vulnerability, protection, and differential susceptibility that ultimately affect the capacity to respond to challenge successfully (i.e., processes of resilience).

Resilience emerges from the interactions of a dynamic system as it transacts with a dynamic context (Lerner, 2006). Within the child who behaves and feels reasonably well despite exposure to adversity, there are functional neural and stress response systems that enable her or him to mobilize attention, behavior, and emotion in the service of successful adaptation. Outside this same child, there may be engaged and supportive adults or caregivers, intact educational settings, a community with basic functionality, and a culture that imbues her or him with a sense of predictability. Thus, any model of resilience must consider the interplay among multiple levels of influence and analysis, and efforts to promote resilience in development must do the same (Cicchetti, 2011).

RESILIENCE AND PRACTICE

The study of resilience inspired a transformation from deficit-based models of intervention to those that acknowledge and promote resources and protective processes in development. Resilience research has informed prevention science by clarifying multilevel goals, identifying mechanisms expected to bring about positive change in varied systems, informing the measurement of key variables, and providing a conceptual framework to guide the form and application of dynamic and contextually sensitive intervention efforts.

## RESILIENCE-GUIDED GOALS

In contrast to traditional medical models that seek to eradicate disease or distress, resilience models aim to promote health and well-being. The study of resilience has inspired interventions with broad appeal by emphasizing attainable goals of competence, rather than optimal performance, and focusing on positive goals, rather than avoiding problems and pitfalls (Masten, 2011). Moreover, by supporting contextualized models of competence in which definitions of "doing okay" are situated within a cultural, developmental, and historical context, resilience-guided practice has garnered the support of consumers and community stakeholders, particularly those from underrepresented and marginalized groups that bore the brunt of the deficit emphasis in classical models of intervention (Bryan, 2005).

The overarching goal of resilience-informed practice is to foster positive adaptation and development in contexts of high risk or adversity. Thus, efforts to define competence are critical to the design and implementation of applied practices that will support it. As the successful negotiation of developmentally, culturally, and contextually relevant issues, competence demands applied goals that change in response to the developing system. For example, interventions to support competence in infancy necessarily focus on different capacities (e.g., behavioral and state regulation) and contexts (e.g., caregiver–child relationships) than those targeting competence during the transition to adulthood (e.g., opportunities for apprenticeship or mentoring, romantic relationships). Some of these capacities will generalize across cultures, while others will vary (Ungar et al., 2013). For example, issues confronting a country wrestling with the challenges of potable water delivery and universal access to primary education may differ from those confronting a country struggling to promote universal access to health care and higher education. Resilience-guided goals for practice share an emphasis on competence promotion and an appreciation for the variation in specific indicators of successful adaptation across systems and settings.

## MECHANISMS OF RESILIENCE PROMOTION

Fifty years of resilience research converge on a set of core resources and protective processes that feature prominently in individual, group, and structural competence in contexts of risk or adversity (i.e., resilience) (Luthar, 2006; Masten, 2013; Wright, Masten, & Narayan, 2013). These factors emerge with a high degree of consistency across varied study designs, samples, and settings, though the majority of resilience research derives from (and correspondingly focuses on) human (particularly child) development in Western nations. For children, these factors center on relationships with caring adults, individual difference variables that confer regulatory and relational flexibility, and community-level structures that support opportunities for safety and growth. Comparable lists of promotive and protective factors can be developed for families, schools, communities, or nations to guide practical efforts to improve the odds of successful adaptation within those settings and, by extension, the systems that interact with them. For example, at the level of community, factors associated with the built environment (e.g., public transport, street design and maintenance), social capital (e.g., community networks and social norms), and services and institutions (e.g., local government, schools) support the capacity for community resilience to disadvantage (Davis et al., 2005; Norris et al., 2008).

Joining the wealth of literature on the many ways development can go awry in adverse contexts, resilience researchers have identified several approaches to facilitate competence, particularly in contexts of adversity (Masten, 2011; Yates & Masten, 2004). As a first line of defense, *risk-focused techniques* aim to improve developmental outcomes by attenuating or eliminating initial adversity exposure; these strategies constitute a primary prevention approach to practice that is well-suited to contexts where risks are identifiable, modifiable, and avoidable (e.g., providing nutrition and medication to prevent intestinal parasites; Grigorenko et al., 2007). *Resource-focused techniques* complement primary prevention efforts by improving access to assets that promote competence and counteract or counterbalance risks, especially those that are intractable or chronic (e.g., perinatal home-based visitation to provide parenting information and support to impoverished families; Olds, 2002). Finally, *process-focused techniques* seek to protect, activate, or restore basic adaptive systems that support development. These systems and corresponding support processes have been specified with greatest clarity in human resilience. Examples include attachment-focused strategies, such as providing safe, supportive, and consistent adult caregivers and mentors (Berlin, Ziv, Amaya-Jackson, & Greenberg, 2005); bolstering mastery motivation, often by providing opportunities for successful engagement with challenge to support natural proclivities toward mastery and personal effectance (Kahana, Kelley-Moore, & Kahana, 2012); and improving self-regulation capabilities to build the capacity to modulate attention, emotion, behavior, and arousal in accord with contextual demands (Blair & Diamond, 2010). It is important to note, however, that core adaptive systems can be targeted in other systems and settings, such as neighborhoods where social cohesion and trust constitute central processes underlying relative vulnerability or resilience (Zautra et al., 2008).

Most effective interventions operate through multiple mechanisms and at multiple levels of action. Cumulative risk is best met by cumulative protection efforts that prevent risk, promote resources, and buffer adaptive functioning (Wyman et al., 2000; Yoshikawa, 1994). For example, the Seattle Social Development Program (Hawkins, Kosterman, Catalano, Hill, & Abbott, 2005) is built on a model of prevention with a focus on promoting positive change in children's bonding to school and family. The program is implemented across the elementary school years, but includes both classroom and family components. Teachers are trained in mastery teaching strategies, learn how to improve classroom management, and teach social skills in the classroom. Parents are trained in effective parenting techniques, such as monitoring and consistent discipline. Long-term evidence points to enduring effects of this program on developmental task achievements, as well as reductions in antisocial behavior and other negative outcomes. Such efforts capitalize on developmental cascades of influence (Masten & Cicchetti, 2010), wherein positive change in one system (e.g., family) may influence adjustment at other levels (e.g., child, school).

SETTINGS FOR APPLIED RESILIENCE

Prior research has elucidated specific principles and practices to support positive development among adversity-exposed individuals. However, these same processes can operate in a range of settings beyond individuals, often with cascading implications for child and youth development. Although an exhaustive review of resilience-informed approaches to practice in varied settings is beyond the scope of this chapter, we provide a few examples of resilience-informed practice to illustrate the broad applicability of resilience theory and research, as well as some challenges when taking these efforts to scale.

Applied efforts to support resilience capacities through individual-level interventions have focused on varied processes, including problem solving skills and social-emotional learning (Aber, Brown, Jones, Berg, & Torrente, 2011); developing and maintaining healthy relationships with parents, peers, and partners (Hawkins et al., 2005); and strengthening executive and regulatory functions (Blair & Diamond, 2010). Although these interventions may be implemented in familial or educational settings, they share an emphasis on individual capacities as the target of change. Importantly, these core adaptive systems are critical for healthy development in all contexts, but may take on increased salience as protective factors in risky environments.

As a central context for the development of both children and adults, the family setting, and patterns of interaction therein, is a common focus for resilience-informed interventions. High-quality relationships between parents and children are implicated in virtually every study of resilience in children (Luthar, 2006; Masten, 2013), and positive romantic relationships are implicated in adult resilience (Conger, Schofield, Neppl, & Merrick, 2013; Ronka, Oravala, & Pulkinen, 2002). A large body of evidence indicates that parenting and parent–child relational dynamics are modifiable mechanisms through which interventions can contribute to improved child outcomes (Belsky & de Haan, 2011; Patterson, Forgatch, & DeGarmo, 2010; Sandler, Schoenfelder, Wolchik, & MacKinnon, 2011). Promising applications of resilience have also been employed to support positive relationship functioning among vulnerable groups, such as couples facing military deployment (Gewirtz, Erbes, Polusny, Forgatch, & DeGarmo, 2011) or serious illness (Badr & Taylor, 2008).

Consistent with a relational view of developmental systems (Lerner & Overton, 2008; Overton, 2013), lives are nested within multiple, often overlapping institutions. As noted earlier, many interventions that target individuals are administered via institutions where people spend a lot of time (e.g., school, work). However, institutions themselves may serve as sites for resilience-enhancing intervention efforts, and these efforts can manifest at multiple levels. For example, within a given employment sector, applied efforts to support resilience could focus on individual workers, managers, central administrators, or training and safety protocols. In schools, interventions may target students, classrooms, teachers, administrators, curricula, individual schools, or school districts. Research consistently points to the critical importance of providing safe and supportive contexts entailing multiple levels of support for successful adaptation, relative to the more modest impact of efforts to change individual capacities directly (Ungar et al., 2013).

Resilience-informed practice may target neighborhoods and communities as well. Norris and colleagues (2008) have developed models to promote community resilience in the context of disaster, and similar approaches have been developed to address public health issues (Paton, Parkes, Daly, & Smith, 2008). Importantly, community-level interventions may have positive effects that are mediated by individual-level factors. For example, social capital, residential stability, and neighborly connections, which are all features of neighborhood resilience (Zautra et al., 2008), may foster hope or security in individuals and, by extension, positive coping and adjustment.

At the grandest scale, resilience may guide practice and policy within or across nations. In these instances, interventions often incorporate multiple settings for applied resilience. Finland's successful educational recovery in the wake of World War II constitutes a striking example of national resilience. For decades following the war, Finland's educational system was problem focused and problem riddled. Once known for its remarkably low rate of school attendance, Finland now boasts one of the world's most educated populations with 99% of children completing compulsory education and 94% completing upper secondary school (Välijärvi & Sahlberg, 2008). Despite shorter school days that are relatively few in number, Finland's youth consistently outperform those in the United States, the European Union, and other nations with comparable ethnic and economic demographics (e.g., Norway; Organisation for Economic Co-operation and Development [OECD], 2011).

An outgrowth of nearly 40 years of carefully constructed educational reform involving students, teachers, administrators, and government officials, Finland's educational resilience is a source of national pride and global influence (OECD, 2011; Sahlberg, 2007). Beginning in 1972, educational reform policies established a standard core compulsory education, but this national standard was implemented at the local level using teacher-selected practices that were best suited to the needs and resources of a particular school or community. Comparative evaluations across schools (and even across students and teachers within schools) were supplanted by school- and teacher-specific evaluation practices for the sole purpose of instructional development and refinement for individual teachers.

In addition to curricular reform for children, Finland enacted a systematic over-haul of its teacher education system and valuation. Teaching, which once ranked among the least desirable professions in Finland, rose to prominence as teachers were required to obtain at least a master's degree before leading their own classroom and teacher curricula were revised to incorporate cutting-edge educational theory and research (Sahlberg, 2010).

With heightened prestige and protected autonomy in the classroom, teaching now ranks among the most valued occupations in Finland and their professional satisfaction and sophistication cascades to influence student learning outcomes. Uniform expectations for success regardless of family background, class, or circumstance encourages Finnish students to take responsibility for their own education (OECD, 2011). Finland's explicit commitment to educational equity in terms of opportunity, obligation, and potential for success guided the design and implementation of education reform efforts at multiple levels, which, in turn, have combined to transform the nation.

Integration of multiple techniques and levels will yield the most effective interventions to support resilience. At the same time, however, these multifaceted and large-scale efforts are among the most challenging models of applied resilience. As illustrated in the Finnish case, true transformation in human development and institutional function requires buy in from all stakeholders, ranging from individual community members to broader systems of policy and governance (Aber et al., 2011).

## A DYNAMIC MODEL OF RESILIENCE IN PRACTICE

Just as resilience emerges in the context of dynamic exchanges between an adaptive system and the broader context, so, too, must practice efforts to support competence in contexts of adversity (i.e., resilience) accommodate and respond to the dynamic nature of development. The influence of a given factor as either protective- or vulnerability-enhancing is moderated by the context in which it is embedded, and the developmental stage of the system at the time when it is introduced. Thus, certain goals (e.g., promoting positive peer relationships) may be best suited to particular settings (e.g., schools) or age periods (e.g., middle childhood and adolescence, when peer relationships are most salient). Similarly, the structure of obesity prevention practices in a neighborhood with minimal green space and high levels of community violence necessarily differs from applied efforts in comparatively benign community settings with ample parks and public recreation areas, though all seek to promote positive nutrition and health.

Whether in children, groups, or social structures, current adaptive organizations within a system build on (and often embody or encompass) prior organizations of that system (Sroufe, Egeland, & Kreutzer, 1990). Thus, early interventions tend to have the greatest developmental and economic impact (Heckman, 2006). Yet adaptive processes wax and wane in influence across development, and, although there may be considerable adaptive continuity, there remains a capacity for change throughout the life course, for better and for worse. This capacity for change is magnified during periods of transition, as when puberty changes an individual body or elections change a system of governance. Individuals, families, and communities may be more open to intervention-induced transformational change when destabilized by transition or crisis (e.g., disaster). In these moments, interventions may provide powerful inducements to change, and precipitate turning-point experiences (Ronka et al., 2002; Rutter, 1996). Similarly, it is during these periods of relative instability that ongoing supports are needed to ensure the maintenance of positive trajectories.

A developmental view of resilience encourages early yet sustained intervention efforts in recognition that ongoing supports and protections are needed to maintain fledgling trajectories of competence. Moreover, targeting periods of rapid transition or heightened sensitivity may guide seemingly counterintuitive decisions about the most appropriate timing of intervention. For example, efforts to promote positive adjustment during the school years may begin with intervention applications prior to birth given evidence that the sensitivity of adaptive systems may be organized and tuned prenatally (Boyce, 2007).

Just as resilience is developmentally contextualized, it is also culturally situated. Thus, it is important to clarify the ways in which adversity and competence vary across different ecological and cultural contexts (Ungar et al., 2013). Applied efforts to promote resilience that incorporate culturally congruent values, norms, and resources will be more readily accepted and utilized by individuals, groups, and communities (Black & Krishnakumar, 1998; Parsai, Castro, Marsiglia, Harthun, & Valdez, 2011).

A TRANSACTIONAL MODEL OF RESILIENCE IN PRACTICE

With a growing body of research illuminating the processes by which systems negotiate salient developmental challenges despite adversity, a resilience framework can guide practice, even as research continues to build a better knowledge base about processes of protection, vulnerability, and differential susceptibility. In turn, efficacy studies of interventions guided by resilience science offer powerful tests of theories about resilience processes. These include investigations of prevention and intervention efforts that deliberately aim to alter the course of development in favorable directions and natural experiments where a naturally occurring change in circumstance (e.g., adoption) can reveal mechanisms of developmental deviation and recovery (Masten, 2011; Rutter, 2007).

Scientific progress emerges from the bidirectional influences of theory and practice in a recursive process of theory formulation, testing, data collection, and theory revision (Sameroff, 1983). Although prevention scientists are increasingly incorporating resilience theory into their missions and models of intervention, there remains a wealth of untapped information awaiting translation from practice to research (Howe, Reiss, & Yuh, 2002). Carefully conducted evaluation research with randomized group assignment and appropriate comparison groups allows investigators to experiment with altering the course of human development in the context of identifiable and quantifiable adversity, and to evaluate causal hypotheses about resilience and development (Masten, 2011). Studies that demonstrate the mediating function of conceptually predicted variables (e.g., improved parental discipline practices) in the relation between intervention (e.g., parent education curricula) and outcome (e.g., reduced antisocial behavior) yield important data for theory testing. However, interventions that were highly successful in elegant university experiments can be difficult to implement successfully in more typical real-world ecological settings.

The divide between the empirical efficacy of resilience interventions in clinical research designs and the real-world effectiveness of resilience interventions in everyday practice constitutes a major barrier to bidirectional exchanges between resilience research and practice. In an effort to bridge this translational divide, investigators are teaming up with field-based experts and consumers to design and test interventions that are informed by frontline knowledge and tailored to real-world contexts to maximize the potential for effectiveness in everyday practice from the outset. Casey and colleagues (2014) describe an iterative process of designing and testing the components of a new intervention to promote executive function skills and academic resilience in homeless and highly mobile preschool children. Their design team included faculty experts in executive function, resilience, and teacher training; teachers and staff from community preschools serving high-risk children; and master teachers from a university-based early childhood training program. Parents also contributed their expertise via focus groups and feedback about each iteration of the intervention. Incorporating the expertise of scientists, practitioners, and consumers yields a translational synergy that strengthens and accelerates the reciprocal influences of science and practice in the design, implementation, evaluation, and dissemination of interventions to promote resilience (Masten, 2011).

In an elegant illustration of translational synergy, Aber and colleagues (2011) initiated an empirical investigation of social-emotional learning and development. They began with a careful explication of theories of change that were implicit in the design and implementation of an applied effort to support children's efforts to resolve conflict creatively. Subsequent evaluations of the theories underlying the Resolving Conflict Creatively Program were translated from practice to research and back again to guide the development of a modified school-based intervention centered on reading, writing, respect, and resolution (4Rs). The 4Rs program incorporates multiple levels of intervention (e.g., individuals, classrooms, schools) and harnesses developmental cascades of influence across schools, classrooms, and children. While acknowledging the many difficulties that thwart synergistic translations between practice and research, the work of Aber and colleagues (2011) also demonstrates the incontrovertible value of confronting these challenges.

Challenges that hinder efforts to integrate the science and practice of resilience are manifold. First, good interventions and the research on which they are based take time, but there is a constant press for immediate action to support children, families, schools, and neighborhoods that are struggling in the present moment and cannot abide by the time course of rigorous science (Ager, Stark, Akesson, & Bootby, 2010; Masten, 2011). Second, effective interventions are, almost by definition, multifaceted, prompting a need to identify the salient facets or active ingredients of successful interventions to best inform future science. Third, theory testing in the context of resilience-guided interventions necessitates a complementary shift in our evaluative lens away from symptom remission toward competence promotion. A legacy of interest in the problems of adaptation has produced far fewer tools to assess competence and positive dimensions of development. As efforts to promote the health and competence of future generations expand, they must be met with commensurate evaluative research to ascertain the specific features of interventions that are effective, and to test the theoretical hypotheses upon which they were grounded. Beyond the individual level, tools to evaluate broader systems, such as communities, governments, and nations, are particularly scarce (see Sherrieb, Norris, & Galea, 2010, for exception). Fourth, there is a dearth of practice-based research networks through which multiple providers in applied settings can collaborate to develop a living laboratory to generate and evaluate knowledge in the context of everyday practice (McMillen, Lenze, Hawley, & Osborne, 2009).

## CONCLUSION

Positive psychology emphasizes the study of human strength and virtue with the aim of understanding and facilitating positive developmental outcomes (Seligman & Csikszentmihalyi, 2000). A resilience framework offers a powerful tool for realizing the goals of positive psychology in contexts of adversity. Contemporary models of resilience highlight the incremental information and impact that derives from integrating multiple levels of analysis and application. Similarly, translational synergy between the practice and science of resilience will best be realized by harnessing dynamic and cascading influences across developing systems and in collaboration with scientists, practitioners, and consumers.

## SUMMARY POINTS

- Resilience refers to the capacity of a dynamic system to adapt successfully to disturbances that threaten system function, viability, or development (Masten, 2014).
- Resilience is supported or thwarted by direct effects of risks and resources, as well as by moderating processes of protection, vulnerability, and differential susceptibility.
- Resilience is dynamic; it emerges from many interactions within and between systems in a given cultural, developmental, and historical context that collectively influence the capacity of an individual system to adapt successfully to challenge.
- Although resilience research often has focused on the behavior of individuals, contemporary models of resilience encompass multiple levels of function and acknowledge the interdependence of interacting systems, ranging from molecular to societal levels of analysis across individuals, families, peer groups, schools, communities, governments, and cultures.
- Cultural influences on resilience are gaining traction amid growing recognition that interventions should be tailored to the unique strengths, vulnerabilities, and values of specific contexts, and also that different cultures may have traditions and practices that can inform resilience theory.
- Resilience remains an inspiring and informative framework for implementing positive psychology in practice.

- Recent efforts to expand the study of resilience across levels of analysis have complementary implications for applying this knowledge to multilevel interventions.
- Likewise, multilevel applications of resilience theory hold considerable potential for testing core theories regarding developmental cascades underlying adaptive continuity and change.
- Careful evaluations of resilience-informed interventions may refine extant efforts to support positive development.
- Interventions and research designed by fully collaborative teams of field-based practitioners, academically based scientists, and consumers have the potential to advance practice and science by accelerating the bidirectional transfer of knowledge and strengthening the mutual trust and respect that facilitate the generation of practice-based evidence and the implementation of evidence-based practice.

## REFERENCES

Aber, L., Brown, J. L., Jones, S. M., Berg, J., & Torrente, C. (2011). School-based strategies to prevent violence, trauma, and psychopathology: The challenges of going to scale. *Development and Psychopathology, 23*, 411–421.

Ager, A., Stark, L., Akesson, B., & Bootby, N. (2010). Defining best practice in care and protection of children in crisis-affected settings: A Delphi study. *Child Development, 81*(4), 1271–1286.

Allenby, B., & Fink, J. (2005). Toward inherently secure and resilient societies. *Science, 309*(5737), 1034–1036.

Badr, H., & Taylor, C. L. C. (2008). Effects of relationship maintenance on psychological distress and dyadic adjustment among couples coping with lung cancer. *Health Psychology, 27*(5), 616.

Barber, B. K. (Ed.). (2009). *Adolescents and war: How youth deal with political violence.* New York, NY: Oxford University Press.

Becvar, D. S. (Ed.). (2013). *Handbook of family resilience.* New York, NY: Springer.

Belsky, J., Bakermans-Kranenburg, M. J., & van IJzendoorn, M. H. (2007). For better and for worse: Differential susceptibility to environmental influences. *Current Directions in Psychological Science, 16*(6), 300–304.

Belsky, J., & de Haan, M. (2011). Annual research review: Parenting and children's brain development: The end of the beginning. *Journal of Child Psychology and Psychiatry, 52*(4), 409–428.

Berlin, L. J., Ziv, Y., Amaya-Jackson, L. M., & Greenberg, M. T. (Eds.). (2005). *Enhancing early attachments: Theory, research, intervention, and policy.* New York, NY: Guilford Press.

Birkmann, J. (2006). Measuring vulnerability to promote disaster-resilient societies: Conceptual frameworks and definitions. In J. Birkmann (Ed.), *Measuring vulnerability to natural hazards: Towards disaster resilient societies* (pp. 9–54). New York, NY: United Nations University.

Black, M. M., & Krishnakumar, A. (1998). Children in low-income, urban settings: Interventions to promote mental health and well-being. *American Psychologist, 53*(6), 635–646.

Blair, C., & Diamond, A. (2010). Biological processes in prevention and intervention: The promotion of self-regulation as a means of preventing school failure. *Development and Psychopathology, 20*(3), 899.

Boxer, P., Huesmann, L. R., Dubrow, E. F., Landau, S., F., Gvisman, S. D., Shikaki, K., & Ginges, J. (2013). Exposure to violence across the social ecosystem and the development of aggression: A test of ecological theory in the Israeli-Palestinian conflict. *Child Development, 84*, 163–177. doi:10.1111/j.1467–8624.2012.01848.x

Boyce, W. T. (2007). A biology of misfortune: Stress reactivity, social context, and the ontogeny of psychopathology in early life. In A. S. Masten (Ed.), *Minnesota symposia on child psychology—Multilevel dynamics in developmental psychopathology: Pathways to the future.* (pp. 45-82). New York, NY: Taylor & Francis Group/ Erlbaum.

Boyce, W. T., & Ellis, B. J. (2005). Biological sensitivity to context: I. An evolutionary-developmental theory of the orgins and functions of stress reactivity. *Development & Psychopathology, 17,* 271–301.

Brody, G. H., Yu, T., Chen, E., Miller, G. E., Kogan, S. M., & Beach, S. R. H. (2013). Is resilience only skin deep? Rural African Americans' socioeconomic status-related risk and competence in preadolescence and psychological adjustment and allostatic load at age 19. *Psychological Science, 24*(7), 1285–1293. doi:10.1177/0956797612471954

Bryan, J. (2005). Fostering educational resilience and achievement in urban schools through school-family-community partnerships. *Professional School Counseling, 8*(3), 219–227.

Casey, E. C., Finsaas, M., Carlson, S. M., Zelazo, P. D., Murphy, B., Durkin, F., . . . Masten, A. S. (2014). Promoting resilience through executive function training for homeless and highly mobile preschoolers. In S. Prince-Embury & D. H. Saklofske (Eds.), *Resilience interventions for youth in diverse populations.* (pp. 133-158). New York, NY: Springer.

Cicchetti, D. (2010). Resilience under conditions of extreme stress: A multilevel perspective. *World Psychiatry, 9*(3), 145–154.

Cicchetti, D. (2011). Pathways to resilience in maltreated children: From single-level to multi-level investigations. In D. Cicchetti & G. I. Roisman (Eds.), *The Minnesota symposia on child psychology: Vol. 36. The origins and organization of adaptation and maladaptation* (pp. 423–459). Hoboken, NJ: Wiley.

Cicchetti, D. (2013). Annual research review: Resilient functioning in maltreated children: Past, present, and future perspectives. *Journal of Child Psychiatry and Psychology, 54,* 402–422. doi:10.1111/j.1469–7610.2012.02608.x

Conger, R. D., Schofield, T. J., Neppl, T. K., & Merrick, M. T. (2013). Disrupting intergenerational continuity in harsh and abusive parenting: The importance of a nurturing relationship with a romantic partner. *Journal of Adolescent Health, 53*(4), S11–S17.

Davis, R., Cook, D., & Cohen, L. (2005). A community resilience approach to reducing ethnic and racial disparities in health. *American Journal of Public Health, 95*(12), 2168–2173.

Doll, B. (2013). Enhancing resilience in classrooms. In S. Goldstein & R. B. Brooks (Eds.), *Handbook of resilience in children* (pp. 399–410). New York, NY: Springer.

Ellis, B. J., & Boyce, W. T. (2011). Differential susceptibility to the environment: Toward an understanding of sensitivity to developmental experiences and context. *Development and Psychopathology, 23*(1), 1.

Gettinger, M., & Stoiber, K. (2009). Effective teaching and effective schools. In C. R. Reynolds & T. B. Gutkin (Eds.), *The handbook of school psychology* (4th ed., pp. 769–790). Hoboken, NJ: Wiley.

Gewirtz, A. H., Erbes, C. R., Polusny, M. A., Forgatch, M. S., & DeGarmo, D. S. (2011). Helping military families through the deployment process: Strategies to support parenting. *Professional Psychology: Research and Practice, 42*(1), 56.

Goldstein, S., & Brooks, R. B. (Eds.). (2013). *Handbook of resilience in children* (2nd ed.). New York, NY: Springer.

Grigorenko, E. L., Jarvin, L., Kaani, B., Kapungulya, P. P., Kwiatkowski, J., & Sternberg, R. J. (2007). Risk factors and resilience in the developing world: One of many lessons to learn. *Development and Psychopathology, 19*(3), 747–765.

Havighurst, R. J. (1972). *Developmental tasks and education.* New York, NY: David McKay.

Hawkins, J. D., Kosterman, R., Catalano, R. F., Hill, K. G., & Abbott, R. D. (2005). Promoting positive adult functioning through social development intervention in childhood: Long-term effects from the Seattle Social Development Project. *Archives of Pediatrics & Adolescent Medicine, 159*(1), 25.

Heckman, J. J. (2006). Skill formation and the economics of investing in disadvantaged children. *Science, 312*, 1900–1902.

Howe, G. W., Reiss, D., & Yuh, J. (2002). Can prevention trials test theories of etiology? *Development and Psychopathology, 14*, 673–694.

Kahana, E., Kelley-Moore, J., & Kahana, B. (2012). Proactive aging: A longitudinal study of stress, resources, agency, and well-being in late life. *Aging & Mental Health, 16*(4), 438–451.

Kim-Cohen, J., & Turkewitz, R. (2012). Resilience and measured gene–environment interactions. *Development and Psychopathology, 24*(4), 1297–1306.

Lerner, R. M. (2006). Resilience as an attribute of the developmental system. *Annals of the New York Academy of Sciences, 1094*(1), 40–51.

Lerner, R. M., & Overton, W. F. (2008). Exemplifying the integrations of the relational developmental system: Synthesizing theory, research, and application to promote positive development and social justice. *Journal of Adolescent Research, 23*(3), 245–255. doi:10.1177/0743558408314385

Luthar, S. S. (2006). Resilience in development: A synthesis of research across five decades. In D. Cicchetti & D. Cohen (Eds.), *Developmental psychopathology: Risk, disorder, and adaptation* (2nd ed., Vol. 3, pp. 739–795). Hoboken, NJ: Wiley.

Masten, A. S. (2011). Resilience in children threatened by extreme adversity: Frameworks for research, practice, and translational synergy. *Development and Psychopathology, 23*(2), 493–506.

Masten, A. S. (2013). Risk and resilience in development. In P. D. Zelazo (Ed.), *The Oxford handbook of developmental psychology: Vol. 2. Self and other* (pp. 579–607). New York, NY: Oxford University Press.

Masten, A. S. (2014). Global perspectives on resilience in children and youth. *Child Development, 85*(1), 6–20.

Masten, A. S., Burt, K. B., & Coatsworth, J. D. (2006). Competence and psychopathology in development. In D. Cicchetti & D. Cohen (Eds.), *Developmental psychopathology* (2nd ed., Vol. 3, pp. 696–738). Hoboken, NJ: Wiley.

Masten, A. S., & Cicchetti, D. (2010). Editorial: Developmental cascades. *Development and Psychopathology, 22*, 491–495.

Masten, A. S., & Monn, A. R. (in press). Resilience in children and families: A call for integrated science, practice, and professional training. *Family Relations*.

Masten, A. S., & Powell, J. L. (2003). A resilience framework for research, policy, and practice. In S. S. Luthar (Ed.), *Resilience and vulnerability: Adaptation in the context of childhood adversities* (pp. 1–25). New York, NY: Cambridge University Press.

Masten, A. S., & Wright, M. O. (1998). Cumulative risk and protection models of child maltreatment. *Journal of Aggression, Maltreatment & Trauma, 2*(1), 7–30.

McMillen, J. C., Lenze, S. L., Hawley, K. M., & Osborne, V. A. (2009). Revisiting practice-based research networks as a platform for mental health services research. *Administration and Policy in Mental Health and Mental Health Services Research, 36*(5), 308–321.

Norris, F. H., Stevens, S. P., Pfefferbaum, B., Wyche, K. F., & Pfefferbaum, R. L. (2008). Community resilience as a metaphor, theory, set of capacities, and strategy for disaster readiness. *American Journal of Community Psychology, 41*(1–2), 127–150.

Obradović, J., Bush, N. R., Stamperdahl, J., Adler, N. A., & Boyce, W. T. (2010). Biological sensitivity to context: The interactive effects of stress reactivity and family adversity on socio-emotional behavior and school readiness. *Child Development, 81*(1), 270–289.

Obradović, J., Shaffer, A., & Masten, A. S. (2012). Risk and adversity in developmental psychopathology: Progress and future directions. In L. C. Mayes & M. Lewis (Eds.), *The Cambridge handbook of environment in human development* (pp. 35–57). New York, NY: Cambridge University Press.

Organisation for Economic Co-operation and Development. (2011). Finland: Slow and steady reform for consistently high results. In *Lessons from PISA for the United States* (pp. 117–135). Paris, France: Author. doi:10.1787/9789264096660-6-en

Olds, D. L. (2002). Prenatal and infancy home visiting by nurses: From randomized control trials to community replication. *Prevention Science, 3,* 153–172.

Overton, W. F. (2013). A new paradigm for developmental science: Relationism and relational-developmental systems. *Applied Developmental Science, 17*(2), 94–107.

Panter-Brick, C., & Leckman, J. F. (2013). Editorial commentary: Resilience in child development–interconnected pathways to wellbeing. *Journal of Child Psychology and Psychiatry, 54*(4), 333–336.

Parsai, M. B., Castro, F. G., Marsiglia, F. F., Harthun, M. L., & Valdez, H. (2011). Using community based participatory research to create a culturally grounded intervention for parents and youth to prevent risky behaviors. *Prevention Science, 12*(1), 34–47.

Paton, D., Parkes, B., Daly, M., & Smith, L. (2008). Fighting the flu: Developing sustained community resilience and preparedness. *Health Promotion Practice, 9*(4 Suppl.), 45S–53S.

Patterson, G. R., Forgatch, M. S., & DeGarmo, D. S. (2010). Cascading effects following intervention. *Development and Psychopathology, 22*(4), 949–970.

Pianta, R. C. (1999). *Enhancing relationships between children and teachers.* Washington, DC: American Psychological Association.

Reich, J. W., Zautra, A. J., & Hall, J. S. (Eds.). (2010). *Handbook of adult resilience.* New York, NY: Guilford Press.

Ronka, A., Oravala, S., & Pulkinen, L. (2002). "I met this wife of mine and things got onto a better track": Turning points in risk development. *Journal of Adolescence, 25,* 47–63.

Russo, S. J., Murrough, J. W., Han, M.-H., Charney, D. S., & Nestler, E. J. (2012). Neurobiology of resilience. *Nature Neuroscience, 15*(11), 1475–1484.

Rutter, M. (1996). Transitions and turning points in developmental psychopathology: As applied to the age span between childhood and mid-adulthood. *International Journal of Behavioral Development, 19,* 603–626.

Rutter, M. (2007). Proceeding from observed correlation to causal inference: the use of natural experiments. *Perspectives on Psychological Science, 2*(4), 377–395.

Rutter, M. (2012). Resilience as a dynamic concept. *Development and Psychopathology, 24*(2), 335.

Sahlberg, P. (2007). Education policies for raising student learning: The Finnish approach. *Journal of Education Policy, 22*(2), 147–171.

Sahlberg, P. (2010). The secret to Finland's success: Educating teachers. *Stanford Center for Opportunity Policy in Education (Research Brief),* 1–8.

Sameroff, A. J. (1983). Developmental systems: Contexts and evolution. In P. H. Mussen & W. Kessen (Eds.), *Handbook of child psychology: Vol. 1. History, theory, methods* (pp. 237–294). New York, NY: Wiley.

Sandler, I., Schoenfelder, E., Wolchik, S., & MacKinnon, D. (2011). Long-term impact of prevention programs to promote effective parenting: Lasting effects but uncertain processes. *Annual Review of Psychology, 62,* 299.

Seifer, R., & Sameroff, A. J. (1987). Multiple determinants of risk and vulnerability. In E. J. Anthony & B. J. Cohler (Eds.), *The invulnerable child* (pp. 51–69). New York, NY: Guilford Press.

Seligman, M. E. P., & Csikszentmihalyi, M. (2000). Positive psychology: An introduction. *American Psychologist, 55,* 5–14.

Sherrieb, K., Norris, F. H., & Galea, S. (2010). Measuring capacities for community resilience. *Social Indicators Research, 99*(2), 227–247.

Sroufe, L. A., Egeland, B., & Kreutzer, T. (1990). The fate of early experience following developmental change: Longitudinal approaches to individual adaptation in childhood. *Child Development, 61,* 1363–1373.

Ungar, M., Ghazinour, M., & Richter, J. (2013). Annual research review: What is resilience within the social ecology of human development. *Journal of Child Psychology and Psychiatry, 54*(4), 348–366.

Välijärvi, J., & Sahlberg, P. (2008). Should "failing" students repeat a grade? Retrospective response from Finland. *Journal of Educational Change, 9*(4), 385–389.

Walsh, F. (2006). *Strengthening family resilience* (2nd ed.). New York, NY: Guilford Press.

Wright, M. O. D., Masten, A. S., & Narayan, A. J. (2013). Resilience processes in development: Four waves of research on positive adaptation in the context of adversity. *Handbook of resilience in children* (pp. 15–37). New York, NY: Springer.

Wyman, P. A., Sandler, I., Wolchik, S., & Nelson, K. (2000). Resilience as cumulative competence promotion and stress protection: Theory and intervention. In D. Cicchetti, J. Rappaport, I. Sandler, & R. P. Weissberg (Eds.), *The promotion of wellness in children and adolescents* (pp. 133–184). Washington, DC: Child Welfare League of America.

Yates, T. M., & Grey, I. K. (2012). Adapting to aging out: Profiles of risk and resilience among emancipated foster youth. *Development and Psychopathology, 24*, 475–492.

Yates, T. M., & Masten, A. S. (2004). The promise of resilience research for practice and policy. In T. Newman (Ed.), *What works? Building resilience: Effective strategies for child care services* (pp. 6–15). Ilford, England: Barnardo's.

Yoshikawa, H. (1994). Prevention as cumulative protection: Effects of early family support and education on chronic delinquency and its risks. *Psychological Bulletin, 115*(1), 28–54.

Zautra, A., Hall, J., & Murray, K. (2008). Community development and community resilience: An integrative approach. *Community Development, 39*(3), 130–147.

# PART XI

# SIGNPOSTS FOR THE PRACTICE OF POSITIVE PSYCHOLOGY

# CHAPTER 45

# The Role of Embodiment in Optimal Functioning

KATE HEFFERON

T
HE BODY MAY BE a "marvel of nature," but it is the one marvel of nature that we "least stop to observe" (Aldersey-Williams, 2013, p. xviii). This is no more so than within the area of positive psychology. Despite rapid growth and advancement over the past decade (Rusk & Waters, 2013; Wong, 2011), the body is still overlooked within positive psychology, which tends to be a "neck-up focused discipline" (Peterson, 2012; Seligman, 2008) preoccupied by cognitive and emotional phenomena. This lack of interest in the physical self has been a critique of positive psychology since its conception (Anderson, 2001; Resnick, Warmoth, & Serlin, 2001). Furthermore, most of what we do know about the body and its effects on well-being has been from a pathological perspective (e.g., anomalous bodily experiences, disorders of self-image; MacLachlan, 2004). Thus, the aim of this chapter is to introduce the concept of embodiment and to argue that positive psychology has an opportunity to go beyond this deficiency in research and practice toward a more holistic, embodied approach to human flourishing. Indeed, how we "treat our body; move our body; soothe our body; feed our body; dress our body; decorate our body and connect to our body, all have an impact on our hedonic and eudaimonic well being" (Hefferon, 2013, p. ix). First, I discuss the research area of embodied cognition and its effects on emotions and overall well-being. Second, I review research on the newly defined construct of positive body image (PBI) and how it impacts our subjective perceptions of flourishing. Finally, evidence-based embodied interventions that have been found to have a positive influence on our optimal human functioning are described.

## UNDERSTANDING EMBODIMENT

Embodiment is an area of research that has been dissected across many disciplines ranging from sociology to cognitive neuroscience (Kontra, Goldin-Meadow, & Beilock, 2012). Embodiment has been defined in various ways, with the consensus being that it is "an awareness of and responsiveness to bodily sensations" (Impett, Daubenmier, & Hirschman, 2006, p. 40) as well as the belief that "thoughts, feelings and behaviours are grounded in sensory experiences and bodily states" (Meier, Schnall, Schwartz, & Bargh, 2012, p. 2). Understanding our body's sensations and signals is imperative for self-knowledge, enhancing positive emotional experiences and psychological well-being (Anderson, 2006; Impett et al., 2006).

There are two approaches to embodiment: simple and radical. Simple embodiment adheres to the more cognitive scientific view of the body, stating that although the body plays an important role, it is just another "add on feature" (Meier et al., 2012, p. 7). The radical view, however, challenges this computation perspective, stating that the body, the brain, and the outer world are complexly intertwined. Thus, all mental processes are grounded in bodily experiences, and it is not possible to remove the mental processing from the body and the body from the self—it is the means of perception (Merleau-Ponty, 1964).

## EMBODIMENT AND WELL-BEING

Embodiment is important to positive psychology for two major reasons. First, the body and its physical state can have a significant effect on shaping our emotions, and second, the body plays an important role during social interactions and the perceived quality of relationships. We know this from the burgeoning field of *embodied cognition* that aims to assess how cognition is influenced by bodily states, actions, and the environment (Kontra et al., 2012) as well as how the perception of and thought processing of emotions involves "perceptual, somato-visceral and motor re-experiencing (collectively referred to as embodiment) of the relevant emotion in one's self" (Niedenthal, 2007, p. 1002). Thus, a significant amount of focus targets how people's body state (temperature, position, gestures, facial expressions) affects how they interpret their social and personal surroundings (e.g., interaction with others, emotions, etc.; Vacharkulksemsuk & Fredrickson, 2012).

To be sure, the area of hedonic well-being focuses heavily on the experience of positive emotions and their role in the pleasurable life (Diener, Suh, Lucas, & Smith, 1999). From the current research, there is evidence to support the role of the body (postures, gestures, and facial expressions) directly affecting the experience of positive mood, feelings of success, and achievement (Stepper & Strack, 1993; Strack, Martin, & Stepper, 1988) as well as anger (Chandler & Schwartz, 2009) and guilt (Rotella & Richeson, 2013; see Barsalou, Niedenthal, Barbey, & Ruppert, 2003). For example, manipulations of back posture during lab experiments (slumped versus straight) subsequently affected the interpretation of achievement scores such that individuals manipulated into straight condition reported better moods and more pride in their achievements than peers within the slumped category (Stepper & Strack, 1993). Researchers have also studied the links between physical and moral cleanliness (physical purity), with the act of washing one's hands reducing feelings of guilt and intensity of moral judgments (Schnall, Benton, & Harvey, 2008; Zhong & Liljenquist, 2006). Furthermore, embodiment can also influence the perception of duration of emotional experiences, such that individuals who are free to spontaneously imitate other persons' facial expressions (angry and happy) overestimate the duration of exposure to the stimuli relative to neutral stimuli (Effron, Niedenthal, Gil, & Droit-Volet, 2006).

The same embodied connections have been linked to simply thinking about emotions, such that when one is engaging in a task exposed to words that have direct and indirect associations with emotions, there is an immediate evoked embodied response within associated muscles, influencing subsequent personal judgments (Niedenthal, 2007; Niedenthal, Winkielman, Mondillon, & Vermeulen, 2009). The researchers argue that using stored emotional information requires embodiment. Furthermore, Foroni & Semin (2009) found increased activation in facial muscles when individuals read actions words for positive emotional expressions (e.g., smile) versus nonaction words (e.g., funny). These and several other body manipulation/emotion tasks have supported the argument that body states can have an influence on the subsequent attention and interpretation of emotions (Niedenthal, 2007).

EMBODIMENT AND INTRAPERSONAL RELATIONSHIPS

Body awareness is one of the key components to embodiment and refers to one's ability to correctly and confidently identify and engage with body sensations as well as link these sensations to emotions (Mehling et al., 2009). Although an overlooked area in positive psychology, the importance of body awareness has been touted across several domains and should be an additional component to the flourishing agenda. Body awareness can be broken down into four dimensions, including *perceived body sensation* (ability to correctly identify sensations); *attention quality* (willingness to engage with these sensations versus overlook them); *attitude* (level of trust in correct identification of sensations and use of these for adaptive future decision making); and *mind–body integration* (level of connection between sensations and emotions and overall embodiment; Mehling et al., 2009). Currently, the Body Awareness Questionnaire (BAQ; Shields, Mallory, & Simon, 1989) is the most widely used measurement tool within research and practice. Another tool is the Body Intelligence Scale (BIS), which aims to measure three different forms of body awareness (energy, comfort, and inner) that potentially contribute to wellness (Anderson, 2006).

Traditionally, heightened body awareness and identification of bodily sensations has been associated with maladaptive functioning within chronic physical and mental illness (e.g., pain, depression, eating disorders; Mehling et al., 2009, 2011). Despite an earlier pathological focus on body awareness, a new wave of research indicates the benefits of body awareness in relation to both hedonic and eudaimonic well-being (Anderson, 2006; Mehling et al., 2009). For example, Brani, Hefferon, Lomas, Ivtzan, and Painter (in press) found a predictive relationship between individuals' self-reported body awareness and subjective well-being (SWB; Diener et al., 1999) within the normal population. This was one of the first findings that suggested that individuals could benefit from becoming more body aware as a potential route to SWB.

From a more eudaimonic perspective, research has shown a link between trauma, the realization of mortality, and heighted body awareness (Frank, 2002; Meier et al., 2012). For example, my own work into embodiment and posttraumatic growth (PTG) has shown that the body plays an important role in the process and facilitation of PTG (Hefferon, 2012, 2013; Hefferon, Grealy, & Mutrie, 2008, 2009, 2010). PTG is the notion that through the struggle of adversity people may change in ways that propel them to higher levels of functioning (psychological, physical) than existed before the event occurred. Survivors can express several notable changes, including *perceived changes in self; improved relationships; changed life philosophy with increased existential awareness; changed priorities;* and *enhanced spiritual beliefs* (Calhoun, Tedeschi, Cann, & Hanks, 2010; see also Tedeschi, Calhoun, & Groleau, Chapter 30, this volume). Research shows that illness and physical trauma can lead to more corporeal awareness and the elimination of the taken-for-granted body (Frank, 1995; Hefferon, 2012; Hefferon et al., 2009, 2010). These corporeal circumstances can enable us to become more embodied and aware of our physical, psychological, and spiritual existence and awaken us to the here and now (Burkeman, 2012; Yalom, 2008). The mission for positive psychology is to learn how we can help individuals live more below their shoulders on an everyday basis, not only when trauma and illness occur.

In terms of future research and practice, positive psychologists could start to include measurement tools such as the BAQ (Shields, Mallory, & Simon, 1989) or BIS (Anderson, 2006) when researching interventions, (e.g., mindfulness meditation, yoga, etc.) as the development of interoceptive body awareness has been shown to improve via meditative practices (Mehling et al., 2009; Siegel, 2010). Similarly, those working in more therapeutic environments can take heed from practices such as body psychotherapy, which literally uses the body as a tool within its sessions, engaging in somatic exercises and encouraging the reconnection of body and mind.

## POSITIVE BODY IMAGE: A NEW FRONTIER FOR POSITIVE PSYCHOLOGY

There is one relationship that can arguably impact our well-being the most, and that is the relationship we have with our body (Cash & Smolak, 2011). This intrapersonal relationship (a.k.a. personal body image) is a notoriously complex construct that encompasses "self-perceptions and attitudes (i.e. thoughts feelings and behaviours) with regards to the body" (Avalos, Tylka, & Wood-Barcalow, 2005, p. 285) as well as "how people experience their own embodiment" (Cash, 2008, p. 1). Body image consists of several dimensions, including:

> *Perceptual*—how the body is pictured in one's own mind.
> *Affective*—the feelings one has about the body's appearance and function (pride and happiness vs. anxiety and shame).
> *Cognitive*—attitudes and thoughts about one's body (value placed on image and investment in appearance).
> *Behavioral*—how one displays outwardly his or her relationship with his or her body (e.g., revealing clothes).
> *Subjective satisfaction*—one's overall and specific satisfaction with her or his body and body parts (Martin-Ginis, Bassett, & Conlin, 2012).

Historically, the area of body image research has taken a pathological approach, focusing on the alleviation of body dissatisfaction. Through decades of study, there is strong evidence to link the presence of a negative body image with increased incidences of eating disorders, higher rates of depression, negative affect, social anxiety, lower confidence in relationships, and lower overall psychological well-being (Avalos et al., 2005; Swami, Begum, & Petrides, 2010).

Despite this previous pathological preoccupation, body image has been found to have both negative and positive features, and the absence of a negative body image does not necessitate a positive body image (Tylka, 2011). For example, not hating your body is not the same as "appreciating, respecting, celebrating and honouring the body" (Tylka, 2011, p. 63). Williams, Cash, and Santos (2004) further demonstrated that body image could be divided into three types—negative, positive, and neutral—with those displaying higher levels of PBI reporting higher levels of psychological and social well-being (e.g., optimism, self-esteem, and adaptive coping). Ultimately, a PBI begins with love and respect for the body. From this foundation, individuals can begin to appreciate the uniqueness of their body and its functionality. PBI is about (1) accepting the body and all its imperfections; (2) being aware of and focusing on assets of the body rather than on the negatives (protective filtering); (3) having a mindful connection with the body and the body's needs; (4) making a conscious effort to absorb positive information and reject or reframe negative information (Tylka, 2011; Wood-Barcalow, Tylka, & Augustus-Horvath, 2010); and (5) feeling "beautiful, comfortable, confident and happy with their body"

(Tylka, 2011, p. 58). Ultimately, people with a PBI are in tune with and mindful of their body's needs, listen to and respect their own bodies, and take care of them when needed.

There are several preconditions that have been identified as facilitators of PBI (Tylka, 2011), including (a) the experience of unconditional acceptance of who they are from loved ones; (b) a comprehension of media images (photo-shopping, lighting, etc.); (c) environments or cultures that broadly define beauty; (d) a belief in a higher power that creates all to be unique; and (e) surrounding themselves in a social circle that also has a PBI (Wood-Barcalow et al., 2010). The body appreciation scale (BAS) was developed to measure PBI and encompasses the aforementioned conditions, as well as including several other components, such as "(a) favourable opinions of the body (regardless of actual physical appearance); (b) acceptance of the body in spite of weight, body shape and imperfections; (c) respect of the body by attending to its needs and engaging in healthy behaviours; and (d) protection of the body by rejecting unrealistic body image portrayed in the media" (Avalos et al., 2005, p. 286). For young adolescents, PBI has been characterized by a functional view of the body and acceptance of imperfections as well as engagement in physical activity for the purpose of experiencing positive emotions and health benefits (Frisén & Holmqvist, 2010). Further inquiry by the same researchers found that adolescents who expressed having a PBI viewed appearance ideals via the media with criticality, as well as holding a flexible view of beauty (Holmqvist & Frisén, 2012).

Individuals with higher levels of PBI have been found to report several positive outcomes, such as intuitive eating, higher levels of self-esteem and optimism, adaptive coping, and better sexual functioning (Tiggemann & McCourt, 2013; Williams et al., 2004). However, as the area is very new, the research has predominantly been restricted to younger, female populations. Thus, there have been mixed and inconsistent results regarding gender differences within PBI as well as the degree to which ethnicity and culture can influence PBI (Swami, Hadji-Michael, & Furnham, 2008; Webb, Warren-Findlow, Chou, & Adams, 2013).

PROMOTING POSITIVE BODY IMAGE

Whilst recognizing that this area of research is still in its infancy, there are current suggestions from researchers on how to promote PBI within young adolescent and young adult populations. Ideally, successful programs should include a media literacy approach, where adolescents are taught lessons surrounding the tricks of the trade within media advertising, including airbrushing, photoshopping, external supports (e.g., tape, bras), and so on, as well as promoting critical discussion behind the motives of the media agencies. PBI programs can also consider using a feminist approach to ideals by providing adolescents with alternatives to the ideals of media advertising in order to enable a more flexible perception of beauty. This would also help adolescents to challenge the sexual objectification of the body and promote engagement in nonobjectifying activities (e.g., physical activity, yoga). Finally, administrators could include a focus on ways to enhance self-esteem and body image (including acceptance of weight and body shape) as well as strategies for healthy eating and exercise (McVey et al., 2010). Physical activity is also a fantastic way to become more embodied, increase positive body image, and enhance our subjective and psychological well-being (see Faulkner, Hefferon, & Mutrie, Chapter 12, this volume).

Within therapeutic environments, therapists can help individuals to not only eliminate their negative body image, but also enhance their positive body image via supporting the use of "protective filtering, interpersonal support, associating with and modelling others who are proud of their body and embracing an inclusive definition of beauty" (Tylka, 2011, p. 61). Furthermore, therapists should suggest activities that promote embodiment, body functionality, and body acceptance such as yoga or physical activity (LePage & Crowther, 2010; Tylka, 2011). It is important to note that people can still have bad body image days where they internalize negative information; however, it can be recorrected via the aforementioned facilities, particularly by reframing negative information.

As a final point, the future research between positive psychology and PBI is rife with possibility. For example, Swami et al. (2010) found a significant relationship between trait emotional intelligence (EI) scores and body appreciation in undergraduate females. More specifically, they found that the well-being factor (self-esteem, positive outlook, and subjective happiness) within the trait EI measurement tool significantly predicted body appreciation scores and actual-ideal weight discrepancy, suggesting that enhancing well-being may also enhance body appreciation. Furthermore, researchers could also employ the use of positive psychological interventions (PPIs; Sin & Lyubomirksy, 2009) to enhance PBI. For example, Geraghty, Wood, and Hyland (2010) found that the use of a daily gratitude diary for 2 weeks was as effective as the treatment as usual (monitoring and reframing) group in decreasing body dissatisfaction. Future research could test different PPIs or contextualize the PPIs to focus on enhancing PBI rather than simply decreasing body dissatisfaction. Finally, Avalos et al. (2005) affirm that the PBI area would benefit from investigation into specific character strengths (Peterson & Seligman, 2004) that prevent body image disturbances and/or promote body appreciation.

### Embodiment and Interpersonal Relationships

Not only are our bodies important for our intrapersonal relationships, they are crucial for creating and maintaining interpersonal connections. Over the past decade, one of the strongest findings from positive psychology is the relationship between social support, health, and overall well-being (Vacharkulksemsuk & Fredrickson, 2012). This connection has led to an increase in relationship science research (Fincham & Beach, 2010), which aims to understand how the quality of our interpersonal relationships (with both loved ones and strangers) influences our overall well-being. *Embodied social cognition* (e.g., simulation, mimicry, synchrony) enables us to not only think about what other humans might be thinking, but to actually experience their bodily states in order to give us a better insight into their intentions and needs (Cacioppo & Cacioppo, 2012). Embodied simulation is an area of research that claims that when we observe another carrying out actions, emotions, or even sensations (e.g., experiencing pain), the same associated bodily states are activated, creating an experience understanding of others (Gallese, 2006). For example, research has found that the same areas of the brain (anterior insula and anterior cingulate cortex) are activated when an individual personally experiences a disgusting smell as well as when she or he watches another person experiencing such a smell (Wicker et al., 2003). By physically simulating the experience, it is argued that we are better able to understand the intentions of others and better able to take the perspective of the person we are observing, thereby increasing levels of empathy. We are also able to feel the pain or touch of others, simply by watching others have the experience. This connection derived via embodied simulation can therefore help with the connection between strangers and other individuals.

Rapport is another concept within relationship science that has been studied in order to understand quality of interactions; however, rapport as a bodily experience has been underrepresented. Embodied rapport is shared feelings not just shared feelings of positivity and mutuality, but of vitality and aliveness (which stem from shared movements; Vacharkulksemsuk & Fredrickson, 2012). Embodied rapport can be achieved via *behavioral synchrony*, defined as "coordination of movement that occurs between individuals during a social interaction, featuring similarity of (1) form, the manner and style of movements and (2) time, the temporal rhythm of movements" (Vacharkulksemsuk & Fredrickson, 2012, p. 399). Synchrony is an important feature of interaction as it can create a sense of oneness as well as compassion, cooperation affiliation, emotional support satisfaction, and even elevated pain thresholds (Niedenthal, 2007). Researchers have also found that behavioral synchrony can mediate the direct effect of self-disclosure among strangers and enhance interaction quality (Vacharkulksemsuk & Fredrickson, 2012).

One of the most recent (and embodied) progressions in the area of positive psychology and relationship science is Fredrickson's new theory on love and positivity resonance (Fredrickson, 2013). Following on from her early research into positive emotions, Fredrickson has ascertained that love is a supreme emotion (more so than gratitude, joy, etc.) and is vital for flourishing. Fredrickson's theory of love is not reflective of the mainstream understanding of love (e.g., as a committed, long-lasting bond between two people, usually spouses or family members or friends). Instead, Fredrickson proposes love from a bodily perspective—as an embodied way of being. Love is momentary experiences that change the physiological nature of the two individuals experiencing micro-moments. Love, therefore, consists of three elements:

1. "A sharing of one or more positive emotions between you and another."
2. "A synchrony between you and the other person's biochemistry and behaviours."
3. "A reflective motive to invest in each other's well being that brings mutual care" (Fredrickson, 2013, p. 17).

Together, these three events are coined as *positivity resonance*, where individuals mirror each other and deepen the interpersonal resonance. However, in order for positivity resonance to occur, there must exist several preconditions, including perception of safety and sensory and temporal connection.

In sum, this theory of love is an embodied perspective—one in which your body and another body are imperative for connection to occur. Fredrickson argues that talking on the telephone, e-mailing, or not being in the physical presence of the other person inhibits love from occurring. From an applied perspective, preliminary research findings have linked the effects of loving kindness meditation interventions to increased experiences of positive emotions and physical health (e.g., increased activation of the vagus nerve; Kok et al., 2013; Kok, Waugh, & Fredrickson, 2013). Ultimately, this new area is among the first positive psychological theories to prioritize the body as a main mechanism for well-being.

## BECOMING EMBODIED: PRACTICAL APPLICATIONS

There are wide individual differences in how much people are aware of their bodies (Nettleton & Watson, 1998). There are many evidence-based practices that can be used to enhance people's connections to their bodies (see Table 45.1). Furthermore,

**Table 45.1**
Body-Based Interventions (see Hefferon, 2013)

| Body-Based Interventions | Overview of Research and Applications |
| --- | --- |
| Body awareness therapies | • Enhancing a person's body awareness is at the heart of mind–body therapies (Mehling et al., 2011).<br>• Body psychotherapy posits that the body itself can be used as a tool for healing and well-being.<br>• Body awareness therapies use several body-based interventions (e.g., body diary) so clients can learn to make friends with their body, emotions, and associated sensations (Rothschild, 2000). |
| Physical activity | • Physical activity is a fantastic way to become more embodied, increase positive body image, and enhance our subjective and psychological well-being (see Faulkner, Hefferon, & Mutrie, Chapter 12, this volume).<br>• Physical activity should be incorporated into most well-being programs in order to create a more embodied approach to flourishing. |
| Yoga | • Yoga is one of the most renowned mind–body exercises, which promotes engagement with body sensations and awareness (Impett et al., 2006).<br>• Engagement can increase positive mood, energy, satisfaction, confidence, mindfulness, self-compassion, sleep quality, and overall quality of life.<br>• Yoga can also decrease stress, anxiety, anger, depression, and back pain and reduce the experience of symptoms of clinical treatments (e.g., cancer; Field, 2011).<br>• Increased frequency of yoga engagement increases levels of embodiment (body awareness + body responsiveness), positive affect, and satisfaction with life and reduces negative affect and body objectification (Impett et al., 2006).<br>• Embodiment may be a key mediator between yoga and well-being. |
| Mindfulness | • Mindfulness-based interventions have also been at the forefront of embodiment therapies and can enhance PBI (Cash, 2008).<br>• Mindfulness aims to connect the body and the mind, using several body-based techniques in order to reassociate people with their bodily sensations (Hanson & Mendius, 2009).<br>• The body scan asks individuals find a quiet place and run through a body scan of sensations, temperatures, and pressures throughout the body.<br>• The purpose of the body scan is not necessarily for relaxation, but to heighten the connection and attention to the body and its sensations. |
| Progressive muscle relaxation (PMR) | • PMR is a well-studied and utilized form of relaxation training that involves the systematic tensing and relaxation of isolated muscles over a period of time (Manzoni, Pagnini, Castelnuovo, & Molinari, 2008).<br>• The aim is to learn how to relax tensed muscles that can be associated with anxiety (Jacobsen, 1938).<br>• The process is similar to the body scan except instead of simply noting sensations, individuals are asked to tense a chosen muscle for approximately 10 seconds and then relax for 20 seconds.<br>• They are then asked to note the difference in body sensation, from tense to relaxed, and then repeat on all major muscle groups. |

**Table 45.1**
*(Continued)*

| Body-Based Interventions | Overview of Research and Applications |
| --- | --- |
| Touch | • As embodied humans, touch with and by others is imperative for optimal functioning (Gallace, 2012; Weiss, Wilson, & Morrison, 2004).<br>• Society is becoming less and less tactile, perpetuating a sense of touch hunger, which is arguably having a very real, negative effect (Field, 2001).<br>• Touch, whether from strangers or loved ones, can influence people's perceptions of trust, intimacy, and overall relational interactions (Gallace, 2012).<br>• Individuals derive a great deal of joy and contentment, as well as reduced stress, from physical interaction with others (Grewen, Anderson, Girdler, & Light, 2003; Grewen, Girdler, Amico, & Light, 2005; Light, Grewen, & Amico, 2005).<br>• Researchers are now focusing on the role of oxytocin (a peptide molecule found in the brain and released when touched), well-being, and social bonding.<br>• Higher levels of oxytocin have been linked to enhanced trust and emotional support within couples as well as increased positive affect and reduced stress, fear, and anxiety (Carter, 2009; Rasmussen & Pressman, 2009). |
| Nutrition | • The role of diet and nutrition in optimal functioning has been overlooked within positive psychology.<br>• Diets full of whole foods (e.g., vegetable, fish, fruits) have been found to predict lower levels of depression 5 years later (Akbaraly et al., 2009) and Mediterranean diets have been found to enhance energy, vigor, and contentment, even after short interventions (10 days; McMillan, Owen, Kras, & Scholey, 2011).<br>• Blanchflower, Oswald, and Stewart-Brown (2012) reported a link between well-being (across a range of measures) and the consumption of fruit and vegetables, indicating seven pieces as the optimal portion size.<br>• White, Horwath, and Conner (2013) conducted a microlongitudinal, correlational design using diaries to assess the effects of diet on positive and negative affect on young adults.<br>• Participants reported higher positive affect on the days where they ate more fruits and vegetables and this predicted their positive mood the following day.<br>• Similar to Blanchflower et al. (2012), they reported that seven to eight servings were the optimal dosage for notable change. |

the main evidence-based PPIs—*gratitude* (letter, counting blessings), *random acts of kindness, cultivating strengths, visualizing best possible selves,* and *meditation* (mindfulness, loving kindness)—can be manipulated to incorporate more corporeal elements to them, thereby providing more opportunity to enhance personality/activity fit (see Table 45.2 for theoretical manipulations and suggestions). Offering individuals variety and choice, from a suite of both cognitive and physical (embodied) interventions, will help support the person in sustaining his or her efforts to attain and maintain well-being (Lyubomirksy & Layous, 2013). Furthermore, with current positive psychology research implementation findings proclaiming the use of varied

**Table 45.2**
Embodied Adaptations to the Main Positive Psychological Interventions

| Intervention | Embodied Adaptation |
| --- | --- |
| Gratitude | For 1 week, individuals are asked to write down three things that they are grateful for in relation to body functionality (what their body did well). If desired, participants can reflect on other aspects they are grateful for that are connected to PBI (e.g., support system, uniqueness; see Holmqvist & Frisén, 2012). |
| Best Possible Self | Individuals can adapt this writing exercise in many ways. First, they can focus on writing about a best possible embodied self (e.g., future aspirations about activity levels, health, body awareness, etc.). Second, participants can engage in this exercise by utilizing embodied writing techniques, which challenge participants to write from the inside out (see Anderson, 2001). |
| Random Acts of Kindness | On 1 day this week, individuals are asked to commit five different random acts of kindness where they explicitly set up the environment for the possibility of positivity resonance (see Fredrickson, 2013). |
| Character Strengths | For 1 week, individuals are asked to use their top five strengths in order to manipulate their physical activity routine. For example, if a top strength is love and be loved, they can try to join an exercise class with a friend, thereby supporting their need for connection. If one of the top strengths is spirituality, they can move their activity outdoors to be closer to nature (see Hefferon & Mutrie, 2012). |
| Mindfulness | This exercise asks participants to move away from viewing their body as something to objectify. Over the next week, individuals are asked to take 10 minutes out to engage in a body scan, connecting sensations to emotions and increasing body awareness (see Cash, 2008). |

and multimodal methods of delivery, there is a tremendous amount of potential for a new wave of embodied positive psychological interventions (Layous, Nelson, & Lyubomirksy, 2012).

## CONCLUSION

In conclusion, the aim of the chapter was to introduce embodiment research and urge positive psychologists to reconceptualize wellness beyond the cognitive and emotional to include the body. Positive psychology is defined as the "scientific study of virtue, meaning, resilience and well being, as well as evidence based applications to improve the life of individual's and society in the totality of life" (Wong, 2011, p. 72). The task of improving the lives of individuals becomes unfeasible if those we are trying to understand do not and cannot make sense of and connect to their own bodies. Areas of research such as embodied cognition, positive body image, and body-based interventions redirect the focus of positive psychology from a neck-up discipline to a more holistic and embodied approach.

## SUMMARY POINTS

- The body plays a crucial role in our ability to experience both hedonic and eudaimonic well-being.
- It is essential for positive psychology to start thinking about well-being from a wider perspective, one that includes the body not as an add-on feature but as part of the overall experience of well-being.

- Embodiment can be integrated in many current positive psychological topics, such as emotion research and relationship science.
- PPIs should contain somatic and visceral components (e.g., body awareness), which will encourage an understanding of the body and its impact on well-being.
- Traditional PPIs can be adapted from their original structure to include more embodied features.
- Additional research is needed into the mechanisms by which the body plays a role in the interpretation of emotions.
- Further neurological research is needed to understand the connections between embodied social cognition and emotions (e.g., empathy).
- Research is needed within the area of embodiment after trauma and the link between the taken-for-granted body, corporeal awareness, and gratitude.

## REFERENCES

Akbaraly, T. N., Brunner, E. J., Ferrie, J. E., Marmot, M. G., Kivimaki, M., & Singh-Manoux, A. (2009). Dietary pattern and depressive symptoms in middle age. *British Journal of Psychiatry, 195*(5), 408–413.

Aldersey-Williams, H. (2013). *Anatomies: The human body, its parts and the stories they tell*. London, UK: Penguin Press.

Anderson, R. (2001). Embodied writing and reflections on embodiment. *Journal of Transpersonal Psychology, 33*(2), 83–98.

Anderson, R. (2006). Body intelligence scale: Defining and measuring the intelligence of the body. *The Humanistic Psychologist, 34*(4), 357–367.

Avalos, L., Tylka, T. L., & Wood-Barcalow, N. (2005). The body appreciation scale: Development and psychometric evaluation. *Body Image, 2*(3), 285–297.

Barsalou, L. W., Niedenthal, P. M., Barbey, A. K., & Ruppert, J. A. (2003). Social embodiment. *Psychology of Learning and Motivation, 43*, 43–92.

Blanchflower, D. G., Oswald, A. J., & Stewart-Brown, S. (2012). Is psychological well-being linked to the consumption of fruit and vegetables? *Social Indicators Research*, 1–17.

Brani, O., Hefferon, K., Lomas, T., Ivtzan, I. & Painter, J. (in press). The impact of body awareness on subjective wellbeing: The role of mindfulness. *International Journal of Body Psychotherapy*.

Burkeman, O. (2012). *The antidote: Happiness for people who can't stand positive thinking*. London, England: Cannongate.

Cacioppo, S., & Cacioppo, J. T. (2012). Decoding the invisible forces of social connections. *Frontiers in Integrative Neuroscience, 6*, 1–7.

Calhoun, L. G., Tedeschi, R. G., Cann, A., & Hanks, E. A. (2010). Positive outcomes following bereavement: Paths to posttraumatic growth. *Psychologica Belgica, 50* (1–2), 125–143.

Carter, S. (2009). Oxytocin. In S. Lopez (Ed.), *The encyclopedia of positive psychology* (pp. 38–40). Chichester, England: Blackwell.

Cash, T. F. (2004). Body image: Past, present, and future. *Body Image, 1*(1), 1–5.

Cash, T. F. (2008). *The body image workbook: An 8-step program for learning to like your looks* (2nd ed.). Oakland, CA: New Harbinger.

Cash, T. F., & Smolak, L. (Eds.). (2011). *Body image: A handbook of science, practice, and prevention* (2nd ed.). New York, NY: Guilford Press.

Chandler, J., & Schwarz, N. (2009). How extending your middle finger affects your perception of others: Learned movements influence concept accessibility. *Journal of Experimental Social Psychology, 45*(1), 123–128.

Diener, E., Suh, E. M., Lucas, R. E., & Smith, H. L. (1999). Subjective well-being: Three decades of progress. *Psychological Bulletin, 125*(2), 276.

Effron, D. A., Niedenthal, P. M., Gil, S., & Droit-Volet, S. (2006). Embodied temporal perception of emotion. *Emotion, 6*(1), 1–9.

Field, T. (2001). *Touch.* Cambridge, MA: MIT Press.

Field, T. (2011). Yoga clinical research review. *Complementary Therapies in Clinical Practice, 17*(1), 1–8.

Fincham, F. D., & Beach, S. R. (2010). Of memes and marriage: Toward a positive relationship science. *Journal of Family Theory & Review, 2*(1), 4–24.

Foroni, F., & Semin, G. R. (2009). Language that puts you in touch with your bodily feelings: The multimodal responsiveness of affective expressions. *Psychological Science, 20*(8), 974–980.

Frank, A. W. (1995). *The wounded storyteller: Body, illness and ethics.* London, England: University of Chicago Press.

Frank, A. W. (2002). *At the will of the body: Reflections on illness.* New York, NY: Mariner Books.

Fredrickson, B. L. (2013). *Love: 2.0.* New York, NY: Hudson Street Press.

Frisén, A., & Holmqvist, K. (2010). What characterizes early adolescents with a positive body image? A qualitative investigation of Swedish girls and boys. *Body Image, 7*(3), 205–212.

Gallace, A. (2012). Living with touch. *The Psychologist, 25*(12), 896–899.

Gallese, V. (2006). Embodied simulation: From mirror neuron systems to interpersonal relations. In Novartis Foundation (Ed.), *Empathy and fairness* (pp. 3–12). Chichester, UK: Wiley.

Geraghty, A. W., Wood, A. M., & Hyland, M. E. (2010). Attrition from self-directed interventions: Investigating the relationship between psychological predictors, intervention content and dropout from a body dissatisfaction intervention. *Social Science & Medicine, 71*(1), 30–37.

Grewen, K. M., Anderson, B. J., Girdler, S. S., & Light, K. C. (2003). Warm partner contact is related to lower cardiovascular reactivity. *Behavioral Medicine, 29*(3), 123–130.

Grewen, K. M., Girdler, S. S., Amico, J., & Light, K. C. (2005). Effects of partner support on resting oxytocin, cortisol, norepinephrine, and blood pressure before and after warm partner contact. *Psychosomatic Medicine, 67*(4), 531–538.

Hanson, R., & Mendius, R. (2009). *Buddha's brain: The practical neuroscience of happiness, love, and wisdom.* Oakland, CA: New Harbinger.

Hefferon, K. (2012). Bringing back the body into positive psychology: The theory of corporeal posttraumatic growth in breast cancer survivorship. *Psychology, 3,* 12, 1238–1242.

Hefferon, K. (2013). *Positive psychology and the body: The somatopsychic side to flourishing.* London, England: McGraw-Hill.

Hefferon, K., Grealy, M., & Mutrie, N. (2008). The perceived influence of an exercise class intervention on the process and outcomes of posttraumatic growth. *Journal of Mental Health and Physical Activity, 1*(2), 47–88.

Hefferon, K., Grealy, M., & Mutrie, N. (2009). Posttraumatic growth and life threatening physical illness: A systematic review of the qualitative literature. *British Journal of Health Psychology, 14*(2), 343–378.

Hefferon, K., Grealy, M., & Mutrie, N. (2010). Transforming from cocoon to butterfly: The potential role of the body in the process of posttraumatic growth. *Journal of Humanistic Psychology, 50*(2), 224–247.

Hefferon, K., & Mutrie, N. (2012). Physical activity as a "stellar" positive psychology intervention. In E. Acevedo (Ed.), *Oxford handbook of exercise psychology* (pp. 117–128). Oxford, England: Oxford University Press.

Holmqvist, K., & Frisén, A. (2012). "I bet they aren't that perfect in reality": Appearance ideals viewed from the perspective of adolescents with a positive body image. *Body Image, 9*(3), 388–395.

Impett, E. A., Daubenmier, J. J., & Hirschman, A. L. (2006). Minding the body: Yoga, embodiment, and well-being. *Sexuality Research & Social Policy, 3*(4), 39–48.

Jacobson, E. (1938). *Progressive relaxation*. Chicago, IL: University of Chicago Press.

Kok, B. E., Coffey, K. A., Cohn, M. A., Catalino, L. I., Vacharkulksemsuk, T., Algoe, S. B., & Fredrickson, B. L. (2013). How positive emotions build physical health perceived positive social connections account for the upward spiral between positive emotions and vagal tone. *Psychological Science, 24*(7), 1123–1132.

Kok, B. E., Waugh, C. E., & Fredrickson, B. L. (2013). Meditation and health: The search for mechanisms of action. *Social and Personality Psychology Compass, 7*(1), 27–39.

Kontra, C., Goldin Meadow, S., & Beilock, S. L. (2012). Embodied learning across the life span. *Topics in Cognitive Science, 4*(4), 731–739.

Layous, K., Nelson, S. K., & Lyubomirsky, S. (2012). What is the optimal way to deliver a positive activity intervention? The case of writing about one's best possible selves. *Journal of Happiness Studies, 14*(12), 1–20.

LePage, M., & Crowther, J. (2010). The effects of exercise on body satisfaction and affect. *Body Image, 7*, 124–130.

Light, K. C., Grewen, K. M., & Amico, J. A. (2005). More frequent partner hugs and higher oxytocin levels are linked to lower blood pressure and heart rate in premenopausal women. *Biological Psychology, 69*(1), 5–21.

Lyubomirsky, S., & Layous, K. (2013). How do simple positive activities increase well-being? *Current Directions in Psychological Science, 22*(1), 57–62.

MacLachlan, M. (2004). *Embodiment: Clinical, critical and cultural perspectives on health and illness.* New York, NY: Open University Press.

Manzoni, G., Pagnini, F., Castelnuovo, G., & Molinari, E. (2008). Relaxation training for anxiety: A ten years systematic review with meta-analysis. *BMC Psychiatry, 8*, 41.

Martin-Ginis, K., Bassett, R., & Conlin, C. (2012). Body image and exercise. In E. Acevedo (Ed.), *The Oxford handbook of exercise psychology* (pp. 55–75). New York, NY: Oxford University Press.

McMillan, L., Owen, L., Kras, M., & Scholey, A. (2011). Behavioural effects of a 10-day Mediterranean diet. *Appetite, 56*(1), 143–147.

McVey, G. L., Kirsh, G., Maker, D., Walker, K. S., Mullane, J., Laliberte, M., . . . Banks, L. (2010). Promoting positive body image among university students: A collaborative pilot study. *Body Image, 7*(3), 200–204.

Mehling, W. E., Gopisetty, V., Daubenmier, J., Price, C. J., Hecht, F. M., & Stewart, A. (2009). Body awareness: construct and self-report measures. *PLoS One, 4*(5), e5614.

Mehling, W. E., Wrubel, J., Daubenmier, J. J., Price, C. J., Kerr, C. E., Silow, T., . . . Stewart, A. L. (2011). Body Awareness: A phenomenological inquiry into the common ground of mind-body therapies. *Philosophy, Ethics, and Humanities in Medicine, 6*(1), 1–12.

Meier, B. P., Schnall, S., Schwarz, N., & Bargh, J. A. (2012). Embodiment in social psychology. *Topics in Cognitive Science, 4*(4), 705–716.

Merleau-Ponty, M. (1964). *The phenomenology of perception*. New York, NY: Routledge.

Nettleton, S., & Watson, J. (1998). *The body in everyday life*. London, England: Routledge.

Niedenthal, P. M. (2007). Embodying emotion. *Science, 316*(5827), 1002–1005.

Niedenthal, P. M., Winkielman, P., Mondillon, L., & Vermeulen, N. (2009). Embodiment of emotion concepts. *Journal of Personality and Social Psychology, 96*(6), 1120.

Peterson, C. (2012). *Pursuing the good life: 100 reflections on positive psychology*. New York, NY: Oxford University Press.

Peterson, C., & Seligman, M. (2004). *Character strengths and virtues: A handbook and classification*. New York, NY: Oxford University Press.

Rasmussen, H., & Pressman, S. (2009). Physical health. In S. Lopez (Ed.), *The encyclopedia of positive psychology* (pp. 695–701). Chichester, England: Blackwell.

Resnick, S., Warmoth, A., & Serlin, I. A. (2001). The humanistic psychology and positive psychology connection: Implications for psychotherapy. *Journal of Humanistic Psychology, 41*(1), 73–101.

Rotella, K. N., & Richeson, J. A. (2013). Body of guilt: Using embodied cognition to mitigate backlash to reminders of personal & ingroup wrongdoing. *Journal of Experimental Social Psychology, 49*, 643–650.

Rothschild, B. (2000). *The body remembers*. New York, NY: Norton.

Rusk, R. D., & Waters, L. E. (2013). Tracing the size, reach, impact, and breadth of positive psychology. *Journal of Positive Psychology, 8*(3), 207–221.

Schnall, S., Benton, J., & Harvey, S. (2008). With a clean conscience cleanliness reduces the severity of moral judgments. *Psychological Science, 19*(12), 1219–1222.

Siegel, D. (2010). *Mindsight: The new science of personal transformation*. New York, NY: Random House.

Seligman, M. E. (2008). Positive health. *Applied Psychology, 57*(s1), 3–18.

Shields, S. A., Mallory, M. E., & Simon, A. (1989). The body awareness questionnaire: Reliability and validity. *Journal of Personality Assessment, 53*(4), 802–815.

Sin, N. L., & Lyubomirsky, S. (2009). Enhancing well-being and alleviating depressive symptoms with positive psychology interventions: A practice-friendly meta-analysis. *Journal of Clinical Psychology, 65*, 467–487.

Stepper, S., & Strack, F. (1993). Proprioceptive determinants of emotional and nonemotional feelings. *Journal of Personality and Social Psychology, 64*(2), 211.

Strack, F., Martin, L., & Stepper, S. (1988). Inhibiting and facilitating conditions in the human smile: A non-obtrusive test of facial feedback hypothesis. *Journal of Personality and Social Psychology, 54*, 768–777.

Swami, V., Begum, S., & Petrides, K. V. (2010). Associations between trait emotional intelligence, actual–ideal weight discrepancy, and positive body image. *Personality and Individual Differences, 49*(5), 485–489.

Swami, V., Hadji-Michael, M., & Furnham, A. (2008). Personality and individual difference correlates of positive body image. *Body Image, 5*(3), 322–325.

Tiggemann, M., & McCourt, A. (2013). Body appreciation in adult women: Relationships with age and body satisfaction. *Body Image, 10*(4), 624–627.

Tylka, T. L. (2011). Positive psychology perspectives on body image. *Body image: A handbook of science, practice, and prevention* (2nd ed., pp. 56–64). New York, NY: Guilford Press.

Vacharkulksemsuk, T., & Fredrickson, B. L. (2012). Strangers in sync: Achieving embodied rapport through shared movements. *Journal of Experimental Social Psychology, 48*(1), 399–402.

Webb, J. B., Warren-Findlow, J., Chou, Y. Y., & Adams, L. (2013). Do you see what I see? An exploration of inter-ethnic ideal body size comparisons among college women. *Body Image, 10*(3), 369–379.

Weiss, W., Wilson, P., & Morrison, D. (2004). Maternal tactile stimulation and the neurodevelopment of low birth weight infants. *Infancy, 5*, 85–107.

White, B. A., Horwath, C. C., & Conner, T. S. (2013). Many apples a day keep the blues away—Daily experiences of negative and positive affect and food consumption in young adults. *British Journal of Health Psychology, 18*, 782–798.

Wicker, B., Keysers, C., Plailly, J., Royet, J. P., Gallese, V., & Rizzolatti, G. (2003). Both of us disgusted in my insula: The common neural basis of seeing and feeling disgust. *Neuron, 40*(3), 655–664.

Williams, E. F., Cash, T. F., & Santos, M. T. (2004). *Positive and negative body image: Precursors, correlates and consequences*. Paper presented at the 38th annual meeting of the Association for Advancement of Behaviour Therapy, New Orleans, LA.

Wong, P. T. (2011). Positive psychology 2.0: Towards a balanced interactive model of the good life. *Canadian Psychology/Psychologie Canadienne, 52*(2), 69–81.

Wood-Barcalow, N. L., Tylka, T. L., & Augustus-Horvath, C. L. (2010). "But I like my body": Positive body image characteristics and a holistic model for young-adult women. *Body Image*, 7(2), 106–116.

Yalom, I. (2008). *Staring at the sun: Overcoming the terror of death*. London, England: Piatkus Books.

Zhong, C. B., & Liljenquist, K. (2006). Washing away your sins: Threatened morality and physical cleansing. *Science*, 313(5792), 1451–1452.

# CHAPTER 46

# The Uneasy—and Necessary—Role of the Negative in Positive Psychology

BRIAN G. PAUWELS

T THE MOST GENERAL LEVEL, this chapter argues that from its inception, positive psychology has had a substantial negative core that at various points has clouded positive psychology's definition while also modifying and challenging the field in important ways. Organized into two broad sections, this chapter first examines positive psychology's definition and the extent to which negative phenomena have historically been included in it. The second section discusses how negative phenomena continue to confront positive psychology, suggesting possible modifications for its future. This second section specifically addresses work on (a) the role of negative emotions in coping with, and potentially growing from, traumatic events; (b) the importance of context as illustrated by recent challenges to attempts at characterizing certain psychological traits or processes as inherently positive; and (c) how students' unpleasant emotions in the educational process might be integrated more thoroughly into a positive psychology approach to education. Many of the issues in the chapter have been previously addressed to some extent by those inside and outside positive psychology. The chapter draws substantially upon and benefits greatly from these efforts (e.g., Held, 2002, 2004, 2005; Kristjánsson, 2010, 2012; Lazarus, 2003a, 2003b; Linley, Joseph, Harrington, & Wood, 2006; McNulty & Fincham, 2012; Norem & Chang, 2002; E. Taylor, 2001) and in part attempts to assemble in one place critiques that underscore the challenges still confronting positive psychology.

Numerous traits, institutions, outcomes, emotions, and psychological processes are studied under positive psychology's umbrella, resulting in a field so complex that even the task of marking its boundaries is a topic of study (e.g., Hart & Sasso, 2011; Yen, 2010). However, Linley et al. (2006) do offer a set of distinctions, or levels of analysis, that may help inform a discussion regarding negative phenomena's place in this endeavor.

First, and of lesser concern for the present chapter, Linley et al. (2006) note that positive psychologists may study the "wellsprings" (p. 7) or antecedent factors such

The author gratefully acknowledges Sabrina Plouzek for her assistance in the preparation of this chapter.

as genetics and environmental influences in early life that ultimately contribute to individuals' happiness, well-being, virtues, and strengths.

Second, positive psychologists may study "processes," which are "those psychological ingredients (for example, strengths and virtues) that lead to the good life, or equally the obstacles to leading a good life" (Linley et al., 2006, p. 7). This level of analysis includes a wide range of variables that can help facilitate desirable, positive outcomes or, alternatively, impede progress toward such outcomes. To illustrate, a given trait such as optimism may be a psychological ingredient that in one context can contribute to the good life (e.g., optimism can enable better coping with disease), and in another context impede that good life (e.g., optimism may promote reckless investment strategies). As noted later in the discussion of context, McNulty and Fincham (2012) argue that evidence shows "psychological traits and processes are not inherently positive or negative" (p. 101), but can be viewed as such only with reference to precise circumstances.

Third, Linley et al. (2006) identify "mechanisms" of positive psychology as "those extra-psychological factors that facilitate (or impede) the pursuit of a good life" (p. 7) and can include "personal and social relationships, working environments, organizations and institutions" (p.7), a category that extends more broadly to include social, economic, and other macro-level systems. Thus, *mechanisms* might be regarded as the context(s), both immediate and distal, in which the psychological ingredients such as traits, virtues, strengths, psychological tendencies, and so on, operate. Such contexts may moderate how beneficial a given trait or psychological process actually turns out to be for that individual.

The fourth level of analysis is that of positive "outcomes," which are the "subjective, social, and cultural states that characterize a good life" (Linley et al., 2006, p. 8). These are end points or goals that positive psychologists intentionally seek to promote via an understanding of the wellsprings, processes, and mechanisms that contribute to them. They may include subjective states such as happiness or well-being, interpersonal states such as communities, or public policies that "promote harmony and sustainability" (p. 8).

The authors offer this framework not as an inflexible, unchanging classification for all the variables positive psychologists may address. In contrast, for a given study, a particular variable may serve as a process, a mechanism (i.e., context), or an outcome. Thus *happiness* might be conceived of as an outcome to be facilitated for its own sake, or it may be regarded as a mechanism that contributes to other desired outcomes (Linley et al., 2006). The framework's value for incorporating negative phenomena within positive psychology is that it encourages researchers to be explicit regarding the negative phenomenon's relationship to other constructs being studied. For example, *worry* may be conceptualized in a given study as an outcome to be avoided or minimized, or alternatively as a psychological process that in particular circumstances allows some individuals to prepare more effectively for future challenges (e.g., see Norem & Chang, 2002, on defensive pessimism). In the chapter's second half, the importance of distinguishing between processes (i.e., psychological ingredients), mechanisms (i.e., contexts), and outcomes is illustrated in discussions of research on relationships (e.g., McNulty & Fincham, 2012), the consequences of cultural endorsement of extroversion (e.g., Cain, 2013), and the role of negative emotion in education. The general point is that as positive psychology gradually incorporates the negative into its enterprise, understanding how the positive and the negative aspects relate to each other will require more deliberate explication of these relationships, benefiting both individual studies and the field as a whole.

# THE HAZY PLACE OF THE NEGATIVE IN POSITIVE PSYCHOLOGY

Negative aspects of human experience have occupied a shifting position within positive psychology's often hazy boundaries, reflecting ambiguity regarding whether its definition should include topics such as anxiety, loss, and coping. Although numerous advocates of positive psychology explicitly acknowledge the value of studying the so-called negative topics, whether these topics are properly considered inside or outside the field has never been clearly resolved.

## Prioritizing the Positive for Its Own Sake

Some early proponents defined positive psychology's purview as distinct from the negative, arguing that psychology had traditionally pursued a disease or pathology model that, while illuminating how people experience adversity, had offered relatively little regarding their pursuit of happiness and flourishing once freed of dire circumstances (e.g., Seligman & Csikszentmihalyi, 2000; Sheldon & King, 2001). In this view, positive psychology's primary purpose was to address this deficit while rightfully acknowledging past efforts. As Folkman and Moskowitz (2003) put it,

> Those who advocate the study of positive aspects of psychology do not intend that it replace concern with its negative aspects. What appears to be an overemphasis may instead be indicative of a catch-up phase for an area that has been underemphasized in recent years. (p. 121)

Such a position provided a clear vision for this new set of priorities. Csikszentmihalyi (2003), referring to his and his collaborators' pioneering efforts, provides one of the strongest statements for studying the positive relatively independently of the negative:

> Basically, we intended to do our best to legitimize the study of positive aspects of human experience in their own right—not just as tools for prevention, coping, health, or some other desirable outcome. We felt that as long as hope, courage, optimism, and joy are viewed simply as useful in reducing pathology, we will never go beyond the homeostatic point of repose and begin to understand those qualities that make life worth living in the first place. (pp. 113–114)

Positive psychology would therefore advocate for deliberately studying human happiness and prosperity in and of itself. Still, some early evaluations of positive psychology expressed concern that although such an effort may be valuable, the movement had failed to appreciate how the most meaningful positive aspects of life are frequently inspired by negative circumstances, suggesting that attempts to separate the positive from the negative may be counterproductive (e.g., Harvey & Pauwels, 2003; Lazarus, 2003a).

## The Boundary Blurs

Emphasis on studying the positive in its own right, if not entirely new (e.g., Ryff, 2003; E. Taylor, 2001), provided momentum for those seeking to understand the positive without necessarily anchoring their work in the negative. However, the boundary between positive and negative proved to be diffuse, as various lines of research initially included under the positive psychology umbrella had roots in the study of pathology and adversity. For example, in the January 2000 issue of *American Psychologist* that helped launch positive psychology, several articles engaged at length with presumably negative topics. These include coping strategies and defenses to alleviate distress (Vaillant, 2000), the role of optimism and feelings of personal control in inhibiting physical disease (S. E. Taylor, Kemeny, Reed, Bower, & Gruenewald, 2000), and how considerable distress can result when individuals are overwhelmed by choice (Schwartz, 2000). Commenting on much of the early literature, Held (2004, 2005) noted that while some proponents strongly advocate an apparent separation of the positive and the negative, contributions from those writing under the auspices of positive psychology often illustrated to varying degrees the importance of including negative phenomena. Such scholars demonstrated what Held (2004) termed a "second-wave/nondominant message" (p. 15) that incorporates negative experiences and emotions into positive psychology, and by doing so highlights the limitations of a psychology that attempts to separate the positive from the negative (Held, 2004, 2005). Thus, the practice of positive psychology was perhaps at odds with some of its advocates' intentions, as at least in some circles it continued to study the negative alongside the positive.

## Explicit Calls for Integration

As positive psychology evolved, some proponents, such as the editors of this volume's first edition, explicitly called for integrating the positive and negative (Linley & Joseph, 2004). Similarly, in proposing a taxonomy for a revised, more balanced approach, Wong (2011, pp. 71–72) included as legitimate topics "bad living conditions" and "lack of resources" and "negative traits" such as despair and depression, further enlarging positive psychology's scope. Hames and Joiner (2011) called for comparable integration between positive psychology and the ostensibly negative field of experimental psychopathology.

Recommendations for an integrative positive psychology raise larger questions about its proper identity and purview. Positive psychology's advocates might emphasize that including such negative topics illustrates a movement that reflects life's difficult realities. Furthermore, such integration would build upon existing research traditions with foundations in negative topics, and therefore would constitute a strength (Harvey & Pauwels, 2003). However, some have argued that if positive psychology were to embrace the study of the negative, such a move would illustrate a lack of distinctiveness from psychology overall, and the very necessity of positive psychology would therefore have to be called into question (see Held, 2004, 2005; Kristjánsson, 2010).

## Should the Negative Be Included? Should We Care? Implications

Perhaps Lyubomirsky and Abbe (2003, p. 132) are correct in suggesting, "Debating what is truly positive and what is not, however, is not terribly productive." At one level, this is true—all new paradigms or movements necessarily have ambiguous boundaries as they incrementally determine which pursuits are more or less fruitful. However, positive psychology operates in the public eye more so than other endeavors, in part because of its potential relevance to that public. Such visibility has surely helped with garnering needed resources, but has also left it open to skepticism regarding what positive psychology has contributed, skepticism that may become more pointed if the field lacks a coherent identity.

Beyond such public concerns, prioritizing the positive in and of itself can perhaps lead, at least temporarily, to a constricted understanding for some topics. For example, initial enthusiasm among scholars and the general public for the possible benefits of self-esteem resulted in a costly, time-consuming, and frequently ineffective endeavor. Only gradually, as evidence on the limitations of self-esteem accumulated, did psychology offer a more nuanced, if somewhat disappointing, view of the construct (e.g., Baumeister, Campbell, Krueger, & Vohs, 2003). This is in part the nature of the scientific endeavor, with initial conclusions gradually revised over time. But it seems that a purely positive approach to positive psychology may, at least in the early stages of investigation, be particularly vulnerable to overly optimistic claims.

If in practice a "purely positive" positive psychology is rarely advocated (i.e., some integration of the positive and negative is valued), then this problem should be limited. However, to the extent that the allocation of scarce resources is affected by whether a topic is more or less positive, the popular view of what constitutes positive psychology among those who set priorities in funding agencies will likely affect the types of work pursued. Admittedly, an integrative positive psychology may not generate the enthusiasm (i.e. the funding) garnered by a "purely positive" positive psychology. This is certainly a familiar predicament in academia, but given its popularity (and in some circles, notoriety), it is of perhaps particular concern for positive psychology.

## INTEGRATING THE NEGATIVE INTO TODAY'S POSITIVE PSYCHOLOGY

Just as the positive can take many forms, there are numerous ways to conceptualize the forms of negative phenomena addressed by positive psychologists and its critics. One can emphasize choice of research topics, positive psychology's differences with humanistic psychology or psychology as a whole, or other notions of negative to evaluate positive psychology (see Held, 2004, for one detailed analysis). This section takes up how the negative is relevant to three broad issues or areas of work in positive psychology. First, the potential for positive growth in response to severe life events will be discussed, an area that includes stress, posttraumatic stress disorder (and growth), and coping. Second, the extent to which psychological traits or processes can be defined as positive or negative in a general sense, with relatively little emphasis on context, is addressed. Third, a discussion of positive psychology's approach to education is presented, emphasizing how negative emotions, and specifically their relationship to students' general beliefs about learning, may be integrated into positive education.

### Positive Outcomes From Negative Events: Adjustment and Growth After Trauma

In the study of trauma, adjustment, and growth, a central issue from a positive psychology perspective is whether traditional medical models that assume a relatively dichotomous relationship between the positive and negative should be significantly modified. For example, Joseph and Wood (2010) argue that in clinical settings, the deliberate assessment of positive functioning may enhance outcomes by enabling clinicians to promote positive functioning that can serve to thwart future distress. Therefore, the typically strong distinction between assessing negative and positive outcomes is replaced with a more continuous model in which both are routinely measured. Consistent with this model, posttraumatic stress and posttraumatic growth (PTG) are viewed not as two separate possible responses to severe adversity. Instead, under certain conditions, posttraumatic stress is recognized as a normal pattern of thoughts and emotions that "can be conceptualized as the engine of post-traumatic growth" (Joseph, Murphy, & Regel, 2012, p. 319). In this approach, stressful ruminations that can follow trauma, frequently viewed as a disorder or pathology to be treated, are instead conceptualized as a component of the normal process of adjustment that can lead to significant psychological growth (Joseph & Linley, 2005). In sum, the authors argue that rather than separating clinicians' tasks into positive or negative categories, such tasks should be integrated in research, assessment, and treatment.

Given the possibility of substantial benefit finding in the aftermath of trauma, positive psychology may help encourage in clinical research the inclusion of measures that assess not only negative outcomes such as stressful ruminations and posttraumatic stress disorder (PTSD), but also positive outcomes such as posttraumatic growth. Currently, studies that deliberately assess both PTSD and PTG are still relatively rare (Schuettler & Boals, 2011). However, as scholars attempt to identify the conditions under which PTSD and PTG (or related outcomes) occur independently of each other, are inversely related to each other, or fail to occur at all, an emphasis on assessing the full range of positive and negative as a matter of course would seem to facilitate such efforts.

*Implications*   Posttraumatic growth seems to be a particularly appropriate arena for positive psychologists to integrate the negative and positive aspects of human experiences (Joseph, 2011). However, as clinical psychology places more importance on examining positive outcomes, scholars have acknowledged that such an approach would alter the agenda of therapy and thus the responsibilities of practitioners and perhaps psychologists in general (e.g., Joseph & Wood, 2010; Schwartz, 2000). Gone would be the primary emphasis on the removal of distress, replaced by a broader mandate that would include the active promotion of growth even after pathology has ceased.

To the degree that a positive psychology seeks to identify the specific mechanisms by which trauma leads to (or fails to lead to) psychological growth, such efforts are valuable. However, this agenda could also lead to two problematic consequences. First, psychologists should be careful not to infer that because trauma and adversity *can* (under circumstances not yet fully understood) lead to psychological growth, that trauma and adversity *should* lead to such growth, resulting in a situation where clients who do not show adequate progress toward the good life after trauma are left believing that they are doing something wrong. As Tedeschi and Calhoun (2004) put it, "The widespread assumptions that traumas often result in disorder should not be replaced with expectations that growth is an inevitable result" (p. 2). Certainly, responsible practitioners would recognize how uncertain the road to psychological growth can be and communicate that reality to patients. Given the visibility of positive psychology, and the hope it can engender within and beyond the scientific community, this particular point is worth reemphasizing.

A second concern is the greater mandate envisioned by some for clinicians in particular and psychologists in general. Although few would disagree with the desirability of promoting psychological growth (and happiness more broadly), even in the early days of positive psychology some expressed concerns about psychology as a whole taking on this greater responsibility. For example, Schwartz (2000) argued that a truly positive psychology must be willing to offer broad prescriptions for behavior and choices as individuals pursue more meaningful lives, that "if psychologists are serious about turning psychology's power to developing a theory of optimal functioning, they can no longer avoid *shoulds*" (p. 87; emphasis in original). At the same time, Schwartz (2000) rightfully noted how such an approach conflicts with the American "ideology of liberal individualism—let people decide for themselves what is good" (p. 87), and provided the following caution:

> What will psychologists call the recipients of their services if and when a positive psychology comes to fruition? I don't think that either *patients* or *clients* does justice to the grand vision that informs these beginnings of a positive psychology. The right term, I think, is *students*. Are psychologists prepared to argue that it is future generations of psychologists who should be society's teachers? I think that unless we are prepared to say *yes* to this question and to develop arguments about the content of a good human life, the potential achievements of a future positive psychology will always be limited. I also believe that the time to be thinking and talking about this very big and difficult issue is now, at the beginning, and not later, in the face of angry critics trying to put psychologists in their place. (Schwartz, 2000, pp. 87–88)

Has psychology sufficiently acknowledged this "very big and difficult issue?" I am not sure, but with regard to the present topic, any answer must be informed by a clear evaluation of our discipline's knowledge base, and its limitations. As additional work attempts to clarify complex constructs such as posttraumatic growth, positive psychologists should exert caution so that the expanded role for psychologists (envisioned by some) does not obscure our view of those limitations. Overly enthusiastic claims of what psychologists can actually provide, versus what they would like to provide, will indeed invite critics to put psychologists in their place.

CONTEXT COUNTS: DEFINING TRAITS AND PROCESSES AS POSITIVE OR NEGATIVE

Some scholars have questioned the goal of discerning which traits, processes, or institutions are inherently positive, arguing that such a task cannot be achieved in any meaningful sense unless contextual factors are consistently taken into account. Thus, the negative inserts itself into positive psychology, perhaps in uninvited fashion, by challenging the notion that particular psychological processes or traits can be consistently identified as positive outcomes for their own sake. For example, McNulty and Fincham (2012), in reviewing research on optimism, forgiveness, benevolent attributions, and kindness within personal relationships, demonstrate that these constructs and behaviors can be beneficial or detrimental depending on particular features of a relationship. They therefore suggest that an approach to relationship research, and psychology in general, that seeks from the outset to identify positive traits and processes without clear reference to context or potential limiting conditions may be counterproductive.

Outside the relationships field, other scholars also emphasize the importance of context. Friedman and Robbins (2012) note that "positive psychologists have tended to argue that resiliency be classified as a virtue, whether or not it involves a healthy adaptive response" (p. 92), pointing out that individuals or organizations can exert resilience to achieve either benevolent or harmful purposes. An individual with the goal of harming others may indeed confront numerous obstacles, especially if considerable planning is required to carry out the harm. The ability to overcome such obstacles and persevere, even in the pursuit of an abhorrent goal, would appear to reflect resilience as it is often understood, yet is seemingly inconsistent with a positive psychology's intended focus. Accordingly, approaching resilience as an intrinsically positive phenomenon has considerable limitations.

Personality traits and their behavioral manifestations can also be culturally valued in such a way that some are generally deemed desirable and encouraged, while others are considered undesirable, and thus perhaps targeted for remediation. For example, in a broad treatment of how Western cultures place great value on behaviors characteristic of extroverts compared to introverts, Cain (2013) notes that common practices in workplaces and classrooms, such as the use of open spaces and collaborative groups, may often hurt performance on tasks that require more solitary efforts (such as writing, reading, and computer programming, among others). Such deliberately designed physical and social environments, which reflect an underlying cultural assumption that more overt activity and social interaction promotes success (in myriad meanings of that word), can overwhelm introverts who would be more productive in quieter environments (Cain, 2013). From this perspective, a culture that prioritizes extroversion across settings creates conditions that inhibit success on tasks that by their very nature require less social interaction, not more. Thus, just as an academic field, by treating particular relationship behaviors or personality traits as intrinsically positive can obscure the contexts under which they produce undesirable outcomes, cultural beliefs that overstate the desirability of extroversion also do so with unacknowledged costs (see Held, 2002, for a discussion of the possible negative consequences associated with a broad cultural endorsement of maintaining a positive attitude). Whether it is a culture that spontaneously decides which traits are positive or negative, or an academic field that deliberately uses valence to organize and prioritize scholarly efforts, the importance of context in moderating the adaptive value of a given psychological trait should not be overlooked.

*Implications*   For both theorists and practitioners, a research agenda that implicitly or explicitly identifies a given construct as primarily "positive" may prematurely narrow the understanding of that construct and perhaps lead to its over-promotion. Indeed, non-valenced approaches to studying other phenomena in psychology have often been quite productive. For example, group polarization may lead to positive or negative outcomes, as discussion among likeminded individuals can intensify hate in one group or promote generosity in another. Similarly, conformity processes can stifle admirable creativity in one context, but in another provide comforting predictability. Certainly, research on these topics was inspired in part by the desire to understand negative behavior. But systematic attempts to pursue them from an exclusively (or even primarily) positive or negative framework would have likely inhibited psychologists' understanding of them. It is reasonable to ask whether adopting a positive orientation for studying particular psychological processes may systematically result in overlooking the nuance and context sensitivity that necessarily characterizes them (e.g., Friedman & Robbins, 2012; McNulty & Fincham, 2012; Norem & Chang, 2002).

Perhaps some of the difficulty in identifying specific traits or processes as inherently positive lies in a tendency to treat them as outcomes to be pursued in and of themselves rather than as processes that may promote or inhibit desirable outcomes, depending upon context (Linley et al., 2006). Drawing on this distinction, researchers and practitioners of positive psychology should clarify whether the variable of interest—for example, a particular personality trait, behavior, thought pattern, and so on—is best understood as an outcome to be promoted/inhibited or, alternatively, as an intermediate process that promotes desirable outcomes in some circumstances, but undesirable outcomes in others. If the latter is the case, explicitly acknowledging this from the outset may help positive psychology avoid overemphasizing the inherent positivity of the variable in question.

The work of McNulty and Fincham (2012) seems consistent with this notion. Conceptualizing forgiveness as a generally desirable goal or outcome, even implicitly, could potentially lead counselors, therapists, and researchers to promote it in relationships where doing so is not fully adaptive or even harmful (e.g., in abusive relationships). Likewise, viewing extroverted behaviors as inherently desirable in the workplace to the point where it undermines worker performance on particular tasks (e.g., Cain, 2013) may result in part from failing to distinguish between extroversion as an outcome (to be pursued for its own sake) and extroversion as a process (which may generate positive or negative outcomes depending on context). Norem and Chang (2002) make a similar argument about attempts to characterize optimism as inherently good and pessimism as inherently bad. In sum, positive psychology would add valuable nuance by consistently accounting for how context modifies notions of what is desirable or undesirable, thus recognizing the ways in which context counts.

## A ROLE FOR THE NEGATIVE IN POSITIVE EDUCATION?

A positive psychology approach to education can take various forms. Some efforts emphasize teaching students specific skills to promote their own happiness and well-being, an outcome that would presumably facilitate more learning and creative thinking (e.g., Seligman, Ernst, Gillham, Reivich, & Linkins, 2009; see also Kibe & Boniwell, Chapter 18, this volume). Others suggest incorporating into specific psychology courses research inspired by or consistent with positive psychology. For example, Magyar-Moe (2011) advocates teaching positive empathy in introductory counseling courses and utilizing the concept of flow in personality courses. The table of contents for the *Handbook of Positive Psychology in Schools* (Gilman, Huebner, & Furlong, 2009) lists chapters dedicated to topics frequently found in the general positive psychology literature, such as optimism, gratitude, satisfaction, flow, and adaptation. In a detailed critique of positive education, Kristjánsson (2012) asserts that as a whole positive education tends to stress the promotion of particular traits and positive emotions, partly as goals unto themselves, and partly as conditions for improving other learning goals. As with other topics infused with positive psychology, the positive within positive education is of a diverse nature.

However, to the extent that education involves challenging students to improve when their efforts fall short, a complete understanding of how presumably positive concepts can improve education will only come about if they are examined concurrently with the aversive experiences that can accompany hard-earned academic accomplishments. The notion of academic challenge implies the possibility of failure, and by extension the unpleasant emotions that result from negative feedback. If it is to avoid the criticism that it promotes an unrealistic view of learning, positive education will have to actively integrate the negative with the positive, delineating when positive or negative emotions fuel academic success and when they undermine it.

The role of negative emotions in education has received relatively little empirical attention within positive education (Kristjánsson, 2012). In a helpful discussion of several research programs outside positive psychology that have examined emotions' role in education, Kristjánsson (2012) argues that such endeavors, compared to the positive education approach, more effectively take into account the complex nature of both positive and negative emotions relevant to education. Such complexity is also illustrated in Huang's (2011) meta-analysis of studies examining the relationship between goals and emotions in achievement contexts, as the author notes that one cannot assume negative and positive emotions have a simple inverse relationship with each other. A positive psychology orientation for education, if not thoroughly integrated with the so-called negative or aversive aspects of students' experience, may conceal important complexities as much as it reveals them.

How might a positive psychology approach to education meaningfully incorporate those negative or aversive aspects of learning? Many avenues are possible, but I would suggest examining how unexpected failure or critical feedback (and its accompanying negative emotion) can serve as an opportunity to challenge and ultimately improve students' general beliefs about learning. Indeed, some scholars have sought to document the conditions under which negative emotion results from failure and how such an experience can either enhance or inhibit academic motivation and achievement (e.g., Clifford, 1984; J. C. Turner, Thorpe, & Meyer, 1998; J. E. Turner & Husman, 2008; see also Kristjánsson's [2012] overview of related work). In addition to such efforts, I draw on recent thinking in positive psychology's approach to adjustment and posttraumatic growth, discussing how negative emotion in the context of academic failure can perhaps serve as a springboard to modify students' general beliefs about learning. To be sure, the brief outline provided here is necessarily speculative and does not fully reflect the complex interplay of cognitions, emotions, and goals that characterizes student learning. But as Kristjánsson (2012) asserts, an effective positive psychology approach to education should incorporate the growing body of evidence that documents the important role negative emotions play in the learning process. I offer the following as one tentative possibility for doing so.

Clearly, in terms of severity, the discomfort students experience when encountering an academic failure is not comparable to that experienced by individuals coping with genuine traumas. However, the underlying psychological processes that can lead a trauma victim to either psychological growth, or alternatively, simply a return to pre-trauma levels of well-being, may, perhaps, provide insight into how students may respond to a less severe, if more common, challenge. The crucial shared element is that in order for positive outcomes to occur, *beliefs must be altered*. Just as individuals responding to serious trauma often seek to understand why the trauma occurred and the significance of the trauma in moving forward with their lives (e.g., Joseph & Linley, 2006), students receiving negative feedback in the form of a failing grade or critical comments may seek to understand why their efforts failed to produce the outcome desired. Of particular concern here is how students make sense of a negative outcome in a way that may challenge their beliefs about academic learning *in general* (as opposed to beliefs specific to the academic project, problem, or task at hand), and thus ultimately lead them to change their approach to academics in a way that facilitates long-term academic success.

Students bring to the educational setting broad beliefs about learning and academic success, not all of which may be accurate or helpful. For example, beliefs in the importance of matching individual students' learning styles to modes of instruction are quite prevalent despite much research to the contrary (Pashler, McDaniel, Rohrer, & Bjork, 2008). In addition, students may wrongfully believe that instructional approaches that they personally enjoy are more conducive to their learning than approaches they do not enjoy, even when the opposite may be true (Clark, Kirschner, & Sweller, 2012). Finally, students who have frequently received inflated grades may have unrealistic, overly positive beliefs regarding their own general approach to academic work, making them particularly sensitive to critical feedback when it is actually encountered (Twenge, 2006). The present issue centers on the role negative emotions elicited by academic failure play in challenging, and ultimately changing, such general beliefs so that more positive educational outcomes emerge in the future.

As long as students experience positive feedback there would seem to be little impetus to modify beliefs. However, in the face of negative feedback, students may consider a variety of responses as they are forced to examine their beliefs regarding why the negative outcome occurred in order to prepare more effectively in the future. Some of these beliefs are fairly specific to the class or test that generated the negative feedback. For example, J. E. Turner and Husman (2008) suggest that students feeling shame after an academic setback may reconsider how much effort is needed for the class, or whether additional study strategies would improve their performance, among other possible adjustments. In addition to such responses, I would also add the possibility that some instances of negative feedback could serve as an impetus for changing students' broader beliefs about the nature of learning, extending beyond the immediate difficulties presented by a specific exam, course, or instructor.

Certainly, not all negative feedback will alter beliefs in ways that will facilitate learning or performance; indeed, in many contexts, negative emotions in the academic environment can undermine motivation and achievement (e.g., Meyer & Turner, 2002). In addition, the degree to which negative emotion is experienced in light of failure may depend on numerous factors, such as whether a student has a learning oriented focus or a performance oriented focus (J. C. Turner et al., 1998). Thus, there is likely no simple direct correspondence between the experience of negative emotion in certain contexts and the adoption of new beliefs about learning that promote improved academic performance. However, just as the positive experiences of benefit finding and meaning making in the aftermath of trauma may be intricately related to (and even driven by) the negative emotions that challenge broader beliefs and assumptions (Joseph et al., 2012), desirable changes in students' general, broader beliefs about learning may occur under those unpleasant conditions when academic failure is encountered.

*Implications*   First, as J. E. Turner and Husman (2008) advise, students feeling shame in the face of academic failure should be encouraged by instructors to "turn the global focus of their failure into more discrete behaviors for which they can control" (p. 166). Thus, instructors can suggest specific study strategies, emphasizing the necessity of making changes to one's approach when previous efforts have been unsuccessful. I would add that such advice may be received with skepticism or even resistance if a student had previously been able to employ his or her own strategies in less demanding academic contexts and receive high grades. An instructor might note that new, demanding circumstances do not require a student to give up previously held beliefs about self-worth or personal intelligence, but rather that a student's general beliefs about what works in school must necessarily change as the demands presented by school change.

Second, the role of occasional unpleasant emotions may be communicated to students as a normal part of the educational process. To be sure, the excitement of learning something new and the positive feelings that accompany success are important. However, most endeavors that include complexity and challenge can also involve moments of frustration, confusion, anxiety, or anger. Emphasizing to students that such emotions can indicate deep cognitive and emotional engagement offers an interpretation for negative emotions that does not prescribe avoiding them. Indeed, when engaging in a truly demanding and valuable academic endeavor, such emotions can serve to not only realistically signify when a goal has not been met, but may also potentially act as an energizing force for changing one's approach to the task at hand (e.g., see Clifford's [1984] notion of "constructive failure") and perhaps to one's broader beliefs about learning.

A final implication is that unpleasant emotions must often, at least temporarily, accompany the traits, habits, or values for which positive psychologists may advocate. A student may heartily agree with an instructor's suggestion that a presumably positive trait such as persistence is necessary for success. But acting upon such advice may be difficult if the student does not anticipate the negative emotions that can accompany academic challenges over the long term. This may be particularly true for students consistently trying to balance academic obligations with work and other responsibilities (e.g., J. E. Turner & Husman, 2008). Acknowledging the reality of these competing challenges and the negative emotions they can elicit may better enable students to anticipate and overcome them. Essentially, a positive psychology approach to education that promotes traits or habits conducive to academic success in the long run must also alert students to the genuine negative emotions that can attend that journey in the short run.

## CONCLUSION

As illustrated by the contributions of positive psychology's proponents and skeptics, the negative has occupied an uneasy, dynamic, but ultimately useful place in positive psychology. It has served to question the priorities and very definition of positive psychology, illuminate its assumptions and limitations, and eventually integrate itself into positive psychology as the field continues to evolve. In many ways, positive psychology has necessarily had a negative component from its very beginning, albeit one that has occasionally been, and perhaps will continue to be, in conflict with the priorities advocated by some of positive psychology's proponents. Whatever positive psychology ultimately contributes to psychology in general, that contribution will be both molded and challenged by the negative side of human nature and the scholars who study and value it.

## SUMMARY POINTS

- The negative aspects of human experience have held a shifting, ambiguous place within positive psychology.
- Substantive critiques of positive psychology that have emphasized the negative have helped to modify and improve positive psychology.
- Attempts to integrate the positive and the negative have both improved positive psychology and also blurred its boundaries.
- Positive psychologists should clarify whether a given psychological construct in a research or applied setting is being regarded as an outcome in and of itself, or as a variable that inhibits or facilitates desired goals.
- The hoped-for benefits of positive psychology must be clearly evaluated with respect to psychology's knowledge base and the admitted limitations of that knowledge base.
- Contextual factors can limit which psychological traits or behaviors should be regarded as positive.
- Disregarding context can lead to unnecessary or harmful promotion of particular traits, processes, or behaviors.
- Positive psychology approaches to education might consider how negative academic experiences can change students' general beliefs about learning for the better.

# REFERENCES

Baumeister, R. F., Campbell, J. D., Krueger, J. I., & Vohs, K. D. (2003). Does high self-esteem cause better performance, interpersonal success, happiness, or healthier lifestyles? *Psychological Science in the Public Interest, 4,* 1–44. doi:10.1111/1529-1006.01431

Cain, S. (2013). *Quiet: The power of introverts in a world that can't stop talking.* New York, NY: Broadway Paperbacks.

Clark, R. E., Kirschner, P. A., & Sweller, J. (2012). Putting students on the path to learning: The case for fully guided instruction. *American Educator, 36,* 6–11.

Clifford, M. M. (1984). Thoughts on a theory of constructive failure. *Educational Psychologist, 19,* 108–120.

Csikszentmihalyi, M. (2003). Legs or wings? A reply to R. S. Lazarus. *Psychological Inquiry, 14,* 113–115.

Folkman, S., & Moskowitz, J. T. (2003). Positive psychology from a coping perspective. *Psychological Inquiry, 14,* 121–125.

Friedman, H. L., & Robbins, B. R. (2012). The negative shadow cast by positive psychology: Contrasting views and implications of humanistic and positive psychology on resiliency. *The Humanistic Psychologist, 40,* 87–102. doi: 10.1080/08873267.2012.643720

Gilman, R., Huebner, E. S., & Furlong, M. J. (2009). *Handbook of positive psychology in schools.* New York, NY: Routledge.

Hames, J. L., & Joiner, T. E. (2011). The dog woman, Addie Bundren, and the ninth circle of hell: Positive psychology should be more open to the negative. In K. M. Sheldon, T. B. Kashdan, & M. F. Steger (Eds.), *Designing positive psychology: Taking stock and moving forward* (pp. 313–323). New York, NY: Oxford University Press.

Hart, K. E., & Sasso, T. (2011). Mapping the contours of contemporary positive psychology. *Canadian Psychology/Psychologie Canadienne, 52,* 82–92. doi:10.1037/a0023118

Harvey, J. H., & Pauwels, B. G. (2003). The ironies of positive psychology. *Psychological Inquiry, 14,* 125–128.

Held, B. S. (2002). The tyranny of the positive attitude in America: Observation and speculation. *Journal of Clinical Psychology, 58,* 965–992. doi:10.1002/jclp.10093

Held, B. S. (2004). The negative side of positive psychology. *Journal of Humanistic Psychology, 44,* 9–46. doi:10.1177/0022167803259645

Held, B. S. (2005). The "virtues" of positive psychology. *Journal of Theoretical and Philosophical Psychology, 25,* 1–34. doi:10.1037/h0091249

Huang, C. (2011). Achievement goals and achievement emotions: A meta-analysis. *Educational Psychology Review, 23,* 359–388. doi:10.1007/s10648-011-9155-x

Joseph, S. (2011). *What doesn't kill us: The new psychology of posttraumatic growth.* New York, NY: Basic Books.

Joseph, S., & Linley, P. A. (2005). Positive adjustment to threatening events: An organismic valuing theory of growth through adversity. *Review of General Psychology, 9,* 262–280. doi: 10.1037/1089-2680.9.3.262.

Joseph, S., & Linley, P. A. (2006). Growth following adversity: Theoretical perspectives and implications for clinical practice. *Clinical Psychology Review, 26,* 1041–1053. doi:10.1016/j.cpr.2005.12.006

Joseph, S., Murphy, D. & Regel, S. (2012). An affective-cognitive processing model of post-traumatic growth. *Clinical Psychology and Psychotherapy, 19,* 316–325. doi: 10.1002/cpp.1798

Joseph, S., & Wood, A. (2010). Assessment of positive functioning in clinical psychology: Theoretical and practical issues. *Clinical Psychology Review, 30,* 830–838. doi:10.1016/j.cpr.2010.01.002

Kristjánsson, K. (2010). Positive psychology, happiness, and virtue: The troublesome conceptual issues. *Review of General Psychology, 14,* 296–310. doi:10.1037/a0020781

Kristjánsson, K. (2012). Positive psychology and positive education: Old wine in new bottles? *Educational Psychologist, 47*, 86–105. doi:10.1080/00461520.2011.610678

Lazarus, R. S. (2003a). Does the positive psychology movement have legs? *Psychological Inquiry, 14*, 93–109. doi:10.1207/S15327965PLI1402_04

Lazarus, R. S. (2003b). The Lazarus manifesto for positive psychology and psychology in general. *Psychological Inquiry, 14*, 173–189. doi:10.1207/S15327965PLI1402_04

Linley, P. A., & Joseph, S. (2004). Toward a theoretical foundation for positive psychology in practice. In P. A. Linley & S. Joseph (Eds.), *Positive psychology in practice* (pp. 713–731). Hoboken, NJ: Wiley.

Linley, P. A., Joseph, S., Harrington, S., & Wood, A. M. (2006). Positive psychology: Past, present, and (possible) future. *Journal of Positive Psychology, 1*, 3–16. doi:10.1080/17439760500372796

Lyubomirsky, S., & Abbe, A. (2003). Positive psychology's legs. *Psychological Inquiry, 14*, 132–136.

Magyar-Moe, J. L. (2011). Incorporating positive psychology content and applications into various psychology courses. *Journal of Positive Psychology, 6*, 451–456. doi:10.1080/17439760.2011.634821

McNulty, J. K., & Fincham, F. D. (2012). Beyond positive psychology? Toward a contextual view of psychological processes and well-being. *American Psychologist, 67*, 101–110. doi:10.1037/a0024572

Meyer, D. K., & Turner, J. C. (2002). Discovering emotion in classroom motivation research. *Educational Psychologist, 37*, 107–114.

Norem, J. K., & Chang, E. C. (2002). The positive psychology of negative thinking. *Journal of Clinical Psychology, 58*, 993–1001. doi:10.1002/jclp.10094

Pashler, H., McDaniel, M., Rohrer, D., & Bjork, R. (2008). Learning styles: Concepts and evidence. *Psychological Science in the Public Interest, 9*, 105–119.

Ryff, C. D. (2003). Corners of myopia in the positive psychology parade. *Psychological Inquiry, 14*, 153–159.

Schuettler, D., & Boals, A. (2011). The path to posttraumatic growth versus posttraumatic stress disorder: Contributions of event centrality and coping. *Journal of Loss and Trauma, 16*, 180–194. doi:10.1080/15325024.2010.519273

Schwartz, B. (2000). Self-determination: The tyranny of freedom. *American Psychologist, 55*, 79–88. doi:10.1037//0003-066X.55.1.79

Seligman, M. E. P., & Csikszentmihalyi, M. (2000). Positive psychology: An introduction. *American Psychologist, 55*, 5–14. doi:10.1037//0003-066X.55.1.5

Seligman, M. E. P., Ernst, R. M., Gillham, J., Reivich, K., & Linkins, M. (2009). Positive education: positive psychology and classroom interventions. *Oxford Review of Education, 35*, 293–311. doi: 10.1080/03054980902934563

Sheldon, K. M., & King, L. (2001). Why positive psychology is necessary. *American Psychologist, 56*, 216–217. doi:10.1037//0003-066X.56.3.216

Taylor, E. (2001). Positive psychology and humanistic psychology: A reply to Seligman. *Journal of Humanistic Psychology, 41*, 13–29. doi:10.1177/0022167801411003

Taylor, S. E., Kemeny, M. E., Reed, G. M., Bower, J. E., & Gruenewald, T. L. (2000). Psychological resources, positive illusions, and health. *American Psychologist, 55*, 99–109. doi:10.1037/0003-066X.55.1.99

Tedeschi, R. G., & Calhoun, L. G. (2004). Posttraumatic growth: Conceptual foundations and empirical evidence. *Psychological Inquiry, 15*, 1–18.

Turner, J. C., Thorpe, P. K., & Meyer, D. K. (1998). Students' reports of motivation and negative affect: A theoretical and empirical analysis. *Journal of Educational Psychology, 90*, 758–771.

Turner, J. E., & Husman, J. (2008). Emotional and cognitive self-regulation following academic shame. *Journal of Advanced Academics, 20*, 138–173.

Twenge, J. M. (2006). *Generation Me: Why today's young Americans are more confident, assertive, entitled—and more miserable than ever before*. New York, NY: Free Press.

Vaillant, G. E. (2000). Adaptive mental mechanisms: Their role in a positive psychology. *American Psychologist, 55*, 89–98. doi:10.1037/0003-066X.55.1.89

Wong, P. T. P. (2011). Positive psychology 2.0: Towards a balanced interactive model of the good life. *Canadian Psychology, 52*, 69–81.

Yen, J. (2010). Authorizing happiness: Rhetorical demarcation of science and society in historical narratives of positive psychology. *Journal of Theoretical and Philosophical Psychology, 30*, 67–78.

# CHAPTER 47

# The Future of Positive Psychology in Practice

STEPHEN JOSEPH

THE BIG IDEA of positive psychology was to change the focus of psychology from its preoccupation with the worst things in life to also include what makes life worth living. As the chapters in this volume show, there has been substantial progress in positive psychology and its applications. Empirical evidence shows that well-being can be increased and approaches to the promotion of human flourishing are developing in educational settings, clinics, workplaces, and communities. In this concluding chapter my aim is to draw together some of the issues that have arisen for me in editing the preceding chapters and to consider the challenges ahead for positive psychology in practice. First, I discuss whether the goal of positive psychology is to integrate with mainstream psychology or to be a separate branch of psychology. Second, I consider how positive psychology relates to negative states and the need for new theoretical developments that dissolve boundaries between the positive and the negative. Third, I discuss the need for greater attention to the theoretical and philosophical underpinnings of practice.

## INTEGRATION AND ISOLATION

Ten years ago, while editing the first edition of this volume, my view was that the success of positive psychology would be marked by its integration into mainstream psychology. As the chapters in this volume show, the practice of positive psychology has attracted interest within various areas of applied psychology, notably clinical (Maddux & Lopez, Chapter 25), counseling (Vossler, Steffen, & Joseph, Chapter 26), forensic (Fortune, Ward, & Mann, Chapter, 37), health (Salsman & Moskowitz, Chapter 24), and organizational psychology (Lewis, Chapter 20). The argument for the relevance of positive psychology is well made in each case. Scholars in other areas are also examining their practices in light of positive psychology, such as in rehabilitation medicine (Peter, Geyh, Ehde, Müller, & Jensen, Chapter 27), the recovery movement (Resnick & Leddy, Chapter 40) and social work (Dekel & Taubman–Ben-Ari, Chapter 39). One of the areas beyond psychology that has proved to be most successful is education as evidenced by the rapidly developing interest in positive education (Kibe & Boniwell, Chapter 18).

It is also clear from these chapters that despite significant progress, positive psychology has much yet to contribute, and its connections within other fields could be more entrenched, before concluding that integration has been achieved.

It seems certain, however, that interest in positive psychology will continue to grow. It is just too good an idea. As practitioners dig down into the positive psychology research they will find much to engage with, such as the work on well-being therapy (Ruini & Fava, Chapter 28), hope interventions (Magyar-Moe & Lopez, Chapter 29), posttraumatic growth (Tedeschi, Calhoun, & Groleau, Chapter 30), emotional intelligence (Caruso, Salovey, Brackett, & Mayer, Chapter 32), gratitude (Bono, Krakauer, & Froh, Chapter 33), wisdom (Kunzmann & Thomas, Chapter 34), choice (Schwartz, Chapter 8), forgiveness (Fincham, Chapter 38), and time perspective (Boniwell & Zimbardo, Chapter 13). What is so vital about these topics is that they cut across the branches of applied psychology.

Likewise the work of Sagy, Eriksson, and Braun-Lewensohn on the sense of coherence concept (Chapter 5); Sagiv, Roccas, and Oppenheim-Weller, on the role of values (Chapter 7); Layous, Sheldon, and Lyubomirsky on how happiness can be increased (Chapter 11); or Parks (Chapter 14) on activities that people can do for themselves, transcend the interests of any single group of practitioners. In each of these chapters there are applications that could be taken up by educationalists, clinicians, leaders, and other practitioners regardless of their contexts of practice. Positive psychology is about thinking differently about what we already do.

In its early days positive psychology grew from the work of scholars and practitioners who were themselves already established in their own fields of abnormal, clinical, social, and personality psychology. It provided a common language that brought people together from these different branches of psychology and stimulated much-needed research into what makes life worth living.

Since then, new scholars and practitioners have been attracted to the ideas of positive psychology. But unlike the first generation of positive psychologists who had already existing identities within their specialist fields, many of the newer generation may now identify themselves first and foremost as a positive psychologist. As such, this seems to be leading to the emergence of positive psychology as a separate branch of psychology. This raises the question of how a separate discipline of positive psychology will coexist with the ambition toward integration.

Paradoxically, it may be that the development of positive psychology as a separate discipline implies that other traditional areas of applied psychology are not concerned with positive functioning and that there is a natural dividing line between the negative and the positive. To me it seems that the field of positive psychology is at a crossroads in which it is not clear whether its mission is ultimately to establish itself as a separate branch of applied psychology or to transform the face of mainstream psychology. It is likely that these two competing paths will continue for some time as those scholars and practitioners interested in becoming part of a new separate discipline organize themselves professionally, and others whose main professional identity is elsewhere as clinical, health, personality, social psychologists, and so on, adopt ideas of positive psychology into their work. Eventually, one path will be more trodden than the other.

## FROM LANGUISHING TO FLOURISHING

Ten years on I still believe that the greatest power of positive psychology is to be an idea that transforms mainstream psychology rather than to become a new and separate discipline of applied psychology. The reason is that I do not view the positive as theoretically separable from the negative.

The very language of positive and negative hinders integration by creating a dichotomy in which practice is seen to be naturally divided between those who specialize from −5 to 0 and those who specialize from 0 to +5.

I would certainly agree that there was a range of professional activity that was not taking place before positive psychology came along, but I would disagree that the theories of psychology were not already up to that job. In many cases the fundamental premise of positive psychology seems to date back to the humanistic theories of scholars such as Abraham Maslow and Carl Rogers. To me it seems that the profession of psychology did not fully grasp the implications of its own theories and put them into practice across the spectrum of human functioning. Instead, it was influenced by the illness ideology in its development, and now finds itself as a profession looking back to these original core ideas through the lens of positive psychology. If there is no illness ideology, the distinction between −5 to 0 and 0 to +5 dissolves. Positive psychology can offer an alternative to the illness ideology as discussed by Maddux and Lopez (Chapter 25).

Language is important. If positive psychology is to be truly transformational it must transcend the dichotomous language of negative and positive. As Pauwels (Chapter 46), discusses, it is important that positive psychology clarifies its position in relation to the negative.

Our starting point for scholars must be to examine the concepts in business-as-usual psychology and their relation to positive psychology. Rashid (Chapter 31) points to some of the recent developments in strength-based assessment that reconceptualize psychological disorders as the absence, excess, or opposite of strengths. In this way we can begin to see how the problems and issues of traditional psychology might be accommodated within a positive psychological framework.

Not only do we need to question the concepts we are used to, we also need to consider alternative ways of thinking about human experience. We need to begin to develop new theoretical approaches that are able to accommodate the problems and issues of traditional psychology within a positive psychological framework. One example of such an approach is the new way of thinking about human reactions to adversity in which posttraumatic stress and posttraumatic growth are seen not as two separate responses, each with their own theoretical frameworks, but as interrelated concepts within one single theoretical framework (see Pauwels, Chapter 46). Such an integrative framework is neither a positive psychology nor a negative psychology.

In a similar way, positive psychologists have begun to talk about human *flourishing*. By this I do not mean any one theorist's view of what this word means, but its use more generally to describe positive functioning. The dictionary definition of flourishing invokes the metaphor of growth as a way to understand human experience. Not growth in the sense that economics uses the term to mean a never ending increase, but growth in the biological sense in which things are born, develop to their best potential, and eventually die.

In the metaphor of growth it is the absence of the conditions that lead to flourishing that lead to languishing. Flourishing and languishing are but descriptions of the same process. We are concerned with both the negative and the positive simultaneously because the focus is on the process not just one outcome of that process. We are also reminded when we think of growth, a biological metaphor instead of a mechanistic one, that we are embodied creatures and that flourishing implies an authentic and organismic connection with our physical selves (Hefferon, Chapter 45).

Integrative thinking that does not assume a natural division between traditional conceptions of the negative and the positive, but seeks to carve human nature at its joints, will deliver new and more productive scientific theories. As such the concept of flourishing, and other integrative ways of thinking, are helpful not only in avoiding a dichotomous message but also in overcoming the simplistic notion that human qualities can be easily divided into those that are positive and negative. Of course, it may turn out that some human experiences may best be considered part of a new separate discipline of positive psychology, but only good theorizing and research that starts by challenging this notion can tell us.

Consistent with the shift in language has been the realization that there is much in common between positive psychology and some aspects of humanistic psychology (see Robbins, Chapter 3). Initially, positive psychologists distanced themselves from humanistic psychology. Perhaps this was advantageous in maintaining credibility for the fledging positive psychology movement. But in so doing, early positive psychology overlooked the rich theoretical development associated with some of the pioneering humanistic psychologists such as Maslow and Rogers.

Maslow and Rogers were ahead of their time. Today there is greater recognition of their work and positive psychology is beginning to catch up. Most notably, there has been a shift from an initial focus on hedonistic well-being to eudaimonic well-being (see Huta, Chapter 10). Maslow used the term *self-actualization*. Rogers used the term *fully functioning*. Nonetheless, theirs was a eudaimonic psychology.

Humanistic psychologists, by and large, have always been positive psychologists in the sense that their interest was always in self-actualization, fully functioning, and living an optimal life. But positive psychologists have not necessarily been humanistic insofar as their core assumptions have not always been consistent with the notions of growth, holism, responsibility and intentionality, and so on. But this seems to be changing. Some of the best humanistic psychology now happening is under the umbrella of positive psychology.

Maslow and Rogers, as Robbins (Chapter 3) points out, had a vision consistent with the Aristotelian view now attracting attention from positive psychologists (see Nafstad, Chapter 2). As such, positive psychology has begun to offer a more humanistic vision of the person as endeavoring to realize their core nature. A challenge for positive psychology is whether it will be possible to converge around a set of agreed principles and whether the Aristotelian perspective currently attracting attention will prove to provide cohesion.

A related perspective that has become a core topic of positive psychology, is self-determination theory (Brown & Ryan, Chapter 9). Self-determination theory also views the person as an active growth-oriented organism, attempting to actualize his or her potentialities within the environment he or she functions in, but provides stronger empirical evidence.

One can see why many humanistic psychologists looked on with surprise at positive psychology as it seemed to be a reinvention of what they had long been advocating. And one can also see how the impetus of positive psychology has succeeded in putting these ideas back on the mainstream agenda when humanistic psychology struggled to do so. However, it is worth reflecting on the history of humanistic psychology and how it once promised to transform business as usual, as positive psychology now does, but lost its impetus, becoming instead isolated as a separate specialist area. It may be that positive psychology will similarly lose its influence if it becomes too inward looking and does not continue to promote its ideas outwardly to all corners of the profession of psychology.

## THEORY INTO PRACTICE

All practice is ultimately grounded in some philosophical viewpoint. A growth model is radically different in its implications for practice than the medical model.

A growth model implies that the organism has the resources within it to flourish if the nutrient conditions are right. Farmers do not grow the corn; it grows itself, even where there are no farmers. What farmers do is cultivate and nurture the corn. Flourishing, in this sense, therefore describes a process that takes place within people. But this is not automatic. We cannot make people flourish; we can only provide the conditions that enable them to flourish.

We now have the evidence that we flourish when connected in close, supportive relationships (Myers, Chapter 41). As already noted, self-determination theory offers a contemporary and empirically supported view of how relationships lead to flourishing (see Sagiv, Roccas, & Oppenheim-Weller, Chapter 7; Brown & Ryan, Chapter 9). Relationships that support peoples' basic needs and that foster their intrinsic motivation are important determinants of human flourishing. The implications of such an approach are considered in relation to youth (Larson & Dawes, Chapter, 19), at work (Henry, Chapter 22) and life coaching (Tarragona, Chapter 15). Leaders need to cultivate resources within the person (Clarke, Arnold, & Connelly, Chapter 21) as do coaches (Kauffman, Joseph, & Scoular, Chapter 23).

The same applies even when working with clinical patients (Delle Fave, Fianco, & Sartori, Chapter 36) and even those some may consider beyond compassion (Fortune, Ward, & Mann, Chapter, 37). We know how to help people flourish and what it takes to lead a longer healthier life (Vaillant, Chapter 35).

Much of positive psychology to date has been concerned with interventions with populations already languishing in some way and seeking to develop their capacity to flourish. As well as these downstream activities, we now need to also think in terms of what positive psychology can do upstream. Increasingly, attention is being paid to the development of public policies that can foster flourishing societies (Thin, Chapter 43). In one example, Kasser (Chapter 6) shows us the dangers of consumer culture and offers valuable suggestions for how we might weaken the vision of the goods life reflected in our money-driven, consumer culture. The ideas of positive psychology can be built into policy, planning, and systems, as discussed by Myers (Chapter 41), Veenhoven (Chapter 42), and Yates, Tyrell, and Masten (Chapter 44).

The most important upstream activity is education (Fineburg & Monk, Chapter 16). Facilitating resilience and well-being as part of school activities (Kibe & Boniwell, Chapter 18) and fostering young people's ability to think for themselves (Reznitskaya & Wilkinson, Chapter 17) are vital if we want to promote flourishing in the next generation.

## CONCLUSION

Imagine a world in which positive psychology was built into public policy, education, organizational systems, and health care. Editing this book has convinced me that so far we have seen but a fraction of what could be achieved by positive psychology. I hope within this book you will have found something to support your practice and feel inspired to make positive psychology part of your own vision.

## SUMMARY POINTS

- A wealth of empirical evidence shows that well-being can be increased.
- Approaches to the promotion of human flourishing are developing in educational settings, clinics, workplaces, and communities.
- Positive psychology is at a crossroads as to whether its aim is to transform traditional areas of practice or to be a new specialty in its own right.
- Positive psychology must examine its deepest philosophical principles and notions about human nature.
- Positive psychology needs theoretical perspectives that can dissolve the dichotomy between the positive and negative.
- Applications in positive psychology have been both upstream and downstream, but the balance now needs to be shifted toward upstream activities, to build human flourishing into public policy, education, organizational systems, and health care.

# About the Editor

STEPHEN JOSEPH, PhD, studied psychology at the University of Ulster on the northern coast of Ireland before going on to study social psychology at the London School of Economics and London's Institute of Psychiatry, where he obtained his PhD, for which he investigated emotional processing in survivors of disaster. For the past 25 years, he has continued researching psychological trauma but has become more interested in the positive psychology of how people can overcome adversity. As a practitioner, he is a health and counseling psychologist with interests in psychotherapy and coaching. He has worked at the Universities of Ulster, Essex, and Warwick, and is now at the University of Nottingham, where he is professor in the School of Education and convenor for the human flourishing research group. When he is not working, Stephen likes to retreat to the hills of Donegal in Ireland, where he spends time looking out to sea and pondering the mysteries of life. He has published many scholarly papers and books, including *Trauma, Recovery, and Growth* (Wiley, 2008) and, most recently, *What Doesn't Kill Us: The New Psychology of Posttraumatic Growth* (Basic Books, 2011).

# Contributors

**Kara A. Arnold**
Memorial University
St. John's, Newfoundland
  and Labrador, Canada

**Ilona Boniwell**
Positran
Goupillières, France
and
Anglia Ruskin University
Cambridge, United Kingdom

**Giacomo Bono**
California State University,
  Dominguez Hills
Carson, California

**Marc Brackett**
Yale University
New Haven, Connecticut

**Orna Braun-Lewensohn**
Ben-Gurion University of the Negev
Be'er Sheva, Israel

**Roger Bretherton**
University of Lincoln
Lincoln, United Kingdom

**Kirk Warren Brown**
Virginia Commonwealth University
Richmond, Virginia

**Lawrence G. Calhoun**
University of North Carolina Charlotte
Charlotte, North Carolina

**David R. Caruso**
Yale University
New Haven, Connecticut

**Heather M. Clarke**
Memorial University
St. John's, Newfoundland
  and Labrador, Canada

**Catherine E. Connelly**
McMaster University
Hamilton, Ontario, Canada

**Nickki Pearce Dawes**
University of Massachusetts, Boston
Boston, Massachusetts

**Rachel Dekel**
Bar Ilan University
Ramat Gan, Israel

**Antonella Delle Fave**
University of Milano
Milano, Italy

**Dawn M. Ehde**
University of Washington
Seattle, Washington

**Monica Eriksson**
University Väst
Trollhättan, Sweden

**Guy Faulkner**
University of Toronto
Toronto, Ontario, Canada

**Giovanni A. Fava**
University of Bologna
Bologna, Italy

**Andrea Fianco**
University of Milano
Milano, Italy

**Frank D. Fincham**
Florida State University
Tallahassee, Florida

**Amy C. Fineburg**
Alabaster City Schools
Alabaster, Alabama

**Clare-Ann Fortune**
Victoria University of Wellington
Wellington, New Zealand

**Jeffrey J. Froh**
Hofstra University
Hempstead, New York

**Szilvia Geyh**
Swiss Paraplegic Research
Nottwil, Switzerland
and
University of Lucerne
Luzern, Switzerland

**Jessica M. Groleau**
University of North Carolina at
    Charlotte
Charlotte, North Carolina

**Kate Hefferon**
University of East London
London, United Kingdom

**Jane Henry**
The Open University
Milton Keynes, United Kingdom

**Veronika Huta**
University of Ottawa/Université
    d'Ottawa
Ottawa, Ontario, Canada

**Mark P. Jensen**
University of Washington
Seattle, Washington

**Stephen Joseph**
University of Nottingham
Nottingham, United Kingdom

**Tim Kasser**
Knox College
Galesburg, Illinois

**Carol Kauffman**
Institute of Coaching
Harvard Medical School
Belmont, Massachusetts

**Chieko Kibe**
Ochanomizu University
Tokyo, Japan

**Mikki Krakauer**
Hofstra University
Hempstead, New York

**Ute Kunzmann**
University of Leipzig
Leipzig, Germany

**Reed W. Larson**
University of Illinois
Urbana, Illinois

**Kristin Layous**
University of California, Riverside
Riverside, California

**Meaghan A. Leddy**
VA Connecticut Healthcare System
West Haven, Connecticut
and
Yale University School of Medicine
New Haven, Connecticut

**Sarah Lewis**
Jemstone Consultancy Ltd.
London, United Kingdom

**Shane J. Lopez**
Clifton Strengths Institute/Gallup
Omaha, Nebraska
and
University of Kansas School of Business
Lawrence, Kansas

**Sonja Lyubomirsky**
University of California, Riverside
Riverside, California

**James E. Maddux**
Center for the Advancement of
    Well-Being
George Mason University
Fairfax, Virginia

**Jeana L. Magyar-Moe**
University of Wisconsin–Stevens Point
Stevens Point, Wisconsin

**Ruth Mann**
Offender Behaviour Programmes Unit
London, United Kingdom

**Ann S. Masten**
University of Minnesota
Minneapolis, Minnesota

**John D. Mayer**
University of New Hampshire
Durham, New Hampshire

**Andrew Monk**
Monivae College
Hamilton, Victoria, Australia

**Judith T. Moskowitz**
Northwestern University
Chicago, Illinois

**Rachel Müller**
Swiss Paraplegic Research
Nottwil, Switzerland
and
University of Washington
Seattle, Washington

**Nanette Mutrie**
University of Edinburgh
Edinburgh, Scotland

**David G. Myers**
Hope College
Holland, Michigan

**Hilde Eileen Nafstad**
University of Oslo
Oslo, Norway

**Shani Oppenheim-Weller**
University of Haifa
Haifa, Israel

**Acacia C. Parks**
Hiram College
Hiram, Ohio

**Brian G. Pauwels**
Doane College
Crete, Nebraska

**Claudio Peter**
Swiss Paraplegic Research
Nottwil, Switzerland

**Tayyab Rashid**
University of Toronto Scarborough
Toronto, Ontario, Canada

**Sandra G. Resnick**
VA New England MIRECC
West Haven, Connecticut
and
Yale University School of Medicine
New Haven, Connecticut

**Alina Reznitskaya**
Montclair State University
Montclair, New Jersey

**Brent Dean Robbins**
Point Park University
Pittsburgh, Pennsylvania

**Sonia Roccas**
The Open University of Israel
Ra'anana, Israel

**Chiara Ruini**
Università di Bologna
Bologna, Italy

**Richard M. Ryan**
Institute for Positive Psychology and
  Education
Australian Catholic University
Strathfield, Australia
and
University of Rochester
Rochester, New York

**Lilach Sagiv**
The Hebrew University of Jerusalem
Jerusalem, Israel

**Shifra Sagy**
Ben-Gurion University of the Negev
Be'er Sheva, Israel

**Peter Salovey**
Yale University
New Haven, Connecticut

**John M. Salsman**
Northwestern University
Chicago, Illinois

**Raffaela D. G. Sartori**
University of Milano
Milano, Italy

**Barry Schwartz**
Swarthmore College
Swarthmore, Pennsylvania

**Anne Scoular**
Meyler Campbell
Kent, United Kingdom

**Kennon M. Sheldon**
University of Missouri
Columbia, Missouri

**Edith Steffen**
University of East London
London, United Kingdom

**Margarita Tarragona**
Universidad TecMilenio
Monterrey, Mexico

**Orit Taubman–Ben-Ari**
Bar Ilan University
Ramat Gan, Israel

**Richard G. Tedeschi**
University of North Carolina
    Charlotte
Charlotte, North Carolina

**Neil Thin**
University of Edinburgh
Edinburgh, Scotland

**Stefanie Thomas**
Arxhof Forensic Center for Young Adults
Basel, Switzerland

**Fanita A. Tyrell**
University of California, Riverside
Riverside, California

**George E. Vaillant**
Harvard Medical School
Boston, Massachusetts

**Ruut Veenhoven**
Erasmus University Rotterdam
Rotterdam, The Netherlands
and
North-West University
Potchefstroom, South Africa

**Andreas Vossler**
The Open University
Milton Keynes, United Kingdom

**Tony Ward**
Victoria University of Wellington
Wellington, New Zealand

**Ian A. G. Wilkinson**
The Ohio State University
Columbus, Ohio

**Tuppett M. Yates**
University of California, Riverside
Riverside, California

**Philip Zimbardo**
Stanford University
Stanford, California

# Author Index

Abbe, A., 810
Abbott, R. D., 778
Abdel-Khalek, A., 486
Abe, Y., 566
Abello, K. M., 240
Aber, L., 779, 780, 782
Abernethy, C., 229
Abrahamse, W., 86
Abramson, L. Y., 130
Abuhamdeh, S., 169
Achor, S., 331
Ackerman, S. J., 638
Acree, M., 197
Adam, M., 48
Adams, C. M., 151
Adams, L., 795
Adams, M., 52, 53
Adams, V., III, 413
Adler, N. A., 776
Adolphs, R., 553
Affleck, G., 434, 497, 504, 619
Ager, A., 300, 782
Agras, W. S., 662
Ahmad, N., 16, 761
Ahmed, M., 699
Ahuvia, A. C., 85, 104
Akbaraly, T. N., 799
Akesson, B., 782
Aknin, L. B., 191, 399, 758
Albee, G. W., 415
Albertsen, K., 343
Albieri, E., 474
Alcover, C. M., 350
Aldwin, C. M., 504
Alexander, R. J., 280, 283, 285, 286
Algoe, S. B., 198, 561, 562, 567
Ali, S., 618
Alkire, S., 766
Allemand, M., 660
Allenby, B., 773
Allison, P. D., 244
Allport, G., 32, 34

Allport, G. W., 18, 21, 464
Almeida, D. M., 584
Almond, R., 175
Alper, C. M., 197
Alvaro, C., 506
Alvermann, D. E., 283, 286, 290
Amabile, T. M., 141
Amaya-Jackson, L. M., 778
Amberg, I., 660
Amico, J., 799
Amodeo, J., 56
Analayo, B., 149
Anastasi, A., 401
Andalib, M., 217
Anders, P., 286
Anderson, B. J., 799
Anderson, C. L., 172, 196
Anderson, D., 647
Anderson, G., 240
Anderson, H., 258
Anderson, J. R., 487
Anderson, K., 684
Anderson, N., 364
Anderson, R., 791, 792, 793, 800
Anderson, R. C., 284, 286, 288, 290–291, 292
Andreasen, N. L., 503
Andree, A., 288
Andrews, C., 92
Andrews, D. A., 635, 639, 653
Andrews, F. M., 732
Andrews, G., 267
Andrykowski, M. A., 508
Angel, E., 33, 49
Angst, J., 130, 133
Angus, R. M., 319, 320
Anic, P., 162, 163
Anielski, M., 756
Anthony, J. L., 420
Anthony, W. A., 688, 696, 701, 704
Antoni, M. H., 512

Antonovsky, A., 61, 62, 63, 65, 66, 67, 68, 70, 72, 494, 619
Antonovsky, H., 67, 68, 69, 70, 71
Apers, S., 68
Apfel, R. J., 548
Apostoleris, N. H., 144, 145, 146
Applebee, A. N., 283, 285
Ardelt, M., 578, 579, 580, 585
Argyle, M., 714, 741
Argyris, C., 366
Arias, B., 520
Aridas, C., 142
Arieli, S., 114
Ariely, D., 172, 196, 722
Aristotle, 168
Arkin, R. M., 88
Armbruster, B. B., 292
Armelius, K., 343
Armstrong, K., 54
Arndt, J., 51, 166
Arnett, R. A. M., 562
Arnhart, L., 641
Arnold, D., 514
Arnold, K. A., 341, 343, 344, 350, 351, 831
Arnold, R., 618
Aron, D., 697
Aronson, E., 91
Arregni, J. L., 652
Arthur, M. C., 367
Asendorpf, J. B., 198
Asher, E. R., 172
Ashforth, B. E., 350
Ashkanasy, N. M., 552
Ashkenas, R., 367
Aspinwall, L. G., 618
Assmann, A., 577
Assor, A., 114
Asterhan, C. S. C., 286
Atherton, J. R., 764
Atienza, A., 402
Atkinson, M., 567
Auerbach, J., 250

Augustus-Horvath, C. L., 794
Aureli, F., 659
Avalos, L., 794, 795, 796
Avanzi, L., 346
Averill, A. J., 89
Averill, J. R., 546
Avey, J. B., 361, 703
Avolio, B., 338
Avolio, B. J., 301, 346, 361, 703
Axford, S., 303
Ayers, S., 451

Ba, G., 619
Baard, P. P., 142
Babyak, M., 211
Bach, P., 397
Bachkirova, T., 251, 252, 385
Bacon, F., 718
Badr, H., 779
Baer, R. A., 167
Bagby, R. M., 548
Baker, B. L., 620
Baker, I., 467
Baker, R., 450
Baker, W., 333
Bakermans-Kranenburg, M. J., 306, 776
Bakker, A. B., 358
Baldassare, M., 194
Baldessarini, R. J., 473
Baldwin, A. S., 396
Baliousis, M., 174, 384
Baltes, M. M., 584, 604
Baltes, P. B., 505, 577, 578, 579, 580, 583, 584, 585, 586, 587, 595, 604
Bandura, A., 64, 88, 228, 315, 319, 343, 344, 361, 362, 396, 421, 422, 484, 494, 618
Banerjee, R., 90
Banks, K. H., 498
Barber, B. K., 775
Barbey, A. K., 792
Bargh, J. A., 147, 148, 150, 791
Barkeley, R. A., 420
Barker, G. T., 437
Barkshire, C. T., 568
Barling, J., 341, 343, 345
Barlow, J., 306, 700
Barnes, J., 16
Barnett, J., 216
Barnett, O. W., 685
Barni, S., 619
Baron, J., 584
Baron, J. A., 608
Baron, M. W., 14
Barone, D. F., 413, 414

Barsade, S. G., 361, 545
Barsalou, L. W., 792
Barskova, T., 397
Bartels, J. M., 717
Bartlett, M. Y., 560, 561
Basabe, N., 106
Baskin, T. W., 664
Bass, B. M., 342, 350, 619
Bassett, R., 794
Bassi, M., 159, 160
Bassman, R., 695
Bastian, B., 107
Batson, C. D., 16, 761
Battista, J., 175
Baucom, D. H., 670
Bauer, D. J., 566
Bauer, D. R., 567
Bauer, J. J., 160
Bauer, M. A., 85
Bauer, R., 617
Baumann, J., 561
Baumann, K., 465
Baumeister, R. F., 51, 55, 88, 147, 148, 254, 300, 417, 420, 673, 716, 717, 754, 811
Baumgarten-Tramer, F. F., 559
Baumrind, B., 17
Baun, W. B., 703
Baxter, D., 163, 168
Bayne, R., 363
Beach, S. R., 660, 670, 796
Beach, S. R. H., 660, 662, 663, 666, 670
Beall, A. E., 418
Beattie, J., 124
Beaumont, E., 22
Bech, P., 464, 472
Beck, A. T., 49, 124, 467, 475, 700
Beck, J. S., 165
Beck, R. W., 124
Beck, W., 755
Becker, B., 301
Becker, D. R., 698
Becker, H. S., 418
Becker, I., 465, 475
Becker, S., 618
Beckett, R., 643
Beckham, J. C., 396
Becvar, D. S., 773
Bedell, B. T., 547
Bedi, R. P., 437
Beech, A., 652
Beermann, U., 13, 162
Beersma, B., 384
Begum, S., 794
Beilock, S. L., 791
Belaise, C., 474
Belbin, R. M., 364

Bell, D. E., 126
Bell, N. E., 358
Bellah, R. N., 55, 721–722, 723
Belluardo, P., 472
Belsky, J., 306, 776, 779
Bempechat, J., 315
Benedict, R., 19
Ben-kiki, T., 242, 243
Bennett, J. L., 385
Bennett, L., 568
Benson, P. L., 568
Bental-Israeli, A., 68
Bentall, R. P., 49
Bentham, J., 731
Bentley, K. A., 687
Benton, J., 792
Berg, J., 779
Berg, M., 743
Berger, M., 300
Bergin, A. E., 667
Bergler, E., 559
Bergsma, A., 697
Berkowitz, M. W., 169
Berlia, N., 126
Berlin, L. J., 778
Bernstein, D. M., 568
Bernstein, J. H., 95, 142
Bernstein, R. J., 12
Berry, J. W., 662, 664
Berry, L. L., 703
Berry, M., 397
Berscheid, E., 716, 754
Best, J., 761
Biddle, S. J. H., 205, 216–217, 220
Bielaczye, K., 287
Bier, M. C., 169
Biglan, A., 669
Bilbao, M. A., 106
Billings, L., 285
Bilsky, W., 106, 164
Bird, E., 109
Bird, T., 620
Bird, V., 532
Bird, V. J., 525, 532
Birditt, K. S., 584
Birkmann, J., 773
Birren, J. E., 577
Biswas-Diener, R., 23, 52, 132, 253, 254, 256, 384, 465, 533, 704, 757
Bitner, J., 229
Bjork, B., 816
Blacher, J., 620
Black, B., 331
Black, C. H., 464
Black, C. J., 686
Black, M. M., 781
Blair, C., 778
Blair-Broeker, C. T., 267

Blanchflower, D. G., 799
Blessing, C., 447
Bliese, P. D., 343, 344
Blobel, B., 245
Block, J. H., 301
Block, R. A., 224
Blount, J. P., 647
Bluck, S., 582, 584
Blum, C. A., 16
Blumenthal, J. A., 211
Blundo, R., 684
Blythe, B. J., 681
Blythe, K., 303
Boals, A., 812
Boat, T., 299
Bobowick, M., 106
Boddana, P., 471
Bodde, A. E., 617
Bodenhausen, G. B., 85
Bodhi, B., 149
Boehm, J. K., 187, 190–191,
    194, 198, 238, 259, 385,
    452, 565, 569
Bohan, J., 417
Bohart, A. C., 31, 471, 696
Bo Homley, P., 93
Boisvert, C. M., 699
Boivin, J., 398
Bolier, L., 240, 241, 452, 465,
    697
Bolino, M. C., 348
Bonanno, G. A., 448, 620
Bond, F. W., 433
Bond, M., 225
Bond, R., 85, 86
Bond, R. W., 165
Boniwell, I., 1, 2, 223, 229,
    230, 231, 232, 253, 254,
    268, 273, 297, 303, 305,
    831
Bono, G., 2, 267, 273, 559,
    562, 565, 566, 569, 831
Bono, J. E., 347, 349,
    359, 368
Bonta, J., 635, 639, 653
Boomsma, D. I., 210
Boorse, C., 443
Bootby, N., 782
Bordia, P., 568
Bordin, E. S., 488, 489
Borg, M., 688
Borg, V., 344
Borgonovi, F., 758
Borsheim-Black, C., 290
Bortoft, H., 41
Bortol, K. M., 85
Bortz, W. M., 596
Bosco, J. S., 554
Boswell, W. R., 187
Botti, S., 122
Bottomley, P., 93

Boudreau, J. W., 187
Boujbel, L., 92
Boulet, D. B., 51
Boulton-Lewis, G., 290
Bouskila-Yam, O., 336
Bowen, M., 753
Bower, J. E., 504, 810
Bowlby, J., 144
Bowles, S., 718
Bowling, N. A., 197
Boxer, P., 775–776
Boyatzis, R. E., 552
Boyce, W. T., 306, 776, 781
Boyd-Wilson, B. M., 230
Brackett, M., 545, 831
Brackett, M. A., 546, 549,
    550, 551, 552, 554
Bradburn, N. M., 733
Bradley, R. T., 567
Brady, M. J., 401
Braithwaite, S., 663
Brand, S., 306
Bränholm, I.-B., 446
Brani, O., 793
Branstetter-Rost, W., 103
Bränström, R., 397
Braslow, J. T., 696, 701
Braten, I., 286
Braun, J. D., 362
Braun, O. L., 88
Braungart, J. M., 186
Braun-Lewensohn, O., 61,
    64, 67, 68, 69, 70, 71, 73,
    831
Brdar, I., 20, 160, 164
Brenner, L., 127–128
Brenner, S.-O., 344, 345
Bretherton, I., 145
Bretherton, R., 47, 831
Brewer, W. F., 285
Brewerton, P., 336
Brickman, P., 128, 187, 739
Bridges, L., 144
Bright, D., 338
Bright, D. A., 652
Brinen, A. P., 700
Brody, C., 445, 447, 452
Brody, G. H., 775
Broemer, P., 105
Brombin, C., 474
Bronfenbrenner, U., 17, 18,
    74
Bronikowski, M., 69
Brook, J., 336
Brooks, R. B., 773
Brooks-Gunn, J., 313
Brown, G. D. A., 565
Brown, G. W., 194
Brown, J. D., 185, 504,
    511
Brown, J. H. L., 38

Brown, J. L., 779
Brown, K. M., 753
Brown, K. W., 86, 89, 92, 95,
    139, 141, 142, 148, 149,
    150, 151, 831
Brown, N. J. L., 331
Brown, S. L., 447
Brownlee, J., 290
Bruner, J., 17, 19
Brunhart, S. M., 618
Bruni, L., 764
Brunker, B., 619
Brunstein, J. C., 108, 109, 192
Brunwasser, S. M., 272
Brusilovskiy, E., 698
Bruyere, S. M., 447
Bryan, J., 777
Bryant, F. B., 172, 233
Buber, M., 37, 55
Bubriski-McKenzie, A., 687
Buck, A. C., 397
Buck, S., 213
Buckingham, M., 336, 377,
    383
Buckles, B., 688
Buckley, K. E., 717
Buijzen, M., 91
Buliung, R. N., 217
Burbules, N., 281
Burkeman, O., 793
Burker, E. J., 396
Burman, B., 662
Burnes, B., 329
Burns, D., 240
Burns, G. W., 465
Burns, J. M., 267
Burns, M. N., 245
Burnstein, E., 134
Burroughs, J. E., 90, 111
Burt, K. B., 775
Burtt, E. A., 34
Buschor, C., 163
Bush, M. W., 384
Bush, N. R., 776
Buss, A. H., 148
Busse, E. W., 604
Butcher, J. N., 519, 537
Butler, E. A., 757
Butler, N., 213
Butollo, W., 503
Butterworth, G., 13
Buunk, A., 761
Buzzell, S., 343

Cable, D. M., 110
Cacioppo, J. T., 111, 471, 721,
    796
Cacioppo, S., 796
Cadell, S., 619
Caffo, E., 474
Cain, S., 808, 814, 815

Caistor-Arendar, L., 758
Calhoun, K. S., 513
Calhoun, L. G., 50, 435, 447, 503, 504, 505, 506, 507, 508, 509, 510, 511, 512, 513, 514, 619, 812, 831
Camacho, T. C., 209–210
Cameron, K., 331, 332, 336, 338
Cameron, K. S., 368, 757
Camino, L., 320
Campbell, A., 215, 732
Campbell, D. T., 128, 187, 739
Campbell, J., 148, 170
Campbell, J. D., 300, 811
Campion, J., 349
Camus, A., 53
Cann, A., 503, 506, 508, 514, 793
Cantanzaro, S. J., 549
Cantor, N., 192
Cantore, S., 329
Cantril, H., 733
Caplan, G., 72, 503
Caplovitz, D., 733
Caponigro, J. M., 400
Carbonneau, H., 618
Card, N. A., 562, 569
Carelli, M. G., 229
Carless, D., 209, 214, 215
Carlson, C. R., 508
Carmelli, D., 402
Carneiro, I. G., 343
Carolan, B., 281
Caron, C., 618
Carpenter, J., 688
Carr, M. A., 225
Carrico, A. W., 396
Carroll, J. B., 545
Carson, J. W., 197
Carstensen, L. L., 172
Carta, J., 299
Carter, A. J., 364
Carter, S., 799
Caruso, D., 302, 304
Caruso, D. R., 545, 547, 550, 551, 831
Carver, C. S., 109, 124, 147, 171, 190, 484, 504, 507
Casey, E. C., 782
Cash, T. F., 794, 798, 800
Caspar, F. H., 532
Caspersen, C. J., 207
Caspi, A., 306
Castelnovo, G., 798
Castro, F. G., 781
Catalano, D., 447
Catalano, R. F., 778
Catalino, L. I., 436

Catanese, K. R., 717
Caughlan, S., 290
Cavanagh, M., 249, 250, 252, 253, 261
Cawley, M. J., 522
Caza, A., 338, 368
Cazzaro, M., 453, 466, 468, 472
Cecen, A. R., 67
Celinski, M. J., 64
Cella, D., 401
Cemalcilar, Z., 106
Chafonleas, S. M., 298
Chalder, T., 448
Chamberlin, J., 695
Chambless, D. L., 307
Chan, D. W., 162
Chan, R., 85
Chancellor, J., 191, 197, 198, 254
Chandler, C. L., 142
Chandler, J., 792
Chandler, M. J., 586
Chang, E. C., 470, 498
Chang, L., 88
Chang, M., 404
Chaplin, L., 564
Chaplin, L. N., 91
Chapman, A. R., 673
Charney, D. S., 475, 776
Chatman, C. M., 323
Chatman, J. A., 110
Che, H., 111
Cheadle, A. C. D., 661
Cheavens, J., 484, 490, 493, 699
Chen, G., 162
Chen, S., 348
Chernev, A., 123
Cherniss, C., 552
Cheung, W.-Y., 86
Cheung-Judge, M., 329
Chida, Y., 396, 465
Childre, D., 567, 568
Chilton, G., 453
Chilton, P., 86, 87
Chinn, C. A., 288, 290–291
Chirkov, V., 140
Chiu, C.-Y., 20
Choi, I., 191
Choi, Y., 745
Chokel, J. T., 717
Chou, C. C., 447, 453
Chou, Y. Y., 795
Chow, R. M., 565
Chow, S.-C., 404
Christensen, A., 314, 671
Christenson, G. M., 207
Christiansen, N. D., 552
Ciarelli, R., 486
Ciarocco, N. J., 717

Cicchetti, D., 301, 773, 776, 778
Cieslak, R., 448
Cieza, A., 448
Ciftci, A., 347
Cirillo, L., 17
Claridge, G., 420
Clark, A. E., 187
Clark, H. B., 568
Clark, K., 367
Clark, L. A., 384
Clark, R. E., 816
Clarke, H. M., 341, 831
Clausen, J. A., 358
Clayton, V., 577
Clifford, M. M., 816, 818
Clifton, D. O., 267, 331, 377, 383
Clinkinbeard, S. S., 68
Clonan, S. M., 298
Clore, G. L., 548
Close, H. T., 664
Clow, A., 209
Clutterbuck, D., 251, 252, 385
Coates, D., 128
Coatsworth, J. D., 775
Cobb, N. K., 242
Coffey, C. S., 404
Coffey, K. A., 185
Coffman, C., 336, 362
Coffman, L., 486
Cohen, A. D., 670
Cohen, G. L., 103
Cohen, J., 85, 90, 551, 753
Cohen, J. L., 508
Cohen, L., 504, 773
Cohen, P., 85, 90
Cohen, R. D., 209–210
Cohen, S., 83, 111, 196, 197, 368, 396, 401, 403, 720
Cohn, H. W., 49, 52
Cohn, M., 397
Cohn, M. A., 185
Coker, L. A., 420
Colbert, A. E., 341
Colby, A., 22
Coleman, J., 272
Coleman, P. T., 755
Coll, E., 761
Collin, C., 619
Collins, A., 287, 548
Collins, J., 380
Colquitt, J. A., 345
Combs, G. M., 703
Comos, D., 689
Compton, W. C., 37, 38, 397
Conchie, S. M., 346
Conde-Sala, J. L., 617
Condon, P., 561
Condor, S., 9

Conger, R. D., 779
Conley-Ayers, A., 1
Conlin, C., 794
Conn, V. S., 213
Connell, J., 142
Connell, J. P., 142
Connelly, C. E., 341, 350, 831
Connelly, J., 331
Connor, M. K., 618
Connor, T. S., 799
Conoley, C. W., 433, 757
Conoley, J. C., 433
Conrad, P., 681
Conroy, R. M., 617
Constanti, P., 349
Conti, S., 453, 466, 472
Conway, C., 471
Cook, C. L., 447
Cook, D., 773
Cook, J. A., 696
Cook, W., 495
Cooke, D., 329
Cooney, G. M., 211
Cooper, H., 198
Cooper, M., 48, 51, 431
Cooper, R. K., 552
Cooperrider, D., 329, 337
Cooperrider, D. L., 364, 365
Copeland, M. E., 695, 700
Corbin, J., 317
Cordischi, C., 659
Cordner, C., 637
Cordovo, M. J., 508
Corngold, J., 22
Cornish, K. A., 37
Cornum, R., 23
Coronado, G., 668
Corrigan, P., 521
Corrigan, P. W., 349
Cortinovis, I., 619, 628
Costa, P. T., 186, 363
Costakis, M. J., 396
Costello, C. G., 420
Côté, S., 550, 552
Cottle, T. J., 225
Couchman, C. E., 145
Courtwright, S. H., 341
Coutu, D., 383
Coutu, D. L., 362, 378
Covey, L. S., 290
Covey, S. R., 365–366
Covington, M. V., 484
Cowger, C. D., 684, 686
Cowles, E., 210
Cox, A., 300
Cox, E., 251, 252
Cox, J., 753
Cox, M., 647
Coyle, A., 435
Coyle, C. T., 670

Coyle, S., 217
Cozzolino, P., 89
Cozzolino, R., 659
Crabtree, S., 492
Craig, A., 448
Craig, C. M., 696
Craig, N., 380
Craik, K. H., 18
Cramm, J. M., 628
Crandall, R., 175
Crane, K., 618
Creswell, J. D., 148, 151
Crews, D. J., 213
Crits-Cristoph, P., 465
Crnic, K. A., 620
Crompton, T., 86
Croom, A. M., 453
Cropanzano, R., 197
Cross, R., 333
Cross, S. E., 417
Crowell, A., 286
Crowther, J., 796
Cruz, J., 561
Cryan, M., 617
Cryer, B., 568
Csikszentmihalyi, I. S., 1, 358, 360
Csikszentmihalyi, M., 1, 9, 10, 11, 12, 19–20, 32, 83, 149–150, 169, 170, 195, 223, 230, 256, 275, 301, 315, 319, 321, 330, 358, 360, 380, 414, 422, 432, 444, 467, 559, 577, 619, 621, 682, 763, 783, 809
Cui, X. J., 606, 608
Cuijpers, P., 240
Cummings, J., 122
Cummings, S., 617
Cummins, R. A., 641, 741
Cunha, T., 761
Cunningham, L. L. C., 508
Curtis, L., 701
Cushing, C., 103
Cushman, P., 19, 417
Cutler, H., 765
Cutrona, C. E., 720
Czapinski, J., 520


Dahlsgaard, K. A., 14
Dahlstrom, W. G., 537
Daigre, S., 486
Dalai Lama, 765
Dal Bo, P., 704
Dalrymple, J., 567
Daly, M., 779
Damasio, A., 553
Damasio, A. R., 553
Danbenmeier, J. J., 791
Daniels, K., 343

Danner, D. D., 747
Danoff-Burg, S., 619
Danovsky, M., 486
Daoud, N., 73
Darley, J. M., 16
Darling-Hammond, L., 288
Darwin, C., 18
Dasborough, M. T., 552
Dasen, P. R., 21
d'Astous, A., 92
Daus, C. S., 552
Davey, G., 20, 23
David, S., 1, 385
Davidov, E., 106
Davidson, L., 688, 704
Davidson, O. B., 494
Davies, M., 474
Davila, J., 660, 663
Davis, C. G., 437, 507
Davis, J. H., 345
Davis, K., 381
Davis, M. K., 489
Davis, R., 773, 778
Davis, W. W., 688, 695
Davy, J., 335
Dawber, T. R., 595, 608
Dawes, L., 286
Dawes, N. P., 313, 315–316, 317, 320, 831
Day, J., 286
Dean, B., 382
Dear, K., 131, 133
de Beauvoir, S., 596
Decarvalho, R. J., 32, 33
De Charms, R., 141
DeChiro, J., 686
Deci, E. L., 37, 83, 84, 87, 88, 104, 109, 121, 139, 140, 141, 142, 143, 144, 145, 146, 147, 149, 150, 159, 160, 167, 169, 172, 190, 215, 302, 317, 320, 330, 343, 360, 379, 463, 617, 640, 666, 716
Decker, S. K., 761
Deckop, J. R., 105
De Cuyper, N., 347, 348
Deegan, P. E., 695
DeFillippi, R. J., 367
DeFries, J. C., 186, 306
DeGarmo, D. S., 779
DeGeus, E. C., 210
de Graaf, J., 95, 96
de Graaf, R., 697
de Haan, M., 779
De Hoogh, A. H. P., 341
De Jongste, M., 618
Dekel, R., 681, 831
Dekker, P., 217
Della Porta, M., 195

Della Porta, M. D., 191, 195, 238
Delle Fave, A., 20, 21, 160, 164, 358, 467, 615, 619, 621, 622, 623, 628, 831
DeLuga, R. J., 197
Demerouti, E., 358
Demir, M., 761
Demoncada, A. C., 450
DeMoor, M. M., 210
Demot, L., 67
Dendato, K. M., 381
Deneulin, S., 84
Den Hartog, D. N., 341
Denkla, D. A., 672
Dennett, D., 150
Dennison, L., 448, 453
Denton, F., 90
De Rivera, J., 755
de St. Aubin, E., 168
de Shazer, S., 437
Desrosiers, J., 618
DeSteno, D., 560, 561
Detweiler, J. B., 302, 547
Deutsch, M., 755
DeVoe, S. E., 122, 126, 132
DeWall, C. N., 561, 717
De Witte, H., 86, 348
Dhont, K., 86
Diamond, A., 778
DiBlasio, W., 664
Dickerhoof, R., 191, 238, 259, 385, 452, 569
Dickerhoof, R. M., 193
Dickerson, S. S., 147
DiClemente, C. C., 171, 382
Didion, L. M., 514
Dienberg Love, G., 465
Diener, C., 132
Diener, D., 358, 381
Diener, E. D., 37, 83, 95, 105, 106, 124, 132, 164, 176, 185, 186, 187, 188, 192, 198, 230, 231, 254, 302, 342, 348, 359, 384, 401, 446, 463, 465, 713, 714, 716, 718, 720, 722, 740, 741, 757, 761, 792, 793
Diener, M., 132, 358
DiGeronimo, T. F., 133
Di Girolamo, S., 688
Dijksterhuis, A. P., 148
Dijksterhuis, B., 103
Dillard, J. P., 718
Dillon, D. R., 283
Dimeo, F. C., 451
Dinnie, E., 753
Dinsen, M. S., 336
Dirks, K. T., 345
Dishman, R. K., 214

Ditchman, N., 447
Dittmar, H., 85, 86, 87, 90
Diwan, S., 349
Dixon, D., 617
Dixon, L. J., 662
Dixon, R. A., 577
Dockray, S., 402
Doggett, L., 379
Dolan, P., 357
Dole, J. A., 288
Doll, B., 773
Dollwet, M., 703
Dominguez, J., 91
Donaghue, N., 761
Donahue, E. M., 124, 561
Donald, I. J., 346
Donaldson, S., 757
Donaldson, S. I., 331, 705
Dong, T., 286
Donker, T., 240
Donocan, M. A., 197
Doraiswamy, P. M., 191
Dornan, D. H., 688
Dotan, N., 67
Dougherty, S. B., 445, 447, 452
Douglas, K., 209
Douleh, T., 103
Dovidio, J. F., 16
Dowling, G. A., 400
Downer, J., 151
Doyle, M., 378
Doyle, W. J., 197, 721
Drake, C. R., 647
Drake, L., 229
Drake, R. E., 698
Dreher, D. E., 493, 494
Driscoll, C., 343
Droit-Volet, S., 792
Du Bois, C., 68
Duckworth, 267
Duckworth, A. L., 171, 267, 396, 397, 402, 422, 423, 450, 566
Duffy, R. D., 169
Duggan, M., 690
DuHamel, K., 509
Dulewicz, V., 552
Dumas, T., 306
Dumont, J. M., 688
Duncan, B., 252
Duncan, B. L., 40
Duncan, E., 229
Duncan, G., 23
Duncan, L. G., 397, 618
Duncan, T., 288
Dunlap, G., 299
Dunn, D. S., 445, 447, 452
Dunn, E., 715
Dunn, E. W., 191, 399, 758

Dunn, J. R., 561
Dunton, G. F., 217
Durand, C. P., 217
Duriez, B., 86, 104
Durkheim, E., 132
Durlak, J. A., 300, 551
Durrett, C. A., 420
Dutton, J., 333
Dutton, J. E., 351, 757
Dvir, T., 347
Dweck, C. S., 169, 170, 275, 319, 484
Dworkin, J., 321
Dymnicki, A. B., 300, 551
Dyrdal, G. M., 160
Dyrenforth, P. S., 187

Eack, S. M., 553
Eakman, A. M., 345
Eaphy, E. D., 351
Early, T. J., 690
Easterbrook, J. A., 548
Easterlin, R., 714
Easterlin, R. A., 187
Eaton, J., 660
Eaton, W. W., 722
Ebert, J. E. J., 132
Eccles, J. S., 314, 315, 318
Eckersley, R., 131, 133, 764
Eden, D., 348
Edgar, L., 397
Edlis-Matityahou, M., 661
Edmondson, K., 397
Edmundowicz, D., 397
Edmunds, S., 209
Edwards, J. R., 110, 111
Edwards, L., 661
Edwards, L. M., 488, 490
Effron, D. A., 792
Efrati, M., 67
Egeland, B., 781
Eghrari, H., 146
Egloff, B., 583
Ehde, D., 443, 445, 831
Ehde, D. M., 445, 452
Ehrenreich, B., 269
Ehrlich, T., 22
Eid, M., 187
Eifert, G. H., 420
Eisemann, M., 70
Eisenberg, N., 16, 761
Eisikovits, Z., 686
Ekin-Wood, A., 619
Ekkekakis, P., 209, 212, 216
Eklund, M., 345
Ekman, P., 738
Ekvall, G., 369
Ekwall, A. K., 619
Elbertson, N. A., 551

Elger, C. E., 448
Elgin, D., 91
Elias, M. J., 551
Ellenberger, H. R., 33
Elliot, A. J., 88, 139, 190, 193
Elliot, M. K., 232
Elliott, S., 214
Elliott, T. R., 451, 452, 453
Ellis, A., 465, 467, 475
Ellis, B. J., 306, 776
Ellis, S., 366
Elmore, R. F., 288, 290, 292
Elster, A., 103
Elwick, H., 618
Embretson, S. E., 401
Emery, G., 49, 467
Emler, N., 300
Emmelkamp, P. M., 466
Emmons, K., 668
Emmons, R. A., 14, 50, 51, 52, 84, 105, 111, 124, 176, 190, 191, 197, 230, 240, 259, 267, 384, 390, 401, 436, 559–560, 561, 562, 564, 569, 570, 640, 641, 645, 647
Enders, T., 506
Engdahl, B. E., 503
Engel, G. L., 616
Enosh, G., 686
Enright, R. D., 660, 662, 664, 666, 670, 671
Epel, E., 228, 229
Epel, E. S., 197
Epstein, M. H., 521
Erbes, C. R., 779
Erekson, D. M., 433
Erikson, E. H., 168, 169, 577, 578, 583, 590
Eriksson, M., 61, 64, 67, 68, 72, 73, 74, 831
Ernst, R. E., 267
Ernst, R. M., 270, 298, 815
Eschleman, K. J., 197
Escobar, M. D., 420
Esterling, B. A., 670
Esterson, A., 49
Estes, R., 756, 759
Etchegoyen, R. H., 565
Ethington, L. L., 431
Etzioni, A., 91, 723, 724
Evans, D. R., 89
Evans, G. W., 720
Evans, I. M., 522, 525
Evans, L. A., 51
Evans, P. B., 760
Evans, W. P., 68
Ewart, C. K., 662
Exline, J. J., 55, 660, 672

Eysenbach, G., 239
Eysenck, H. J., 19

Faber, R. J., 87, 88
Fabes, R. A., 761
Fahey, J. L., 504
Faircloth, B. S., 315
Fallon, B. J., 761
Farig, J., 85
Farkas, M., 706
Farrow, T. F. D., 661
Farwell, L., 565
Faulkner, G., 207, 209, 212, 214, 215, 216–217, 218
Faulkner, G. E. J., 217
Fava, G. A., 165, 452, 463, 464, 465, 466, 468, 470, 471, 472, 473, 474, 477, 700, 831
Fava, M., 475
Fava, R. G., 464
Feather, N., 225
Feather, N. T., 110
Feeney, J. A., 396
Fehr, R., 673
Feigenson, N. R., 672
Feinberg, O., 114
Feld, S., 733
Feldman, D., 699
Feldman, D. B., 413, 423, 493, 494
Feldman, M. E., 396
Felfe, J., 345
Felner, R., 306
Femia, E. E., 618
Fenell, D., 662
Fenigstein, A., 148
Ferguson, M. J., 148
Ferguson, Y., 196
Fernandez, Y. M., 643, 647
Ferrans, C., 446
Ferrario, N., 619
Ferrin, D. L., 345
Festinger, L., 123
Fetchenhauer, D., 761
Feuerstein, M., 450
Fianco, A., 615, 831
Field, T., 798, 799
Fincham, F. D., 561, 564, 659, 660, 661, 662, 663, 666, 670, 672, 673, 796, 807, 808, 813, 814, 815, 832
Fineburg, A., 269
Fineburg, A. C., 267, 268, 270, 832
Fingerman, K. L., 584
Fink, J., 773
Fink, J. K., 620
Finkel, N. J., 504

Finkel, S. M., 185
Fischer, S. A., 494
Fisher, D., 643
Fisher, G. K., 346
Fiske, A. P., 15
Fitchett, G., 401
Fitoussi, J. E., 755
Fitzgerald, J., 285
Fitzpatrick, R., 616
Flache, A., 761
Flak, V. E., 652
Flaschner, A. B., 341
Fletcher, J. M., 420
Flett, G. L., 124
Flett, R., 230
Flor, H., 451, 498, 499
Flores, N., 520
Floyd, R. K., 488
Flückiger, C., 532, 537
Flum, H., 314
Foldes, H. J., 349
Folkman, S., 66, 197, 394, 395, 398, 504, 617, 618, 809
Fong, G. W., 151
Fook, J., 323
Ford, B. Q., 196, 400
Ford, T., 298
Fordyce, M. W., 38, 171, 193, 465
Forgatch, M. S., 779
Forman, B. S., 225
Foroni, F., 792
Forresi, B., 474
Forrett, R., 273
Förster, J., 584
Fortune, C.-A., 635, 653, 832
Foster, A., 704
Foster, J. H., 67
Foster, J. M., 760
Foucault, M., 17
Fowers, B. J., 160
Fowler, D., 699
Fox, K. R., 214, 215
Fox, L., 299
Fox Eades, J. M., 304
Fox-Genovese, E., 721
Fraccaroli, F., 346
Fraley, R. C., 420
Frances, A., 413, 416, 419
Frances, A. J., 415, 418, 420
Frank, A. W., 793
Frank, J. B., 40
Frank, J. D., 40, 464
Frank, R. C., 451
Frank, R. H., 714
Frankl, V., 16, 20
Frankl, V. E., 164, 165, 503
Frattarole, J., 721
Frazier, P., 175, 401

Frazier, P. A., 431
Frederick, C., 174, 176
Frederick, S., 128, 187
Fredrickson, B. L., 11, 168,
    171, 185, 191, 197, 198,
    233, 260, 301, 366, 395,
    435, 436, 463, 465, 466,
    521, 567, 618, 747, 792,
    796, 797, 800
Freedman, S., 660
Freedman, S. R., 671
Freire, T., 20, 160
Fremming, R., 618
Freres, D. R., 303
Frese, F. J., 688, 695
Freud, S., 739
Freund, A. M., 505, 584
Frey, B. S., 357, 733
Fried, C., 91
Friedberg, J. P., 661
Friedman, H., 31, 38, 40, 696
Friedman, H. L., 38, 331,
    434, 521, 813, 814
Fries, J. F., 595
Friessen, W. V., 747
Frisch, M. B., 165, 452, 465,
    533
Frisén, A, 795, 800
Fritz, H. L., 720
Frodi, A., 144
Froh, J. J., 2, 31, 191, 267,
    268, 559, 562, 564, 565,
    566, 569, 832
Fromm, E., 56
Fugl-Meyer, A. R., 446
Fugl-Meyer, K. S., 446
Fuhrer, M. J., 446
Fuhrman, A., 146
Fujimoto, T., 367
Fujita, F., 186, 192, 718
Fukui, S., 688, 689
Fulker, D. W., 186
Fuller, J. A. K., 191
Fulmer, D., 503
Funder, D. C., 186
Furlong, M. J., 757, 815
Furnham, A., 52, 110, 795

Gable, S. F., 681
Gable, S. L., 1, 172, 561
Gagnon, A. J., 397
Gal, A., 103
Galea, S., 783
Galile, R., 70
Gallace, A., 799
Gallese, V., 796
Galnoor, I., 763
Galvin, K., 450
Galvin, L. R., 448
Gambrell, E., 682
Gamoran, A., 281, 283

Gandek, B., 446
Gannon, T., 652
Gannon, T. A., 641, 652, 653
Garcea, N., 52
Garcia-Moya, I., 68, 69
Garde, A. H., 343
Gardiner, P., 367
Gardner, H., 300, 382
Garland, E. L., 471
Garmezy, N., 300, 620
Garnefski, N., 69
Garre-Olme, J., 617
Garrison, C. Z., 298
Garske, J. P., 489
Gassman, D., 436
Gatersleben, B., 86
Gauffin, H., 69
Gay, C., 214
Gebauer, J. E., 105
Geckova, A. M., 68
Gelfand, M. J., 20, 111, 673
Gelso, C. J., 433, 437
Gemmell, I., 217
Georgaca, E., 418
George, B., 380
George, M. S., 475
Georgellis, Y., 187
Geraghty, A., 566
Geraghty, A. W., 191, 796
Geraghty, A. W. A., 465, 471,
    566
Gerber, P. D., 608
Gergen, K. J., 19, 416
Gergen, R. J., 17, 19
Gerlic, I., 553
Gershon, R. C., 400
Gerson, E. M., 735
Gerstein, E. D., 620
Gerstein, L. H., 432, 435,
    437, 438
Gettinger, M., 773
Getzels, J. W., 111
Geva, N., 618
Gewirtz, A. H., 779
Geyer, S., 64
Geyh, S., 443, 448, 832
Ghaedi, G., 106
Ghazinour, M., 775
Giacalone, R. A., 105
Giannopoulos, V., 698
Gibson, J., 110
Gick, 284
Gil, I. B., 687
Gil, S., 792
Gilbert, D. T., 132, 173
Gill, A. S., 341, 342
Gillett, R., 465
Gillham, J., 270, 298, 301,
    815
Gillham, J. E., 32, 267, 272,
    303, 465

Gillham, J. M., 303
Gilman, R., 270, 757, 815
Gilman, S. L., 420
Gilovich, T., 126
Gilpin, M., 331
Gilson, L., 358
Gingerich, S., 700
Gingras, I., 85
Gino, F., 561
Ginsburg, G. S., 474
Girdler, S. S., 799
Gittell, J., 331, 332
Givvin, K. B., 286
Gladdis, M. M., 465
Glass, G. V., 191, 452
Glassman, A. H., 290, 448
GlenMaye, L. F., 690
Glina, M., 281, 288
Glück, J., 579, 580, 582,
    584
Glueck, E., 597
Glueck, S., 597
Goddard, A. W., 475
Godfrey, H. P., 448
Goldberg, L. R., 186
Golden, T. P., 447
Golding, S., 791
Goldman, D., 549
Goldstein, E., 451
Goldstein, S., 773
Goleman, D., 300, 361, 382,
    545, 552
Gollwitzer, P. M., 148, 171,
    267
Gomes, R., 761
Gomez-Fraguela, J. A., 85
Gonzalez, A., 226, 227
Gonzalez, E., 720
Gonzalez, R., 508
Gonzalez-Molina, G., 362
Goode, M. R., 86
Gooding, P. A., 525
Goodman, P., 49
Goodman, R., 298
Goodwin, E. M., 532
Goossens, E., 69
Gootman, J. A., 318
Gorczynski, P., 212
Gordon, A. K., 567
Gordon, A. M., 561
Gordon, C. L., 562
Gordon, G., 492
Gordon, G. W., 186
Gordon, K. C., 662, 670
Gordon, S. E., 696
Gordon, W. A., 444
Gorgievski, M. J., 348
Gorman, B. S., 224
Gorsuch, R. L., 525
Gosch, E. A., 465
Goscha, R. J., 525, 532

Gosney, J. L., 212
Gosselin, J. T., 411, 420
Gotlib, I. H., 718
Gottfredson, G. D., 111
Gottman, J. M., 55, 331
Gouldner, A. W., 559
Govier, T., 288, 637, 638
Govindji, R., 23, 304, 465
Gow, K. M., 64
Graham, E., 764
Graham, J. R., 537
Grandi, S., 453, 464, 466, 472, 473
Grant, A., 114, 249, 250, 251, 252, 253, 261, 273
Grant, A. M., 122, 378–379, 466, 561
Grant, H., 267
Grant, P. M., 700
Grassmann, R., 108, 192
Grawe, K., 436
Gray, J. A. M., 307
Grealy, M., 213, 214, 793
Greeff, A. P., 67
Green, H., 298
Green, L. S., 273
Green, M., 13
Greenberg, I. S., 489
Greenberg, J., 51
Greening, T., 31, 696
Greenstein, F. I., 553
Greenwald, A. G., 150
Greenwood, G., 549
Gregory, R. J., 240
Greifeneder, R., 123
Grewen, K. M., 799
Grey, I. K., 775
Griffeth, J., 338
Griffin, S., 124, 176, 230, 384, 401
Griffith, A., 319
Griffiths, C. A., 67
Grigorenko, E. L., 778
Grogan, J. L., 32, 832
Groleau, J. M., 503, 832
Grolnick, W. S., 141, 144, 145, 146
Grooms, A. N., 722
Gropper, D. M., 759, 761
Gross, J. J., 585
Grosse, M., 532
Grossman, I., 590
Grossman, P., 151, 451
Grouzet, F. M. E., 84, 164
Gruber, J., 400, 404
Gruenewald, T. L., 810
Grugulis, I., 367
Guan, Y., 216
Guidi, J., 470, 471, 472
Guillen-Royo, M., 84, 85
Gum, A., 699

Guo, W., 684, 690
Gupta, N., 111
Gurin, G., 733
Gurka, V., 198
Gustafsson, P. A., 69–70
Gustafsson, P. E., 69–70
Gwaltney, J. M., Jr., 721

Haasova, M., 216
Hackman, J. R., 360, 366
Hadley, S., 471
Hage, S. M., 430, 433, 436
Hagelskamp, C., 551
Hagerty, M. R., 722
Haggerty, R. J., 668
Haidt, J., 1, 11, 240, 561
Haidt, J. T., 83
Hainsworth, J., 700
Hakanen, J. J., 358
Halama, P., 486
Halbesleben, J. R. B., 348
Hale, D., 272
Hale, R. L., 267
Halji-Michael, M., 795
Hall, E. E., 216
Hall, J., 773
Hall, J. H., 660
Hall, J. S., 776
Hall, R., 270
Hallal, P. C., 208, 215
Hallberg, R., 619
Halpern, R., 314
Hambrick-Dixon, P. J., 90
Hames, J. L., 810
Hamey, P., 487
Hamilton, S. F., 568
Hampson, S. E., 186
Han, M.-H., 776
Hanaway, M., 48
Handy, C., 362, 366
Hanke, K., 673
Hanks, E. A., 793
Hannah, S. T., 350
Hanoch, Y., 122
Hansen, D., 314
Hanson, R., 798
Harackiewicz, J. M., 192
Hardman, F., 283
Hare, R., 643
Harford, R. A., 148
Harker, L., 198, 653
Harkins, L., 652
Harlan, D., 503
Harper, D., 418, 443
Harrington, S., 22, 31, 47, 53, 61, 444, 689, 807
Harris, C., 487
Harris, D. V., 208
Harris, J. R., 186
Harris, R., 94
Harrison, R. A., 217

Hart, K. E., 807
Hart, S., 645
Härtel, C. E., 552
Harter, J., 331
Harter, J. K., 331, 703
Harter, S., 152
Harthun, M. L., 781
Hartnell, C. A., 350
Hartner, J. K., 358
Hartner, L. M., 358
Harvey, J., 348
Harvey, J. H., 809, 810
Harvey, S., 792
Harzer, C., 162
Haslam, N., 107
Haslam, S. A., 346
Hassmen, P., 213
Hasson-Ohayon, I., 689
Hastings, S., 304, 490
Haupt, A. L., 717
Havighurst, R. J., 463, 733, 775
Hawkes, A., 453
Hawkins, J. D., 778, 779
Hawkins, L., 323
Hawley, K. M., 783
Hawley, L., 525
Hawley, W. D., 288
Haworth, J., 357, 358
Haybron, D. M., 13
Hayden, A., 95
Hayes, D. A., 290
Hayes, S. C., 165, 397, 433
Hayes, T., 331
Hayes, T. C., 703
Haynes, R. B., 307
Hayward, R. D., 51
Hazan, O., 103, 115
Hazler, R. J., 39
Headey, B., 186, 198
Heaphy, E., 331
Heath, S. B., 315
Heatherton, T. F., 147
Heathfield, S., 367
Hebl, J. H., 664
Hecht, S. A., 420
Heckhausen, J., 577
Heckman, J. J., 781
Hedstrom, L. J., 566
Hefferline, R. F., 49, 148
Hefferon, K., 2, 207, 208, 209, 213, 214, 215, 305, 331, 791, 793, 798, 800, 832
Heider, F., 559
Heiman-Patterson, T., 620
Heimpel, H., 596
Heintz, A., 290
Held, B. S., 31, 36, 470, 807, 810, 811, 814

Helgeson, V. S., 447, 508, 720
Heller, D., 358
Heller, R. F., 217
Helliwell, J., 752, 756, 757, 763
Helliwell, J. F., 761
Hellstrom, I., 618
Helson, R., 578, 579, 586
Hemmeter, M. L., 299
Hemmings, A., 320
Henckmann, W., 34
Henderson, A. S., 194
Henderson, J. D., 436
Henderson, M. E., 753
Hendrick, C., 719
Hendrick, S. S., 719
Henry, C., 229
Henry, J., 357, 359, 367, 368, 369, 370, 832
Heppner, P. P., 484
Hepworth, D. H., 682
Herman, J. L., 686
Hernandez, B., 652
Hernandez, J. A., 652
Hernandez, L., 401
Hernandez-Fernaud, E., 652
Hertzberg, F., 359
Hewitt, J. P., 417
Hewitt, P. L., 124
Hicks, B. M., 190
Hicks, J. A., 166
Hidi, S., 315, 323
Higgins, E. T., 584
Higgins, P., 504
Higgins, R. L., 417
Higgs, M., 334, 552
Hill, K. G., 778
Hill, L., 290
Hill, P., 660
Hillier, C., 450
Hilsenroth, M. J., 638
Hirsch, B. J., 320
Hirsch, S. K., 363
Hirschfeld, R., 298
Hirschi, A., 163
Hirschman, A. L., 791
Hitlin, S., 103
Hobfoll, S. E., 347, 348, 350
Hobman, E. V., 341, 346
Hockemeyer, J. R., 508
Hodgekins, J., 699
Hodges, T. D., 267
Hodgins, H. S., 148, 470
Hofer, B. K., 284, 290
Hoffman, M. L., 16
Hofmann, S. G., 151
Hofmann, W., 187
Hofstede, G., 370, 721
Hogan, M. F., 701
Holbecke, L., 329
Holland, J. L., 111, 114

Holleran, S. A., 487
Holliday, S. G., 586
Hollin, C. R., 639
Hollingshead, A. B., 605
Holman, D., 350
Holmgren, M. R., 660
Holmqvist, K., 795, 800
Holohan, D. R., 514
Holt-Lunstad, J., 525, 721
Holub, S. C., 567
Holyoak, 284
Hommer, D., 151
Honey, P., 363
Hong, Y.-Y., 20
Hoogwegt, M. T., 396
Hooke, A., 346
Hopke, D. R., 451
Hopkins, B., 13
Hopkins, J., 167
Hoppe, C., 448
Hopper, K., 696, 701
Hops, H., 298
Horejsi, C. R., 684
Horner, R. H., 300
Horney, K., 689
Hornick, J., 224
Horowitz, M. J., 465
Horrell, S. C. V., 514
Horselenberg, R., 474
Horvath, A. O., 489
Horvath, C. C., 799
Horwitz, A. V., 418
House, J. S., 720
Houser-Marko, L., 109
Hovsto, A., 245
Howard, G. S., 14, 23
Howard, K., 252
Howard, K. I., 484
Howe, G. W., 782
Howell, J. M., 346
Howell, R. T., 196, 197, 229, 231, 463
Hoza, B., 486
Huang, C., 815
Huang, H., 761
Huang, J.-W., 341
Huang, S. T., 662, 666
Hubble, M., 252
Hubble, M. A., 40, 438
Huberman, G., 122
Hudson, S. M., 639
Huebner, E. S., 270, 401, 492, 757, 815
Huffman, J., 255, 259
Huffman, J. C., 237, 399
Hufford, M. R., 402
Hughes, F. M., 662
Hulfand, J., 123
Hull, G. H., 684
Humphrey, A., 300, 302
Hung, T., 689

Hunt, M., 668
Hunter, L., 551
Huppert, F. A., 275
Hurling, R., 685
Hurst, C., 521
Hurst, M., 85, 86
Husman, J., 816, 817, 818
Huta, V., 159, 160, 161, 162, 163, 164, 165, 166, 168, 174, 175, 176, 525, 832
Hutchinson, J., 433, 435
Hutchinson, T. S., 566
Huxley, A., 732, 746
Hwang, J., 618
Hyatt-Edwards, L., 662
Hyland, M. E., 191, 465, 566, 616, 619, 796
Hyman, S. E., 419

Ichasky, A. D., 566
Ickovics, J. R., 504
Ilardi, S., 465, 484, 488
Ilies, R., 347, 349, 368
Impett, E. A., 172, 561, 791, 792, 798
Inglehart, R., 718, 752
Inhelder, B., 284
Intini, S., 619
Irving, L. M., 487, 493
Isen, A., 331
Isen, A. M., 394, 618
Ishida, R., 397
Islam, M. M., 343
Ivanchenko, G., 229
Ivanoff, A., 681
Iveson, C., 521
Ivgi, I., 112
Ivtzan, I., 793
Iwanski, C., 237, 699
Iwasaki, Y., 213
Iwata, O., 92
Iyengar, S., 125
Iyengar, S. M., 122
Iyengar, S. S., 122, 126, 132

Jackson, C. J., 341
Jackson, P. Z., 365
Jackson, T., 86, 95
Jacobs, G. A., 525
Jacobs Bao, K., 187, 191
Jacobsen, B., 51
Jacobsen, E., 451, 798
Jacobson, L. J., 619
Jacobson, N., 701
Jacoby, J., 94
Jahoda, M., 358, 397, 522, 733
James, W., 149
Jang, H., 140, 143
Janoff-Bulman, R., 128, 504, 506

Janovics, J., 552
Jansovec, N., 553
Jarrett, R. L., 320
Jarvis, P., 584
Jasinski, J. L., 687
Jaspers, K., 54
Jausovec, K., 553
Jaycox, L., 301
Jeffery, R. W., 396
Jelinek, M., 369
Jenaro, C., 520
Jenkins, J. M., 420
Jennings, D. J., 664
Jensen, A. L., 304
Jensen, M., 443, 832
Jensen, M. P., 451
Jepson, R., 212
Jex, S. M., 343, 344
Jiang, W., 122
Jick, T., 367
Jiménez , A., 106
Jiménez-Iglesias, A., 68, 69
Jimmieson, N. L., 341
Jiranek, P., 761
Joel, S., 561
Johar, G. V., 94
John, D. R., 91, 564
John, O. P., 124, 561
Johns, H., 764
Johnson, C. A., 550
Johnson, D., 237, 699
Johnson, D. W., 673
Johnson, E. C., 111
Johnson, H., 319
Johnson, J., 525
Johnson, J. A., 522
Johnson, K. A., 503
Johnson, R. T., 673
Johnston, D., 668
Johnston, L., 148
Johnston, M., 533, 617
Johnston, P., 286
Johnstone, G., 672
Joiner, T., 465
Joiner, T. E., 810
Jonas, K., 350
Jonathan, H., 681
Jones, A., 175
Jones, F., 396
Jones, S. M., 779
Jordan, B., 753
Jordan, J., 577
Jordan, P. J., 552
Jørgensen, I. S., 10, 11, 47
Joseph, D., 287
Joseph, S., 1, 2, 17, 21, 22, 23,
    31, 32, 47, 50, 61, 74, 85,
    166, 174, 267, 377, 379,
    384, 423, 429, 433, 434,
    435, 437, 438, 444, 447,
    464, 465, 477, 503, 504,

514, 524, 525, 537, 618,
    619, 690, 696, 807, 810,
    811, 812, 816, 817, 823,
    829, 832
Joshanloo, M., 106
Judge, T. A., 358, 359, 521
Jung, C. G., 464
Junker, B. W., 288
Jurkiewicz, C. L., 105
Juzwik, M. M., 290

Kabat-Zinn, J., 149
Kadison, R. D., 133
Kaemmer, B., 537
Kafetsios, K., 554
Kahana, B., 231, 778
Kahana, E., 231, 778
Kahler, C. W., 237, 532
Kahn, R. L., 595, 604
Kahne, J., 300
Kahneman, D., 37, 128, 316,
    402
Kaldor, M., 753
Kaler, M., 175, 401
Kallie, C. S., 52
Kalpakjian, C. Z., 661
Kaltreider, N. B., 465
Kammann, R., 230
Kanner, A. D., 83, 93, 394
Kanov, J. M., 704
Kanste, O., 341, 342
Kantz, J. E., 661
Kaplan, A., 314
Kaplan, B. K., 298
Kaplan, G. A., 209–210
Kaplan, H., 114
Kaplan, K., 698
Kaplan, R., 359
Kaplan, S., 359
Kaplan, U., 140
Karabati, S., 106
Karabenick, S. A., 230
Karasek, R. A., 359
Kardash, C. M., 286
Kardiner, A., 68
Karremans, J., 661
Karremans, J. C., 662
Kashdan, T., 240
Kashdan, T. B., 22, 23, 50,
    160, 166, 465, 470, 561,
    566, 685, 704
Kashdan, T. K., 533
Kasindorf, M., 718
Kasri, F., 129
Kasser, T., 83, 84, 85, 86, 87,
    88, 89, 90, 91, 92, 93, 95,
    104, 139, 150, 151, 164,
    168, 190, 193, 565, 714,
    832
Katie, M., 686
Kato, T., 486

Katz, I., 314
Kauffman, C., 250, 251, 253,
    254, 377, 378, 379, 381,
    383, 384, 385, 832
Kawachi, I., 448
Kazakino, E., 225
Kearney, R., 52
Kearns, J. N., 661, 673
Kee, K. S., 553, 554
Keegan, B., 274
Keeling, J., 685, 686
Keenan, B., 148
Kegan, R., 380
Kekes, J., 577, 586, 637, 640,
    642
Kelley, E., 343
Kelley-Moore, J., 778
Kellner, R., 472
Kelloway, E. K., 341, 343,
    345
Kelly, D. R., 171, 402
Kelly, J., 224
Kelman, H. C., 464
Keltner, D., 198, 561, 585
Kemeny, M. E., 89, 147, 504,
    810
Kemp, T., 273
Kempton, O., 753
Kendler, K. S., 567
Kennedy, P., 619
Kenny, C., 752, 764
Kenny, D., 451
Kentle, R. L., 124, 561
Kerig, P. K., 307
Kern, M. L., 196, 463
Kerr, S., 367
Kesebir, S., 722
Ketteringham, J., 360
Keyes, C. L. M., 37, 83, 160,
    185, 275, 302, 342, 343,
    347, 358, 384, 420, 424,
    464, 466, 468, 536, 615,
    617, 697
Khanna, S., 86
Kibe, C., 297, 832
Kiecolt-Glaser, J. K., 111,
    471, 662, 720, 721
Kiel, F., 378
Kierkegaard, S., 18, 53, 55
Kilbourne, J., 90
Kilburg, R., 382
Kilpatrick, S. D., 559–560
Kim, A., 140
Kim, E. S., 272
Kim, H. S., 194
Kim, I., 286
Kim, J. K., 85
Kim, J. S., 684
Kim, Y., 84, 85, 88, 139, 140,
    190
Kim-Cohen, J., 776

Kimes, L. A., 416, 417
Kimsey-House, H., 250, 378, 379
Kimsey-House, K., 250, 378
Kimura, Y., 566
King, L., 169, 185, 199, 258, 260, 619, 809
King, L. A., 22, 23, 37, 50, 111, 166, 191, 704
King, P. M., 287, 290
King, T., 652
Kinicki, A. J., 344
Kinnunen, U., 348
Kirk, A. F., 216
Kirk, S., 362
Kirk, S. A., 418, 419
Kirk, U., 151
Kirkpatrick, K. L., 402
Kirschner, P. A., 816
Kirst-Ashman, K. K., 684
Kirton, M. J., 363
Kisthardt, W., 684
Kitayama, S., 126, 132, 316, 317, 318, 320
Kitchener, K. S., 287, 290
Klausner, E. J., 493
Klein, B., 241
Klein, G., 316, 323
Klentz Davis, C., 436
Klerman, G. L., 130, 133
Klinger, E., 397, 647
Klubben, L. M., 437
Kluckhohn, C., 103
Kluger, A. N., 336
Knafo, A., 106
Knee, C. R., 148
Knee, R., 470
Knight, C., 346
Knight, J., 273
Knoll, N., 448
Knutson, B., 151
Ko, D., 194
Ko, I., 331, 705
Koban, R., 681, 683
Kobasa, S., 64
Koepke, F., 617
Koesk, G., 362
Koestner, R., 5, 104, 141, 143, 150
Koëter, G., 618
Kohlberg, L., 169
Kohn, A., 714
Koivula, N., 213
Kok, B. E., 436, 797
Kolts, R. L., 436, 561
Konermann, L., 396
König, S., 584
Kontra, C., 791, 792
Koole, S., 103
Koposov, R. A., 70
Kopp, M. S., 85

Kopperud, K. H., 50
Koptka, S. M., 484
Korchin, S. J., 413
Korek, S., 345
Kosinski, M., 446
Kosterman, R., 778
Kottler, J., 87–88
Kottler, J. A., 39
Kovjanic, S., 350
Kraaij, V., 69
Kraemer, D. T., 549
Kraemer, H. C., 662
Krakauer, M., 559, 832
Kramer, D. A., 577, 578, 586
Kras, M., 799
Krause, C., 73
Krause, M. S., 484
Krause, N., 51, 397
Kravetz, S., 689
Krech, G., 566
Kreider, H., 323
Kress, J. S., 551
Kreutzer, T., 781
Krieshok, T., 491
Krietemeyer, J., 167
Kring, A. M., 400
Krishnakumar, A., 781
Kristjánsson, K., 807, 810, 815, 816
Kristof-Brown, A. L., 111
Kropp, P. R., 645
Kross, E., 590
Krueger, A. B., 402
Krueger, J. I., 300, 811
Krueger, R. F., 52, 190
Kruger, A., 687
Krumholz, H. M., 605
Kubzansky, I. D., 448
Kuhl, J., 146
Kuhn, B. W., 279
Kuhn, D., 284, 285, 286
Kuller, L. H., 397
Kumano, M., 162
Kumar, S., 126
Kunzmann, U., 577, 578, 579, 580, 585, 587, 588, 832
Küpers, W., 590
Kupper, S., 451
Kurman, J., 108
Kurylo, M., 452
Kurzbau, R., 659
Kutchins, H., 418, 419
Kuziemko, I., 724
Kvale, S., 19
Kyngäs, H., 341


L'Abate, L., 670
Labouvie-Vief, G., 578
Lackaye, T. D., 69
Lagerstrom, M., 69

La Guardia, J. G., 142, 145
Laing, R. D., 49
Laizner, A. M., 397
Lakey, B., 761
Lamb, P., 346
Lamb, S., 465
Lambert, J., 568
Lambert, M., 520
Lambert, M. J., 433
Lambert, N. M., 561, 563, 564, 666
Lancastle, D., 398
Landenberg, S., 761
Landers, D. M., 213
Landis, K. R., 720
Landman, J., 126, 127
Landtblom, A. M., 69
Lane, R., 130, 132, 133
Lane, R. E., 738
Langdridge, D., 48, 51
Langer, E., 149
Langer, J. A., 283
Lantieri, L., 551
LaPoint, V., 90
Larkin, G. R., 567
Larsen, J., 682
Larsen, R. J., 124, 176, 230, 384, 401, 466
Larson, D. B., 559–560
Larson, J., 507, 509
Larson, P. C., 445
Larson, R., 315, 316, 318, 320, 321, 323
Larson, R. W., 313, 314–315, 318, 319, 320, 322, 832
Laske, O. E., 382
Latack, J. C., 344
Latendresse, S. J., 133
Latham, G. P., 254
Lauermann, F., 230
Lavin, J., 348
Lawlor, E., 758
Lawlor, M. S., 304
Lawlor-Row, K., 661
Lawlor-Row, K. A., 662
Lawrence-Webb, C., 690
Laws, D. R., 639, 641, 644, 645, 646
Lawson, K. J., 359
Lawson, R. A., 759
Layard, R., 272, 359, 752
Layous, K ., 185, 191, 192, 195, 254, 255, 256, 259, 260, 799, 800, 832
Layton, J. B., 525, 720
Lazaris, A., 381
Lazarus, N. B., 209–210
Lazarus, R. S., 37, 66, 269, 394, 395, 398, 434, 618, 807, 809

Leamy, M., 532
Leary, M. R., 88, 716, 717, 754
Le Boutillier, C., 532
Leckman, J. F., 773, 776
Leddy, M. A., 695, 832
Le Doux, J. E., 553
Ledrich, J., 486
Lee, E., 447
Lee, H., 84
Lee, H. C., 191
Lee, I. M., 208, 218
Lee, L., 397
Lee, R. M., 431
Lee, S. W.-Y., 288
Lee, T. W., 240
Lee, V., 397
Leeper, R. W., 548
Lefcourt, H. M., 402
Lefstein, A., 281
Legate, N., 150
Legault, C., 568
Legge, K., 369
Leggett, E. L., 169
Legh-Jones, H., 217
Lehmann, P., 536
Leidner, O., 242, 243
Leighton, D., 758
Leiter, M., 233
Leith, L., 209
Lekes, N., 85
Lema, J. C., 435
Lema, V., 433
Lemer, R. M., 779
Lendrum, A., 302
Lennings, C. J., 224, 225
Lennon, J., 718
Lens, W., 87
Lenze, S. L., 783
Leonard-Barton, D., 92
Leone, D. R., 146
LePage, M., 796
LePine, J. A., 358
LePine, M. A., 358
Lepore, S. J., 508, 720
Lepper, H., 384
Lepper, H. S., 124, 176
Lepper, M., 126, 132
Leppert, J., 68
Lerner, N., 549
Lerner, R. M., 568, 776
Lester, D., 52
Leuner, B., 546
Levak, R. W., 536
Levenson, J. A., 475
Leveson, J., 652
Levesque, C. S., 150
Levesque, D. A., 383
Levin, D. E., 90
Levy-Storms, L., 465
Lewandowski, A. M., 417

Lewandowski-Romps, L., 348
Lewin, K., 2, 18, 445
Lewinsohn, P. M., 191, 240, 298, 494
Lewis, A., 329
Lewis, K., 370
Lewis, M., 509
Lewis, S., 329, 331, 832
Lexell, J., 619
Li, J., 240
Li, Y., 286
Liberatore, V., 697
Liberman, N., 584
Libet, B., 150
Lieberei, B., 465
Lieberman, M. A., 504
Light, K. C., 799
Lilienfeld, S. O., 421
Liljenquist, K., 792
Lillis, J., 165, 433
Lim, S., 331
Lin, K., 753, 755
Linde, J. A., 396
Linden, M., 465
Lindström, B., 64, 68, 72, 74
Linehan, M. M., 149
Linkins, M., 270, 298, 815
Linley, P. A., 17, 21, 22, 31, 32, 47, 52, 53, 61, 64, 74, 89, 151, 166, 174, 229, 267, 304, 384, 432, 433, 434, 437, 438, 444, 465, 503, 504, 505, 514, 533, 619, 685, 689, 696, 807, 808, 810, 812, 814, 816
Linn, S., 90, 93, 94, 95
Linton, R., 68
Lipman, M., 279, 281
Lipset, S. M., 724
Lishner, D. A., 16, 761
Litaker, D., 697
Little, B. R., 37, 507
Littleton, K., 279, 285
Litzinger, S. C., 662
Liu, J., 343, 345, 346
Livneh, H., 448, 453
Lloyd, C., 286
Locke, E. A., 85, 254
Lockerbie, L., 652
Loevinger, J., 169, 175
Loew, B., 267
Loewenstein, G., 128, 172, 187, 196
Lofy, M. M., 224
Lomas, T., 793
Long, D. A., 281
Lonigan, C. J., 420
Lönnqvist, J. E., 106, 110
Loomes, G., 126

Lopata, H. Z., 503
Lopes, P. N., 550, 552
Lopez, D. F., 587
Lopez, M. E., 323
Lopez, S. J., 1, 11, 22, 74, 254, 267, 304, 411, 420, 422, 423, 424, 432, 434, 483, 485, 486, 488, 490, 491, 492, 493, 498, 499, 525, 536, 703, 763, 832
Lopez-Bastida, J., 617
Lopez-Pousa, S., 617
Lord, H., 314
Lorenz, C., 465
Losada, M., 331, 465
Losada, M. F., 466
Loseke, D., 687
Loughlin, C., 345
Louis, M. C., 267
Loumidis, K., 514
Lowery, B. S., 565
Lu, L., 112
Lubinski, D., 420
Lucas, R. E., 106, 132, 185, 186, 187, 198, 302, 342, 446, 463, 741, 792
Ludlow, A., 307
Ludwig, T. E., 566, 662
Luhmann, M., 187
Lumley, M. A., 508
Lundh, U., 618
Lundhal, B. W., 664
Luoma, J. B., 165, 433
Luraschi, E., 619
Lushene, R., 525
Lustig, D. C., 347
Luszczynska, A., 448
Lutgendorf, A. K., 508
Luthans, F., 301, 361, 366, 703
Luthar, S. S., 133, 301, 620, 773, 775, 777, 779
Luther, L., 700
Luyckx, K., 69
Lykins, E. L. B., 89
Lykken, D., 186, 713
Lynch, J., 145
Lynch, M. F., 145
Lytle, B. L., 396
Lytton, S., 370
Lyubomirsky, S., 2, 83, 124, 125, 129, 165, 171, 172, 173, 176, 185, 187, 188, 189, 190–191, 192, 193, 195, 196, 198, 199, 233, 237, 238, 240, 243, 254, 255, 256, 259, 260, 384, 385, 445, 452, 463, 465, 565, 569, 697, 700, 756, 796, 799, 800, 810, 832

Macagno, F., 280
MacCauley, M. H., 363
MacDonald, D. A., 521
MacDonald, G., 561
MacGivers, V. L., 286
MacIntyre, A., 14, 53
Mackay, R., 620
MacKuen, M., 553
MacLachlan, M., 791
MacLeod, A. K., 466, 471, 475
Macquarrie, J., 54
Macrae, C. N., 148
Maddi, S. R., 626
Maddox, G. L., 604
Maddux, J. E., 11, 23, 171, 411, 412, 413, 415, 417, 420, 423, 521, 696, 832
Madjalli, S., 67
Madsen, R., 721–722
Maercker, A., 447
Magaletta, P. R., 484
Magasi, S., 447
Magnus, P., 186
Magrin, E., 619
Magyar-Moe, J., 433, 434, 438, 465, 483
Magyar-Moe, J. L., 237, 302, 488, 536, 815, 833
Maheux, B., 568
Mahoney, J. L., 314
Mahrer, A. R., 51
Maier, S. F., 130
Maio, G., 86
Maio, G. R., 86, 103, 105
Maisel, N., 561
Mäkikangas, A., 348
Makuch, R., 420
Malec, J. F., 619
Mallery, R., 214
Mallory, M. E., 793
Maltby, J., 174, 384, 465, 565, 685
Mammen, G., 209
Mana, A., 67, 71
Mancini, A. D., 448
Mancuso, C. A., 399, 400
Mandler, G., 548
Mangelli, L., 466
Mania, E. W., 662–663
Mann, R., 635, 647, 833
Mann, R. E., 641, 643, 645, 646, 647, 652
Mannell, R. C., 213
Manno, S., 348
Manzoni, G., 798
Marangos, J., 757
Marano, H. E., 720
Marcel, G., 55
Marcia, J. E., 166
Marcus, G. E., 553

Margalit, A., 638
Margalit, M., 67, 69, 494
Margerison, C., 364
Margolin, G., 662
Mariame, B., 686
Marino, L., 421
Marinoff, L., 50
Markland, D., 146
Markowitz, J. C., 475
Marks, I. M., 474
Marks, N., 359, 360
Markus, H. R., 126, 132, 316, 317, 318, 320, 417
Marmot, M. G., 604, 608
Marques, S. C., 267, 486, 492, 493
Marsh, S. C., 68
Marshall, W. L., 636, 638, 643, 647
Marsiglia, F. F., 781
Martin, A. M., 652
Martin, D. J., 489
Martin, J. E., 522, 720
Martin, L., 792
Martin, L. L., 507, 508
Martin, M. W., 39, 172
Martin, R., 341
Martin, R. A., 402
Martinez-Inigo, D., 350
Martin-Ginis, K., 350, 794
Martinsen, E., 170, 174
Martos, T., 85
Martz, E., 448, 453
Maruna, S., 230, 639
Maslach, C., 233
Maslow, A., 169
Maslow, A. H., 16, 20, 21, 32, 33, 38, 88, 164, 165, 230, 464, 522
Mason, L., 286
Mason, S., 197
Massimini, F., 159, 160, 170, 467, 615, 619
Mastekaasa, A., 719
Masten, A., 620
Masten, A.S., 299, 300, 301, 773, 774, 775, 776, 777, 778, 779, 781, 782, 783, 833
Masuda, A., 165, 433
Mather, M., 172
Mathias, M., 451
Matthews, K. A., 63, 397
Matthews, M. D., 23, 171, 402
Mattila, M., 69
Mauger, P. A., 665
Mauss, I. B., 172, 196, 400
Maxwell, M., 212
May, 35
May, D. R., 358

May, R., 16, 20, 21, 33, 35, 40, 49, 51, 54, 56
Mayer, J., 545
Mayer, J. D., 300, 302, 304, 361, 546, 547, 550, 553, 554, 833
Mayer, K. V., 595
Mayer, M., 360
Mayer, R. C., 345
Mayle, D., 367
Mayor, K. V., 604
McAdams, D. P., 160, 168, 505, 507, 509, 567, 584
McAteer, D., 430–431
McCann, D., 364
McCarthy, G. M., 617
McCartney, P., 718
McCauley, C. R., 167
McClelland, D. C., 150
McClern, G. E., 306
McClure, J., 230
McCombs, B. L., 381
McCormack, E., 420
McCourt, A., 795
McCown, K. S., 304
McCrae, R., 363
McCrae, R. R., 186, 504
McCrate, F., 616
McCraty, R., 567
McCullar, B., 652
McCullough, M. E., 51, 190, 191, 197, 240, 362, 398, 436, 559–560, 562, 566, 569, 660, 661, 663, 665, 670
McDaniel, M., 816
McDermott, D., 304, 490, 495
McDougal, J. L., 298
McDougall, W., 15–16
McEniff, S., 617
McFarland, C., 506
McGhee, D. E., 150
McGinnity, A., 298
McGrath, H., 271, 298, 300, 301, 303, 305
McGrath, J. E., 224
McGrath, R. E., 524
McGregor, H., 87
McGregor, I., 37
McGregor, J. A., 84
McGue, M., 190
McGuffin, P., 306
McGuire, W. J., 9
McHoskey, J. W., 86
McInerney, R. G., 32, 33, 34
McKee, A., 552
McKee, M. C., 343, 347, 349
McKergrow, M., 365
McLaughlin, T., 418
McLean, A., 380

McLeod, J., 215, 431
McMahon, K., 399
McMillan, J., 508
McMillan, L., 799
McMillen, C., 504
McMillen, J. C., 447, 783
McMurray, A. J., 343
McNally, R. J., 503
McNulty, J. K., 663, 807, 808, 813, 814, 815
McVey, G. L., 795
McWilliams, N., 520
Mead, N. L., 86
Mead, S., 695
Meadows, J., 86
Meara, N. M., 429, 433, 436
Medvec, V. H., 126
Meehl, P. E., 467
Megginson, D., 385
Mehan, H., 286
Mehling, W. E., 793, 794, 798
Meier, B. P., 791, 792, 793
Meltzer, H., 298
Mendel, R., 366
Mendius, R., 798
Mendola, R., 504
Mercer, N., 279, 285, 286
Meredith, P., 396
Merleau-Ponty, M., 40, 792
Merrick, M. T., 779
Messer, S., 252
Messias, E., 722
Meyer, D. K., 316, 816, 817
Meyer, J. E., 664
Meyer, P., 237, 699, 700
Meyer, S. E., 597
Meyers, L. S., 89
Mezzina, R., 688
Mguni, N., 758
Mhatre, K., 361
Mhatre, K. H., 703
Miao, Q., 346
Michael, S., 699
Michael, S. T., 465, 484, 488, 490
Michaels, S., 288
Michalos, A. C., 129
Mickler, C., 579, 580, 583
Middleton, J., 448
Mikulincer, M., 16
Miles, H., 652
Miller, A. H., 382
Miller, A. J., 661
Miller, D. T., 9
Miller, N., 566
Miller, S., 252
Miller, S. D., 40, 438
Miller, S. R., 761
Miller, W. R., 146, 671
Miller-Perrin, C. L., 685
Milyavskaya, M., 716

Miner, K., 619
Minhas, G., 465, 533
Mintzberg, H., 368
Mirabito, A. M., 703
Mischel, W., 758
Mishra, P., 285
Missotten, M. A., 69
Mitchell, J., 241
Mitchell, R., 360
Mitra, R., 217
Mittelmark, M. B., 61
Moeenizaheh, M., 700
Moen, P., 399
Mogilner, C., 95
Molinari, E., 798
Mollen, D., 431, 433
Mollica, C. O., 160
Moltzen, K., 346
Molyneux, G. J., 617
Mondillon, L., 792
Mongrain, M., 239, 567, 698
Monk, A., 267, 273, 833
Monn, A. R., 775
Montgomery, M., 87–88
Moons, P., 69
Moore, 506
Moore, R., 466, 475
Moore, S., 217
Moran, E. K., 400
Moreno, C., 68, 69
Morgan, M. L., 12, 13, 14, 18, 19
Morishita, S., 566
Morrell, R. W., 503
Morrin, M., 94, 123
Morris, A., 672
Morris, B. A., 619
Morris, I., 303
Morris, S., 753
Morrison, D., 799
Morrow, W. R., 414
Mosher, C. E., 619
Moskowitz, J. T., 197, 393, 396, 397, 400, 404, 504, 617, 809, 833
Mosley-Hänninen, P., 67
Moss-Morris, R., 448
Motl, R. W., 212
Mount, M. K., 358
Moyers, B. D., 170
Mrazek, P. J., 668
Mroczek, D. K., 403
Mroz, M., 283
Muehlenhard, C. L., 416, 417
Mueser, K., 700
Mukamal, K., 597, 598, 607
Müller, R., 443, 448, 833
Mumford, A., 363
Mundell, C. E., 420
Munir, F., 343, 344, 347, 349

Muñoz, R. F., 191, 240, 671
Murayama, K., 141
Murch, R., 504
Muris, P., 474
Muros, J. P., 349
Murphy, D., 22, 434, 690, 812
Murphy, H., 215
Murphy, J., 620
Murphy, M. C., 641
Murphy, P. K., 290
Murray, E. J., 670
Murray, J. E., 720
Murray, K., 773
Murray, K. E., 620
Murrough, J. W., 776
Musher-Eizenman, D. R, 567
Musick, M. A., 397, 399
Mutrie, N., 207, 209, 213, 214, 215, 216, 218, 800, 833
Myers, D., 130, 132, 133
Myers, D. G., 23, 83, 228, 267, 359, 713, 714, 833
Myers, I. B., 363
Myers, R. A., 429, 433, 436
Myrin, B., 69

Nadler, D. A., 369
Nafstad, H. E., 9, 10, 11, 15, 16, 47, 833
Nag, M., 673
Naidu, N. V. R., 126
Nairn, A., 93
Nakamura, J., 10, 32, 170, 256, 275
Napa, C. K., 37
Narayan, A. J., 777
Nave, C. S., 186
Nayak, R. M., 360
Nebling, L., 402
Neff, K., 402
Neff, K. D., 402
Neimark, J., 52
Neitzert, E., 758
Nelson, C., 433, 436, 533
Nelson, K., 774
Nelson, N., 69–70, 720
Nelson, S. K., 191, 195, 800
Nemas, C. R., 565
Nenkov, G. Y., 123
Nenova, M., 509
Neppl, T. K., 779
Nesse, R. M., 447, 519
Nestler, E. J., 776
Nettleton, S., 797
Neuchterlein, K., 300
Neugarten, B. L., 463, 733, 737
Neuman, W. R., 553

Neuner, B., 69
Newman, A., 346
Newton, T. L., 720
Neyer, F. J., 198
Ngai, F. W., 67
Ngu, S. F., 67
Nicholls, J., 758
Nichols, C. P., 87
Nichols, S. N., 536
Nickerson, C., 105, 112
Nieboer, A. P., 628
Niedenthal, P. M., 792, 793, 797
Nielsen, K., 343, 344, 345, 347, 349
Niemann, L., 151, 451
Niemiec, C. P., 88, 148, 150, 302, 716
Niemiec, R. M., 53, 525, 538
Nietzsche, F. W., 53
Nikkilä, J., 341
Nilsson, K., 68
Nir, M., 366
Noam, G. G., 14
Noble, T., 271, 298, 300, 301, 303, 305
Noblet, A. J., 359
Nolan, A., 86
Nolan, M., 618
Nolen-Hoeksema, S., 437, 507, 508, 509
Norcross, J. C., 382
Norem, J. K., 470, 807, 808, 814, 815
Norman, G. R., 401
Norman, S. M., 703
Norris, A. S., 503
Norris, F. H., 773, 778, 779, 783
Northrop, J. T., 568
Norton, D. L., 166, 170
Norton, M., 399, 715
Norton, M. I., 191, 722, 758
Nortvedt, P., 16
Nowak, A., 186
Nunley, E. P., 546
Nuss, C. K., 717
Nussbaum, M. C., 641
Nygaard, R. L., 672
Nystrand, M., 281, 283, 286

Oatley, K., 420
Oberleitner, L. M., 508
Oberli, E., 191
Obradovic, A. J., 301
Obradovic, J., 774, 775, 776
O'Brien, D. G., 283
O'Connell, M. E., 299
O'Connell, M. J., 704
O'Connor, C., 288
O'Connor, P. J., 214

Oelmans, H. I., 160
Oelofsen, N., 619
Oesterreich, R., 397
Oettingen, G., 267
Offidani, E., 473, 474
Ogden, J., 394
Ogedegbe, G. A., 399
Ogihara, R., 396
Oh, D., 151
Oh, I.-S., 341
O'Heeron, R. C., 721
Ohida, T., 396
Oishi, S., 106, 107, 109, 160, 175, 302, 401, 714, 722
Okada, M., 397
Okamura, L., 198
Okundaye, J. N., 690
Olafson, L., 286, 290
Oldham, G. R., 360
Olds, D. L., 778
O'Leary, V. E., 504
Oliver, J. M., 484
Ollendick, T. H., 307
Oman, D., 399
Omar, R. Z., 396
Ones, D., 213
Ong, A. D., 536
Onken, S. J., 688, 696
Onraet, E., 86
Oppenheim, S., 103
Oppenheim-Weller, S., 103, 108, 109, 833
Oreskovich, J., 617
Orevala, S., 779
Orlans, V., 430, 431
Orlick, T., 169
Orlinsky, D., 250, 252
Orlinsky, D. E., 386
Ormerod, P., 764
Ormrod, J., 93
Orphanos, S., 288
Ortony, A., 284, 548
Orzech, K., 89, 151
Osbaldiston, R., 86
Osborn, R. L., 450
Osborne, V. A., 783
Osin, E., 229, 232
Ostermann, R. F., 533
Oswald, A. J., 799
Otake, K., 168
Otsui, K., 168
Ottolini, F., 474
Overing, J., 759
Overmier, J. B., 130
Overton, W. F., 776, 779
Overwien, P., 170, 174
Owen, A. D., 661
Owen, L., 799
Owens, J. F., 397
Owens, R. L., 433
Ownsworth, T., 453

Oyler, J., 288
Ozaki, A., 396
Ozer, E. J., 315
Ozimkowski, K. M., 566

Pace, J. L., 320
Padesky, C. A., 465
Páezi, D., 106
Pagnini, F., 798
Painter, J., 793
Pais-Reibero, J., 267
Pais-Reibero, J. L., 486, 492
Pakizeh, A., 86
Paleari, F. G., 660, 662
Palfai, T. P., 548
Palsane, M. N., 720
Panter-Brick, C., 773, 776
Parente, M. E., 314
Parfitt, G., 212
Pargament, K. I., 51, 504
Paris, J., 416, 418, 419
Park, C. L., 50, 503, 504, 505, 506
Park, N., 13, 32, 38, 47, 160, 162, 166, 172, 191, 240, 259, 446, 452, 465, 524, 563, 681, 683, 697
Parker, I., 418
Parker, J. D. A., 548
Parker, M., 369
Parkes, B., 779
Parkes, C. M., 66, 506
Parks, A., 191, 195, 699
Parks, A. C., 172, 237, 238, 239, 240, 241, 242, 243, 244, 268, 465, 532, 566, 833
Parloff, M. B., 464
Parsai, M. B., 781
Partridge, C., 396
Pascale, R., 368, 369
Pascale, R. T., 382
Pashler, H., 816
Passes, A., 759
Passmore, J., 329
Patera, J. L., 703
Paton, D., 779
Patrick, B. C., 146
Patrick, H., 142
Patten, A. H., 509
Patterson, G. R., 779
Patterson, J., 620
Patterson, M. M., 433
Patterson, T., 379
Patti, J., 551
Patton, G. K., 359
Pauleen, D., 590
Paulson, A. S., 381
Pauwels, B. G., 807, 810, 833
Pava, J. A., 475
Pavot, W., 718

Pawelski, J., 254, 257, 259
Pawlowska, I., 448
Paykel, E. S., 472
Payne, R., 720
Payne, W. L., 546, 549
Payton, J. W., 551
Peak, P. K., 758
Pearce, K., 163
Pearce, N., 318
Pearce [Dawes], N., 316, 320
Peasgood, T., 357
Pedrotti, J. T., 491
Peeters, G., 520
Pek, J, 185
Peled, D., 68
Peled, E., 686, 687
Pelham, W. E., 486
Pelled, L. H., 197
Pelletier, L., 163
Pelletier, L. G., 142, 168
Peng, A. C., 350
Penn, D., 699
Penn, D. L., 237, 689
Pennebaker, J. W., 508, 670, 721
Penner, L. A., 16
Pennix, B. W., 618
Pentz, M. A., 217
Perkins, H. W., 714
Perkins, R., 689
Perls, F., 49
Perrin, R. D., 685
Peter, C., 443, 448, 833
Peterman, A. H., 401
Peters, T., 369
Petersen, F., 245
Peterson, C. H., 2, 13, 14, 32, 38, 47, 52, 130, 160, 161, 162, 163, 166, 171, 172, 191, 209, 240, 253, 254, 259, 301, 306, 383, 402, 445, 446, 452, 465, 484, 520, 522, 523, 524, 525, 533, 537, 563, 681, 683, 684, 697, 754, 791, 796
Peterson, C. P., 83
Peterson, J. C., 399, 400
Petit, P., 14
Petrides, C. V., 794
Petruzello, S. J., 212, 216
Pettigrew, T. F., 18
Pettinger, R., 360
Pfefferbaum, B., 773
Pfefferbaum, R. L., 773
Pharow, P., 245
Phillips, F. L., 85
Phillips, R., 753
Philpot, A., 368
Pi, S., 447
Piaget, J., 21, 284
Pianta, R. C., 776

Piccolo, R. F., 345
Pickett, K., 722
Piel, J. A., 13
Pierce, P. F., 348
Pierce, R. S., 195, 238
Pietrini, P., 661
Pilgrim, D., 437
Piliavin, J. A., 16, 103
Pinker, S., 752, 758
Pipher, M. B., 717
Pirola-Merlo, A., 343
Pithers, W. D., 635
Plomin, R., 186, 306
Pluess, M., 305, 306
Podsakoff, N. P., 358
Poirier, J., 242
Polland, B., 617
Pollard, C., 619
Polusny, M. A., 779
Pond, R. S., 561
Pool, A. G., 724
Poortinga, W., 217
Pope, K. S., 520
Porporino, F. J., 640
Porras, J. I., 369
Post, M. W., 447
Post, S. G., 52, 398
Postman, N., 279
Postmus, J. L., 686
Potter, N. N., 638
Powell, A. A., 761
Powell, J. L., 774
Powell, K. E., 207
Powell, S., 503
Powell, T., 619
Powers, G., 51
Powers, M., 446
Pressman, S., 799
Pressman, S. D., 196, 396, 401, 403
Pretelt, V., 435
Price, R. H., 18
Prilleltensky, I., 757, 761
Prilleltensky, O., 757
Primeau, J., 343
Print, B., 653
Prizmic, Z., 466
Procacci, E. N., 160
Prochaska, J. M., 383
Prochaska, J. O., 170, 171, 382, 383
Proctor, C., 304
Proctor, E. K., 702, 704
Profitt, D. H., 514
Profitt, N. J., 686
Pröpper, F., 451
Proyer, R. T., 162, 163
Przybylski, A. K., 146
Pulkinen, L., 779
Pulla, V., 685, 690
Purdie, N., 290

Purvis, M., 653
Puschel, K., 668
Putnam, R., 722
Putnam, R. D., 194, 761
Putnam, R. J., 764
Putterman, L., 704
Pyles, L., 686

Qian, Z., 286
Qualls, D. L., 37
Quart, A., 90
Quinn, R. E., 757

Raabe-Menssen, C., 451
Rabin, B. S., 721
Radloff, L., 524
Rafanelli, C., 452, 463, 464, 465, 466, 468, 471, 472, 473, 475, 477
Rahman, A., 396
Rahtz, D., 753
Railton, P., 254
Ralph, R., 688
Ralph, R. O., 696
Ramana, R., 464
Ranchor, A., 618
Rand, K. L., 484
Randall, R., 344, 345
Raphael, J., 686
Rapoff, M., 486, 495
Rapp, C., 684
Rapp, C. A., 525, 532, 640, 687, 690
Rappaport, H., 225, 232
Rashid, F., 349
Rashid, T., 53, 172, 237, 465, 519, 521, 524, 532, 533, 535, 537, 566, 833
Raskin, J. D., 417
Rasmussen, H., 799
Raspin, C., 258
Rath, J. F., 453
Rath, N., 739, 746
Rathunde, K., 10, 31
Raty, L., 69
Rawls, J., 12
Reasoner, R. W., 753
Reber, J. S., 9
Redd, W. H., 509
Reddich, F. C., 605
Redman, B. K., 451
Redzanowski, U., 580
Reed, E., 396
Reed, G. M., 810
Reed, J., 213
Reed, S. K., 284
Rees, K. J., 86
Reeve, C. L., 508
Reeve, J., 140
Regalia, C., 660, 662
Regehr, C., 617

Regel, S., 812
Register, E., 685
Reich, J. W., 776
Reichard, R., 361
Reichard, R. J., 703
Reid, F., 396
Reid, J., 144
Reis, H. T., 172
Reise, S. P., 401
Reisman, J. M., 413
Reiss, D., 782
Reisweber, J., 700
Reivich, K., 270, 298, 301, 303, 815
Reivich, K. J., 303
Reninger, K. B., 288
Rennie, D. L., 434
Renninger, A., 315, 323
Repper, J., 689
Rescher, N., 641
Reschly, A. L., 270
Resick, P. A., 513
Resnick, L. B., 288
Resnick, S., 31, 791
Resnick, S. G., 695, 696, 705, 706, 833
Rethorst, C. D., 213
Revenson, T. A., 448
Reveslot, C., 617
Reyes, M. R., 551, 552
Reynolds, D. K., 566
Reynolds, J., 509
Reynolds, K. A., 447
Reznek, L., 411, 418, 421
Reznitskaya, A., 279, 280, 281, 285, 286, 288, 304, 833
Rice, T., 122
Rich, G. J., 31
Richard, J., 381
Richardson, F. C., 9
Richardson, G. E., 306
Richardson, M., 401
Richardson, N., 288
Richardson, P., 619
Richardson, V., 286, 290
Richardson, W. S., 307
Richeson, J. A., 792
Richter, J., 775
Ricks, D. F., 231, 737
Riddle, M. A., 474
Rideout, G., 504
Rideout, M. G., 304
Ridgway, P., 688, 696
Ridley, C. R., 431
Riek, B. M., 662–663
Rigby, C. S., 142, 146
Riggio, R. E., 350
Riketta, M., 105
Riley-Tillman, T. C., 298

Rimmer, E., 378
Rinaldi, P., 617
Rind, B., 568
Rindfleisch, A., 90, 111, 564
Rini, C., 509
Ripley, J. S., 495, 670
Rique, J., 660
Rivas, J., 618
Rivera, F., 68
Rivera, P., 452
Rivers, S. E., 549, 550, 551, 552
Rives, M., 618
Robbins, A., 133
Robbins, B., 833
Robbins, B. D., 31, 32, 33, 34, 35, 36, 37, 40, 41, 434
Robbins, B. R., 813, 814
Roberts, D. E., 687
Roberts, D. L., 689
Roberts, D. R., 369
Roberts, K. D., 664
Roberts, R., 298
Roberts, R. D., 545
Roberts, R. E., 209–210
Robertson, A., 212
Robertson, D., 451
Robertson, P. J., 369
Robertson, R., 212
Robertson, S. M., 618
Robin, V., 91
Robin Cohen, S., 397
Robins, R. W., 175
Robinson, C., 267
Robinson, J., 93
Robinson, M., 105
Robitschek, C., 433
Roccas, S., 103, 106, 108, 115, 833
Roche, S. F., 686
Rodin, G. C., 146
Rodriguez-Hanley, A., 489
Rodwell, J. J., 359
Roe, D., 689
Roese, N. J., 127
Roeser, R. W., 314, 315
Roets, A., 126
Roffey, S., 300, 754, 761
Rogers, C. R., 3, 16, 20, 21, 38, 40, 49, 149, 165, 166, 379, 431, 464
Rogoff, B., 320
Rohan, M. J., 103, 105
Rohde, P., 494
Rohner, R. P., 18
Rohrer, D., 816
Rokeach, M., 84, 103, 522
Rollnick, S., 146
Romero, E., 85
Romm, K. L., 699

Ronka, A., 779, 781
Rønnestad, M. H., 386
Rook, K. S., 194, 721
Rooney, G. D., 682
Rooney, R. H., 682
Root, L. M., 665, 670
Rosch, E., 147
Rose, G., 668
Rose, S., 267
Rosebud Yellow Robe, 282
Rosenberg, M., 124
Rosenberg, W. M. C., 307
Rosenblatt, A., 697
Rosenblum, K. E., 417, 418
Rosenfield, S., 194
Rosenhek, R. A., 696, 705, 706
Rosenthal, M., 446
Rosner, R., 503
Rosnick, D., 95
Ross, K., 323
Ross, L., 125, 129
Ross, M. W., 568
Rotella, K. N., 792
Roth, J., 313
Rothbard, N. P., 111
Rothbart, M., 301
Rothenberg, B., 686
Rothman, A. J., 302, 396
Rothschild, B., 798
Rottenberg, J., 470
Rottenstreich, Y., 127–128
Rotter, J., 65
Rotter, M., 465
Roudinesco, E., 20
Rousseau, J.-J., 15
Routh, D. K., 413
Rovine, M. J., 618
Rowe, J. W., 595, 604
Rowland, R., 334
Rowley, D., 617
Røysamb, E., 160, 186, 188
Rozin, P., 167
Rubel, T., 106
Ruch, W., 13, 162, 163
Ruchkin, V. V., 70
Rude, S. S., 402
Ruini, C., 463, 465, 466, 468, 472, 473, 474, 475, 477, 833
Rumelhart, D. E., 284
Ruotsalainen, P., 245
Ruppert, J. A., 792
Rusbult, C. E., 659
Rush, A. J., 49, 467
Rusk, N., 313
Russell, G., 384
Russo, S. J., 776
Rutherford, J., 764

Rutter, M., 300, 301, 306, 620, 773, 781
Rutterford, N. A., 618
Ryan, L., 268, 273, 303, 305
Ryan, M., 323
Ryan, P., 67
Ryan, R. M., 37, 83, 84, 85, 88, 89, 90, 95, 104, 121, 139, 140, 141, 142, 143, 144, 145, 146, 147, 148, 149, 150, 151, 159, 160, 161, 162, 163, 164, 167, 172, 174, 175, 176, 190, 215, 302, 314, 315, 318, 320, 321, 322, 330, 342, 343, 360, 379, 463, 617, 640, 666, 714, 716, 833
Ryan, S., 586
Ryff, C. D., 13, 37, 83, 160, 175, 185, 214, 302, 342, 343, 347, 384, 394, 396, 452, 463, 464, 465, 466, 468, 470, 475, 477, 504, 522, 689, 754, 809
Rynsaardt, J., 273

Sabato, H., 70
Sabine, R., 347
Sachs, J., 752
Sachs, J. D., 761
Sachs, P. R., 445
Sackett, D. L., 307
Safran, J. D., 149
Sagiv, L., 103, 106, 110, 112, 113, 114, 115, 833
Sagy, S., 61, 64, 66, 67, 68, 69, 70, 71, 72, 73, 74, 75, 833
Sahlberg, P., 780
Sakaeda, A. R., 160
Sakuta, T., 566
Salagame, K., 700
Saleebey, D., 521, 684, 685, 690
Salerno, A., 700
Salmon, J. M., 286
Salovey, P., 300, 302, 304, 361, 545, 547, 548, 549, 550, 551, 552, 834
Salsman, J., 401
Salsman, J. M., 393, 834
Salter, A. C., 643
Salyers, M. P., 689
Salzer, M. S., 698
Samboceti, J., 89
Sameroff, A. J., 90, 775, 781
Sandage, S. J., 664
Sandahl, P., 250, 378
Sanderman, R., 618
Sanders, P., 49
Sandler, I., 774

Sandvik, E., 358
Sangsue, J., 306
Sansone, C., 192
Santelli, A. G., 660
Santerve, C., 566
Santos, M. T., 794
Sapyta, J. J., 164
Sarason, B. S., 492
Sarchielli, G., 346
Saris, W. E., 740
Sarker, U., 618
Sarros, J. C., 343
Sartori, R. D. G., 615, 834
Sartre, J., 50, 53
Saslow, L. R., 397, 400
Sasso, T., 807
Saunders, S. M., 484
Savani, K., 126, 132
Savino, N., 172
Savino, N. S., 196
Sawaf, A., 552
Sawyer, A. T., 151
Scales, P. C., 568
Scarløss, B., 288
Schaabroek, J. M, 350
Scheel, M. J., 436, 437, 438
Scheibehenne, B., 123
Scheier, M., 401
Scheier, M. F., 124, 147, 148, 171, 190, 484, 504
Schellinger, K. B., 300, 551
Schepens, R., 303
Scher, S. J., 420
Schimmack, U., 740
Schkade, D., 128, 172, 185, 243, 700
Schkade, D. A., 400
Schlegel, R. J., 166
Schluchter, M. D., 298
Schmaling, K. B., 662
Schmidt, F., 331
Schmidt, F. L., 358, 703
Schmidt, P., 106
Schmidt, S., 451
Schmotkin, D., 37
Schmuck, P., 84, 85, 104, 640
Schmuckle, S. C., 583
Schnall, S., 791, 792
Schneider, B., 111
Schneider, J. W., 681
Schneider, K., 31, 269, 434
Schnurr, P. P., 608
Schoenbach, V. J., 298
Schofield, C., 647
Schofield, T. J., 779
Schöhofer, K. S., 396
Scholey, A., 799
Scholz, U., 448
Schonert-Reichl, K. A., 191, 304

Schooler, J. W., 172, 196
Schoonhaven, C. B., 369
Schoorman, F. D., 345
Schopenhauer, A., 230
Schopp, L. H., 617
Schor, J. B., 85, 90, 93, 94, 95, 722
Schraw, G., 286, 290
Schroeder, D. A., 16
Schroeder, L. L., 413
Schueller, S. M., 162, 163, 193, 237, 239, 241
Schuettler, D., 812
Schuh, S. C., 350
Schultheiss, O. C., 108, 192
Schultz, P. P., 150
Schulz, D. P., 33
Schulz, S. E., 33
Schwartz, B., 39, 83, 121, 122, 123, 124, 125, 126, 128, 131, 132, 133, 134, 167, 358, 466, 533, 559, 810, 812, 813, 834
Schwartz, G. E. R., 566
Schwartz, J. L. K., 150
Schwartz, N., 37, 791, 792
Schwartz, R. M., 466
Schwartz, S. H., 103, 105, 106, 110, 111, 112, 113, 114, 164
Schwartz, S. J., 166, 169
Schwarz, B. B., 286
Schwarz, N., 105, 402, 548
Schweitzer, M. E., 561
Schwer Canning, S., 240
Schwerdtfeger, A., 396
Scirica, F., 286
Scollon, C. N., 187
Scott, P., 661
Scoular, A., 251, 377, 834
Scouler, P. A., 379, 380, 383
Scrignaro, M., 619
Scucchi, S., 659
Sedlacek, W. E., 169
Seekins, T., 617
Seeley, J., 298
Seeley, J. R., 494
Seeman, T. E., 465, 471
Sefick, W. J., 191, 564
Segal, Z., 148, 149
Segal, Z. V., 149
Segall, M. H., 110
Segerstrom, S. C., 89
Seidlitz, L., 358
Seifer, R., 775
Seitsinger, A., 306
Selby, E., 663
Selby, J. W., 507
Selby, L. E., 507
Seligman, E., 446

Seligman, M. E. P., 1, 2, 9, 10, 11, 12, 13, 14, 16, 17, 19–20, 21, 23, 31, 32, 39, 47, 63, 64, 74, 83, 95, 121, 130, 160, 162, 163, 164, 165, 166, 167, 169, 171, 172, 191, 198, 207, 208, 209, 213, 215, 223, 231, 237, 240, 241, 243, 253, 254, 257, 259, 260, 267, 268, 270, 272, 298, 301, 303, 330, 383, 384, 396, 414, 421, 422, 432, 444, 445, 446, 450, 452, 465, 520, 521, 522, 523, 525, 532, 533, 537, 559, 563, 565, 566, 577, 666, 681, 682, 683, 684, 685, 697, 700, 716, 754, 763, 791, 796, 809, 815
Selin, H., 20, 23
Semaan, I., 687
Semiatin, A. M., 618
Semin, G. R., 792
Semler, R., 366, 370
Semmer, N., 343
Semprini, F., 470
Semsa, A., Jr., 568
Sen, A., 735, 755, 760
Senge, P. M., 382
Seo, D., 617
Sergeant, S., 239, 567
Serlin, I. A., 31, 791
Serrano-Aguilar, P. E., 617
Sessa, M., 619
Shachar, M., 341
Shafer, J. L., 323
Shaffer, A., 774
Shaffer, J. B. P., 32, 35
Shaftoe, H., 753
Shakespeare-Finch, J., 506, 619
Shalker, T. E., 394
Shamir, B., 347
Shandra, J. S., 95
Shapira, L., 698
Shapiro, P. A., 448
Shapiro, S. B., 31
Shapiro, S. L., 566
Shapley, K., 288
Sharma, J. M., 521
Sharoff, K., 451
Sharpe, K. E., 39, 533
Shatté, A., 303
Shaver, P. R., 16
Shaw, B. A., 397
Shaw, B. F., 49
Shaw, J. D., 111
Shaw, S., 653
Shaywitz, B. A., 420
Shaywitz, S. E., 420

Sheafor, B. W., 684
Sheasby, J., 700
Sheldon, K. M., 10, 11, 22, 85, 86, 87, 88, 95, 104, 109, 139, 172, 174, 185, 187, 188, 189, 190–191, 193, 195, 196, 198, 238, 243, 259, 379, 385, 452, 565, 569, 640, 700, 716, 809, 834
Sheldon, M. S., 86
Shelov, D. V., 661
Shepard, D., 87–88
Sher, T. G., 662
Sherman, D. K., 103, 194
Sherman, R. A., 186
Shernoff, D. J., 314, 315, 316
Sherrieb, K., 783
Sherry, M. B., 290
Shew, B. F., 467
Shi, D., 91
Shi, K., 343
Shields, S. A., 793, 794
Shiffman, S., 402, 549
Shim, M., 306
Shimai, S., 168
Shin, J. Y., 164, 165
Shingler, J., 645, 646
Shipley, M. C., 396
Shiratsuchi, T., 566
Shlien, J. M., 432
Shmotkin, D., 343
Shock, N., 604
Shoda, V., 758
Sholomskas, D. E., 701
Shotter, J., 19
Shryack, J., 52
Shum, D., 453
Siegel, D., 794
Siegel, L., 536
Sifneos, P. E., 548
Sigmon, D. R., 484
Sigmon, S. T., 487
Silberman, J., 253, 254
Silburn, R., 618
Silver, N., 319
Silver, R., 508
Silvia, P., 166
Simmel, G., 559, 570
Simmons, C., 536
Simmons, R. G., 568
Simon, A., 793, 794
Simon, H. A., 123, 548
Simon, J., 620
Simons, D. A., 652, 653
Simons, J., 87, 104
Simonsson, B., 68
Sin, N. L., 185, 190, 191, 193, 237, 254, 259, 452, 465, 697, 700, 796
Sinatra, G. M., 286

Singer, B., 452, 522, 754
Singer, B. F., 397
Singer, B. H., 13, 214, 463, 464, 465, 468, 470, 475, 689
Singer, B. S., 504
Singer, C. H., 477
Singer, J. A., 397
Sircova, A., 229
Sirgy, M. J., 753
Sitarenios, G., 550
Sitkin, S. B., 350
Siu, O.-L., 343, 345
Sivanathan, N., 340, 341, 342, 343, 344, 346, 349, 351
Sivberg, B., 619
Skevington, S., 616
Skoner, D. P., 197, 720
Slade, M., 532, 706
Slavin-Spenny, O. M., 508
Slee, P. T., 302
Slife, B. D., 9, 32, 34, 36
Sloan, D., 521
Slote, M, 14
Sluss, D. M., 350
Smeets, K., 103
Smith, C., 758
Smith, D. M., 447
Smith, F., 283
Smith, G. T., 167
Smith, H. L., 132, 185, 446, 463, 741, 792
Smith, J., 577, 578
Smith, J. C., 566
Smith, L., 779
Smith, M. L., 37, 191, 452
Smith, P., 690
Smith, S., 620
Smith, T. B., 525, 720
Smithenry, D. W., 316
Smolak, L., 794
Smyth, J. M., 508
Snibbe, A. C., 126, 132
Snipes, S. A., 668
Snively, C. A., 684
Snow, K. K., 446
Snowden, A. D., 747
Snyder, C. R., 1, 22, 51, 74, 171, 267, 413, 417, 422, 423, 465, 483, 484, 485, 486, 487, 488, 489, 490, 492, 494, 495, 525, 536, 699, 763
Snyder, D. K., 670
Snyder, M., 192
So, T. T., 275
Sodergren, S. C., 616, 619
Soenens, B., 86, 104
Søholt, Y., 50
Sokal, A. D., 38, 331

Solberg, E. C., 105
Soldz, S., 597
Solomon, R. C., 565
Sommers, R., 128
Sonam, P., 767
Sonino, N., 465, 470
Sonnentag, S., 364
Sood, S., 127–128
Sorensen, G., 668, 669
Sortheix, F. M., 106, 110
Sosik, J. J., 350
Soter, A., 285, 288, 290
Sourani, T., 67
Sowers, W., 701
Sparks, A., 212
Sparrow, P., 361
Specht, J., 583
Spector, P. E., 111
Spencer, H., 15
Spering, C., 433
Spielberger, C. D., 525
Spiessel, H., 617
Spinella, M., 53
Spinelli, E., 48
Spinhoven, P., 69
Spini, D., 106
Spreitzer, G., 336
Srinivas, V. S., 661
Sripada, C., 254
Srivastava, A., 85
Srivastava, S., 586
Sroufe, L. A., 781
Srour, A., 67
Stahl, B., 451
Stahl, K. J., 486
Stairs, M., 52, 331
Stajkovic, A. D., 361
Stamperdahl, J., 776
Stange, K. C., 697
Stangier, U., 473
Stanimirovic, R., 241
Stantcheva, S., 725
Stanton, A. L., 198, 448, 453, 567
Staples, A. D., 89
Stark, L., 782
Starrin, B., 68
Staub, E., 761
Staudinger, U. M., 166, 577, 578, 579, 580, 582, 583, 586, 587
Stauge, A., 579
Staw, B., 570
Steedman, I., 764
Steele, C., 103
Steen, T., 259
Steen, T. A., 32, 172, 191, 240, 396, 422, 450, 452, 465, 563, 566, 681, 697
Steffen, E., 429, 435, 834
Steger, M., 254

Steger, M. F., 22, 23, 52, 160, 164, 165, 175, 401, 431
Steginga, S., 453
Stein, T. A., 47
Stelter, R., 249, 250, 251, 253, 261
Stephens, T., 213
Stepper, S., 792
Steptoe, A., 213, 396, 465
Stern, L., 384
Stern, R., 551
Sternberg, R. J., 280, 304, 577, 578, 581, 586, 588, 590
Sterne, A., 689
Sternthal, M. J., 397
Sterzinger, L., 617
Stetner, F., 298
Stetter, F., 451
Stevens, S. P., 773
Stevenson, B., 714, 764
Stevenson, R., 664
Steward, W. T., 302
Stewart, C. A., 642, 644, 648
Stewart-Brown, S., 306, 799
Stiglitz, J. E., 755, 759
Stiller, J., 144
Stillman, T. F., 561, 666
Stillwell, A. M., 673
Stipek, D. J., 286
Stober, D., 250, 252, 253
Stocks, E. L., 761
Stolarski, M., 229
Stone, A. A., 402
Stone, J., 91
Stone, M., 486
Stone, M. R., 217
Stone, T., 436, 561
Storr, A., 377
Stout-Rostron, S., 384
Stowell-Smith, M., 418
Strack, F., 792
Strain, P., 299
Straus, R., 550
Strauss, A., 317
Strausser, D. R., 347
Strausser, K. S., 717
Straw, B. M., 358, 361
Streiner, D. L., 401
Stroebe, M., 549
Stroebe, W., 549
Strom-Gottffried, K., 682
Stromso, H. I., 286
Strong, J., 396
Strosahl, K. D., 433–434
Struthers, C. W., 660
Stuart Hall, J., 620
Stubbe, J. H., 210
Stucke, T. S., 717
Stutzer, A., 357
Suchday, S., 661

Sue, E., 106
Sugai, G., 300
Sugarman, J., 31
Sugden, R., 126
Suh, E., 164
Suh, E.M., 132, 185, 186, 446, 463, 741, 757, 792
Sullivan, P. J., 320
Sullivan, W. P., 684, 688, 690, 721–722
Summers, R., 521
Sundararajan, L., 31
Sunderland, R., 568
Sunstein, C. R., 133
Sussman, T., 617
Sutherland, F., 229
Sutzer, A., 733
Suwaki, H., 566
Suzette, G., 686
Suzuki, T., 132
Swami, V., 794, 795, 796
Swan, G. E., 402
Swedberg, R., 760
Sweller, J., 816
Swidler, A., 721–722
Sympson, S., 465
Szabo, M., 267
Szanto, R. K., 191, 240
Szasz, T., 415, 419, 520
Szymanska, K., 167

Tabachinick, B. G., 520
Tabak, B., 665
Tabak, B. A., 659
Tafarodi, R. W., 164
Tafvelin, S., 343, 347
Tagaya, H., 396
Tajfel, H., 346
Taku, K., 503
Tal, K., 114
Tambs, K., 186
Tamir, M., 172, 196
Tan, K., 720
Tanaka-Matsumi, J., 168
Tarragona, M., 249, 257, 258, 834
Tarrier, N., 422, 423, 437, 525
Tashakkori, A., 21
Tate, D. G., 661
Taubman–Ben-Ari, O., 681, 834
Tavel, P., 68
Tay, L., 713, 714, 720
Taylor, A., 209
Taylor, A. M., 213
Taylor, B., 91
Taylor, C., 132, 757
Taylor, C. B., 662
Taylor, C. L. C., 779
Taylor, E., 31, 807, 809
Taylor, G. J., 548

Taylor, J., 664
Taylor, J. D., 413
Taylor, P. J., 346
Taylor, R., 368
Taylor, R. D., 300, 551
Taylor, S., 362
Taylor, S. E., 185, 194, 504, 511, 719, 810
Teasdale, J. D., 130, 148, 149
Teddlie, C., 21
Tedeschi, R. G., 50, 435, 447, 503, 504, 505, 506, 508, 509, 510, 511, 512, 513, 514, 619, 812, 834
Tellegen, A., 186, 384, 537, 713
ten Have, M., 697
Tennant, R., 384
Tennen, H., 434, 448, 497, 504, 619
Tesser, A., 507, 508
Tetlock, P. E., 111
Thaler, R. H., 133
Theeboom, T., 384
Theodore, K., 699
Thieme, K., 451
Thin, N., 752, 754, 761, 765, 766, 834
Thomae, H., 604
Thomas, F., 451
Thomas, M., 562
Thomas, P. W., 450
Thomas, R. M., 68
Thomas, S., 450, 577, 580, 583, 584, 588, 834
Thomés, F., 755
Thompson, A., 163
Thompson, B., 668
Thompson, E., 147
Thoresen, C. E., 51, 399
Thorne, B., 49
Thorne, J. T., 759
Thornton, D., 643, 648, 651
Thorpe, P. K., 816
Thorson, C. J., 359
Thunedborg, K., 464
Tiberius, Y., 23
Tice, D. M., 147, 717
Tichy, J., 187
Tidwell, D., 286
Tiggemen, M., 795
Tillich, P., 50
Tipton, S. M., 721–722
Tobin, S., 463
Tobin, S. S., 733
Tobin, V., 146
Todd, P. M., 123
Tolman, R. M., 686
Tomasino, D., 567
Tomba, E., 165, 464, 470, 471, 474, 477, 700

Tomcizk, N. D., 662
Tomich, P. L., 447
Tomolo, A., 697
Toncic, M., 162, 163
Tondo, L., 473
Tondora, J., 704
Tonry, L., 167
Topor, A., 688
Torrente, C., 779
Totterdell, P., 350
Toulmin, S. E., 285
Toussaint, L., 661
Toussaint, L. L., 661
Tov, W., 761
Traci, M. A., 617
Tracy, J. L., 175
Tran, Y., 448
Trapnell, P. D., 148
Travis, T. C., 417, 418
Treanor, J. J., 197
Treynor, W., 508
Trinidad, D. R., 550
Triplett, K. N., 508
Tripodi, T., 681
Trivers, R. L., 559
Trull, T. J., 420
Tsang, J., 190, 559, 560, 561, 569, 660
Tsang, J. A., 16
Tsui, M., 684, 690
Tucker, K. L., 129
Tuckman, B. W., 364
Tugade, M. M., 567
Tulloch, H., 508
Tulsky, D. S., 446
Tunariu, A., 305
Tupling, C., 300
Turkewitz, R., 776
Turner, A., 700
Turner, B. S., 35
Turner, J. C., 314, 346, 816, 817
Turner, J. E., 816, 817, 818
Turner, N., 341, 343, 345
Turner, R. B., 197
Turro-Garnje, O., 617
Turte, D. C., 451
Twenge, J. M., 90, 93, 300, 717, 816
Tyler, C., 652
Tyler, L., 414
Tyler, L. E., 429, 433
Tylka, T. L., 794, 795, 796
Tyrell, F., 773, 834

Uchino, B. N., 111, 471, 721
Uchiyama, M., 396
Udell, W., 284
Ullrich, P. M., 508
Ulrich, D., 367
Ulven, J. C., 485

Umberson, D., 720
Umbreit, M. S., 672
Underwood, M., 396
Ungar, M., 775, 777, 779, 781
Urai, K., 766
Urbina, S., 401
Urdan, T., 314
Urrows, S., 504
Uslaner, E. M., 217
Uutela, A., 213

Vacharkulksemsuk, T., 792, 796, 797
Vagg, P. R., 525
Vaillant, C. O., 599, 608
Vaillant, G. E., 11, 595, 597, 598, 599, 604, 606, 607, 608, 720, 810, 834
Valdez, H., 781
Välijärvi, J., 780
Valkenburg, P. M., 91
Vallacker, R. R., 186
Vallerand, R. J., 144, 146, 470
Valli, L. E., 288
Vance, G. T., 514
Vandell, D. L., 313–314
Van der Heijden, B. I. J. M., 347
Van der Laan, K. L., 662
van der Maesen, L. J. G., 753, 755
van Deurzen, E., 48, 49, 50, 52, 55, 433, 434
van Deurzen-Smith, E., 48
Van de Wetering, A., 336
van Dick, R., 346, 350
Van Dijk, J., 68
Van Dulmen, M., 536
Van Hiel, A., 86
van IJzendoorn, M. H., 306, 776
van Knippenberg, D., 350
van Knippenburg, A., 103
van Knippenburg, A. D., 148
VanLanduyt, L. M., 216
Van Looey, S., 447
VanPraag, B. N., 741
van Quaquebeke, N., 350
Van Scoyoc, S., 430, 431
Vansteenkiste, M., 86, 87, 104, 105, 141, 147
Vansteenwegen, A., 67
van Straten, A., 240
van Vianen, A. E. M., 384
Van Wormer, K., 685
Varela, F. J., 147
Vázquez, G., 473
Veenhoven, R., 20, 198, 616, 697, 731, 733, 734, 736,

738, 740, 741, 742, 743, 744, 745, 746, 764, 834
Velicer, W. F., 170
Vella-Brodrick, D., 20, 160, 241, 698
Vella-Brodrick, D. A., 38, 162
Vergunst, R., 742
Verma, N., 336
Vermeer, E., 474
Vermeulen, N., 792
Veroff, J., 172, 233, 733
Vetlesen, A. J., 16, 17, 20
Vigano, C., 619
Vilalta-Franch, J., 617
Villar, P., 85
Vincent, P. J., 471
Vinokur, A. D., 348, 447
Vinson, G., 349
Visani, D., 474
Vittersø, J., 50, 160, 161, 170, 172, 174, 186
Vohs, K. D., 86, 300, 811
Voloaca, M., 163
Vorpe, G., 306
Vossler, A., 429, 437, 834
Vygotsky, L. S., 284

Wachs, T. D., 301
Wade, N. G., 664, 671
Waggoner, M., 288, 290–291
Wagner, S., 17
Wakefield, J. C., 411
Walach, H., 151, 451
Walker, A., 753, 755
Walker, A. C., 755
Walker, D., 453
Walker, K., 318
Walker, K. C., 314, 315, 318, 320, 322, 323
Walkey, F. H., 230
Wall, K., 283
Wallace, D. H., 596
Waller, N. G., 420
Walsh, F., 620, 773
Walsh, S., 292
Walsh, W. B., 18
Waltman, M. A., 661
Walton, D., 280, 285
Walumbwa, F. O., 338, 346, 350
Walzer, M., 753
Wampold, B., 252
Wampold, B. E., 40
Wang, A. L., 160
Wang, G., 341
Wang, L., 191
Wang, Q., 197
Wang, X.-H., 346
Wangdi, K., 766
Ward, A., 123, 358

Ward, T., 635, 636, 639, 640, 641, 642, 644, 645, 646, 647, 648, 652, 653, 834
Ware, J., 652
Ware, J. E., 446
Ware, L., 486
Warmoth, A., 31, 791
Warner, K. E., 299
Warner, R. M., 550, 554
Warnock, M., 48, 167
Warr, P., 447, 720
Warr, P. B., 358, 362
Warren-Findlow, J., 795
Warzon, K. B., 314
Wasre, J. E., Jr., 733
Wasserman, R. H., 31
Wasylyshyn, K., 378
Watanabe, S., 358
Waterman, A. S., 11, 13, 21, 22, 31, 32, 50, 160, 166, 169, 174, 434
Waterman, R. M., 369
Watkins, C., 552
Watkins, N. D., 320
Watkins, P. C., 436, 561, 562, 565, 569
Watson, D., 384
Watson, J., 797
Waugh, C. E., 567, 797
Wayman, H. A., 508
Wearing, A., 186, 198
Webb, S., 759
Webb, T. R., 661
Weber, M., 163, 228, 520
Webster, S. D., 645, 647
Wecking, C., 346
Wedding, R. M., 538
Wegerif, R., 279, 286
Wegge, J., 346
Wegner, D. M., 150
Wei, R. C., 288
Weick, A., 684
Weinberger, J., 150
Weiner, B., 131
Weinstein, N., 146
Weintraub, J. K., 504
Weisbrot, M., 95
Weiss, H. B., 323
Weiss, L., 335
Weiss, T., 506
Weiss, W., 799
Weissberg, R. P., 300, 551
Weissman, M. M., 130, 133, 475
Wells, G., 173
Wells, J., 306
Wells, J. D., 348
Wells, R. E., 125
Welzel, C., 752
Wentworth, K., 56
Wentzell, K. R., 320

Werner, H., 19
Wernsing, T. S., 338
Wertz, F. J., 40
Wessman, A. E., 224, 225, 231, 738
West, J., 68
West, M., 364
West, M. A., 364
Westerberg, K., 343
Westerberg, M., 619
Westerhoff, G. J., 275
Westerman, A. S., 159, 160, 161
Westman, M., 348
Westphal, M., 448
Whalley, B., 450
Whelan, J., 107
Whisman, M., 663
White, B. A., 799
White, M., 258, 357, 368
White, M. A., 303
Whitmore, J., 378, 379
Whitney, D., 329, 364, 365
Whitworth, L., 250, 253
Whodey, M. A., 618
Wiberg, B., 229
Wiberg, M., 229
Wicker, B., 796
Wicklund, R. A., 88
Widiger, T., 415, 418, 420
Widiger, T. A., 420
Wieczorkowska, G., 134
Wigelsworth, M., 302
Wilbur, K., 149
Wiley, D., 596
Wilkie, J. E. B., 85
Wilkinson, I. A. G., 279, 288, 290, 834
Wilkinson, R., 722
Wilkinson, R. A., 453
Willars, J., 52, 384, 533
Willemsen, G., 210
Williams, D. R., 397
Williams, E. F., 794
Williams, G. C., 142, 146
Williams, J., 532
Williams, J. M. G., 148, 149
Williams, K., 378
Williams, K. D., 717
Williams, R. M., 399
Williams, R. N., 9, 32, 34, 36
Williams, S. L., 416, 420
Williams, T. D., 36
Willis, G., 652
Willis, G. M., 652
Willis, T. A., 172
Wills, T. A., 111
Willutzke, U., 532
Wilner, A., 133
Wilson, C., 451, 758
Wilson, C. M., 720

Wilson, J., 399, 562
Wilson, K. G., 433–434
Wilson, L. M ., 447
Wilson, M., 413, 419
Wilson, P., 799
Wilson, T. D., 173
Winar, C., 307
Windschitl, M., 284
Wink, P., 578, 579
Winkielman, P., 792
Winstead, B. A., 411
Winstok, Z., 686
Wipfli, B. M., 213
Wise, J. C., 240
Wissing, M., 160
Wissing, M. P., 20
Withey, S. B., 732
Witt, A. A., 151
Wittekind, A., 347
Witvliet, C. V., 362, 566, 662
Witvliet, C. V. D., 661, 665
Wohlwend-Lloyd, R., 565
Wolch, J., 217
Wolchik, S., 774
Wolfers, J., 764
Wolfers, R. H., 714, 764
Wong, P. T., 791, 800
Wong, P. T. P., 31, 51, 167, 169, 810
Wong, Y. J., 13, 17
Wood, A. M., 22, 31, 47, 61, 174, 191, 384, 422, 423, 437, 444, 464, 465, 477, 524, 525, 537, 565, 566, 685, 796, 807, 811, 812
Wood, C., 758
Wood, R., 618
Wood, S., 122
Wood-Barcalow, N., 794
Wood-Barcalow, N. L., 795
Woodhams, J., 652
Woodhouse, S., 433, 437
Woodruff, P., 53
Woodside-Jiron, H., 286
Woodson, S. J., 433

Woodward, K., 436, 561
Woolfolk, R. L., 31, 37
Woolston, L., 23
Wooten, M., 333
Worrell, F. C., 267
Worsley, R., 438
Worthington, E. L., 495, 660, 661, 662, 664
Wortman, C. B., 508
Wright, B. A., 423, 445, 452, 536
Wright, M. O., 775
Wright, M. O. D., 299, 777
Wright, R., 758
Wright, T. A., 197, 570
Wright,C., 700
Wrzesniewski, A., 167, 169
Wu, I., 281
Wuench, K. L., 662
Wuthnow, R., 714
Wyatt, L., 486
Wyche, C. F., 773
Wyman, P. A., 774, 778

Xanthopoulou, D., 358
Xin, K. R., 197

Yalom, I., 49, 51, 793
Yalom, I. D., 504
Yamhure, L., 465
Yanes-Lopez, V., 617
Yang, B., 350
Yang, L. Q., 111
Yang, Y., 346
Yarker, J., 344, 345
Yates, P., 644, 645, 652
Yates, T. M., 773, 774, 775, 778, 834
Yen, J., 807
Yi, H., 288
Yip, J. A., 552
Yip, K. S., 690
Yoon, K. S., 288
Yoshikawa, H., 778
Young, M. E., 566

Young, S., 48
Young, W., 672
Youngren, M. A., 191, 240
Youssef, C. M., 301, 361
Yovetich, N. A., 659
Yuh, J., 782
Yule, W., 300

Zadrow, L., 717
Zaepernick-Rothe, U., 345
Zairi, M., 369
Zakay, D., 224
Zangmo, T., 766
Zarit, S. H., 618
Zautra, A., 773, 778, 779
Zautra, A. J., 620, 776
Zax, M., 90
Zeelenberg, M., 124
Zeiser, S., 281
Zeiss, A. M., 191, 240
Zemon, V., 509
Zhang, J. W., 229, 231
Zhang, L., 230
Zhong, C. B., 792
Zhu, R., 346
Zhu, W., 346, 350
Zilberfeld, T., 112
Zilca, R., 195
Zimbardo, P., 834
Zimbardo, P. G., 223, 226, 227, 228, 229
Zimbardo, P. R., 232
Zimmerman, B. J., 381
Zimmerman, R. D., 111
Zimmermann, A. C., 187
Zimprich, D., 660
Ziv, Y., 778
Zoellner, T., 447
Zonderman, A. B., 186
Zopiatis, A., 349
Zuravin, S., 504
Zuroff, D. C., 142, 168
Zuzanek, J., 213
Zvolensky, M. J., 420

# Subject Index

Acceptance commitment therapy, 165, 433–434
Acts of kindness, 194, 195, 256, 260, 398–399, 700
Adaptation, 128, 187. *See also* Resilience
Adolescents. *See also* Children
  consumer culture and values among, 90–91, 93–95
  gratitude in, 562, 564, 565–566, 568–569, 570
  hope accentuation strategies for, 486, 490–493
  motivation cultivation in, 313–324
  positive body image of, 795
  positive youth development theory for, 568–569
  sense of coherence among, 67, 69–70, 71–72, 73
  as sex offenders, 653
  social relationship importance to, 718
  suicide among, 130–131
  well-being therapy for, 474–475
Adolescents' motivation cultivation:
  art of, 321–323
  context for motivation strategies, 314–316, 321–323
  factors influencing motivation, 315–316, 317–318, 322
  individual and collective efficacy support in, 318–319, 322
  overview of, 313–315, 323
  ownership influencing, 317–318, 322
  relationship support in, 316, 320, 322
  research methods for studying, 316–318, 323
  self-doubt addressed in, 318–319
  structure of activities impacting, 318, 321–322
  summary of, 323–324
  work-fun balance in, 321, 322
Advertising and marketing:
  body image influenced by, 795
  children and adolescents as targets of, 90–91, 93–95
  consumer culture use of, 90–91, 93–95
  forgiveness campaign through, 669
  public policy on, 94–95

Affective disorders. *See* Anxiety and anxiety disorders; Depression and depressive disorders
Age and aging:
  life span throughout (*see* Life span development)
  positive, 595–610
  wisdom in relation to, 577–578, 582–584, 589
Aggression, 227, 561
Agoraphobia, 527
American Association for Humanistic Psychology (AAHP), 33
American Psychiatric Association, *Diagnostic and Statistical Manual of Mental Disorders*, 88, 415–416, 418–419, 520
American Psychological Association:
  7-day unit teaching plan by, 269
  clinical psychology training standards, 415
  research guidelines, 307
  Society for Humanistic Psychology, 33
  Society of Counseling Psychology, 429
  Teachers of Psychology in Secondary Schools, 267
Anger, 227
Anxiety and anxiety disorders:
  agoraphobic, 527
  assessment of, 466, 524–525, 527–529, 535, 536
  body dysmorphic, 528
  forgiveness impacting, 663
  generalized, 473, 527, 700
  gratitude correlation with, 566–567
  hoarding-related, 528
  hope accentuation strategies for, 493
  obsessive-compulsive, 475–476, 528, 531, 700
  physical activity impacting, 213
  positive education in response to, 298, 303
  posttraumatic, 474, 528–529, 700, 812
  prevalence of, 298
  rehabilitation psychology addressing, 450
  relapse and recurrence in, 464
  resilience training for, 303
  separation, 527
  social, 527

Anxiety and anxiety disorders (*Continued*)
  strength-based assessment of, 524–525,
    527–529, 535, 536
  time perspectives associated with, 227
  well-being therapy for, 464, 472–474,
    475–476, 700
Aristotelian foundations:
  of humanistic psychology, 33–34, 37, 39
  of positive psychology, 12–14, 16–17, 18,
    19, 20
  of virtue ethics, 53
Assessment:
  of anxiety and anxiety disorders, 466,
    524–525, 527–529, 535, 536
  of bipolar disorder, 526
  of choice goals, 123–126
  computerized adaptive testing in, 401
  Day Reconstruction Method of, 401–402
  of depression and depression disorders,
    472, 524–525, 526, 535, 536
  *Diagnostic and Statistical Manual of Mental
    Disorders* for, 88, 415–416, 418–419, 520
  of disability-related impacts, 616–617,
    618, 621, 624
  Ecological Momentary Assessment, 402
  of embodiment, 793, 795
  of emotional intelligence, 549–550
  of eudaimonic and hedonic
    orientation/practices, 161–163, 166,
    174–176
  in executive or leadership coaching,
    383–384
  of gratitude, 560–562
  of happiness and well-being, 273, 343, 401,
    446, 466, 468, 472, 737–738
  of hope, 485–487, 490, 492, 493
  item-response theory in, 401
  of meaning and purpose, 401
  of mindfulness, 149–150, 151
  of personality, 124, 363, 383, 529–532, 587
  of positive aging, 596–597, 598
  of positive constructs in health settings,
    400–402, 403
  of posttraumatic growth, 504
  of quality of life, 446, 465
  of sense of coherence, 67
  of sex offenders, 643–646
  strength-based approach to, 519–539
  of time perspective, 225–227, 228, 229,
    230–231
  of virtues and strengths, 53, 163, 446, 522,
    523–524, 684–685, 754
  of wisdom, 523, 579, 580–581, 587
  of work strengths and styles, 363
Assessment instruments:
  Adult Carers Quality of Life
    Questionnaire (AC-QoL), 618
  Adult Dispositional Hope Scale, 486, 487,
    493
  Adult Needs and Strengths Assessment,
    533

Australian Early Development Index
    (AEDI), 273
Beck Depression Inventory, 124
Big Five personality inventory, 363
Body Appreciation Scale (BAS), 795
Body Awareness Questionnaire (BAQ),
    793
Body Intelligence Scale (BIS), 793
Center for Epidemiologic Studies
    Depression Scale–Revised (CES-D),
    524, 537
Children's Hope Scale (CHS), 485–486,
    490, 492
Children's Sense of Coherence Scale
    (CSOC), 67
Circles Test, 225
Classification of Virtues and Strengths
    (CVS), 522
Clinical Interview for Depression (CID),
    472
Family Sense of Coherence Scale (FSOC),
    67
Flow Questionnaire (FQ), 621
Gallup's StrengthsFinder, 383
GQ-6, 561, 562
Gratitude Adjective Checklist (GAC), 562
Gratitude Resentment and Appreciation
    Test (GRAT), 561, 562
Hedonic and Eudaimonic Motives for
    Activities (HEMA) scale, 161–162
Implicit Association Test (IAT), 150
Instrumental Activities of Daily Living,
    598
Kirton Adaption Innovation Inventory
    (KAI), 363
Learning Styles Inventory (LSI), 363
Life History Questionnaire, 537
Life Orientation Test, 124
Life Satisfaction Index (LSI), 737
Life Satisfaction Questionnaire (LISAT),
    446
Life Theme Questionnaire (LT), 621
Maximization Scale, 123–124, 125–126
Mayer-Salovey-Caruso Emotional
    Intelligence Test (MSCEIT), 549–550,
    552–553
Medical Outcomes Study Short-Form
    Health Survey, 446
Middle Years Development Instrument
    (MDI), 273
Mindfulness Attention Awareness Scale
    (MAAS), 149
Minnesota Multiphasic Personality
    Inventory-2 (MMPI-2), 537
Multidimensional Perfectionism Scale, 124
Myers-Briggs Type Indicator (MBTI), 363,
    383
NIH Toolbox, 401, 402
Orientations To Happiness Questionnaire
    (OTHQ), 161–162

Orientations to Happiness Scale (OTH), 446
Orientation to Life Questionnaire, 67
Posttraumatic Growth Inventory, 504
Psychological Well-Being Scales (PWB), 466, 468, 472
Quality of Life Index (QLI), 446
Quality of Life Inventory (QOLI), 533
Realize 2, 384
Satisfaction with Life Scale, 124
Sense of Coherence questionnaire (SOC-13 or -29), 67
Spielberger State-Trait Anxiety Inventory (STAI), 524, 537
Stanford Time Perspective Inventory (STPI), 225
Strengths Assessment Worksheet (SAW), 525
Subjective Happiness Scale, 124
Time Lines, 225
Time Structure Questionnaire, 225
Values in Action scale, 53, 163, 166, 383–384, 446, 523–524, 525, 533, 537, 684, 754
Zimbardo Time Perspective Inventory (ZTPI), 225–226, 227, 228, 231
Association for Supervision and Curriculum Development (ASCD), Whole-Child Initiative, 271, 275
Attachment theory, 144, 145, 716
Attention:
  attention-deficit/hyperactivity disorder, 529
  mindfulness of (*see* Mindfulness practices)
  self-regulation relationship to, 147–151
Authenticity:
  Authentic Happiness website, 537
  authentic leadership, 334, 338, 380
  eudaimonia and hedonia on, 161, 166–167, 174
  values related to, 88
Autonomy:
  autonomous regulation, 140–151
  choice relationship to, 121–122, 130–133
  happiness relationship to, 745
  health impacts of, 396
  humanistic psychology on, 35
  motivated behavior based on, 139–152, 318, 322
  physical activity enhancing, 215
  values related to, 88, 95, 104, 105, 114–115
  well-being therapy on, 471
  work-related, 360, 366–368, 370
Axial Age, 54

Berlin wisdom paradigm, 578–579, 581–582
Bhutan's Gross National Happiness, 766–767
Bipolar disorder, 526

Body dysmorphic disorder, 528
Body image and awareness. *See* Embodiment
Bounce Back! program, 303
*Brave New World* (Huxley), 732, 746, 747
Broaden-and-Build model, 395, 436, 521

Children. *See also* Adolescents
  consumer culture and values among, 90–91, 93–95
  gratitude in, 562, 564, 565–566, 568–569, 570
  hope accentuation strategies for, 485–486, 490–493
  parent-child attachment with, 144, 145, 716
  positive youth development theory for, 568–569
  sense of coherence among, 67, 69–70
  social relationship importance to, 717, 718
  well-being therapy for, 474–475
Choice:
  adaptation effects on, 128
  autonomy relationship to, 121–122, 130–133
  cultural influences on, 126, 132
  depression and suicide relationship to, 130–131
  eudaimonic and hedonic orientation of, 161–162
  freedom relationship to, 121–122, 131–134
  future research in, 134
  high expectations influencing, 129, 131
  maximizing and satisficing goals of, 123–126
  missed opportunities influencing, 127–128
  motivation relationship to, 139–152, 317
  overview of, 121–122, 133–134
  paradox of, 121–134
  paralysis from overload of, 122–123
  regret influencing, 124, 126–127
  self-blame due to, 130, 131
  self-identity options based on, 131–132
  self-regulation of, 139–152
  social comparison influencing, 128–129
  social relationship options based on, 132–133
  summary of, 134
Cisco Systems Serious Health Notification System, 704–705
Civic responsibilities, 96
Client-centered psychotherapy and counseling, 433
Clinical practice:
  balancing time perspective in, 231–233
  complexity of well-being in, 465–466
  disability-related resource-focused programs in, 627–628
  emotional intelligence in, 553–554

Clinical practice (*Continued*)
  eudaimonic and hedonic pursuit in,
    165–173, 174–176, 463–464, 467
  extrinsic *vs.* intrinsic values in, 87–90
  gratitude interventions in, 566–567
  hope accentuation strategies as, 483–500
  life coaching distinction from, 250
  physical activity in, 210–212
  positive aging examples in, 595, 600–603
  positive psychology growth influencing,
    465
  posttraumatic growth applications in,
    503–514
  quality of life assessment in, 465
  rehabilitation psychology in, 444
  response *vs.* recovery in, 464 (*see also*
    Recovery-oriented service systems)
  self-help approaches *vs.*, 237–238, 240,
    245–246
  social work strength perspective in,
    687–689
  strength-based assessment in, 519–539
  well-being therapy as, 463–477, 699–700
Clinical psychology:
  categorical *vs.* dimensional models of
    health in, 419–420
  conceptions of wellness and illness in,
    411–412
  disease classifications in, 411–412,
    415–416, 418–419
  essentialist perspective on, 417
  historical roots of, 413–416
  illness ideology in, 412–421
  overview of, 411–412, 423
  positive psychology vision and mission
    in, 411–412, 421–424
  practice applications of (*see* Clinical
    practice)
  psychoanalytic theory in, 413–414
  science of, 420–421
  social-constructivist perspective on, 412,
    416–419, 420–421, 422
  summary of, 423–424
  training and education in, 413–414, 415
Coaching. *See* Executive or leadership
  coaching; Life coaching
Cognitive-behavioral therapy (CBT):
  affective disorder clinical treatment via,
    472–474
  eudaimonic and hedonic pursuits via, 165
  executive or leadership coaching based
    on, 381
  mindfulness in (*see* Mindfulness practices)
  multimodal integrative cognitive
    stimulation therapy in, 699
  positive activities for happiness *vs.*, 191
  recovery-oriented service systems
    adaptations of, 699–700
  rehabilitation psychology including,
    450–452
  resilience programs based on, 303, 305

  self-help approaches based on, 240
  strengths focus in, 437
  well-being therapy relationship to,
    472–476, 699–700
Cognitive evaluation theory (CET), 143–144
Collaborative for Academic, Social, and
  Emotional Learning (CASEL), 300
Communitarian movement, 723–724
Community:
  civic responsibilities to, 96
  disability-related support resources in,
    615–629
  forgiveness facilitation in, 659–674
  physical activity encouraged in, 216, 217
  positive organizational psychology in,
    335–336
  public policy individuality-community
    balancing, 713–725
  recovery-oriented service systems in,
    695–706
  resilience practices in, 777–778, 779–780,
    781
  safety in, 217
  sex offender rehabilitation in, 635–654
  social work in, 681–691
  time systems in, 223–224
  work organization engagement in, 368
Computerized functions. *See*
  Internet-related functions
Conduct disorders, 529
Conservation of resources theory, 347–349
Consumer culture:
  advertising and marketing of, 90–91,
    93–95
  children and adolescents as targets for,
    90–91, 93–95
  clinical issues involving, 87–90
  ecological well-being in, 86–87
  overview of, 83–84, 96
  personal well-being in, 85
  practice implications of values in, 87–96
  prevention practices in response to, 90–92
  public policy on, 92–96
  social well-being in, 86
  summary of, 97
  time affluence *vs.*, 95–96
  values in, 83–97
  voluntary simplicity interventions
    rejecting, 91–92
Coping and coping skills, 395, 451, 567–568,
  606–607
Cougar Automation, 336–337
Counseling psychology:
  acceptance commitment therapy as,
    433–434
  client-centered psychotherapy and
    counseling as, 433
  cultural influences and perspectives on,
    430–431, 432
  definition and description of, 430
  development and identity of, 429–431, 435

disease or illness ideology in, 432–433, 436–437
gratitude focus in, 436, 437
humanistic psychology roots of, 431–432, 434
overview of, 429, 438
positive affect focus in, 435–436
positive psychology relationship to, 429, 431–439
posttraumatic growth focus in, 435, 437
practice applications of positive psychology in, 435–438
resilience focus in, 435–436
summary of, 438–439
training and education in, 437, 438
Cultural influences and perspectives:
on choice goals, 126, 132
consumer culture as, 83–97
on counseling psychology, 430–431, 432
on embodiment, 795
gender-related, 68, 552–553, 764, 795
on gratitude, 565
on happiness and well-being, 194, 713, 738, 740–744, 745, 746, 757, 759–760
on hope accentuation strategies, 498–499
on individuality-community balancing, 713, 721–722, 723–724
on motivation, 316, 317
on negative perspective, 814
on personality, 814
on positive activities, 194
on resilience, 775, 777, 780, 781
on sense of coherence, 68, 72–73
social-constructivist perspective reflecting, 284, 412, 416–419, 420–421, 422
on social relationships, 721–722
socioeconomic, 68, 714–715, 722–724, 741–743, 746, 757–760, 763–764
on time perspectives, 223–224, 225, 228
Universalistic perspective on, 17–20
value congruency with, 112–113
on wisdom, 578
work or corporate culture as, 369, 370
Cyclothymic disorder, 473–474

*Daily Challenge,* 241–242, 244
Davy, Jim, 333–335
Day Reconstruction Method, 401–402
Depression and depressive disorders:
assessment of, 472, 524–525, 526, 535, 536
choice relationship to, 131
forgiveness impacting, 662–663, 665
gratitude correlation with, 561, 566–567
hope accentuation strategies for, 493
pharmacological interventions for, 211, 472, 473
physical activity impacting, 209–210, 211–212
positive education in response to, 298, 303, 305

prevalence of, 130–131, 298
rehabilitation psychology addressing, 450
relapse and recurrence in, 464, 472–473
resilience training for, 272, 303, 305
self-help approaches to, 238, 239, 240
social relationships impacting, 717, 718
strength-based assessment of, 524–525, 526, 535, 536
time perspectives associated with, 227, 231–232
well-being therapy for, 464, 472–474, 476, 700
*Diagnostic and Statistical Manual of Mental Disorders (DSM),* 88, 415–416, 418–419, 520
Dialogic teaching:
classroom practice transformation via, 279–292
definition and description of, 280
epistemology and theory underlying, 283–285
overview of, 279–280, 291–292
professional development in, 287–291
recitation teaching *vs.,* 282–283
research on, 285–286
summary of, 292
teacher-student relations in, 281–282
teaching through, 280–283
Dignity, 36–37
Disability-impacted people and caregivers:
assessment of, 616–617, 618, 621, 624
caregivers, specifically, 617–627
daily experiences and future expectations of, 620–623
disability, defined, 443
hereditary spastic paraparesis impacting, 620–623
optimal experiences or flow of, 619–620, 621–623, 628
overview of issues for, 615–616, 629
perceived facilitators and barriers for, 623–627
person and resources shift in focus on, 616–617
positive emotions of, 618–619
posttraumatic growth in, 619
prevalence of, 444
psychological and relational resources for, 617–620
rehabilitation for, 443–455
resilience of, 620, 628
resource-focused intervention programs for, 627–628
resources for, 615–629
self-efficacy of, 618
sense of coherence of, 619
social barriers for, 625, 628
summary of issues for, 629
theoretical framework for, 616–620
Domestic violence, 685–687
Dutton, 370

Ecological Momentary Assessment (EMA), 402
Ecological well-being, 86–87
Education. *See* School settings; Teaching and learning methods and processes; Training and education
Embodiment:
   body awareness, 793–794
   body-based interventions, 797–800
   cultural influences and perspectives on, 795
   definition and description of, 791–792
   emotional intelligence relationship to, 796
   interpersonal relationships and, 796–797
   intrapersonal relationships and, 793–796
   optimal functioning role of, 791–801
   overview of, 791, 800
   positive activities enhancing, 796, 799–800
   positive body image, 794–796
   practical applications of, 797–800
   radical and simple view of, 792
   summary of, 800–801
   understanding, 791–797
   well-being and, 792–793, 796
Emotional intelligence:
   ability model of, 546, 547–554
   applications of, 551–554
   clinical applications of, 553–554
   competency approach to, 546
   definition and description of, 545, 546
   embodiment relationship to, 796
   executive or leadership coaching focus on, 382
   life span development of, 545–554
   managing emotions in, 547, 548–549, 550
   measuring, 549–550
   outcome predictions based on, 550
   overview of, 545–546, 554
   perceiving emotions in, 547, 548, 550
   personality relationship to, 546, 550
   political use of, 553
   positive education promoting, 300, 302, 304, 551–552
   precursors to theory of, 546–547
   professional development focus on, 361
   social and emotional learning through, 300, 302, 304, 551–552
   summary of, 554
   understanding emotions in, 547–548, 550
   using emotions to facilitate thought in, 547, 548, 550
   wisdom relationship to, 582, 585–590
   work organization applications of, 361, 382, 552–553
Emotional prosperity program, 52
Environmental factors:
   community factors as (*see* Community)
   cultural factors as (*see* Cultural influences and perspectives)
   environmental affordances as, 110
   familial factors as (*see* Families)
   livability of environment for happiness, 735, 741–744
   mastery and control of, 396, 470
   person-environment value congruency, 110–113, 114–115
   rehabilitation psychology consideration of, 443, 445
   resilience practice response to, 778–780
   social systems as (*see* Social relationships)
   social work person-environment focus, 682, 683, 685, 688, 689
   socioeconomic, 68, 714–715, 722–724, 741–743, 746, 757–760, 763–764
   work environment factors, 358, 359 (*see also* Work organizations)
Ethical issues. *See also* Morality; Values; Virtues
   eudaimonic conception of, 39
   organizational approaches to, 337–338
   positive social planning consideration of, 752, 757–760, 766
   self-help approaches creating, 245–246
   sex offender rehabilitation consideration of, 636
   virtue theory on, 38–41
Eudaimonia and hedonia:
   assessment of orientation/practice of, 161–163, 166, 174–176
   authenticity in, 161, 166–167, 174
   clinical practice pursuit of, 165–173, 174–176, 463–464, 467
   complementary roles of, 159–176
   definitions and descriptions of, 37, 159–161, 342–343
   distinction between, 163–165
   empirical findings on, 162–163
   eudaimonic-specific steps toward, 166–171
   excellence in, 161, 168–169, 175
   growth in, 161, 169–171, 175
   hedonic adaptation to happiness, 187
   hedonic-specific steps toward, 171–173
   humanistic psychology views of, 37–38, 39
   meaning in, 37–38, 161, 167–168, 175
   orientations of, 160, 161–162
   overview of, 159, 173
   positive education perspectives on, 302
   positive psychology foundations in, 2–3, 37
   Present-Hedonistic time perspective, 227, 230
   rehabilitation psychology approach to, 446
   summary of, 173–174
   wisdom in relation to, 578
Every Child Matters initiative, 298
Executive or leadership coaching:
   authentic leadership coaching as, 380
   coaches providing, 378–379, 385–386

cognitive and behavioral techniques in, 381
core assumption of, 379–380
definition and description of, 249, 377–378
emotional intelligence in, 382
flow states and optimal performance in, 380
generational changes in, 377–379
multimodal therapy in, 381–382
overview of, 377, 386–387
positive psychology in, 377–387
psychometric assessment in, 383–384
reasons to engage in, 378
research in, 384–386
self-determination theory compatibility with, 380
structure of, 378
summary of, 387
systems theory in, 382
techniques used in, 381–383
time perspective coaching in, 232
Transtheoretical Model of Change in, 382–383
Existential psychology:
definition and description of, 35
diffuse influence of, 49–50
history of, 33
humanistic psychology roots in, 33, 35
internal diversity of, 48–49
methodology in, 51–52
motivation theories in, 20–21
overview of, 47, 56
positive psychology dimensions of, 20–22, 33, 35, 47–56
practical collaboration with positive psychology and, 52–56
summary of, 56
tragedy emphasis in, 50–51
values in, 52–54
virtues and strengths in, 52–56
Expectations, 129, 131

Families. *See also* Adolescents; Children; Marriage or partnerships
consumer culture impacting, 90–91, 93–95
disability-related caregiving by, 617–627
domestic violence in, 685–687
eudaimonic and hedonic parenting variables in, 163
health impacted by, 719–721
parent-child attachment in, 144, 145, 716
parenting skills in, 687
resilience of, 620, 628, 778–779
sense of coherence in, 67, 70–71, 72
strength-based assessment including, 537–538
values reflected in, 90–91, 93–95, 111, 112
Finland, educational resilience in, 780
Flow and flow states:

disability-related impacts on, 619–620, 621–623, 628
executive or leadership coaching focus on, 380
forgiveness contribution to, 666
humanistic psychology roots of, 32
life coaching addressing, 257
mindfulness correlation to, 149
motivation relationship to, 315, 318, 320, 330
personal growth and, 170
work-related, 330, 358, 360
Forgiveness:
adverse effects of, 663
applied research on, 664–665
benevolence and, 666
community-level interventions for, 667–668, 672–673
definition and description of, 660–661
delivery format for facilitation of, 671
education and psychoeducation on, 669–670, 673
enhancement through, 670
facilitation of, 659, 665–674
forgiveness interventions, 566, 659, 665–674
gratitude relationship to, 566
health and well-being relationship to, 661–664, 665
intensity of interventions on, 668
legal/justice system focus on, 672
limitations of interventions on, 673
marital or partner-related, 659–660, 662, 663, 665, 670
motivation for, 662, 666, 668
overview of, 659, 673
peer mediation focus on, 672–673
positive and negative views of, 815
positive psychology approach to, 665–666
prevention practices involving, 667, 668
reach of interventions on, 667–668
reconciliation and, 661
religious influences on, 662, 666, 667
revenge and retaliation *vs.*, 659, 660, 666
sex offender rehabilitation including, 637–638
summary of, 674
Freedom. *See also* Autonomy
choice relationship to, 121–122, 131–134
existential concept of, 48, 54, 55, 56
humanistic psychology on, 35, 36
motivation impacted by, 317
social well-being relationship to, 760
work-related, 360, 366–368, 370

Geelong Grammar School, 272, 302
Gender influences, 68, 552–553, 764, 795
Generalized anxiety disorder (GAD), 473, 527, 700
Genetic factors, 186, 188, 306, 713

Global Advocacy Council for Physical
    Activity, Toronto Charter for Physical
    Activity, 207
Gratitude:
    adult-specific, 561–562, 563–564, 568
    child/adolescent, 562, 564, 565–566,
        568–569, 570
    clinical applications of, 566–567
    coping and resilience improvements
        through, 567–568
    counseling psychology focus on, 436, 437
    creative applications of, 566–567
    cultural influences and perspectives on,
        565
    emotional prosperity program based on,
        52
    existential approaches to, 50
    good life relationship to, 568–569
    health impacts of, 398
    interventions to promote, 562–564
    life span development of, 559–571
    measures and correlates of, 560–562
    moral affect conceptualization of, 559–560
    obstacles to promoting, 564–566
    overview of, 559, 570
    personality correlates with, 561–562, 565
    positive activities through expression of,
        190, 191, 197, 198, 259, 260, 398,
        563–564, 700, 796
    recovery-oriented service systems
        including, 700
    research on, 559, 560–562, 569–570
    self-help approaches to, 241, 243–244
    summary of, 570–571
    work organization benefits of, 569–570
Gratitude Bucket, 241
Gratitude Journal, 243–244
Gratitude Tree, 244
Gratitude Visit intervention, 563
Great Transformation, 54
Gross National Happiness, 766–767
Group settings, 513, 647–648. See also
    Community

Haberdasher's Academies, 302–303
Happify, 242–243, 244
Happiness and well-being:
    assessment of, 273, 343, 401, 446, 466, 468,
        472, 737–738
    Bhutan's Gross National Happiness,
        766–767
    conditions for, 741–745
    counseling psychology focus on, 435–436
    cultural influences and perspectives on,
        194, 713, 738, 740–744, 745, 746, 757,
        759–760
    definition and description of, 185,
        682–683, 734–737
    demographics of happy people, 713–714
    as desirable outcome, 746–748
    disability-related impacts on, 618–619
        embodiment and, 792–793, 796
        empirical evidence and research on,
            189–191, 196, 732–734
        genetic influences on, 186, 188
        greatest happiness principle, 731–732
        health relationship to, 196–197, 394–395,
            396, 399–400, 745
        hedonic adaptation to, 187
        hedonic pursuit of, 171–173 (see also
            Eudaimonia and hedonia)
        manufacturing of, 741–745
        money relationship to, 714–715, 722–723,
            741–743, 746, 757–760, 763–764
        optimal conditions for increasing,
            192–196
        overview of, 185–186, 199, 748
        personality relationship to, 186, 713, 745
        pessimism and optimism on intentional
            pursuit of, 186–187
        positive activities increasing, 188–199,
            254–255, 700
        positive social planning focus on, 751–767
        possibility of, 739–741
        practicable goal of, 734–741
        as public policy priority, 731–748
        pursuit of, practices for, 185–199
        quality of life and, 734–736
        religious and spiritual influences on,
            713–714, 739
        satisfaction and, 735–737, 739–740, 746
        self-help approaches for, 237–246
        social relationships impacting, 198,
            716–722, 744, 796
        summary of, 199, 748
        theoretical perspectives in, 188
        time perspective and, 230–231
        values relationship to, 85–86, 747–748,
            757–760
        work relationship to, 197–198, 341–352,
            357–360, 702–703
    World Database of Happiness, 734, 738,
        741
Health and well-being:
    categorical vs. dimensional models of,
        419–420
    clinical psychology on, 411–424
    definition of, 597
    disabilities impacting, 443–455, 615–629
    disease classifications in, 411–412,
        415–416, 418–419
    eudaimonic view of (see Eudaimonia and
        hedonia)
    forgiveness relationship to, 661–664, 665
    happiness relationship to, 196–197,
        394–395, 396, 399–400, 745
    health psychology on, 383–404
    illness ideology of, 412–421, 432–433,
        436–437
    mastery and control impacting, 396
    meaning and purpose impacting, 397

mental health, specifically (*see* Mental health)

positive activity consequences for, 196–197, 397–400

positive affect impacting, 196–197, 394–395, 396, 399–400

positive aging in relation to, 595–610

positive psychology on (*see* Positive psychology)

practices for (*see* Health and well-being practices)

rehabilitation for disabilities impacting, 443–455

salutogenic continuum of illness and, 61–75, 275

sense of coherence and, 65–73

social-constructivist perspective of, 412, 416–419, 420–421, 422

social relationships impacting, 719–721, 796

social work strength perspective on, 687–689

stress impacting (*see* Stress)

Health and well-being practices:

balancing time perspective as, 223–234

happiness pursuit as, 185–199

life coaching as, 249–261

physical activity as, 207–218

positive psychology interventions as, 397–400

self-help approaches as, 237–246

Health psychology:

assessment of positive constructs in, 400–402, 403

Broaden-and-Build model in, 395

definition and description of, 394

future directions in, 402–404

health outcome mediators in, 395–397

mastery and control in, 396

meaning and purpose in, 397

overview of, 393, 404

positive affect in, 394–395, 396, 399–400

positive psychology interventions in, 397–400

positive psychology synergy with, 383–404

Revised Stress and Coping Theory in, 395

stress and health focus in, 394–397

summary of, 404

Hedonia. *See* Eudaimonia and hedonia

Hereditary spastic paraparesis (HSP), 620–623

Historical and philosophical foundations:

agenda of positive psychology, 11

Aristotelian foundations as, 12–14, 16–17, 18, 19, 20, 33–34, 37, 39, 53

assumptions of positive psychology, 10

existential psychology as, 20–22, 33, 35, 47–56

humanistic psychology as, 20–22, 31–42, 431–432, 434, 696, 826

overview of, 9–10, 31–32, 41, 47, 56, 61–62, 74–75

of positive psychology, 9–24, 31–42, 47–56, 61–75, 431–432, 434, 696, 826

psychology subdiscipline application history in, 22–23

research approaches in, 21–22, 22–23, 38, 51–52

salutogenic paradigm as, 61–75

social and moral motivation as, 14–17

summary of, 24, 41–42, 56, 75

Universalistic perspective as, 17–20

Hoarding disorders, 528

Hope accentuation strategies:

adult-specific, 493–497

child/adolescent, 485–486, 490–493

clinical applications of, 483–500

cultural influences and perspectives on, 498–499

formal, 485–487, 489, 490–495, 497

hope as change agent in, 484–485

hope bonding as, 485, 488–489

hope enhancing as, 485, 489–497

hope finding as, 485–488

hope profiling as, 488

hope reminding as, 485, 497–498

hope theory on, 483–485

informal, 487–488, 489, 495–497, 497–498

overview of, 483, 499

summary of, 499–500

*The How of Happiness* (Lyubormirsky), 240, 244

Humanistic-experimental approaches, 437

Humanistic psychology:

Aristotelian foundations of, 33–34, 37, 39

counseling psychology roots in, 431–432, 434

epistemology in, 38

eudaimonia *vs.* hedonia in, 37–38, 39

existentialism in, 33, 35

history of, 32–37

key themes in, 35–37

methodology in, 38

motivation theories in, 20–21

overview of, 31–32, 41

personalism in, 34

phenomenology in, 33–34

positive psychology bridges with, 3, 20–22, 31–42, 431–432, 434, 696, 826

psychoanalytic theory *vs.*, 20–21, 32–33

summary of, 41–42

virtue theory in, 38–41

Humanistic therapies, 165

Illness Management and Recovery, 700

Individuality-community balancing:

close relationships and happiness in, 718–722

communitarian movement on, 723–724

Individuality-community balancing
 (*Continued*)
  cultural influences and perspectives on,
   713, 721–722, 723–724
  demographics of happy people for,
   713–714
  health considerations in, 719–721
  money and happiness role in, 714–715,
   722–724
  need to belong in, 716–718, 721–722
  overview of, 713, 724
  in public policy, 713–725
  radical individualism impacts in,
   721–722
  social toxicity of inequality in,
   722–724
  summary of, 724–725
  vision of connected future in, 722–723
Inner resources. *See* Emotional intelligence;
  Gratitude; Positive aging; Wisdom
Institute of Coaching, 379
*International Classification of Disease,* 415
*International Classification of Functioning,*
 *Disability and Health,* 443, 616–617
International Positive Psychology
 Association (IPPA), 379
International Society for Quality of Life
 Studies (ISQOLS), 733
Internet-related functions:
  computerized adaptive testing as, 401
  context sensing via, 245
  emerging technology impacting, 245
  forgiveness facilitation intervention
   delivery via, 671
  self-help approaches via, 240–244, 245
Interventions and practices:
  clinical (*see* Clinical practice)
  community-related (*see* Community)
  health and well-being (*see* Health and
   well-being practices)
  mindfulness (*see* Mindfulness practices)
  pharmacological (*see* Pharmacological
   interventions)
  positive activities as (*see* Positive
   activities)
  prevention-focused (*see* Prevention
   practices)
Investors in People (IIP), 360–361
Item-response theory (IRT), 401

*Journal of Abnormal and Social Psychology,* 414
*Journal of Humanistic Psychology,* 32

KidsMatter program, 302
Knox Grammar School, 273

Leadership behavior:
  authentic, 334, 338, 380
  characteristics of positive, 338, 342
  conservation of resources theory on,
   347–349

definition and description of, 342
emotional intelligence influence on, 382,
 553
ethical and virtuous organization
 behavior influenced by, 338
executive or leadership coaching on, 232,
 249, 377–387
future research on, 349–351
identification fostering relationship to,
 346, 348
meaningful work relationship to,
 344–345, 348
mediators of effects of, 343–347, 348
organizational values exhibited through,
 704–705
overview of, 341–342, 351
political, 553
practice implications of, 351
self-efficacy relationship to, 343–344,
 348
summary of, 351–352
transformational, 341–352
trust in management relationship to,
 345–346, 348
workplace wellness program support
 through, 702–703
Life coaching:
  approaches to, 252
  definition and description of, 249–252
  development of, 250–251
  eudaimonic and hedonic pursuits
   via, 165
  information sources for, 258–259
  meta-theory for, 252
  orientation of, 257–258
  overview of, 249, 261
  PERMA model for, 257
  positive activities/interventions in,
   254–256, 259–260
  Positive Psychology Coaching as, 254–
   256
  positive psychology compatibility with,
   253–256
  positive psychology integration with,
   257–261
  psychotherapy and counseling distinction
   from, 250
  research on, 252–253
  self-help tools for, 260–261
  summary of, 261
  time perspective coaching in, 232–233
Life span development:
  of emotional intelligence, 545–554
  forgiveness changes over, 673
  of gratitude, 559–571
  inner resources for positive, 545–554,
   559–571, 577–591, 595–610
  of positive aging, 595–610
  of resilience, 780–781
  of sense of coherence, 68
  of wisdom, 577–591
*LiveHappy,* 244

Loving-kindness meditation, 197, 260
Luckey, Richard, 595, 602–603

Making Hope Happen for Kids program,
490–492
Marriage or partnerships. *See also* Families
"Call for a New Conversation on
Marriage," 725
divorce or separation in, 718
emotional intelligence in, 554
existential psychology on, 55–56
forgiveness in, 659–660, 662, 663, 665, 670
gratitude in, 562
happiness and well-being in, 718–719
health impacts of, 720
hope accentuation strategies for, 495
positive activity consequences for, 198
positive aging impacts of, 603, 608
resilience in, 779
wisdom related to conflict in, 580–581, 584
Meaning or meaningfulness:
assessment, 401
autonomous regulation and, 140, 142, 146
eudaimonia and hedonia on, 37–38, 161,
167–168, 175
existential psychology on, 50–51
forgiveness contribution to, 666
happiness relationship to, 185, 735
health impacts of, 397
humanistic psychology on, 33–34,
37–38
life coaching on, 254, 257
meaningful work, 344–345, 348
phenomenology focus on, 33–34
posttraumatic growth as meaningful
change (*see* Posttraumatic growth)
quality of life through, 735
salutogenic paradigm on, 65–66, 67, 73
teaching and learning focus on, 302, 305
well-being therapy on, 470–471
Medication, 165, 211, 472, 473
Meditation:
body awareness in, 794, 799
eudaimonia development via, 167
executive or leadership coaching
including, 381
gratitude in, 566
loving-kindness, 197, 260
positive activities through, 197, 260
Mental health. *See also* Health and
well-being
anxiety impacting (*see* Anxiety and
anxiety disorders)
bipolar disorder impacting, 526
body dysmorphic disorder impacting, 528
clinical responses to (*see* Clinical practice;
Clinical psychology)
conduct disorders impacting, 529
depression impacting (*see* Depression and
depressive disorders)
obsessive-compulsive disorder impacting,
475–476, 528, 531, 700

personality disorders impacting, 529–532
positive psychology on (*see* Positive
psychology)
posttraumatic stress disorder impacting,
474, 528–529, 700, 812
psychosis impacting, 699
recovery movement in, 695–706
schizophrenia impacting, 212, 420,
553–554, 699
social work strength perspective on,
687–689
Mindfulness practices:
body awareness in, 794, 799
eudaimonia development via, 167
executive or leadership coaching
including, 381
gratitude in, 566
intentional systematic mindfulness as, 566
intrinsic value focus in, 89, 150–151
meditation as, 167, 197, 260, 381, 566, 794,
799
mindfulness cultivation through, 151
self-regulation shaped through, 148–151
Money. *See* Socioeconomic status
Morality. *See also* Ethical issues; Values;
Virtues
gratitude as moral affect, 559–560
moral motivation for, 14–17
public policy on, 723–724
utilitarianism as moral principle, 731–732,
747–748
MORE model of wisdom, 582
Motivation and motivation theories:
autonomy of motivated behavior,
139–152, 318, 322
choice relationship to, 139–152, 317
context for motivation strategies,
314–316, 321–323
cultivation of adolescents' motivation,
313–324
cultural influences and perspectives on,
316, 317
factors influencing motivation, 315–316,
317–318, 322
forgiveness relationship to, 662, 666, 668
hope as motivating force, 484
humanistic and existential theory
relationship to, 20–21
individual and collective efficacy support
in, 318–319, 322
intrinsic and extrinsic motivation,
139–152, 313–314, 321–323, 380
organizational motivation challenges and
improvements, 330, 336, 360
ownership influencing, 317–318, 322
positive psychology foundations of, 14–17
relationship support facilitating, 320, 322
self-determination theory as, 139–152,
320, 380
self-doubt relationship to, 318–319
wisdom relationship to, 586–590
work-fun balance in, 321, 322

Mount Barker High School, 274
Multimodal therapy:
  executive or leadership coaching
    including, 381–382
  multimodal integrative cognitive
    stimulation therapy as, 699
  multimodal pain management as, 451
  recovery-oriented service systems
    including, 699
Multiple sclerosis, 212

Naikan therapy, 566, 568
National Institute of Mental Health (NIMH),
  414
Negative perspectives:
  context influencing view of, 813–815
  cultural influences and perspectives on,
    814
  hazy boundaries between positive and,
    809–811
  integration of positive with, 810–818,
    825–826
  overview of, 807–808, 818
  positive education role of, 815–818
  positive psychology role of, 807–818,
    825–826
  posttraumatic growth as positive after
    negative events, 811–813
  prioritizing the positive vs., 809, 811
  psychoanalytic theory as, 20–21
  strengths-based assessment impacted by
    negativity bias, 519–520
  summary of, 818

Obsessive-compulsive disorder, 475–476,
  528, 531, 700
Online functions. See Internet-related
  functions
Opportunity costs, 127–128
Oppositional defiant disorder, 529
Optimal experiences. See Flow and flow
  states; Meaning or meaningfulness
Organismic integration theory, 140–142,
  145
Organizational psychology. See also Work
  organizations
  appreciative inquiry in, 329–330, 331,
    334–335
  case studies of, 333–336
  decision-making speed and authority in,
    333, 704
  economies of strengths in, 337
  ethical considerations in, 337–338
  leadership behavior in, 334, 338, 702–703,
    704–705
  motivation challenges and improvements
    in, 330, 336
  organizational compassion in, 704–705
  organizational resilience in, 331–332
  overview of, 329–330, 338
  positive deviance in, 335–336

positive psychology in, 329–339, 702–705
positivity benefits to performance in, 331,
  336–337
recovery-oriented service systems
  including, 702–705
social networks and relationships in, 333
step-change application of positive
  psychology in, 336
strengths contributions to performance in,
  330–331, 336–337
summary of, 338–339
transformational applications of positive
  psychology in, 336–337
virtuous organizational behavior in, 332,
  338
Oswal, Shri Paul, 335–336

Paine, Alfred, 595, 600–602
Penn Resiliency Program (PRP), 272, 274,
  275, 303
PERMA (positive, engagement,
  relationships, meaning, achievement)
  model of well-being, 257, 446–447, 683,
  754
Personalism, 34, 565
Personality:
  agreeableness in, 561
  assessment of, 124, 363, 383, 529–532, 587
  cultural influences and perspectives on,
    814
  emotional intelligence relationship to, 546,
    550
  extraversion in, 186, 358, 561, 814, 815
  gene-environment interactions
    in, 306, 713
  gratitude correlates with, 561–562, 565
  happiness and well-being relationship to,
    186, 713, 745
  humanistic and existential theories on,
    20–21
  neuroticism in, 186, 358, 561
  openness to experience in, 582, 583, 587
  positive and negative views of, 814–815
  psychoanalytic theory on, 20–21
  strength-based assessment of, 529–532
  time perspective as characteristic of, 225
  Universalist perspective on, 18–19
  wisdom relationship to, 577, 579, 582, 583,
    586–587
  work satisfaction and performance
    relationship to, 358, 363
Personality disorders:
  antisocial, 529, 532
  avoidant, 531
  borderline, 529–530
  dependent, 531–532
  histrionic, 530–531
  narcissistic, 530
  obsessive-compulsive, 531
  paranoid, 529
  strength-based assessment of, 529–532

Personal well-being, 85, 111–113
Pharmacological interventions, 165, 211, 472, 473
Phenomenology, 33–34
Physical activity:
    barriers to, 215
    body image/embodiment enhancement via, 795
    community encouragement for, 216, 217
    "feel good" function of, 212–214
    guidelines for dosage of, 207–208, 216–217
    health and well-being practice of, 207–218
    increasing prevalence of, 215–217
    mechanisms for impacts of, 214–215
    mental health relationship to, 209–214, 216–217
    overview of, 207–209, 218
    positive aging impacted by, 608
    preventative function of, 209–210
    process orientation on benefits of, 214–215
    quality of life function of, 212
    somatopsychic principles of, 208–209
    summary of, 218
    therapy function of, 210–212
Politics, 553, 722–724. *See also* Public policy
Positive activities:
    acts of kindness as, 194, 195, 256, 260, 398–399, 700
    assessment of, 400–402, 403
    circumstances creating, 189–190
    counting blessings as, 195, 256, 259–260, 563–564
    cultural influences and perspectives on, 194
    dosage and timing of, 195–196, 256
    embodiment enhancement via, 796, 799–800
    empirical evidence and research on, 189–191, 196, 255–256
    gratitude expression as, 190, 191, 197, 198, 259, 260, 398, 563–564, 700, 796
    happiness increased through, 188–199, 254–255, 700
    health impacts of, 196–197, 397–400
    intentional, 189–191
    life coaching including, 254–256, 259–260
    meditation on positive feelings as, 197, 260
    motivation and effort for, 193–194
    multi-component, 399–400
    optimal conditions for success of, 192–196, 256
    optimism practice as, 260
    overview of, 199
    person-activity fit with, 192–193, 256
    positive reappraisal as, 398
    recovery-oriented service systems including, 700
    rehabilitation psychology including, 452, 453

    relationship impacts of, 198
    selection of, 192–193
    social support for, 194–195
    strengths use in new ways as, 260
    summary of, 199
    theoretical perspectives on, 188
    values affirmation as, 260
    variety of, 195, 256
    visualization of future self as, 260
    well-being therapy focus on, 468
    work impacts of, 197–198
Positive affect. *See* Happiness and well-being
Positive aging:
    assessment of, 596–597, 598
    clinical examples of, 595, 600–603
    definition of, 600
    life span development of, 595–610
    mission of, 596
    non-predictive factors for, 604–606
    overview of, 595–600, 609–610
    physical health and, 596–597, 598–599, 601, 602, 605, 607
    physical reserves and, 596
    predictors of, 604, 606–609
    psychosocial health and, 597, 599–600, 601–602, 603, 605, 607
    research on, 596–600
    sexual relations and, 596
    social supports for, 599, 602–603
    sociodemographics and, 597, 600–601, 604, 605, 608–609
    summary of, 610
Positive education:
    current primary and secondary school initiatives in, 301–305
    definition and description of, 298–299
    effective utilization of, 306
    empirical validation of, 307
    eudaimonic and hedonic perspectives on, 302
    historical perspective on, 299–301
    negative role in, 815–818
    optimization of initiatives in, 305–307
    overview of, 297, 307
    positioning of, 299
    Positive Educational Practices (PEPs) Framework for, 305
    qualitative evaluation in, 306–307
    reasons for, 298
    resilience building through, 297, 300–301, 303, 305, 306
    self-esteem promotion through, 299–300
    social and emotional learning promotion through, 300, 302, 304, 551–552
    summary of, 307–308
Positive Living intervention, 699
Positive psychology:
    agenda of, 11
    assumptions of, 10

Positive psychology (*Continued*)
chapter overview on, 3–6
choice in (*see* Choice)
clinical psychology relationship to, 411–424 (*see also* Clinical practice)
community integration of (*see* Community)
counseling psychology relationship to, 429, 431–439
cultural perspectives in (*see* Cultural influences and perspectives)
definition and description of, 1, 11, 47, 681, 682–683
embodiment role in, 791–801
epistemology in, 38
eudaimonic foundations of, 2–3, 37 (*see also* Eudaimonia and hedonia)
existential dimension of, 20–22, 33, 35, 47–56
future of, in practice, 823–828
growth of, 1–2
health psychology relationship to, 383–404 (*see also* Health and well-being)
historical and philosophical foundations of, 9–24, 31–42, 47–56, 61–75, 431–432, 434, 696, 826
humanistic psychology bridges with, 3, 20–22, 31–42, 431–432, 434, 696, 826
inner resources in (*see* Emotional intelligence; Gratitude; Positive aging; Wisdom)
interventions/practices in (*see* Interventions and practices)
methodology in, 38, 51–52
negative role in, 807–818, 825–826
posttraumatic growth in, 50, 213–214, 435, 437, 447, 503–514, 619, 793, 811–813
psychology subdisciplines application of, 22–23, 823–824
public policy influenced by (*see* Public policy)
recovery-oriented service systems built through, 695–706
rehabilitation psychology relationship to, 443–455, 635–654
research in (*see* Research)
social work interface with, 681–691
training and education related to (*see* Teaching and learning methods and processes; Training and education)
values in (*see* Values)
well-being in (*see* Happiness and well-being; Health and well-being; Well-being)
work organizations impacted by (*see* Work organizations)
Positive Psychology Center (PPC), 271, 272, 273
Positive social planning:
Bhutan's Gross National Happiness as, 766–767

ethical considerations and transparency in, 752, 757–760, 766
global outbreak of social positivity, 752–753
intrinsic value of positive social appreciation in, 764–766
mental thriving considered in, 762–763
normative considerations in, 763–764
overview of, 751–752
positive psychology foundations in, 754, 756–757
public policy of, 751–767
social progress conceptions for, 753–754, 755–756
social quality in, 754, 756–757, 760–764
social values and prosperity in, 757–760
social well-being matrix in, 760–762
summary of, 767
Positive youth development theory, 568–569
Posttraumatic growth:
clinical applications of, 503–514
clinicians' facilitation of, 509–513
clinicians' gain from, 514
cognitive engagement and processing in, 507–508, 509, 510, 511
concept of, 504
counseling psychology focus on, 435, 437
deliberate *vs.* intrusive rumination in, 508
disability-related impacts on, 619
disclosure for, 508–509
embodiment and, 793
existential themes in, 50
expert companion assistance with, 510–513
growth-oriented trauma therapy for, 513–514
narratives of, 509
nonbeneficial nature of trauma despite, 506, 514
overview of, 503
paradoxical changes of, 504–506
physical activity relationship to, 213–214
positive and negative integration in, 811–813
process of, 506–509
psychological comfort and, 504–505
rehabilitation psychology outcome of, 447
self-enhancing bias in, 506
social relationships and support in, 504–505, 508–509
summary of, 514
Posttraumatic stress disorder (PTSD), 474, 528–529, 700, 812
Practices. *See* Interventions and practices
Prevention practices:
child and family focus in, 90–91
counseling psychology as, 430, 435–436
forgiveness facilitation as, 667, 668
intrinsic *vs.* extrinsic values focus in, 90–92
physical activity as, 209–210

positive education as, 300–301, 303, 305
resilience practice as, 776–783
sex offender relapse prevention as, 635, 636, 639
voluntary simplicity intervention as, 91–92
well-being therapy as, 464, 472–473
Problem-solving training, 451, 538–539
Psychoanalytic theory, 20–21, 32–33, 413–414
Psychosis, 699
*Psyfit*, 242
Public policy:
  on advertising and marketing, 94–95
  on civic responsibilities, 96
  on consumer culture and values, 92–96
  on economics, 715, 722, 723–724
  happiness as priority in, 731–748
  individuality-community balancing in, 713–725
  on morality, 723–724
  positive social planning in, 751–767
  resilience theory and practice in, 773–784
  on time affluence, 95–96
Purpose. *See* Meaning or meaningfulness

Quality of life. *See also* Well-being
  clinical practice consideration of, 465
  happiness and classification of, 734–736
  physical activity improving, 212
  rehabilitation psychology focus on, 446–447, 452

Realise2, 362
Recovery-oriented service systems:
  application of combined interventions in, 700–701
  delivery format of, 700–701
  expansion beyond deficit focus in, 698
  individual differences considered in, 698
  mainstream movement of, 696–697
  mental health and well-being continua in, 697–698
  mental health-specific, 701–705
  multimodal integrative cognitive stimulation therapy in, 699
  organizational psychology in, 702–705
  overview of, 695, 706
  positive interventions in, 697–701
  Positive Living intervention in, 699
  positive psychology foundations of, 695–706
  provider-specific focus in, 702–704
  recovery definition and description, 695–696
  research on, 705
  summary of, 706
  system-level focus in, 704–705
  training and education in, 701–702, 703
  well-being therapy in, 699–700
Regret, 124, 126–127

Rehabilitation psychology:
  biomedical deficit model of, 445
  cognitive-behavioral therapy in, 450–452
  definition and description of, 443, 444
  environmental factors considered in, 443, 445
  growth/posttraumatic growth outcomes in, 447
  multiple factors mediating, 448
  outlook and future directions in, 452–454
  overview of, 443–444, 454
  positive principles of, 444–445
  positive psychology in, 443–455, 635–654
  practice applications of positive psychology in, 450–452, 452–453
  psychosocial interventions in, 450–452
  research on, 448–450, 453–454, 652–653
  sex offender rehabilitation in, 635–654
  social relationships and participation considered in, 445, 447, 451
  strengths and resources focus in, 445–446
  summary of, 454–455
  well-being/quality of life as outcome of, 446–447, 452
Relationships. *See* Social relationships
Relativistic thinking, 363
Relaxation training, 381, 451, 566
Religion and spirituality:
  forgiveness related to, 662, 666, 667
  happiness and well-being relationship to, 713–714, 739
Research:
  on adolescent motivation, 316–318, 323
  on choice, 134
  design methodology for, 21–22, 38, 51–52, 196
  on dialogic teaching, 285–286
  on eudaimonia and hedonia, 162–163
  on executive or leadership coaching, 384–386
  on forgiveness, 664–665
  on gratitude, 559, 560–562, 569–570
  on happiness and well-being, 189–191, 196, 732–734
  on health psychology, 402–404
  on life coaching, 252–253
  on positive activities/interventions, 189–191, 196, 255–256
  on positive aging, 596–600
  on positive education, 307
  on positive psychology, 1–2, 21–22
  on recovery-oriented service systems, 705
  on rehabilitation psychology, 448–450, 453–454, 652–653
  self-help approach translation of, 238–239, 244–245
  on sex offender rehabilitation, 652–653
  on strength-based assessment, 525, 532
  teaching and learning approaches impacted by, 274–275, 285–286, 307, 316–318, 323

Research (*Continued*)
  on time perspective, 226–228
  on transformational leadership, 349–351
  on well-being therapy, 472–475
  on wisdom, 582–584, 586–590
Resilience:
  adversity leading to, 774–775
  competence and, 775, 777
  context of, 813–814
  counseling psychology focus on, 435–436
  cultural influences and perspectives on,
    775, 777, 780, 781
  definition and description of, 301
  disability-related impacts on, 620, 628
  dynamic model of, 780–781
  in dynamic systems, 776
  gratitude improving, 567–568
  mechanisms for promoting, 777–778
  organizational, 331–332
  overview of, 773–774, 783
  positive education focus on, 297, 300–301,
    303, 305, 306
  practice applications of, 776–783
  psychological capital including, 361
  public policy related to, 773–784
  related concepts to, 774–776
  resilience-guided goals, 777
  risks, resources, and processes
    underlying, 775–776, 778
  sense of coherence relationship to, 69
  settings for applied resilience, 778–780
  summary of, 783–784
  teaching and learning approaches to, 272,
    274, 275, 297, 300–301, 303, 305, 306
  transactional model of, 781–783
Resolving Conflict Creatively Program, 782
RULER (recognizing, understanding,
    labeling, expressing, and regulating
    emotions) program, 551–552
Rule-utilitarianism, 732

St. Peter's School, 273–274
Salutogenic paradigm:
  overview of, 61–62, 74–75
  pathogenic paradigm *vs.*, 62–64
  positive psychology foundations in, 61–75
  practical implications of, 73–74
  sense of coherence concept in, 64–74
  summary of, 75
  teaching and learning approaches
    addressing, 275
Satisfaction, 735–737, 739–740, 746
Schema theory, 284–285
Schizophrenia, 212, 420, 553–554, 699
School settings:
  cultivation of adolescents' motivation in,
    313–324
  dialogic teaching in, 279–292
  education in (*see* Training and education)
  forgiveness facilitation in, 672–673
  gratitude interventions in, 570

hope accentuation strategies in, 490–493
  peer mediation in, 672–673
  physical activity in, 215
  positive education in, 297–308, 551–552,
    815–818
  resilience practices in, 778–780, 782
  sense of coherence in, 69
  teaching and learning methods in,
    267–276, 279–292, 297–308, 313–324,
    551–552, 815–818
  teaching approaches in, 267–276
  value fulfillment and congruency in, 112,
    114
  violence in, 718
  well-being therapy in, 474–475
Scotch College Adelaide, 273
Seattle Social Development Program, 778
Self-acceptance, 471
Self-blame, 130, 131
Self-determination theory (SDT):
  cognitive evaluation theory in, 143–144
  eudaimonic autonomy-supportive
    principles in, 167
  executive or leadership coaching
    compatibility with, 380
  internal facilitation of autonomous
    regulation in, 146–151
  intrinsic and extrinsic motivation in,
    139–152, 320, 380
  nature of autonomous regulation in,
    140–142
  organismic integration theory in, 140–142,
    145
  organizational psychology application of,
    704
  self-regulation perspective in, 139–152
  social support facilitating autonomous
    regulation in, 143–146
  values in, 104–105, 106, 107
Self-doubt, 318–319
Self-efficacy:
  disability-related impacts of, 618
  health impacts of, 396
  motivational support for, 318–319, 322
  psychological capital including, 361
  transformational leadership relationship
    to, 343–344, 348
Self-esteem, 299–300, 699, 717
Self-help approaches:
  book-based, 240
  challenges of real world use of, 244–246
  context sensing for, 245
  emerging technology impacting, 245
  empirical validation of, 244–245
  ethical considerations with, 245–246
  existing, examples of, 239–244
  life coaching use of, 260–261
  overview of, 237–238, 246
  person-activity fit of, 239
  positive psychology interventions via,
    237–246

research translation to, 238–239, 244–245
smartphone-based, 243–244, 245
social support for, 239
summary of, 246
web-based, 240–243
Self-regulation:
  attention relationship to, 147–151
  eudaimonic growth based on, 171
  internal facilitation of autonomous, 146–151
  intrinsic and extrinsic motivation in, 139–152
  managing emotions as, 547, 548–549, 550
  mindfulness impacting, 148–151
  nature of autonomous, 140–142
  overview of, 139–140, 151–152
  self-determination theory perspective on, 139–152
  social support facilitating autonomous, 143–146
  summary of, 152
Semco, 370
Sense of coherence (SOC):
  child and adolescent, 67, 69–70, 71–72, 73
  collective sense of, 70–71
  concept of, 64–65
  cultural influences and perspectives on, 68, 72–73
  disability-related impacts on, 619
  health and, 65–73
  life span development of, 68
  measurement of, 67
  non-significance findings on, 71–73
  practical implications of, 73–74
  salutogenic paradigm view of, 64–74
Separation anxiety disorder, 527
Sex offender rehabilitation:
  assessment of offenders in, 643–646
  ethical issues in, 636
  forgiveness in, 637–638
  goals and priorities of offenders in, 644–645
  Good Lives Model of, 635–636, 638, 640–654
  good lives plan for, 641–642
  human nature viewpoints in, 637, 638, 640
  internal and external conditions impacting, 641–642
  overview of, 635–636, 653–654
  personal identity of offenders in, 639, 641
  probation case management application of, 653
  relapse prevention approach to, 635, 636, 639
  research on, 652–653
  revenge avoidance in, 638
  risk-need-responsivity approach to, 635, 636, 639–640
  summary of, 654
  theoretical framework for, 636–640

therapist's view of offenders in, 636–638, 642–643
treatment principles, goals, and structure in, 646–652
youth offenders in, 653
Social and Emotional Aspects of Learning (SEAL) program, 302
Social and emotional learning, 300, 302, 304, 551–552
Social-constructivist perspective:
  on clinical psychology, 412, 416–419, 420–421, 422
  on dialogic teaching, 284
Social phobia, 527
Social relationships:
  choice in relation to, 132–133
  cultural influences and perspectives on, 721–722
  disability-related social barriers, 625, 628
  embodiment and, 796–797
  emotional intelligence relationship to, 549, 550, 554
  extrinsic *vs.* intrinsic values impacting, 86
  familial (*see* Families; Marriage or partnerships)
  gratitude impacting, 560, 561–562, 566
  happiness and well-being relationship to, 198, 716–722, 744, 796
  health impacts of, 719–721, 796
  hope accentuation strategies impacting, 489, 495
  motivation influenced by interpersonal experiences in, 14–17, 316, 320, 322
  need to belong addressed through, 716–718, 721–722
  organizational benefits of, 333, 358, 364–365
  positive activity consequences for, 198
  positive social qualities of, 754, 756–757, 760–764
  posttraumatic growth impacted by, 504–505, 508–509
  rehabilitation psychology consideration of, 445, 447, 451
  social comparisons in, 128–129
  social environment for physical activity affecting, 215, 217
  social environment values, 110–113, 114–115
  social isolation from, 717–718
  social motivation for, 14–17
  social sanctions in, 110–111
  social support facilitating autonomous regulation, 143–146
  social support for positive activities via, 194–195
  social support for positive aging via, 599, 602–603
  social support for self-help approaches, 239

Social relationships (*Continued*)
  social support interventions impacting, 451
  social toxicity of inequality, 722–724
  social well-being and, 86, 760–762
  team building including, 364–365
  well-being therapy on, 471–472
  wisdom consideration of, 586–587, 588
Social work:
  assessment of strengths in, 684–685
  definitions and missions in, 681–684
  on domestic violence, 685–687
  future directions in, 689–690
  on mental health, 687–689
  overview of, 681, 690–691
  person-environment focus in, 682, 683, 685, 688, 689
  positive psychology interface with, 681–691
  strength perspective in, 684–689
  summary of, 691
Socioeconomic status:
  happiness relationship to, 714–715, 722–723, 741–743, 746, 757–760, 763–764
  inequality of, 722–724
  positive aging relationship to, 604, 605
  sense of coherence influenced by, 68
  work income impacting, 358–359
Solution-focused therapy, 437
SPARK Resilience Programme, 305
Strength-based assessment:
  accessibility of tools for, 537
  advantages of, 521–522
  of anxiety and anxiety disorders, 524–525, 527–529, 535, 536
  of attention-deficit/hyperactivity disorder, 529
  of bipolar disorder, 526
  of body dysmorphic disorder, 528
  clinical applications of, 519–539
  clinical interviews including, 537
  collateral information for, 537–538
  of conduct disorders, 529
  courage in, 523
  deficit-based assessment *vs.*, 519–521
  definition and description of, 519
  of depression and depressive disorders, 524–525, 526, 535, 536
  early administration of, 538
  empirical evidence for, 525, 532
  existing inclusion of, 537
  four-front approach to, 536
  of hoarding disorders, 528
  humanity in, 523
  icons of strengths used in, 538
  illustrations of, 533–537
  justice in, 523
  narrative strategy for, 538
  negativity bias complicating, 519–520
  of obsessive-compulsive disorder, 528, 531

  of oppositional defiant disorder, 529
  overview of, 519–521, 539
  of personality disorders, 529–532
  positive activity pursuit based on, 538
  positive psychology foundations of, 521, 522
  of posttraumatic stress disorder, 528–529
  problem solving tactics based on, 538–539
  recommendations for clinical practice regarding, 537–539
  summary of, 539
  temperance in, 524
  theoretical foundations of, 522, 524–525
  transcendence in, 524
  wisdom and knowledge in, 523
Strengthscope, 362
Stress:
  definition and description of, 394
  health psychology focus on, 394–397
  physical activity for coping with, 213
  positive affective impacting, 394–395, 396
  positive aging not predicted by, 606
  posttraumatic stress disorder, 474, 528–529, 700, 812
  Revised Stress and Coping Theory on, 395
  salutogenic view of, 64, 69–70, 71–72
  stress management interventions for, 451
  (*see also* Relaxation training)
Suicide, 130–131
Systemic family therapy, 437
Systems theory, 382

Teaching and learning methods and processes:
  cultivation of adolescents' motivation as, 313–324
  dialogic teaching as, 279–292
  future directions in, 274–275
  instructional materials for, 268, 288
  levels of positive psychology curricula integration in, 269–274
  overview of, 267–268, 276, 279–280, 291–292, 297, 307, 313–315, 323
  positive education as, 297–308, 551–552, 815–818
  summary of, 276, 292, 307–308, 323–324
  teaching approaches as, 267–276
*Thnk4.org,* 241
Three Good Things intervention, 563
Time-based issues:
  time affluence as, 95–96
  time perspective balancing as, 223–234
  timing of positive activities as, 195–196, 256
  Universalist perspective on social and historical time, 17–20
Time Paradox, 232

Time perspective:
  balanced, 228–231
  cultural influences and perspectives on,
    223–224, 225, 228
  definition and description of, 224
  flexibility in, 229
  future-oriented, 226–227, 230–231
  measurement of, 225–227, 228, 229,
    230–231
  optimal functioning pursuit via balanced,
    223–234
  overview of, 223–225, 233–234
  past-oriented, 227, 230
  practical applications of, 231–233
  present-oriented, 227, 230
  research on, 226–228
  summary of, 234
  time-management interventions based on,
    233
  well-being and, 230–231
Toronto Charter for Physical Activity, 207
Tragedy, 50–51
Training and education:
  in clinical psychology, 413–414, 415
  in counseling psychology, 437, 438
  in dialogic teaching, 287–291
  in forgiveness facilitation, 669–670, 673
  in humanistic psychology, 33
  in mindfulness, 151 (*see also* Mindfulness
    practices)
  positive aging predicted by years of,
    608–609
  in positive body image, 795
  in positive psychology, 2, 22–23, 271–272
  professional development through,
    287–291, 360–363
  in recovery-oriented service systems,
    701–702, 703
  in resilience practices, 778
  school settings for (*see* School settings)
  sense of coherence relationship to, 69
  teaching and learning methods and
    processes for, 267–276, 279–292,
    297–308, 313–324, 551–552, 815–818
  in transformational leadership, 351
  in wisdom, 590
  in work organizations, 351, 360–363
Transformational leadership:
  conservation of resources theory on,
    347–349
  definition and description of, 342
  follower well-being improvements due to,
    341–352
  future research on, 349–351
  identification fostering relationship to,
    346, 348
  meaningful work relationship to,
    344–345, 348
  mediators of effects of, 343–347, 348
  overview of, 341–342, 351
  practice implications of, 351

  self-efficacy relationship to, 343–344, 348
  summary of, 351–352
  trust in management relationship to,
    345–346, 348
Transtheoretical Model of Change, 382–383
Trauma:
  posttraumatic growth following, 50,
    213–214, 435, 437, 447, 503–514, 619,
    793, 811–813
  posttraumatic stress disorder following,
    474, 528–529, 700, 812
Tully State High School, 274

United Nations:
  Declaration of Universal Human Rights,
    36, 753
  Declaration on Social Progress and
    Development, 753
  "Happiness: Towards a Holistic Approach
    to Development" resolution, 767
  social progress defined by, 753
Universalistic perspective, 17–20
University of Illinois, Collaborative for
    Academic, Social, and Emotional
    Learning, 300
University of Melbourne, Australia, Master
    of Applied Positive Psychology, 272
University of Pennsylvania:
  Authentic Happiness website, 537
  Penn Resiliency Program, 272, 274, 275,
    303
  Positive Psychology Center, 271, 272, 273
  Witmer psychological clinic at, 413
Utilitarianism, 731–732, 747–748

Values. *See also* Virtues
  conservation, 105
  consumer culture-related, 83–97
  ecological well-being impacted by, 86–87
  eudaimonia focus on, 161, 166–167
  existential psychology on, 52–54
  extrinsic *vs.* intrinsic, 84–97, 104–107, 109,
    113–114, 115, 150–151
  goal attainment perspective on, 107–110,
    114
  good life association with, 83, 84–87
  happiness relationship to, 85–86,
    747–748, 757–760
  healthy and unhealthy, 104–107, 113–114
  humanistic psychology value-laden
    worldview, 35–36
  internal conflict over, 111–113
  mindfulness practice focus on, 89,
    150–151
  openness to change, 105
  organizational, 95–96, 111–113, 704–705
  overview of, 83–84, 96, 103–104, 115
  personal well-being impacted by, 85
  person-environment value congruency,
    110–113, 114–115
  positive activities affirming, 260

Values (*Continued*)
    positive social planning on social values, 757–760
    practice implications of, 87–96
    prevention practices focus on, 90–92
    public policy reflecting, 92–96
    self-determination theory on, 104–105, 106, 107
    self-enhancement, 105
    self-transcendence, 105
    social well-being impacted by, 86
    summary of issues related to, 96, 115–116
    time affluence reflection of, 95–96
    virtues distinction from, 53–54
    voluntary simplicity interventions based on, 91–92
    well-being and, 85–86, 103–116, 747–748, 757–760
    wisdom in relation to, 578–579, 588
Values in Action website, 537
Veterans Administration, U.S., 414
Victim-offender mediation (VOM), 672
Virtues. *See also* Ethical issues; Morality; Values
    assessment of, 53, 163, 446, 522, 523–524, 684–685, 754
    character strengths based on, 445–446
    existential psychology on, 52–56
    humanistic psychology on, 38–41
    traditions of virtue, 54–56
    values distinction from, 53–54
    virtue theory on, 38–41
    virtuous organizational behavior, 332, 338, 368
Voluntary simplicity interventions, 91–92

Well-being:
    choice impacting, 121–134
    definition and description of, 342–343, 683
    ecological, 86–87
    embodiment and, 792–793, 796
    eudaimonic and hedonic (*see* Eudaimonia and hedonia)
    forgiveness relationship to, 661–664, 665
    goal attainment impacting, 107–110, 114
    happiness and (*see* Happiness and well-being)
    health and (*see* Health and well-being)
    inner resources for (*see* Emotional intelligence; Gratitude; Positive aging; Wisdom)
    internal conflict impacting, 111–113
    PERMA model of, 257, 446–447, 683, 754
    personal, 85, 111–113
    person-environment value congruency impacting, 110–113, 114–115
    positive education focus on, 297–308
    rehabilitation psychology outcome of, 446–447, 452
    social, 86, 760–762
    subjective, 446

    time perspective and, 230–231
    values and, 85–86, 103–116, 747–748, 757–760
    work-related, 197–198, 341–352, 357–360, 702–703
*Well-Being Curriculum,* 303
Well-being therapy:
    autonomy in, 471
    case studies of, 475–476
    child/adolescent, 474–475
    clinical applications of, 463–477, 699–700
    cognitive-behavioral therapy relationship to, 472–476, 699–700
    complexity of well-being for, 465–466
    conceptual framework of, 468–472
    developments modifying use of, 464–465
    environmental mastery in, 470
    eudaimonic and hedonic pursuits via, 165, 463–464, 467
    mechanisms of action in, 475
    optimal-balanced well-being goal in, 468–469
    overview of, 463–465, 476–477
    personal growth in, 470
    positive interpersonal relations in, 471–472
    protocol or structure of, 466–468
    purpose in life in, 470–471
    recovery-oriented service systems including, 699–700
    rehabilitation psychology including, 452
    relapse and recurrence prevention through, 464, 472–473
    self-acceptance in, 471
    summary of, 477
    validation studies of, 472–475
Wellington College, 302
Wellness Recovery Action Planning (WRAP), 700, 705
Wellness Self-Management, 700
Whole-Child Initiative, 271, 275
Wisdom:
    age relationship to, 577–578, 582–584, 589
    assessment of, 523, 579, 580–581, 587
    Berlin wisdom paradigm on, 578–579, 581–582
    cognition relationship to, 585–586, 587
    conflict management based on, 580–581, 584, 588
    cultural influences and perspectives on, 578
    definition and description of, 578–581
    development of, 581–582
    emotional intelligence relationship to, 582, 585–590
    expert knowledge as, 578–579
    gain and loss of, 583–584
    humanistic psychology on, 40
    integration of factors for, 585–590
    life span development of, 577–591
    MORE model of, 582

motivation relationship to, 586–590
overview of, 577–578, 590
personality relationship to, 577, 579, 582, 583, 586–587
personal *vs.* general, 579–580, 583
professional development of, 363
research on, 582–584, 586–590
social or interpersonal factors of, 586–587, 588
strength-based assessment of, 523
summary of, 590–591
theoretical models of, 581–582
Work organizations:
appreciative inquiry in, 329–330, 331, 334–335, 364–365
autonomy, freedom and control in, 360, 366–368, 370
case studies of, 333–336
community engagement of, 368
conservation of resources theory on, 347–349
corporate culture of, 369, 370
decision-making speed and authority in, 333, 704
economies of strengths in, 337
emotional intelligence in, 361, 382, 552–553
ethical considerations in, 337–338
executive or leadership coaching in, 232, 249, 377–387
gratitude in, 569–570
human resources management in, 552–553
identification fostering in, 346, 348
income from, 358–359
job satisfaction and performance in, 358, 359–360, 363
leadership behavior in, 232, 249, 334, 338, 341–352, 377–387, 553, 702–703, 704–705
meaningful work in, 344–345, 348
motivation challenges and improvements in, 330, 336, 360
organizational compassion in, 704–705
organizational development of, 368–370
organizational psychology of, 329–339, 702–705
organizational resilience in, 331–332

overtime policies in, 95–96
overview of, 329–330, 338, 341–342, 351, 370–371, 377, 386–387
paid leave policies in, 95–96
participatory working in, 366–368, 370
personality influences in, 358, 363
positive activity consequences in, 197–198
positive approach applications in, 357–371
positive deviance in, 335–336
positive psychology in, 329–339, 341–352, 357–371, 377–387, 702–705
positivity benefits to performance in, 331, 336–337
professional development in, 360–363
psychological capital in, 361–362, 703
public policy impacting, 95–96
resilience practices in, 779
self-efficacy in, 343–344, 348, 361
social networks and relationships in, 333, 358, 364–365
step-change application of positive psychology in, 336
strengths contributions to performance in, 330–331, 336–337, 362–363
summary of, 338–339, 351–352, 371, 387
teamwork in, 364–365
time affluence and perspective in, 95–96, 232, 233
transformational applications of positive psychology in, 336–337
trust in management in, 345–346, 348
values reflected in, 95–96, 111–113, 704–705
virtuous organizational behavior in, 332, 338, 368
well-being in, 197–198, 341–352, 357–360, 702–703
work style assessments in, 363
World Database of Happiness, 734, 738, 741
World Health Organization:
health defined by, 597, 616
*International Classification of Disease*, 415
*International Classification of Functioning, Disability and Health*, 443, 616–617
physical activity recommendations by, 207

Youth. *See* Adolescents; Children

Printed in the USA
CPSIA information can be obtained
at www.ICGtesting.com
LVHW060919070923
757354LV00023B/54

9 781118 756935